DESIGNING EXPERIMENTS AND ANALYZING DATA

A MODEL COMPARISON PERSPECTIVE

Second Edition

DESIGNING EXPERIMENTS AND ANALYZING DATA

A Model Comparison Perspective

Second Edition

Scott E. Maxwell
University of Notre Dame

Harold D. Delaney
University of New Mexico

LEA

2004

LAWRENCE ERLBAUM ASSOCIATES, PUBLISHERS

Mahwah, New Jersey   London

Senior Editor:	Debra Reigert
Editorial Assistant:	Jason Planer
Cover Design:	Kathryn Houghtaling Lacey
Textbook Production Manager:	Paul Smolenski
Full-Service Compositor:	TechBooks
Text and Cover Printer:	Hamilton Printing Company

This book was typeset in 10/12 pt. Times, Italic, Bold, and Bold Italic.
The heads were typeset in Americana, Americana Italic, and Americana Bold.

Lawrence Erlbaum Associates, Inc., Publishers
10 Industrial Avenue
Mahwah, New Jersey 07430
www.erlbaum.com

Library of Congress Cataloging-in-Publication Data

Maxwell, Scott E.
    Designing experiments and analyzing data : a model comparison
perspective / Scott E. Maxwell, Harold D. Delaney.—2nd ed.
        p.   cm.
    Includes bibliographical references and indexes.
    ISBN 0-8058-3718-3 (acid-free paper)
    1. Experimental design.   I. Delaney, Harold D.   II. Title.

    QA279 .M384   2003
    519.5′3—dc21   2002015810

To our parents, and
To Katy, Melissa, Cliff,
Nancy, Ben, Sarah, and Jesse

Contents

IV ALTERNATIVE ANALYSIS STRATEGIES

15 An Introduction to Multilevel Models for Within-Subjects Designs

Preface

This book is written to serve as either a textbook or a reference book on designing experiments and analyzing experimental data. Our particular concern is with the methodology appropriate in the behavioral sciences but the methods introduced can be applied in a variety of areas of scientific research. The book is centered around the view of data analysis as involving a comparison of models. We believe that this model comparison perspective offers significant advantages over the traditional variance partitioning approach usually used to teach analysis of variance. Instead of approaching each experimental design in terms of its own unique set of computational formulas, the model comparison approach allows us to introduce a few basic formulas that can be applied with the same underlying logic to every experimental design. This establishes an integrative theme that highlights how various designs and analyses are related to one another. The model comparison approach also allows us to cover topics that are often omitted in experimental design texts. For example, we are able to introduce the multivariate approach to repeated measures as a straightforward generalization of the approach used for between-subjects designs. Similarly, the analysis of nonorthogonal designs (designs with unequal cell sizes) fits nicely into our approach. Further, not only is the presentation of the standard analysis of covariance facilitated by the model comparison perspective, but we are also able to consider models that allow for heterogeneity of regression across conditions. In fact, the underlying logic can be applied directly to even more complex methodologies such as hierarchical linear modeling (discussed in this edition) and structural equation modeling. Thus, our approach provides a conceptual framework for understanding experimental design and it builds a strong foundation for readers who wish to pursue more advanced topics.

The focus throughout the book is conceptual, with our greatest emphasis being on promoting an understanding of the logical underpinnings of design and analysis. This is perhaps most evident in the first part of the book dealing with the logic of design and analysis, which touches on relevant issues in philosophy of science and past and current controversies in statistical reasoning. But the conceptual emphasis continues throughout the book, where our primary concern is with developing an understanding of the logic of statistical methods. This is why we present definitional instead of computational formulas, relying on statistical packages to perform actual computations on a computer. This emphasis allows us to concentrate on the meaning of what is being computed instead of worrying primarily about how to perform the calculation. Nevertheless, we recognize the importance of doing hand calculations on occasion to better understand what it is that is being computed. Thus, we have included a number of exercises at the end of each chapter that give the reader the opportunity to calculate quantities by hand on small data sets. We have also included many thought questions, which are intended to develop a deeper understanding of the subject and to help the reader draw out logical connections in the materials. Finally, realistic data sets allow the reader to experience an analysis of data from each design in its entirety. These data sets are included on the CD packaged with the book, as are all other data sets that appear in the text. Every data set is available in three forms: a SAS system file, an SPSS system file, and an ascii file, making it easy for students to practice their understanding by using their preferred statistical package. Solutions to numerous selected (starred) exercises are provided at the back of the book. Answers for the remaining exercises are available in a solutions manual for instructors who adopt the book for classroom use.

Despite the inclusion of advanced topics such as hierarchical linear modeling, the necessary background for the book is minimal. Although no mathematics beyond high school algebra is required, we do assume that readers will have had at least one undergraduate statistics course. For those readers needing a refresher, a Review of Basic Statistics is included on the book's CD. Even those who have had more than a single statistics course may find this Review helpful, particularly in conjunction with beginning the development of our model comparison approach in Chapter 3. The other statistical tutorial on the CD, which could most profitably be read upon the completion of Chapter 3, provides a basic discussion of regression for those who have not previously studied or need a review of regression.

There is a companion web site for the book:

www.designingexperiments.com

This web site contains examples of SAS and SPSS instructions for analyzing the data sets that are analyzed in the various chapters of the book. The data sets themselves are contained on the CD for ease of access, while the instructions are placed on the web site so they can be modified as new versions of SAS and SPSS are released. Our intent is that these instructions can serve as models for students and other readers who will usually want to apply similar analyses to their own data. Along these lines, we have chosen not to provide SAS or SPSS instructions for end-of-chapter exercises, because we believe that most instructors would prefer that students have the opportunity to develop appropriate instructions for these exercises themselves based on examples from the chapters instead of being given all of the answers. Thus we have intentionally left open an opportunity for practice and self-assessment of students' knowledge and understanding of how to use SAS and SPSS to answer questions presented in end-of-chapter exercises.

Organization

The organization of the book allows chapters to be covered in various sequences or omitted entirely.

Part I (Chapters 1 and 2) explains the logic of experimental design and the role of randomization in the conduct of behavioral research. These two chapters attempt to provide the philosophical and historical context in which the methods of experimental design and analysis may be understood. Although Part I is not required for understanding statistical issues in the remaining chapters of the book, it does help the reader see the "big picture."

Part II provides the core of the book. Chapter 3 introduces the concept of comparing full and restricted models. Most of the formulas used throughout the book are introduced in Chapters 3 and 4. Although most readers will want to follow these two chapters by reading at least Chapters 5, 7, and 8 in Part II, it would be possible for more advanced readers to go straight to Chapters 13 and 14 on the multivariate approach to repeated measures. Chapter 9, on Analysis of Covariance, is written in such a way that it can be read either immediately following Chapter 8 or deferred until after Part III.

Part III describes design and analysis principles for within-subjects designs (that is, repeated measures designs). These chapters are written to provide maximum flexibility in choosing an approach to the topic. In our own one-semester experimental design courses, we find it necessary to omit one of the four chapters on repeated measures. Covering only Chapters 11, 13, and 14 introduces the univariate approach to repeated measures but covers the multivariate approach in greater depth. Alternatively, covering only Chapters 11, 12, and 13 emphasizes the univariate approach. Advanced readers might skip Chapters 11 and 12 entirely and read only Chapters 13 and 14.

Part IV, consisting of Chapters 15 and 16, presents a basic introduction to hierarchical linear modeling. This methodology has several advantages over traditional ANOVA approaches, including the possibility of modeling data at individual and group levels simultaneously as well as permitting the inclusion of participants with incomplete data in analyses of repeated measures designs. In a two-quarter or two-semester course, one might cover not only all four chapters on ANOVA approaches to repeated measures but also Chapters 15 and 16. Alternatively, these final two chapters might be used in the first part of a subsequent course devoted to hierarchical linear modeling.

As in the first edition, discussion of more specialized topics is included but set off from the main text in a variety of ways. Brief sections explicating specific ideas within chapters are marked with an "Optional" heading and set in a smaller font. A more involved discussion of methods relevant to a whole chapter are appended to the chapter and denoted as an Extension. Detailed notes on individual ideas presented in the text is provided in the Endnotes in Appendix C.

We have taken several steps to make key equations interpretable and easy to use. The most important equations are numbered consecutively in each chapter as they are introduced. If the same equation is repeated later in the chapter, we use its original equation number followed by the designation "repeated," to remind the reader that this equation was already introduced and to facilitate finding the point where it was first presented. Cross-references to equations in other chapters are indicated by including the chapter number followed by a period in front of the equation number. For example, a reference in Chapter 5 to Equation 4.35 refers to Equation 35 in Chapter 4. However, within Chapter 4 this equation is referred to simply as Equation 35. Finally, we have frequently provided tables that summarize important equations for a particular design or concept, to make equations easier to find and facilitate direct comparisons of the equations to enhance understanding of their differences and similarities.

Changes in This Edition

Especially for those who used the first edition of the book, we want to highlight important changes included in this edition. The most extensive revision is the greatly increased attention given to measures of effects. Briefly introduced in the first edition, we now have discussion of confidence intervals, measures of strength of association, and other measures of effect size throughout the book. Other general changes include a more thorough integration of information on statistical packages and an increased use of graphics.

In terms of the most important changes in individual chapters, Chapter 1 incorporates important recent discussions of validity such as those by Shadish, Cook and Campbell (2002) and Abelson (1996), as well as alluding to recent influences on philosophy of science such as postmodernism. Chapter 2 was extensively re-worked to address past and present controversies regarding statistical reasoning, including disputes ranging from Fisher's disagreements with Neyman and Pearson up through the recent debates about hypothesis testing that motivated the formation of the APA Task Force on Statistical Inference (Wilkinson et al., 1999). Chapter 2 is now considerably less sanguine about the pervasiveness of normally distributed data. Also added to this chapter is an overview of experimental designs to be covered in the book.

Chapter 3 now opens with a data plot to stress the importance of examining one's data directly before beginning statistical analyses. An extended treatment of transformations of data is now presented. The treatment of power analyses was updated to include an introduction to computerized methods. Chapters 4, 5 and 6 on contrasts, like the rest of the book, include more on measures of effect and confidence intervals, with Chapter 5 now stressing simultaneous confidence intervals and introducing concepts such as the false discovery rate.

Chapter 7, which introduces two-way ANOVA, extends the treatment of measures of effect to alternative ways of accommodating the influence of the other factor included in the design in addition to the one whose effects you wish to characterize. The greatly expanded development of interaction contrasts is now illustrated with a realistic data set. In Chapter 8, which discusses designs with three or more factors, the presentation of three-way interactions has been expanded. More extensive use is now made of plots of simple interaction effects as a way of explaining three-way interactions.

A numerical example with realistic data was added to Chapter 9 on covariates. A new section on choosing covariates is also included.

Chapter 10 on designs with random or nested factors was revised extensively. The rationale for the model used for testing effects in designs with random factors is contrasted with alternative approaches used by some computer packages. Application of rules for determining the effects that can be tested and the appropriate error terms to use in complex designs is discussed in greater detail. The intraclass correlation as a measure of effect size is now introduced for use with random factors.

Chapters 11 through 14 on univariate and multivariate approaches to repeated measures designs, like the previous chapters, now incorporate various measures of effects, both in terms of standardized mean differences as well as measures of association such as omega squared. Sample size considerations are also dealt with in greater detail.

Chapters 15 and 16 on hierarchical linear modeling (HLM) are entirely new. Chapter 15 extends Chapters 11 through 14 by developing additional models for longitudinal data. We explicitly describe how these new models (sometimes called multilevel models, mixed models or random coefficient models) are related to the traditional ANOVA and MANOVA models covered in Chapters 11–14. This contrasts with many other presentations of HLM, which either relate these new models to regression but not ANOVA or present the new models in isolation from any form of more traditional models. Chapter 16, an extension of Chapter 10, applies HLM to nested designs. In both Chapters 15 and 16, numerous examples of SAS syntax are presented, and the advantages of these newer methods for dealing with designs with unequal n or missing data are stressed.

This edition features two new appendices that discuss more global aspects of the model comparison theme of our book. One of these (Appendix B, Part I), designed for readers who have previously studied multiple regression, details the relationship between ANOVA and regression models, and illustrates some advantages of the ANOVA approach. The other (Appendix B, Part II) deals with general principles of formulating models including such considerations as specification errors, or the implications of not having the appropriate factors included in one's statistical model.

Finally, this new edition also includes a CD as well as a web site to accompany the book. The CD contains:

(1) a Review of Basic Statistics tutorial
(2) a Regression tutorial
(3) data files in 3 formats (SAS, SPSS, and ascii) for all data sets that appear in the book (including end-of-chapter exercises as well as data presented in the body of chapters)

The accompanying web site (www.designingexperiments.com) contains:

(1) a brief description of the research question, the design, and the data for each data set that appears in the body of a chapter
(2) SAS and SPSS instructions (i.e., syntax or examples of menu choices) for how to perform analyses described in the book itself

Acknowledgments

The number of individuals who contributed either directly or indirectly to this book's development defies accurate estimation. The advantages of the model comparison approach were first introduced to us by Elliot Cramer when we were graduate students at the University of North Carolina at Chapel Hill. The excellent training we received there provided a firm foundation on which to build. Much of the philosophy underlying our approach can be traced to Elliot and our other mentors at the L. L. Thurstone Psychometric Lab (Mark Appelbaum, John Carroll, Lyle Jones, and Tom Wallsten). More recently we have benefited from insightful comments from colleagues who used the first edition, as well as many current and former students and teaching assistants. One former teaching assistant, John Moulton, was great assistance in completing the index for the current volume. Similarly, current graduate students Ken Kelley and Joe Rausch assisted in the creation of datasets for the book's CD and computer syntax for the web page. We are also indebted to the University of Notre Dame and the University of New Mexico for providing us with sabbatical leaves to work on the book. The encouragement of our colleagues must be mentioned, especially that of David Cole, George Howard, Tim Goldsmith, Paul Amrhein, Bill Miller, and John Oller. We appreciate the support of the staff at Lawrence Erlbaum Associates, especially editor Debra Riegert. Excellent secretarial support provided by Judy Spiro was again extremely helpful, and the efficient clerical assistance of Louis Carrillo and Nancy Chavez appreciated.

The current edition, like the first, benefited from the many worthwhile suggestions of a number of reviewers. We are indebted to the following individuals who provided comments either on the first edition or on a draft of the current edition: David A. Kenny, University of Connecticut; David J. Francis, University of Houston; Richard Gonzalez, University of Michigan; Sam Green and Stephen West, Arizona State University; Howard M. Sandler, Vanderbilt University; András Vargha, Eötvös Lóránd University (Budapest); Ron Serlin, University of Wisconsin; James E. Carlson, Auburn University at Montgomery; James Jaccard, State University of New York at Albany; Willard Larkin, University of Maryland, College Park; K. J. Levy, State University of New York at Buffalo; Marjorie Marlin, University of Missouri, Columbia; Ralph G. O'Brien, Cleveland Clinic; Edward R. Stearns, California State University, Fullerton; Rand Wilcox, University of Southern California; Rhanda K. Kowalchuk, University of Wisconsin, Milwaukee; Keith F. Widaman, University of California, Davis; and Jon Williams, Kenyon College.

Finally, and most importantly, we thank our families for providing us with the warmth, love, and understanding that have helped us not just to complete projects such as this but also to appreciate what is most important in life. Most critical are the roles played by Katy Brissey Maxwell and Nancy Hurst Delaney who, among many other things, made it possible in the midst of busy family lives for us to invest the tremendous amount of time required to complete the book. Our parents, Lylton and Ruth Maxwell, and Hugh and Lee Delaney, and our children, Melissa and Clifford Maxwell, and Ben, Sarah, and Jesse Delaney, have also enriched our lives in ways we cannot begin to express. It is to our families that we dedicate this book.

DESIGNING EXPERIMENTS AND ANALYZING DATA

A MODEL COMPARISON PERSPECTIVE

Second Edition

I

Conceptual Bases
of Experimental Design
and Analysis

Man, being the servant and interpreter of Nature, can do and understand so much, and so much only, as he has observed, in fact or in thought, of the course of Nature....Human knowledge and human power meet in one; for where the course is not known, the effect cannot be produced. Nature, to be commanded, must be obeyed.

—FRANCIS BACON, *NOVUM ORGANUM*, 1620

1

The Logic
of Experimental Design

Methods of experimental design and data analysis derive their value from the contributions they make to the more general enterprise of science. To appreciate what design and analysis can and cannot do for you, it is necessary to understand something of the logic of science. Although we do not attempt to provide a comprehensive introduction to the philosophy of science, we believe it is necessary to present some of the difficulties involved in attempting to draw valid inferences from experimental data regarding the truth of a given scientific explanation of a particular phenomenon.

We begin with a discussion of the traditional view of science and mention some of the difficulties inherent in this view. Next, we consider various responses that have been offered to the critique of the traditional view. Finally, we discuss distinctions that can be made among different types of validity and enumerate some specific types of threats to drawing valid inferences from data.

THE TRADITIONAL VIEW OF SCIENCE

The perspective on science that emerged in the West around 1600 and that profoundly shaped and defined the modern era (Whitehead, 1932) can be identified in terms of its methodology: empirical observation and, whenever possible, experimentation. The essence of experimentation, as Shadish, Cook, and Campbell (2002) note, is an attempt "to discover the effects of presumed causes" (p. 3). It is because of their contribution to the understanding of causal processes that experiments play such a central role in science. As Schmidt (1992) suggests, "The major task in any science is the development of theory. . . . Theories are causal explanations. The goal in every science is explanation, and explanation is always causal" (p. 1177). The explication of statistical methods that can assist in the testing of hypothesized causes and estimating their effects via experiments is the primary concern of this book. Such an emphasis on technical language and tools is characteristic of modern science and perhaps contributes to the popular perception of science as a purely objective, rule-governed process. It is useful to review briefly how such a view arose historically and how it must be qualified.

Many trace the origins of modern science to British statesman and philosopher Sir Francis Bacon (1561–1626). The context in which Bacon was writing was that of a culture that for

3

centuries had been held in the grips of an Aristotelian, rationalistic approach to obtaining knowledge. Although Aristotle had considered induction, the "predominant mode of his logic was deduction, and its ideal was the syllogism" (Durant & Durant, 1961, p. 174). Bacon recognized the stagnation that had resulted in science because of this stress on deduction rather than observation and because the ultimate appeal in scientific questions was to the authority of "the Philosopher," Aristotle. Bacon's complaint was thus not so much against the ancients as with their disciples, particularly the Scholastic philosophers of the late Middle Ages (Robinson, 1981, p. 209). Bacon's *Novum Organum* (1620/1928a) proposed that this old method be replaced with a new organ or system based on the inductive study of nature itself. In short, what Bacon immodestly attempted was to "commence a total reconstruction of sciences, [practical] arts, and all human knowledge, raised upon the proper foundations" (Bacon, 1620/1928b, p. 4). The critical element in this foundation was the method of experimentation. Thus, a deliberate manipulation of variables was to replace the "noting and naming" kind of empiricism that had characterized the Aristotelian approach when it did lower itself to observation (Robinson, 1981, p. 212).

The character of Bacon's reconstruction, however, was to have positive and negative consequences for the conception of science that predominated for the next 3 centuries. The Baconian ideal for science was as follows: At the start of their research, experimenters are to remove from their thinking all the "'idols' or time-honored illusions and fallacies, born of [their] personal idiosyncrasies of judgment or the traditional beliefs and dogmas of [their] group" (Durant & Durant, 1961, p. 175). Thus, in the Baconian view, scientific observations are to be made in a purely objective fashion by individuals having no loyalties to any hypotheses or beliefs that would cause them to be blind to any portion of the empirical evidence. The correct conclusions and explanatory principles would then emerge from the evidence relatively automatically, and without the particular philosophical presuppositions of the experimenter playing any part. Thus, the "course of Nature" could be observed clearly if the experimenter would only look at Nature as it is. Nature, as it were, unambiguously dictated the adoption of true theories. The whole process of science, it was thought, could be purely objective, empirical, and rational.

Although this view of science is regarded as passé by some academics (cf. Gergen, 2001), particularly in the humanities, its flaws need to be noted because of its persistence in popular thought and even in the treatment of the scientific method in introductory texts in the sciences. Instead of personal judgment playing no role in science, it is critical to the whole process. Whether one considers the data collection, data analysis, or interpretation phases of a study, the process is not purely objective and rule governed. First, the scientist's preexisting ideas about what is interesting and relevant undeniably guide decisions about what data are to be collected. For example, if one is studying the effects of drug treatments on recovery of function following brain injury, one has decided in advance that the drugs present in the bloodstream may be a relevant factor, and one has likely also decided that the day of the week on which the drug treatment is administered is probably not a relevant factor. Data cannot be collected without some preexisting ideas about what may be relevant, because it is those decisions that determine the variables to be manipulated or assessed in a particular experimental design. There are no logical formulas telling the scientist which particular variables must be examined in a given study.

Similarly, the patterns observed in a set of data are influenced by the ideas the investigator brings to the research. To be sure, a great deal can be said about what methods of analysis are most appropriate to aid in this pattern-detection process for a particular experimental design. In fact, much of this book is devoted to appropriate ways of describing causal relationships observed in research. However, both experiments in cognitive psychology and examples from the history of science suggest that, to a large extent, what one sees is determined by what one expects to see (see Kuhn, 1970, especially Chapter VI). Although statistical analysis can objectify to some extent the process of looking for patterns in data, statistical methods, as Koch (1981) and others point out, even when correctly applied, do not assure that the most appropriate ways of organizing the data will be found. For example, in a simple four-group experimental design, there are, at least in theory, an infinite number of comparisons of the four group means that could be tested for significance. Thus, even assuming that the most appropriate data had been collected, it is entirely possible that a researcher might fail to examine the most illuminating comparison. Admittedly, this problem of correctly perceiving at least approximately what the patterns in your data are is less serious than the problem of collecting the relevant data in the first place or the problem of what one makes of the pattern once it is discerned. Nonetheless, there are no absolutely foolproof strategies for analyzing data.

The final step in the inductive process is the most troublesome. Once data relevant to a question are collected and their basic pattern noted, how should the finding be explained? The causal explanations detailing the mechanisms or processes by which causes produce their effects are typically much harder to come by than facts to be explained (cf. Shadish et al., 2002, p. 9). Put bluntly, "there is no *rigorous logical* procedure which accounts for the birth of theories or of the novel concepts and connections which new theories often involve. There is no 'logic of discovery'" (Ratzsch, 2000, p. 19). As many a doctoral candidate knows from painful experience after puzzling over a set of unanticipated results, data sometimes do not clearly suggest any theory, much less dictate the "correct" one.

RESPONSES TO THE CRITICISMS OF THE IDEA OF PURE SCIENCE

Over the years, the pendulum has swung back and forth regarding the validity and implications of this critique of the allegedly pure objectivity, rationality, and empiricism of science. We consider various kinds of responses to these criticisms. First, it is virtually universally acknowledged that certain *assumptions* must be made to do science at all. Next, we consider three major alternatives that figured prominently in the shaping of *philosophy of science* in the 20th century. Although there were attempts to revise and maintain some form of the traditional view of science well into the 20th century, there is now wide agreement that the criticisms were more sound than the most influential revision of the traditional view. In the course of this discussion, we indicate our views on these various perspectives on philosophy of science and point out certain of the inherent limitations of science.

Assumptions

All rational argument must begin with certain assumptions, whether one is engaged in philosophical, scientific, or competitive debating. Although these assumptions are typically present only implicitly in the practice of scientific activities, there are some basic principles essential to science that are not subject to empirical test but that must be presupposed for science to make sense. Following Underwood (1957, pp. 3–6), we consider two assumptions to be most fundamental: the lawfulness of nature and finite causation.

Lawfulness of Nature

Although possibly itself a corollary of a more basic philosophical assumption, the assumption that the events of nature display a certain lawfulness is a presupposition clearly required by science. This is the belief that nature, despite its obvious complexity, is not entirely chaotic: regularities and principles in the outworking of natural events exist and wait to be discovered. Thus, on this assumption, an activity like science, which has as its goal the cataloging and understanding of such regularities, is conceivable.

There are a number of facets or corollaries to the principle of the lawfulness of nature that can be distinguished. First, at least since the ancient Greeks, there has been agreement on the assumption that *nature is understandable*, although not necessarily on the methods for how that understanding should be achieved. In our era, with the growing appreciation of the complexities and indeterminacies at the subatomic level, the belief that we can understand is recognized as not a trivial assumption. At the same time, the undeniable successes of science in prediction and control of natural events provide ample evidence of the fruitfulness of the assumption and, in some sense, are more impressive in light of current knowledge. As Einstein said, the most incomprehensible thing about the universe is that it is comprehensible[1] (Einstein, 1936, p. 351; see Koch, 1981, p. 265).

A second facet of the general belief in the lawfulness of nature is that *nature is uniform*—that is, processes and patterns observed on only a limited scale hold universally. This is obviously required in sciences such as astronomy if statements are to be made on the basis of current observations about the characteristics of a star thousands of years ago. However, the validity of the assumption is questionable, at least in certain areas of the behavioral sciences. Two dimensions of the problem can be distinguished. First, relationships observed in the psychology of 2005 may not be true of the psychology of 1955 or 2055. For example, the social psychology of attitudes in some sense must change as societal attitudes change. Rape, for instance, was regarded as a more serious crime than homicide in the 1920s but as a much less serious crime than homicide in the 1960s (Coombs, 1967). One possible way out of the apparent bind this places one in is to theorize at a more abstract level. Rather than attempting to predict attitudes toward the likely suitability for employment of a rapist some time after a crime, one might instead theorize about the possible suitability for future employment of someone who had committed a crime of a specified level of perceived seriousness and allow which crime occupied that level to vary over time. Although one can offer such abstract theories, it is an empirical question as to whether the relationship will be constant over time when the particular crime occupying a given level of seriousness is changing.

A second dimension of the presupposition of the uniformity of nature that must be considered in the behavioral sciences pertains to the homogeneity of experimental material (individuals, families) being investigated. Although a chemist might safely assume that one hydrogen atom will behave essentially the same as another when placed in a given experimental situation, it is not at all clear that the people studied by a psychologist can be expected to display the same sort of uniformity. Admittedly, there are areas of psychology—for example, the study of vision—in which there is sufficient uniformity across individuals in the processes at work that the situation approaches that in the physical sciences. In fact, studies with very small numbers of subjects are common in the perception area. However, it is generally the case that individual differences among people are sufficiently pronounced that they must be reckoned with explicitly. This variability is, indeed, a large part of the need for behavioral scientists to be trained in the areas of experimental design and statistics, in which the focus is on methods for accommodating to this sort of variability. We deal with the logic of this accommodation at numerous points, particularly in our discussion of external validity in this chapter and randomization in Chapter 2. In addition, Chapter 9 on control variables is devoted to methods for incorporating variables assessing individual differences among participants into one's design and analysis, and the succeeding chapters relate to methods designed to deal with the systematic variation among individuals.

A third facet of the assumption of the lawfulness of nature is the *principle of causality*. One definition of this principle, which was suggested by Underwood, is that "every natural event (phenomenon) is assumed to have a cause, and if that causal situation could be exactly reinstituted, the event would be duplicated" (1957, p. 4). At the time Underwood was writing, there was fair agreement regarding causality in science as a deterministic, mechanistic process. Since the 1950s, however, we have seen the emergence of a variety of views regarding what it means to say that one event causes another and, equally important, regarding how we can acquire knowledge about causal relationships. As Cook and Campbell put it, "the epistemology of causation, and of the scientific method more generally, is at present in a productive state of near chaos" (1979, p. 10).

Cook and Campbell admirably characterized the evolution of thinking in the philosophy of science about causality (1979, Chapter 1). We can devote space here to only the briefest of summaries of that problem. Through most of its first 100 years as an experimental discipline, psychology was heavily influenced by the view of causation offered by the Scottish empiricist philosopher David Hume (1711–1776). Hume argued that the inference of a causal relationship involving unobservables is never justified logically. Even in the case of one billiard ball striking another, one does not observe one ball causing another to move. Rather, one simply observes a correlation between the ball being struck and its moving. Thus, for Hume, correlation is all we can know about causality. These 18th-century ideas, filtered through the 19th-century positivism of Auguste Comte (1798–1857), pushed early 20th-century psychology toward an empiricist monism, a hesitancy to propose causal relationships between hypothetical constructs. Rather, the search was for functional relationships between observables or, only slightly less modestly, between theoretical terms, each of which was operationally defined by one particular measurement instrument or set of operations in a given study. Thus, in 1923, Boring would define *intelligence* as what an intelligence test measures. Science was to give us sure knowledge of relationships that had been confirmed rigorously by empirical observation.

These views of causality have been found to be lacking on a number of counts. First, as every elementary statistics text reiterates, causation is now regarded as something different from mere correlation. This point must be stressed again here, because in this text we describe relationships with statistical models that can be used for either correlational or causal relationships. This is potentially confusing, particularly because we follow the convention of referring to certain terms in the models as "effects." At some times, these effects are the magnitude of the change an independent variable causes in the dependent variable; at other times, the effect is better thought of as simply a measure of the strength of the correlational relationship between two measures. The strength of the support for the interpretation of a relationship as causal, then, hinges not on the statistical model used, but on the nature of the design used. For example, in a correlational study, one of the variables may be dichotomous, such as high or low anxiety, rather than continuous. That one could carry out a t test[2] of the difference in depression between high- and low-anxiety groups, rather than computing a correlation between depression and anxiety, does *not* mean that you have a more secure basis for inferring causality than if you had simply computed the correlation. If the design of the study were such that anxiety was a measured trait of individuals rather than a variable independently manipulated by the experimenter, then that limits the strength of the inference rather than the kind of statistic computed.

Second, using a single measurement device as definitional of one's construct entails a variety of difficulties, not least of which is that meters (or measures) sometimes are broken (invalid). We have more to say about such construct validity later. For now, we simply note that, in the behavioral sciences, "one-variable, 'pure' measuring instruments are an impossibility. *All* measures involve many known theoretical variables, many as yet unknown ones, and many unproved presumptions" (Cook & Campbell, 1979, p. 14).

Finally, whereas early empiricist philosophers required causes and effects to occur in *constant conjunction*—that is, the cause was necessary and sufficient for the effect—current views are again more modest. At least in the behavioral sciences, the typical view is that all causal relationships are contingent or dependent on the context (cf. Shadish et al., 2002). The evidence supporting behavioral "laws" is thus probabilistic. If 90 of 100 patients in a treatment group, as opposed to 20 of 100 in the control group, were to be cured according to some criterion, the reaction is to conclude that the treatment caused a very large effect, *instead* of reasoning that, because the treatment was not sufficient for 10 subjects, it should not be regarded as the cause of the effect.

Most scientists, particularly those in the physical sciences, are generally realists; that is, they see themselves as pursuing theoretical truth about hidden but real mechanisms whose properties and relationships explain observable phenomena. Thus, the realist physicist would not merely say, as the positivist would, that a balloon shrinks as a function of time. Rather, he or she would want to proceed to make a causal explanation, for example, the leakage of gas molecules caused the observed shrinkage. This is an assertion that not just a causal relationship was constructed in the physicist's mind, but that a causal relationship really exists among entities outside of any human mind. Thus, in the realist view, theoretical assertions "have objective contents which can be either right or wrong" (Cook & Campbell, 1979, p. 29).

Others have wanted to include human volition under their concept of cause, at least in sciences studying people. For example, Collingwood (1940) suggested "that which is 'caused' is the free and deliberate act of a conscious and responsible agent, and 'causing' him to do it means affording him a motive for doing it" (p. 285). This is the kind of attribution for the cause of action presupposed throughout most of the history of Western civilization, but that came to represent only a minority viewpoint in 20th-century psychology, despite persisting as the prevailing view in other disciplines such as history and law. In recent years, several prominent researchers such as Roy Baumeister (Baumeister, Bratslavsky, Muraven, & Tice, 1998), Joseph Rychlak (2000), and George Howard (Howard & Conway, 1986; Howard, Curtin & Johnson, 1991) have argued that research in experimental psychology can proceed from such an agentic or teleological framework as well.

Thus, we see that a variety of views are possible about the kind of causal relationships that may be discovered through experimentation: the relationship may or may not be probabilistic, the relationship may or may not be regarded as referring to real entities, and the role of the participant (subject) may or may not be regarded as that of an active agent. This last point makes clear that the assumption of the lawfulness of nature does not commit one to a position of philosophical determinism as a personal philosophy of life (Eacker, 1972). Also, even though many regard choosing to do science as tantamount to adopting determinism as a working assumption in the laboratory, others do not see this as necessary even there. For example, Rychlak (2000) states that traditional research experiments provide a means of his putting his teleological theories of persons as free agents to the test. Similarly, George Howard and colleagues argue (Howard et al., 1991) that it is the individual's freedom of choice that results in the unexplained variation being so large in many experiments. Given that the algebraic models of dependent variables we use throughout this book incorporate both components reflecting unexplained variability and components reflecting effects of other variables, their use clearly does not require endorsement of a strictly deterministic perspective. Rather, the commitment required of the behavioral scientist, like that of the physicist studying subatomic particles, is to the idea that the consistencies in the data will be discernible through the cloud of random variation (see Meehl, 1970b).

It should perhaps be noted, before we leave the discussion of causality, that in any situation there are a variety of levels at which one could conduct a causal analysis. Both nature and science are stratified, and properties of entities at one level cannot, in general, be reduced to constellations of properties of entities at a lower level. For example, simple table salt (NaCl) possesses properties that are different from the properties of either sodium (Na) or chloride (Cl) (see Manicas & Secord, 1983). To cite another simple example, consider the question of what causes a room to suddenly become dark. One could focus on what causes the light in the room to stop glowing, giving an explanation at the level of physics by talking about what happens in terms of electric currents when the switch controlling the bulb is turned off. A detailed, or even an exhaustive, account of this event at the level of physics would not do away with the need for a psychological explanation of why a person flipped off the switch (see Cook & Campbell, 1979, p. 15). Psychologists are often quick to argue against the fallacy of reductionism when it is hinted that psychology might someday be reduced to physics or, more often, to biology. However, the same argument applies with equal force to the limitations of the causal relationships that behavioral scientists can hope to discover through empirical investigation. For example, a detailed, or even an exhaustive, psychological account of how someone came to hold a particular belief says nothing about the philosophical question of whether such a belief is true.

Having considered the assumption of the lawfulness of nature in some detail, we now consider a second fundamental assumption of science.

Finite Causation

Science presupposes not only that there are natural causes of events, but also that these causes are finite in number and discoverable. Science is predicated on the belief that generality of some sort is possible; that is, it is not necessary to replicate the essentially infinite number of elements operating when an effect is observed initially in order to have a cause sufficient for producing the effect again. Now, it must be acknowledged that much of the difficulty in arriving at the correct interpretation of the meaning of an experimental finding is deciding *which* elements are critical to causing the phenomenon and *under what conditions* they are likely to be sufficient to produce the effect. This is the problem of causal explanation with which much of the second half of this chapter is concerned (cf. Shadish et al., 2002).

A statistical analogy may be helpful in characterizing the principle of finite causation. A common challenge for beginning statistics students is mastering the notion of an interaction whereby the effect of a factor depends or is contingent on the level of another factor present. When more than two factors are simultaneously manipulated (as in the designs we consider in Chapter 8), the notion extends to higher-order interactions whereby the effect of a factor depends on combinations of levels of multiple other factors. Using this terminology, a statistician's way of expressing the principle of finite causation might be to say that "the highest-order interactions are not always significant." Because any scientific investigation must be carried out at a particular time and place, it is necessarily impossible to re-create exactly the state of affairs operating then and there. Rather, if science is to be possible, one must assume that the effect of a factor does not depend on the levels of all the other variables present when that effect is observed.

A corollary of the assumption of finite causation has a profound effect on how we carry out the model comparisons that are the focus of this book. This corollary is the bias toward simplicity. It is a preference we maintain consistently, in test after test, until the facts in a given situation overrule this bias.

Many scientists stress the importance of a strong belief in the ultimate simplicity of scientific laws. As Gardner points out, "this was especially true of Albert Einstein. 'Our experience,' he wrote, 'justifies us in believing that nature is the realization of the simplest conceivable mathematical ideas'" (Gardner, 1979, pp. 169–170; see Einstein, 1950, p. 64). However, as neuroscientists studying the brain know only too well, there is also an enormous complexity to living systems that at least obscures if not makes questionable the appropriateness of simple models. Indeed, the same may be true in some sense in all areas of science. Simple first approximations are, over time, qualified and elaborated: Newton's ideas and equations about gravity were modified by Einstein; Gall's phrenology was replaced by Flourens's views of both the unity and diversification of function of different portions of the brain.

Thus, we take as our guiding principle that set forward for the scientist by Alfred North Whitehead: "Seek simplicity and distrust it"; or again, Whitehead suggests that the goal of science "is to seek the simplest explanation of complex facts" while attempting to avoid the error of concluding nature is simpler than it really is (1920/1964, p. 163).

Admittedly, the principle of parsimony is easier to give lip service to than to apply. The question of how to measure the simplicity of a theory is by no means an easy one. Fortunately, within mathematics and statistics the problem is somewhat more tractable, particularly if you restrict your attention to models of a particular form. We adopt the strategy in this text of restricting our attention for the most part to various special cases of the general linear model. Although this statistical model can subsume a great variety of different types of analyses, it takes a fundamentally simple view of nature in that such models assume the effects of various causal factors simply cumulate or are added together in determining a final outcome. In addition, the relative simplicity of two competing models in a given situation may easily be described by noting how many more terms are included in the more complex model. We begin developing these ideas in much greater practical detail in Chapter 3.

Modern Philosophy of Science

Having considered two fundamental assumptions of science, we continue our discussion of responses to the critique of the traditional view of science by considering four alternative philosophies of science. We begin by considering an attempt to revise and maintain the traditional view that has played a particularly important role in the history of psychology.

Positivism

In our discussion of the principle of causality as an aspect of the assumption of the lawfulness of nature, we previously alluded to the influence of Humean empiricism and 19th-century positivism on 20th-century psychology. This influence was so dominant over the first 75 years of the 20th century that something more must be said about the principal tenets of the view of science that developed out of positivism and the opposing movements that in the latter part of the 20th century continued to grow in strength to the point of overtaking this view.

A positivistic philosophy of science was crystallized by the "Vienna Circle," a group of philosophers, scientists, and mathematicians in Vienna who, early in the 20th-century, set forth a view of science known as *logical positivism*. Rudolph Carnap and Herbert Feigl were two of the principal figures in the movement, with Carl Hempel and A. J. Ayer also being among those whose writings heavily influenced psychology. Their logical positivism represented a wedding of Comte's positivism with the logicism of Whitehead and Russell's *Principia Mathematica*.

The aim of Auguste Comte's positive philosophy was to advance the study of society beyond a theological or metaphysical stage, in which explanations for phenomena were sought at the level of supernatural volition or abstract forces, to a "positive" stage. The stage was conceived to be positive in two distinct senses. First, all knowledge in the positive stage would be based on the positive (i.e., certain, sure) methods of the physical sciences. Rather than seeking a cause or an essence, one is content with a law or an empirical generalization. Second, Comte expected that the philosophical unity that would be effected by basing all knowledge on one method would result in a religion of humanity uniting all men and women (Morley, 1955).

The logical positivists combined this positivism with the logicism of Bertrand Russell's mathematical philosophy (Russell, 1919a). Logicism maintains that mathematics is logic. "All pure mathematics deals exclusively with concepts definable in terms of a very small number of fundamental concepts, and . . . all its propositions are deducible from a very small number of logical principles" (Russell, 1937, p. xv). Thus, all propositions in mathematics can be viewed as the result of applying truth functions to interpret various combinations of elementary or atomic propositions—that is, one determines the implications of the fundamental propositions according to a set of strictly logical rules. The meaning or content of the elementary propositions plays no role in the decision concerning whether a particular molecular proposition constructed out of elementary propositions by means of operators is true or false. Thus, like logic, mathematics fundamentally "is concerned solely with syntax, i.e., with formal relations between symbols in accordance with precise rules" (Brown, 1977, p. 21).

The modern logical positivism, which played such a dominant role in the way academic psychologists thought about their field, is a form of positivism that takes such symbolic logic as its primary analytic tool. This is seen in the central doctrine of logical positivism, known as the *Verifiability Criterion of Meaning*. According to this criterion, a proposition is meaningful "if and only if it can be empirically verified, i.e., if and only if there is an empirical method for deciding if it is true or false" (Brown, 1977, p. 21). (The only exception to this rule is the allowance for analytical propositions, which are propositions that assert semantic identities or that are true just in virtue of the terms involved, e.g., "All bachelors are unmarried.") Thus, scientific terms that could not be defined strictly and completely in terms of sensory observations were regarded as literally meaningless. Any meaningful statement must reduce then to elementary propositions that can literally be seen to be true or false in direct observation. The bias against statistical tests and in favor of black-or-white, present-or-absent judgment of relationships in data was only one practical outworking of this philosophical view.

The goal of the logical positivists was then to subsume the rationale and practice of science under logic. The central difficulty preventing this was that scientific laws are typically stated as universal propositions that cannot be verified conclusively by any number of observations. One cannot show, for example, that all infants babble simply by observing some critical number of babbling babies. In addition, there are a number of paradoxes of confirmation about which no consensus was ever achieved as to how they should be resolved (Brown, 1977, Chapter 2). Hempel's "paradox of the ravens" illustrates the most famous of these (1945). As Wesley Salmon succinctly summarized in *Scientific American*,

> If all ravens are black, surely non-black things must be non-ravens. The generalizations are logically equivalent, so that any evidence that confirms one must tend to confirm the other. Hence the observation of a green vase seems to confirm the hypothesis that all ravens are black. Even a black raven finds it strange. (1973, p. 75)

Such paradoxes were especially troublesome to a philosophical school of thought that had taken the purely formal analysis of science as its task, attempting to emulate Whitehead and Russell's elegant symbolic logic approach that had worked so well in mathematics.

Although the dilemmas raised because the contrapositive of an assertion is logically equiv-alent to the original assertion [i.e., (raven → black) ↔ (nonblack → nonraven)] may not seem relevant to how actual scientific theories come to be accepted, this is typical of the logical positivist approach. Having adopted symbolic logic as the primary tool for the analysis of science, then proposition forms and their manipulation became the major topic of discussion. The complete lack of detailed analysis of major scientific theories or research efforts is thus understandable, but unfortunate. When psychologists adopted a positivistic approach as the model of rigorous research in the physical sciences, they were, in fact, adopting a method that bore virtually no relationship to the way physicists actually approached research.

The most serious failing of logical positivism, however, was the failure of its fundamental principle of the Verifiability Criterion of Meaning. A number of difficulties are inherent in this principle (Ratzsch, 2000, p. 31ff.), but the most critical problems include the following: First, as we have seen in our discussion of the assumptions of science, some of the basic principles needed for science to make sense are not empirically testable. One cannot prove that events have natural causes, but without such assumptions, scientific research is pointless.

Second, attempts such as operationism to adhere to the criterion resulted in major difficulties. The operationist thesis, so compatible with behaviorist approaches, was originally proposed by P. W. Bridgman: "In general, we mean by any concept nothing more than a set of operations; the concept is synonymous with the corresponding set of operations" (1927, p. 5). However, this was taken to mean that if someone's height, much less their intelligence, were to be measured by two different sets of operations, these are not two different ways of measuring height, but are definitional of different concepts, which should be denoted by different terms (see the articles in the 1945 Symposium on Operationism published in *Psychological Review*, especially Bridgman, 1945, p. 247). Obviously, rather than achieving the goal of parsimony, such an approach to meaning results in a proliferation of theoretical concepts and, in some sense, "surrender of the goal of systematizing large bodies of experience by means of a few fundamental concepts" (Brown, 1977, p. 40). Finally, the Verifiability Criterion of Meaning undercuts itself. The criterion itself is neither empirically testable nor obviously analytic. Thus, either it is itself meaningless, or meaningfulness does not depend on being empirically testable—that is, it is either meaningless or false.

Thus, positivism failed in its attempts to subsume science under formal logic, did not allow the presuppositions necessary for doing science, prevented the use of generally applicable theoretical terms, and was based on a criterion of meaning that was ultimately incoherent. Unfortunately, its influence on psychology long outlived its relatively brief prominence within philosophy itself.

Popper

An alternative perspective that we believe holds considerably more promise for appropri-ately conceptualizing science is provided by Karl Popper's falsificationism (1968) and sub-sequent revisions thereof (Lakatos, 1978; Newton-Smith, 1981). These ideas have received increasing attention of late in the literature on methodology for the behavioral sciences (see Cook & Campbell, 1979, p. 20ff.; Dar, 1987; Gholson & Barker, 1985; Rosenthal & Rosnow, 1991, p. 32ff.; Serlin & Lapsley, 1985; Shadish et al., 2002, p. 15ff.; see also Klayman & Ha, 1987). Popper's central thesis is that deductive knowledge is logically possi-ble. In contrast to the "confirmationist" approach of the logical positivists, Popperians believe progress occurs by falsifying theories. Although this may seem counterintuitive, it rests on the logic of the compelling nature of deductive as opposed to inductive arguments.

What might *seem* more plausible is to build up support for a theory by observing that the predictions of the theory are confirmed. The logic of the seemingly more plausible confirmationist approach may be expressed in the following syllogism:

Syllogism of Confirmation

If theory T is true, then the data will follow the predicted pattern P.
The data follow predicted pattern P.
Therefore, theory T is true.

This should be regarded as an invalid argument but perhaps not as a useless one. The error of thinking that data prove a theory is an example of the logical fallacy known as "affirming the consequent." The first assertion in the syllogism states that T is sufficient for P. Although such if–then statements are frequently misunderstood to mean that T is necessary for P (see Dawes, 1975), that does not follow. This is illustrated in the Venn diagram in Figure 1.1(a). As with any Venn diagram, it is necessary to view the terms of interest (in this case, theory T and data pattern P) as sets, which are represented in the current diagram as circles. This allows one to visualize the critical difference between a theory's being a sufficient explanation for a data pattern and its being necessarily correct. That theory T is sufficient for pattern P is represented by T being a subset of P. However, in principle at least, there are a number of other theories that also could explain the data, as illustrated by the presence of theories T_x, T_y, and T_z in Figure 1.1 (b). Just being "in" pattern P does not imply that a point will be "in" theory T, that is, theory T is not necessarily true. In fact, the history of science provides ample support for what has been termed the *pessimistic induction*: "Any theory will be discovered to be false within, say 200 years of being propounded" (Newton-Smith, 1981, p. 14).

Popper's point, however, is that under certain assumptions, *rejection* of a theory, as opposed to confirmation, may be done in a deductively rigorous manner. The syllogism now is:

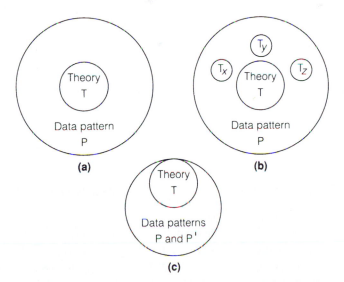

FIG. 1.1.   Venn diagrams illustrating that theory T is sufficient for determining data pattern P (see (a)), but that data pattern P is not sufficient for concluding theory T is correct (see (b)). The Venn diagram in (c) is discussed later in this section of the text.

Syllogism of Falsification

If theory T is true, then the data will follow the predicted pattern P.
The data do not follow predicted pattern P.
Therefore, theory T is false.

The logical point is that although the converse of an assertion is *not* equivalent to the assertion, the contrapositive, as we saw in the paradox of the ravens, *is*. That is, in symbols $(T \rightarrow P)$ $\not\rightarrow (P \rightarrow T)$, but $(T \rightarrow P) \leftrightarrow (\text{not } P \rightarrow \text{not } T)$. In terms of Figure 1.1, if a point is in P, that does not mean it is in T, but if it is outside P, it is certainly outside T. Thus, although one cannot prove theories correct, one can, by this logic, prove them false.

Although it is hoped that this example makes the validity of the syllogism of falsification clear, it is important to discuss some of the assumptions implicit in the argument and raise briefly some of the concerns voiced by critics of Popper's philosophy, particularly as it applies to the behavioral sciences. First, consider the first line of the falsification syllogism. The one assumption pertinent to this, about which there is agreement, is that it is possible to derive predictions from theories. Confirmationists assume this as well. Naturally, theories differ in how well they achieve the desiderata of good theories regarding predictions—that is, they differ in how easily empirical predictions may be derived and in the range and specificity of these predictions. Unfortunately, psychological theories, particularly in recent years, tend to be very restricted in scope. Also, unlike physics, the predictions that psychological theories do make are typically of a nonspecific form ("the groups will differ") rather than being point predictions ("the light rays will bend by x degrees as they go past the sun") (see Meehl, 1967, 1986). However, whether specific or nonspecific, as long as it is assumed that a rather confident judgment can be made—for example, by a statistical test—about whether the results of an experiment are in accord with the predictions, the thrust of the argument maintains its force.[3]

More troublesome than the lack of specificity or generality of the predictions of psychological theories is that the predictions depend not only on the core ideas of the theory, but also on a set of additional hypotheses. These often have to do with the particular way in which the theoretical constructs of interest are implemented in a given study and may actually be more suspect than the theory itself (cf. Smedslund, 1988). As expressed in the terminology of Paul Meehl, "[I]n social science the auxiliaries A and the initial and boundary conditions of the system C are frequently as problematic as the theory T itself" (1978, p. 819). For example, suppose a community or health psychologist wants to investigate the effect of perceived risk and response efficacy on self-protection. Funding is obtained to investigate the effectiveness of such a theoretically driven intervention in decreasing the use of alcohol and illegal drugs as the criterion behavior in a population of at-risk youth. In her study, the psychologist attempts to impress groups of middle school youth from local economically disadvantaged areas with the dangers of drug use by taking them to hospitals or detention centers to talk with young adults who have been injured or arrested as a result of their use of alcohol or illegal drugs. She also attempts to increase the middle schoolers' belief in their ability to avoid alcohol or drug use by having them participate in discussion groups on the subject led by undergraduate research assistants. A negative result (or worse yet, increased drug use in the treated group) causes one to question if the core substantive theory (T) of the impact of risk perception and response efficacy on self-protection has been falsified or if one or more of the auxiliary hypotheses (A) have been falsified. For example, perhaps the visits with the hospitalized or jailed youths served to tacitly validate them as role models to be emulated rather than increasing the students' perceived risk of drug use, or perhaps the fact that a large majority of the undergraduate assistants leading the discussions were themselves binge drinkers or users of illegal drugs did not facilitate their ability to persuade the middle schoolers of how easily and efficaciously they could make responses to avoid such risky behaviors. Or perhaps even the presumed boundary condition (C) that the motivation to avoid danger in the form of health or legal consequences was present at a high level, particularly in comparison to other motivations such as peer approval, was not satisfied in this population. We consider such difficulties further when we discuss construct validity later in this chapter.

Turning now to the second line of the falsification syllogism, much also could be said about caveats. For one thing, some philosophers of science, including Popper, have philosophical reservations about whether one can know with certainty that a predicted pattern has not been obtained because that knowledge is to be obtained through the fallible inductive method of empirical observation (see Newton-Smith, 1981, Chapter III). More to the point for our purposes is the manner in which empirical data are to be classified as conforming to one pattern or another. Assuming one's theory predicts that the pattern of the data will be that people in general will perform differently in the treatment and control conditions, how does one decide on the basis of a sample of data what is true of the population? That, of course, is the task of inferential statistics and is the sort of question to which the bulk of this book is addressed. First, we show in Chapter 2 how one may derive probability statements rigorously for very simple situations under the assumption that there is no treatment effect. If the probability is sufficiently small, the hypothesis of no difference is rejected. If the probability fails to reach a conventional level of significance, one might conclude the alternative hypothesis is false. (More on this in a moment.) Second, we show beginning in Chapter 3 how to formulate such questions for more complicated experiments using standard parametric tests. In sum, because total conformity with the exact null hypotheses of the social and behavioral sciences (or, for that matter, with the exact point predictions sometimes used—e.g., in some areas of physics) is never achieved, inferential statistics serves the function of helping scientists classify data patterns as being confirmed predictions, falsified predictions, or, in some cases, ambiguous outcomes.

A final disclaimer is that Popper acknowledges that, in actual scientific practice, singular discordant facts alone rarely do or should falsify theories. Hence, in practice, as hinted at previously, a failure to obtain a predicted data pattern may not *really* lead to a rejection or abandonment of the alternative hypothesis the investigator wanted to support. In all too many behavioral science studies, the lack of statistical power is a quite plausible explanation for failure to obtain predicted results.[4] Also, such statistical reasons for failure to obtain predicted results are only the beginning. Because of the existence of the other explanations we have considered (e.g., "Some auxiliary theory is wrong") that are typically less painful to a theorist than rejection of the principal theory, in practice a combination of multiple discordant facts *and* a more viable alternative theory are usually required for the refutation of a theoretical conjecture (see Cook & Campbell, 1979, p. 22ff.).

We pause here to underscore some of the limitations of science that have emerged from our consideration of Popper and then highlight some of the general utility of his ideas. Regarding science's limitations, we have seen that not only is there no possibility of proving any scientific theory with logical certainty, but also that there is no possibility of falsifying one with logical certainty. That there are no proven theories is a well-known consequence of the limits of inductive logic. Such difficulties are also inherent to some extent in even the simplest empirical generalization (the generalization is not logically compelled, for reasons including the fact that you cannot be certain what the data pattern is because of limited data and potential future counterexamples to the current pattern and that any application of the generalization requires reliance on principles like uniformity). In short, "the data do not drive us inevitably to correct theories, and even if they did or even if we hit on the correct theory in some other way, we could not prove its correctness conclusively" (Ratzsch, 2000, pp. 76–77). Furthermore, theories cannot be proved false because of the possibility of explaining away purported refutations via challenges based on the fallibility of statistical evidence or of the auxiliary hypotheses relied on in testing the theory. In addition, there is the practical concern that despite the existence of discordant facts, the theory may be the best available.

On the positive side of the ledger, Popper's ideas have much to offer, both practically and philosophically. Working within the limitations of science, the practical problem for the scientist is how to eliminate explanations other than the theory of interest. We can see the utility of the Popperian conceptual framework in Figure 1.1. The careful experimenter proceeds, in essence, by trying to make the shaded area as small as possible, thereby refuting the rival theories. We mentioned previously that the syllogism of confirmation, although invalid, was not useless. The way in which rival hypotheses are eliminated is essentially by confirming the predictions of one's theory in more situations, in at least some of which the rival hypotheses make contrary predictions. Figure 1.1(c) illustrates this. The outer circle now represents the intersection or joint occurrence of obtaining the predicted data P and also predicted data P'. For example, if a positive result had been obtained in the self-protection study with middle schoolers, the interpretation that increased perception of risk was the causal variable could be strengthened by including control conditions in which plausible other causes were operating. One possible rival hypothesis (which might be represented by T_x in Figure 1.1) could be that the increased monitoring of the middle schoolers involved in the study might itself serve to suppress drug use regardless of the treatment received. Having a control group that was assessed as often and in as much detail as the treatment group but that did not manifest the decreased use seen in the treatment group essentially eliminates that rival explanation. The plausibility of the causal explanation would be enhanced further by implementing the construct in different ways, such as attempting to increase the perceived risk of smoking or sun exposure as a means of trying to induce other self-protective behaviors in other populations.

Indeed, part of the art of experimental design has to do with devising control conditions for which the theory of interest would make a different prediction than would a plausible rival hypothesis. (As another example, the rival: "The deficit is a result of simply the operation, not the brain area destroyed" is discounted by showing no deficit in a sham surgery condition.) If the rival hypothesis is false, part of the credo of science is that with sufficient investigation, ultimately, it will be discovered. As Kepler wrote regarding rivals to the Copernican hypothesis that made some correct predictions,

> And just as in the proverb liars are cautioned to remember what they have said, so here false hypotheses which together produce the truth by chance, do not, in the course of a demonstration in which they have been applied to many different matters, retain this habit of yielding the truth, but betray themselves. (Kepler, 1601)

Although in principle an infinite number of alternative hypotheses always remain, it is of little concern if no *plausible* hypotheses can be specified. We return to this discussion of how rival hypotheses can be eliminated in the final section of this chapter.

Regarding other, more philosophical considerations, for Popper, the aim of science is truth. However, given that he concurs with Hume's critique of induction, Popper cannot claim to know the truth of a scientific hypothesis. Thus, the reachable goal for science in the real world is to be that of a closer approximation to the truth, or in Popper's terms, a higher degree of *verisimilitude*. The method of achieving this is basically a rational one by way of the logically valid refutation of alternative conjectures about the explanation of a given phenomenon. Although the details of the definition of the goal of verisimilitude and the logic of the method are still evolving (see Popper, 1976; Meehl, 1978; Newton-Smith, 1981), we find ourselves in basic agreement with a neo-Popperian perspective, both in terms of ontology and of epistemology. However, we postpone further discussion of this until we have briefly acknowledged some of the other major positions in contemporary philosophy of science.

Kuhn

Thomas Kuhn, perhaps the best-known contemporary philosopher of science, is perceived by some as maintaining a position in *The Structure of Scientific Revolutions* (1970) that places him philosophically at the opposite pole from Karl Popper. Whereas Popper insists that science is to be understood logically, Kuhn maintains that science should be interpreted psychologically (Robinson, 1981, p. 24) or sociologically. Once a doctoral student in theoretical physics, Kuhn left the field to carry out work in the history and philosophy of science. Spending 1958–1959 at the Center for Advanced Studies in the Behavioral Sciences helped crystallize his views. Whereas his major work is based on the history of the physical sciences, his rationale draws on empirical findings in behavioral science, and others (e.g., Gholson & Barker, 1985; see also Gutting, 1980) apply Kuhn's views to psychology in particular.

Kuhn's basic idea is that psychological and sociological factors are the real determinants of change in allegiance to a theory of the world, and in some sense actually help determine the characteristics of the physical world that is being modeled. The notion is quasi-Kantian in that characteristics of the human mind, or at least of the minds of individual scientists, determine in part what is observed.

Once we have described four of Kuhn's key ideas—paradigms, normal science, anomalies, and scientific revolutions—we point out two criticisms commonly made of his philosophy of science.

For Kuhn, *paradigms* are "universally recognized scientific achievements that for a time provide model problems and solutions to a community of practitioners" (Kuhn, 1970, p. viii). Examples include Newton's *Principia* and Lavoisier's *Chemistry*, "works that served for a time implicitly to define the legitimate problems and methods of a research field" (1970, p. 10). The period devoted to solving the unresolved puzzles within an area following publication of such landmark works as these is what constitutes *normal science*. Inevitably, such periods of normal science turn up *anomalies*, or data that do not fit perfectly within the paradigm (1970, Chapter VI). Although such anomalies may emerge slowly because of the difficulties in perceiving them shared by investigators working within the *Weltanschaung* of a given paradigm, eventually a sufficient number of anomalies are documented to bring the scientific community to a crisis state (1970, Chapter VII). The resolution of the crisis eventually may require a shift to a new paradigm. If so, the transition to the new paradigm is a cataclysmic event. Although some may view the new paradigm as simply subsuming the old, according to Kuhn, the transition—for example, from "geocentrism to heliocentrism, from phlogiston to oxygen, or from corpuscles to waves . . . from Newtonian to Einsteinian mechanics"—necessitated a "revolutionary reorientation," a conceptual transformation that is "decisively destructive of a previously established paradigm" (1970, p. 102).

Although his contributions have been immensely useful in stressing the historical development of science and certain of the psychological determinants of the behavior of scientists, there are, from our perspective, two major related difficulties with Kuhn's philosophy. Kuhn, it should be noted, has attempted to rebut such criticisms [see especially points 5 and 6 in the Postscript added to *The Structure of Scientific Revolutions* (1970, pp. 198–207)]; however, in our view, he has not done so successfully. First, paradigm shifts in Kuhn's system do not occur, because of the objective superiority of one paradigm over the other. In fact, such cannot be demonstrated, because for Kuhn, paradigms are incommensurable. Thus, attempts for proponents of different paradigms to talk to each other result in communication breakdown (Kuhn, 1970, p. 201). Although this view is perhaps not quite consensus formation via mob psychology, as Lakatos (1978) characterizes it, it certainly implies that scientific change is not rational (see Manicas & Secord, 1983; Suppe, 1977). We are too committed to the real effects of psychological variables to be so rash as to assume that all scientific change is rational with regard to the goals of science. In fact, we readily acknowledge not only the role of psychological factors, but also the presence of a fair amount of fraud in science (see Broad & Wade, 1982). However, we believe that these are best understood as deviations from a basically rational model (see Newton-Smith, 1981, pp. 5–13, 148ff.).

Second, we share with many concerns regarding what appears to be Kuhn's relativism. The reading of his work by a number of critics is that Kuhn maintains that there is no fixed reality of nature for science to attempt to more accurately describe. For example, he writes:

> [W]e may . . . have to relinquish the notion, explicit or implicit, that changes of paradigm carry scientists and those who learn from them closer and closer to the truth. . . . The developmental process described in this essay has been a process of evolution *from* primitive beginnings—a process whose successive stages are characterized by an increasingly detailed and refined understanding of nature. But nothing that has been or will be said makes it a process of evolution *toward* anything. (Kuhn, 1970, pp. 170–171)

Kuhn elaborates on this in his Postscript:

> One often hears that successive theories grow ever closer to, or approximate more and more closely to, the truth. Apparently generalizations like that refer not to the puzzle–solutions and the concrete predictions derived from a theory but rather to its ontology, to the match, that is, between the entities with which the theory populates nature and what is "really there."

> Perhaps there is some other way of salvaging the notion of "truth" for application to whole theories, but this one will not do. There is, I think, no theory-independent way to reconstruct phrases like "really there"; the notion of a match between the ontology of a theory and its "real" counterpart in nature now seems to me illusive in principle. (Kuhn, 1970, p. 206)

Perhaps it is the case, as the pessimistic induction suggests, that all theories constructed in this world are false. However, it seems clear that some are less false than others. Does it not make sense to say that the earth revolves around the sun is a closer approximation to the truth of how things really are than to assert that the sun revolves around the earth or that the sun is made of blue cheese? Is it not reasonable to believe that the population mean score on the Wechsler Adult Intelligence Scale is really closer to 100 than it is to 70 or 130? In Kuhn's system, there is no standard to allow such judgments. We concur with Popper (1972) and Newton-Smith (1981, pp. 34–37, 102–124) that this relativism about the nature of the world is unreasonable. In recent years, it has been the postmodernists who have advanced arguments against an objectively knowable world and against a view of science as attempting to use language, including numerical language, to make true statements about the world (Gergen, 2001). Yet the very advancing of an argument for the truth of the position that there is no truth undercuts itself. One is reminded of Socrates' refutation of the self-stultifying nature of the Sophists' skepticism (cf. Robinson, 1981, p. 51); in effect, you claim that no one has any superior right to determine whether any opinion is true or false—if so, why should I accept your position as authoritative?

Although the relativistic position of the postmodernists has certainly attracted numerous followers since the early 1980s, particularly in the humanities, for the most part the sciences, including academic psychology, continue to reject such views (see Haig, 2002; Hofmann, 2002) in favor of the realist perspective we consider next.

Realism

Although there are a multitude of different realist positions in the philosophy of science, certain core elements of realism can be identified (Fine, 1987, p. 359ff.). First, realism holds that a definite world exists, a world populated by entities with particular properties, powers, and relations and "the way the world is" is largely independent of the observer (Harré & Madden, 1975). Second, realist positions maintain that it is possible to obtain a substantial amount of accurate, relatively observer-independent information about the world (Rosenthal & Rosnow, 1991, p. 9), including information about structures and relations among entities as well as what may be observed more superficially. Third, the aim of science is to achieve such knowledge. Fourth, as touched on in our earlier discussion of causality, realist positions maintain that scientific propositions are true or false by virtue of their correspondence or lack or correspondence with the way the world is, independently of ourselves (Newton-Smith, 1981, pp. 28–29). Finally, realist positions tend to be optimistic in their view of science by claiming that the historically generated sequence of theories of a mature science reflect an improvement in terms of the degree of approximation to the truth (Newton-Smith, 1981, p. 39).

These tenets of realism can be more clearly understood by contrasting these positions with alternative views. Although there have been philosophers in previous centuries (e.g., Berkeley, 1685–1753) and in modern times (e.g., Russell, 1950) who question whether the belief in the existence of the physical world was logically justified, not surprisingly, most find arguments for the existence of the world compelling (Russell's argument and rebuttals thereof are helpfully juxtaposed by Oller, 1989). As Einstein tells it, the questioning of the existence of the world is the sort of logical bind one gets oneself into by following Humean skepticism to its logical conclusion (Einstein, 1944, pp. 279–291). Hume correctly saw that our inferences about causal connections, for example, are not logically necessitated by our empirical experience. However, Russell and others extended this skepticism to any knowledge or perception we might have of the physical world. Russell's point is that, assuming causality exists (even though we cannot know it does), our perception represents the end of a causal chain. Trying to reconstruct what "outside" caused that perception is a hazardous process. Even seeing an object such as a tree, if physics is correct, is a complicated and indirect affair. The light reaching the eye comes ultimately from the sun, not the tree, yet you do not say you are seeing the sun. Thus, Russell concludes that "from what we have been saying it is clear that the relation of a percept to the physical object which is supposed to be perceived is vague, approximate and somewhat indefinite. There is no *precise* sense in which we can be said to perceive physical objects" (Russell, 1950, p. 206). And, not only do we not know the true character of the tree we think we are seeing, but also "the colored surfaces which we see cease to exist when we shut our eyes" (Russell, 1914, p. 64). Here, in effect, Russell throws the baby out with the bathwater. The flaw in Russell's argument was forcefully pointed out by Dewey (1916). Dewey's compelling line of reasoning is that Russell's questioning is based on the analysis of perception as the end of a causal chain; however, this presupposes that there is an external object that is initiating the chain, regardless of how poorly its nature may be perceived.

Moving to a consideration of the other tenets of realism, the emphasis on accurate information about the world and the view that scientific theories come to more closely approximate a true description of the world clearly contrasts with relativistic accounts of science that see it as not moving toward anything. In fact, one early realist, C. S. Peirce, developed an influential view of truth and reality that hinges on there being a goal toward which scientific investigations of a question must tend (see Oller, 1989, p. 53ff.). Peirce wrote:

> The question therefore is, how is true belief (or belief in the real) distinguished from false belief (or belief in fiction). . . . The ideas of truth and falsehood, in their full development, appertain exclusively to the scientific method of settling opinion. . . . All followers of science are fully persuaded that the processes of investigation, if only pushed far enough, will give one certain solution to every question to which it can be applied. . . . The opinion which is fated to be ultimately agreed to by all who investigate, is what we mean by the truth and the object represented in this opinion is the real. . . . Our perversity and that of others may indefinitely postpone the settlement of opinion; it might even conceivably cause an arbitrary proposition to be universally accepted as long as the human race should last. Yet even that would not change the nature of the belief, which alone could be the result of investigation, that true opinion must be the one which they would ultimately come to. (Peirce, 1878, pp. 298–300)

Thus, in Peirce's view, for any particular scientific question that has clear meaning, there was one certain solution that would be obtained if only scientific investigation could be carried far enough. This view of science is essentially the same as Einstein's, who likened the process of formulating a scientific theory to the task facing

> a man engaged in solving a well designed word puzzle. He may, it is true, propose any word as the solution; but, there is only one word which really solves the puzzle in all its forms. It is an outcome of faith that nature—as she is perceptible to our five senses—takes the character of such a well formulated puzzle. (Einstein, 1950, p. 64)

Scientific realism may also be contrasted with instrumentalist views. Instrumentalists argue that scientific theories are not intended to be literally true, but are simply convenient summaries or calculational rules for deriving predictions. This distinction is illustrated particularly well by the preface that Osiander added to Copernicus's *The Revolutions of the Heavenly Spheres*:

> It is the duty of the astronomer to compose the history of the celestial motions through careful and skillful observation. Then turning to the causes of these motions or hypotheses about them, he must conceive and devise, since he cannot in any way attain to the true causes, such hypotheses as, being assumed, enable the motions to be calculated correctly from the principles of geometry, for the future as well as the past. The present author [Copernicus] has performed both these duties excellently. For these hypotheses need not be true nor even probable; if they provide a calculus consistent with the observations that alone is sufficient. (Rosen, 1959, pp. 24–25)

Osiander recognized the distinction between factual description and a convenient formula for making predictions and is suggesting that whether the theory describes reality correctly is irrelevant. That is the instrumentalist point of view. However, many scientists, particularly in the physical sciences, tend to regard their theories as descriptions of real entities. This was the case for Copernicus and Kepler regarding the heliocentric theory and more recently for Bohr and Thomson regarding the electron. Besides the inherent plausibility of the realist viewpoint, the greater *explanatory power* of the realist perspective is a major argument offered in support of realism. Such explanatory power is perhaps most impressive when reference to a single set of entities allows predictions across different domains or allows predictions of phenomena that have never been observed but that, subsequently, are confirmed.

Some additional comments must be made about realism at this point, particularly as it relates to the behavioral sciences. First, scientific realism is not something that is an all-or-nothing matter. One might be a realist with regard to certain scientific theories and not with regard to others. Indeed, some have attempted to specify the criteria by which theories should be judged, or at least have been judged historically, as deserving a realistic interpretation (Gardner, 1987; Gingerich, 1973). Within psychology, a realistic interpretation might be given to a brain mechanism that you hypothesize is damaged on the basis of the poor memory performance of a brain-injured patient. However, the states in a mathematical model of memory, such as working memory, may be viewed instrumentally, as simply convenient fictions or metaphors that allow estimation of the probability of recall of a particular item.

A second comment is that realists tend to be emergentists and stress the existence of various levels of reality. Nature is viewed as stratified, with the higher levels possessing new entities with powers and properties that cannot be explained adequately by the lower levels (Bhaskar, 1982, especially Sections 2.5 and 3.3). "From the point of view of emergence, we cannot reduce personality and mind to biological processes or reduce life to physical and chemical processes without loss or damage to the unity and special qualities of the entity with which we began" (Titus, 1964, p. 250). Thus, psychology from the realist perspective is not in danger of losing its field of study to ardent sociobiologists any more than biologists would lose their object of inquiry if organic life could be produced by certain physical and chemical manipulations in the laboratory. Neither people nor other living things would cease to be real, no matter what the scientific development. Elements of lower orders are just as real, no more or less, than the comprehensive entities formed out of them. Both charged particles and thunderstorms, single cells and single adults exist and have powers and relations with other entities at their appropriate levels of analysis.

Because of the many varieties of realism—for example, critical realism (Cook & Campbell, 1979), metaphysical realism (Popper, 1972), and transcendental realism (Bhaskar, 1975)—and because our concern regarding philosophy of science is less with ontology than with epistemological method, we do not attempt to summarize the realist approach further. The interested reader is referred to the article by Manicas and Secord (1983) for a useful summary and references to the literature.

Summary

As is perhaps already clear, our own perspective is to hold to a realist position ontologically and a temperate rationalist position epistemologically of the neo-Popperian variety. The perspective is realist because it assumes phenomena and processes exist outside of our experience and that theories can be true or false, and among false theories, false to a greater or lesser extent, depending on the degree of correspondence between the theory and the reality. Naturally, however, our knowledge of this reality is limited by the nature of induction—thus, it behooves us to be critical of the strength of our inferences about the nature of that reality (see Cook & Campbell, 1979).

We endorse a rational model as the ideal for how science should proceed. Given the progress associated with the method, there is reason to think that the methodology of science has, in general, resulted in choices between competing theories primarily on the strength of the supporting evidence. However, our rationalism is temperate in that we recognize that there is no set of completely specifiable rules defining the scientific method that can guarantee success and that weight should be given to empirically based inductive arguments even though they do not logically compel belief (see Newton-Smith, 1981, especially p. 268ff.).

We believe the statistical methods that are the primary subject matter of this book are consistent with this perspective and more compatible with this perspective than with some others. For example, thinking it is meaningful to attempt to detect a difference between fixed-population means seems inconsistent with a relativistic perspective. Similarly, using statistical methods rather than relying on one's ability to make immediate judgments about particular facts seems inconsistent with a logical positivist approach. In fact, one can view the primary role of statistical analysis as an efficient means for summarizing evidence (see Abelson, 1995; Rosenthal & Rubin, 1985; Scarr, 1997): Rather than being a royal road to a positively certain scientific conclusion, inferential statistics is a method for accomplishing a more modest but nonetheless critical goal, namely quantifying the evidence or uncertainty relevant to a particular statistical conclusion. Doing this well is certainly not all there is to science, which is part of what we are trying to make clear, but it is a first step in a process that must be viewed from a broader perspective. Because there is no cookbook methodology that can take you from a data summary to a correct theory, it behooves the would-be scientist to think through the philosophical position from which the evidence of particular studies is to be viewed. Doing so provides you with a framework within which to decide if the evidence available permits you to draw conclusions that you are willing to defend publicly. That the result of a statistical test is only one, albeit important, consideration in this process of reaching substantive conclusions and making generalizations is something we attempt to underscore further in the remainder of this chapter.

THREATS TO THE VALIDITY OF INFERENCES FROM EXPERIMENTS

Having reviewed the perils of drawing inductive inferences at a philosophical level, we now turn to a consideration of threats to the validity of inferences at a more practical level. The classic treatment of the topic of how things can go wrong in attempting to make inferences from experiments was provided in the monograph by Campbell and Stanley (1963). Generations of graduate students around the country memorized their "threats to validity." An updated and expanded version of their volume addressing many of the same issues, but also covering the details of certain statistical procedures, appeared 16 years later authored by Cook and Campbell (1979). Very recently, the third instantiation of a volume on quasi-experimentation co-authored by Donald Campbell appeared (Shadish et al., 2002), which Campbell worked on until his death in 1996. Judd and Kenny (1981) and Krathwohl (1985) have provided very useful and readable discussions of these validity notions of Campbell and his associates. Cronbach's (1982) book also provides a wealth of insights into problems of making valid inferences, but like Cook and Campbell (1979), it presumes a considerable amount of knowledge on the part of the reader. (For a brief summary of the various validity typologies, see Mark, 1986).

For our part, we begin the consideration of the practical problems of drawing valid inferences by distinguishing among the principal types of validity discussed in this literature. Then, we suggest a way for thinking in general about threats to validity and for attempting to avoid such pitfalls.

Types of Validity

When a clinician reads an article in a journal about a test of a new procedure and then contemplates applying it in his or her own practice, a whole series of logical steps must all be correct for this to be an appropriate application of the finding. (Krathwohl, 1985, offers the apt analogy of links in a chain for these steps.) In short, a problem could arise because the conclusion or design of the initial study was flawed or because the extrapolation to a new situation is inappropriate. Campbell and Stanley (1963) referred to these potential problems as threats to internal and external validity, respectively. Cook and Campbell (1979) subsequently suggested that, actually, four types should be distinguished: statistical conclusion validity, internal validity, construct validity, and external validity. Recently, Shadish et al. (2002) suggested refinements but maintained this fourfold validity typology. We discuss each in turn, but first a word or two by way of general introduction.

Validity means essentially truth or correctness, a correspondence between a proposition describing how things work in the world and how they really work (see Russell, 1919b; Campbell, 1986, p. 73). Naturally, we never know with certainty if our interpretations are valid, but we try to proceed with the design and analysis of our research in such a way to make the case for our conclusions as plausible and compelling as possible.

The propositions or interpretations that abound in the discussion and conclusion sections of behavioral science articles are about how things work in general. As Shadish et al. (2002) quip, "Most experiments are highly local but have general aspirations" (p. 18). Typical or modal experiments involve particular people manifesting the effects of particular treatments on particular measures at a particular time and place. Modal conclusions involve few, if any, of these particulars. Most pervasively, the people (or patients, children, rats, classes, or, most generally, units of analysis) are viewed as a sample from a larger population of interest. The conclusions are about the population. The venerable tradition of hypothesis testing is built on this foundational assumption: One unit of analysis differs from another. The variability among units, however, provides the yardstick for making the statistical judgment of whether a difference in group means is "real."

What writers such as Campbell have stressed is that not just the units or subjects, but also the other components of our experiments should be viewed as representative of larger domains, in somewhat the same way that a random sample of subjects is representative of a population. Specifically, Cronbach (1982) suggested that there are four building blocks to an experiment: units, treatments, observations or measures, and settings. We typically want to generalize along all four dimensions, to a larger domain of units, treatments, observations, and settings, or as Cronbach puts it, we study "utos" but want to draw conclusions about "UTOS." For example, a specific multifaceted treatment program (t) for problem drinkers could have involved the same facets with different emphases (e.g., more or less time with the therapist) or different facets not represented initially (e.g., counseling for family members and close friends) and yet still be regarded as illustrating the theoretical class of treatments of interest, controlled drinking (T). (In Chapter 10, we discuss statistical procedures that assume the treatments in a study are merely representative of other treatments of that type that could have been used, but more often the problem of generalization is viewed as a logical or conceptual problem, instead of a statistical problem.)

Turning now to the third component of experiments—namely the observations or measures—it is perhaps easier because of the familiarity of the concepts of "measurement error" and "validity of tests," to think of the measures instead of the treatments used in experiments as fallible representatives of a domain. Anyone who has worked on a large-scale clinical research project has probably been impressed by the number of alternative measures available for assessing the various psychological traits or states of interest in that study. Finally, regarding the component of the setting in which experiments take place, our comments about the uniformity of nature underscore what every historian or traveler knows but that writers of discussion sections sometimes ignore: What is true about behavior for one time and place may not be universally true. In sum, an idea to remember as you read about the various types of validity is how they relate to the question of whether a component of a study—such as the units, treatments, measures, or setting—truly reflects the domain of theoretical interest.

Statistical Conclusion Validity

The question to be answered in statistical conclusion validity is, "Was the original statistical inference correct?" That is, did the investigators reach a correct conclusion about whether a relationship between the variables exists in the population or about the extent of the relationship? Thus, statistical conclusions are about population parameters—such as means or correlations—whether they are equal or what their numerical values are. So in considering statistical conclusion validity, we are not concerned with whether there is a causal relationship between the variables, but whether there is any relationship, be it causal or not.

One of the ways in which a study might be an insecure base from which to extrapolate is that the conclusion reached by that study about a statistical hypothesis it tested might be wrong. As you likely learned in your first course in statistics, there are two types of errors or ways in which this can happen: Type I errors, or false positives—that is, concluding there is a relationship between two variables when, in fact, there is none—and Type II errors, or false negatives—that is, failing to detect a relationship that in fact exists in the population. One can think of Type I errors as being gullible or overeager, whereas Type II errors can be thought of as being blind or overly cautious (Rosnow & Rosenthal, 1989). Because the nominal alpha level or probability of a Type I error is fairly well established by convention within a discipline—for example, at .05—the critical issue in statistical conclusion validity is power. The power of a test is its sensitivity or ability to detect relationships that exist in the population, and so it is the complement of a Type II error. As such, *power* in a statistical sense means sensitivity or ability to detect what is present. Studies with low power are like "trying to read small type in dim light" (Rosnow & Rosenthal, 1989). In conventional terms, power is the probability of rejecting the null hypothesis when it is false and equals 1 minus the probability of a Type II error.

The threats to the validity of statistical conclusions are then of two general kinds: a liberal bias, or a tendency to be overly optimistic about the presence of a relationship or exaggerate its strength; and a conservative bias, or a tendency to be overly pessimistic about the absence of a relationship or underestimate its strength.

As Cohen (1988) stresses, one of the most pervasive threats to the validity of the statistical conclusions reached in the behavioral sciences is low power. It is critical in planning experiments and evaluating results to consider the likelihood that a given design would detect an effect of a given size in the population. As discussed in detail beginning in Chapter 3, there are a variety of ways to estimate how strong the relationship is between the independent variable and the dependent variable, and using this, to compute a numerical value of the power of a study. Our concern here, however, is with why statistical conclusions are often incorrect; several reasons can be enumerated.

Studies typically have low power because sample sizes used are too small for the situation. Because the number required depends on the specifics of the research problem, one cannot specify in general a minimum number of subjects to have per condition. However, although other steps can be taken, increasing the number of participants is the simplest solution, conceptually at least, to the problem of low power.

Another important reason for low power is the use of an unreliable dependent variable. Reliability, of course, has to do with consistency and accuracy. Scores on variables are assumed to be the result of a combination of systematic or true score variation and random error variation. For example, your score on a multiple-choice quiz is determined in part by what you know and in part by other factors, such as your motivation and your luck in guessing answers you do not know. Variables are unreliable, in a psychometric sense, when the random error variation component is large relative to the true score variation component (see Judd & Kenny, 1981, p. 111ff., for a clear introduction to the idea of reliability).

We acknowledge, as Nicewander and Price (1983) point out, that there are cases in which the less reliable of two possible dependent variables can lead to greater power, for example, because a larger treatment effect on that variable may more than offset its lower reliability. However, other things being equal, the lower the reliability of a dependent measure is, the less sensitive it will be in detecting treatment effects. Solving problems of unreliability is not easy, in part because there is always the possibility that altering a test in an attempt to make it more reliable might change what it is measuring as well as its precision of measurement. However, the rule of thumb, as every standard psychometrics text makes clear (e.g., Nunnally, 1978; see Maxwell, 1994), is that increasing the length of tests increases their reliability. The longer the quiz, the less likely you can pass simply by guessing.

Other reasons why unexplained variability in the dependent variable and hence the probability of a Type II error may be unacceptably high include implementing the treatment in slightly different ways from one subject to the next and failure to include important explanatory variables in your model of performance for the situation. Typically, in behavioral science studies, who the participant happens to be is a more important determinant of how he or she performs on the experimental task than the treatment to which the person is assigned. Thus, including a measure of the relevant individual differences among participants in your statistical model, or experimentally controlling for such differences, can often greatly increase your power. (Chapters 9 and 11–14 discuss methods for dealing with such individual differences.)

Maxwell, Cole, Arvey, and Salas (1991) provide a helpful discussion of these issues, comparing alternative methods of increasing power. In particular, they focus on the relative benefits of lengthening the posttest and including a pretest in a design. These are complementary strategies for reducing unexplained variability in the dependent variable. When the dependent measure is of only moderate or low reliability, as may be the case with a locally developed assessment, greater gains in power are realized by using a longer and hence more reliable posttest. When the dependent measure has high reliability, then including a pretest that can be used to control for individual differences among subjects will increase power more.

The primary cause of Type I error rates being inflated over the nominal or stated level is that the investigator has performed multiple tests of the same general hypothesis. Statistical methods exist for adjusting for the number of tests you are performing and are considered at various points in this text (see, for example, Chapter 5 on multiple comparisons). Violations of statistical assumptions can also affect Type I and Type II error rates. As we discuss at the end of Chapter 3, violating assumptions can result in either liberal or conservative biases. Finally, sample estimates of how large an effect is, or how much variability in the dependent variable is accounted for, tend to overestimate population values. Appropriate adjustments are available and are covered in Chapters 3 and 7. A summary of these threats to statistical conclusion validity and possible remedies is presented in Table 1.1.

TABLE 1.1
THREATS TO STATISTICAL CONCLUSIONS AND SOME REMEDIES

Threats Causing Overly Conservative Bias	Remedies and References	
Low power as a result of small sample size	Increase sample size	Chapters 3ff; Cohen, 1988
Low power due to increased error because of unreliability of measures	Improve measurement (e.g., by lengthening tests)	Chapter 9; Maxwell, 1994; Maxwell, Cole, Arvey, & Salas, 1991
Low power as a result of high variability because of diversity of subjects	Control for individual differences: In analysis by controlling for covariates In design by blocking, matching, or using repeated measures	Chapters 9 and 11ff.; Maxwell, Delaney, & Dill, 1984
Low power due to violation of statistical assumptions	Transform data or use different method of analysis	Chapter 3; McClelland, 2000
Threats Causing Overly Liberal Bias		
Repeated statistical tests	Use adjusted test procedures	Chapter 5
Violation of statistical assumptions	Transform data or use different method of analysis	Chapter 3
Biased estimates of effects	Use corrected values to estimate effects in population	Chapters 3ff.

Internal Validity

Statistical tests allow one to make conclusions about whether the mean of the dependent variable (typically referred to as variable Y) is the same in different treatment populations. If the statistical conclusion is that the means are different, one can then move to the question of what caused the difference, with one of the candidates being the independent variable (call it variable X) as it was implemented in the study. The issue of internal validity is, "Is there a causal relationship between variable X and variable Y, regardless of what X and Y are theoretically supposed to represent?" If variable X is a *true* independent variable and the statistical conclusion is valid, then internal validity is to a large extent assured (appropriate caveats follow). By a *true independent variable,* we mean one for which the experimenter can and does independently determine the level of the variable that each participant experiences— that is, assignment to conditions is carried out independently of any other characteristic of the participant or of other variables under investigation. Internal validity is, however, a serious issue in quasi-experimental designs in which this condition is not met. Most commonly, the problem is using intact or self-selected groups of subjects. For example, in an educational psychology study, one might select the fifth-grade class in one school to receive an experimental curriculum and use the fifth-grade class from another school as a control group. Any differences observed on a common posttest might be attributed to preexisting differences between students in the two schools rather than your educational treatment. This threat to internal validity is termed *selection bias* because subjects were selected from different intact groups. A selection bias is an example of the more general problem of a *confound*, defined as an extraneous variable that is correlated with or, literally, "found with" the levels of the variable of interest. Perhaps less obvious is the case in which an attribute of the subjects is investigated as one of the factors in an experiment. Assume that depressed and nondepressed groups of subjects were formed by scores on an instrument such as the Beck Depression Inventory; then, it is observed that the depressed group performs significantly worse on a memory task. One might like to claim that the difference in memory performance was the result of the difference in level of depression;

however, one encounters the same logical difficulty here as in the study with intact classrooms. Depressed subjects may differ from nondepressed subjects in many ways besides depression that are relevant to performance on the memory task.

Internal validity threats are typically thus "third" variable problems. Another variable besides X and Y may be responsible for either an apparent relationship or an apparent lack of a relationship between X and Y.

A number of other threats to internal validity arise when subjects are assessed repeatedly over time,[5] or participate in what is called a *longitudinal* or *repeated measures design*. The most intractable difficulties in making a causal inference here arise when there is just a single group whose performance in being monitored over time, in what Campbell has referred to as a *one-group pretest–posttest design*, denoted $O_1 X O_2$ to indicate a treatment intervenes between two assessments. One of the most common threats to internal validity is *attrition*, or the problem that arises when possibly different types of people drop out of various conditions of a study or have missing data for one or more time periods. The threats to validity caused by missing data are almost always a concern in longitudinal designs. Chapter 15 presents methodology especially useful in the face of missing data in such designs. *Cross-sectional designs* or designs that involve only one assessment of each subject can often avoid problems of missing data, especially in laboratory settings. However, the internal validity of even cross-sectional designs can be threatened by missing data, especially in field settings, for example, if a subject fails to show up for his or her assigned treatment or refuses to participate in the particular treatment or measurement procedure assigned. Attempts to control statistically for variables on which participants are known to differ can be carried out, but face interpretational difficulties, as we discuss in Chapter 9. West and Sagarin (2000) present a very readable account of possible solutions for handling missing data in randomized experiments, including subject losses that arise from noncompliance as well as attrition.

Other threats arising in longitudinal designs include *testing*. This threatens internal validity when a measurement itself might bring about a change in performance, such as when assessing the severity of participants' drinking problem affects their subsequent behavior. Such measures are said to be *reactive*. *Regression* is a particular problem in remediation programs in which subjects may be selected based on their low scores on some variable. *History* threatens the attribution of changes to the treatment when events outside the experimental setting occur that might cause a change in subjects' performance. *Maturation* refers to changes that are not caused by some external event, but by processes such as fatigue, growth, or natural recovery. So, when only one group experiences the treatment, the appropriate attribution may be that "time heals." Thus, the potential remedy for these last four artifacts shown in Table 1.2 that are characteristic of one-group longitudinal designs is the addition of a similarly selected and measured but randomly assigned group of control participants who do not experience the treatment.

Estimating the internal validity of a study is largely a thought problem in which you attempt to systematically think through the plausibility of various threats relevant to your situation.[6] On occasion, one can anticipate a given threat and gather information in the course of a study relevant to it. For example, questionnaires or other attempts to measure the exact nature of the treatment and control conditions experienced by subjects may be useful in determining whether extra-experimental factors differentially affected subjects in different conditions.

Finally, a term from Campbell (1986) is useful for distinguishing internal validity from the other types remaining to be considered. Campbell suggests it might be clearer to call internal validity "local molar (pragmatic, atheoretical) causal validity" (p. 69). Although a complex phrase, this focuses attention on points deserving of emphasis. The concern of internal validity is causal in that you are asking what was responsible for the change in the dependent variable. The view of causes is molar—that is, at the level of a treatment package, or viewing the

TABLE 1.2
THREATS TO INTERNAL VALIDITY

Threats	Definition
Selection bias	Participant characteristics confounded with treatment conditions because of use of intact or self-selected participants; or more generally, whenever predictor variables represent measured characteristics as opposed to independently manipulated treatments.
Attrition	Differential drop out across conditions at one or more time points that may be responsible for differences.
Testing	Altered performance as a result of a prior measure or assessment instead of the assigned treatment.
Regression	The changes over time expected in the performance of subjects, selected because of their extreme scores on a variable, that occur for statistical reasons but might incorrectly be attributed to the intervening treatment.
Maturation	Observed changes as a result of ongoing, naturally occurring processes rather than treatment effects.
History	Events, in addition to an assigned treatment, to which subjects are exposed between repeated measurements that could influence their performance.

treatment condition as a complex hodgepodge of all that went on in that part of the study—thus emphasizing that the question is *not* what the "active ingredient" of the treatment is. Rather, the concern is pragmatic, atheoretical—did the treatment, for whatever reason, cause a change, did it work? Finally, the concern is local: Did it work here? With internal validity, one is not concerned with generalization.

Construct Validity

The issue regarding construct validity is, Given there is a valid causal relationship, is the interpretation of the constructs involved in that relationship correct?[7] Construct validity pertains to both causes and effects. That is, the question for both the independent and dependent variables as implemented in the study is, Can I generalize from this one set of operations to a referent construct? What one investigator labels as construct *A* causing a change in construct *C*, another may interpret as an effect of construct *B* on construct *C*, or of construct *A* on construct *D*, or even of *B* on *D*. Showing a person photographs of a dying person may arouse what one investigator interprets as death anxiety and another interprets as compassion. Threats to construct validity are a pervasive and difficult problem in psychological research. We addressed this issue implicitly earlier in this chapter in commenting on the meaning of theoretical terms. Since Cronbach and Meehl's (1955) seminal paper on construct validity in the area of assessment, something approaching a general consensus has been achieved that the specification of constructs in psychology is limited by the richness, generality, and precision of our theories. Given the current state of psychological theorizing, it is understandable why a minority continue to argue for strategies such as adopting a strict operationalism or attempting to avoid theorizing altogether. However, the potential for greater explanatory power offered by theoretical constructs places most investigators in the position of having to meet the problem of construct validity head-on rather than sidestepping it by abandoning theoretical constructs.

The basic problem in construct validity is the possibility "that the operations which are meant to represent a particular cause or effect construct can be construed in terms of more than one construct, each of which is stated at the same level of reduction" (Cook & Campbell, 1979, p. 59). The qualifier regarding the level of reduction refers to the fact that alternative explanations of a phenomenon can be made at different levels of analysis, and that sort of multiplicity of explanation does not threaten construct validity. This is most clearly true across disciplines. One's support for a political position could be explained at either a sociological level or by invoking a psychological analysis, for example, of attitude formation. Similarly, showing there is a physiological correlate of some behavior does not mean the behavioral phenomenon is to be understood as nothing but the outworking of physiological causes.

Some examples of specific types of artifacts serve to illustrate the confounding that can threaten construct validity. A prime example of a threat to construct validity is the experimenter-bias effect demonstrated by Rosenthal (1976). This effect involves the impact of the researcher's expectancies and, in particular, the transmission of that expectancy to the subject in such a way that performance on the dependent variable is affected. Thus, when the experimenter is not blind to the hypothesis under investigation, the role of experimenter bias must be considered, as well as the nominal treatment variable, in helping to determine the magnitude of the differences between groups.

Another set of threats to construct validity arises in situations in which there are clear, unintended by-products of the treatment as implemented that involve causal elements that were not part of the intended structure of the treatment (cf. Shadish et al., 2002, p. 95). One example is *treatment diffusion*, which can occur when there is the possibility of communication during the course of a study among subjects from different treatment conditions. Thus, the mixture of effects of portions of different treatments that subjects functionally receive, filtered through their talkative friends, can be quite different from the single treatment they were nominally supposed to receive. This type of threat can be a particularly serious problem in long-term studies such as those comparing alternative treatment programs for clinical populations. Another such threat is termed *resentful demoralization.* For example, a waiting-list control group may be demoralized by learning that others are receiving effective treatments while they are receiving nothing. Furthermore, in a variety of other areas of psychology in which studies tend to involve brief treatment interventions but in which different people may participate over the course of an academic semester, the character of a treatment can be affected greatly by dissemination of information over time. Students who learn from previous participants the nature of the deception involved in the critical condition of a social psychology study may experience a considerably different condition than naive subjects would experience. These participants may well perform differently than participants in other conditions, but the cause may have more to do with the possibly distorted information they received from their peers than the nominal treatment to which they were assigned.

Two major pitfalls to avoid in one's attempt to minimize threats to construct validity can be cited: *inadequate preoperational explication* of the construct and *mono-operation bias* or using only one set of operations to implement the construct (Cook & Campbell, 1979, p. 64ff.; Shadish et al., 2002, p. 73ff.). First, regarding explication, the question is, "What are the essential features of the construct for your theoretical purposes?" For example, if you wish to study social support, does your conceptual definition include the perceptions and feelings of the recipient of the support or simply the actions of the provider of the support? Explicating a construct involves consideration not only of the construct you want to assess, but also the other similar constructs from which you hope to distinguish your construct (see Campbell & Fiske, 1959; Judd & Kenny, 1981). Second, regarding mono-operation bias, using only a single dependent variable to assess a psychological construct typically runs the risk of both underrepresenting the construct and containing irrelevancies. For example, anxiety is typically regarded as a multidimensional construct subsuming behavioral, cognitive, and physiological components. Because measures of these dimensions are much less than perfectly correlated, if one's concern is with anxiety in general, then using only a single measure is likely to be misleading. The structural equation modeling methods that have become popular since the early 1980s provide a means for explicitly incorporating such fallible indicators of latent constructs into one's analytical models (see Appendix B).

External Validity

The final type of validity we consider refers to the stability across other contexts of the causal relationship observed in a given study. The issue in external validity is, "Can I generalize this finding across populations, or settings, or time?" As mentioned in our discussion of the uniformity of nature, this is more of an issue in psychology than in the physical sciences.

A central concern with regard to external validity is typically the heterogeneity and representativeness of the sample of people participating in the study. Unfortunately, most research in the human sciences is carried out using the sample of subjects that happens to be conveniently available at the time. Thus, there is no assurance that the sample is representative of the initial target population, not to mention some other population to which another researcher may want to generalize. In Chapter 2, we consider one perspective on analyzing data from convenience samples that, unlike most statistical procedures, does not rely on the assumption of random sampling from a population.

For now, it is sufficient to note that the concern with external validity is that the effects of a treatment observed in a particular study may not be obtained consistently. For example, a classroom demonstration of a mnemonic technique that had repeatedly shown the mnemonic method superior to a control condition in a sophomore-level class actually resulted in worse performance than the control group in a class of students taking a remedial instruction course. Freshmen had been assigned to take the remedial course in part on the basis of their poor reading comprehension, and apparently failed to understand the somewhat complicated written instructions given to the students in the mnemonic condition.

One partial solution to the problem of external validity is, where possible, to take steps to assure that the study uses a heterogeneous group of persons, settings, and times. Note that this is at odds with one of the recommendations we made regarding statistical conclusion validity. In fact, what is good for the precision of a study, such as standardizing conditions and working with a homogeneous sample of subjects, is often detrimental to the generality of the findings. The other side of the coin is that although heterogeneity makes it more difficult to obtain statistically significant findings, once they are obtained, it allows generalization of these findings with greater confidence to other situations. In the absence of such heterogeneity or with a lack of observations with the people, settings, or times to which you wish to apply a finding, your generalization must rest on your ideas of what is theoretically important about these differences from the initial study (Campbell, 1986). Much more in-depth discussion of the issues of causal generalization across settings is presented by Shadish et al. (2002).

Conceptualizing and Controlling for Threats to Validity

As discussed by Campbell (1969), a helpful way to think about most of the artifacts that we have considered is in terms of incomplete designs or of designs having more factors than originally planned. For example, consider a two-group study in which a selection bias was operating. Because the two treatment groups involved, in essence, subjects from two different populations, one could view the groups as but two of the four possible combinations of treatment and population. Similarly, when a treatment is delivered, there are often some incidental aspects of the experience that are not an inherent part of the treatment, but that are not present in the control condition. These instrumental incidentals may be termed the *vehicle* used to deliver the treatment. Once again, a two-group study might be thought of as just two of the four possible combinations: the "pure" treatment being present or absent combined with the vehicle being present or absent (Figure 1.2).

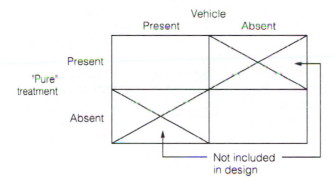

FIG. 1.2.   Original design.

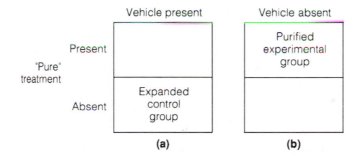

FIG. 1.3.   Preferred designs.

In the case of such confoundings, a more valid experimental design may be achieved by using two groups that differ along only one dimension, namely that of the treatment factor. In the case of selection bias, this obviously would mean sampling subjects from only one population. In the case of the vehicle factor, one conceivably could either expand the control group to include the irrelevant details that were previously unique to the experimental group or "purify" the experimental group by eliminating the distinguishing but unnecessary incidental aspects of the treatment (Figure 1.3). Both options may not be available in practice. For example, in a physiological study involving ablation of a portion of the motor cortex of a rat, the surgical procedure of opening the skull may be a part of the ablation treatment that cannot be eliminated practically. In such a case, the appropriate controls are not untreated animals, but an expanded control group: animals who go through a sham surgery involving the same anesthetic, opening of the skull, and so on, but who do not experience any brain damage.

Regarding the issues having to do with increasing the generality of one's findings, viewing simple designs as portions of potentially larger designs is again a useful strategy. One might expand a two-group design, for example, by using all combinations of the treatment factor and a factor having levels corresponding to subpopulations of interest (Figures 1.4 and 1.5). If, in your psychology class of college sophomores, summer school students behave differently on your experimental task than regular academic year students, include both types to buttress the generality of your conclusions.

Finally, with regard to both construct validity and external validity, the key principle for protecting against threats to validity is *heteromethod replication* (Campbell, 1969, p. 365ff.). Replication of findings is, of course, a desirable way of demonstrating the reliability of the effects of an independent variable on a dependent variable. Operationism would suggest that

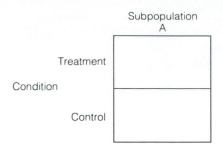

FIG. 1.4.   Original design.

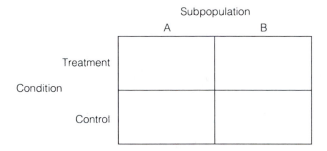

FIG. 1.5.   Expanded design.

one should carry out the details of the original design in exactly the same fashion as was done initially. The point we are making, however, is that construct and external validity are strengthened if the details of procedure deemed theoretically irrelevant are varied from one replication to the next. (In Chapter 3, we cover how statistical tests may be carried out to determine if the effects in one study are replicated in another.) Campbell (1969, p. 366) even goes so far as to entertain the idea that every Ph.D. dissertation in the behavioral sciences be required to implement the treatment in at least two different ways and measure the effects of the treatment using two different methods. Although methodologically a good suggestion for assuring construct and external validity, Campbell rejects this idea as likely being too discouraging in practice, because, he speculates, "full confirmation would almost never be found" (1969, p. 366).

Whether simple or complex, experimental designs require statistical methods for summarizing and interpreting data, and it is toward the development and explication of those methods that we move in subsequent chapters.

EXERCISES

*1. Cite three flaws in the Baconian view that science can proceed in a purely objective manner.

2. a. Are there research areas in psychology in which the assumption of the uniformity of nature regarding experimental material is not troublesome? That is, in what kinds of research is it the case that between-subject differences are so inconsequential that they can be ignored?
   b. In other situations, although how one person responds may be drastically different from another, there are still arguments in favor of doing single-subject research. Cite an example of such a situation and suggest certain of the arguments in favor of such a strategy.

*3. Regarding the necessity of philosophical assumptions, much of 20th-century psychology was dominated by an empiricist, materialist monism—that is, the view that matter is all that exists—the only way one can come to know is by empirical observation. Some have even suggested that this position is necessitated by empirical findings. In what sense does attempting to prove materialism by way of empirical methods beg the question?

4. How might one assess the simplicity of a particular mathematical model?

5. Cite an example of what Meehl terms an *auxiliary theory* that must be relied on to carry out a test of a particular content theory of interest.

6. Explain why, in Popper's view, falsification of theories is critical for advancing science. Why are theories not rejected immediately on failure to obtain predicted results?

7. Assume a study finds that children who watch more violent television programs are more violent themselves in a playground situation than children who report watching less violent television programs. Does this imply that watching violence on television causes violent behavior? What other explanations are possible in this situation? How could the inference of the alleged causal relationship be strengthened?

8. Regarding statistical conclusion validity, sample size, as noted in the text, is a critical variable. Complete the following:
   a. Increasing sample size _____ the power of a test.
      increases   decreases   does not affect
   b. Increasing sample size _____ the probability of a Type II error.
      increases   decreases   does not affect
   c. Increasing sample size _____ the probability of a Type I error.
      increases   decreases   does not affect

*9. A learning theorist asserts, "If frustration theory is correct, then partially reinforced animals will persist longer in responding during extinction than will continuously reinforced animals." What is the contrapositive of this assertion?

*10. A national study involving a sample of more than two thousand individuals included a comparison of the performance of public and Catholic high school seniors on a mathematics achievement test. (Summary data are reported by Wolfle, L. M. (1987). "Enduring cognitive effects of public and private schools." *Educational Researcher, 16*(4), 5–11.) The statistics on the mathematics test for the two groups of students were as follows:

	High School	
	Public	*Catholic*
Mean	12.13	15.13
SD	7.44	6.52

Would you conclude from such data that Catholic high schools are doing a more effective job in educating students in mathematics? What additional information could make this explanation of the difference in mean scores more or less compelling?

2

Introduction to the Fisher Tradition

Discussion of potential threats to the validity of an experiment and issues relating to philosophy of science may, at first blush, seem unrelated to statistics. And, in fact, some presentations of statistics may border on numerology—whereby certain rituals performed with a set of numbers are thought to produce meaningful conclusions, with the only responsibility for thought by the investigator being the need to avoid errors in the calculations. This nonthinking attitude is perhaps made more prevalent by the ready availability of computers and statistical software. For all their advantages in terms of computational speed and accuracy, these conveniences may mislead some into thinking that, because calculations are no longer an issue, there is nothing more to statistics than learning the syntax for your software or which options to "click." It thus becomes easier to avoid facing the central issue squarely: How do I defend my answers to the scientific questions of interest in this situation?

However, statistical decisions, appropriately conceived, are essentially organized arguments. This is perhaps most obvious when the derivations of the statistical tests themselves are carried out in a mathematically rigorous fashion. (Although the point of the argument might be totally obscure to all but the most initiated, that it is a highly structured deductive argument is clear enough.) Thus, in a book on linear models, one could begin from first principles and proceed to prove the theorems necessary for use of the F tests and the associated probability tables. That is the approach taken in mathematical statistics texts (see, e.g., one of the standard sources such as the book by Freund & Walpole, 1980; Hogg & Craig, 1978; Mood, Graybill, & Boes, 1974). It is, of course, possible to derive the theory without showing that it has any practical utility for analyzing data, although certain texts attempt to handle both (e.g., Graybill, 1976). However, rigorous treatment of linear models requires mastery of calculus at a level that not many students of the behavioral sciences have achieved. Fortunately, this does not preclude acquiring a thorough understanding of how statistics in general and linear models in particular can be used effectively in behavioral science research.

The view of statistics as a kind of rational argument was one that the prime mover in the area, Sir Ronald A. Fisher (1890–1962), heartily endorsed. In fact, Fisher reportedly was dismayed that, by the end of his life, statistics was being taught "essentially as mathematics" with an overelaborate notation apparently designed to make it appear difficult (Cochran, 1967, p. 1461). Fisher, however, saw statistics as being much more closely related to the experimental sciences in which the methods actually were to be used. He developed new methods in response to the practical needs he saw in serving as a consultant to researchers in various departments related to the biological sciences. A major portion of Fisher's contributions to mathematical statistics and to the design and analysis of experiments came early in his career, when he was chief statistician at the Rothamsted Agricultural Station. Fisher, who later served as Galton Professor at the University of London and as professor of genetics at the University of Cambridge, was responsible for laying the foundations for a substantial part of the modern discipline of statistics. Certainly, the development and dissemination of the analysis of variance and the *F* test named for him were directly due to Fisher. His writings, which span half a century, provide masterful insights into the process of designing and interpreting experiments. His *Design of Experiments* (1935/1971) in particular can be read with great profit, regardless of mathematical background, and illustrates very effectively the close link that should exist between logical analysis and computations. It is the purpose of this chapter to provide a brief introduction to the kind of statistical reasoning that characterizes the tradition that Fisher set in motion.

We should note that the Fisherian approach has not been without its detractors, either in his day or in ours. Although current widely used procedures of testing statistical hypotheses represent an amalgam of Fisher's approach with that of others (namely Jerzy Neyman and Egon Pearson; see Gigerenzer, 1993), Fisher was the most important figure in the modern development of statistics, if not the prime mover in the area (cf. Huberty, 1991), and thus it is useful to gain an appreciation for some of his basic ideas regarding statistical reasoning. One purpose in tracing the rationale of hypothesis testing to its origins is to place our presentation of statistical methods in some broader historical context, in something of the same way that Chapter 1 attempted to locate statistical reasoning within a broader philosophical context. By highlighting some of the past and present controversy regarding statistical reasoning, we hope to communicate something of the dynamic and evolving nature of statistical methodology.

We begin by examining one of the most fundamental ideas in statistics. A critical ingredient in any statistical test is determining the probability, assuming the operation of only chance factors, of obtaining a more extreme result than that indicated by the observed value of the test statistic. For example, in carrying out a one-sample z test manually in an elementary statistics course, one of the final steps is to translate the observed value of z into a probability (e.g., using a table like that in Appendix A-12). The probability being sought, which is called a *p value*, is the probability of obtaining a z score more extreme than that observed. Whenever the test statistic follows a continuous distribution like the z, t, or F, any treatment of this problem that goes deeper than "you look it up in the table" requires the use of rather messy mathematical derivations. Fortunately, the same kind of argument can be developed in detail quite easily if inferences are based on a discrete probabilistic analysis of a situation rather than by making reference to a continuous distribution. Thus, we illustrate the development of a statistical test by using an example relying on a discrete probability distribution.[1] First, however, let us consider why any probability distribution is an appropriate tool for interpreting experiments.

"INTERPRETATION AND ITS REASONED BASIS"

What Fisher hoped to provide was an integrated methodology of experimental design and statistical procedures that together would satisfy "all logical requirements of the complete process of adding to knowledge by experimentation" (Fisher, 1935/1971, p. 3). Thus, Fisher was a firm believer in the idea that inductive inferences, although uncertain, could be made rigorously, with the nature and degree of uncertainty itself being specified. Probability distributions were used in this specification of uncertainty. However, as we have indicated, in Fisher's view, statistics was not a rarefied mathematical exercise. Rather, it was part and parcel of experimentation, which in turn was viewed not merely as the concern of laboratory scientists, but also as the prototypical avenue by which people learn from experience. Given this, Fisher believed that an understanding of scientific inference was the appropriate concern of any intelligent person.

Experiments, Fisher wrote, "are only experience carefully planned in advance and designed to form a secure basis of new knowledge" (1935/1971, p. 8). The goal is to design experiments in such a way that the inferences drawn are fully justified and logically compelled by the data, as Fisher explained in *Design of Experiments*. When Fisher advised experimenters in a section entitled "Interpretation and Its Reasoned Basis" to know in advance how they will interpret any possible experimental outcome, he was not referring to the theoretical or conceptual mechanism responsible for producing an effect. The theoretical explanation for why a particular effect should be observed in the population is quite different from the statistical conclusion itself. Admittedly, the substantive interpretation is more problematic in the behavioral sciences than in the agricultural sciences, where the experimental manipulation (e.g., application of kinds of fertilizer) is itself the treatment of substantive interest rather than being only a plausible representation of a theoretical construct (Chow, 1988, p. 107). However, the details of the preliminary argument from sample observations to general statistical conclusions about the effectiveness of the experimental manipulation had not been worked out prior to Fisher's time. His key insight, which solved the problem of making valid statistical inferences, was that of randomization. In this way, one is assured that no uncontrolled factor would bias the results of the statistical test. The details of how this works out in practice are illustrated in subsequent sections.

For the moment, it is sufficient to note that the abstract random process and its associated probabilities are merely the mathematical counterparts of the use of randomization in the concrete experimental situation. Thus, in any true experiment, there are points in the procedure when the laws of chance are explicitly introduced and are in sole control of what is to be done. For example, one might flip a coin to determine what treatment a particular participant receives. The probability distribution used in the statistical test makes sense only because of the use of random assignment in the conduct of the experiment. By doing so, one assures that, if the null hypothesis of no difference between treatments is correct, the results of the experiment are determined entirely by the laws of chance (Fisher, 1935/1971, p. 17). One might imagine, for example, a wide variety of factors that would determine how a particular phobic might respond on a posttest of performance in the feared situation after receiving one of an assortment of treatments. Assuming the treatments have no effect, any number of factors—such as the individual's conditioning history, reaction to the experiment, or indigestion from a hurried lunch—might in some way affect performance. If, in the most extreme view, the particular posttest performance of each individual who could take part in your experiment was thought to be completely determined from the outset by a number of, for your purposes, irrelevant factors, the random assignment to treatment conditions assures that, in the long run, these would balance out. That is, *randomization* implies that the population means in the various treatments are, under these conditions, exactly equal, and that even the form of the distribution of scores in the various conditions is the same.

Next, we show how this simple idea of control of irrelevant factors by randomization works in a situation that can be described by a discrete probability distribution. Thus, we are able to derive (by using only simple counting rules) the entire probability distribution that can be used as the basis for a statistical test.

A DISCRETE PROBABILITY EXAMPLE

Fisher introduced the principles of experimentation in his *Design of Experiments* (1935/1971) with an appropriately British example that has been used repeatedly to illustrate the power of randomization and the logic of hypothesis testing (see, e.g., Kempthorne, 1952, pp. 14–17, 120–134). We simply quote the original description of the problem:

> A lady declares that by tasting a cup of tea made with milk, she can discriminate whether the milk or the tea infusion was first added to the cup. We will consider the problem of designing an experiment by means of which this assertion can be tested. (Fisher, 1935/1971, p. 11)

[Those enamored with single-subject experimentation might be bemused to note that the principles of group experimentation were originally introduced with an *N*-of-1 design. In fact, to be accurate in assigning historical priority, it was the distinguished American philosopher and mathematician Charles S. Peirce, working on single-subject experiments in psychophysics in the 1880s, who first discussed the advantages of randomization (Stigler, 1999, p. 192ff.). However, it was a half century later before Fisher tied these explicitly to methods for arriving at probabilistic inferences.] If you try to come up with an exemplary design appropriate for this particular problem, your first thought might be of the variety of possible disturbing factors over which you would like to exert experimental control. That is, you may begin by asking what factors could influence her judgment and how could these be held constant across conditions so that the only difference between the two kinds of cups is whether the milk or tea was added first. For example, variation in the temperature of the tea might be an important clue, so you might carefully measure the temperature of the mixture in each cup to attempt to assure they were equally hot when they were served. Numerous other factors could also influence her judgment, some of which may be susceptible to experimental control. The type of cup used, the strength of the tea, the use of sugar, and the amount of milk added merely illustrate the myriad potential differences that might occur among the cups to be used in the experiment. The logic of experimentation until the time of Fisher dictated that to have a valid experiment here, all the cups to be used "must be exactly alike," except for the independent variable being manipulated. Fisher rejected this dictum on two grounds. First, he argued that exact equivalence was logically impossible to achieve, both in the example and in experimentation in general. The cups would inevitably differ to some degree in their smoothness, the strength of the tea and the temperature would change slightly over the time between preparation of the first and last cups, and the amounts of milk or sugar added would not be exactly equal, to mention only a few problems. Second, Fisher argued that, even if it were conceivable to achieve "exact likeness" or, more realistically, "imperceptible difference" on various dimensions of the stimuli, it would in practice be too expensive to attempt. Although one could, with a sufficient investment of time and money, reduce the irrelevant differences between conditions to a specified criterion on any dimension, the question of whether it is worth the effort must be raised in any actual experiment. The foremost concern with this and other attempts at experimental control is to arrive at an appropriate test of the hypothesis of interest. Fisher argued that, because the validity of the experiment could be assured by the use of randomization, it was not the best use of inevitably limited resources to attempt to achieve exact equality of stimuli on all dimensions. Most causes of fluctuation in participants' performance "ought to be deliberately ignored" (1935/1971, p. 19).

Consider now how one might carry out and analyze an experiment to test our British lady's claim. The difficulty with asking for a single judgment, of course, is that she might well correctly classify it just by guessing. How many cups then would be needed to constitute a sufficient test? The answer naturally depends on how the experiment is designed, as well as the criterion adopted for how strong the evidence must be in order to be considered compelling.

One suggestion might be that the experiment be carried out by mixing eight cups of tea, four with the milk added to the cup first (milk-first, or MF, cups) and four with the tea added first (tea-first, or TF, cups), and presenting them for classification by the subject in random order. Is this a sufficient number of judgments to request?

> In considering the appropriateness of any proposed experimental design, it is always needful to forecast all possible results of the experiment, and to have decided without ambiguity what interpretation shall be placed upon each one of them. Further, we must know by what argument this interpretation is to be sustained. (Fisher, 1935/1971 p. 12)

Thus, Fisher's advice translated into the current vernacular might be, "If you can't analyze an experiment, don't run it." To prescribe the analysis of the suggested design, we must consider what the possible results of the experiment are and the likelihood of the occurrence of each. To be appropriate, the analysis must correspond exactly to what actually went on in the experiment.[2] Assume the subject is told that the set of eight cups consists of four MF and four TF cups. The measure that indicates how compelling the evidence could be is the probability of a perfect performance occurring by chance alone. If this probability is sufficiently small, say less than 1 chance in 20, we conclude it is implausible that the lady has no discrimination ability. There are, of course, many ways of dividing the set of eight cups into two groups of four each, with the participant thinking that one group consists of MF cups and the other group TF cups. However, if the participant cannot discriminate at all between the two kinds of cups, each of the possible divisions into two groups would be equally likely.

Thus, the probability of a correct performance occurring by chance alone could be expressed simply as the proportion of the possible divisions of the cups that are correct:

$$\text{Pr (being correct by chance)} = \frac{\text{Number of divisions that are exactly correct}}{\text{Total number of possible divisions}} \quad (1)$$

Naturally, only one division would match exactly the actual breakdown into MF and TF cups, which means the numerator of the fraction in Equation 1 would be 1. The only problem, then, is to determine the total number of ways of splitting up eight things into two groups of four each. Actually, we can solve this by determining only the number of ways the subject could select a particular set of four cups as being the MF cups; because once four are chosen as being of one kind, the other four must be put into the other category. Formulating the solution in terms of a sequence of decisions is easiest. Any one of the eight cups could be the first to be classified as an MF cup. For each of the eight possible ways of making this first decision, there are seven cups from which to choose the second cup to be classified as an MF cup. Given the 8×7, or 56, ways of making the first two decisions, there are six ways of choosing the third MF cup. Finally, for each of these $8 \times 7 \times 6$ orderings of three cups, there would be five possible ways of selecting the fourth cup to be assigned to the MF category. Thus, there are $8 \times 7 \times 6 \times 5$, or 1680, ways of choosing four cups out of eight in a particular order. However, each set of four particular cups would appear $4 \times 3 \times 2 \times 1$, or 24, times in a listing of the 1680 orderings, because any set of four objects could be ordered in 24 ways. We are not concerned with the particular sequence in which the cups in a set of four were selected, only with which set was selected. Thus, we can find the number of distinct sets of cups by dividing the number of orderings, 1680, by the number of ways, 24, that each distinct set could be ordered. In summary,

$$\text{Total number of possible divisions} = \frac{8 \times 7 \times 6 \times 5}{4 \times 3 \times 2 \times 1} = \frac{1680}{24} = 70 \qquad (2)$$

Those who have studied what is known as *counting rules*, or "permutations and combinations" may recognize the above solution as the number of combinations of eight things taken four at a time, which may be denoted $_8C_4$. In general, if one is selecting r objects from a larger set n, by the reasoning followed previously, we write

$$_nC_r = \frac{n(n-1)(n-2)\cdots(n-r+1)}{r(r-1)(r-2)\cdots 1} = \frac{n!}{r!(n-r)!} \qquad (3)$$

The solution here, of there being 70 distinct combinations or sets of four cups, which could possibly be designated as MF cups, is critical to the interpretation of the experiment. Following Equation 1, because only 1 of these 70 possible answers is correct, the probability of the lady being exactly right by chance alone is $1/70$. Because this is less than the $1/20$, or .05, probability we adopted as our criterion for being so unlikely as to be convincing, if the lady were to correctly classify all the cups, we would have a sufficient basis for rejecting the null hypothesis of no discrimination ability.

Notice that in essence, we have formulated a statistical test of our null hypothesis, and instead of looking up a p value for an outcome of our experiment in a table, we have derived that value ourselves. Because the experiment involved discrete events rather than scores on a continuous variable, we were able simply to use the definition of probability and a counting rule, which we also developed "from scratch" for our situation, to determine a probability that could be used to judge the statistical significance of one possible outcome of our experiment.

Although no mean feat, we admittedly have not yet considered "all possible results of the experiment," deciding "without ambiguity what interpretation shall be placed on each one." One plausible outcome is that the lady might get most of the classifications correct, but fall short of perfect performance. In the current situation, this would necessarily mean that three of the four MF cups would be correctly classified. Note that, because the participant's response is to consist of putting four cups into each category, misclassifying one MF cup necessarily means that one TF cup was inappropriately thought to be a MF cup. Note also that the decision about which TF cup is misclassified can be made apart from the decision about which MF cup is misclassified. Each of these two decisions may be thought of as a combinatorial problem: How many ways can one choose three things out of four? How many ways can one be selected out of four? Thus, the number of ways of making one error in each grouping of cups is

$$\text{Number of ways of making one error of each kind} = {_4C_3} \cdot {_4C_1}$$

$$= \frac{4!}{3!1!} \cdot \frac{4!}{1!3!} = 4 \cdot 4 = 16 \qquad (4)$$

It may seem surprising that there are as many as 16 ways to arrive at three out of four correctly classified MF cups. However, any one of the four could be the one to be left out, and for each of these, any one of four wrong cups could be put in its place.

Making use again of the definition of the probability of an event as the number of ways that event could occur over the total number of outcomes possible, we can determine the probability of this near-perfect performance arising by chance. The numerator is what was just determined, and the denominator is again the number of possible divisions of eight objects into two sets of four each, which we previously (Equation 2) determined to be 70:

$$\text{Pr (three MF and one TF classified as MF)} = \frac{{}_4C_3 \cdot {}_4C_1}{{}_8C_4} = \frac{4 \cdot 4}{70} = \frac{16}{70} \tag{5}$$

The fact that this probability of 16/70, or .23, is considerably greater than our criterion of .05 puts us in a position to interpret not only this outcome, but all other possible outcomes of the experiment as well. Even though three out of four right represents the next best thing to perfect performance, the fact that performance that good or better could arise $(16 + 1)/70 = .24$, or nearly one fourth, of the time when the subject had no ability to discriminate between the cups implies it would not be good enough to convince us of her claim. Also, because all other possible outcomes would be less compelling, they would also be interpreted as providing insufficient evidence to make us believe that the lady could determine which were the MF cups.

Let us now underscore the major point of what we have developed in this section. Although we have not made reference to any continuous distribution, we have developed from first principles a statistical test appropriate for use in the interpretation of a particular experiment. The test is in fact more generally useful and is referred to in the literature as the *Fisher–Irwin exact test* (Marascuilo & Serlin, 1988, p. 200ff.), or more commonly as *Fisher's exact test* (e.g., Hays, 1994, p. 863).

Many statistical packages include Fisher's exact test as at least an optional test in analyses of cross-tabulated categorical data. In SPSS, both one-tailed and two-tailed p levels for Fisher's exact test are automatically computed for 2×2 tables in the Crosstabs procedure. Although our purpose in this section primarily is to illustrate how p values may be computed from first principles, we comment briefly on some other issues that we develop more fully in later chapters. In general, in actual data analysis situations it is desirable not just to carry out a significance test, but also to characterize the magnitude of the effect observed. There are usually multiple ways in which this can be done, and that is true in this simple case of analysis of a 2×2 table, as will be the case in more complicated situations. One way of characterizing the magnitude of the effect is by using the phi coefficient, which is a special case for a 2×2 table of the Pearson product–moment correlation coefficient, well known to most behavioral researchers. For example, in the case in which one error of each kind was made in the classification of eight cups, the effect size measure could be computed as the correlation between two numerical variables, say Actual and Judged. With only two levels possible, the particular numerical values used to designate the level of TF or MF are arbitrary, but one would have eight pairs of scores [e.g., (1,1), (1,1), (1,1), (1,2), (2,1), (2,2), (2,2), (2,2)], which would here result in a correlation or phi coefficient between Actual and Judged of .50. Small, medium, and large effect sizes may be identified with phi coefficients of .10, .30, and .50, respectively.

An alternative approach to characterizing the effect size is to think of the two rows of the 2×2 table as each being characterized by a particular probability of "success" or probability of an observation falling in the first column, say p_1 and p_2. Then, one could describe the magnitude of the effect as the estimated difference between these probabilities, or $\hat{p}_1 - \hat{p}_2$. However, one difficulty with interpreting such a difference is that the relative chances of success can be very different with small as opposed to large probabilities. For example, a difference of .1 could mean the probability of success is 11 times greater in one condition than in the other if $p_1 = .01$ and $p_2 = .11$, or it could mean that one probability is only 1.2 times the other if $p_1 = .50$ and $p_2 = .60$. To avoid this difficulty, it is useful for some purposes to measure the effect size in terms of the ratio of the odds of success in the two rows. The odds ratio is defined as

$$\frac{p_1/(1 - p_1)}{p_2/(1 - p_2)}$$

Methods for constructing confidence intervals around estimates of the odds ratio are discussed by Rosner (1995, pp. 368–370) and Good (2000, p. 100).

Regarding power, Fisher's exact test may be regarded as the "uniformly most powerful among all unbiased tests for comparing two binomial populations" in a variety of situations such as where the marginals are fixed (Good, 2000, p. 99). As is usually the case, one can increase the power of the test by increasing the total N and by maintaining equal numbers in the marginals under one's control, for example, the number of TF and MF cups presented. Power of Fisher's exact test against specific alternatives defined by a given odds ratio can be determined by computations based on what is called the *noncentral hypergeometric distribution*[3] (cf. Fisher, 1934, pp. 48–51). A helpful discussion of the test with references to relevant literature is given in Good (2000, Chapter 6). Alternative methods of estimating power illustrated with numerical examples are provided by O'Brien and Muller (1993), Rosner (1995, p. 384ff.), and Cohen (1977).

Readers wishing to determine power should be aware, as noted by O'Brien (1998), of the large number of different methods for carrying out computations of p values and power for the case of data from a 2×2 design. One common situation, different from the current case, is that in which one carries out analyses under the assumption that one is comparing two independent proportions, such as the proportion of successes in each of the two rows of the table. In contrast to situations such as the present one where the subject is constrained to produce equal numbers of responses in the two classifications, in many experimental situations the total number of responses of a given kind is not constrained. The appropriate power analysis can be considerably different under such an assumption.[4]

It perhaps should be mentioned that Fisher's exact test, besides illustrating how one can determine the probability of an outcome of an experiment, can be viewed as the forerunner of a host of other statistical procedures. Recent years have seen the rapid development of such techniques for categorical data analysis. These are particularly useful in those research areas—for example, some types of public health or sociological research—in which all variables under investigation are categorical. A number of good introductions to such methods are available (see, e.g., Bishop, Fienberg, & Holland, 1975).

Although these methods have some use in the behavioral sciences, it is much more common for the dependent variable in experiments to be quantitative instead of qualitative. Thus, we continue our introduction to the Fisher tradition by considering another example from his writing that makes use of a quantitative dependent variable. Again, however, no reference to a theoretical population distribution is required.

RANDOMIZATION TEST

Assume that a developmental psychologist is interested in whether brief training can improve performance of 2-year-old children on a test of mental abilities. The test selected is the Mental Scale of the Bayley Scales of Infant Development, which yields a mental age in months. To increase the sensitivity of the experiment, the psychologist decides to recruit sets of twins and randomly assigns one member of each pair to the treatment condition. The treatment consists simply of watching a videotape of another child attempting to perform tasks similar to those

TABLE 2.1
SCORES ON BAYLEY MENTAL SCALE (IN MONTHS) FOR 10 PAIRS OF TWINS

Twin Pair	Condition		Difference
	Treatment	*Control*	*(Treatment – Control)*
Week 1 data			
1	28	32	−4
2	31	25	6
3	25	15	10
4	23	25	−2
5	28	16	12
Sum for Week 1	**135**	**113**	**22**
Week 2 data			
6	26	30	−4
7	36	24	12
8	23	13	10
9	23	25	−2
10	24	16	8
Sum for Week 2	**132**	**108**	**24**
Sum for 2 weeks	**267**	**221**	**46**
Mean for 2 weeks	**26.7**	**22.1**	**4.6**

making up the Bayley Mental Scale. The other member of each pair plays in a waiting area as a time-filling activity while the first is viewing the videotape. Then both children are individually given the Bayley by a tester who is blind to their assigned conditions. A different set of twins takes part in the experiment each day, Monday through Friday, and the experiment extends over a 2-week period. Table 2.1 shows the data for the study in the middle columns.

Given the well-known correlations between twins' mental abilities, it would be expected that there would be some relationship between the mental ability scores for the two twins from the same family, although the correlation is considerably lower at age 2 than at age 18. (Behavior of any 2-year-old is notoriously variable from one time to another; thus, substantial changes in even a single child's test performance across testing sessions are common.) The measure of treatment effectiveness that would commonly be used then in such a study is simply the difference between the score of the child in the treatment condition and that of his or her twin in the control condition. These are shown on the right side of Table 2.1.

A *t* test would typically be performed to make an inference about the mean of these differences in the population. For this particular data set, some hesitation might arise because the sample distribution is U-shaped[5] rather than the bell-shaped distribution that would be expected if the assumption made by the *t* test of a normal population were correct. The *t* test might in practice be used despite this (see the discussion of assumptions at the end of Chapter 3). However, it is not necessary to make any assumptions about the form of the population distribution in order to carry out certain tests of interest here. In fact, one can use all the quantitative information available in the sample data in testing what Fisher referred to as "the wider hypothesis" (1935/1971, p. 43) that the two groups of scores are samples from the same, possibly nonnormal population.

The test of this more general hypothesis is based simply on the implications of the fact that subjects were randomly assigned to conditions. Hence, the test is referred to as a *randomization test*. The logic is as follows: If the null hypothesis is correct, then subjects' scores in the experiment are determined by factors other than what treatment they were assigned (that is, the treatment did not influence subjects' scores). In fact, one may consider the score for each subject to be predetermined prior to the random assignment to conditions. Thus, the difference between any two siblings' scores would have been the same in absolute value regardless of the assignment to conditions. For example, under the null hypothesis, one subject in Pair 1 was going to receive a score of 28 and the other subject a score of 32; the random assignment then simply determined that the higher-scoring subject would be in the control condition here, so that the difference of "treatment minus control" would be -4 instead of $+4$. Because a random assignment was made independently for each of the 10 pairs, 10 binary decisions were in effect made as to whether a predetermined difference would have a plus or minus sign attached to it. Thus, there were 2^{10} possible combinations of signed differences that could have occurred with these subjects, and the sum of the signed differences could be used to indicate the apparent benefit (or harm) of the treatment for each combination. The distribution of these 2^{10} sums is the basis for our test. The sum of the differences actually observed, including the four negative differences, was 46. A randomization test is carried out simply by determining how many of the 2^{10} combinations of signed differences would have totals equal to or exceeding the observed total of 46. Because under the null hypothesis each of these 2^{10} combinations is equally likely, the proportion of them having sums at least as great as the observed sum provides directly the probability to use in assessing the significance of the observed sum.

In effect, one is constructing the distribution of values of a test statistic (the sum of the differences) over all possible reassignments of subjects to conditions. Determining where the observed total falls in this distribution is comparable to what is done when one consults a table in a parametric test to determine the significance of an observed value of a test statistic. However, now the distribution is based directly on the scores actually observed rather than on some assumed theoretical distribution.

That one uses all the quantitative information in the sample and gets a statistical test without needing to make any distributional assumptions makes an attractive combination. There are disadvantages, however. A major disadvantage that essentially prevented use of randomization tests until recent years in all but the smallest data sets is the large number of computations required. To completely determine the distribution of possible totals for even the set of 10 differences in Table 2.1 would require examining $2^{10} = 1024$ sets of data. We summarize the results of this process later, but illustrate the computations for the smaller data set consisting only of the five scores from week 1.

With five scores, there are $2^5 = 32$ possible assignments of positive and negative signs to the individual scores. Table 2.2 lists the scores in rank order of their absolute value at the top left. Then, 15 other sets, including progressively more minus signs, are listed along with the sum for each. The sums for the remaining 16 sets are immediately determined by realizing that when the largest number of 12 is assigned a negative rather than a positive sign, the sum would be reduced by 24.

If the first week constituted the entire experiment, these 32 sums would allow us to determine the significance of the observed total Bayley difference for the first week of 22 ($= -4 + 6 + 10 - 2 + 12$, see Table 2.1). Figure 2.1 shows a grouped, relative frequency histogram for the possible sums, with the shaded portion on the right indicating the sums greater than or equal to the observed sum of 22. (An ungrouped histogram, although still perfectly symmetrical, appears somewhat less regular.) Thus, the probability of a total at least as large as and in the same direction as that observed would be 5/32 ($= 3/32 + 2/32$), or .16, which would not be sufficiently small for us to claim significance.

The same procedure could be followed for the entire set of 10 scores. Rather than listing the 1024 combinations of scores or displaying the distribution of totals, the information needed to perform a test of significance can be summarized by indicating the number of totals greater than or equal to the observed sum of 46. Fortunately, it is clear that if five or more numbers

TABLE 2.2

POSSIBLE SUMS OF DIFFERENCES RESULTING FROM REASSIGNMENTS OF FIRST-WEEK CASES

Assignment

	1	2	3	4	5	6	7	8	9	10	11	12	13	14	15	16
	12	12	12	12	12	12	12	12	12	12	12	12	12	12	12	12
	10	10	10	10	10	10	10	10	-10	-10	-10	-10	-10	-10	-10	-10
	6	6	6	6	-6	-6	-6	-6	6	6	6	6	-6	-6	-6	-6
	4	4	-4	-4	4	4	-4	-4	4	4	-4	-4	4	4	-4	-4
	2	-2	2	-2	2	-2	2	-2	2	-2	2	-2	2	-2	2	-2
Sum	**34**	**30**	**26**	**22**	**22**	**18**	**14**	**10**	**14**	**10**	**6**	**2**	**2**	**-2**	**-6**	**-10**

Assignment[a]

	17	18	19	20	21	22	23	24	25	26	27	28	29	30	31	32
	-12	-12	-12	-12	-12	-12	-12	-12	-12	-12	-12	-12	-12	-12	-12	-12
	10	10	10	10	10	10	10	10	-10	-10	-10	-10	-10	-10	-10	-10
	6	6	6	6	-6	-6	-6	-6	6	6	6	6	-6	-6	-6	-6
	4	4	-4	-4	4	4	-4	-4	4	4	-4	-4	4	4	-4	-4
	2	-2	2	-2	2	-2	2	-2	2	-2	2	-2	2	-2	2	-2
Sum	**10**	**6**	**2**	**-2**	**-2**	**-6**	**-10**	**-14**	**-10**	**-14**	**-18**	**-22**	**-22**	**-26**	**-30**	**-34**

[a] Note that assignments 17–32 are the same as assignments 1–16 except that 12 is assigned a negative sign rather than a positive sign, and so each sum is 24 less than the sum for the corresponding assignment above.

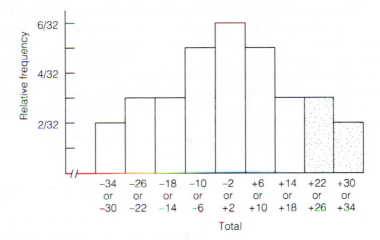

FIG. 2.1. Distribution of possible totals of difference scores using data from Week 1.

TABLE 2.3
NUMBER OF COMBINATIONS OF SIGNED DIFFERENCES WITH SUMS EQUAL TO OR
GREATER THAN THE OBSERVED SUM

Number of Negative Values	Total Number of Combinations	Number of Combinations with		
		Sum > 46	Sum = 46	Sum < 46
0	1	1		
1	10	8	2	
2	45	12	6	27
3	120	5	5	110
4	210		1	209
5	252			252
6	210			210
7	120			120
8	45			45
9	10			10
10	1			1
Totals	**1024**	**26**	**14**	**984**

were assigned negative signs, the total would necessarily be less than 46. Table 2.3 shows the breakdown for the other possible combinations.

We now have the needed information to address the question with which we began this section: Does brief training improve the performance of 2-year-olds on a test of mental abilities? Under the null hypothesis that the scores from the subjects receiving training and those not receiving training represent correlated samples from two populations having identical population distributions, the random assignment to conditions allows us to generate a distribution of possible totals of 10 scores based on the data actually observed. As shown in Table 2.3, we find that only 40 of 1024, or .039, of the possible combinations of signed differences result in totals as large or larger than that actually observed. Thus, we conclude that we have significant evidence that our training resulted in improved performance among the children tested in the experiment.

Two points about this conclusion are noteworthy. First, we performed a one-tailed test. A one-tailed test might be warranted in an applied setting in which one is interested in the treatment only if it helps performance. If a two-tailed test had been performed, a different con-clusion would have been reached. To see this, we make use of the symmetry of the distributions used in randomization tests (every combination of signed differences is matched by one in which every sign is reversed, so every positive total has a corresponding negative total of the same absolute value). Thus, there would be exactly 40 cases totaling -46 or less. This yields a combined probability of $80/1024$, or .078, of observing a total as extreme or more extreme in either direction than that observed; hence, we would fail to reject the null hypothesis in favor of a nondirectional alternative hypothesis.

Second, it should be pointed out that the hypothesis tested by the randomization test is not identical to that tested by the t test. The hypothesis in the t test concerns the population mean of a continuous random variable. The hypothesis in the randomization test concerns the presumption that each of the observed difference scores could have been preceded by a positive or negative sign with equal likelihood. The p value yielded by performing a t test would be exact only if the theoretical distribution prescribed by its density formula were perfectly matched by the actual distribution of the test statistic given the current population, which it certainly is not here. However, in part because of the factors summarized by the central limit theorem (discussed in the next section), the p value in the table generally is a very good approximation to the exact p value even with nonnormal data, such as we have in the current example. Similarly, the p value in the randomization test is the exact probability only for the distribution arising from hypothetical reassignments of the particular cases used in the study (Edgington, 1966, 1995). However, the closeness of the correspondence between the p value yielded by the randomization test and that yielded by the t test can be demonstrated mathematically under certain conditions (Pitman, 1937).

We can illustrate this correspondence in the current example as well. If we perform a t test of the hypothesis that the mean difference score in the population is 0, we obtain a t value of 2.14 with 9 degrees of freedom. This observed t value is exceeded by .031 of the theoretical t distribution, which compares rather closely with the .039 we obtained from our randomization test previously. The correspondence is even closer if, as Fisher suggested (1935/1971, p. 46), we correct the t test for the discontinuous nature of our data.[6] Hence, with only 10 cases, the difference between the probabilities yielded by the two tests is on the order of 1 in 1000. In fact, one may view the t test and the randomization test as very close approximations to one another (cf., Lehman, 1986, pp. 230–236). Deciding to reject the hypothesis of the randomization test is tantamount to deciding to reject the hypothesis of the t test.

As with the Fisher's exact test, our purpose with the randomization test is primarily to emphasize the meaning of p values rather than to fully develop all aspects of the methodology. When such a method is used in actual research, one may want to construct a confidence interval around a parameter indicating the location or central tendency of the distribution. Methods for doing so are discussed briefly in Good (2000, pp. 34–35) and in more theoretical detail in Lehmann (1986, pp. 245–248). Power of randomization tests is considered by Bradbury (1987), Robinson (1973), and Good (2000, p. 36), and is often similar to that of the standard t test. We consider measures of effect size and power for group comparisons in the context of the linear models introduced in subsequent chapters. With the ready availability of increasingly powerful computers in recent years, randomization tests have become much more feasible. A number of specialized, commercially available programs perform such tests (e.g., StatXact, 1995, from Cytel Software), and one has the option of obtaining programs for free from "shareware" sources, such as NPSTAT (May, Hunter, & Masson, 1993) or from published program listings (Edgington, 1995). Although these procedures are not yet available as of this writing in packages such as SPSS and SAS, sets of commands that allow one to carry out these procedures have been published for both of these packages (Chen & Dunlap, 1993; Hayes, 1998).

OF HYPOTHESES AND *p* VALUES: FISHER
VERSUS NEYMAN–PEARSON

To this point, we have dealt with only a single hypothesis, namely the null hypothesis. This was Fisher's strong preference (Huberty, 1987). The familiar procedure of simultaneously considering a null and an alternative hypothesis, which became standard practice in psychology in the 1940s (Huberty, 1991; Rucci & Tweney, 1980), is actually a modification of Fisherian practice that had been advocated by statisticians Jerzy Neyman and Egon Pearson. One particularly memorable version of the historical debates regarding statistical methods and how they manifest themselves currently is that offered in Freudian terms by Gigerenzer (1993).

In the Neyman–Pearson view, statistical inference was essentially an exercise in decision making. Whereas Fisher had viewed significance testing as a means of summarizing data to aid in advancing an argument for a position on a scientific question, Neyman and Pearson emphasized the practical choice between two statistical hypotheses, the null hypothesis and its complement, the alternative hypothesis. The benefit of this approach was to make clear that one could not only make a Type I error (with probability α) of rejecting the null hypothesis when it is true, but also a Type II error, or failing to reject the null hypothesis when it is false (with probability β). In practical situations in business or medicine, one could adjust the probabilities of these errors to reflect the relative costs and benefits of the different kinds of errors. Of course, determining a particular value of β required one to specify an exact alternative hypothesis (e.g., $\mu = 105$, not just $\mu \neq 100$).

One disadvantage of the Neyman–Pearson approach was the overemphasis on the accept–reject decision. Although a 5% level of significance was acknowledged as "usual and convenient" by even Fisher (1935/1971, p. 13), thinking that an up-or-down decision is a sufficient summary of the data in all situations is clearly misguided. For one, an effect of identical size might be declared significant in one study but not another simply because of differences in the number of subjects used. Although abandoning significance tests, as some advocate (e.g., Cohen, 1994; Oakes, 1986), would avoid this problem, one thereby would lose this critical screen that prevents researchers from interpreting what could reasonably be attributed to chance variation (cf. Frick, 1996; Hagen, 1997). However, viewing the alpha level established before the experiment as the only probability that should be reported suppresses information. Some researchers apparently believe that what statistical correctness requires is to report all significant p values only as significant at the alpha level established before the experiment. Thus, the "superego" of Neyman–Pearson logic might seem to direct that if α is set at 5% before the experiment, then .049 and .003 should both be reported only as "significant at the .05 level" (Gigerenzer, 1993). But, as Browner and Newman (1987) suggest, all significant p values are not created equal. Although there is value in retaining the conventions of .05 and .01 for declaring results significant or highly significant, any published report of a statistical test, in our view and that of groups of experts asked to make recommendations on the issue, should be accompanied by an exact p value (Greenwald, Gonzalez, Harris, & Guthrie, 1996, p. 181; Wilkinson & the APA Task Force on Statistical Inference, 1999, p. 599). As Fisher saw it, this is part of the information that should be communicated to others in the spirit of freedom that is the essence of the Western tradition. Reporting exact p values recognizes "the right of *other* free minds to utilize them in making *their own* decisions" [Fisher, 1955, p. 77 (italics Fisher's)].

Because we emphasize relying on and reporting p values, it is critical to be clear about what they are and what they are not. As we tried to make clear by our detailed development of the p values for the Fisher's exact and randomization tests, a p value is the probability of data as extreme or more extreme as that obtained, computed under the presumption of the truth of the null hypothesis. In symbols, if we let D stand for data as or more extreme as that obtained, and H_o stand for the null hypothesis, then a p value is a conditional probability of the form $Pr(D \mid H_o)$.

Unfortunately, erroneous interpretations of p values by academic psychologists, including textbook authors and journal editors, are very common and have been well documented, often by those raising concerns about hypothesis testing. Two misunderstandings seem to be most prevalent. The first has been termed the *replication fallacy*, which is erroneously thinking that a significant p value is the complement of the probability (i.e., $1 - p$) that a replication of the study would also yield significance. However, the probability of obtaining significance in a replication when the null hypothesis is false refers to the concept of *power*, which can be computed only under the assumption of a specific alternative hypothesis, and in any event is only indirectly related to the p value. Gigerenzer (1993) provides a number of examples of the replication fallacy, including an example from Nunnally's (1975) *Introduction to Statistics for Psychology and Education*, which asserted " 'If the statistical significance is at the 0.05 level ... the investigator can be confident with odds of 95 out of 100 that the observed difference will hold up in future investigations' (Nunnally, 1975, p. 195)" (Gigerenzer, 1993, p. 330). More recently, one study conducted by a British psychologist of 70 university lecturers, research fellows, and postgraduate students elicited endorsement by 60% of a statement to the effect that a result significant at $p = .01$ meant that "You have a reliable experimental finding in the sense that if, hypothetically, the experiment were repeated a great number of times, you would obtain a significant result on 99% of occasions" (Oakes, 1986, pp. 79–80). In point of fact, an experiment that yields a p value of .05 would lead to a probability of a significant replication of only about .50, not .95 (Greenwald et al., 1996; Hoenig & Heisey, 2001). So, neither the exact p value nor its complement can be interpreted as the probability of a significant replication. However, the point that some strident critics of null hypothesis testing overlook but that contributes to the enduring utility of the methodology is "replicability of a null hypothesis rejection is a continuous, increasing function of the complement of its p value" (Greenwald et al., 1996, p. 181). The exact probability of a successful replication depends on a number of factors, but some helpful guidance is provided by Greenwald et al. (1996), who show that under certain simplifying assumptions, p values can be translated into a probability of successful replication (power) at $\alpha = .05$ as follows: $p = .05 \rightarrow$ power $\cong .5$, $p = .01 \rightarrow$ power $\cong .75$, $p = .005 \rightarrow$ power $\cong .8$, and $p = .001 \rightarrow$ power $> .9$.

The second prevalent misinterpretation of p values is as indicating an inverse probability, that is, the probability that a hypothesis is true or false given the data obtained [e.g., $Pr(H_o \mid D)$], instead of the probability of data given the null hypothesis is assumed true. Again, textbooks as well as research psychologists provide numerous examples of this fallacy (Cohen, 1994, p. 999, lists various sources reporting examples). For example, when hypothesis testing was first being introduced to psychologists in the 1940s and 1950s, the leading text, Guilford's *Fundamental Statistics in Psychology and Education*, included headings such as " 'Probability of hypotheses estimated from the normal curve' (p. 160)" (cited in Gigerenzer, 1993, p. 323). That psychologists have gotten and believe this wrong message is illustrated by Oakes' (1986) study, which found that each of three statements of inverse probability, such as, "You have found the probability of the null hypothesis being true" (p. 79), were endorsed by between 36% and 86% of academic psychologists, with 96% of his sample endorsing at least one of these erroneous interpretations of a p value of .01 (pp. 80, 82). Although one can construct plausible scenarios of combinations of power, alpha levels, and prior probabilities of the hypotheses being true, where the p value turns out to be reasonably close numerically to the posterior probability of the truth of the null hypothesis given the data (Baril & Cannon, 1995), the conceptual difference cannot be stressed too strongly.

However, in our view, the solution to the problem of misuse and misunderstanding of p values is not to abandon their use, but to work hard to get things correct. The venerable methods of null hypothesis testing need not be abandoned, but they can be effectively complemented by additional methods, such as confidence intervals, meta-analyses, and Bayesian approaches (Howard, Maxwell, & Fleming, 2000). The future holds the promise of the emergence of use of multiple statistical methodologies, including even Bayesian procedures that allow statements regarding the truth of the null hypotheses—what the id, as Gigerenzer (1993) termed it, in statistical reasoning really wants.

TOWARD TESTS BASED ON DISTRIBUTIONAL ASSUMPTIONS

Although this chapter may in some ways seem an aside in the development of analysis of variance procedures, in actuality, it is a fundamental and necessary step. First, we have shown the possibility of deriving our own significance levels empirically for particular data-analysis situations. This is a useful conceptual development to provide an analogy for what follows, in which we assume normal distribution methods. Second, and perhaps more important, the close correspondence between the results of randomization and normal theory-based tests provides a justification for using the normal theory methods. This justification applies in two important respects, each of which we discuss in turn. First, it provides a rationale for use of normal theory methods regardless of whether subjects are, in fact, randomly *sampled* from a population. Second, it is relevant to the justification of use of normal theory methods regardless of the actual shape of the distribution of the variable under investigation.

Statistical Tests with Convenience Samples

The vast majority of psychological research uses subject pools that can be conveniently obtained rather than actually selecting subjects by way of a random sampling procedure from the population to which the experimenter hopes to generalize. Subjects may be those people at your university who were in Psychology 101 and disposed to volunteer to participate in your experiment, or they may be clients who happened to come to the clinic or hospital at the time your study was in progress. In no sense do these individuals constitute a simple random sample from the population to which you would like to generalize, for example, the population of all adults or all mental health clinic clients in the United States.

If your goal is to provide normative information that could be used in classifying individuals—for example, as being in the top 15% of all college freshmen on a reading comprehension test—then a sample obtained exclusively from the local area is of little help. You have no assurance that the local students have the same distribution of reading comprehension scores as the entire population. Although one can compute standard errors of the sample statistics and perhaps maintain that they are accurate for the hypothetical population of students for which the local students could be viewed as a random sample, they do not inform you of what you probably want to know—for example, how far is the local mean from the national mean, or how much error is probable in the estimate of the score on the test that would cut off the top 15% of the population of all college freshmen? Such misinterpretations by psychologists of the standard errors of statistics from nonrandom samples have been soundly criticized by statisticians (see Freedman, Pisani, & Purves, 1998, p. 388, A-84).

The situation is somewhat, although not entirely, different with between-group comparisons based on a convenience sample in which subjects have been randomly assigned to conditions.

A randomization test could always be carried out in this situation and is a perfectly valid approach. The p value yielded by such a test, as we have shown, refers to where the observed test statistic would fall in the distribution obtained by hypothetical redistributions of subjects to conditions. Because the p value for a t test or F test is very close to that yielded by the randomization test, and because the randomization test results are cumbersome to compute for any but the smallest data sets,[7] one may compute the more standard t or F test and interpret the inference as applying either to possible reassignments of the currently available subjects or to an imaginary population for which these subjects might be thought to be a random sample. The generalization to a real population or to people in general that is likely of interest is then made on nonstatistical grounds. Thus, behavioral scientists in general must make use of whatever theoretical knowledge they possess about the stability of the phenomena under investigation across subpopulations in order to make accurate and externally valid assertions about the generality of their findings.

The Assumption of Normality

The F tests that are the primary focus in the following chapters assume that the population distribution of the dependent variable in each group is normal in form. In part because the dependent-variable distribution is never exactly normal in form, the distribution of the test statistic is only approximately correct. However, as we discuss in Chapter 3, if the only assumption violated is that the shape of the distribution of individual scores is not normal, generally, the approximation of the distribution of the test statistic to the theoretical F is good. Not only that, but the correspondence between the p value yielded by an F test and that derived from the exact randomization test is generally very close as well. Thus, the F tests that follow can actually be viewed as approximations to the exact randomization tests that could be carried out. The closeness of this approximation has been demonstrated both theoretically (Wald & Wolfowitz, 1944) and by numerical examples (Kempthorne, 1952, pp. 128–132; Pitman, 1937) and simulations (e.g., Boik, 1987; Bradbury, 1987). In the eyes of some, it is this correspondence of F tests to randomization tests that is a more compelling rationale for their use than the plausibility of a hypothetical infinitely large population, for example, "Tests of significance in the randomized experiment have frequently been presented by way of normal law theory, whereas their validity stems from randomization theory" (Kempthorne, 1955, p. 947). Similarly, Scheffé (1959, p. 313) notes that the F test "can often be regarded as a good approximation to a permutation [randomization] test, which is an exact test under a less restrictive model."

Of course, if data tend to be normally distributed, either rationale could be used. Historically, there has been considerable optimism about the pervasiveness of normal distributions, buttressed by both empirical observations of bell-shaped data patterns as well as arguments for why it is plausible that data should be approximately normally distributed.

Researchers have been noting since the early 1800s that data are often normally distributed. Although the normal curve was derived as early as 1733 by Abraham De Moivre as the limit of the binomial distribution (Stigler, 1986, pp. 70–77), it was not until the work of Laplace, Gauss, and others in the early 1800s that the more general importance of the distribution was recognized. A first step in the evolution of the normal curve from a mathematical object into an empirical generalization of natural phenomena was the comparison with distributions of errors in observations (Stigler, 1999, p. 190ff., p. 407ff.). Many of the early applications of statistics were in astronomy, and it was an astronomer, F. W. Bessel, who in 1818 published the first comparison of an empirical distribution with the normal. [Bessel is known in the history of psychology for initiating the scientific study of individual differences by

TABLE 2.4

BESSEL'S COMPARISON OF THE DISTRIBUTION OF THE
ABSOLUTE VALUES OF ERRORS WITH THE NORMAL
DISTRIBUTION FOR **300** ASTRONOMICAL OBSERVATIONS

Range in Seconds	Frequency of Errors	
	Observed	Estimated (Based on Normal Distribution)
0.0–0.1	114	107
0.1–0.2	84	87
0.2–0.3	53	57
0.3–0.4	24	30
0.4–0.5	14	13
0.5–0.6	6	5
0.6–0.7	3	1
0.7–0.8	1	0
0.8–0.9	1	0

developing "the personal equation" describing interastronomer differences (Boring, 1950).]
From a catalog of 60,000 individual observations of stars by British Astronomer Royal James
Bradley, Bessel examined in detail a group of 300 observations of the positions of a few
selected stars. These data allowed an empirical check on the adequacy of the normal curve
as a theory of the distribution of errors. The observations were records of Bradley's judgments of the instant when a star crossed the center line of a specially equipped telescope.
The error of each observation could be assessed; Table 2.4 portrays a grouped frequency
distribution of the absolute value of the errors in tenths of a second. Bessel calculated the
number of errors expected to fall in each interval by using an approximation of the proportion of the normal distribution in that interval. In short, the fit was good. For example, the
standard deviation for these data was roughly 0.2 s, and thus approximately two thirds of
the cases (i.e., 200 of the 300 observations) were expected to fall within 1 standard deviation of the mean (i.e., absolute values of errors <.2), and in fact they did (see Stigler, 1986,
p. 202ff.).

Two important figures in the history of psychology played pivotal roles in changing how
the normal distribution was viewed. In 1873, C. S. Peirce was apparently the first to refer to
the mathematical formula as the *normal curve*, with the connotation that it describes the way
errors are usually or ordinarily distributed (Stigler & Kruskal, 1999, p. 411). However, the true
believer in the ubiquity of normal distributions in nature was Francis Galton, who, extending
the pioneering work of the Belgian sociological statistician Adolpe Quetelet, became an advocate of the remarkable fit of the normal distribution to distributions of human abilities and
characteristics. At his Anthropometric Laboratory outside London in the late 1800s, Galton
amassed data showing how both physical characteristics (e.g., height) and mental characteristics (e.g., examination scores) could be fit reasonably well with a normal curve (Stigler, 1986,
Chapters 5, 8). Galton's "well-known panegyric" to the normal curve suggests the devotion
felt by him and others: "I know of scarcely anything so apt to impress the imagination as the
wonderful form of cosmic order expressed by the 'Law of Frequency of Error.' The law would
have been personified by the Greeks and deified, if they had known it" (Galton, 1889a, p. 66,
cited in Stigler, 1999, p. 414).

Later psychological research also revealed many situations in which normality is reasonably
approximated (although in recent years many have argued that this is the exception rather
than the rule). We cite two historically important examples to illustrate the point, one from
experimental psychology, the other from clinical psychology.

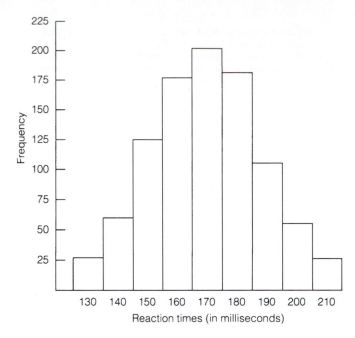

FIG. 2.2.   Group frequency distribution of simple reaction times.

One of the most frequently used measures in current human experimental psychology is that of reaction time. Reaction time is used, for example, in a chronometric approach to cognitive psychology to assess the effects of manipulations such as priming (presenting a cue word immediately before a trial) on the mean time it takes to detect the presentation of a target word. Although over repeated trials a single individual's reaction time tends to follow a positively skewed distribution (more on this in a moment), it has been known for many years that *across* individuals, the distribution of individual's average reaction time conforms very closely to the normal distribution. Figure 2.2 presents data originally reported by Fessard (1926) and cited by Woodworth and Schlosberg (1954, p. 37). Fessard measured the reaction time to sound for each of a group of 1000 men who were applicants for jobs as machinists in Paris. Each man was measured on 30 trials, and the mean of these was used in determining the frequencies shown in the figure. A few extreme cases (35 of 1000) were excluded by Fessard (1926, p. 218) from the table reporting his data. Although the correspondence between the data as plotted and the normal distribution is quite close, the complete data may have provided an even better fit because of the long tails of the normal distribution. Nonetheless, allowing for sampling variability, the data as presented correspond reasonably well to the theoretical normal distribution.

A second empirical example of normally distributed data in psychology is provided by scores on the Minnesota Multiphasic Personality Inventory (MMPI). Figure 2.3 shows the distribution of scores of 699 Minnesotans on the Hypochondriasis scale of the MMPI, as reported by McKinley and Hathaway (1956). The respondents, originally described in Hathaway and McKinley (1940), were individuals who were not ill, but who accompanied relatives or friends to the University of Minnesota Hospital. Again, a distribution that corresponds quite closely to a theoretical normal distribution is yielded by these test scores from "Minnesota normals."

Although the data in these two examples are perhaps more nearly normal than most, many measures of aptitude, personality, memory, and motor skill performance are often

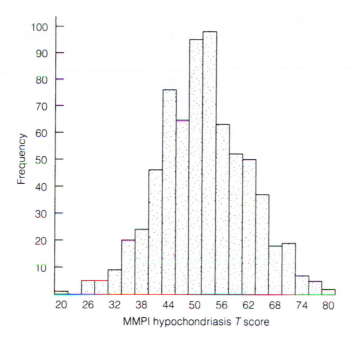

FIG. 2.3.   MMPI hypochondriasis scores.

approximately normally distributed. In part, this has to do with the global level at which constructs within the behavioral sciences are typically assessed. In a sense, the further the analysis of a phenomenon into its basic, elementary components has been carried, the less likely the data are to follow a normal distribution. Within some areas of physiological psychology, this is the case. The interest may, for example, be simply in the occurrence or nonoccurrence of a discrete event: Did the neuron fire?

Perhaps the most extensively modeled nonnormal, continuous processes are temporal ones. Mathematical psychologists theorize in detail about the specific nonnormal form of, for instance, the distribution of simple reaction times within an individual to repeated presentations of a tone, or the distribution of interresponse times in the recordings of a single nerve fiber (see McGill, 1963). However, most areas of psychology have not progressed to having theories about the form of distributions. Nor do we have many valid binary measures of elementary processes. Instead, the dependent variable is most often a composite of a number of measures, for example, the total of the responses to 40 items on a questionnaire. Although the questionnaire may be of interest because it is thought to indicate the presence or absence of a particular psychological state such as clinical depression, the distribution of the observed variable probably is not such that it can be indicated by the frequency of two particular scores on the scale (for example, 0 and 40). Rather, its distribution is determined largely by the fact that the score on the questionnaire is the sum of the responses to 40 different items, which are far from all being perfectly correlated. Because it is not unusual for the dependent variable in a behavioral science study to be of this composite nature, a remarkable theorem can give a reasonable basis for expecting data in some situations to follow a bell-shaped curve.

This theorem, arguably the most important in statistics, is the *central limit theorem*. In its simplest form, the theorem states that the sum of a large number of independent random variables is approximately normally distributed. What is remarkable about the result is that there are almost no constraints placed on the individual distributions of the original random variables. Some could be discrete, others continuous; some could be U-shaped, some skewed, some flat; some could have large variances, some small; and still their sum would be normally distributed.

This theorem can be relied on in two ways in constructing an argument for why broad classes of behavioral science data might be expected to be normally distributed[8] (Bailey, 1971, p. 199ff.). First, theory may suggest that numerous *independent factors* are the causes of a particular phenomenon. For example, the keenness of an individual's vision may be viewed as the product of a series of partial causes, most of which are related to genetic background, although some environmental factors such as quality of diet or amount of eyestrain experienced might also be posited in a particular theoretical account. If these various partial causes were to occur independently in nature and summate to determine the quality of an individual's vision, then the central limit theorem tells us that the distribution of visual acuity over individuals would follow a bell-shaped distribution.

A second way in which the central limit theorem could be used to justify the expectation of a normal distribution is through conceptualizing behavioral observations for various individuals as being the result of a distribution of *errors around one true value*. This approach fits nicely with the way in which we express statistical models in Chapter 3. Instead of there being a distribution of true values across individuals as a result of specified causes, now there is assumed to be one true value around which individuals vary for unspecified reasons. To continue with another perceptual example, assume individuals are being asked to reproduce a line segment of a given length that they are shown briefly. Then, we might say that $Y_i = \tau + \varepsilon_i$, where Y_i is the measured length of the line drawn by individual i, τ is the true length of the line, and ε_i is the error term for individual i. Each of these ε_i scores may be viewed as each being a composite of a number of factors that cause the measured line length for an individual to depart from the true length. These would include both errors of measurement in recording the length of the line the subject draws and the momentary fluctuations in the individual that affect the perception of the length of the presented line and the exact length of the line the individual produces. This latter category might include the effects of slight changes in the point where the eyes are fixated at the time of exposure, fluctuations in attention, and variations in the hosts of neural processes involved in programming a response and muscular actions required to execute it. If each of these small factors independently contributes to the composite error score for each of the individuals performing the task, then the central limit theorem shows that the composite error scores, and hence the observed Y scores, will be normally distributed. [This view of errors as themselves being composites, and hence approximately normally distributed according to the central limit theorem, was first conceived by Laplace in 1810, and played a major role in the development of inferential statistics (Stigler, 1986, p. 143).]

Either or both of these factors may be at work to make the data in any particular study tend toward a normal distribution. However, there are any number of countervailing factors that may prevent this from happening. First, although it is the case that measures in the behavioral sciences are usually composites or totals of numerous items, and those items are generally not perfectly correlated, they also are not independent. Indeed, psychological instruments generally are constructed so that items on a scale have at least moderate positive intercorrelations. Second, although there are situations in which individual observations are appropriately modeled as random variation around a group mean, in fact, it is probably much more common when the observations are coming from different people that they represent different true scores across people as well as random measurement error. For example, scores on a Beck Depression Inventory may be systematically different across different subgroups of participants (e.g., representing different personality types). The random variation model may be most appropriate only when most important causal factors have been included in one's model. This is just one of many reasons for including relevant individual difference measures as predictors in one's statistical model in addition to any manipulated variables in a study (more on this in Chapter 9). Third, more mundane constraints preventing reasonable approximations to normality, such as the fact that only a very small number of scale values are possible, say a 5-point scale is used to rate treatment outcome, or floor or ceiling effects are operating whereby a substantial proportion of participants receive either the lowest or highest value on the scale.

The point is that it is an empirical question as to whether data are in fact normally distributed in any study. One extensive study of large data sets in psychology argued for the conclusion that normal distributions are as hypothetical as the proverbial unicorn. Micceri (1989) examined 440 large-sample achievement and psychometric measures and found in every case that their distributions were significantly nonnormal at the .01 α level. The majority of the distributions were moderately to extremely asymmetric, and most also had a greater proportion in the tails of the distribution than expected in a normal distribution. A variety of other problems such as distributions that were "lumpy" (relative frequencies not consistently increasing or decreasing) or multimodal were also noted. In short, the world certainly is not as universally normal as reading Galton might suggest.

Yet whatever the empirical and conceptual reasons or evidence for expecting data to be normally distributed, in the historical development of statistics, assuming normality made it easier to solve a number of difficult mathematical problems. This increased tractability no doubt contributed to the rise to prominence of statistical methods based on the normal distribution. For example, working independently, Gauss in 1809 showed that a particular estimation problem could be solved if errors were assumed to be normally distributed, and Laplace's central limit theorem of 1810 provided good reasons for expecting normal distributions to occur. As Stephen Stigler tells the story in his excellent book on the history of statistics, "the remarkable circumstance that the curve that led to the simplest analysis also had such an attractive rationale was conceptually liberating" (1986, p. 145). The result was a synthesis of ideas and a development of techniques representing "one of the major success stories in the history of science" (1986, p. 158).

Although behavioral data often may not be closely approximated by the normal distribution, we have argued that normal theory-based tests are close approximations to randomization tests regardless of the shape of the distribution. Furthermore, to anticipate a related argument for the use of normal theory-based procedures that we explore in more detail at the end of Chapter 3 when we discuss the statistical assumptions made in linear model tests, even when one is sampling from extremely nonnormal distributions, such as some of those highlighted by Micceri (1989), tests assuming normality can often still perform well [e.g., when sample sizes are large and equal, and homogeneity of variance is satisfied (Sawilowsky & Blair, 1992)].

Even so, recent years have seen a profusion of so-called robust or sturdy statistical procedures, which are offered as an alternative to normal theory procedures. We consider some of these in the extension at the end of Chapter 3. However, for reasons such as those discussed regarding the reasonableness of the normal distribution assumption and the hard fact of a historical context in which normal theory-based procedures have been dominant (Huberty, 1987, 1991), statistical methods based on the general linear model assuming normally distributed data are expected to continue as some of the most important analytic methods in the behavioral sciences. Also, although alternative methods such as robust methods are expected to continue to proliferate, one must understand normal theory-based methods both because they are most powerful in situations in which their assumptions hold and as a point of departure for considering alternative methods when their assumptions are violated in important ways. Thus, in subsequent chapters, it is such normal theory-based methods that are our primary focus.

OVERVIEW OF EXPERIMENTAL DESIGNS
TO BE CONSIDERED

Having surveyed some of the conceptual considerations relevant to hypothesis testing and statistical analysis in psychology, and having stressed that the statistical analysis of any experiment must flow from the nature of the experimental design used, it is now time to provide a brief overview of the various types of designs we consider in this book.

First, however, a word is in order about the goals of scientific investigation and distinctions among the kinds of factors one might investigate. Science has to do with relationships among variables. At a descriptive level, the goal might be characterized as accounting for variability by predicting the values of one variable on the basis of the values of one or more other variables. At a conceptual level, however, the goal is explanation. Explanations of phenomena posit not only predictive but causal relations as well (cf. Schmidt, 1992, p. 1177ff.). Discovering causal relationships carries the greatest import for theory and also confers the practical power of insight into how a phenomenon may be controlled, or, as Bacon termed it, commanded.

Predictor variables or factors may be manipulated by the experimenter or simply measured. In trying to predict scores of an undergraduate psychology major on the Psychology Area test of the Graduate Record Exam, one may find that such scores are predicted by variables such as the student's cumulative grade point average (GPA), GPA in psychology courses, and the quality of the student's undergraduate institution. Yet, from the point of view of controlling or increasing a student's score on the Psychology Area test, these do not immediately give insight into how that might be done. Perhaps much of the variance in these predictors is the result of the intelligence of the student, which might also independently contribute to the determination of the Graduate Record Exam (GRE) score. Thus it may be the case either that some of these predictors could not be readily changed, or that changing one of them, such as the value of a student's GPA, would not cause a change in the score the student achieves on the GRE. However, if students randomly assigned to an intensive instructional program were shown to have significantly higher GRE Psychology test scores than students randomly assigned to a control condition, one has gained insight into how one could increase GRE psychology scores, even though the strength of the relationship with the dependent variable may be considerably weaker than the relationship between the dependent variable and the continuous individual difference variables. How to characterize such varying strength of effects is one of the major concerns of this book, beginning with the Chapter 3.

Factors that are manipulated in studies are almost always discrete variables, whereas factors that are measured, although sometimes discrete, are more often relatively continuous. From the perspective only of accounting for variability in the dependent variable, the most important factors to include in a model are usually continuous measures of preexisting individual differences among subjects. We deal with considerations bearing on incorporating such variables into your models in Chapter 9. (For readers who have not been exposed previously to multiple regression, we have included a tutorial on the data disk to provide a brief introduction. For those who are familiar with multiple regression, a more in-depth discussion of the relationship between regression and analysis of variance, as well as how they relate to more advanced techniques, is included in Appendix B). Yet the effects of manipulated variables are clearer to interpret theoretically and apply practically, and constitute the primary focus of this book.

Some critical distinctions among types of experimental designs are introduced now that will structure much of the rest of the book. Designs differ in how many factors are being investigated, the number of levels of each factor and how those levels are selected, how the levels of different factors are combined, and whether participants in the study experience only one treatment or more than one treatment.

The simplest experimental design is one involving only a single factor. Among single-factor designs, the simplest situation to model, although not to interpret, occurs when there is only a single group of participants who may experience an experimental treatment, but there is no similar control group and no measured variable other than the dependent variable. This consitutes, to use Campbell and Stanley's (1963) terminology, a *one-shot case study* and permits only limited testing of hypotheses. For example, if one were to have available a national random sample of undergraduate psychology majors and have them experience a GRE psychology preparation course, one could compare their group mean to normative information on a typical score on the test. Because discrepancies from past averages might be the result either of the study program or because of differences between the participants in your study and the individuals in the norming group used to determine the typical score on the test, such one-shot case studies are seldom done. Instead, the more conventional design would include one or more control groups whose performance could be compared with that of the group of interest. When more than two groups are involved, one is typically interested not only in whether there are differences among the groups overall, but also in specific comparisons among combinations of group means. Designs in which the various groups are defined by the particular level of a single factor they experience are referred to as *one-way designs*, because the groups differ in one way or along one dimension. Note that this is the convention even when the levels of the factor correspond to conditions that differ qualitatively, not just quantitatively. A design with three groups that receive 5 hours, 10 hours, or 15 hours of classroom instruction is a one-way design, but so is a design that involves a group that receives classroom instruction, a group that receives a self-study manual, and a no-treatment control group.

For various practical or theoretical reasons, an experimenter may prefer to include multiple factors in a single study rather than in separate experiments. When an added factor represents a breakdown of participants ignored in a single-factor study (e.g., including gender along with treatment condition as a factor), typically the result is to increase power to detect the effect of the treatment factor, as well as to allow a check on the consistency of the effect of that factor across male and female subgroups. When the various conditions included in a study represent combinations of levels of two different factors, the design is referred to as a *two-way design*. One-way designs can be represented with a schematic involving a group of cells differing along one dimension, and in the usual case, two-way designs can be represented as a two-dimensional table as shown in Figure 2.4.

In cases of designs with multiple factors, designs differ in which combinations of levels of the different factors are used. In most cases, all possible combinations of levels of the factors

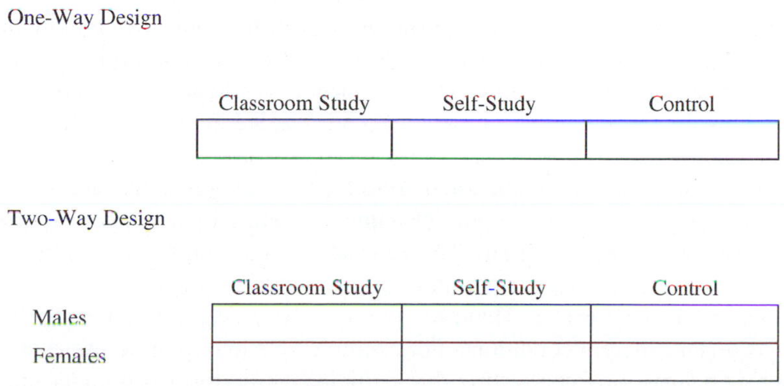

One-Way Design

Classroom Study	Self-Study	Control

Two-Way Design

	Classroom Study	Self-Study	Control
Males			
Females			

FIG. 2.4. Schematic diagrams of one-way and two-way designs.

Crossed Design

	Rogerian	Behavior Analytic
Therapist 1		
Therapist 2		
Therapist 3		
Therapist 4		

Nested Design

	Rogerian	Behavior Analytic
Therapist 1		missing
Therapist 2		missing
Therapist 3	missing	
Therapist 4	missing	

FIG. 2.5.   Diagrams of crossed and nested designs.

occur. The factors in such a design are said to be crossed, with all levels of one factor occurring in conjunction with every level of the other factor or factors. Thus, if there are a levels of Factor A and b levels of factor B, there would be $a \times b$ combinations of levels in the design. Each combination of levels corresponds to a different cell of the rectangular schematic of the design. Alternatively, in certain designs, not all of the possible combinations of levels occur. Among such incomplete designs, the most common is one where nonoverlapping subsets of levels of one factor occur in conjunction with the different levels of the other factor. For example, in a comparison of Rogerian and Behavior Analytic therapies, therapists may be qualified to deliver one method or the other, but not both. In such a case, therapists would be said to be *nested* within therapy methods. In contrast, if all therapists used both methods, therapists would be said to be *crossed* with method. Diagrams of these structures are shown in Figure 2.5.

Although it is not apparent from the groups that are ultimately included in a design, one can also make distinctions based on how the levels of a particular factor were selected for inclusion. In most instances, the levels are included because of an inherent interest in that particular level. One might be interested in a particular drug treatment or patient group, and thus would include the same condition in any replication of the study. Such factors are said to be *fixed*, and any generalization to other levels or conditions besides those included in the study must be made on nonstatistical grounds. Alternatively, if one wanted to provide a statistical argument for such generalizations, one could do so by selecting the levels for inclusion in a study at random from some larger set of levels. When this is done, the factor is designated as *random*, and how the statistical analysis of the data is carried out may be affected, as well as the interpretation.

Perhaps the most important distinction among types of design is between-subjects versus within-subjects designs. Here, the important point is whether each subject experiences only one or multiple experimental conditions. The basic advantage of the between-subjects design is that one need not be concerned about possible carryover effects from other conditions, because only one condition is experienced. However, one may be specifically interested in using the same subjects under different conditions. For example, one may want to use each participant as his or her own control by contrasting that participant's performance under one condition with his or her performance under another condition. In many cases in psychology, the various conditions experienced by a given subject correspond to observations at different points in

Between-subjects design

Condition 1	Condition 2	Condition 3
S_1 S_2 S_3 S_4 S_5	S_6 S_7 S_8 S_9 S_{10}	S_{11} S_{12} S_{13} S_{14} S_{15}

Within-subjects design

Condition 1	Condition 2	Condition 3
S_1	S_1	S_1
S_2	S_2	S_2
S_3	S_3	S_3
S_4	S_4	S_4
S_5	S_5	S_5

FIG. 2.6. Between-subjects vs. within-subjects designs.

time. For example, a test of clinical treatments may assess clients at each of several follow-up time points. If so, the same subjects would serve in multiple conditions. Denoting the different subjects in an experiment by the letter "S" with a different subscript for each person, we can diagram a basic between-subjects design as in Figure 2.6 and contrast that with the structure of a within-subject design.

Part II of this book, which includes Chapters 3 through 10, concerns various between-subjects designs, beginning with single-factor designs in Chapter 3, and considering tests of contrasts among the levels in Chapters 4 and 5. Chapters 7 and 8 extend this to multiple-factor designs. Chapter 9 considers the implications of having a continuous predictor variable, as well as a grouping variable in the analysis. Chapter 10 concludes the discussion of between-subjects designs with a consideration of designs with random and nested factors.

Parts III and IV of the book, which include Chapters 11 through 16, focus primarily on designs involving within-subject factors. Chapters 11 and 13 consider the case in which there is only one within-subject factor. Chapters 12 and 14 consider cases in which there are multiple factors, either all within-subjects factors or one or more within-subjects factors in conjunction with one or more between-subjects factors. Chapters 15 and 16 present an introduction to some new methods developed largely since the 1980s for dealing with correlated data, such as that obtained in repeated measures designs and with random factors to which you are introduced in Chapter 10. Chapter 15 explains how these models, which we term *multilevel hierarchical mixed models*, can be used with repeated measures designs, and Chapter 16 develops how they can be used with nested designs.

EXERCISES

1. True or False: The observed value of a test statistic, and hence the observed p value, depend on the data collected in a study.

2. True or False: If a p value indicates the results of a study are highly statistically significant, the null hypothesis cannot be true.

3. True or False: Other things being equal, the smaller the p value, the stronger the evidence against the null hypothesis.

4. True or False: The p value in a randomization test can be 0.

*5. True or False: The p value associated with the observed value of a test statistic is the probability the results are due to chance.

6 Assume a cognitive psychologist is planning an experiment involving brief presentations of letter strings that satisfy certain constraints. There are 14 such letter strings that satisfy the constraints, but only 6 can be used in a particular paradigm.
   a. How many combinations of 6 letter strings can be chosen from the set of 14?
   b. Given that 6 letter strings have been selected, in how many different sequences could they conceivably be presented?

*7. Assume a staff member at the local state mental hospital who has been doing intake interviews for years claims that he can tell on the basis of his interviews whom the psychiatrists will judge to be sufficiently healthy to release from the hospital within the first week and whom the psychiatrists will require to stay longer than a week. As a young clinical intern at the hospital who is taken with actuarial as opposed to intuitive predictions, you are eager to prove the staff member wrong. You bet him that he will perform no differently than could be explained by chance (with alpha of .05, two-tailed) in his predictions about the next 12 patients. He agrees to the bet on the condition that you first provide him information at the end of the week about how many of the 12 patients were released so that he will know how many such patients to name. With this figure, he thinks he can determine who the released patients were, just on the basis of his earlier interview (he has no subsequent contact with the patients). To your surprise, he correctly names 5 of the 6 patients released early. Do you owe him any money? Would it have made any difference if he had named 5 of 6 early release patients out of a set of 15 intake interviews rather than 12? Support your answers.

8. A police officer in an urban police department alleges that minorities are being discriminated against in promotion decisions. The difference in promotion rates in 1984 is offered as evidence. In that year, among those eligible for promotion to the rank of sergeant, 20 officers, including 7 members of minority groups, passed an objective exam to qualify them for consideration by the review board. The number of officers that can be promoted is determined by the number of vacancies at the higher rank, and in 1984, there were 10 vacancies at the rank of sergeant that needed to be filled. Eight of the 13 nonminority officers were promoted, for a promotion rate of 61.5%, whereas only 2 of the 7 minority officers were promoted, for a promotion rate of 28.5%. If one assumes that the decisions about whom to promote were made independently of minority status, what is the probability that the discrepancy between proportions being promoted would be at least this different by chance alone, given the total number of officers under consideration and the total number of promotions possible?

9. Fisher (1934) illustrated his exact test for a 2×2 table with data on criminal twins in his first paper read before the Royal Statistical Society. The study identified 30 male criminals known to have a same-sex twin. The twin pairs were classified as monozygotic or dizygotic, and each of the 30 twin brothers of the identified criminals were then classified as to whether he was also a convicted criminal. As shown in the following table, 10 of the 13 monozygotic criminals had brothers who had been convicted, whereas only 2 of 17 dizygotic criminals had brothers who had been convicted. What is the probability that so large a discrepancy in proportions would have arisen under the assumption that the difference observed is due to chance?

Convictions of Twin Brothers of Identified Criminals

	Monozygotic	Dizygotic	Total
Convicted	10	2	12
Not convicted	3	15	18
Total	**13**	**17**	**30**

*10. Biological changes that result from psychological manipulations, although typically not well understood, have captured attention in many areas such as health psychology. One early study examined the effects of the social environment on the anatomy of the brain in an effort to find evidence for the kinds of changes in the brain as a result of experience demanded by learning theories. The experiments are described in Bennett, E. L., Diamond, M. C., Krech, D., & Rosenzweig, M. R. (1964). "Chemical and anatomical plasticity of the brain" *Science 146*, 610–619, and some of the raw data are presented in Freedman et al. (1998, p. 501). Pairs of male rats from a litter were used as subjects, with one member of each litter being chosen at random to be reared with other rats in an enriched environment, complete with playthings and novel areas to explore on a regular basis, whereas another member of the litter was randomly selected to be reared in isolation in a relatively deprived environment. Both groups were permitted to consume as much as they wanted of the same kinds of food and drink. After a month, the deprived environment animals were heavier and had heavier brains overall. Of critical interest though was the size of the cortex, or gray matter portion, of the brain in the two groups. The experiment was replicated a number of times. However, in the current exercise, we are considering the data from only one of the replications (labeled Experiment 3 in Freedman et al., 1998, p. 501). The weights of the cortex (in milligrams) for the pairs of experimental (enriched) and control (deprived) subjects are shown in the following table:

Experiment #3

Experimental	Control
690	668
701	667
685	647
751	693
647	635
647	644
720	665
718	689
718	642
696	673
658	675
680	641

Test for the effect of the treatment in this experiment by doing a randomization test. That is, perform a test of the hypothesis that the sum of the difference scores is no different than you would expect if the + and − signs had been assigned with probability .5 to the absolute values of the obtained difference scores. Although a large number of rerandomizations are possible with 12 pairs of subjects, the randomization test can be carried out here with even less computation than a *t* test by thinking a bit about the possibilities. To carry out the test, you should answer the following questions:

a. What is the observed sum of differences here?

b. How many assignments of signs to differences are possible?

c. What proportion of these would result in a sum at least as large in absolute value as that observed? To answer this question, use the following approach:

  (i) What is the largest possible positive sum that could be achieved, given the observed absolute values of the differences?

  (ii) By considering how much this largest sum would be reduced by changing one or two of the signs of the absolute differences from positive to negative, determine which assignments of signs to differences would result in sums between (or equal to) the maximal sum and the observed sum.

  (iii) Considering the symmetry of the distribution of sums resulting from rerandomizations, what is the total number of sums as extreme or more extreme, either positive or negative, as the observed sum?

*11. In 1876 Charles Darwin reported the results of a series of experiments on "The Effects of Cross- and Self-Fertilisation in the Vegetable Kingdom." The description of his experiment and the table of data for this problem are based on Fisher's discussion of "A Historical Experiment on Growth Rate"

(Fisher, 1935/1971, Chapter III). The experimental method adopted by Darwin was to pit each self-fertilized plant against a cross-fertilized one under conditions that were as similar as possible for the two plants. Darwin emphasized this similarity by indicating "my crossed and self-fertilised plants . . . were of exactly the same age, were subjected from first to last to the same conditions, and were descended from the same parents" (as quoted in Fisher, 1935/1971, p. 28). One of the ways Darwin used to equalize conditions for the two members of a pair was to plant them in the same pot. The dependent measure was the height of the plant. (Darwin did not specify when this was measured, other than to say that all plants were of the same age when their height was measured.) Although sample sizes were relatively small, Darwin indicated in his report that the experiment required 11 years to complete. To be certain that his analysis of these valuable data was correct, Darwin requested and obtained statistical consulting from his half-cousin, Francis Galton. Darwin's data and Galton's rearrangements of the data are shown in Table 2.5. Darwin's paired data are shown in columns II and III, where the reader sees that varying numbers of pairs of plants were put in each pot. For example, there were three pairs in Pot I, five pairs in Pot III, and so on. Galton complained that the data had no "prima facie appearance of regularity." He attempted to rectify this problem by arranging the data by rank ordering according to heights, first within pots in columns IV and V, and then collapsing across pots in columns VI and VII. Galton's differences between the reordered lists are shown in column VIII.

a. Criticize Darwin's experimental design.

b. Perform appropriate analyses of these data.

   (i) Begin simply. Determine how many of the within-pair differences in heights in the original data of columns II and III favor cross-fertilization. If the cross-fertilization had no effect, how many differences would you expect on the average out of 15 to favor the cross-fertilized member of a pair? Is the observed number of differences favoring cross-fertilization significantly different from what you would expect by chance?

TABLE 2.5
ZEA MAYS (YOUNG PLANTS)

			Arranged in Order or Magnitude				
	As Recorded by Mr. Darwin		In Separate Pots		In a Single Series		
Column I	II	III	IV	V	VI	VII	VIII
	Crossed	Self-Fertilized	Crossed	Self-Fertilized	Crossed	Self-Fertilized	Difference
	Inches	Inches	Inches	Inches	Inches	Inches	Inches
Pot I	$23\frac{4}{8}$	$17\frac{3}{8}$	$23\frac{4}{8}$	$20\frac{3}{8}$	$23\frac{4}{8}$	$20\frac{3}{8}$	$-3\frac{1}{8}$
	12	$20\frac{3}{8}$	21	20	$23\frac{2}{8}$	20	$-3\frac{2}{8}$
	21	20	12	$17\frac{3}{8}$	23	20	-3
					$22\frac{1}{8}$	$18\frac{5}{8}$	$-3\frac{4}{8}$
Pot II	22	20	22	20	$22\frac{1}{8}$	$18\frac{5}{8}$	$-3\frac{4}{8}$
	$19\frac{1}{8}$	$18\frac{3}{8}$	$21\frac{4}{8}$	$18\frac{5}{8}$	22	$18\frac{3}{8}$	$-3\frac{5}{8}$
	$21\frac{4}{8}$	$18\frac{5}{8}$	$19\frac{1}{8}$	$18\frac{3}{8}$	$21\frac{5}{8}$	18	$-3\frac{5}{8}$
					$21\frac{4}{8}$	18	$-3\frac{4}{8}$
Pot III	$22\frac{1}{8}$	$18\frac{5}{8}$	$23\frac{2}{8}$	$18\frac{5}{8}$	21	18	-3
	$20\frac{3}{8}$	$15\frac{2}{8}$	$22\frac{1}{8}$	18	21	$17\frac{3}{8}$	$-3\frac{5}{8}$
	$18\frac{2}{8}$	$16\frac{4}{8}$	$21\frac{5}{8}$	$16\frac{4}{8}$	$20\frac{3}{8}$	$16\frac{4}{8}$	$-3\frac{7}{8}$
	$21\frac{5}{8}$	18	$20\frac{3}{8}$	$16\frac{2}{8}$	$19\frac{1}{8}$	$16\frac{2}{8}$	$-2\frac{7}{8}$
	$23\frac{2}{8}$	$16\frac{2}{8}$	$18\frac{2}{8}$	$15\frac{2}{8}$	$18\frac{2}{8}$	$15\frac{4}{8}$	$-2\frac{6}{8}$
					12	$15\frac{2}{8}$	$+3\frac{2}{8}$
Pot IV	21	18	23	18	12	$12\frac{6}{8}$	$+0\frac{6}{8}$
	$22\frac{1}{8}$	$12\frac{6}{8}$	$22\frac{1}{8}$	18	—	—	—
	23	$15\frac{4}{8}$	21	$15\frac{4}{8}$	—	—	—
	12	18	12	$12\frac{6}{8}$	—	—	—

    (ii) Perform the simplest possible parametric statistical test appropriate for analyzing Darwin's data. How does the p value for this test compare to that in part (i)? Why is the difference between the p values in this case in the direction it is?

    (iii) What assumptions are required for your analyses in parts (i) and (ii)?

    (iv) One could, and Fisher, in fact, did, carry out a randomization test on these data. What assumptions does that test require, and what hypothesis would it test here?

c. Criticize Galton's analysis. How differently would the strength of the evidence have appeared if the data in columns VI and VII had been used for analysis rather than that in columns II and III?

II

Model Comparisons for Between-Subjects Designs

The aim of science is, on the one hand, a comprehension as complete as possible ... and, on the other hand, the accomplishment of this aim by the use of a minimum of primary concepts and relations.

—ALBERT EINSTEIN, *PHYSICS AND REALITY*, 1936

3

Introduction to Model Comparisons: One-Way Between-Subjects Designs

The basic purpose of analysis of variance (ANOVA) is to assist the researcher in formulating a linear model that is appropriate for describing the data obtained in a study. The most appropriate model is one that is as simple as possible, yet still provides an adequate description of the data. Although the simplicity and adequacy of a particular model could be evaluated on an absolute basis, typically models are judged on a relative basis by comparisons with other possible models. This notion of searching for a simple yet adequate model is pervasive. It informs not only all applications of ANOVA, but also many other kinds of hypothesis testing.

We begin our discussion of ANOVA and linear models by approaching the problem from a purely descriptive point of view. We define a model in this context, as we develop shortly, as simply an algebraic statement of how the scores on the dependent variable arose. *Linear* is used in the sense of linear combination; that is, the models portray the dependent variable as being the result of the additive combination of various effects. We estimate the unknowns in each model in such a way that the model appears as adequate as possible; that is, the error of the model is minimized given a particular set of data. Statistical tests can then be developed as a comparison of the minimal errors associated with two competing models. To perform a hypothesis test is essentially to ask if a more complex model results in a substantially better fit to the data than does a simpler model.

To give an overview of the direction our discussion, we first present the rationale and form of the general linear model. In the remainder of the chapter, our discussion proceeds from the simplest case of this general linear model to more and more complex forms. We consider a one-group situation, a two-group situation, and then situations involving three or more groups of subjects. To ensure that the model-comparison approach is clear, we begin with experimental designs that are one or two steps simpler than those considered in typical ANOVA texts. Besides easing the introduction to linear models, this illustrates the generality of the linear models approach.

When considering the situation involving a single population, typically the primary question to answer is, "Is the mean of the population equal to a particular value?" Naturally, any attempt to answer such a question involves estimating the population mean for the dependent variable on the basis of a sample of data. After analyzing this situation descriptively, we develop an intuitively reasonable test statistic and relate this to a statistical test with which you are probably already familiar. (If you need a review of elementary parametric statistical tests, see the Tutorial on the data disk.)

In the two-group situation, our approach is similar, and our concern is to use the model-comparison procedure to address the question, Are the two population means equal? In other designs involving three or more populations, which is the simplest case in which most researchers would use ANOVA, the question simply generalizes to, Are all the population means the same?

Thus, our tactic is to consider first the general form of linear models and then one-sample tests, two-sample tests, and several-sample tests as special cases of the general approach. Once the general approach has been introduced for the tests in these different situations, we discuss other topics, including methods for characterizing the effects observed in a study and the assumptions underlying the tests.

In each case considered in this chapter, we assume that the samples represent independent groups of participants and that these groups differ along a single dimension or factor. Hence, the experimental designs under consideration here are termed *one-way between-subject designs*. Once you understand the linear model approach in these simple situations, extensions to multiple-factor designs or topics such as regression or analysis of covariance should come relatively easily.

Obviously, our concern in this chapter is primarily going to be with statistical models, tests, and indices. These are extremely useful ways of summarizing or condensing data. However, before beginning to summarize one's data, the individual data points themselves should be examined. For example, Figure 3.1 displays the data on 30 individuals in a mood induction study. Participants were assigned at random to one of three conditions designed to influence their mood, and their overall affect was rated by an observer who saw a videotape of their facial expressions but did not know to what condition participants were assigned. We analyze these data later in the chapter when we discuss three-group designs. Although we want to develop

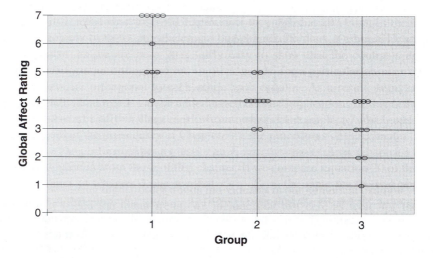

FIG. 3.1. Individual scores on a 7-point rating scale of global affect in three treatment groups (1 = Pleasant Mood Induction, 2 = Neutral Mood Induction, 3 = Unpleasant Mood Induction).

ways of making inferences about population means based on such samples of data, the first priority in understanding results is to try to get a feel for the individual values themselves. As the APA Task Force on Statistical Inference advised, "before you compute any statistics, *look at your data*" (Wilkinson et al., 1999, p. 597). This allows you to screen for errors in data entry or coding, examine the form of the distributions, and see whether it is plausible to view the data as conforming to the assumptions of the statistical procedures you plan to use. In the current situation, for example, it appears the individual scores are roughly equally spread out within each group. However, the typical level of scores on the dependent variable seems to differ across group. Much of this chapter is devoted to developing methods for validating and quantifying, but not substituting for, such preliminary impressions.

THE GENERAL LINEAR MODEL

The basic assumption underlying all models considered in this book is that any phenomenon is affected by multiple factors. Although our assumption of finite causation postulates that the number of factors causing any event is not infinitely large (hence, causes can be replicated and science is possible), we also must realistically acknowledge that many factors enter into why a particular subject obtains a particular score on any dependent variable that is likely to be of interest in behavioral science research. In any one research project, we can hope to manipulate or measure only a small number of the likely causal factors of any event. The remainder we either fail to recognize or recognize but do not account for in our model. Thus at the simplest level, the basic structure of our models of data is as follows:

$$
\begin{array}{l}
\text{observed value} \\
\text{on dependent} \\
\text{variable}
\end{array}
=
\begin{array}{l}
\text{sum of effects} \\
\text{of "allowed-for"} \\
\text{factors}
\end{array}
+
\begin{array}{l}
\text{sum of effects} \\
\text{of other} \\
\text{factors}
\end{array}
$$

or as John Tukey (1977) succinctly expressed it: data = fit + residual.

We "allow for" the effect of a factor by explicitly incorporating a term into our statistical model for that factor. The other factors can be dealt with in one of two ways. First, variables that we know are important but that are not the immediate concern of our research can be held constant. We can thus "control for" the effect of age by selecting all subjects from the same age range or the effect of the location in which an experiment is run by using the same laboratory room for all subjects. Unrecognized factors such as certain common historical events could also conceivably be constant across all subjects in a sample. Second, we can allow certain other factors to vary across subjects. This may arise because we explicitly decide that it is not desirable to control for a particular factor. For example, characteristics of a person's skin may influence galvanic skin response (GSR) readings in a psychophysiological study, but be too expensive in time and resources to measure independently. Or, intelligence may be recognized as an important factor in performance on a problem-solving task, but we may choose not to select subjects on the basis of intelligence so as to increase the generality of our findings. Furthermore, variation occurs without our knowledge in a host of factors besides those we allow for in our model. Most obviously, the history of individual subjects is, for the most part, beyond our knowledge. Other factors such as minor differences in environmental conditions vary from subject to subject and may influence performance in some way. The effects of all these other varying factors are lumped together in our statistical model in an error or residual term that is allowed to assume a unique value for each subject.

Thus, we can refine slightly the structure of our model to distinguish between other factors that are held constant and those that vary randomly over subjects:

$$
\begin{array}{c}
\text{observed value} \\
\text{on dependent} \\
\text{variable}
\end{array}
=
\begin{array}{c}
\text{effect of} \\
\text{constant} \\
\text{factors}
\end{array}
+
\begin{array}{c}
\text{sum of effects} \\
\text{of allowed-for} \\
\text{factors}
\end{array}
+
\begin{array}{c}
\text{randomly} \\
\text{varying} \\
\text{other factors}
\end{array}
$$

To give a concrete example, there are obviously any number of factors exerting an influence on an individual child's performance on a particular IQ test. In one research project, we might be interested in concentrating on assessment of how various parental characteristics such as socioeconomic status (SES), parents' IQ, and time spent with the child are related to their child's IQ score. Thus, our model might be

$$
\begin{array}{rl}
\text{child's IQ score} = & \text{a baseline IQ score} + \text{the effect of parents' SES} \\
& + \text{the effect of parents' IQ} \\
& + \text{the effect of amount of time spent with parents} \\
& + \text{the effect of other factors}
\end{array}
$$

As you can see, it quickly becomes cumbersome, even for just three specific factors, to write out the labels for each in an equation. Some sort of shorthand obviously is needed.

We follow the convention of using Y to denote the dependent variable and using Xs for the various "accounted-for" factors. We can then translate the verbal equation into a more typical algebraic form:

$$
Y_i = \beta_0 X_{0_i} + \beta_1 X_{1_i} + \beta_2 X_{2_i} + \beta_3 X_{3_i} + \varepsilon_i
$$

Here, Y_i represents the score of individual i on the dependent variable, and the Xs provide information about the level of individual i on the factors for which we are allowing. The βs are unknowns that we must estimate. Each β indicates something of the relationship between a particular X factor and the dependent variable. [Frequently, as noted in Chapter 1 (p. 7), we refer to these unknowns as *effect parameters*. However, whether one's interpretation should be that of a causal rather than a correlational relationship hinges on one's theory of the process. One's ability to persuade others of the causal nature of the relationship often hinges on the design of the study—for example, whether the experimenter independently determined the level of a factor experienced by a particular individual.]

The first unknown parameter and X variable listed in the model typically play the special role of reflecting the effect of the constant factors, that is, those factors that are common to all subjects. Thus, X_0 is usually simply a 1 for every individual, indicating that 1 times the constant is part of the equation for each individual; the constant β_0 is usually the mean of the population from which we are sampling (cf. the following section). The final term in the equation also plays a special role. Epsilon (ε)—that is, the "e" of the Greek alphabet—designates error, or the randomly varying other factors, with ε_i being the error for individual i. In a sense, ε_i is a nonvariable because it simply takes up whatever "slack" is left in Y after you predict as well as you can with the X variables. However, this term, which makes up the difference between the predictions and reality, is a very important component of the model, because it is the magnitude of these errors that is the means by which we assess the adequacy of each model.[1]

The only change we must make to arrive at a very general form of the previously described model is to allow for some arbitrarily large number of factors in the model. If we say that p is the number of factors, then we have

$$Y_i = \beta_0 X_{0_i} + \beta_1 X_{1_i} + \beta_2 X_{2_i} + \beta_3 X_{3_i} + \cdots + \beta_p X_{p_i} + \varepsilon_i \tag{1}$$

All univariate (single dependent measure) tests we consider in this text can be viewed as comparisons of various special cases of this general linear model.

ONE-GROUP SITUATION

Basics of Models

Consider the case in which there is just a single group of scores that result from a particular study. For example, we might use the IQ score from the Wechsler Intelligence Scale for Children–Revised (WISC-R) as a dependent measure, but not know anything that would allow different predictions to be made for the different individuals within the group. In such a situation, we clearly cannot be allowing for the variation of any factors across groups—there's just one group. Thus, if we eliminate allowed-for factors from our model, we are left with just the effect of constant factors and the effects of factors that randomly vary from one subject to the next. Such a random-variation model is typically expressed

$$Y_i = \mu + \varepsilon_i \tag{2}$$

That is, our model postulates that variable Y has some unknown typical value in the population and that deviations from this typical value are due to random, uncontrolled factors; ε_i denotes this random error and is the sole source of variance in the Y scores. The typical value of Y in the population is usually denoted by the Greek letter mu (μ), and is generally unknown, although we might have some a priori ideas about its value.

We could just as well have used some other symbol, such as β_0, for this typical value. We could also make explicit that this value is to be used as a prediction for every subject by saying that it is to be multiplied by 1 for every subject. You can see, then, that this random-variation model could be expressed more explicitly as a special case of the general linear model (see Equation 1):

$$Y_i = \beta_0 X_{0_i} + \varepsilon_i \tag{3}$$

where $X_0 = 1$ for every subject.

However, to use μ and presume it is clear that our model implies a prediction equation for each subject is more common. Thus, we could view Equation 2 as being a shorthand for a set of n equations, where n is the number of subjects in our group. That is,

$$\begin{aligned} Y_1 &= \mu + \varepsilon_1 \\ Y_2 &= \mu + \varepsilon_2 \\ &\vdots \\ Y_n &= \mu + \varepsilon_n \end{aligned} \tag{4}$$

The Y scores are values we observe for our sample, but μ and the n values of ε_i are unknown. From a pragmatic viewpoint, we typically are much more interested in finding the most appropriate value of μ than in determining the exact error for each subject. However, technically we have n equations in $n + 1$ unknowns (even if one unknown is of more interest than the others). This means that there are any number of possible values of μ and ε_i that we could use and still satisfy the equations. To obtain a unique solution for the unknowns in the equations in (4), we must impose some additional constraint, or, in the terminology used by statisticians, *side condition.*

To see what might be a reasonable constraint or criterion to adopt to estimate the unknowns in any model, we might view the model as a prediction equation. Generally, in prediction you want to make your guesses as close to the observed values as possible. The εs then could be viewed as the errors of prediction for each subject, which would be estimated by e_i, the difference between the observed value and your predicted value of μ. That is,

$$e_i = \hat{\varepsilon}_i = Y_i - \hat{\mu} \tag{5}$$

(We follow the convention of using a caret over a symbol—which here you read as "mu hat"—to indicate a predicted or estimated value.) Because your model constrains you to guess the same value for every score in your sample, you obviously will be wrong generally. However, you likely would want to choose your predicted value so that on the average your errors would balance out—that is, you might like the expected value of $Y_i - \hat{\mu}$ to be zero. In addition, you would probably not want systematic large positive errors simply to be canceled out by systematic large negative errors, but would think it more desirable if your errors in general, irrespective of sign, were small. Thus, you might hit on using squared errors, $(Y_i - \hat{\mu})^2$, to indicate the lack of accuracy of your predictions, because squaring is a mathematically convenient way of ignoring the sign and emphasizes the importance of large errors. Simply specifying that we want the sum or average of these squared deviations to be as small as possible is sufficient to obtain a unique solution to the equations in (4). Furthermore, we use this simple desideratum any time we want to estimate parameters in any linear model. Choosing parameter estimates to minimize squared errors of prediction is known as the *least-squares criterion.* Least-squares estimates possess a number of desirable statistical properties, such as always being unbiased. In addition, they are minimum variance unbiased linear estimators, which means that over replications of a study, the least-squares estimates of the population parameter would be more efficient (have less variability) than would any other estimator that also is a linear combination of the observations in the sample. Incidentally, note that this holds true regardless of whether ε_i is normally distributed. However, if normality is approximated, several important statistical results follow; the most important is that we can legitimately do standard parametric statistical tests and justifiably consult statistical tables to determine the probability that the results of a study, or more extreme results, would have arisen, presuming only chance variation is operating.

In the one-group situation, the least-squares criterion implies that we should choose the estimate of the mean in such a way that we minimize the sum of squared errors; that is, we choose $\hat{\mu}$ to minimize

$$\sum_{i=1}^{n} e_i^2 = \sum_{i=1}^{n} (Y_i - \hat{\mu})^2 \tag{6}$$

You may well recall from a previous statistics course that the sample mean $\overline{Y}$ has the property that the sum of squared deviations from it is smaller than around any other value. This is proved in the following section. (The material in the paragraph that follows requires somewhat more use of mathematical arguments than does most of the text. Such sections marked "Optional" can be skipped on initial reading of the chapter without loss of continuity.)

OPTIONAL

Proof That $\overline{Y}$ Is the Least-Squares Estimate of μ

We can easily demonstrate algebraically that $\overline{Y}$ is the least-squares estimate of μ, and doing so has the additional pedagogical value of illustrating a little mathematical trick that is often useful in seeing the relationship between different sums of squared errors. The algebraic proof is as follows: Assume that we want to use some constant value C, possibly different from $\overline{Y}$, as our estimate of μ. Then, our sum of squared errors would be

$$\sum_{i=1}^{n} e_i^2 = \sum_{i=1}^{n}(Y_i - C)^2 \tag{7}$$

Clearly, we would not change the expression on the right if we were to add a zero to it. The "trick" is that a very useful form of zero to add in is $-\overline{Y} + \overline{Y}$. This lets us see the relationship between these squared errors and something with which we are already familiar. Adding in $-\overline{Y} + \overline{Y}$, grouping terms and expanding, we have

$$\sum(Y_i - \overline{Y} + \overline{Y} - C)^2 = \sum[(Y_i - \overline{Y}) + (\overline{Y} - C)]^2 \tag{8}$$

$$= \sum[(Y_i - \overline{Y})^2 + 2(Y_i - \overline{Y})(\overline{Y} - C) + (\overline{Y} - C)^2] \tag{9}$$

$$= \sum(Y_i - \overline{Y})^2 + \sum 2(Y_i - \overline{Y})(\overline{Y} - C) + \sum(\overline{Y} - C)^2 \tag{10}$$

When we factor out constants, note that the cross-product term—that is, the second summation in Equation 10—becomes $2(\overline{Y} - C)\Sigma(Y_i - \overline{Y})$, which equals 0, because $\Sigma(Y_i - \overline{Y}) = 0$. Furthermore, you may recognize the term on the left in Equation 10 as the numerator of the familiar definitional formula for the unbiased sample variance s^2. That is,

$$s^2 = \left[\sum(Y_i - \overline{Y})^2\right] \Big/ (n - 1) \tag{11}$$

so,

$$\sum(Y_i - \overline{Y})^2 = (n - 1)s^2 \tag{12}$$

Making this substitution for the term on the left in Equation 10 and dropping the middle term, we have

$$\sum(Y_i - C)^2 = (n - 1)s^2 + \sum(\overline{Y} - C)^2 \tag{13}$$

Because the term on the right is a constant value and adding up n such values is equivalent to multiplying the value by n, we see that the sum of squared deviations from C can be expressed as a function of two squared quantities:

$$\sum(Y_i - C)^2 = (n - 1)s^2 + n(\overline{Y} - C)^2 \tag{14}$$

Because on the right we have the sum of multiples of two squared quantities, we know neither can be negative and that $\Sigma(Y_i - C)^2$ must be at least as large as $(n - 1)s^2$. Furthermore, $\Sigma(Y_i - C)^2$ is a minimum when $n(\overline{Y} - C)^2$ is zero, which can only occur if $C = \overline{Y}$. Thus, we have proved that the way to minimize our errors of prediction—that is, the way to satisfy the least-squares criterion—is to use the sample mean as our estimate of the unknown parameter in our model.

Adopting $\overline{Y}$ as the best estimate of the parameter μ—that is, as the best value for $\hat{\mu}$—virtually completes the estimation problem: Once $\hat{\mu}$ is determined, we can get the values of the errors associated with individual subjects immediately because $e_i = Y_i - \hat{\mu}$. Furthermore, a very important by-product of using the least-squares criterion to estimate parameters is that it yields a measure of the adequacy of the model that is as fair as possible. That is, we know the sum of squared errors of prediction

$$\sum_{i=1}^{n} e_i^2 = \sum_{i=1}^{n}(Y_i - \overline{Y})^2$$

is as small as it could be for this model.

Naturally, other models for this one-group situation are also possible. One might be interested in how well a specific a priori value might do as an estimate of the observed scores. For example, we may wonder if it is plausible to model the IQ of a group of hyperactive children with the value of 100, which we know is representative of the population of all children. The appropriate model for such a supposition might be written

$$Y_i = \mu_0 + \varepsilon_i \tag{15}$$

where μ_0 is understood to be some prespecified constant value. This means that the values of e_i for this model are determined without any parameter estimation; that is, in this case,

$$e_i = \varepsilon_i = Y_i - \mu_0 \tag{16}$$

Thus, the total error (that is, the sum of squared errors) made by a model incorporating the restriction that $\mu = \mu_0$ is $\Sigma(Y_i - \mu_0)^2$. Typically, imposing such a restriction results in increased error relative to a model that is not so constrained. Examining the error associated with the current, restricted model allows us to see just what the increase in error will be. In fact, using the same technique that worked in proving $\overline{Y}$ was the least-squares estimator of μ—that is, adding and subtracting $\overline{Y}$—it can easily be shown[2] that

$$\sum(Y_i - \mu_0)^2 = \sum(Y_i - \overline{Y})^2 + n(\overline{Y} - \mu_0)^2 \tag{17}$$

When we compare this with the minimal error made with our unrestricted model $\Sigma(Y_i - \overline{Y})^2$, we see the magnitude of the increase in error associated with going to the restricted model is simply $n(\overline{Y} - \mu_0)^2$. This makes sense, because it should depend on how far $\overline{Y}$ is from our hypothesized value of μ_0.

The question that logically follows is, How much must the error be increased for us to consider our supposition (hypothesis) to be false? Because the increase in error we just developed is in squared Y units, it is difficult to evaluate directly. However, an intuitively reasonable relative measure of its magnitude is achieved by looking at the proportional increase in error—that is, how large the increase is relative to the best we can do with the unconstrained model:

$$\text{proportional increase in error} = \frac{\text{increase in error}}{\text{minimal error}} \tag{18}$$

Development of the General Form
of the Test Statistic

In the following paragraphs, we develop this idea of proportional increase in error into a test statistic. Our development does not proceed in the way the test statistic would be introduced in a mathematical statistics text. However, our goal is like the mathematician's in that we strive for generality, not just the solution to a single problem. We develop the test statistic rationally, not mathematically, as a reasonable index of the relative adequacy yet simplicity of two competing models. However, instead of developing things in a way that would work only in a one-sample situation, we introduce a method that works in essentially all cases we consider in this book. Doing so takes a few more lines than developing a test for only one sample. However, in so doing, we are providing a perspective and a general procedure that together serve as a unifying theme for the book.

To carry out our development more succinctly, consider the following terminology. We call the unconstrained model the *full model* because it is "full" of parameters, with the number of parameters in the full model frequently equaling the number of groups in the design. In the full model for the one-group case, we have one unknown parameter μ, which is to be estimated on the basis of the data. The general method used to arrive at a second model is to place restrictions on the parameters of the first model. The restrictions are essentially our null hypothesis and serve to delete some of the parameters from the set used by the full model. We call the resultant constrained model simply the *restricted model*. In the one-group case, the restricted model does not require the estimation of any parameters. Although that is not usually the case in other designs, it is true that the restricted model always involves the estimation of fewer parameters than does the full model. Thus, we have the following models, least-squares estimates, and errors, in the one-group case:

Model		Least-Squares Estimates	Errors
Full:	$Y_i = \mu + \varepsilon_{i_F}$	$\hat{\mu} = \overline{Y}$	$\sum e_{i_F}^2 = \sum (Y_i - \overline{Y})^2$
Restricted:	$Y_i = \mu_0 + \varepsilon_{i_R}$	No parameters estimated	$\sum e_{i_R}^2 = \sum (Y_i - \mu_0)^2$

We use E_F to designate the sum of squared errors $\sum e_{i_F}^2$ in the full model, and E_R to designate the analogous quantity $\sum e_{i_R}^2$ for the restricted model.[3] Letting PIE stand for the proportional increase in error, we can express our verbal equation comparing the adequacy of the two models in algebraic form as

$$\text{PIE} = \frac{E_R - E_F}{E_F} \qquad (19)$$

Substituting, we have

$$\text{PIE} = \frac{\sum e_{i_R}^2 - \sum e_{i_F}^2}{\sum e_{i_F}^2}$$

$$= \frac{\sum (Y_i - \mu_0)^2 - \sum (Y_i - \overline{Y})^2}{\sum (Y_i - \overline{Y})^2}$$

and using Equation 17 to simplify the numerator, we obtain

$$\text{PIE} = \frac{n(\overline{Y} - \mu_0)^2}{\sum(Y_i - \overline{Y})^2} \tag{20}$$

Hopefully, the final way PIE is expressed looks at least vaguely familiar. One of the first hypothesis tests you likely encountered in your first statistics course was a one-sample t test. Recall that the form of a one-sample t test assessing the null hypothesis $H_0 : \mu = \mu_0$ looks at the deviation of a sample mean from the hypothesized value relative to the standard error of the mean

$$
\begin{aligned}
t &= \frac{\overline{Y} - \mu_0}{\hat{\sigma}_{\overline{Y}}} = \frac{\overline{Y} - \mu_0}{s/\sqrt{n}} \\
&= \frac{\sqrt{n}(\overline{Y} - \mu_0)}{\sqrt{\sum(Y_i - \overline{Y})^2/(n-1)}}
\end{aligned}
\tag{21}
$$

where $\hat{\sigma}_{\overline{Y}}$ is the standard error of the mean (that is, the standard deviation of the sampling distribution of $\overline{Y}$) and s is the square root of the unbiased sample variance. Note that if we were to square the form of the one-sample t given on the right in Equation 21, we would have something very much like our PIE. In fact, all we would have to do to change PIE into t^2 is to divide the denominator[4] of the PIE by $(n-1)$. (Note that we have said nothing about distributional assumptions; we are simply pointing out the similarity between how we would compute an intuitively reasonable statistic for comparing two models and the form of the test statistic for the one-sample t. We consider assumptions about the distribution of Y scores shortly.)

We began our discussion of the model-comparison approach by noting that we want models that are simple yet adequate. You may wonder if we could not incorporate both of these aspects into a summary measure for comparing models. We must, in fact, do so. PIE simply compares the adequacy of the models (actually, in comparing errors of prediction, it does so by contrasting the inadequacy of the models) without regard to their complexity. To make PIE a more informative summary of the relative desirability of the models, we really want to take into account the simplicity of the models. We know in advance that our simpler, restricted model is necessarily less adequate than our full model (see Equation 17). Thus, intuitively, we would like our summary measure to indicate something such as, Is the loss in adequacy per additional unit of simplicity large? However, how could we assess the simplicity of a model?

The simplicity of a linear model is determined by the number of parameters: the fewer parameters, the simpler the model. As we illustrate momentarily, each parameter that we must estimate entails the loss of a degree of freedom. In fact, we define the degrees of freedom (df) resulting from using a particular equation as a model for an experiment as the number of independent observations in the study minus the number of independent parameters estimated. Thus, the df associated with a model can be used as our index of its simplicity. Given that, for a study having a fixed number of observations, the number of df associated with a model is inversely related to the number of parameters in the model, the df can be taken as a direct indicator of the model's simplicity: the more df, the simpler the model.

This allows us to construct a very useful summary measure for comparing models. The error of our more adequate model relative to its df gives us a basis for evaluating the size of the increase in error entailed by adopting a simpler model relative to the corresponding increase in df.

We can easily incorporate this consideration of the models' simplicity into our measure of the proportional increase in error.

Specifically, we need only divide the denominator and numerator of PIE in Equation 19 by the *df* of the model(s) involved in each. That is, in the denominator we divide the error of the full model (E_F) by the degrees of freedom of the full model (df_F), and in the numerator we divide the difference between the error of the restricted model and the error of the full model ($E_R - E_F$) by the difference in the degrees of freedom associated with the two models ($df_R - df_F$). This yields a revised measure, which we denote by F, of the relative adequacy yet simplicity of the two models:

$$F = \frac{(E_R - E_F)/(df_R - df_F)}{E_F/df_F} \tag{22}$$

This simple comparison measure is in fact extremely useful and general. We can use it for carrying out all the hypothesis tests we need for the various special cases of the general linear model we will consider. All tests in ANOVA, analysis of covariance, bivariate regression, and multiple regression can be computed using this formula. The models being compared may differ widely from one situation to the next, but our method of comparing them can always be the same.

If there is no difference between the two models' descriptive accuracy except for the additional free parameter(s) in the full model, then the numerator (the increase in error per additional degree of freedom associated with using the simpler, restricted model) would be expected to be approximately the same as the denominator (the baseline indication of error per degree of freedom). Thus, values of F near 1 would indicate no essential difference in the accuracy of the models, and the simpler model would be preferred on grounds of parsimony. However, if the increase in error associated with using the simpler model is larger than would be expected given the difference in parameters, then larger F values result, and we tend to reject the simpler model as inadequate.

For the two models we are considering for a design involving only one group of subjects, we can determine the degrees of freedom to use in our general formula quite easily. In the full model, we are estimating just one parameter, μ; thus, if we have n independent observations in our sample, the degrees of freedom associated with the full model is $n - 1$. In the restricted model, we do not have to estimate any parameters in this particular case; thus, $df_R = n$. When we subtract df_F from df_R, the number of subjects "drops out," and the difference is only the difference in the numbers of parameters estimated by the two models. Thus, for the one-group situation, we have

$$F = \frac{(E_R - E_F)/(df_R - df_F)}{E_F/df_F}$$

$$= \frac{n(\overline{Y} - \mu_0)^2/[n - (n - 1)]}{\sum(Y_i - \overline{Y})^2/(n - 1)} = t^2 \tag{23}$$

To make this intuitively developed descriptive statistic useful for inferential purposes (i.e., hypothesis testing), we need only assume that the individual errors have certain characteristics. Specifically, if we assume the error terms ε_i in our models are independently distributed as normal random variables with zero mean and variance σ^2, then it can be shown that the F in our general formula does in fact follow a theoretical F distribution with $df_R - df_F$ and df_F degrees of freedom.

TABLE 3.1
HYPERACTIVE CHILDREN'S WISC-R SCORES

Full-Model Analysis

IQ Scores Y_i	Prediction Equations	Parameter Term $\hat{\mu}$	Error Scores $e_{i_F} = Y_i - \hat{\mu}$	Squared Errors $e_{i_F}^2$
96	$= \hat{\mu} + e_1$	104	−8	64
102	$= \hat{\mu} + e_2$	104	−2	4
104	$= \hat{\mu} + e_3$	104	0	0
104	$= \hat{\mu} + e_4$	104	0	0
108	$= \hat{\mu} + e_5$	104	+4	16
110	$= \hat{\mu} + e_6$	104	+6	36
$\sum = 624$ $\overline{Y} = 104$			$\sum = 0$	$E_F = 120$

Restricted-Model Analysis

IQ Scores Y_i	Prediction Equations	Parameter Term μ_0	Error Scores $e_{i_R} = Y_i - \mu_0$	Squared Errors $e_{i_R}^2$
96	$= \mu_0 + e_1$	98	−2	4
102	$= \mu_0 + e_2$	98	4	16
104	$= \mu_0 + e_3$	98	6	36
104	$= \mu_0 + e_4$	98	6	36
108	$= \mu_0 + e_5$	98	10	100
110	$= \mu_0 + e_6$	98	12	144
				$E_R = 336$

$$F = \frac{(E_R - E_F/(df_R - df_F)}{E_F/df_F} = \frac{(366 - 120)/(6 - 5)}{120/5} = \frac{216}{24} = 9$$

$$t = \frac{\overline{Y} - \mu_0}{\hat{\sigma}_{\overline{Y}}} = \frac{\overline{Y} - \mu_0}{s/\sqrt{n}} = \frac{\overline{Y} - \mu_0}{\sqrt{\frac{\sum(Y - \overline{Y})^2}{n - 1}}/\sqrt{n}} = \frac{104 - 98}{\sqrt{\frac{120}{5}}/\sqrt{6}} = \frac{6}{\sqrt{\frac{24}{6}}} = 3$$

Numerical Example

Assume that you work in the research office of a large school system. For the last several years, the mean score on the WISC-R, which is administered to all elementary school children in your district, has been holding fairly steady at about 98. A parent of a hyperactive child in one of your special education programs maintains that the hyperactive children in the district are actually brighter than this average. To investigate this assertion, you randomly select the files of six hyperactive children and examine their WISC-R scores. Table 3.1 shows these scores.

The unconstrained, or full, model does not make any a priori judgments about the mean IQ of hyperactive children. Rather, the estimate of μ is chosen so that $E_F = \Sigma e_{i_F}^2$ is minimized for this set of data. As we know, the sample mean, which here equals $624/6 = 104$, minimizes this sum of squared errors. Computing the deviations from this estimated population mean, we note that they sum to zero. This is, of course, always going to be the case because

$$\sum e_{i_F} = \sum (Y_i - \overline{Y}) = \sum \left(Y - \sum Y/N \right)$$

$$= \sum Y - \sum \left(\sum Y/N \right) = \sum Y - N \left(\sum Y/N \right) = 0$$

We square each of these error scores and sum to obtain what we use as our index of the inadequacy of the model, that is, $E_F = 120$.

The degrees of freedom, which is the number of data values you would be free to choose once all parameter estimates have been specified, reflects the model's simplicity, as we indicated. For example, in the full model, once the sample mean is determined to be 104, you could choose five of the data values to be whatever you like, but the sixth must be the value that would bring the total to 624 so that the mean of the six scores will in fact be 104, that is, $Y_6 = 6(104) - \Sigma_{i=1}^{5} Y_i$. As indicated in Table 3.1, the *df* for our full model is 5—that is, the number of independent observations in the sample (6) minus the number of parameters estimated (1, which here is μ). In general, the degrees of freedom associated with a model for a particular set of data is the total number of independent observations minus the number of parameters to be estimated in that model.

The analysis for the restricted model proceeds similarly. However, in this simplest case, there are no parameters to estimate, the average of the population having been hypothesized to be exactly 98. Thus, the error scores associated with this model can be computed directly by subtracting 98 from each score. When these error scores are squared and summed, we get a total error ($E_R = 336$) that is considerably larger than that associated with the full model ($E_F = 120$). Recall that the restricted model always has as great or greater summed errors than that associated with the full model. In fact, as shown (see Equations 17 and 20), the increase in error here depends simply on how far $\overline{Y}$ is from μ_0, that is,

$$
\begin{aligned}
E_R - E_F &= n(\overline{Y} - \mu_0)^2 \\
&= 6(104 - 98)^2 = 6(6)^2 = 6(36) = 216 \\
&= 336 - 120
\end{aligned}
\tag{24}
$$

Finally, the degrees of freedom for the restricted model is simply equal to the number of observations—that is, 6—because no parameters had to be estimated.

Dividing our error summary measures by the corresponding degrees of freedom, as shown in our basic equation for the F near the bottom of Table 3.1, we obtain the values of the numerator and denominator of our test statistic. The value of 24 in the denominator is the squared error per degree of freedom for our full model (often referred to as *mean square error*). The value of 216 in the numerator is the increase in error per additional degree of freedom gained by adopting the restricted model. Computing their ratio, we get a value of 9 for F, which can be viewed, as we have indicated, at a descriptive level as an "adequacy yet simplicity" score. Its value here indicates that the additional error of the simpler restricted model per its additional degree of freedom is nine times larger than we would expect it to be on the basis of the error of the full model per degree of freedom. That is, the restricted model is considerably worse per extra degree of freedom in describing the data than is the full model relative to its degrees of freedom. Thus, intuitively it would seem that the restricted model should be rejected. We need, however, a statistical criterion for judging how large the F is.

To determine if the probability of obtaining an F this extreme is sufficiently small to justify rejecting the restricted model, we can consult the tabled values of the F distribution shown in Appendix Table A.2. To obtain a critical F value from the table, we consult the column corresponding to the degrees of freedom from the numerator of our test statistic—that is, $df_R - df_F$—and the main row of the table corresponding to the denominator degrees of freedom, that is, df_F. The third factor to be considered is the α level, that is, the probability of obtaining an F value larger than the tabled value, assuming that the restricted model is in fact correct. Critical F values are provided for six different α levels, namely .25, .10, .05, .025,

.01, and .001, on six adjacent rows of the table for each denominator df. When the observed F value of 9 is compared against the tabled values of the F distribution with numerator and denominator degrees of freedom of $df_R - df_F = 1$ and $df_F = 5$, respectively, we find it exceeds the critical value of 6.61 for $\alpha = .05$. The conclusion would then be that there is significant reason to doubt that the population of hyperactive children has the same mean IQ as the other students in your district. The parent who brought the matter to your attention apparently was correct.

Relationship of Models and Hypotheses

As may be clear, the two models being compared are the embodiments of two competing hypotheses. The full model corresponds to the alternative hypothesis, and the restricted model to the null hypothesis. In the full model and the alternative hypothesis, the population parameter is not constrained to equal any particular value. The restricted model is obtained from the full model by imposing the restriction on its parameters stated in the null hypothesis. As indicated below, restricting the μ in the full model to a particular value, μ_0, such as 98, yields the restricted model:

Hypothesis	**Model**	
$H_1 : \mu \neq \mu_0$	Full: $Y_i = \mu + \varepsilon_i$	(25)
$H_0 : \mu = \mu_0$	Restricted: $Y_i = \mu_0 + \varepsilon_i$	(26)

TWO-GROUP SITUATION

Development in Terms of Models

Designs involving a single group are rare in psychology and for good reason. Although it might be the case that there is one condition or treatment you are interested in, to evaluate that condition alone in an absolute sense in a compelling way is difficult. You may want to show that biofeedback is an effective way of reducing anxiety associated with public speaking. Trying the treatment with a group of volunteers and showing that after treatment their anxiety regarding public speaking was in the normal range would, of course, not constitute proof of the effectiveness of the biofeedback: their anxiety scores may have been normal to begin with. Selecting individuals for participation because they were very anxious about public speaking may seem like the obvious solution; but with only one group, improvement after biofeedback training could be attributed to regression toward the mean or to any of a number of other potential confounding variables (Campbell & Stanley, 1963; also see Chapter 1). Thus, using at least one comparison group is expected practice in psychological research. The model-comparison approach we developed for the one-group case can easily be extended for analysis of two-group designs.

We extend our statistical analysis to help us decide again between two alternative conceptions of the world. These competing viewpoints could be described verbally, or in terms of statistical hypotheses, or in terms of models of how the data arose. Typically, the question to be addressed is "Is there evidence that the two groups differ?" Thus, we want to compare a view that says the groups differ with one that says they do not. These views would correspond, respectively, to a statistical hypothesis that the population means of the two groups differ and to a hypothesis that they are equal. A model embodying the first hypothesis (which is the hypothesis you usually want to find evidence to support) would indicate that each score equals the population mean for its group plus some random error. A model embodying the second hypothesis would differ only in that it would use a single parameter for the population mean because it is to embody the restriction that the two groups are drawn from the same population. We can express these hypotheses and models in symbols:

Hypothesis	**Model**	
Alternative hypothesis: $\mu_1 \neq \mu_2$	Full model: $Y_{ij} = \mu_j + \varepsilon_{ij_F}$	(27)
Null hypothesis: $\mu_1 = \mu_2 = \mu$	Restricted model: $Y_{ij} = \mu + \varepsilon_{ij_R}$	(28)

Here, μ_1 and μ_2 are, of course, the population means of groups 1 and 2; more generally, we use μ_j to denote the population mean of the jth group. Note that the scores on the dependent variable Y now have two subscripts, i and j: the j designates groups and here takes on the values 1 and 2; the i, as before, indicates the individuals within a group. We allow the number of subjects in groups 1 and 2, designated n_1 and n_2, respectively, to differ. Thus, the ranges of the subscripts can be indicated succinctly as $j = 1, 2$ and $i = 1, 2, 3, \ldots, n_j$. Like the one-group case, the error score for each individual ε_{ij} indicates how much the dependent-variable score deviates from the parameter value. The errors for the simpler, restricted model are again larger in general than those for the full model, and the subscripts R and F are used when necessary to distinguish between them.

We see the generality of the model-comparison approach when we raise the question of how to decide between these two competing accounts of the data. The question in terms of model comparisons is "Will a restricted model involving fewer parameters be a significantly less adequate representation of the data than a full model with a parameter for each group?" This is the kind of question we address repeatedly in this book, and the method of resolving the trade-off between simplicity and adequacy is in terms of the general form of our F test, that is, $F = [(E_R - E_F)/(df_R - df_F)]/(E_F/df_F)$, where E_R and E_F are, as before, the sums of squared errors and df_R and df_F are the degrees of freedom associated with the two models.

Once again, we want to determine the errors associated with a model so that each model is placed in the best possible light. Using the least-squares criterion, as we have seen, not only gives us parameter estimates that are in many ways optimal, but also yields a measure of the model's adequacy, as we have defined it, that makes the model appear as adequate as possible. Let us work through the steps for determining the least-squares estimates of the parameters for the models, beginning with the restricted model.

A comparison of the restricted model in the two-group case, with the full model for the one-group situation (see Equations 28 and 25), reveals that they both involve using a single parameter to model the data. This suggests that the solution to the least-squares estimation problem should be the same, and, in fact, it is. That is, when one parameter estimate is to be used as the guess or prediction for all observations, the sum of squared errors is minimized when the mean of all observations is used as the estimate. Expressing this with symbols, the error associated with the restricted model for the two-group situation is

$$E_R = \sum_j \sum_i e_{ij_R}^2 = \sum_j \sum_i (Y_{ij} - \hat{\mu})^2 \qquad (29)$$

Following the identical reasoning to that used in the one-group case, it is easily shown that E_R is minimized when

$$\hat{\mu} = \sum_j \sum_i Y_{ij}/N \qquad (30)$$

that is, when $\hat{\mu}$ is set equal to the grand mean of all observations, which we denote $\overline{Y}$. For the full model, the estimation problem appears more complicated, because there are now two parameters to be estimated. However, the problem can be translated into a form where the same kind of solution can be used. Specifically, in the full model, we wish to minimize

$$E_F = \sum_j \sum_i e_{ij_F}^2 = \sum_{j=1}^{2} \sum_i (Y_{ij} - \hat{\mu}_j)^2 \qquad (31)$$

Because there are only two groups, we can express E_F simply as the sum of the total squared errors in group 1 and the total squared errors in group 2:

$$E_F = \sum_i (Y_{i1} - \hat{\mu}_1)^2 + \sum_i (Y_{i2} - \hat{\mu}_2)^2 \qquad (32)$$

Because each of the two terms on the right side of the equation is the sum of a set of squared numbers, each term must be positive, and the way in which E_F can be minimized is to minimize each of these separately. Thus, we have two minimization problems, but each is identical to the problem we addressed in the one-group case, namely "What number for a single group of scores results in the sum of squared deviations from that number being as small as possible?" The answer, you recall, is to use the mean of the observed scores in whatever group is being considered. Thus, the least-squares estimate of the population mean for each group is the sample mean for that group. That is, $\hat{\mu}_1 = (\Sigma_i Y_{i1})/n_1 = \overline{Y}_1$, and $\hat{\mu}_2 = (\Sigma_i Y_{i2})/n_2 = \overline{Y}_2$.

We now see how these measures of the adequacy of our two competing models for the two-group situation combine when they are entered into our general form of the F test:

$$F = \frac{(E_R - E_F)/(df_R - df_F)}{E_F/df_F} \qquad \text{(22, repeated)}$$

Noting that $df_R = N - 1$ because we estimate a single parameter in the restricted model and $df_F = N - 2$ because we estimate a population mean for each of the two groups in the full model, we see that $df_R - df_F = (N - 1) - (N - 2) = 2 - 1 = 1$, thus obtaining

$$F = \frac{\left(\sum \sum e_{ij_R}^2 - \sum \sum e_{ij_F}^2\right)/1}{\sum \sum e_{ij_F}^2/(N - 2)} \qquad (33)$$

$$= \frac{\sum_j \sum_i (Y_{ij} - \overline{Y})^2 - \sum_j \sum_i (Y_{ij} - \overline{Y}_j)^2}{\sum_j \sum_i (Y_{ij} - \overline{Y}_j)^2/(N - 2)} \qquad (34)$$

It turns out that E_R, the term on the left in the numerator in Equation 34, can be expressed[5] as the total of two quantities: (1) the sum of the squared deviations of the scores within a group from their group mean $\Sigma_j \Sigma_i (Y_{ij} - \overline{Y}_j)^2$, and (2) the sum of squared deviations of the group means from the grand mean $\Sigma_j \Sigma_i (\overline{Y}_j - \overline{Y})^2$. Because the former of these two quantities is how E_F is defined here, the difference between E_R and E_F used in the numerator of our test may be expressed as just the latter of these quantities, that is,

$$E_R - E_F = \left[\sum_j \sum_i (Y_{ij} - \overline{Y}_j)^2 + \sum_j \sum_i (\overline{Y}_j - \overline{Y})^2 \right] - \sum_j \sum_i (Y_{ij} - \overline{Y}_j)^2$$

$$= \sum_j \sum_i (\overline{Y}_j - \overline{Y})^2 \tag{35}$$

Also, because how much the group mean deviates from the grand mean is a constant for all subjects within a group, we have

$$E_R - E_F = \sum_j n_j (\overline{Y}_j - \overline{Y})^2 \tag{36}$$

Thus, the general form of our F test for the two-group situation reduces to

$$F = \frac{\sum\limits_j n_j (\overline{Y}_j - \overline{Y})^2}{\sum\limits_j \sum\limits_i (Y_{ij} - \overline{Y}_j)^2 / (N - 2)} \tag{37}$$

Alternative Development and Identification with Traditional Terminology

Traditionally within psychology, statistics texts have presented F tests in ANOVA not as a method for comparing models, but as a measure of the degree to which the data depart from what would be expected if chance alone were operating. This traditional approach can also be characterized by focusing on the question, Is the variability between groups greater than that expected on the basis of the within-group variability? That is, one asks if the variability among the group means is greater than would be expected given the variability observed among the individual scores within each of the groups.

The logic here is that if all scores in both groups were simply randomly selected from a single population of scores, the sample means of the two groups would still almost certainly differ because of sampling variability. Just how much the means would be expected to differ would depend on the variability of the population. This in turn can be estimated by either of the sample variances observed or, better, by a pooled estimate or weighted average of the two variances. If we use s_j^2 to denote the unbiased sample variance of the jth group of scores, that is,

$$s_j^2 = \frac{\sum\limits_i (Y_{ij} - \overline{Y}_j)^2}{n_j - 1} \tag{38}$$

then the pooled estimate of the population variance σ^2, based on these within-group sample variances, can be expressed as

$$\text{estimated } \sigma^2 = \frac{(n_1 - 1)s_1^2 + (n_2 - 1)s_2^2}{n_1 + n_2 - 2} \tag{39}$$

The numerator in Equation 39 is typically expressed for computational convenience in terms of the raw scores, with the contribution of the jth group to this numerator being

$$(n_j - 1)s_j^2 = \sum_i (Y_{ij} - \overline{Y}_j)^2 \tag{40}$$

Hence, we see that the numerator consists of a sum of squared deviations from the group means; thus, the numerator is denoted *sum of squares within groups*, or SS_{Within}. When the division by $n_1 + n_2 - 2$ is carried out, one obtains something like a mean or average squared deviation, and so the estimate of the population variance is denoted *mean square within* (MS_{Within}):

$$MS_{\text{Within}} = \frac{\sum_j \sum_i (Y_{ij} - \overline{Y}_j)^2}{\sum_j (n_j - 1)} \tag{41}$$

If the null hypothesis that all scores are drawn from the same population is true, then the variability between the sample means could be used to derive a separate estimate of population variance. This would provide a variance estimate that, under certain assumptions, is independent of the within-group variance MS_{Within}. Each sample mean, of course, has more stability than the individual scores in the sample. In fact, one of the most important results in statistics is the statement of just how much less variable means are than the scores on which they are based. (For a review of this point, see Tutorial 1 on the data disk.) Recall that the relationship depends solely on the number of scores on which the mean is based with the variance of sample means $\sigma_{\overline{Y}}^2$ equaling σ_Y^2/n. The variance of the distribution of sample means $\sigma_{\overline{Y}}^2$ can be estimated by the variability of the observed sample means, even when there are only two means present. When there are only two groups with the same number of subjects in each group, an unbiased estimate of the variance of the sampling distribution would be

$$\text{estimated } \sigma_{\overline{Y}}^2 = \left[\sum_{j=1}^{2} (\overline{Y}_j - \overline{Y})^2 \right] \Big/ (2 - 1) \tag{42}$$

That is, divide the squared deviations of the group means from the grand mean by the number of groups minus 1. To obtain an estimate of the population variance from this estimated variance of means, we need only multiply by n so that it is on the appropriate scale:

$$\text{estimated } \sigma^2 = n \sum_{j=1}^{2} (\overline{Y}_j - \overline{Y})^2 / 1 \tag{43}$$

This estimate is also an average squared deviation, but its magnitude is determined solely by the difference between the group means rather than by the variability within a group. Hence, the numerator is denoted SS_{Between}, and the variance estimate is denoted MS_{Between}. Here, SS_{Between} and MS_{Between} happen to be the same because there are only two groups (in which case the denominator of MS_{Between}, as shown in Equation 43, is 1). When there are more than two groups, MS_{Between} and SS_{Between} differ.

We can generalize these estimates, based on group differences, somewhat. First, if there are unequal numbers of observations in the groups, then the deviation for a group is weighted by the number in the group, that is,

$$SS_{\text{Between}} = \sum_j n_j (\overline{Y}_j - \overline{Y})^2 \tag{44}$$

Note that here $\overline{Y}$ is still the grand mean—that is, the mean of all the observations, not the mean of the group means. Second, if there were more than two groups, then the divisor to convert this from a sum of squares to a mean square would be greater than 1. If we designate the number of groups as a, then we can write a general form for MS_{Between} as

$$MS_{\text{Between}} = \left[\sum_{j=1}^{a} n_j (\overline{Y}_j - \overline{Y})^2 \right] \Big/ (a - 1) \tag{45}$$

The situation with more than two groups is developed more fully from a model-comparison perspective in a subsequent section.

Thus, we have two separate estimates of population variance. MS_{Within} is an unbiased estimate regardless of the presence of treatment effects or systematic differences between the groups. MS_{Between} is an unbiased estimate of σ^2 only if there are no treatment effects. When systematic differences between the groups exist along with the random variability among individuals, MS_{Between} tends to be larger than σ^2 and hence larger than MS_{Within}. The ratio of these two variance estimates then is used in the traditional approach to construct a test statistic, that is,

$$F = \frac{MS_{\text{Between}}}{MS_{\text{Within}}} \tag{46}$$

Now we are ready to identify these mean squares with the measures of error associated with models on which we focus in this book. The *minimal error*—that is, E_{F}, the error associated with our full model—is the squared deviations of the scores around their group means and hence can be identified with SS_{Within}. The difference in the errors associated with our two models—that is, $E_{\text{R}} - E_{\text{F}}$—depends on how much the group means vary around the grand mean and hence can be identified with SS_{Between}. The error associated with our restricted model, we have seen, is the total of SS_{Within} and SS_{Between} (see the discussion of Equations 34 and 35). Thus, E_{R} here[6] is identified with what is traditionally called SS_{Total}. (Rather than spelling out "Within" and "Between" in the subscripts of these sums of squares, we economize our notation by referring to them as SS_{W} and SS_{B}, and similarly denote the mean squares MS_{W} and MS_{B}.)

OPTIONAL

Tests of Replication

Up to this point, we have assumed that the only comparison of interest in the two-group case is that between a cell mean model and a grand mean model. That is, we have compared the full model of

$$Y_{ij} = \mu_j + \varepsilon_{ij} \tag{27, repeated}$$

with the model obtained when we impose the restriction that $\mu_1 = \mu_2 = \mu$. However, this is certainly not the only restriction on the means that would be possible. Occasionally, you can make a more specific statement of the results you expect to obtain. This is most often true when your study is replicating previous research that provided detailed information about the phenomena under investigation. As long as you can express your expectation as a restriction on the values of a linear combination of the parameters of the full model, the same general form of our F test allows you to carry out a comparison of the resulting models.

For example, you may wish to impose a restriction similar to that used in the one-group case in which you specify the exact value of one or both of the population means present in the full model. To extend the numerical example involving the hyperactive-children data, we might hypothesize that a population of hyperactive children and a population of nonhyperactive children would both have a mean IQ of 98, that is,

$$\mu_1 = \mu_2 = 98 \tag{47}$$

In this case, our restricted model would simply be

$$Y_{ij} = 98 + \varepsilon_{ij} \tag{48}$$

Thus, no parameters need to be estimated, and hence the degrees of freedom associated with the model would be $n_1 + n_2$.

As a second example, one may wish to specify numerical values for the population means in your restriction but allow them to differ between the two groups. This also would arise in situations in which you are replicating previous research. Perhaps you carried out an extensive study of hyperactive children in one school year and found the mean IQ of all identified hyperactive children was 106, whereas that of the remaining children was 98. If 2 years later you wondered whether the values had remained the same and wanted to make a judgment on the basis of a sample of the cases, you could specify these exact values as your null hypothesis or restriction. That is, your restricted model would be

$$\begin{aligned} Y_{i1} &= 106 + \varepsilon_{i1} \\ Y_{i2} &= 98 + \varepsilon_{i2} \end{aligned} \tag{49}$$

Once again, no parameters must be estimated, and so $df_R = n_1 + n_2$. As with any model, the sum of squared deviations from the specified parameter values could be used as a measure of the adequacy of this model and compared with that associated with the full model.

In general, if we let c_j stand for the constant specified in such a restriction, we could write our restricted model

$$\begin{aligned} Y_{i1} &= c_1 + \varepsilon_{i1} \\ Y_{i2} &= c_2 + \varepsilon_{i2} \end{aligned}$$

or equivalently,

$$Y_{ij} = c_j + \varepsilon_{ij}$$

The error term used as a measure of the adequacy of such a model would then be

$$E_R = \sum_j \sum_i e_{ij_R}^2 = \sum_j \sum_i (Y_{ij} - c_j)^2 \tag{50}$$

As a third example, you may wish to specify only that the difference between groups is equal to some specified value. Thus, if the hyperactive-group mean had been estimated at 106 and the normal-group mean at 98, you might test the hypothesis with a new sample that the hyperactive mean would be 8 points higher than the normal mean. This would allow for the operation of factors such as changing demographic characteristics of the population being sampled, which might cause the IQ scores to generally increase or decrease. The null hypothesis could still be stated easily as $\mu_1 - \mu_2 = 8$. It is a bit awkward to state the restricted model in this case, but thinking through the formulation of the model illustrates again the flexibility of the model-comparison approach. In this case, we do not wish to place any constraints on the grand mean, yet we wish to specify the magnitude of the between-group difference at 8 points. We can accomplish this by specifying that the hyperactive-group mean will be 4 points above the grand mean and that the normal-group mean will be 4 points below the grand mean, that is,

$$
\begin{aligned}
Y_{i1} &= \mu + 4 + \varepsilon_{i1} \\
Y_{i2} &= \mu - 4 + \varepsilon_{i2}
\end{aligned}
\tag{51}
$$

Arriving at a least-squares estimate of μ in this context is a slightly different problem than encountered previously. However, we can solve the problem by translating it into a form we have considered. By subtracting 4 from both sides of the equation for the Y_{i1} scores and adding 4 to both sides of the equation for the Y_{i2} scores in Equation 51, we obtain

$$
\begin{aligned}
Y_{i1} - 4 &= \mu + \varepsilon_{i1} \\
Y_{i2} + 4 &= \mu + \varepsilon_{i2}
\end{aligned}
\tag{52}
$$

This is now essentially the same estimation problem that we used to introduce the least-squares criterion in the one-sample case. There we showed that the least-squares estimate of μ is the mean of all scores on the left side of the equations, which here would imply taking the mean of a set of transformed scores, with the scores from group 1 being 4 less than those observed and the scores in group 2 being 4 greater than those observed. In the equal-n case, these transformations cancel each other, and the estimate of μ would be the same as in a conventional restricted model. In the unequal-n case, the procedure described would generally result in a somewhat different estimate of the grand mean, with the effect that the predictions for the larger group are closer to the mean for that group than is the case for the smaller group. In any event, the errors of prediction are generally different for this restricted model than for a conventional model. In this case, we have

$$
E_R = \sum_i (Y_{i1} - 4 - \hat{\mu})^2 + \sum_i (Y_{i2} + 4 - \hat{\mu})^2
\tag{53}
$$

where $\hat{\mu}$ is the mean of the transformed scores, as described previously.

This test, like the others considered in this chapter, assumes that the population variances of the different groups are equal. We discuss this assumption in more detail in the section entitled "Statistical Assumptions" and present procedures there for testing the assumption. In the case in which it is concluded that the variances are heterogeneous, refer to Wilcox (1985) for an alternative procedure for determining if the difference between two-group means differ by more than a specified constant. Additional techniques for imposing constraints on combinations of parameter values are considered in following chapters.

To try to prevent any misunderstanding that might be suggested by the label *test of replication*, we should stress that the tests we introduce in this section follow the strategy of identifying the constraint on the parameters with the restricted model or the null hypothesis being tested. This allows one to detect if the data depart significantly from what would be expected under this null hypothesis. A significant result then would mean a *failure* to replicate. Note that the identification here of the theoretical expectation with the null hypothesis is different from the usual situation in psychology, and instead approximates that in certain physical sciences. As mentioned in Chapter 1, p. 14, Meehl (1967) calls attention to how theory testing in psychology is usually different from theory testing in physics. In physics, one typically proceeds by making a specific point prediction and assessing whether the data depart significantly from that theoretical prediction, whereas in psychology, one typically lends support to a theoretical hypothesis by rejecting a null hypothesis of no difference. On the one hand, the typical situation in psychology is less precise than that in physics in that the theoretical prediction is often just that "the groups will differ" rather than specifying by how much. On the other hand, the identification of the theoretical prediction with the null hypothesis raises a different set of problems, in that the presumption in hypothesis testing is in favor of the null hypothesis. Among the potential disadvantages to such an approach, which applies to the tests of replication introduced here, is that one could be more likely to confirm one's theoretical expectations by running fewer subjects or doing other things to lower power. It is possible to both have the advantages of a theoretical point prediction and give the presumption to a hypothesis that is different from such theoretical expectations, but doing so requires use of novel methods beyond what we introduce here. For a provocative discussion of a method of carrying out a test in which the null hypothesis is that data depart by a prespecified amount or more from expectations so that a rejection would mean significant support for a theoretical point prediction, see Serlin and Lapsley (1985).

■

THE GENERAL CASE OF ONE-WAY DESIGNS

Formulation in Terms of Models

The consideration of the general case of ANOVA in which we have an arbitrarily large number of groups can now be done rather easily, because it is little different from the model comparisons we carried out in the two-group case. Of course, psychological experiments typically involve more than two groups. Most theoretical and empirical questions of interest involve the use of multiple treatment groups and may require multiple control groups as well. As noted at the end of Chapter 2, we will subsequently consider cases in which the several groups in a study arise from the "crossing" of different factors. However, for now, we proceed as if each of the groups is of unique interest rather than being one of the groups that results from simultaneously crossing factors that are of more interest than any one group. However, we can anticipate later developments somewhat by noting here that all crossed factorial designs may, in fact, be viewed as special cases of the one-factor or one-way design with which we are now concerned.

Whatever the groups represent, we can designate them as different levels of a single factor. For example, in a behavior modification study investigating different methods of helping people stop smoking, a researcher might compare a condition using aversive conditioning with one involving positive reinforcement for not smoking. These might be compared with two control conditions: One group is told to try to stop smoking using whatever methods they think best, and the other group is a "waiting list" control, that is, during the actual experiment, they are told that they are on a waiting list for treatment but they do not receive treatment until after the actual study is over. Although we can designate a group by a particular number—for example, Group 1, Group 2, Group 3, and Group 4—the numbers, of course, do not rank the groups but simply name them. Thus, we might say we have a single factor here of "Smoking Condition" with four levels.

In general, to designate a factor by a single capital letter and the number of levels of the factor by the corresponding lowercase letter is frequently convenient. Hence, the general case of one-factor ANOVA might be designated by saying "Factor A was manipulated," or "We had a groups in our study." The models being compared in an overall test of Factor A are essentially identical to the two-group case, that is,

$$\text{Full model:} \quad Y_{ij} = \mu_j + \varepsilon_{ij_F} \tag{54}$$

$$\text{Restricted model:} \quad Y_{ij} = \mu + \varepsilon_{ij_R} \tag{55}$$

with the only difference being that now the subscript j, which designates groups, can take on more than two values, with a being its maximal value—that is, $j = 1, 2, 3, \ldots, a$. Once again, the least-squares estimate of μ_j would be the sample mean of observations in the jth group, and the least-squares estimate of μ would be the mean of all scores observed in the study. Using these as our "guesses" of the observations in the two models, we can compute error scores for each individual, as we have done before, and compare the sum of squared errors to compare the adequacy of the two models. We would then substitute these into our general form of the F test:

$$F = \frac{(E_R - E_F)/(df_R - df_F)}{E_F/df_F} \qquad (22, \text{repeated})$$

$$= \frac{\left(\sum\sum e_{ij_R}^2 - \sum\sum e_{ij_F}^2\right)/(df_R - df_F)}{\sum\sum e_{ij_F}^2/df_F}$$

$$= \frac{\left[\sum_j \sum_i (Y_{ij} - \overline{Y})^2 - \sum_j \sum_i (Y_{ij} - \overline{Y}_j)^2\right]/(df_R - df_F)}{\sum_j \sum_i (Y_{ij} - \overline{Y}_j)^2/df_F}$$

The difference between E_R and E_F can be expressed more simply. Following the identical logic to that used in the two-sample case (see the development of Equation 35) we again have

$$E_R - E_F = \sum_{j=1}^{a} \sum_i (\overline{Y}_j - \overline{Y})^2 \qquad (56)$$

with the only difference from the previous case being that we are now summing over a groups instead of two groups. As usual, because the term being summed in Equation 56 is a constant with respect to the summation over individuals within a group, we can simply multiply the constant by the number of individuals in that group:

$$E_R - E_F = \sum_{j=1}^{a} n_j(\overline{Y}_j - \overline{Y})^2 \qquad (57)$$

In the special case in which there are equal numbers of subjects per group, n would also be a constant with respect to the summation over j, and so we could factor it out to obtain

$$E_R - E_F = n \sum_{j=1}^{a} (\overline{Y}_j - \overline{Y})^2 \qquad (58)$$

Regarding degrees of freedom, because in our restricted model we are estimating only one parameter just as we did in the two-group case, $df_R = N - 1$. In the full model, we are estimating as many parameters as we have groups; thus, in the general case of a groups, $df_F = N - a$. The degrees of freedom for the numerator of the test can be written quite simply as $a - 1$, because the total number of subjects drops out in computing the difference:

$$df_R - df_F = (N - 1) - (N - a) = N - 1 - N + a = a - 1 \qquad (59)$$

The difference in degrees of freedom is thus just the difference in the number of parameters estimated by the two models. This is generally true. In the case of one-way ANOVA, this means $df_R - df_F$ is one less than the number of groups. Thus, the general form of our F test for the a-group situation reduces to

$$F = \frac{\sum_j n_j(\overline{Y}_j - \overline{Y})^2/(a - 1)}{\sum_j \sum_i (Y_{ij} - \overline{Y}_j)^2/(N - a)} \tag{60}$$

We can use this form of our F test to carry out the ANOVA for any one-way design.

Before proceeding to a numerical example, let us make two comments about developments to this point. First, regarding E_F, although the link between the within-group standard deviations and the denominator of the F statistic was noted in our discussion of the two-group case (see the development of Equation 41), it is useful to underscore this link here. In general, in one-way ANOVA, E_F can be determined by computing the sum of within-group variances, each weighted by its denominator, that is, by the number of subjects in that group less one. In symbols we have

$$E_F = \sum_j (n_j - 1)s_j^2 \tag{61}$$

In the equal-n case, notice that we can factor out $(n - 1)$:

$$E_F = (n - 1) \sum_j s_j^2 \tag{62}$$

and thus the denominator of the F statistic can be expressed very simply as the average within-group variance:

$$\frac{E_F}{df_F} = \frac{(n - 1) \sum s_j^2}{N - a} = \frac{(n - 1) \sum s_j^2}{a(n - 1)} = \frac{\sum s_j^2}{a} \tag{63}$$

This is a useful approach to take in computing E_F when standard deviations are available, for example, when reanalyzing data from articles reporting means and standard deviations.

Second, a general pattern can be seen in the special cases of the general linear model we have considered. All model comparisons involve assessing the difference in the adequacy of two models. In the major special cases of one-way ANOVA treated in this chapter—namely, the one-group case, the two-group case, and the a-group case—we began by determining the best estimates of the models' parameters, then used these to predict the observed values of the dependent variable. When we compared the errors of prediction for the two models under consideration to compute a value for the numerator of our tests, in each case all terms involving the individual Y scores have dropped out of our summaries. In fact, as shown in Table 3.2, we can express the difference in the adequacy of the models solely in terms of the differences in the two models' predictions. Indeed, this is true not only in one-way ANOVA but also in factorial ANOVA, analysis of covariance and regression. The sum-of-squares term for the numerator of the F test can always be written, as shown at the bottom of Table 3.2, simply as the sum over all observations in the study of the squared difference in the predictions of the two models, that is,

$$E_R - E_F = \sum_{\text{all obs}} (\hat{Y}_F - \hat{Y}_R)^2 \tag{64}$$

TABLE 3.2
COMPARISON OF THE DIFFERENCE IN SUM OF SQUARED ERRORS FOR
VARIOUS DESIGNS

Situation	Predictions		Difference in Adequacy of Models (i.e., $E_R - E_F$)
	Full Model	Restricted Model	
One-group case	$\overline{Y}$	μ_0	$\sum_{i=1}^{n}(\overline{Y} - \mu_0)^2$
Two-group case	$\overline{Y}_j$	$\overline{Y}$	$\sum_{j=1}^{2}\sum_{i=1}^{n_j}(\overline{Y}_j - \overline{Y})^2$
a-group case	$\overline{Y}_j$	$\overline{Y}$	$\sum_{j=1}^{a}\sum_{i=1}^{n_j}(\overline{Y}_j - \overline{Y})^2$
In general	$\hat{Y}_F$	$\hat{Y}_R$	$\sum_{\text{all obs}}(\hat{Y}_F - \hat{Y}_R)^2$

TABLE 3.3
GLOBAL AFFECT RATINGS FROM
MOOD-INDUCTION STUDY

	Assigned Condition		
	Pleasant	Neutral	Unpleasant
	6	5	3
	5	4	3
	4	4	4
	7	3	4
	7	4	4
	5	3	3
	5	4	1
	7	4	2
	7	4	2
	7	5	4
$\overline{Y}_j$	6.000	4.000	3.000
s_j	1.155	0.667	1.054

Numerical Example

Although different mood states have, of course, always been of interest to clinicians, recent years have seen a profusion of studies attempting to manipulate mood states in controlled laboratory studies. In such induced-mood research, participants typically are randomly assigned to one of three groups: a depressed-mood induction, a neutral-mood induction, or an elated-mood induction. One study (Pruitt, 1988) used selected videoclips from several movies and public television programs as the mood-induction treatments. After viewing the video for her assigned condition, each participant was asked to indicate her mood on various scales. In addition, each subject was herself videotaped, and her facial expressions of emotion were rated on a scale of 1 to 7 (1 indicating sad; 4, neutral; and 7, happy) by an assistant who viewed the videotapes but was kept "blind" regarding the subjects' assigned conditions. Table 3.3 shows representative data[7] of these Global Affect Ratings for 10 observations per group, along with the means and standard deviations for the groups. These are the data displayed in Figure 3.1 on page 68.

As had been predicted, the mean Global Affect Rating is highest in the pleasant condition, intermediate in the neutral condition, and lowest in the unpleasant. We need to carry out a statistical test to substantiate a claim that these differences in sample means are indicative of real differences in the population rather than reflecting sampling variability. Thus, we wish to compare the models shown in Equations 54 and 55:

$$\text{Full model: } Y_{ij} = \mu_j + \varepsilon_{ij_F} \tag{54, repeated}$$

$$\text{Restricted model: } Y_{ij} = \mu + \varepsilon_{ij_R} \tag{55, repeated}$$

To compute the value in this situation of our general form of the F statistic

$$F = \frac{(E_R - E_F)/(df_R - df_F)}{E_F/df_F} \tag{22, repeated}$$

we begin by computing E_F, that is, the sum of squared errors for the full model or the sum of squared deviations of the observations from their group means:

$$E_F = \sum \sum e_{ij_F}^2 = \sum_j \sum_i (Y_{ij} - \overline{Y}_j)^2 \tag{65}$$

As shown in Table 3.4, this involves computing an error score for each subject by subtracting the group mean from the observed score, for example, $e_{11} = Y_{11} - \overline{Y}_1 = 6 - 6 = 0$. When

TABLE 3.4
COMPUTATIONS FOR ONE-WAY ANOVA ON MOOD-INDUCTION DATA

| | | | | Condition | | | | |
| | Pleasant | | | Neutral | | | Unpleasant | |
Y_{i1}	e_{i1}	e_{i1}^2	Y_{i2}	e_{i2}	e_{i2}^2	Y_{i3}	e_{i3}	e_{i3}^2
6	0	0	5	1	1	3	0	0
5	−1	1	4	0	0	3	0	0
4	−2	4	4	0	0	4	1	1
7	1	1	3	−1	1	4	1	1
7	1	1	4	0	0	4	1	1
5	−1	1	3	−1	1	3	0	0
5	−1	1	4	0	0	1	−2	4
7	1	1	4	0	0	2	−1	1
7	1	1	4	0	0	2	−1	1
7	1	1	5	1	1	4	1	1
$\overline{Y}_1 = 6$		$\sum = 12$	$\overline{Y}_2 = 4$		$\sum = 4$	$\overline{Y}_3 = 3$		$\sum = 10$

$$\overline{Y} = 4.333$$

$$E_F = \sum \sum e_{ij}^2 = \sum \sum (Y_{ij} - \overline{Y}_j)^2 = 12 + 4 + 10 = 26 (= SS_w)$$

$$E_R - E_F = n \sum_j (\overline{Y}_j - \overline{Y})^2 = 10[(6 - 4.333)^2 + (4 - 4.333)^2 + (3 - 4.333)^2]$$

$$= 10[2.778 + 0.111 + 1.778] = 46.67 (= SS_B)$$

$$df_F = N - a = 30 - 3 = 27 (= df_w)$$

$$df_R - df_F = (N - 1) - (N - a) = a - 1 = 3 - 1 = 2 (= df_B)$$

$$F = \frac{(E_R - E_F)/(df_R - df_F)}{E_F/df_F} = \frac{46.67/2}{26/27} = \frac{23.33}{.963} = 24.23, \, p < .001$$

each is squared and summed within each group, we obtain values of 12, 4, and 10 for the pleasant, neutral, and unpleasant conditions, respectively. Thus, E_F, or what would usually be denoted SS_W, is 26.

To compute the numerator of our F, we can use the form of $E_R - E_F$ shown in Equation 58 to determine how much more error our restricted model would make:

$$E_R - E_F = n \sum_{j=1}^{a} (\overline{Y}_j - \overline{Y})^2 \qquad \text{(58, repeated)}$$

As shown in Table 3.4, this sum of squared deviations of group means around the grand mean, weighted by number per group, is 46.67. This value of $E_R - E_F$ is usually called SS_B.

The values of our degree-of-freedom terms are as usual dependent on the number of observations and the number of parameters estimated in each model. The degrees of freedom for the denominator of our test statistic is the total number of observations in the study, 30, less the number of parameters estimated in the full model, 3. This df_F of 27 is usually denoted df_W. The degrees of freedom for the numerator is simply the number of groups less 1, or 2. This $df_R - df_F$ is usually denoted df_B.

We are now ready to combine the values we computed to determine the value of our test statistic. As shown at the bottom of Table 3.4, the numerator of our F, usually denoted MS_B, is 23.33, and the denominator of our F, usually denoted MS_W, is .963. Note that we could have computed this denominator directly from the within-group standard deviations of Table 3.3 by using Equation 63:

$$\frac{E_F}{df_F} = \frac{\sum s_j^2}{a} \qquad \text{(63, repeated)}$$

$$= \frac{(1.155)^2 + (0.667)^2 + (1.054)^2}{3}$$

$$= \frac{1.334 + 0.444 + 1.111}{3}$$

$$= \frac{2.890}{3} = .963$$

Combining our values of MS_B and MS_W, we obtain an F value of 24.23. Consulting Appendix Table A.2, we note that there is not an entry for denominator df of 27. In such a case, we would use the entries for the closest smaller value of denominator degrees of freedom. This means using the critical value for an F with 2 and 26 degrees of freedom, which is 9.12 for $p = .001$. Naturally, for most actual analyses, you will likely be using a computer program that yields exact p values for your particular degrees of freedom. In any case, the obtained F of 24.23 is highly significant. In a report of this analysis, this would be indicated as $F(2, 27) = 24.23$, $p < .001$. Thus, we would conclude that the restricted model should be rejected. We do have statistical grounds for arguing that the mood-induction treatments would produce different population means on the Global Affect Rating Scale.

A Model in Terms of Effects

Models can be written in different ways. Until now, we have used cell mean or μ_j models. Our full models have had one parameter for each cell of the design, with the parameter being the population mean for that condition. Although this type of model works well in the one-way case, it proves unwieldy in the case of factorial designs; thus, in later chapters, we generally use a different approach that makes it easier to talk about the effects of the factors under investigation. To anticipate those developments, we introduce here a full model in terms of effects, or an α_j model. Note that α_j (read "alpha sub j") is used here as a parameter in a model, and as such is totally unrelated to the use of α as a symbol for the probability of a Type I error.

We present the effects model for the general one-way situation in which a treatment conditions or groups are being compared. The full model for this situation can be written

$$Y_{ij} = \mu + \alpha_j + \varepsilon_{ij} \tag{66}$$

where, as before, Y_{ij} and ε_{ij} are, respectively, the observed score and error of the model for the ith subject in the jth group. The unknown parameters are now μ, which represents a grand mean term common to all observations, and the a $\alpha_j s$—that is, $\alpha_1, \alpha_2, \alpha_3, \ldots, \alpha_a$, each of which represents the effect of a particular treatment condition. We combine these $a + 1$ parameters to arrive at predictions for each of the a groups. Because we have more parameters than predictions, we must impose some additional constraint to arrive at unique estimates of the parameters. Simply requiring the effect parameters to sum to zero is the constraint that results in the parameters having the desired interpretation. This condition that the parameters are required to meet, namely,

$$\sum_{j=1}^{a} \alpha_j = 0 \tag{67}$$

is what is termed a *side condition* (see discussion of Equation 4), a technical constraint adopted to get a desired unique solution to an estimation problem. This is in contrast to a restriction with substantive meaning like our null hypotheses.

As you know, deviations from a mean sum to zero, and it is as deviations from a mean that our effect parameters are defined. This can be seen easily by comparing the effects full model with the cell mean model:

$$Y_{ij} = \mu + \alpha_j + \varepsilon_{ij} \tag{66, repeated}$$

$$Y_{ij} = \mu_j + \varepsilon_{ij} \tag{54, repeated}$$

The grand mean term plus the effect parameter of Equation 66 is equivalent to the cell mean parameter of Equation 54, that is,

$$\mu + \alpha_j = \mu_j \tag{68}$$

Subtracting μ from both sides of Equation 68, we have

$$\alpha_j = \mu_j - \mu \tag{69}$$

Thus, the effect of a particular treatment is defined here as the extent to which the population mean for that condition departs from the grand mean term. Furthermore, the constraint in

TABLE 3.5
POPULATION MEANS AND EFFECT
PARAMETERS FOR FOUR TREATMENTS

Condition	Mean μ_j	Effect α_j
1. Educational program	32	+9
2. Standard abstinence program	20	−3
3. Antabuse therapy	18	−5
4. Controlled drinking	22	−1
Mean of means μ	23	

Equation 67 that the effects sum to zero can be stated in terms of the deviations of Equation 69, that is,

$$\sum_{j=1}^{a}(\mu_j - \mu) = 0 \tag{70}$$

which, when one solves for μ, implies that the grand mean term in the effects model is just the mean of treatment population means, that is,

$$\mu = \frac{\sum_{j=1}^{a} \mu_j}{a} \tag{71}$$

To illustrate, assume that the population means were for four treatments for alcohol abuse. The dependent variable is number of drinks per week, which is assessed 1 year after the end of treatment. Assume that the population means for the four treatments are as shown in Table 3.5. The mean of the treatment-population means, which here is 23 drinks per week, serves as the value of μ in Equation 66 for this domain and is the baseline against which the effects of the treatments are evaluated. For example, the effect of treatment 3, Antabuse therapy, was to lower the mean 5 drinks per week below this baseline, that is, $\alpha_3 = \mu_3 - \mu = 18 - 23 = -5$.

Parameter Estimates

As usual, we estimate the parameters of our model to minimize the squared errors of prediction. For the effects model, the predictions are

$$\hat{Y}_{ij} = \hat{\mu} + \hat{\alpha}_j$$

which means that the least-squares estimates of μ and α_j are arrived at by minimizing

$$\sum_j \sum_i e^2_{ij_F} = \sum_j \sum_i (Y_{ij} - \hat{Y}_{ij})^2 = \sum_j \sum_i [Y_{ij} - (\hat{\mu} + \hat{\alpha}_j)]^2 \tag{72}$$

Because we have enough free parameters to have a different prediction for each cell (i.e., for each group), it should not be surprising that the way to minimize these squared errors of prediction is to choose our parameters in such a way that they combine to equal the observed cell means, that is,

$$\hat{Y}_{ij} = \overline{Y}_j = \hat{\mu} + \hat{\alpha}_j \tag{73}$$

Because the effects are required to sum to zero across groups, adding these predictions over the a groups indicates that the least-squares estimate of μ is the average of the observed cell means, that is,

$$\hat{\mu} = \frac{\sum\limits_{j=1}^{a} \overline{Y}_j}{a} \tag{74}$$

We designate this sample mean $\overline{Y}_u$, that is,

$$\overline{Y}_u = \frac{\sum\limits_{j} \overline{Y}_j}{a} \tag{75}$$

with the subscript u being used to indicate it is a grand mean computed as an *unweighted* average of the group means. In cases in which the same number of subjects is observed in each group, this mean of the means, $\overline{Y}_u$, equals the conventional grand mean of all the observations, $\overline{Y}$. In the case in which there are different numbers of observations per group, these values can differ.[8] From the viewpoint of the restricted model, each subject, regardless of his or her group assignment, is sampled from one and the same population and thus should contribute equally to the estimate of the population's mean. However, in the full model, the logic is that there are as many populations as there are groups, each with its own mean. Thus the "grand mean" is more reasonably thought of as a mean of the different group means. Substituting this value into Equation 73 and solving for $\hat{\alpha}_j$ yields

$$\hat{\alpha}_j = \overline{Y}_j - \overline{Y}_u \tag{76}$$

Notice that these least-squares estimates of μ and α_j indicated in Equations 74 and 76 are equivalent to the definitions in Equations 71 and 69, respectively, with sample means substituted for population means.

Computation of the Test Statistic

The observed F value for a model comparison involving a model stated in terms of effects is identical to that for a model comparison using the equivalent cell means model. For a one-way ANOVA, the models to be compared using an effects approach are

$$\text{Full model}: Y_{ij} = \mu + \alpha_j + \varepsilon_{ij} \tag{66, repeated}$$

$$\text{Restricted model}: Y_{ij} = \mu + \varepsilon_{ij} \tag{55, repeated}$$

The predictions of the full model, as shown in Equation 73, are the observed group means, just as was true for the cell means full model of Equation 54. The restricted models are identical in the effects and cell means cases; thus, the predictions are, of course, identical, namely the grand mean of all observations. The degrees of freedom associated with this common restricted model is $N - 1$.

The one point of possible confusion concerns degrees of freedom of the full effects model. Although as written in Equation 66, this model appears to require $a + 1$ parameters (a αs and 1μ), implicit in the model is the side condition that the sum of the α_js is zero. This implies that one of these parameters could be eliminated. For example, we could say that an arbitrarily chosen one of the αs—for example, the final one—is equal to the negative of the sum of the remaining αs:

$$\alpha_a = -\sum_{j=1}^{a-1} \alpha_j \tag{77}$$

Thus, in reality there are a parameters in our full model, one μ parameter, and $a - 1$ independent α_js. Because all terms making up the general form of our F statistic—namely E_R, E_F, df_R, and df_F—are the same in the effects and cell mean cases, the observed Fs must be the same.

Furthermore, in the case in which there are an equal number of observations in each group, the sum of squares, $E_R - E_F$, for the numerator of our F test can be expressed simply in terms of the estimated effect parameters. In particular, this difference in errors for our two models is just the sum over all observations of the estimated effects squared, that is,

$$E_R - E_F = \sum_{j=1}^{a}\sum_{i=1}^{n} \hat{\alpha}_j^2 \tag{78}$$

Because the estimated effect is the same for all individuals within a group, we can replace the summation over i by a multiplier of n:

$$E_R - E_F = n\sum_{j=1}^{a} \hat{\alpha}_j^2 \tag{79}$$

For example, if the means shown in Table 3.5 were sample means and estimated effects from a study based on 10 observations per cell, we could compute $E_R - E_F$ directly from the estimated effects:

$$E_R - E_F = 10[9^2 + (-3)^2 + (-5)^2 + (-1)^2]$$
$$= 10(81 + 9 + 25 + 1) = 10(116)$$
$$= 1160$$

In the unequal-n case, we still use the general principle that the difference in the models' adequacy can be stated in terms of the difference in their predictions:

$$E_R - E_F = \sum_{\text{all obs}} (\hat{Y}_F - \hat{Y}_R)^2 \tag{64, repeated}$$

Because the predictions of the effects full model are the group means (see Equation 73), this can be written in terms of means in exactly the same way as in the cell mean model:

$$E_R - E_F = \sum_{j=1}^{a} n_j(\overline{Y}_j - \overline{Y})^2 \tag{57, repeated}$$

Having now developed our model-comparison procedure using parameters reflecting the effects of the treatments, we now turn to alternative ways of characterizing the strength of effects of the treatments being investigated.

ON TESTS OF SIGNIFICANCE AND MEASURES OF EFFECT

Up to this point, we have more or less presumed that conducting a test of significance is an effective way of summarizing the results of an experiment. We must now explicitly consider this presumption and discuss alternative approaches to summarizing results.

As noted in Chapter 2, there has been controversy surrounding hypothesis testing since the days of Fisher. Although there have been critics expressing concerns within the methodological literature about statistical hypothesis testing for decades (cf. Morrison & Henkel, 1970), more recently it seems that both the prevalence and intensity of the criticisms have increased (cf. Cohen, 1994; Schmidt, 1996). Some of the criticisms offered have been as mundane as asserting that aspects of the approach are not well understood by some of its users. The prime example cited is the misunderstanding of a test's p value as the probability that the results were due to chance. That is, some researchers (and textbook writers!) occasionally have made the mistake of saying that the p value is the probability that the null hypothesis is true, given the obtained data. Instead, as we tried to make clear by our development of p values through the discrete probability examples in Chapter 2, the p value is the probability of obtaining a test statistic as extreme or more extreme than that observed, given that the null hypothesis (or restricted model) is assumed to be true. Granted, chance *is* involved, but that is in the sampling variability inherent in obtaining data from only a sample. Thus, a p value from a standard hypothesis test is always a conditional probability of data given the null hypothesis, not a conditional probability of the null hypothesis being true given the data. (Conditional probabilities of the hypotheses given the data can be yielded by a *Bayesian* analysis, but such analyses require one to specify in advance the prior probability of the truth of different hypotheses; see Howard, Maxwell, & Fleming, 2000.) We believe that the appropriate response to a misunderstanding of p values is simply to try to prevent such misunderstanding in the future, not to abandon the statistical testing methodology.[9]

Several other more forceful criticisms of hypothesis testing have been advanced as well. (Among the more helpful reviews and responses to these criticisms are those offered by Abelson, 1997; Baril & Cannon, 1995; Chow, 1988; Frick, 1996; Greenwald et al., 1996; Hagen, 1997; Nickerson, 2000; and Wainer, 1999.) The major difficulty, in the eyes of some, is the role played by the size of the sample in determining the outcome of a test. As we develop more explicitly later in this chapter, other things being equal, the magnitude of a test statistic is directly related to the size of the sample. Thus, a treatment condition and a control condition could result in means differing by the same amount in each of two studies, yet the effect could be declared "highly significant" in one study, while not approaching significance in the other study, simply because the first study included more participants. Given the fact that the number of participants in a study is arbitrary, it is reasonable to ask whether something does not need to be done to prevent this arbitrariness from affecting the directions in which significance tests push science. Regularly reporting one or more of the measures introduced in the following sections would help considerably in telling the rest of the story about an effect besides the statistical conclusion about the difference in population means.

The "sample-size problem" relates to the validity of these statistical conclusions. However, from our viewpoint, that smaller and smaller differences can be detected with larger and larger samples is not so much a problem as the way it should be. As more members of each population are sampled, it makes sense that your estimate of each mean should be more precise and that your ability to discriminate among differing means increases. Again, what is needed is avoiding confusing statistical significance with something else, namely how big the effect or difference between groups is.

Another common criticism is that the process of hypothesis testing is necessarily arbitrary because the null hypothesis is never true (Bakan, 1966; Cohen, 1994), and proposals have been offered in response regarding how the logic of hypothesis testing could be modified (e.g., Harris, 1997; Jones & Tukey, 2000; Serlin & Lapsley, 1985). The concern is that the restriction of certain population parameters being exactly equal will virtually never be satisfied, so the only question in doing a significance test is whether the investigator invested enough effort recruiting subjects to detect the particular inequality. Although it is plausible that any treatment will produce a detectible difference on some variable, it is not clear that that difference will be on the particular dependent variable whose population means are being investigated in a study. As Hagen suggested,

> A few years ago, visual imagery therapists were treating AIDS patients by asking the patients to imagine little AIDS viruses in their bodies being eaten by monsters. Under such a treatment, both psychological and physiological changes would take place. . . . But many would question whether or not such changes would be reflected in the participant's T-cell count. (1997, p. 21)

A somewhat different line of attack is to fault significance tests for diverting attention from other questions. For example, significance testing conventionally has focused on whether the p value meets the accepted probability of a Type I error, while virtually ignoring the probability of a Type II error or conversely the power of the test (cf. Cohen, 1977). Although admittedly low power is a common problem, it is the machinery of inferential statistics that provides methods for assessing the extent of the problem or for determining appropriate sample sizes so as to address the problem.

These various concerns about p values, sample size, effect size, and power relate to the more general question of the role of statistical tests in science. Various kinds of tests certainly can be a part of the reasoned arguments advanced in support of a theoretical conclusion. In those areas of science where theory is refined to the point of making mathematically precise predictions, the statistical tests can be tests for goodness-of-fit rather than tests of null hypotheses. Even given the imprecision of most psychological theorizing and recognizing that experiments necessarily involve imperfect embodiments of theoretical constructs, nonetheless, tests of null hypotheses shed light on the plausibility of explanatory theories by providing a basis for choosing between two alternative assertions. The assertions concern whether the data follow the pattern predicted by the theory, such as, "The mean in the experimental group will be higher than in the control" (see the discussion of the syllogisms of confirmation and falsification in Chapter 1), and it is the significance test that permits the decision of whether the data conform to the predicted pattern (cf. Chow, 1988; Frick, 1996; Wainer, 1999). As Abelson (1997) argues, the categorical statements hypothesis tests encourage permit us as a field to talk about novel and interesting phenomena. They help buttress the claims of credibility and reliability researchers wish to make for their findings, and thus form part of a principled argument for consideration by a community of scholars. The results of the test, of course, are not the only dimensions along which to evaluate the quality of a research-based claim,[10] but nonetheless have a place.

It must be acknowledged that despite one's best efforts to control Type I and Type II errors that the accept–reject decisions are at times in error. Although perhaps not fully offsetting the costs of such errors, research studies can at least ameliorate them to some extent by reporting measures of effect in conjunction with statistical tests. Such measures can then contribute to the building up of cumulative knowledge by becoming input for meta-analyses that combine estimates of the magnitude of effects across studies, regardless of the correctness of the decision reached in any individual hypothesis test (cf. Schmidt, 1996).

Of course, experiments serve other purposes besides theory testing. Generally, the empirical question itself is of interest apart from the question of why the effect occurs. Perhaps most obviously in applied research such as evaluation of clinical or educational treatments, the empirical questions of which treatment is most effective and by how much are, in fact, of primary interest. To have an estimate of the magnitude of the effect is critical particularly if decisions are to be made on the basis of an experiment about whether it would be cost effective to implement a particular program (Kirk, 1996).

Thus, for both theoretical and practical reasons, the consensus that seems to have emerged from the debate in recent years has been in favor of maintaining hypothesis tests but supplementing them with an indication of the magnitude of the effect (e.g., Abelson, 1997; Estes, 1997; Frick, 1996; Hagen, 1997; Nickerson, 2000; Rosnow & Rosenthal, 1989; Scarr, 1997; Wainer, 1999). As the APA Task Force recommended, "always provide some effect-size estimate when reporting a p value" (Wilkinson et al., 1999, p. 599).

Thus, it is to a discussion of such measures of effects that we now turn.

MEASURES OF EFFECT

As mentioned previously, the numerical value of a test statistic is determined as much by the number of participants in the study as it is by any absolute measure of the size of the treatment effect. In particular, the two factors multiply together to determine the test statistic:

$$\text{Test statistic} = \text{Size of effect} \times \text{Size of study} \tag{80}$$

The size-of-study term is some function of the number of participants and is often a degrees-of-freedom term. The size-of-effect term can be expressed in different ways in different contexts. Rosenthal (1987, pp. 106–107) presents several forms of the general equation shown in Equation 80 for χ^2, z, independent-groups t, dependent-groups t, and F tests. We illustrate first the size-of-effect term with our general form of the F test. Recall that we began the development of the F test in the one-sample case by using the proportional increase in error, which was defined as follows:

$$\text{proportional increase in error} = \frac{\text{increase in error}}{\text{minimal error}} = \frac{E_R - E_F}{E_F} \tag{81}$$

Using this measure of how much more adequate the full model is as a size-of-effect index, we express our F in the form of Equation 80 as follows:

$$F = \frac{E_R - E_F}{E_F} \times \frac{df_F}{df_R - df_F} \tag{82}$$

This form of the F underscores the general principle that one can get larger test statistics either by increasing the effect size or by increasing the study size.

There are a number of different ways of assessing effects. Yeaton and Sechrest (1981) make a useful distinction between two broad categories of such measures: those that measure effect size and those that measure association strength. Measuring effect size involves examining differences between means. Measuring association strength, however, involves examining proportions of variance and is perhaps most easily described using the terminology of correlational research. One perspective on the distinction between these kinds of measures is that "a difference between means shows directly how much effect a treatment has; a measure of association shows the dependability or uniformity with which it can be produced" (Yeaton & Sechrest, 1981, p. 766). The proportional increase in error of our F test would be considered an association measure. Although association measures are closely related to test statistics (Kirk, 1996, reports that more than 80% of the articles reporting a measure of effect use some kind of association measure), often the simpler, more direct effect-size measures are more useful in interpreting and applying results. We consider such effect-size measures first.

Measures of Effect Size

Mean Difference

The simplest measure of the treatment effect is the difference between means. Such a simple measure is most appropriate when there are only two groups under study. The treatment effect in the population then could be described simply as $\mu_1 - \mu_2$. The difference between the sample means $\overline{Y}_1 - \overline{Y}_2$ is an unbiased estimate of the population difference. One advantage of this effect measure is that it is on the same meaningful scale as the dependent variable.

For example, Gastorf (1980) found a $\overline{Y}_1 - \overline{Y}_2$ difference of 3.85 minutes in a comparison of when students who scored high on a scale of Type A behavior arrived for an appointment as opposed to the later-arriving, low scorers on the scale. As Yeaton and Sechrest (1981) point out, this sort of effect measure can easily be translated in a meaningful way into applied settings. A difference of 3.85 minutes in arrival time is of a magnitude that, for a firm employing 1,000 workers at $10 an hour, would translate into $150,000 of additional work per year, assuming the difference manifested itself only once daily.

When there are more than two conditions in a one-way design, then there are, of course, multiple mean differences that may be considered. Often, the range of means is used as the best single indicator of the size of the treatment effect. For example, using the data from the mood-induction study presented in Table 3.3—in which the means for the pleasant, neutral, and unpleasant conditions were 6, 4, and 3, respectively—we could easily compute the difference between the largest and smallest means, $\overline{Y}_{max} - \overline{Y}_{min}$:

$$\overline{Y}_{max} - \overline{Y}_{min} = 6 - 3 = 3$$

Thus, the effect of receiving a pleasant-mood induction as opposed to an unpleasant-mood induction amounted to a difference of 3 points on the 7-point Global Affect Rating Scale. Chapter 5 considers various ways of testing differences between pairs of means chosen like these to reflect the range of effects present in a study.

Estimated Effect Parameters

An alternative solution when there are more than two groups is to describe the effects in terms of the estimates of the α_j parameters in the full model written in terms of effects:

$$Y_{ij} = \mu + \alpha_j + \varepsilon_{ij} \qquad \text{(66, repeated)}$$

As you know, these effect parameters are defined as deviations of the treatment means from the mean of the treatment means. They are then smaller on the average than the pairwise differences between means we considered in the previous section. For example, in the mood-induction study, the mean of the treatment means was 4.333, resulting in estimated effects of $+1.667$, $-.333$ and -1.333 for the pleasant, neutral, and unpleasant conditions, respectively. Thus, the neutral condition is seen to be somewhat more like the unpleasant treatment than the pleasant treatment in that its effect is to produce a mean Global Affect Rating that is .333 units below the grand mean of the study.

If a single measure of treatment effect is desired, the standard deviation of the α_j parameters could be used to indicate how far, on the scale of the dependent variable, the typical treatment causes its mean to deviate from the grand mean. In fact, we use this measure in developing a standardized measure of effect size in our discussion of power at the end of the chapter.

The Standardized Difference Between Means

The measures of effect size considered thus far have the advantage of being expressed in the units of the dependent variable. That is also their weakness. In most areas of the behavioral sciences, there is not a single universally accepted dependent variable. Even within a fairly restricted domain and approach, such as depression as assessed by the individual's self-report, there typically are various measures being used in different research laboratories and clinics across the country. As a result, to compare effect sizes across measures, it is necessary to transform them to a common scale. In fact, part of the motivation for developing standardized measures of effects was to permit their use in quantitative research integration studies or meta-analyses, as suggested by Glass (1976) and others. The goal then is to have a standard scale for effects like the z-score scale, and the solution is achieved in the same way as with z scores; that is, divide by the standard deviation so that differences can be expressed in standard deviation units. Following Cohen (1988, p. 20), we denote this standardized difference between two population means as d:

$$d = (\mu_1 - \mu_2)/\sigma_\varepsilon \qquad (83)$$

where σ_ε is the common within-group population standard deviation. We can estimate this standardized effect measure by substituting sample statistics for the corresponding population parameters, and we denote this estimate $\hat{d}$:

$$\hat{d} = (\overline{Y}_1 - \overline{Y}_2)/S \qquad (84)$$

where, following Hedges (1981, p. 110), S is the pooled within-group standard deviation estimate. That is, S^2 is the weighted average of the sample within-group variances:

$$S^2 = \frac{\sum(n_j - 1)s_j^2}{\sum(n_j - 1)} \qquad (85)$$

We first encountered such pooled variance estimates in the two-group case (see Equation 39). As discussed there, we can express such within-group variances estimates either in terms of the full model's sum of squared error or in terms of traditional terminology, that is,

$$S^2 = \frac{E_F}{df_F} = \frac{SS_w}{df_w} = MS_w \tag{86}$$

For the mood-induction data in Table 3.3, we found the average variance to be .963 (see bottom of Table 3.4, p. 92), implying $S = .981$. With this as the metric, we can say that the pleasant condition resulted in a mean Global Affect Rating that was two standard deviations higher than that in the neutral condition: $\hat{d} = (\overline{Y}_1 - \overline{Y}_2)/S = (6 - 4)/.981 = 2.038$. Given Cohen has suggested that in a two-group study a d value of .2 constitutes a *small effect*, a d value of .5 is a *medium effect*, and a d value of .8 is a *large effect* (1988, p. 24ff.), this represents a very large effect.

Hedges (1981) determined the mathematical distribution of $\hat{d}$ values[11] and extended this work in several subsequent publications (see, e.g., Hedges, 1982, 1983). The use of a standardized effect-size measure in research integration is illustrated by Smith and Glass's (1977) review of psychotherapy outcome studies, by Rosenthal and Rubin's (1978) discussion of interpersonal expectancy effects—for example, the effect of teachers' expectations on students' gains in intellectual performance—and by Bien, Miller, and Tonigan's (1993) review of brief interventions for alcohol problems, among a host of other quantitative reviews.

Like the previous measures we have considered, standardized differences can be adapted for use as summary measures when there are more than two treatment conditions. Most simply, one can use the standardized difference between the largest and smallest means as the overall summary of the magnitude of effects in an a-group study. Again following Cohen (1988), we denote the standardized difference that is large enough to span the range of means d. This is estimated by the standardized range of sample means:

$$\hat{d} = (\overline{Y}_{max} - \overline{Y}_{min})/S \tag{87}$$

For the mood-induction study, we would have $\hat{d} = (6 - 3)/.981 = 3.058$. This is an unusually large effect.

We use d in the final section of the chapter as part of a simplifying strategy for approximating the power of a study. In addition, a multiple of d proves useful in follow-up tests after an a-group ANOVA (see the discussion of the studentized range in Chapter 5).

There is a second way of adapting standardized differences for a-group studies, besides ignoring all but the two most extreme means. As mentioned in the "Estimated Effect Parameters" section, one could use the standard deviation of the group means as an indicator of the typical effect and divide that by the within-group standard deviation to get an overall standardized effect. Because the conditions included in a study are regarded as all that are of interest, we can treat the a levels as the population of levels of interest and define

$$\sigma_m = \sqrt{\frac{\sum(\mu_j - \mu)^2}{a}} = \sqrt{\frac{\sum \alpha_j^2}{a}} \tag{88}$$

Then a standardized treatment standard deviation, which Cohen (1988, p. 274) denotes f, would be

$$f = \frac{\sigma_m}{\sigma_\varepsilon} \tag{89}$$

This particular summary measure figures prominently in our upcoming discussion of power.

Measures of Association Strength

Describing and understanding relationships constitute a major goal of scientific activity. As discussed in Chapter 1, causal relationships are of special interest. The clearest example of a causal relationship is one in which the cause is necessary and sufficient for the effect to occur. Unfortunately, in the behavioral sciences, we have few examples of such infallible, deterministic relationships. Rather, most phenomena of interest are related only probabilistically to the causes to which we have access. Furthermore, the causes that we can manipulate or control in an experiment may be only a small subset of the determinants of the scores on the dependent variable. It is easy to lose sight of this, however, if one focuses exclusively on hypothesis testing. Computing a measure of the association strength between your independent variable and dependent variable often provides a safeguard against overestimating the importance of a statistically significant result.

Measures of association strength can be thought of as proportions. The goal is to indicate, on a 0-to-1 scale, how much of the variability in the dependent variable is associated with the variation in the independent-variable levels.

Our models' perspective allows us to arrive at such a proportion immediately in terms of the measures of inadequacy of our two models. The proportion is to indicate how much knowledge of group membership improves prediction of the dependent variable. That is, we want to express the reduction in error that results from adding group membership parameters to our model as a proportion of the error we would make without them in the model. This proportionate reduction in error (PRE) measure is most commonly designated R^2:

$$R^2 = \frac{E_R - E_F}{E_R} \tag{90}$$

where the restricted model is a grand mean model and the full model is a cell means model, as in Equations 55 and 54, respectively. This ratio is a descriptive statistic indicating the proportion of variability in the observed data that is accounted for by the treatments. R^2 is very commonly used in the context of multiple regression, which we develop in second statistical Tutorial on the data disk, to indicate directly a model's adequacy in accounting for the data. As we develop there, R^2 is the square of the correlation between observed scores and predicted scores. It is sometimes denoted $\hat{\eta}^2$ (lowercase Greek eta, hat, squared) (Maxwell, Camp, & Arvey, 1981, p. 527).

There is no question of the legitimacy of R^2 as a descriptive index for sample data (cf. Hays, 1994, p. 402). Because of its clear interpretation and the fact that, unlike a test statistic, it does not tend to increase with sample size, R^2 has much to recommend it as a useful supplement to the p value of a test. However, other measures of association, most notably $\hat{\omega}^2$ (lowercase Greek omega, hat, squared), are available; their rationale and advantages relative to R^2 merit consideration. One can argue, as Hays (1994, p. 332) does, that what is of most interest is the proportion of variance in the population that would be accounted for by the treatments. If this is granted, then characteristics of R^2 as an estimator must be considered. In this regard, recall that the numerator of R^2 depends on the variability among the group means:

$$E_R - E_F = \sum_j \sum_i (\overline{Y}_j - \overline{Y})^2 \qquad \text{(see 56)}$$

However, even if the population-group means were identical, the sample means would almost certainly differ from each other. Thus, although in the population the treatments may account for no variance, R^2 would nonetheless be expected to be greater than zero because of this sampling variability in the observed means. This positive bias of R^2, or tendency to systematically overestimate the population proportion, in fact is present whether the population-treatment means are equal. It turns out that the extent of positive bias of R^2 can be estimated and is a decreasing function of sample size.

The other measures of association like $\hat{\omega}^2$ attempt to correct for this positive bias by shrinking the numerator in Equation 90. Thus, the formula for $\hat{\omega}^2$ for an a-group one-way ANOVA can be written

$$\hat{\omega}^2 = \frac{(E_R - E_F) - (a-1)(E_F/df_F)}{E_R + (E_F/df_F)} \tag{91}$$

or in terms of the traditional ANOVA notation in which $\hat{\omega}^2$ is typically described:

$$\hat{\omega}^2 = \frac{SS_B - (a-1)MS_W}{SS_{Total} + MS_W} \tag{92}$$

Although it is clear from comparing Equations 90 and 91 that $\hat{\omega}^2$ is smaller than R^2, it is not obvious how much less. For all practical purposes, the amount of shrinkage of R^2 can be estimated using some early work by Wherry (1931). Wherry showed that the proportion of unexplained variability in the population is actually larger than $1 - R^2$ by a factor of approximately df_R/df_F. From this, we can estimate the adjusted (or shrunken) R^2, which we denote $\tilde{R}^2$, as follows:

$$\tilde{R}^2 = 1 - \frac{df_R}{df_F}(1 - R^2) = 1 - \frac{N-1}{N-a}(1 - R^2) \tag{93}$$

Maxwell et al. (1981) review work showing that the value of $\tilde{R}^2$ is typically within .02 of $\hat{\omega}^2$.

We illustrate numerically how these association-strength measures compare using the mood-induction data in Table 3.4 (p. 92). From the values of $E_R = 72.67$, $E_F = 26$, $df_R = 29$, and $df_F = 27$, we can easily compute the value of R^2 from Equation 90

$$R^2 = \frac{E_R - E_F}{E_R} = \frac{72.67 - 26.00}{72.67} = \frac{46.67}{72.67} = .642$$

the value of $\hat{\omega}^2$ from Equation 91

$$\hat{\omega}^2 = \frac{(E_R - E_F) - (a-1)(E_F/df_F)}{E_R + (E_F/df_F)}$$

$$= \frac{(72.67 - 26.00) - (2)(26/27)}{72.67 + 26/27} = \frac{46.67 - 1.926}{72.67 + .963} = .608$$

and the value of $\tilde{R}^2$ from Equation 93

$$\tilde{R}^2 = 1 - \frac{N-1}{N-a}(1 - R^2) = 1 - \frac{29}{27}(1 - .642)$$

$$= 1 - 1.074(.358) = 1 - .384 = .616$$

In this case, the mood-induction treatments appear to account for more than 60% of the variability in the population as well as the sample. Although the differences among the three association-strength measures are small here, R^2 can be considerably larger than $\hat{\omega}^2$ or $\tilde{R}^2$ if the sample sizes are small, especially when $1 - R^2$ is relatively large. In fact, $\hat{\omega}^2$ and $\tilde{R}^2$ can yield values that are less than zero, in which case the estimated population proportion would be set equal to zero.

Evaluation of Measures

Measures of association strength provide an additional perspective on the amount of control your treatment manipulation has over the dependent variable. Like the measures of effect size, association measures cannot be made to look impressive simply by running more subjects. However, unlike the effect size indices, association measures are assessed on a bounded, unitless metric (that is, a 0–1 scale); further, they clearly reflect how much variability remains unaccounted for, besides reflecting the treatment effects.

Despite these advantages, association measures have been criticized on a variety of fronts (e.g., Abelson, 1985; O'Grady, 1982; Rosenthal & Rubin, 1982; Yeaton & Sechrest, 1981). First, the measures are borrowed from correlational research and are less appropriate for an experimental situation where certain fixed levels of an independent variable are investigated (Glass & Hakstian, 1969). As O'Grady (1982, p. 771ff.) notes, the number and choice of levels of the factor under investigation are decided on by the experimenter and can greatly influence the PRE measures. Including only extreme groups in a study of an individual difference variable would tend to exaggerate the PRE. Conversely, failing to include an untreated control group in a clinical study comparing reasonably effective treatments might greatly reduce PRE, but would not alter the actual causal powers of the treatments. (Alternative ways of estimating the proportion of variance accounted for by a factor that adjust for the effects of other causes is introduced in Chapter 7 in the context of two-way designs.)

Thus, the arbitrary-choice-of-levels problem relates to the more general difficulty of attempting to infer the importance of a factor as a cause of an outcome from a PRE measure. The conventional wisdom is that correlations that indicate a factor accounts for, say, 10% or less of the variability in an outcome are of trivial importance practically or theoretically. For example, this was the rationale of Rimland (1979) in suggesting that a review of 400 psychotherapy outcome studies showing such an effect sounded the "death knell" for psychotherapy. Similarly, the Type A effect on arrival time mentioned previously was noted by Strahan (1981) as corresponding to an R^2 of about .02.

In fact, if one pursues research in the human sciences, one is forced in many areas to proceed by the cumulation of knowledge based on effects of this magnitude. The most important reason for this is that the effects of interest—for example, psychological adjustment—are determined by a large number of factors. In addition, the measure of the construct of interest may be of low reliability or validity. These points have been illustrated in a compelling fashion by authors who have cited effects of factors recognized to be important despite their low PREs. For example, Rosenthal (1987, p. 115) notes that a placebo-controlled study of propranolol was halted by the National Heart, Lung, and Blood Institute because "the results were so favorable to the treatment that it would be unethical" to withhold the treatment from the placebo-controlled patients. The effect of the drug was to increase survival rate of patients by 4%, a statistically significant effect in a study of 2108 patients. The compelling argument to make the drug available to all patients is hardly offset by the fact that it accounted for only 0.2% of the variance in the treatment outcome (living or dying). Many psychological variables of interest may have as many potential causes as living or dying, thus limiting correlations to similarly low levels as in the propranolol study. What is more, our constructs are generally measured with much lower reliability or validity than the outcome variable in that study, which further limits the strength and interpretability of the effects that can be observed. Such psychometric issues regarding association measures have been helpfully reviewed by O'Grady (1982).

A final difficulty with the measures of explained variability is the nature of the scale. The benefit of having a 0-to-1 scale is achieved at the cost of working from ratios of squared units. The practical implications of a value on such a scale are not as immediately obvious as one on the scale of the dependent variable. The squaring tends further to make the indices take on values close to zero, which can result in effects being dismissed as trivial. An alternative measure that can alleviate these difficulties in certain situations is discussed in the next section.

With these caveats in mind, PRE measures can be a useful adjunct to a test of significance. Because the population is typically of more interest than the sample, and because the bias in the sample R^2 can be substantial if N is, say, less than 30, some type of adjusted R^2 is preferred for general use. The $\hat{\omega}^2$ measure satisfies this and seems to be more widely used than the $\tilde{R}^2$ measure. In addition, general algorithms have been developed to calculate $\hat{\omega}^2$ in complex designs. Thus, we recommend $\hat{\omega}^2$ for inferential purposes. (We defer until Chapter 10 discussion of the related idea of an intraclass correlation, which is useful when a factor is treated as a random rather than a fixed effect.)

Alternative Representations of Effects

Various other tabular, numerical, and graphical methods have been suggested for communicating information about treatment effects. We describe some of these briefly and refer the reader to other sources for more detailed treatments.

Confidence Intervals

Thus far in our discussion of measures of effect, we have used the sample mean in a condition as the indicator of the population mean. Although $\overline{Y}_j$ is always an unbiased estimator of μ_j, it is important to remember that as an estimator $\overline{Y}_j$ can also be characterized by its variance. That the variance of a sample mean $\sigma^2_{\overline{Y}_j}$ is directly related to the variance of the population and inversely related to the number of scores in the sample is one of the most fundamental ideas in statistics, that is,

$$\sigma^2_{\overline{Y}_j} = \sigma^2_\varepsilon / n_j \tag{94}$$

The population variance may be estimated by substituting our observed value of mean square error $E_F/df_F = MS_W$ for σ^2_ε. Dividing this estimated population variance by n_j in turn yields an estimate of $\sigma^2_{\overline{Y}_j}$, the variance of the sampling distribution of $\overline{Y}_j$, which we denote by $s^2_{\overline{Y}_j}$; that is,

$$s^2_{\overline{Y}_j} = (E_F/df_F)/n_j \tag{95}$$

A very useful way of characterizing the imprecision in your sample mean as an estimator of the population mean is to use the standard error of the mean, that is, the square root of the quantity in Equation 95, to construct a confidence interval for the population mean. Under the standard ANOVA assumptions, this interval is the one centered around $\overline{Y}_j$ and having as its limits the quantities

$$\overline{Y}_j \pm \sqrt{F_{1, df_F}} s_{\overline{Y}_j} \tag{96}$$

where F_{1, df_F} is the critical value from Appendix Table A.2 for the α level corresponding to the desired degree of confidence $(1 - \alpha) \times 100$. For example, if the critical values for $\alpha = .05$ were to be used, the interpretation of the confidence interval is that if repeated samples of size n_j were observed under treatment j and such a confidence interval were constructed for each sample, 95% of them would contain the true value of μ_j.

In estimating the standard error of the mean used in Equation 96, we were implicitly relying on the assumption of homogeneity of variance, as we do throughout most of this chapter. That is, the variance of the errors σ_ε^2 in Equation 94 is assumed to be the same in all a populations, so that the sample variances in the groups can just be averaged to arrive at a pooled estimate of within-group variability (see Equations 39 and 63). As indicated in the next section, data should be examined to see if this assumption is plausible, and if not, it may be more appropriate to estimate the standard error of each group mean based only on the variance in that group (i.e., $s_{\overline{Y}_j}^2 = s_j^2/n_j$). (Some computer programs, such as SPSS (as of this writing), use such separate variance estimates automatically when confidence intervals are requested in graphs.)

Indicators of the variability of the estimates of the difference between combinations of means are considered in Chapters 4 through 6. These often are of as much interest as the variability of the individual means.

Binomial Effect Size Display (BESD)

Rosenthal and Rubin (1982) suggest the Binomial Effect Size Display (BESD) as a simple summary of results that would be easier to understand than the proportion-of-variance measures. In a sense, the measure represents a compromise: Like the measures of effect size, it uses the dependent-variable scale (albeit in dichotomized form); like the measures of association, it is based on a measure of relationship (albeit R instead of R^2).

The BESD presents results in a 2×2 table. Table 3.6 shows an example. The virtual doubling of the success rate as the result of the experimental treatment is one most would agree is substantial, particularly if the outcome categories corresponded to "alive" and "dead." Surprisingly, the effect shown is one where the treatment condition accounts for 10% of the variance. In fact, simply taking the difference in success rates here immediately gives the value of R—that is, $R = .66 - .34 = .32$—which, when squared, yields the proportion of variance accounted for, for example, $R^2 = (.32)^2 = .10$.

The limitations on the method are that you can consider only two conditions and two possible outcomes. Because most outcomes of behavioral interventions are continuous variables, it is necessary to artificially dichotomize the scores on the dependent variable—for example, those above or below the overall median—to create a BESD. Rosenthal and Rubin (1982, p. 168)

TABLE 3.6
A BINOMIAL EFFECT SIZE DISPLAY

		Outcome		
		Success	*Failure*	
Condition	Treatment	66	34	100
	Control	34	66	100
		100	100	200

make suggestions concerning refinements of the display, which depend on the form of the dependent-variable distribution and the value of R. However, technicalities aside, in many applied settings such a comparison of success rates may be the most meaningful supplement to the hypothesis test for communicating clearly the treatment effect.

Common Language (CL) Effect Size

Like the BESD, the common language (CL) effect size and its variants attempt to summarize the magnitude of a treatment effect on a standard unit scale ranging from 0 to 1. Whereas the number between 0 and 1 that the BESD arrives at based on the difference in success rates is taken as an estimate of a correlation, CL measures estimate a probability. As proposed by McGraw and Wong (1992), CL is an estimate of the probability p that "a score sampled at random from one distribution will be greater than a score sampled from some other distribution" (1992, p. 361).

Assuming there are no ties, one can compute CL from two samples of data simply as the proportion of times a score from the first group, Y_{i1}, is less than a score from the second, $Y_{i'2}$. With n_1 scores in Group 1 and n_2 scores in Group 2, this involves making $n_1 \times n_2$ comparisons of scores. If there are ties across the two groups, then the estimate of p is improved by increasing the proportion of times Y_{i1} is less than $Y_{i'2}$ by one half the proportion of times Y_{i1} equals $Y_{i'2}$.

Assessing the magnitude of an estimate of p is aided by having a rough idea of what constitutes a large effect. As mentioned above, Cohen's (1988) rule of thumb is that a standardized difference d between two population means (see Equation 83) of .2 might be termed a *small effect*, a d value of .5 constitutes a *medium effect*, and a d value of .8 a *large effect*. Assuming the population distributions are normal and have equal standard deviations, one can determine by referring to a normal distribution table that the corresponding values of p would be approximately .56 for a small effect, .64 for a medium effect, and .71 for a large effect.

A closely related measure championed by Norman Cliff (e.g., 1996, p. 124) is δ, which is defined as the difference between the $\Pr(Y_{i1} > Y_{i'2})$ and $\Pr(Y_{i1} < Y_{i'2})$. It can be shown that this measure is a linear transformation of p that measures effect size on a scale from -1 to $+1$ instead of 0 to 1.

Graphical Methods

Plots of data are, of course, useful in helping you and others gain an understanding of the trends in your data. Rough, hand-drawn plots showing the individual data points in each condition, as in Figure 3.1 (page 68), may bring to your attention differences in variability across conditions or the occurrence of individual aberrant scores. (Statistical methods for testing for heterogeneity of variance are considered in the following section.) Final plots in the published reports of findings typically show only the means in the various conditions. The informativeness of these plots can be increased by adding a vertical line going through the point corresponding to the group mean to points one standard error above and below the mean.

Recent years have seen the development of a number of graphical methods (e.g., Tukey, 1977; Cleveland, 1985) that can be used to supplement standard plots of means. Most newer methods involve plotting medians or other percentiles. For example, Tukey's box graph includes five horizontal lines for each group corresponding to the 10th, 25th, 50th, 75th, and 90th percentiles for that group. An example of such a box plot is shown in Tutorial 1 on "Review of Basic Statistics." Refer to the book by Cleveland (1985, pp. 129ff.) for details.

As is perhaps obvious from the wide-ranging discussion of ways of characterizing effects, the methods available are not nearly as standardized as the methods of testing for significance. However, the message you have hopefully received is that, whether through graphs, tables, or numerical methods, measures of effect can carry useful information over and above that contained in the p value of the test.

STATISTICAL ASSUMPTIONS

The F test for comparing two models is a very flexible procedure in that it can be used in a wide variety of circumstances. However, for the expression

$$F_{obs} = \frac{(E_R - E_F)/(df_R - df_F)}{E_F/df_F}$$

to follow an F distribution, certain assumptions must be met. If these assumptions fail to hold for one's data, it is possible that the use of the F table in Appendix A (Table A.2) is inappropriate. For example, suppose that an experiment is conducted comparing three groups of six subjects each (18 subjects in all). Inspection of the F table shows that the critical F value here is 3.68 for an α level of .05. In other words, the observed F value (F_{obs}) exceeds 3.68 only 5% of the time (in the long run) if the null hypothesis is true. Using the value of 3.68 as a critical value thus ensures that we make a Type I error only 5% of the time.

However, the assurance that F_{obs} exceeds 3.68 5% of the time depends on a set of statistical assumptions. Without these assumptions, F_{obs} can exceed 3.68 either more or less than 5% of the time, in which case our statistical analysis may produce either too many or too few Type I errors.

Three assumptions must be met for F_{obs} to follow an F distribution:

1. The population distribution of scores on the dependent variable (Y) must be normal within each group. In other words, if an entire population of scores were obtained in a particular condition, it is assumed that those scores would be normally distributed
2. The population variances of scores on Y must be equal for all a groups. In symbols, $\sigma_1^2 = \sigma_2^2 = \cdots = \sigma_a^2$, where σ_j^2 represents the variance of Y scores for group j, and $j = 1, 2, \ldots, a$.
3. The scores must be statistically independent of each other. More is said about this assumption later.

These assumptions are often stated in terms of the errors (εs) of the ANOVA model instead of in terms of Y. In fact, these two formulations are identical for our model because the Y scores are independent and normal and equally variable within groups if and only if the error components in the model are themselves normal, equally variable, and independent of each other.

Implications for Expected Values

These assumptions imply certain things about what population value is being estimated by the numerator and denominator of our test statistic. Beginning with the denominator, as we have noted (see Equation 63), E_F/df_F or MS_w is an average of the sample variances for the groups in the design. Within any given group j, the sample variance, s_j^2 computed by dividing the sum of squared deviations from the group mean by $n - 1$, is an unbiased estimator of the population variance for that group σ_j^2 and hence of the population variance of the errors σ_ε^2. Using $\mathcal{E}$ to indicate expected value (see the Appendix on "Review of Basic Statistics" or other standard sources such as Hays, 1994, p. 912ff.), we can write this as

$$\mathscr{E}(s_j^2) = \sigma_\varepsilon^2 \tag{97}$$

This in turn implies that the average of the sample variances in the denominator of our test is also an unbiased estimator of population error variance, that is,

$$\mathscr{E}\left[\frac{E_F}{df_F}\right] = \mathscr{E}(MS_w) = \mathscr{E}\left[\frac{\sum_j (n_j - 1)s_j^2}{\sum_j (n_j - 1)}\right]$$

$$= \frac{\sum_j (n_j - 1)\mathscr{E}(s_j^2)}{\sum_j (n_j - 1)}$$

$$= \frac{\sum_j (n_j - 1)\sigma_e^2}{\sum_j (n_j - 1)} = \sigma_\varepsilon^2 \tag{98}$$

Under our assumptions, it is the case that E_F/df_F or MS_W is an unbiased estimator of population error variance regardless of whether the null hypothesis of equal population means is true or false.

However, the numerator of our test statistic estimates one value when the null hypothesis is true and other values when it is false. In particular, it can be shown (e.g., Kirk, 1995, pp. 89–91) that the expected value of MS_B, the numerator of the F, is

$$\mathscr{E}\left[\frac{E_R - E_F}{df_R - df_F}\right] = \mathscr{E}(MS_B) = \sigma_\varepsilon^2 + \frac{\sum_j n_j \alpha_j^2}{a - 1} \tag{99}$$

That is, when the hypothesis that all the treatment effects are zero is exactly true, the numerator of the F estimates only population error variance. Otherwise, the numerator is estimating some larger value, with the particular value depending on just how large the treatment effects are.

Under our assumption that the groups of scores represent samples from a normal population distribution, the numerator and denominator of our test statistic are statistically independent. Also, if the null hypothesis is true, their ratio is distributed as an F under our assumptions of normality, homogeneity of variance, and independence.

Robustness of ANOVA

In many ANOVA applications, these assumptions are reasonably well satisfied. For example, as discussed in Chapter 2, both theoretical suggestions (cf. Hays, 1994, pp. 247–249) and empirical experience suggest that data sometimes at least approximate normality. Also, the assumption of homogeneous (equal) variances is often plausible because different treatments may be expected to affect the mean level of response but not the variability. Whether the independence-of-errors assumption is met is determined largely by the experimental design used, as discussed later.

Even if a researcher's data are not perfectly normally distributed, they may be close enough to normal (e.g., unimodal, symmetric, most scores centrally located, few scores at the extremes) that there would seem to be little cause for concern. Of course, in the real world, the question inevitably arises, How close is close enough? Statisticians have conducted a number of studies to answer this question for ANOVA. These studies allow us to characterize the robustness of ANOVA (*robustness* is the term used to denote the extent to which a statistical method produces correct results even when its assumptions fail to hold).

We simply summarize findings concerning the robustness of ANOVA. References that provide additional details are cited where relevant. We discuss robustness to violations of each of the three previously mentioned assumptions in turn.

1. ANOVA is generally robust to violations of the normality assumption, in that even when data are nonnormal, the actual Type I error rate is usually close to the nominal (i.e., desired) value. For example, even if the data in our study comparing three groups of six subjects are not normally distributed, the percentage of observed F values exceeding 3.68 is still very close to 5%. Thus, many do not regard lack of normality as a serious impediment to the use of ANOVA. For example, Scheffé's (1959, p. 345) summary of relevant mathematical work was, "Nonnormality has little effect on inferences about means" in fixed effects analysis of variance. Recent simulation studies with nonnormal data confirm this. As discussed in Tutorial 1: nonnormality is indicated by nonzero values of skewness (indicating asymmetry) or kurtosis (indicating "peakedness", i.e., distributions with unusually heavy or light tails). A meta-analysis of simulation studies with very nonnormal data (skewness = 2, kurtosis = 6) reported alpha levels tended to be reasonably close to nominal .05 alpha levels with equal sample sizes (mean actual alpha of .059 with a standard deviation of .026), but less so with unequal sample sizes (mean alpha of .069 with a standard deviation of .048) (Lix, Keselman, & Keselman, 1996, pp. 599–600).

Two additional points should be considered. First, robustness is not really "either/or," but rather is a matter of degree. As data get farther from normality, the actual Type I error rate tends to get farther from the nominal value. It is possible for data to deviate so wildly from normality that the actual Type I error rate is rather different from the nominal value (e.g., an actual rate of .10 when the nominal level is .05), but it is questionable how often such data occur in practice (for conflicting views, see Bradley, 1978; Glass, Peckham, & Sanders, 1972). Even when samples were drawn from the clearly nonnormal distributions of real data documented by Micceri (1989), actual Type I levels were generally very close to nominal levels, and departures observed even under unfavorable conditions such as small and unequal sample sizes tended to be in the direction of being moderately conservative (e.g., actual alpha of .041 for the extremely asymmetric psychometric measure) (Sawilowsky & Blair, 1992). Second, most studies of robustness have focused on Type I error instead of Type II error (or power). The available evidence suggests that ANOVA is also generally robust in terms of power to violations of normality (Glass, Peckham, & Sanders, 1972; Scheffé, 1959, p. 350; Sawilowsky & Blair, 1992). When normality and the other assumptions hold, ANOVA is the most powerful test of the omnibus null hypothesis, that is, the null hypothesis that $\mu_1 = \mu_2 = \cdots = \mu_a$. Although its power is relatively unaffected by violations of normality, the power of alternate approaches (e.g., nonparametric methods) changes considerably under nonnormality. As a consequence, some of these alternate approaches may be more powerful than ANOVA when normality fails to hold (Blair, 1981; Wilcox, 1996). The extension to the current chapter presents approaches that might be preferable in such a situation.

2. ANOVA is generally robust to moderate violations of homogeneity of variance as long as the sample sizes in each group are equal to each other and are not unreasonably small (e.g., less than five per group). However, when ns are unequal, even moderate heterogeneity of

variance can produce actual Type I error rates considerably different from the nominal value. When the groups with smaller population variances have larger samples, the pooled estimate of population variance in the denominator of the F tends to be smaller than it would be in the equal-n case, with the result that the actual Type I error rate will be greater than .05. For example, mathematical results indicate that when variances are in the ratio of 1 : 1 : 3 and corresponding sample sizes are 7, 5, and 3, respectively, the actual probability of a Type I error is .11 instead of the nominal value of .05 (Scheffé, 1959, p. 354). If the sample sizes were even more unbalanced, the departure would be even more pronounced. Sample sizes of 9, 5, and 1, respectively, for example, would produce an actual Type I error rate of .17 when the variances are in the 1 : 1 : 3 ratio (Scheffé, 1959, p. 354). However, when the groups with smaller population variances are represented by smaller samples, the pooled variance estimate tends to be larger than it would be in the equal-n case, and the actual Type I error rate is less than .05. For example, when variances are in the ratio of 1 : 1 : 3 and corresponding sample sizes are 1, 5, and 9, respectively, the actual probability of a Type I error is .013 instead of the nominal value of .05 (Scheffé, 1959, p. 354). Although a lower probability of making a Type I error might not sound so bad, it is in fact a serious problem, because it implies an increase in the probability of a Type II error. In other words, the price to be paid here for a conservative test is a decrease in power. The general pattern Scheffé noted has been confirmed repeatedly by simulation studies under a wide variety of conditions. Such simulations also show that heterogeneity of variance influences Type I error rates much more than does nonnormality (cf. Lix et al., 1996).

When sample sizes are equal, heterogeneity of variance must be more pronounced to produce a substantial distortion in the probability of a Type I error, but it can still occur. For example, Wilcox (1987a) reviews studies showing that in a four-group case with 12 observations in each group when the variances are in the ratio of 1 : 1 : 1 : 16, the probability of a Type I error is .101 instead of the nominal value of .05. When sample sizes are larger, the effect of unequal variances is reduced.

When sample sizes are unequal and population variances are heterogeneous, the standard F test of this chapter is inappropriate. Nonparametric approaches such as the Kruskal–Wallis test (described in the extension of this chapter) have sometimes been recommended when variances are heterogeneous. However, as pointed out by Vargha and Delaney (1998), when the Kruskal–Wallis test is used as a test of equal central tendencies, one must still assume that the variances are equal, just as in a standard analysis of variance. Thus, transformations of the data or modifications of our standard parametric test are generally preferable to the Kruskal–Wallis test in this situation. The chapter extension presents two such parametric modifications, the Brown-Forsythe F^* and Welch's W, either of which is preferable to the standard F test when sample sizes are unequal and variances are heterogeneous. It should be noted that these approaches are preferable only when population variances are unequal. Procedures for testing this hypothesis of homogeneity of variance are described later in this chapter.

3. ANOVA is not robust to violations of the independence-of-errors assumption. The actual probability of a Type I error may depart dramatically from the nominal level when errors are correlated. As stated earlier, the reasonableness of this assumption depends primarily on the design used. The meaning of this assumption can perhaps best be understood by considering a couple of examples in which the assumption is not met. First, suppose that a researcher wants to test whether relaxation training lowers subjects' blood pressure. To answer this question, the researcher measures pretest blood pressure on a group of 15 subjects, exposes them to relaxation training, and then obtains posttest readings on these subjects. Thus, 30 scores in all are obtained, 2 from each subject. However, these 30 scores are not all independent of each other, because only 15 subjects were tested. It is highly likely that a subject with a high pretest reading will

also have a high posttest reading, so that pretest and posttest scores will be correlated. Such an occurrence violates the independence-of-scores (errors) assumption. Chapters 11–14 describe procedures for analyzing such data, which represent a repeated measures (or within-subjects) design.

In between-subjects designs, such as those we have been considering in this chapter, what violations of the assumption of independent errors would mean is somewhat more difficult to understand. As Kenny and Judd (1986) suggest, instead of thinking of the assumption in terms of a correlation between variables, one should think of the assumption in terms of the conditional probability of one observation given another observation. For example, suppose that an educational psychologist wants to compare a structured classroom environment versus an open classroom for teaching arithmetic to second-grade children. One class of 30 children is randomly assigned to the structured condition, and a second class of 30 children is assigned to the open condition. The researcher reports that an ANOVA on posttest arithmetic knowledge reveals a statistically significant group difference, $F(1, 58) = 6.83$. Once again, the independence assumption has likely been violated because children influence each other within the classroom setting. As Glass and Stanley (1970) point out, one unruly child in one of the classrooms may lower the scores of all children in that classroom. Thus, even if the instructional treatment being manipulated had no effect, observing a particular score of one child in a classroom could alter the conditional probability of observing particular scores from other children in the classroom. One alternative that avoids this problem is to regard the experimental design of such a study as a nested design. As Chapter 10 shows, when such an approach is taken, it is imperative to assign several classrooms (not just one) to each of the treatment conditions being compared.

Checking for Normality and Homogeneity of Variance

A number of procedures have been developed for assessing the adequacy of the normality and homogeneity-of-variance assumptions in ANOVA. Perhaps the most useful is a good graph that, as John Tukey remarked, "forces us to notice what we never expected to see" (quoted in Wainer & Thissen, 1993, pp. 395, 448). Gross violations of normality can be detected easily through graphical procedures, especially with large samples. Useful references are Chambers, Cleveland, Kleiner, and Tukey (1983), Iman and Conover (1983), and Wainer and Thissen (1993, pp. 408–413). Statistical packages often can generate Q–Q plots, which display the data values having a given rank order or quantile against the values expected according to the normal distribution. Nonnormality is indicated when the points in the Q–Q plot depart from a straight line, but the exact form of the plot can vary from package to package and it takes some instruction and practice to master interpretation of the plots (cf. Wilk & Gnanadesikan, 1968). However, it is critical, as Wilkinson et al. (1999) argue, to examine graphical displays of the data for evaluating distributional assumptions, if not in P–P plots, then in some simpler format. It is sufficient for most purposes simply to examine a histogram of the data, perhaps with a normal curve overlaid. For example, a plot of the drinking at intake (mean number of standard drinks) for a sample of 105 homeless alcoholics (Smith, Meyers, & Delaney, 1998) shown in Figure 3.2 makes clear the data are positively skewed rather than bell shaped.

Statistical tests for assessing normality are also available. SPSS provides the information needed for testing skewness and kurtosis because standard errors of both statistics are reported. SAS performs the Shapiro–Wilk test when sample size is 50 or less and a modified

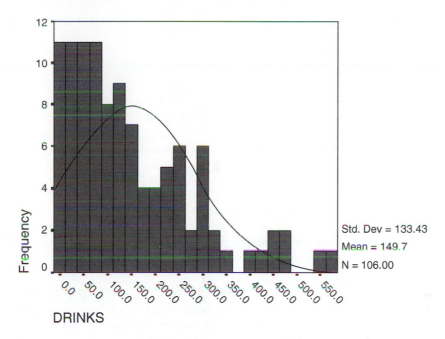

FIG. 3.2.   Distribution of average number of standard drinks per week at intake for a sample of homeless alcoholics (Smith, Meyers, & Delaney, 1998). Distribution has skewness =1.16 and kurtosis = .98.

Kolmogorov–Smirnov test when sample size is greater than 50. We do not discuss such tests, however, because when you have enough observations to have an accurate picture of the form of an empirical distribution, you probably have enough power to reject the hypothesis of normality. Micceri (1989), after finding that tests indicated that all 440 data sets he examined, each being based on 400 or more cases, were significantly nonnormal, concluded that "it therefore appears meaningless to test either ability or psychometric distributions for normality" (1989, p. 161). (Micceri's "psychometric" category consisted of the sorts of scales commonly used in clinical and social psychology research, e.g., MMPI subscales, measures of locus of control, anxiety, masculinity/femininity.) Even the frequency distributions presented in Chapter 2 of data that generally appear normal, all resulted when tested in highly significant departures from normality, $p < .001$. Thus, it may be more useful to have an idea of the typical range of skewness and kurtosis measures. These obviously vary across domains, with some studies (e.g., Pearson & Please, 1975) of empirical distributions reporting more modest departures from normality (skewness of their data sets were always less than .8) than the largest study to date of distributions of behavioral variables (Micceri, 1989). Although more than two thirds of Micceri's distributions had absolute values of skewness less than .70, about 10% had values greater than 2.00. Psychometric measures were somewhat more extreme with just under half having skewness measures less than .70, and perhaps as many as 18% having skewness more than 2.00. Kurtosis values, which correlated .78 with the skewness values, ranged from −1.7 to 37.37 for these 440 distributions, with 8% being greater than 3.0. The distribution shown in Figure 3.2 has a skewness of 1.16 and a kurtosis of .98, indicating, according to Micceri's criteria, an extreme level of skewness and a moderate degree of "contamination" in the right-hand tail (i.e., more than twice the expected number of scores more than two standard deviations above the mean).

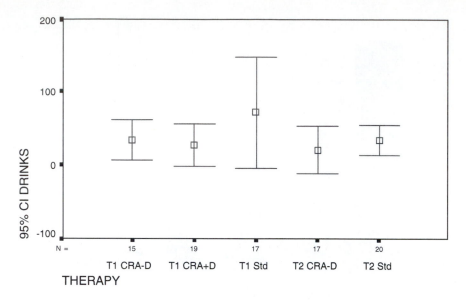

FIG. 3.3.   Confidence intervals around means for number of drinks per week for five groups at 9-month follow-up (Smith, Meyers & Delaney, 1998). Clients were initially assigned to one of two tracks (T1 or T2) and then were assigned randomly to receive therapy utilizing the Community Reinforcement Approach with disulfiram (CRA+D), therapy utilizing the Community Reinforcement Approach without disulfiram (CRA−D), or Standard therapy (Std). Clients in Track 2 were not eligible to receive disulfiram.

Graphical methods can also be helpful in drawing one's attention to possible violations of the assumption of homogeneity of variance in your data. For example, Figure 3.3 shows the 95% confidence intervals around the group means, computed using the different standard deviations for the various groups, for one of the follow-up assessments in a five-group clinical trial of therapy methods for homeless alcoholics (Smith et al., 1998). Given the sample sizes were approximately equal, the fact that the longest confidence interval is three times longer than the shortest one alerts the researcher to the fact that homogeneity of variance is likely violated in these data.

If one wants to carry out a formal statistical test of the homogeneity of variance assumption, there are more than 50 different tests that could be used (Kuehl, 2000, p. 128). The more familiar tests include the Bartlett–Box F test and Hartley's F_{max} (Neter, Wasserman, & Kutner, 1985, p. 618ff.). Hartley's test is particularly simple in that the test statistic is just the ratio of the largest within-group variance to the smallest within-group variance. Unfortunately, both tests assume the data are normally distributed and are very sensitive to departures from normality (Neter et al., 1985, pp. 622–623; O'Brien, 1981). Thus, if the data are nonnormal, results of these tests can be quite misleading. Some of the best procedures for testing homogeneity of variance involve computing a transformation of the original scores and then doing a standard analysis of variance on the new scores. One such method introduced by O'Brien (1981) involves computing the transformation in such a way that the group mean of the new variable equals the variance of the original variable for that group. Because it uses a standard F test to test for differences on the transformed variable, O'Brien's test is robust to violations of normality. For a one-way design, the steps of this procedure are as follows:

1. For each group, compute the sample mean $\overline{Y}_j$ and the unbiased sample variance:

$$s_j^2 = \sum_i (Y_{ij} - \overline{Y}_j)^2 / (n_j - 1)$$

2. For each observation Y_{ij}, compute a transformed score,

$$r_{ij} = \frac{(n_j - 1.5)n_j(Y_{ij} - \overline{Y}_j)^2 - .5s_j^2(n_j - 1)}{(n_j - 1)(n_j - 2)}$$

3. Verify that for each group, the mean of r is equal to the variance of the original Y scores, that is $\overline{r}_j = s_j^2$.
4. Perform an ANOVA using r as the dependent variable. When sample sizes are very unbalanced [the largest sample size max (n_j) is four or more times larger than the smallest min (n_j)], O'Brien recommends that a Welch-type ANOVA be used (see chapter extension, p. 134). Not only is this procedure robust, but it also generalizes easily to factorial designs.

The test of homogeneity of variance used by SPSS as of this writing is one from Levene (1960). Like O'Brien's test, Levene's test involves computing a transformed variable and doing an ANOVA on the transformed scores. However, the transformation used in Levene's test is simply the absolute value of the deviation of the score from the mean for its group, that is,

$$L_{ij} = |Y_{ij} - \overline{Y}_j|$$

For the drinking data shown in Figure 3.2, neither O'Brien's test, $F(4, 83) = 0.953$, $p = .438$, nor Levene's test, $F(4, 83) = 1.756$, $p = .146$, reaches significance. Perhaps somewhat ironically, one of the reasons why these tests fail to reach significance here is that in the transformed data, like in the original drinking data, the standard deviations tend to be larger than and proportional to the means. In such a situation, as we explain in the next section, it may be helpful to consider computing a transformation of the dependent variable to use in the primary analysis.

Transformations

When data are nonnormal and/or variances are unequal, it is often possible to transform the data so that the new scores more nearly approximate normality and equality of variances. For example, when data are positively skewed, either a square root or a logarithmic transformation often produces data that are more nearly normal; in some circumstances, the same transformation also achieves equality of variances.

However, there are potential disadvantages to transforming one's data. Primary among these is that interpretation of results may be less clear. For example, most individuals find it difficult to understand the mean value of the square root of their original scores. Also, in general, the null hypothesis that groups have the same mean on Y does not imply and is not implied by the null hypothesis that group means on a transformed variable are equal. As Games (1983, p. 382) says, "the use of curvilinear transformations in data analysis is a rather complex topic that involves philosophy of science considerations as well as statistical considerations."

However, it sometimes turns out to be the case that a transformation that makes theoretical sense also tends to stabilize the variances and make the distributions more nearly normally

TABLE 3.7
DESCRIPTIVE STATISTICS ON DRINKS PER WEEK AT 9-MONTH FOLLOW-UP IN FIVE
THERAPY GROUPS

Group	Mean	n	Median	Minimum	Maximum	SD	Skewness	Kurtosis
T1 CRA−D	33.80	15	11.89	0	169.29	49.39	1.84	3.10
T1 CRA+D	26.42	19	0.00	0	237.28	60.94	2.78	8.10
T1 Std	71.51	17	28.80	0	624.62	148.87	3.59	13.73
T2 CRA−D	20.31	17	0.00	0	257.32	62.87	3.78	14.76
T2 Std	33.77	20	13.47	0	164.06	44.82	1.64	2.43

distributed. We will illustrate with the drinking data shown in Figure 3.3. Table 3.7 shows descriptive statistics on the dependent variable of drinks per week at a 9-month follow-up assessment for each of five treatment groups.

The fact that the means are always greater than the medians and the standard deviations are greater than the means corroborates the information in the last two columns on the right that indicate the scores within each group are extremely positively skewed and heavy tailed. Most troublesome for the analysis of variance is the heterogeneity of variance across groups (the ratio of the largest to the smallest variance is $\frac{148.87^2}{44.82^2} = 3.32^2 = 11.03$) and the strong relationship that exists between the group means and standard deviations (which here correlate .90).

In deciding on a transformation, both theoretical and empirical considerations come into play. The theoretical or "philosophy of science" consideration here has to do with the meaning of the dependent variable. From one perspective, as a variable arrived at by counting, number of drinks is a ratio scale variable with an absolute zero point and equal intervals everywhere on the scale. However, the theoretical construct the investigators wanted this measure to reflect is severity of an individual's drinking problem, which is probably related to number of drinks in a nonlinear fashion. To illustrate, consider the drinking levels of three selected individuals who reported drinking 53.91, 257.31, and 624.62 drinks per week. The first individual who is drinking nearly 8 standard drinks per day would be regarded as a heavy drinker, but the other two, at more than 30 and 80 drinks per day, respectively, are both extremely heavy drinkers. In terms of the severity of the drinking problem, one could argue that the difference between the first and second individuals is likely a greater difference than the difference between the second and third individuals. A transformation that shrinks the differences between the most extreme drinkers would perhaps result in a dependent variable that is more directly related to the construct of interest.

Now from an empirical perspective there are a range of transformations that are available. One possible strategy would be simply to try different transformations and see which one results in distributions that more nearly conform to assumptions (i.e., less heterogeneity of variance, less relationship between the means and standard deviations, and lower skewness and kurtosis). Yet even with such a brute-force approach, it is helpful to realize that a number of the most useful transformations can be ordered along a "ladder of powers" (Tukey, 1977). The steps in the ladder are the powers or exponents to which the original scores are to be raised in computing the new scores, as shown in Table 3.8.

In a situation with three or more groups, one can estimate empirically the value of p that tends to equate variances across groups by doing a regression of the log of the standard deviations on the log of the means (cf. Kuehl, 2000, p. 136ff.). If b is the estimated slope in this regression, then one can estimate the appropriate power for your transformation as $\hat{p} = 1 - b$. For the five groups in the study with the homeless alcoholics, the slope of the regression of

TABLE 3.8
THE "LADDER OF POWERS" FOR TRANSFORMING SCORES WHERE $Y' = Y^p$

Power, p	Transformation	Name and Remarks
2	Y^2	Square, useful when need to increase spread among higher scores relative to lower scores, e.g. with negatively skewed data
1	Y	Raw data, no transformation
$\frac{1}{2}$	$\sqrt{Y}$	Square root, helpful with positively skewed distributions
0	$\log_{10} Y$	Logarithmic, use when p estimated to be near zero, e.g., with extremely positively skewed distributions. Use $Y' = \log_{10}(Y + 1)$ if there are any zeros in data.
−1	$1/Y$	Reciprocal, e.g., transforming latency to speed. Use $Y' = 1/(Y + 1)$ if there are any zeros in data.

TABLE 3.9
DESCRIPTIVE STATISTICS ON LOG TRANSFORMED DRINKS PER WEEK AT 9-MONTH
FOLLOW-UP IN FIVE THERAPY GROUPS

Group	Mean	n	Median	Min.	Max.	SD	Skewness	Kurtosis
T1 CRA−D	1.01	15	1.08	0	2.23	0.80	−0.03	−1.46
T1 CRA+D	0.54	19	0.00	0	2.38	0.83	1.37	0.32
T1 Std	1.23	17	1.47	0	2.80	0.87	−0.24	−0.87
T2 CRA−D	0.39	17	0.00	0	2.41	0.74	1.94	1.06
T2 Std	1.05	20	1.15	0	2.22	0.78	−0.21	−1.39

the log standard deviations on the log means was 0.742, and so p was estimated as .258, or approximately $\frac{1}{4}$. Because this was approximately midway between the levels for the square root and log transformation, both transformations were tried and resulting heterogeneity of variance examined. With the square root, the ratio of largest to smallest variance was 2.5 to 1, down dramatically from the 11 to 1 ratio in the raw data. However, with the log transform, this ratio was reduced still further to 1.2 to 1. In terms of the three illustrative individuals mentioned previously, their scores on the log scale were 1.732, 2.410, and 2.796, respectively. So now the difference between the first and second of these individuals, .678, was considerably larger than that between the two extremely heavy drinkers, .385, as desired. Summary statistics using a log transform are shown in Table 3.9, and confidence intervals around the means of the transformed variable are shown in Figure 3.4. One can see at a glance at these confidence intervals that they are now much more nearly equal in length than the intervals for the original data in Figure 3.3.

One added benefit of this variance stabilizing transformation with positively skewed distributions is that shrinking the influence of the few heaviest drinkers greatly reduced the variability within groups relative to the variability between groups. As seen in Figure 3.4, the confidence intervals around the individual group means now show much less overlap across groups than was the case before the transformation. In terms of results of a statistical test, whereas an ANOVA of the original scores did not approach significance, $F(4, 83) = 1.02$, $p = .400$, an ANOVA of the log drinks per week is now significant, $F(4, 83) = 3.48$, $p = .011$. One reason for this dramatic change is that the power of the F test is adversely affected by nonnormality (McClelland, 2000). As seen in Table 3.9, not only are the variances now much more homogeneous, but the skewness and kurtosis of the distributions, although still in some groups departing substantially from the zero values for normal distributions, have been markedly reduced from their previous maximum values of 3.78 and 14.76, respectively.

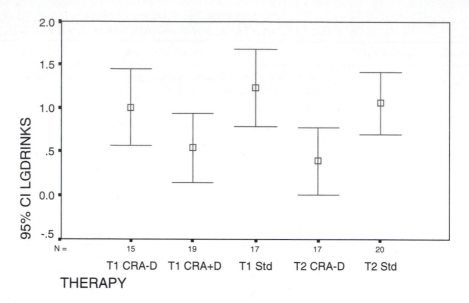

FIG. 3.4. Confidence intervals around mean of log transformed drinks per week at 9-month follow-up for five therapy conditions.

As suggested previously, data transformations are a topic about which reasonable people differ. One perspective on this debate is seen in the spirited exchange between Levine and Dunlap (1982, 1983) and Games (1983, 1984).

POWER OF THE F TEST: ONE-WAY ANOVA

As noted in Chapter 1, the power of a test is its sensitivity in detecting real differences between groups. That is, *power*, denoted $1 - \beta$, is defined as the probability of rejecting the null hypothesis (or the restricted model) given that it is false (or given that the full model is the correct description of the data). Power analyses are useful for determining how sensitive a particular experimental design is. Most often, such analyses are performed to determine the sample size required to give an experiment adequate power.

Besides the assumptions about the independence, variability, and normality of the scores in various groups, to determine the power of the F test one must also specify the magnitude of the treatment effects in the population. In the preceding section, we considered those statistical assumptions that are necessary for the observed F statistic to have the distributional shape presumed by the probability values indicated in a conventional F table. It bears repeating that it is also necessary for the null hypothesis to be true for the observed F to have this distribution over replications. If the statistical assumptions are met, but the null hypothesis is false, the test statistic follows what is termed a *noncentral F distribution*. Such a distribution depends not only on the typical degrees of freedom associated with a central F but also on a noncentrality parameter, λ (lowercase Greek letter lambda), which combines information about the magnitude of the difference among the population means, the within-group population variance, and the sample size: $\lambda = n \Sigma_{j=1}^{a} \alpha_j^2 / \sigma_\varepsilon^2$.

Working with noncentral F distributions to determine power may seem like a difficult computational challenge. However, as with most standard statistical problems, a variety of computer programs are currently available to do the necessary computations (e.g., including both commercially marketed programs such as Power and Precision, as well as "shareware" programs such as UnifyPow, which handles power analyses for a wide variety of designs and tests, available at www.bio.ri.ccf.org/power.html). Actually, the most difficult part of power analysis is usually conceptual rather than computational. In part, this is because research is almost never an exact replication of what has been done before. Yet to perform a power analysis one must make projections about the magnitude of the effect or even the exact numerical values of the means and standard deviations one is going to obtain. Even when somewhat similar work has been reported in the literature, such projections necessarily rely on one's judgment about the difference that the details of a proposed experimental design will make. For example, what difference will it make if a motivational intervention in a clinical treatment program is used as an adjunct to a computer-based intervention rather than to a standard outpatient program using a therapist? What will be the impact of using one set of materials rather than another in a study of reading comprehension? What difference does it make that a study is run in Albuquerque rather than South Bend or using college students rather than older adults as participants? Clearly these questions concern the generalizability of findings, and answering them for purposes of a power analysis requires not only a general appreciation of construct and external validity issues, but also making numerical projections about how these will affect population parameters, a more daunting task than learning to read a power chart. The best-case scenario might be where one has pilot data in hand based on the actual implementations of the independent and dependent variable constructs that will be used in the current study. Methods for using pilot data rather than projected populations parameters in a power analysis are considered shortly.

Determining Sample Size Using f and Power Charts

To turn now to how to carry out the calculations if one is doing the power analysis by hand, the standard procedure is to use a chart or a table that relates power to some function of the noncentrality parameter. However, because noncentrality parameters depend on the sample size, which is typically what you are doing a power analysis to determine, it is easier to begin thinking about the magnitude of the expected effect using an alternative measure. Most useful perhaps is f, one of the standardized measures of effect size that we introduced previously:

$$f = \sigma_m/\sigma_\varepsilon \qquad \text{(89, repeated)}$$

Recall that σ_ε is the square root of the population within-cell error variance and that σ_m can be viewed as the standard deviation of the population means for the various groups in your design or equivalently as the standard deviation of the effect parameters:

$$\sigma_m = \sqrt{\frac{\sum(\mu_j - \mu)^2}{a}} = \sqrt{\frac{\sum \alpha_j^2}{a}} \qquad \text{(88, repeated)}$$

Here, μ is the mean of the population means, that is, $\mu = (\Sigma_j\mu_j)/a$. The projections about reasonable values for σ_ε and μ_j are typically made on the basis of a combination of prior work and informed judgment. Some guidance about typical values of the f index was provided by Cohen (1977, Chapter 8), who suggested that a "small" effect size be defined as $f = .10$, a "medium" effect size as $f = .25$, and a "large" effect size as $f = .40$. Thus, for a medium effect size, the standard deviation of the population means would be one quarter of the within-group standard deviation. In a two-group study, because the standard deviation of two population means is just half the difference between them, this definition of medium effect size would imply that the expected value of the difference between the means in your study would be half of the expected within-group standard deviation.

Cohen (1988, pp. 289–354) provides tables that allow you to read off the power for particular combinations of the degrees of freedom of the numerator of your test ($df_R - df_F$), the Type I error rate (α), the effect-size parameter (f), and the number of subjects per group. With four factors varying, it perhaps should not be surprising that the tables require 66 pages.

Some simplifying strategy is clearly needed. The one most often used is to summarize the information about the noncentral F distribution in a series of charts (such as those found in Appendix Table A.11) and, if necessary, use "visual interpolation" between lines on the graphs to approximate the power for your situation. The information required to read a power value from these charts is

1. The numerator degrees of freedom for your test—that is, $df_R - df_F$—denoted df_{num} in the charts
2. The Type I error rate α
3. The denominator degrees of freedom df_F denoted df_{denom}
4. An effect-size parameter ϕ, which reflects the sample size and the magnitude of the effects.

The effect size parameter ϕ (lowercase Greek phi) can be defined in terms of the noncentrality parameter as $\phi = \sqrt{\lambda/a}$, but we use a definition in terms of the following simple transformation of f:

$$\phi = f \sqrt{n} \tag{100}$$

where n is the number of subjects per group. Note that you must use a value of n to determine both ϕ and df_F. Thus, if you are planning a study, a power analysis proceeds in a trial-and-error fashion where you test out different values of n.

For example, assume that you are planning a reaction-time study involving three groups. Pilot research and data from the literature suggest that the means in your three groups might be 400, 450, and 500 ms with a within-group standard deviation of 100 ms. Thus, substituting these values in the formula defining σ_m (Equation 88), we obtain

$$\sigma_m = \sqrt{\frac{(400 - 450)^2 + (450 - 450)^2 + (500 - 450)}{3^2}}$$

$$= \sqrt{\frac{2500 + 0 + 2500}{3}} = \sqrt{\frac{5000}{3}} = \sqrt{1666.66} = 40.82$$

This means that here, f is in the large range:

$$f = \frac{\sigma_m}{\sigma_\varepsilon} = \frac{40.82}{100} = .4082$$

Suppose that you want to have power of .8 for $\alpha = .05$, so that if the population parameters are as you hope, four times out of five your study allows you to declare your results significant.

You might hope that you can get by with only 10 subjects per group. This would mean a total N of 30, and hence the values required to enter the charts would be

$$df_{num} = df_R - df_F = (N - 1) - (N - a) = a - 1 = 3 - 1 = 2$$
$$df_{denom} = df_F = N - a = 30 - 3 = 27$$

and,

$$\phi = f\sqrt{n} = .4082\sqrt{10} = 1.29$$

From the chart for $df_{num} = 2$, following the curve for $df_{denom} = 30$ (the closest value to 27), we find the power for our parameter values by determining the height of the curve directly above the point on the horizontal axis that seems to approximate a ϕ value of 1.29 for $\alpha = .05$. This indicates the power here is approximately .45, which is unacceptably small. Thus, we might next try 25 subjects per group. This would change df_{denom} to 72, and ϕ would be .4082 $\sqrt{25} = .4082(5) = 2.041$. Following the curve for $df_{denom} = 60$ to our value of ϕ suggests a power of .87, which is more than we required. Eventually, we could iterate[12] to $n = 21$, yielding $df_{denom} = 60$ and $\phi = 1.8706$ and a power of essentially .8.

Determining Sample Size Using d and Table 3.10

A second strategy that simplifies things still further is to define the effect size simply in terms of the number of standard deviations between the largest and smallest population means anticipated. Recall that we designated this measure of effect size d (see Equations 83 and 87):

$$d = \frac{\mu_{max} - \mu_{min}}{\sigma_\varepsilon}$$

Table 3.10, which is similar to tables published by Bratcher, Moran, and Zimmer (1970), allows one to read directly the sample size required for detecting an effect for various values of d. The price paid for this simplicity is that the anticipated value of all other means except the two most extreme means does not affect the value of d. In fact, the tables are computed by presuming that all other means except the two extremes are exactly equal to the grand mean μ. If this is not the case, somewhat greater power results than is indicated by the table. The relationship between f and d, as Cohen (1988) notes, depends on what the particular pattern of means is, but in most cases d is between two and four times as large as f.

For our particular data, the "other" (nonextreme) mean was exactly at the grand mean (450), so the results of Table 3.10 are exact for our case. One enters the table with a desired value of power $(1 - \beta)$, a standardized effect size d, and the number of groups a. For our hypothesized data

$$d = \frac{\mu_{max} - \mu_{min}}{\sigma_\varepsilon} = \frac{500 - 400}{100} = 1.0$$

Reading from the column labeled 1.00 from the section of the table for power $= .80$, we find the entry for the row for $a = 3$ indicates the required n for $\alpha = .05$ to be 21, the same value we determined earlier by use of the charts.

TABLE 3.10
MINIMUM SAMPLE SIZE PER GROUP NEEDED TO ACHIEVE SPECIFIED LEVELS OF
POWER WITH $\alpha = .05$

Number of Levels	d					
a	0.25	0.50	0.75	1.00	1.25	1.50

Power $= 1 - \beta = .50$

a	0.25	0.50	0.75	1.00	1.25	1.50
2	124	32	15	9	7	5
3	160	41	19	11	8	6
4	186	48	22	13	9	7
5	207	53	24	14	10	7
6	225	57	26	15	10	8

Power $= 1 - \beta = .80$

a	0.25	0.50	0.75	1.00	1.25	1.50
2	253	64	29	17	12	9
3	310	79	36	21	14	10
4	350	89	40	23	15	11
5	383	97	44	25	17	12
6	412	104	47	27	18	13

Power $= 1 - \beta = .95$

a	0.25	0.50	0.75	1.00	1.25	1.50
2	417	105	48	27	18	13
3	496	125	56	32	21	15
4	551	139	63	36	23	17
5	596	150	67	39	25	18
6	634	160	72	41	27	19

Pilot Data and Observed Power

As noted previously, the best-case scenario conceptually for doing a power analysis is when you have pilot data in hand using the treatments and measures that will be used in the actual study. Computationally, however, a slight modification in the effect size measure is needed to adjust for the effects of sampling variability in the group means observed in the pilot study. The reason this is needed is suggested by the fact that even if the null hypothesis of no difference in population means were true, we would not expect the sample means to be exactly equal. Thus, the variability of the sample means is something of an overestimate of the variability of the population means. Just how much of an adjustment is needed can be derived from the expressions for the expected values of the numerator and denominator of the F test (see Equations 98 and 99). There we saw that the denominator of the test MS_W estimates the population error variance and that, when the null hypothesis is true, the numerator of the test MS_B also estimates the population error variance. Heuristically, one might say that the implication is that nonzero values of MS_B can be unambiguously attributed to true treatments effects only to the extent that MS_B exceeds MS_W. More specifically, it turns out that one can adjust for this by estimating the variance of the population means as

$$\hat{\sigma}_m^2 = \frac{(a-1)}{N}(MS_B - MS_W) \tag{101}$$

This, in turn, implies that the adjusted estimate of effect size appropriate for use in determining sample size in a power analysis would be

$$f_{\text{adj}} = \sqrt{\frac{(a-1)}{N} \frac{(MS_B - MS_W)}{MS_W}} = \sqrt{\frac{(a-1)}{N}(F-1)} \tag{102}$$

As suggested by the right side of Equation 102, a convenient way of arriving at an adjusted effect size measure to use in a power analysis is to begin with the value of the F test statistic yielded by an ANOVA on the pilot data.[13] How much of a difference this adjustment makes in the estimated effect size depends on how large the observed F statistic is. When F is less than 1, the formula would yield a negative adjusted effect size, in which case it would be presumed to be zero. As the observed value of F increases, the proportionate reduction declines, until when F exceeds 10, the reduction in f is 5% or less.

We want to stress that the power computed based on this sort of adjusted effect derived from pilot data for purposes of planning a future study is different from what has come to be known as *observed power*, which can be computed as an adjunct to one's data analysis for purposes of interpreting a completed study (e.g., this is currently available as an option in SPSS's General Linear Model procedures such as UNIANOVA for univariate analysis of variance). Observed power is computed by simply assuming the population means are exactly equal to the observed sample means. As Hoenig and Heisey (2001) summarize, a number of journals advocate the reporting of observed power. We believe this is misguided for several reasons.

First, as we have just seen, the variability among the sample means is not the best estimate of the variability among the population means because of the inflation due to sampling variability. The smaller the sample, the bigger this problem is. Second, to report observed power in addition to the p value of a test is to appear to report additional information, whereas in reality there is a one-to-one correspondence between the two: the smaller the p value, the higher the observed power. Third, the logic of the argument of some advocates of observed power is misguided. The reasoning is that if observed power is high and yet the null hypothesis was not rejected, then the evidence against the null hypothesis is stronger than if observed power is low. One problem with this line of reasoning is that observed power in a situation with nonsignificant results can never be high. In particular, saying $p > .05$ is tantamount to saying that observed power is less than .5 (cf. Greenwald et al., 1996; Hoenig & Heisey, 2001).

Note that we are not in any way questioning the legitimate uses of power analyses in *designing* studies. Failing to reject the null hypothesis because of low power to detect what would constitute an important difference is a pervasive problem, and using power analyses as an aid to planning experiments so as to make such misses less likely is something we certainly advocate. Yet using observed power as a way of analyzing or interpreting data is quite different. Although it is true that the higher the power to detect a *meaningful, prespecified difference*, the more one should think that a nonrejection is *not* the result of low power and hence the stronger the evidence that the null hypothesis is true, or at least approximately true. However, the higher the *observed* power, computed based on the obtained results, the stronger the evidence is *against*, not in favor of, the null hypothesis. This is because higher observed power necessarily means a lower p value and hence stronger evidence against the null. Thus, reporting observed power is not recommended.

This completes the introduction of the model-comparison approach to one-way ANOVA. As indicated, an advantage of this approach is that the logic of searching for an adequate yet simple model is the same for all other applications of the general linear model that we consider. In fact, in a sense, it is the case that in terms of between-groups designs we have already covered the most complex design we must consider, because all other designs can be considered to be special cases of the one-way design. However, to appreciate the sense in which this is true and to develop the follow-up tests that are likely of interest in multiple-group designs, we must develop methods that allow particular combinations of means of interest to be tested. We apply the model-comparison approach to these issues of testing specific contrasts of interest in the chapters that follow.

EXERCISES

1. The full model is _____ than the restricted model.
   a. simpler   b.   less simple

2. The full model corresponds to the _____ hypothesis.
   a. null   b.   alternative

3. True or False: The restricted model is a special case of the full model.

4. True or False: For a fixed total N, the simpler the model, the greater the degrees of freedom.

*5. True or False: When the null hypothesis is true, MS_B estimates the variance of the sampling distribution of sample means.

6. True or False: The sum of squared errors for the restricted model (E_R) is always less than the sum of squared errors for the full model (E_F).

*7. True or False: The sum of squared errors associated with the restricted model E_R is always SS_{Total}.

*8. Gauss said, "The estimation of a magnitude using an observation [that is] subject to a larger or smaller error can be compared not inappropriately to a game of chance in which one can only lose and never win and in which each possible error corresponds to a loss." (See LeCam, L., & Neyman, J. (1965). Bayes–Bernoulli–Laplace Seminar. New York: Springer, p. viii.) What "loss function" is used in the solution of the estimation problems in this book?

9. Assume that a psychologist has performed a study to compare four different treatments for alleviating agoraphobia. Three subjects have been randomly assigned to each of four types of therapy: rational–emotive (R–E), psychoanalytic (P), client–centered (C–C), and behavioral (B). The following posttest scores were obtained on a fear scale, where higher scores indicate more severe phobia:

R–E	P	C–C	B
2	10	4	8
4	12	6	10
6	14	8	12

   a. Carry out the model comparison necessary to test whether there is a statistically significant difference between the means of the four groups. State the models, estimate their parameters, calculate the predicted scores and errors for each individual subject, compute the summary measures E_R and E_F, and finally determine the value of F and its significance.

   b. Calculate the t value for comparing each pair of means. You should have six such t values. Note that with equal n,

$$t = \frac{\overline{Y}_1 - \overline{Y}_2}{\sqrt{(s_1^2 + s_2^2)/n}}$$

Hint: There is a peculiar relationship among the four s_j^2 values for these data. This should simplify your task considerably.

c. Square each of the t values you calculated in part b. Do you see any relationship between these six t^2 values and the F value you calculated in part a?

*10. As described in the Chapter 2 exercises, an important series of studies by Bennett et al. (1964) attempted to find evidence for changes in the brain as a result of experience. Posttreatment weights of the cortex of animals reared in an enriched environment or in a deprived environment are shown below for three replications of the study done at different times of year. Cortex weights (in milligrams) for experimental and control animals are as follows:

Experiment 1		Experiment 2		Experiment 3	
Experimental	Control	Experimental	Control	Experimental	Control
688	655	707	669	690	668
655	623	740	650	701	667
668	652	745	651	685	647
660	654	652	627	751	693
679	655	649	656	647	635
663	646	676	642	647	644
664	600	699	698	720	665
647	640	696	648	718	689
694	605	712	676	718	642
633	635	708	657	696	673
653	642	749	692	658	675
676	661	691	618	680	641

(Raw data are adapted from those reported in Freedman, Pisani, & Purves, 1978, p. 452.) Twelve pairs of rats served as subjects in each study, with one member of each pair assigned randomly to the enriched environment and the other to the deprived environment. The two scores on the same row above for a given experiment came from two male rats taken from the same litter. The experimental hypothesis was that, even though both groups were permitted to feed freely, animals reared in the more stimulating environment would develop heavier cortexes. In Chapter 2, you were asked to test this hypothesis using a randomization test. Now, a series of parametric analyses are requested.

First Analysis, Experiment 2 Data Only

a. How many independent observations are there in Experiment 2?
b. What full model should be used to describe these independent observations?
c. What constraint on this model is of interest to test? What restricted model incorporates this constraint?
d. What is the sum of squared errors associated with the full model? With the restricted model?
e. Carry out the statistical test comparing these two models.
f. What is your conclusion?

Second Analysis, Data from Experiments 1, 2, and 3

g. Now use the data from all three experiments. Assume that you are interested in whether the three experiments revealed the same advantage for the experimental animals within sampling error regardless of the time of year when the experiment was run. State the models appropriate for testing this hypothesis and carry out the analysis, again providing parameter estimates and sums of squared errors for your models as well as stating your conclusion.

*11. Again using the data from the previous problem, reanalyze the data from Experiment 2 under a different set of assumptions about what went on. Assume that the treatment and control subjects all came from different litters so that there was no pairing of observations.

   a. Under this assumption, state the models that are likely of interest and carry out the test comparing these two models, stating the estimated parameter values and sum of squared errors for each model.

   b. How does the strength of the evidence against the restricted model in this analysis compare to that in your analysis in parts a–f of Exercise 10?

*12. For the Experiment 2 data analyzed as a two independent-groups design as in Exercise 11, characterize the magnitude of the effect in the following ways:

   a. As a standardized difference between means, $\hat{d}$.

   b. By computing the following measures of the proportional reduction in error: R^2 and $\hat{\omega}^2$.

13. For your master's thesis you are doing a study that in part replicates previous research. You plan to use three groups and expect the means on the dependent variable to be 55, 67, and 79. On the basis of previous research, you have evidence that leads you to expect the population within-group variance to be about 3600. How many subjects are required per cell to achieve a power of .80 with $\alpha = .05$?

*14. Assume that you are planning a study and that you are at the point of trying to determine how many subjects are needed for your four-group design. You decide that all groups will have the same number of subjects. Assume the following group means of 21, 24, 30, and 45 are the actual population means instead of sample statistics. Under this hypothesis and assuming the population within-group standard deviation is 20, how many subjects would be needed per group in order to have a power of .8 in a one-way ANOVA with $\alpha = .05$?

15. Suppose that we are planning a study to compare three treatments for depression. Group 1 subjects receive weekly therapy sessions using client-centered therapy. Group 2 subjects also receive client-centered therapy but are seen only every two weeks. Group 3 subjects serve as a waiting list control group. Posttest assessment occurs 3 months into the study. The dependent measure is the Center for Epidemiology Studies' Depression Scale (CES-D).

   a. Our best guess as to the likely magnitude of group differences is reflected in the following population means: $\mu_1 = 15$, $\mu_2 = 18$, and $\mu_3 = 24$. We expect the population standard deviation (within-groups) to be around 10. Naturally, we set α at .05. What is the total number of subjects we should include in our study, assuming equal n per group in order to have a power of .8?

   b. Suppose that our estimate of the population standard deviation in part a is too small. Specifically, assume that the true value is 14 instead of 10. Because we planned our study using the value of 10, the number of subjects we use is still the number you found in part a. If we use this many subjects, but in fact 14 is the true standard deviation, what is the actual value of our power?

16. Throughout this book, we make extensive use of the principle of least squares. In this chapter, we have proved mathematically that the sample mean $\overline{Y}$ is the least-squares estimator of a population mean μ. This exercise explores this fact in additional detail from an empirical (as opposed to a mathematical) perspective.

   a. Suppose we have a sample of five scores: 43, 56, 47, 61, and 43. Calculate the sum of squared deviations from the mean for these five scores. Also, calculate the sum of squared deviations from the median for the five scores. Which is less? Will this always be true? Why or why not?

   b. Suppose that we were to choose our estimator not to minimize the sum of squared errors, but instead to minimize the sum of the absolute values of the errors. Calculate the sum of absolute deviations from the mean and from the median. Which is less? Do you think this will always be true? Why or why not?

17. You are planning a large-scale replication of a study of a treatment for problem drinkers that previously has been shown in a different location to be significantly more effective than a control

condition. You begin by conducting a pilot study with five subjects per group. Your results for this pilot study are shown below, where the dependent variable is the estimated number of days of problem drinking per year after treatment.

Group	
Treatment	**Control**
41	214
23	199
20	194
16	189
0	174

a. The previous researchers had found means of 12 and 174 on this dependent variable for their implementations of the treatment and control conditions, respectively. Conduct a test of whether your pilot results replicate this previous research by comparing a model that allows for different population means in the two conditions with one that assumes means of 12 and 174.

b. Alternatively, you could have simply asked the question of whether the difference between your means was significantly different from the 162-point difference obtained by the previous investigators. Perform the test comparing the models relevant to this question.

c. What do you conclude on the basis of the results of the tests in parts a and b?

*18. In a study of a behavioral self-control intervention for problem drinkers, one of the less sensitive dependent variables was number of drinking days per week [Hester, R. K., & Delaney, H. D. (1997). Behavioral Self-Control Program for Windows: Results of a controlled clinical trial. *Journal of Consulting and Clinical Psychology*, *65*, 686–693]. Forty participants were assigned randomly to either receive the intervention immediately or be in a waiting list control group (i. e., $n = 20$ per group). At the initial follow-up assessment, the means and standard deviations on Drinking Days per Week were as follows:

Condition	Mean	SD
Immediate	3.65	1.57
Delayed	4.80	2.55

Assume this set of data is being viewed as a pilot study for a proposed replication.

a. Conduct an ANOVA on these data, and compute as descriptive measures of the effect size observed both d and f.

b. Determine the sample size that would be required to achieve a power of .80 using an α of .05 if one used the value of f arrived at in part a as the effect size measure in the power analysis.

c. Now compute f_{adj}, the corrected effect size measure that adjusts for the sampling variability in the observed means. Carry out a revised power analysis based on this adjusted effect size measure. How many more subjects are required to achieve 80% power than would have been thought to be required if the power analysis had been based on the uncorrected effect size estimate as in part b?

EXTENSION: ROBUST METHODS FOR ONE-WAY BETWEEN-SUBJECT DESIGNS

In Chapter 3, we state that ANOVA is predicated on three assumptions: normality, homogeneity of variance, and independence of observations. When these conditions are met, ANOVA is a "uniformly most powerful" procedure. In essence, this means that the F test is the best possible test when one is interested uniformly (i.e., equally) in all possible alternatives to the null hypothesis. Thus, in the absence of planned comparisons, ANOVA is the optimal technique to use for hypothesis testing whenever its assumptions hold. In practice, the three assumptions are often met at least closely enough so that the use of ANOVA is still optimal.

Recall from our discussion of statistical assumptions in Chapter 3 that ANOVA is generally robust to violations of normality and homogeneity of variance, although robustness to the latter occurs only with equal n (more on this later). *Robustness* means that the actual rate of Type I errors committed is close to the nominal rate (typically .05) even when the assumptions fail to hold. In addition, ANOVA procedures generally appear to be robust with respect to Type II errors as well, although less research has been conducted on Type II error rate.

The general robustness of ANOVA was taken for granted by most behavioral researchers during the 1970s, based on findings documented in the excellent literature review by Glass, Peckham, and Sanders (1972). Because both Type I and Type II error rates were only very slightly affected by violations of normality or homogeneity (with equal n), there seemed to be little need to consider alternative methods of hypothesis testing.

However, the 1980s saw a renewed interest in possible alternatives to ANOVA. Although part of the impetus behind this movement stemmed from further investigation of robustness with regard to Type I error rate, the major focus was on Type II error rate, that is, on issues of power. As Blair (1981) points out, robustness implies that the power of ANOVA is relatively unaffected by violations of assumptions. However, the user of statistics is interested not in whether ANOVA power is unaffected, but in whether ANOVA is the most powerful test available for a particular problem. Even when ANOVA is robust, it may not provide the most powerful test available when its assumptions have been violated.

Statisticians are developing possible alternatives to ANOVA. Our purpose in this extension is to provide a brief introduction to a few of these possible alternatives. We warn you that our coverage is far from exhaustive; we simply could not cover in the space available the wide range of possibilities already developed. Instead, our purpose is to make you aware that the field of statistics is dynamic and ever-changing, just like all other scientific fields of inquiry. Techniques (or theories) that are favored today may be in disfavor tomorrow, replaced by superior alternatives.

Another reason we make no attempt to be exhaustive here is that further research yet needs to be done to compare the techniques we describe to usual ANOVA methods. At this time, it is unclear which, if any, of these methods will be judged most useful. Although we provide evaluative comments where possible, we forewarn you that this area is full of complexity and controversy. The assumption that distributions are normal and variances are homogeneous simplifies the world enormously. A moment's reflection should convince you that "nonnormal" and "heterogeneous" lack the precision of "normal" and "homogeneous." Data can be nonnormal in an infinite number of ways, rapidly making it very difficult for statisticians to find an optimal technique for analyzing "nonnormal" data. What is good for one form of nonnormality may be bad for another form. Also, what kinds of distributions occur in real data? A theoretical statistician may be interested in comparing data-analysis techniques for data from a specific nonnormal distribution, but if that particular distribution never underlies behavioral data, the comparison may have no practical import to behavioral researchers. How far do actual data depart from normality and homogeneity? There is no simple answer, which partially explains why comparing alternatives to ANOVA is complicated and controversial.

The presentation of methods in this extension is not regularly paralleled by similar extensions on robust methods later in the book because many of the alternatives to ANOVA in the single-factor between-subjects design have not been generalized to more complex designs.

Two possible types of alternatives to the usual ANOVA in between-subjects designs have received considerable attention in recent years. The first type is a parametric modification of the F test that does not assume homogeneity of variance. The second type is a nonparametric approach that does not assume normality. Because the third ANOVA assumption is independence, you might expect there to be a third type of alternative that does not assume independence. However, as we stated earlier, independence is largely a matter of design, so modifications would likely involve changes in the design instead of changes in data analysis (see Kenny & Judd, 1986). Besides these two broad types of alternatives, several other possible approaches are being investigated. We look at two of these after we examine the parametric modifications and the nonparametric approaches.

Parametric Modifications

As stated earlier, one assumption underlying the usual ANOVA F test is homogeneity of variance. Statisticians have known for many years that the F test can be either very conservative (too few Type I errors and hence decreased power) or very liberal (too many Type I errors) when variances are heterogeneous and sample sizes are unequal. In general, the F test is conservative when large sample sizes are paired with large variances. The F is liberal when large sample sizes are paired with small variances. The optional section at the end of this extension shows why the nature of the pairing causes the F sometimes to be conservative and other times to be liberal. Obviously, either occurrence is problematic, especially because the population variances are unknown parameters. As a consequence, we can never know with complete certainty whether the assumption has been satisfied in the population. However, statistical tests of the assumption are available (see Chapter 3), so one strategy might be to use the standard F test to test mean differences only if the homogeneity of variance hypothesis cannot be rejected. Unfortunately, this strategy seems to offer almost no advantage (Wilcox, Charlin, & Thompson, 1986). The failure of this strategy has led some statisticians (e.g., Tomarken & Serlin, 1986; Wilcox, Charlin, & Thompson, 1986) to recommend that the usual F test routinely be replaced by one of the more robust alternatives we present here, especially with unequal n.

Although these problems with unequal n provide the primary motivation for developing alternatives, several studies have shown that the F test is not as robust as had previously been thought when sample sizes are equal. Clinch and Keselman (1982), Rogan and Keselman (1977), Tomarken and Serlin (1986), and Wilcox, Charlin, and Thompson (1986) show that the F test can become somewhat liberal with equal n when variances are heterogeneous. When variances are very different from each other, the actual Type I error rate may reach .10 or so (with a nominal rate of .05), even with equal n. Of course, when variances are less different, the actual error rate is closer to .05.[1] In summary, there seems to be sufficient motivation for considering alternatives to the F test when variances are heterogeneous, particularly when sample sizes are unequal.

We consider two alternatives: The first test statistic was developed by Brown and Forsythe (1974) and has a rather intuitive rationale. The second was developed by Welch (1951). Both are available in SPSS (one-way ANOVA procedure), so in our discussion we downplay computational details.[2]

The test statistic developed by Brown and Forsythe (1974) is based on the between-group sum of squares calculated in exactly the same manner as in the usual F test:

$$SS_{\text{B}} = \sum_{j=1}^{a} n_j (\overline{Y}_j - \overline{Y})^2 \tag{E.1}$$

where $\overline{Y} = \sum_{j=1}^{a} n_j \overline{Y}_j / N$. However, the denominator is calculated differently from the denominator of the usual F test. The Brown–Forsythe denominator is chosen to have the same expected value as the numerator if the null hypothesis is true, even if variances are heterogeneous. (The rationale for finding a denominator with the same expected value as the numerator if the null hypothesis is true is discussed in Chapter 10.) After some tedious algebra, it can be shown that the expected value of SS_B under the null hypothesis is given by

$$\mathscr{E}(SS_B) = \sum_{j=1}^{a} [1 - (n_j/N)]\sigma_j^2 \tag{E.2}$$

Notice that if we were willing to assume homogeneity of variance, Equation E.2 would simplify to

$$\mathscr{E}(SS_B) = \sum_{j=1}^{a} [1 - (n_j/N)]\sigma^2 = \sigma^2 \left[a - \sum_{j=1}^{a} (n_j/N) \right] = (a-1)\sigma^2$$

where σ^2 denotes the common variance. With homogeneity, $\mathscr{E}(MS_W) = \sigma^2$, so the usual F is obtained by taking the ratio of MS_B (which is SS_B divided by $a-1$) and MS_W. Under homogeneity, MS_B and MS_W have the same expected value under the null hypothesis, so their ratio provides an appropriate test statistic.[3]

When we are unwilling to assume homogeneity, it is preferable to estimate the population variance of each group (i.e., σ_j^2) separately. This is easily accomplished by using s_j^2 as an unbiased estimate of σ_j^2. A suitable denominator can be obtained by substituting s_j^2 for σ_j^2 in Equation E.2, yielding

$$\sum_{j=1}^{a} [1 - (n_j/N)]s_j^2 \tag{E.3}$$

The expected value of this expression equals the expected value of SS_B under the null hypothesis, even if homogeneity fails to hold. Thus, taking the ratio of SS_B and the expression in Equation E.3 yields an appropriate test statistic:

$$F^* = \frac{\sum_{j=1}^{a} n_j (\overline{Y}_j - \overline{Y})^2}{\sum_{j=1}^{a} [1 - (n_j/N)]s_j^2} \tag{E.4}$$

The statistic is written as F^* instead of F because it does not have an exact F distribution. However, Brown and Forsythe show that the distribution of F^* can be approximated by an F distribution with $a-1$ numerator degrees of freedom and f denominator degrees of freedom. Unfortunately, the denominator degrees of freedom are tedious to calculate and are best left to a computer program. Nevertheless, we present the formula for denominator degrees of freedom as follows:

$$f = \frac{1}{\sum_{j=1}^{a} \dfrac{g_j^2}{(n_j - 1)}} \tag{E.5}$$

where

$$g_j = \frac{[1 - (n_j/N)]s_j^2}{\displaystyle\sum_{j=1}^{a} [1 - (n_j/N)]s_j^2}$$

It is important to realize that, in general, F^* differs from F in two ways. First, the denominator degrees of freedom for the two approaches are different. Second, the observed values of the test statistics are typically different as well. In particular, F^* may be either systematically smaller or larger than F. If large samples are paired with small variances, F^* tends to be smaller than F; however, this reflects an advantage for F^*, because F tends to be liberal in this situation. Conversely, if large samples are paired with large variances, F^* tends to be larger than F; once again, this reflects an advantage for F^*, because F tends to be conservative in this situation. What if sample sizes are equal? With equal n, Equation E.4 can be rewritten as

$$F^* = \frac{n \displaystyle\sum_{j=1}^{a} (\overline{Y}_j - \overline{Y})^2}{\displaystyle\sum_{j=1}^{a} [1 - (1/a)]s_j^2} = \frac{n \displaystyle\sum_{j=1}^{a} (\overline{Y}_j - \overline{Y})^2}{\displaystyle\sum_{j=1}^{a} [(a-1)/a]s_j^2}$$

$$= \frac{n \displaystyle\sum_{j=1}^{a} (\overline{Y}_j - \overline{Y})^2}{(a-1) \displaystyle\sum_{j=1}^{a} s_j^2/a} = \frac{n \displaystyle\sum_{j=1}^{a} (\overline{Y}_j - \overline{Y})^2/(a-1)}{\displaystyle\sum_{j=1}^{a} s_j^2/a}$$

$$= \frac{MS_B}{MS_W} = F$$

Thus, with equal n, the observed values of F^* and F are identical. However, the denominator degrees of freedom are still different. It can be shown that with equal n, Equation E.5 for the denominator degrees of freedom associated with F^* becomes

$$f = \frac{(n-1)\left(\displaystyle\sum_{j=1}^{a} s_j^2 \right)^2}{\displaystyle\sum_{j=1}^{a} \left(s_j^2\right)^2} \tag{E.6}$$

Although it may not be immediately apparent, f is an index of how different sample variances are from each other. If all sample variances were identical to each other, f would equal $a(n-1)$, the denominator degrees of freedom for the usual F test. At the other extreme, as one variance becomes infinitely larger than all others, f approaches a value of $n-1$. In general, then, f ranges from $n-1$ to $a(n-1)$ and attains higher values for more similar variances.

We can summarize the relationship between F^* and F with equal n as follows. To the extent that the sample variances are similar, F^* is similar to F; however, when sample variances are different from each other, F^* is more conservative than F because the lower denominator degrees of freedom for F^* imply a higher critical value for F^* than for F. As a consequence, with equal n, F^* rejects the null hypothesis less often than does F. If the homogeneity of variance assumption is valid, the implication is that F^* is less powerful than F. However, Monte Carlo studies by Clinch and Keselman (1982) and Tomarken and Serlin (1986) suggest that the power advantage of F over F^* rarely exceeds .03 with equal n.[4] On the other hand, if the homogeneity assumption is violated, F^* tends to maintain α at .05, whereas F becomes somewhat liberal. However, the usual F test tends to remain robust as long as the population variances are not widely different from each other. As a result, in practice any advantage that F^* might offer over F with equal n is typically slight, except when variances are extremely discrepant from each other.

However, with unequal n, F^*, and F may be very different from one another. If it so happens that large samples are paired with small variances, F^* maintains α near .05 (assuming that .05 is the nominal value), whereas the actual α level for the F test can reach .15 or even .20 (Clinch & Keselman, 1982; Tomarken & Serlin, 1986), if population variances are substantially different from each other. Conversely, if large samples happen to be paired with large variances, F^* provides a more powerful test than does the F test. The advantage for F^* can be as great as .15 or .20 (Tomarken & Serlin, 1986), depending on how different the population variances are and on how the variances are related to the sample sizes. Thus, F^* is not necessarily more conservative than F.

Welch (1951) also derived an alternative to the F test that does not require the homogeneity of variance assumption. Unlike the Brown and Forsythe alternative, which was based on the between-group sum of squares of the usual F test, Welch's test uses a different weighting of the sum of squares in the numerator. Welch's statistic is defined as:

$$W = \frac{\sum_{j=1}^{a} w_j (\overline{Y}_j - \tilde{Y})^2 \Big/ (a-1)}{\left[1 + \frac{2}{3}(a-2)\Lambda\right]}$$

where

$$w_j = n_j / s_j^2$$

$$\tilde{Y} = \frac{\sum_{j=1}^{a} w_j \overline{Y}_j}{\sum_{j=1}^{a} w_j}$$

$$\Lambda = \frac{3 \sum_{j=1}^{a} \left\{ \left[1 - \left(w_j \Big/ \sum_{j=1}^{a} w_j\right)\right]^2 \Big/ (n_j - 1) \right\}}{a^2 - 1}$$

When the null hypothesis is true, W is approximately distributed as an F variable with $a - 1$ numerator and $1/\Lambda$ denominator degrees of freedom. (Notice that Λ is used to represent the value of Wilks' lambda in Chapter 14. Its meaning here is entirely different, and reflects the unfortunate tradition among statisticians to use the same symbol for different expressions. In any event, the meaning here should be clear from the context.) It might alleviate some concern to remind you at this point that the SPSS program for one-way ANOVA calculates W as well as its degrees of freedom and associated p value.

The basic difference between the rationales behind F^* and W involves the weight associated with a group's deviation from the grand mean, that is, $\overline{Y}_j - \overline{Y}$. As Equation E.1 shows, F^* weights each group according to its sample size. Larger groups receive more weight because their sample mean is likely to be a better estimate of their population mean. W, however, weights each group according to n_j/s_j^2, which is the reciprocal of the estimated variance of the mean. Less variable group means thus receive more weight, whether the lesser variability results from a larger sample size or a smaller variance. This difference in weighting causes W to be different from F^*, even though neither assumes homogeneity of variance. As an aside, notice also that the grand mean is defined differently in Welch's approach than for either F or F^*; although it is still a weighted average of the group means, the weights depend on the sample variances as well as the sample sizes.

Welch's W statistic compares to the usual F test in a generally similar manner as F^* compares to F. When large samples are paired with large variances, W is less conservative than F. When large samples are paired with small variances, W is less liberal than F. Interestingly, when sample sizes are equal, W differs more from F than does F^*. Whereas F and F^* have the same observed value with equal n, in general, the observed value of W is different. The reason is that, as seen earlier, W gives more weight to groups with smaller sample variances. When homogeneity holds in the population, this differential weighting is simply based on chance, because in this situation sample variances differ from one another as a result of sampling error only. As a result, tests based on W are somewhat less powerful than tests based on F. Based on Tomarken and Serlin's (1986) findings, the difference in power is usually .03 or less, and would rarely exceed .06 unless sample sizes are very small. However, when homogeneity fails to hold, W can be appreciably more powerful than the usual F test, even with equal n. The power advantage of W was often as large as .10, and even reached .34 in one condition in Tomarken and Serlin's simulations. This advantage stems from W giving more weight to the more stable sample means, which F does not do (nor does F^*). It must be added, however, that W can also have less power than F with equal n. If the group that differs most from the grand mean has a large population variance, W attaches a relatively small weight to the group because of its large variance. In this particular case, W tends to be less powerful than F because the most discrepant group receives the least weight. Nevertheless, Tomarken and Serlin found that W is generally more powerful than F for most patterns of means when heterogeneity occurs with equal n.

The choice between F^* and W when heterogeneity is suspected is difficult given the current state of knowledge. On the one hand, Tomarken and Serlin (1986) found that W is more powerful than F^* across most configurations of population means. On the other hand, Clinch and Keselman (1982) found that W becomes somewhat liberal when underlying population distributions are skewed instead of normal. They found that F^* generally maintains a close to a nominal value of .05 even for skewed distributions. In addition, Wilcox, Charlin, and Thompson (1986) found that W maintained an appropriate Type I error rate better than F^* when sample sizes are equal, but that F^* was better than W when unequal sample sizes are paired with equal variances. Choosing between F^* and W is obviously far from clear cut, given the complex nature of findings. Further research is needed to clarify their relative strengths. Although the choice between F^* and W is unsettled, it is clear that both are preferable to F when population variances are heterogeneous and sample sizes are unequal.

Table 3E.1 summarizes the properties of F, F^*, and W as a function of population variances and sample sizes. Again, from a practical standpoint, the primary point of the table is that F^* or W should be considered seriously as a replacement for the usual F test when sample sizes are unequal and heterogeneity of variance is suspected.

TABLE E.1
PROPERTIES OF F, F^*, AND W AS A FUNCTION OF SAMPLE SIZES AND
POPULATION VARIANCES

	Test Statistic		
	F	F^*	W
Equal Sample Sizes			
Equal variances	Appropriate	Slightly conservative	Robust
Unequal variances	Robust, except can become liberal for very large differences in variances	Robust, except can become liberal for extremely large differences in variances	Robust
Unequal Sample Sizes			
Equal variances	Appropriate	Robust	Robust, except can become slightly liberal for very large differences in sample sizes
Large samples paired with large variances	Conservative	Robust, except can become slightly liberal when differences in sample sizes and in variances are both very large	Robust, except can become slightly liberal when differences in sample sizes and in variances are both very large
Large samples paired with small variances	Liberal	Robust, except can become slightly liberal when differences in sample sizes and in variances are both very large	Robust, except can become slightly liberal when differences in sample sizes and in variances are both very large

Nonparametric Approaches

The parametric modifications of the previous section were developed for analyzing data with unequal population variances. The nonparametric approaches of this section were developed for analyzing data whose population distributions are nonnormal. As we discuss in some detail later, another motivating factor for the development of nonparametric techniques in the behavioral sciences has been the belief held by some researchers that they require less stringent measurement properties of the dependent variable. The organizational structure of this section consists of first, presenting a particular nonparametric technique, and second, discussing its merits relative to parametric techniques.

There are several nonparametric alternatives to ANOVA for the single-factor between-subjects design. We present only one of these, the Kruskal–Wallis test, which is the most frequently used nonparametric test for this design. For information on other nonparametric methods, consult such nonparametric textbooks as Bradley (1968), Cliff (1996), Gibbons (1971), Marascuilo and McSweeney (1977), Noether (1976), or Siegel (1956).

The Kruskal–Wallis test is often called an "ANOVA by Ranks" because a fundamental distinction between the usual ANOVA and the Kruskal–Wallis test is that the original scores are replaced by their ranks in the Kruskal–Wallis test. Specifically, the first step in the test is to rank order all observations from low to high (actually, high to low yields exactly the same result) in the entire set of N subjects. Be certain to notice that this ranking is performed across all a groups, independently of group membership. When scores are tied, each observation is assigned the average (i.e., mean) rank of the scores in the tied set. For example, if three scores are tied for 6th, 7th, and 8th place in order, all three scores are assigned a rank of 7.

Once the scores have been ranked, the test statistic is given by

$$H = \frac{12}{N(N+1)} \sum_{j=1}^{a} n_j \{ \overline{R}_j - [(N+1)/2] \}^2 \tag{E.7}$$

where $\overline{R}_j$ is the mean rank for group j. Although Equation E.7 may look very different from the usual ANOVA F statistic, in fact, there is an underlying similarity. For example, $(N+1)/2$ is simply the grand mean of the ranks, which we know must have values of $1, 2, 3, \ldots, N$. Thus, the term $\Sigma_{j=1}^{a} n_j \{ \overline{R}_j - [(N+1)/2] \}^2$ is a weighted sum of squared deviations of group means from the grand mean, as in the parametric F test. It also proves to be unnecessary to estimate σ^2, the population error variance, because the test statistic is based on a finite population of size N (cf. Marascuilo & McSweeney, 1977, for more on this point). The important point for our purposes is that the Kruskal–Wallis test is very much like an ANOVA on ranks.

When the null hypothesis is true, H is approximately distributed as a χ^2 with $a - 1$ degrees of freedom. The χ^2 approximation is accurate unless sample sizes within some groups are quite small, in which case tables of the exact distribution of H should be consulted in such sources as Siegel (1956) or Iman, Quade, and Alexander (1975). When ties occur in the data, a correction factor T should be applied:

$$T = 1 - \frac{\sum_{i=1}^{G}(t_i^3 - t_i)}{N^3 - N}$$

where t_i is the number of observations tied at a particular value and G is the number of distinct values for which there are ties. A corrected test statistic H' is obtained by dividing H by $T : H' = H/T$. The correction has little effect (i.e., H' differs very little from H) unless sample sizes are very small or there are many ties in the data, relative to sample size. Most major statistical packages (e.g., SAS, and SPSS) have a program for computing H (or H') and its associated p value. Also, it should be pointed out that when there are only two groups to be compared (i.e., $a = 2$), the Kruskal–Wallis test is equivalent to the Wilcoxon Rank Sum test, which is also equivalent to the Mann–Whitney U.

Choosing Between Parametric and Nonparametric Tests

Statisticians have debated the relative merits of parametric versus nonparametric tests ever since the inception of nonparametric approaches. As a consequence, all too often behavioral researchers are told either that parametric procedures should always be used (because they are robust and more powerful) or that nonparametric methods should always be used (because they make fewer assumptions). Not surprisingly, both of these extreme positions are oversimplifications. We provide a brief overview of the advantages each approach possesses in certain situations. Our discussion is limited to a comparison of the F, F^*, and W parametric tests and the Kruskal–Wallis nonparametric test.

Nevertheless, even with this limitation, do not expect our comparison of the methods to provide a definitive answer as to which approach is "best." The choice between approaches is too complicated for such a simple answer. There are certain occasions where parametric tests are preferable and others where nonparametric tests are better. A wise data analyst carefully weighs the advantages in his or her situation and makes an informed choice accordingly.

A primary reason the comparison of parametric and nonparametric approaches is so difficult is that they do not always test the same null hypothesis. To see why they do not, we must consider the assumptions associated with each approach. As stated earlier, we consider specifically the F test and Kruskal–Wallis test for one-way between-subjects designs.

As discussed in Chapter 3, the parametric ANOVA can be conceptualized in terms of a full model of the form

$$Y_{ij} = \mu + \alpha_j + \varepsilon_{ij}$$

ANOVA tests a null hypothesis

$$H_0 : \alpha_1 = \alpha_2 = \cdots = \alpha_a = 0$$

where it is assumed that population distributions are normal and have equal variances. In other words, under the null hypothesis, all a population distributions are identical normal distributions if ANOVA assumptions hold. If the null hypothesis is false, one or more distributions are shifted either to the left or to the right of the other distributions. Figure 3E.1 illustrates such an occurrence for the case of three groups. The three distributions are identical except that $\mu_1 = 10$, $\mu_2 = 20$, and $\mu_3 = 35$. When the normality and homogeneity assumptions are met, the distributions still have the same shape, but they have different *locations* when the null hypothesis is false. For this reason, ANOVA is sometimes referred to as a *test of location* or as *testing a shift hypothesis*.

Under certain conditions, the Kruskal–Wallis test can also be conceptualized as testing a shift hypothesis. However, although it may seem surprising given it has been many years since Kruskal and Wallis (1952) introduced their test, there has been a fair amount of confusion and variation in textbook descriptions even in recent years about what assumptions are required and what hypothesis is tested by the Kruskal–Wallis test (a summary is provided by Vargha & Delaney, 1998). As usual, what one can conclude is driven largely by what one is willing to assume. If one is willing to assume that the distributions being compared are identical except possibly for their location, then the Kruskal–Wallis test can lead to a similar conclusion as an ANOVA. Like other authors who adopt these restrictive "shift model" assumptions, Hollander and Wolfe (1973) argue that the Kruskal–Wallis test can be thought of in terms of a full model

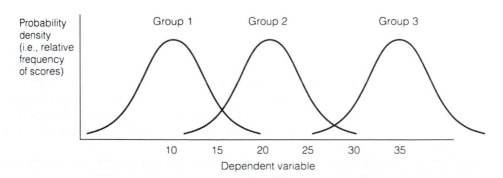

FIG. 3E.1.   Shifted distributions under ANOVA assumptions.

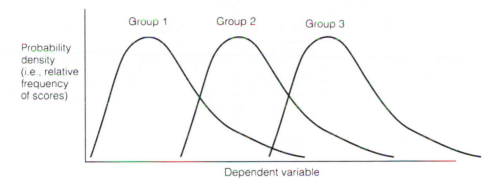

FIG. 3E.2.   Shifted distributions under Kruskal–Wallis assumptions.

of the form

$$Y_{ij} = \mu + \alpha_j + \varepsilon_{ij}$$

and that the null hypothesis being tested can be represented by

$$H_0 : \alpha_1 = \alpha_2 = \cdots = \alpha_a = 0$$

just as in the parametric ANOVA. From this perspective, the only difference concerns the assumptions involving the distribution of errors (ε_{ij}). Whereas the parametric ANOVA assumes both normality and homogeneity, the Kruskal–Wallis test assumes only that the population of error scores has an identical continuous distribution for every group. As a consequence, in the Kruskal–Wallis model, homogeneity of variance is still assumed, but normality is not. The important point for our purposes is that, under these assumptions, the Kruskal–Wallis test is testing a shift hypothesis, as is the parametric ANOVA, when its assumptions are met. Figure 3E.2 illustrates such an occurrence for the case of three groups. As in Figure 3E. 1, the three distributions of Figure 3E.2 are identical to each other except for their location on the X axis. Notice, however, that the distributions in Figure 3E.2 are skewed, unlike the distributions in Figure 3E.1 that are required to be normal by the ANOVA model. Under these conditions, both approaches are testing the same null hypothesis, because the α_j parameters in the models are identical. For example, the difference $\alpha_2 - \alpha_1$ represents the extent to which the distribution of Group 1 is shifted either to the right or to the left of Group 2. Not only does $\alpha_2 - \alpha_1$ equal the difference between the population means, but as Figure 3E.3 shows, it also equals the difference between the medians, the 5th percentile, the 75th percentile, or any other percentile. Indeed, it is fairly common to regard the Kruskal–Wallis test as a way of deciding if the population medians differ (cf. Wilcox, 1996, p. 365). This is legitimate when the assumption that all distributions have the same shape is met. In this situation, the only difference between the two approaches is that the parametric ANOVA makes the additional assumption that this common shape is that of a normal distribution. Of course, this difference implies different properties for the tests, which we discuss momentarily. To summarize, when one adopts the assumptions of the shift model (namely identical distributions for all a groups, except for a possible shift under the alternative hypothesis), the Kruskal–Wallis test and the parametric ANOVA are testing the same null hypothesis. In this circumstance, it is possible to compare the two approaches and state conditions under which each approach is advantageous.[5]

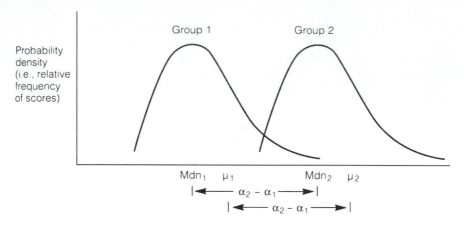

FIG. 3E.3.   Meaning of $\alpha_2 - \alpha_1$ for two groups when shift hypothesis holds.

However, there are good reasons for viewing the Kruskal–Wallis test differently. Although it is widely understood that the null hypothesis being tested is that the groups have identical population distributions, the most appropriate alternative hypothesis and required assumptions are not widely understood. One important point to understand is that the Kruskal–Wallis test possesses the desirable mathematical property of consistency only with respect to an alternative hypothesis stated in terms of whether individual scores are greater in one group than another.

This is seen most clearly when two groups are being compared. Let p be defined as the probability that a randomly sampled observation from one group on a continuous dependent variable Y is greater than a randomly sampled observation from the second group (e.g., Wilcox, 1996, p. 365). That is,

$$p = \Pr (Y_1 > Y_2)$$

If the two population distributions are identical, $p = \frac{1}{2}$, and so one could state the null hypothesis the Kruskal–Wallis is testing in this case as $H_0 : p = \frac{1}{2}$. The mathematical reason doing so makes most sense is that the test is consistent against an alternative hypothesis if and only if it implies $H_1 : p \neq \frac{1}{2}$ (Kendall & Stuart, 1973, p. 513). Cases in which $p = \frac{1}{2}$ have been termed cases of *stochastic equality* (cf. Mann & Whitney, 1947; Delaney & Vargha, 2002), and the consistency property means that if the two populations are stochastically unequal ($p \neq \frac{1}{2}$), then the probability of rejecting the null hypothesis approaches 1 as the sample sizes get larger.

When the populations have the same shape, ANOVA and Kruskal–Wallis are testing the same hypothesis regarding location, although it is common to regard the ANOVA as a test of differences between population means, but regard the Kruskal–Wallis test as a test of differences between population medians.[6] However, when distributions have different asymmetric shapes, it is possible for the population means to all be equal and yet the population medians all be different, or vice versa. Similarly, with regard to the hypothesis that the Kruskal–Wallis test is most appropriate for, namely stochastic equality, with different asymmetric distributions, the population means might all be equal, yet the distributions be stochastically unequal, or vice versa. The point is that, in such a case, the parametric ANOVA may be testing a true null hypothesis, whereas the nonparametric approach is testing a false null hypothesis. In such a circumstance, the probabilities of rejecting the null hypothesis for the two approaches cannot be compared meaningfully because they are answering different questions.

In summary, when distributions have different shapes, the parametric and nonparametric approaches are generally testing different hypotheses. Different shapes occur fairly often, in part because of floor and ceiling effects such as occur with Likert-scale dependent variables. In such conditions, the basis for choosing between the approaches should probably involve consideration of whether the research question is best formulated in terms of population means or in terms of comparisons of individual scores. When these differ, we would argue that more often than not, the scientist is interested in the comparison of individuals. If one is interested in comparing two methods of therapy for reducing depression, or clients' daily alcohol consumption, one is likely more interested in which method would help the greater number of people rather than which method produces the greater mean level of change—if these are different. In such situations, stochastic comparison might be preferred to the comparison of means.

Suppose that, in fact, population distributions are identical—which approach is better, parametric or nonparametric? Although the question seems relatively straightforward, the answer is not. Under some conditions, such as normal distributions, the parametric approach is better. However, under other conditions, such as certain long-tailed distributions (in which extreme scores are more likely than in the normal distribution), the nonparametric approach is better. As usual, the choice involves a consideration of Type I error rate and power.

If population distributions are identical and normal, both the F test and the Kruskal–Wallis test maintain the actual α level at the nominal value, because the assumptions of both tests have been met (assuming, in addition, as we do throughout this discussion, that observations are independent of one another). On the other hand, if distributions are identical but nonnormal, only the assumptions of the Kruskal–Wallis test are met. Nevertheless, the extensive survey conducted by Glass and colleagues (1972) suggests that the F test is robust with respect to Type I errors to all but extreme violations of normality.[7] Thus, with regard to Type I error rates, there is little practical reason to prefer either test over the other if all population distributions have identical shapes.

While on the topic of Type I error rate, it is important to dispel a myth concerning nonparametric tests. Many researchers apparently believe that the Kruskal–Wallis test should be used instead of the F test when variances are unequal, because the Kruskal–Wallis test does not assume homogeneity of variance. However, we can see that this belief is misguided. Under the shift model, the Kruskal–Wallis test assumes that population distributions are identical under the null hypothesis, and identical distributions obviously have equal variances. Even when the Kruskal–Wallis is treated as a test of stochastic equality, the test assumes that the *ranks* of the scores are equally variable across groups (Vargha & Delaney, 1998), so homogeneity of variance in some form is, in fact, an assumption of the Kruskal–Wallis test. Furthermore, the Kruskal–Wallis test is not robust to violations of this assumption with unequal n. Keselman, Rogan, and Feir-Walsh (1977) as well as Tomarken and Serlin (1986) found that the actual Type I error rate of the Kruskal–Wallis test could be as large as twice the nominal level when large samples are paired with small variances (cf., Oshima & Algina, 1992). It should be added that the usual F test was even less robust than the Kruskal–Wallis test. However, the important practical point is that neither test is robust. In contrast, Tomarken and Serlin (1986) found both F^* and W to maintain acceptable α levels even for various patterns of unequal sample sizes and unequal variances.[8] Thus, the practical implication is that F^* and W are better alternatives to the usual F test than is the standard Kruskal–Wallis test when heterogeneity of variance is suspected, especially with unequal n. Robust forms of the Kruskal–Wallis test have now been proposed, but are not considered here (see Delaney & Vargha, 2002).

A second common myth surrounding nonparametric tests is that they are always less powerful than parametric tests. It is true that if the population distributions for all a groups are normal with equal variances, then the F test is more powerful than the Kruskal–Wallis test. The size of the difference in power varies as a function of the sample sizes and the means, so it is impossible to state a single number to represent how much more powerful the F test is. However, it is possible to determine mathematically that as sample sizes increase toward infinity, the efficiency of the Kruskal–Wallis test to the F test is 0.955 under normality.[9] In practical terms, this means that for large samples, the F test can achieve the same power as the Kruskal–Wallis test and yet require only 95.5% as many subjects as would the Kruskal–Wallis test. It can also be shown that for large samples, the Kruskal–Wallis test is at least 86.4% as efficient as the F test for distributions of any shape, as long as all a distributions have the same shape. Thus, at its absolute worst, for large samples, using the Kruskal–Wallis instead of the F test is analogous to failing to use 13.6% of the subjects one has observed. We must add, however, that the previous statement assumes that all population distributions are identical. If they are not, the Kruskal–Wallis test in some circumstances has little or no power for detecting true mean differences, because it is testing a different hypothesis, namely stochastic equality.

So far, we have done little to dispel the myth that parametric tests are always more powerful than nonparametric tests. However, for certain nonnormal distributions, the Kruskal–Wallis test is, in fact, considerably more powerful than the parametric F test. Generally speaking, the Kruskal–Wallis test is more powerful than the F test when the underlying population distributions are symmetric but heavy-tailed, which means that extreme scores (i.e., outliers) are more frequent than in the normal distribution. The size of the power advantage of the Kruskal–Wallis test depends on the particular shape of the nonnormal distribution, sample sizes, and the magnitude of separation between the groups. However, the size of this advantage can easily be large enough to be of practical importance in some situations. It should also be added that the Kruskal–Wallis test is frequently more powerful than the F test when distributions are identical but skewed.

As mentioned earlier, another argument that has been made for using nonparametric procedures is that they require less stringent measurement properties of the data. In fact, there has been a heated controversy ever since Stevens (1946, 1951) introduced the concept of "levels of measurement" (i.e., nominal, ordinal, interval, and ratio scales) with his views of their implications for statistics. Stevens argues that the use of parametric statistics requires that the observed dependent variable be measured on an interval or ratio scale. However, many behavioral variables fail to meet this criterion, which has been taken by some psychologists to imply that most behavioral data should be analyzed with nonparametric techniques. Others (e.g., Gaito, 1980; Lord, 1953) argue that the use of parametric procedures is entirely appropriate for behavioral data.

We cannot possibly do justice in this discussion to the complexities of all viewpoints. Instead, we attempt to describe briefly a few themes and recommend additional reading. Gardner (1975) provides an excellent review of both sides of the controversy through the mid-1970s. Three points raised in his review deserve special mention here. First, parametric statistical tests do not make any statistical assumptions about level of measurement. As we stated previously, the assumptions of the F test are normality, homogeneity of variance, and independence of observations. A correct numerical statement concerning population mean differences does not require interval measurement. Second, although a parametric test can be performed on ordinal data without violating any assumptions of the test, the meaning of the test could be damaged. In essence, this can be thought of as a potential construct validity problem (see Chapter 1). Although the test is correct as a statement of mean group differences on the observed variable, these differences might not reflect true differences on the underlying construct. Third, Gardner cites two empirical studies (Baker, Hardyck, & Petrinovich, 1966; Labovitz, 1967) that showed that, although in theory construct validity might be problematic, in reality, parametric tests produced meaningful results for constructs even when the level of measurement was only ordinal.

Recent work demonstrates that the earlier empirical studies conducted prior to 1980 were correct as far as they went, but it has become clear that these earlier studies were limited in an important way. In effect, the earlier studies assumed that the underlying population distributions on the construct not only had the same mean, but were also literally identical to each other. However, a number of later studies (e.g., Maxwell & Delaney, 1985; Spencer, 1983) show that, when the population distributions on the construct have the same mean but different variances, parametric techniques on ordinal data can result in very misleading conclusions. Thus, in some practical situations, nonparametric techniques may indeed be more appropriate than parametric approaches. Many interesting articles continue to be written on this topic. Recent articles deserving attention are Davison and Sharma (1988), Marcus-Roberts and Roberts (1987), Michell (1986), and Townsend and Ashby (1984).

In summary, the choice between a parametric test (F, F^*, or W) and the Kruskal–Wallis test involves consideration of a number of factors. First, the Kruskal–Wallis test does not always test the same hypothesis as the parametric tests. As a result, in general, it is important to consider whether the research question of interest is most appropriately formulated in terms of comparisons of individual scores or comparisons of means. Second, neither the usual F test nor the Kruskal–Wallis test is robust to violations of homogeneity of variance with unequal n. Either F^* or W, or robust forms of the Kruskal–Wallis test, are preferable in this situation. Third, for some distributions, the F test is more powerful than the Kruskal–Wallis test; whereas for other distributions, the reverse is true. Thus, neither approach is always better than the other. Fourth, level of measurement continues to be controversial as a factor that might or might not influence the choice between parametric and nonparametric approaches.

OPTIONAL

Two Other Approaches

As if the choice between parametric and nonparametric were not already complicated, there are yet other possible techniques for data analysis, even in the relatively simple one-way between-subjects design. As we stated at the beginning of this extension, statisticians are constantly inventing new methods of data analysis. In this section, we take a brief glimpse at two methods that are still in the experimental stages of development. Because the advantages and disadvantages of these methods are largely unexplored, we would not recommend as of this writing that you use these approaches as your sole data-analysis technique without first seeking expert advice. Nevertheless, we believe that it is important to expose you to these methods because they represent the types of innovations currently being studied. As such, they may become preferred methods of data analysis during the careers of those of you who are reading this book as students.

The first innovation, called a *rank transformation approach*, has been described as a bridge between parametric and nonparametric statistics by its primary developers, Conover and Iman (1981). The rank transformation approach consists of simply replacing the observed data with their ranks and then applying the usual parametric test. Conover and Iman (1981) discuss how this approach can be applied to such diverse problems as multiple regression, discriminant analysis, and cluster analysis. In the case of the one-way between-subjects design, the parametric F computed on ranks (denoted F_R) is closely related to the Kruskal–Wallis test. Conover and Iman show that F_R is related to the Kruskal–Wallis H by the formula:

$$F_R = [H/(a - 1)]/[(N - 1 - H)/(N - a)]$$

The rank transformation test compares F_R to a critical F value, whereas the Kruskal–Wallis test compares H to a critical χ^2 value. Both methods are large-sample approximations to the true critical value. Iman and Davenport (1976) found the F approximation to be superior to the χ^2 approximation in the majority of cases they investigated (see Delaney & Vargha, 2002, for discussion of a situation where using rank transformations did not work well).

A second innovation involves a method of parameter estimation other than least squares. Least squares forms the basis for comparing models in all parametric techniques we discuss in this book. In one form or another, we generally end up finding a parameter estimate $\hat{\mu}$ to minimize an expression of the form $\Sigma(Y - \hat{\mu})^2$. Such an approach proves to be optimal when distributions are normal with equal variances. However, as we have seen, optimality is lost when these conditions do not hold. In particular, least squares tends to perform poorly in the presence of outliers (i.e., extreme scores) because the squaring function is very sensitive to extreme scores. For example, consider the following five scores: 5, 10, 15, 20, 75. If we regard these five observations as a random sample, we could use least squares to estimate the population mean. It is easily verified that $\hat{\mu} = 25$ minimizes $\Sigma(Y - \hat{\mu})^2$ for these data. As we know, the sample mean, which here equals 25, is the least-squares estimate. However, only one of the five scores is this large. The sample mean has been greatly influenced by the single extreme score of 75. If we are willing to assume that the population distribution is symmetric, we could also use the sample median as an unbiased estimator of the population mean.[10] It is obvious that the median of our sample is 15, but how does this relate to least squares? It can be shown that the median is the estimate that minimizes the sum of the absolute value of errors: $\Sigma|Y - \hat{\mu}|$. Thus, the sample mean minimizes the sum of squared errors, whereas the sample median minimizes the sum of absolute errors. The median is less sensitive than the mean to outliers—for some distributions, this is an advantage; but for others, it is a disadvantage. In particular, for heavy-tailed distributions, the median's insensitivity to outliers makes it superior to the mean. However, in a normal distribution, the median is a much less efficient estimator than is the mean. The fact that neither the median nor the mean is uniformly best has prompted the search for alternative estimators.

Statisticians developed a class of estimators called M estimators that in many respects represent a compromise between the mean and the median. For example, one member of this class (the Huber M estimator) is described as acting "like the mean for centrally located observations and like the median for observations far removed from the bulk of the data" (Wu, 1985, p. 339). As a consequence, these robust estimators represent another bridge between parametric and nonparametric approaches. These robust estimators are obtained once again by minimizing a term involving the sum of errors. However, M estimators constitute an entire class of estimators defined by minimizing the sum of some general function of the errors. The form of the function determines the specific estimator in the general class. For example, if the function is the square of the error, the specific estimation technique is least squares. Thus, least-squares estimators are members of the broad class of M estimators. The median is also a member of the class because it involves minimizing the sum of a function of the errors, the particular function being the absolute value function.

Although quite a few robust estimators have been developed, we describe only an estimator developed by Huber because of its relative simplicity.[11] Huber's estimator requires that a robust estimator of scale (i.e., dispersion, or variability) have been calculated prior to determining the robust estimate of location (i.e., population mean). Note that the scale estimate need not actually be based on a robust estimator; however, using a robust estimator of scale is sensible, if one believes that a robust estimator of location is needed in a particular situation. Although a number of robust estimators of scale are available, we present only one: the median absolute deviation (MAD) from the median. MAD is defined as MAD = median

$\{|Y - Mdn|\}$, where Mdn is the sample median. Although at first reading, the definition of MAD may resemble double-talk, its calculation is actually very straightforward. For example, consider again our hypothetical example of five scores: 5, 10, 15, 20, and 75. As we have seen, the median of these scores is 15, so we can write $Mdn = 15$. Then the absolute deviations are given by $|5 - 15| = 10$, $|10 - 15| = 5$, $|15 - 15| = 0$, $|20 - 15| = 5$, and $|75 - 15| = 60$. MAD is defined to be the median of these five absolute deviations, which is 5 in our example.[12] MAD can be thought of as a robust type of standard deviation. However, the expected value of MAD is considerably less than σ for a normal distribution. For this reason, MAD is often divided by 0.6745, which puts it on the same scale as σ for a normal distribution. We let S denote this robust estimate of scale, so we have $S = \text{MAD}/0.6745$.

With this background, we can now consider Huber's M estimator of location. To simplify our notation, we define u_i to be $(Y_i - \hat{\mu})/S$, where S is the robust estimate of scale (hence we already know its value) and $\hat{\mu}$ is the robust estimate of location whose value we are seeking. Then, Huber's M estimator minimizes the sum of a function of the errors $\sum_{i=1}^{n} f(u_i)$, where the function f is defined as follows:

$$f(u_i) = \begin{cases} \frac{1}{2}u_i^2 & \text{if } |u_i| \leq 1 \\ |u_i| - \frac{1}{2} & \text{if } |u_i| > 1 \end{cases}$$

Notice that function f involves minimizing sums of squared errors for errors that are close to the center of the distribution but involves minimizing the sum of absolute errors for errors that are far from the center. Thus, as our earlier quote from Wu indicated, Huber's estimate really does behave like the mean for observations near the center of the distribution but like the median for those farther away. At this point you may be wondering how the $\hat{\mu}$ that minimizes the sum of Huber's function is determined. It turns out that the value must be determined through an iterative procedure. As a first step, a starting value for $\hat{\mu}$ is chosen; a simple choice for the starting value would be the sample median. We might denote this value $\hat{\mu}_0$, the zero subscript indicating that this value is the optimal value after zero iterations. Then, a new estimate is computed that minimizes the function $\sum_{i=1}^{n} f(u_i)$, where $u_i = (Y_i - \hat{\mu}_0)/S$. This yields a new estimate $\hat{\mu}_1$, where the subscript 1 indicates that one iteration has been completed. The process continues until it converges, meaning that further iterations would make no practical difference in the value.[13]

Not only does M estimation produce robust estimates, but it also provides a methodology for hypothesis testing. Schrader and Hettmansperger (1980) show how full and restricted models based on M estimates can be compared to arrive at an F test using the same basic logic that underlies the F test with least squares. Li (1985) and Wu (1985) describe how M estimation can be applied to robust tests in regression analysis.

In summary, we have seen two possible bridges between the parametric and nonparametric approaches. It remains to be seen whether either of these bridges will eventually span the gap that has historically existed between proponents of parametrics and proponents of nonparametrics.

OPTIONAL

Why Does the Usual F Test Falter with Unequal ns When Population Variances Are Unequal?

Why is the F test conservative when large sample sizes are paired with large variances, yet liberal when large sample sizes are paired with small variances? The answer can be seen by comparing the expected values of MS_W and MS_B when the null hypothesis is true, but variances are possibly unequal. In this situation, the expected values of both MS_B and MS_W are weighted averages of the a population variances. However, sample sizes play different roles in the two weighting schemes.

Specifically, it can be shown that if the null hypothesis is true, MS_B has an expected value given by

$$\mathcal{E}(MS_B) = \frac{\sum\limits_{j=1}^{a} w_j \sigma_j^2}{\sum\limits_{j=1}^{a} w_j} \qquad (E.1)$$

where $w_j = N - n_j$. Thus, the weight a population variance receives in MS_B is inversely related to its sample size. Although this may seem counterintuitive, it helps to realize that MS_B is based on $\overline{Y}_j - \overline{Y}$, and larger groups contribute proportionally more to $\overline{Y}$.

Similarly, it can be shown that MS_W has an expected value equal to

$$\mathcal{E}(MS_W) = \frac{\sum\limits_{j=1}^{a} w_j^* \sigma_j^2}{\sum\limits_{j=1}^{a} w_j^*} \qquad (E.2)$$

where $w_j^* = n_j - 1$. Thus, the weight a population variance receives in MS_W is directly related to its sample size.

What are the implications of Equations 3E.1 and 3E.2? Let's consider some special cases.

Case I.   Homogeneity of Variance

If all σ_j^2 are equal to each other, Equations 3E.1 and 3E.2 simplify to $\mathcal{E}(MS_B) = \sigma^2$ and $\mathcal{E}(MS_W) = \sigma^2$, because the weights are irrelevant when all the numbers to be averaged are identical. In this case, the F ratio of MS_B to MS_W works appropriately, regardless of whether the sample sizes are equal or unequal.

Case II.   Unequal Variances but Equal n

If all n_j are equal to each other, Equations 3E.1 and 3E.2 simplify to $\mathcal{E}(MS_B) = \sum_{j=1}^{a} \sigma_j^2 / a$ and $\mathcal{E}(MS_W) = \sum_{j=1}^{a} \sigma_j^2 / a$. Because the weights are equal to one another, in both cases the weighted averages become identical to simple unweighted averages. Thus, MS_B and MS_W are equal to one another in the long run. Although the ANOVA assumption has been violated, the F test is typically only slightly affected here.

Case III.   Unequal Variances: Large Samples Paired with Small Variances

In this situation, we can see from Equation 3E.1 that $\mathcal{E}(MS_B)$ receives more weight from the smaller samples, which have larger variances. Thus, the weighted average used to calculate $\mathcal{E}(MS_B)$ is larger than the unweighted average of the σ_j^2 terms. However, $\mathcal{E}(MS_W)$ receives more weight from the larger samples, which have smaller variances. Thus, the weighted average used to calculate $\mathcal{E}(MS_W)$ is smaller than the unweighted average of the σ_j^2 terms. As a consequence, $\mathcal{E}(MS_B) > \mathcal{E}(MS_W)$, even when the null hypothesis is true. F values tend to be too large, resulting in too many rejections of the null hypothesis when it is true. Thus, the Type I error rate is too high.

Case IV. Unequal Variances: Large Samples Paired with Large Variances

This situation is just the opposite of Case III. Now, $\mathscr{E}(MS_B)$ gives more weight to the groups with small variances because they are smaller in size. In contrast, $\mathscr{E}(MS_W)$ gives more weight to the groups with large variances because they are larger in size. As a result, $\mathscr{E}(MS_B) < \mathscr{E}(MS_W)$ when the null hypothesis is true. The F test is conservative and rejects the null hypothesis too infrequently. Thus, power suffers.

EXERCISES

*1. True or False: Although the parametric modification F^* is more robust than the usual F test to violations of homogeneity of variance in between-subjects designs, the F^* test is always at least slightly less powerful than the F test.

2. True or False: The parametric test based on Welch's W statistic can be either more or less powerful than the usual F test in equal-n designs.

3. True or False: When sample sizes are unequal and heterogeneity of variance is suspected in one-way between-subjects designs, either F^* or W should seriously be considered as a replacement for the usual F test.

4. True or False: If one is willing to assume distributions have identical shapes, the Kruskal–Wallis test can be regarded as testing a "shift" hypothesis in location without requiring an assumption that scores are distributed normally.

5. True or False: The nonparametric Kruskal–Wallis test and the parametric F test always test the same hypothesis, but they require different distributional assumptions.

6. True or False: Although the F test is more powerful than the Kruskal–Wallis test when the normality and homogeneity of variance assumptions are met, the Kruskal–Wallis test can be more powerful than the F test when these assumptions are not met.

*7. True or False: When sample sizes are unequal and heterogeneity of variance is suspected in one-way between-subjects designs, the nonparametric Kruskal–Wallis test should be considered seriously as a replacement for the usual F test.

*8. How do the values of F, F^*, and W compare to each other when samples are of different sizes and variances are considerably different from one another? Consider the following summary statistics:

Group 1	Group 2	Group 3
$n_1 = 20$	$n_2 = 20$	$n_3 = 50$
$\overline{Y}_1 = 10$	$\overline{Y}_2 = 12$	$\overline{Y}_3 = 14$
$s_1^2 = 10$	$s_2^2 = 10$	$s_3^2 = 50$

a. Calculate an observed F value for these data.

b. Calculate the F^* value for these data (however, you need not compute the denominator degrees of freedom).

c. Calculate the W value for these data.

d. Are your answers to parts a–c consistent with the assertion made in Table 3E.1 that when large samples are paired with large variances the F is conservative, whereas F^* and W are more robust?

9. Suppose that, as in Exercise 8, samples are of different sizes and variances are considerably different from each other. Now, however, the large variance is paired with a small sample size:

Group 1	Group 2	Group 3
$n_1 = 20$	$n_2 = 20$	$n_3 = 50$
$\overline{Y}_1 = 10$	$\overline{Y}_2 = 12$	$\overline{Y}_3 = 14$
$s_1^2 = 50$	$s_2^2 = 10$	$s_3^2 = 10$

a. Calculate an observed F value for these data.
b. Calculate the F^* value for these data (however, you need not compute the denominator degrees of freedom).
c. Calculate the W value for these data (however, you need not compute the denominator degrees of freedom).
d. Are your answers to parts a–c consistent with the assertion made in Table 3E.1 that when large samples are paired with small variances, the F is liberal, whereas F^* and W are more robust?
e. Are the F, F^*, and W values of this exercise higher or lower than the corresponding F, F^*, and W values of Exercise 8? Is the direction of change consistent with Table 3E.1?

*10. Assume the following data are from a one-way between-subjects design (these data are also used in Exercise 16 at the end of Chapter 5):

Group 1	Group 2	Group 3
48	59	68
54	46	62
47	49	53
54	63	59
62	38	67
57	58	71

Perform a nonparametric test of the difference among these three groups.

4

Individual Comparisons
of Means

In Chapter 3, you learned how to test a null hypothesis that all a groups have the same mean. A global test such as this one that is sensitive to any differences among the levels of the factor is often referred to as *testing an omnibus null hypothesis*. Although the importance of this methodology cannot be overemphasized, it must also be recognized that it has certain limitations. Specifically, anytime a is three or greater and the null hypothesis is rejected, the precise inference to be made is unclear. For example, if $a = 3$, all that the statistical test has informed us at this point is that the statement $\mu_1 = \mu_2 = \mu_3$ is false. However, it is not necessarily true that all three means are different from each other. For example, one possible inference is that $\mu_1 = \mu_2$, but both μ_1 and μ_2 differ from μ_3. However, perhaps $\mu_2 = \mu_3$, but both differ from μ_1. Obviously, we need a way to decide which individual means do indeed differ from each other. The name given to this topic is *individual comparisons*.

For example, suppose that a researcher is interested in treatments to reduce hypertension. Consider a hypothetical study with four independent groups of subjects, each of whom is assigned randomly to one of the following treatments: drug therapy, biofeedback, dietary modification, and a treatment combining all aspects of the other treatments. For simplicity, suppose the dependent variable is a single blood pressure reading taken 2 weeks after the termination of treatment. In Chapter 3, you learned how to test an omnibus null hypothesis that all four treatments are equally effective. However, there are a number of other questions that might be addressed here, either in addition to or instead of the omnibus null hypothesis. For example, Is there a difference in the effectiveness of drug therapy versus biofeedback? Drug therapy versus diet? Biofeedback versus diet? Is the combination treatment more effective than any of the individual treatments? Is it more effective than the average of the individual treatments? In this chapter, you learn how to answer these questions and others like them.

To preview Chapters 4 and 5 for you, we first show how to use a model-comparisons approach to test hypotheses concerning individual comparisons. Then a more traditional but mathematically equivalent approach to individual comparisons is developed. Chapter 5 considers issues that arise when more than one individual comparison is performed in a single study. As we show, in most studies, several comparisons are indeed tested, leading to the topic of multiple comparisons. The desire to test multiple comparisons can arise in either of two circumstances. First, there are occasions in which a researcher may decide to test several specific comparisons either instead of or in addition to performing a test of the omnibus null hypothesis that all a population means are equal. Such an approach is called *planned comparisons* because the specific comparisons to be investigated are decided on at the beginning of the study. Second, on other occasions, the omnibus null hypothesis is tested. If it is rejected, further data analyses are conducted to explore which groups contributed to the statistically significant result. This approach is called *post hoc comparisons* because the comparisons to be tested are decided on after having examined the data. The distinction between these two situations is described in detail in Chapter 5.

A MODEL COMPARISON APPROACH
FOR TESTING INDIVIDUAL COMPARISONS

Preview of Individual Comparisons

The next two sections present the rationale for formulas for testing individual comparisons (i.e., questions regarding a specific difference among the groups included in the study). We see that the model comparison approach allows us to use many of the same formulas we develop in Chapter 3. In particular, we continue to use the same general expression to obtain an F test to compare the sums of squared errors of full and restricted models. Moreover, the full model we develop in Chapter 3 continues as the full model for Chapter 4. From this perspective, the only difference is that the restricted model of Chapter 4 is different from the restricted model of Chapter 3 because we test a different null hypothesis. As a consequence, the specific expression for the F test is also different. For example, the next section shows in detail that an F test for comparing the means of the first and second groups in a study can be written as

$$F = \frac{(\overline{Y}_1 - \overline{Y}_2)^2}{\left(\dfrac{1}{n_1} + \dfrac{1}{n_2}\right) MS_{\mathrm{W}}} \tag{1}$$

where n_1 and n_2 are the sample sizes of the first and second groups, $\overline{Y}_1$ and $\overline{Y}_2$ are the sample means of the first and second groups, and MS_{W} is mean square within, just as in Chapter 3. We now show how this expression can be derived by comparing appropriate full and restricted models.

Relationship to Model Comparisons

Recall from Chapter 3 that we learned how to test the null hypothesis that all a groups in an a-group study have the same population mean. Symbolically, this corresponds to

$$H_0 : \mu_1 = \mu_2 = \cdots = \mu_a \tag{2}$$

Using the principle of model comparisons, we began with a full model

$$Y_{ij} = \mu_j + \varepsilon_{ij} \tag{3}$$

We obtained the restricted model from our null hypothesis that all μ_j parameters in fact equal a single value, which we denoted μ. Thus, our restricted model was given by

$$Y_{ij} = \mu + \varepsilon_{ij} \tag{4}$$

At this point, our purpose is to consider a different null hypothesis. Instead of testing that all a groups have the same mean, suppose that we simply want to test a null hypothesis that the population means of the first and second groups are equal, that is, our null hypothesis now is

$$H_0 : \mu_1 = \mu_2 \tag{5}$$

Once again, we can use the principle of model comparisons to test this hypothesis. Our full model remains the same as our previous full model, namely

$$Y_{ij} = \mu_j + \varepsilon_{ij} \tag{6}$$

According to H_0, however, this model is too complex. Instead, a restricted model, where $\mu_1 = \mu_2$, provides a simpler but (according to H_0) just as adequate a description of scores on the dependent variable. It is difficult to represent this restricted model compactly with symbols. One solution is simply to write the restricted model as

$$Y_{ij} = \mu_j + \varepsilon_{ij} \tag{7}$$

where $\mu_1 = \mu_2$. However, for greater clarity, we might write

$$Y_{i1} = \mu^* + \varepsilon_{i1} \tag{8}$$
$$Y_{i2} = \mu^* + \varepsilon_{i2}$$
$$Y_{ij} = \mu_j + \varepsilon_{ij} \qquad j = 3, 4, \ldots, a$$

where μ^* represents the common population mean of the first and second groups. Notice that Equation 8 allows groups 3 through a to each have their own potentially unique population mean, but groups 1 and 2 are restricted to having equal population means.

In a moment, we see that as usual in order to form an F test, we must know the degrees of freedom of our full and restricted models. These degrees of freedom depend on (1) sample size, and (2) the number of parameters in the models. Thus, it is helpful at this point to establish how many parameters each model has. Notice that the full model of Equation 3 has a separate parameter for each group, so with a total of a groups, the model includes a parameters. However, the restricted model of Equation 8 does not include a separate parameter for each and every group. Instead, as a consequence of the restriction imposed by the null hypothesis that the first two groups have the same population mean, there are now only $a - 1$ parameters in the restricted model. For example, if we had 4 groups, the restricted model would include 3 parameters: μ^*, μ_3, and μ_4. Notice that μ^* does "double duty" here because it serves as the population mean for both group 1 and group 2, which is exactly what the null hypothesis implies. We return to the topic of degrees of freedom after we develop expressions for the sums of squared errors of the full and restricted models.

Now that the full and restricted models have been identified, it is possible to perform a test of the null hypothesis by comparing the sums of squared errors of the two models as we did in Chapter 3. Finding the sum of squared errors for the full model here is easy because it is simply the full model of Chapter 3. As we saw there,

$$E_F = \sum_{j=1}^{a} \sum_{i=1}^{n_j} (Y_{ij} - \bar{Y}_j)^2 = SS_W \tag{9}$$

Finding the sum of squared errors for the restricted model here is similar to the process used in Chapter 3. As before, the principle of least squares is used. We now have $a - 1$ parameters to estimate in the restricted model: $\mu^*, \mu_3, \mu_4, \ldots, \mu_a$. You should realize that there are only $a - 1$ parameters to be estimated in the restricted model because the separate μ_1 and μ_2 parameters of the full model have been replaced by the single parameter μ^* in the restricted model. The only new wrinkle here is estimating μ^*, because the least-squares estimates of μ_3 through μ_a are again the corresponding sample means, that is, $\overline{Y}_3$ through $\overline{Y}_a$, respectively. Intuitively, it seems reasonable that the estimate of μ^* should be based on the sample means of the first two groups. Indeed, with equal n, we see momentarily that

$$\mu^* = (\overline{Y}_1 + \overline{Y}_2)/2 \tag{10}$$

So, for example, if $\overline{Y}_1 = 6$ and $\overline{Y}_2 = 10$, our best single guess is that the common value of the population mean for groups 1 and 2 is 8. A more general formula involving weighted means can be used when sample sizes are unequal. The following section derives the expressions for these parameter estimates and also shows that the difference between the sum of squared errors of the restricted model and the sum of squared errors of the full model can be written as

$$E_R - E_F = \frac{n_1 n_2}{n_1 + n_2}(\overline{Y}_1 - \overline{Y}_2)^2 \tag{11}$$

OPTIONAL

Derivation of Parameter Estimates and Sum of Squared Errors

We now show algebraically that the intuitive reasoning about using the average of the first two sample means as the estimate of μ^* (see Equation 10) is correct, and we also develop a more general formula that can be used when sample sizes are unequal.

The goal in estimating μ^* is to choose as an estimate whatever value minimizes the following expression:

$$\sum_{i=1}^{n_1}(Y_{i1} - \hat{\mu}^*)^2 + \sum_{i=1}^{n_2}(Y_{i2} - \hat{\mu}^*)^2 \tag{12}$$

which is the sum of squared errors for subjects in the first and second groups. However, this expression is equivalent to

$$\sum_{j=1}^{2}\sum_{i=1}^{n_j}(Y_{ij} - \hat{\mu}^*)^2 \tag{13}$$

Notice that in this expression we are summing over $n_1 + n_2$ individual scores. Although in fact these scores come from two distinct groups, the sum would be the same if we had a single group of $n_1 + n_2$ scores. We saw previously that the sample mean of a group provides the best (in a least-squares sense) estimate in this case. Thus, to minimize Equation 10, we should choose $\hat{\mu}^*$ equal to the sample mean of the $n_1 + n_2$ scores in the first and second groups. Symbolically,

$$\hat{\mu}^* = \sum_{j=1}^{2}\sum_{i=1}^{n_j}Y_{ij} \left/ (n_1 + n_2) \right. \tag{14}$$

Equivalently, it can be shown that the estimate $\hat{\mu}^*$ is a weighted mean of $\overline{Y}_1$ and $\overline{Y}_2$:

$$\hat{\mu}^* = (n_1\overline{Y}_1 + n_2\overline{Y}_2)/(n_1 + n_2) \tag{15}$$

which, in the special case of equal sample sizes ($n_1 = n_2$), simplifies to

$$\hat{\mu}^* = (\overline{Y}_1 + \overline{Y}_2)/2 \tag{16}$$

As stated earlier, this expression for estimating μ^* should make sense intuitively because according to the restricted model, $\mu_1 = \mu_2 = \mu^*$. If this is actually true, $\overline{Y}_1$ and $\overline{Y}_2$ differ from one another only because of sampling error, and the best estimate of the single population mean is obtained by averaging $\overline{Y}_1$ and $\overline{Y}_2$.

To test the null hypothesis that $\mu_1 = \mu_2$, it is necessary to find E_R. This turns out to be easy conceptually now that we know the least-squares parameter estimates for the model of Equation 7 (or, equivalently, Equation 8). That it is also easy computationally becomes apparent shortly. If we let $\overline{Y}^*$ represent our estimate $\hat{\mu}^*$, we have

$$E_R = \sum_{j=1}^{2} \sum_{i=1}^{n_j} (Y_{ij} - \overline{Y}^*)^2 + \sum_{j=3}^{a} \sum_{i=1}^{n_j} (Y_{ij} - \overline{Y}_j)^2 \tag{17}$$

Recall that our real interest is in the increase in error brought about by the restricted model, $E_R - E_F$. To help make it easier to see what this difference equals, we can rewrite Equation 9 as

$$E_F = \sum_{j=1}^{2} \sum_{i=1}^{n_j} (Y_{ij} - \overline{Y}_j)^2 + \sum_{j=3}^{a} \sum_{i=1}^{n_j} (Y_{ij} - \overline{Y}_j)^2 \tag{18}$$

Now, by subtracting the terms in Equation 18 from those in Equation 17, we see that the difference $E_R - E_F$ equals

$$E_R - E_F = \sum_{j=1}^{2} \sum_{i=1}^{n_j} (Y_{ij} - \overline{Y}^*)^2 - \sum_{j=1}^{2} \sum_{i=1}^{n_j} (Y_{ij} - \overline{Y}_j)^2 \tag{19}$$

After some straightforward but tedious algebra, Equation 19 simplifies to

$$E_R - E_F = \frac{(\overline{Y}_1 - \overline{Y}_2)^2}{\left(\dfrac{1}{n_1} + \dfrac{1}{n_2}\right)}$$

$$= \frac{n_1 n_2}{n_1 + n_2}(\overline{Y}_1 - \overline{Y}_2)^2 \tag{20}$$

Expression of F Statistic

The increase in error associated with the restricted model is a function of the sample sizes and the magnitude of the difference between $\overline{Y}_1$ and $\overline{Y}_2$. In particular, as we have just derived in the immediately preceding optional section,

$$E_R - E_F = \frac{n_1 n_2}{n_1 + n_2}(\overline{Y}_1 - \overline{Y}_2)^2 \tag{20, repeated}$$

Larger discrepancies between $\overline{Y}_1$ and $\overline{Y}_2$ suggest that μ_1 may not equal μ_2, as reflected by the larger increase in error. This should seem reasonable, because in the long run the magnitude of the difference between $\overline{Y}_1$ and $\overline{Y}_2$ should reflect the magnitude of the difference between μ_1 and μ_2. Once again, the problem arises of, "How large is large?" The answer is provided by the same form of the F statistic we encountered in Chapter 3:

$$F = \frac{(E_R - E_F)/(df_R - df_F)}{E_F/df_F} \tag{21}$$

The only term in this expression yet to be found for our problem is $df_R - df_F$. Recall that the degrees of freedom for a model equals the number of independent observations in the study minus the number of parameters estimated. In the current problem, a parameters were estimated in the full model, because each group has its own population mean in the full model. Recall that $a - 1$ parameters were estimated in the restricted model; unlike the full model, not every group is allowed its own mean in the restricted model. Instead, the means of the first two groups are allowed only a single parameter (i.e., μ^*), so that in total a groups are presumed to be describable in terms of $a - 1$ parameters. Hence,

$$df_F = N - a \tag{22}$$

so $df_F = df_W$, as in Chapter 3.

$$df_R = N - (a - 1) = N - a + 1 \tag{23}$$

where N represents the total number of subjects in the study (summed over all groups). Subtracting Equation 22 from Equation 23 yields

$$df_R - df_F = 1 \tag{24}$$

As demonstrated in Equation 24, an individual comparison has 1 degree of freedom associated with it, that is, the test of a single restriction on means involves 1 degree of freedom in the numerator. Finally, for testing the null hypothesis of $H_0 : \mu_1 = \mu_2$, we obtain the following test statistic by making the appropriate substitutions into Equation 18:

$$F = \frac{\dfrac{n_1 n_2}{n_1 + n_2}(\overline{Y}_1 - \overline{Y}_2)^2/1}{SS_W/df_W} \tag{25}$$

When the first two groups have the same number of subjects (so that $n_1 = n_2$), Equation 25 can be written as

$$F = \frac{\dfrac{n}{2}(\overline{Y}_1 - \overline{Y}_2)^2}{SS_W/df_W} \tag{26}$$

where n is the common sample size.

Equations 25 and 26 are messy because they involve ratios of fractions. We have nevertheless chosen to write them in this form because in both cases, the numerator represents the sum of squares for the effect (i.e., the difference between the sum of squared errors of the restricted and full models), whereas the denominator represents the sum of squared errors of the full model divided by the degrees of freedom of the full model.

For computational purposes, Equation 25 can be written more simply as[1]

$$F = \frac{n_1 n_2 (\overline{Y}_1 - \overline{Y}_2)^2}{(n_1 + n_2) MS_W} \qquad (27)$$

Similarly, in the case of equal n, Equation 26 can be written more simply as

$$F = \frac{n(\overline{Y}_1 - \overline{Y}_2)^2}{2 MS_W} \qquad (28)$$

Although Equations 27 and 28 are admittedly easier to read than their counterparts of Equations 25 and 26, we typically write formulas to correspond with the form of Equations 25 and 26, so that sums of squares for effects appear in the numerator and sums of squares for error appear in the denominator. The only exception to this rule is in the t test formulation, to be presented shortly, in which the established convention is to write only means in the numerator with all remaining terms in the denominator.

Numerical Example

It may be instructive here to consider a numerical example. Table 4.1 displays hypothetical data for four groups of subjects, corresponding to the four treatments for hypertension introduced at the beginning of the chapter. Specifically, we assume that a group of 24 mild hypertensives have been independently and randomly assigned to one of four treatments: drug therapy, biofeedback, dietary modification, and a treatment combining all aspects of the other treatments. The scores shown in Table 4.1 are systolic blood pressure readings for each subject taken 2 weeks after the termination of treatment.

Two preliminary remarks must be made. First, we said that 24 subjects were assigned to treatment groups, but Table 4.1 shows scores for only 20 subjects. In general, we can proceed with a meaningful analysis of such data only if we can reasonably assume that the reasons for the missing subjects are unrelated to the treatments themselves, that is, the treatment did not cause these subjects to be missing. We act as if such an assumption is reasonable here. In fact, these hypothetical data were created with unequal sample sizes to illustrate the most general situation for testing comparisons. Second, we could use the principles of Chapter 3 to perform an omnibus test. If we were to do so, we would obtain an observed F value of 1.66 for these data, which is nonsignificant at the .05 level. However, we assume that our real interest is in testing contrasts among the groups. The relationship between contrasts and the omnibus test is discussed more fully in Chapter 5.

TABLE 4.1
HYPOTHETICAL SYSTOLIC BLOOD PRESSURE DATA

	Drug Therapy	Biofeedback	Diet	Combination
	84	81	98	91
	95	84	95	78
	93	92	86	85
	104	101	87	80
		80	94	81
		108		
Mean $(\overline{Y}_j)$	94.0	91.0	92.0	83.0
Var (s_j^2)	67.3	132.0	27.5	26.5

TABLE 4.2
ILLUSTRATIVE TEST OF A PAIRWISE COMPARISON FOR DATA
IN TABLE 4.1

Test of $H_0: \mu_1 = \mu_2$

Approach of Equation 27

$$
\begin{aligned}
F &= \frac{n_1 n_2 (\overline{Y}_1 - \overline{Y}_2)^2}{(n_1 + n_2) MS_W} \\
&= \frac{(4)(6)(94 - 91)^2}{(4 + 6)(67.375)} \\
&= 0.32
\end{aligned}
$$

because

$$
\begin{aligned}
MS_W &= \frac{\sum\limits_{j=1}^{a}(n_j - 1)s_j^2}{N - a} \\
&= \frac{3(67.3) + 5(132.0) + 4(27.5) + 4(26.5)}{20 - 4} \\
&= 67.375
\end{aligned}
$$

Approach of Equation 21

$$
F = \frac{(E_R - E_F)/(df_R - df_F)}{E_F/df_F}
$$

$$
\begin{aligned}
E_F &= \sum_{j=1}^{a} \sum_{i=1}^{n_j} (Y_{ij} - \overline{Y}_j)^2 \\
&= \sum_{i=1}^{n_1}(Y_{i1} - 94)^2 + \sum_{i=1}^{n_2}(Y_{i2} - 91)^2 + \sum_{i=1}^{n_3}(Y_{i3} - 92)^2 + \sum_{i=1}^{n_4}(Y_{i4} - 83)^2 \\
&= 1078.00
\end{aligned}
$$

$$
\begin{aligned}
E_R &= \sum_{i=1}^{n_1}(Y_{i1} - \overline{Y}^*)^2 + \sum_{i=1}^{n_2}(Y_{i2} - \overline{Y}^*)^2 + \sum_{i=1}^{n_3}(Y_{i3} - \overline{Y}_3)^2 + \sum_{i=1}^{n_4}(Y_{i4} - \overline{Y}_4)^2 \\
&= \sum_{i=1}^{n_1}(Y_{i1} - 92.2)^2 + \sum_{i=1}^{n_2}(Y_{i2} - 92.2)^2 + \sum_{i=1}^{n_3}(Y_{i3} - 92)^2 + \sum_{i=1}^{n_4}(Y_{i4} - 83)^2 \\
&= 214.96 + 668.64 + 110.00 + 106.00 \\
&= 1099.60
\end{aligned}
$$

Then,

$$
F = \frac{(1099.60 - 1078.00)/(17 - 16)}{1078.00/16} = 0.32
$$

In an actual study, we would probably test several contrasts. However, to keep things simple, we illustrate a test for only one contrast. Specifically, we suppose that the hypothesis to be tested is whether there is a difference in the effectiveness of drug therapy and biofeedback.

Table 4.2 shows two equivalent ways to test this hypothesis. Although Equation 27 is easier to use in practice, the approach based on Equation 21 is also shown, primarily for pedagogical reasons. With either approach, the observed F value is 0.32, with 1 and 16 degrees of freedom. The observed value is less than the critical F value of 4.49 (see Appendix Table A.2) for $\alpha = .05$, so the difference between the means is nonsignificant at the .05 level. Thus, the hypothesis that drug therapy and biofeedback are equally effective cannot be rejected at the .05 level.

COMPLEX COMPARISONS

Models Perspective

The approach we have just developed is adequate for testing hypotheses of the form $H_0 : \mu_1 = \mu_2$. More generally, any hypothesis of the form

$$H_0 : \mu_l = \mu_m \tag{29}$$

where μ_l and μ_m are the population means of any two groups is said to involve a pairwise comparison because it involves an equality of only two groups' means. Equation 27 provides a computationally simple method for testing hypotheses of this form.

Although research questions often center on pairwise comparisons, there are occasions in which hypotheses concern a difference involving more than two means. For example, in the hypothetical blood pressure study we have been discussing, one question we raised at the beginning of the chapter was whether the combination treatment is more effective than the average of the other three treatments. We could write the null hypothesis for this question as

$$H_0 : \tfrac{1}{3}(\mu_1 + \mu_2 + \mu_3) = \mu_4 \tag{30}$$

Notice that this null hypothesis does not necessarily stipulate that all four population means are equal to each other. For example, if $\mu_1 = 88$, $\mu_2 = 87$, $\mu_3 = 83$, and $\mu_4 = 86$, the null hypothesis would be true, because the average of 88, 87, and 83 is 86. Also notice that, as Equation 30 shows, the null hypothesis being tested here involves more than two groups. Such a hypothesis involves a *complex comparison*.

When a complex comparison is to be tested, it is not at all intuitively obvious how least-squares estimates of parameters are obtained in the appropriate restricted model. In fact, it is difficult even to write down an appropriate expression for the restricted model, unless we simply say it is

$$Y_{ij} = \mu_j + \varepsilon_{ij} \tag{31}$$

where

$$\tfrac{1}{3}(\mu_1 + \mu_2 + \mu_3) = \mu_4$$

Given this formulation of the restricted model, the least-squares estimates are still not apparent.[2] Although it is possible to describe a procedure that yields the least-squares estimates, we instead take a different approach. The primary rationale for this approach is that we are typically not interested in the parameter estimates themselves; rather, we are interested in the difference between the sum of squared errors for the restricted and full models, $E_R - E_F$, just as we were when we tested pairwise comparisons. There is a general procedure for finding this difference for any contrast we might wish to test. In particular, a contrast such as that expressed by the null hypothesis of Equation 30 can be tested rather easily with the approach we now develop.

It is convenient to rewrite the hypothesis expressed in Equation 30 in the following manner:

$$H_0 : \tfrac{1}{3}\mu_1 + \tfrac{1}{3}\mu_2 + \tfrac{1}{3}\mu_3 - \mu_4 = 0 \tag{32}$$

The expression on the left side of the equals sign—that is, $\tfrac{1}{3}\mu_1 + \tfrac{1}{3}\mu_2 + \tfrac{1}{3}\mu_3 - \mu_4$—is a linear combination of the group population means. In general, we might express a hypothesis concerning the means as

$$H_0 : c_1\mu_1 + c_2\mu_2 + c_3\mu_3 + c_4\mu_4 = 0 \tag{33}$$

where c_1, c_2, c_3, and c_4 are coefficients (or weights) chosen by the experimenter to test a hypothesis of substantive interest. Notice that Equation 32 is a special case of Equation 33, where $c_1 = 1/3$, $c_2 = 1/3$, $c_3 = 1/3$, and $c_4 = -1$. An expression of the form

$$c_1\mu_1 + c_2\mu_2 + c_3\mu_3 + c_4\mu_4 \tag{34}$$

is called a *contrast* or a *comparison* (the terms are used interchangeably). The general definition of a contrast is that it is a linear combination of population means in which the coefficients of the means add up to zero. In the general case of a groups, we can represent a contrast quite compactly with Σ notation as

$$\sum_{j=1}^{a} c_j\mu_j \tag{35}$$

Instead of writing this expression every time we refer to a contrast, it is conventional to use a lowercase Greek psi (ψ) to represent the numerical value of a contrast. In other words,

$$\psi = \sum_{j=1}^{a} c_j\mu_j \tag{36}$$

Several points need mentioning here. First, the general concept of a comparison as exemplified in Equation 36 is very powerful because this formulation permits a wide range of hypotheses to be tested. The primary reason for this tremendous flexibility is that a researcher is free to choose contrast coefficients (the c_j terms) in whatever manner that corresponds to the substantive hypothesis of interest. For example, we see in a moment that the general expression in Equation 36 enables us to test whether the combination hypertension treatment (group 4) is more effective than the average of the other three treatments. We accomplish this by choosing c_1, c_2, and c_3 to equal $1/3$, and c_4 to equal -1. Alternatively, as a second example, suppose that we want to test the difference between drug therapy and biofeedback, as we did earlier in the chapter. This null hypothesis could be written as

$$H_0 : \mu_1 - \mu_2 = 0$$

To test this hypothesis, then, we can choose coefficients as follows: $c_1 = 1$, $c_2 = -1$, $c_3 = 0$, and $c_4 = 0$. The resultant contrast ψ is given by

$$\psi = (1)\mu_1 + (-1)\mu_2 + (0)\mu_3 + (0)\mu_4 = \mu_1 - \mu_2$$

Thus, testing a null hypothesis that ψ as defined in this manner equals zero is equivalent to testing whether $\mu_1 = \mu_2$. The general point to be understood here is that by choosing c_j values appropriately, it is possible to define ψ to test any particular comparison, either pairwise or complex, that may be of interest. Second, realize that ψ is simply a number because it is a linear combination of the population means. For example, consider the following definition of ψ:

$$\psi = \tfrac{1}{3}\mu_1 + \tfrac{1}{3}\mu_2 + \tfrac{1}{3}\mu_3 - \mu_4$$

If $\mu_1 = 88$, $\mu_2 = 87$, $\mu_3 = 83$, and $\mu_4 = 86$, then $\psi = 0$. Notice here that the null hypothesis is true. However, if $\mu_1 = 88$, $\mu_2 = 87$, $\mu_3 = 83$, but $\mu_4 = 80$, then $\psi = -6$. In this case, the null hypothesis is false because the combination treatment is better than the average of the other treatments (remember that lower blood pressure readings are better—at least until they approach zero!). Admittedly, in actual research we do not know what number ψ represents because it is a population parameter, but nevertheless, it is a number. Because we cannot know the population value of ψ, we must use sample data to estimate and test hypotheses about ψ. Third, as the previous example illustrates, ψ equals zero when the null hypothesis is true and is nonzero when it is false. For this reason, we can rewrite our null hypothesis as

$$H_0 : \psi = 0 \tag{37}$$

More formally, Equation 37 follows from substituting ψ from Equation 36 into Equation 33.[3] Fourth, the mathematics for forming F tests would work even if the coefficients did not sum to zero. However, we refer to the set of coefficients in this case as defining a particular linear combination rather than a contrast or comparison (e.g., $\mu_1 + \mu_2$ combines two means but does not contrast or compare their values with one another). Typically, linear combinations that are not contrasts do not address theoretically meaningful questions. Fifth, as we again see later, we are usually interested in several different contrasts in one study. To avoid confusion, we often use subscripts for ψ; for example, we might have ψ_1, ψ_2, and ψ_3 in a particular study. Each ψ would have its own coefficients and would represent a hypothesis of interest to the experimenter. For example, with four groups, we might be interested in the following three contrasts:

$$\psi_1 = \mu_1 + \mu_2 - \mu_3 - \mu_4 \tag{38}$$
$$\psi_2 = \mu_1 - \mu_2$$
$$\psi_3 = \mu_3 - \mu_4$$

For the moment, we continue to focus our attention on testing a hypothesis about a particular contrast, for example ψ_1. (In Chapter 5, we consider issues that arise in testing more than one contrast.)

In general, our purpose is to develop a test of a null hypothesis of the form expressed in Equation 37, namely $\psi = 0$. Once again, we use our expression for an F test:

$$F = \frac{(E_R - E_F)/(df_R - df_F)}{E_F/df_F} \tag{21, repeated}$$

However, Equation 21 can be simplified here because it is possible to develop a general expression for $E_R - E_F$ when testing a hypothesis that $\psi = 0$. It can be shown (see the extension at the end of this chapter) in this case that a general expression for the difference between the sum of squared errors of the restricted and full models is given by

$$E_R - E_F = (\hat{\psi})^2 \bigg/ \sum_{j=1}^{a} \left(\frac{c_j^2}{n_j} \right) \tag{39}$$

where $\hat{\psi}$ is a sample estimate of the population parameter ψ. Because $E_R - E_F$ represents a difference in sum of squared errors associated with ψ, we often use $SS(\psi)$ to represent $E_R - E_F$ for a contrast, that is, $SS(\psi) = E_R - E_F$. Because $\overline{Y}_j$ is the least-squares estimate of

μ_j, the least-squares estimate of ψ is obtained by simply replacing each population mean in Equation 36 by the corresponding sample mean. Thus,

$$\hat{\psi} = \sum_{j=1}^{a} c_j \overline{Y}_j \tag{40}$$

We see throughout the book that Equation 39 is important. We want to test contrasts for statistical significance in a variety of designs and continually return to Equation 39 to find the sum of squares associated with the contrast of interest. For this reason, we digress momentarily to help you develop an intuitive appreciation of the formula. From the numerator, we can see that the restricted model is inferior to the full model to the extent that $\hat{\psi}$ differs from zero (either positively or negatively). This makes sense because our null hypothesis is that ψ is zero. If ψ really is zero, $\hat{\psi}$ has a mean of zero and differs from zero only because of sampling error; however, if ψ is nonzero, $\hat{\psi}$ differs from zero both because of sampling error and because its mean is nonzero. Thus, $\hat{\psi}^2$, and hence the difference in errors $E_R - E_F$, tends to be larger when the null hypothesis is false than when it is true. Also, notice that the n_j term appears in the denominator of the denominator. As a result, all other things being equal, larger sample sizes produce larger sums of squares, just as we would expect based on the discussion of power in Chapter 3. The final term in the formula is c_j. The intuitive justification for including the coefficients in the denominator of Equation 39 is to compensate for the fact that the numerator, $(\hat{\psi})^2$, could be made arbitrarily larger or smaller simply by multiplying all of the c_j coefficients by a constant. To illustrate this point, consider two hypotheses that might be tested in a four-group study:

$$H_0 : \mu_1 + \mu_2 = \mu_3 + \mu_4$$
$$H_0 : .5(\mu_1 + \mu_2) = .5(\mu_3 + \mu_4)$$

These two hypotheses are logically equivalent because the .5 values on either side of the second hypothesis cancel one another. However, what happens if we translate these hypotheses into contrasts? We could define

$$\psi_1 = \mu_1 + \mu_2 - \mu_3 - \mu_4$$

for the first hypothesis, and

$$\psi_2 = .5\mu_1 + .5\mu_2 - .5\mu_3 - .5\mu_4$$

for the second. Now, suppose that we obtain the following sample means based on 10 subjects in each group

$$\overline{Y}_1 = 10, \overline{Y}_2 = 12, \overline{Y}_3 = 10, \text{ and } \overline{Y}_4 = 8$$

Then, the sample value of ψ_1 equals

$$\hat{\psi}_1 = 1(10) + 1(12) - 1(10) - 1(8) = 4$$

The sample value of ψ_2 equals

$$\hat{\psi}_2 = .5(10) + .5(12) - .5(10) - .5(8) = 2$$

If we considered only the $\hat{\psi}$ values, we might mistakenly conclude that there is more evidence against the null hypothesis for the first contrast than for the second. However, the sum of squared coefficients $\Sigma_{j=1}^{a} c_j^2$ is also relevant because for ψ_1,

$$\sum_{j=1}^{a} c_j^2 = (1)^2 + (1)^2 + (-1)^2 + (-1)^2 = 4$$

whereas for ψ_2,

$$\sum_{j=1}^{a} c_j^2 = (.5)^2 + (.5)^2 + (-.5)^2 + (-.5)^2 = 1$$

Thus, $\Sigma_{j=1}^{a} c_j^2$ is four times larger for the first contrast than the second, just as $(\hat{\psi})^2$ is four times larger for the first contrast than the second. As a result, substituting the values for $(\hat{\psi})^2$, $\Sigma_{j=1}^{a} c_j^2$ and n_j into Equation 39 produces a value of 40 for the sum of squares for both contrasts. Because the contrasts are logically equivalent, it is sensible that the two sums of squares should also be equivalent. The inclusion of the squared-coefficients term in the denominator of Equation 39 ensures that logically equivalent contrasts yield the same sum of squares, regardless of the absolute size of the coefficients.

The only remaining term in Equation 21 to be discussed is the difference in degrees of freedom, $df_R - df_F$. To find df_R, we must determine the number of independent parameters in the restricted model. Consider the null hypothesis of Equation 32 when $a = 4$:

$$H_0 : \tfrac{1}{3}\mu_1 + \tfrac{1}{3}\mu_2 + \tfrac{1}{3}\mu_3 - \mu_4 = 0 \tag{32, repeated}$$

The corresponding restricted model was

$$Y_{ij} = \mu_j + \varepsilon_{ij} \tag{31, repeated}$$

where $1/3\mu_1 + 1/3\mu_2 + 1/3\mu_3 - \mu_4 = 0$. This model has four parameters when $a = 4$, but it has only three independent parameters because we know that the four parameters must obey the restriction that

$$\tfrac{1}{3}\mu_1 + \tfrac{1}{3}\mu_2 + \tfrac{1}{3}\mu_3 - \mu_4 = 0$$

For example, suppose that $\mu_1 = 88$, $\mu_2 = 87$, and $\mu_3 = 83$. Then, according to the model, we know it should be true that $\mu_4 = 86$. Once the values of any three population means have been determined, the fourth is fixed. In the general case of a groups, there would be one restriction on the parameter values, implying that there would be $a - 1$ independent parameters. Thus, in the general case,

$$df_R - df_F = [N - (a - 1)] - (N - a)$$
$$= 1$$

Because E_F/df_F is MS_W, Equation 21 becomes

$$F = \frac{(\hat{\psi})^2 \Big/ \displaystyle\sum_{j=1}^{a} (c_j^2/n_j)}{MS_W} \tag{41}$$

which may be used for testing any null hypothesis that can be expressed as

$$H_0 : \psi = \sum_{j=1}^{a} c_j \mu_j = 0$$

Numerical Example

To illustrate calculations for testing a complex comparison, we return to the hypertension data shown in Table 4.1. Recall that Table 4.2 showed two equivalent approaches for testing a pairwise comparison, one based on Equation 27 and one based on Equation 21. Similarly, Table 4.3 shows two equivalent approaches for testing complex comparisons, one based on Equation 41 and one based on Equation 21. Notice that Equation 27 is not illustrated because it is appropriate only for pairwise comparisons.

For purposes of illustration, we continue to assume that we are interested in testing whether the combined treatment is more effective than the average of the other treatments. As the top half of Table 4.3 shows, the observed F value for this contrast is 4.82, which exceeds the critical F value of 4.49 for 1 and 16 degrees of freedom. Thus, we can assert that the combined treatment is in fact more effective than the average of the other treatments.

The bottom half of Table 4.3 shows the calculations using Equation 21. The primary reason for presenting these calculations is to demonstrate that they produce the same result as Equation 41. However, as should be obvious from comparing the two halves of Table 4.3, Equation 41 is much simpler, so it is used in the remainder of the book, instead of going back

TABLE 4.3
ILLUSTRATIVE TEST OF A COMPLEX COMPARISON FOR DATA IN TABLE 4.1

Test of $H_0 : 1/3(\mu_1 + \mu_2 + \mu_3) = \mu_4$

Approach of Equation 41

$$F = \frac{(\hat{\psi})^2}{MS_W \sum_{j=1}^{a} (c_j^2/n_j)}$$

$$= \frac{[1/3(94 + 91 + 92) - 83]^2}{67.375\{[(1/3)^2/4] + [(1/3)^2/6] + [(1/3)^2/5] + [(-1)^2/5]\}}$$

$$= \frac{(92.33 - 83)^2}{67.375(0.2685)}$$

$$= 4.82$$

Approach of Equation 21

$$F = \frac{(E_R - E_F)/(df_R - df_F)}{E_F/df_F}$$

$$E_F = \sum(Y_{i1} - 94)^2 + \sum(Y_{i2} - 91)^2 + \sum(Y_{i3} - 92)^2 + \sum(Y_{i4} - 83)^2$$

$$= 1078.00$$

$$E_R = \sum(Y_{i1} - 91.103)^2 + \sum(Y_{i2} - 89.069)^2 + \sum(Y_{i3} - 89.683)^2 + \sum(Y_{i4} - 89.952)^2$$

$$= 235.57 + 682.37 + 136.84 + 347.65$$

$$= 1402.43$$

Then,

$$F = \frac{(1402.43 - 1078.00)/(17 - 16)}{1078.00/16} = 4.82$$

to first principles of model comparisons using Equation 21. Nevertheless, it is important for you to understand that Equation 41 is also based on a comparison of models.

In fact, the approach based on Equation 21 is even more tedious than the bottom half of Table 4.3 implies. The reason for this additional complication is that the least-squares estimates for the parameters in the restricted model are tedious to find.[4] In our example, the parameter estimates subject to the constraint $1/3\mu_1 + 1/3\mu_2 + 1/3\mu_3 - 1\mu_4 = 0$ are given by

$$\hat{\mu}_1 = 91.103$$
$$\hat{\mu}_2 = 89.069$$
$$\hat{\mu}_3 = 89.683$$
$$\hat{\mu}_4 = 89.952$$

Notice that the constraint requires that the average of the first three means minus the fourth mean must equal zero. In symbols, this implies that

$$\tfrac{1}{3}\hat{\mu}_1 + \tfrac{1}{3}\hat{\mu}_2 + \tfrac{1}{3}\hat{\mu}_3 - \hat{\mu}_4 = 0$$

Indeed, the parameter estimates we have obtained obey this restriction because

$$\tfrac{1}{3}(91.103) + \tfrac{1}{3}(89.069) + \tfrac{1}{3}(89.683) - 89.952 = 0$$

(within rounding error). Thus, by doing all this additional work, as Table 4.3 shows, we can use Equation 21 to duplicate the results of Equation 41. However, even though the general model comparison approach exemplified in Equation 21 produces an appropriate result, we prefer Equation 41 for the specific problem of testing a contrast because it is simpler as a result of being derived specifically for this type of problem.

One other point must be made here. Although in some situations a researcher may be interested only in pairwise comparisons, in many studies hypotheses involving complex comparisons are also of interest. In particular, complex comparisons potentially reveal interesting features of the data that may be hidden from pairwise comparisons. For example, in the hypothetical hypertension data in Table 4.1, it turns out that none of the six pairwise differences between means is significant at the .05 level. However, we have just seen that a complex comparison is significant at the .05 level. If we had only tested pairwise comparisons, this finding would have gone undetected. However, it might be argued that if we test a large number of hypotheses, some will inevitably be statistically significant, even if every null hypothesis is true. This problem is discussed in detail in Chapter 5. The general point to understand here is that you should not always restrict your testing to pairwise comparisons. In some studies, complex comparisons should also be tested. In general, formulate comparisons that correspond to the hypotheses you want to test, remembering that the resultant contrasts may be either pairwise or complex.

THE t TEST FORMULATION OF HYPOTHESIS TESTING FOR CONTRASTS

To summarize the chapter to this point, we have seen that testing hypotheses concerning contrasts can be thought of as a comparison of models. As in Chapter 3, least squares is used to estimate parameters in full and restricted models. Then, the sums of squared errors of the two models are compared adjusting for degrees of freedom, yielding an F value. This F value is then compared to the table of the F distribution to determine whether the null hypothesis should be rejected.

Some textbooks do not present the test of a contrast as an F test, but rather as a t test. Although at first this may seem disconcerting, it should be remembered that the t is a special case of the F. Specifically, when the F has a single numerator degree of freedom, $t^2 = F$. Indeed, this relationship holds for testing a contrast because $df_R - df_F = 1$, so the F has 1 numerator degree of freedom.

Practical Implications

There are two practical implications here of the relationship between the t test and the F test. First, so far in our discussion of contrasts, we have implicitly been conducting two-tailed tests. However, we might very well want to conduct a one-tailed test in certain situations. For example, we might want to test

$$H_0 : \mu_1 \geq \mu_2 \qquad \text{versus} \qquad H_1 : \mu_1 < \mu_2$$

A one-tailed t test is straightforward because tables are readily available (see Appendix Table A.1). If $\alpha = .05$, instead of finding a critical value corresponding to an area of .025 in each tail, we find the critical value that has an area of .05 in the one relevant tail. If $\overline{Y}_1 < \overline{Y}_2$ and the resulting t value exceeds the critical t in absolute value, the null hypothesis is rejected at the .05 level. A one-tailed test can also be performed using F tables. Instead of using the critical F in the .05 table, the critical F is found in the .10 table, although the actual α is .05. If the direction of the difference corresponds to H_1 (here, $\overline{Y}_1 < \overline{Y}_2$) and the F exceeds the .10 critical F, the null hypothesis is rejected at the .05 level, one-tailed. Thus, the first practical implication is that researchers can choose between one-tailed and two-tailed tests of contrasts, according to whichever provides a more appropriate test of their theory. Also, either a t test or an F test can be used to perform each type of hypothesis test. The second practical implication is that a t test for testing $H_0 : \mu_1 = \mu_2$ is developed in Chapter 3. How are the procedures of this chapter different from those of Chapter 3, if they differ at all? First, in the Chapter 3 t test, there were only two groups, whereas in this chapter there are a groups. Hence, testing a contrast such as

$$\tfrac{1}{3}\mu_1 + \tfrac{1}{3}\mu_2 + \tfrac{1}{3}\mu_3 - \mu_4$$

requires the procedures of this chapter. However, what about $\mu_1 - \mu_2$? We could test $H_0 : \mu_1 = \mu_2$ using either the procedures of Chapter 3 or the procedures of this chapter. Although in either case we can perform either a t test or an F test, the results of the Chapter 3 test are at least somewhat different from those of this chapter. If we compare Equation 20 of this chapter with the procedures of Chapter 3, we see that $E_R - E_F$ is the same for the two approaches. Also, with both approaches, $df_R - df_F = 1$. However, E_F and df_F are not the same in the two approaches. In Chapter 3, E_F was the sum of squared errors for the full model, which was based on the two groups of subjects being compared. However, in this chapter, E_F is based on all a groups, regardless of which groups are being compared in a particular contrast. The same difference exists for the degrees of freedom.

To ensure that this difference is clear, consider the numerical example of Table 4.1 once again. Suppose we want to test $H_0 : \mu_1 = \mu_2$ versus $H_1 : \mu_1 \neq \mu_2$. We saw earlier that using the procedures of this chapter, the observed F is 0.32, with 1 and 16 degrees of freedom.

However, if we were to use the approach of Chapter 3, the F would be 0.20 with 1 and 8 degrees of freedom. Naturally, the question arises as to which approach is better. As it happens, the correct answer to this question is, "It depends." Specifically, it depends on the validity of the homogeneity-of-variance assumption. The obvious difference between the two approaches is that in the numerical example, the third and fourth groups contribute to E_F for the approach of this chapter, but are completely irrelevant for the Chapter 3 approach. At this point, we must ask ourselves whether the third and fourth groups contain information pertinent to the comparison of the first two groups. At first blush, it would seem that if the goal is simply to compare groups 1 and 2, then groups 3 and 4 should be irrelevant. However, if the homogeneity-of-variance assumption is true, all four population variances are equal. Under this condition, E_F/df_F of Chapter 3 and E_F/df_F of this chapter both provide unbiased estimates of the common population variance. However, E_F/df_F of this chapter provides a more precise estimate because it is based on more observations than is E_F/df_F of Chapter 3.

The practical import is that, if the assumption is met, in the long run the average value of the F using the Chapter 3 approach approximately equals the F of this chapter; however, the F of Chapter 3 is more variable from sample to sample because it is based on fewer observations, as reflected by its lower denominator degrees of freedom. Inspection of the F table shows that as the denominator degrees of freedom decrease, the critical F required for significance increases. Thus, to obtain a significant result, the F from the Chapter 3 approach must be larger than the F of the approach of this chapter. For this reason, the method of this chapter is more powerful than the method of Chapter 3 when homogeneity of variance holds.

UNEQUAL POPULATION VARIANCES

What if the homogeneity-of-variance assumption is not met? After the discussion of robustness of Chapter 3, it would not be surprising to learn that this assumption is not really important for testing contrasts. However, it turns out that the homogeneity assumption is in fact very important for testing contrasts. After some reflection, this should make intuitive sense. For example, if a contrast of the form $\mu_1 - \mu_2$ is tested when $a = 4$ and if the variances of the third and fourth groups are very different from those of the first and second groups, it seems reasonable that information from the third and fourth groups should be ignored. If we mistakenly assume homogeneity of variance, our resulting test may be either too liberal or too conservative. If the within-group population variance of the third and fourth groups is less than that of the first and second groups, MS_W underestimates the actual variability of $\overline{Y}_1 - \overline{Y}_2$. Because MS_W is in the denominator of the F, the observed F value in this situation is, on the average, larger than it should be; thus, the observed F exceeds the critical F more than 5% of the time, creating a liberal test. However, if the third and fourth groups have larger variances than the first and second groups, just the opposite occurs, and the test is conservative. Although an α level below .05 is not a problem in and of itself, here it is accompanied by lower power, lessening the ability to detect a true difference if one exists.

The problem of testing mean differences when variances are unequal has plagued statisticians for several decades. This problem is often referred to as the *Behrens–Fisher problem*, because Behrens and Fisher studied the problem extensively in the 1930s. A number of alternative approaches have been proposed over the years. The approach described here is a generalization of a method derived independently by Welch (1938) and Satterthwaite (1946) as a solution to the Behrens–Fisher problem of testing the difference between two population means when population variances are unequal. The numerator term of the F remains the same as under the homogeneity assumption. However, both the denominator of the F and the critical value against which the observed F is compared are adjusted. Specifically, in the denominator of Equation 41, MS_W is replaced by

$$\text{denom} = \sum_{j=1}^{a} \left[\left(c_j^2/n_j \right) s_j^2 \right] \bigg/ \sum_{j=1}^{a} \left(c_j^2/n_j \right) \tag{42}$$

where s_j^2 is the unbiased variance estimate for the jth group. The observed test statistic, which is distributed approximately as an F variable, is obtained by dividing the expression in Equation 39 by the expression in Equation 42. Because the denominator of the test statistic is now different, the denominator degrees of freedom are also different. The ratio of the expression in Equation 39 divided by the expression in Equation 42 is compared to a critical F whose numerator degrees of freedom equal 1 and whose denominator degrees of freedom are given by

$$df = \frac{\left(\sum\limits_{j=1}^{a} c_j^2 s_j^2 \big/ n_j \right)^2}{\sum\limits_{j=1}^{a} \left[\left(c_j^2 s_j^2/n_j \right)^2 \big/ (n_j - 1) \right]} \tag{43}$$

This expression for the denominator degrees of freedom is, at best, tedious and, at worst, terrifying. Fortunately, there is little reason ever to compute these degrees of freedom by hand because most statistical packages do this computation for you. For most purposes, all you need to know is that (1) the value of Equation 43 typically changes from one contrast to another, because it depends on c_j; (2) only those variances and sample sizes for groups having nonzero coefficients influence the final value; (3) the value is always less than or equal to $N - a$, the denominator degrees of freedom under the homogeneity assumption; and (4) all other things being equal, larger discrepancies in sample variances lead to smaller denominator degrees of freedom.

What is perhaps more important to realize is that the denominator of the F test is a weighted mean of the sample variances s_j^2 of the a groups, whether the denominator is derived from Equation 38 or is based on MS_W. In other words, in either case, the denominator is of the general form

$$\text{denom} = \left(\sum_{j=1}^{a} w_j s_j^2 \right) \bigg/ \sum_{j=1}^{a} w_j \tag{44}$$

However, the two possible denominators differ in the weights w_j to be used because one denominator does not assume homogeneity of variance, whereas the other does. As Equation 42 shows, the denominator when variances are not assumed to be equal is based on weights given by

$$w_j = c_j^2/n_j \tag{45}$$

We can understand the reason for these weights by considering the variance of $\hat{\psi}$. Because $\hat{\psi}$ is defined to be $\hat{\psi} = \Sigma_{j=1}^{a} c_j \overline{Y}_j$, the variance of $\hat{\psi}$ is given by

$$\text{Var}\left(\hat{\psi} \right) = \sum_{j=1}^{a} c_j^2 \text{Var}\left(\overline{Y}_j \right)$$

$$= \sum_{j=1}^{a} c_j^2 \sigma_j^2/n_j$$

We can rewrite this as

$$\text{Var}(\hat{\psi}) = \sum_{j=1}^{a} (c_j^2/n_j)\sigma_j^2,$$

to get an expression that shows that weights of the form (c_j^2/n_j) should be applied to each variance, as claimed in Equation 45. However, because σ_j^2 is unknown, we must estimate it with s_j^2, yielding as an estimate of $\text{Var}(\hat{\psi})$:

$$\text{estimated Var}(\hat{\psi}) = \sum_{j=1}^{a} (c_j^2/n_j)s_j^2 \tag{46}$$

Notice then that when we divide the numerator of the F (from Equation 39) by the denominator (from Equation 42), we obtain

$$F = \frac{(\hat{\psi})^2 \Big/ \sum_{j=1}^{a}(c_j^2/n_j)}{\sum_{j=1}^{a}(c_j^2/n_j)s_j^2 \Big/ \sum_{j=1}^{a}(c_j^2/n_j)}$$

which equals

$$F = \frac{(\hat{\psi})^2}{\sum_{j=1}^{a}(c_j^2/n_j)s_j^2}$$

However, we have just seen from Equation 42 that the denominator here is the estimated variance of $\hat{\psi}$. Thus, effectively, this F statistic is of the form

$$F = \frac{(\hat{\psi})^2}{\text{estimated Var}(\hat{\psi})} \tag{47}$$

where no assumption of equal variances has been made. Equation 47 shows explicitly that the denominator of the F statistic using Equation 42 is the estimated variance of the particular contrast being tested. Notice that each individual contrast is thus allowed to have its own particular variance, in keeping with the desire not to assume equal variances across groups. We encounter this separate variance approach for testing contrasts again when we discuss within-subject designs (i.e., repeated measures designs) in Chapters 11–14.

If we are willing to assume equal variances, the variance of the contrast can be written as $\text{Var}(\hat{\psi}) = \Sigma_{j=1}^{a}c_j^2\sigma^2/n_j$. We can factor out σ^2, yielding $\text{Var}(\hat{\psi}) = \sigma^2\Sigma_{j=1}^{a}c_j^2/n_j$. Now the problem is that we must estimate the common population variance σ^2. The best estimate is given by MS_W, which equals

$$MS_W = \frac{\sum_{j=1}^{a}(n_j - 1)s_j^2}{\sum_{j=1}^{a}(n_j - 1)}$$

Notice then that MS_W is a special case of Equation 44, where $w_j = n_j - 1$. Thus, both the pooled error term of MS_W and the separate error term of Equation 42 are based on estimating the variance of the contrast to be tested. They differ from one another in how they weight the sample variances of each group.

What are the practical implications of this difference in weighting? When the homogeneity-of-variance assumption is valid, both approaches provide an unbiased estimate of the variance of the contrast. However, the estimate using MS_W is somewhat more efficient, so tests based on MS_W are at least slightly more powerful than tests based on a separate error term. However, when population variances are unequal, only the separate variance approach provides an unbiased estimate of the variance of the contrast to be tested.[5] As a result, tests of contrasts based on MS_W can either be quite liberal or quite conservative, depending on whether MS_W underestimates or overestimates the variance of the particular contrast being tested. For some contrasts, the hypothesis test using MS_W as the error term may have a Type I error rate badly in excess of .05, whereas for other contrasts, the test may be conservative and hence lack power to detect true mean differences.

Although the separate variance approach provides a tremendous improvement over the traditional one when variances are heterogeneous, it has received little attention to date for a number of reasons. First, in many experimental studies, the homogeneity-of-variance assumption is reasonably well met. Even if the population variances are not literally identical, they are close enough to one another that the traditional approach suffices. However, Wilcox (1987a), who surveyed educational research studies, and Fenstad (1983) argue that large discrepancies in variances are more common than most researchers realize. Second, these approaches are difficult and tedious to implement by hand, as should be obvious from Equation 43. Fortunately, SPSS computes the appropriate statistic (by selecting "Compare Means" followed by "One-Way ANOVA" at this time), alleviating the need for hand calculations. As of this writing, SAS provides procedures that can be used only in the special case of pairwise comparisons. Third, these procedures have been ignored because many researchers mistakenly believe that tests of contrasts are robust to violations of homogeneity of variance. It should be emphasized that, although the omnibus test tends to be robust when sample sizes are equal (as we discussed in Chapter 3 and in the Extension to Chapter 3), in general, tests of contrasts are not robust to heterogeneity even with equal n.

Numerical Example

Because testing contrasts without assuming homogeneity of variance is best done on the computer, we call on SPSS to illustrate the calculations behind this approach by using the data in Table 4.1 once again. Recall that Table 4.2 illustrates a test of a pairwise comparison (group 1 versus group 2) and Table 4.3 illustrates a test of a complex comparison (group 4 versus the average of the other three groups). Both of these previous tests assumed homogeneity of variance, as illustrated by the use of MS_W as an error term.

Table 4.4 shows SPSS output for testing each of these contrasts. The first section of the table simply shows the coefficients we specified as input to the program in order to obtain tests of the desired contrasts. Notice that "Contrast 1" has coefficients of 1, −1, 0, and 0 and thus corresponds to the pairwise comparison of the first two groups. Similarly, "Contrast 2" has coefficients of 1, 1, 1, and −3 and thus represents the complex comparison of the fourth group versus the average of the first three groups. The second section of the table, labeled "Contrast Tests," presents the results of performing these tests on our data. This section is itself divided into two halves. The top half shows results based on MS_W as an error term, assuming homogeneity of variance. The lower half shows results based on a separate error term, without assuming homogeneity of variance.

Notice that this output presents results in terms of t statistics instead of F values. However, as must be the case, squaring each t value produces the corresponding F value. For example,

TABLE 4.4
SPSS OUTPUT OF A PAIRWISE COMPARISON AND A COMPLEX COMPARISON
FOR DATA IN TABLE 4.1

| | Contrast Coefficients GROUP | | | |
Contrast	1.00	2.00	3.00	4.00
1	1	−1	0	0
2	1	1	1	−3

| | | | Contrast Tests | | | | |
		Contrast	Value of Contrast	Standard Error	t	df	Significance (Two Tailed)
SBP	Assume equal	1	3.0000	5.2984	.566	16	.579
	variances	2	28.0000	12.7602	2.194	16	.043
	Does not assume	1	3.0000	6.2316	.481	7.885	.643
	equal variances	2	28.0000	9.5934	2.919	11.034	.014

squaring the t value of 0.566 shown in Table 4.4 for the first contrast yields an F value of 0.32, identical to the value we calculated earlier in Table 4.2. Similarly, squaring 2.194 results in an F value of 4.81, which differs only slightly from the Table 4.3 value of 4.82 because of rounding error.

Now let us consider what happens when we relax the homogeneity of variance assumption. The pairwise comparison remains nonsignificant, just as it was when homogeneity was assumed. Both the observed t and the degrees of freedom for the denominator have decreased for this contrast. As Table 4.4 shows, the complex comparison is again statistically significant, as it was when homogeneity is assumed. Interestingly, the observed t value has increased appreciably, from 2.19 to 2.92. As a result, the p value has decreased from .04 to .01. How can this happen if the approach that does not assume homogeneity is more conservative? The answer is that this approach is not necessarily more conservative. The denominator from Equation 42 is smaller than MS_W for some contrasts and larger than MS_W for others. For the contrast of group 4 versus the other three groups, Equation 42 weights group 4 more heavily than each of the other three groups because its contrast coefficient is three times larger than the others. In these particular data, group 4 has a small variance (i.e., $s_4^2 = 26.5$), so giving it a larger weight produces a smaller value for the denominator. The smaller number in the denominator yields a larger t (or F) value than is obtained with MS_W in the denominator. However, another contrast might show just the opposite pattern. The only sense in which the approach of Equation 42 is necessarily "conservative" is that the denominator degrees of freedom are less than with MS_W. This reflects the fact that when the homogeneity assumption is true, MS_W is a more efficient estimate of the population variance, so a lower critical value can be used. However, when homogeneity fails to hold, only the denominator of Equation 42 yields an accurate test.

MEASURES OF EFFECT

We emphasized in Chapter 3 that hypothesis tests are influenced not only by the size of the treatment effect but also by the number of participants in the study. For this reason, it is usually important to supplement hypothesis tests with additional indices that directly reflect the size of the treatment effect. As we discussed in Chapter 3, there are a variety of such indices. We once again follow Yeaton and Sechrest's (1981) distinction between measures of effect size and measures of association strength. We now proceed to present examples of each type of index for contrasts. We hasten to add that rarely would a researcher report all of these measures. Nevertheless, we present a variety of measures for two reasons. First, you may encounter each of these measures at some point in reading empirical studies, so it is important to understand what a measure reflects and, for that matter, what it does not reflect. Second, by being exposed to a variety of measures, you are better positioned to choose an appropriate measure in your own data to reflect the characteristics of those data you deem to be important. Once we present each type, we illustrate them with our numerical example, examining treatments for hypertension.

Measures of Effect Size

Confidence Intervals

Hypothesis tests tell us whether we can be certain beyond a reasonable doubt that some hypothesized difference between means is different from zero. However, the test by itself does not tell us how far from zero this difference may be. Confidence intervals provide this additional information. Recall that we have expressed the population value of a contrast as

$$\psi = \sum_{j=1}^{a} c_j \mu_j \qquad \text{(36, repeated)}$$

So far, we have presented procedures for testing whether the population parameter ψ can be shown to differ from zero. We now show how to form a confidence interval for ψ. There is a direct relationship between the alpha level of a test and the corresponding confidence level of a confidence interval. Forming an interval with a confidence level of $1 - \alpha$ corresponds to setting the Type I error rate at α. For example, a 95% confidence interval corresponds directly to a hypothesis test with an alpha level of .05. Just as an alpha level of .05 is a common convention for statistical tests, a confidence level of 95% is a common convention for confidence intervals.

A confidence interval for the parameter ψ can be formed with confidence level $1 - \alpha$ through the following expression:

$$\hat{\psi} \pm \sqrt{F_{\alpha;1,N-a} \; MS_W \sum_{j=1}^{a} \left(c_j^2/n_j\right)} \qquad (48)$$

Several additional points must be made. First, $F_{\alpha;1,N-a}$ is a critical value, and as such is obtained from Table A.2. It is important to notice that this is not the observed value of the test statistic for testing the contrast, and in fact has nothing whatsoever to do with the data except insofar as the value depends on a and N. Second, this interval is intended to represent a difference between means. In order to do so, the sum of the absolute values of the contrast coefficients should equal 2. For example, suppose we have four groups and want to compare the average of the first three groups with the final group. An appropriate set of contrast coefficients would then be $1/3, 1/3, 1/3$, and -1. Notice that finding the absolute value of each coefficient and summing yields a value of 2, as it should. Although the mathematics continues to work correctly even if this condition is not satisfied, the resulting confidence interval would be difficult to interpret because it would not reflect a difference in means. Third, Equation 48 assumes homogeneity of variance. An expression for forming a confidence interval without having to assume equal variances is given by

$$\hat{\psi} \pm \sqrt{F_{\alpha;1,df}} \sqrt{\sum_{j=1}^{a} [(c_j^2/n_j)s_j^2]} \tag{49}$$

where df is found from Equation 43, which generally involves use of a statistical computer package. Fourth, confidence intervals using either Equation 48 or 49 are often useful for assessing equivalence between groups. Even if we do not believe that the population value ψ of some contrast is literally zero (theoretically to an infinite number of decimal points), we may believe that the value of ψ is so close to zero that for all practical purposes we can regard it as being zero. Although there are a variety of ways of establishing whether a contrast is essentially zero (see Feinstein, 2002, for further discussion), one method involves forming a confidence interval. Specifically, the first step is to specify on theoretical grounds prior to collecting data a value of ψ to be regarded as a boundary between equivalent and nonequivalent. In principle, we could have only one boundary, but in practice it is more typical to establish both a lower and an upper boundary. In fact, most typical is to center the upper and lower boundary around zero. For example, in an intervention study designed to affect GRE scores, we might regard a 10-point effect as being equivalent to no effect, in which case our lower boundary would be -10 and our upper boundary would be 10. Of course, the value chosen for this boundary is necessarily somewhat subjective, but at least it operationalizes a meaning for "equivalent." After having chosen boundary values, the next step is to form a confidence interval for ψ. The contrast is then regarded as consistent with equivalence if the entire confidence interval is between the upper and lower theoretical bounds. In the GRE example, we would regard the groups as equivalent if the entire confidence interval for ψ lies between -10 and 10.

We return to the blood pressure data shown originally in Table 4.1 to illustrate confidence intervals for contrasts. Suppose we want to form confidence intervals for both the pairwise comparison and the complex comparison we have formulated for these data. As Equations 48 and 49 show, we must decide whether to assume homogeneity of variance. We begin by making this assumption, and then show the corresponding intervals relaxing the assumption. Current software packages differ in their ability to form confidence intervals. Some packages calculate intervals only for pairwise comparisons, and some calculate intervals only under the homogeneity of variance assumption. We use intermediate calculations obtained from SPSS to show how intervals can be formed even if an available package does not provide complete flexibility to form all desired intervals directly. Table 4.4 shows the output obtained from SPSS.

For the pairwise comparison, the value of $\hat{\psi}$ is shown in Table 4.4 to equal 3.00. Assuming homogeneity, the standard error of the contrast, which is the second term under a square root sign in Equation 48, equals 5.2984. Appendix Table A.2 shows that the critical F value for an alpha level of .05 with 1 numerator and 16 denominator degrees of freedom in equals 4.49. Substituting these three values into Equation 48 produces

$$3.00 \pm 11.23$$

Thus, we can be 95% confident that the true value of the contrast (i.e., the population mean blood pressure with drug therapy minus the population mean for biofeedback) is between -8.23 and 14.23 units. The large width of this interval underscores the fact that considerable uncertainty about the difference between these two groups remains even after conducting our study. Also notice that the interval contains zero, consistent with the nonsignificant test of the contrast.

The interval for the complex comparison follows exactly the same logic. However, we have to realize that the contrast coefficients we have used here exaggerate the actual difference between means because the sum of the absolute value of the coefficients is 6, not 2. Thus, we need to divide both the value of the contrast and its standard error by 3 to establish a proper metric. Doing so and following the same procedure as for the pairwise contrast produces an interval of

$$9.33 \pm 9.01$$

Thus, we can be 95% confident that the combined therapy is at least 0.32 points and at most 18.34 points better than the average of the other three therapies. Notice that this interval is somewhat narrower than that for the pairwise comparison, which reflects one advantage of a complex comparison and that, furthermore, this interval does not contain zero, once again consistent with the significant difference found in Table 4.3. Assuming equal variances and equal sample sizes, complex comparisons yield narrower intervals than pairwise comparisons because complex comparisons evaluate pooled means that have smaller standard errors because they are based on more subjects.

The same basic logic applies even if we do not assume homogeneity of variance. We simply find the value of the contrast and its standard error in the "does not assume equal variances" section of the output and then remember that the critical F value must take into account the smaller degrees of freedom than we had when we assumed homogeneity. Taking this approach (and being slightly conservative by using 7 denominator degrees of freedom instead of 7.885) shows that the 95% interval for the pairwise comparison is now

$$3.0 \pm 14.73$$

Notice that this interval is approximately 30% wider than the corresponding interval when homogeneity was assumed. For the complex comparison, when we do not assume homogeneity, the interval becomes

$$9.33 \pm 7.04$$

Unlike the pairwise comparison, this interval is about 20% narrower than the interval based on homogeneity. The explanation for this difference is that the largest weight in the complex comparison is for group 4, which has the smallest variance in this data set (see Table 4.1), and hence a variance estimate computed as a weighted average of variances (see Equation 46) is considerably smaller than one based on MS_W.

Standardized Difference

Recall that Chapter 3 defined the standardized difference between two population means as

$$d = (\mu_1 - \mu_2)/\sigma_\varepsilon \qquad \text{(3.83, repeated)}$$

With two groups, this population parameter can be estimated from sample data by

$$\hat{d} = (\overline{Y}_1 - \overline{Y}_2)/\sqrt{MS_W} \qquad \text{(50)}$$

In the case of two or more groups, we can define a standardized difference for a contrast of population means as

$$d = 2\psi \Bigg/ \left[\sigma_\varepsilon \left(\sum_{j=1}^{a} |c_j| \right) \right] \tag{51}$$

Note that the 2 in the numerator and the sum of absolute value of coefficients in the denominator cancel one another when the coefficients are chosen to represent a mean difference. However, the inclusion of these "extra" terms in the numerator and denominator ensures that the population parameter is meaningful even if coefficients were to be chosen in a manner that their absolute values did not sum to 2.

Of course, we can never know the precise value of d as defined by Equation 51, because in order to know d, we would have to also know the value of σ_ε as well as the values of the population means involved in the contrast. Instead, we must use sample data to estimate the population value of d. We can do so through the following equation:

$$\hat{d} = 2\hat{\psi} \Bigg/ \left[\sqrt{MS_W} \left(\sum_{j=1}^{a} |c_j| \right) \right] \tag{52}$$

If the homogeneity of variance assumption is questionable, MS_W in Equation 52 can be replaced by the expression we saw earlier in Equation 42.

Standardized mean differences can be calculated very easily based on the Table 4.4 SPSS output. The only necessary value not included in this table is MS_W. However, we saw in Table 4.2 that MS_W for our data equals 67.375, a value that would also be obtained easily with any statistical package. Simply substituting the relevant values into Equation 52 shows that the standardized mean difference between drug therapy and biofeedback is 0.37, whereas the standardized mean difference between the combined therapy and the average of the other therapies is 1.14. Based on conventions originally suggested by Cohen (1977), the pairwise comparison represents a small to medium effect, whereas the complex comparison represents a large effect. However, it is important to keep in mind that these standardized differences are simply estimates based on our sample data and hence do not convey any information about the precision of those estimates. In particular, the confidence intervals we have formed show that it is plausible that the population difference between the drug therapy and biofeedback may be zero, so we must be very careful in any claim that the difference is "small to medium."

Measures of Association Strength

As we discussed in Chapter 3, measures of association strength reflect how much of the variability in the dependent variable is associated with the variation in the independent-variable levels. In the context of the omnibus hypothesis for a one-way between-subjects design, the simplest measure of association strength is the ratio of between-group sum of squares to total sum of squares:

$$R^2 = SS_B / SS_{Total} \tag{53}$$

Although the same essential logic applies when we begin to consider measures of association strength for contrasts, two differences emerge. First, the numerator is no longer SS_B, but instead is the sum of squares for the specific contrast of interest. Second, it turns out that there are now a variety of different ways we might conceptualize the denominator variability that forms the basis of comparison for the numerator. We illustrate three possibilities, each of which provides a unique perspective of the data.

First, one question of potential interest is the extent to which a specific contrast captures the essence of the entire difference among groups. A measure answering this question is given by

$$R^2_{\text{alerting}} = SS(\psi)/SS_{\text{Between}} \tag{54}$$

We have followed Rosenthal, Rosnow, and Rubin's (2000) terminology by designating this squared correlation as "alerting" the researcher of the extent to which this contrast has succeeded in capturing between-group differences. The value of R^2_{alerting} can range from 0 to 1, because $SS(\psi)$ can be as small as zero or as large as SS_{Between}.

Keppel (1973) provides another perspective that helps clarify the meaning and usefulness of R^2_{alerting}. In particular, he shows that in the case of equal sample sizes, R^2_{alerting} is equivalent to the squared correlation between the contrast coefficients and the actual sample means of the groups.[6] This equivalence implies that the R^2_{alerting} and hence the sum of squares for a contrast depend on the extent to which the coefficients for that contrast match the pattern of sample means. For example, suppose that the following three sample means are obtained in a three-group study: $\overline{Y}_1 = 10$, $\overline{Y}_2 = 8$, and $\overline{Y}_3 = 15$. The sample grand mean here is 11, which implies that the group deviations from the grand mean are -1, -3, and 4, respectively. It then follows that a contrast with coefficients of -1, -3, and 4 correlates perfectly with the pattern of sample means, producing an R^2_{alerting} value of 1.0. Looking back at Equation 54, we can see that this value of 1.0 implies that $SS(\psi)$ must equal SS_{Between}. In other words, this single contrast has completely captured the entirety of the between-group difference. We should immediately caution that this does not necessarily make it the "best" possible contrast, because these coefficients may not correspond to an interesting theoretical question. Furthermore, in real data, the contrast coefficients are rarely integers, complicating interpretation yet further. However, as suggested by the terminology adopted by Rosenthal, Rosnow, and Rubin (2000), these coefficients alert the researcher to the pattern that maximizes the sum of squares accounted for and thus may form the basis of further selection of coefficients. For example, in the three-group case discussed previously, the researcher may decide that a more interpretable contrast is the pairwise comparison of groups 2 and 3, which would then have coefficients of 0, -1, and 1. It can be shown that the R^2_{alerting} value for this contrast (with equal n) is 0.94, which means that this pairwise contrast accounts for 94% of the entire between-group variability. The slight decrease from 100% may well be outweighed by an increase in interpretability. The last section of this chapter as well as the entirety of Chapter 5 discusses issues involved in selecting multiple contrasts in one's data.

In our blood pressure example, we have seen (Table 4.2) that the pairwise difference between drug therapy and biofeedback has a sum of squares of 21.60. Similarly, the sum of squares for the complex comparison of combined versus the average of all other therapies equals 324.41. The between-group sum of squares for these data is 334.55. Incidentally, these sums of squares are trivial to find with SAS PROC GLM, but as of this writing are available in SPSS only through the MANOVA procedure. Substituting the relevant pair of values into Equation 54 shows that our pairwise contrast accounts for 6.46% of the between-group variability, whereas the complex contrast accounts for 96.97%. Thus, almost all of the variability among the four groups can be explained by the fact that the combined group is different from the other three groups. Also, you may notice that if we were to add 6.46% and 97.97%, we would obtain a value greater than 100%. Later in the chapter we delineate situations in which it is meaningful to sum percentages versus other situations in which it is not. As you might suspect, we see that the current situation is one in which it is not meaningful to add percentages.

Our first strength of association measure, R^2_{alerting}, is useful for describing how much of the between-group variability is associated with a specific contrast. However, we must be careful to realize that it does not take into account how much of the total variability is between-groups and how much is within-groups. As a result, a contrast might account for 94% of the between-group variability, but only a tiny proportion of the total variability, because SS_{Between} might be much smaller than SS_{Within}. For this reason, it is sometimes useful to adopt a different perspective, one in which the question of interest is the proportion of total variability associated with the contrast. This leads to a second measure of strength of association, which Rosenthal et al. (2000) call $R^2_{\text{effect size}}$. This measure is defined as

$$R^2_{\text{effect size}} = SS(\psi)/SS_{\text{Total}} \tag{55}$$

Comparing $R^2_{\text{effect size}}$ from Equation 55 to R^2_{alerting} from Equation 54 shows that they have the same numerator but different denominators. Whereas R^2_{alerting} describes the proportion of between-group variability associated with a particular contrast, $R^2_{\text{effect size}}$ describes the proportion of total variability associated with the contrast. Neither measure is necessarily better than the other; instead, they simply convey different perspectives on the data. In general, R^2_{alerting} is more useful for describing the extent to which a single contrast completely accounts for between-group differences, whereas $R^2_{\text{effect size}}$ is more useful for describing the extent to which a single contrast accounts for total variability in the data. Notice in particular that R^2_{alerting} is often much larger than $R^2_{\text{effect size}}$ and may be close to 1.0 even when $R^2_{\text{effect size}}$ is close to 0.0, so it is important not to overinterpret large values of R^2_{alerting} as implying that a contrast has accounted for a sizable proportion of the total variability in the data.

We already found $SS(\psi)$ for the two contrasts we have been discussing in our blood pressure data. We can easily calculate SS_{Total}, because we have already seen that SS_{Between} is 334.55, and SS_W is simply the sum of squares of our full model. From either Table 4.2 or 4.3, we can see that E_F equals 1078.00, which implies that SS_W is also 1078.00. SS_{Total} then equals the sum of SS_{Between} and SS_W, or 1412.55. $R^2_{\text{effect size}}$ for the difference between drug therapy and biofeedback is 0.0153 (i.e., the ratio of 21.60 to 1412.55). Thus, this difference explains 1.53% of the total variability in the data. Similarly, $R^2_{\text{effect size}}$ for our complex comparison is 0.2297. Thus, the difference between the combined therapy and the average of the other therapies explains 22.97% of the total variability in the data. Notice that this is a much smaller percentage than we found for R^2_{alerting} because the two indices are intended to reflect different aspects of the data.

There is yet a third strength of association measure that may also be of interest. To motivate this third measure, we return to our three-group study, in which we observed means of 10, 8, and 15. Suppose we add the new information that the sample size per group is 20 and $SS_W = 2850$. It then follows that $SS_{\text{Between}} = 520$ and $SS_{\text{Total}} = 3370$. Let's reconsider the pairwise comparison of the second group versus the third group. As we have seen, the R^2_{alerting} value for this contrast is 0.94 (i.e., 490 divided by 520). The corresponding value of $R^2_{\text{effect size}}$ is not surprisingly much lower, 0.15 (i.e., 490 divided by 3370), because SS_{Total} is much larger than SS_{Between}. Although the values of 0.94 and 0.15 are dramatically different from one another, they both provide valid descriptions of how different the second group is from the third group. Now, however, suppose that a researcher replicates this study, but changes the nature of the first group. Perhaps the researcher was disappointed that the first group was not very different from either the second or the third groups, so a different manipulation is introduced in the first condition. For simplicity, suppose that the only change is that the new manipulation was successful in creating a larger difference, so that the sample mean for the first group is 1 instead of 10. We continue to assume that there are 20 participants per group, that the second and third groups have sample means of 8 and 15, and that SS_W equals 2850. Because the first group in this replication is so different from the second and third groups, the new between-group sum of squares is now 1960, as compared to 520 in the original study. As a consequence, R^2_{alerting} now falls from 0.94 in the original study to 0.25 in this new study. Similarly, $R^2_{\text{effect size}}$ falls from 0.15 to 0.10. Our intent with both R^2_{alerting} and $R^2_{\text{effect size}}$ is to describe how different the second and third groups are from one another. Now we reach the crucial question. Should this description depend on the mean of the first group? There is no simple answer to this question, but notice that neither R^2_{alerting} nor $R^2_{\text{effect size}}$ reflect the pure difference we would expect to see in a two-group study comparing only groups 2 and 3. The need for such a measure leads to our third measure of strength of association. We define R^2_{contrast} as follows:

$$R^2_{\text{contrast}} = SS(\psi)/(SS(\psi) + SS_W) \qquad (56)$$

Let us now consider the value of R^2_{contrast} in each of our two studies. In the first study, the sum of squares for the pairwise contrast of the second and third groups equals 490, and the within-group sum of squares equals 2850, so R^2_{contrast} equals 0.15 (rounded to two decimal places). However, it is also the case that R^2_{contrast} equals 0.15 in the replication study, because both $SS(\psi)$ and SS_W are presumed to remain the same in the second study. Of course, in an actual pair of studies, these values would change somewhat simply because of sampling error, but the important point is that there is no systematic reason to expect R^2_{contrast} to depend on the other conditions included in the study.[7]

In our blood pressure example, we have already determined that the sum of squares for the pairwise difference between drug therapy and biofeedback is 21.60. Similarly, the sum of squares for the complex comparison of combined versus the average of all other therapies equals 324.41. We also know that SS_W for these data is 1078.00. It immediately follows that R^2_{contrast} for the pairwise comparison equals 0.02, whereas while R^2_{contrast} for the complex comparison equals 0.23. Notice that in both cases R^2_{contrast} is somewhat larger than the corresponding value of $R^2_{\text{effect size}}$ as must happen by definition.

The logic underlying R^2_{contrast} can be extended yet one further step. We have just seen that one potential reason for favoring R^2_{contrast} over either R^2_{alerting} or $R^2_{\text{effect size}}$ is that only R^2_{contrast} remained the same value when we changed the nature of the first group in the study. However, suppose we now changed the study even more dramatically. In particular, what if we retained the second and third groups from the original study, but now added three additional groups, yielding a five-group study in all? All else being equal, we might well expect $SS(\psi)$ to remain the same, but we would expect SS_W to increase, simply because the total sample size has increased. We could attempt to rectify this problem by redefining our effect size measure so that SS_W was calculated based only on the groups involved in the contrast. In our blood pressure example, the difference between drug therapy and biofeedback accounts for 2.44% of the variance using only the data from these two groups, as compared to 1.53% based on $R^2_{\text{effect size}}$ and 1.96% based on R^2_{contrast} using all four groups. Although the differences for this specific contrast in these data are small in an absolute sense, they reflect a sizable relative difference. In some data sets, the difference between these three measures can be quite large even in an absolute sense. For that reason, our general preference is to base this measure only on the groups actually involved in the comparison. However, the more general point is that strength of association measures are prone to misinterpretation because the concept of variance is often ambiguous in experimental designs. Largely for that reason, we generally prefer measures of effect size, but as we outlined in Chapter 3, each type of measure has its own set of advantages and disadvantages.[8]

TESTING MORE THAN ONE CONTRAST

In most studies, it is rarely the case that an investigator is interested in testing only a single contrast. Instead, there typically are several comparisons of interest. When this is true, a number of questions arise. For example, is there a limit to the number of contrasts that should be tested in a study? Is it permissible to perform multiple tests using an α level of .05 for each? Does it matter whether the contrasts were planned prior to conducting the study or were arrived at after inspecting the data? These and other questions are considered in this section and in Chapter 5.

How Many Contrasts Should Be Tested?

How many contrasts is it reasonable to test in a single study? There is no simple answer to this question, because the "correct" number depends on substantive as well as statistical considerations. In some experiments, there may be only a few explicit questions of interest, so only a small number of contrasts are tested. In other studies, the questions to be addressed may be broader in scope, necessitating the testing of many different contrasts. Thus, the number of contrasts that should be tested depends primarily on the nature of the research endeavor. Nevertheless, there are some statistical considerations that should be remembered when deciding how many contrasts to test. It is to these considerations that we now turn.

A natural place to begin is to consider from a purely mathematical standpoint the number of contrasts that might possibly be tested in a study. Let's consider the simplest case of $a = 3$ (why not $a = 2$?). There are three pairwise contrasts that might be tested:

$$\mu_1 - \mu_2, \qquad \mu_1 - \mu_3, \quad \text{and} \quad \mu_2 - \mu_3,$$

In addition, various complex comparisons could be tested. For example, possible candidates are

$$\frac{1}{2}(\mu_1 + \mu_2) - \mu_3$$
$$\frac{1}{2}(\mu_1 + \mu_3) - \mu_2$$
$$\frac{1}{2}(\mu_2 + \mu_3) - \mu_1$$

It might seem that this list exhausts the supply of possible contrasts, but this is far from true, at least mathematically. For example, some other possibilities are

$$\frac{1}{3}\mu_1 + \frac{2}{3}\mu_2 - \mu_3$$
$$\frac{4}{5}\mu_1 + \frac{1}{5}\mu_2 - \mu_3$$
$$\frac{1}{10}\mu_1 + \frac{9}{10}\mu_2 - \mu_3$$

and so forth. Some reflection should convince you that the "and so forth" goes on forever. Our only stipulation for a contrast is that the coefficients sum to zero, that is, $\Sigma c_j = 0$. Mathematically, there are an infinite number of contrasts that satisfy this rule, even when a is as low as 3. In fact, for $a \geq 3$, there are always infinitely many contrasts that might be tested.

Of course, not all these tests may answer meaningful questions, but from a purely statistical perspective, they are all possible to perform.

It might be suspected that with three groups, some of the information contained in the infinite number of contrasts is redundant, and indeed, this is true. We use an example to consider the maximum number of contrasts that might be tested without introducing redundancy when $a = 3$. Suppose that an investigator expresses an interest in the following contrasts:

$$\psi_1 = \mu_1 - \mu_2 \tag{57}$$
$$\psi_2 = \mu_1 - \mu_3$$
$$\psi_3 = \tfrac{1}{2}(\mu_1 + \mu_2) - \mu_3$$

Are these three contrasts providing redundant information? We can see that the answer is Yes by realizing that $\psi_3 = \psi_2 - 1/2\psi_1$. In other words, the value of ψ_3 is completely determined if we already know the values of ψ_1 and ψ_2. In this sense, ψ_3 provides no new information over that contained in ψ_1 and ψ_2. Alternatively, we could say that ψ_1 is redundant with ψ_2 and ψ_3 because $\psi_1 = 2(\psi_2 - \psi_3)$. The basic point here is that once we know the values of any two of the contrasts, the third is determined precisely. It can be shown that in the general case of a groups, there can be no more than $a - 1$ contrasts without introducing redundancy. Indeed, this is one way of conceptualizing why it is that the omnibus test of mean differences between a groups has $a - 1$ numerator degrees of freedom; in a sense, there are $a - 1$ different ways in which the groups might differ.

Linear Independence of Contrasts

In the previous example, we say that the set of three contrasts ψ_1, ψ_2, and ψ_3 is linearly dependent because the set contains redundant information. More formally, a set of contrasts is linearly dependent if it is possible to express at least one member of the set as a linear combination of the other contrasts. Conversely, any set that is not linearly dependent is said to be *linearly independent*.[9] Notice that this is exactly what we did when we found that ψ_3 was equal to $\psi_2 - 1/2\psi_1$. The concept of linear dependence is important for using some statistical packages such as SPSS MANOVA for testing the significance of contrasts, because this program requires the user to create a set of $a - 1$ linearly independent contrasts, even if only a single contrast is to be tested. Unfortunately, that all sets of $a - 1$ contrasts are linearly independent is not true. Suppose the following three contrasts are to be tested when $a = 4$:

$$\psi_1 = \mu_1 - \mu_2, \quad \psi_2 = \mu_1 - \mu_3, \quad \text{and} \quad \psi_3 = \mu_2 - \mu_3$$

It is easily verified that $\psi_3 = \psi_2 - \psi_1$, so that the contrasts are linearly dependent, even though there are only three contrasts in the set. This illustration simply serves as a warning that determination of linear independence can be complicated, especially for large values of a. The most general procedure for assessing linear independence involves matrix algebra. The interested reader is referred to Kirk (1995) for more detail.

Let's return to our earlier example in which $a = 3$. Our three contrasts were

$$\psi_1 = \mu_1 - \mu_2 \tag{57, repeated}$$
$$\psi_2 = \mu_1 - \mu_3$$
$$\psi_3 = \tfrac{1}{2}(\mu_1 + \mu_2) - \mu_3$$

Suppose for the moment that we were to limit our tests to ψ_1 and ψ_2; that is, we would simply ignore ψ_3. The contrasts ψ_1 and ψ_2 are not redundant with one another because ψ_2 includes information about μ_3, which is not included in ψ_1. However, a careful examination of the coefficients for ψ_1 and ψ_2 suggests that, although the two contrasts are not completely redundant with one another, there is some overlap in the information they provide because in each case we compare the mean of group 1 with the mean of another group. The statistical term for such overlap is nonorthogonality. This means that the information in ψ_1 is correlated with the information in ψ_2.

Orthogonality of Contrasts

Two topics demand attention now: First, how can we assess whether two contrasts are orthogonal to one another? Second, what are the implications of orthogonality versus nonorthogonality? The determination of orthogonality is straightforward from the definition, which we now introduce. Suppose that we have two contrasts ψ_1 and ψ_2 such that

$$\psi_1 = \sum c_{1j}\mu_j \qquad \text{and} \qquad \psi_2 = \sum c_{2j}\mu_j$$

(Notice that the coefficients now have two subscripts. The first subscript indexes which contrast the coefficients are for, whereas the second subscript indexes the group. For example, c_{23} would be the coefficient for ψ_2 for the third group.) The two contrasts ψ_1 and ψ_2 are defined as orthogonal when sample sizes are equal if and only if their coefficients satisfy the following property:

$$\sum c_{1j}c_{2j} = 0 \tag{58}$$

When sample sizes are unequal, the orthogonality condition is that

$$\sum c_{1j}c_{2j}/n_j = 0 \tag{59}$$

To ensure understanding of Equation 58, consider the three contrasts of Equation 57. Earlier we argued intuitively that ψ_1 and ψ_2 were nonorthogonal. To see that this is true mathematically, let's apply the definition of Equation 58, assuming equal n. It is helpful first to write out the individual coefficients of each contrast. In this case, we have

$$c_{11} = 1 \qquad c_{12} = -1 \qquad c_{13} = 0$$
$$c_{21} = 1 \qquad c_{22} = 0 \qquad c_{23} = -1$$

According to Equation 58, we now must multiply the ψ_1 coefficients times the ψ_2 coefficients for each group and then sum the products. This yields $(1)(1) + (-1)(0) + (0)(-1) = 1$. The nonzero result means that the contrasts are nonorthogonal.

Consider a second example. Are ψ_1 and ψ_3 of Equation 57 orthogonal? Writing out the coefficients yields

$$c_{11} = 1 \qquad c_{12} = -1 \qquad c_{13} = 0$$
$$c_{31} = 1/2 \qquad c_{32} = 1/2 \qquad c_{33} = -1$$

Multiplying and adding the products results in $(1)(1/2) + (-1)(1/2) + (0)(-1) = 0$. Thus, ψ_1 and ψ_3 are orthogonal to one another.

In the general case of a groups, one might be interested in whether several contrasts considered together are orthogonal. A set of contrasts is orthogonal if and only if every pair of contrasts in the set is orthogonal to one another. Consider an example in which $a = 4$, with equal n:

$$\psi_1 = \mu_1 - \mu_2$$
$$\psi_2 = \tfrac{1}{2}(\mu_1 + \mu_2) - \mu_3$$
$$\psi_3 = \tfrac{1}{3}(\mu_1 + \mu_2 + \mu_3) - \mu_4$$

Do these three contrasts form an orthogonal set? To answer this question, we must consider three pairs of contrasts: ψ_1 and ψ_2, ψ_1 and ψ_3, and ψ_2 and ψ_3. Using Equation 58 shows that ψ_1 and ψ_2 are orthogonal, ψ_1 and ψ_3 are orthogonal, and ψ_2 and ψ_3 are orthogonal. Thus, the three contrasts form an orthogonal set because every pair of contrasts in the set is orthogonal to one another. Notice that it is meaningless to try to apply the condition of Equation 58 to all three contrasts simultaneously. Instead, Equation 58 considers only two contrasts at a time. To evaluate the orthogonality of a set, the equation is applied $C(C-1)/2$ times, where C is the number of contrasts in the set. [The expression $C(C-1)/2$ equals the number of distinct pairs of C objects.]

If a study has a groups, how many contrasts might be in an orthogonal set? It can be proved that there can be at most $a - 1$ contrasts in an orthogonal set. In other words, any set with a or more contrasts is by mathematical necessity nonorthogonal. Note carefully that there are many (actually, infinitely many) possible sets of $a - 1$ orthogonal contrasts. The limit of $a - 1$ pertains to the number of contrasts in a set but says nothing about how many sets of orthogonal contrasts may exist. Recall that we encountered a limit of $a - 1$ in our earlier discussion of linear independence. It turns out that orthogonal contrasts are by mathematical necessity linearly independent, so they also must obey this limit. In fact, orthogonal contrasts represent a special case of linear independence. With linearly independent contrasts, we argued that the information gained from the set is nonredundant. When the contrasts are orthogonal as well, the information contained in the contrasts has additional properties that we now consider.

What difference does it make whether contrasts are orthogonal to one another? The primary implication is that orthogonal contrasts provide nonoverlapping information about how the groups differ. More formally, when two contrasts ψ_1 and ψ_2 are orthogonal, the sample estimates (e.g., $\hat{\psi}_1$ and $\hat{\psi}_2$) are statistically independent of one another.[10] In other words, there is no relationship between $\hat{\psi}_1$ and $\hat{\psi}_2$, and in this sense, each provides unique information about group differences.

OPTIONAL

Example of Correlation Between Nonorthogonal Contrasts

We explore this idea more fully with an example using the contrasts of Equation 57. Suppose that unbeknown to us, $\mu_1 = \mu_2 = \mu_3 = 10$. In this case, it follows that $\psi_1 = \psi_2 = \psi_3 = 0$. Although the population means are equal for the three groups, the sample means, of course, vary from group to group and from replication to replication. According to our assumptions, the $\overline{Y}_j$ values are normally distributed across replications. For simplicity in this example, we assume that $\overline{Y}_j$ can take on only three values:

TABLE 4.5
ORTHOGONALITY

$\overline{Y}_1$	$\overline{Y}_2$	$\overline{Y}_3$	$\hat{\psi}_1$	$\hat{\psi}_2$	$\hat{\psi}_3$
8	8	8	0	0	0
8	8	10	0	−2	−2
8	8	12	0	−4	−4
8	10	8	−2	0	1
8	10	10	−2	−2	−1
8	10	12	−2	−4	−3
8	12	8	−4	0	2
8	12	10	−4	−2	0
8	12	12	−4	−4	−2
10	8	8	2	2	1
10	8	10	2	0	−1
10	8	12	2	−2	−3
10	10	8	0	2	2
10	10	10	0	0	0
10	10	12	0	−2	−2
10	12	8	−2	2	3
10	12	10	−2	0	1
10	12	12	−2	−2	−1
12	8	8	4	4	2
12	8	10	4	2	0
12	8	12	4	0	−2
12	10	8	2	4	3
12	10	10	2	2	1
12	10	12	2	0	−1
12	12	8	0	4	4
12	12	10	0	2	2
12	12	12	0	0	0

$\mu_j - 2$, μ_j, and $\mu_j + 2$. In effect, we are assuming that the error for a group mean is either -2, 0, or 2 in any sample. We also assume that these three values are equally likely. (Although this assumption for the error term is unrealistic, it makes the implications of orthogonality much easier to show than does the normality assumption.) According to our simple model, then, each $\overline{Y}_j$ is 8, 10, or 12, and these three values occur equally often. What is the relationship between $\overline{Y}_1$, $\overline{Y}_2$, and $\overline{Y}_3$? They are independent of one another because the three groups of subjects are independent. This means, for example, that knowing $\overline{Y}_1 = 8$ says nothing about whether $\overline{Y}_2$ is 8, 10, or 12. The first three columns of Table 4.5 show the 27 possible combinations of $\overline{Y}_1$, $\overline{Y}_2$, and $\overline{Y}_3$ that can occur, given our assumptions. As a result of the independence between groups, each of these 27 combinations is equally likely to occur, that is, each has a probability of 1/27. The next three columns show for each combination of $\overline{Y}_j$ values the resulting values for $\hat{\psi}_1$, $\hat{\psi}_2$, and $\hat{\psi}_3$, where

$$\hat{\psi}_1 = \overline{Y}_1 - \overline{Y}_2$$

$$\hat{\psi}_2 = \overline{Y}_1 - \overline{Y}_3$$

$$\hat{\psi}_3 = \tfrac{1}{2}(\overline{Y}_1 + \overline{Y}_2) - \overline{Y}_3$$

The primary purpose for obtaining the values in Table 4.5 is to investigate the relationships among the different contrasts. Earlier we argued intuitively that ψ_1 and ψ_2 were related to one another. Specifically, it would seem reasonable that if $\hat{\psi}_1$ large, then $\hat{\psi}_2$ would be large also because both involve comparing $\overline{Y}_1$ with another group. This possibility can be explored systematically by forming a contingency

TABLE 4.6
CONTINGENCY TABLES ILLUSTRATING RELATIONSHIP
OF $\hat{\psi}_1$ TO $\hat{\psi}_2$ AND $\hat{\psi}_1$ TO $\hat{\psi}_3$

	$\hat{\psi}_2$				
$\hat{\psi}_1$	-4	-2	0	2	4
4			1	1	1
2		1	2	2	1
0	1	2	3	2	1
-2	1	2	2	1	
-4	1	1	1		

	$\hat{\psi}_3$								
$\hat{\psi}_1$	-4	-3	-2	-1	0	1	2	3	4
4			1		1		1		
2		1		2		2		1	
0	1		2		3		2		1
-2		1		2		2		1	
-4			1		1		1		

table relating the $\hat{\psi}_1$ and $\hat{\psi}_2$ values of Table 4.5. The top half of Table 4.6 is such a contingency table. Each entry in this table equals the number of times that a particular combination of $\hat{\psi}_1$ and $\hat{\psi}_2$ values occurs in Table 4.5. For example, the combination $\hat{\psi}_1 = 4$ and $\hat{\psi}_2 = 4$ occurs once in Table 4.5, whereas $\hat{\psi}_1 = 0 = \hat{\psi}_2 = 0$ occurs three times. The combination $\hat{\psi}_1 = 4$ and $\hat{\psi}_2 = -4$ never occurs. If we were to divide each entry in the contingency table by 27, the result would be a bivariate probability distribution, but this degree of formality is unnecessary for our purposes. Instead, the important point here is simply that $\hat{\psi}_1$ and $\hat{\psi}_2$ are correlated. Specifically, they are positively correlated because higher values of $\hat{\psi}_1$ tend to be associated with higher values of $\hat{\psi}_2$. Thus, samples in which $\hat{\psi}_1$ exceed zero have a systematic tendency to yield $\hat{\psi}_2$ values that are in excess of zero. Is this also true of ψ_1 and ψ_2? We saw earlier that according to the definition of orthogonality, ψ_1 and ψ_3 are orthogonal. The bottom half of Table 4.6 displays the contingency table for ψ_1 and ψ_3. Are $\hat{\psi}_1$ and $\hat{\psi}_3$ correlated? Can we predict $\hat{\psi}_3$ from $\hat{\psi}_1$ (or vice versa)? Suppose that $\hat{\psi}_1 = 4$. When $\hat{\psi}_1 = 4$, the best guess concerning $\hat{\psi}_3$ is zero, because zero is the mean value of $\hat{\psi}_3$ when $\hat{\psi}_1 = 4$. Suppose that $\hat{\psi}_1 = 2$. The best guess for $\hat{\psi}_3$ is still zero. In fact, for any given value of $\hat{\psi}_1$, the best guess for $\hat{\psi}_3$ is zero. Knowledge of $\hat{\psi}_1$ does not improve prediction of $\hat{\psi}_3$. Thus, $\hat{\psi}_1$ and $\hat{\psi}_3$ are uncorrelated. In this example, $\hat{\psi}_1$ and $\hat{\psi}_3$ are not statistically independent because the errors were distributed as -2, 0, and 2 instead of normally. With normally distributed errors, $\hat{\psi}_1$ and $\hat{\psi}_3$ would have been statistically independent as well as uncorrelated. Thus, orthogonal contrasts possess the beneficial property of being uncorrelated with one another.

Another Look at Nonorthogonal Contrasts: Venn Diagrams

Another property of orthogonal contrasts can best be illustrated by example. Consider the data for three groups in Table 4.7. It can easily be shown that the sum of squares for the test of the omnibus null hypothesis is given by $SS_B = 190$ for these data. Let's reconsider our three contrasts of Equation 57:

$$\psi_1 = \mu_1 - \mu_2$$

$$\psi_2 = \mu_1 - \mu_3$$

$$\psi_3 = \tfrac{1}{2}(\mu_1 + \mu_2) - \mu_3$$

TABLE 4.7
HYPOTHETICAL DATA FOR THREE GROUPS

	1	2	3	
	12	10	6	
	10	8	2	
	11	12	3	
	9	14	4	
	13	6	0	
$\overline{Y}_j$	**11**	**10**	**3**	$\overline{Y} = 8$
$\sum_{i=1}^{n_j}(\overline{Y}_{ij} - \overline{Y}_j)^2$	10	40	20	
$\sum_{i=1}^{n_j}(\overline{Y}_{ij} - \overline{Y})^2$	55	60	145	

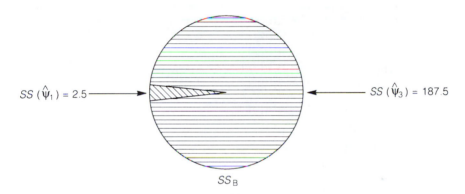

$SS(\hat{\psi}_1) = 2.5 \longrightarrow \qquad \longleftarrow SS(\hat{\psi}_3) = 187.5$

SS_B

FIG. 4.1.   Venn diagram of relationship between $SS(\hat{\psi}_1)$, $SS(\hat{\psi}_3)$, and SS_B.

We can test each contrast in turn by forming an appropriate restricted model and comparing its error sum of squares to the error sum of squares of the full model. After some computation, it turns out that

$$SS(\psi_1) = 2.5$$

$$SS(\psi_2) = 160.0$$

$$SS(\psi_3) = 187.5$$

Interestingly enough, the sum of $(SS\psi_1) + SS(\psi_3) = 190$, which was the between-group sum of squares. As you might suspect, this occurrence is not accidental. Given three groups, two orthogonal contrasts partition the sum of squares between groups, that is, the sum of the sum of squares for the contrasts equals SS_B. More generally, for a groups, $a - 1$ orthogonal contrasts partition the between-group sum of squares. This fact provides another perspective on the unique information provided by each member of a set of orthogonal contrasts. If we decide to test ψ_1 and ψ_3 as given here, then we have completely accounted for all differences between the three groups. In this sense, ψ_1 and ψ_3 together extract all available information concerning group differences. Venn diagrams are sometimes used to depict this situation visually. Figure 4.1 shows how ψ_1 and ψ_3 together account for SS_B, which is represented by the entire circle. However, suppose we test ψ_1, and ψ_2. The sum of $SS(\psi_1)$ and $SS(\psi_2)$ fails to account for all of

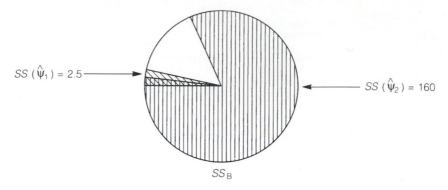

FIG. 4.2.   Venn diagram of relationship between $SS(\hat{\psi}_1)$, $SS(\hat{\psi}_2)$, and SS_B.

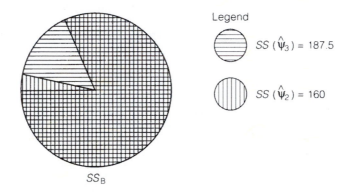

FIG. 4.3.   Venn diagram of relationship between $SS(\hat{\psi}_2)$, $SS(\hat{\psi}_3)$, and SS_B.

the between-group sum of squares because these two contrasts are nonorthogonal. Figure 4.2 shows that ψ_1 and ψ_2 overlap. At this point, you might think that the combination of ψ_1 and ψ_2 is inferior to ψ_1 and ψ_3 because $2.5 + 160$ is less than the 190 sum of $2.5 + 187.5$. Consider, however, the possibility of testing ψ_2 and ψ_3 together. It would seem that these two contrasts, which are nonorthogonal, somehow account for more of a difference between the groups than actually exists. That this is not true can be seen from Figure 4.3. Because ψ_2 and ψ_3 are nonorthogonal, there is substantial overlap in the areas they represent. Thus, they do not account for more between-group variability than exists. This illustrates an important principle: The sums of squares of nonorthogonal contrasts are not additive—for example, the sum of $160 + 187.5$ has no meaning here. However, the sums of squares of orthogonal contrasts can be added to determine the magnitude of the sum of squares they jointly account for.

One additional point concerning orthogonality is of interest. Why is a contrast defined to have the restriction that the sum of its coefficients must equal zero, that is, $\Sigma_{j=1}^{a} c_j = 0$? The reason for this restriction is that it guarantees that the contrast is orthogonal to the grand mean μ. Notice that μ is like a contrast in the sense that it is a linear combination of the population means. With equal n for a groups,

$$\mu = \sum_{j=1}^{a} \mu_j / a = \sum_{j=1}^{a} (1/a)\mu_j$$

Consider a general contrast of the form

$$\psi = \sum_{j=1}^{a} c_j \mu_j$$

Is ψ orthogonal to μ? Applying Equation 58 yields

$$(1/a)(c_1) + (1/a)(c_2) + \cdots + (1/a)(c_a)$$

as the sum of the products. Because $1/a$ is a common term, it can be factored out, resulting in

$$(1/a)(c_1 + c_2 + \cdots + c_a),$$

which equals $1/a \sum_{j=1}^{a} c_j$. This must equal zero for ψ to be orthogonal to μ, but we know $\sum_{j=1}^{a} c_j$ does equal zero, given the definition of a contrast. The $\sum_{j=1}^{a} c_j = 0$ condition also can be shown to apply for unequal n, given the more general definition of nonorthogonality. If we allowed contrasts in which $\sum_{j=1}^{a} c_j$ was nonzero, such a contrast would not be orthogonal to μ. Why should a contrast be orthogonal to μ? Contrasts should represent differences between the groups and should thus be insensitive to the mean score averaged over all groups. By requiring that $\sum_{j=1}^{a} c_j = 0$, the information obtained from ψ is independent of the grand mean and hence reflects pure differences between the groups. If a contrast in which $\sum_{j=1}^{a} c_j \neq 0$ is allowed, the information then reflects some combination of group differences and the size of the grand mean. For example, consider a four-group problem in which the experimenter decides to test a linear combination of population means with coefficients given by $c_1 = 2$, $c_2 = -1$, $c_3 = 0$, and $c_4 = 0$. Then, ψ can be written as

$$\psi = 2\mu_1 - \mu_2$$

However, we can re-express ψ as

$$\psi = (0.25 + 1.75)\mu_1 + (0.25 - 1.25)\mu_2 + (0.25 - 0.25)\mu_3 + (0.25 - 0.25)\mu_4$$

Rearranging terms yields

$$\begin{aligned} \psi &= (0.25\mu_1 + 0.25\mu_2 + 0.25\mu_3 + 0.25\mu_4) + 1.75\mu_1 - 1.25\mu_2 - 0.25\mu_3 - 0.25\mu_4 \\ &= \mu + (1.75\mu_1 - 1.25\mu_2 - 0.25\mu_3 - 0.25\mu_4) \end{aligned}$$

Thus, this linear combination equals the sum of the grand mean and a contrast whose coefficients sum to zero. Although statistical statements about the population magnitude of this linear combination could be made, the meaning of the results would be uninterpretable.

From the previous discussion, it might seem that researchers who want to test several contrasts involving a groups should be certain that these contrasts form an orthogonal set. However, this viewpoint is overly restrictive. Although there are statistical advantages to forming contrasts in an orthogonal manner, an investigator might nevertheless decide to test contrasts that are nonorthogonal. The reason for such a decision is very simple—when the investigator contemplates all hypotheses of scientific interest, the corresponding contrasts may be nonorthogonal. To answer the questions of interest, these contrasts should be tested. At the same time, the investigator should be aware that he or she is not extracting information on group differences as efficiently as could be done with orthogonal contrasts. Further guidelines for choosing an appropriate set of contrasts to be tested are developed in Chapter 5.

■

EXERCISES

*1. Write out the coefficients for contrasts to be used for testing each of the following hypotheses in a four group study.
   a. $H_0 : \mu_1 = \mu_2$
   b. $H_0 : \mu_1 = .5(\mu_2 + \mu_3)$
   c. $H_0 : \mu_2 = \mu_4$
   d. $H_0 : \mu_4 = 1/3(\mu_1 + \mu_2 + \mu_3)$

2. Which of the contrasts in Exercise 1 are pairwise? Which are complex?

*3. A psychologist collected data for three groups. The sample means are as follows: $\overline{Y}_1 = 12, \overline{Y}_2 = 10$, and $\overline{Y}_3 = 6$. The value of MS_W is 25, and there are 10 subjects in each group. The psychologist is interested in comparing the average of the Group 1 and 2 means to the Group 3 mean.
   a. The psychologist forms a contrast whose coefficients are given by .5, .5, and -1. Test this contrast for statistical significance.
   b. A colleague has suggested that it would be simpler to test a contrast with coefficients of 1, 1, and -2. Does this produce the same result as part a?
   c. What is the relationship between $(\hat{\psi})^2$ of part a and $(\hat{\psi})^2$ of part b? What is the relationship of $\Sigma_{j=1}^{a} c_j^2$ in part a to $\Sigma_{j=1}^{a} c_j^2$ in part b? Does this explain why the Σc_j^2 term is needed in Equation 41? Justify your answer.

4. Yet another contrast that might be used in Exercise 3 is one with coefficients of $-1, -1$, and 2. How does the F value for this contrast compare with the F value obtained in Exercise 3? What general rule does this illustrate?

5. Exercises 3 and 4 asked you to test a complex comparison in a three-group study. This exercise asks you to form a confidence interval for the same complex comparison. As before, the sample means are: $\overline{Y}_1 = 12, \overline{Y}_2 = 10$, and $\overline{Y}_3 = 6$. The value of MS_W is 25, and there are 10 subjects per group. Continue to assume that the psychologist is interested in comparing the average of the Group 1 and 2 means to the Group 3 mean.
   a. Form a 95% confidence interval for the contrast of interest. (Notice that with the available information, you must assume homogeneity of variance.)
   b. Does the confidence interval you found in part a agree with the results of the hypothesis test in Exercise 3? Explain your answer.
   c. Express the mean difference for this contrast as a standardized difference. How would you interpret this result?
   d. We saw in Exercise 3 that we could use coefficients of 1, 1, and -2 without changing the result of the hypothesis test. Can we also use these coefficients for forming a confidence interval without changing the result? Why or why not?

6. A psychologist conducted a study to compare several treatments for hyperactivity in children. Eleven subjects are randomly assigned to each condition, and the following data are obtained:

Group	Mean	Var (s^2)
Behavior therapy	12	11
Drug therapy	11	8
Placebo	7	12
Waiting list control	6	9

   a. Find the sum of squares for the comparison that contrasts the average of the two therapies with the average of Placebo and Waiting list.

   b. Test the comparison in part a for statistical significance.

   c. Find the value of R^2_{alerting} for the comparison in part a.

   d. Find the value of $R^2_{\text{effect size}}$ for the comparison in part a.

   e. Find the value of R^2_{contrast} for the comparison in part a.

   f. Explain the different meanings of each measure of association you calculated in parts c–e.

7. A study was conducted to compare four approaches for alleviating agoraphobia: placebo, cognitive, behavioral, and cognitive plus behavioral. The researcher's hypothesis is that the "cognitive plus behavioral" approach will be the most effective of the four approaches. Can a contrast with coefficients of $-1, -1, -1$, and 3 be used to test this hypothesis? Why or why not?

*8. A graduate student designed her master's thesis study with three groups: a cognitive intervention, a behavioral intervention, and a control group. A total of 50 subjects are randomly assigned to groups: 20 to each intervention and 10 to the control group. The following data are obtained:

	Cognitive	Behavioral	Control
Sample size	20	20	10
Mean	6.0	4.0	3.8
S.D. (s)	3.2	2.9	3.3

   a. Is there a statistically significant difference between the means of the Cognitive and the Behavioral groups?

   b. Is there a statistically significant difference between the means of the Cognitive and the Control groups?

   c. Which pair of means is more different—Cognitive and Behavioral or Cognitive and Control? How can you reconcile this fact with your answers to parts a and b?

9. Consider the data in Exercise 8 from the perspective of confidence intervals. You may assume homogeneity of variance throughout the problem.

   a. Form a 95% confidence interval for the difference between the means of the Cognitive and the Behavioral groups.

   b. Form a 95% confidence interval for the difference between the means of the Cognitive and the Control groups.

   c. Which interval is centered further away from zero? Why?

   d. Which interval is narrower?

   e. Which interval contains zero, and which interval excludes zero?

   f. How do your results in parts a–e help explain the hypothesis test results found in Exercise 8?

10. A psychologist is planning a three-group study in which he wants to test the following two comparisons: Group 1 versus Group 3 (ψ_1) and Group 2 versus Group 3 (ψ_2).

   Sixty subjects are available to participate in the study. His initial thought was to assign 20 subjects at random to each condition. However, after further thought, he has decided to assign twice as many subjects to the third group as to the first two groups because the third group is involved in both comparisons. (Notice that subjects are still randomly assigned to conditions.) Is this a good idea? To explore the answer to this question, we must consider the variances of the two contrasts. Why the variances? Both sample size–allocation schemes produce unbiased estimates of the population value ψ of the contrast in question. However, the two schemes differ in the imprecision—that is, the variance—of the estimate. It can be shown that (assuming homogeneity of variance) the population variance of a contrast is given by $\sigma^2 \Sigma_{j=1}^{a} c_j^2 / n_j$.

   a. Find an expression for the variance of $\hat{\psi}_1$ and $\hat{\psi}_2$, when 20 subjects are assigned to each treatment.

   b. Find an expression for the variance of $\hat{\psi}_1$ and $\hat{\psi}_2$ when 15 subjects are assigned to Group 1, 15 to Group 2, and 30 to Group 3.

   c. Which method of allocating subjects to groups is better for testing ψ_1 and ψ_2 if homogeneity holds?

   d. Will any allocation scheme yield a smaller variance than the two schemes already proposed? Consider the possibility of assigning 18 subjects to Group 1, 18 subjects to Group 2, and 24 subjects to Group 3. Find the variance of $\hat{\psi}_1$ and $\hat{\psi}_2$ and compare your answer to the answers you obtained in parts a and b.

e. All other things being equal, variance is minimized by assigning an equal number of subjects to each group. How does this help explain why the 18, 18, 24 scheme results in a lower variance than does the 15, 15, 30 scheme?

11. I. B. Normal, a graduate student at Skew U., conducted a study with four groups. The first three groups are treatment groups, and the fourth group is a control group. The following data are obtained:

Treatment 1	Treatment 2	Treatment 3	Control
9	7	5	4
8	8	7	5
7	7	6	2
10	4	7	7
5	5	4	5
9	5	7	7

a. Normal's adviser says that the first question Normal should address is whether the mean of the treatment subjects differs from the mean of the control subjects. The adviser tells her to perform a t test comparing the 18 treatment subjects to the 6 control subjects. In other words, the adviser recommends that the three treatment groups be combined into one group, ignoring (for this analysis) the distinction among the three treatment groups. What did Normal find? (HINT: It will be helpful for parts c and d that follow if you analyze these data as a one-way ANOVA, using the principles discussed in Chapter 3.)

b. Normal was rather disappointed with the result she obtained in part a. Being the obsessive type, she decided also to test a contrast whose coefficients were 1, 1, 1, and −3. What did she find?

c. Why are the results to parts a and b different? After all, they both compare treatment subjects to control subjects. To see why the results differ, we look at the numerator and the denominator of the F statistic individually. How does the value of the sum of squares for the contrast in part b compare to the value of the sum of squares between groups in part a?

d. How does the value of the within-group sum of squares in part b compare to the value of the within-group sum of squares in part a? Notice that the within-group sum of squares in part b is based on four groups, whereas the within-group sum of squares in part a is based on only two groups. As a consequence, the full model in part b has four parameters to be estimated, whereas the full model in part a has only two parameters.

e. Verify that the following expressions provide the correct sums of squares (within rounding error) for the full models in parts a and b. For part a:

$$E_F = \sum_{\substack{\text{Treatment} \\ \text{subjects}}} (Y_{ij} - 6.67)^2 + \sum_{\substack{\text{Control} \\ \text{subjects}}} (Y_{ij} - 5)^2$$

For part b:

$$E_F = \sum_{\text{Group 1}} (Y_{ij} - 8)^2 + \sum_{\text{Group 2}} (Y_{ij} - 6)^2 + \sum_{\text{Group 3}} (Y_{ij} - 6)^2 + \sum_{\text{Group 4}} (Y_{ij} - 5)^2$$

f. The between-group sum of squares for differences among the three treatment groups equals 16 for these data. How does this relate to the difference in the two approaches? Why?

g. Which approach do you think would generally be preferable—that of part a or part b? Why?

12. A graduate student has conducted a treatment study involving three treatments to alleviate depression. The first two groups are active treatment groups and the third group is a placebo control group. The following data are obtained:

Active Treatment 1	Active Treatment 2	Control
10	6	13
13	12	16
14	8	13
8	13	19
9	10	11
12	16	13

You may assume homogeneity of variance throughout all parts of this exercise.

a. Test whether the mean of Active Treatment 1 is different from the mean of the Control group.

b. Test whether the mean of Active Treatment 2 is different from the mean of the Control group.

c. Test whether the mean of the two Active Treatment groups combined is different from the mean of the Control group (i.e., form a complex comparison).

d. Form a 95% confidence interval for the mean difference between Active Treatment 1 and the Control group.

e. Form a 95% confidence interval for the mean difference between Active Treatment 2 and the Control group.

f. Form a 95% confidence interval for the difference between the mean of the two Active Treatment groups and the mean of the Control group.

g. Which of your intervals in parts d–f contain zero and which exclude zero? How does this relate to the tests you performed in parts a–c?

h. Where is the center of your intervals in parts d and e? Where is the center of your interval in part f? How can you reconcile these patterns with the results you reported in part g?

*13. The following data are obtained in a four-group study (to be done on computer or by hand).

	1	2	3	4
	3	7	9	11
	4	5	2	7
	5	6	5	11
	5	5	9	7
	3	7	5	4
Mean	4	6	6	8
Var (s^2)	1	1	9	9

This exercise asks you to compare the results of using MS_W to the results of using separate error terms when sample variances differ widely from one another.

a. Test a comparison of Group 3 versus Group 4, first using MS_W and then using a separate error term. How do the results compare?

b. Test a comparison of Group 1 versus Group 2, first using MS_W and then using a separate error term. How do the results compare? Do they support the common belief that the use of a separate error term is conservative? Explain your answer.

c. Test a comparison of the average of Groups 1 and 2 versus the average of Groups 3 and 4, first using MS_W and then using a separate error term. How do the results compare? In interpreting the relationship between the two approaches here, it is helpful to know that the test of an individual comparison is robust to violations of homogeneity of variance with equal n if and only if the absolute values of the coefficients for every group are equal to one another (see Note 5).

14. This exercise continues to examine the data in Exercise 13, but now from the perspective of confidence intervals.

a. Form a 95% confidence interval for the mean difference between Groups 3 and 4, assuming homogeneity of variance.

b. Form a 95% confidence interval for the mean difference between Groups 3 and 4, without assuming homogeneity of variance.

c. How do your results in parts a and b compare to one another? Explain your answer.

d. How does your answer to part c relate to your answer to part a of Exercise 13?

e. Form a 95% confidence interval for the mean difference between Groups 1 and 2, assuming homogeneity of variance.

f. Form a 95% confidence interval for the mean difference between Groups 1 and 2, without assuming homogeneity of variance.

g. How do your results in parts e and f compare to one another? Explain your answer.

h. How does your answer to part g relate to your answer to part b of Exercise 13?

i. Form a 95% confidence interval for the mean difference between the average of Groups 1 and 2 as compared to the average of Groups 3 and 4, assuming homogeneity of variance.

j. Form a 95% confidence interval for the mean difference between the average of Groups 1 and 2 as compared to the average of Groups 3 and 4, without assuming homogeneity of variance.

k. How do your results in parts i and j compare to one another? Explain your answer.

15. A psychologist designs a study with four independent groups. However, the number of subjects in each group is very unequal: $n_1 = 10$, $n_2 = 50$, $n_3 = 50$, and $n_4 = 10$. One specific comparison of interest is the contrast of Groups 1 and 4. Believing that homogeneity of variance holds here, he decides to use MS_W as the error term for his comparison. However, his research assistant argues that even with homogeneity, the data in Groups 2 and 3 should be completely ignored because Groups 1 and 4 are so much smaller. In other words, the research assistant maintains that the large samples for Groups 2 and 3 make the observed F for comparing Groups 1 and 4 much larger than it would be if a separate error term were used (i.e., an error term based just on Groups 1 and 4). Thus, even with homogeneity, the test should be based only on the 10 subjects in Group 1 and 10 subjects in Group 4 to avoid an inflated F from the large sample in Groups 2 and 3.

a. Would you expect the observed F to be larger using MS_W instead of a separate error term, if homogeneity holds? Why or why not? (HINT: How would you expect MS_W to compare to the error term given by Equation 42, if homogeneity holds?)

b. How does the critical F based on MS_W compare to the critical F based on a separate error term?

c. Which approach is preferable, if homogeneity holds?

16. Is the following set of contrasts among four groups (i.e., $a = 4$) orthogonal?

	1	2	3	4
ψ_1	1	−1	0	0
ψ_2	1	1	0	−2
ψ_3	1	1	−3	1
ψ_4	0	0	−1	1

Show your work or explain your answer.

17. In a six-group study, an investigator wants to test the following two comparisons:

$$\mu_1 + \mu_2 + \mu_3 - \mu_4 - \mu_5 - \mu_6 \quad \text{and} \quad \mu_1 + \mu_2 - 2\mu_3$$

Construct three additional comparisons that yield an orthogonal set. Assume equal n.

EXTENSION: DERIVATION OF SUM OF SQUARES FOR A CONTRAST

Chapter 4 presents a very general expression for the sum of squares associated with a specific individual comparison. Specifically, the chapter claims that such a sum of squares can be written as

$$E_R - E_F = (\hat{\psi})^2 \bigg/ \sum_{j=1}^{a} \left(c_j^2/n_j\right) \tag{E.1}$$

The purpose of this extension is to derive this expression. Arguably, the simplest method of derivation relies on matrix algebra. However, it is also possible to obtain the derivation without resorting to matrices, an approach we use here.

We begin by writing an expression for the sum of squared errors for the restricted model. We then see that part of this expression contains the formula for the sum of squared errors of the full model, which naturally leads to an easy way to write the difference between the sums of squared errors of the two models.

Each subject's error in the restricted model is the difference between the subject's actual score and the score predicted by the model. Thus, the sum of squared errors of the restricted model equals

$$E_R = \sum_{j=1}^{a} \sum_{i=1}^{n_j} (Y_{ij} - \hat{\mu}_j)^2 \tag{E.2}$$

Under the null hypothesis, the predicted score for an individual in group j can be written as

$$\hat{\mu}_j = \overline{Y}_j - \left(1 \bigg/ \sum_{j=1}^{a} \left(c_j^2/n_j\right)\right)(c_j/n_j)(\hat{\psi}) \tag{E.3}$$

The notation of Equation E.3 can be simplified by realizing that the sum of squared contrast coefficients divided by sample size is a constant for any given contrast. We arbitrarily use the letter k to represent this sum. In other words, we simply establish the following notation:

$$k = \sum_{j=1}^{a} \left(c_j^2/n_j\right) \tag{E.4}$$

in which case Equation E.3 can be rewritten as

$$\hat{\mu}_j = \overline{Y}_j - (1/k)(c_j/n_j)(\hat{\psi}) \tag{E.5}$$

Substituting for $\hat{\mu}_j$ from Equation E.5 into Equation E.2 yields

$$E_R = \sum_{j=1}^{a} \sum_{i=1}^{n_j} [Y_{ij} - \overline{Y}_j + (1/k)(c_j/n_j)(\hat{\psi})]^2 \tag{E.6}$$

Expanding the square and regarding the expression to the left of the plus sign as one term and the expression to the right as a second term allows Equation E.6 to be rewritten as

$$E_R = \sum_{j=1}^{a} \sum_{i=1}^{n_j} (Y_{ij} - \overline{Y}_j)^2 + \sum_{j=1}^{a} \sum_{i=1}^{n_j} (1/k)^2 \left(c_j^2/n_j^2\right)(\hat{\psi})^2 + 2\sum_{j=1}^{a} \sum_{i=1}^{n_j} (Y_{ij} - \overline{Y}_j)(1/k)(c_j/n_j)(\hat{\psi})$$

$$\tag{E.7}$$

Equation E.7 can be simplified in three ways: (1) The very first term is identical to the sum of squared errors for the full model, so this term can be rewritten as E_F; (2) k and $(\hat{\psi})$ are constants, so they can be moved outside the summation over both individuals and groups; and (3) c_j and n_j are constants within a group, so they can be moved outside the summation over individuals. Incorporating these simplifications yields

$$E_R = E_F + (1/k)^2(\hat{\psi})^2 \left(\sum_{j=1}^{a} n_j (c_j^2/n_j^2) \right) + 2(1/k)(\hat{\psi}) \left(\sum_{j=1}^{a} c_j/n_j \sum_{i=1}^{n_j} (Y_{ij} - \overline{Y}_j) \right) \qquad \text{(E.8)}$$

Notice that Equation E.8 expresses E_R as the sum of three components. However, we can simplify this expression greatly by realizing that the third component must equal zero, because the sum of deviations around the mean is always zero. We can also simplify the middle component by canceling the n_j in the numerator with one of the n_j squared terms in the denominator. As a consequence, Equation E.8 reduces to

$$E_R = E_F + (1/k)^2(\hat{\psi})^2 \left(\sum_{j=1}^{a} c_j^2/n_j \right) \qquad \text{(E.9)}$$

Looking back at Equation E.4, we see that the final term in parentheses is identical to what we chose to label as k, so we could rewrite Equation E.9 as

$$E_R = E_F + (1/k)^2(\hat{\psi})^2(k) \qquad \text{(E.10)}$$

which then reduces to

$$E_R = E_F + (\hat{\psi})^2/k \qquad \text{(E.11)}$$

Finally, we move E_F to the left side of the equation, and we substitute from Equation E.4 for k, which leads to

$$E_R - E_F = (\hat{\psi})^2 \left/ \sum_{j=1}^{a} (c_j^2/n_j) \right. \qquad \text{(E.12)}$$

Thus, we have shown that the sum of squares associated with a contrast can indeed be written as shown in Equation E.1, as claimed in the body of Chapter 4.

5

Testing Several Contrasts: The Multiple-Comparisons Problem

In Chapter 4, you learned how to test individual comparisons among means and assess their practical significance through such procedures as confidence intervals and effect size measures. You were also introduced to the concepts of linear independence and orthogonality. As these two concepts demonstrate, several contrasts are often tested on the same set of data. Linear independence and orthogonality concern the degree of overlap in information obtained from testing several contrasts among a groups. In this chapter, another issue that arises in testing several contrasts is considered. We will approach this issue primarily from the perspective of hypothesis testing, but we will see that the issue is also relevant for confidence intervals.

MULTIPLE COMPARISONS

Experimentwise and Per-Comparison Error Rates

We begin by considering the example from the beginning of the previous chapter, where there are four treatments for hypertension to be compared. Suppose it was decided to test the following three contrasts:

$$\psi_1 = \mu_1 - \mu_2$$
$$\psi_2 = \tfrac{1}{2}(\mu_1 + \mu_2) - \mu_3$$
$$\psi_3 = \tfrac{1}{3}(\mu_1 + \mu_2 + \mu_3) - \mu_4$$

Assuming equal n, these three contrasts form an orthogonal set, as we verified near the end of Chapter 4. Suppose that each of these contrasts is tested using an alpha level of .05. If the four treatments are in fact equally effective, how likely are we to obtain at least one significant result in our study? In other words, how probable is it that we will make at least one Type I error? The answer is obviously a number greater than .05 because we are performing three different tests at the .05 level. At first glance, the answer might seem to be .05 × 3, or .15. Although .15 is a number we return to momentarily, it is not the answer to this question. Recall from probability theory that probabilities of events cannot be summed unless the events are mutually exclusive, that is, unless the occurrence of one event rules out the occurrence of another. This is not the case here, because if the H_0 for ψ_1 is mistakenly rejected, the hypotheses for ψ_2 and ψ_3 might or might not be rejected. It turns out that for orthogonal contrasts, the binomial formula provides an answer to our question:

$$\Pr\,(\text{at least one Type I error}) = 1 - \Pr\,(\text{no Type I errors}) \tag{1}$$

$$= 1 - (1 - \alpha)^C$$

where α is the alpha level for a single contrast and C is the number of contrasts tested. For our example, then, $\alpha = .05$ and $C = 3$. Substituting into Equation 1, we find that the probability of at least one Type I error in our study is .143.

Before we comment further on this number, several comments on Equation 1 are in order. First, the expression $1 - (1 - \alpha)^C$ is obtained from the binomial formula for the probability of at least one success in C trials, when the probability of a success on a single trial is α. It may be necessary to remind oneself that here a "success" is a Type I error. Second, Equation 1 is only appropriate when the C contrasts to be tested form an orthogonal set, because the binomial requires an assumption that the C trials be statistically independent. This assumption is not met for nonorthogonal contrasts, so Equation 1 is inappropriate unless the contrasts are orthogonal. Third, strictly speaking, Equation 1 holds only for large n, because although the $\hat{\psi}$ values of orthogonal contrasts are uncorrelated, the F tests all use the same denominator term—namely, MS_W, assuming homogeneity of variance. Thus, the F tests are not strictly independent. However, this is a technical point and need not concern us.

Let's return to our value of .143. Remember that this is the probability of committing at least one Type I error in the study. Is this a problem? After all, it seemed that our alpha level was .05, but now we are saying that our probability of a Type I error is almost three times as large as .05. To clarify this issue, it is helpful to develop some terminology. First, the *error rate per contrast* (α_{PC}) is the probability that a particular contrast will be falsely declared significant. In other words, if a contrast whose true population value is zero were to be tested over and over again in repeated studies, α_{PC} is the proportion of times that the contrast would be found to be statistically significant. Second, the *expected number of errors per experiment* (ENEPE) is the expected number of contrasts that will be falsely declared significant in a single experiment.[1] Notice that ENEPE is not a probability and in fact can exceed one under some circumstances. Third, the *experimentwise error rate* (α_{EW}) is the probability that one or more contrasts will be falsely declared significant in an experiment. In other words, if an experiment were to be conducted repeatedly, α_{EW} is the proportion of those experiments (in the long run) that would contain at least one Type I error. Fourth, in designs with more than one factor, it is necessary to define yet another error rate, called the *familywise error rate* (α_{FW}). As discussed in more detail in Chapter 7, in multifactor designs, significance tests involving different factors are usually regarded as constituting different families. For this reason, a single experiment may contain several families of tests, in which case α_{FW} and α_{EW} are different. However, in single-factor designs, which is all that we have discussed until now, α_{FW} and α_{EW} are identical, so we will wait until Chapter 7 to discuss familywise error rate.

The distinctions among these three types of error rates (i.e., α_{PC}, α_{EW}, and ENEPE) can perhaps best be understood by returning to our example, with four groups and three contrasts to be tested. In this example, α_{PC} is equal to .05, because each comparison was tested at an alpha level of .05. For any single comparison, there is a 5% chance of a Type I error. What is the value of ENEPE? ENEPE will equal .15 because the expected number of Type I errors per contrast is .05 and there are three contrasts tested in the experiment. In general, with C contrasts each tested at an alpha level of α_{PC}, ENEPE equals $C\alpha_{PC}$. Finally, α_{EW} is the probability of at least one Type I error being made in the experiment. Earlier, we found that this probability equals .143.

That there are three types of error rates and that each has a different numerical value here poses a problem. Even though the value of .05 is somewhat arbitrary, at least it provides an objective standard for making decisions in most disciplines that employ inferential statistics. So, suppose that we can agree that .05 is the standard we wish to use. The problem that immediately confronts us is: Which error rate should be .05? In our four-group example, α_{PC} was .05, but ENEPE and α_{EW} exceeded .05. What if we were to have chosen either ENEPE or α_{EW} to be .05? In this case, it turns out that α_{PC} must be less than .05 whenever more than a single contrast is tested in an experiment. Thus, when multiple contrasts are tested, it is impossible to achieve a .05 value for all three types of error. Instead, a decision must be made regarding which type of error is to be controlled at the 5% level.

Although this is an issue about which reasonable people may choose to differ, our preference is to control α_{EW} at .05. The basic argument in favor of this approach is that there must be an explicit control on the number of studies in the literature that contain Type I errors. By keeping α_{EW} at .05, the probability of a Type I error occurring anywhere in a given experiment is at most .05. If instead we were to control α_{PC} or ENEPE at .05, studies with multiple tests would produce Type I errors more than 5% of the time. Many of these studies might then report statistically significant results in the published literature. Even though the error rate for the study as a whole may be inflated, these studies may be accepted for publication unless journals require that α_{EW} instead of α_{PC} be controlled at .05. As Greenwald (1975) pointed out, allowing such studies to be published without controlling α_{EW} is a major problem, because it is difficult in many fields to publish studies claiming to demonstrate the lack of an effect. As a consequence, studies that unbeknownst to us report Type I errors are likely to go uncorrected because subsequent studies of the phenomenon will likely produce nonsignificant results. Although failing to reject the null hypothesis is obviously appropriate when it is in fact true, there is nevertheless a problem if journals tend not to publish papers claiming to support the null hypothesis. Controlling the alpha level for the study instead of for the individual comparison makes it less likely that studies will report Type I errors in the first place. This is one reason that most methodologists advocate controlling the alpha level for the study instead of for the individual comparison. However, in so doing, it does not necessarily follow that 5% of published findings represent Type I errors. (See Greenwald, 1975, for an interesting discussion of this issue.) If, instead, α_{PC} were controlled at .05, studies with multiple contrasts would have a higher Type I-error rate than .05. In this situation, an experimenter could increase his or her chances of obtaining a statistically significant result simply by testing many contrasts. By choosing to set α_{EW} rather than α_{PC} at .05, this problem is avoided. Of course, it might be argued that the structure imposed by a single experiment is rather arbitrary. Miller (1981, pp. 31–32) provides a humorous discussion along these lines:

> Two extremes of behavior are open to anyone involved in statistical inference. A non-multiple comparisonist regards each separate statistical statement as a family, and does not give increased protection to any group of statements through group error rates. At the other extreme is the ultraconservative statistician who has just a single family consisting of every statistical statement he might make during his lifetime. If all statisticians operated in this latter fashion at the 5 percent level, then 95 percent of the world's statisticians would never falsely reject a null hypothesis, and 5 percent would be guilty of some sin against nullity. There are a few statisticians who would adhere to the first principle, but the author has never met one of the latter variety.

Why do you suppose Miller has never met such an ultraconservative statistician—after all, aren't statisticians stereotypically considered to be rather conservative? Suppose there was such a statistician somewhere. Further suppose he or she figures that the total number of statistical hypotheses he or she might test in a lifetime is 1,000. This set of 1,000 hypotheses then can be thought of as an "experiment" in terms of Type I error. Algebraic manipulation of Equation 1 shows that

$$\alpha_{PC} = 1 - \sqrt[c]{1 - \alpha_{EW}} \tag{2}$$

for unrelated hypotheses. If, for simplicity, we assume that the 1,000 hypothesis tests are independent and that α_{EW} is to be kept at .05, Equation 2 tells us that α_{PC} must be set at .0000513, or, essentially, .05 divided by 1,000. If you remember that there is an inverse relationship between Type I and Type II errors, it should be obvious that in lowering the alpha level from .05 to .00005, we are inevitably increasing the probability of a Type II error. In other words, if we decide to control α_{EW} rather than α_{PC} at .05, we must set α_{PC} at .00005. As a result, the power to detect real effects (differences) in the population is greatly diminished. The same effect occurs anytime we decide to control α_{EW} at .05, although the magnitude of the effect is much weaker when the number of hypotheses in the experiment is not so large. Indeed, in this sense, the decision about controlling α_{EW} or α_{PC} at .05 really involves a trade-off between Type I and Type II errors.

SIMULTANEOUS CONFIDENCE INTERVALS

Although much of the focus of this chapter will be on hypothesis testing, the concept of multiple comparisons is also relevant for confidence intervals. Consider an example where $a = 3$, and the goal is to form three 95% confidence intervals, one for each pairwise difference between means, that is, $\mu_1 - \mu_2$, $\mu_1 - \mu_3$, and $\mu_2 - \mu_3$. Because more than one interval is being formed, the 95% figure could take on either of two meanings. First, the confidence level might be 95% for each interval considered individually. In other words, for a single pairwise difference, 95% of such intervals would contain the true difference. Second, the 95% figure might pertain to the entire collection of intervals, in which case it is referred to as a 95% simultaneous confidence interval. In other words, (in this case) 95% of the time that three such intervals were constructed, all three would contain the true difference. A 95% confidence interval for a single contrast is directly analogous to a hypothesis test where $\alpha_{PC} = .05$, whereas a 95% simultaneous confidence interval is directly analogous to a collection of hypothesis tests where $\alpha_{EW} = .05$.

We will see that simultaneous confidence intervals can be constructed for many but not all multiple comparisons procedures. For the methods we recommend in this book, the formation of simultaneous confidence intervals follows one basic formula. To form a confidence interval for a contrast ψ, under the assumption of homogeneity, the interval is given by

$$\hat{\psi} \pm w \sqrt{MS_w \sum_{j=1}^{a} \left(c_j^2 / n_j\right)} \tag{3}$$

where w depends on the multiple comparison procedure employed. Looking back at Chapter 4, you might realize that Equation 3 bears a striking resemblance to Equation 4.48:

$$\hat{\psi} \pm \sqrt{F_{\alpha;1,N-a}} \sqrt{MS_w \sum_{j=1}^{a} \left(c_j^2 / n_j\right)} \tag{4.48}$$

Recall that we developed this equation as a confidence interval for a single contrast. This implies that choosing w equal to $\sqrt{F_{\alpha;1,N-a}}$ is equivalent to controlling confidence at the per-interval level. In other words, this choice does not produce simultaneous confidence intervals. However, we will see momentarily that by choosing w differently we can obtain simultaneous confidence intervals. We will also see that similar but slightly more complicated expressions can be used when homogeneity is questionable.

For these recommended procedures, there is a direct correspondence between the confidence interval and the hypothesis test. The null hypothesis is rejected if and only if the simultaneous confidence interval fails to contain the hypothesized value of ψ (which in almost all applications is zero). Thus, proper interpretation of a simultaneous confidence interval conveys the information contained in a hypothesis test for each of these multiple-comparison procedures. However, a simultaneous confidence interval is often more informative than the corresponding hypothesis test because the interval shows both the magnitude of the difference and the precision with which the magnitude is estimated.

Levels of Strength of Inference

Anytime multiple inferences are to be made, researchers face a choice about how to control the error rate. So far we have seen that two choices are to control either α_{EW} or α_{PC} at .05. In fact, there are yet other choices we will now describe. Once a researcher has chosen a desired level of control (also referred to as a level of inference), the next step is to choose a statistical technique to provide the appropriate level of control. Unfortunately, in practice, there is the appearance that all too often the statistical technique is chosen first, and only later (if at all) does the researcher seriously think about level of inference. Thus, our presentation here has two related goals. First, we need to describe the pros and cons of each of the levels of inference, so you can make an informed choice about which level you believe is most appropriate for your situation. Second, we need to describe statistical techniques that allow you to control your Type I error rate at the desired level of inference.

Hsu (1996) describes five levels of strength of inference, each of which corresponds to a choice of how best to control the error rate. Table 5.1 lists these levels from weakest to strongest (top to bottom). The weakest level of inference is simply to control the per comparison alpha level and thus make no adjustment whatsoever for multiple tests. A statistically significant result obtained by a researcher who chooses this level of inference allows a conclusion that this specific contrast is truly nonzero, but provides absolutely no protection against inflating the Type I error rate with regard to the set of contrasts being tested. The next weakest level of inference controls the alpha level for a "test of homogeneity." A statistically significant result at this level allows a researcher to state that a difference exists among a set of population means, but it does not allow a statement about which specific means differ from one another. Hsu's third level is "confident inequalities." This level is stronger than the previous level because it allows a statement about specific means that differ from one another. However, only at the fourth level, "confident directions," is there justification for a statement that one mean is larger or smaller than another. In other words, at Levels 2 and 3, a researcher can legitimately claim only that some form of difference exists, but cannot legitimately proclaim the direction of any such differences. The fifth and strongest level, "confidence intervals," not only allows a statement of direction, but also allows a statement about the size of the difference between means.

Thus, one step in choosing how to proceed in the face of multiple inferences is to choose a level of strength of inference from Table 5.1. Our general recommendation, which agrees with Hsu (1996), is to choose techniques (to be described momentarily) that provide inference

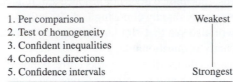

TABLE 5.1
HSU'S (1996) LEVELS OF INFERENCE
FOR MULTIPLE COMPARISONS

1. Per comparison	Weakest
2. Test of homogeneity	
3. Confident inequalities	
4. Confident directions	
5. Confidence intervals	Strongest

at either the confidence intervals or confident directions level. Anything less than this simply tells us that means are different, but does not tell us in what direction they differ. Except in rare cases, knowledge of direction seems essential, both scientifically and practically.

You might wonder why we are spending so much time on this topic. One reason is that many researchers have failed to appreciate the distinctions among the levels shown in Table 5.1. All too often in the published literature, one finds a journal article where the author has used a statistical technique that provides inference only at level 2 or 3, yet the author has gone right ahead and interpreted his or her results in terms of direction of mean differences. However, such an interpretation demands a technique appropriate for level 4 or 5.

Thus, although we stressed that many of the choices in this chapter are more subjective than simple "right versus wrong," it is also true that some interpretations of results are literally wrong in the sense that the technique chosen to analyze the data does not answer the true question of interest. As Tukey (1991) states:

> Statisticians classically asked the wrong question—and were willing to answer with a lie, and one that was often a downright lie. They asked "Are the effects of *A* and *B* different?" and they were willing to answer "no."
>
> ... asking "Are the effects different?" is foolish.
>
> What we should be answering first is "Can we tell the direction in which the effects of *A* differ from the effects of *B*?"

We agree with both Tukey and Hsu, and thus emphasize techniques at the highest level of inference. In any event, the most important point may be that researchers who choose to use techniques corresponding to lower levels must realize the limitations of the statements that they are justified in making based on their choice of technique.

Types of Contrasts

Hsu (1996) classifies techniques for handling multiple inferences in terms of two dimensions. We have just seen that one of these dimensions is level of strength of inference. The second dimension is the type of contrast to be tested. We will consider four types of contrasts: (1) pairwise, (2) complex, (3) comparisons with a control, and (4) comparisons with the best. We will describe each of these in detail as we progress through the chapter, so for the moment we will provide only a brief preview. The important point for now is that the choice of an appropriate technique to address multiple inference should depend on the type of questions being asked. For example, different techniques are appropriate when all contrasts to be examined are pairwise than when some complex contrasts are also of interest. In some situations, a preselected set of contrasts may be of interest. For example, the specific goal of a study may be to compare each of several treatment groups to a control group, leading to the third type of contrast in Hsu's conceptualization. Or, an example of the fourth type of contrast occurs when the goal is to determine the best treatment based on data obtained in an experiment. As we will see shortly, each of these situations calls for a particular technique to analyze data appropriately.

Overview of Techniques

Not only is the choice of a multiple comparison technique somewhat arbitrary, but the choice is complicated by the great variety of available options. As of this writing, both SAS and SPSS offer at least a dozen choices, any one of which can be instantly selected by a simple click of a computer mouse. Although the instant availability of these techniques is obviously convenient, it also can lead to researchers reporting results based on a choice that does not really correspond to their situation. The choice may not reflect an appropriate level of strength of inference, or the choice may not correspond to the type of contrast examined by the researcher. Thus, while we will describe how to perform a variety of tests, our primary goal in this chapter is to delineate situations where different types of techniques are appropriate. Table 5.2 is a variation of a table presented by Hsu (1996), showing where the most popular multiple comparison procedures fit into a two-dimensional framework of (1) level of strength of inference and (2) type of contrast.

As we stated previously, we believe that with rare exception, techniques must provide information about the direction of differences in group means if they are to be useful. Thus, we largely restrict our attention to techniques that satisfy this requirement. Readers who are convinced that their specific situation does not demand this level of inference may want to consult such sources as Hsu (1996) and Toothaker (1991) for descriptions of other techniques.

To provide a structure for reading the rest of the chapter, we present a brief overview of the multiple-comparisons procedures we recommend. First, when a researcher plans to test a small number of contrasts based on theoretical hypotheses prior to data collection, a technique known as the Bonferroni adjustment is appropriate. Second, when all pairwise comparisons are of potential interest, Tukey (1953) developed a procedure to maintain α_{EW} at .05. Third, Scheffé's procedure can be used when an investigator decides to test complex comparisons

TABLE 5.2
TWO-DIMENSIONAL CONCEPTUALIZATION OF MULTIPLE COMPARISON PROCEDURES[†]

	Planned	All Pairwise	Some Complex	Comparisons With a Control	Comparisons With the Best
Per comparison		Duncan			
Test of homogeneity		Newman–Keuls			
		LSD			
		Tukey's-b			
Confident inequalities		REGW-Q			
		REGW-F			
Confident directions				See Hsu (1996)	
Confidence intervals	Bonferroni*	Tukey WSD*	Scheffe*	Dunnett*	Edwards–Hsu*
	Sidak*	Dunnett's T3*			Hsu*
		Games–Howell*			
		Hochberg's GT2			
		(or SMM)			
		Gabriel			

[†] Rows indicate strength of inference and columns indicate type of contrasts of interest.

*We recommend this technique in certain situations, see the text for details.

suggested by the data. In other words, Scheffé's method permits "data snooping," so that even after having examined the data, multiple tests can be performed, and α_{EW} will be maintained at .05. Fourth, occasionally, the only questions of interest involve comparing a control group to each of several treatment groups. Dunnett developed a procedure appropriate for this situation. Fifth, especially in applied studies, the major goal may be to determine the best treatment. Hsu has shown how Dunnett's method can be modified in this situation. As of this writing, this method has been greatly underutilized in the behavioral sciences and is not yet widely available in statistical software. However, we believe it deserves much more attention than it has received to date, so we will feature it later in the chapter.

We first consider why it is important whether contrasts to be tested have been selected prior to or after having collected the data. Then we present the Bonferroni, Tukey, Scheffé, and Dunnett procedures. Besides describing the mechanics of how to perform each test, we also develop the logic behind each technique. This discussion of logical underpinnings is especially important because we have seen that the literature is filled with many more multiple-comparisons procedures than just these four. As a result, you need to understand what it is that these four methods accomplish that many competing methods do not. To further attain this goal, after presenting the four techniques we recommend, we also briefly discuss liabilities of some of the more popular competitors. Finally, we also present a flowchart (i.e., a decision tree) to help you decide which technique should be used in a particular situation.

Planned Versus Post Hoc Contrasts

As might be expected, controlling α_{EW} at .05 is considerably more difficult than simply deciding to use an alpha level of .05 for each contrast to be tested. The first step in our task distinguishes between planned and post hoc contrasts. A *planned contrast* is a contrast that the experimenter decided to test prior to any examination of the data. A *post hoc contrast*, on the other hand, is a contrast that the experimenter decided to test only after having observed some or all of the data. For this reason, it is often said that a post hoc contrast is a contrast suggested by the data.

Why is the distinction between planned and post hoc contrasts important? The importance can be illustrated by the following example. Suppose that a researcher obtains the following means in a four-group study: $\overline{Y}_1 = 50$, $\overline{Y}_2 = 44$, $\overline{Y}_3 = 52$, and $\overline{Y}_4 = 60$. Consider the single contrast $\mu_2 - \mu_4$. There is an important difference between deciding in advance to compare Groups 2 and 4 versus deciding after having looked at the data to compare these two groups. The difference can be exemplified most easily by supposing that unbeknown to the researcher all four population means are equal, that is

$$\mu_1 = \mu_2 = \mu_3 = \mu_4 \tag{4}$$

If the comparison of Groups 2 and 4 has been planned and $\alpha_{PC} = .05$ is used, then (in the long run) 5 out of every 100 times the experiment would be conducted, the contrast would be statistically significant and a Type I error would have been committed. However, suppose that this contrast had not been planned. How would things change? Suppose that the study were repeated, yielding a different set of sample means: $\overline{Y}_1 = 46$, $\overline{Y}_2 = 57$, $\overline{Y}_3 = 49$, and $\overline{Y}_4 = 54$. From inspecting these data, it is doubtful that an experimenter would decide to compare Groups 2 and 4. Instead, this time the data suggest that the comparison of Groups 1 and 2 should be investigated. In other words, if the contrast to be tested is suggested by the data, it is only natural that the largest difference between means be tested because the usual goal of hypothesis testing is to obtain a statistically significant result. Suppose that a procedure was followed where this largest difference is always tested using an α level of .05 for the contrast. The result would be that the probability of committing a Type I error would greatly exceed .05, especially for large a. The crucial point is that $\overline{Y}_2 - \overline{Y}_4$ has a very different sampling distribution from $\overline{Y}_{max} - \overline{Y}_{min}$, where $\overline{Y}_{max}$ and $\overline{Y}_{min}$ are the largest and smallest sample means, respectively. The critical value of the F distribution that provides an alpha level of .05 for judging the significance of $\overline{Y}_2 - \overline{Y}_4$ is too small for judging the significance of $\overline{Y}_{max} - \overline{Y}_{min}$. The point of this discussion has simply been to convince you that it matters greatly whether a contrast is planned or has been selected post hoc. We now turn to a consideration of procedures for testing more than one planned comparison in a study. In the following section, we consider how to test post hoc contrasts, where such topics as the sampling distribution of $\overline{Y}_{max} - \overline{Y}_{min}$ become relevant.

MULTIPLE PLANNED COMPARISONS

We illustrate the use of multiple planned comparisons by an example. Consider a four-group study whose purpose is to investigate the effects of strategy training on a memory task for children of two age levels. Independent samples of 6-year-olds and 8-year-olds are obtained. One half of the children in each group are assigned to a strategy-training condition, and the other half receive no training and serve as a control group. The general question of interest concerns the effect of strategy training on mean level of memory task performance for the two age groups.

How should the investigator attempt to answer this question? If the investigator has not planned to compare specific groups prior to collecting data, a test of the omnibus null hypothesis for all four groups could be performed. If the test were nonsignificant, no further tests would be performed; if the test were significant, contrasts suggested by the data might be further tested. Although this approach is entirely permissible, we defer discussion of it for the moment. Instead, we discuss an alternative approach whereby the investigator plans to test a number of specific hypotheses instead of the general omnibus hypothesis. For example, suppose that an investigator decides prior to obtaining data that he or she is interested in testing the following contrasts in our four-group study:

$$\psi_1 = \mu_{T6} - \mu_{C6}$$

$$\psi_2 = \mu_{T8} - \mu_{C8}$$

$$\psi_3 = \tfrac{1}{2}(\mu_{T6} + \mu_{C6}) - \tfrac{1}{2}(\mu_{T8} + \mu_{C8})$$

In this instance, the first subscript represents treatment (T) or control (C), and the second subscript represents the child's age group (6 or 8). The first contrast equals the effect of training for 6-year-olds, the second equals the effect for 8-year-olds, and the third equals an age effect averaged over condition. We should hasten to point out that we are not claiming these are the three "correct" contrasts to test. What is "correct" depends on the scientific questions the study is designed to answer. For our purposes, we assume that these three contrasts have been chosen to allow us to address the questions of scientific interest. Keep in mind, however, that a researcher with different goals might formulate a very different set of contrasts. Indeed, even the number of contrasts might be very different from three.

Assuming that these three contrasts have been chosen, how should the investigator proceed? The first step is to compute an F statistic for each contrast. This can be accomplished using any of the approaches described in Chapter 4. For example, if we are willing to assume homogeneity of variance, Equation 4.41 might be used:

$$F = \frac{(\hat{\psi})^2 \Big/ \sum_{j=1}^{a} (c_j^2/n_j)}{MS_W}$$

(4.41, repeated)

Suppose that we have done this calculation for our first contrast, and we obtained an F value equal to 4.23. Let's say there were 11 participants per group, so this F value has 1 and 40 degrees of freedom associated with it. Can we reject the null hypothesis that the population value of the first contrast is zero? If we refer to an F table, the critical F for an alpha of .05 with 1 and 40 degrees of freedom is 4.08. The observed F exceeds the critical F, which would seem to imply a statistically significant result. However, recall our earlier distinction between α_{PC} and α_{EW}. The procedure that was just described used .05 for α_{PC}. However, earlier we demonstrated that if three orthogonal contrasts (with equal n) are each tested with an alpha of .05, then $\alpha_{EW} = .143$. In other words, if we test ψ_1, ψ_2, and ψ_3 using $\alpha_{PC} = .05$ for each, there is a 14.3% chance of committing at least one Type I error. This seems to defeat the primary purpose behind inferential statistics, namely, to avoid a declaration of a difference between groups (or a relationship between variables) where in fact none exists in the population.

Bonferroni Adjustment

Instead of letting α_{EW} be at the mercy of α_{PC}, it seems reasonable to work backward. In other words, it would be preferable to control α_{EW} at .05, but to accomplish this, α_{PC} would have to be lowered by some amount. The problem is to determine an appropriate value of α_{PC} to result in $\alpha_{EW} = .05$. It turns out that there is a remarkably simple and intuitive solution. In the general case of C hypotheses to be tested, set α_{PC} at $.05/C$. It can be proven mathematically that with this procedure, α_{EW} will be .05 or less. To use this approach in our current example, α_{PC} would be set equal to .05/3, or .0167. The critical F for $p = .0167$ with 1 and 40 degrees of freedom is 6.25, which is naturally somewhat larger than the value of 4.08 that we found for α_{PC} equal to .05. In fact, we would now judge our observed F of 4.23 to be nonsignificant because it fails to exceed the critical value of 6.25. In an actual study, the second and third contrasts would also be tested for significance. The use of α_{PC} values other than .05 can sometimes be awkward in practice, because appropriate tables of the F distribution may be unavailable. There are two possible solutions to this problem. Appendix Table A.3 can be used to find critical values for an F distribution with 1 numerator degree of freedom and an α_{PC} equal to $.05/C$ (two-tailed). Each row of the table represents a particular value for denominator degrees of freedom, and each column represents a value of C. It should be noted that the table only applies to F distributions with 1 numerator degree of freedom. This limitation poses no problem for testing a contrast because such a test has 1 degree of freedom in the numerator; however, there are other procedures similar to the method we discuss that involve more than 1 numerator degree of freedom. Appendix Table A.3 could not be used for this situation. Second, if a computer program analyzes your data and if the program provides a p value in the output, the Bonferroni adjustment is extremely easy to apply. All that must be done is to compare the p value from the printout with $.05/C$, because $.05/C$ is the per-comparison alpha level. The contrast is statistically significant if and only if the p value is below $.05/C$. Notice that this procedure works as well in the more general case, where the numerator degrees of freedom exceed 1.

At this point, more detail for the rationale behind the $.05/C$ adjustment must be provided. The procedure was first applied to the problem of multiple contrasts by Dunn (1961), so the

Bonferroni adjustment is also known as Dunn's procedure. She based the procedure on an inequality derived by the Italian mathematician Bonferroni, who proved mathematically that

$$1 - (1 - \alpha)^C \leq C\alpha \tag{5}$$

for any value of C whenever $0 \leq \alpha \leq 1$. The practical importance of this inequality for us can be seen by realizing that the left-hand side of Equation 5 is identical to the expression in Equation 1. Thus, it is true that

$$\text{Pr (at least one Type I error)} \leq C\alpha$$

whenever C orthogonal contrasts are each tested at the same alpha level (indicated simply by α). By setting $\alpha = .05/C$, it follows from Equation 5 that

$$\text{Pr (at least one Type I error)} \leq .05 \tag{6}$$

Indeed, this is precisely what is done in the Bonferroni approach. Several comments are pertinent here. First, because Equation 5 is an inequality, it might happen that the actual probability of a Type I error is much less than .05 when the Bonferroni adjustment is used. However, for orthogonal contrasts and small values of alpha, the inequality is for all practical purposes an equality, as Table 5.3 shows. Thus, the adjustment does not result in a conservative test. Second, so far we have only considered orthogonal contrasts. Remember that $1 - (1 - \alpha)^C$ equals the probability of at least one Type I error only for orthogonal contrasts. It turns out that if the set of contrasts is nonorthogonal, the probability of at least one Type I error will always be less than $1 - (1 - \alpha)^C$. Thus, the Bonferroni procedure maintains α_{EW} at .05 for nonorthogonal and for orthogonal contrasts. However, the procedure is somewhat conservative for nonorthogonal contrasts.

A second way of viewing the rationale for the Bonferroni adjustment is in many ways simpler than the first perspective. Recall that in our discussion of error rates we defined the error rate per experiment ENEPE to be the expected number of Type I errors in an experiment. If we perform C tests of significance, each at an alpha value of α_{PC}, then the expected number

TABLE 5.3
COMPARISON OF $1 - [1 - (.05/C)]^C$ AND .05
FOR ORTHOGONAL CONTRASTS

C	Actual Probability of at Least One Type I Error $1 - [1 - (.05/C)]^c$
1	.050000
2	.049375
3	.049171
4	.049070
5	.049010
⋮	⋮
10	.048889
⋮	⋮
20	.048830
⋮	⋮
50	.048794

of Type I errors is simply

$$\text{ENEPE} = C\alpha_{\text{PC}} \tag{7}$$

If we choose α_{PC} to equal $.05/C$, then obviously ENEPE will equal .05. As a result, the expected number of Type I errors in an experiment will equal .05, regardless of the number of tests that are performed. What is the relationship between α_{EW} and ENEPE? The former equals the proportion of experiments that have Type I errors, whereas the latter equals the number of Type I errors per experiment. In symbols

$$\alpha_{\text{EW}} = \frac{\text{number of experiments with errors}}{\text{number of experiments}} \tag{8}$$

$$\text{ENEPE} = \frac{\text{number of errors}}{\text{number of experiments}} \tag{9}$$

Obviously, α_{EW} and ENEPE share the same denominator. However, the numerator for α_{EW} is less than or equal to the numerator for ENEPE, for the same set of data, because the numerator of Equation 8 is at most 1 per experiment, whereas the numerator of Equation 9 is incremented by 1 or more whenever the numerator of Equation 8 is 1. Thus, it is true that $\alpha_{\text{EW}} \leq \text{ENEPE}$. We showed a moment ago that the Bonferroni approach yields a value of ENEPE equal to .05. Because $\alpha_{\text{EW}} \leq \text{ENEPE}$, the Bonferroni procedure guarantees that $\alpha_{\text{EW}} \leq .05$.

The Bonferroni approach has a straightforward counterpart for simultaneous confidence intervals. We saw earlier in the chapter that the general expression for simultaneous confidence intervals is

$$\hat{\psi} \pm w \sqrt{MS_{\text{W}} \sum_{j=1}^{a} \left(c_j^2 / n_j \right)} \tag{3, repeated}$$

For the Bonferroni method, w is given by

$$w = \sqrt{F\left(.05/C, 1, df_{\text{error}}\right)}$$

Notice that if C were equal to 1, the Bonferroni interval would simply duplicate the interval given by Equation 4.48, which controls confidence at the per-interval level. However, whenever C is greater than 1, w for the Bonferroni interval will be wider than w in Equation 4.48. Thus, the Bonferroni interval will be wider than the per-interval confidence level. This decrease in precision is the price to be paid for obtaining confidence at the simultaneous level.

Two other points are worth mentioning. First, in theory, the α_{EW} of .05 need not be divided into C equal pieces of $.05/C$ in the Bonferroni method. Instead, it is only necessary that the $C \alpha_{\text{PC}}$ values sum to .05. For example, an experimenter testing three contrasts might use α_{PC} values of .03, .01, and .01. This could be done if the first contrast were considered most important. Notice that the larger alpha value for it would increase the power for detecting an effect, if one exists. However, there is a catch that limits the value of such unequal splitting of alpha in practice—the choice about how to divide .05 must be made prior to any examination of data. Otherwise, the experimenter could capitalize on chance and obtain statistically significant findings too often. Second, you might wonder why we did not use Equation 2 to find the value of α_{PC} that would keep α_{EW} at .05:

$$\alpha_{\text{PC}} = \sqrt[C]{1 - \alpha_{\text{EW}}} \tag{2, repeated}$$

Although we derived this equation for C orthogonal contrasts, Sidak (1967) proved that an inequality similar to Bonferroni's holds in the general case of nonorthogonal or orthogonal contrasts. Specifically, if α_{PC} is set equal to $1 - \sqrt[C]{.95}$, then α_{EW} will be .05 or less. It turns out that Sidak's value of α_{PC} is always slightly higher than the Bonferroni value (for $C > 1$), so the Sidak modification is more powerful than the Bonferroni approach. However, the difference in power is very small as long as α_{EW} is low. In addition, the Bonferroni α_{PC} is much easier to calculate. For these reasons, in practice, the Bonferroni approach is usually preferable to Sidak's method (for more detail on the Sidak approach, see Kirk, 1982, or Holland and Copenhaver, 1988).

There is a final point regarding planned multiple comparisons that must be mentioned. The procedure we have described guarantees that α_{EW} will be .05 or less regardless of how many contrasts an experimenter plans. Thus, the overall probability of a Type I error being made somewhere in the experiment is the same as it would be if the researcher were to perform a test of the omnibus null hypothesis instead of planned comparisons. In this way, the chances of obtaining statistical significance in a study are not increased simply by performing multiple tests. At the same time, however, there is a penalty imposed on the investigator who plans a large number of contrasts, because α_{PC} is set at $.05/C$. As C increases, it becomes more difficult to detect each individual true effect, all other things being equal. Although the experiment as a whole has an alpha level of .05, each individual hypothesis is tested at $.05/C$. It could be argued that this puts each hypothesis test at an unfair disadvantage. Indeed, some behavioral statisticians (e.g., Keppel, 1982; Kirk, 1982) used this line of reasoning for planned contrasts. With their approaches, α_{EW} is allowed to exceed .05, because they allow up to $a - 1$ contrasts to be tested with an α_{PC} level of .05. There is disagreement within this camp about whether the $a - 1$ contrasts must form an orthogonal set in order to set α_{PC} at .05. Although this general approach has some appeal, it nevertheless fails to control α_{EW} at .05. We prefer the Bonferroni approach, because it accomplishes this goal.

Modification of the Bonferroni Approach With Unequal Variances

As we discussed in Chapter 4, using MS_W as an error term for testing contrasts is problematic when population variances are unequal. Just as heterogeneous variances affect α_{PC}, they also may affect α_{EW}. However, a rather straightforward solution is available. The Bonferroni procedure is easily modified by using Equations 4.42 and 4.43 when population variances are unequal. As we showed in Chapter 4, the resultant F statistic in this case is given by

$$F = \frac{(\hat{\psi})^2}{\sum\limits_{j=1}^{a} \left(c_j^2 / n_j \right) s_j^2} \tag{10}$$

As we mentioned in Chapter 4, the corresponding denominator degrees of freedom are tedious, so a computer package will invariably be invoked for their calculation. Later in this chapter, Tables 5.16 and 5.17 will show the formula for these degrees of freedom in the context of summarizing our recommended multiple comparisons procedures.

The F value shown in Equation 10 will usually be computed by a statistical package, which will also yield the p value for this F and its corresponding degrees of freedom. As usual with the Bonferroni adjustment, the obtained p value is then compared to α_{EW}/C (usually $.05/C$) to assess the statistical significance of the contrast. Thus, access to a statistical package that computes F values of the form shown in Equation 10 makes it straightforward to test contrasts without having to assume homogeneity of variance.

We saw that a simultaneous confidence interval can be obtained under the homogeneity assumption by generalizing Equation 48 from Chapter 4. When homogeneity is questionable, a simultaneous confidence interval can be formed by generalizing Equation 49 from Chapter 4. Recall that Equation 49 in Chapter 4 was given by

$$\hat{\psi} \pm \sqrt{F_{\alpha;1,df}} \sqrt{\sum_{j=1}^{a} \left[(c_j^2/n_j)s_j^2 \right]} \tag{4.49}$$

The Bonferroni approach simply uses α/C instead of α to find the critical F value in Equation 49. Thus, when homogeneity is questionable, a Bonferroni 95% simultaneous confidence interval has the form

$$\hat{\psi} \pm \sqrt{F_{.05/C;1,df}} \sqrt{\sum_{j=1}^{a} \left[(c_j^2/n_j)s_j^2 \right]} \tag{11}$$

Numerical Example

We will illustrate the Bonferroni procedure by considering the data shown in Table 5.4, which are a slight modification of the blood pressure data we originally encountered in Chapter 4. We will now assume that the experiment successfully obtained blood pressure readings from all intended individuals, so we no longer have to worry about missing data. Although the Bonferroni method easily accommodates unequal sample sizes, we want to use this same data set to illustrate a variety of multiple-comparison procedures, and we will see later in the chapter that some of the procedures yet to come are much simpler with equal sample sizes. We should also emphasize from the outset that we will use the Table 5.4 data to illustrate several different procedures, but in an actual study, a single procedure should be chosen based on an appropriate intersection of the rows and columns of Table 5.2. We will say more at the end of the chapter about choosing an appropriate procedure.

Suppose that before collecting the data shown in Table 5.4, the investigator had decided to examine four planned contrasts: (1) drug versus biofeedback, (2) drug versus diet, (3) biofeedback versus diet, and (4) the average of each of the first three treatments versus the combined treatment. As usual, we are not claiming that these four contrasts are necessarily the only correct contrasts to examine in this data set. On the other hand, we do believe they constitute a plausible set of contrasts that might in fact be examined as planned comparisons in such a study. How should the investigator proceed? To answer this question, look at Table 5.2.

TABLE 5.4
BLOOD PRESSURE DATA FOR FOUR TREATMENT GROUPS

	Group		
1	*2*	*3*	*4*
84	81	98	91
95	84	95	78
93	92	86	85
104	101	87	80
99	80	94	81
106	108	101	76

TABLE 5.5
SPSS OUTPUT FOR PLANNED COMPARISONS

Contrast Coefficients

		GROUP		
Contrast	*1.00*	*2.00*	*3.00*	*4.00*
1	1	−1	0	0
2	1	0	−1	0
3	0	1	−1	0
4	1	1	1	−3

Contrast Tests	*Contrast*	*Value of Contrast*	*Std. Error*	*t*	*df*	*(Sig. 2-tailed)*
SBP assume equal	1	5.8333	4.6676	1.250	20	.226
variances	2	3.3333	4.6676	.714	20	.483
	3	−2.5000	4.6676	−.536	20	.598
	4	35.8333	11.4331	3.134	20	.005
	1	5.8333	5.7237	1.019	8.947	.335
Does not assume	2	3.3333	4.0838	.816	9.222	.435
equal variances	3	−2.5000	5.2836	−.473	7.508	.650
	4	35.8333	9.0955	3.940	13.288	.002

Simultaneous Confidence Intervals

Assuming Homogeneity of Variance

Contrast	*Computation*	*Interval*
1	$5.8333 \pm (\sqrt{7.53})(4.6676)$	−6.97, 18.64
2	$3.3333 \pm (\sqrt{7.53})(4.6676)$	−9.47, 16.14
3	$-2.500 \pm (\sqrt{7.53})(4.6676)$	−15.31, 10.31
4	$(35.83/3) \pm (\sqrt{7.53})(11.4331/3)$	1.49, 22.40

Without Assuming Homogeneity of Variance

Contrast	*Computation*	*Interval*
1	$5.8333 \pm (\sqrt{10.28})(5.7237)$	−12.52, 24.18
2	$3.3333 \pm (\sqrt{9.68})(4.0838)$	−9.37, 16.04
3	$-2.500 \pm (\sqrt{11.12})(5.2836)$	−20.12, 15.12
4	$(35.83/3) \pm (\sqrt{8.39})(9.0955/3)$	3.16, 20.73

Because all comparisons are planned, a procedure can be chosen from the first column of the table. If the investigator follows our recommendation to obtain strength of inference at the level of confidence intervals, either Bonferroni or Sidak is appropriate.

We will see that using SAS or SPSS to test contrasts with the Bonferroni approach is very simple. However, using these packages to form confidence intervals is less straightforward. As of this writing, SAS and SPSS provide proper Bonferroni (or Sidak) confidence intervals only in a very special case, where three conditions are met: (1) All pairwise contrasts are of interest; (2) no complex contrasts are of interest; and (3) homogeneity is assumed. To form confidence intervals for a subset of pairwise contrasts, or for complex contrasts (with or without homogeneity) or for pairwise contrasts without assuming homogeneity, the best one can do with these packages is to obtain intermediate values that can then be used as input to appropriate formulas for final hand calculations. For example, Table 5.5 shows output obtained from SPSS for the four contrasts in question. It is important to stress that the results in this table were obtained without specifying the Bonferroni option in SPSS. Our situation does not conform to the three conditions previously listed. If we had specified the Bonferroni option, SPSS would have provided tests and confidence intervals for pairwise contrasts under a mistaken assumption that C (the number of contrasts of interest) equals 6, because that is the total number of pairwise contrasts with 4 groups. In reality, $C = 4$ in our situation, so asking for the Bonferroni option in either SAS or SPSS would not be appropriate here. Instead, the results shown here implicitly assume a per-comparison alpha level of .05, contrary to our real goal. Thus, we will have to adjust information in the output ourselves instead of relying entirely on the computer package.

The information in Table 5.5 makes it easy to test the null hypothesis that each contrast equals zero using the Bonferroni method. All we need to do is to compare each p value on the printout with an adjusted per-comparison alpha level of $.05/C$. In our case, $C = 4$, so $\alpha_{PC} = .0125$. Table 5.5 shows that regardless of whether we assume homogeneity, the only contrast with a p value less than .0125 is the fourth contrast. Thus, the only statistically significant difference is between the combined treatment and the average of the three individual treatments.

Forming simultaneous confidence intervals for the contrasts is slightly more complicated.[2] However, we can use our computer output by realizing that Equation 3 (assuming homogeneity) and the comparable variation based on Equation 4.49 (without assuming homogeneity) for forming confidence intervals can be written in words as

$$\text{estimate} \pm (\text{critical value})\,(\text{estimated standard error}) \qquad (12)$$

With one possible minor exception to be noted in a moment, the estimate and the estimated standard error can be read directly from the output. Appendix Table A.3 provides the necessary critical value (notice we will usually have to round down for the degrees of freedom to use this table based on computer output). The "minor exception" is that, as we discussed in Chapter 4, we may need to be aware of the scaling (or metric) of the contrast coefficients. As long as the sum of the absolute value of the coefficients equals 2, we can simply proceed. In our example, this is true for the first three contrasts. However, the coefficients that produced the output for the fourth contrast were 1, 1, 1, and -3. To obtain the correct result, we need to divide both the estimate and the estimated standard error shown on the output by 3. Incidentally, SAS allows the user to specify a "divisor" as part of the definition of the contrast, so the output already reflects the division we have to do by hand with SPSS.

The bottom of Table 5.5 shows the simultaneous confidence intervals using the Bonferroni procedure, first when we are willing to assume homogeneity of variance and then when we are not. With or without assuming homogeneity, only the fourth interval does not contain zero, so only this contrast is statistically significantly different from zero. Notice that this result is consistent with comparing the p value in the output with a critical p value of $.05/C$, as it must be. Also notice that in these particular data, it makes little practical difference whether we assume homogeneity. Two of the intervals are appreciably wider when we relax the assumption, but the other two intervals are slightly narrower without the assumption. It is important to keep in mind that in other situations the assumption of homogeneity can make more of a difference, and in particular can be much more problematic.

PAIRWISE COMPARISONS

Frequently, a researcher decides to consider only pairwise differences between groups. In other words, no complex comparisons will be tested. How can α_{EW} be controlled at .05 in this situation? One possible approach would be to use a Bonferroni adjustment. However, care must be taken in using the proper value of C. Most often, $C = a(a - 1)/2$ for testing pairwise comparisons. The reason is that with a levels of the factor, there are $a(a - 1)/2$ pairs of means that can be compared. Thus, when all pairwise comparisons might be tested, the (α_{EW} value of .05 must be divided by $a(a - 1)/2$.

It is important to understand the connection between this section on pairwise comparisons and the previous discussion of planned comparisons. To solidify this connection, suppose that a researcher is conducting a four-group study and is interested for theoretical reasons in comparing the following pairs of means: μ_1 versus μ_2, μ_2 versus μ_3, and μ_3 versus μ_4. As long as these comparisons have been selected prior to collecting data, α_{EW} can be maintained at .05 by using an α_{PC} equal to .05/3. Thus, $C = 3$ in this situation, even though there are a total of six pairs of means; using $C = 3$ restricts the investigator to ignore the other three pairs of means, no matter how interesting such differences might appear after having collected data. For example, it would not be permissible to decide after examining data that μ_1 versus μ_4 should also be tested, and then redefine C to equal 4. Similarly, suppose that the investigator originally planned to test all pairwise comparisons, but after looking at data, decided not to test μ_1 versus μ_3 or μ_2 versus μ_4. Again, it would not be legitimate to define $C = 4$; instead, the value of C must be set at 6.

Thus, when a specific subset of mean differences is chosen in advance of collecting data, C equals the number of comparisons in the subset. However, C must be set equal to $a(a - 1)/2$ if any of the following conditions apply:

1. All pairwise comparisons are to be tested.
2. The original intent was to test all pairwise comparisons, but after looking at the data, fewer comparisons are actually tested.
3. The original intent was to test a subset of all possible pairwise comparisons, but after looking at the data, one or more additional pairwise comparisons are also to be tested.

In any case, the Bonferroni adjustment can be used to control α_{EW} when performing pairwise comparisons. However, when one of the three conditions listed above applies, so that C must be set at $a(a - 1)/2$, the Bonferroni approach is usually not as powerful as other special-purpose techniques that have been developed specifically for testing all pairwise comparisons. The technique we generally recommend for testing pairwise comparisons in between-subjects designs was developed by Tukey (1953) and is referred to as Tukey's WSD (or, interchangeably, Tukey's HSD).[3] This technique generally is more powerful than the Bonferroni approach when $C = a(a - 1)/2$, and yet it allows a researcher to test all possible pairwise comparisons and still maintain the α_{EW} level at .05 (or any other desired level).

Before describing the details of Tukey's WSD, we want to mention that Tukey developed several different multiple comparison procedures, so it is important to be certain that "Tukey" as operationalized in a statistical package is in fact WSD. For example, as of this writing, SPSS provides two "Tukey" options. The option labeled simply as "Tukey" is indeed WSD, but an alternative labeled "Tukey-b" is a variation that does not necessarily control α_{EW} at the intended level, and thus we do not recommend it. On a related point, as of this writing, both SAS and SPSS also present other procedures similar to Tukey's, including a method developed by Hochberg (referred to as either GT2 or SMM) as well as a method developed by Gabriel. Although Hochberg's method succeeds in appropriately controlling α_{EW}, it is always less powerful than Tukey's WSD with equal sample sizes and is generally less powerful for unequal sample sizes as well. Gabriel's method is identical to Hochberg's for equal sample sizes and thus is also always less powerful than Tukey's WSD in this case. With unequal sample sizes, Gabriel's method is more powerful than Hochberg's, but it can fail to control α_{EW}, so once again we prefer Tukey's WSD.

Tukey's WSD Procedure

Tukey's WSD procedure allows a researcher to perform tests of all possible pairwise comparisons in an experiment and still maintain the α_{EW} level at $.05$.[4] This control of α_{EW} is accomplished by adopting a critical value appropriate for testing the significance of that pair of means that is found post hoc to yield a larger F value than any other pair of means. To make things concrete, suppose that $a = 3$. In this situation, there are three pairwise comparisons that can be tested:

$$\psi_1 = \mu_1 - \mu_2$$
$$\psi_2 = \mu_1 - \mu_3$$
$$\psi_3 = \mu_2 - \mu_3$$

For the moment, we restrict ourselves to the case of equal n and homogeneity of variance. (Tukey made both of these assumptions in deriving his procedure; in a later section, we consider modifications when either condition is not satisfied.) To test the significance of the three contrasts, Equation 4.28 can be applied three times. With equal n, this yields

$$F_{\psi_1} = \frac{n(\overline{Y}_1 - \overline{Y}_2)^2}{2MS_W}$$

$$F_{\psi_2} = \frac{n(\overline{Y}_1 - \overline{Y}_3)^2}{2MS_W}$$

$$F_{\psi_3} = \frac{n(\overline{Y}_2 - \overline{Y}_3)^2}{2MS_W}$$

It is obvious from these three equations that the largest F value will be obtained for the pair of sample means whose values are most different from one another. In symbols

$$F_{\text{pairwise maximum}} = \frac{n(\overline{Y}_{\max} - \overline{Y}_{\min})^2}{2MS_W}$$

(Notice that because the difference between means is squared, we could just as well subtract $\overline{Y}_{\max}$ from $\overline{Y}_{\min}$.) How can we achieve our goal of maintaining α_{EW} at $.05$? If we were to use a single critical value (which we will abbreviate as CV) against which to judge each contrast, there would be a statistically significant result in the experiment if and only if $F_{\text{pairwise maximum}} > CV$. Our goal is that the α_{EW} should be $.05$, so we need to determine how large CV must be so that $F_{\text{pairwise maximum}}$ will exceed it only 5% of the time when the null hypothesis is true. The appropriate value of CV can be found from the sampling distribution of $F_{\text{pairwise maximum}}$, which has been derived mathematically. Specifically, it can be shown that the expression $\sqrt{2F_{\text{pairwise maximum}}}$ has a "studentized range" distribution if all assumptions are met. It is traditional to represent the studentized range with the letter q, so we can write $q = \sqrt{2F_{\text{pairwise maximum}}}$.

To obtain an alpha level of $.05$, the critical value CV is chosen to be that value in the right tail of the q distribution beyond which lies 5% of the area. Appendix Table A.4 presents critical

TABLE 5.6

COMPARISON OF CORRESPONDING PER-COMPARISON,
TUKEY, AND BONFERRONI CRITICAL VALUES FOR TESTING
ALL PAIRWISE COMPARISONS WITH $df_{error} = 12$

Number of Groups	Critical Value		
	Per-Comparison	Tukey	Bonferroni
2	4.75	4.75	4.75
3	4.75	7.14	7.73
4	4.75	8.78	9.92
5	4.75	10.17	11.76
6	4.75	11.33	13.32

values of the studentized range distribution for both $\alpha = .05$ and $\alpha = .01$. Before we examine this table, we summarize the mechanics of Tukey's procedure. To employ Tukey's method, an observed F is calculated in the usual way for each pairwise contrast. However, instead of comparing this observed F to a critical F value, we take the square root of $2F$ and compare this number to a critical q value. This procedure is repeated for each contrast to be tested.

What makes Tukey's method different from the previously encountered methods for testing contrasts is the use of a different critical value. Instead of comparing an observed F to a critical F with an alpha level of .05 or $.05/C$, the observed F is compared to $q^2/2$. Notice, then, that the observed test statistic itself is unchanged; what has changed is the critical value for assessing significance. As mentioned earlier, this critical value is chosen to maintain α_{EW} at .05.

Table 5.6 illustrates how the use of $q^2/2$ controls α_{EW} at the desired value. The specific values in the table are for $df_{error} = 12$, but the general pattern would hold for other values as well. For the moment, we concentrate on the first two columns of critical values, which show that whenever $a \geq 3$, the critical value for Tukey's method is larger than the critical value that would be used if α_{PC} were set at .05. The table also shows that the Tukey critical value increases dramatically as a increases. This is not surprising, because the rationale for Tukey's approach is that $F_{pairwise\ maximum}$ exceeds the Tukey critical value only 5% of the time. As a increases, there are more pairs of groups to be contrasted, so that $F_{pairwise\ maximum}$ tends to be larger in the long run. (Of course, it is also true that in Table 5.6, the degrees of freedom for error is 12 regardless of a; as a increases, there are necessarily fewer participants per group.) For this reason, the Tukey critical value is larger for higher values of a. In this way, α_{EW} is maintained at .05. A necessary consequence is that implicitly α_{PC} is less than .05 whenever $a > 2$ for Tukey's method.

This leads us to a comparison of the second and third columns of critical values. Suppose that an investigator plans to test all $a(a - 1)/2$ pairwise contrasts in an a-group study. From our earlier discussion, it would seem that the Bonferroni adjustment could be applied, in which case the third column displays the appropriate critical values. In the four cases where $a > 2$, the Bonferroni critical value is larger than the Tukey critical value. The smaller critical value for Tukey's method illustrates the point made earlier, that Tukey's WSD is more powerful than the Bonferroni procedure for testing all pairwise comparisons. Although both procedures are guaranteed to control α_{EW} at the desired level (as long as necessary statistical assumptions are met), Tukey's technique is preferable in between-subjects designs because it is more powerful. However, in Chapter 13, we will see that the Bonferroni approach may be preferable to Tukey's WSD in within-subjects designs because of the restrictive assumptions required by the WSD approach in such designs.

So far, the presentation of Tukey's method has been restricted to the equal sample size, equal variance condition. We now discuss modifications that can be employed when either or both of these conditions fail to hold.

Modifications of Tukey's WSD

Consider an experiment where the sample sizes of the various groups are unequal, but homogeneity of variance is assumed. The recommended procedure to employ here was developed by Kramer (1956). Recall that we developed Tukey's procedure using Equation 4.28, which is a special case of Equation 4.27 to be used only when $n_1 = n_2$. Kramer's approach for unequal n is simply to compute the observed F using the general form of Equation 4.27 that allows for unequal n. In other words, the F is calculated in exactly the same way as it was calculated for planned contrasts with unequal n. As with Tukey's approach, the observed F for each contrast is compared to a critical value given by $q^2/2$, where q is found in Appendix Table A.4, using the appropriate α, a, and degrees of freedom for error.

When population variances are unequal, the situation is considerably more complicated. As we discussed in Chapter 4, procedures using Equation 4.27 are not robust to violations of homogeneity of variance, so neither Tukey's procedure nor the Kramer modification is appropriate when variances are heterogeneous. A number of modifications of these procedures, which involve different formulas for calculating an observed F value and for calculating a critical value, have been suggested. Our recommendation is based on a synthesis of findings reported in Games, Keselman, and Rogan (1981); Hochberg and Tamhane (1987); and Wilcox (1987b). When a researcher is unwilling to assume homogeneity of variance, the observed F statistic for comparing groups g and h should be calculated as

$$F = \frac{(\overline{Y}_g - \overline{Y}_h)^2}{\dfrac{s_g^2}{n_g} + \dfrac{s_h^2}{n_h}} \tag{13}$$

where the g and h subscripts refer to the two groups involved in the specific comparison. This expression for the F statistic is simply a special case of the more general formula developed in Chapter 4 for dealing with heterogeneity (also see Equation 5.10). Similarly, the appropriate degrees of freedom in this special case can be written as

$$df = \frac{\left(s_g^2/n_g + s_h^2/n_h\right)^2}{s_g^4/n_g^2(n_g - 1) + s_h^4/n_h^2(n_h - 1)} \tag{14}$$

Fortunately, current versions of widely distributed statistical packages calculate a t-statistic analog to Equations 13 and 14. In other words, they calculate the square root of the F in Equation 13; the degrees of freedom are the same for the F and the t statistics. For example, as of this writing, these values are obtained from the separate variance estimate calculations in an SPSS independent samples t test and an SPSS one-way ANOVA and from the unequal variances calculation in SAS PROC TTEST.

Once the observed t (or F) has been obtained, it must be compared to a critical value. Statisticians have proposed numerous critical values as possibilities here. Current evidence suggests that when sample sizes are small (i.e., fewer than 50 per group), a critical value suggested by Dunnett is most appropriate. For larger samples, a different critical value suggested by Games and Howell is better. Dunnett's procedure, which is called Dunnett's T3 (the T comes from a statistician named Tamhane, who developed the predecessor to T3), is based on the studentized maximum modulus distribution.[5] The observed t statistic is compared to a critical value V, obtained from Appendix Table A.5. (Alternatively, F can be compared to V squared.) The columns of Appendix Table A.5 correspond to the number of groups,[6] and the rows correspond to degrees of freedom calculated from Equation 14. When the observed t exceeds the critical V, the contrast is statistically significant:

For larger samples, we recommend a procedure suggested by Games and Howell (1976). To use their procedure, the observed t statistic is compared to $q/\sqrt{2}$ (or, equivalently, F is compared to $q^2/2$), where the degrees of freedom for the studentized range again come from Equation 14. If the observed t exceeds $q/\sqrt{2}$, the contrast is statistically significant. The reason Dunnett's T3 is recommended instead of the Games–Howell procedure for smaller sample sizes is that Dunnett (1980) found that the Games–Howell approach becomes slightly liberal (i.e., α_{EW} is slightly above .05) when sample sizes are small. Fortunately, both Dunnett's T3 and the Games–Howell procedure are currently available as options in an SPSS one-way ANOVA, so these tests (as well as simultaneous confidence intervals) can easily be obtained. As of this writing, SAS does not offer these options, which implies that although PROC TTEST can be used to find the relevant observed F value and its degrees of freedom, the critical value must be calculated by hand using either Appendix Table A.5 (for T3) or A4 (for Games–Howell).

Numerical Example

We will return to the blood pressure data of Table 5.4 to illustrate Tukey's WSD and its modifications. Table 5.7 shows SPSS output for the six pairwise comparisons we can examine in our four-group study. The table actually shows 12 comparisons under the assumption of homogeneity, as well as 12 additional comparisons without the assumption, because the table shows not only $\mu_1 - \mu_2$ but also $\mu_2 - \mu_1$ and so forth.

Table 5.7 shows that under the homogeneity assumption, the only statistically significant pairwise difference is between the drug and combination therapies. We can be 95% confident that the population mean of the combination therapy is at least 2 units (rounding off) and at most 28 units lower than the population mean of the drug therapy. Notice that although this difference is statistically significant, the small sample size has produced a very wide confidence interval, leaving considerable uncertainty about the extent to which the combination therapy is truly superior to the drug therapy. Further, it is plausible that all five other differences may be either positive or negative, so cannot establish which of these therapies are better than the other.[7]

If we decide not to assume homogeneity of variance, an additional pairwise comparison becomes statistically significant. For these data, we can still assert that combination therapy is superior to drug therapy, but we can now also claim that combination therapy is superior to diet. In general, the number of statistically signficant differences can either be larger or smaller when one relaxes the homogeneity assumption. In either case, the decision as to whether to assume homogeneity should clearly be made on grounds other than the number of significant results obtained.

POST HOC COMPLEX COMPARISONS

The previous section provides a method for maintaining α_{EW} at .05 when all pairwise contrasts are tested. Now the Scheffé method is introduced to maintain α_{EW} at .05 when at least some of the contrasts to be tested are complex and suggested by the data. Although in many situations

TABLE 5.7
SPSS OUTPUT FOR PAIRWISE COMPARISONS

Multiple Comparisons
Dependent Variable: SBP

	(I) GROUP	(J) GROUP	Mean Difference (I−J)	Std. Error	Sig.	95% Confidence Interval Lower Bound	Upper Bound
Tukey's HSD	1.00	2.00	5.8333	4.6676	.604	−7.2310	18.8977
		3.00	3.3333	4.6676	.890	−9.7310	16.3977
		4.00	15.0000*	4.6676	.021	1.9356	28.0644
	2.00	1.00	−5.8333	4.6676	.604	−18.8977	7.2310
		3.00	−2.5000	4.6676	.949	−15.5644	10.5644
		4.00	9.1667	4.6676	.235	−3.8977	22.2310
	3.00	1.00	−3.3333	4.6676	.890	−16.3977	9.7310
		2.00	2.5000	4.6676	.949	−10.5644	15.5644
		4.00	11.6667	4.6676	.091	−1.3977	24.7310
	4.00	1.00	−15.0000*	4.6676	.021	−28.0644	−1.9356
		2.00	−9.1667	4.6676	.235	−22.2310	3.8977
		3.00	−11.6667	4.6676	.091	−24.7310	1.3977
Tamhane	1.00	2.00	5.8333	4.6676	.913	−13.3759	25.0425
		3.00	3.3333	4.6676	.967	−10.2644	16.9311
		4.00	15.0000*	4.6676	.027	1.6489	28.3511
	2.00	1.00	−5.8333	4.6676	.913	−25.0425	13.3759
		3.00	−2.5000	4.6676	.998	−21.1741	16.1741
		4.00	9.1667	4.6676	.535	−9.4938	27.8271
	3.00	1.00	−3.3333	4.6676	.967	−16.9311	10.2644
		2.00	2.5000	4.6676	.998	−16.1741	21.1741
		4.00	11.6667*	4.6676	.032	.9112	22.4221
	4.00	1.00	−15.0000*	4.6676	.027	−28.3511	−1.6489
		2.00	−9.1667	4.6676	.535	−27.8271	9.4938
		3.00	−11.6667*	4.6676	.032	−22.4221	−.9112

* The mean difference is significant at the .05 level.

the data may suggest that a researcher compare all pairs of groups, there are times when other comparisons may also be of interest, as we saw in the hypertension example of Chapter 4. To consider another such example, suppose that the effects of different dosage levels of a drug on some aspect of behavior are being investigated. A researcher might conduct a three-group study, where the groups are defined by the dosage level they receive, such as 1 ml, 2 ml, or 3 ml. Assume that on examination of the data, the intermediate dosage seems to be most effective. Then, one contrast of interest might be

$$\psi_1 = \tfrac{1}{2}(\mu_1 + \mu_3) - \mu_2$$

to see whether the average of the effects of 1 and 3 ml equals the effect of 2 ml. Suppose that the researcher also wants to test the three pairwise contrasts:

$$\psi_2 = \mu_1 - \mu_2$$

$$\psi_3 = \mu_1 - \mu_3$$

$$\mu_4 = \mu_2 - \mu_3$$

Although it would be possible to use the Bonferroni approach if these are planned contrasts, we assume for the moment that they have instead been formed post hoc. After developing an appropriate technique for testing these contrasts post hoc, we return to the planned versus post hoc distinction.

If these four contrasts are to be tested post hoc, neither the Bonferroni nor the Tukey method is appropriate. The Bonferroni method is not applicable, because these particular contrasts were not selected prior to examining the data. Thus, it would be incorrect to set C equal to 4 and use the Bonferroni adjustment with $\alpha_{PC} = .05/4$. Tukey's method is not applicable either: not all the contrasts are pairwise, because ψ_1 involves three groups. We now turn to Scheffé's approach for a method that allows all four contrasts to be tested post hoc and yet keep α_{EW} at .05.

Our presentation of the logic underlying Scheffé's method is similar to the presentation of the rationale for Tukey's method. Recall that for Tukey's approach, we considered the sampling distribution of $F_{\text{pairwise maximum}}$. Now, however, we do not want to restrict ourselves to only pairwise contrasts. The logic of Scheffé's method is to consider the sampling distribution of F_{maximum}, which represents the largest possible F value for any contrast in the data, either pairwise or complex. Although finding this distribution would seem to be an extremely difficult task, it actually becomes rather easy with a few additional facts at our disposal.

Proof That $SS_{\text{max}} = SS_{B}$

We detour momentarily to develop these facts. Recall that we are interested in finding the sampling distribution of F_{maximum}. Notice that the contrast that produces the largest F value is whatever contrast yields the largest sum of squares, because the F value is simply the sum of squares divided by mean square within, that is

$$F_{\psi} = SS_{\psi}/MS_{W}$$

It then follows that

$$F_{\text{maximum}} = SS_{\text{max}}/MS_{W} \tag{15}$$

where SS_{max} is the sum of squares of the contrast with the largest sum of squares. We now show that for any set of data, SS_{max} equals the between groups sum of squares SS_{B}.

First, we must convince you that the sum of squares for a contrast must always be less than or equal to the between group sum of squares, that is

$$SS_{\psi} \leq SS_{B} \tag{16}$$

This must be true, because we learned in Chapter 4 that one measure of effect size for comparisons is R^2_{alerting}, which was defined as

$$R^2_{\text{alerting}} = SS(\psi)/SS_{\text{Between}} \tag{4.54}$$

However, as a squared multiple correlation, R^2_{alerting} can be no larger than 1.0, in which case it immediately follows that $SS(\psi)$ can be no larger than SS_{Between}. In other words,

$$SS_{\psi} \leq SS_{B} \tag{16, repeated}$$

which is what we were seeking to prove. Thus, it follows that no contrast can have a sum of squares larger than the between-group sum of squares, implying that

$$SS_{\text{max}} \leq SS_{B} \tag{17}$$

The final step in this argument is to show that it is always possible (after obtaining the data) to find a contrast whose sum of squares will equal SS_B. This is accomplished by defining contrast coefficients to be equal to (or proportional to) the weighted deviations of each group mean from the grand mean, where the weights for the deviations are given by the sample sizes of the groups. In other words, the contrast whose sum of squares equals SS_B has coefficients of the form

$$c_j = n_j(\overline{Y}_j - \overline{Y}) \tag{18}$$

For any sample data, the contrast whose coefficients are defined as in Equation 18 will have an R^2_{alerting} value of 1.0 and a sum of squares equal to SS_B.[8] This contrast is then necessarily the contrast with the largest possible sum of squares, because we saw earlier from Equation 17 that

$$SS_{\text{max}} \leq SS_B \tag{17, repeated}$$

However, as proved in Footnote 8, there is always a contrast whose sum of squares equals SS_B. Combining these two facts allows us to amend Equation 17. We can now say that

$$SS_{\text{max}} = SS_B \tag{19}$$

Earlier, we argued that

$$F_{\text{maximum}} = SS_{\text{max}}/MS_W \tag{15, repeated}$$

Substituting Equation 19 into Equation 15 yields

$$F_{\text{maximum}} = SS_B/MS_W \tag{20}$$

Thus, for a given set of data, the largest F value for a contrast always equals SS_B/MS_W.

Remember that the task at hand was to find the sampling distribution of F_{maximum}. This is made simple now that we know $F_{\text{maximum}} = SS_B/MS_W$, because we can rewrite this as

$$F_{\text{maximum}} = (a - 1)MS_B/MS_W \tag{21}$$

because $SS_B = (a - 1)MS_B$. However, if all necessary assumptions are met, MS_B/MS_W is distributed as an F variable with $a - 1$ and $N - a$ degrees of freedom under the null hypothesis. It follows that F_{maximum} is simply distributed as $(a - 1)$ times such an F variable. Therefore, even if the omnibus null hypothesis is true, so every contrast has a population value of zero, F_{maximum} exceeds

$$(a - 1)F_{.05; a-1, N-a} \tag{22}$$

only 5% of the time. By using $(a - 1)F_{.05; a-1, N-a}$ as a critical value against which to judge the significance of a contrast, we guarantee ourselves of maintaining α_{EW} at .05, regardless of how many contrasts we test, even after having looked at the data. (Of course, as always, the necessary assumptions must be met in order for the actual alpha level to equal the nominal value.) Notice that, once again, in order to use the Scheffé method, the observed F value is calculated from Equation 4.41 (or one of its equivalent forms). What distinguishes this method from the other multiple-comparisons procedures is the use of Equation 22 for the critical value.

A nice feature of Scheffé's method is that it has a direct correspondence to the test of the omnibus null hypothesis. Remember that the omnibus null hypothesis will be rejected if and only if

$$MS_B/MS_W > F_{.05; a-1, N-a} \qquad (23)$$

Suppose that we were to test the contrast corresponding to $F_{maximum}$ with Scheffé's approach. Recall that $F_{maximum} = (a - 1)MS_B/MS_W$. The critical value for Scheffé is $(a - 1)$ $F_{.05; a-1, N-a}$.

This contrast is judged to be statistically significant if and only if its observed F value exceeds the Scheffé critical value, that is, if and only if

$$F_{maximum} > (a - 1)F_{.05; a-1, N-a} \qquad (24)$$

However, from Equation 21

$$F_{maximum} = (a - 1)MS_B/MS_W \qquad (21, \text{repeated})$$

Substituting this result into Equation 24, we see that the contrast is significant if and only if

$$(a - 1)MS_B/MS_W > (a - 1)F_{.05; a-1, N-a}$$

However, we can cancel the $(a - 1)$ terms, implying that the contrast is significant if and only if

$$MS_B/MS_W > F_{.05; a-1, N-a}$$

However, this repeats Equation 23, which is the condition under which the omnibus null hypothesis is rejected. Thus, the maximum contrast is statistically significant by Scheffé's method if and only if the omnibus null hypothesis is rejected.

Thus, if the omnibus null hypothesis is rejected, at least one contrast exists that is significant by Scheffé's method (namely the contrast corresponding to $F_{maximum}$). Conversely, if the omnibus null hypothesis is not rejected, it is impossible to find a significant contrast using Scheffé's method. All this should seem eminently reasonable. After all, if we declare the means to be different from one another, we should be able to specify how they are different. On the other hand, if we declare them to be the same, it makes no sense to turn around and say how they are different. Although this is indeed reasonable, not all multiple-comparison procedures share this property. For example, with Tukey's method, inconsistencies can occur. It is possible to reject the omnibus null hypothesis and yet reject none of the pairwise differences. The opposite can also occur—it is possible to reject one or more of the pairwise contrasts, although the omnibus null hypothesis cannot be rejected.

Comparison of Scheffé to Bonferroni and Tukey

Scheffé's method is very useful in that it allows the researcher to test literally any contrast that may be suggested by the data. Because the critical value is based on the sampling distribution of $F_{maximum}$, all possible contrasts could be tested for an experiment, and α_{EW} would still be maintained at .05. As we have noted before, the number of contrasts that may be tested is infinite. Although many of these may have little or no scientific meaning, they can all be tested

TABLE 5.8
COMPARISON OF BONFERRONI AND SCHEFFÉ
CRITICAL VALUES FOR $a = 4$ AND $df_{error} = 30$

C	Bonferroni	Scheffé
	$F_{.05/C; 1,30}$	$3F_{.05; 3,30}$
1	4.17	8.76
2	5.57	8.76
3	6.45	8.76
4	7.08	8.76
5	7.56	8.76
6	8.01	8.76
7	8.35	8.76
8	8.64	8.76
9	8.94	8.76
10	9.18	8.76

for significance with Scheffé's method. On the other hand, what if we are really interested in testing just a few of these contrasts? In this situation, the Scheffé method is typically quite conservative, in that the actual α_{EW} for the few contrasts we actually test may be considerably less than the .05 that would result from testing all possible contrasts. Indeed, this points out the advantage of planned contrasts. If the experimenter plans the contrasts prior to the study and if the number of contrasts to be tested is relatively small, the Bonferroni critical value will be less than the Scheffé critical value, so the Bonferroni approach will be more powerful. Table 5.8 illustrates this point, where $a = 4$ and $df_{error} = 30$. From the table, we can see that as many as eight planned comparisons could be tested and still use a lower critical value with the Bonferroni than with the Scheffé. Only an investigator who might be interested in more than eight contrasts among the four groups would find the Scheffé method superior.

Table 5.9 provides a more complete view of the choice between Bonferroni and Scheffé. Each entry in the table is the maximum number of contrasts that could be planned and still have the Bonferroni critical value less than the Scheffé. The entries are a function of a and df_{error}. Notice that the entry for $a = 4$ and $df_{error} = 30$ is 8, agreeing with Table 5.8. This table is useful for helping decide whether you should perform planned contrasts or use the Scheffé method for testing your contrasts post hoc. If the number of contrasts you might conceivably test is less than or equal to the number in Table 5.9 for your values of a and df_{error}, the Bonferroni approach is better. On the other hand, if you might test more contrasts than the number in the table, Scheffé's method is better, even if all the contrasts are planned. In the face of this discussion of how the Bonferroni and Scheffé techniques compare, do not forget Tukey's method.

We saw earlier that Tukey's method is generally superior to Bonferroni's for testing all pairwise contrasts. The Scheffé is even less appropriate. Notice that almost all values in Table 5.9 exceed $a(a - 1)/2$ (the number of pairwise contrasts), indicating that the Bonferroni is almost always better than the Scheffé for this number of contrasts. But we have already seen that Tukey is superior to Bonferroni here; Tukey is also superior to Scheffé for this purpose. Thus, using Scheffé's method to test pairwise comparisons sacrifices power. Scheffé's method should not be used unless at least one of the comparisons to be tested is complex.

Modifications of Scheffé's Method

When population variances are unequal, it may be desirable to use a separate variances modification of Scheffé's method for testing comparisons. Such a modification was proposed by

TABLE 5.9
MAXIMUM NUMBER OF CONTRASTS THAT SHOULD BE TESTED IN A STUDY
WITH THE BONFERRONI APPROACH

	Number of Groups							
df_{error}	3	4	5	6	7	8	9	10
5	2	4	8	12	17	24	31	40
6	2	5	9	14	21	30	41	55
7	2	5	10	16	25	37	52	71
8	2	6	11	18	29	44	64	89
9	2	6	12	20	33	51	75	107
10	2	6	12	22	37	58	87	127
12	3	7	13	25	43	70	110	166
14	3	7	14	28	49	82	132	205
16	3	7	15	30	54	93	153	243
18	3	7	16	32	58	103	173	281
20	3	7	17	33	63	112	191	316
30	3	8	18	39	78	147	267	470
40	3	8	20	43	87	170	320	586
50	3	8	20	45	94	187	360	674
60	3	8	21	47	98	199	390	743
70	3	9	21	48	102	209	414	799
80	3	9	21	49	105	217	433	844
90	3	9	22	50	107	223	449	882
100	3	9	22	50	109	228	462	913
110	3	9	22	51	111	232	473	941
120	3	9	22	51	112	236	483	964

Brown and Forsythe (1974). Several simulation studies have suggested that their modification successfully controls α_{EW} when variances are heterogeneous.[9]

The Brown–Forsythe procedure is based on the same F statistic we have repeatedly seen previously when a separate variances approach is taken. Specifically, an observed F is calculated as

$$F = \frac{(\hat{\psi})^2}{\sum_{j=1}^{a} (c_j^2/n_j)s_j^2} \qquad \text{(10, repeated)}$$

As we mentioned in Chapter 4, the corresponding denominator degrees of freedom are arduous, so a computer package will invariably be invoked for their calculation. Later in this chapter, Tables 5.16 and 5.17 will show the formula for these degrees of freedom in the context of summarizing our recommended multiple comparisons procedures. The observed F from Equation 10 is compared to a critical F equal to $(a - 1)F_{.05;\,a-1,\,df}$.

Notice that this is the same critical F as used in Scheffé's method (see Equation 22), except that the denominator degrees of freedom are no longer simply equal to $N - a$.

Numerical Example

We will return once again to our hypertension data to illustrate Scheffé's procedure. Suppose that four contrasts are of interest: (1) drug versus biofeedback, (2) drug versus diet, (3) biofeedback versus diet, and (4) the average of each of the first three treatments versus the combined treatment. You may realize that these are exactly the same contrasts we examined with the

TABLE 5.10
POST HOC CONTRASTS USING SCHEFFÉ'S METHOD

Multiple Comparisons
Dependent Variable: SBP
Scheffé

(I) GROUP	(J) GROUP	Mean Difference (I−J)	Std. Error	Sig.	95% Confidence Interval Lower Bound	95% Confidence Interval Upper Bound
1	2	5.8333	4.6676	.673	−8.3971	20.0638
	3	3.3333	4.6676	.915	−10.8971	17.5638
	4	15.0000*	4.6676	.036	.7696	29.2304
2	1	−5.8333	4.6676	.673	−20.0638	8.3971
	3	−2.5000	4.6676	.962	−16.7304	11.7304
	4	9.1667	4.6676	.307	−5.0638	23.3971
3	1	−3.3333	4.6676	.915	−17.5638	10.8971
	2	2.5000	4.6676	.962	−11.7304	16.7304
	4	11.6667	4.6676	.135	−2.5638	25.8971
4	1	−15.0000*	4.6676	.036	−29.2304	−.7696
	2	−9.1667	4.6676	.307	−23.3971	5.0638
	3	−11.6667	4.6676	.135	−25.8971	2.5638

* The mean difference is significant at the .05 level.

Simultaneous Confidence Intervals

Assuming Homogeneity of Variance

Intervals for pairwise comparisons are shown directly in output.
For our complex comparison of interest, we have:

$$(35.83/3) \pm (\sqrt{9.30})(11.4331/3) \qquad 0.32, 23.57$$

Without Assuming Homogeneity of Variance

Contrast[a]	Computation	Interval
1	$5.8333 \pm (\sqrt{12.21})(5.7237)$	−14.17, 25.83
2	$3.3333 \pm (\sqrt{11.58})(4.0838)$	−10.56, 17.23
3	$-2.500 \pm (\sqrt{13.05})(5.2836)$	−21.59, 16.59
4	$(35.83/3) \pm (\sqrt{10.23})(9.0955/3)$	2.25, 21.64

[a]The first three contrasts are pairwise. In order, they are (1) Group 1 minus Group 2, (2) Group 1 minus Group 3, and (3) Group 2 minus Group 3, The fourth contrast is the average of the first three groups minus the fourth group.

Bonferroni method, as shown in Table 5.5. Now, however, we will suppose that we have chosen these specific contrasts after having seen the data, in which case the Bonferroni method is no longer applicable. Because the contrasts are now post hoc and because they include a complex comparison, Scheffé is the method of choice.

Current versions of SPSS and SAS provide significance tests and confidence intervals for pairwise comparisons using Scheffé's method under an assumption of homogeneity. Ironically, however, neither at the moment provide the capability to apply Scheffé to complex comparisons, despite the fact that this is precisely the situation that calls for Scheffé.

The top portion of Table 5.10 shows SPSS output for all pairwise comparisons. We can obviously use this output to find tests and confidence intervals for our pairwise contrasts of interest. Below the SPSS output are hand calculations needed for forming confidence intervals for the complex contrast as well as for all contrasts when we decide not to assume homogeneity. As in our discussion of the Bonferroni method, we can conceptualize each confidence interval as

$$\text{estimate} \pm (\text{critical value}) (\text{estimated standard error}) \tag{25}$$

Notice that the estimate and the estimated standard error for a contrast do not depend on which multiple-comparison procedure we are using, so these two values are the same for any given contrast as they were for Bonferroni or Tukey. As usual, what we must take into account when using Scheffé is the appropriate critical value. Thus, the calculations seen in Table 5.10 differ from those we saw earlier in Table 5.5 only in that the critical values differ. In particular, the critical value for Scheffé is larger than the critical value for Bonferroni (notice how this is consistent with Table 5.9), so it necessarily follows that Scheffé intervals will be wider than Bonferroni intervals. Indeed, comparing Table 5.10 with Table 5.5 shows that each Scheffé interval is wider than the corresponding Bonferroni interval. This is the price we must pay for choosing our contrasts of interest post hoc instead of planned. Nevertheless, in these particular data, regardless of whether our four contrasts were post hoc or planned, we find that only in the case of the complex contrast can we make a confident statement of directionality, namely that the combined group is more effective than the average of the other three groups.

OTHER MULTIPLE-COMPARISON PROCEDURES

Although the Bonferroni, Tukey, and Scheffé multiple-comparison procedures are probably the most widely used and most generally appropriate techniques, we have already seen that they are far from the only ones that have been developed. In particular, referring back to Table 5.2, notice that we have now described appropriate procedures for establishing direction and magnitude of mean differences for the first three columns of the table, that is, for examining (1) planned, (2) pairwise, and (3) complex comparisons.

We now proceed to describe procedures for the final two columns of Table 5.2. First, Dunnett's procedure is particularly useful when one of the groups in a study is a control group. Second, a variation of Dunnett's method can be used when the purpose of the study is to identify the best treatment group.

Dunnett's Procedure for Comparisons with a Control

In some studies, the primary tests of interest may involve comparing one of the groups with each of the other $a - 1$ groups individually. For example, a researcher might plan to compare each of $a - 1$ different treatments with a control group. Although the Bonferroni procedure could be used, Dunnett (1955) developed a test that is more powerful in this situation, which is often referred to as "many–one" testing because many groups are each compared to one other group. (Do not confuse this procedure with Dunnett's T3, which is an entirely different procedure we presented earlier for performing pairwise comparisons with unequal variances.) This method is used much less often in behavioral research than Bonferroni, Tukey, or Scheffé, primarily because Dunnett's method does not accommodate tests comparing the $a - 1$ treatment groups to one another.

There is no change in the calculation of the observed F test statistic for Dunnett's procedure. As in the methods previously encountered, however, the critical value is altered to maintain the α_{EW} level at .05. Appendix Tables A.6 and A.7 provide the necessary critical values for two-tailed and one-tailed tests, respectively. The columns of the table correspond to the number of groups, including the control group. The entry in the table must be squared to establish a critical value for the F statistic. In other words, the entries in the table are critical t values against which to judge an observed t statistic. Confidence intervals are formed as usual, the only difference being the choice of critical value.

Numerical Example

Suppose the only questions of interest in the hypertension example involved comparing the combined treatment to each of the separate treatments. In other words, suppose we have no interest in comparing the separate treatment groups to one another. Such a "many–one" set of comparisons is exactly the situation where Dunnett's method is appropriate. We will illustrate two-tailed tests and two-sided confidence intervals, although a case could be made for one-tailed tests and one-sided intervals here.

Table 5.11 shows SAS output for comparing the combined treatment against each of the three separate treatments. According to Dunnett's method, we can be 95% confident that the combined treatment is approximately between 3 and 27 units better than drug therapy alone (the first treatment). We cannot unequivocally establish the direction of difference for the combined therapy versus either diet or biofeedback. Notice that the Dunnett intervals shown in Table 5.11 are all narrower than the corresponding Tukey intervals we saw in Table 5.7. The increased precision of the Dunnett intervals reflects the advantage we have gained in being willing to forgo consideration of how the separate therapy conditions compare to one another. Thus, in practice, there is a trade-off here between precision and the number of contrasts we choose to consider. As Exercise 12 at the end of the chapter shows, the Dunnett intervals are also narrower than Bonferroni intervals for this same set of contrasts.

TABLE 5.11
CONTRASTS OF EACH SEPARATE TREATMENT VERSUS
COMBINED TREATMENT

The GLM Procedure

Dunnett's t Tests for SBP

Note. This test controls the Type 1 experimentwise error for comparisons of all treatments against a control.

Alpha	0.05
Error degrees of freedom	20
Error mean square	65.35833
Critical value of Dunnett's t	2.54043
Minimum significant difference	11.858

***Comparisons significant at the 0.05 level.

Group Comparison	Difference Between Means	Simultaneous 95% Confidence Interval	
1–4	15.000	3.142	26.858***
3–4	11.667	−0.191	23.524
2–4	9.167	−2.691	21.024

Procedures for Comparisons With the Best

Especially in applied settings, the fundamental question of interest may be to establish which treatment is best, that is, either the treatment with the largest or the smallest population mean, depending on which end of the scale is most desirable. Hsu (1996) describes a modification of Dunnett's procedure that can be used to answer this question. We will see that we can continue to use the same Dunnett critical value we developed in the immediately preceding discussion. The primary difference is that in the previous use of Dunnett, we knew in advance which group was the control group, whereas in the application we are about to develop, we will not know in advance of collecting the data which single group we should focus on. Thus, the precise details of the procedure must be modified, even though we will continue to use much of what we developed in the previous section.

From another perspective, the goal here is similar to and yet not quite the same as that of examining pairwise comparisons. Tukey's WSD and similar methods in the second column of Table 5.2 implicitly assume that we are interested in comparing every possible pair of groups. However, when the goal is to identify the best group, we are not interested in pairwise differences that do not include the best group. Thus, although we could use Tukey's WSD in an attempt to identify the best group, we would implicitly be including comparisons of no real interest for our specific purpose and therefore considering a larger family of contrasts than necessary. The practical implication is that the method we will present for identifying the best treatment will yield greater power and precision than Tukey's WSD. Thus, Tukey's method is inefficient for identifying the best treatment. Indeed, its inefficiency for this purpose may explain why some researchers have resorted to using such alternatives as Newman–Keuls and Duncan in an effort to increase power and precision. However, if the goal is to identify the best treatment, we should use the modification of Dunnett's method that we will now present.

Our remaining presentation of this method will consist of three sections. First, we will present the rationale for the method in more detail. Second, because most statistical packages do not yet include an explicit option for identifying the best treatment, we will spend more time than usual on the mechanics of performing the test. Third, we will conclude with a numerical example based on our hypertension data.

We will now consider the logic behind the method Hsu (1996) presents for identifying the best treatment group. For example, suppose we wonder whether Group 1 might be the best group in a study. For the moment, let's assume that higher scores are better on the dependent variable. (The same basic logic applies when lower scores are better, but as we will see later, we then have to reverse our comparisons.)

Our question is whether μ_1 is the largest population mean. Equivalently, we could ask whether μ_1 is larger than all other population means in the study. Formally, the question centers around an expression of the form

$$\mu_1 - \max_{j \neq 1} \mu_j$$

The term after the minus sign is to be understood as the largest population mean among the remaining $a - 1$ groups. In theory, it is trivial with this formulation to identify the best treatment. If

$$\mu_1 - \max_{j \neq 1} \mu_j > 0$$

it immediately follows that the first group is in fact the best. On the other hand, if

$$\mu_1 - \max_{j \neq 1} \mu_j < 0$$

it similarly follows that some other group has a larger mean than μ_1, in which case the first group is not the best. Notice that we said that this formulation makes our answer clear—in theory. The complication here is that we do not know the population means, but instead have access only to sample data.

Fortunately, we can solve this problem by forming a confidence interval for the difference between the population mean of Group 1 and the population mean of the best group other than Group 1. As usual, we will be especially interested in discovering whether this interval contains zero. For example, if the interval lies entirely above zero, we can be 95% confident that the population mean of Group 1 is larger than the population mean of any other group, implying that Group 1 is indeed the best treatment. On the other hand, if the interval lies entirely below zero, we can be 95% confident that the population mean of Group 1 is smaller than that of some other group, in which case we can conclude that Group 1 is not the best treatment. Finally, if the interval straddles zero, the mean of Group 1 might be either larger or smaller than the largest mean of the remaining groups, in which case Group 1 may or may not be the best treatment. In this final scenario, we cannot rule out Group 1 as a possibility, but we also cannot be 95% confident that it is truly best.

This same approach is then applied to each group in the study. The end result will be a set of intervals that show plausible values for the difference between each individual group mean and the best of the remaining group means. As a consequence, in the simplest case, we will be able to identify one group as the best with some desired level of confidence (typically 95%). However, in some situations, one group will not stand out from the others, in which case all we can do is to identify a subset of groups, any one of which may be best in the population. In other words, in this scenario, we can eliminate some groups as possibly being best, but we cannot reduce the number of contenders to a single group. Of course, when group differences are all small in the sample, it may happen that we cannot be certain that any groups are truly different from one another, in which case we are left with the unfortunate conclusion that no groups can be eliminated from contention as possibly the best.

Hsu (1996) describes two slightly different techniques for identifying the best treatment, one based on unconstrained intervals and another based on constrained intervals. Unconstrained intervals provide slightly more information but are somewhat wider than constrained intervals. In particular, unconstrained intervals include information about how much better the best group is than other groups, whereas constrained intervals only allow a conclusion that a group is best without estimating the extent to which it is best. Thus, as often happens, there is a trade-off between how much we can say and how precisely we can say it. In our judgment, both variations have their place, so we will present both.

As of this writing, procedures for comparisons with the best are available in Minitab and JMP, but in neither SAS nor SPSS. Even Minitab and JMP do not provide all options we believe you should consider and which we will describe here. Largely for this reason, we will describe the mechanics of these procedures in more detail than has been typical of other procedures. Specifically, we will present four scenarios: (1) unconstrained intervals where high scores on the dependent variable are best, (2) unconstrained intervals where low scores are best, (3) constrained intervals where high scores are best, and (4) constrained intervals where low scores are best. Ideally, our descriptions will allow you not only to use these methods but also to understand them more fully.

TABLE 5.12
COMPARISONS WITH THE BEST: STEPS FOR FORMING
UNCONSTRAINED INTERVALS

When High Scores on the Dependent Variable Are Best

1. Identify the group with the largest sample mean.
2. Use Dunnett's method to form two-sided confidence intervals, comparing the group with the largest sample mean to each of the other $a - 1$ groups. Be certain to calculate the difference so that the largest mean is subtracted from each other mean, in which case the center of each interval should be below zero. This is the current default in the way both SAS and SPSS implement Dunnett when the group with the largest mean is designated to be the "control" group.
3. The first two steps provide an interval for every group except the group with the largest mean. An interval for this group can be obtained from the results in Step 2. Specifically, identify the group with the second largest mean. Then reverse the signs of the lower and upper endpoints of the confidence interval, comparing this group to the group with the largest mean, to obtain the upper and lower endpoints, respectively, for the group with the largest mean.
4. If the interval for the group with the largest mean does not contain zero, this group is deemed to be the best treatment. If this interval does contain zero, all groups with intervals containing zero are included in a set of groups, any one of which is possibly the best treatment. Any group whose interval is entirely below zero is ruled out as the best treatment.

When Low Scores on the Dependent Variable Are Best

1. Identify the group with the smallest sample mean.
2. Use Dunnett's method to form two-sided confidence intervals, comparing the group with the smallest sample mean to each of the other $a - 1$ groups. Be certain to calculate the difference so that the smallest mean is subtracted from each other mean, in which case the center of each interval should be above zero. This is the current default in the way both SAS and SPSS implement Dunnett when the group with the smallest mean is designated to be the "control" group.
3. The first two steps provide an interval for every group except the group with the smallest mean. An interval for this group can be obtained from the results in Step 2. Specifically, identify the group with the second smallest mean. Then reverse the signs of the lower and upper endpoints of the confidence interval, comparing this group to the group with the smallest mean, to obtain the upper and lower endpoints, respectively, for the group with the smallest mean.
4. If the interval for the group with the smallest mean does not contain zero, this group is deemed to be the best treatment. If this interval does contain zero, all groups with intervals containing zero are included in a set of groups, any one of which is possibly the best treatment. Any group whose interval is entirely above zero is ruled out as the best treatment.

Table 5.12 describes the necessary steps for forming unconstrained intervals. The top half of the table pertains to situations where high scores are best, while the bottom half is relevant when low scores are best. These steps follow the same basic logic we developed for using Dunnett's method to compare a set of treatment groups to a control group. For example, suppose that high scores on the dependent variable are best in a three-group study and that the second group has the largest sample mean. Then the second step consists of using Dunnett's method to find confidence intervals based on the sample mean differences $\overline{Y}_1 - \overline{Y}_2$ and $\overline{Y}_3 - \overline{Y}_2$. Step 3 then involves a similar interval, but this time the interval involves subtracting $\overline{Y}_2$ minus the next largest mean. Each of the resulting intervals then provides lower and upper limits for the difference between the population mean in question and the largest of all the other $a - 1$ population means.

Table 5.13 describes the necessary steps for forming constrained intervals. As in Table 5.12, the top half of the table pertains to situations where high scores are best, whereas the bottom half is relevant when low scores are best. Once again, the essential logic follows Dunnett's method, although the precise steps are somewhat more complicated. Notice that the fundamental difference between the unconstrained intervals of Table 5.12 and the constrained intervals of Table 5.13 is that the former use the two-tailed version of Dunnett's method, whereas the latter use the one-tailed version. As a result, constrained intervals will always be narrower than

TABLE 5.13

COMPARISONS WITH THE BEST: STEPS FOR FORMING CONSTRAINED INTERVALS

When High Scores on the Dependent Variable Are Best

1. Identify the group with the largest sample mean.
2. Form the lower limit of each confidence interval by using Dunnett's method to form one-sided confidence intervals, comparing the group with the largest sample mean to each of the other $a - 1$ groups. Choose DUNNETTU in SAS or DUNNETTR in SPSS (shown as "> control" in menu options). Also, be certain to calculate the difference so that the largest mean is subtracted from each other mean, in which case the lower limit of each interval should be below zero. This is the current default in the way both SAS and SPSS implement Dunnett when the group with the largest mean is designated to be the "control" group.
3. The next step is to form the upper limit of each interval. To do so, use Dunnett's method once again to compare the group with the largest sample mean to each of the other $a - 1$ groups. However, this time choose DUNNETTL in SAS as well as SPSS (also shown as "< control" in SPSS menu options). As before, be certain to calculate the difference so that the largest mean is subtracted from each other mean. Again, this is the current default in both SAS and SPSS when the group with the largest mean is designated to be the control group.
4. Consider the value calculated for each upper limit in Step 3. Any interval with a negative upper limit is assigned a new upper limit of zero. Intervals with positive upper limits retain their original upper limit.
5. The preceding steps provide an interval for every group except the group with the largest mean. An interval for this group can be obtained from the results in Step 4. Specifically, identify the group with the second largest mean. Then reverse the signs of the lower and upper endpoints (after having assigned the new upper limit of zero in Step 4, if relevant) of the confidence interval comparing this group to the group with the largest mean, to obtain the upper and lower endpoints, respectively, for the group with the largest mean.
6. If the interval for the group with the largest mean has a lower limit of zero, this group is deemed to be the best treatment. If the interval contains zero, all groups with intervals containing zero are included in a set of groups, any one of which is possibly the best treatment. Any group whose interval has an upper limit of zero is ruled out as the best treatment.

When Low Scores on the Dependent Variable Are Best

1. Identify the group with the smallest sample mean.
2. Form the upper limit of each confidence interval by using Dunnett's method to form one-sided confidence intervals comparing the group with the smallest sample mean to each of the other $a - 1$ groups. Choose DUNNETTL in SAS as well as SPSS (also shown as "< control" in SPSS menu options). Also, be certain to calculate the difference so that the smallest mean is subtracted from each other mean, in which case the upper limit of each interval should be above zero. This is the current default in the way both SAS and SPSS implement Dunnett when the group with the smallest mean is designated to be the control group.
3. The next step is to form the lower limit of each interval. To do so, use Dunnett's method once again to compare the group with the smallest sample mean to each of the other $a - 1$ groups. However, this time choose DUNNETTU in SAS or DUNNETTR in SPSS (shown as "> control" in menu options). As before, be certain to calculate the difference so that the smallest mean is subtracted from each other mean. Again this is the current default in both SAS and SPSS when the group with the smallest mean is designated to be the control group.
4. Consider the value calculated for each lower limit in Step 3. Any interval with a positive lower limit is assigned a new lower limit of zero. Intervals with negative lower limits retain their original lower limit.
5. The preceding steps provide an interval for every group except the group with the smallest mean. An interval for this group can be obtained from the results in Step 4. Specifically, identify the group with the second smallest mean. Then reverse the signs of the lower and upper endpoints (after having assigned the new lower limit of zero in Step 4, if relevant) of the confidence interval, comparing this group to the group with the smallest mean, to obtain the upper and lower endpoints, respectively, for the group with the smallest mean.
6. If the interval for the group with the smallest mean has an upper limit of zero, this group is deemed to be the best treatment. If the interval contains zero, all groups with intervals containing zero are included in a set of groups, any one of which is possibly the best treatment. Any group whose interval has a lower limit of zero is ruled out as the best treatment.

unconstrained intervals. However, only unconstrained intervals allow you to estimate how much better the best treatment is than all other treatments, so when you want to be able to make this type of statement, the increased width of intervals may be a small price to pay for being able to say more about the best treatment.

The steps shown in Tables 5.12 and 5.13 are appropriate when two conditions hold: equal sample sizes and homogeneity of variance. When population variances are equal but sample sizes are unequal, complications emerge in calculating appropriate critical values for the procedure, necessitating a computer package such as Minitab or JMP. Appropriate methods when variances are unequal await further research.

Numerical Example

We will once again rely on our blood pressure data to illustrate how to perform comparisons with the best. We will first show how to form unconstrained intervals, and then we will show how to form constrained intervals. Remember that low blood pressure scores are best, so we will be referring to the bottom portions of Tables 5.12 and 5.13. Readers desiring an opportunity to practice the procedures when high scores are best should know that Exercise 17 at the end of the chapter provides this practice. In addition, we will use SAS to obtain Dunnett intervals for these data, but the same values should be available from any statistical package that will form two-sided and one-sided Dunnett intervals.

We will begin by assuming that we want to form unconstrained confidence intervals to find which treatment produces the lowest mean blood pressure readings. The bottom half of Table 5.12 shows that the first step is to identify the group with the smallest sample mean. In our case, that is the combined treatment group, which has a mean of 81.83. Step 2 requires that we use Dunnett's method to compare this group with each of the other groups. Table 5.14 shows SAS output providing two-sided Dunnett's intervals. Notice that the values shown in Table 5.14 are exactly the same as those we saw earlier in Table 5.11, because in both cases we are comparing the combined group to each of the other groups. However, the remaining

TABLE 5.14
TWO-SIDED DUNNETT INTERVALS TO IDENTIFY
THE BEST TREATMENT FOR HYPERTENSION

The GLM Procedure

Dunnett's t Tests for SBP

Note. This test controls the Type 1 experimentwise error for comparisons of all treatments against a control.

Alpha	0.05
Error degrees of freedom	20
Error mean square	65.35833
Critical value of Dunnett's t	2.54043
Minimum significant difference	11.858

***Comparisons significant at the 0.05 level.

Group Comparison	Difference Between Means	Simultaneous 95% Confidence Interval	
1–4	15.000	3.142	26.858***
3–4	11.667	−0.191	23.524
2–4	9.167	−2.691	21.024

steps and ultimate interpretation of the intervals is somewhat different in the two cases. Step 3 requires that we find the group with the second smallest sample mean, which is the biofeedback group, with a mean of 91.00. Reversing the sign of the limits of this interval in the SAS output yields an additional interval for the combined group, with a lower limit of −21.024 and an upper limit of 2.691. Notice that this interval contains zero, so according to Step 4, all groups with intervals containing zero should be regarded as possibly the best treatment. Given our data, it is plausible that either biofeedback, diet, or the combined treatment is the best treatment. In other words, with 95% confidence, we can only rule out drug therapy as possibly the best treatment. Further, notice we can be 95% confident that the combined therapy is at most 2.69 units less effective than the best treatment, whereas the biofeedback and diet treatments may be as much as 21.02 and 23.52 units less effective, respectively. Even though our single best guess is that the combined treatment is best, the data are not strong enough for us to eliminate biofeedback and diet from consideration. A larger sample size would have given us more power to detect the best treatment.

Suppose we are not interested in estimating the extent to which the best treatment is truly best. In this case, we should form constrained intervals. The bottom half of Table 5.13 shows that the first step is to find the group with the smallest sample mean, which is the combined therapy group in our data. The top half of Table 5.15 shows one-sided Dunnett upper limits obtained from SAS in accordance with Step 2 of Table 5.13. The next section of Table 5.15 shows lower limits obtained as described in Step 3. The final section of the table shows the results of applying Steps 4 and 5, where values of zero are assigned and an interval is formed for the combined treatment group. The intervals for both the combined and the biofeedback groups contain zero, so we can be 95% confident that one of them is the best treatment. In other words, we can rule out drug and diet as possibly being the best treatment. Notice that for these data, forming constrained intervals allowed us to rule out more treatments than we were

TABLE 5.15
ONE-SIDED DUNNETT INTERVALS TO IDENTIFY THE BEST
TREATMENT FOR HYPERTENSION

Upper Limits

Group Comparison	Difference Between Means	Simultaneous 95% Confidence Limits	
1–4	15.000	−Infinity	25.233
3–4	11.667	−Infinity	21.899
2–4	9.167	−Infinity	19.399

Lower Limits

Group Comparison	Difference Between Means	Simultaneous 95% Confidence Limits	
1–4	15.000	4.767	infinity***
3–4	11.667	1.434	infinity***
2–4	9.167	−1.066	infinity

Final Confidence Limits

		Lower Limit	Upper Limit
Group 1	Drug	0.00	25.23
Group 2	Biofeedback	−1.07	19.40
Group 3	Diet	0.00	21.90
Group 4	Combined	−19.40	1.07

able to do with unconstrained intervals. However, if the data had allowed us to identify a single group as best, constrained intervals would not have allowed us to estimate how much better this group is than the remaining groups, reflecting the trade-off we have previously mentioned.

Fisher's LSD (Protected t)

We finish this section with a description of yet one other method, Fisher's least significant difference (LSD). Notice that this method appears in the second row of Table 5.2. Because it does not allow us to establish confident directions, much less confidence intervals, we generally recommend against its use. It may seem strange, therefore, that we have decided to include it in this chapter. Our primary purpose in including it is to illustrate why we believe it suffers from a serious shortcoming. However, another reason for including it is that Levin, Serlin, and Seaman (1994) have shown that this general shortcoming is not a problem in the very special case of three groups. For reasons we will explain momentarily, in this specific situation, Fisher's LSD may be useful.

Fisher (1935) developed a procedure known as Fisher's LSD method or, equivalently, as the protected t-test method. Although this technique was developed nearly 20 years earlier than the other multiple-comparison methods described in this chapter, it is still in use today, partly because of its simplicity. The test proceeds in two stages. First, the omnibus null hypothesis is tested. If it is not rejected, no further tests are performed; if it is rejected, the process continues to the second stage. At this stage, individual contrasts among the groups are tested using an α_{PC} level of .05 for each contrast. Traditionally, only pairwise contrasts are tested in the second step (Fisher developed the procedure for this purpose), but as Keppel (1982) and Levin, Serlin, and Seaman (1994) point out, the logic of the procedure does not rule out complex comparisons in the second stage. The LSD has another advantage besides its simplicity—the critical values at the second stage are less than those for the Bonferroni, Tukey, or Scheffé methods. This is true because the LSD uses an α_{PC} of .05, whereas the others use an α_{EW} of .05. The implication is that the LSD has more power to detect true differences. You may be thinking that this is an unfair comparison, however, because the objective of a multiple-comparisons procedure is to control α_{EW} at .05.

We now consider whether the LSD succeeds in maintaining α_{EW} at .05. The basic logic behind the LSD is that, because it requires a statistically significant omnibus F value, in only 5 of every 100 studies (in the long run) will the process mistakenly lead to Stage 2, when in fact all the population means are equal. Even if the second stage were to always produce a statistically significant result, only 5% of the time would a Type I error be committed, because the omnibus test of Stage 1 protects tests performed in the second stage. It seems that by requiring the omnibus test to be significant before testing individual contrasts, the goal of maintaining α_{EW} at .05 is accomplished. Indeed, the reasoning to this point is valid. As long as all a population means are equal (i.e., the complete null hypothesis is true), α_{EW} is held at .05 by the LSD. However, suppose that some but not all of the null hypothesis is true. For example, with $a = 11$, it might happen that the first 10 groups all have identical population means. The 11th treatment, however, has been included in the study because prior evidence suggests it to be very different from the first 10. If the 11th group is different enough from the first 10, the omnibus null hypothesis will be rejected with a probability approaching 1.0 for a large enough sample size. Conceivably, then, the second stage of the LSD will be reached with a high probability. Now, however, the LSD offers no further protection for contrasts among the first 10 groups. In other words, there is no protection for that part of the complete null hypothesis that is true. If all pairwise contrasts among the 10 truly identical groups are performed, the probability of at least one significant result using

$\alpha_{PC} = .05$ is approximately .60. Thus, in 60 of every 100 such experiments (in the long run), a Type 1 error would be committed. Thus, the LSD fails to maintain α_{EW} at .05, except in the special case where the entire null hypothesis is true. None of the other approaches (Bonferroni, Tukey, Scheffé, or Dunnett) suffer from this limitation—they all maintain α_{EW} at .05 under all circumstances as long as the basic ANOVA assumptions are satisfied. Indeed, as mentioned earlier, Tukey's method is referred to as the wholly significant difference (WSD) precisely because the whole set of pairwise contrasts is protected at .05 with his approach.

Levin, Serlin, and Seaman (1994) realized that the flaw disclosed in the previous paragraph is no longer applicable in the special case of three groups. In particular, they point out that there are three relevant patterns of possible population means with three groups:

1. All population means are equal.
2. Two of the population means are equal to one another (but the third mean is different).
3. All three population means are different from one another.

Levin, Serlin, and Seaman (1994) then explain why the LSD performs satisfactorily in any of these three situations. First, if all population means are equal, the omnibus test will reject only 5% of the time, so the procedure moves to the second stage only 5% of the time, which means that the experimentwise error rate will be at most 5%. Second, if one of the means is different from the other two (i.e., case b), the second stage will generally be reached more than 5% of the time. However, once it is reached, there is only one true null hypothesis, so testing it at the 5% level is perfectly appropriate and succeeds in controlling α_{EW} at .05. Third, if all three population means are different from one another, there are no true null hypotheses to test, so no Type I errors can be committed. Thus, Fisher's LSD successfully controls α_{EW} at .05 in the special case of three groups, and can be recommended in this specific situation. However, even in this favorable situation, it does not allow the formation of appropriate simultaneous confidence intervals, so its use is restricted to hypothesis testing.

Several other methods have been developed that in many ways represent a compromise between the LSD and Tukey's approach for testing pairwise comparisons. Two of the most widely used compromises are the Newman–Keuls and the Duncan procedures. Both are referred to as either multiple-range tests or layered methods, because they involve testing ranges between groups in a layered fashion. Unfortunately, both of these methods suffer from the same liability as Fisher's LSD (with more than three groups) in that they do not necessarily control α_{EW} at .05. Thus, we recommend against their use. More recently, other alternatives, such as REGW-Q and REGW-F, have been developed and included in statistical packages. These methods succeed in properly controlling α_{EW} at .05. Their major liability is that although they succeed in properly identifying true differences in population means, they do not allow a statement of confident directions or the formation of confidence intervals. In this sense, they are appropriate only in a rather special case where the only goal is to establish differences without regard to the direction and magnitude of those differences.

FALSE DISCOVERY RATE

A recurring theme throughout this chapter has been the importance of the distinction between the per-comparison error rate and the experimentwise error rate. In 1995, Benjamini and Hochberg introduced yet another way of conceptualizing error rates in the presence of more than one test per experiment. They called their new conceptualization the "false discovery rate" (FDR). Although as of this writing it is still a newcomer in the long history of multiple comparisons, it has nevertheless begun to attract quite a bit of attention, because in a practical sense it represents a compromise between the more traditional ideas of the per-comparison error rate and the experimentwise error rate.

The motivation behind the FDR stems from a desire to control the proportion of false discoveries that appear in the literature. By "false discoveries," Benjamini and Hochberg (1995) mean false rejections of the null hypothesis (i.e., Type 1 errors). What is different about the FDR is that Benjamini and Hochberg (1995) define it in terms of the total number of discoveries, that is, in terms of the total number of rejected hypotheses, some of which may have been falsely rejected, but others of which may have been correctly rejected. The idea here is to make certain that the proportion of false discoveries relative to total discoveries is kept appropriately small, such as at the 5% level. It turns out that defining error rates in this way leads to methods that are less prone to Type I errors than are methods that simply control the per-comparison alpha level, but are often more powerful than methods that control the experimentwise alpha level. In a moment we will look at FDR in more detail, but its essence can be thought of in terms of the following fraction:

$$\frac{\text{number of false rejections}}{\text{number of total rejections}}$$

The goal of the FDR is to control the average value of this fraction. In other words, we want to use a method that ensures that only a small fraction of the discoveries (i.e., statistically significant results) we report are unbeknownst to us false discoveries.

We need to consider three additional aspects of the FDR:

1. Exactly how is controlling FDR different from controlling α_{EW} ?
2. What methods provide appropriate control of the FDR?
3. Under what types of circumstances might the FDR be most appropriate?

In order to understand the FDR, it is first helpful to revisit exactly what it means to control α_{EW}. Suppose an experiment involves testing m null hypotheses. Define a variable P whose value depends on the outcome of the experiment in the following manner:

$P = 0$ if no true null hypotheses are rejected.
$P = 1$ if one or more true null hypotheses are rejected.

Thus, in any single experiment, P will have a value of either 0 or 1. As a thought experiment, we could contemplate replicating any given study over and over again many times. Each time we will record the value of P. (Of course, in actual research, we never know with certainty which if any null hypotheses are true, but remember that this is a thought experiment.) Across replications, our values of P will be a string of zero's and one's, where we would hope that the zero's predominate. What it means from this perspective to control α_{EW} at .05 is that the average value of P is at most .05. In other words, in the long run, only 1 time out of 20 will an experiment contain a false rejection of the null hypothesis. Thus, from this perspective, if our goal is to control α_{EW} at .05, we need to use a method that leads to an average value of P no larger than .05.

How does this compare to the FDR? Once again, consider an experiment consisting of m hypothesis tests. Now, however, define a variable Q whose value depends on the outcome of the experiment in the following manner:

$Q = 0$ if no true null hypotheses are rejected.

$Q = V/(V + S)$ if V true null hypotheses are rejected and S false null hypotheses are rejected.

Notice the relationship between Q and the fraction we defined a few paragraphs ago. Whenever $V + S$ is greater than zero, Q is literally the fraction of falsely rejected null hypotheses relative to the total number of rejections. In cases where $V + S$ equals 0, the fraction is itself considered to be zero, because no Type I errors have been committed. In general, then, we can regard Q as an index of the number of false rejections relative to the number of total rejections. Whereas α_{EW} is defined as the average value of P, FDR is defined as the average value of Q.

Thus, to better understand the FDR, we need to better understand Q. First, let's consider a situation where (unbeknownst to us) all m null hypotheses we are testing are true. Notice then that $S = 0$ in every replication, because we have no false null hypotheses available to be rejected. Because $S = 0$ in every replication, Q takes on either of two values. If we do not reject any true null hypotheses in a specific replication, $Q = 0$. However, $Q = 1$ anytime we reject one or more true null hypotheses. As a result, in this situation, we will get a string of Q values consisting of zero's and one's. The crucial point to realize is that this string of Q values will be identical to the string of P values we would obtain for the same replications. Thus, FDR and α_{EW} will be the same here. In general, when all null hypotheses being tested are true, FDR and α_{EW} are equal to one another.

What if some of the null hypotheses we are testing are false? In particular, suppose we test 10 null hypotheses, where 7 of them are true and 3 are false. Suppose we decided to use a per-comparison alpha level of .005 in order to control α_{EW}. What would our string of values for P look like? The string necessarily consists of zeros and ones, and in this case the proportion of one's would be something less than .05. What about our string of values for Q? Assuming we still use a per-comparison alpha level of .005, Q will equal zero for any specific replication in the string if and only if $P = 0$ for that same replication. But what about when $P = 1$? In this instance, Q will tend to be less than 1, because S will tend to be greater than 0 to the extent that we have reasonable power for testing our three false null hypotheses. For example, as the power of each of these tests approaches 1.0, S will approach a value of 3 for every replication, which means that the ratio of V to $V + S$ is likely to be 0.25 (except when we falsely reject more than one of the seven true null hypotheses in the same study). The practical point is that the average value of the string of Q values will be noticeably less than the average value of the comparable string of P values. In other words, when some of the hypotheses we are testing are false, FDR will be less than α_{EW}. Thus, we can allow α_{EW} to exceed .05 and yet succeed in controlling FDR at .05 when some of our hypotheses should be rejected because they are false. In such a situation, deciding to control FDR instead of α_{EW} provides more power to detect those hypotheses that should in fact be rejected.

To pursue the difference between FDR and α_{EW} one step further, we will continue to consider our hypothetical study involving a total of 10 hypotheses, 7 of which are true and 3 of which are false. Suppose we used a critical value for each comparison so that 80% of the time none of the true null hypotheses were rejected, but 20% of the time at least one false rejection occurs. In this instance, 80% of our P values would be zero, and 20% would be 1. Thus, α_{EW} would equal 0.20, a rate likely to be deemed too large. Now consider our values of Q using the same critical value. As with P, 80% of our Q values will equal zero. But what about the other 20%? For simplicity, suppose we have power close to 1.00 for rejecting the three false hypotheses. Then the remaining 20% of Q values will tend to equal 0.25 (i.e., $1/(1 + 3)$), because only rarely will we reject more than one of the true nulls, and we will almost always reject all three of the false nulls). What will the overall average of Q equal here? If 80% of values are zero and 20% of values are 0.25, the overall average will equal 0.05. Thus, the same critical value that produces an experimentwise error rate of 0.20 produces an FDR of 0.05. We would almost certainly decide that our decision rule is unacceptable in terms of α_{EW} and thus be forced to increase our critical value, inevitably lowering power to detect true differences. However, the original critical value would presumably be judged as acceptable in terms of FDR, so we would proceed with the smaller critical value and hence enjoy the benefits of greater power.

Suppose we decide to use FDR as the basis for controlling our error rate in the face of multiple hypotheses. What method can we use to ensure proper control of the FDR? Before answering this question, remember that we have seen throughout this chapter that the choice of method depends on two dimensions: the definition of error control and the type of contrast being tested. Recall that these two dimensions are reflected in Table 5.2. The situation is no different when controlling the FDR in the sense that different methods are appropriate for different types of contrasts. However, the situation for the FDR is further complicated by the fact that this is a newly emerging area of research, so new suggestions about ideal methods for controlling the FDR continue to appear. We cannot possibly do justice to the entire topic here, so instead we have chosen to present a single method that is applicable for either of two situations: testing independent (i.e., orthogonal) hypotheses and testing pairwise comparisons.

The name of the specific method we will present is Benjamini and Hochberg's Linear Step Up procedure. Benjamini and Hochberg (1995) have shown that this method controls the FDR for independent tests, and Keselman, Cribbie, and Holland (1999) have shown that it controls FDR for pairwise comparisons. However, other methods are needed for testing other patterns of hypotheses where test statistics may be correlated with one another. Benjamini, Drai, Elmer, Kafkafi, and Golani (2001) describe a slightly more complicated procedure that controls FDR for any arbitrary pattern of correlated test statistics.

The Linear Step Up (LSU) procedure begins by rank ordering the p values obtained from testing each of the m hypotheses. Specifically, the p values are ordered from smallest to largest. The LSU begins with the largest p value. If this p value is less than .05, all null hypotheses are rejected. If this p value is greater than .05, the hypothesis corresponding to this p value is not rejected, and the procedure moves on to consider the next p value in the ordering. If this second largest p value is less than $((m - 1)/m).05$, this hypothesis and all remaining hypotheses are rejected. However, if the p value is greater than $((m - 1)/m).05$, then this hypothesis is not rejected, and the procedure moves on once again to consider the next p value in the ordering. No hypotheses at all are rejected if the procedure reaches the smallest p value and it exceeds $.05/m$.

Notice that the alpha levels of the LSU procedure reveal how it represents a compromise between per-comparison control and experimentwise control. In the LSU, the largest p value is compared against .05, which corresponds to the per-comparison alpha level. The smallest p value is compared against $.05/m$, which corresponds to the experimentwise alpha level. All other p values are compared against intermediate values. The LSU procedure can be described more formally as consisting of the following steps, for testing a total of m hypotheses:

1. Rank order the p values from smallest to largest.
2. Assign an index value i to each p value to represent its rank. The smallest p value is assigned an index value i of 1, the next smallest is assigned an index value i of 2, and so forth, up to the largest p value, which receives an index value of m.
3. Compare each p value to $(i/m)\alpha$, where α is the desired value of the FDR (usually .05).
4. Define k to be the largest value of i for which the observed p value is less than $(i/m)\alpha$.
5. All hypotheses with index values less than or equal to k are rejected, whereas all hypotheses with index values larger than k are not rejected.
6. If all observed p values are larger than $(i/m)\alpha$, no hypotheses are rejected.

To see how the LSU procedure works, let's consider an example where $m = 5$ and we want to control FDR at .05. Suppose we obtained the following five p values: .029, .026, .167, .048, and .001. How can we assess the statistical significance of each corresponding hypothesis? We begin by ranking the p values from smallest to largest, which yields .001, .026, .029, .048, and .167. We then compare the largest p value of .167 to $(5/5).05$. The observed p value is larger than .05, so we do not reject this hypothesis and instead move on to the next p value. We compare this p value of .048 to $(4/5).05$. Once again, the observed p value of .048 is larger than .040, so we again move on to the next p value. This time we compare the p value of .029 to $(3/5).05$. Now .029 is less than .030, so we reject the hypothesis corresponding to this p value. Formally, we have determined that $k = 3$ for these data, so according to Step 5 above, we reject the hypotheses associated with the three smallest p values. Notice that we do so even though the second smallest p value of .026 would not have been less than $(2/5).05$. As soon as we identify a p value smaller than $(i/m).05$, testing stops.

Under what types of circumstances might we prefer to define error control in terms of FDR instead of α_{EW}? Any answer to this question is necessarily somewhat subjective. Before providing any type of answer, it is essential to realize that the FDR is a different way of thinking about error control. Only when all null hypotheses are true is FDR identical to α_{EW}. Thus, whenever at least one null hypothesis is false, choosing to control FDR at .05 necessarily means that α_{EW} is being allowed to exceed .05. Whether this is good or bad depends on one's perspective. At any rate, such authors as Benjamini and Hochberg (1995); Keselman, Cribbie, and Holland (1999); and Williams, Jones, and Tukey (1999) have suggested a variety of situations where FDR might be preferred to α_{EW}. Examples include exploratory studies where discovering unexplored results may be more important than in later stages of confirmatory research. Similarly, in neuroscience, hypotheses involving brain activity may be tested in a very large number of areas of the brain, in which case controlling α_{EW} may wreak havoc with power. Instead of ignoring the problem altogether and using a per-comparison alpha level, FDR may be an appropriate compromise, especially when statistically significant results obtained for regions for a single individual can then be compared across individuals. Yet other examples are designs with multiple subgroups and multiple dependent variables.

CHOOSING AN APPROPRIATE PROCEDURE

The practical implication of this chapter is that we have recommended five multiple-comparisons procedures for general use: Bonferroni, Tukey, Scheffé, Dunnett, and Hsu. Figure 5.1 is a flowchart (i.e., a decision tree) that is intended to provide a general guideline for choosing from among these four procedures in a particular situation. We should stress the phrase "general guideline" here; it is important that you understand the principles we have presented in the chapter so that you can use this flowchart as an aid in choosing a technique without being at the complete mercy of a set of mechanical rules to follow blindly. For example, you may want to consider the FDR as an appropriate measure of error control, but we have not attempted to incorporate this conceptualization into Figure 5.1. Similarly, keep in mind that Fisher's LSD properly controls α_{EW} in the special case of three groups, but even there it does not allow for simultaneous confidence intervals. For this reason, we have excluded it from the figure, but if you are content with hypothesis tests unaccompanied by confidence intervals, you may want to consider the LSD with three groups. For these and other reasons, the flowchart is meant to help you organize some of the issues of this chapter, but it cannot possibly reflect all of the nuances we have discussed.

We would be remiss if we did not take a moment to explain where the omnibus test of Chapter 3 fits into this framework. In particular, it is important that you understand that the

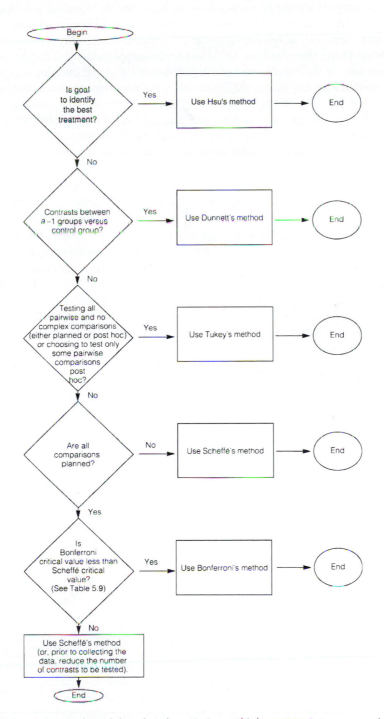

FIG. 5.1.   General guideline for choosing a multiple-comparisons procedure.

omnibus test is not a prerequisite for the Bonferroni, Tukey, Dunnett, or Hsu procedures. Instead, these methods should be viewed as substitutes for the omnibus test because they control α_{EW} at the desired level all by themselves. Requiring a significant omnibus test before proceeding to perform any of these analyses, as is sometimes done, only serves to lower α_{EW} below the desired level (Bernhardson, 1975) and hence inappropriately decreases power.

The proper role of the omnibus test is that it addresses a global question of whether any differences exist among the groups. At times, this is an important question in its own right, independently of the likely desire to proceed by investigating which specific groups differ from one another. In this case, the omnibus test should be viewed as a precursor to Scheffé's method. As discussed earlier, if the omnibus test is statistically significant, there is at least one contrast that will be statistically significant with Scheffé's method, namely a contrast whose coefficients are given by

$$c_j = n_j(\overline{Y}_j - \overline{Y}) \qquad\qquad\qquad \text{(18, repeated)}$$

Thus, a statistically significant omnibus test is a signal that it is worthwhile to search for significant contrasts. On the other hand, if the omnibus test is nonsignificant, searching for any significant contrast is pointless, because none exists. Thus, the omnibus test serves a very definite purpose, but it does so only when neither the Bonferroni, Tukey, Dunnett, or Hsu procedures are appropriate for addressing an investigator's questions.

As further assistance, Tables 5.16 and 5.17 summarize the procedural details for the Bonferroni, Tukey, and Scheffé procedures. Table 5.16 provides formulas for hypothesis

TABLE 5.16
TEST STATISTICS AND CRITICAL VALUES
FOR MULTIPLE-COMPARISONS PROCEDURES

	Test Statistic	*Critical Value*
Assuming Homogeneity of Variance		
Bonferroni	$(\hat{\psi})^2 \Big/ \left[MS_W \sum_{j=1}^{a} \left(c_j^2/n_j\right) \right]$	$F_{.05/C;\,1,\,N-a}$
Tukey	$\dfrac{n_g n_h(\overline{Y}_g - \overline{Y}_h)^2}{(n_g + n_h)MS_w}$	$(q_{.05;\,a,\,N-a})^2/2$
Scheffé	$(\hat{\psi})^2 \Big/ \left[MS_W \sum_{j=1}^{a} \left(c_j^2/n_j\right) \right]$	$(a-1)F_{.05;\,a-1,\,N-a}$
*Without Assuming Homogeneity of Variance**		
Bonferroni	$(\hat{\psi})^2 \Big/ \left[\sum_{j=1}^{a} \left(c_j^2/n_j\right)s_j^2 \right]$	$F_{.05/C;\,1,df}$
Tukey	$\dfrac{(\overline{Y}_g - \overline{Y}_h)^2}{\dfrac{s_g^2}{n_g} + \dfrac{s_h^2}{n_h}}$	large n: $(q_{.05;\,a,df})^2/2$ small n: $V^2_{.05;\,a,df}$
Scheffé	$(\hat{\psi})^2 \Big/ \left[\sum_{j=1}^{a} \left(c_j^2/n_j\right)s_j^2 \right]$	$(a-1)F_{.05;\,a-1,df}$

$$\text{*For all procedures, } df = \frac{\left(\sum\limits_{j=1}^{a} c_j^2 s_j^2/n_j\right)^2}{\sum\limits_{j=1}^{a} \left(c_j^2 s_j^2/n_j\right)^2/(n_j - 1)}$$

TABLE 5.17

FORMULAS FOR FORMING SIMULTANEOUS CONFIDENCE INTERVALS

Assuming Homogeneity of Variance

Bonferroni

$$\hat{\psi} \pm \sqrt{F_{.05/C;1,N-a}}\sqrt{MS_W \sum_{j=1}^{a}\left(c_j^2/n_j\right)}$$

Tukey

$$(\overline{Y}_g - \overline{Y}_h) \pm (q_{.05;a,N-a}/\sqrt{2})\sqrt{MS_W\left(\frac{1}{n_g}+\frac{1}{n_h}\right)}$$

Scheffé

$$\hat{\psi} \pm \sqrt{(a-1)F_{.05;a-1,N-a}}\sqrt{MS_W \sum_{j=1}^{a}\left(c_j^2/n_j\right)}$$

*Without Assuming Homogeneity of Variance**

Bonferroni

$$\hat{\psi} \pm \sqrt{F_{.05/C;1,df}}\sqrt{\sum_{j=1}^{a}\left[\left(c_j^2/n_j\right)s_j^2\right]}$$

Tukey

large *n:* $(\overline{Y}_g - \overline{Y}_h) \pm (q_{.05;a,df}/\sqrt{2})\sqrt{\left(s_g^2/n_g\right)+\left(s_h^2/n_h\right)}$

small *n:* $(\overline{Y}_g - \overline{Y}_h) \pm V_{.05;a,df}\sqrt{\left(s_g^2/n_g\right)+\left(s_g^2/n_h\right)}$

Scheffé

$$\hat{\psi} \pm \sqrt{(a-1)F_{.05;a-1,df}}\sqrt{\sum_{j=1}^{a}\left[\left(c_j^2/n_j\right)s_j^2\right]}$$

*For all procedures, $df = \dfrac{\left(\sum\limits_{j=1}^{a} c_j^2 s_j^2/n_j\right)^2}{\sum\limits_{j=1}^{a}\left(c_j^2 s_j^2/n_j\right)^2/(n_j-1)}$

testing, and Table 5.17 provides formulas for forming simultaneous confidence intervals. Both tables provide procedures to use when homogeneity of variance is assumed, as well as when it is not. Although the entries in the tables assume that α_{EW} has been set at .05, other values of α_{EW} could be substituted for .05.

In closing, we should mention that research on multiple-comparisons procedures is very active in the field of statistics. Readers who are interested in more details are advised to consult Hsu (1996), Toothaker (1991), Hochberg and Tamhane (1987) or Wilcox (1987a, 1987b).

EXERCISES

1. An investigator decides to test the following four contrasts in a five-group study:

	1	*2*	*3*	*4*	*5*
ψ_1	1	−1	0	0	0
ψ_2	0	0	1	−1	0
ψ_3	1	1	−1	−1	0
ψ_4	1	1	1	1	−4

Find the α_{EW} level if each contrast is tested with an α_{PC} level of .05.

*2. A researcher has conducted a five-group study. She plans to test the following pairwise comparisons: μ_1 versus μ_2, μ_2 versus μ_3, and μ_4 versus μ_5.

   a. What multiple comparisons procedure should be used to maintain the α_{EW} level at .05?

b. What will the critical F value be for each contrast, if there are 13 participants per group?

c. Suppose that after looking at the data, the researcher decides to replace the comparison of μ_2 versus μ_3 with a comparison of μ_3 versus μ_4. What multiple-comparisons procedure should be used to maintain the α_{EW} level at .05?

d. What will the critical F value be in part c if there are 13 subjects per group?

e. What implications does the difference in critical values you found in Parts b and d have for revising planned comparisons after having examined the data?

*3. The following summary data are obtained in a four-group study, with 25 participants per group:

$$\overline{Y}_1 = 52 \qquad \overline{Y}_2 = 46 \qquad \overline{Y}_3 = 51 \qquad \overline{Y}_4 = 54$$
$$s_1^2 = 96 \qquad s_2^2 = 112 \qquad s_3^2 = 94 \qquad s_4^2 = 98$$

After examining the data, the experimenter decides to compare the means of Groups 2 and 4. He finds that the mean difference is nonsignificant using Scheffé's method.

a. Is he correct that this mean difference cannot be declared significant using Scheffé's method? (You can assume homogeneity of variance.)

b. Is there a better method available for testing this contrast that will maintain α_{EW} at .05, although the contrast was chosen post hoc? If so, can the contrast be declared significant with this method?

4. The experimenter in Exercise 3 has decided to supplement his hypothesis test comparing Groups 2 and 4 with a confidence interval.

a. Use an appropriate method to form a 95% simultaneous confidence interval for the difference between Groups 2 and 4, where this specific comparison has been chosen from the larger set of all pairwise comparisons. You may assume homogeneity of variance.

b. The experimenter argues that the interval in part a could be formed using Equation 5.3 and setting w equal to 1.99, because he is forming only this single interval. Do you agree? Why or why not?

*5. This problem asks you to reconsider the data from Exercise 13 in Chapter 4. The data are given here once again:

	1	2	3	4
	3	7	9	11
	4	5	2	7
	5	6	5	11
	5	5	9	7
	3	7	5	4
Mean	4	6	6	8
Var (s^2)	1	1	9	9

We assume that all pairwise comparisons are to be tested and that α_{EW} is to be maintained at .05. Although all comparisons are of potential interest, this exercise only requires you to consider two specific comparisons: Group 1 versus Group 2 and Group 3 versus Group 4.

a. Test the difference in the means of Groups 3 and 4, first using MS_W as the error term and then using a separate error term. How do the results compare?

b. Test the difference in the means of Groups 1 and 2, first using MS_W as the error term and then using a separate error term. How do the results compare?

c. Which error term do you think is more appropriate here? Why?

6. This problem uses the same data as Exercise 5. However, we assume here that the goal now is to form confidence intervals instead of testing hypotheses. Assume that a confidence interval is to be formed for each pairwise comparison, but as in Exercise 5, this exercise only requires you to consider two specific comparisons: Group 1 versus Group 2 and Group 3 versus Group 4.

a. Form a 95% simultaneous confidence interval for $\mu_3 - \mu_4$, first using MS_W as the error term and then using a separate error term. How do the results compare?

b. Form a 95% simultaneous confidence interval for $\mu_1 - \mu_2$, first using MS_W as the error term and then using a separate error term. How do the results compare?

c. Based on the respective confidence intervals, which error term do you think is more appropriate here? Why?

*7. A graduate student has conducted a four-group study in which he tested the following three planned comparisons:

	1	2	3	4
ψ_1	1	−1	0	0
ψ_2	.5	.5	−1	0
ψ_3	1/3	1/3	1/3	−1

The sums of squares for the three comparisons are 75, 175, and 125, respectively. The value of MS_W equals 25, and there were 11 participants in each group. The student's adviser wonders whether the omnibus F test of $H_0 : \mu_1 = \mu_2 = \mu_3 = \mu_4$ would be statistically significant for these data. Can you help her?

a. Is it possible to perform the test of the omnibus null hypothesis from the available information? If so, is the test significant? If it is not possible, explain why not.

b. Find the observed F value for each of the planned comparisons tested by the student. Which, if any, are statistically significant with an α_{EW} level of .05?

c. What relationship, if any, is there between the single observed F value of part a and the three observed F values of part b?

8. A researcher has conducted an experiment with six independent groups of 12 participants each. Although the omnibus F test was nonsignificant, he decided to use Scheffé's method of multiple comparisons. He claims that his calculations revealed that the average of the first three groups was significantly different from that of the last three. How would you respond to his claim?

9. A graduate student has designed a study in which she will have four independent groups of seven participants each. Parts a–h ask you to decide which multiple-comparisons procedure (MCP) should be used to achieve maximal power while maintaining experimentwise alpha at .05. For each part, tell which MCP she should use and briefly justify your answer.

a. The student plans to test all pairwise comparisons.

b. The student decides after having looked at the data to test all pairwise comparisons.

c. The student plans to test only four pairwise comparisons.

d. The student decides after having looked at the data to test only four pairwise comparisons.

e. The student plans to test seven planned comparisons.

f. After having looked at the data, the student decides to test seven specific comparisons.

g. The student plans to test 20 planned comparisons. (Hint: The critical t value for $\alpha_{PC} = .05/20$ is 3.376.)

h. After having looked at the data, the student decides to test 20 specific comparisons.

10. The following data were obtained in a four-group study:

	1	2	3	4
	6	6	3	5
	5	9	7	3
	7	9	6	1
	5	4	3	4
	3	5	4	3
	4	6	7	5
Mean	5.0	6.5	5.0	3.5
Var (s^2)	2.0	4.3	3.6	2.3

a. Are the four group means significantly different from each other?

b. Suppose all pairwise comparisons were investigated. If the α_{EW} level is maintained at .05, is the difference between the means of Groups 2 and 4 significant? (You can assume homogeneity of variance).

c. How can you explain the results of Parts a and b? What general pattern of means is most likely to produce this type of result?

d. What does this example imply about the necessity of obtaining a statistically significant omnibus test before using Tukey's WSD method to test all pairwise comparisons?

*11. A professor has obtained the following data for a three-group between-subjects design:

Group	Mean	SDs
1	10	10.00
2	10	14.00
3	22	12.41

There were 11 participants per group (i.e., 33 participants in all).

a. The professor claims that he can reject the omnibus null hypothesis. Do you agree? Show your work.

b. Having allegedly found the three groups to be somewhat different, the professor uses Tukey's WSD method to test all pairwise comparisons. He claims that no differences were significant. Do you agree? Show your work.

c. On the basis of the results found in Parts a and b, the professor argues that the omnibus test is misleading. He concludes that he cannot state that there are any differences among these three groups. Do you agree? Why or why not?

12. This problem uses the same data as Exercise 11. Suppose that the first two groups are active treatment groups, whereas the third group is a placebo control group. Further suppose that the professor who collected these data wants to form two confidence intervals, one comparing the first treatment group to the control, and a second comparing the second treatment group to the control.

a. Because none of the comparisons of interest are complex, the professor uses Tukey's WSD as the basis for maintaining experimentwise alpha. What does the professor find when he forms intervals based on this approach?

b. A colleague suggests to the professor that he should use Bonferroni instead of Tukey to ensure simultaneous confidence here. Do you agree? Whether or not you agree, find the appropriate intervals based on the Bonferroni approach.

c. A student suggests to the professor that another option might be to use Dunnett's method to form his intervals. Find the appropriate intervals using Dunnett's method.

d. How do the intervals you found in Parts a–c compare to one another? Which method is best here? Why?

13. A graduate student used a four-group between-subject design for her thesis. She had $n = 11$ participants per group. Her sample means are $\overline{Y}_1 = 12$, $\overline{Y}_2 = 13$, $\overline{Y}_3 = 20$, and $\overline{Y}_4 = 19$. The value of MS_W was 55.

a. Should she reject an omnibus null hypothesis that $\mu_1 = \mu_2 = \mu_3 = \mu_4$? Show your work.

b. Based on her answer to part a, she decides to investigate which groups are different. She decides to test all pairwise differences, assuming homogeneity of variance and using an appropriate method for controlling familywise error rate. Does she obtain any significant differences? Why or why not?

c. Her adviser asks her to compare the average of Groups 1 and 2 with the average of Groups 3 and 4, again controlling for familywise error rate. She argues in light of part b that testing the complex comparison here is fruitless because tests of complex comparisons are more conservative then tests of pairwise comparisons. Is she correct? Show your work or explain your answer.

    d. She has shown the results of Parts a–c to her adviser, who is thoroughly confused. He argues that according to the results she claims to have obtained, she has shown that $12(\overline{Y}_1)$ and $20(\overline{Y}_3)$ are not significantly different, but that 12.5 and 19.5 are, which is obviously absurd. Is his argument correct?

    e. Approaching this apparent contradiction through confidence intervals may be illuminating. Form appropriate 95% simultaneous confidence intervals for the difference between Groups 1 and 3, as well as for the complex comparison of the average of Groups 1 and 2 versus Groups 3 and 4.

    f. Which interval(s) in part e contain zero? Which of the two intervals is centered farther from zero? Is this the interval that does not contain zero? Explain this pattern of results.

14. In an experiment with five independent groups (5 participants per group), the omnibus F value observed is 3.00, just barely significant at the .05 level. Noticing that the sample means are $\overline{Y}_1 = 10, \overline{Y}_2 = 10, \overline{Y}_3 = 15, \overline{Y}_4 = 20$, and $\overline{Y}_5 = 30$. It is decided to test the following post hoc comparison: $\psi = -7\mu_1 - 7\mu_2 - 2\mu_3 + 3\mu_4 + 13\mu_5$.

    a. Find SS for this comparison. Show your work.

    b. What will the observed F value for this comparison be? Why?

    c. Will the result in part b be significant using Scheffé's method? Why or why not?

    d. What is the value of MS_W here?

15. Dr. S. Q. Skew performed an experiment involving four treatment groups with 16 participants per group. His research assistant performed an SPSS analysis of the data, but it did not answer all of Skew's questions. So far, Skew knows from this analysis that $SS_B = 864$ and $SS_W = 4320$. He also knows that the observed F for the pairwise comparison of Groups 1 and 2 is equal to 1.000 and that the observed F for the pairwise comparison of Groups 3 and 4 is only 0. 111 (i.e., literally 1/9). Because neither of these is significant, Skew wants to compare the average of the first two groups versus the average of the last two groups. Unfortunately, unbeknown to Skew, his assistant has lost the data. Knowing that you are a statistical whiz, the assistant comes to you desperate for help. Your task is to test this third comparison for significance. Show your work. Also, assume that Skew chose this contrast after having examined the data.

16. The following data are from a completely randomized (between-subjects) design:

1	2	3
48	59	68
54	46	62
47	49	53
54	63	59
62	38	67
57	58	71

Five psychologists analyze this data set individually, each with different goals in mind. Your task is to duplicate the results obtained by each.

    a. Psychologist 1 formulates three planned comparisons of interest: Group 1 versus 2, 1 versus 3, and 2 versus 3. Perform these planned comparisons, assuming homogeneity of variance.

    b. Psychologist 2 has no a priori comparisons, so she first performs the omnibus test. Following this, all pairwise comparisons are tested for significance, assuming homogeneity of variance. Once again, provide observed and critical values.

    c. Psychologist 3 differs from psychologist 2 only in that he decides not to assume homogeneity of variance for testing the comparison (don't worry about this assumption for the omnibus test). Once again, provide observed and critical values.

    d. Psychologist 4 differs from psychologist 2 only in that she decides post hoc to test not only all pairwise comparisons but also the average of Groups 1 and 2 versus Group 3. Like psychologist 2, she assumes homogeneity. Once again, provide observed and critical values.

    e. Psychologist 5 performs the same tests as psychologist 4. However, psychologist 5 has planned to conduct these particular tests prior to examining the data. Homogeneity is assumed.

f. Finally, write a brief explanation (one to two paragraphs) of why the various psychologists did not all arrive at the same conclusions regarding group differences. You need not specify one approach as "best," but you should explain the patterns of findings for these data. Also, you need not discuss all findings in relationship to one another; instead, focus your attention on differences that emerge and the reasons for such differences.

17. This problem uses the same data as Exercise 16. Suppose that these data were collected with the specific goal of identifying the best treatment, where higher scores on the dependent variable are considered better.
   a. Assuming homogeneity of variance, use an appropriate method to form two-sided confidence intervals for the best treatment. Write a brief interpretation of your findings.
   b. Assuming homogeneity of variance, use an appropriate method to form one-sided confidence intervals for the best treatment. Write a brief interpretation of your findings.
   c. How do your results in part b compare to your results in part a? Is the difference you found for these data consistent with the general pattern of the difference between one-sided and two-sided intervals for the best treatment? Explain your answer.

18. A psychologist has tested eight independent hypotheses. She has decided she wants to control the false discovery rate for this set of hypotheses. The eight p values she has obtained are as follows: .041, .022, .276, .010, .523, .003, .024, and .165.
   a. Which, if any, hypotheses can she reject using an FDR of .05? Show your work or explain your answer.
   b. Suppose she had decided that it was important to control the experimentwise alpha level at .05 for this set of hypotheses. Which, if, any hypotheses would she be able to reject from this perspective?
   c. Briefly explain types of situations where it might be justifiable to control FDR instead of α_{EW} at .05.

19. A psychologist has tested 10 independent hypotheses. He has decided to control the false discovery rate for this set of hypotheses at .05. The 10 p values he has obtained are as follows: .04, .15, .02, .31, .06, .63, .01, .03, .46, and .08. Which, if any, hypotheses can he reject controlling the FDR at .05? Show your work or explain your answer.

6

Trend Analysis

In the examples considered in Chapters 4 and 5, the factor was qualitative in the sense that the different groups that constituted the factor differed from each other in quality and not just in quantity. For example, at the beginning of Chapter 4, we discussed a study that compared four treatments for hypertension: drug therapy, biofeedback, dietary modification, and a combination of these approaches. Although we could assign the numbers 1, 2, 3, and 4 to the four treatments, it is not at all clear which treatment should be assigned a 1, which a 2, and so forth. In other words, we cannot describe the treatments in terms of differences in magnitude of a single quantity. In this sense, we might say that the treatment levels form a nominal scale. We have simply formed four groups, which serve to classify participants.

QUANTITATIVE FACTORS

Let's now consider a different experiment. Suppose young children are given a fixed length of time to study a list of words to be memorized. One group of children is allowed 1 minute to study the list, another group gets 2 minutes, a third group gets 3 minutes, and a fourth group gets 4 minutes. The distinction among the groups in this study can be described in a purely quantitative manner, unlike the groups in the hypertension study. As a result, we say that we have a quantitative factor in the memory study.

What difference does it make whether we have a quantitative factor? As we will see shortly, up to a point it does not matter because we still typically want to compare group means by testing contrasts, just as we did in Chapters 4 and 5. However, we consider quantitative factors to be a separate topic here because the particular contrast coefficients we will choose (i.e., the c_j terms) will usually be different for quantitative factors than for qualitative factors.

Testing contrasts of levels of a quantitative factor is often referred to as trend analysis. Another term that is frequently used to describe this form of analysis is the *method of orthogonal polynomials*. The meaning behind these terms will become clear as we develop the underlying concepts. For the moment, to keep things in perspective, it is important to remember that what we are about to discuss simply involves testing contrasts. What we will develop is a special case of what we've already developed in Chapter 4. Indeed, the only really new idea to be presented here can be thought of as finding a method for choosing appropriate contrast coefficients to test the hypotheses in which we are interested.

Before we jump into the statistical aspects of trend analysis, it may be helpful to say a bit more about when trend analysis might be used. Trend analysis is almost invariably used anytime the factor under investigation is quantitative. A moment's reflection should convince you that psychologists and other behavioral scientists are often interested in the effects of quantitative factors. Examples of quantitative factors whose effects behavioral scientists might examine are the amount of study time in a memory task, number of hours of food deprivation, number of hours of sleep, number of reinforcements, frequency of reinforcements, drug dosage, and age. We should also stress that this chapter is concerned only with trend analysis in between-subjects designs, that is, designs where each level of the factor consists of different groups of subjects. Beginning with Chapter 11, we consider within-subjects designs, where each subject is observed at every level of the factor. As we will see later in the book, trend analysis is also useful for studying quantitative factors in within-subjects designs. Thus, the concepts we develop now are useful later in the book as well, although some of the specific formulas in the two designs are different from one another.

Readers who are familiar with regression analysis may wonder how the trend analysis methods to be presented in this chapter compare to regression. There are close connections between the two approaches, especially in between-subjects designs. Tutorial 2 on the data disk provides a brief introduction to regression, whereas Appendix B, Part 1 focuses on the relationships between analysis of variance and regression analysis. Although in some ways trend analysis and regression analysis could be regarded as two variations of the same basic method, they can be distinguished in practice. The choice between the two approaches depends primarily on the extent to which the quantitative factor is best regarded as continuous (with many distinct values) versus categorical (with a relatively small number of discrete values). In particular, regression analysis is more useful than trend analysis when the majority of individuals have unique scores on the predictor variable. For example, suppose the predictor is mother's IQ score, and the dependent variable is child's IQ score. In this case, there are likely to be many values of the predictor, and relatively few mothers will have exactly the same IQ score, making regression the method of choice here, instead of trend analysis. On the other hand, if there are relatively few distinct values of the predictor and there are several individuals with scores at each of these values, trend analysis offers advantages over regression analysis. Exercises 11 and 12 at the end of this chapter present an opportunity to compare trend analysis and regression as applied to the same data and show how trend analysis can be advantageous for certain types of data. Even so, we should stress that there are certainly situations where regression analysis is preferable. Along these lines, rarely is it useful to categorize a continuous variable in order to perform a trend analysis. Instead, if the variable is best regarded as continuous, it is almost always preferable to leave it in a continuous form and use regression analysis instead of trend analysis to investigate its relationship to the dependent variable.

STATISTICAL TREATMENT OF TREND ANALYSIS

To motivate the statistical treatment of trend analysis, consider the data shown in Table 6.1. These data are intended to represent recall scores of 24 children assigned to one of four experimental conditions. Each child is allowed a fixed period of time to study a list of 12 words. Six of the children are randomly assigned to a condition where they are given 1 minute to study the words, a second group is given 2 minutes, a third group is given 3 minutes, and the fourth group is given 4 minutes. The dependent variable is the number of words the child recalls after a brief interference task.

TABLE 6.1
HYPOTHETICAL MEMORY DATA

	Study Time			
	1 Minute	*2 Minutes*	*3 Minutes*	*4 Minutes*
	2	6	6	11
	3	8	8	10
	1	5	10	7
	2	3	5	9
	0	7	10	8
	4	7	9	9
Mean	**2**	**6**	**8**	**9**

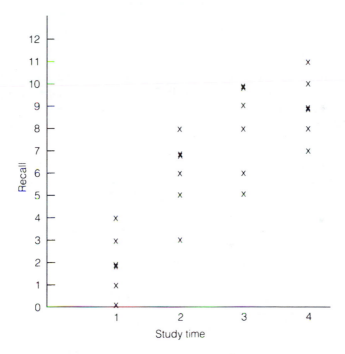

FIG. 6.1. Scatterplot of recall scores as a function of study time.

How should the data of Table 6.1 be analyzed? Although we could certainly apply the analysis of variance (ANOVA) techniques of Chapter 3 to these data, these techniques would not take advantage of the quantitative nature of the experimental manipulation. To capitalize on the quantitative nature of the factor, we instead consider the data from the standpoint of regression, which is introduced in Tutorial 2 on the data disk. We will shortly see that even from a regression perspective, trend analysis of quantitative factors becomes a matter of testing contrasts of group means.

To understand the motivation behind trend analysis, it is helpful to examine a visual representation of the data of Table 6.1. Figure 6.1 shows a scatterplot of recall scores plotted as a function of study time. This figure strongly suggests that recall improves with increases in study time, just as we would expect in an experiment of this sort. To formalize this intuition, we might develop a model that specifies that recall is a linear function of study time. As discussed in Tutorial 2, the equation for a straight line consists of an intercept and a slope. If we let Y_{ij} represent the recall score for Individual i in Group j, and if we let X_{ij} be that same individual's level of study time, an appropriate model is given by

$$Y_{ij} = \beta_0 + \beta_1 X_{ij} + \varepsilon_{ij} \tag{1}$$

where β_0 is the population intercept of the straight line, β_1 is the population slope, and ε_{ij} is an error term. We can immediately simplify this equation by dropping the i subscript from the X_{ij} term because every individual in Group j has the same score on X. For example, in our recall study, $X_{i1} = 1$ for all i, because every participant's X score in group 1 is 1 minute. Thus, we can simply say that $X_1 = 1$. Rewriting Equation 1 in this fashion results in

$$Y_{ij} = \beta_0 + \beta_1 X_j + \varepsilon_{ij} \tag{2}$$

The Slope Parameter

As usual, the task is to estimate parameters and test hypotheses concerning these parameters in our model. In our situation, we are primarily interested in the slope parameter (β_1), because it reflects the extent to which X is linearly related to Y. As shown in most elementary statistics textbooks, the general formula for the least-squares estimate of the slope parameter is given by

$$\hat{\beta}_1 = \left[\sum_{j=1}^{a} \sum_{i=1}^{n_j} (X_{ij} - \overline{X})(Y_{ij} - \overline{Y}) \right] \Big/ \sum_{j=1}^{a} \sum_{i=1}^{n_j} (X_{ij} - \overline{X})^2 \tag{3}$$

where $\overline{X}$ and $\overline{Y}$ are the sample means of X and Y, respectively, averaged across all subjects in the study regardless of group. Equation 3 can be simplified through several steps. First, as we saw before, X_{ij} can be replaced by X_j. This substitution results in

$$\hat{\beta}_1 = \left[\sum_{j=1}^{a} \sum_{i=1}^{n_j} (X_j - \overline{X})(Y_{ij} - \overline{Y}) \right] \Big/ \sum_{j=1}^{a} \sum_{i=1}^{n_j} (X_j - \overline{X})^2$$

Second, to simplify the notation, we represent $X_j - \overline{X}$ as c_j. Notice that c_j is then simply a deviation score on the X variable (i.e., it represents distance from the mean in either a positive or a negative direction). The reason we have chosen c_j as the symbol for this deviation score will become apparent momentarily. With this substitution, the equation simplifies to

$$\hat{\beta}_1 = \left[\sum_{j=1}^{a} \sum_{i=1}^{n_j} c_j (Y_{ij} - \overline{Y}) \right] \Big/ \sum_{j=1}^{a} \sum_{i=1}^{n_j} c_j^2$$

Third, the c_j term can be moved outside the summation over i because c_j is a constant for every i. This yields

$$\hat{\beta}_1 = \left[\sum_{j=1}^{a} c_j \sum_{i=1}^{n_j} (Y_{ij} - \overline{Y}) \right] \Big/ \sum_{j=1}^{a} n_j c_j^2$$

After some additional algebraic manipulation, the numerator of Equation 3 ultimately simplifies to $\sum_{j=1}^{a} c_j n_j \overline{Y}_j$. Making this substitution yields

$$\hat{\beta}_1 = \sum_{j=1}^{a} c_j n_j \overline{Y}_j \bigg/ \sum_{j=1}^{a} n_j c_j^2 \qquad (4)$$

Equation 4 thus provides the formula for estimating the slope relating X and Y. Although applying Equation 4 is relatively straightforward, the conceptual implications of the equation are much clearer if we make a simplifying assumption that each group has the same number of subjects. In other words, we assume that there are the same number of subjects at each level of X, in which case $n_1 = n_2 = \cdots = n_a$, so that n_j can be replaced with just n. Substituting n for n_j in Equation 4 yields

$$\hat{\beta}_1 = \sum_{j=1}^{a} c_j n \overline{Y}_j \bigg/ \sum_{j=1}^{a} n c_j^2$$

We can factor out the n term in both the numerator and the denominator, leaving

$$\hat{\beta}_1 = \frac{\sum_{j=1}^{a} c_j \overline{Y}_j}{\sum_{j=1}^{a} c_j^2} \qquad (5)$$

Several points about Equation 5 must be made here. First, notice that the estimated slope $\hat{\beta}_1$ depends only on the sample means $\overline{Y}_j$ and not on the values of the individual Y_{ij} data points. Thus, the extent to which we estimate X and Y to be linearly related depends in some manner on how the $\overline{Y}_j$ values relate to X. Second, notice that the term $\sum_{j=1}^{a} c_j \overline{Y}_j$ is simply a sample contrast, as shown in Equation 4.40. We typically require that the contrast coefficients sum to zero, that is, $\sum_{j=1}^{a} c_j = 0$. This condition will be met for trend analysis, because $\sum_{j=1}^{a} c_j = \sum_{j=1}^{a} (X_j - \overline{X}) = 0$ as long as we have equal n. In fact, using our earlier notation for contrasts, we could write

$$\hat{\psi}_{\text{linear}} = \sum_{j=1}^{a} c_j \overline{Y}_j \qquad (6)$$

so that

$$\hat{\beta}_1 = \hat{\psi}_{\text{linear}} \bigg/ \sum_{j=1}^{a} c_j^2 \qquad (7)$$

The estimated regression slope simply equals the sample value of the linear contrast divided by the sum of squared c_j values. Thus, the slope can be found by forming a contrast, just as we discussed throughout Chapter 4. Third, as always, the defining characteristic of the contrast comes from the coefficients used to form the contrast. In other words, the slope of a linear trend can be found by forming a contrast of the group means on $\overline{Y}_j$, where the coefficients take on a special form, namely

$$c_j = X_j - \overline{X} \qquad (8)$$

as long as we have equal n. With unequal n, the same idea applies, but the formulas become more complicated, as we will see later in the chapter.

Numerical Example

How can we apply what we have done so far to our numerical example? From Equation 7, the estimated slope for our data is

$$\hat{\beta}_1 = \hat{\psi}_{\text{linear}} \Big/ \sum_{j=1}^{a} c_j^2 \qquad \text{(7, repeated)}$$

where

$$\hat{\psi}_{\text{linear}} = \sum_{j=1}^{a} c_j \overline{Y}_j \qquad \text{(6, repeated)}$$

Table 6.1 shows that $\overline{Y}_1 = 2, \overline{Y}_2 = 6, \overline{Y}_3 = 8$, and $\overline{Y}_4 = 9$ for our data. The contrast coefficients are defined to be

$$c_j = X_j - \overline{X} \qquad \text{(8, repeated)}$$

For our data, $X_1 = 1$, $X_2 = 2$, $X_3 = 3$, and $X_4 = 4$. Thus, the mean X is $\overline{X} = 2.5$. The corresponding contrast coefficients are $c_1 = -1.5$, $c_2 = -0.5$, $c_3 = 0.5$, and $c_4 = 1.5$. Applying these four coefficients to the four $\overline{Y}_j$ values according to Equation 6 yields

$$\hat{\psi}_{\text{linear}} = -1.5(2) - 0.5(6) + 0.5(8) + 1.5(9)$$
$$= 11.5$$

To find the estimated slope, we must also calculate $\sum_{j=1}^{a} c_j^2$, the sum of squared coefficients. Here we have

$$\sum_{j=1}^{a} c_j^2 = (-1.5)^2 + (-0.5)^2 + (0.5)^2 + (1.5)^2$$
$$= 5.0$$

Then, from Equation 7, the estimated slope is given by

$$\hat{\beta}_1 = \hat{\psi}_{\text{linear}} \Big/ \sum_{j=1}^{a} c_j^2$$
$$= 11.5/5.0$$
$$= 2.3$$

What meaning can be attached to this value of 2.3? The interpretation here would be that when we fit a linear trend to the data, we estimate that every additional minute of study time translates into an average gain of 2.3 additional words recalled. To fully appreciate this statement, it is helpful to once again see a graphical depiction of the data. The open circles in

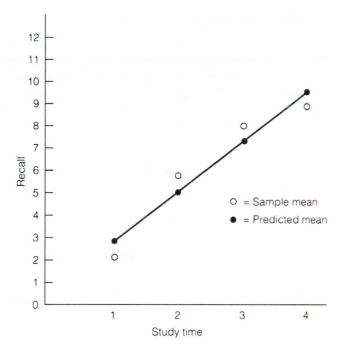

FIG. 6.2. Plot of sample means and estimated linear trend.

Figure 6.2 show the sample mean recall score $\overline{Y}_j$ for each level X_j of study time. The closed circles are the predicted means obtained from the linear trend. The straight line is obtained from the previously determined slope value $\hat{\beta}_1 = 2.3$ and from the intercept, whose least squares estimate is found from the following equation:

$$\hat{\beta}_0 = \overline{Y} - \hat{\beta}_1 \overline{X}$$

For our data, the estimated intercept is

$$\hat{\beta}_0 = 6.25 - (2.3)(2.5)$$
$$= 0.50$$

Thus, the equation of the straight line shown in Figure 6.2 is

$$\hat{Y}_{ij} = 0.50 + 2.3X_j$$

Although this straight line fits the sample means reasonably well, the fit is not perfect in the sense that the sample means do not lie perfectly on the straight line. As we will see later, this "imperfection" could either reflect some nonlinear trend in the data or it might simply reflect sampling error. Also, the estimated slope could have been negative, in which case the straight line would have sloped downward (when moving from left to right) instead of upward.

Hypothesis Test of Slope Parameter

So far we have learned how to estimate the slope coefficient for a linear trend. We have seen that this slope depends solely on the sample means and that it can be formulated in terms of a contrast. The second major topic to consider here is hypothesis testing. Is the estimated slope coefficient statistically significantly different from zero? For example, in our memory study, we estimated the slope coefficient to equal 2.3. Although this value suggests that recall improves with increases in study time, we cannot rule out the possibility that the population value of the slope coefficient is zero.

To address this possibility, we must perform a hypothesis test. As usual, we operationalize our test as a comparison of full and restricted models. The full model here is given by our earlier straight-line model for the data:

$$\text{Full:} \qquad Y_{ij} = \beta_0 + \beta_1 X_j + \varepsilon_{ij} \qquad \text{(2, repeated)}$$

The null hypothesis to be tested is that $\beta_1 = 0$, so an appropriate restricted model is given by

$$\text{Restricted:} \qquad Y_{ij} = \beta_0 + \varepsilon_{ij} \qquad (9)$$

As usual, to compare these two models, we must find the sum of squared errors for each model. It can be shown[2] that for simple linear regression models such as

$$E_R = \sum_{j=1}^{a} \sum_{i=1}^{n_j} (Y_{ij} - \overline{Y})^2.$$

and

$$E_F = \sum_{j=1}^{a} \sum_{i=1}^{n_j} (Y_{ij} - \overline{Y})^2 - \left[\hat{\beta}_1^2 \sum_{j=1}^{a} \sum_{i=1}^{n_j} (X_{ij} - \overline{X})^2 \right]$$

Of particular interest is the difference in the sum of squared errors of the two models, that is, $E_R - E_F$. Simple subtraction shows that

$$E_R - E_F = \hat{\beta}_1^2 \sum_{j=1}^{a} \sum_{i=1}^{n_j} (X_{ij} - \overline{X})^2$$

We can now simplify this expression through three steps. First, recall that X_{ij} can be replaced by X_j because every subject's X score is the same within a group. Second, from Equation 8, $c_j = X_j - \overline{X}$.

Third, c_j^2 is a constant within each group, so we can bring it outside the summation over i (individuals). For simplicity, we continue to assume equal n, in which case applying each of these three steps leads to

$$E_R - E_F = n\hat{\beta}_1^2 \sum_{j=1}^{a} c_j^2 \qquad (10)$$

Although our equation for $E_R - E_F$ is now fairly straightforward, it still does not look familiar. However, we now show that in fact it is equivalent to an equation we developed in

Chapter 4. To approach this more familiar form, we saw in Equation 7 that

$$\hat{\beta}_1 = \hat{\psi}_{\text{linear}} \bigg/ \sum_{j=1}^{a} c_j^2 \qquad \text{(7, repeated)}$$

Substituting this expression for $\hat{\beta}_1$ into Equation 10 produces

$$E_R - E_F = n(\hat{\psi}_{\text{linear}})^2 \left(\sum_{j=1}^{a} c_j^2 \right) \bigg/ \left(\sum_{j=1}^{a} c_j^2 \right)^2$$

This reduces to

$$E_R - E_F = n(\hat{\psi}_{\text{linear}})^2 \bigg/ \sum_{j=1}^{a} c_j^2 \qquad (11)$$

However, Equation 11 is just the formula for the sum of squares of a contrast, with equal n. Thus, the difference in the sum of squared errors for the full and restricted models simply equals the sum of squares of the linear contrast:

$$E_R - E_F = SS_{\psi_{\text{linear}}}$$

An F test can then be performed by dividing the sum of squares due to the contrast by mean square within, as in Chapters 4 and 5:

$$F = SS_{\psi}/MS_W.$$

An appropriate critical value is found as usual. If the observed F exceeds the critical F, the null hypothesis $\beta_1 = 0$ is rejected, and there is a statistically significant linear trend in the data. Of course, consistent with the discussion in Chapter 5, we need to distinguish between α_{PC} and α_{EW} if we perform multiple tests of comparisons instead of just testing the linear trend.

CONFIDENCE INTERVAL AND OTHER EFFECT SIZE MEASURES FOR SLOPE PARAMETER

Having now established how to estimate and test the slope coefficient for a linear trend, we can borrow principles from Chapter 4 to form a confidence interval for the slope coefficient. Recall that the slope $\hat{\beta}_1$ is almost but not quite identical to $\hat{\psi}_{\text{linear}}$:

$$\hat{\beta}_1 = \hat{\psi}_{\text{linear}} \bigg/ \sum_{j=1}^{a} c_j^2 \qquad \text{(7, repeated)}$$

where

$$c_j = X_j - \overline{X} \qquad \text{(8, repeated)}$$

Because we want to form a confidence interval for $\hat{\beta}_1$ instead of for $\hat{\psi}_{\text{linear}}$, we have to alter the expression we developed in Chapter 4 slightly.[3] The specific expression for the confidence interval for $\hat{\beta}_1$ is

$$\hat{\beta}_1 \pm \left(\sqrt{F_{\alpha;1,N-a}} \sqrt{MS_W \sum_{j=1}^{a} (c_j^2/n_j)} \middle/ \sum_{j=1}^{a} c_j^2 \right) \qquad (12)$$

Appropriate adjustments can be applied to the critical F value, if relevant, as we discussed in Chapter 5.

Other effect size measures follow directly from Chapter 4. Although the variety of measures we discussed in Chapter 4 can all be useful at times, R_{alerting}^2 is often of special interest in trend analysis, because we will see later that with equal n, the trend contrasts form an orthogonal set, which means that the sum of their R_{alerting}^2 values will equal 1, so we can describe the relative ability of each trend to account for the entirety of the between-group effect.

Numerical Example

To make the discussion less abstract, let's return to the memory-study data of Table 6.1. Previously, we saw that the least-squares estimate of the slope coefficient is $\hat{\beta}_1 = 2.3$. Can we infer that the population slope β_1 is nonzero? To answer this question, we must test the significance of the contrast corresponding to the linear trend. According to Equation 8, the coefficients for this contrast are given by

$$c_j = X_j - \overline{X} \qquad \text{(8, repeated)}$$

As we saw earlier, this implies $c_1 = -1.5, c_2 = -0.5, c_3 = 0.5,$ and $c_4 = 1.5$ for our data. All that must be done to calculate an observed F statistic is to find the values of SS_ψ and MS_W. From Equation 11, the sum of squares for the contrast is given by

$$SS_\psi = n(\hat{\psi}_{\text{linear}})^2 \middle/ \sum_{j=1}^{a} c_j^2 \qquad \text{(11, repeated)}$$

In our example, $n = 6$ and $\sum_{j=1}^{a} c_j^2 = 5$. Recall that $\hat{\psi} = \sum_{j=1}^{a} c_j \overline{Y}_j$, so that

$$\hat{\psi}_{\text{linear}} = (-1.5)(2) + (-0.5)(6) + (0.5)(8) + (1.5)(9)$$

$$= 11.5$$

Substituting these values into Equation 11 yields

$$SS_\psi = 6(11.5)^2/5 = 158.7$$

Thus, the sum of squares attributable to the linear trend is 158.7 for these data. To obtain an observed F value, we must divide SS_ψ by MS_W. It is easily verified that $MS_W = 2.9$ for these data. As a result, the F statistic for the linear trend equals

$$F = 158.7/2.9 = 54.72$$

which is statistically significant beyond the .001 level. Thus, we can assert that there is a linear trend in the population. In this example, increases in study time lead to increased recall.

Although the hypothesis test enables us to conclude that the slope is nonzero, it does not allow us to establish plausible lower and upper limits for the slope coefficient. We can address this goal by forming a confidence interval. The values we need to provide as input for Equation 12 are as follows: $\hat{\beta}_1 = 2.3$, $F_{05;1,20} = 4.35$, $MS_W = 2.9$, $\Sigma c_j^2 = 5.0$, and $n_j = 6$ for all values of j. Substituting these values into Equation 12 produces a confidence interval of 2.3 plus or minus 0.65. Thus, we can be 95% confident that the population slope parameter has a value between 1.65 and 2.95. In other words, every additional minute of study time leads to an increase of between 1.65 and 2.95 words recalled. As usual, statistical packages can reduce hand calculations considerably. The only catch here is that we need to describe our coefficients to a statistical package in accordance with Equations 7 and 8. For example, in these data the coefficients need to be scaled as -0.3, -0.1, 0.1, and 0.3. Notice that each of these values is the original c_j from Equation 8, which is then divided by the sum of the squared coefficients as shown in Equation 7. In other words, the original values of -1.5, -0.5, 0.5, and 1.5 are each divided by 5 to produce the new values. Depending on the specific statistical package, we may be given the confidence interval directly, or can at least use the resulting standard error of the contrast to form the desired interval. In the latter case, for example, we can use a statistical package to discover that the standard error of $\hat{\beta}_1$ is 0.3109. This value simply needs to be multiplied by the square root of the critical F value (i.e., the square root of 4.35 in our data) to obtain the value of 0.65 as the half width of the confidence interval.

We will defer consideration of measures of association strength until we have presented methods for considering nonlinearity in our data.

Two further interpretational points deserve mention here. First, the alert reader may have noticed that the last sentence three paragraphs ago made it sound as if a claim were being made that increases in study time cause increases in recall. Because participants were randomly assigned to study conditions, a causal inference is in fact legitimate here. Some readers might object that we cannot infer causation because we have tested a regression slope, which is equivalent to testing a correlation, and everyone knows that correlation does not imply causation. Half of this argument is correct. We did test a regression slope, which is equivalent to testing a correlation coefficient. However, as we discussed in Chapter 1, the legitimacy of a causal inference is determined not by how we analyze the data (e.g., regression versus analysis of variance), but instead by the design of the study. The presence of random assignment permits a causal inference to be made here, although the question of why study time increases recall is left open to debate. Second, the meaning of a significant linear trend is sometimes misunderstood by researchers. To consider this issue, reconsider the plots shown earlier in Figures 6.1 and 6.2. The existence of a significant linear trend means that if a straight line is fit to either set of data (i.e., either Figure 6.1 or Figure 6.2), that straight line has a nonzero slope. In other words, there is a general tendency for Y to either decrease on average or increase on average as a function of X. The important point to realize is that the presence of a significant linear trend says absolutely nothing about the possible presence of nonlinear trends. Some researchers mistakenly believe that finding a significant linear trend implies that the relationship between Y and X is strictly linear. However, it is entirely possible for the same data to exhibit both linear and nonlinear trends. Indeed, the plot of sample means in Figure 6.2 suggests such a possibility for the recall data.

Although recall increases as study time increases, there is some indication that an extra minute of study time may not always produce the same average increase in recall. For example, increasing study time from 1 minute to 2 minutes in this sample resulted in an average improvement of four words (see Table 6.1). However, increasing study time from 3 minutes to 4 minutes resulted in an average improvement of only one word. This pattern suggests the possibility of a nonlinear trend, because a strictly linear trend would imply that the change in recall produced by increasing study time 1 minute should always be the same, in our case 2.3 words.

Alternatively, the discrepancies from this value of 2.3 may simply reflect sampling error.[4] In other words, with only six subjects per group, we would not expect sample differences in recall to be exactly the same for every 1-minute change in study time. Not surprisingly, there is a way we can resolve this question of whether the pattern obtained here reflects true nonlinearity or just sampling error.

TESTING FOR NONLINEARITY

The test for nonlinearity is often referred to as a test for deviations (or departures) from linearity. This phrase holds the key for understanding how to test for nonlinearity. For simplicity, we assume equal n throughout our discussion. At the end of the chapter, we briefly discuss the additional complexities that arise with unequal n.

Recall that the model for a linear trend was given by

$$Y_{ij} = \beta_0 + \beta_1 X_j + \varepsilon_{ij} \qquad\qquad (2, \text{repeated})$$

Nonlinear relationships between X and Y can be incorporated into the model by including powers of X (e.g., X squared, X cubed, etc.) on the right-hand side of the equation. For example, we might have a model of the form

$$Y_{ij} = \beta_0 + \beta_1 X_j + \beta_2 X_j^2 + \beta_3 X_j^3 + \varepsilon_{ij}$$

This equation raises a question of how many powers of X should be included, that is, should we stop with X^3, or should we go on to X^4, X^5, and so on? The answer is that with a levels of the factor (i.e., with a values of X), we can include at most terms up to and including X^{a-1} (i.e., X raised to the $a-1$ power) in the model. To understand why, consider the simple case where $a = 2$—that is, we have only two groups of participants. According to the above rule, we can include only X to the first power in the model. Thus, the model would be

$$Y_{ij} = \beta_0 + \beta_1 X_j$$

The reason for this is that with only two groups, there are only two group means we are trying to explain, and the relationship between these two means and X can always be explained with a straight line, because a straight line can always be drawn between any two points. For this reason, terms of the form X^2, X^3, and so on are not needed. The same logic holds for values of a over 2 as well. For example, when $a = 3$, the model allowing for all possible nonlinear trends would be

$$Y_{ij} = \beta_0 + \beta_1 X_j + \beta_2 X_j^2$$

It turns out that with X and X^2 in the model, any three values for the means of Y can be fit perfectly with this model. Terms such as X^3, X^4, and so forth would simply be redundant (i.e., linearly dependent—see Chapter 4). Thus, a general model allowing for nonlinear trends with a levels of the factor includes all powers of X up to and including X to the $a-1$ power. The model then has the general form

$$Y_{ij} = \beta_0 + \beta_1 X_j + \beta_2 X_j^2 + \cdots + \beta_{a-1} X_j^{a-1} + \varepsilon_{ij} \qquad\qquad (13)$$

Departures from linearity are represented by X^2, X^3, and so forth. Thus, to test these departures for significance, we state a null hypothesis that

$$\beta_2 = \beta_3 = \cdots = \beta_{a-1} = 0$$

In other words, the hypothesis to be tested is that in the population, all trends other than the linear trend are zero. This null hypothesis implies a restricted model of the form

$$Y_{ij} = \beta_0 + \beta_1 X_j + \varepsilon_{ij} \qquad \text{(2, repeated)}$$

This is simply the linear trend model with which we have already been working.

As usual, the task is to compare these two models by finding the sum of squared errors and degrees of freedom for each model. Because we have already encountered the restricted model of Equation 2, we begin with it. We claimed earlier that the sum of squared errors for this model is given by

$$E_{\text{R}} = \sum_{j=1}^{a} \sum_{i=1}^{n} (Y_{ij} - \overline{Y})^2 - \left[\hat{\beta}_1^2 \sum_{j=1}^{a} \sum_{i=1}^{n} (X_{ij} - \overline{X})^2 \right]$$

We can simplify this expression in two ways. First, the term $\sum_{j=1}^{a} \sum_{i=1}^{n} (Y_{ij} - \overline{Y})^2$ equals what we referred to in Chapter 3 as SS_{total}. Second, we saw earlier in this chapter that

$$\hat{\beta}_1^2 \sum_{j=1}^{a} \sum_{i=1}^{n} (X_{ij} - \overline{X})^2 = SS_{\text{linear}}$$

Making these two substitutions

$$E_{\text{R}} = SS_{\text{total}} - SS_{\text{linear}} \qquad (14)$$

The degrees of freedom for the restricted model are straightforward because there are two parameters to be estimated (β_0 and β_1). Thus

$$df_{\text{R}} = N - 2 \qquad (15)$$

where N is total sample size.

Next, let's turn our attention to the full model of Equation 13:

$$Y_{ij} = \beta_0 + \beta_1 X_j + \beta_2 X_j^2 + \cdots + \beta_{a-1} X_j^{a-1} + \varepsilon_{ij} \qquad \text{(13, repeated)}$$

The degrees of freedom for this model are again straightforward, because in general there are a parameters to be estimated. Thus

$$df_{\text{F}} = N - a \qquad (16)$$

To understand the sum of squared errors of this model, remember why we stopped adding powers of X at $a - 1$. Including powers up to this point guarantees that the resulting trend passes through the mean value of Y for each group. In other words, the predicted value of Y

at each value of X is the mean value of Y for the group of participants at that particular value of X. As a result, the predicted score on Y for Individual i in Group j is $\overline{Y}_j$, the mean Y score for all participants in that group. Thus, for the full model of Equation 13

$$\hat{Y}_{ij}(F) = \overline{Y}_j$$

where $\hat{Y}_{ij}(F)$ indicates the predicted score from the full model for Subject i in Group j. The sum of squared errors for the model is then given by

$$E_F = \sum_{j=1}^{a} \sum_{i=1}^{n} \left[Y_{ij} - \hat{Y}_{ij}(F)\right]^2$$

This is equivalent to

$$E_F = \sum_{j=1}^{a} \sum_{i=1}^{n} (Y_{ij} - \overline{Y}_j)^2$$

However, the term $\sum_{j=1}^{a} \sum_{i=1}^{n} (Y_{ij} - \overline{Y}_j)^2$ is simply the within-group sum of squares, so we can write

$$E_F = SS_W \tag{17}$$

Indeed, it turns out to be the case that the full model here, that is

$$Y_{ij} = \beta_0 + \beta_1 X_j + \beta_2 X_j^2 + \cdots + \beta_{a-1} X_j^{a-1} + \varepsilon_{ij} \tag{13, repeated}$$

is equivalent to the full cell means model we have previously encountered:

$$Y_{ij} = \mu_j + \varepsilon_{ij}$$

Although the two full models obviously look very different, they both have a parameters, and both allow for a separate predicted Y score for each group. As a result, the two full models are mathematically equivalent. We are now ready to compare the full and restricted models with our usual F statistic:

$$F = \frac{(E_R - E_F)/(df_R - df_F)}{E_F/df_F}$$

Substituting from Equations 14, 17, 15 and 16 for E_R, E_F, df_R, and df_F, respectively, yields

$$F = \frac{(SS_{total} - SS_{linear} - SS_W)/[(N-2)-(N-a)]}{SS_W/(N-a)}$$

All three components of this expression can be simplified. First, consider $SS_{total} - SS_{linear} - SS_W$. From Chapter 3, $SS_{total} = SS_B + SS_W$, so substituting this expression for SS_{total} results in $SS_B + SS_W - SS_{linear} - SS_W$, which is obviously just $SS_B - SS_{linear}$. Similarly, $(N-2)-(N-a)$ simplifies to $a-2$. Finally, the ratio $SS_W/(N-a)$ is just MS_W. Putting the simplified components back together again yields

$$F = \frac{(SS_B - SS_{linear})/(a-2)}{MS_W} \tag{18}$$

Equation 18 thus provides a formula for testing the statistical significance of nonlinear trends.

Numerical Example

To see an example of this test, reconsider the data in Table 6.1. Earlier in the chapter, we found that for these data, $SS_{linear} = 158.7$ and $MS_W = 2.9$. From principles and formulas of Chapter 3, it is easily verified that $SS_B = 172.5$ for these data. Substituting these values along with $a = 4$ into Equation 18 yields

$$F = \frac{(172.5 - 158.7)/(4 - 2)}{2.9} = 2.38$$

which, with 2 and 20 degrees of freedom, is not significant at the .05 level. Thus, the results of this test suggest that the possible nonlinearity observed in Figure 6.2 for these data may simply reflect sampling error. Notice that as always we should not assert that the null hypothesis is true. We have not proved that the nonlinear trends here are zero; instead, we lack sufficient evidence to declare them to be nonzero.

We have just seen the procedure for testing departures from linearity. Although this test is frequently appropriate to address a researcher's questions, at times an alternate strategy is better. Instead of performing one test for any departures from linearity, it may be more informative to test for specific forms of departure. To understand this distinction, recall the null hypothesis we formulated for testing departure from linearity. In the full model

$$Y_{ij} = \beta_0 + \beta_1 X_j + \beta_2 X_j^2 + \cdots + \beta_{a-1} X_j^{a-1} + \varepsilon_{ij} \qquad \text{(13, repeated)}$$

we tested a null hypothesis of the form

$$H_0 : \beta_2 = \beta_3 = \cdots = \beta_{a-1} = 0$$

Notice that the null hypothesis stipulates that each and every one of these $a - 2$ parameters equals zero, which is why the F statistic has $a - 2$ numerator degrees of freedom. In some situations, however, we may be interested in performing separate tests on one or more of these $a - 2$ parameters, much as we performed a separate test on β_1 to test the linear trend.

TESTING INDIVIDUAL HIGHER ORDER TRENDS

Just as the test of the linear trend can be conceptualized as a test of a contrast, tests of the other beta parameters (which are said to reflect higher order trends) can also be formulated in terms of contrasts. There are two issues to consider here. First, what sort of trend do these individual beta parameters represent? That is, what meaning can be attached to those individual beta parameters? Second, how are appropriate contrast coefficients found for testing the significance of these parameters?

To understand the meaning of the individual beta parameters, consider a specific case with four groups, so that $a = 4$. In this case, the full model can be written as

$$Y_{ij} = \beta_0 + \beta_1 X_j + \beta_2 X_j^2 + \beta_3 X_j^3 + \varepsilon_{ij}$$

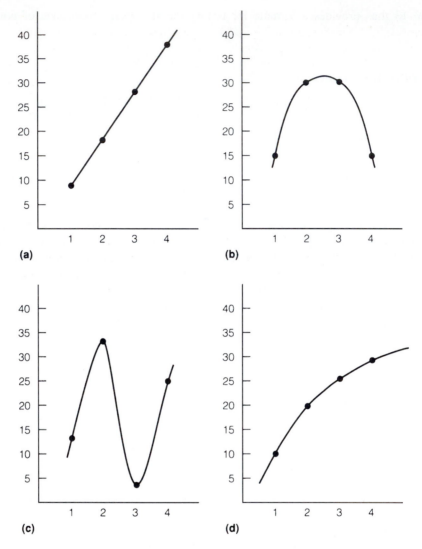

FIG. 6.3. Plots of various trends: (a) linear trend, (b) quadratic trend, (c) cubic trend, and (d) linear and quadratic trends.

Figures 6.3a–6.3c show the types of trends represented by each individual beta parameter. Figure 6.3a shows that the role of β_1 is to account for any straight line relationship between X and Y. As X increases, Y systematically increases also (assuming that the slope of the line is positive; otherwise, Y systematically decreases). Notice that the X variable here is raised to the first power and that there are no (i.e., zero) changes in the direction of the trend. In other words, X to the first power produces a trend with zero bends. Figure 6.3b shows that the inclusion of X^2 in the model allows Y to systematically decrease as X moves away (either higher or lower) from some central point on the x-axis. This pattern is called a quadratic trend. Figure 6.3b corresponds to a plot where the sign of β_2 is negative; if β_2 were positive, the trend would be reversed, and Y would systematically increase as X moves away from the central point. Notice that when X is raised to the second power, there is one change of direction (i.e., bend) in the curve. Figure 6.3c shows that the inclusion of X^3 in the model allows Y to first increase, then decrease, and then increase again as X increases. This pattern is called a cubic trend. Once again, if the sign of β_3 were reversed, the plot would be reversed as well (i.e., it would be flipped over about a horizontal line). Notice that when X is raised to the third power, there are two changes of direction (i.e., bends) in the curve. Regardless of the value of a, this same pattern occurs. Namely if X is raised to some power P, the curve associated with X^P has $P - 1$ bends in it.

Figure 6.3d serves as a reminder that in an actual study, the pattern of means may very well reflect a combination of two or more of the pure forms shown in Figures 6.3a–6.3c. Although the means in Figure 6.3d tend to increase as X increases, the increases themselves are becoming smaller. Such a negatively accelerated curve is fairly common in the behavioral sciences and reflects a model with both linear and quadratic components. Because such combinations of trends are possible, it is usually necessary to test higher order trends regardless of whether the linear trend is statistically significant. We will return to this issue after we discuss the choice of appropriate contrast coefficients.

Contrast Coefficients for Higher Order Trends

Now that we have considered the form that higher order trends take on, it is necessary to consider how to test these trends as contrasts. In other words, we need to determine appropriate contrast coefficients for testing each trend. Recall that we have already shown that with equal n, the appropriate contrast coefficients for testing the linear trend are given by

$$c_j = X_j - \overline{X}$$

Although we could go through similar steps to find the appropriate coefficients for testing higher order trends (e.g., quadratic, cubic, etc.), we will not do so because the steps would be tedious. In addition, many statistical packages calculate the appropriate coefficients and conduct the corresponding significance tests automatically. Thus, what is important is that the concepts underlying trend analysis be understood, as opposed to being able to derive contrast coefficients.

Although calculations are usually best left to the computer, it is helpful to present higher order trend coefficients to better understand the meaning of the trends. Appendix Table A.10 presents contrast coefficients for performing trend analysis whenever two conditions are met. First, equal spacing of the X variable is assumed. Equal spacing implies that the numerical difference between adjacent values of X is a constant. For example, X values of 7, 12, 17, 22, and 27 would be equally spaced, because the difference between adjacent values is always 5. On the other hand, a developmental psychologist who compared children of ages 12 months, 13 months, 15 months, 18 months, and 22 months would have unequally spaced values. A researcher might choose to use such unequal spacing if theoretical considerations implied the possibility of rapid change in the months shortly after month 12, followed by less rapid change in later months (see Keppel, 1982, p. 132, for a good discussion of this issue). Many statistical packages automatically generate appropriate coefficients even when values are unequally spaced. Second, Table A.10 assumes that sample sizes are equal in every group. Whether these coefficients are also appropriate with unequal n is subject to debate, as we discuss at the end of the chapter.

To understand Appendix Table A.10, let's consider the four-group case in some detail. According to the table, the appropriate contrast coefficients for testing the linear trend are given by values of -3, -1, 1, and 3 for Groups 1, 2, 3, and 4, respectively. Are these the same coefficients that we developed in the four-group case earlier in the chapter? No, they are not, because in the word-recall study described earlier, we used contrast coefficients of -1.5, -0.5, 0.5, and 1.5 for the four groups, based on $X_j - \overline{X}$. However, these two sets of coefficients are proportional to one another because we can multiply each recall-study coefficient by two to obtain the coefficients shown in Table A.10. As we saw in Chapter 4, multiplying all coefficients of a contrast by a constant does not change the sum of squares attributable to the contrast. As a result, the observed F value for the contrast also remains the same. Thus, the tabled values of $-3, -1, 1$, and 3 are consistent with the values of $-1.5, -0.5, 0.5$, and 1.5 that we used earlier. Thus, these different metrics are interchangeable for hypothesis testing and for calculating measures of association strength. However, as we have seen, the metric of the coefficients is important for constructing confidence intervals, so in this case we must decide which specific coefficients are appropriate.

According to Appendix Table A.10, the coefficients for testing a quadratic trend among four groups are equal to $1, -1, -1$, and 1. In what sense do these coefficients test a quadratic trend? Instead of attempting to provide a mathematical answer, reconsider Figures 6.3a–6.3c. What happens if we apply these coefficients to the means shown in Figure 6.3a? The resultant contrast has a value of zero, implying no quadratic trend, which is just what we would expect for means that perfectly fit a straight line. Similarly, applying the coefficients to the means shown in Figure 6.3c also yields a value of zero, because these means correspond to a pure cubic trend. However, applying the coefficients to the means of Figure 6.3b produces a nonzero value because these data show a quadratic trend. Similarly, the cubic trend coefficients shown in Table A.10 yield a contrast whose value equals zero for Figures 6.3a and 6.3b, but which is nonzero for Figure 6.3c. Thus, the coefficients shown in Table A.10 provide an appropriate set of values for testing the pure forms of trend shown in Figures 6.3a–6.3c.

Another perspective on higher order trends can be gained by plotting the coefficients themselves on the y-axis, with the corresponding X values on the x-axis. If we do this, we discover that the resultant plot looks exactly like the type of trend those coefficients are designed to detect. Thus, the coefficients for a linear trend form a straight line when we plot them. Similarly, the coefficients for a quadratic trend form a U shape like that shown in Figure 6.3b,[5] and the coefficients for a cubic trend display two bends, as in Figure 6.3c. As you might guess, this equivalence of plots is not a coincidence, but instead results from a fact we developed in Chapter 4. Recall that R^2_{alerting} reflects the extent to which contrast coefficients match the pattern of sample means. With equal n, as we are assuming here, a contrast completely accounts for between-group differences if its coefficients match the pattern of mean differences. As we have seen, this is exactly what the trend coefficients accomplish.

One other property of the contrasts defined in Appendix Table A.10 should be mentioned. Assuming equal n, as we are here, it is fairly easy to show that the contrasts defined by these coefficients form an orthogonal set. In other words, for a particular number of groups, trend components are orthogonal to each other, with equal n. As a result, sums of squares attributable to individual trends can be added together. The implications of this orthogonality can be discussed most easily in the context of our numerical example, to which we now turn.

Numerical Example

We now illustrate testing higher order trends individually in our numerical example. Although we have already tested the linear trend, we include that test here as well, for the sake of completeness and to show results in terms of the coefficients from Appendix Table A.10.

Table 6.2 shows intermediate calculations used to find the sum of squares attributable to each contrast. As always (with equal n), each sum of squares is found from

$$SS_\psi = \frac{n(\hat{\psi})^2}{\sum_{j=1}^{a} c_j^2}$$

TABLE 6.2
INTERMEDIATE CALCULATIONS FOR SUM OF SQUARES FOR EACH
TREND COMPONENT

	Group			
	1	*2*	*3*	*4*
Mean	2	6	8	9

	Contrast Coefficients				$\hat{\psi}$	$\sum_{j=1}^{a} c_j^2$	SS
	1	*2*	*3*	*4*			
Linear	-3	-1	1	3	23	20	158.7
Quadratic	1	-1	-1	1	-3	4	13.5
Cubic	-1	3	-3	1	1	20	0.3

TABLE 6.3
ANOVA TABLE FOR RECALL DATA OF TABLE 6.1

Source	SS		df		MS	F	p
Between	172.5		3		57.5	19.83	.001
Linear		158.7	1		158.7	54.72	.001
Deviation from linearity		13.8	2		6.9	2.38	.118
Quadratic			13.5	1	13.5	4.66	.043
Cubic			0.3	1	0.3	0.10	.751
Within	58.0		20		2.9		

Recall that in this example, $n = 6$. All other quantities needed in the calculation are shown in Table 6.2.

Table 6.3 presents the ANOVA table for these data. The first line of the table shows the between-group sum of squares for the data. The corresponding F test is the test of the omnibus null hypothesis that all four group population means are equal, as we discussed in Chapter 3. Consistent with the discussion in Chapter 5, the omnibus test need not necessarily be performed when testing trends, because we may have planned to test these trends prior to collecting the data; it is presented here primarily to show how it relates to the tests of individual trends. The second line of Table 6.3 shows the results for the linear trend, which as we have already seen is highly statistically significant. The third line presents the sum of squares and corresponding test for departure from linearity. As we have seen, the test is not significant at the .05 level. Notice that as exemplified by Equation 18 earlier in the chapter

$$SS_{\text{deviation from linearity}} = SS_B - SS_{\text{linear}}$$

or, equivalently

$$SS_B = SS_{\text{linear}} + SS_{\text{deviation from linearity}} \tag{19}$$

With equal n, the between-group sum of squares can be partitioned into two additive components: linear and nonlinear. The fourth line of Table 6.3 shows the results for the quadratic trend. When tested individually with $\alpha_{PC} = .05$, this trend is significant. We discuss the apparent inconsistency between this result and the nonsignificant result for departure from linearity momentarily. First, however, notice that the fifth line of Table 6.3 presents the results for the cubic trend, which is nonsignificant for these data. Notice also that with equal n, the sum of squares attributable to nonlinearity can be partitioned into two additive components:

$$SS_\text{deviation from linearity} = SS_\text{quadratic} + SS_\text{cubic} \tag{20}$$

If there were more than four groups, the SS_cubic term would instead be

$$SS_\text{deviation from quadratic}$$

which would represent the sum of squares attributable to trends above the quadratic model, that is, a model that includes linear and quadratic components. Substituting the right-hand side of Equation 20 for $SS_\text{deviation from linearity}$ into Equation 19 yields

$$SS_\text{B} = SS_\text{linear} + SS_\text{quadratic} + SS_\text{cubic}$$

Thus, when $a = 4$ and sample sizes are equal, the three trend contrasts completely account for the variation among the groups. This relationship holds, because the trend contrasts form an orthogonal set as long as sample sizes are equal.

Let's now return to the apparent discrepancy between the significant quadratic trend and the nonsignificant deviation from linearity. How can we assert that the β_2 parameter is nonzero and at the same time fail to reject a hypothesis that both β_2 and β_3 are zero? After all, if β_2 is nonzero, then it cannot be true that both β_2 and β_3 are zero. Equation 20 is helpful for understanding this apparent dilemma:

$$SS_\text{deviation from linearity} = SS_\text{quadratic} + SS_\text{cubic} \tag{20, repeated}$$

The F test for deviation from linearity equals

$$F = \frac{(SS_\text{quadratic} + SS_\text{cubic})/2}{MS_\text{W}} \tag{21}$$

whereas the F statistic for the quadratic trend by itself equals

$$F = \frac{SS_\text{quadratic}}{MS_\text{W}} \tag{22}$$

When SS_cubic is small, as in this example, the F statistic of Equation 22 may be nearly twice as large as the F statistic of Equation 21. This reflects the fact that the test of the quadratic trend by itself is more powerful than the test of deviation from linearity if the population quadratic trend is nonzero but the population cubic trend is zero.

What does this imply about which tests shown in Table 6.3 should be performed and interpreted? In most behavioral studies, trends beyond quadratic are largely uninterpretable. For this reason, one strategy is to test the linear trend separately, the quadratic trend separately, and then to perform a combined test of all remaining trends (i.e., cubic, quartic, etc.). This last test is usually not directly interpreted, except insofar as it indicates whether linear and quadratic components are adequate to explain between-group differences. A slightly different strategy can be employed if theory dictates that any differences between groups should be linear in nature. In this situation, the linear trend can be tested by itself, and all remaining trends are tested together as the departure from linearity. As in our numerical example, these two strategies do not always reach the same conclusion. Which is more appropriate is dictated primarily by theoretical considerations.

TABLE 6.4
MEASURES OF ASSOCIATION STRENGTH FOR RECALL DATA

Trend	R^2_{alerting}	$R^2_{\text{effect size}}$	R^2_{contrast}
Linear	0.92	0.69	0.73
Quadratic	0.08	0.06	0.19
Cubic	0.00	0.00	0.01

Even after we have conducted all hypothesis tests we deemed appropriate, our analysis is typically not complete until we also consider measures of effect size. For example, you may recall that we have already formed a confidence interval for the slope parameter for these data. Although it is mathematically possible to form confidence intervals for nonlinear trends, such intervals are usually difficult to interpret. An alternative is to calculate measures of association strength. Specifically, the same three measures we introduced in Chapter 4 may be of interest with trend analysis:

$$R^2_{\text{alerting}} = SS(\psi)/SS_{\text{Between}} \tag{4.54}$$

$$R^2_{\text{effect size}} = SS(\psi)/SS_{\text{Total}} \tag{4.55}$$

$$R^2_{\text{contrast}} = SS(\psi)/(SS(\psi) + SS_{\text{W}}) \tag{4.56}$$

Table 6.4 shows the values of these three measures for each trend in the recall data. All three measures largely confirm the dominance of the linear trend for these data. For example, R^2_{alerting} shows that the linear trend accounts for 92% of the between-group variance and 69% of the total variance in the recall data. The measures also reaffirm that the cubic trend here is weak. As we have seen from other perspectives, the quadratic trend is much less evident than the linear trend, but nevertheless might be judged as an important aspect of the data. Finally, notice that the three R^2_{alerting} values sum to 1.00, as they must mathematically because the three trends form an orthogonal set. Thus, this measure provides an especially useful method of partitioning the between-group variability into additive components.

FURTHER EXAMINATION
OF NONLINEAR TRENDS

Now, it may be helpful to further examine our numerical example to gain a better understanding of nonlinear trends, especially how both linear and nonlinear trends might exist in the same data. As shown in Figure 6.1, there is a systematic tendency in these data for Y (number of words recalled) to increase as X (study time) increases. This tendency explains why the linear trend is significant, as shown in Figure 6.2.

To understand the meaning of the quadratic trend here, it is helpful to remove the effects of the linear trend from the data. To do this, we must first describe the linear trend. The simplest method relies on the equation we derived earlier in the chapter for the best-fitting straight line for these data:

$$\hat{Y}_{ij} = 0.50 + 2.3X_j \tag{23}$$

Notice from this equation that all participants in Group 1 (i.e., $X_1 = 1$) are predicted by the linear trend model to have a recall score of 2.8. Similarly, predicted scores in the remaining three groups are 5.1, 7.4, and 9.7, respectively.[6]

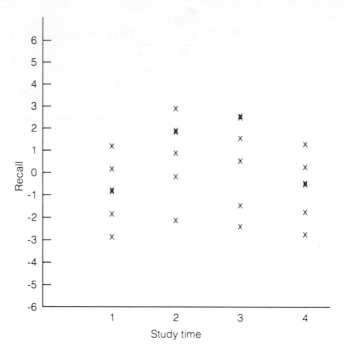

FIG. 6.4.   Scatterplot of Figure 6.1 data with linear trend removed.

We can now look at the errors of the linear trend model. Figure 6.4 shows this error for each of the 24 subjects in the study. Even more useful is Figure 6.5, which shows the mean error for each group. In other words, the mean error in Group 1 is -0.8, because the predicted score for every subject in this group is 2.8, but in fact the actual sample mean for subjects in this group is only 2.0. Notice also that the values plotted in Figure 6.5 correspond to the differences between the actual means and the predicted means shown earlier in Figure 6.2.

The plots in Figures 6.4 and 6.5 display the data with the linear trend removed. If the only true trend in the data is linear, there should be no apparent pattern to the data in Figures 6.4 and 6.5. In fact, however, as seen most clearly in Figure 6.5, these data bear a strong resemblance to the quadratic curve shown in Figure 6.3b. The plot of the data strongly suggests that the linear trend is not sufficient by itself to fully describe the data. This visual impression is consistent with the statistically significant effect of the quadratic trend shown earlier in Table 6.3.

What sort of curve is produced when both linear and quadratic trends are included in the model? To answer this question, we need to consider a model that includes not just X as a linear representation of time, but also X^2 as its quadratic manifestation. It is easily verified (by using a multiple regression routine in any statistical package) for our data that the corresponding predicted scores are given by

$$\hat{Y}_{ij} = -3.25 + 6.05X_j - 0.75X_j^2 \tag{24}$$

resulting in predicted scores of 2.05, 5.85, 8.15, and 8.95 for the four study times, respectively. Notice that the inclusion of the quadratic term increases the predicted scores for Groups 2 and 3 but decreases the predicted scores for Groups 1 and 4, which is exactly what Figure 6.5 suggests needs to be done.

Figure 6.6 shows the actual sample means and the predicted means obtained from the quadratic model of Equation 24, that is, the model that includes both linear and quadratic

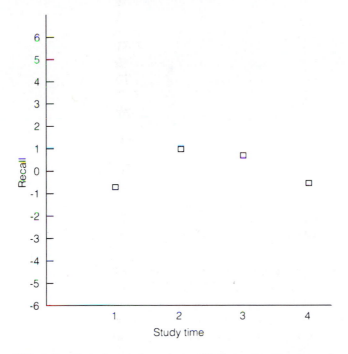

FIG. 6.5.   Plot of sample means with linear trend removed.

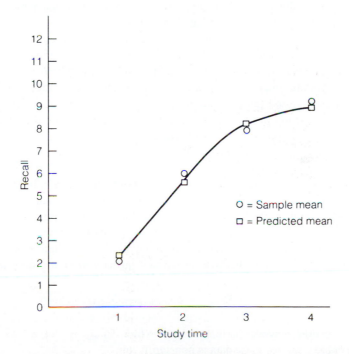

FIG. 6.6.   Plot of sample means and estimated means from quadratic model.

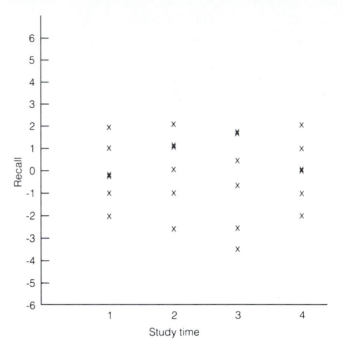

FIG. 6.7. Scatterplot of Figure 6.1 data with linear and quadratic trends removed.

trends. It seems clear from comparing Figure 6.2 for the linear trend model to Figure 6.6 for the quadratic model that the quadratic model fits the data better. Once again, the graphs confirm the statistically significant quadratic trend as shown in Table 6.3.

Just as we looked at errors of the linear trend model, we can also look at the errors of the quadratic trend model. Figure 6.7 shows this error for each of the 24 subjects in the study, and Figure 6.8 shows the mean error for each group. Two things must be said about Figure 6.8. First, and most important, the means in Figure 6.8 all hover close to zero. Unless the within-group variance is very small (and we can tell from Figure 6.7 that it is not), this suggests that the remaining variation in sample means is likely to be random rather than systematic. Once again, this visual impression is corroborated by the statistical test of the cubic trend, which as we saw in Table 6.3 was nonsignificant. Second, obsessive-compulsives may have noticed that although the means in Figure 6.8 hover around zero, it is nevertheless true that the pattern of these means fits the pattern of means shown in Figure 6.3c for a cubic trend. Doesn't this similarity suggest that there is in fact a cubic trend to the data, regardless of what the significance test might say? The answer is no, it does not, because the only pattern that the means can possibly display is one like Figure 6.3c (or its negative), once the linear and quadratic trends have been removed. After their removal, the only source of between-group variance remaining must be cubic because, as we saw earlier with four groups and equal n

$$SS_B = SS_{linear} + SS_{quadratic} + SS_{cubic}$$

The important question, however, is the extent to which SS_{cubic} is "large." As suggested by Figure 6.7, the cubic trend for these data is nonsignificant.

Although we have decided that the cubic trend is unnecessary for these data, it is instructive to see what would happen if we were to add the cubic trend component to our model. Predicted

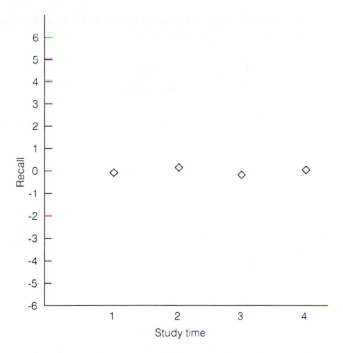

FIG. 6.8. Plot of sample means with linear and quadratic trends removed.

scores can be found from the following equation:

$$\hat{Y}_{ij} = -5.000 + 8.833X_j - 2.000X_j^2 + 0.167X_j^3 \tag{25}$$

The predicted means of 2, 6, 8, and 9 are literally identical to the observed sample means.[7] Thus, the inclusion of the cubic trend has resulted in a model that completely accounts for all between-group variation. Although at first glance this may seem impressive, it is in fact a mathematical necessity of the trend-analysis model. As we discussed previously, with a groups, it is always the case that a model with $a - 1$ trend components completely explains the between-group variance, and, as a consequence, predicted means equal actual sample means. The important practical point to be understood in the numerical example is that as Figure 6.6 shows, the quadratic trend model provides a very close fit to the sample means. As a consequence, there is no evidence for needing to include the cubic trend in the model.

TREND ANALYSIS WITH UNEQUAL SAMPLE SIZES

Trend analysis becomes more complicated when sample sizes are unequal. In essence, the reason for the additional complication is that the contrasts defined by the trend coefficients of Appendix Table A.10 are no longer orthogonal when sample sizes are unequal. As a result, trend components as defined by these coefficients no longer partition the between-group sum of squares additively. We do not attempt to deal with all the implications of this added complexity. Instead, we briefly present two alternate strategies for dealing with unequal n.

The first approach involves a hierarchical approach to model comparisons. With this approach, individual trend components are added to the model in successive steps, in a prespecified theoretical order. The first component to enter the model is the linear trend. The two models to be compared are thus defined to be

$$\text{I} \qquad Y_{ij} = \beta_0 + \varepsilon_{ij}$$

$$\text{II} \qquad Y_{ij} = \beta_0 + \beta_1 X_j + \varepsilon_{ij}$$

The sum of squares attributable to the linear trend then equals $E_I - E_{II}$. Second, a quadratic term is added to Model II, yielding

$$\text{III} \qquad Y_{ij} = \beta_0 + \beta_1 X_j + \beta_2 X_j^2 + \varepsilon_{ij}$$

The sum of squares attributable to the quadratic trend then equals $E_{II} - E_{III}$. Additional terms are added to the model in this fashion until all possible terms have been entered.

The second approach simply continues to use the contrast coefficients of Appendix Table A.10 despite the fact that sample sizes are unequal. The sum of squares attributable to any particular trend is given by

$$SS_\psi = (\hat{\psi})^2 \left/ \sum_{j=1}^{a} \left(c_j^2 / n_j \right) \right.$$

Which of these two approaches is preferable? Fortunately, with equal n, the two approaches yield identical results, so no choice is necessary. With unequal n, however, the two approaches do not necessarily lead to the same conclusion. To make the choice more difficult, sometimes one approach is better, and at other times the other approach is better. To understand this dilemma, it is helpful to compare contrast coefficients. It can be shown that the hierarchical approach is equivalent to testing contrasts whose coefficients are influenced by the sample size of each group. For example, the contrast coefficients for testing the linear trend with the hierarchical approach can be shown to equal

$$c_j = n_j (X_j - \overline{X}_w) \tag{26}$$

where $\overline{X}_W$ is the weighted sample mean of the X values. On the other hand, the second approach is often called an unweighted approach, because it continues to use unweighted contrast coefficients of the form

$$c_j = X_j - \overline{X}_U \tag{27}$$

where $\overline{X}_U$ is the unweighted sample mean of the X values.[8] Notice that the coefficients of Equation 27 differ from those of Equation 26 in that groups implicitly receive equal weights of 1.0 instead of weights dependent on sample size.

Which approach is better—weighted or unweighted coefficients? The answer is, "It depends." For example, if the only true trend in the population is linear, then the weighted coefficients of Equation 26 are superior because the test of the linear trend will be more powerful than the test using unweighted coefficients. The hierarchical approach also produces additive sums of squares, unlike the unweighted approach. However, if there are in fact nonlinear trends in the population, the weighted coefficients of Equation 26 may result in a biased estimate of the true population slope coefficient. For this reason, a linear trend deemed to be statistically significant by the weighted coefficients may in fact be reflective of a true quadratic trend in the population means. The linear trend for the population means may very well be zero. Exercise 13 at the end of the chapter explores this point in more detail. Because the use of weighted coefficients potentially leads to bias, our general recommendation is to continue to use unweighted coefficients, as shown in Appendix Table A.10 for equally spaced intervals of X. However, when there are strong theoretical reasons to believe that the only true population trend is linear, the use of weighted coefficients may be justified. Perhaps most important is simply to be aware of the distinction and to know which type of coefficient your favorite statistical package uses. With most packages, either type of coefficient can be used, although to do so may require overriding certain default values built into the program. In addition, you might be reassured to know that the distinction between weighted and unweighted means is discussed in greater detail in Chapter 7, when we discuss two-way ANOVA with unequal sample sizes.

CONCLUDING COMMENTS

We conclude the presentation of trend analysis with brief mention of four miscellaneous points. First, we introduced trend analysis as a valuable tool for studying group differences whenever the defining characteristic of groups is quantitative. Hale (1977), in an article directed primarily toward developmental psychologists, argues persuasively that many psychologists tend to underutilize trend analysis. He describes potential benefits of the trend-analysis approach, particularly when the form of the trend is expected to be monotonic. Second, researchers using trend analysis must be careful to avoid extrapolating beyond the data. Statistical inferences regarding trends pertain only to the values of X (the factor) actually used in the study. For example, suppose a four-group study with X values of 1, 2, 3, and 4 yields a linear trend of the form

$$Y_{ij} = 0.50 + 2.3X_j$$

It is inappropriate to use this equation to predict that if X were equal to 10, the mean Y value would be 23.50. Even if the trend appears to be purely linear throughout the range from 1 to 4, there is no guarantee that the trend would remain linear beyond X values of 4. Third, interpolation must also be used carefully and thoughtfully. For example, in the four-group study, it may be reasonable to predict that if X were equal to 3.5, the mean value of Y would be 8.55. However, such a prediction requires some theoretical justification, because there are no data that can directly be used to predict Y when X is between 3 and 4. However, in many practical situations, interpolation, unlike extrapolation, is probably reasonably well justified. Fourth, there is a whole host of techniques available for curve fitting beyond the use of orthogonal polynomial trends. Although trend analysis is typically the methodology of choice for analyzing data with quantitative factors, theoretical considerations sometimes suggest other methodologies. The interested reader is referred to Lewis's (1960) classic book on curve fitting.

EXERCISES

1. Appendix Table A.10 shows that the trend coefficients for four equally spaced levels of a quantitative factor are given by

	Level			
	1	*2*	*3*	*4*
Linear	−3	−1	1	3
Quadratic	1	−1	−1	1
Cubic	−1	3	−3	1

Show that the contrasts defined by these coefficients form an orthogonal set with equal n.

*2. The plot in Figure 6.3a represents a pure linear trend for four groups. The purpose of this exercise is to verify that the figure does in fact reflect a pure form. Assume $n = 10$ participants per group throughout. The means shown in Figure 6.3a are $\overline{Y}_1 = 10$, $\overline{Y}_2 = 20$, $\overline{Y}_3 = 30$, and $\overline{Y}_4 = 40$.
   a. Find the sum of squares for the linear trend.
   b. Find the sum of squares for the quadratic trend.
   c. Find the sum of squares for the cubic trend.
   d. Does Figure 6.3a reflect a pure linear trend?

3. This problem uses the same data as Exercise 2. In particular, $n = 10$ for each of four groups, with sample means of 10, 20, 30, and 40, respectively. We stated in Chapter 4 that R^2_{alerting} is equivalent to the squared correlation between the contrast coefficients and the actual sample means of the groups. Further, the sum of squares for a contrast equals the product of R^2_{alerting} and the between-group sum of squares.
   a. Find the correlation between the sample means and the contrast coefficients for the linear trend for these data. What does this tell you about how much of the between-group sum of squares is attributable to the linear trend for these data?
   b. Find the correlation between the sample means and the contrast coefficients for the quadratic trend for these data. What does this tell you about how much of the between-group sum of squares is attributable to the quadratic trend for these data?
   c. Find the correlation between the sample means and the contrast coefficients for the cubic trend for these data. What does this tell you about how much of the between-group sum of squares is attributable to the cubic trend for these data?

4. The plot in Figure 6.3b represents a pure quadratic trend for four groups. The purpose of this exercise is to verify that the figure does in fact reflect a pure form. Assume $n = 10$ participants per group throughout. The means shown in Figure 6.3b are $\overline{Y}_1 = 15$, $\overline{Y}_2 = 30$, $\overline{Y}_3 = 30$, and $\overline{Y}_4 = 15$.
   a. Find the sum of squares for the linear trend.
   b. Find the sum of squares for the quadratic trend.
   c. Find the sum of squares for the cubic trend.
   d. Does Figure 6.3b reflect a pure quadratic trend?

5. The plot in Figure 6.3c represents a pure cubic trend for four groups. The purpose of this exercise is to verify that the figure does in fact reflect a pure form. Assume $n = 10$ participants per group throughout. The means shown in Figure 6.3c are $\overline{Y}_1 = 15$, $\overline{Y}_2 = 35$, $\overline{Y}_3 = 5$, and $\overline{Y}_4 = 25$.
   a. Find the sum of squares for the linear trend.
   b. Find the sum of squares for the quadratic trend.
   c. Find the sum of squares for the cubic trend.
   d. Does Figure 6.3c reflect a pure cubic trend?

*6. An investigator conducted a five-group study where the groups represent equally spaced levels of a quantitative factor. Data are obtained for 15 participants in each group. The following sample means are obtained: $\overline{Y}_1 = 80$, $\overline{Y}_2 = 83$, $\overline{Y}_3 = 87$, $\overline{Y}_4 = 89$, and $\overline{Y}_5 = 91$. The value of mean square within (MS_W) equals 150.
   a. Assume that the investigator has planned to test only the linear trend. Is the trend statistically significant at the .05 level?
   b. Is the omnibus test of group differences statistically significant? In other words, can the null hypothesis $H_0 : \mu_1 = \mu_2 = \mu_3 = \mu_4 = \mu_5$ be rejected?
   c. Why is the observed F value so much larger for the linear trend than for the omnibus test? (Hint: Compare SS_{linear} to SS_B for these data. If SS_{linear} equals SS_B, how would the respective F values compare?)
   d. What are the implications of your answer to part c for the potential benefits of testing a planned linear trend instead of testing the omnibus null hypothesis?
   e. Is it legitimate to claim a planned linear trend as statistically significant if the omnibus test for the data is nonsignificant?

7. We saw that the estimated slope parameter for the data in Table 6.1 is $\hat{\beta}_1 = 2.3$. However, slopes between adjacent levels of the factor differ appreciably from 2.3. In particular, the slope of the line

connecting the 1-minute and 2-minute means is 4, the slope from 2 minutes to 3 minutes is 2, and the slope from 3 minutes to 4 minutes is 1. Verify the statement made in Note 4, that the slope $\hat{\beta}_1$ is a weighted average of these individual slopes. Specifically, show that the value of $\hat{\beta}_1$ here equals $\hat{\beta}_1 = .3d_1 + .4d_2 + .3d_3$, where $d_1 = \overline{Y}_2 - \overline{Y}_1$, $d_2 = \overline{Y}_3 - \overline{Y}_2$, and $d_3 = \overline{Y}_4 - \overline{Y}_3$.

8. A graduate student used a three-group study employing equally spaced levels of a quantitative factor for her thesis. Her theory suggests that the relationship between her factor and her dependent variable should be linear. She obtains the following data ($n = 10$ per group): $\overline{Y}_1 = 10$, $\overline{Y}_2 = 50$, and $\overline{Y}_3 = 30$. Her test of the linear trend yields an F value of 10.0, which is significant at the .01 level. Does this finding support her theory? Why or why not?

*9. A developmental psychologist is interested in the extent to which childrens' memory for facts improves as children get older. Ten children each of ages 4, 7, and 10 are randomly selected to participate in the study. The three-group means on the dependent measure of accuracy are 5.5, 7.7, and 10.2. To estimate the slope parameter, the psychologist finds linear trend coefficients of -1, 0, and 1 for three groups from Appendix Table A.10. Equation 7 is used to find the estimated slope. Specifically, $\hat{\psi} = 4.7$ and $\sum_{j=1}^{a} c_j^2 = 2$, so the estimated slope appears to be $\hat{\beta}_1 = 4.7/2 = 2.35$. However, this seems to imply an average increase of 2.35 units on the dependent measure for every increase of 1 year in age. Thus, we might expect 10-year-olds to outperform 4-year-olds by approximately 14.10 units (note that 14.10 equals the product of 6 and 2.35). In fact, however, 10-year-olds outperform 4-year-olds by only 4.7 units in the study. Is the psychologist's estimated slope of 2.35 accurate? Why or why not?

10. An interesting question to developmental psychologists is whether children's generosity (or altruism) steadily increases with age. The following study is modeled after an experiment reported in Zarbatany, L., Hartmann, D. P., & Gelfand, D. M. (1985). Why does children's generosity increase with age: Susceptibility to experimenter influence or altruism? *Child Development, 56,* 746–756. First-, third-, and fifth-grade children were allowed to select from among four alternatives what they would do if a fixed amount of money were donated to their school. A separate group of children of similar ages was used to create a generosity scale, using a paired-comparisons format. (It is interesting that in the actual study, the experimenters also used a scale with rational weights and obtained different results for the two weighting schemes.) Consider the following data, where each score represents the rating of the child's chosen alternative on the generosity scale:

First Graders	Third Graders	Fifth Graders
0	2	3
1	1	2
0	3	3
2	0	1
0	0	2
1	2	0
3	0	3
2	1	1
2	0	1
1	1	2
3	1	3
0	2	0
2	1	2
2	2	1
1	0	3

a. Suppose that the experimenter plans to test both the linear and the quadratic trends. Perform these tests for these data.
b. Plot the predicted means based on a linear trend model, that is, a model without a quadratic component. How do these means compare to the actual sample means?

c. Plot the predicted means based on a model that includes both linear and quadratic trend components. How do these means compare to the actual sample means? Why?

d. The experimenter is interested in knowing how much ratings tend to change for every additional year of school. Form a 95% confidence interval for the population slope. (Hint: Be careful how you code your coefficients.)

e. Calculate the three measures of association strength presented in this chapter. How would you interpret your findings for these data?

*11. A physiological psychologist is interested in the differential effects of four dosage levels of a particular drug on the ability of rats to learn how to find their way through a maze. The dependent variable for each animal is the mean number of incorrect turns made over five trials after exposure to the drug and an initial acquaintance with the maze. The following data are obtained:

	Level		
1	2	3	4
6.6	4.8	3.4	4.2
7.2	5.0	3.6	4.8
5.0	3.8	3.8	5.0
6.2	4.2	3.2	4.6
5.8	4.4	3.2	5.2

Assume that the levels of drug dosage are equally spaced in units of size 1 (as in 1, 2, 3, 4), throughout the remainder of the problem.

a. Starting with the coefficients shown in Appendix Table A.10, modify them as required by Equations 7 and 8 to obtain an estimated slope parameter.

b. Using standard procedures for testing the statistical significance of a contrast, test the linear trend for significance.

c. Use the regression routine of a statistical package to regress number of errors Y on drug dosage X. What is the least-squares estimate of the slope parameter? How does this value compare with the answer you obtained in part a? (This is to be done by computer.)

d. As part of the output you obtained in part c, you should have a significance test of the slope parameter. Depending on the specific program, the test statistic should be either $t = -2.70$ or, equivalently, $F = 7.28$. How does this value compare to the F value you calculated in part b?

e. To explore why the answers to Parts b and d are different, we first consider the difference between the sum of squared errors of the full and restricted models of the two approaches. Is this value (i.e., the numerator sum of squares) identical in the two approaches?

f. Now consider the denominator of the F statistic in the two approaches. Is the error sum of squares identical in the two approaches? What about the degrees of freedom of the error term (i.e., the degrees of freedom of the denominator)?

g. The reason the error sums of squares of the two approaches are different is that the error term is based on a different full model in the two approaches. In the regression analysis of part d, the error term is based on a full model of the form $Y_{ij} = \beta_0 + \beta_1 X_{ij} + \varepsilon_{ij}$. However, the error term of the contrast approach of part b is based on a cell means model of the form: $Y_{ij} = \mu_j + \varepsilon_{ij}$. Why is the sum of squared errors larger for the error term of the regression approach than for the error term used to test the contrast? (Hint: What role do the nonlinear trends play in the difference between these two models, that is, the models on which the error terms are based?)

h. Based on your answer to part g, which approach do you think would generally be preferable for testing a linear trend? Why?

12. This problem uses the same data as Exercise 11. As in Exercise 11, this problem compares regression and ANOVA analyses of these data, but now we will compare these two approaches in terms of confidence intervals.

a. Use the procedures of this chapter to form a 95% confidence interval for the slope coefficient where number of errors Y is regressed on drug dosage X, where X is coded as 1, 2, 3, and 4.

b. Use the regression routine of a statistical package to regress number of errors Y on drug dosage X, where X is once again coded as 1, 2, 3, and 4. Form a 95% confidence interval for the slope coefficient.

c. Are your answers to Parts a and b identical? How are the two intervals the same? How are they different?

d. Which approach provides a more precise estimate here? Why?

13. Two different methods are presented in the chapter for testing trends with unequal n. This exercise explores how these methods differ. Consider a four-group study where the groups represent equally spaced levels of a quantitative factor. Assume that the following data have been obtained:

$$n_1 = 30 \qquad n_2 = 30 \qquad n_3 = 5 \qquad n_4 = 5$$

$$\overline{Y}_1 = 2 \qquad \overline{Y}_2 = 4 \qquad \overline{Y}_3 = 4 \qquad \overline{Y}_4 = 2$$

Further assume that mean square within (MS_W) = 2.

a. One approach described in the text is a hierarchical approach. Find the contrast coefficients for testing the statistical significance of the linear trend for these data using this approach.

b. Based on the coefficients of part a, test the linear trend for statistical significance.

c. The other approach described in the text is an unweighted approach. What are the contrast coefficients for the linear trend using this approach?

d. Based on the coefficients of part c, test the linear trend for statistical significance.

e. Plot the sample means obtained here as a function of the level of the quantitative factor. Which plot of those shown in Figure 6.3 does your plot most resemble? Does your plot suggest the existence of a linear trend?

f. Which approach, hierarchical or unweighted, seems preferable here? Why?

g. Explain why the linear trend is significant here with the hierarchical approach.

14. A question currently being studied by developmental psychologists is how parent–infant play changes as infants get older. The following study is modeled after an experiment reported in Power, T. G. (1985). Mother- and father-infant play: A developmental analysis. *Child Development, 56,* 1514–1524. Parents of 16 children at each of three ages (7, 10, and 13 months) were videotaped during toy-play interactions with their infants. Raters judged the number of seconds over a 10-minute period during which parents encouraged different types of infant play. One dependent variable of interest was the proportion of time parents encouraged pretend play in their children. Suppose that the following data were obtained:

7-month-olds	10-month-olds	13-month-olds
.02	.15	.09
.01	.11	.03
.07	.22	.18
.04	.05	.12
.01	.09	.18
.09	.05	.43
.05	.15	.24
.06	.11	.40
.05	.14	.02
.01	.21	.19
.04	.06	.15
.03	.12	.07
.02	.11	.45
.02	.19	.20
.13	.12	.49
.06	.04	.19

a. Suppose that the experimenter plans to test both the linear and the quadratic trends. Perform these tests for these data.

b. Plot the predicted means based on a linear trend model, that is, a model without a quadratic component. How do these means compare to the actual sample means?

c. Plot the predicted means based on a model that includes both linear trend and quadratic trend components. How do these means compare to the actual sample means? Why?

d. Suppose the experimenter is interested in the average change in proportion of time parents encourage pretend play as a function of the child's age in months. Form a 95% confidence interval for the population slope relating these two variables.

e. Calculate the three measures of association strength presented in this chapter. How would you interpret your findings for these data?

f. When the dependent measure is a proportion, as it is here, it is sometimes recommended to transform the dependent variable before performing the analysis. The particular transformation usually recommended is an inverse sine transformation that defines a new dependent variable Y' in terms of the original variable Y as follows:

$$Y' = 2\arcsine(\sqrt{Y})$$

Perform the trend tests of part a using Y' as the dependent variable. (Hint: This transformation is straightforward to apply using many statistical packages. For example, both SAS and SPSS have SQRT and ARSIN functions to perform the necessary transformation.)

7

Two-Way Between-Subjects Factorial Designs

So far, we have seen how to compare the means of a groups of individuals. This chapter continues this theme but in a more general context. We now consider designs where the groups are defined by two or more factors (independent variables). For example, suppose that a psychologist wants to evaluate the effectiveness of biofeedback and drug therapy for treating hypertension, that is, for lowering blood pressure. The psychologist might design a study with four groups: both biofeedback training and drug therapy, biofeedback but no drug therapy, drug therapy but no biofeedback, and neither biofeedback nor drug therapy. We will see later in this chapter that such a design provides efficient tests of the individual effects of biofeedback and drug therapy, as well as the effect of the two in combination. As before, each subject selected to participate in the study would be assigned to one of the four groups, ideally at random.

THE 2 × 2 DESIGN

To explore this design and analysis in detail, consider the hypothetical data of Table 7.1. As usual in our data sets, the number of subjects is kept small to minimize the computational burden. For the sake of discussion, we assume that the scores in the table represent systolic blood pressure readings taken at the end of the treatment period. Based on what we have learned so far, we might analyze these data in either of two ways. First, we might perform an omnibus test to compare all four groups. Table 7.2 shows the ANOVA table that would result from this approach. There is a statistically significant difference among the four groups, but, of course, the omnibus test does not reveal which specific groups are different.

Second, instead of performing the omnibus test, we might have decided to test planned comparisons. Naturally, the comparisons of most interest should assess the effectiveness of biofeedback and drug therapy. There are several reasonable ways in which we might define such contrasts, but for the moment we will only consider one. To evaluate the biofeedback effect, notice that Groups 1 and 2 received biofeedback training, whereas Groups 3 and 4 did not. Thus, a contrast we could form to test the biofeedback effect would have coefficients of 1, 1, −1, and −1. Similarly, the effect of drug therapy could be tested by a contrast with coefficients of 1, −1, 1, and −1.

If we apply Chapter 4 principles to the data of Table 7.1, we find that the sum of squares attributable to the biofeedback contrast is 500, whereas that for drug therapy is 720. The

TABLE 7.1
BLOOD PRESSURE DATA FOR 2 × 2 FACTORIAL DESIGN

	Group			
	1: Biofeedback and Drug	2: Biofeedback Alone	3: Drug Alone	4: Neither
	158	188	186	185
	163	183	191	190
	173	198	196	195
	178	178	181	200
	168	193	176	180
Mean	168	188	186	190
s	7.91	7.91	7.91	7.91

TABLE 7.2
ANOVA FOR DATA IN TABLE 7.1

Source	SS	df	MS	F	p
Between	1540.00	3	513.33	8.21	.002
Within	1000.00	16	62.50		
Total	2540.00	19			

respective F values, obtained by dividing each sum of squares by MS_W (which equals 62.50, from Table 7.2), are 8.00 and 11.52. Both are statistically significant if we use an α_{PC} level of .05 (more on this later in the chapter). Thus, our two tests suggest that both biofeedback and drug therapy have an effect.

At this point, there is a question we should ponder. Have the tests we performed completely explained the differences among our four groups? To answer this question, we can compare SS_B in Table 7.2 with the sum of squares associated with each of our contrasts. From Table 7.2, we see that the between-group sum of squares is 1,540 for our data; the sums of squares for our two contrasts are 500 and 720. Can we say here that the two contrasts together account for a sum of squares equal to $500 + 720 = 1,220$? Recall from Chapter 4 that the sum of squares for contrasts are additive if the contrasts are orthogonal. Indeed, our biofeedback and drug therapy contrasts are orthogonal, as we can see from applying Equation 4.58:

$$(1)(1) + (1)(-1) + (-1)(1) + (-1)(-1) = 0$$

For future reference, notice that this formula requires equal n, which we have here. Thus, so far with two contrasts, we have accounted for a sum of squares of 1,220. However, this means that we have failed to account for a sum of squares equal to 320 (i.e., $1540 - 1220$). Notice that although we have used two contrasts and hence 2 degrees of freedom to examine group differences, with four groups we have 3 degrees of freedom in all for assessing group differences. Thus, there is 1 degree of freedom yet to be examined.

It can be shown that there is only one contrast orthogonal to the two we have formed so far and that its coefficients are 1, −1, −1, and 1 (of course, coefficients of −1, 1, 1, and −1 would also work, as would .5, −.5, −.5, and .5, but these are all really the same contrast).[1] Indeed, if we calculate the sum of squares for this contrast, it equals 320, as it must. The corresponding F value is 5.12, which is significant at the .05 level. Thus, this contrast has detected a significant effect. But what does this effect mean?

Before answering this question, recall the meaning of our other two contrasts. One of these tested the effectiveness of biofeedback, whereas the other tested the effectiveness of drug therapy. However, if we look carefully at the contrasts, a more specific interpretation emerges. The first contrast compared the difference between the means of the two groups that received biofeedback versus the two groups that did not. However, notice that there were two groups in each case because one half of the groups received drug therapy, whereas the other half did not. In other words, the first contrast averages over the drug condition. As a result, it tests the average effect of biofeedback by comparing group means with biofeedback versus those without, giving equal weight to groups receiving drug therapy as those not receiving it. Notice that the second contrast similarly tests an average effect of drug therapy. These average effects are referred to as *main effects*, that is, the effect that each factor has in the main or on the average.

The Concept of Interaction

Thus, our first two contrasts tested main effects, the average effect of biofeedback and drug therapy, respectively. The possibility remains, however, that the biofeedback effect in the presence of drug therapy is different from the average effect of biofeedback. Indeed, this is precisely what the third contrast tests. This test is referred to as an interaction test. To say that an interaction exists in our data means that the biofeedback effect in the presence of drug therapy is different from the average effect of biofeedback.

This can be clarified by looking at the means shown in Table 7.3. The four group means are arranged in a 2×2 table, where the two rows represent the presence or absence of drug therapy and the two columns represent the presence or absence of biofeedback. The average of each row (called the row marginal mean, because it is placed at the margin of the table) and of each column (the column marginal mean) is also presented, as is the grand mean (the average of all the scores). What have we tested with our three planned comparisons? The first comparison combined the means of 168 and 188 in the first column and compared them to the means of 186 and 190 in the second column. This is equivalent to testing the difference between 178 and 188, the two column marginal means. When we average over the rows, do the two columns differ? As previously stated, this tests the average effect of biofeedback. Similarly, the second contrast tested the difference between 177 and 189, the two row marginal means.

The third contrast, the test of the interaction, is more complicated. Remember that it tests whether the biofeedback effect in the presence of drug therapy is the same as the average effect of biofeedback. Here, the biofeedback effect in the presence of drug therapy is to lower blood pressure 18 points ($186 - 168$). The average effect, however, is to lower blood pressure only 10 points ($188 - 178$). The F value of 5.12 was statistically significant at the .05 level for these data, implying that the effect of 18 is discernibly different from the average effect of 10. Thus, biofeedback has a larger effect in the presence of drug therapy than it has on the average. There is yet one other way of viewing this test. Notice that the average effect of 10 is the average of 18; the biofeedback effect in the presence of drug therapy; and 2, the biofeedback effect

TABLE 7.3
FACTORIAL ARRANGEMENT OF MEANS
FROM TABLE 7.1

		Biofeedback		
		Present	Absent	Average
Drug Therapy	Present	168	186	177
	Absent	188	190	189
	Average	178	188	183

in the absence of drug therapy. We are claiming that the effect of 18 is significantly different from the average of the 18 itself and 2. But this simply amounts to saying that the effect of 18 is significantly different from the effect of 2. That is, a significant interaction here means that the biofeedback effect in the presence of drug therapy is significantly different from the biofeedback effect in the absence of drug therapy. In terms of the means in Table 7.3, the difference between columns 1 and 2 is not the same in row 1 as in row 2.

Additional Perspectives on the Interaction

So far, we have only considered whether the biofeedback effect is the same in the presence of drug therapy as in the absence of drug therapy. However, it may be just as interesting to determine whether the drug therapy effect is the same in the presence of biofeedback as in the absence of biofeedback. Table 7.3 shows that the magnitude of the drug therapy effect is 20 in the presence of biofeedback but only 4 in its absence. The difference in effectiveness is thus 16, the same difference that was found for biofeedback. That the same number resulted for both differences is not a coincidence—instead, it is a mathematical necessity. We can see why first algebraically and then geometrically. Recall that the coefficients of the interaction contrast were $1, -1, -1$, and 1. Thus, this contrast tests the following null hypothesis:

$$H_0 : \mu_{\text{drug \& biofeedback}} - \mu_{\text{drug}} - \mu_{\text{biofeedback}} + \mu_{\text{neither}} = 0 \tag{1}$$

We can rewrite this expression in either of two ways. First, the equation is equivalent to

$$H_0 : \mu_{\text{drug \& biofeedback}} - \mu_{\text{drug}} = \mu_{\text{biofeedback}} - \mu_{\text{neither}} \tag{2}$$

This statement, if true, implies that the biofeedback effect in the presence of drug therapy equals the biofeedback effect in the absence of drug therapy. Alternatively, the equation can be written as

$$H_0 : \mu_{\text{drug \& biofeedback}} - \mu_{\text{biofeedback}} = \mu_{\text{drug}} - \mu_{\text{neither}} \tag{3}$$

This asks whether the drug therapy effect in the presence of biofeedback equals the drug therapy effect in the absence of biofeedback.

Because all three equations are equivalent mathematically, they are in fact all testing the same null hypothesis. Thus, the interaction test addresses the question of whether the effect of one factor is the same for each level of the other factor. If the answer is yes for one factor, it must also be yes for the other factor as well.

The meaning of an interaction is often clarified by a graphic display (the geometric approach mentioned earlier). Figure 7.1 presents pictorial representations of the group means of Table 7.3. Figure 7.1a shows clearly that biofeedback lowers blood pressure an average of 18 units when drug therapy is present but only 2 units when drug therapy is absent. Recall that the significant interaction here means that the 18 and 2 are significantly different from one another. Geometrically, this implies that the two lines shown in Figure 7.1a depart significantly from parallelism. If the lines were parallel, the vertical distance between them would be the same at every level of drug therapy. However, in these data, the distances are unequal, and the lines are not parallel. This provides another way of conceptualizing the significance test for interaction. If the group means are plotted as in Figure 7.1a, is there a significant departure from parallelism? In other words, is there evidence "beyond a reasonable doubt" that lines connecting population means would also not be parallel?

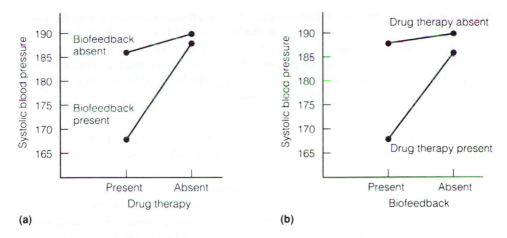

FIG. 7.1. Geometric depiction of group means shown in Table 7.3.

Notice that Figure 7.1b simply reverses the roles of biofeedback and drug therapy. Once again, the lines are not parallel because the same four means are plotted as in Figure 7.1a. Although Figure 7.1b is mathematically redundant with Figure 7.1a, it is often useful visually to draw both figures, because the biofeedback effect is visually highlighted in Figure 7.1a, whereas the drug therapy effect is clearer in Figure 7.1b. In addition, an interaction that is disordinal in one figure (meaning that the lines cross one another besides not being parallel) may not be disordinal in the other figure (meaning that although the lines may not be parallel, they do not cross).[2]

The concept of an interaction is extremely important in statistics and represents the most novel idea in this chapter. For this reason, at the risk of beating a dead horse, one more perspective is provided on the meaning of an interaction. It is sometimes said that if two factors interact, their effects are not additive. What does it mean to test whether two factors combine in an additive manner? To answer this question, reconsider Equation 1:

$$H_0 : \mu_{\text{drug \& biofeedback}} - \mu_{\text{drug}} - \mu_{\text{biofeedback}} + \mu_{\text{neither}} = 0 \qquad \text{(1, repeated)}$$

This can be rewritten as

$$H_0 : \mu_{\text{drug \& biofeedback}} = \mu_{\text{drug}} + \mu_{\text{biofeedback}} - \mu_{\text{neither}}$$

If we subtract a μ_{neither} term from both sides of the equation, we obtain

$$H_0 : \mu_{\text{drug \& biofeedback}} - \mu_{\text{neither}} = \mu_{\text{drug}} + \mu_{\text{biofeedback}} - \mu_{\text{neither}} - \mu_{\text{neither}}$$

Rearranging terms on the right-hand side yields

$$H_0 : \mu_{\text{drug \& biofeedback}} - \mu_{\text{neither}} = (\mu_{\text{drug}} - \mu_{\text{neither}}) + (\mu_{\text{biofeedback}} - \mu_{\text{neither}}) \qquad (4)$$

The left-hand side of the equation represents the combined effect of the two factors, that is, how the combination of both differs from the absence of both. On the right-hand side, the first term represents the drug therapy effect in isolation, that is, in the absence of biofeedback. Similarly, the second term represents the biofeedback effect in isolation. Thus, the null hypothesis states that the combined effect of drug therapy and biofeedback equals the sum of their separate effects individually. In other words, the hypothesis states that the effect of combining drug therapy and biofeedback equals the sum of their individual effects, so the two individual effects literally add together to produce the combined effect. Because Equation 4 is mathematically equivalent to Equation 1, the null hypothesis of Equation 4 expresses a statement that the two factors do not interact. Thus, the lack of an interaction corresponds to an additive effect, whereas the presence of an interaction implies a nonadditive effect.

A MODEL COMPARISON APPROACH TO THE GENERAL TWO-FACTOR DESIGN

In the previous section, we performed three hypothesis tests in our two-factor design: drug therapy main effect, biofeedback main effect, and interaction. In this section, we see how these three tests can be conceptualized in terms of model comparisons. Our earlier example was restricted to a 2×2 design, where each factor had only two levels. In general, however, each factor may have two or more levels. For ease of discussion, we refer to the two factors as A and B, where in general A has a levels and B has b levels. For example, A might be presence or absence of biofeedback (so $a = 2$), and B might represent three types of drug therapy (so $b = 3$) for treating hypertension.

The full model in the general situation of an $a \times b$ design can be written in either of two equivalent ways. First, the model can be written as

$$Y_{ijk} = \mu_{jk} + \varepsilon_{ijk} \tag{5}$$

where Y_{ijk} represents the score on the dependent variable of the ith subject at level j of the A factor and level k of the B factor, μ_{jk} is the population mean of Y for level j of A and level k of B, and ε_{ijk} is an error term associated with the ith subject at level j of A and level k of B. Notice that the value of the j subscript ranges from 1 to a, the value of the k subscript ranges from 1 to b, and the value of i ranges from 1 to n_{jk}, where n_{jk} is the number of subjects in the jk cell (i.e., the jth level of A and kth level of B). The model is often referred to as a cell means model, because just like the full model for the one-way design in Chapter 3, it states that any subject's score is dependent only on the cell of the design in which the subject resides and an error component. Indeed, mathematically, this full model for the two-way design is no different from the full model we developed earlier for the one-way design. In particular, we will see later that the least-squares parameter estimates and error sum of squares can be found using the same logic as before.

Alternate Form of Full Model

Although this form of the full model is perfectly valid mathematically, it is often convenient[3] to rewrite it in the following form:

$$Y_{ijk} = \mu + \alpha_j + \beta_k + (\alpha\beta)_{jk} + \varepsilon_{ijk} \tag{6}$$

where μ represents a grand mean term common to all observations, α_j is the effect of the jth level of A, β_k is the effect of the kth level of B, and $(\alpha\beta)_{jk}$ is the interaction effect of level j of A and level k of B in combination with one another. We have chosen to represent this effect with the combination of α and β instead of with some other single Greek letter, because the effect represents the interaction of A and B.[4] However, as we will see momentarily, $(\alpha\beta)_{11}$ (we have arbitrarily picked row 1 and column 1 as an example) is a single parameter

TABLE 7.4
POPULATION MEANS IN A 3×4 DESIGN

		B				Marginal Means
		1	2	3	4	
	1	10	15	20	11	14
A	2	15	10	5	14	11
	3	8	5	14	5	8
Marginal Means		11	10	13	10	11

and as a consequence $(\alpha\beta)_{11}$ ultimately equals some number, just as α_1 (for example) did in one-way designs. It is particularly important to realize that $(\alpha\beta)_{jk}$ does not mean the product of multiplying α_j by β_k. Although $(\alpha\beta)_{jk}$ is related to α_j and β_k in a way that we will soon see, the relationship is not multiplicative.

To understand the meaning of an effect, it is helpful to return to the concept of a marginal mean. The idea of a sample marginal mean was introduced in the discussion of Table 7.3; the focus now is on the notion of a population marginal mean. Consider the hypothetical 3×4 design shown in Table 7.4. Each cell entry represents a population mean (in an actual study, we obviously would not know precise values of population means, but here we assume that population values are known, for pedagogical purposes). Population marginal means (PMM) are defined for each row, each column, and rows and columns combined in the following manner. The PMM for the jth row (i.e., jth level of A) is

$$\mu_{j.} = \sum_{k=1}^{b} \mu_{jk} / b \tag{7}$$

which tells us to sum the cell means across columns in row j and then divide by the number of columns. The period following the j in $\mu_{j.}$ is a reminder that we have averaged over the second subscript k, which represents columns. For the means of Table 7.4, we would then have

$$\mu_{1.} = (10 + 15 + 20 + 11)/4 = 14$$

$$\mu_{2.} = (15 + 10 + 5 + 14)/4 = 11$$

$$\mu_{3.} = (8 + 5 + 14 + 5)/4 = 8$$

These numbers simply tell us that the mean score in the first row is 14, the mean in the second row is 11, and so on. It should be noted that the mean here is an unweighted mean, in that each column is weighted equally. (We will return to the importance of weights later in the chapter.) The PMM for the kth column is defined as

$$\mu_{.k} = \sum_{j=1}^{a} \mu_{jk} / a \tag{8}$$

For the data in Table 7.4, then, the column means are given by $\mu_{.1} = 11$, $\mu_{.2} = 10$, $\mu_{.3} = 13$, and $\mu_{.4} = 10$. Finally, the population grand mean is defined as

$$\mu_{..} = \sum_{j=1}^{a} \sum_{k=1}^{b} \mu_{jk} / ab \tag{9}$$

This equals 11 for the data in Table 7.4. Notice that $\mu_{..}$ is simply the unweighted mean of all individual cell means in the population.

We are now finally ready to define the effects in the full model as represented by Equation 6:

$$Y_{ijk} = \mu + \alpha_j + \beta_k + (\alpha\beta)_{jk} + \varepsilon_{ijk} \qquad \text{(6, repeated)}$$

First, μ in Equation 6 is simply the $\mu_{..}$ term defined in Equation 9. Second, α_j is defined as

$$\alpha_j = \mu_{j.} - \mu_{..} \qquad (10)$$

which represents the difference between the marginal mean in row j and the grand mean. For example, for the data in Table 7.4, α_1 would equal 3, α_2 would equal 0, and α_3 would equal -3. On the average, the effect of row 1 is to raise scores 3 points, the second row has no effect, and the third row lowers scores 3 points.[5] Third, β_k is defined as

$$\beta_k = \mu_{.k} - \mu_{..} \qquad (11)$$

This represents the difference between the marginal mean in column k and the grand mean. For example, for the data in Table 7.4, $\beta_1 = 0$, $\beta_2 = -1$, $\beta_3 = 2$, and $\beta_4 = -1$. Finally, the $(\alpha\beta)_{jk}$ terms are defined by

$$(\alpha\beta)_{jk} = \mu_{jk} - (\mu_{..} + \alpha_j + \beta_k) \qquad (12)$$

This represents the difference between a cell mean and the additive effect of the two factors. In other words, the $(\alpha\beta)_{jk}$ parameters reflect the extent to which the cell means fail to conform to an additive pattern. Notice that there is one $(\alpha\beta)_{jk}$ parameter for each cell in the design. To be certain that Equation 12 is clear, let's find the value of $(\alpha\beta)_{11}$ for the data in Table 7.4. From the equation

$$(\alpha\beta)_{11} = \mu_{11} - (\mu_{..} + \alpha_1 + \beta_1)$$

We saw earlier that for these data, $\mu_{..} = 11$, $\alpha_1 = 3$, and $\beta_1 = 0$. Thus

$$(\alpha\beta)_{11} = 10 - (11 + 3 + 0) = -4$$

The nonzero value for $(\alpha\beta)_{11}$ indicates an interactive (i.e., nonadditive) effect for this cell. If the effects of A and B were strictly additive, the population mean in the (1,1) cell would be 14, because row 1 raises scores 3 units on the average and column 1 has no effect on the average, so together the mean should be 3 points above 11, or 14. The fact that the population mean is actually 10 reflects that the particular combination of A_1 and B_1 lowers scores, contrary to their average effects separately. Applying Equation 12 to all 12 of the cells of Table 7.4 shows that

$(\alpha\beta)_{11} = -4$	$(\alpha\beta)_{12} = 2$	$(\alpha\beta)_{13} = 4$	$(\alpha\beta)_{14} = -2$
$(\alpha\beta)_{21} = 4$	$(\alpha\beta)_{22} = 0$	$(\alpha\beta)_{23} = -8$	$(\alpha\beta)_{24} = 4$
$(\alpha\beta)_{31} = 0$	$(\alpha\beta)_{32} = -2$	$(\alpha\beta)_{33} = 4$	$(\alpha\beta)_{34} = -2$

Equations 9–12 are important for two reasons. First, they provide formal definitions of the A main effect, B main effect, and interaction parameters. It is important to understand what

these parameters mean because we formulate hypothesis tests in terms of these parameters. Second, the algebraic expressions we have developed are helpful for developing least-squares parameter estimates and the corresponding sum of squared errors of various models.

We have now discussed in some detail two forms of the full model for a two-way design. Before we introduce a restricted model and subsequent hypothesis testing, we first compare the two different forms of the full model. Recall that the first form was

$$Y_{ijk} = \mu_{jk} + \varepsilon_{ijk} \qquad\qquad (5, \text{repeated})$$

and the second form was

$$Y_{ijk} = \mu + \alpha_j + \beta_k + (\alpha\beta)_{jk} + \varepsilon_{ijk} \qquad\qquad (6, \text{repeated})$$

We now demonstrate that these two forms are mathematically equivalent. Remember that the interaction parameters $(\alpha\beta)_{jk}$ of Equation 6 were defined as

$$(\alpha\beta)_{jk} = \mu_{jk} - (\mu_{..} + \alpha_j + \beta_k) \qquad\qquad (12, \text{repeated})$$

Making this substitution into Equation 6 and remembering that $\mu_{..} = \mu$, we obtain

$$Y_{ijk} = \mu_{jk} + \varepsilon_{ijk}$$

which of course is exactly the same as Equation 5. How can these two forms be equivalent when they look so different? After all, they do not even appear to have the same number of parameters. The model in Equation 5 has ab parameters, whereas the model in Equation 6 has $1 + a + b + ab$ parameters. However, it turns out that the parameters in the Equation 6 model are not all independent. For example, it can be shown algebraically that $\sum_{j=1}^{a} \alpha_j = 0$, given the definition of each α_j in Equation 10.[6] For the data in Table 7.4, the α_j parameters add to zero (as they must) because $\alpha_1 = 3$, $\alpha_2 = 0$, and $\alpha_3 = -3$. If the effect of row 1 is $+3$ and the effect of row 2 is 0, then the effect of row 3 must be -3 because the effects are all defined relative to the grand mean and the average of the row means must be the grand mean. Hence, there are only two independent α_j parameters for these data; once we know any two values, the third is completely determined. Similarly, it turns out that as a consequence of our definitions of β_k and $(\alpha\beta)_{jk}$ that they possess the following properties:

$$\sum_{k=1}^{b} \beta_k = 0$$

$$\sum_{j=1}^{a} (\alpha\beta)_{jk} = 0 \qquad \text{for each value of } k$$

$$\sum_{k=1}^{b} (\alpha\beta)_{jk} = 0 \qquad \text{for each value of } j$$

As a consequence of these constraints, the model of Equation 6 has $1 + (a - 1) + (b - 1) + (a - 1)(b - 1)$ independent parameters. However, multiplying the terms of this expression and performing the necessary subtraction shows that the number of independent parameters is simply ab, the same as Equation 5. Thus, the models of Equations 5 and 6 are indeed equivalent.

Comparison of Models for Hypothesis Testing

We are now ready to consider tests of hypotheses in terms of model comparisons in the $a \times b$ factorial design. As we have seen earlier in this chapter, there are three null hypotheses to be tested. Each of these null hypotheses leads to a restricted model, which then is compared to the full model. In each case, to test a hypothesis, we use our usual F test for comparing two models, namely

$$F = \frac{(E_R - E_F)/(df_R - df_F)}{E_F/df_F}$$

The primary challenge is finding E_F and E_R, the error sum of squares for the full and restricted models. Notice that the specific form of the restricted model depends on the hypothesis being tested (A main effect, B main effect, or AB interaction). The full model, on the other hand, is the same for every hypothesis. Because the full model remains the same, it is easiest to consider its error sum of squares first.

The error sum of squares for the full model (E_F) can be found most easily by writing the full model in the form of Equation 5:

$$Y_{ijk} = \mu_{jk} + \varepsilon_{ijk}$$

Recall that E_F is given by

$$E_F = \sum_{\substack{\text{all} \\ \text{obs}}} [Y_{ijk} - \hat{Y}_{ijk}(F)]^2$$

Here, $\hat{Y}_{ijk}(F)$ is a subject's predicted score when the parameters of the model are estimated using least squares. The parameters of the full model are simply the population means of each cell. Least-squares estimates these population means by their respective sample means, so that

$$\hat{Y}_{ijk}(F) = \overline{Y}_{jk} \tag{13}$$

Thus

$$E_F = \sum_{\substack{\text{all} \\ \text{obs}}} (Y_{ijk} - \overline{Y}_{jk})^2 \tag{14}$$

which we have previously seen as the within-cell (or within-group) sum of squares in the single-factor design. As in the one-way design, we can represent E_F as SS_W. As before, E_F simply measures the magnitude of variation within cells, that is, the extent to which scores within a group differ from each other. Also keep in mind that when we divide E_F by df_F, the resultant ratio is simply MS_W.

Although E_F can be found most easily by writing the full model in the form of Equation 5, it can also be found by writing it in the form of Equation 6. We also present the least-squares estimation of parameters for the Equation 6 model because this form of the model translates more easily to restricted models. The least-squares estimates can be found simply by substituting sample means for the corresponding population means in Equations 9–12.[7] Thus

$$\hat{\mu} = \overline{Y}_{..} = \sum_{j=1}^{a} \sum_{k=1}^{b} \overline{Y}_{jk}/ab \tag{15}$$

$$\hat{\alpha}_j = \overline{Y}_{j.} - \overline{Y}_{..} \tag{16}$$

$$\hat{\beta}_k = \overline{Y}_{.k} - \overline{Y}_{..} \tag{17}$$

$$\widehat{\alpha\beta}_{jk} = \overline{Y}_{jk} - (\overline{Y}_{..} + \overline{Y}_{j.} - \overline{Y}_{..} + \overline{Y}_{.k} - \overline{Y}_{..})$$

$$= \overline{Y}_{jk} - \overline{Y}_{j.} - \overline{Y}_{.k} + \overline{Y}_{..} \tag{18}$$

In case it is not clear $\overline{Y}_{j.}$ is the sample mean of all scores at the jth level of A. (We will consider alternate meanings of $\overline{Y}_{j.}$ with unequal n later in the chapter.) Similarly, $\overline{Y}_{.k}$ is the sample mean of all scores at the kth level of B. With this formulation, a predicted score from the full model is given by

$$\hat{Y}_{ijk}(F) = \hat{\mu} + \hat{\alpha}_j + \hat{\beta}_k + \widehat{\alpha\beta}_{jk} \tag{19}$$

Substituting for $\hat{\mu}$, $\hat{\alpha}_j$, $\hat{\beta}_k$, and $\widehat{\alpha\beta}_{jk}$ from Equations 15–18 yields $\overline{Y}_{ijk}(F) = \overline{Y}_{jk}$, the same as Equation 13. This simply underscores the equivalence of the models of Equations 5 and 6.

Next, we must consider the restricted model to be compared with the full model. Recall that the restricted model depends on the null hypothesis to be tested. First, consider the null hypothesis that the A main effect is zero in the population. We can conceptualize the implications of this hypothesis by considering the full model written according to Equation 6:

$$\text{Full:} \quad Y_{ijk} = \mu + \alpha_j + \beta_k + (\alpha\beta)_{jk} + \varepsilon_{ijk}$$

According to the null hypothesis, all the marginal means of the levels of the A factor are equal to one another, that is, the effect of each and every level of the A factor is zero. Symbolically, the null hypothesis can be written as

$$H_0 : \alpha_1 = \alpha_2 = \cdots = \alpha_a = 0 \tag{20}$$

This null hypothesis then leads to the following restricted model:

$$Y_{ijk} = \mu + \beta_k + (\alpha\beta)_{jk} + \varepsilon_{ijk} \tag{21}$$

The error sum of squares of this restricted model (E_R) can be found by once again using least squares to estimate the parameters of the model. With equal n per cell (as we are assuming here), parameter estimates for μ, β_k, and $(\alpha\beta)_{jk}$ are once again obtained from Equations 15, 17, and 18, just as they were in the full model. The omission of the α_j parameters does not change the estimates of the other parameters, because the effects are orthogonal to one another with equal n (this orthogonality was demonstrated earlier in the chapter in the case of the 2×2 design). Notice that a predicted score from the restricted model is given by

$$\hat{Y}_{ijk}(R) = \hat{\mu} + \hat{\beta}_k + \widehat{(\alpha\beta)}_{jk} \tag{22}$$

Substituting for $\hat{\mu}$, $\hat{\beta}_k$, and $\widehat{\alpha\beta}_{jk}$ from Equations 15, 17, and 18 yields

$$\hat{Y}_{ijk}(R) = \overline{Y}_{jk} - \hat{\alpha}_j \tag{23}$$

where $\hat{\alpha}_j = \overline{Y}_{j.} - \overline{Y}_{...}$.

Before formally finding E_R, it is instructive to compare Equations 13 and 23 for the predicted scores from the full and restricted models, respectively. To the extent that the α_j parameters differ from zero, the predicted scores of the full model are superior to those of the restricted model, that is, they are closer to the actual scores (when the error in prediction is squared). This must be true because the sample means minimize the sum of squared deviations.

What is the formula for the error sum of squares E_R of the model given by Equation 21? As usual,

$$E_R = \sum_{k=1}^{b} \sum_{j=1}^{a} \sum_{i=1}^{n} [Y_{ijk} - \hat{Y}_{ijk}(R)]^2$$

When $\overline{Y}_{jk} - \hat{\alpha}_j$ is substituted for $\hat{Y}_{ijk}(R)$, simple algebra reveals that E_R can be written as

$$E_R = E_F + nb \sum_{j=1}^{a} (\overline{Y}_{j.} - \overline{Y}_{..})^2 \tag{24}$$

where n is the number of observations per cell and b is the number of levels of the B factor. Obviously, then, the difference in the error sum of squares of the full and restricted models equals

$$E_R - E_F = nb \sum_{j=1}^{a} (\overline{Y}_{j.} - \overline{Y}_{..})^2 \tag{25}$$

Before finishing the necessary details of the F test, several comments are in order concerning Equation 25. First, the numerical value obtained for $E_R - E_F$ here is referred to as the sum of squares attributable to the A main effect and is usually written as SS_A. Second, notice that this sum of squares is a measure of the extent to which the sample marginal means of A differ from the grand mean. In other words, it reflects the degree to which some levels of A have higher mean scores than other levels of A, averaging across the B factor. Third, it is interesting to compare Equation 25 with the expression we obtained in Chapter 3 (see Equation 3.58) for $E_R - E_F$ in the single-factor design, which (for equal n) was given by

$$E_R - E_F = n \sum_{j=1}^{a} (\overline{Y}_j - \overline{Y})^2 \tag{26}$$

Although Equations 25 and 26 look rather different, there is in fact an underlying equivalence. The equivalence can be seen most clearly by realizing that Equations 25 and 26 are actually both special cases of a formula we presented earlier in Chapter 3:

$$E_R - E_F = \sum_{j=1}^{a} \sum_{i=1}^{n} \hat{\alpha}_j^2 \tag{3.78, repeated}$$

which can be written more generally as

$$E_R - E_F = \sum_{\text{all obs}} \hat{\alpha}_j^2$$

In both the one-way design and the factorial design (with equal n), $\hat{\alpha}_j$ is given by

$$\hat{\alpha}_j = \overline{Y}_j - \overline{Y}$$

Then, in the factorial design

$$E_R - E_F = \sum_{\text{all obs}} (\overline{Y}_j - \overline{Y})^2$$

To sum over all observations, we must sum over rows, columns, and subjects within cells, so that

$$E_R - E_F = \sum_{j=1}^{a} \sum_{k=1}^{b} \sum_{i=1}^{n} (\overline{Y}_j - \overline{Y})^2$$

However, the squared deviation term $(\overline{Y}_j - \overline{Y})^2$ is a constant within a cell and within a row, so that we can write

$$E_R - E_F = \sum_{j=1}^{a} \sum_{k=1}^{b} n(\overline{Y}_j - \overline{Y})^2$$

$$= \sum_{j=1}^{a} nb(\overline{Y}_j - \overline{Y})^2$$

$$= nb \sum_{j=1}^{a} (\overline{Y}_j - \overline{Y})^2$$

which is equivalent to Equation 25. In the one-way design, the difference in sum of squared errors is also given by

$$E_R - E_F = \sum_{\text{all obs}} (\overline{Y}_j - \overline{Y})^2$$

However, to sum over all observations, we must sum over groups and subjects within groups, so that

$$E_R - E_F = \sum_{j=1}^{a} \sum_{i=1}^{n} (\overline{Y}_j - \overline{Y})^2$$

As before, the squared deviation term is a constant for every subject within a group, so

$$E_R - E_F = \sum_{j=1}^{a} n(\overline{Y}_j - \overline{Y})^2$$

$$= n \sum_{j=1}^{a} (\overline{Y}_j - \overline{Y})^2$$

in agreement with Equation 26. As a result of this equivalence, in equal n designs, the sum of squares due to A in the factorial design exactly equals the sum of squares due to A in a single-factor design when the data are analyzed as if the B factor never existed. This should seem reasonable: Remember that the sum of squares due to A—that is, the A main effect—considers only the marginal means of A because the calculations average over the B factor. (Exercise 5 at the end of the chapter asks you to demonstrate this empirically on the numerical example presented in Table 7.5.)

We are now ready to finalize the details of the F test for the main effect of the A factor. Recall that the formula for the F statistic is given by

$$F = \frac{(E_R - E_F)/(df_R - df_F)}{E_F/df_F}$$

We have derived formulas for E_F (Equation 14) and $E_R - E_F$ (Equation 25). All that remains is to find df_R and df_F, the degrees of freedom of the two models. Remember that the degrees of freedom for a model equals the total number of observations (subjects) minus the number of independent parameters in the model. We saw earlier that the full model (Equation 5 or 6) has ab independent parameters. The restricted model (Equation 21) is the same as the full model, except that the α_j parameters have been omitted. Although there are a levels of A, there are only $a - 1$ independent α_j parameters, because, as we saw earlier, the sum of the α_j parameters is constrained to equal zero. Thus, with a total of nab subjects in the design

$$df_F = nab - ab$$
$$= ab(n - 1) \tag{27}$$

and

$$df_R - df_F = a - 1 \tag{28}$$

Substituting Equations 14, 25, 27, and 28 into the formula for the F statistic yields

$$F = \frac{nb \sum_{j=1}^{a} (\overline{Y}_{j.} - \overline{Y}_{..})^2/(a - 1)}{\sum_{j=1}^{a} \sum_{k=1}^{b} \sum_{i=1}^{n} (Y_{ijk} - \overline{Y}_{jk})^2/ab(n - 1)} \tag{29}$$

The observed F value obtained from Equation 29 is compared to a critical F value with $a - 1$ numerator degrees of freedom and $ab(n - 1)$ denominator degrees of freedom. If the observed F exceeds the critical F, there is a statistically significant main effect for the A factor.

Although it may be tempting to heave a sigh of relief at this point, we must remind you that we have only accomplished one third of our task. The B main effect and the AB interaction remain to be tested. However, the underlying logic for these tests is the same as for the A main effect. For this reason, instead of presenting the derivation of E_F and E_R in detail, we can consider these tests much more rapidly. This is especially true because the full model remains the same for all three hypothesis tests.

The restricted model to be used in testing the B main effect is given by

$$Y_{ijk} = \mu + \alpha_j + (\alpha\beta)_{jk} + \varepsilon_{ijk} \tag{30}$$

If we were to follow the same steps as we did for the A main effect, we would find that the F statistic for testing the B main effect is given by

$$F = \frac{na \sum_{k=1}^{b} (\overline{Y}_{.k} - \overline{Y}_{..})^2/(b - 1)}{\sum_{j=1}^{a} \sum_{k=1}^{b} \sum_{i=1}^{n} (Y_{ijk} - \overline{Y}_{jk})^2/ab(n - 1)} \tag{31}$$

The observed F value is compared to a critical F value with $b-1$ numerator degrees of freedom and $ab(n-1)$ denominator degrees of freedom. Notice that Equation 31 for testing the B main effect bears a strong resemblance to Equation 29, which provides the F statistic for testing the A main effect. The denominators of the two equations are identical because they both equal MS_W. The numerator of Equation 31 has the same basic form as the numerator of Equation 29, but Equation 31 is based on differences among the marginal means of the B factor instead of the A factor.

Finally, the restricted model to be used in testing the AB interaction is given by

$$Y_{ijk} = \mu + \alpha_j + \beta_k + \varepsilon_{ijk} \tag{32}$$

Predicted scores from the restricted model equal

$$\hat{Y}_{ijk}(R) = \overline{Y}_{..} + (\overline{Y}_{j.} - \overline{Y}_{..}) + (\overline{Y}_{.k} - \overline{Y}_{..}) = \overline{Y}_{j.} + \overline{Y}_{.k} - \overline{Y}_{..}$$

It can then be shown that the difference in the sum of squared errors of the restricted and full models is given by

$$E_R - E_F = n \sum_{j=1}^{a} \sum_{k=1}^{b} (\overline{Y}_{jk} - \overline{Y}_{j.} - \overline{Y}_{.k} + \overline{Y}_{..})^2 \tag{33}$$

Equation 33 provides what is referred to as the interaction sum of squares, because its magnitude reflects the extent to which the A and B effects are nonadditive. The sum of squares for the interaction is also a special case of the general formula we developed in Chapter 3 for $E_R - E_F$, just as we found earlier for the main effects sums of squares. Specifically, by substituting $\widehat{\alpha\beta}_{jk}$ from Equation 18 into Equation 33, we can see that

$$SS_{AB} = E_R - E_F$$

$$= n \sum_{j=1}^{a} \sum_{k=1}^{b} (\widehat{\alpha\beta})_{jk}^2$$

$$= \sum_{\text{all obs}} (\text{estimated parameter})^2$$

To find the expression for the F statistic to test the interaction for statistical significance, we must find $df_R - df_F$. The restricted model has $a + b - 1$ independent parameters; recall that the full model has ab parameters. Thus

$$df_R - df_F = ab - (a + b - 1),$$

which after some algebraic manipulation can be shown to be equal to

$$df_R - df_F = (a-1)(b-1) \tag{34}$$

Thus, the F statistic for testing the interaction equals

$$F = \frac{n \sum_{j=1}^{a} \sum_{k=1}^{b} (\overline{Y}_{jk} - \overline{Y}_{j.} - \overline{Y}_{.k} + \overline{Y}_{..})^2 / (a-1)(b-1)}{\sum_{j=1}^{a} \sum_{k=1}^{b} \sum_{i=1}^{n} (Y_{ijk} - \overline{Y}_{jk})^2 / ab(n-1)} \tag{35}$$

TABLE 7.5
BLOOD PRESSURE DATA FOR 2 × 3 DESIGN

	Biofeedback and Drug X	Biofeedback and Drug Y	Biofeedback and Drug Z	Drug X Alone	Drug Y Alone	Drug Z Alone
	170	186	180	173	189	202
	175	194	187	194	194	228
	165	201	199	197	217	190
	180	215	170	190	206	206
	160	219	204	176	199	224
Mean	170	203	188	186	201	210
S	7.91	13.91	13.84	10.84	10.93	15.81

TABLE 7.6
CELL MEANS AND MARGINAL MEANS FOR TABLE 7.5 DATA

		B (Drug)			
		1 (X)	2 (Y)	3 (Z)	Marginal Means
A (Biofeedback)	1 (Present)	170	203	188	187
	2 (Absent)	186	201	210	199
	Marginal Means	178	202	199	193

This observed F is compared to a critical F with $(a - 1)(b - 1)$ numerator degrees of freedom and $ab(n - 1)$ denominator degrees of freedom.

Numerical Example

Instead of proceeding with further theory development, it would probably be helpful to consider a numerical example at this point. Table 7.5 presents hypothetical data from a study investigating the effects of biofeedback and drug therapy on hypertension. We (arbitrarily) refer to the presence or absence of biofeedback as factor A and to the type of drug as factor B. Hence, we have a 2 × 3 design. Also notice that $n = 5$: that is, there are five subjects in each cell of the design. (Power considerations might dictate a larger n, but only five will be used here to simplify computations.)

Table 7.6 shows the cell means for these data displayed in a 2 × 3 form. We have (arbitrarily) chosen to display the A factor in terms of rows and the B factor in terms of columns. The table also shows the sample marginal means for these data.

Table 7.7 shows the full model and the three restricted models to be compared, as well as the error sum of squares of each model. The bottom third of Table 7.7 presents an ANOVA table for these data. This type of table is often used for summarizing results in a journal article and is the type of table produced by most statistical packages. This table shows that both main effects are significant but that the interaction is nonsignificant at the .05 level. The meaning of these tests is best understood by referring to the means shown in Table 7.6. The significant A main effect implies that biofeedback has a nonzero effect, averaging over type of drug. Specifically, the marginal mean of 187 is significantly different from the mean of 199. Similarly, the significant B main effect implies that the marginal means of Drugs X, Y, and Z are not all equal to each other. Notice that this does not mean that they are all different, but rather that there is a difference somewhere. The precise location of the difference remains to be

TABLE 7.7
ANALYSIS OF TABLE 7.5 DATA

Models Underlying Hypothesis Tests

$$
\begin{aligned}
F: \quad & Y_{ijk} = \mu + \alpha_j + \beta_k + (\alpha\beta)_{jk} + \varepsilon_{ijk} \\
R1: \quad & Y_{ijk} = \mu + \beta_k + (\alpha\beta)_{jk} + \varepsilon_{ijk} \\
R2: \quad & Y_{ijk} = \mu + \alpha_j + (\alpha\beta)_{jk} + \varepsilon_{ijk} \\
R3: \quad & Y_{ijk} = \mu + \alpha_j + \beta_k + \varepsilon_{ijk}
\end{aligned}
$$

Error Sum of Squares for Models

$$
\begin{aligned}
E_F &= 3738 \\
E_{R1} &= 4818 \\
E_{R2} &= 7158 \\
E_{R3} &= 4518
\end{aligned}
$$

ANOVA Table

Source	SS	df	MS	F	p
A	1080	1	1080.00	6.93	.014
B	3420	2	1710.00	10.98	.001
AB	780	2	390.00	2.50	.101
Within cells	3738	24	155.75		

found, using contrasts as in the single-factor design. The nonsignificant interaction implies that (within sampling error) the biofeedback effect is the same for every drug, which is equivalent to saying that differences among the drugs are the same in the presence of biofeedback as in its absence. As usual, however, we cannot claim to have proved that the null hypothesis is true. In other words, we cannot be certain that the effects of biofeedback and drug are really additive. Instead, there may be a true interaction in the population, which we had little power to detect with only five subjects per cell.

Familywise Control of Alpha Level

The careful reader may have noticed that we have performed three statistical tests on our data (one each for the A main effect, the B main effect, and the interaction), and yet we seem to have forgotten Chapter 5 because we have said nothing about preventing the inflation of Type I errors when multiple tests are performed. The reason for our lack of attention to this potential problem until now is that, although three tests are being performed in the experiment, these tests are conceptualized as each constituting a separate family of tests. In other words, we regard questions of the A main effect (biofeedback in our example) as representing one family of questions to be addressed. The alpha level is held at .05 for this family. Questions of the drug main effect and the interaction are considered separately, because they represent conceptually distinct questions. Recall that in Chapter 5 we briefly distinguished between α_{EW}, experimentwise alpha level, and α_{FW}, familywise alpha level. In the factorial design, each type of major effect (A, B, and AB) is defined to represent a family, and traditional practice is to control α_{FW} at .05.[8] Thus, although the alpha level for the experiment as a whole (the α_{EW} level) is allowed to exceed .05, the α_{FW} rate is set at .05 for each of the three families under consideration.

Measures of Effect

Measures of effect are just as relevant in factorial designs as in single-factor designs. The only real difference is that the presence of multiple factors leads to yet additional ways of conceptualizing measures of effect. Our general preference is to recommend interpretation of these measures for single degree of freedom contrasts instead of for omnibus effects. However, we will briefly mention some examples of measures of effect for omnibus effects in factorial designs before proceeding to consider other issues, including a consideration of measures of effects for single degree of freedom contrasts.

Suppose we want to report a measure of effect to describe the influence of type of drug on blood pressure in the data already shown in Table 7.5. Chapter 3 presented several possible measures for the single-factor design. For example, we could report an R^2 value for the drug effect much as we described in Chapter 3. You may recall that we defined R^2 in Chapter 3 as

$$R^2 = \frac{E_R - E_F}{E_R} \tag{3.90, repeated}$$

An immediate complication in the factorial design is that as we have just seen in Table 7.7, there is more than one restricted model. We will see momentarily that the existence of more than one restricted model leads to more than one way of defining an R^2 measure. However, for the moment we will proceed by noting that because we want to calculate R^2 for the drug factor (labeled B in our example), it follows that a reasonable restricted model of interest here would be the model that restricts all beta parameters to be zero, which is model $R2$ in Table 7.7. Thus, we can rewrite our expression for R^2 for the B main effect as

$$R^2_{B,\text{partial}} = \frac{E_{R2} - E_F}{E_{R2}} \tag{36}$$

where we have added the B subscript to R^2 as a reminder that the R^2 for other effects would be different. We will see shortly why we have also designated this R^2 as a "partial R^2." Also notice that similar expressions can be written for the A main effect and the AB interaction simply by replacing E_{R2} in both the numerator and the denominator with either E_{R1} (for the A main effect)or E_{R3} (for the AB interaction). Further notice that R^2 of Equation 36 could be rewritten equivalently as

$$R^2_{B,\text{partial}} = \frac{SS_B}{SS_W + SS_B} \tag{37}$$

because the numerator of Equation 36 is literally SS_B, whereas the denominator reflects two sources of error, SS_W as well as SS_B. Comparable expressions for the R^2 for the A main effect and the AB interaction are given by

$$R^2_{A,\text{partial}} = \frac{SS_A}{SS_W + SS_A} \tag{38}$$

and

$$R^2_{AB,\text{partial}} = \frac{SS_{AB}}{SS_W + SS_{AB}} \tag{39}$$

Notice that Equations 37, 38, and 39 are all special cases of a more general expression that applies to any factorial fixed effects design:

$$R^2_{\text{partial}} = \frac{SS_{\text{effect}}}{SS_W + SS_{\text{effect}}} \tag{40}$$

In our data, we can calculate R^2 for the type of drug directly from the numerator of Equation 31. Substituting 3,420 for SS_{effect} and 3,738 for SS_W yields an R^2 value of 0.48. The ultimate interpretation of this value goes beyond pure statistical considerations, but in most situations this would be regarded as a sizable effect.

We now need to consider two aspects of Equations 37 through 40. The first issue is unique to designs with more than one factor. To motivate this issue, let's return to the R^2 for type of drug, the B factor in our design. Now suppose we learn that another researcher has also investigated the effects of these same three drugs on blood pressure, the only difference being that this researcher did not manipulate the presence or absence of biofeedback. In other words, this researcher used a single-factor design to study drug differences. Would we expect this researcher's value of R^2 from her single-factor design to have approximately the same value as our own value of R^2 for drug in our factorial design? A compelling case can be made that this would be a desirable feature of any R^2 measure. For example, suppose that a few years after these various studies had been completed, a different researcher decides to conduct a meta-analysis comparing these three drugs to one another. We would hope that the R^2 value this meta-analyst might use would not vary from study to study simply because some studies were based on one factor, whereas other studies were based on multiple factors. So the question arises as to whether we would expect the R^2 value obtained in a factorial design to be at least approximately the same as an R^2 value obtained in a single-factor design.

The answer depends (and sometimes strongly depends) on exactly how this other researcher conducted her single-factor design. Suppose she had randomly assigned 10 individuals to Drug X, 10 to Drug Y, and 10 to Drug Z. The critical question is how she chooses to handle the biofeedback factor. We will consider two different ways she might have handled this second factor. First, one possibility is that she designs her study so as to compare the three drugs in a way that holds biofeedback constant. In other words, either none of her 30 individuals receives biofeedback or everyone receives biofeedback in this version of her design. What might we expect to find in this single-factor design? The column marginal means provide reasonable estimates of the means we might expect to observe if biofeedback were held constant. (Technically, this is true only when there is no interaction in the population, but we will proceed under that assumption for the remainder of our comparison of single-factor and factorial designs.) We might once again expect to obtain means of 178, 202, and 199 for the three drugs. Based on 10 participants per group, this would yield a between group sum of squares equal to 3,420 in this single-factor design. To complete the picture, we need to consider what value we would expect to obtain for SS_W. To the extent that homogeneity of variance holds here, we would expect MS_W to equal 155.75, as it does in the factorial design, because homogeneity implies that the population variance is the same value in every cell of the design. The corresponding value of SS_W would be 4,205.25 (i.e., 155.75 times 27), because with 30 participants and three groups, there are 27 degrees of freedom for the within cells source of variance. Thus, in this single-factor design, $E_R - E_F = 3,420$, whereas $E_R = 7,625.25$ (i.e., the sum of 3,420 and 4,205.25). Substituting the values of 3,420 and 7,625.25 into Equation 3.90 shows that the R^2 value for this single factor design would equal 0.45.

What is the relationship between the R^2 we have calculated in the factorial design and the R^2 in the single-factor design? The numerator values of both expressions equal 3,420. The only difference is a slight difference in the denominator values because of the difference in denominator degrees of freedom. Thus, the partial R^2 value in the factorial design is essentially equivalent to the R^2 value we would have obtained in a single-factor design where the other factor in the design is held constant.

Now consider a different way in which our hypothetical researcher might have conducted a single-factor design comparing the drugs. Instead of conducting the study so that either no one received biofeedback or everyone received biofeedback, suppose that some individuals received biofeedback but others did not. In particular, for simplicity, we will suppose that within each drug condition, one half of the participants received biofeedback but the other half did not. Thus, whereas we previously assumed that biofeedback was being held constant, we are now assuming that biofeedback was not constant and in fact varied from person to person. At this point, you may be thinking that this sounds exactly like the study depicted in Tables 7.5 through 7.7. In fact, it is exactly the same study. So how can it be a single-factor design? We will simply suppose that the study was designed in such a manner that both drug and biofeedback vary from person to person, but the data will be analyzed ignoring any variability due to the presence or absence of biofeedback. Specifically, instead of using the models shown in Table 7.7 to analyze the data, we will return to full and restricted models for a single-factor design. Namely the single-factor design uses a full model of the form

$$Y_{ij} = \mu + \alpha_j + \varepsilon_{ij} \qquad \text{(3.66, repeated)}$$

However, the factorial design uses a full model of the form

$$Y_{ijk} = \mu + \alpha_j + \beta_k + (\alpha\beta)_{jk} + \varepsilon_{ijk} \qquad \text{(6, repeated)}$$

It can be shown that the between-group sum of squares in the single-factor design is 3,420, exactly the same value as the sum of squares for the drug main effect in the factorial design (Exercise 5 at the end of the chapter asks you to demonstrate this equivalence for the biofeed-back effect). This equivalence will always hold in equal-n factorial designs. However, the within-group sum of squares for the single-factor design is almost 50% larger than the within-group sum of squares for the factorial design. The reason can be understood by comparing Equations 3.66 and 7.6. In equal-n designs, the μ and α_j parameters have exactly the same meaning, population values, and estimated sample values in the two models. Thus, the only difference is that the model for the factorial design represents any additional variability not accounted for by the α_j parameters as being due to a combination of β_k, $(\alpha\beta)_{jk}$, and error. However, the model for the single-factor design regards all variability beyond that due to the α_j parameters as being due to error. In other words, any variability attributable to β_k and to $(\alpha\beta)_{jk}$ in the factorial design is unaccounted for in the single-factor model. As a consequence, the B and AB effects manifest themselves in the error term of the model for the single-factor design and contribute to the error sum of squares for the model. In our data, then, the error sum of squares for the full model in the single-factor design would equal 5,598 (the sum of 1,080, 780, and 3,738, the SS for A, AB, and Within, respectively, shown at the bottom of Table 7.7, because in this case we have omitted A and AB effects from our model). The sum of squared errors for the restricted model will then equal 9,018 (the sum of 3,420 and 5,598). Substituting 3,420 and 9,018 into Equation 3.90 yields an R^2 value of 0.38. Remember that the R^2 value for type of drug based on Equation 37 for the factorial design is 0.48. Realize that the difference between 0.38 and 0.48 can reflect only whether we construe the data of Table 7.5 in terms of one factor or two factors, because we calculated both 0.48 and 0.38 on exactly these same data.

So which value is correct? It turns out that this is not really an appropriate question. It's not a matter of right versus wrong, but instead what question we want to answer. To understand this issue, we need to keep in mind why we are calculating R^2 in the first place. Presumably, we want to know how much of the variability in the data is due to differences between drugs. The complication that emerges here is that the denominator of R^2 reflects total variance, and the magnitude of total variance depends on what other factors, if any, vary in the data. If biofeedback is held constant, total variance is smaller, so the value of R^2 is larger, whereas if biofeedback varies, total variance is larger, so the value of R^2 is smaller. Thus, for R^2 to have a meaningful interpretation and to compare R^2 values from study to study (as in meta-analysis), it is vital to agree on what other potential sources of variance should be regarded as fixed and which should be regarded as varying.

Ideally, this framework clearly identifies the issue, but even so, the solution can sometimes be debatable. The key issue usually involves the extent to which the "off factor" is an "intrinsic" factor. For example, is biofeedback "intrinsic" to comparisons of drug effects? Or would it be entirely reasonable to design a study comparing drugs for hypertension without varying presence or absence of biofeedback? It seems reasonable here to argue that such a study would indeed be reasonable, so it follows that it is also reasonable to interpret the size of drug effects holding biofeedback constant. In this case, we would maintain that the "off factor" of biofeedback is extrinsic to questions of drug effects, and the partial R^2 expressions shown in Equations 36 through 40 provide meaningful indices of effect size.

To consider a situation where we might arrive at a different conclusion, suppose we are still interested in assessing the effect of type of drug, but now suppose that the second factor is gender instead of presence or absence of biofeedback. What difference does this make? Would we usually examine drug effects holding gender constant? Although we certainly could take this approach, it seems more natural to regard gender as an intrinsic factor, in which case variability due to gender would be included in the denominator of the R^2 measure. Equations 36 through 40 would overestimate the intended measure of effect in this case. Instead, when we want to allow variance accounted for by other factors to be included in the total variance, a different expression is necessary for R^2. The general expression for this type of R^2 is

$$R^2_{\text{effect}} = SS_{\text{effect}}/SS_{\text{T}} \tag{41}$$

where SS_{T} is simply total sum of squares, adding over all sources of variance, including SS_{W}. Just for illustration, if we were to regard biofeedback as an intrinsic factor in our two-way design, we would obtain an R^2 value of 0.38 using Equation 41. Notice that this is exactly the same value we illustrated a few moments ago when we regarded biofeedback as varying instead of being held constant.

Another perspective on this issue is provided by considering R^2 in terms of F values. In particular, when we regard "off factors" as extrinsic, we can calculate R^2_{partial} as

$$R^2_{\text{partial}} = \frac{df_{\text{effect}} F_{\text{effect}}}{df_{\text{effect}} F_{\text{effect}} + df_{\text{W}}} \tag{42}$$

whereas when we regard the off factor as intrinsic, R^2 can be found from

$$R^2 = \frac{df_{\text{effect}} F_{\text{effect}}}{\displaystyle\sum_{\text{all effects}} (df_{\text{effect}} F_{\text{effect}}) + df_{\text{W}}} \tag{43}$$

Comparing Equations 42 and 43 makes it clear that the two versions of R^2 have the same numerator but different denominators. From this perspective, the question ultimately comes down to whether the F values for other effects in the design should influence the R^2 value we choose to interpret for the effect of interest. For example, should the R^2 value for representing the magnitude of the drug effect be influenced by the size of the biofeedback effect? Probably not, in which case we would prefer the partial R^2 measure of Equation 42. On the other hand, should we be allowed to increase our measure of R^2 by controlling for gender, and thus use Equation 42 in this instance also? Probably not, but now this suggests that Equation 43 is likely to provide the more interpretable index. The bottom line is that the choice between the two types of R^2 measures depends on how we want to conceptualize total variance, and the answer to that question stretches beyond statistics into the subject matter itself. At the very least, it is important to be aware of the difference between the two types of measures.

We are finally ready to consider the second issue we alluded to several paragraphs ago. We now need to realize that each of these expressions we have been considering accurately depicts the proportion of variance accounted for by the relevant effect in this particular sample. However, as we discussed in Chapter 3, the sample R^2 is a biased estimator of the population R^2. Thus, we might prefer to compute an omega squared value much as we considered in Chapter 3. Once again, we must decide whether to regard "off factors" as intrinsic or extrinsic. When "off factors" are conceptualized as extrinsic, the general expression for partial omega squared in a fixed effects factorial design is given by

$$\hat{\omega}^2_{\text{partial}} = \frac{SS_{\text{effect}} - df_{\text{effect}}MS_W}{SS_{\text{effect}} + (N - df_{\text{effect}})MS_W} \tag{44}$$

Similarly, when "off factors" are regarded as intrinsic, the general expression for omega squared is

$$\hat{\omega}^2 = \frac{SS_{\text{effect}} - (df_{\text{effect}}MS_W)}{SS_T + MS_W} \tag{45}$$

Once again, it is instructive to rewrite Equations 44 and 45 in terms of F values. For extrinsic "off factors," this yields

$$\hat{\omega}^2_{\text{partial}} = \frac{df_{\text{effect}}(F_{\text{effect}} - 1)}{df_{\text{effect}}(F_{\text{effect}} - 1) + N} \tag{46}$$

However, the comparable expression for intrinsic "off factors" is

$$\hat{\omega}^2 = \frac{df_{\text{effect}}(F_{\text{effect}} - 1)}{\displaystyle\sum_{\text{all effects}} (df_{\text{effect}}F_{\text{effect}}) + df_W + 1} \tag{47}$$

Notice that the primary difference between these two expressions for omega squared and our previous expressions for R^2 involves the numerator. Descriptive R^2 measures of variance accounted for will be positive anytime the F value for an effect is not zero, which essentially implies that in real data, R^2 will always be at the very least slightly positive. On the other hand, omega squared measures become positive only when the observed F value exceeds 1.0, so only in cases where F is larger than 1.0 would we infer that the effect truly accounts for variance in the population.

Table 7.8 shows R^2, $\hat{\omega}^2$, partial R^2, and partial $\hat{\omega}^2$ values for the three omnibus effects of our blood pressure data. By mathematical necessity, for any given effect, the largest measure is given by R^2_{partial} and the smallest by $\hat{\omega}^2$. Of course, the choice of which measure to interpret should depend not on the magnitude of the measure, but instead on which is judged

TABLE 7.8
STRENGTH OF ASSOCIATION MEASURES FOR
BLOOD PRESSURE DATA

Effect	R^2	$\hat{\omega}^2$	R^2_{partial}	$\hat{\omega}^2_{\text{partial}}$
A	.12	.10	.22	.17
B	.38	.34	.48	.40
A B	.09	.05	.17	.09

to answer the appropriate question. In these blood pressure data, the drug effect is strongest and the interaction weakest by all accounts. Even though the interaction effect was not statistically significant, Table 7.8 suggests that it may still account for a noticeable proportion of variance in the data. On the one hand, the small sample size in our hypothetical example may not have been enough to give us reasonable power to detect an interaction. We will have more to say on the topic of power later in the chapter. On the other hand, the small sample size also suggests that our estimates of strength of association may themselves be subject to considerable sampling error. For example, our single best estimate of the partial variance accounted for by the interaction in the population is 9%, but we need to regard this precise value with a fair amount of skepticism, because the true population value might be very different from the value we obtained in our small sample. One solution to this problem is to report a confidence interval for the measure. Interested readers are referred to Steiger and Fouladi (1997) and Fidler and Thompson (2001) for descriptions of such confidence intervals.

FOLLOW-UP TESTS

Further Investigation of Main Effects

Let's return to the data shown in Table 7.5. As we saw in Table 7.7, both main effects are significant. However, the precise meaning of the drug main effect is unclear, because we do not know which specific column marginal means are different from each other. As in Chapter 4, we can address this question by forming contrasts of the means. (Notice that we do not need to worry about contrasts for the A main effect in our numerical example—why not?) Indeed, contrasts are formed and tested in exactly the same manner as in the one-way design. The sum of squares for a contrast of the levels of the B factor is given by

$$SS_\psi = na\,(\hat{\psi})^2 \Big/ \sum_{k=1}^{b} c_k^2 \qquad (48)$$

where $\hat{\psi}$ is the sample value of the contrast. The na term appears in the numerator, because each B marginal mean is based on n times a observations. Similarly, if we wanted to contrast marginal means of the A factor, the sum of squares would be

$$SS_\psi = nb\,(\hat{\psi})^2 \Big/ \sum_{j=1}^{a} c_j^2 \qquad (49)$$

In either case, the contrast would be tested for statistical significance by calculating an observed F value:

$$F = SS_\psi / MS_W \tag{50}$$

The critical value against which to compare this observed F would depend on the same decisions as discussed in Chapter 5 on multiple-comparisons procedures. In other words, the critical value might be obtained through either the Bonferroni, Tukey, or Scheffé methods, keeping in mind that the number of levels potentially being compared equals the number of levels for that factor.

To see an example of testing contrasts, reconsider the sample means in Table 7.6. So far, we know that the drug main effect is statistically significant, implying that the population means of drugs X, Y, and Z are not all equal to each other. Let's suppose we have decided to compare drug X versus drug Y. From Table 7.6, we can see that the corresponding marginal means are 178 and 202. Formally, we can represent the test of their difference as a comparison of population marginal means (as defined earlier in Equation 8):

$$\psi = 1\mu_{.1} - 1\mu_{.2} + 0\mu_{.3}$$

The population value of the contrast is estimated with $\hat{\psi}$:

$$\hat{\psi} = 1\overline{Y}_{.1} - 1\overline{Y}_{.2} + 0\overline{Y}_{.3}$$

which for these data corresponds to

$$\hat{\psi} = 1\,(178) - 1\,(202) + 0\,(199)$$

so that $\hat{\psi}$ equals -24. Substituting this value along with $n = 5$, $a = 2$, and $\sum_{k=1}^{b} c_k^2 = 2$ into Equation 48 yields

$$SS_\psi = 5(2)(-24)^2/2 = 2880$$

As shown in Equation 50, the observed F value is obtained by dividing the sum of squares for the contrast by the value of mean square within, which equals 155.75 for these data. Thus, for our contrast, the observed F equals

$$F = 2880/155.75 = 18.49$$

Because we are testing a pairwise comparison, we should use Tukey's WSD to control α_{FW}, unless this contrast is one of a small number we planned prior to collecting the data. As in the one-way design (see Table 5.16), the observed F must be compared to a critical value of the form $(q_{.05,\,b,\,df_{error}})^2/2$. Notice that here we have used b instead of a to subscript q, because we are comparing marginal means of the B factor. With this in mind, we have here that $b = 3$, and $df_{error} = 24$, so from Appendix Table A.4, the critical q value is 3.53. Thus, the critical value against which we should compare the observed F equals 6.23 (i.e., 3.53 squared and then divided by 2). The observed value exceeds the critical value, so we can conclude that the marginal means of Drugs X and Y are significantly different from one another. Remember, as we pointed out at the end of Chapter 5, if our interest lies solely in pairwise comparisons, in fact, the B main-effect test need not be performed, because Tukey's WSD by itself controls α_{FW}. Nevertheless, the main-effect test might be reported, because it provides a context for the pairwise comparisons and because most behavioral researchers traditionally do report main-effect tests in this situaton.

As usual, we might want to supplement our hypothesis test with a confidence interval or even use the interval instead of the test. In either case, the procedure follows exactly from Table 5.17. For example, the Tukey solution for a simultaneous 95% interval for the difference between the population means of drugs X and Y would be computed from Table 5.17 as

$$(178 - 202) \pm (3.53/\sqrt{2})\sqrt{155.75\left(\frac{1}{10} + \frac{1}{10}\right)} \qquad (51)$$

Before proceeding, we need to be clear about why we have used values of 10 for n_1 and n_2. At first glance, it might seem that the appropriate values are 5, because we have 5 participants per cell. However, we need to remember that we are comparing column marginal means, and each column has 10 participants. In other words, the mean of 178 is computed from the 10 participants who received Drug X; 5 of these participants received biofeedback and 5 did not, but the crucial point is that the value we use for n_g should correspond to the number of participants we used to compute $\overline{Y}_g$, which in these data is 10.

Carrying out the arithmetic yields an interval of -37.93 to -10.07. Thus, although our single best guess is that Drug X is 24 points better than Drug Y, it is plausible that in the population Drug X is as much as 38 points better or as little as 10 points better. Keep in mind that this interval does not contain zero, so using Tukey's method, we can reject the null hypothesis that there is no population difference between Drugs X and Y. As usual, this conclusion can be reached either by noticing that the confidence interval does not contain zero or by directly testing the null hypothesis.

An approximate standardized interval can be formed by dividing the lower and upper limits of the interval by the square root of mean square within, because mean square within is an estimate of within-cells variance, and we want to divide by a standard deviation in order to standardize the data. In our data, MS_W equals 155.75, so an estimate of the within-cell standard deviation is 12.48 (i.e., the square root of 155.75). Dividing the limits of the raw score confidence interval by 12.48 yields an interval given by -3.04 and -0.81. From the perspective of this standardized metric, we can be confident that the advantage of Drug X over Drug Y is large by conventional criteria (recall that Cohen identified a value of .80 as large). The width of this interval emphasizes that we have not pinpointed the precise advantage with great accuracy. To obtain a more precise estimate would require considerably more participants than the 10 per drug we used here. Also keep in mind that the interval we formed is approximate. As we have mentioned previously, several sources (e.g., Steiger & Fouladi, 1997) describe more complicated methods for obtaining exact intervals. Finally, we also need to point out that proper interpretation of standardized intervals requires that we once again confront the question of whether the "off factor" in the design should be regarded as extrinsic or intrinsic. By choosing MS_W as our estimate of variance, we have implicitly treated the biofeedback factor as extrinsic. If instead we decided to treat it as intrinsic, we would need to use a variance estimate that did not control for biofeedback. We could obtain such an estimate by summing all sources in Table 7.7 other than the drug effect and then dividing the resultant sum of squares by the resultant degrees of freedom. In our data, this would yield a value of 5,598 for the sum of squares (remember that we saw this value in our discussion of strength of association measures) and a value of 27 for degrees of freedom. An estimate of the relevant standard deviation would equal 14.40 (the square root of 5,598 divided by 27). An approximate standardized interval would now range from -2.63 to -0.70. In this example, the different standard deviations do not result in greatly different intervals, but that is not always the case, so researchers who decide to report standardized intervals must carefully consider how they want to conceptualize the appropriate standard deviation.

OPTIONAL

Marginal Mean Comparisons Without Homogeneity Assumption

It is often helpful in working with contrasts of marginal means to realize that in effect the factorial design is reduced to a one-way design when marginal means are being examined. Thus, the same principles we developed there also apply here. This conceptualization is especially helpful if we are concerned about possible violations of homogeneity of variance. For example, suppose that we want to test the difference between Drug X and Drug Y, just as we did in the preceding section, except now we are unwilling to assume homogeneity of variance. We can express the contrast in terms of the six cell means as

$$\psi = .5\mu_{11} + .5\mu_{21} - .5\mu_{12} - .5\mu_{22} + 0\mu_{13} + 0\mu_{23}$$

For our data, $\hat{\psi}$ is given by

$$
\begin{aligned}
\hat{\psi} &= .5\overline{Y}_{11} + .5\overline{Y}_{21} - .5\overline{Y}_{12} - .5\overline{Y}_{22} \\
&= .5(170) + .5(186) - .5(203) - .5(201) \\
&= -24
\end{aligned}
$$

The corresponding sum of squares for the contrast can be found from Equation 4.39:

$$SS_\psi = E_R - E_F = (\hat{\psi})^2 \Big/ \sum_{j=1}^{ab} (c_j^2/n_j) \qquad \text{(see 4.39)}$$

The j subscript ranges from 1 to the number of cells in the original factorial design. For these data, the sum of squares equals

$$SS_\psi = (-24)^2/[(.25/5) + (.25/5) + (.25/5) + (.25/5)] = 2880$$

Notice that this is precisely the value we obtained when we used Equation 48 (of this chapter) to calculate the sum of squares directly from the marginal means. As in the one-way design, the only difference that emerges, if we are unwilling to assume homogeneity, is that we do not use MS_W as the error term. Instead, the separate variance approach uses an error term of the form

$$\text{denom} = \left(\sum_{j=1}^{ab} (c_j^2/n_j)s_j^2\right) \Big/ \sum_{j=1}^{ab} (c_j^2/n_j) \qquad \text{(see 4.42)}$$

In our example, the appropriate error term equals

$$
\text{denom} = \frac{(.25/5)(62.5) + (.25/5)(117.5) + (.25/5)(193.5) + (.25/5)(119.5)}{(.25/5) + (.25/5) + (.25/5) + (.25/5)}
$$

$$= 123.25$$

The resultant F value is thus given by $F = 2{,}880/123.25 = 23.37$. Assuming that we wish to use Tukey's WSD to control α_{FW},[9] from Table 5.16, we can see that the appropriate critical value equals $(q_{.05,b,df})^2/2$, where

$$df = \frac{\left(\sum\limits_{j=1}^{ab} c_j^2 s_j^2 / n_j\right)^2}{\sum\limits_{j=1}^{ab} \left[\left(c_j^2 s_j^2 / n_j\right)^2 / (n_j - 1)\right]}$$

(see 4.43)

For our data, it turns out that $df = 14$, or just over half the degrees of freedom we had when we assumed homogeneity. From Appendix Table A.4, the critical q value is 3.70 (remember that $b = 3$, even though there are six individual cell means). The critical value for the F is then 6.84 (i.e., 3.70 squared and then divided by 2). As happened when we assumed homogeneity, the observed F exceeds the critical value, so we can conclude that there is a difference in the population marginal means of Drug X and Drug Y.

Further Investigation of an Interaction—Simple Effects

If a statistically significant interaction had occurred in the data shown in Table 7.5, we probably would have wanted to interpret the data differently. Specifically, the interpretation of the main effects is changed when an interaction is found, because an interaction implies that the effects of a factor are not consistent across the levels of another factor. Although the marginal mean still reflects an average, the average itself may be misleading because the interaction is a signal that the individual effects are significantly different from the average effect.[10] For this reason, it is usually more meaningful to test the significance of these individual effects of a factor at each level of the other factor separately rather than test the main effect.

To discuss this argument further, reconsider the data of Table 7.5. Suppose that there were in fact six participants per group: the five per group already shown in Table 7.5 plus one additional observation per group, shown in Table 7.9. The cell means based on all six scores per group are shown in Table 7.10. Performing our usual three tests of significance for these data reveals that all three effects are significant: For the A main effect, $F = 9.49$, $p = .0046$; for the B main effect, $F = 15.02$, $p = .0001$; and for the AB interaction, $F = 4.22$, $p = .0237$. Even in the presence of a significant interaction, the significant main effects imply that marginal means are significantly different from one another. For example, the two marginal means for A, which equal 187 and 199 in the sample, are significantly different. Average blood pressure readings are lower in the presence of biofeedback than in its absence. On the average, the difference is estimated to be 12 points. However, is this 12 points an accurate indication of the effect under each of the three drugs? No, it is not. Why not? Because of the significant interaction, which means that the 20-point difference under Drug X, the -4-point difference under Drug Y, and the 20-point difference under Drug Z are not all the same. Notice that the mean of these effects (20, -4, and 20) is indeed 12, the difference in the marginal means. However, we can be certain (at the .05 level) that the sample values of 20, -4, and 20 do not all come from the

TABLE 7.9
ADDITIONAL OBSERVATIONS FOR TABLE 7.5 DATA

Biofeedback and Drug X	Biofeedback and Drug Y	Biofeedback and Drug Z	Drug X Alone	Drug Y Alone	Drug Z Alone
158	209	194	198	195	204

TABLE 7.10
CELL MEANS AND MARGINAL MEANS BASED ON
SIX OBSERVATIONS PER CELL

	1 (X)	2 (Y)	3 (Z)	Marginal Means
1 (Present)	168	204	189	187
2 (Absent)	188	200	209	199
Marginal Means	178	202	199	193

same population. Using one number (i.e., 12 for these data) to estimate a single population effect in this situation is usually misleading.

A reasonable alternative to interpreting the marginal mean difference of 12 is to interpret the individual effects whose average is 12. In other words, we need to consider each of the three effects individually. Is there a biofeedback effect for Drug X? Drug Y? Drug Z? These effects are referred to as simple effects. Tests of simple effects of A proceed by examining the effect of A at a fixed level of B. In our example, there are three simple effects tests of A, the biofeedback factor: (1) A at B_1 (the biofeedback effect in the presence of Drug X); (2) A at B_2 (the biofeedback effect in the presence of Drug Y): and (3) A at B_3 (the biofeedback effect in the presence of Drug Z). Similarly, there are two simple effects tests of B: (1) B at A_1 (the drug effect when biofeedback is present) and (2) B at A_2 (the drug effect when biofeedback is absent). Notice that in each case we have reduced the two-factor design to a one-factor design. For this reason, we can test the significance of a simple effect by treating the data as if they came from a single-factor design. For example, consider the effect of A at B_1. Are the sample means of 168 and 188 significantly different from one another? We can calculate a sum of squares for this effect using the same formula we used in the single-factor design:

$$SS_{\text{effect}} = n \sum_{j=1}^{a} (\overline{Y}_j - \overline{Y})^2 \tag{52}$$

For our data, $n = 6$, $\overline{Y}_1 = 168$, $\overline{Y}_2 = 188$, and $\overline{Y} = 178$. Performing the arithmetic yields $SS = 1{,}200$ for the A within B_1 effect. Because we are comparing two means, the degree of freedom for the effect is just 1 (in general, $df = $ number of groups -1). If we are willing to assume homogeneity of variance, E_F/df_F (which is simply MS_W) continues to be an appropriate error term. Hence, we can obtain an observed F value from

$$F = \frac{SS_{\text{effect}}/df_{\text{effect}}}{MS_W} = \frac{1200/1}{136.6} = 8.78$$

The p value associated with this F for 1 and 30 df is .0060, indicating a statistically significant biofeedback effect with Drug X. Similar calculations for the other two drugs show $F = 0.35$ ($p = .5644$) for Drug Y and $F = 8.78$ ($p = .0060$) for Drug Z. Thus, biofeedback has a significant effect when used together with Drug X or Drug Z but not with Drug Y.

Just as we have tested the biofeedback effect within each type of drug, we can also test the drug effect within each level of the biofeedback factor. For example, consider the effect of B (drug) at A_1 (biofeedback present). Are the sample means of 168, 204, and 189 significantly different from each other? Using Equation 52, we find that $SS = 3{,}924$ for the B-within-A_1 effect. Because we are comparing three means, this effect has two degrees of freedom. The

F for this effect thus equals

$$F = \frac{SS_{\text{effect}}/df_{\text{effect}}}{MS_W} = \frac{3924/2}{136.6} = 14.36$$

This has an associated p value of .0001. Thus, the three drugs are significantly different from each other in the presence of biofeedback. It turns out that the drugs also differ in the absence of biofeedback; the observed F value is 4.88, $p = .0145$. In both cases, we must keep in mind that we have not necessarily shown that all three drugs are different; instead, we have only shown that they are not all the same. To determine which specific drugs are different, we would need to test comparisons just as we did in the single-factor design. In factorial designs, such comparisons are usually referred to as cell mean comparisons because we are literally comparing means of individual cells to one another. For example, suppose we want to compare Drugs Y and Z in the presence of biofeedback. Are the sample means of 189 and 204 significantly different from one another? To answer this question, we must find the sum of squares associated with the relevant contrast. Recall that (with equal n) the SS for a contrast is given by

$$SS_\psi = n(\hat{\psi})^2 \Big/ \sum_{j=1}^{a} c_j^2$$

For our data, $n = 6$, $\hat{\psi} = -15$, and $\sum_{j=1}^{a} c_j^2 = 2$, so the SS for the contrast equals 675. The corresponding degree of freedom equals 1 because we are testing a single contrast. Thus, the observed F value is given by

$$F = \frac{SS_{\text{contrast}}/df_{\text{contrast}}}{MS_w} = \frac{675/1}{136.6} = 4.94,$$

This has a p value of .0320. With an α_{PC} of .05, this would be significant. However, if we are to be consistent with the principles we developed in Chapter 5 for the one-way design, we should use an appropriate multiple-comparisons procedure to control the familywise error rate.

As usual, we might also want to report a confidence interval for the difference between Drugs Y and Z in the presence of biofeedback. We can continue to rely on Table 5.17, although in order to use this table we must decide how we intend to control familywise alpha level. For example, suppose we decide to conceptualize questions involving drug differences in the presence of biofeedback as a separate family (we believe this is a reasonable decision, but not the only reasonable way to proceed, as we discuss further in the next section). Then we can use Tukey's method to control alpha for all pairwise comparisons. Based on Table 5.17, the 95% simultaneous confidence interval for the difference in population means of Drugs Y and Z in the presence of biofeedback is given by

$$(189 - 204) \pm (3.53/\sqrt{2})\sqrt{155.75\left(\frac{1}{5} + \frac{1}{5}\right)} \tag{53}$$

Notice that this is very similar to the expression we developed in Equation 51 for comparing marginal means. However, the sample sizes are different here (namely 5) than they were when we compared marginal means (where we used 10 for the sample size) because each cell mean is based on only 5 participants, whereas each column marginal mean is based on 10 participants. Carrying out the arithmetic yields an interval ranging from -34.70 to 4.70. Thus, we cannot be reasonably certain which drug is more effective, because the interval contains zero. Notice that this interval is wider than our previous interval for marginal mean comparisons, because the cell means are based on fewer participants. For a fixed sample size, power is less and intervals are wider for cell mean comparisons than for marginal mean comparisons. Thus, researchers anticipating analyses of cell means need to be prepared to use larger samples than in situations where marginal means are of most interest. Also, it would be possible to convert this raw score confidence interval to a standardized interval.

As a further note on cell mean comparisons, we should note that certain computer programs (such as PROC GLM in SAS, as of this writing) require such effects to be specified in terms of model parameters from the full model shown originally in Equation 6:

$$Y_{ijk} = \mu + \alpha_j + \beta_k + (\alpha\beta)_{jk} + \varepsilon_{ijk} \qquad\qquad (6, \text{repeated})$$

To see what this means, let's return to our example comparing Drugs Y and Z in the presence of biofeedback. From Table 7.10, notice that this is a comparison of the cell in row 1 and column 2 versus the cell in row 1 and column 3. We can write the mean for row 1 and column 2 in terms of our model parameters as

$$\mu_{12} = \mu + \alpha_1 + \beta_2 + (\alpha\beta)_{12}$$

Similarly, we can write the mean for row 1 and column 3 as

$$\mu_{13} = \mu + \alpha_1 + \beta_3 + (\alpha\beta)_{13}$$

Thus, the difference $\mu_{12} - \mu_{13}$ between the means can be written as

$$(\mu + \alpha_1 + \beta_2 + (\alpha\beta)_{12}) - (\mu + \alpha_1 + \beta_3 + (\alpha\beta)_{13}),$$

This simplifies to

$$\beta_2 - \beta_3 + (\alpha\beta)_{12} - (\alpha\beta)_{13}$$

Three further points are worth noting. First, notice that the row effect parameter α_j does not appear in this cell mean comparison, because both cells being compared are in the first row. Thus, any effect attributable to row differences is moot for this particular comparison. Second, notice that this cell mean comparison consists of a combination of main effect parameters and interaction parameters. In this sense, this cell mean comparison reflects a mixture of main effect and interaction effects as opposed to being a pure indicator of a single type of effect. Third, this comparison can be tested (and estimated—more about this later) using an "estimate" statement in SAS PROC GLM with the following syntax:

estimate 'cell 12 versus cell 13' B 0 1 $-$ 1 A^*B 0 1 $-$ 1 0 0 0;

The words inside the single quotes are simply a label. Notice that the values after "B" reflect the β_k column effect parameters (including β_1, which we must explicitly tell PROC GLM is to be weighted zero), whereas the values after "A^*B" reflect the $(\alpha\beta)_{jk}$ interaction parameters— once again being explicit that $(\alpha\beta)_{11}$, for example, is given a weight of zero in this particular comparison.

Relationships of Main Effect, Interaction, and Simple Effects

We have just seen that cell mean comparisons as follow-up tests to simple effects involve a combination of main effect and interaction parameters. More generally, there is a definite relationship among these three types of tests. One way of capturing these relationships is through sums of squares. For example, in equal n designs, the sums of squares for simple effects always obey the following equation:

$$\sum_{k=1}^{b} SS_{AwB_k} = SS_A + SS_{AB} \tag{54}$$

In words, the left side of the equation represents the sum of b simple effects, namely, the sum of squares for a row simple effect within each and every column of the design. A comparable expression can be written for the column simple effects:

$$\sum_{j=1}^{a} SS_{BwA_j} = SS_B + SS_{AB} \tag{55}$$

The practical implications of these two equations are easiest to understand in the special case of a 2×2 design. Assuming that MS_W is used as the error term for all effects (we will describe other possible options shortly), Abelson (1995) has shown that the following relationship always holds between the interaction and the simple effects in an equal n 2×2 factorial design:

$$t(AB) = \frac{t(Aw\,B_1) - t(Aw\,B_2)}{\sqrt{2}} \tag{56}$$

where $t(AB)$ is the observed t value for the interaction, and $t(Aw\,B_k)$ is the observed t value for the row simple effect in column k. A comparable expression also holds for the column effect within rows:

$$t(AB) = \frac{t(Bw\,A_1) - t(Bw\,A_2)}{\sqrt{2}} \tag{57}$$

Although Equations 56 and 57 look different from one another, they will always yield the same observed t value for the interaction. You may wonder why Abelson (and we) chose to write these expressions in terms of t values instead of our usual F values. The reason is that it is important here to retain information about the direction of the effect, which t values (unlike F values) allow us to do, because they may be either positive or negative. For example, if row 1 has a higher mean than row 2 within column 1, but row 2 has a higher mean than row 1 within column 2, the two t values in the numerator of Equation 56 would necessarily have opposite signs.

What are the practical implications of Equations 56 and 57? Notice that the signs of the t values will agree with one another if the interaction is ordinal and will disagree if the interaction is disordinal. This immediately shows why all other things being equal, ordinal interactions are much more difficult to detect than disordinal interactions—the interaction t value for an ordinal interaction in a 2×2 design will always be smaller than at least one (and possibly both) of the simple effect t values. On the other hand, the interaction t value for a disordinal interaction may well be larger than even the larger t value for the simple effects. Also notice that when one simple effect is expected to be close to zero (and thus the t statistic itself will be close to zero in the long run), the interaction t value will tend to be about 70% as large as the other simple effect. In this case, it will usually be preferable statistically to test the simple effects directly instead of testing the interaction effect.

Abelson (1995) has also shown a relationship between the main effect and the simple effects in an equal n 2×2 factorial design:

$$t(A) = \frac{t(A w B_1) + t(A w B_2)}{\sqrt{2}} \tag{58}$$

Once again, a comparable expression could be written for the B main effect

$$t(B) = \frac{t(B w A_1) + t(B w A_2)}{\sqrt{2}} \tag{59}$$

Notice the key difference between these equations (either for A or for B) and the previous equations for the interaction is that the simple effects are now added together instead of subtracted from one another. Thus, the t value for the A main effect (or the B effect) will be larger than the t value for the interaction if and only if the t values for the two simple effects have the same sign. Said differently, when the two simple effects are in a consistent direction, the t value for the main effect will be larger than the t value for the interaction. On the other hand, when the two simple effects are in opposite directions, the t value for the interaction will be larger than the t value for the main effect. We can also think about how the t value for the main effect compares to the t values for the simple effects. In particular, the t value for the main effect will be increased to the extent that the simple effects are similar to one another and of the same sign. In fact, if the t values for the simple effects were exactly equal to one another, the t value for the A main effect would be 141% as large as the common t value of the simple effects. From a statistical perspective, this is a primary reason for favoring the main effect test instead of the simple effect tests in this situation. What if the two t values for the simple effects were of equal magnitudes but of opposite signs? In this case, the t value for the main effect would clearly equal zero, in which case the main effect is insensitive to any effects in the data. Fortunately, this pattern is ideally suited to detection by the interaction effect.

Consideration of Type I Error Rate in Testing Simple Effects

When simple effects tests are performed in an attempt to interpret the meaning of a significant interaction, it is inevitable that multiple significance tests will be conducted. If each test is conducted with $\alpha = .05$, the overall Type I error rate may be considerably greater than .05. Some researchers maintain that this inflation should not be regarded as problematic, because they will conduct these tests only if the interaction is significant, which will happen only 5% of the time if in fact there is no interaction. Although this logic holds if there is literally no interaction in the population, it fails when the interaction null hypothesis is partially true. Indeed, the problem with this logic is the same as the problem with the logic of Fisher's LSD (the protected t test), discussed in Chapter 5.

Even if it is agreed that it is inappropriate to conduct every test at $\alpha = .05$, there can still be legitimate disagreement over what constitutes a family (see Keppel, 1982; Kirk, 1982, for two examples). The approach advocated here is to consider all tests regarding differences among rows (biofeedback, in our example) as one family and all tests regarding differences among columns (drugs, in our example) as a second family. The goal is to maintain alpha at .05 for each family. We can accomplish this goal in the following manner. First, consider tests of row effects, that is, tests of the A factor, which in our example is biofeedback. We will conduct three tests of biofeedback, one for each level of drugs. The familywise alpha can be maintained at .05 by performing each of these tests at an alpha level of .05/3. In general, we would use an alpha level of .05/b for each test. Second, consider tests of the B factor. By the same logic, using an alpha level of .05/a for each test would maintain the α_{FW} at .05.

In addition, if a simple effects test yields a significant result, it typically is necessary to test comparisons of individual cell means unless the factor in question has only two levels (in which case the precise nature of the difference is already identified). Again, the alpha level can be maintained by using the principles of Chapter 5. However, it must be kept in mind that the alpha level for the simple effects test that preceded the cell means comparison was not .05, but .05/b for simple effects tests of A, and .05/a for simple effects tests of B. Thus, it is this smaller alpha level that should be used in performing subsequent multiple comparisons. It should be noted that this can create practical difficulties because it necessitates finding Tukey and Scheffé critical values for alpha levels other than .05 or .01. This problem can be circumvented by using the computer. As of this writing, SAS ANOVA and SAS GLM both allow specification of any value between 0 and 1 for the alpha level with Tukey's or Scheffé's method.

Figure 7.2 is a flowchart that summarizes approaches to understanding effects either in the presence or the absence of an interaction. It should be stressed that the flowchart is meant to be used only as a guideline—not as a rigid structure that must always be obeyed. In particular, when enough theoretical background is available, a researcher may plan certain tests to be performed that deviate from the flowchart. Also, it may not be of theoretical interest to test both simple effects of A within B and of B within A when a significant interaction is found. Other exceptions to the flowchart undoubtedly could be uncovered as well. Data analysis should not follow a formula but instead should correspond to theoretical questions; nevertheless, the flowchart is a useful guide toward appropriate analyses as long as it is not interpreted too strictly.

Error Term for Testing Simple Effects

Throughout the previous discussion, it was implicitly assumed that the denominator (error term) to be used for testing simple effects would be mean square within. Is this a reasonable error term? To answer this question, consider our numerical example. One simple effects test we performed was the test of Drug B differences in the presence of biofeedback (i.e., within the first level of A). We calculated a sum of squares for this effect as if we had a one-way design with three groups. Not surprisingly, data from the three groups that did not receive biofeedback have no influence on the sum of squares for B within A_1. However, data from these three groups do influence the value for MS_W, because MS_W is simply the average variance within each of the six cells in the design. Should data from the biofeedback-absent groups be included in the error term if we want to compare only the differences among the biofeedback-present groups? It depends. If the homogeneity of variance assumption is met, using MS_W as the error term for all tests is appropriate. Statistical power is maximized because the estimate of the population error variance is most efficient when all relevant data are combined to form the estimate.

On the other hand, if variances are heterogeneous, using MS_W for testing all effects may be quite misleading. Some tests will be too liberal, whereas others will be too conservative. When heterogeneity of variance is suspected, we thus recommend that MS_W not be used as the error term. Instead, the error term should be based only on the groups actually being compared. For example, if we are testing the simple effect of B at A_1, the error term could be based only on

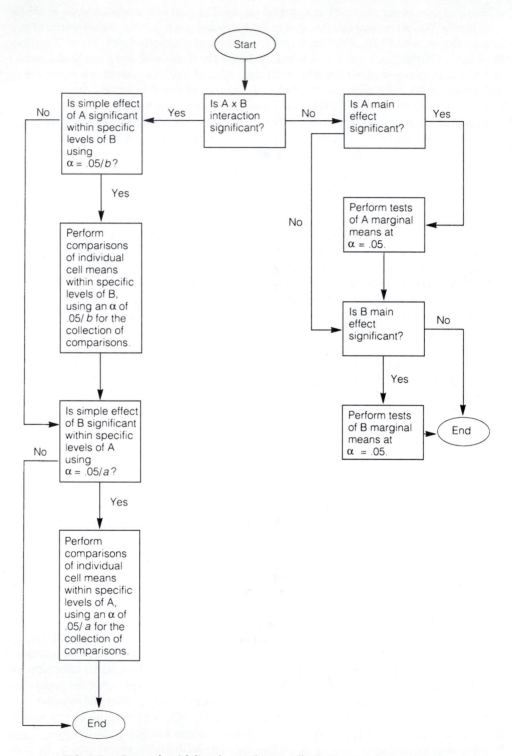

FIG. 7.2.   General guideline for analyzing effects in a two-factor design.

the three biofeedback-present groups. In this case, the analysis is literally a one-way ANOVA with three groups. As before, tests of comparisons can be performed without assuming homogeneity by using appropriate procedures from Chapters 4 and 5.

An Alternative Method for Investigating an Interaction—Interaction Contrasts

Most researchers follow up a significant interaction by testing simple effects. However, there is an alternative approach, which some behavioral statisticians recommend (e.g., Levin & Marascuilo, 1972). To introduce this approach, remember how we interpret the meaning of a main effect, which we designate as the A effect for convenience. When the factor has more than two levels, we form comparisons of the marginal means. The comparisons are called subeffects because each comparison represents one specific way in which the means might differ. Each comparison has 1 df, whereas the effect as a whole has degrees of freedom equal to $a - 1$. How might we interpret an interaction in a similar manner? Recall that the interaction as a whole has $(a - 1)(b - 1)$ degrees of freedom. We could again form single degree-of-freedom comparisons to investigate which subeffects are contributing to the overall example.

Consider our earlier numerical example, with the cell means shown in Table 7.10. Recall that we obtained a significant interaction, implying that the biofeedback effect is not the same for every drug. Does this imply that the biofeedback effect is different for all three drugs? No, as we can easily tell just by "eyeballing" these artificial data. The biofeedback effect in the sample is 20 for both Drug X and Drug Z. The effect appears to be different for Drug Y. We could test a null hypothesis that the biofeedback effect for Drug Y is different from that for Drug X or Z. For example, suppose we wanted to compare the biofeedback effect for Drug Y to that for Drug X. The null hypothesis could be written formally as

$$H_0 : \mu_{12} - \mu_{22} = \mu_{11} - \mu_{21}$$

where the cells are labeled to correspond to the rows and columns shown in Table 7.10. We could rewrite this as

$$H_0 : \mu_{12} - \mu_{22} - \mu_{11} + \mu_{21} = 0$$

This has the form of a comparison. Using principles from Chapter 4, the sum of squares for this comparison equals 864, which corresponds to an F value of 6.33 (using MS_W as the error term). If we were to use an alpha level of .05 for this test, the result would be significant. If this comparison has been chosen post hoc, however, we can maintain our α_{FW} at .05 by using a Scheffé critical value given by $(a - 1)(b - 1)F_{.05,(a-1)(b-1),N-ab}$ For our example, the appropriate Scheffé critical value would equal $(2 - 1)(3 - 1)F_{.05,(2-1)(3-1),36-6}$, which is $2F_{.05,2,30} = 2(3.32) = 6.64$. Thus, if we have indeed chosen this comparison post hoc, we cannot assert it to be significant.

The lack of a significant comparison here might seem puzzling, because the interaction as a whole was significant. It turns out, however, that we have not identified the optimal subeffect, which here contrasts the biofeedback effect for Drug Y with the average of the biofeedback effects for Drugs X and Z. You should verify that this subeffect produces a sum of squares of 1,152, which corresponds to an F value of 8.43, which is significant even with the Scheffé critical value. Kirk (1982, pp. 378–379) presents formulas for determining the coefficients of the optimal subeffect, that is, the particular interaction contrast that maximally accounts for the entire interaction sum of squares.

Two other comments are pertinent here. First, Levin and Marascuilo (1972) argue that interaction contrasts rather than simple effects should be used to interpret a significant interaction, because the simple effects are not subeffects of the interaction. Games (1973), on the other hand, argues that the simple effects tests more often answer the theoretical questions raised by most researchers. The interested reader is referred to Marascuilo and Levin (1976), which includes references to both sides of the debate. Second, yet one other method of interpreting an interaction is to test several interaction contrasts simultaneously. Such tests are called partial interaction or treatment-contrast interaction tests. The interested reader is referred to Boik (1979), Keppel (1982), or Kirk (1995) for details.

We motivated the use of interaction contrasts for our hypertension data by pointing out a pattern in the observed sample cell means. In this specific case, we might not have had any particular theoretical reason before collecting the data to expect this pattern, which is why we discussed Scheffé's method for maintaining the familywise alpha level. In other situations, however, there may be clear theoretical reasons for expecting a specific pattern for the interaction parameters, in which case a researcher would typically want to formulate one or more planned interaction contrasts.

Abelson and Prentice (1997) argue that psychologists have historically failed to capitalize on possible advantages of testing a priori interaction contrasts even when theory dictates the relevance of this approach. In particular, they describe three types of contrast tests. They call their first type a "matching" pattern, where, for example, higher scores might be expected along the diagonal cells of the design than in the off-diagonal cells. Their other two types pertain to situations where at least one factor is quantitative. In this case, they describe a "qualitative quadratic" pattern, where means are monotonic in the same direction but differ in being concave upward in some rows (or columns) but concave downward in other rows (or columns). Their third type is "differential curvilinearity," where the general shape of the curve for the quadratic factor is the same for all groups, but the curves differ in amplitude.

Abelson and Prentice (1997) provide excellent examples of all three types of interaction patterns they define, so instead of merely duplicating one of their examples, we will present a slightly different example of a situation where theoretical considerations may call for testing planned interaction contrasts. In particular, we want to emphasize that such tests may preclude the need for an omnibus interaction test and may be more informative than following the more typical path of testing simple effects.

Consider an example of a cognitive neuroscience study of patient groups. Specifically, suppose that a certain theory implies that amnesic patients will have a deficit in explicit memory but not on implicit memory. According to this theory, Huntington patients, on the other hand, will be just the opposite: They will have no deficit in explicit memory, but will have a deficit in implicit memory. We might design a study yielding a 3×3 factorial design to test this theory. The rows of this study will represent three types of individuals: amnesic patients, Huntington patients, and a control group of individuals with no known neurological disorder. Each research participant will be randomly assigned to one of three tasks: (1) artificial grammar task, which consists of classifying letter sequences as either following or not following grammatical rules; (2) classification learning task, which consists of classifying hypothetical patients as either having or not having a certain disease based on symptoms probabilistically related to the disease; and (3) recognition memory task, which consists of recognizing particular stimuli as stimuli that have previously been presented during the task. Table 7.11 presents hypothetical data for 15 amnesiacs, 15 Huntington individuals, and 15 controls. Keep in mind that each person has been randomly assigned to one of the three tasks, so there are five observations per cell of the design.

TABLE 7.11
PERFORMANCE DATA FOR THREE TYPES OF
INDIVIDUALS ON THREE TYPES OF TASKS

	Grammar	Classification	Recognition
Amnesic	44	72	70
	63	66	51
	76	55	82
	72	82	66
	45	75	56
Huntington's	24	53	107
	30	59	80
	51	33	98
	55	37	82
	40	43	108
Control	76	92	107
	98	65	80
	71	86	101
	70	67	82
	85	90	105

As an aside, we should acknowledge that a variation on this design would entail assessing each person on all three tasks. The task factor in such a design would then be a within-subjects design. We will consider such designs in Chapter 14 (where an interaction contrast would still be relevant), but for now we will assume that each person is assessed on only one task, in which case both factors are between-subjects. We should also note that in either design the various tasks need to be scaled similarly to interpret the interaction meaningfully.

The key point to understand before proceeding is that these tasks have been chosen so as to map onto the theoretical differences between the three types of research participants. Namely the first two tasks are known to reflect implicit memory processes, whereas the third task is known to reflect explicit memory processes. Thus, if the theory is correct, we would expect to see relatively higher scores on the first two tasks for the amnesic group but relatively higher scores on the third task for the Huntington group. At first glance, it might sound as if we could simply perform simple effect tests of task within each group to test our theory. However, Equation 55 shows that such tests would not truly test the theory, because they would reflect main effects of task as well as the interaction of true theoretical interest. Instead, we need to test an interaction contrast.(Exercise 16 at the end of the chapter pursues the question of why simple effects are less well suited than an interaction contrast for answering the theoretical question of interest in this situation.)

The next step in testing our hypothesis is to formulate the appropriate contrast coefficients. We will begin by looking at each factor separately. In terms of the diagnostic groups, recall that we want to compare the amnesics to the Huntington individuals. This corresponds to a contrast with coefficients of 1, −1, and 0 for amnesiacs, Huntingtons, and control, respectively. Similarly, in terms of the tasks, we want to compare the average of the two implicit memory tasks with the explicit memory task. This corresponds to a contrast with coefficients of 0.5, 0.5, and −1 for the three tasks. Statistical software often is capable of generating the appropriate interaction contrast after we have specified the contrasts for each factor separately. Nevertheless, we will proceed to show how to construct the interaction contrast in terms of the nine cells of our 3×3 design. We do this for two reasons. First, we believe it will deepen your understanding of exactly what an interaction contrast represents. Second, some statistical software may require you to specify the interaction contrast in terms of all cells of the factorial design, especially

		Grammar 0.5 ↓	Classification 0.5 ↓	Recognition −1 ↓
Amnesic	1 →			
Huntington's	−1 →			
Control	0 →			

FIG. 7.3.   Interaction contrast coefficients for each row and column separately.

		Grammar 0.5	Classification 0.5	Recognition −1
Amnesic	1	0.5	0.5	−1
Huntington's	−1	−0.5	−0.5	1
Control	0	0	0	0

FIG. 7.4.   Interaction contrast coefficients for 9 cells in 3 × 3 design.

if you are interested not just in testing the contrast for statistical significance, but also want to form a confidence interval for the contrast.

Figure 7.3 shows the 3×3 structure of our factorial design. Notice that also shown for each row as well as for each column is the contrast coefficient corresponding to each row and column. We can now find the coefficients of the corresponding interaction contrast using a straightforward algorithm. Namely the coefficient for each cell can be found simply from the row and column that define that cell. In particular, the interaction contrast coefficient for each cell can be found by multiplying the row coefficient to the left of the cell by the column coefficient above the cell. For example, consider the group of amnesiacs performing the grammar task, which is the cell in the first row and first column. The interaction contrast coefficient for this cell can be found by multiplying the value of 1 to the left of this cell by the value of 0.5 above this cell. Figure 7.4 shows that the result is an interaction contrast coefficient of 0.5 for this cell. This figure also shows the interaction contrast coefficients for the remaining cells of the design. This figure makes it clear that the control participants are not involved in this contrast and that the first two columns are effectively combined into a single column to be compared with the third column.

We will make one more comment before proceeding to an interpretation of the results for our data. If we sum the absolute values of the nine contrast coefficients shown in Figure 7.4, we obtain a value of 4. Although this sum is irrelevant for testing a contrast, we saw in Chapters 4, 5, and 6 that the sum is important if we want to form a confidence interval. However, in those chapters, we stated that the appropriate sum in this case should be 2, not the value of 4 we now have in Figure 7.4. Have we made a mistake here? No, because an interaction contrast (in a two-factor design) is a contrast of contrasts. For example, we could say that our interaction contrast here compares two different task contrasts to one another. Specifically, we are comparing: (a) a task contrast with coefficients of 0.5, 0.5, and −1 for amnesiacs to (b) a task contrast with coefficients of 0.5, 0.5, and −1 for Huntingtons. Notice that the sum of the absolute values of the coefficients for each of these contrasts is 2, just as we would expect from previous chapters. However, when we form a contrast of contrasts, the resulting sum will always be 4. This issue frequently takes care of itself with statistical software, but it is crucial in forming confidence intervals to be certain that the metric of the contrast coefficients is appropriate.

Now that we have formulated the coefficients for the contrast we want to test, we can proceed to conduct the test and also to form a confidence interval for the contrast if that is of

TABLE 7.12
SPSS MANOVA OUTPUT FOR INTERACTION CONTRAST

Analysis of Variance

45 cases accepted.
 0 cases rejected because of out-of-range factor values.
 0 cases rejected because of missing data.
 9 nonempty cells.
 1 design will be processed.

Analysis of Variance—Design 1
Tests of Significance for Y Using UNIQUE Sums of Squares

Source of Variation	SS	DF	MS	F	Sig. of F
Within Cells	5680.00	36	157.78		
Diagnose (1) by task (1)	4593.75	1	4593.75	29.12	.000

Estimates for Y Individual univariate .9500 confidence intervals

Diagnose (1)
by Task (1)

Parameter	Coeff.	Std. Error	t Value	Sig. t	95% CL Lower	Upper
2	52.5000000	9.72968	5.39586	.00000	32.76730	72.23270

interest here. For example, by conceptualizing our data in terms of nine groups, we could use the coefficients shown in Figure 7.4 to define a contrast. We could as usual use Equation 4.39 to find the sum of squares for this contrast, and (assuming homogeneity) could use MS_W to form the appropriate F test. Because the calculations are literally no different than what we have already seen in Chapter 4, we will not bother to repeat them here, but will instead simply show you relevant computer output.

Table 7.12 shows a portion of the output generated by SPSS MANOVA to assess this interaction contrast. The sum of squares for our interaction contrast is 4,593.75, which yields an F value of 29.12 and a corresponding p value less than .001. Thus, there is strong evidence that the contrast is not zero in the population. In other words, amnesiacs and Huntington's differ in the difference between implicit and explicit recognition memory tasks. Examining the cell means or even better the plot of cell means (i.e., Figure 7.5) shows that amnesiacs perform relatively better on implicit memory tasks, whereas Huntington individuals perform relatively better on explicit memory tasks, just as expected from our theory.

It may be useful to supplement this hypothesis test with some indication of effect size. Although many types of effect size measures can be defined for this purpose, our recommendation is typically to form a confidence interval, either for the raw score metric of the dependent variable or for a standardized metric. We will illustrate both types of confidence intervals for these data.

By conceptualizing our data in terms of nine groups and using the contrast coefficients shown in Figure 7.4, a raw score confidence interval can be found using Equation 48 from Chapter 4:

$$\hat{\psi} \pm \sqrt{F_{\alpha;1,N-a}} \sqrt{M S_W \sum_{j=1}^{a} \left(c_j^2 / n_j \right)} \qquad \text{(4.48, repeated)}$$

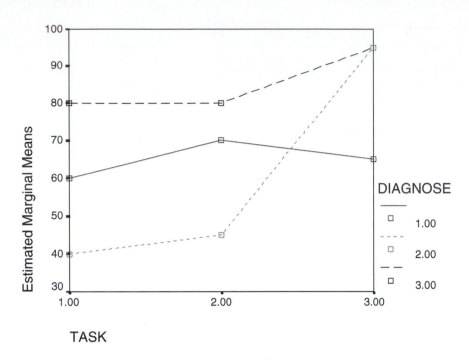

TASK

FIG. 7.5.   Interaction plot of diagnosis and task.

The lower portion of SPSS output in Table 7.12 shows the result of this calculation. First, notice that the estimated value of the contrast (i.e., $\hat{\psi}$) equals 52.50. To see where this value comes from, recall that the contrast is the difference between amnesiacs and Huntingtons on the difference between implicit and explicit memory tasks. The task difference for amnesiacs turns out to be zero in our data (the average of 60 and 70 compared to 65), whereas the task difference for Huntingtons is -52.50 (the average of 40 and 45 compared to 95). Thus, the task difference for amnesiacs minus the task difference for Huntingtons equals 52.50 (i.e., 0 minus -52.50). Even if our ultimate interest is in the confidence interval, it is always a good idea to make sure the estimated value of the contrast itself is reasonable, because, as we will see momentarily, this value becomes the center of the confidence interval. Second, the table shows that the estimated standard error of this contrast is 9.73. This value is what we obtain when we compute the square root of the multiple of MS_W shown on the right in Equation 4.48. Multiplying the value of 9.72968 by the square root of the critical F value of 4.11 (for 1 numerator and 36 denominator degrees of freedom; for example, see Appendix Table A.3 where $C = 1$) yields an interval of the form 52.50 ± 19.73. The table presents this interval by showing that a 95% confidence interval stretches from 32.77 to 72.23.

We need to make several points here. First, notice that this interval does not contain zero. Thus, we can be 95% confident that the task difference is not the same for amnesiacs as for Huntingtons, which is why we can reject the null hypothesis that the difference in differences is zero. Second, remember that Equation 4.48 assumes homogeneity of variance. In situations where this assumption may be questionable, it may be preferable to use Equation 4.49, which, as we mentioned in Chapter 4, usually involves the use of a computer program. Third, notice also that we have made no attempt here to control familywise alpha level. This is perfectly appropriate as long as our contrast is a single planned comparison. If, however, this were one of several planned comparisons within the same family or if this contrast were chosen after having examined the data, we should usually use a confidence interval of the form shown in Table 5.17.

How should we react to an interval with a lower limit of 32.77 and an upper limit of 72.23? Does this reflect an important difference of differences? To answer this question, we have to be aware of what constitutes an important difference on the scale of the dependent variable. If differences on the raw scale metric are not easily interpreted, it may be preferable to form a confidence interval for a standardized difference in means, just as we have discussed in earlier chapters. In particular, be sure you understand that our goal here is to form a confidence interval for the population value of d for a contrast, as discussed in Chapter 4. The definition of d for an interaction contrast is identical to the definition we have seen earlier, except that the 2 in the numerator must be replaced by a 4 because, as we pointed out a few paragraphs ago, the sum of coefficients for an interaction contrast in a two-factor design is 4 instead of 2. Thus, the population d value of an interaction contrast can be expressed as

$$d = 4\psi \left/ \left[\sigma_\varepsilon \left(\sum_{j=1}^{a} |c_j| \right) \right] \right. \tag{60}$$

Notice that if coefficients are already formed so that their absolute values sum to 4, this expression simplifies to

$$d = \psi / \sigma_\varepsilon \tag{61}$$

This can be estimated easily by

$$\hat{d} = \hat{\psi} / \sqrt{MS_W} \tag{62}$$

as long as coefficients have been formed so that the sum of their absolute values is 4.

An approximate confidence interval for an interaction contrast can be formed in either of two ways. First, the data can be converted to z scores by dividing each original value on the dependent variable by the square root of MS_W. In our data, we would divide each score by the square root of 157.78. Then the usual interval is formed for these transformed scores. The result is shown in Table 7.13. Notice that the F value for the contrast has remained exactly the same, as it must if all we have done is to rescale the dependent variable through a linear transformation. However, also notice that the value of MS_W for the rescaled scores is 1.0, indicating that we have succeeded in scaling scores so that the variance (within cells) is now 1.0. Further notice that the values for the center of the interval and the estimated standard error are different from the values we previously saw for the raw score metric. As a consequence, we have a new interval with limits of 2.61 and 5.75. Thus, the population difference in differences is likely to be somewhere between 2.61 and 5.75 standard deviation units. This would usually be regarded as a very large difference. Of course, large does not necessarily mean important, but at least we now know that the difference in differences is sizable. Second, we could also obtain this confidence interval simply by taking the limits of our original raw score interval and dividing each limit by the square root of MS_W. Regardless of which way we obtain the limits of the interval, recall from our discussion in Chapter 4 that the resulting interval is approximate, and that more complicated procedures are required to obtain exact limits for the interval.

It is also possible to form measures of association strength for an interaction contrast. Although there are a variety of such measures each of which provides its own perspective on the data, we will focus on R^2_{alerting}, because we believe that it is often the most useful measure of association strength for interpreting an interaction contrast. Recall from Chapter 4 that we

TABLE 7.13
SPSS MANOVA OUTPUT FOR STANDARDIZED CONFIDENCE INTERVAL
OF INTERACTION CONTRAST

Analysis of Variance

45 cases accepted.
 0 cases rejected because of out-of-range factor values.
 0 cases rejected because of missing data.
 9 nonempty cells.
 1 design will be processed.

Analysis of Variance—Design 1
Tests of Significance for Z Using UNIQUE Sums of Squares

Source of Variation	SS	DF	MS	F	Sig. of F
Within Cells	36.00	36	1.00		
Diagnose (1) by task (1)	29.12	1	29.12	29.12	.000

Estimates for Z: Individual univariate .9500 confidence intervals

Diagnose (1)
by Task (1)

Parameter	Coeff.	Std. Error	t Value	Sig. t	95% CL Lower	Upper
2	4.17961684	.77460	5.39586	.00000	2.60866	5.75057

defined R^2_{alerting} in a single factor design as

$$R^2_{\text{alerting}} = SS(\psi)/SS_{\text{Between}} \qquad \text{(4.54, repeated)}$$

We could use exactly this same expression in the two-factor design to tell us what proportion of the entire difference among all group means can be attributed to our interaction contrast. Although there is nothing mathematically wrong with using Equation 4.54 for an interaction contrast, in most cases it will probably be more meaningful to find out what proportion of the interaction sum of squares can be attributed to this specific contrast. Keep in mind that we have already partitioned the between-group sum of squares into three orthogonal components: SS_A, SS_B, and SS_{AB}. We know that an interaction contrast is a subeffect of the interaction effect, so it usually will be most informative to determine how much of the interaction effect we have succeeded in detecting with our interaction contrast. This perspective leads to the following definition of R^2_{alerting} for an interaction contrast:

$$R^2_{\text{alerting}} = SS(\psi)/SS_{AB} \qquad (63)$$

To illustrate the calculation and interpretation of R^2_{alerting} for an interaction contrast, let's return to our example comparing amnesiacs and Huntington patients on implicit and explicit memory tasks. We saw in Table 7.12 that the interaction contrast we defined for these data (in the original metric of the dependent variable) yielded a sum of squares equal to 4,593.75. The interaction sum of squares for these data is 5,000.00, so from Equation 63 R^2_{alerting} for this contrast equals 0.92. Thus, this contrast captures approximately 92% of the sample variance attributable to the interaction of diagnosis and task. Such a large value suggests that we have succeeded in anticipating the primary source of any interaction between diagnosis and task in this 3×3 design.

Our single degree of freedom interaction contrast accounts for 92% of the overall interaction effect. Realizing that there are 4 df for the interaction in a 3×3 design, it follows that the three remaining degrees of freedom account for 8% of the overall interaction effect, or, equivalently, the sum of squares corresponding to these 3 degrees of freedom equals 406.25 (notice that this is 5,000 minus 4,593.75). We can test the statistical significance of these 3 df by converting the sum of squares to a mean square and then dividing by MS_W. The resultant F statistic for our data equals 0.86, which corresponds to a p value of .47. Thus, it is plausible that our single degree of freedom contrast reflects the entirety of the true population interaction effect between diagnosis and task.

More generally, Abelson and Prentice (1997) point out that in some situations it is important not just to demonstrate that the interaction contrast of theoretical interest is in fact statistically significant, but in addition that any remaining subeffects of the overall interaction effect are nonexistent or at least trivially small. Such a combination suggests that (1) the hypothesized pattern exists in the cell means and (2) any other apparent patterns in the cell means may plausibly reflect sampling error instead of true patterns in the population. If both conditions hold, the interaction contrast has completely accounted for the overall interaction in the population. Abelson and Prentice (1997) call such an outcome a "canonical outcome."

They point out that there are two rather different ways in which a noncanonical outcome can occur: (1) The theoretical contrast may be weak and nonsignificant, and (2) even if the theoretical contrast is strong and significant, it may fail to account for the overall interaction effect. The first way might result for any of several reasons: (1) there may simply be little interaction of any sort; (2) if a substantial overall interaction effect exists, the pattern of cell means may not conform to theoretical expectations; or (3) statistical power may be low. The second way indicates that the theoretical expectation has received less than full support. However, this is not necessarily such a bad thing, because as Abelson and Prentice (1997) suggest, this opens the door to further exploration and explanation of these additional components of the interaction effect. For this reason, they refer to this type of outcome as "ecumenical."

STATISTICAL POWER

Researchers should, of course, be concerned about the statistical power of their studies. As in the one-way design, it is possible to determine power if alpha level, sample size, and effect size are known. A general formula for the ϕ value of an effect in a fixed-effects design (which is all that we will consider until Chapter 10) can be written as

$$\phi_{\text{effect}} = \sqrt{\left[\sum_{\text{all obs}} (\text{effect parameter})^2 \right] \Big/ (df_{\text{effect}} + 1)\sigma_\varepsilon^2}$$

The numerator of this expression requires some additional explanation. Notice that it is very similar to the general formula we have seen for the sum of squares due to an effect:

$$SS_{\text{effect}} = \sum_{\text{all obs}} (\text{estimated parameter})^2$$

The only difference is that the numerator of ϕ is based on the parameter value itself, as opposed to an estimate. Table 7.14 provides a specific expression for the numerator for all three effects

TABLE 7.14
EXPLANATION OF ϕ^2 IN AN A $\times$ B
FACTORIAL DESIGN

Effect	Numerator Expression	df_{effect}
A	$nb \sum_{j=1}^{a} \alpha_j^2$	$a - 1$
B	$nb \sum_{k=1}^{b} \beta_k^2$	$b - 1$
A $\times$ B	$n \sum_{j=1}^{a} \sum_{k=1}^{b} [(\alpha\beta)_{jk}]^2$	$(a - 1)(b - 1)$

(A, B, and $A \times B$) in the two-way design, as well as for df_{effect}. The ϕ value for an effect is referred to power charts as in the one-way design to determine power.

One of the most important implications of the expressions we have just given for power in factorial designs is that the power to detect an interaction will often be less than the power to detect a main effect. Or, stated differently, the sample size needed to have adequate power for detecting an interaction will frequently be larger than the sample size needed to detect a main effect. Thus, when interactions are of theoretical interest, there is a special need to consider whether the sample size is adequate.

Why does detection of interactions often require larger samples? There are three potential reasons. We should stress at the outset that these reasons are labeled as "potential" reasons because in theory it is possible to define situations where tests of interactions will be more powerful than tests of main effects. However, in practice, it is much more often the case that for a fixed sample size, interaction tests will be less powerful than tests of main effects. In particular, we will present two reasons for this phenomenon.

First, effect sizes for interactions are often (but not always) smaller than effect sizes for main effects. Although it is possible mathematically for an interaction to have a larger effect size than does a main effect, in many actual situations, the effect size for the interaction will be smaller than the effect size for the main effect. One reason for this is that interactions are often ordinal (remember that this means that lines do not cross in a graph of the interaction plot). Recall from our discussion of Equations 56 and 59 that the t value for the interaction will be smaller than the t value for the main effect unless the simple effects have the same sign. But this is precisely what it means to say that the interaction is ordinal, in which case the effect size of the ordinal interaction is necessarily smaller than the effect size of this main effect. Of course, if the interaction is disordinal, it is entirely possible for the interaction effect size to be larger than the effect size for either of the main effects, but disordinal interactions are probably less frequent than ordinal interactions in many areas of the behavioral sciences. Further, McClelland and Judd (1993) have shown that the effect size for an interaction is usually deflated in observational field studies. The essential reason is that the interaction test depends on observations in the corners of the design, but such observations tend to be rare in field studies, especially when the factors themselves are correlated. We will have much more to say later in the chapter about analyzing data from this type of design, where cell sizes are unequal, but the general point for the moment is that the typical lack of observations in the corners of such a design contributes yet further to difficulties in detecting interactions without very large sample sizes.

Second, even if a particular interaction effect size happens to be as large as an effect size for a main effect, it may nevertheless be the case that the power for the interaction is less than the power for the main effect. To see why, we need to realize that an important implication of the formula for ϕ is that whenever $a > 2$ and $b > 2$, the power for testing an interaction of a particular effect size is less than the power for testing a main effect of that same effect size. As a consequence, larger samples (i.e., more subjects per cell) are typically required for having sufficient power to test interactions. Consider, for example, a 3×4 design (A has three levels; B has four levels). It can be shown that to achieve a power of .8 for detecting an A main effect of "medium" size as defined by Cohen (1977), a study should use 14 participants per cell, or 168 participants in all. However, to achieve a power of .8 for detecting an $A \times B$ interaction of "medium" size requires 20 participants per cell, or 240 participants in all, more than a 40% increase in sample size. The intuitive explanation for this discrepancy is that the A main-effect test is based on the A marginal means, which themselves are based on nb observations, which in this specific design equals $4n$. However, the interaction test is based on individual cell means and hence requires more participants per cell to achieve the same power, all other things being equal.

ADVANTAGES OF FACTORIAL DESIGNS

Continuing the theme of our numerical example, suppose that we were interested in the effectiveness of various treatments for hypertension. Specifically, we wonder whether biofeedback reduces blood pressure, and we are also interested in comparing Drugs X, Y, and Z. Would it be better to conduct a 2×3 factorial study or to perform two separate single-factor studies?

The most obvious advantage of the factorial design is that it enables us to test the existence of an interaction. With two single-factor studies, we could never learn that differences between drugs might differ depending on the presence or absence of biofeedback. In particular, stop and think about the single-factor study to compare the three drugs. This study most likely would be conducted in the absence of biofeedback, so in effect we are performing what would be a simple effects test in the factorial design. However, the simple effects test may convey only one-half of the relevant ways in which drugs differ. In summary, it may be of theoretical interest to discover an interaction, which implies the necessity of a factorial design.

What if an interaction is not expected? Is there still any advantage to the factorial design? Yes, because the factorial design enables greater generalizability. If our hypertension study is conducted as a factorial design and there is no interaction, we can conclude that drug differences are the same in the presence of biofeedback as in its absence. (However, an alternate explanation, especially with small sample sizes, is that the power to detect an interaction was inadequate. Even with sufficient power, one should really conclude that any differences that may exist are so small that we can regard them as nonexistent for all practical purposes because we should not literally accept the null hypothesis.) In other words, we can generalize drug effects across two levels of the biofeedback factor. If we had instead conducted a single-factor study, we could not assess the extent of generalizability.

So far we have seen that a factorial design may be preferable to a series of single-factor studies because we can test interaction effects and we can assess generalizability (notice that these two advantages are really opposite perspectives on one advantage). However, don't factorial designs require larger sample sizes? Let's consider two hypothetical psychologists: Dr. Single and Dr. Multiple. Dr. Single decides to conduct two single-factor studies. The first study investigates the relative effectiveness of Drugs X, Y, and Z. Thirty subjects are assigned at random to each of the three drugs. In the second study, biofeedback is compared to a control. Forty-five individuals are assigned at random to each of the two groups. In the two studies combined, Dr. Single has used 180 participants. Dr. Multiple conducts a 2×3 factorial study investigating the effect of biofeedback and drug effects simultaneously. Fifteen individuals are assigned at random to each of the six groups. Of course, Dr. Multiple can test an interaction that Dr. Single cannot, but how else will their tests be different? Both will test whether biofeedback has an effect. Dr. Single's comparison involves 45 individuals in each group. But so does Dr. Multiple's, because there were 15 individuals at each level of drug, implying that 45 individuals received biofeedback whereas 45 others did not. Both investigators will also test for drug differences. By the same logic, both Dr. Single and Dr. Multiple will have exposed 30 individuals to each type of drug. Thus, it should be the case that Dr. Multiple's statistical power for assessing biofeedback and drug effects should be equivalent to Dr. Single's. Does this mean that Dr. Single's and Dr. Multiple's approaches are equally good in how efficiently participants are used? Recall that Dr. Single used 180 individuals in all. However, Dr. Multiple used a total of $6 \times 15 = 90$ participants. Dr. Multiple's factorial design produced the same power with half as many subjects as Dr. Single's two separate studies! The implication is that the factorial design uses participants more efficiently than would a series of single-factor studies.[11]

Does this mean that researchers should strive to design studies with as many factors as they can imagine? This issue and problems in analyzing designs with three or more factors are considered in Chapter 8. Before proceeding, however, there is one other topic to be covered in the two-factor design.

NONORTHOGONAL DESIGNS

So far in this chapter, we have only considered designs where there are the same number of participants in each cell in the design. Although this condition is not an assumption of the model, it simplifies calculations of sums of squares. This section considers designs where this condition is not met. However, we assume throughout that the factors are completely crossed; that is, there are no missing cells. For a discussion of designs with missing cells, see Searle (1987). When the number of observations (participants) varies from cell to cell, the design is said to be nonorthogonal (or unbalanced).

This use of the term *nonorthogonal* appears to be at odds with the meaning we developed in Chapter 4. In fact, however, the usage here is entirely consistent. Unequal-n factorial designs are said to be nonorthogonal because contrasts representing the A main effect, B main effect, and $A \times B$ interaction are no longer orthogonal with unequal n. Recall that one of the first things we did at the beginning of this chapter was to show that the biofeedback main-effect contrast was orthogonal to the drug therapy main-effect contrast in our 2×2 design. The respective contrast coefficients were 1, 1, -1, and -1 for biofeedback, and 1, -1, 1, and -1 for drug therapy. We saw that these two contrasts are orthogonal by applying Equation 4.58: $(1)(1) + (1)(-1) + (-1)(1) + (-1)(-1)$, which equals zero, the condition for orthogonality. However, with unequal n, the test for orthogonality (see Equation 4.59) is given by

$$\frac{(1)(1)}{n_{11}} + \frac{(1)(-1)}{n_{21}} + \frac{(-1)(1)}{n_{12}} + \frac{(-1)(-1)}{n_{22}}$$

This expression equals zero if and only if

$$\frac{1}{n_{11}} + \frac{1}{n_{22}} = \frac{1}{n_{21}} + \frac{1}{n_{12}}$$

Although unequal cell sizes might obey this requirement (e.g., 10 participants in both cells of row 1 and 8 participants in both cells of row 2), in general they do not. Thus, unequal cell sizes typically yield nonorthogonal effects. As we saw in Chapter 4, sums of squares of nonorthogonal contrasts are not additive, which leads to complications in data analysis.

One sign of the increased difficulty in analyzing data from nonorthogonal designs is that the proper analysis method is still the source of some controversy. Our approach essentially consists of providing an understanding of the logic behind the various approaches that we believe are most often preferable. However, at the outset, we should state that we agree with Herr and Gaebelein's (1978) statement that different approaches may be optimal in different situations.

Design Considerations

Before considering issues of analysis, it is important to discuss reasons that a nonorthogonal design may have arisen. It is useful to distinguish designs involving classification factors from designs involving experimental factors. As an example of the former, we might randomly sample the employees of a business organization and classify each individual according to gender and level of educational attainment (e.g., college graduates versus noncollege graduates). There is no reason in general to believe that the number of individuals who would be placed in each cell of the 2×2 design would be equal. Thus, when the factors of the design are classificatory in nature, it typically is the case that a nonorthogonal design occurs.

On the other hand, the factors may represent experimental variables, where the experimenter assigns participants to specific cells of the design. In such a situation, the experimenter usually assigns an equal number of participants to each cell. (This assignment process typically maximizes robustness and power, as well as simplifies the analysis.) However, the number of individuals on whom data are obtained may be reduced because of participant attrition. If data are not obtained for all participants, the resulting design is likely to be nonorthogonal, because the number of participants with missing data will likely vary from cell to cell.

Relationship Between Design and Analysis

The analysis methods to be presented do not necessarily yield meaningful answers when cell sizes are unequal. Whether any of the analysis methods yield meaningful information depends on why the design is nonorthogonal. If the factors are classification factors, the methods to be presented do yield meaningful data as long as individuals are randomly sampled from the population of interest. If the factors are experimental factors, the picture is less clear. The analysis methods yield meaningful information only if it can be assumed that the reasons for participant attrition are independent of the treatments. In other words, it is necessary to assume that the treatments are not differentially responsible for participants failing to complete the study. This assumption may be unrealistic, especially if some treatments are more aversive or more rewarding than others. If the treatments have indeed differentially affected participant attrition, none of the analysis methods presented here yields meaningful answers. When treatments have such differential effects, the individuals for whom scores are available in one cell are systematically different from those with scores in another cell. Any comparison of scores is likely to confound true treatment effects with preexisting differences between individuals because there is a "selection bias" that threatens internal validity, as discussed in Chapter 1. On the other hand, if the treatments have not differentially caused participant attrition, then within each cell, the individuals for whom data are available are for all practical purposes a random sample of the original random sample. In this case, groups of participants are not systematically different except insofar as the treatments truly have different effects, so analysis can proceed unambiguously.

In summary, the analysis methods to be represented are appropriate in either of two situations. First, the factors may be classification factors, where unequal cell sizes reflect true

TABLE 7.15
HYPOTHETICAL SALARY DATA (IN THOUSANDS) FOR
FEMALE AND MALE EMPLOYEES

	Females		*Males*	
	College Degree	No College Degree	College Degree	No College Degree
	24	15	25	19
	26	17	29	18
	25	20	27	21
	24	16		20
	27			21
	24			22
	27			19
	23			
Mean	25	17	27	20

differences in population sizes. Second, the factors may be experimental factors, where the treatments have not differentially caused participant attrition.

Analysis of the 2 × 2 Nonorthogonal Design

Just as we did for the equal-*n* case, we begin with the 2 × 2 design because the concepts are easier to grasp in this simpler case. Once the concepts have been developed for the 2 × 2 design, we consider a general two-factor design where both factors may have more than two levels.

To illustrate the 2 × 2 design, we examine data from a hypothetical organization that has been accused of salary discrimination against female employees. Specifically, the allegation is that newly hired females are underpaid relative to newly hired males. Table 7.15 presents hypothetical data for 12 females and 10 males who have just been hired by the organization. The mean salary for the 12 females is $22,333, whereas the mean for the 10 males is $22,100. These numbers would certainly seem to argue that females have not been discriminated against, because not only does the small difference of $233 turn out to be statistically nonsignificant,[12] but its direction favors females. If anything, females seem slightly overpaid, although their "advantage" is within the bounds of sampling error. However, Table 7.15 contains information about an additional characteristic of employees, namely whether they received a college degree. It is obvious from glancing at the table that a majority of the new female employees are college graduates, whereas a majority of the males are not. How should this affect our interpretation that there is no discrimination?

To begin to address this question, notice that we can conceptualize these data in terms of a 2 × 2 design, where one factor is the employee's gender and the other factor is the employee's educational attainment.[13] It is immediately apparent that this design is nonorthogonal because there is an unequal number of observations in the four cells.

Test of the Interaction

Our substantive interest here is primarily in the gender main effect, although the gender by education interaction may also help us understand the nature of any possible discrimination in pay. Because it may be difficult to interpret the main effect if the interaction is significant, we first consider how to test the interaction in a 2 × 2 nonorthogonal design. Recall from the beginning of the chapter that the interaction in a 2×2 design can be tested via a contrast with coefficients of $1, -1, -1,$ and 1 for the $(1, 1), (1, 2), (2, 1)$ and $(2, 2)$ cells, respectively. Further, recall that the sum of squares for a contrast is given by

$$SS_\psi = (\hat{\psi})^2 \Big/ \sum_{j=1}^{a} c_j^2/n_j \qquad \text{(4.39, repeated)}$$

Here, $\hat{\psi}$ is the value of the contrast, c_j is the contrast coefficient for Group j, and n_j is the sample size for Group j. In our specific problem, we can simplify this formula by noting that

$$\hat{\psi} = \overline{Y}_{11} - \overline{Y}_{12} - \overline{Y}_{21} + \overline{Y}_{22}$$

and

$$c_1^2 = c_2^2 = c_3^2 = c_4^2 = 1$$

Making these substitutions yields

$$SS_{AB} = (\overline{Y}_{11} - \overline{Y}_{12} - \overline{Y}_{21} + \overline{Y}_{22})^2/(1/n_{11} + 1/n_{12} + 1/n_{21} + 1/n_{22})$$

This can be rewritten as

$$SS_{AB} = \tilde{n}(\overline{Y}_{11} - \overline{Y}_{12} - \overline{Y}_{21} + \overline{Y}_{22})^2/4 \qquad (64)$$

where $\tilde{n}$ denotes the harmonic mean of $n_{11}, n_{12}, n_{21},$ and n_{22}.

Three points deserve mention here. First, because the harmonic mean is probably unfamiliar, we take a moment to explain it briefly. The harmonic mean of a set of numbers is an average value, similar to the usual arithmetic mean. In general, the harmonic mean of a set of scores $X_1, X_2, \ldots, X_a$ is defined to be

$$\tilde{X} = a \Big/ \left[\sum_{j=1}^{a} (1/X_j) \right]$$

Thus, the harmonic mean of the four cell sizes $n_{11}, n_{12}, n_{21},$ and n_{22} is

$$\tilde{n} = 4/(1/n_{11} + 1/n_{12} + 1/n_{21} + 1/n_{22})$$

For our data, the harmonic mean of the cell sizes equals

$$\tilde{n} = 4/(1/8 + 1/4 + 1/3 + 1/7) = 4.699$$

Notice that this value is close to, but somewhat less than, the arithmetic mean of the cell sizes, which equals 5.5. The reason the harmonic mean appears in the formula instead of the arithmetic mean is that the variance of each cell mean is proportional to the reciprocal of the number of participants in that cell.[14] Second, notice the similarity to the formula for SS_{AB} in the 2×2 design with equal n, in which case SS_{AB} is given by

$$SS_{AB} = n(\overline{Y}_{11} - \overline{Y}_{12} - Y_{21} + \overline{Y}_{22})^2/4$$

TABLE 7.16
SAMPLE MEANS FOR SALARY DATA IN TABLE 7.15

		Educational level (B)	
		College Degree	No College Degree
Sex (A)	Female	$n_{11} = 8$ $\overline{Y}_{11} = 25$	$n_{12} = 4$ $\overline{Y}_{12} = 17$
	Male	$n_{21} = 3$ $\overline{Y}_{21} = 27$	$n_{22} = 7$ $\overline{Y}_{22} = 20$

Thus, with unequal n, the only complication in the formula is that an average cell size (specifically, the harmonic mean) is used instead of the single cell size common to all cells in the equal-n design. Third, it turns out that this modification is restricted to designs where all factors have only two levels. When some factors have more than two levels, we will see later that additional complications arise because the sum of squares for effects cannot be calculated as the sum of squares of a single contrast.

The interaction sum of squares for the data in Table 7.15 can be calculated as

$$SS_{AB} = 4.699(25 - 17 - 27 + 20)^2/4$$

Performing the necessary arithmetic yields $SS_{AB} = 1.1748$. The interaction can be tested for significance as usual by dividing the interaction mean square by the mean square within. The mean square within is calculated for unequal n in exactly the same manner as it was calculated for equal n. For the data in Table 7.15, this yields $MS_W = 2.7778$, so the F value for the interaction is 0.4229. This value is nonsignificant at the .05 level, so there is no evidence that gender and education interact. Thus, the difference between female and male salaries is the same for those with a college degree as for those without, at least within sampling error.

We can now consider whether this consistent gender difference is a true difference or whether it is within sampling error of zero. To do this, we need to consider the main effect of gender. As we learned at the beginning of this chapter, a main effect involves a comparison of marginal means, averaging across the other factor. To help conceptualize the marginal means for our data, consider Table 7.16, which shows the four cell means of Table 7.15 arranged in a 2×2 design.

Unweighted Marginal Means and Type III Sum of Squares

To find the marginal mean for females, we should average the two cell means in the first row, that is, 25 and 17. An obvious solution would be to add 25 and 17 and divide by 2, yielding a marginal mean of 21. Following the same logic for males would produce a marginal mean of 23.5. Notice that we have calculated the marginal mean in each case by taking an unweighted average of the relevant cell means. For this reason, the marginal means we have calculated are referred to as unweighted marginal means. We will see momentarily that this is indeed a reasonable method for calculating a marginal mean, but there are two other reasonable possibilities as well. Before considering these other possibilities, let's see how we can test whether the difference between the two unweighted marginal means is statistically significant.

When the factor in question has two levels (as in our example), the test of a difference between unweighted marginal means can be accomplished easily, because once again the difference can be stated in terms of a single comparison. The difference in A marginal means (where A represents gender, the row factor in Table 7.16) can be represented as a contrast with coefficients of .5, .5, $-.5$, and $-.5$, for the (1, 1), (1, 2), (2, 1), and (2, 2) cells, respectively.[15] Once again, the usual formula for the sum of squares of a contrast applies:

$$SS_\psi = (\hat{\psi})^2 \bigg/ \sum_{j=1}^{a} c_j^2/n_j \qquad \text{(4.39, repeated)}$$

In our specific case, the formula becomes

$$SS_\psi = (.5\overline{Y}_{11} + .5\overline{Y}_{12} - .5\overline{Y}_{21} - .5\overline{Y}_{22})^2/(1/4n_{11} + 1/4n_{12} + 1/4n_{21} + 1/4n_{22})$$

Rearranging terms yields

$$SS_\psi = \tilde{n}(.5\overline{Y}_{11} + .5\overline{Y}_{12} - .5\overline{Y}_{21} - .5\overline{Y}_{22})^2$$

If we let $\overline{Y}_{1.(U)}$ and $\overline{Y}_{2.(U)}$ represent the unweighted sample marginal means, the formula simplifies yet further to

$$SS_\psi = \tilde{n}(\overline{Y}_{1.(U)} - \overline{Y}_{2.(U)})^2$$

Finally, the sum of squares for the difference between unweighted marginal means is often called the Type III sum of squares (remember that there are two other ways of defining marginal means yet to be discussed). Thus, when the A factor has two levels, we can write the sum of squares as

$$\text{Type III} \qquad SS_A = \tilde{n}(\overline{Y}_{1.(U)} - \overline{Y}_{2.(U)})^2 \qquad (65)$$

We should emphasize again that this formula is restricted to a two-level factor; additional complications arise when the factor has three or more levels.

At this point, let's calculate the Type III sum of squares due to A for our data. Substituting $\tilde{n} = 4.699$ (as before for testing the interaction), $\overline{Y}_{1.(U)} = 21.0$, and $\overline{Y}_{2.(U)} = 23.5$ yields a sum of squares equal to 29.3706. Dividing by the MS_W value of 2.7778 produces an F value of 10.5734, which has an associated p value of .0044. Thus, we can say that females' and males' unweighted marginal means are significantly different at the .05 level. Further note that the female mean is the smaller of the two, by $2,500.

Unweighted Versus Weighted Marginal Means

This result appears to contradict the earlier statement that females are paid more than males, although the earlier difference was nonsignificant. Specifically, we stated earlier that females were favored by $233. Now we seem to be saying that males are favored by $2,500. Which is correct? As we will see, both differences are numerically correct, but they address different questions.

The $2,500 difference in favor of males occurred when we compared a female salary of $21,000 versus a male salary of $23,500. The $2,500 difference is literally an average (unweighted) of the $2,000 difference for college graduates and the $3,000 difference for nongraduates (refer to Table 7.16 to see where the figures $2,000 and $3,000 come from). Thus, if we compare an average female to an average male—both of whom have the same educational level—the mean difference in their salary is $2,500. Recall that the nonsignificant interaction told us that the $2,000 difference for graduates is not significantly different from the $3,000 difference for nongraduates, so in this sense the $2,500 difference can be regarded as a correct estimate within sampling error both for graduates and nongraduates. The most important point to realize here is that the difference between the rows is being calculated within each column, and then an unweighted average is calculated across the columns.

The $233 difference in favor of females was arrived at in a rather different manner. This value is the difference between the mean of $22,333 for the 12 females and the mean of $22,100 for the 10 males. Notice that these means were calculated ignoring educational level. In effect, what we have done here is to calculate a weighted marginal mean, where the weights are a function of the number of observations at each educational level. For example, the female marginal mean of $22,333 was obtained from $(8/12)(25,000) + (4/12)(17,000)$. Similarly, the weighted marginal mean for males was obtained from $(3/10)(27,000) + (7/10)(20,000)$. The unweighted marginal means were calculated as $(1/2)(25,000) + (1/2)(17,000)$ for females and $(1/2)(27,000) + (1/2)(20,000)$ for males. The reason that the weighted mean for females ($22,333) is greater than the unweighted mean for females ($21,000) is because a majority of the females in the sample have a college degree and employees with such a degree tend to be paid more than those without. The same logic explains why the weighted mean for males ($22,100) is less than the unweighted mean for males ($23,500). Thus, it is because a greater proportion of females than males have college degrees in this sample that for weighted means, females are paid more than males (although the difference is nonsignificant), but for unweighted means, females are paid less than males.

It is important to emphasize that testing differences in weighted marginal means answers a different question from testing differences in unweighted marginal means. When we test differences in weighted marginal means, we are testing whether the rows (for example) have different means irrespective of any association between the rows and columns. In our example, the 12 females are paid slightly more than the 10 males on the average, as reflected by the weighted marginal means. (Again, the difference is nonsignificant.) This is an entirely correct statement, but it may or may not answer the question in which we are interested. In particular, differences in the weighted marginal means do not tell us whether females and males of similar educational attainment tend to be paid equally. This question can be answered by comparing unweighted marginal means. For our data, females are paid significantly less than males of the same educational level. To summarize for our data, females are paid slightly more than males on the whole, but once we take educational level into account (i.e., allow for the effects of educational level on salary), females are significantly underpaid. In this sense, although females are paid slightly more than males overall, their apparent advantage is significantly less than it should be, given their average superior educational level in this sample.

Three further points merit attention here regarding weighted and unweighted means. First, notice that the distinction was unnecessary in an equal-n design, because the weights used to calculate weighted means would all be equal to one another. As a result, in an equal-n design, weighted and unweighted means are identical to one another. Second, although we may be tempted to conclude in our example that females are indeed being discriminated against, we should also consider other qualifications that might differentiate the females from the males in this sample. For example, years of work experience might be an important factor, which potentially could either favor the females in the sample (increasing the actual discrimination) or the males (decreasing the actual discrimination). Third, although we stated earlier in the discussion that the difference between the weighted marginal means of $22,333 for females and $22,100 for males is nonsignificant, we did not provide the computational details. Once again, when the factor has two levels, the sum of squares for the difference between weighted marginal means can be calculated as the sum of squares for a contrast. In general, the coefficients for testing the difference in weighted row marginal means are given by $n_{11}/n_{1+}, n_{12}/n_{1+}, -n_{21}/n_{2+}$, and $-n_{22}/n_{2+}$, where n_{1+} and n_{2+} are the total number of participants in rows 1 and 2, respectively. For our data, the resulting coefficients are 8/12, 4/12, -3/10, and -7/10. Applying the usual formula for the sum of squares due to a contrast (Equation 4.39) yields a value of 0.2970. Dividing this value by the MS_W of 2.7778 yields an F value of 0.1069, which is nonsignificant at the .05 level.

The sum of squares for the difference in row marginal means is called a Type I sum of squares, where effects due to row have been included in the model but effects due to column have not.[16] This terminology is discussed more fully momentarily, when we consider nonorthogonal designs beyond the 2×2.

Type II Sum of Squares

At this point, we have discussed two different types of sums of squares—Type I and Type III. Not surprisingly, there is also a Type II sum of squares.[17] Before introducing the Type II sum of squares, it is relevant to reconsider the question addressed by the Type III sum of squares, which you should recall was used to test differences in unweighted marginal means. The difference in unweighted row marginal means averages differences between the rows within each column, giving equal weight to the columns. To understand the rationale for the Type II sum of squares, consider a situation where there is no interaction of rows and columns in the population and there are more observations in the first column than in the second column. The lack of an interaction implies that the difference between the population mean in row 1 versus row 2 is the same in both columns. Thus, the quantities $\overline{Y}_{11} - \overline{Y}_{21}$ and $\overline{Y}_{12} - \overline{Y}_{22}$ are both estimates of the same population parameter. If there are more observations in the first column than in the second column, $\overline{Y}_{11} - \overline{Y}_{21}$ will probably be a better estimate than $\overline{Y}_{12} - \overline{Y}_{22}$. The rationale behind the Type II sum of squares is to give the better estimate more weight than the other estimate. Notice that the Type III sum of squares does not capitalize on the opportunity in this situation, because its value is based on a difference where $\overline{Y}_{12} - \overline{Y}_{22}$ receives the same weight as $\overline{Y}_{11} - \overline{Y}_{21}$.

It can be shown that in this situation the optimal weights are $n_{11}n_{21}/n_{+1}$ for $\overline{Y}_{11} - \overline{Y}_{21}$ and $n_{12}n_{22}/n_{+2}$ for $\overline{Y}_{12} - \overline{Y}_{22}$.[18] Once again, when the factor has two levels, the test can be performed by testing the significance of a contrast. The contrast coefficients are given by $n_{11}n_{21}/n_{+1}$ (for the 11 cell), $n_{12}n_{22}/n_{+2}$ (for the 12 cell), $-n_{11}n_{21}/n_{+1}$ (for the 21 cell), and $-n_{12}n_{22}/n_{+2}$ (for the 22 cell). For our data, the contrast coefficients are given by 2.1818, 2.5455, -2.1818, and -2.5455. Alternatively, we can divide each weight by 4.7273 (the sum of 2.1818 and 2.5455) to obtain units comparable to the original metric, in which case the weights are 0.4615, 0.5385, -0.4615, and -0.5385. Notice that the gender difference for nongraduates receives a little more weight than the gender difference for graduates. The reason is that a difference between means based on samples of size 4 and 7 is less variable than a difference based on samples of size 3 and 8 (the harmonic mean of 4 and 7 is larger than the harmonic mean of 3 and 8; see Note 14). For our data, the difference in marginal means equals .4615(27,000 - 25,000) + .5385(20,000 - 17,000), which equals $2,538.50, only slightly larger than the $2,500 difference in unweighted marginal means. Application of Equation 4.39 yields a Type II sum of squares of 30.4615, which corresponds to an F value of 10.9662 and a p value of .0039. Thus, for our data, the Type II and Type III sum of squares yield very similar conclusions. Although this is quite often the case, particularly if the interaction is nonexistent, in other circumstances substantial differences can occur. We will return to comparing these two approaches after we have considered the general $a \times b$ nonorthogonal design.

TABLE 7.17

CONTRAST COEFFICIENTS FOR THE A (ROW) MAIN EFFECT IN A
2 × 2 DESIGN

	Cell			
	11	*12*	*21*	*22*
Type I SS^*	n_{11}/n_{1+}	n_{12}/n_{1+}	$-n_{21}/n_{2+}$	$-n_{22}/n_{2+}$
Type II $SS^\dagger$	$n_{11}n_{21}/n_{+1}$	$n_{12}n_{22}/n_{+2}$	$-n_{11}n_{21}/n_{+1}$	$-n_{12}n_{22}/n_{+2}$
Type III SS	$1/2$	$1/2$	$-1/2$	$-1/2$

*The A factor is entered into the model first.

†These coefficients are not on the same scale as the original metric, which can be preserved by dividing each coefficient shown here by $\frac{1}{2}(\tilde{n}_{.1} + \tilde{n}_{.2})$, where $\tilde{n}_{.1}$ and $\tilde{n}_{.2}$ are the harmonic means of the cell sizes in the first and second columns, respectively.

TABLE 7.18

HYPOTHESES TESTED BY THREE TYPES OF SUMS OF SQUARES FOR
A MAIN EFFECT IN A 2 × 2 DESIGN

		General Expression
Type I	SS^*	$H_0 : \frac{1}{n_{1+}}(n_{11}\mu_{11} + n_{12}\mu_{12}) = \frac{1}{n_{2+}}(n_{21}\mu_{21} + n_{22}\mu_{22})$
Type II	$SS^\dagger$	$H_0 : \frac{1}{(\tilde{n}_{.1}+\tilde{n}_{.2})}(\tilde{n}_{.1}\mu_{11} + \tilde{n}_{.2}\mu_{12}) = \frac{1}{(\tilde{n}_{.1}+\tilde{n}_{.2})}(\tilde{n}_{.1}\mu_{21} + \tilde{n}_{.2}\mu_{22})$
Type III	SS	$H_0 : 1/2(\mu_{11} + \mu_{12}) = 1/2(\mu_{21} + \mu_{22})$

	Specific Expression for Table 7.15 Data
Type I	$H_0 : .6667\mu_{11} + .3333\mu_{12} = .3000\mu_{21} + .7000\mu_{22}$
Type II	$H_0 : .4615\mu_{11} + .5385\mu_{12} = .4615\mu_{21} + .5385\mu_{22}$
Type III	$H_0 : .5000\mu_{11} + .5000\mu_{12} = .5000\mu_{21} + .5000\mu_{22}$

*The A factor is entered into the model first

$^\dagger\tilde{n}_{.1}$ and $\tilde{n}_{.2}$ are the harmonic means of the cell sizes in the first and second columns, respectively.

Summary of Three Types of Sum of Squares

Table 7.17 summarizes the differences between the coefficients of Type I, Type II, and Type III sums of squares for the row main effect in a 2 × 2 design. Table 7.18 presents the corresponding hypothesis being tested by each type of sum of square. As we emphasized earlier, this table shows clearly that the three types of sums of squares are generally answering different questions. However, there are three special circumstances where some of the hypotheses (and also the sums of squares) converge. First, if $n_{11} = n_{12}$ and $n_{21} = n_{22}$, all three types test the same hypothesis, and all three yield identical sums of squares. Second, if $n_{11} = n_{21}$ and $n_{12} = n_{22}$, Types I and II are the same, but Type III is different. Third, if the population interaction is zero (so $\mu_{11} - \mu_{21}$ equals $\mu_{12} - \mu_{22}$), Types II and III test the same hypothesis, but their sums of squares are still generally somewhat different. We have more to say about which type of sum of squares is "best" after we discuss the general $a \times b$ design.

Although our discussion has focused on the row main effect, the same logic obviously applies to the column main effect, because it is arbitrary which factor is represented as rows and which as columns to begin with. Also, notice that the different types of sums of squares were not discussed for the interaction, because the interaction is a test of cell mean differences instead of marginal mean differences. Thus, the various approaches to "averaging" across the other factor are not an issue for testing the interaction.

ANALYSIS OF THE GENERAL $a \times b$ NONORTHOGONAL DESIGN

The concepts we developed in the 2×2 design are also applicable in the general $a \times b$ design. For example, there is still a distinction among Type I, Type II, and Type III sum of squares for a main effect. Although the concepts remain the same, the necessary calculations become considerably more difficult because the sum of squares for an effect cannot be obtained from a single contrast when the effect has more than 1 df.

To consider the $a \times b$ design, we return to our model-comparisons strategy. In the process, we see how the various types of sums of squares we initially encountered in the 2×2 design can be conceptualized in terms of model comparisons.

You may remember that earlier in the chapter we presented a flowchart (Figure 7.2) to be used as a guideline for analyzing effects in a two-factor design. Although this flowchart was presented in the context of equal-n designs, it is also applicable for unequal-n designs. According to the flowchart, the first step in analyzing two-way designs is generally to test the interaction.

Test of the Interaction

The test of the interaction in the general $a \times b$ design with unequal n involves the same full and restricted models as in the equal-n design:

$$\text{Full:} \qquad Y_{ijk} = \mu + \alpha_j + \beta_k + (\alpha\beta)_{jk} + \varepsilon_{ijk} \qquad \text{(6, repeated)}$$

$$\text{Restricted:} \qquad Y_{ijk} = \mu + \alpha_j + \beta_k + \varepsilon_{ijk} \qquad \text{(32, repeated)}$$

Least-squares estimates of the parameters of the full model are easy to obtain, even with unequal n, because as we saw earlier in the chapter, this model is a cell means model. As a consequence, the sum of squared errors for the full model is given by

$$E_F = \sum_{k=1}^{b} \sum_{j=1}^{a} \sum_{i=1}^{n_j} (Y_{ijk} - \overline{Y}_{jk})^2$$

$$= SS_W \qquad (66)$$

where SS_W denotes the within-group sum of squares. Unfortunately, there is no correspondingly simple expression for the sum of squared errors of the restricted model, because formulas for the least-squares estimates of its parameters have no simple form without resorting to matrix algebra (Searle, 1987, p. 102). As a consequence, there is no simple expression for the interaction sum of squares, SS_{AB}, which equals $E_R - E_F$, the difference in the sum of squared errors of the restricted and full models.[19] Thus, for all practical purposes, computations must be performed on a computer, except in the 2×2 design. However, what is important for our purposes is to realize that the test of the $A \times B$ interaction is based on comparing the same models in the unequal-n design as in the equal-n design. Although calculations are much more formidable with unequal n, the meaning of the test does not change, because the interaction parameters continue to have the same meaning that we developed at some length at the beginning of the chapter. It is also important to realize that there is a single numerical value for the interaction sum of squares, that is, the Type I, Type II, and Type III sums of squares are all equal to each other for the interaction.[20]

According to the flowchart in Figure 7.2, if the interaction is statistically significant, we would typically perform simple-effect tests. These tests are relatively straightforward to conduct, even with unequal n, because the sum of squares for a simple effect is based on a single level of the other factor. As a result, the sum of squares can be calculated using appropriate formulas from Chapter 3 for a one-way design. The presence of unequal cell sizes presents no special problems here, because there is no need to average over levels of another factor.

Test of Unweighted Marginal Means

If the interaction is not significant, the next step would typically involve testing main effects. We arbitrarily focus on the A main effect (at the end of this section, we present comparable formulas for B). With equal n, we found the sum of squares due to A by comparing the following pair of models:

$$\text{Full:} \qquad Y_{ijk} = \mu + \alpha_j + \beta_k + (\alpha\beta)_{jk} + \varepsilon_{ijk} \qquad\qquad \text{(6, repeated)}$$
$$\text{Restricted:} \qquad Y_{ijk} = \mu + \beta_k + (\alpha\beta)_{jk} + \varepsilon_{ijk} \qquad\qquad \text{(21, repeated)}$$

These same two models can also be compared with unequal n. It can be shown that the null hypothesis being tested here is of the form

$$H_0 : \mu_{1.(U)} = \mu_{2.(U)} = \cdots = \mu_{a.(U)} \qquad\qquad (67)$$

where $\mu_{1.(U)}$ is the unweighted marginal means of row 1, $\mu_{2.(U)}$ is the unweighted marginal mean of row 2, and so forth. Notice that the unweighted marginal mean for row j would be defined as

$$\mu_{j.(U)} = \sum_{k=1}^{b} \mu_{jk}/b$$

The important point to realize here is that comparing Equations 6 and 21 with unequal n provides a test of whether unweighted row marginal means are equal to one another. As usual, the test is performed by finding the difference in the sum of squared errors of the two models, that is, $E_R - E_F$. Searle (1987, p. 90) shows[21] that this difference equals

$$E_R - E_F = \sum_{j=1}^{a} b\tilde{n}_{j.}(\overline{Y}_{j.(U)} - \overline{Y}_{G(A)})^2 \qquad\qquad (68)$$

where

$$b = \text{number of levels of the B factor}$$

$$\tilde{n}_{j.} = b \left/ \sum_{k=1}^{b}(1/n_{jk}) \right.$$

$$\overline{Y}_{j.(U)} = \sum_{k=1}^{b} \overline{Y}_{jk}/b$$

and

$$\overline{Y}_{G(A)} = \sum_{j=1}^{a} \tilde{n}_{j.}\overline{Y}_{j.(U)} \left/ \sum_{j=1}^{a} \tilde{n}_{j.} \right.$$

To make Equation 68 more understandable, it might help to compare it to Equation 25, which provided the formula for SS_A with equal n :

$$E_R - E_F = nb \sum_{j=1}^{a} (\overline{Y}_{j.} - \overline{Y}_{..})^2 \qquad \text{(25, repeated)}$$

It will be helpful to move the nb term in Equation 25 inside the summation and to place b before n, in which case we have (for equal n):

$$E_R - E_F = \sum_{j=1}^{a} bn(\overline{Y}_{j.} - \overline{Y}_{..})^2 \qquad (69)$$

Notice that each term in Equation 69 for equal n has a corresponding term in Equation 68 for unequal n. However, some of the specific terms differ. In particular, the cell size n in Equation 69 has been replaced by $\tilde{n}_{j.}$ in Equation 68. The $\tilde{n}_{j.}$ term is the harmonic mean of the cell sizes in row j. As such, it equals the "effective" cell size (see Note 14, referred to earlier, for more detail) for cells in the jth row. In this sense, the $\tilde{n}_{j.}$ term reflects sample size in Equation 68, just as n does in Equation 69. Also, the marginal mean $\overline{Y}_{j.}$ in Equation 69 is written as $\overline{Y}_{j.(U)}$ in Equation 68, because with unequal n we must distinguish between weighted and unweighted marginal means. Finally, $\overline{Y}_{G(A)}$ in Equation 68 is a grand mean similar to $\overline{Y}_{..}$ in Equation 69. However, $\overline{Y}_{G(A)}$ is calculated as a weighted average of the row marginal means, with the weights given by the "effective" sample sizes of the rows. Thus, although Equation 68 is somewhat more tedious to calculate than is Equation 69, in many respects, their underlying rationales are the same.

Recall that when we tested a null hypothesis of equality among unweighted means in the 2×2 unequal-n design, we referred to the corresponding sum of squares as Type III (see Table 7.18, for a reminder). The same terminology is used in the general $a \times b$ design. Thus, we can say that the Type III sum of squares for the A main effect is obtained when we compare models of the form

Full:	$Y_{ijk} = \mu + \alpha_j + \beta_k + (\alpha\beta)_{jk} + \varepsilon_{ijk}$	(6, repeated)
Restricted:	$Y_{ijk} = \mu + \beta_k + (\alpha\beta)_{jk} + \varepsilon_{ijk}$	(21, repeated)

Because Equation 68 provides the formula for the difference in the sums of squared errors of these two models, it follows that the Type III sum of squares for the A main effect can be written as

$$\text{Type III} \quad SS_A = \sum_{j=1}^{a} b\tilde{n}_{j.}(\overline{Y}_{j.(U)} - \overline{Y}_{G(A)})^2 \qquad (70)$$

where all terms are defined just as they were in Equation 68. As a final point, notice that the Type III sum of squares is obtained by allowing for all of the other effects in the model. In other words, both the restricted and the full models allow for the possibility of a B main effect as well as an $A \times B$ interaction. In a sense, then, B and $A \times B$ effects are "controlled for" when the Type III sum of squares is used to test the A main effect.

Test of Marginal Means in an Additive Model

Notice, however, that Figure 7.2 generally recommends testing (and interpreting) main effects only when the interaction is nonsignificant. It might be argued that if the interaction is nonsignificant, the interaction parameters can be (or even should be) dropped from our model. The resultant full model would be an additive model and could be written as

$$\text{Full}: \qquad Y_{ijk} = \mu + \alpha_j + \beta_k + \varepsilon_{ijk} \qquad\qquad \text{(32, repeated)}$$

In fact, as we saw earlier, the additive model of Equation 32 is the restricted model for the interaction test; a nonsignificant F test implies that this restricted model is not significantly worse at explaining our data than is the model that also includes interaction parameters. By the principle of parsimony, as discussed in Chapter 1, we might then prefer to consider the additive model of Equation 32 as a new full model.

From this perspective, we can test the A main effect by testing a null hypothesis that all of the α_j parameters in the full model of Equation 32 equal zero. Thus, we need to compare the following pair of models:

$$\text{Full}: \qquad Y_{ijk} = \mu + \alpha_j + \beta_k + \varepsilon_{ijk} \qquad\qquad \text{(32, repeated)}$$
$$\text{Restricted}: \qquad Y_{ijk} = \mu + \beta_k + \varepsilon_{ijk} \qquad\qquad \text{(71)}$$

The resultant difference in the sums of squared errors of the full and the restricted models produces the Type II sum of squares for the A main effect. Unfortunately, there is no simple expression for the Type II sum of squares in the $a \times b$ design. It is possible, however, to write a general expression for the hypothesis being tested by the Type II sum of squares for A in the general $a \times b$ design:

$$H_0 : \sum_{k=1}^{b} \left[n_{jk} - \left(n_{jk}^2 / n_{+k} \right) \right] \mu_{jk} = \sum_{j \neq j'} \sum_{k=1}^{b} (n_{jk} n_{j'k} / n_{+k}) \mu_{j'k} \qquad (72)$$

where $j = 1, 2, \ldots, a - 1$. Comparing this null hypothesis to the null hypothesis for the Type III sum of squares (see Equation 67) makes it clear that interpreting Type II sums of squares may be much less straightforward than interpreting Type III sums of squares. However, just as we showed earlier in the 2×2 design, it turns out here as well that the Type II sum of squares for A can be conceptualized as testing the more straightforward hypothesis of Equation 67 if there is no interaction in the population. This lack of interaction is consistent with our decision to drop the $(\alpha\beta)_{jk}$ parameters from our model in the first place. When the population interaction is truly zero, omitting the $(\alpha\beta)_{jk}$ parameters increases power, so Type II sums of squares are preferable to Type III sums of squares. However, when the population interaction is not zero, the decision to omit $(\alpha\beta)_{jk}$ parameters is incorrect, and Type II sums of squares are considerably more difficult to interpret than are Type III sums of squares. Of course, the real problem here is that we never know with absolute certainty whether there is an interaction in the population, even after we have tested the interaction in our sample. We discuss this issue in more detail at the end of the chapter.

Test of Weighted Marginal Means

Remember that we began our consideration of the A main effect by comparing two models, both of which allowed for both B and A by B effects. The resultant comparison produced the Type III SS for A. Then we compared two models both of which allowed for B, but not for A by B. The resultant comparison produced the Type II SS for A. Suppose that we were to omit not just the interaction parameters but also the B main-effect parameters from our model. Our models would then be

$$\text{Full}: \quad Y_{ijk} = \mu + \alpha_j + \varepsilon_{ijk}$$

$$\text{Restricted}: \quad Y_{ijk} = \mu + \varepsilon_{ijk}$$

Not surprisingly, the difference in the sums of squared errors of these two models equals the Type I sum of squares for A (when A is entered first in the hierarchical sequence). By ignoring B and A by B effects, the Type I sum of squares attributes any differences among rows to the A factor, irrespective of potential column effects (i.e., any effects involving the B factor). Recall that this phenomenon was illustrated in our numerical example of the 2×2 design, where the Type I sum of squares ignored the effects of educational level and thus attributed any difference between females' and males' average salaries to the gender factor itself. By ignoring possible B and A by B effects, the Type I sum of squares for A is testing a null hypothesis that the weighted marginal means for all rows are equal to one another. We can write this in symbols as

$$H_0 : (1/n_{1+}) \sum_{k=1}^{b} n_{1k}\mu_{1k} = (1/n_{2+}) \sum_{k=1}^{b} n_{2k}\mu_{2k} = \cdots = (1/n_{a+}) \sum_{k=1}^{b} n_{ak}\mu_{ak} \quad (73)$$

If we use $\overline{Y}_{j.(\text{W})}$ to represent the weighted sample mean for row j (where the weights applied to $\overline{Y}_{jk}$ equal n_{jk}/n_{j+}), the Type I sum of squares for A can be written as

$$\text{Type I } SS_A = \sum_{j=1}^{a} n_{j+}(\overline{Y}_{j.(\text{W})} - \overline{Y}_{..(\text{W})})^2 \quad (74)$$

where $\overline{Y}_{..(\text{W})}$ is defined as

$$\overline{Y}_{..(\text{W})} = \sum_{j=1}^{a} n_{j+}\overline{Y}_{j.(\text{W})} \Big/ \sum_{j=1}^{a} n_{j+}$$

Summary of Types of Sum of Squares

At this point, it probably is helpful to summarize what we have learned about the nonorthogonal $a \times b$ design. First, the sum of squares for the interaction is unambiguous because it does not involve averaging over any of the cells in the design. Second, there are three possible ways to test a main effect. In particular, we could test the A main effect by any of the following:

1. Ignoring both B and A by B (Type I)
2. Allowing for B, but ignoring A by B (Type II)
3. Allowing for possible B and A by B effects (Type III).

The most important thing to understand here is that with unequal n, these three approaches generally test different hypotheses. Thus, the investigator's responsibility is to clearly formulate a hypothesis and choose the corresponding type of sum of squares. We will say more about this choice shortly. Third, Tables 7.19 to 7.22 summarize these approaches by presenting in each case the models being compared, the hypotheses being tested, and the sums of squares for both the A main effect and the B main effect. Although our theoretical development focuses exclusively on the A main effect, as these tables show, corresponding formulas are obtained for the B main effect simply by interchanging rows and columns. Also, notice that two versions of Type I sums of squares are presented, because in the hierarchical approach either A effects or B effects can enter the model first. In other words, model building can either first include α_j parameters and then add β_k parameters at a second step or vice versa. Fourth, we should mention that it is conventional to use mean square within as the error term for all of these model comparisons. Thus, in all cases, an F statistic is formed as

$$F = \frac{SS_{\text{effect}}/df_{\text{effect}}}{MS_{\text{W}}}$$

Which Type of Sum of Squares Is Best?

In an equal-n design, Type I, Type II, and Type III sums of squares are all identical. The reason is that the A, B, and AB factors are orthogonal to each other in an equal-n design. Thus, with equal n, when testing A (for example), it does not matter whether B parameters are included in the model. However, in an unequal-n design, the factors are typically correlated. Usually, the three types of sum of squares are at least somewhat different in this situation. Which one should be used? This is a complicated question that has been debated extensively in the psychological statistics literature. Not surprisingly, the correct answer is, "It depends".

Type I sums of squares are usually not appropriate, because the test of differences in weighted marginal means obviously depends on cell sizes. Such an approach is meaningful only if the cell sizes themselves are thought to represent population sizes, as they may when the factors in question are classificatory rather than experimental. In this situaton, Type I sums of squares are meaningful, but even here it must be kept in mind that the other factor is being ignored. Thus, in our salary data example, it may be of interest to discover that females are paid slightly more than males and that the difference is nonsignificant. However, this result must be interpreted extremely carefully, because it ignores any effects of educational level. Howell and McConaughy (1982) provide additional examples of situations where differences in weighted marginal means may be informative. However, the crucial point is that tests based on Type I sum of squares ignore the effects of the other factor in the design, which usually defeats the purpose behind including multiple factors.

Type II and Type III sums of squares are based on differences within the levels of the other factor, unlike Type I sums of squares. Thus, they are usually more appropriate than Type I sums of squares for interpreting a main effect. Which of these two is better, Type II or Type III? As stated earlier, it depends on whether the interaction is zero in the population. If it is, the Type II approach is more powerful, because stable differences are weighted more heavily than unstable differences. If the interaction is nonzero, the Type III approach is preferable, because it is more easily interpreted. To see why, let's return to our hypothetical salary data. The Type III sum of squares always provides a test of unweighted marginal means. In our example, this corresponds to averaging the gender difference in salaries for college graduates with the difference for nongraduates. The important point is that we are giving the same weight to the difference we observe for graduates as to the weight we observe for nongraduates. Thus, the "average" is easy to interpret. However, the Type II approach is estimating .4615 times the difference for graduates plus .5385 times the difference for nongraduates. If the two differences are the same, this weighted average is easily interpreted, because it simply equals the constant difference that exists for both graduates and nongraduates. Of course, the two differences are the same in the population if and only if the interaction is zero in the population. On the other hand, if there is an interaction in the population, whatever difference exists for nongraduates is receiving more weight than the difference for graduates. This complicates interpretation, especially because the differential weights are entirely a function of the cell sizes, which may be unequal for reasons we are not interested in interpreting. However, as Tables 7.18 and 7.20 show, the cell sizes influence not only the F test but also the null hypothesis being tested with Type II sum of squares if there is an interaction in the population.

What should we do? One approach would be to test the interaction. If it is nonsignificant, we could proceed with Type II sum of squares. However, we would have to concern ourselves here with the probability that we have made a "Type II error."[22] That is, the interaction might be nonzero in the population, but our statistical test failed to detect its presence. Because of this difficulty, our general recommendation is to test marginal means based on Type III sum of squares. However, it should be recognized that some researchers prefer Type II sums of squares, particularly in situations where there are strong theoretical reasons to suspect the lack of an interaction and the empirical test of the interaction results in a p value substantially above .05 (e.g., above .20 or .25). As implied earlier, there is a long history of debate on this topic. The interested reader is referred to Cramer and Appelbaum (1980); Herr and Gaebelein (1978); Overall, Spiegel, and Cohen (1975); and the references they cite for further information.

To end this discussion on a less controversial note, we mention two further approaches to handling nonorthogonal data, neither of which is recommended. First, earlier textbooks often recommended an "unweighted means analysis." In this approach, equal-n formulas are used to calculate sums of squares, except that n (the sample size assumed to be equal for each cell) is replaced by the harmonic mean of the cell sizes. Although this approach is simple to implement, the resulting mean squares do not generally have chi-square distributions, so dividing them by MS_W results in distributions that are only approximately F distributions. The one situation where the resulting ratios have exact F distributions is when every factor has two levels. In this special case, unweighted means analysis produces Type III sums of squares. Otherwise, the results are only approximate, so this method should be avoided. Its primary appeal was ease of calculation, but with the advent of statistical packages to perform calculations on computers, computational simplicity is no longer relevant. Nevertheless, you need to be aware that some statistical packages (see Dallal, 1988) may still use an unweighted means analysis for nonorthogonal designs, because this type of analysis is easier to write for the author of the program. Second, some researchers when faced with unequal n randomly delete observations from all but the smallest cell to achieve equal n. Such an approach obviously lowers power and may tempt researchers to delete a few observations nonrandomly if they fail to conform to expectations. Better yet, why not delete observations randomly but try the randomization process repeatedly until the "erroneous" observations have been "randomly" selected for deletion? This is obviously inappropriate and would create a bias, making any statistical analysis uninterpretable.

In summary, least-squares analysis performed by comparing models provides appropriate hypothesis tests for factorial designs, both in equal n- and unequal n-conditions. However, the choice of models to be compared in unequal-n designs is complicated, because there are three potentially reasonable ways of calculating a marginal mean.

A Note on Statistical Packages for Analyzing Nonorthogonal Designs

Once we have decided which type of sum of squares is appropriate for testing hypotheses in which we are interested, we still have to worry about performing the actual calculations. Although even with unequal n we may be able to calculate sums of squares for main effects by

TABLE 7.19
TYPE III SUMS OF SQUARES

A Main Effect

Models

Full : $Y_{ijk} = \mu + \alpha_j + \beta_k + (\alpha\beta)_{jk} + \varepsilon_{ijk}$

Restricted : $Y_{ijk} = \mu + \beta_k + (\alpha\beta)_{jk} + \varepsilon_{ijk}$

Null Hypothesis

$H_0 : \mu_{1.(U)} = \mu_{2.(U)} = \cdots = \mu_{a.(U)}$

Sum of Squares

$SS_A = \sum_{j=1}^{a} b\tilde{n}_{.j.}(\overline{Y}_{j.(U)} - \overline{Y}_{G(A)})^2$

B Main Effect

Models

Full : $Y_{ijk} = \mu + \alpha_j + \beta_k + (\alpha\beta)_{jk} + \varepsilon_{ijk}$

Restricted : $Y_{ijk} = \mu + \alpha_j + (\alpha\beta)_{jk} + \varepsilon_{ijk}$

Null Hypothesis

$H_0 : \mu_{.1(U)} = \mu_{.2(U)} = \cdots = \mu_{.b(U)}$

Sum of Squares

$SS_B = \sum_{k=1}^{b} a\tilde{n}_{..k}(\overline{Y}_{.k(U)} - \overline{Y}_{G(B)})^2$

TABLE 7.20
TYPE II SUM OF SQUARES

A Main Effect

Models

Full : $Y_{ijk} = \mu + \alpha_j + \beta_k + \varepsilon_{ijk}$

Restricted : $Y_{ijk} = \mu + \beta_k + \varepsilon_{ijk}$

Null Hypothesis

$H_0 : \sum_{k=1}^{b} [n_{jk} - (n_{jk}^2/n_{+k})]\mu_{jk} = \sum_{j\neq j'} \sum_{k=1}^{b} (n_{jk}n_{j'k}/n_{+k})\mu_{j'k}$

where $j = 1, 2, \ldots, a - 1$

Sum of Squares

No simple expression (see text and Note 19)

B Main Effect

Models

Full : $Y_{ijk} = \mu + \alpha_j + \beta_k + \varepsilon_{ijk}$

Restricted : $Y_{ijk} = \mu + \alpha_j + \varepsilon_{ijk}$

Null Hypothesis

$H_0 : \sum_{j=1}^{a} [n_{jk} - (n_{jk}^2/n_{j+})]\mu_{jk} = \sum_{k\neq k'} \sum_{j=1}^{a} (n_{jk}n_{jk'}/n_{j+})\mu_{jk'}$

where $k = 1, 2, \ldots, b - 1$

Sum of Squares

No simple expression (see text and Note 19)

TABLE 7.21
TYPE I SUM OF SQUARES—A ENTERED FIRST

A Main Effect

Models

Full: $Y_{ijk} = \mu + \alpha_j + \varepsilon_{ijk}$
Restricted: $Y_{ijk} = \mu + \varepsilon_{ijk}$

Null Hypothesis

$H_0: (1/n_{1+})\sum_{k=1}^{b} n_{1k}\mu_{1k} = (1/n_{2+})\sum_{k=1}^{b} n_{2k}\mu_{2k} = \cdots = (1/n_{a+})\sum_{k=1}^{b} n_{ak}\mu_{ak}$

Sum of Squares

$SS_A = \sum_{j=1}^{a} n_{j+}(\bar{Y}_{j\cdot(W)} - \bar{Y}_{\cdot\cdot(W)})^2$

B Main Effect

Models

Full: $Y_{ijk} = \mu + \alpha_j + \beta_k + \varepsilon_{ijk}$
Restricted: $Y_{ijk} = \mu + \alpha_j + \varepsilon_{ijk}$

Null Hypothesis

Same as H_0 for Type II SS for B (see Table 7.20)

Sum of Squares

Same as Type II SS for B (see Table 7.20)

TABLE 7.22
TYPE I SUM OF SQUARES—B ENTERED FIRST

A Main Effect

Models

Full: $Y_{ijk} = \mu + \alpha_j + \beta_k + \varepsilon_{ijk}$
Restricted: $Y_{ijk} = \mu + \beta_k + \varepsilon_{ijk}$

Null Hypothesis

Same as H_0 for Type II SS for A (see Table 7.20)

Sum of Squares

Same as Type II SS for A (see Table 7.20)

B Main Effect

Models

Full: $Y_{ijk} = \mu + \beta_k + \varepsilon_{ijk}$
Restricted: $Y_{ijk} = \mu + \varepsilon_{ijk}$

Null Hypothesis

$H_0: (1/n_{+1})\sum_{j=1}^{a} n_{j1}\mu_{j1} = (1/n_{+2})\sum_{j=1}^{a} n_{j2}\mu_{j2} = \cdots = (1/n_{+b})\sum_{j=1}^{a} n_{jb}\mu_{jb}$

Sum of Squares

$SS_B = \sum_{k=1}^{b} n_{+k}(\bar{Y}_{\cdot k(W)} - \bar{Y}_{\cdot\cdot(W)})^2$

hand (see Tables 7.18–7.22), the only practical way to calculate the interaction sum of squares with unequal n is with a computer (except in the case of a 2×2 design). Of course, using an computer is no guarantee of accuracy. For example, a decade or so ago, the ANOVA program of one widely distributed statistical package would sometimes report that the interaction sum of squares was negative in nonorthogonal designs. The program, as computers are wont to do, was unconcerned with this impossible result and proceeded to report a negative F value as well. The problem was that the computational algorithm used by the programmer was appropriate only for equal-n designs.

One way to avoid this problem is to use a multiple-regression program. Although multiple regression is an extremely flexible methodology worthy of intensive study, most regression programs are clumsy for actually performing an ANOVA. In any event, all major statistical packages include programs that analyze data from nonorthogonal factorial designs. The default type of sum of squares is typically Type III. However, it is also possible to override default specifications to obtain other types of sums of squares that may be more appropriate for the hypotheses you want to test. The most important point here is that in a nonorthogonal design, you cannot necessarily assume that the statistical package you are using is really testing the hypothesis you want to test. Such a failure is especially likely if you are using a microcomputer program that your adviser or a colleague stumbled on with unknown origins (see Dallal, 1988). If you cannot tell from reading the manual what type(s) of sums of squares the program computes, it is probably wise to run some test data (where you already know what the answers are supposed to be) through the program. To facilitate this process and to put all our abstract theoretical developments into practice, we conclude our presentation of nonorthogonal designs with a numerical example.

Numerical Example

Suppose that a clinical psychologist is interested in comparing the relative effectiveness of three forms of psychotherapy for alleviating depression. Fifteen individuals are randomly assigned to each of three treatment groups: cognitive-behavioral, Rogerian, and assertiveness training. The Depression Scale of the MMPI serves as the dependent variable. A one-way ANOVA of the data yields an observed F value of 2.35, which fails to exceed the critical F value of 3.23 for 2 and 40 df (the actual denominator degrees of freedom equal 42, but the critical F is based on 40 df, because 42 df are not included in Appendix Table A.2). As a result, the null hypothesis cannot be rejected, so insufficient evidence of differential effectiveness has been found.

However, it occurs to the psychologist that subjects were classified according to the severity of their depression as mild, moderate, or severe. What would happen if a severity factor were incorporated into the design, along with type of therapy? Table 7.23 shows hypothetical MMPI scores for 45 participants, each of whom is placed in one cell of a 3×3 design. One factor (A, the row factor) is type of therapy. The other factor (B, the column factor) is degree of severity.

We must make three comments before embarking on the analysis of these data. First, as Table 7.23 shows, we are faced with a nonorthogonal design, because cell sizes are unequal (they range from 3 to 7). Such an imbalance is not surprising, even though subjects have been randomly assigned to groups. Although random assignment guarantees that in the long run one third of the individuals at each severity level would be assigned to each treatment, with a total of only 45 participants, some departure from strict equality would inevitably occur due to sampling error. Second, if we were to totally ignore the severity factor and analyze these data with a one-way ANOVA, we would obtain an observed F value of 2.35, which, as we already

TABLE 7.23
MMPI DEPRESSION SCALE SCORES

		Degree of Severity (B)		
		Mild	Moderate	Severe
Type of Therapy (A)	Cognitive-Behavioral	41 43 50	51 43 53 54 46	45 55 56 60 58 62 62
	Rogerian	56 47 45 46 49	58 54 49 61 52 62	59 55 68 63
	Assertiveness Training	43 56 48 46 47	59 46 58 54	55 69 63 56 62 67

discussed, is nonsignificant. Third, an analysis of these data, which includes severity level as a second factor, may provide a more powerful test of the treatment effect than the one-way ANOVA. This use of a second factor is called post hoc blocking. We will have much more to say about blocking in Chapter 9. For the moment, we simply say that in some circumstances, post hoc blocking provides an appropriate method for increasing power.[23]

We are now ready to consider the analysis of the data shown in Table 7.23. To facilitate interpretations of the data, Table 7.24 presents cell sizes, cell means, and marginal means. The cell sizes and cell means follow naturally from Table 7.23, but some explanation of the marginal means is probably required. The Type I marginal means (labeled as I in the table) are the weighted marginal means for the levels of the factor if that factor is entered first in the model. As such, they are sample estimates of the population marginal means being tested when the sum of squares for a main effect is calculated while ignoring both the other main effect and the interaction (see Table 7.21, for a reminder). For example, the Type I sum of squares for A is based on comparing weighted marginal means of the form

$$\overline{Y}_{j.(W)} = \sum_{k=1}^{b} n_{jk}\overline{Y}_{jk}/n_{j+}$$

Thus, the Type I marginal mean for the first row in our data equals

$$\overline{Y}_{1.(W)} = [3(44.67) + 5(49.40) + 7(56.86)]/15 = 51.93$$

The Type II marginal means, like the Type II sum of squares, have no simple form. Thus, for all practical purposes, they must be calculated by computer.[24] The Type III marginal means are simply unweighted means, averaging over the other factor. For example, the Type III marginal

TABLE 7.24

CELL SIZES, CELL MEANS, AND MARGINAL MEANS FOR TABLE 7.23 DATA

		Degree of Severity (B)			Marginal Means
		Mild	Moderate	Severe	
	Cognitive-Behavioral	$n_{11} = 3$ $\overline{Y}_{11} = 44.67$	$n_{12} = 5$ $\overline{Y}_{12} = 49.40$	$n_{13} = 7$ $\overline{Y}_{13} = 56.86$	I: 51.93 II: 50.18 III: 50.31
Type of Therapy (A)	Rogerian	$n_{21} = 5$ $\overline{Y}_{21} = 48.60$	$n_{22} = 6$ $\overline{Y}_{22} = 56.00$	$n_{23} = 4$ $\overline{Y}_{23} = 61.25$	I: 54.93 II: 55.39 III: 55.28
	Assertiveness Training	$n_{31} = 5$ $\overline{Y}_{31} = 48.00$	$n_{32} = 4$ $\overline{Y}_{32} = 54.25$	$n_{33} = 6$ $\overline{Y}_{33} = 62.00$	I: 55.27 II: 54.81 III: 54.75
	Marginal Means	I: 47.46 II: 46.96 III: 47.09	I: 53.33 II: 53.29 III: 53.22	I: 59.71 II: 60.13 III: 60.04	

mean for row j is of the form

$$\overline{Y}_{j.(U)} = \sum_{k=1}^{b} \overline{Y}_{jk}/b$$

Thus, the Type III marginal mean for the first row in our data equals

$$\overline{Y}_{1.(U)} = (44.67 + 49.40 + 56.86)/3 = 50.31$$

It is important to remember that none of these marginal means are "right" or "wrong"; instead, as we discussed earlier, they address different hypotheses.

What does an ANOVA of these data reveal? First, the interaction of treatment and degree of severity is nonsignificant ($SS_{A \times B} = 14.19$, $F = 0.13$, $p = .97$). Thus, we have some justification for interpreting main-effect tests. As discussed in the previous section, our general recommendation is to report and interpret Type III sums of squares. In any event, we would normally only report whichever type corresponds to the hypotheses of interest. However, for pedagogical purposes, we report all three types here.

Table 7.25 presents all three possible tests of both the A main effect and the B main effect. Of particular interest is the fact that the A main effect is statistically significant for both Type III and Type II sums of squares. Notice that both F values here (3.67 for Type III and 4.27 for Type II) are appreciably larger than the F value of 2.35 we obtained in the one-way ANOVA where severity level was entirely ignored. As we discuss in more detail in Chapter 9, the primary reason for the larger F values in the two-way design is that the error term (MS_W) is smaller because individual differences in MMPI scores that are attributable to severity level no longer contribute to the error term, as they did in the one-way design. The reduction in error is substantial here because, as Table 7.25 shows, the effect of severity level on the MMPI depression score is highly significant for these data.

At this point, we illustrate the calculations of Type III and Type I sums of squares using the formulas we presented earlier in the chapter. We focus our attention on the therapy main effect, because it is the effect of primary interest. Similar steps could be undertaken for the

TABLE 7.25
MAIN EFFECT TESTS FOR TABLE 7.23 DATA

TABLE 7.25
MAIN EFFECT TESTS FOR TABLE 7.23 DATA

	Sum of Squares	F	p
A Main Effect			
Type III	204.76	3.67	.04
(allowing for B and AB)			
Type II	238.48	4.27	.02
(allowing for B, but ignoring AB)			
Type I—B entered first	238.48	4.27	.02
(allowing for B, but ignoring AB)			
Type I—A entered first	101.11	1.81	.18
(ignoring B and AB)			
B Main Effect			
Type III	1181.11	21.15	<.01
(allowing for A and AB)			
Type II	1253.19	22.44	<.01
(allowing for A, but ignoring AB)			
Type I—A entered first	1253.19	22.44	<.01
(allowing for A, but ignoring AB)			
Type I—B entered first	1115.82	19.98	<.01
(ignoring A and AB)			

severity main effect. The Type III sum of squares for the *A* main effect was presented earlier in Equation 70:

$$\text{Type III} \quad SS_A = \sum_{j=1}^{a} b\tilde{n}_{j.}(\overline{Y}_{j.(U)} - \overline{Y}_{G(A)})^2 \tag{70, repeated}$$

The first step in using this formula is to calculate the "effective" cell size $\tilde{n}_{j.}$ for each row, where

$$\tilde{n}_{j.} = b \Big/ \sum_{k=1}^{b}(1/n_{jk})$$

For our data

$$\tilde{n}_{1.} = 3/(1/3 + 1/5 + 1/7) = 4.4366$$

$$\tilde{n}_{2.} = 3/(1/5 + 1/6 + 1/4) = 4.8649$$

$$\tilde{n}_{3.} = 3/(1/5 + 1/4 + 1/6) = 4.8649$$

Although we have already calculated the unweighted marginal means for each row, we repeat the calculations here and report results to four decimal places to reduce rounding error in subsequent calculations:

$$\overline{Y}_{1.(U)} = (44.6667 + 49.4000 + 56.8571)/3 = 50.3079$$

$$\overline{Y}_{2.(U)} = (48.6000 + 56.0000 + 61.2500)/3 = 55.2833$$

$$\overline{Y}_{3.(U)} = (48.0000 + 54.2500 + 62.0000)/3 = 54.7500$$

Next, we can calculate $\overline{Y}_{G(A)}$ from the following formula:

$$\overline{Y}_{G(A)} = \sum_{j=1}^{a} \tilde{n}_{j.} \overline{Y}_{j.(U)} \Bigg/ \sum_{j=1}^{a} \tilde{n}_{j.}$$

$$= (4.4366)(50.3079) + (4.8649)(55.2833)$$
$$+ \frac{(4.8649)(54.7500)}{(4.4366 + 4.8649 + 4.8649)}$$

$$= 53.5420$$

Now that we have completed intermediate calculations, we can substitute appropriate values into Equation 70:

$$\text{Type III} \quad SS_A = (3)(4.4366)(50.3079 - 53.5420)^2$$
$$+ (3)(4.8649)(55.2833 - 53.5420)^2$$
$$+ (3)(4.8649)(54.7500 - 53.5420)^2$$
$$= 204.76$$

This is in agreement with the value shown in Table 7.25.

Although Type I sums of squares are often of little interest, for the sake of completeness, we also illustrate the Type I sum of squares for the therapy main effect. From Equation 74

$$\text{Type I} \quad SS_A = \sum_{j=1}^{a} n_{j+}(\overline{Y}_{j.(w)} - \overline{Y}_{..(w)})^2 \qquad \text{(74, repeated)}$$

For the Table 7.23 data

$$n_{1+} = 3 + 5 + 7 = 15$$
$$n_{2+} = 5 + 6 + 4 = 15$$
$$n_{3+} = 5 + 4 + 6 = 15$$
$$\overline{Y}_{1.(w)} = [3(44.6667) + 5(49.4000) + 7(56.8571)]/15 = 51.9333$$
$$\overline{Y}_{2.(w)} = [5(48.6000) + 6(56.0000) + 4(61.2500)]/15 = 54.9333$$
$$\overline{Y}_{3.(w)} = [5(48.0000) + 4(54.2500) + 6(62.0000)]/15 = 55.2667$$
$$\overline{Y}_{..(w)} = [15(51.9333) + 15(54.9333) + 15(55.2667)]/(15 + 15 + 15) = 54.0444$$

Substituting these values into Equation 74, we have

$$\text{Type I} \quad SS_A = 15(51.9333 - 54.0444)^2 + 15(54.9333 - 54.0444)^2$$
$$+ 15(55.2667 - 54.0444)^2$$
$$= 101.11$$

Once again, this is in agreement with the value shown in Table 7.25.

Final Remarks

In closing, it is undoubtedly obvious now that unequal cell sizes tremendously complicate the analysis of factorial designs. Indeed, Appelbaum and Cramer (1974, p. 335) state that "the nonorthogonal multifactor analysis of variance is perhaps the most misunderstood analytic technique available to the behavioral scientist, save factor analysis." As if the complications we have already described are not bad enough, we feel compelled to mention yet another potential problem. As you might anticipate from our discussion of the effects of heterogeneity of variance in earlier chapters, unequal population variance can create substantial problems in nonorthogonal factorial designs (see Milligan, Wong, & Thompson, 1987, for further details). Some readers may be tempted to conclude from all of the discussion that the best lesson to be learned here is never to have unequal-n designs. Although we agree that equal-n designs are strongly preferable whenever possible, there are nevertheless some circumstances where unequal-n designs are inevitable. The message on nonorthogonal designs we would like for you to come away with is twofold. First, think carefully about precisely what null hypotheses you want to test. Second, choose an appropriate method for testing your hypotheses.

EXERCISES

*1. Consider the following sets of population means in a 3×3 two-way design. For each set of means, your task involves answering four questions: (1) Find the values of α_1, α_2, and α_3. (2) Find the values of β_1, β_2, and β_3. (3) Find the value of each interaction parameter $\alpha\beta_{jk}$. (4) Which effects (A, B, or A by B) are nonzero in the population?

a.

			B	
		1	2	3
	1	10	10	10
A	2	12	12	12
	3	17	17	17

b.

			B	
		1	2	3
	1	10	15	20
A	2	10	15	20
	3	10	15	20

c.

			B	
		1	2	3
	1	26	22	21
A	2	23	19	18
	3	17	13	12

d.

			B	
		1	2	3
	1	26	23	20
A	2	18	19	23
	3	13	15	14

e.

			B	
		1	2	3
	1	26	22	21
A	2	25	17	18
	3	15	15	12

2. Consider the following hypothetical population means in a 2×2 design:

		B	
		1	2
A	1	10	8
	2	12	18

a. Plot the cell means in a manner similar to that shown in Figure 7.1 (*a* and *b*), using levels of *A* on the horizontal axis.
b. Based on the figure you have drawn in part a, is there an interaction in the population? If so, is the interaction ordinal or disordinal?
c. Repeat part a, but this time use levels of *B* on the horizontal axis of the figure.
d. Based on the figure you have drawn in part c, is there an interaction in the population? If so, is the interaction ordinal or disordinal?
e. Which main-effect test do you think would be less misleading for this population? Why?

3. A graduate student conducted a two-factor design to investigate children's learning performance. One factor was form of practice, either massed or spaced. The second factor was presence or absence of feedback to the children. The following cell means were obtained:

		Feedback	
		Present	*Absent*
Practice	Massed	62	47
	Spaced	75	68

There are 15 participants per cell, and $MS_W = 400$.
a. The student claims that the difference between massed and spaced practice is smaller when feedback is present than when it is absent. Do you agree?
b. A friend of the student's claims that the effect of feedback is weaker when practice is spaced than when it is massed. Do you agree?
c. Are the effects of feedback and type of practice additive in this situation?

*4. The following sample means were obtained in an equal-*n* design with 8 individuals per cell:

		B		
		1	2	3
	1	8	10	15
A	2	9	14	10
	3	13	9	11

a. Find $\hat{\alpha}_j$ for each row (i.e., for each value of j).
b. Based on your answer to part a, calculate SS_A.
c. Find $\hat{\beta}_k$ for each column (i.e., for each value of k).
d. Based on your answer to part c, calculate SS_B.
e. Find $\widehat{\alpha\beta}_{jk}$ for each cell (i.e., for each pair of j and k values).
f. Based on your answer to part e, calculate SS_{AB}.

*5. The purpose of this exercise is to compare the meaning of a main effect in a two-way design to the comparable omnibus effect in a one-way design. Consider the data shown in Table 7.5 for a 2×3 design.

a. Find the sum of squares for the biofeedback main effect using Equation 25:

$$SS_A = E_R - E_F = nb \sum_{j=1}^{a} (\overline{Y}_{j.} - \overline{Y}_{..})^2$$

b. Suppose that the drug factor was not included in the design, so the design was conceptualized as a single-factor design. Specifically, 15 participants are in the biofeedback-present condition, and 15 participants are in the biofeedback-absent condition. Find the sum of squares for biofeedback in this one-way design using Equation 26:

$$SS_A = E_R - E_F = n \sum_{j=1}^{a} (\overline{Y}_j - \overline{Y})^2$$

c. How do your answers to Parts a and b compare to one another? What implication does this have for interpreting a main effect in an equal-n two-way design?

6. A counseling psychologist is interested in three types of therapy for modifying snake phobia. However, she does not believe that one type is necessarily best for everyone; instead, the best type may depend on degree (i.e., severity) of phobia. Undergraduate students enrolled in an introductory psychology course are given the Fear Schedule Survey (FSS) to screen out subjects showing no fear of snakes. Those displaying some degree of phobia are classified as either mildly, moderately, or severely phobic on the basis of the FSS. One third of subjects within each level of severity are then assigned to a treatment condition: systematic desensitization, implosive therapy, or insight therapy. The following data are obtained, using the Behavioral Avoidance Test (higher scores are better):

Desensitization			Implosion			Insight		
Mild	Moderate	Severe	Mild	Moderate	Severe	Mild	Moderate	Severe
14	15	12	10	12	10	8	9	6
17	11	10	16	14	3	10	6	10
10	12	10	19	10	6	12	7	8
13	10	9	20	11	8	14	12	9
12	9	11	19	13	2	11	11	7

Your task is to analyze these data, to answer any questions you believe would be of theoretical interest. Don't feel compelled to perform an analysis just because it would be possible statistically. Longer is not necessarily better. On the other hand, you probably will not want to stop after testing only main effects and the interaction.

You should describe your findings in a manner consistent with the results section of an American Psychological Association journal. If it seems appropriate, you may want to briefly justify your choice of alpha level, error term, and so on, but do not let this discussion overshadow what the results mean. Also, you may not want to focus exclusively on significance tests; descriptive statistics may also be useful.

7. A psychologist is interested in evaluating the effectiveness of behavioral treatments for hypertension. Specifically, he is interested in comparing a cognitive therapy to a form of relaxation therapy. He also is interested in the effects of diet. A subject pool of 120 participants is available to him. He is debating between two different designs. The first design would involve randomly assigning 40 participants to each of three conditions: cognitive, relaxation, and relaxation plus diet. The second design would involve randomly assigning 30 participants to each of four conditions: cognitive, relaxation, relaxation plus diet, and cognitive plus diet.

a. Which, if either, design will allow the psychologist to assess whether the difference between the psychological approaches (cognitive and relaxation) interacts with diet?

b. The psychologist is leaning toward the first design, because he believes that it will provide a more powerful test of the difference between the cognitive and relaxation approaches than would the second design. Do you agree? Why or why not?

*8. A commonly heard rule of thumb for choosing sample size is "10 participants per cell of the design." The purpose of this exercise is to determine the magnitude of statistical power that results from following this rule of thumb for various designs.

We assume throughout that we are interested in the power associated with a large effect size, as defined by Cohen (1977). It can be shown that the value of ϕ for a large effect size in a one-way design is given by

$$\phi = .40\sqrt{n},$$

where n is the number of participants per group. For factorial designs, this formula generalizes to

$$\phi = .40\sqrt{\frac{df_F}{df_R - df_F + 1} + 1}$$

or, equivalently

$$\phi = .40\sqrt{\frac{df_{denominator}}{df_{effect} + 1} + 1}$$

where df_{effect} and $df_{denominator}$ are the numerator and denominator degrees of freedom, respectively, for the F test. Use the Pearson–Hartley power charts (Appendix Table A.11) to calculate the power of detecting a large effect for each of the following designs, assuming 10 participants per cell.

a. Omnibus effect in a one-way design with two groups
b. Omnibus effect in a one-way design with five groups
c. Main effect in a 2×2 design
d. Interaction effect in a 2×2 design
e. Main effect in a 3×3 design
f. Interaction effect in a 3×3 design
g. It is often recommended that the power of a test to be performed be at least .8. For which of the above effects is the power this high for detecting a large effect with 10 participants per cell?
h. In light of your answers to Parts a through g, what is your reaction to the general utility of the "10 participants per cell" rule?

9. A clinical psychologist is interested in comparing three types of therapy for modifying snake phobia. However, she does not believe that one type is necessarily best for everyone; instead, the best type may depend on degree (i.e., severity) of phobia. Undergraduate students enrolled in an introductory psychology course are given the Fear Schedule Survey (FSS) to screen out subjects showing no fear of snakes. Those displaying some degree of phobia are classified as either mildly or severely phobic on the basis of the FSS. One third of the participants within each level of severity are then randomly assigned to a treatment condition: systematic desensitization, implosive therapy, or insight therapy. The following data are obtained, using the Behavioral Avoidance Test (higher scores indicate less phobia):

Desensitization		Implosion		Insight	
Mild	*Severe*	*Mild*	*Severe*	*Mild*	*Severe*
16	16	14	13	15	15
13	10	16	7	15	10
12	11	17	3	12	11
15	12	15	10	14	7
11	6	13	4	13	5
12	8	17	2	11	12
14	14	15	4	11	6
13	12	16	9	12	8

a. Test the main effects and interaction. Which effects, if any, are statistically significant?

b. Find the values of R^2, $\hat{\omega}^2$, partial R^2, and partial $\hat{\omega}^2$ for the main effects and interaction. Which do you think is more meaningful here, the partial association measures or the unpartialled measures? Why?

c. Test the simple effect of therapy within each level of severity, using a pooled error term. Are there statistically significant therapy effects at either level of severity?

d. Continue part c by performing pairwise tests of therapy differences within each level of severity, again using a pooled error term. Maintain the α_{FW} level at .05 within each level of severity.

e. Test the simple effect of therapy within each level of severity as in part c, but this time use a separate error term specific to the particular level of severity. How do your results compare to the results you obtained in part c? If the results are different, explain why.

f. Perform pairwise tests of therapy difference within each level of severity, as in part c, but this time use a separate error term specific to the particular contrast. As before, maintain the α_{FW} level at .05 within each level of severity. How do your results compare to the results you obtained in part d? If the results are different, explain why.

10. A graduate student obtained the following sample means in an equal-n 3×2 factorial design:

		B	
		1	2
	1	11	13
A	2	8	12
	3	5	11

He performed an ANOVA on these data, but his 6-year old daughter spilled sulfuric acid on a portion of the ANOVA table. What remains is the following:

Source	SS	df	MS	F
A				
B				
A × B	44			
Within	1,620	60		

Knowing that you are a statistics whiz, the graduate student asks you (in the questions below) to fill in the remainder of his table.

a. Find the value of SS_A.

b. Find the value of SS_B.

c. Fill in the missing degree of freedom entries in the table.

d. Calculate the mean square for each source in the table.

e. Calculate the F value for each effect. Which effects are significant at the .05 level?

f. The graduate student claims that the interaction is nonsignificant here. Because he is primarily interested in the A main effect, he decides to reanalyze the data as a one-way design with three groups, simply ignoring B. What will he find? Show your work.

*11. A clinical psychologist conducted a study to compare two forms of therapy. Ten females and 10 males were randomly assigned to each form of therapy (i.e., each cell contains 10 participants). The following sample means are obtained:

	Females	Males
Therapy A	60	40
Therapy B	80	60

Mean square within for these data equals 800. The psychologist presented these data to four different graduate students and asked each to analyze the data and report back to her. As it turned out, each student analyzed the data somewhat differently. Your task is to reproduce each of these analyses, which are described in Parts a–d below.

a. Student 1 compared the two therapies within each gender, that is, separate analyses were performed for females and males. The pooled MS_W was used as the error term for each analysis.

b. Student 2 used the same approach as Student 1, but used a separate error term for each gender. Assume that $MS_W = 800$ for the females and that $MS_W = 800$ for the males. (We would expect MS_W for females to equal MS_W for males in the long run if homogeneity of variance holds. In an actual study, however, MS_W for females would inevitably be somewhat different from MS_W for males, if for no other reason than sampling error. We have chosen to act as if there were no sampling error here to make the difference between the approaches of Student 1 and Student 2 clearer, when homogeneity is met.)

c. Student 3 tested the two main effects and the interaction in the 2×2 design. Is the difference between the therapies statistically significant?

d. Student 4 ignored the gender factor altogether and simply performed a *t* test comparing the 20 participants who received Therapy A to the 20 participants who received Therapy B.

e. Which of the four approaches do you think is best for these data?

12. The theoretical importance of a statistically significant interaction is sometimes difficult to interpret, because the nature of the interaction may depend on the scale of the dependent variable. In particular, a significant interaction may become nonsignificant when a monotonic transformation is performed on the dependent variable. This exercise illustrates how this apparent inconsistency can occur. For further reading, see Busemeyer (1980). A cognitive psychologist measured subjects' reaction times in identifying a stimulus in a 2×2 design. The data are as follows:

	A_1		A_2	
B_1	B_2	B_1	B_2
340	508	635	608
503	535	540	745
375	468	551	1,022
456	592	648	982
413	580	592	822
402	524	568	783
426	546	623	755
434	516	574	851

a. Test the statistical significance of the two-way interaction for these data.

b. Because reaction times are often positively skewed, it is common (as discussed in Chapter 3) to perform a logarithmic transformation of the dependent variable. Test the interaction using the log of reaction time as the dependent variable.

c. Another possibility here is to analyze each participant's speed of response. Speed is inversely proportional to reaction time, so speed of response can be operationalized as the reciprocal of reaction time. In other words, speed can be defined as Speed = 1/Reaction Time. Test the interaction using speed as the dependent variable.

d. How do the results of Parts a–c compare? Can it clearly be stated that *A* and *B* interact in this study?

13. In Chapter 6 (Exercise 14), we introduced a study investigating how parent–infant play changes as infants get older. The current exercise expands on the earlier exercise by introducing a second factor into the design. Whereas the Chapter 6 exercise studied proportion of pretend play as a function of the child's age, the current exercise investigates the same hypothetical data as a function of the

child's gender as well as age. Consider the following hypothetical data:

7-Month-Olds		10-Month-Olds		13-Month-Olds	
Girls	Boys	Girls	Boys	Girls	Boys
.02	.05	.15	,14	.09	.02
.01	.01	.11	.21	.03	.19
.07	.04	.22	.06	.18	.15
.04	.03	.05	.12	.12	.07
.01	.02	.09	.11	.18	.45
.09	.02	.05	.19	.43	.20
.05	.13	.15	.12	.24	.49
.06	.06	.11	.04	.40	.19

a. Test the significance of the age main effect, the gender main effect, and the age-by-gender interaction.
b. Based on your answer to part a, what follow-up tests should be performed here? Should cell means or marginal means be compared?
c. Test the significance of the linear and quadratic trends of the marginal means for age.
d. Suppose that it was deemed important to compare all pairs of the age marginal means. Test all of these pairwise comparisons and maintain the α_{FW} level at .05.
e. Form 95% simultaneous confidence intervals for the pairwise comparisons of age marginal means you tested in part d. Which if any intervals do not contain zero? How does this compare to your results from part d?

14. Manuck, Kaplan, Adams, and Clarkson (1988) report a series of studies investigating behavioral influences on coronary artery disease in monkeys. In one study, they examined the effects of a psychosocial manipulation (periodic group reorganization) on the development of atherosclerosis in animals of dominant or subordinate social status. (Manuck, S. B., Kaplan, J. R., Adams, M. R., & Clarkson, T. B. (1988). Studies of psychosocial influences on coronary artery atherogenesis in cynomolgus monkeys. *Health Psychology*, 7, 113–124.) In one condition ("unstable"), animals are redistributed every 1 to 3 months into new social groups. In the other condition ("stable"), animals remain in the same social group throughout the course of the investigation. The following data are modeled after data reported by Manuck and colleagues (1988):

Social Condition			
Stable		Unstable	
Social Status		Social Status	
Dominant	Subordinate	Dominant	Subordinate
.23	.34	.54	.39
.17	.62	.68	.23
.26	.54	.70	.27
.32	.30	.76	.49
.41	.51	.58	.53
.38	.44	.87	.42
.49	.41	.81	.34

The above scores reflect coronary intimal area measurements (in mm^2); higher scores indicate greater disease.
a. Test the significance of the condition main effect, the status main effect, and the condition-by-status interaction.

b. Based on your answer to part a, what follow-up tests should be performed here? Should cell means or marginal means be compared?

c. Test the simple effect of condition within each level of status, maintaining α_{FW} at .05 for condition effects.

d. Test the simple effect of status within each level of condition, maintaining α_{FW} at .05 for status effects.

e. Test the difference between the dominant unstable cell and the average of the other three cells.

f. What percentage of the between cells sum of squares does each of the contrasts you tested in parts c through e account for? What does this tell you about $R^2_{alerting}$ (defined in terms of $SS_{Between}$) for each of these contrasts?

g. Which contrast of all those you tested in Parts c–e has the property that its coefficients best match the pattern of cell means? What implications does this have for interpreting the results of this study? Explain your answer.

15. Brehm (1981) reports the results of a study investigating the extent to which children diminish or enhance the attractiveness of objects taken away from them. (Brehm, S. S. (1981). Psychological reactance and the attractiveness of unobtainable objects: Sex differences in children's responses to an elimination of freedom. *Sex Roles*, 7, 937–949.) Half of female and male elementary school children were led to believe that they would be asked to choose between two objects; the other half were told that they would receive one of two objects, but were not led to believe that they would be asked to make a choice between the objects. After each child ranked the attractiveness of 10 objects, each was given his or her third-ranked object and denied his or her fourth-ranked object. Children were then asked to rerank the attractiveness of the 10 objects. One dependent variable of interest was the new rank of the denied object, which was initially ranked fourth for each participant. The following data are modeled after the data reported by Brehm (1981; higher scores indicate less attractiveness on reranking):

	Females		Males	
	Choice	*No Choice*	*Choice*	*No Choice*
	4	5	4	5
	3	3	3	4
	6	4	3	4
	4	4	5	6
	7	3	6	3
	5	2	4	7
	4	5	4	6
	5	3	5	5
	5	6	3	6

a. Test the significance of the gender main effect, the choice-condition main effect, and the gender-by-choice-condition interaction.

b. Based on your answer to part a, what follow-up tests should be performed here? Should cell means or marginal means be compared?

c. Test the simple effect of gender within each choice condition. Perform each test at an alpha level of .05.

d. Is there a choice-condition effect for females? For males? Answer each question using an alpha level of .05.

e. Form a 95% confidence interval for the effect of choice for females. Also form the comparable interval for males. Does either of these intervals contain zero? How does this finding relate to the result of the hypothesis you tested in part d?

f. Formulate the two separate tests you performed in part d of the choice-condition effect for females and males as t tests. How does the difference between the two t values you obtain here relate to the F value for the interaction in part a? (Hint: See Equation 56.)

16. This exercise explores different approaches toward analyzing the data originally presented in Table 7.11. Recall that this study was motivated by a theory predicting that amnesic patients have a deficit in explicit memory but not implicit memory, whereas Huntington's patients will be just the opposite.

    (a) Suppose we decided to test this theory by examining simple effects. Specifically, test the simple effect of task for amnesic patients. Does your result appear to support or contradict the theory?
    (b) To what extent is the test you conducted in part a really a test of the relevant theory? Why might this simple-effects test be nonsignificant even if the theory is correct? (Hint: See Equation 55.)
    (c) Explain how testing an interaction contrast provides a more appropriate test of the underlying theory by avoiding the interpretational difficulties embedded in the simple effects test you performed in part a.

*17. For your master's thesis, you undertake a correlational study of personality types, environmental stress, and blood pressure. Twenty individuals are selected who are Type As and 20 who are Type Bs. Each participant's environment is classified as either high stress or low stress. (In reality, it might be preferable to regard stress as a continuous variable. We describe such an approach in Chapter 9, which covers analysis of covariance models.) Mean blood pressure and sample sizes for the four cells of the design are shown below:

		Stress	
Type		*High*	*Low*
	A	170	150
		$n = 14$	$n = 6$
	B	140	120
		$n = 6$	$n = 14$

    a. If you want to separate the stress effects from the personality-type effects, what kind of marginal means should you use? What are their numerical values here?
    b. Is the estimated magnitude of the mean blood pressure difference between personality types greater, different, or smaller when the effect of stress is taken into account than when it is not?

18. The psychology department at a hypothetical university has been accused of underpaying female faculty members. The following data represent salary (in thousands of dollars) for every assistant professor and associate professor in the department:

Assistant Professors		Associate Professors	
Females	*Males*	*Females*	*Males*
33	39	42	43
36	38	40	40
35	40	44	49
38	44	43	47
42			48
37			51
			48
			45

    a. Is the interaction of gender and rank (i.e., assistant versus associate) statistically significant? What does this result imply about the advisability of interpreting main effects?
    b. Write each of the null hypotheses for the gender main effect using Type I, Type II, and Type III sums of squares. Which of these hypotheses is (are) most pertinent to the question of possible sex discrimination? Why?

c. Test the gender main effect null hypotheses associated with Type I, Type II, and Type III sums of squares.

d. Form a 95% confidence interval for the contrast corresponding to the Type I sum of squares main effect for gender.

e. Form a 95% confidence interval for the contrast corresponding to the Type II sum of squares main effect for gender. Be certain to use coefficients that preserve the original metric.

f. Form a 95% confidence interval for the contrast corresponding to the Type III sum of squares main effect for gender.

g. How do the confidence intervals of Parts d–f compare to each other? What do they suggest about the extent to which females are underpaid?

h. Can you conclude beyond a reasonable doubt that the department is discriminating? Why or why not? (Hint: Can you unequivocally conclude that gender is a cause of pay in this department?)

19. During the 1980s, findings from the National Assessment of Educational Progress have shown that the size of average achievement differences between White and Black students has been steadily decreasing. In Jones, L. V. (1984). White-black achievement differences: The narrowing gap. *American Psychologist*, 39, 1207–1213, national data are reported suggesting that some of the existing difference between Blacks' and Whites' average mathematics achievement test scores may be due to differences in enrollment patterns in high school math courses. The following hypothetical data are modeled after the data reported by Jones (1984). Suppose that a group of high school seniors who have taken zero, one, two, or three high school math courses have received the following scores on a standardized math achievement test:

		Blacks				Whites	
	Number of Courses				*Number of Courses*		
0	1	2	3	0	1	2	3
45	51	61	71	42	61	63	77
34	59	73	82	51	48	68	68
51	53	55	70	39	46	78	79
54	49	77		55	63	60	66
40	60				55	73	85
46	65						80
	59						

a. Find the mean achievement test score for all Black students, irrespective of number of courses. Find the comparable mean for White students. How large is the difference between the means?

b. Find the unweighted marginal mean for Black students in the two-way design. Find the comparable mean for White students. How large is the difference between the means?

c. Why is the difference in part b much smaller than the difference in part a?

d. Test the significance of the race main effect allowing for a "number-of-courses" main effect and a "number of courses" by race interaction.

*20. A clinical psychologist conducted a study comparing cognitive-behavioral therapy (CBT) and client-centered therapy (CCT). Participants were randomly assigned to a therapy condition. The psychologist is also interested in gender differences, so gender is included as a second factor in the design. However, the resultant cell sizes are somewhat unequal (reflecting sampling error and/or attrition, presumed to be random here). The following cell sizes and cell means are obtained:

	Females	Males
CBT	$n_{11} = 6$	$n_{12} = 4$
	$\overline{Y}_{11} = 52$	$\overline{Y}_{12} = 46$
CCT	$n_{21} = 8$	$n_{22} = 5$
	$\overline{Y}_{21} = 48$	$\overline{Y}_{22} = 42$

Notice that the mean score for *CBT* is 4 points higher than the mean for *CCT* for both females and males. Thus, our single best estimate is that *CBT* is 4 points better than *CCT*. However, it may be important to know the margin of error in this estimate. The precision of the estimate is revealed by forming a confidence interval. We suppose throughout the remainder of this problem that mean square within $(MS_W) = 19$.

a. From Table 7.17, we can see that the Type III sum of squares for the therapy main effect here is based on a contrast of the form

$$\psi = .5\mu_{11} + .5\mu_{12} - .5\mu_{21} - .5\mu_{22}$$

Form a 95% confidence interval for ψ. Explain in one sentence what this interval means.

b. From Table 7.17, we can see that the Type II sum of squares for the therapy main effect is based on a contrast of the form

$$\psi = (n_{11}n_{21}/n_{+1})\mu_{11} + (n_{12}n_{22}/n_{+2})\mu_{12}$$

$$- (n_{11}n_{21}/n_{+1})\mu_{21} - (n_{12}n_{22}/n_{+2})\mu_{22}$$

Form a 95% confidence interval for the corresponding contrast that preserves the original metric of the dependent variable.

c. Which contrast can be estimated more precisely, the one corresponding to Type III sum of squares or the one corresponding to Type II sum of squares? What does this result suggest about which type of sum of square is preferable when there is no true interaction. (Notice in these data that there is literally no interaction, even in the sample.)

d. Some investigators would take an entirely different approach here. Instead of dealing with the nonorthogonal design, observations might be randomly deleted to produce 4 participants in each cell. Although the subsequent analysis is undoubtedly simpler, is there a cost associated with this approach? To answer this question, we again consider the precision of our estimated treatment effect. Suppose that after participants are randomly deleted, the data are as follows:

	Females	Males
CBT	$n_{11} = 4$	$n_{12} = 4$
	$\overline{Y}_{11} = 52$	$\overline{Y}_{12} = 46$
CCT	$n_{21} = 4$	$n_{22} = 4$
	$\overline{Y}_{21} = 48$	$\overline{Y}_{22} = 42$
	$MS_W = 19$	

Notice that the cell means and MS_W are unchanged from their previous values, which is what we would expect in the long run when observations are randomly deleted. The therapy main effect is represented by the following contrast:

$$\psi = .5\mu_{11} + .5\mu_{12} - .5\mu_{21} - .5\mu_{22}$$

Find a 95% confidence interval for this contrast.

e. How does the confidence interval you found in part d compare to the intervals you found in Parts a and b? What does this result imply about the wisdom of randomly deleting observations to obtain an equal-*n* design?

8

Higher Order Between-Subjects Factorial Designs

In Chapter 7, we extended the presentation of one-way designs in Chapter 3 to designs with two factors. In this chapter, we extend our presentation further, by considering designs with more than 2 factors. We focus the great majority of our attention on designs with 3 factors, because once we understand the extension from 2 to 3 factors, generalizations to designs with even more factors should be relatively straightforward.

We saw in Chapter 7 that consideration of factorial designs introduces the concept of interaction. With the addition of a third factor, we can generalize the concept of an interaction, because it may happen that all three factors interact. Alternatively, one or more pairs of the factors might interact, although the three factors together do not. The primary purpose of this chapter is to explore these various ways in which factors can interact with one another. Once we have developed the concepts, we consider their implications for analyzing data from higher order factorial designs.

THE 2 × 2 × 2 DESIGN

We begin our discussion of three-way (i.e., three-factor) designs by restricting ourselves to the case where each factor has only 2 levels, in which case we have a 2 × 2 × 2 design. The reason we begin with this design is that the concepts we need to develop are easier to illustrate when each factor has only 2 levels. Once we have introduced concepts in the 2 × 2 × 2 design, we will consider more general $a \times b \times c$ designs. We should also mention that we only consider equal-n designs until the end of the chapter, at which time we discuss the additional issues that arise in nonorthogonal designs.

To make our discussion more concrete, we continue with one of the examples we introduced in Chapter 7. Specifically, suppose that a psychologist wants to examine the effectiveness of various therapies for treating hypertension. In Chapter 7, we considered a 2 × 2 design. Each factor (biofeedback training and drug therapy) had two levels, because each form of therapy was either present or absent in the treatment combination presented to a particular subject. We now add a third factor, diet therapy, to the design. Specifically, we suppose that one half of all subjects receive individualized dietary plans, which they are to follow, whereas the remaining participants receive no dietary instructions. We further suppose that participants

354

TABLE 8.1
TABLE 8.1
HYPOTHETICAL POPULATION MEANS FOR A $2 \times 2 \times 2$ HYPERTENSION STUDY

	Diet Absent		Diet Present	
	Biofeedback Present	Biofeedback Absent	Biofeedback Present	Biofeedback Absent
Drug Present	180	205	170	190
Drug Absent	200	210	185	190

have been randomly and independently assigned to each of the eight possible combinations of biofeedback, drug therapy, and diet therapy.

At this point, we could consider how to obtain F tests for analyzing sample data. However, we defer this topic until we reach the general $a \times b \times c$ design, because the F tests for a three-way design follow exactly the same logic as F tests for a two-way design. The new feature of the three-way design involves the meaning of the effects being tested, which can be made clearest through population means instead of sample data. For this reason, we consider hypothetical population means that might occur in our hypertension study. Table 8.1 presents 8 population means, one for each cell of the $2 \times 2 \times 2$ design. Our interest here is to describe what effects exist in the population. Be certain you understand that tests of statistical significance are irrelevant here, because we are pretending that we have population data. Thus, any nonzero effect is a true effect, because these population means are not affected by sampling error. Also, the discussion for the moment is restricted to equal-n designs, so we need not concern ourselves with differences between weighted and unweighted means.

Recall from Chapter 7 that in a two-way factorial design there are 3 effects of interest: an A main effect, a B main effect, and an $A \times B$ interaction. Not surprisingly, there are additional effects in a three-way design. Kirk (1995, pp. 437–438) provides an especially clear explanation of how to determine all interactions as well as main effects in factorial designs where the factors are completely crossed (i.e, every level of each factor is combined with every level of each other factor in the design). If we label the third factor as C, the seven omnibus effects in a three-way design can be found by forming all possible combinations of treatment letters while maintaining the alphabetical order of the letters. With factors A, B, and C, following this procedure yields an A main effect, a B main effect, a C main effect, an $A \times B$ interaction, an $A \times C$ interaction, a $B \times C$ interaction, and an $A \times B \times C$ interaction. We typically refer to interactions involving 2 factors as "two-way interactions" or "first-order interactions." The ABC interaction is referred to as a three-way or second-order interaction. The same basic logic applies in higher order designs. For example, notice that in a 4-factor design, we would have 15 effects: 4 main effects (A, B, C, and D), 6 two-way interactions (AB, AC, AD, BC, BD, and CD), 4 three-way interactions (ABC, ABD, ACD, and BCD), and 1 four-way interaction ($ABCD$). We will briefly return to higher order designs with more than 3 factors near the end of the chapter, but for now our initial goal is to understand the meaning of each type of effect in a three-way design. We begin with the main effects, then the two-way interactions, and finally the three-way interaction.

The Meaning of Main Effects

We saw in Chapter 7 that a main effect in a two-way design involves averaging over the levels of the other factor. For example, the A main effect compares levels of A after we have averaged over levels of B. In a three-way design, the A main effect compares levels of A after averaging over levels of both B and C. In general, the main effect for a factor in any factorial design involves comparing the levels of that factor after having averaged over all other factors in the design. To consider this point in detail, consider the data in Table 8.1. We designate the biofeedback factor as A, the drug factor as B, and the diet factor as C. To determine whether a nonzero A main effect exists in the population, it is necessary to average over levels of B and C. The resultant marginal mean when biofeedback is present is given by

$$(180 + 200 + 170 + 185)/4$$

This equals 183.75 for our data. Similarly, the marginal mean for the biofeedback-absent condition is given by

$$(205 + 210 + 190 + 190)/4$$

This equals 198.75. The fact that these two marginal means are different implies the existence of a nonzero biofeedback main effect in the population. What this means is that the mean blood pressure score is different when biofeedback is present than when it is absent, when we average across the four combinations of drug and diet as well as across subjects.

The B and C main effects are found in exactly the same manner. Specifically, the B effect is found by averaging over levels of A and C, whereas the C effect is found by averaging over levels of A and B. Following the same logic used for A, you should be able to convince yourself that the main effects for B and C are also both nonzero in the population. (Exercises 3 and 4 at the end of the chapter ask the reader to perform the relevant calculations.)

The Meaning of Two-Way Interactions

Next, we consider the three different two-way interactions: $A \times B$, $A \times C$, and $B \times C$. Let's begin with the $A \times B$ interaction. We just saw that the main effect for a factor is found by first averaging over all other factors in the design and then comparing the resultant marginal means. The concept of a two-way interaction in a higher order factorial design (i.e., a design with 3 or more factors) follows the same general logic in that it is necessary to average over the factor(s) not involved in the interaction effect. For example, the $A \times B$ interaction averages over the levels of C. The result is a two-way table of population means, which is shown in Table 8.2 for our data. Each cell mean in this table is the average of two of the original cell means from Table 8.1. For example, the value of 175.0 in Table 8.2 is simply the average of 180 and 170, the means for diet absent and diet present, respectively, when both biofeedback and drug therapy are present.

We can determine whether an $A \times B$ interaction exists in these population data directly from Table 8.2. Recall that an $A \times B$ interaction in the two-way design meant that the A effect differed at different levels of B. The meaning of an $A \times B$ interaction is precisely the same in a three-way design, except that we must first average across levels of C, as we have already done in Table 8.2. From the table, we can see that the effect of a drug is 17.5 when biofeedback

TABLE 8.2
POPULATION MEANS FOR BIOFEEDBACK AND DRUG
FACTORS AVERAGING ACROSS LEVELS OF DIET

	Biofeedback Present	Biofeedback Absent
Drug Present	175.0	197.5
Drug Absent	192.5	200.0

TABLE 8.3
POPULATION MEANS FOR DRUG AND DIET
FACTORS AVERAGING ACROSS BIOFEEDBACK

	Diet Absent	Diet Present
Drug Present	192.5	180.0
Drug Absent	205.0	187.5

TABLE 8.4
POPULATION MEANS FOR BIOFEEDBACK AND DIET
FACTORS AVERAGING ACROSS LEVELS OF DRUG FACTOR

	Diet Absent	Diet Present
Biofeedback Present	190.0	177.5
Biofeedback Absent	207.5	190.0

is present, but the effect of a drug is only 2.5 when biofeedback is absent. Thus, the magnitude of the drug effect differs at different levels of biofeedback, implying an interaction. Thus, there is a two-way Drug × Biofeedback interaction in this population. Tables 8.3 and 8.4 show the population means used to assess the Drug × Diet and Biofeedback × Diet interactions, respectively. By the same logic used in examining Tables 8.2, 8.3, and 8.4 show that there are also nonzero Drug × Diet and Biofeedback × Diet interactions in this population.

The major point to be made so far is that the logic of main effects and two-way interactions in a three-way design is basically the same as in a two-way design. The only difference is that there is an additional factor to average across in the three-way design. This brings us to the one new type of effect in a three-way design, namely the three-way interaction.

The Meaning of the Three-Way Interaction

Before considering the meaning of a three-way interaction, let's review the meaning of a two-way interaction in a two-way design. An $A \times B$ interaction in a two-way design-means that the A effect differs at different levels of B or, equivalently, that the B effect differs at different levels of A. How could we extend this logic to apply to an $A \times B \times C$ interaction in a three-way design? An $A \times B \times C$ interaction means that the two-way $A \times B$ effect differs at different levels of C, just as an $A \times B$ interaction means that the A effect differs at different levels of B.

To better understand the meaning of a three-way interaction, let's return to our hypothetical population data. To assess the existence of a Drug × Biofeedback × Diet interaction, we must consider whether the Drug × Biofeedback interaction is the same when the diet is absent as when it is present. Table 8.5 presents 2 sets of drug and biofeedback means, first when the diet is absent and second when the diet is present. The 2 × 2 table when the diet is absent shows that the drug effect is 20 when biofeedback is present, but the drug effect when biofeedback is absent is only 5. Thus, there is a two-way Drug × Biofeedback interaction when the diet is absent, because the drug effect is 15 units larger when biofeedback is present than when it is absent. Let's now consider the 2 × 2 table of population means when the diet is present. This table shows that the drug effect is 15 when biofeedback is present, but the drug effect when biofeedback is absent is 0. Thus, there is a two-way Drug × Biofeedback interaction when the diet is present, because the drug effect is 15 units larger when biofeedback is present

TABLE 8.5
POPULATION MEANS FOR DRUG AND BIOFEEDBACK COMBINATIONS,
SEPARATELY BY DIET

	Diet Absent		Diet Present	
	Biofeedback Present	Biofeedback Absent	Biofeedback Present	Biofeedback Absent
Drug Present	180	205	170	190
Drug Absent	200	210	185	190
Drug Effect	20	5	15	0
Difference in Drug Effect	15		15	

TABLE 8.6
POPULATION MEANS FOR DRUG AND DIET COMBINATIONS,
SEPARATELY BY LEVELS OF BIOFEEDBACK

Biofeedback Present

	Diet Absent	Diet Present	Diet Effect	Difference in Diet Effect
Drug Present	180	170	10	5
Drug Absent	200	185	15	
Drug Effect	20	15		
Difference in Drug Effect	5			

Biofeedback Absent

	Diet Absent	Diet Present	Diet Effect	Difference in Diet Effect
Drug Present	205	190	15	5
Drug Absent	210	190	20	
Drug Effect	5	0		
Difference in Drug Effect	5			

than when it is absent. Notice that this difference of 15 units for the drug effect is the same when diet is present as when diet is absent. This equality implies that the two-way Drug × Biofeedback interaction is the same at both levels of the diet factor. Because the magnitude of the two-way interaction is the same at every level of the third factor, there is no three-way interaction in this population. In other words, the null hypothesis of no three-way interaction is true for these data.

So far, we have conceptualized the three-way Drug × Biofeedback × Diet interaction in terms of the consistency of the magnitude of the Drug × Biofeedback interaction at the various levels of diet. It turns out that there are two other conceptualizations that are mathematically equivalent to this one. First, we could consider the consistency of the magnitude of the two-way Drug × Diet interaction at the various levels of the Biofeedback factor. Table 8.6 shows the population means of Table 8.1 from this perspective. We can see from Table 8.6 that the difference in the drug effect for the diet absent versus present conditions is 5 units when biofeedback is present. However, the difference in the drug effect for diet absent versus present is also 5 units when biofeedback is absent. Thus, the magnitude of the Drug × Diet interaction

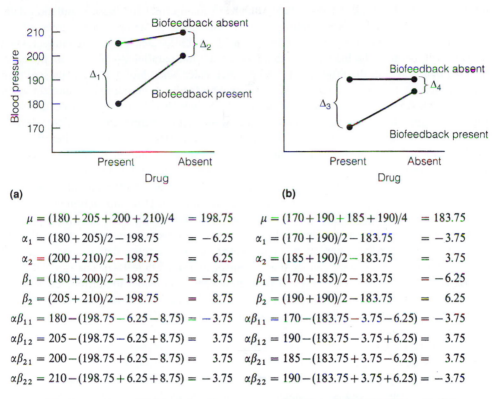

$$\mu = (180 + 205 + 200 + 210)/4 = 198.75 \qquad \mu = (170 + 190 + 185 + 190)/4 = 183.75$$

$$\alpha_1 = (180 + 205)/2 - 198.75 = -6.25 \qquad \alpha_1 = (170 + 190)/2 - 183.75 = -3.75$$

$$\alpha_2 = (200 + 210)/2 - 198.75 = 6.25 \qquad \alpha_2 = (185 + 190)/2 - 183.75 = 3.75$$

$$\beta_1 = (180 + 200)/2 - 198.75 = -8.75 \qquad \beta_1 = (170 + 185)/2 - 183.75 = -6.25$$

$$\beta_2 = (205 + 210)/2 - 198.75 = 8.75 \qquad \beta_2 = (190 + 190)/2 - 183.75 = 6.25$$

$$\alpha\beta_{11} = 180 - (198.75 - 6.25 - 8.75) = -3.75 \qquad \alpha\beta_{11} = 170 - (183.75 - 3.75 - 6.25) = -3.75$$

$$\alpha\beta_{12} = 205 - (198.75 - 6.25 + 8.75) = 3.75 \qquad \alpha\beta_{12} = 190 - (183.75 - 3.75 + 6.25) = 3.75$$

$$\alpha\beta_{21} = 200 - (198.75 + 6.25 - 8.75) = 3.75 \qquad \alpha\beta_{21} = 185 - (183.75 + 3.75 - 6.25) = 3.75$$

$$\alpha\beta_{22} = 210 - (198.75 + 6.25 + 8.75) = -3.75 \qquad \alpha\beta_{22} = 190 - (183.75 + 3.75 + 6.25) = -3.75$$

FIG. 8.1. Plots of Table 8.1 cell means as a function of diet condition: (a) diet absent and (b) diet present.

is the same at both levels of the Biofeedback factor, implying that the three-way interaction is zero. Alternatively, Table 8.6 also shows that the difference in the diet effect when the drug is present versus absent is 5 units, both when biofeedback is present and when it is absent. This equality also simply affirms that the two-way Drug × Diet interaction is the same at both levels of biofeedback. Thus, we reach the same conclusion by examining the consistency of the two-way Drug × Diet interactions at each level of biofeedback as we did by examining the consistency of the two-way Drug × Biofeedback interactions at each level of the diet factor. Second, yet another equivalent conceptualization is to consider the consistency of the two-way Biofeedback × Diet interactions at each level of the drug factor. Instead of presenting a table of cell means to represent this conceptualization, we leave this as an exercise for the reader. Specifically, Exercise 5 at the end of the chapter asks whether the Biofeedback × Diet interaction is consistent at both levels of the drug factor for the data in Table 8.1.

Graphical Depiction

As we saw in the two-way design (Chapter 7), yet another way of viewing main effects and interactions is to graph cell means. Figure 8.1 provides a graphical depiction of the population means given earlier in Table 8.1. Figure 8.1a plots cell means for biofeedback and drug combinations when diet is absent. Figure 8.1b presents corresponding cell means when diet is present. This figure reveals a number of important aspects of the data. First, if we were to consider main effects here (thereby averaging over all other factors), blood pressure values are lower when biofeedback is present than when it is absent. The same holds true for drug and diet as well. Thus, all 3 factors have a nonzero main effect for these population data. However, we must qualify interpretations of main effects due to the presence of interactions. In particular, we can tell from the plot in Figure 8.1a that biofeedback and drug interact when diet is absent, because the lines shown in the figure are not parallel. As we saw in Table 8.5 when the diet is absent, the drug effect is 15 points greater when biofeedback is present than when it is absent. The plot in Figure 8.1b shows that biofeedback and drug also interact when diet is present. A three-way interaction is determined by whether the two-way biofeedback by drug interaction is the same when diet is absent as when diet is present. In a $2 \times 2 \times 2$ design, the three-way interaction involves a comparison of 4 simple effects with one another. We have inserted 4 brackets in Figure 8.1 to illustrate visually the 4 simple effects in question here. Notice that Δ_1 represents the effect of biofeedback when drug is present and diet is absent. Similarly, Δ_2 represents the effect of biofeedback when drug is absent and diet is absent. The difference between Δ_1 and Δ_2 is literally the two-way Biofeedback $\times$ Drug interaction when diet is absent. The difference between Δ_3 and Δ_4 is the same two-way interaction when diet is present. The three-way interaction asks whether these 2 two-way interactions have the same value. In other words, the three-way interaction is represented by the difference between $\Delta_1 - \Delta_2$ and $\Delta_3 - \Delta_4$. From Figure 8.1a we can see that Δ_1 equals 25 (i.e., $205 - 180$). The value of Δ_2 is 10 (i.e., $210 - 200$). Thus, $\Delta_1 - \Delta_2 = 15$. We now need to consider the difference between Δ_3 and Δ_4. From Figure 8.1b we can see that $\Delta_3 = 20$ (i.e., $190 - 170$). Similarly, $\Delta_4 = 5$ (i.e., $190 - 185$). Thus, the difference between Δ_3 and Δ_4 is 15. However, we have just shown that both $\Delta_1 - \Delta_2$ and $\Delta_3 - \Delta_4$ equal 15. The fact that both differences equal the same value is precisely what it means to say that there is no three-way interaction in the population. Although the plot in Figure 8.1a is not identical to the plot in Figure 8.1b (even moving the plots upward or downward), there is nevertheless an underlying equivalence. The form of nonparallelism is the same in both cases, because the extent to which the biofeedback effect is larger when the drug is present than when the drug is absent is 15 in both plots (i.e., $25 - 10 = 20 - 5$). Thus, Figure 8.1 implies the lack of a three-way interaction for these population data.

The correspondence between the two plots is formalized in the calculations of parameter values shown underneath each plot. The parameters shown here are not the parameters of the three-way full model, but instead are the parameters corresponding to two separate two-way full models, one when the diet is absent and one when the diet is present. As such, the values have been calculated using Equations 7.9–7.12. What is important for our purposes is to notice that each $\alpha\beta$ parameter has the same value when diet is absent as when diet is present. Formally, this implies that the Biofeedback $\times$ Drug interaction when diet is absent is equivalent to the Biofeedback $\times$ Drug interaction when diet is present. Thus, there is no three-way interaction in these data. Finally, we should add that, just as we saw in Chapter 7 for the two-way design, there is more than one way to plot the cell means in a three-way design. For example, we might plot means for biofeedback absent in Figure 8.1a and means for biofeedback present in Figure 8.1b, with diet present versus absent on the x-axis. Some effects are easier to see with certain plots than with others, so how we decide to plot the data should be determined largely by which effects we want to feature most clearly.

Notice that the null hypothesis for the three-way interaction requires that the magnitude of the two-way $A \times B$ effect at C_1 (the first level of C) must exactly equal the magnitude of the two-way effect at all other levels of C. To illustrate this point, consider the population means shown in Table 8.7. These data show a different possible configuration of population means that might exist in our hypothetical study. Specifically, the only change from Table 8.5 is that the mean blood pressure when drug, biofeedback, and diet are all present is now presumed to be 175 instead of 170, as in Table 8.5. Naturally, the difference in the drug effect is still 15 when diet is absent. However, the difference in the drug effect when diet is present is now only

TABLE 8.7
ALTERNATE POPULATION MEANS FOR DRUG AND BIOFEEDBACK
COMBINATIONS, SEPARATELY BY DIET

	Diet Absent		Diet Present	
	Biofeedback Present	Biofeedback Absent	Biofeedback Present	Biofeedback Absent
Drug Present	180	205	175	190
Drug Absent	200	210	185	190
Drug Effect	20	5	10	0
Difference in Drug Effect	15		10	

10 units, because the drug effect when biofeedback and diet are present is 10 in Table 8.7. For these population means, there is a nonzero three-way Drug × Biofeedback × Diet interaction. The reason is that, as we have seen, the magnitude of the Drug × Biofeedback interaction is not the same when diet is present as when it is absent. Although it is true for both levels of diet that the drug is more effective when biofeedback is present than when it is absent, the exact magnitude of the difference in the drug effect is not the same when diet is present as when it is absent. Specifically, for the data of Table 8.7, there is a stronger two-way Drug × Biofeedback interaction when the diet is absent than when the diet is present. This inequality implies the existence of a three-way Drug × Biofeedback × Diet interaction for the population means shown in Table 8.7.

Further Consideration of the Three-Way Interaction

We will present two additional examples to solidify your understanding of the three-way interaction and to highlight its importance in interpreting effects in three-way designs. We will present two new examples of cell means as well. The data are unrelated to blood pressure data, but we will continue to assume in each case that the means available to us are population means, so that we do not have to deal with the complication of figuring out which differences are real and which reflect only sampling error.

Consider the new cell means shown in Figure 8.2. Figure 8.2a shows an interaction plot for A and B at the first level of C. Figure 8.2b shows the comparable plot at the second level of C. Do these plots suggest the existence of a three-way interaction? Recall that a three-way interaction exists when the $A \times B$ interaction at the first level of C is different from the $A \times B$ interaction at the second level of C. In these data, we can easily tell that A and B interact at the first level of C, because the lines of the interaction plot are clearly not parallel. However, it is also clear that there is no interaction between A and B at the second level of C, because the lines in Figure 8.2b are indeed parallel. The existence of a two-way $A \times B$ interaction at C_1, together with the lack of a two-way $A \times B$ interaction at C_2, immediately implies that the two-way $A \times B$ interaction at C_1 cannot be equal to the comparable $A \times B$ interaction at C_2. However, this is exactly what it means to have a three-way interaction.

How does the presence of a three-way interaction affect our interpretation of these data? We will present a detailed answer to this question in the context of the general $A \times B \times C$ design, but we will briefly preview the more general answer here. For example, suppose we want to know whether A and B interact in the Figure 8.2 data. We might be tempted to create an interaction plot for A and B averaging over C, because this corresponds to the meaning of the two-way interaction in the three-way design. Figure 8.3 shows this plot for our data.

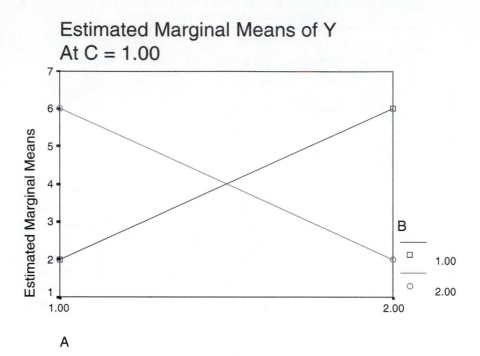

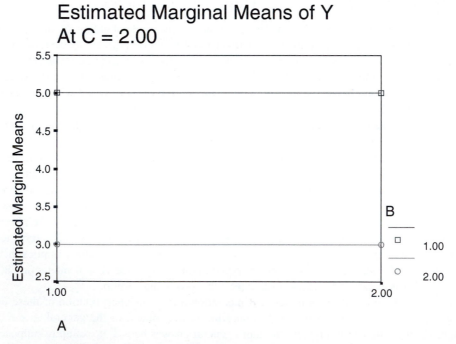

FIG. 8.2. Interaction plots for *A* and *B* at (a) C_1 and (b) C_2.

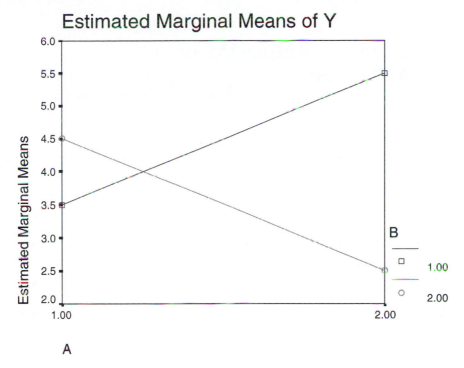

FIG. 8.3.   Interaction plot for A and B averaging over levels of C.

The fact that the lines in this plot cross tells us that we have a two-way $A \times B$ interaction. Although this is a correct statement mathematically, it may be misleading to offer this interpretation of our data. As Figure 8.2b shows, A and B do not interact at the second level of C. Nevertheless, the interaction that does exist at the first level of C (as shown in Figure 8.2a), when averaged with the lack of interaction at the second level of C, yields an interaction between A and B averaging over C. Even though this average interaction is weaker than the interaction at C_1 by itself, the average interaction is nonzero. Instead of stating that A and B interact and leaving it at that, it probably is better to offer an interpretation that makes it clear that A and B do interact at C_1 but do not interact at C_2. More generally, the existence of a three-way interaction typically qualifies our interpretation of all lower order effects, so that we will usually want to interpret various types of simple effects instead of average effects.

The previous example showed that it is possible to have a nonzero two-way $A \times B$ interaction even if the two-way $A \times B$ interaction is literally zero at a specific level of C. We will now consider what in some respects is the opposite question. Is it possible to have no two-way $A \times B$ interaction even if the two-way $A \times B$ interaction is nonzero at a specific level of C? To answer this question, begin by examining the interaction plots shown in Figures 8.4a and 8.4b. We need to be clear from the outset that although we are still considering a $2 \times 2 \times 2$ design, these are different data unrelated to those we just considered in Figures 8.2 and 8.3.

We can see from Figure 8.4a that A and B interact at the first level of C, because the lines in the interaction plot are clearly not parallel. Similarly, Figure 8.4b shows that there is also an $A \times B$ interaction at the second level of C. What would we find if we were to examine the $A \times B$ interaction averaging over levels of C? Figure 8.5 provides the graphical answer to this question. Your first reaction to this figure may be that something is missing, because there is only one line. There is only one line, because the line for B_1 is identical to the line for B_2

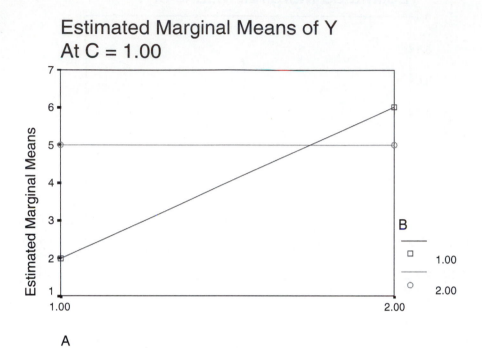

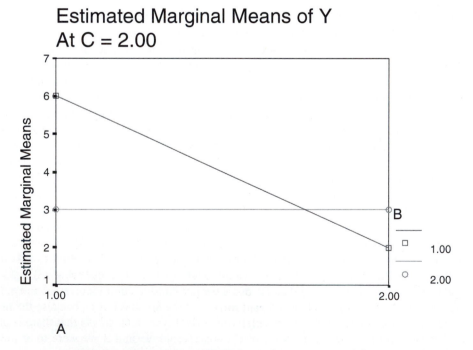

FIG. 8.4.   Interaction plots for *A* and *B* at (a) C_1 and (b) C_2.

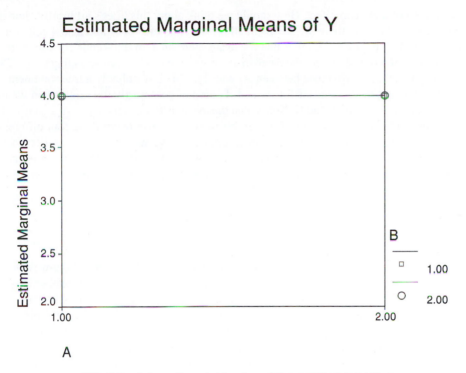

FIG. 8.5.   Interaction plot for A and B averaging over C.

for these cell means. This happens because when we average over C in Figures 8.4a and 8.4b, the resultant four cell means in the 2×2 $A \times B$ design all equal 4. Thus, after we average over C, there are no effects whatsoever for A or B. In this sense, there is no A main effect, no B main effect, and no $A \times B$ interaction. Would we then want to infer that A and B have no effect on Y? To think further about how we might want to answer this question, let's first consider the two-way $A \times B$ interaction.

Because there is only one line in the Figure 8.5 interaction plot, the lines for B_1 and B_2 must be parallel (because these two potentially different lines are in fact the same line here), so there is no $A \times B$ interaction when we average over C. Would we want to interpret these data as suggesting that A and B do not interact? Although this is a correct statement mathematically in the sense of the average $A \times B$ interaction, it obscures the reality that A and B do interact at both levels of C. It's just that in this particular case, the $A \times B$ interaction at C_1 exactly cancels the $A \times B$ interaction at C_2. Although this may be an interesting phenomenon in its own right, we probably do not want our ultimate interpretation of these data to be that A and B do not interact. Thus, once again, we see that the existence of a three-way $A \times B \times C$ interaction typically alters any interpretation we might offer for the $A \times B$ two-way interaction. We should emphasize that this is true whether the two-way interaction is statistically significant or nonsignificant. Figures 8.2 and 8.3 show that a three-way interaction means that we need to be careful interpreting statistically significant two-way interactions, because they may exist at some but not all levels. On the other hand, Figures 8.4 and 8.5 show that a three-way interaction means that we need to be careful interpreting a nonsignificant two-way interaction, because the individual two-way interactions at every level of the third factor may be nonzero.

Figures 8.4 and 8.5 show that we must also be careful interpreting main effects in the presence of a three-way interaction. Figure 8.5 shows that after we average over C, there is neither an A nor a B main effect. How should we think about this? Let's arbitrarily choose A as our focus. Notice that there are 4 cells in all for the first level of A and also 4 cells for the second level of A. Figure 8.5 implies that the mean score on Y in the 4 cells corresponding to A_1 has a value of 4.0, and so does the mean in the remaining 4 cells corresponding to A_2. Thus, on average, there is no difference between A_1 and A_2. This is absolutely a true statement, but it obscures the fact that the means for A_1 and A_2 are not necessarily the same when we look within any combination of B and C. Notice that the mean difference for $A_1 - A_2$ equals -4, 0, 4, and 0 for B_1C_1, B_2C_1, B_1C_2, and B_2C_2, respectively. The average of these four differences is in fact 0, which is why there is no A main effect, but we would not necessarily want to conclude that there is no difference whatsoever between A_1 and A_2. Thus, the presence of a three-way interaction typically implies that we need to qualify our interpretation of main effects as well as two-way interactions.

Summary of Meaning of Effects

It may be helpful at this point to summarize the meaning of effects in a three-way design. Table 8.8 describes the meaning of the three main effects, the three two-way interactions, and the single three-way interaction in an $A \times B \times C$ design. It is important to understand that the seven effects described in Table 8.8 are logically independent of each other. In other words, the presence or absence of any particular effect in the population has no particular implications for the presence or absence of any other effect. In other words, any possible combination of the seven effects can conceivably exist in a population. However, as in the two-way design, our interpretation of certain effects may be colored by the presence or absence of other effects in our data. For example, we might refrain from interpreting a statistically significant A main effect if we also obtain a significant $A \times B$ interaction. We deal further with such interpretational issues later in the chapter.

TABLE 8.8
MEANING OF EFFECTS IN A THREE-WAY $A \times B \times C$ DESIGN

	Meaning
Main Effects	
A	Comparison of marginal means of A factor, averaging over levels of B and C
B	Comparison of marginal means of B factor, averaging over levels of A and C
C	Comparison of marginal means of C factor, averaging over levels of A and B
Two-Way Interactions	
A × B	Examines whether the A effect is the same at every level of B, averaging over levels of C (equivalently, examines whether the B effect is the same at every level of A, averaging over levels of C)
A × C	Examines whether the A effect is the same at every level of C, averaging over levels of B (equivalently, examines whether the C effect is the same at every level of A, averaging over levels of B)
B × C	Examines whether the B effect is the same at every level of C, averaging over levels of A (equivalently, examines whether the C effect is the same at every level of B, averaging over levels of A)
Three-Way Interaction	
A × B × C	Examines whether the two-way A × B interaction is the same at every level of C (equivalently, examines whether the two-way A × C interaction is the same at every level of B; equivalently, examines whether the two-way B × C interaction is the same at every level of A)

Although our discussion to this point has been limited to the special case of a $2 \times 2 \times 2$ design, it turns out that the concepts generalize directly to the more general $A \times B \times C$ design. For example, the meaning of effects depicted in Table 8.8 is equally appropriate for the $A \times B \times C$ design. The only difference is that in the $2 \times 2 \times 2$ design, each effect accounts for only 1 df, whereas in the $A \times B \times C$ design, effects generally account for more than 1 df.

THE GENERAL $A \times B \times C$ DESIGN

We examine the general case of an $A \times B \times C$ design using model comparisons. For the moment, we restrict ourselves to the situation where the number of participants is the same in each cell of the design. Later in the chapter, we consider the additional complications that arise with unequal n.

The Full Model

As in the two-factor design, the full model for the three-factor design can be written in either of two equivalent ways. First, the full model can be written as

$$Y_{ijkl} = \mu_{jkl} + \varepsilon_{ijkl} \tag{1}$$

where Y_{ijkl} represents the score on the dependent variable of the ith subject at the jth level of A, the kth level of B, and the lth level of C; μ_{jkl} is the population cell mean of Y for level j of A, level k of B, and level l of C; and ε_{ijkl} is an error term associated with the ith subject at level j of A, level k of B, and level l of C. Notice that the value of the i subscript ranges from 1 to n, the value of j ranges from 1 to a, the value of k ranges from 1 to b, and the value of l ranges from 1 to c. Thus, the full model reflects an attempt to understand the score of all n subjects within every cell of the $A \times B \times C$ design. Further, notice that this full model is a cell means model because, like the full models we have considered in previous chapters, it states that any subject's score is dependent only on the cell of the design the participant appears in plus an error component.

Although the form of the full model given in Equation 1 is perfectly valid, it is convenient to rewrite it in another form, just as we did for the one-way and two-way designs of Chapters 3 and 7, respectively. This alternate form of the full model is given by

$$Y_{ijkl} = \mu + \alpha_j + \beta_k + \gamma_l + (\alpha\beta)_{jk} + (\alpha\gamma)_{jl} + (\beta\gamma)_{kl} + (\alpha\beta\gamma)_{jkl} + \varepsilon_{ijkl} \tag{2}$$

where Y_{ijkl} represents the score on the dependent variable of the ith subject at the jth level of A, the kth level of B, and the lth level of C; μ is the grand mean parameter; α_j is the effect associated with the jth level of A; β_k is the effect associated with the kth level of B; γ_l is the effect associated with the lth level of C; $(\alpha\beta)_{jk}$ is the effect of the interaction of the jth level of A and the kth level of B; $(\alpha\gamma)_{jl}$ is the effect of the interaction of the jth level of A and the lth level of C; $(\beta\gamma)_{kl}$ is the effect of the interaction of the kth level of B and the lth level of C; $(\alpha\beta\gamma)_{jkl}$ is the effect of the three-way interaction of the jth level of A, the kth level of B, and the lth level of C; and ε_{ijkl} is the error for the ith participant at level j of A, level k of B, and level l of C.

The meaning of the parameters in the full model of Equation 2 is very similar to the meaning of parameters in the two-way design of Chapter 7. (For a review, see Equations 7.6–7.12.) Table 8.9 shows the algebraic representation of these population parameters for the

TABLE 8.9
ALGEBRAIC EXPRESSIONS FOR PARAMETERS IN A FULL MODEL
OF THREE-WAY A × B × C DESIGN

Parameter	Expression

$$\mu = \sum_{j=1}^{a} \sum_{k=1}^{b} \sum_{l=1}^{c} \mu_{jkl}/abc$$

$$\alpha_j = \mu_{j..} - \mu$$

$$\beta_k = \mu_{.k.} - \mu$$

$$\gamma_l = \mu_{..l} - \mu$$

$$(\alpha\beta)_{jk} = \mu_{jk.} - (\mu + \alpha_j + \beta_k)$$

$$(\alpha\gamma)_{jl} = \mu_{j.l} - (\mu + \alpha_j + \gamma_l)$$

$$(\beta\gamma)_{kl} = \mu_{.kl} - (\mu + \beta_k + \gamma_l)$$

$$(\alpha\beta\gamma)_{jkl} = \mu_{jkl} - [\mu + \alpha_j + \beta_k + \gamma_l + (\alpha\beta)_{jk} + (\alpha\gamma)_{jl} + (\beta\gamma)_{kl}]$$

model in Equation 2. It may be helpful to compare the algebraic representation of parameters in Table 8.9 to the verbal representation of effects shown earlier in Table 8.8, because these two tables are essentially two different ways of conveying the same information.

As shown in Tables 8.8 and 8.9, as well as in Equation 2, there are 7 effects in the full model, each of which we are typically interested in testing. In other words, there are 7 different null hypotheses we may want to test. Each of these null hypotheses leads to a restricted model, that is, a restricted version of the full model depicted in Equation 2. We use our usual F test to compare the full and restricted models to one another:

$$F = \frac{(E_R - E_F)/(df_R - df_F)}{E_F/df_F} \tag{3}$$

As this point, we have two tasks confronting us. First, we must identify a restricted model for each null hypothesis we wish to test. Second, we must calculate the sum of squared errors and degrees of freedom for both the full and the restricted models.

Formulation of Restricted Models

The task of identifying appropriate restricted models turns out to be trivial. To test one of the 7 null hypotheses of interest, a restricted model is formed simply by omitting from the full model those parameters that equal zero according to the null hypothesis. For example, suppose that we want to test the A main effect. If the null hypothesis is true that there is no A main effect in the population, then every α_j parameter in the full model equals zero. Thus, a restricted model for testing the A main effect is obtained by omitting the α_j parameters from the full model, in which case we are left with a model of the form

$$Y_{ijkl} = \mu + \beta_k + \gamma_l + (\alpha\beta)_{jk} + (\alpha\gamma)_{jl} + (\beta\gamma)_{kl} + (\alpha\beta\gamma)_{jkl} + \varepsilon_{ijkl}$$

Table 8.10 shows the restricted models used to test each of the 7 null hypotheses of interest. Notice that each of these restricted models has omitted the parameters of one effect, namely the effect to be tested.

The second task is to compute the sum of squared errors and degrees of freedom for the full model and for the 7 models shown in Table 8.10. The sum of squared errors for the full model (E_F) can as usual be found most easily by expressing the full model in the form of Equation 1:

$$Y_{ijkl} = \mu_{jkl} + \varepsilon_{ijkl} \tag{1, repeated}$$

TABLE 8.10

RESTRICTED MODELS FOR TESTING MAIN EFFECTS, TWO-WAY INTERACTIONS,
AND THREE-WAY INTERACTION IN A THREE-WAY A × B × C DESIGN

Effect to Be Tested	Restricted Model
A	$Y_{ijkl} = \mu + \beta_k + \gamma_l + (\alpha\beta)_{jk} + (\alpha\gamma)_{jl} + (\beta\gamma)_{kl} + (\alpha\beta\gamma)_{jkl} + \varepsilon_{ijkl}$
B	$Y_{ijkl} = \mu + \alpha_j + \gamma_l + (\alpha\beta)_{jk} + (\alpha\gamma)_{jl} + (\beta\gamma)_{kl} + (\alpha\beta\gamma)_{jkl} + \varepsilon_{ijkl}$
C	$Y_{ijkl} = \mu + \alpha_j + \beta_k + (\alpha\beta)_{jk} + (\alpha\gamma)_{jl} + (\beta\gamma)_{kl} + (\alpha\beta\gamma)_{jkl} + \varepsilon_{ijkl}$
A × B	$Y_{ijkl} = \mu + \alpha_j + \beta_k + \gamma_l + (\alpha\gamma)_{jl} + (\beta\gamma)_{kl} + (\alpha\beta\gamma)_{jkl} + \varepsilon_{ijkl}$
A × C	$Y_{ijkl} = \mu + \alpha_j + \beta_k + \gamma_l + (\alpha\beta)_{jk} + (\beta\gamma)_{kl} + (\alpha\beta\gamma)_{jkl} + \varepsilon_{ijkl}$
B × C	$Y_{ijkl} = \mu + \alpha_j + \beta_k + \gamma_l + (\alpha\beta)_{jk} + (\alpha\gamma)_{jl} + (\alpha\beta\gamma)_{jkl} + \varepsilon_{ijkl}$
A × B × C	$Y_{ijkl} = \mu + \alpha_j + \beta_k + \gamma_l + (\alpha\beta)_{jk} + (\alpha\gamma)_{jl} + (\beta\gamma)_{kl} + \varepsilon_{ijkl}$

As in the other designs we have considered, E_F is defined to be

$$E_F = \sum_{j=1}^{a}\sum_{k=1}^{b}\sum_{l=1}^{c}\sum_{i=1}^{n}\left[Y_{ijkl} - \hat{Y}_{ijkl}(F)\right]^2$$

where $\hat{Y}_{ijkl}(F)$ is a subject's predicted score when the parameters of the model are estimated using least squares. Notice that the full model has as many parameters as there are cells in the design, namely $a \times b \times c$. In fact, each parameter is simply the population mean of a cell. Not surprisingly, the least-squares estimate of a population mean is, as before, the corresponding sample mean. Thus, the full model predicts a subject's score to be the sample mean of that subject's cell. In terms of symbols, this implies that

$$\hat{Y}_{ijkl}(F) = \overline{Y}_{jkl}$$

Thus, the sum of squared errors is given by

$$E_F = \sum_{j=1}^{a}\sum_{k=1}^{b}\sum_{l=1}^{c}\sum_{i=1}^{n}(Y_{ijkl} - \overline{Y}_{jkl})^2 \tag{4}$$

which is the within-cell sum of squares. Thus, E_F is an index of the extent to which scores vary within each cell in the design.

To obtain the degrees of freedom of the full model, we must calculate the number of independent parameters included in the model. We just saw that there is one parameter for each cell in the design, so there are abc independent parameters in the model.[1] As in earlier chapters, the ratio E_F/df_F, which forms the denominator of the F statistic, is referred to as the mean square within and is often written as MS_W. As in previous designs, MS_W is simply an average within-group variance. Specifically, it can be shown that in the three-way design with equal n, MS_W is given by

$$MS_W = \sum_{j=1}^{a}\sum_{k=1}^{b}\sum_{l=1}^{c} s_{jkl}^2 / abc \tag{5}$$

where s_{jkl}^2 is the variance of scores within the cell represented by the jkl combination of A, B, and C. Thus, the error term for testing an effect in the three-way design simply reflects an average within-group variance.

To complete the F test for an effect, we must consider E_R and df_R, the sum of squared errors and degrees of freedom for the relevant restricted model. Although it is useful conceptually to realize that the sum of squared errors for a restricted model can be calculated by using least squares to estimate the parameters of the model and then finding the squared error for each subject, there is a simpler approach in practice. It turns out that after some tedious algebra similar to that demonstrated for the two-way design in Chapter 7, it is possible to write general expressions for the sums of squares attributable to each effect in the three-way design.

Table 8.11 shows two equivalent expressions for the sum of squares of each of the seven effects to be tested. The general expressions demonstrate that the sum of squares for any effect equals the sum of squared parameter estimates for that effect in the full model, where the sum is computed across all $abcn$ observations. That this is true should come as no surprise, because we have previously seen the same relationship in Chapter 3 for the one-way design and in Chapter 7 for the two-way design. The specific expressions show the sum of squares for each effect in terms of sample means instead of estimated parameters. However, the general and specific expressions for an effect are equivalent, because parameter estimates are simply a function of sample means. For example, consider the A main effect. Its general expression is given by

$$SS_A = \sum_{j=1}^{a}\sum_{k=1}^{b}\sum_{l=1}^{c}\sum_{i=1}^{n} \hat{\alpha}_j^2 \tag{6}$$

Where does the specific expression come from? We know from Table 8.9 that the population α_j effect is defined as

$$\alpha_j = \mu_{j..} - \mu \tag{7}$$

The estimated α_j effect is obtained by estimating the population means on the right-hand side of Equation 7 by their respective sample means, which leads to

$$\hat{\alpha}_j = \overline{Y}_{j..} - \overline{Y}_{...}$$

(The estimated parameter values for the other effects shown in Table 8.11 are similarly obtained by estimating population values in Table 8.9 with corresponding sample means.) Thus, Equation 6 is equivalent to

$$SS_A = \sum_{j=1}^{a}\sum_{k=1}^{b}\sum_{l=1}^{c}\sum_{i=1}^{n} (\overline{Y}_{j..} - \overline{Y}_{...})^2 \tag{8}$$

Because $(\overline{Y}_{j..} - \overline{Y}_{...})^2$ does not contain an i, k, or l subscript, it is a constant for all levels of i (participants), k (the B factor), and l (the C factor). We know that there are n participants, b levels of B, and c levels of C, so that Equation 8 can be written as

$$SS_A = bcn \sum_{j=1}^{a} (\overline{Y}_{j..} - \overline{Y}_{...})^2$$

which is the specific expression for the sum of squares due to the A main effect, as shown in Table 8.11. The same type of relationship holds for the other effects listed in the table.

TABLE 8.11

SUM OF SQUARES AND DEGREES OF FREEDOM FOR EACH EFFECT IN THREE-WAY BETWEEN-SUBJECT DESIGN

Effect	General Expression for SS	Specific Expression for SS	df
A	$\sum_{j=1}^{a}\sum_{k=1}^{b}\sum_{l=1}^{c}\sum_{i=1}^{n}\hat{\alpha}_j^2$	$bcn\sum_{j=1}^{a}(\overline{Y}_{j..}-\overline{Y}_{...})^2$	$a-1$
B	$\sum_{j=1}^{a}\sum_{k=1}^{b}\sum_{l=1}^{c}\sum_{i=1}^{n}\hat{\beta}_k^2$	$acn\sum_{k=1}^{b}(\overline{Y}_{k.}-\overline{Y}_{...})^2$	$b-1$
C	$\sum_{j=1}^{a}\sum_{k=1}^{b}\sum_{l=1}^{c}\sum_{i=1}^{n}\hat{\gamma}_l^2$	$abn\sum_{l=1}^{c}(\overline{Y}_{.l}-\overline{Y}_{...})^2$	$c-1$
$A \times B$	$\sum_{j=1}^{a}\sum_{k=1}^{b}\sum_{l=1}^{c}\sum_{i=1}^{n}(\widehat{\alpha\beta})_{jk}^2$	$cn\sum_{j=1}^{a}\sum_{k=1}^{b}(\overline{Y}_{jk.}-\overline{Y}_{j..}-\overline{Y}_{k.}+\overline{Y}_{...})^2$	$(a-1)(b-1)$
$A \times C$	$\sum_{j=1}^{a}\sum_{k=1}^{b}\sum_{l=1}^{c}\sum_{i=1}^{n}(\widehat{\alpha\gamma})_{jl}^2$	$bn\sum_{j=1}^{a}\sum_{l=1}^{c}(\overline{Y}_{j.l}-\overline{Y}_{j..}-\overline{Y}_{.l}+\overline{Y}_{...})^2$	$(a-1)(c-1)$
$B \times C$	$\sum_{j=1}^{a}\sum_{k=1}^{b}\sum_{l=1}^{c}\sum_{i=1}^{n}(\widehat{\beta\gamma})_{kl}^2$	$an\sum_{k=1}^{b}\sum_{l=1}^{c}(\overline{Y}_{kl}-\overline{Y}_{k.}-\overline{Y}_{.l}+\overline{Y}_{...})^2$	$(b-1)(c-1)$
$A \times B \times C$	$\sum_{j=1}^{a}\sum_{k=1}^{b}\sum_{l=1}^{c}\sum_{i=1}^{n}(\widehat{\alpha\beta\gamma})_{jkl}^2$	$n\sum_{j=1}^{a}\sum_{k=1}^{b}\sum_{l=1}^{c}(\overline{Y}_{jkl}-\overline{Y}_{jk.}-\overline{Y}_{j.l}-\overline{Y}_{kl}+\overline{Y}_{j..}+\overline{Y}_{k.}+\overline{Y}_{.l}-\overline{Y}_{...})^2$	$(a-1)(b-1)(c-1)$

Table 8.11 also shows the degrees of freedom associated with each effect, which equals the number of independent parameters omitted from the full model. For example, as Table 8.10 shows, to test the A main effect, the α_j parameters were omitted from the full model. Although there are a such parameters (i.e., there is an α_j value for each of the a levels of A), only $a - 1$ of these parameters are independent. Thus, the difference in the number of independent parameters in the full and restricted models equals $a - 1$. In terms of symbols

$$df_R - df_F = a - 1$$

From Table 8.11 and Equation 5, it is possible to test any of the 7 null hypotheses of interest. Our usual F statistic is given by

$$F = \frac{(E_R - E_F)/(df_R - df_F)}{E_F/df_F} \qquad (3, \text{repeated})$$

From Table 8.11, for testing any effect, the difference in the error sum of squares of the restricted and full models is

$$E_R - E_F = SS_{\text{effect}}$$

Similarly

$$df_R - df_F = df_{\text{effect}}$$

We also know that the ratio of SS_{effect} divided by df_{effect} is simply the mean square for the effect:

$$MS_{\text{effect}} = SS_{\text{effect}}/df_{\text{effect}}$$

Finally, from Equation 5, we know that the ratio of E_F divided by df_F for the full model being used here is mean square within:

$$MS_W = E_F/df_F$$

Substituting these expressions into Equation 3 yields

$$F = MS_{\text{effect}}/MS_W$$

The observed F can be compared to a critical F with df_{effect} numerator degrees of freedom and $N - abc$ denominator degrees of freedom to assess its statistical significance.

NUMERICAL EXAMPLE

At this point, it will probably be helpful to consider a numerical example for the general three-way $a \times b \times c$ design. This example builds from the hypertension example used in Chapter 7 for the two-way design. Table 8.12 presents hypothetical data from a study investigating the effects of biofeedback, drug therapy, and diet therapy on hypertension. For purposes of comparison, the data for the diet-absent condition in Table 8.12 are identical to the data shown in Tables 7.5 and 7.9 to illustrate a two-way design. Thus, the data for the current example

TABLE 8.12
BLOOD PRESSURE DATA

Biofeedback and Drug X	Biofeedback and Drug Y	Biofeedback and Drug Z	Drug X Alone	Drug Y Alone	Drug Z Alone
Diet Absent					
170	186	180	173	189	202
175	194	187	194	194	228
165	201	199	197	217	190
180	215	170	190	206	206
160	219	204	176	199	224
158	209	194	198	195	204
Diet Present					
161	164	162	164	171	205
173	166	184	190	173	199
157	159	183	169	196	170
152	182	156	164	199	160
181	187	180	176	180	179
190	174	173	175	203	179

TABLE 8.13
CELL MEANS FOR DATA SHOWN IN TABLE 8.12

		Diet Absent			
		Drug X	Drug Y	Drug Z	Marginal Means
	Present	168	204	189	187
Biofeedback	Absent	188	200	209	199
	Marginal Means	178	202	199	193

		Diet Present			
		Drug X	Drug Y	Drug Z	Marginal Means
	Present	169	172	173	171.33
Biofeedback	Absent	173	187	182	180.67
	Marginal Means	171	179.5	177.5	176

differ only in that data have been added for the diet-present condition. We (arbitrarily) refer to the presence or absence of biofeedback as factor A, to the type of drug as factor B, and to the presence or absence of diet as factor C. Thus, we have a $2 \times 3 \times 2$ design. As in Chapter 7, $n = 6$, that is, there are only 6 individuals per cell. As before, power considerations would typically dictate a larger sample size, but we work with $n = 6$ to make computations more manageable.

Table 8.13 shows the cell means for these data, displayed as two 2×3 tables, one for diet absent and one for diet present. The table also shows some but not all marginal means for these data. For example, the marginal mean for biofeedback and Drug X averaging over diet would be 168.5 (the mean of 168 and 169), but this value is not shown in the table. We will see momentarily that the marginal means that are in fact shown in the table are the ones in which we are most interested for this particular study.

Table 8.14 shows the ANOVA table for these data. From this table, we can see that all three main effects are highly statistically significant. None of the three two-way interactions are statistically significant at the .05 level, although the Drug $\times$ Diet interaction just misses .05. Because none of the two-way interactions are significant, it might seem that the main effects

TABLE 8.14
ANOVA TABLE FOR DATA SHOWN IN TABLE 8.12

Source	SS	df	MS	F	p
A (biofeedback)	2048	1	2048.0	13.07	<.001
B (drug)	3675	2	1837.5	11.73	<.001
C (diet)	5202	1	5202.0	33.20	<.001
A × B	259	2	129.5	0.83	.44
A × C	32	1	32.0	0.20	.65
B × C	903	2	451.5	2.88	.06
A × B × C	1075	2	537.5	3.43	.04
Within cells	9400	60	156.7		

can be interpreted unambiguously. In fact, however, it is necessary to consider not only the two-way interactions but also the three-way interaction. Table 8.14 shows that the Biofeedback × Drug × Diet interaction is statistically significant at the .05 level for these data.

Before considering in some detail the implication of this three-way interaction, we will momentarily point out that it may be useful to supplement significance tests such as those shown in Table 8.14 with measures of effect. The same general choices as we have seen in previous designs once again are available for the three-factor design. For example, suppose we want to estimate how much variance each of our effects accounts for in the population. We could then report omega-squared values. As we discussed in Chapter 7, in a factorial design, we must decide whether to regard "off factors" in the design as intrinsic or extrinsic. For intrinsic off factors, we can express omega squared in terms of F values as

$$\hat{\omega}^2 = \frac{df_{\text{effect}}(F_{\text{effect}} - 1)}{\displaystyle\sum_{\text{all effects}} (df_{\text{effect}} F_{\text{effect}}) + df_{\text{W}} + 1} \qquad (7.47, \text{repeated})$$

However, the comparable expression for extrinsic off factors is

$$\hat{\omega}^2_{\text{partial}} = \frac{df_{\text{effect}}(F_{\text{effect}} - 1)}{df_{\text{effect}}(F_{\text{effect}} - 1) + N} \qquad (7.46, \text{repeated})$$

In our blood pressure example, we would probably regard each pair of off factors as extrinsic to any specific factor of interest, because it would be sensible to design a study examining any one of these factors in isolation from the others. Thus, we could use Equation 7.46 to calculate values of partial omega squared. Table 8.15 shows partial omega squared values for our data. Notice that the values for the $A \times B$ and $A \times C$ interactions have been set at zero, because the observed F values for each of these effects was less than 1. The partial omega squared values for these data might tempt us into dismissing the importance of the interactions, none of which are estimated to account for as much variance as any of the main effects. However, we believe that dismissing the interactions would lead to an overly simplistic understanding of the data. Instead, we maintain that a more complete interpretation of the data should begin by considering the implications of the statistically significant interaction.

Implications of a Three-Way Interaction

What are the implications of a statistically significant three-way interaction? First, as we have discussed earlier in the chapter, the significant three-way interaction implies that two-way interactions cannot be interpreted unambiguously. To see why, let's consider the

TABLE 8.15
PARTIAL OMEGA SQUARED VALUES
FOR DATA SHOWN IN TABLE 8.12

Effect	$\omega^2_{partial}$
A	.14
B	.23
C	.31
$A \times B$	.00
$A \times C$	.00
$B \times C$	.05
$A \times B \times C$	.06

Biofeedback $\times$ Drug interaction. We know from Table 8.14 that this interaction ($A \times B$) does not even approach significance at the .05 level. However, the fact that the three-way interaction is significant implies that the Biofeedback $\times$ Drug interaction when diet is absent is significantly different from the Biofeedback $\times$ Drug interaction when diet is present. As a result, instead of interpreting the average Biofeedback $\times$ Drug interaction effect, we should interpret 2 individual Biofeedback $\times$ Drug interaction effects, one for each level of diet. Although the average Biofeedback $\times$ Drug interaction is nonsignificant, it is entirely possible that either or both of the individual Biofeedback $\times$ Drug interaction effects within the two levels of the diet factor are statistically significant. We will have more to say about performing such tests momentarily. The important point for now is that we should generally not attempt to interpret two-way interactions when the three-way interaction is statistically significant.

The second implication of a significant three-way interaction is that we should generally not interpret main effects, either. To see why this is so, let's consider the drug main effect. Because the three-way interaction is significant, the Biofeedback $\times$ Drug interaction is not the same when the diet is absent as when it is present. However, this implies that the Biofeedback $\times$ Drug interaction cannot be null both when diet is absent and when it is present, or else it would then be the same for both. In other words, there is a Biofeedback $\times$ Drug interaction either when diet is absent, when it is present, or both.[2] However, the existence of a nonzero two-way interaction for at least one level of the diet factor implies that the effect of drugs varies as a function of the level of biofeedback, for that level of the Diet factor. Thus, the effect of drugs is not consistent and generally cannot be interpreted unambiguously.

In general, then, a significant three-way interaction implies that the effect of one factor is not consistent at all combinations of the other two factors. Thus, for example, it may be misleading to conclude on the basis of the significant drug main effect shown in Table 8.14 that the difference between the three drugs included in this study can be interpreted on the basis of their marginal means. For the sake of illustration, if we were to attempt to make such an interpretation, we would calculate the marginal means for Drugs X, Y, and Z, averaging over biofeedback and diet. From Table 8.13, we can see that the appropriate values of these marginal means are 174.5 for Drug X, 190.75 for Drug Y, and 188.25 for Drug Z. Remembering that lower blood pressure values are better, we would probably conclude that Drug X is better than either Drug Y or Drug Z. Of course, we would want to verify our impression by conducting a formal test of a contrast. However, the point we are trying to make here concerns the meaning of such a statement. Although it would be correct that Drug X truly does have a lower mean than Drugs Y or Z for these data, such a statement is true only if we average across both biofeedback and diet. However, we will see momentarily that in fact there is not a significant drug effect at all when diet is present. In addition, there is a Biofeedback $\times$ Drug interaction when diet is absent, implying that the differences between Drugs X, Y, and Z vary as a function of presence or absence of biofeedback when diet is absent. As a result, although it may be true that Drug X is the most effective drug of these three drugs on the average, it may be much more important to realize that its superiority is not at all consistent across different levels of diet and biofeedback. In general, it is important to remember that main effects represent effects that are averaged over all other factors in the design, as we showed earlier in Table 8.8. However, a statistically significant three-way interaction is a signal that these average effects are not consistent and thus are not representative of the effects at individual levels of the other factors. As a result, when a significant three-way interaction is obtained, it is generally preferable to consider effects within such individual levels of other factors instead of interpreting the main effects themselves.

General Guideline for Analyzing Effects

How should we proceed with the interpretation of the data in our hypothetical study? Figure 8.6 presents a flowchart, which serves as a general guideline for analyzing effects in a three-way design. We orient the discussion of data analysis in our hypothetical example around this flowchart. Three cautions should be mentioned before proceeding. First, as with the flowcharts we have seen in previous chapters, this flowchart also is intended to be used only as a guideline. For example, the flowchart does not include the possibility of performing certain planned comparisons instead of omnibus tests. Nevertheless, the flowchart is a useful guide as long as it is used flexibly. Second, not all parts of the flowchart are self-explanatory. At several points, it will be necessary to expand on or clarify the figure. Thus, it is important to read and understand the following pages of text. Third, the flowchart provides no assistance for choosing an error term or for defining a family when considering Type I error rates. The logic underlying these issues is the same as it was in Chapter 7 for the two-way design. In the following analysis, we use MS_W as the error term for all tests, and we use $\alpha = .05$ for each test until we consider comparisons of cell means. We have made these choices not necessarily because they are "correct," but quite frankly because they simplify the presentation and allow the reader to concentrate on understanding the necessary steps to analyze data from a three-way design.

With these cautions in mind, we can now consider the analysis of our data, using Figure 8.6 as a guideline. According to Figure 8.6, we must begin by ascertaining whether the three-way interaction is statistically significant. From Table 8.14, we can see that $A \times B \times C$ is significant at the .05 level, so the answer to the question in the flowchart is yes. Thus, we branch to the left in the flowchart.

Because the three-way $A \times B \times C$ interaction was significant, the next step is to determine whether $A \times B$ is significant at C_l. Before attempting to answer this question, we must understand what is being asked. As we saw earlier in the chapter, a significant three-way interaction implies that the two-way interaction is not the same at every level of the third factor. Thus, the flowchart suggests that we test the two-way $A \times B$ interaction separately at each individual level of C (recall that C_l refers to level l of factor C).

At this point, we must discuss an important issue that is not revealed in the flowchart. From a statistical standpoint, a significant three-way interaction can be viewed from any of three perspectives:

1. The $A \times B$ interaction is different at individual levels of C.
2. The $A \times C$ interaction is different at individual levels of B.
3. The $B \times C$ interaction is different at individual levels of A.

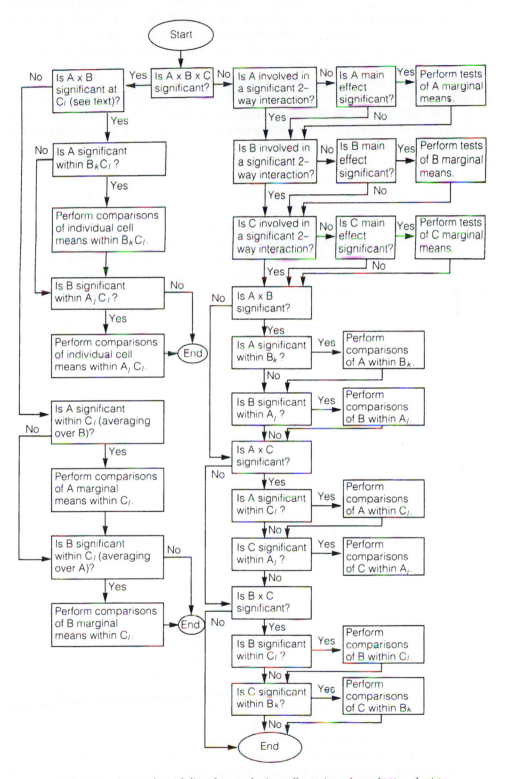

FIG. 8.6.   General guideline for analyzing effects in a three-factor design.

These three perspectives are equivalent and thus equally valid statistically. However, in most research situations, one of these three perspectives is more interesting than the other two. In our example, we assume that the investigator is most interested in examining the Biofeedback $\times$ Drug interaction separately for each level of the Diet factor. From a statistical perspective, we could also investigate the Biofeedback $\times$ Diet interaction for each drug and the Drug $\times$ Diet interaction for both levels of biofeedback. Although it would be legitimate to perform all three tests, we will only test Biofeedback $\times$ Drug at each level of the diet factor. We would also suggest that in practice it is usually best not to perform all three tests, but instead to test only the question of most interest and importance. There are essentially two reasons not to perform all three tests. First, attempting to describe all three tests may become overbearing, in light of the potential follow-up tests to be conducted. The number of potential tests can be appreciated most easily by referring again to Figure 8.6 and realizing that the left-hand side of the figure only shows tests corresponding to $A \times B$ at one level of C. If we test not only $A \times B$ at multiple levels of C, but also $A \times C$ at all levels of B, and $B \times C$ at all levels of A, the resultant number of tests may be overwhelming. Second, the three tests ($A \times B$ within C, $A \times C$ within B, and $B \times C$ within A) are somewhat redundant, because they all involve $SS_{A \times B \times C}$. Stated another way, the contrasts underlying these various tests are not orthogonal to each other, which can additionally complicate the interpretation. Although these two reasons should not be viewed as prohibiting the testing of all three effects, in most situations one of the effects stands out for theoretical reasons as the single effect to be tested.

Thus, in our example, we will test the Biofeedback $\times$ Drug interaction at each level of the diet factor, that is, $A \times B$ within C_l. Such a test is often called a simple interaction test, because it pertains to a single level of one factor (viz., C), much like the simple effects test we encountered in Chapter 7. Be sure to understand that we will test the $A \times B$ interaction here at each and every level of C. In other words, although we will test $A \times B$ at an individual level of C, we will conduct the test not only for C_1 but also for C_2, because C has two levels in our example. In general, there would be as many "simple $A \times B$ interaction tests" as there were levels of C in the design. We should also mention that the sums of squares for these effects can be found by regarding the data as a two-way design and using the computational formulas of Chapter 7. For example, to find $SS_{A \times BwC_1}$, the $A \times B$ interaction sum of squares at the first level of C, we could literally ignore the data from the other levels of C. The resultant design would be a two-way $A \times B$ design and could be analyzed accordingly. As usual, careful thought should be given concerning whether the error term for testing this effect should also ignore data from the other levels of C (if heterogeneity of variance is suspected) or should incorporate data from all participants (under the assumption of homogeneity of variance).

Table 8.16 shows the results of testing Biofeedback $\times$ Drug at each level of the diet factor. From the table, it is clear that there is a significant (at the .05 level) Biofeedback $\times$ Drug interaction when diet is absent but not when it is present. Notice that such a discrepancy is consistent with, although not required by, the significant three-way effect we had already observed. Because $A \times B$ is significant at C_1 (diet absent) but nonsignificant at C_2 (diet present), the next test to be performed is different for the two levels of the diet factor. Before actually performing the tests, however, it is helpful to realize that conceptually we have two two-way designs here, one when diet is absent and one when diet is present. Because A and B interact when diet is absent but not when it is present, the subsequent tests to be performed will not be the same for the two levels of the diet factor.

Let's first consider what further tests should be performed when diet is absent. So far we know that biofeedback and drug interact when diet is absent. Thus, the effect of biofeedback is not the same for every drug; similarly, the differences among drugs are not the same when biofeedback is present as when it is absent. For this reason, we must test the effect of biofeedback at each individual level of the drug factor and the drug effect at each level of

TABLE 8.16
SIMPLE INTERACTION TESTS PERFORMED ACCORDING TO
GUIDELINES OF FIGURE 8.2

Source	SS	df	MS	F	p
$A \times B$ w C_1 (biofeedback $\times$ drug for diet absent)	1152	2	576.0	3.68	.03
$A \times B$ w C_2 (biofeedback $\times$ drug for diet present)	182	2	91.0	0.58	.57
Within cells	9400	60	156.7		

TABLE 8.17
SIMPLE, SIMPLE MAIN EFFECTS WHEN DIET IS ABSENT

Source	SS	df	MS	F	p
$Aw B_1 C_1$ (biofeedback for drug X when diet is absent)	1200	1	1200.0	7.66	.007
$Aw B_2 C_1$ (biofeedback for drug Y when diet is absent)	48	1	48.0	0.31	.589
$Aw B_3 C_1$ (biofeedback for drug Z when diet is absent)	1200	1	1200.0	7.66	.007
$Bw A_1 C_1$ (drugs for biofeedback present when diet is absent)	3924	2	1962.0	12.52	<.001
$Bw A_2 C_1$ (drugs for biofeedback absent when diet is absent)	1332	2	666.0	4.25	.018
Within cells	9400	60	156.7		

biofeedback.[3] On the one hand, we have tests of A at each level of B; on the other hand, we have tests of B at each level of A. However, throughout these tests, we are restricting our attention to the diet-absent condition, so that all tests are performed at the first level of C. As a result, the tests of A are of the form A within $B_1 C_1$, A within $B_2 C_1$, and A within $B_3 C_1$. The two tests of B are B within $A_1 C_1$, and B within $A_2 C_1$. Notice that in each case, we effectively have a one-way design, so that the sum of squares for any of these effects can be found using formulas from Chapter 3. The results of these tests, which are commonly called *simple, simple main effects*, because we are fixing the levels of two other factors, are shown in Table 8.17. We can see from this table that in the absence of the diet, biofeedback has an effect when combined with Drug X or Drug Z but not Drug Y. In addition, when diet is absent, there is a significant difference among the drugs whether biofeedback is present or absent. At this point, you may want to refer back to the cell means shown in Table 8.13 to better understand these results. Table 8.17 tells us that, for the diet-absent condition, column differences are significant within the first row (biofeedback present) and within the second row (biofeedback absent) and that row differences are significant within the first column (Drug X) and the third column (Drug Z) but not the second column (Drug Y).

According to the flowchart, we now should perform comparisons of individual cell means within $B_1 C_1$ and within $B_3 C_1$ because A within $B_1 C_1$ and A within $B_3 C_1$ are both significant.

TABLE 8.18
INDIVIDUAL CELL MEAN COMPARISONS WHEN DIET IS ABSENT

Source	SS	df	MS	F
X vs. YwA_1C_1 (drug X vs. drug Y when biofeedback is present and diet is absent)	3888	1	3888.0	24.82
X vs. ZwA_1C_1 (drug X vs. drug Z when biofeedback is present and diet is absent)	1323	1	1323.0	8.44
Y vs. ZwA_1C_1 (drug Y vs. drug Z when biofeedback is present and diet is absent)	675	1	675.0	4.31
X vs. YwA_2C_1 (drug X vs. drug Y when biofeedback is absent and diet is absent)	432	1	432.0	2.76
X vs. ZwA_2C_1 (drug X vs. drug Z when biofeedback is absent and diet is absent)	1323	1	1323.0	8.44
Y vs. ZwA_2C_1 (drug Y vs. drug Z when biofeedback is absent and diet is absent)	243	1	243.0	1.55
Within cells	9400	60	156.7	

In general, the idea here is that when the A simple, simple main effect is significant, we must compare the individual levels of A to determine which levels are different from each other. However, in our example, A has only two levels, so such comparisons are unnecessary. When the simple, simple main effect of A is significant in our example, it must be the case that mean blood pressure is different when biofeedback is present than when it is absent.

The drug factor, on the other hand, has three levels. Thus, we do need to perform comparisons of individual cell means, both within A_1C_1 and within A_2C_1, to understand the nature of drug differences. These comparisons can be of any form discussed in Chapter 4, with an appropriate adjustment to the critical value as discussed in Chapter 5. For illustrative purposes, we suppose that pairwise comparisons are of interest here.[4] Table 8.18 shows the results of performing pairwise comparisons of cell means (as shown earlier in Table 8.13) to our data. We define a family to be a particular combination of A and C. To keep the α_{FW} at .05, Tukey's WSD can be used. The critical q from Appendix Table A.4 is 3.40 for $\alpha = .05$, $df = 60$, and three means. To be statistically significant, an observed F must exceed $q^2/2$, which equals 5.78 here. Three of the observed F values in Table 8.18 exceed this value, and thus the corresponding comparisons are statistically significant. For our data, when diet is absent, Drug X differs significantly from Drug Y as well as Drug Z when biofeedback is present, and Drug X differs significantly from Drug Z when biofeedback is absent.

We have obtained a thorough analysis of the effects of biofeedback and drugs when the diet is absent. However, the analysis when the diet is present is still stranded near the top of the flowchart. The last analysis we performed for the diet-present condition showed that the Biofeedback × Drug interaction is nonsignificant for diet present (see Table 8.16). Because these two factors do not interact when diet is present, we can interpret their main effects unambiguously, within the second level of the diet factor. As a result, we do not follow the same strategy as we did for the diet-absent condition, where simple, simple main effects were tested. Instead, as Figure 8.6 shows, we test the A (biofeedback) effect within C_2 (diet present) by averaging over levels of B (drug). Similarly, we will test the B (drug) effect within C_2 (diet present) by averaging over levels of A (biofeedback).

TABLE 8.19
SIMPLE MAIN-EFFECT TESTS WHEN DIET IS PRESENT

Source	SS	df	MS	F	p
AwC_2	784	1	784.0	5.00	.027
(biofeedback when diet is present)					
BwC_2	474	2	237.0	1.51	.227
(drugs when diet is present)					
Within cells	9400	60	156.7		

TABLE 8.20
CELL MEANS FOR HYPOTHETICAL DATA

		Diet Absent			
		Drug X	Drug Y	Drug Z	Marginal Means
	Present	168^a	204^{be}	189^b	187
Biofeedback	Absent	188^c	200^{cde}	209^d	199
		178	202	199	193

		Diet Present			
		Drug X	Drug Y	Drug Z	Marginal Means
	Present	169	172	173	171.33^f
Biofeedback	Absent	173	187	182	180.67^g
		171^h	179.5^h	177.5^h	176

We first test the A (biofeedback) effect within the second level of the diet factor (i.e., within C_2, diet present). Table 8.19 shows that this effect is significant at the .05 level. In general, as the flowchart shows, we would next perform comparisons of A marginal means within C_2. However, because A has only two levels in our example, further comparisons are unnecessary. We already know which specific means are different—the marginal mean of 171.33 for biofeedback present is significantly different from the marginal mean of 180.67 for biofeedback absent when diet is present (see Table 8.13 to understand from where these values come).

The second test to be performed is a test of B within C_2, that is, the drug effect when the diet is present. As Table 8.19 shows, this effect is nonsignificant. Thus, further investigation of specific differences among the three drugs is unwarranted. The marginal means of 171, 179.5, and 177.5 (see Table 8.13) are not significantly different from each other, so there is no evidence of differential effectiveness of the three drugs when diet is present.

Summary of Results

At this point, it may be helpful to summarize what we have discovered about our data. Table 8.20 repeats the means shown earlier in Table 8.13. However, Table 8.20 also includes superscripts (small letters a–g) to designate which means are significantly different from one another and which are not. Means that are in the same row or column as each other but do not share a superscript in common are significantly different from each other. Means that are in the same row or column as each other and that do share a superscript in common are not significantly different from each other. Differences between means that are in different rows and different columns have not been tested, so their superscripts cannot be compared.

To see what all of this means, look at Table 8.20. We'll begin with the diet-present condition, because findings here are less complicated. The first thing to notice is that superscripts are associated with the marginal means instead of the cell means. The reason is that biofeedback and drug did not interact when diet is present, so we can unambiguously interpret marginal means. Next, notice that the superscript for the biofeedback-present marginal mean is f, whereas the superscript for the biofeedback-absent marginal mean is g. The fact that the two superscripts are different signifies that the two marginal means are significantly different; that is, there is a statistically significant biofeedback effect in the diet-present condition (see Table 8.19). Next, consider the column marginal means. The fact that all three superscripts here are h implies that these means are not significantly different from each other (recall from Table 8.19 that the drug effect when the diet is present is nonsignificant). Finally, be certain you understand that comparing superscripts of row marginal means to superscripts of column marginal means has no meaning, because we never performed such tests. Thus, do not be misled into thinking that the row 1 marginal mean (171.33) is significantly different from the column 1 marginal mean (171). Such a test could be performed, in which case we could incorporate it into our subscripts; however, in the great majority of cases, only comparisons within a row or within a column are interpretable. For this reason, the notational system adopted here is meaningful only for comparisons within a row or within a column.

The situation is more complicated when diet is absent. First, notice that the superscripts here are associated with individual cell means, not marginal means, as they were in the diet-present condition. The reason is that biofeedback and drug were found to interact when diet is absent. Thus, we interpret row differences within each column and column differences within each row. Let's start with the row differences. Table 8.20 shows that there is a significant biofeedback effect for Drug X (a and c are different) and for Drug Z (b and d are different) but not for Drug Y (be and cde share the e superscript in common). What about the column differences? Within the first row, Drug X differs from both Drug Y and Drug Z, but Drugs Y and Z do not differ from one another. Within the second row, Drug X differs from Drug Z (c and d are different). However, Drug Y is not significantly different from either Drug X (c and cde share c in common) or Drug Z (d and cde share d in common). As in the diet-present condition, comparing superscripts of means that differ in both their row and their column is not meaningful. For example, the values of 189 and 188 have different superscripts (b and c, respectively), but they obviously would not be different from one another if we were to test them. However, the notational system simply reflects the fact that such differences have not been tested and typically would not be interpretable or interesting. Also notice that it is meaningless here to compare means when diet is absent to means where diet is present, because we performed tests within each level of the diet factor individually. This does not mean that such tests could not be performed, but rather that they were judged not to be interesting in the context of this study.

Graphical Depiction of Data

A table like that given in Table 8.20 is certainly not the only way in which data analyses from a three-way design might be summarized. For example, an alternative might be to plot the cell means, as shown in Figure 8.7. This plot aids understanding of the statistically significant results we have obtained for these data. For example, the plot shows clearly that the three-way interaction we obtained can be conceptualized as due to the existence of a strong Biofeedback × Drug interaction when diet is absent, but little or no such interaction when diet is present. Notice that this interpretation is consistent with the F tests reported earlier in Table 8.16. The figure is also consistent with Table 8.20. For example, the figure and the table together imply that when diet is present, biofeedback has an effect, but there are no significant differences among the drugs. On the other hand, when diet is absent, biofeedback has an effect only for Drugs X and Z. In addition, when diet is absent, Drugs X and Z differ both when biofeedback is present and when

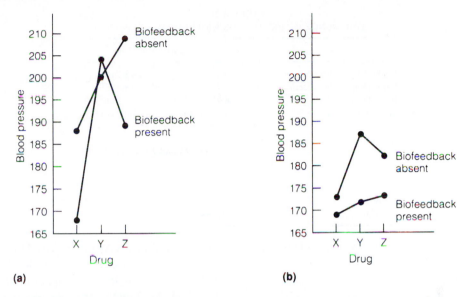

FIG. 8.7.   Plot of Table 8.13 cell means as a function of diet condition: (a) diet absent and (b) diet present.

it is absent; Drugs X and Y differ only when biofeedback is present; and, Drugs Y and Z do not differ in either case. As usual, remember that the plot could have been constructed differently, if we wanted to emphasize different effects. The most important point to be made here is that our interpretation should ultimately hinge not only on the F and p values of Tables 8.14 and 8.16–8.19 but also on the cell means themselves, which, after all, are what the F and p values are derived from.

Confidence Intervals for Single Degree of Freedom Effects

Yet another approach to interpreting effects is to form confidence intervals. As we discussed in Chapter 7, confidence intervals can be formed for single degree of freedom effects, such as contrasts, using the same approach we developed in Chapter 5. In particular, Table 5.17 shows appropriate formulas depending on how we choose to control our error rate when we may be forming more than one interval for the same family of effects.

It would be extremely laborious and largely redundant to provide a detailed presentation of every confidence interval we might form in our blood pressure data. Instead, we have chosen to illustrate a few different examples of types of intervals we might form. In particular, we will present output from SAS and SPSS showing confidence intervals that correspond to the significance tests shown in Tables 8.17, 8.18, and 8.19. For each type of interval, we will also show how the values generated by SAS and SPSS are consistent with the expressions shown in Table 5.17.

First, let's consider the effects tested in Table 8.17. Notice that the biofeedback tests have a single degree of freedom, whereas the drug effects have 2 df. This implies that we can form a confidence interval corresponding to each of the biofeedback effects, but that we will need to consider individual contrasts for the drug effects. In fact, you may recall that Table 8.18 displayed precisely this type of test, and we will turn our attention to intervals corresponding to contrasts between the drugs in a moment. However, our immediate focus is on the biofeedback effect within each level of drug when diet is absent.

TABLE 8.21
CONFIDENCE INTERVALS FOR BIOFEEDBACK EFFECT

Parameter	95% Confidence Limits	
bio w Drug X, diet absent	−34.4551411	−5.5448589
bio w Drug Y, diet absent	−10.4551411	18.4551411
bio w Drug Z, diet absent	−34.4551411	−5.5448589
bio w diet present	−17.6790130	−0.9876537

	Standardized Effects	
Parameter	95% Confidence Limits	
bio w Drug X, diet absent	−2.75274338	−0.44299843
bio w Drug Y, diet absent	−0.83529829	1.47444666
bio w Drug Z, diet absent	−2.75274338	−0.44299843
bio w diet present	−1.41243902	−0.07890716

Table 8.21 presents SAS output for three such intervals, one for Drug X, a second for Drug Y, and a third for Drug Z. For example, a 95% confidence interval for the effect of biofeedback in the presence of Drug X when diet is absent has a lower limit of −34.46 and an upper limit of −5.54. In other words, we can be 95% confident that biofeedback in the presence of Drug X and the absence of diet lowers systolic blood pressure somewhere between 34.46 and 5.54 units.

Six further comments are relevant. First, notice that this interval does not contain zero, consistent with the p value less than .05 for this effect in Table 8.17. Second, notice that the center of the interval equals −20.00 (i.e., the mean of −34.46 and −5.54 is −20.00). Looking back at Table 8.13 shows us that −20.00 is exactly the difference between the row means for Drug X when diet is absent. In other words, it makes sense that our single best guess about the effect of biofeedback in this condition is that it lowers blood pressure 20 points (i.e., the difference between 168 and 188), so it is reasonable that this value is at the center of our interval. Third, because the units of the dependent variable are intrinsically meaningful, we might not need to calculate a standardized interval. However, for completeness, the lower half of Table 8.21 shows approximate intervals formed by first dividing each score in the data by the square root of mean square within and then using SAS as usual to form an interval. As mentioned previously, a more precise method is described by Steiger and Fouladi (1997) as well as Fidler and Thompson (2001). Fourth, these intervals provide 95% confidence only at the level of the individual interval. Extending confidence to a set of intervals would entail basing the interval width on an appropriate multiple comparisons procedure, as shown in Table 5.17. Fifth, speaking of this table, the interval limits of −34.46 and −5.54 can be calculated from Table 5.17 as

$$(168 - 188) \pm \sqrt{4.00}\sqrt{156.7\left(\frac{1}{6} + \frac{1}{6}\right)}$$

This produces (within rounding error) an interval from −34.46 to −5.54, in agreement with the SAS output shown in Table 8.21. Sixth, the table also shows comparable intervals for the biofeedback effect for Drugs Y and Z when diet is absent.

Table 8.21 also shows a 95% confidence interval for the biofeedback effect when diet is present. Notice that this corresponds to the test reported in Table 8.19 and is not reported separately for each drug because the biofeedback and drug factors did not interact in the presence of diet. The same comments we made about the other intervals shown in Table 8.21

generally apply here, but it is important to realize that this last interval is effectively based on 18 observations because we have averaged over levels of drug. Thus, from Table 5.17, the interval for the biofeedback effect when diet is present is given by

$$(171.33 - 180.67) \pm \sqrt{4.00} \sqrt{156.7 \left(\frac{1}{18} + \frac{1}{18} \right)}$$

Here, 171.33 and 180.67 are the marginal means for biofeedback when diet is present, and 18 is the number of individuals on which each of these means is based. The resulting interval once again agrees within rounding error with the result shown in Table 8.21 from SAS.

Notice that the interval for the effect of biofeedback when diet is present is substantially narrower than the three intervals for the effect of biofeedback when diet is absent. The reason is that the former interval averages over levels of drug and thus effectively increases the sample size from 6 to 18. More generally, when forming confidence intervals, it is obviously crucial to be careful that the sample size used in the formula corresponds to the number of individuals on whom each relevant sample mean is based.

Table 8.22 shows confidence intervals corresponding to the drug effects tested in Table 8.18. You may recall that we used Tukey's WSD to control familywise alpha in the tests shown in Table 8.18. To be consistent, we have used SPSS to form confidence intervals with a

TABLE 8.22

CONFIDENCE INTERVALS FOR DRUG DIFFERENCES WHEN DIET IS ABSENT

Biofeedback Present
Multiple Comparisons
Dependent Variable: SBP
Tukey's HSD

(I) DRUG	(J) DRUG	Mean Difference (I–J)	Std. Error	Sig.	95% Confidence Interval	
					Lower Bound	Upper Bound
1	2	−36.000000	7.226495	.000	−53.366879	−18.633121
	3	−21.000000	7.226495	.014	−38.366879	−3.633121
2	1	36.000000	7.226495	.000	18.633121	53.366879
	3	15.000000	7.226495	.104	−2.366879	32.366879
3	1	21.000000	7.226495	.014	3.633121	38.366879
	2	−15.000000	7.226495	.104	−32.366879	2.366879

Biofeedback Absent
Multiple Comparisons
Dependent Variable: SBP
Tukey's HSD

(I) DRUG	(J) DRUG	Mean Difference (I–J)	Std. Error	Sig.	95% Confidence Interval	
					Lower Bound	Upper Bound
1	2	−12.000000	7.226495	.229	−29.366879	5.366879
	3	−21.000000	7.226495	.014	−38.366879	−3.633121
2	1	12.000000	7.226495	.229	−5.366879	29.366879
	3	−9.000000	7.226495	.431	−26.366879	8.366879
3	1	21.000000	7.226495	.014	3.633121	38.366879
	2	9.000000	7.226495	.431	−8.366879	26.366879

simultaneous confidence level of 95%. Once again, each of the intervals calculated by SPSS can also be calculated from Table 5.17. For example, consider the difference between Drugs X and Y when biofeedback is present and diet is absent. The table shows that this confidence interval has a lower limit of -53.37 and an upper limit of -18.63. The same limits (within rounding error) can be calculated from Table 5.17 as

$$(168 - 204) \pm (3.40/\sqrt{2})\sqrt{156.7\left(\frac{1}{6} + \frac{1}{6}\right)}$$

where 168 and 204 are the relevant cell means (see Table 8.13), 3.40 is the critical value for the studentized range distribution (from Appendix Table A.4), 156.7 is MS_W, and each mean is based on six observations. The other intervals shown in Table 8.22 can be calculated in the same manner.

Other Questions of Potential Interest

We do not want to leave the impression that the analyses we have presented exhaust the range of questions we might address with these data. For example, from a clinical perspective, the microscopic analyses reported here may not have directly addressed a fundamental question, namely what combination of therapies is most effective. Should biofeedback, drug, and diet therapies all be combined into one package? The main-effects tests reported earlier in Table 8.14 would seem to suggest that they should be combined, because all three factors had highly significant main effects. In particular, Table 8.23 shows the marginal means associated with each main effect. For example, the value of 179.17 for biofeedback present is the (unweighted) average of the six cell means from Table 8.13 when biofeedback is present. Also shown in Table 8.23 is the deviation from the grand mean (which equals 184.50) for each effect. As shown earlier in Tables 8.9 and 8.11, these deviations are estimates of the effect parameters associated with each main effect. For example, $\hat{\alpha}_1 = -5.33$, which implies that the effect of biofeedback averaged over all conditions is to lower blood pressure 5.33 units relative to the grand mean. Similarly, Drug X lowers blood pressure by 10.00 units, and the diet lowers blood pressure by 8.50 units. We might then expect that biofeedback, Drug X, and diet in combination would lower blood pressure by 23.83 units (notice that 23.83 is the sum of 5.33, 10.00, and 8.50). Such a reduction from the grand mean (184.50) would produce a mean of 160.67.

However, as we have seen (in Tables 8.13 and 8.20 and in Figure 8.7), the actual mean for this condition is 169, considerably higher than we might have thought. What has gone wrong here? The reason these two values do not agree is that the value of 160.67 was obtained based on the assumption that the three factors combine additively. However, we know that in fact there are significant interactions for these data. The value of 160.67 was based on the

TABLE 8.23
MARGINAL MEANS FOR MAIN EFFECTS

	Marginal Mean	Deviation from Grand Mean
Biofeedback present	$\overline{Y}_{1..} = 179.17$	-5.33
Biofeedback absent	$\overline{Y}_{2..} = 189.83$	5.33
Drug X	$\overline{Y}_{.1.} = 174.50$	-10.00
Drug Y	$\overline{Y}_{.2.} = 190.75$	6.25
Drug Z	$\overline{Y}_{.3.} = 188.25$	3.75
Diet present	$\overline{Y}_{..1} = 176.00$	-8.50
Diet absent	$\overline{Y}_{..2} = 193.00$	8.50

assumption that μ_{112} would equal the sum of $\mu_{...}$, α_1, β_1, and γ_2, but this happens only if the factors do not interact. In general, the equation for μ_{112} comes from Equation 2 earlier in the chapter, and is given by

$$\mu_{112} = \mu_{...} + \alpha_1 + \beta_1 + \gamma_2 + (\alpha\beta)_{11} + (\alpha\gamma)_{12} + (\beta\gamma)_{12} + (\alpha\beta\gamma)_{112}$$

Of course, with sample data, we can only estimate these parameters, in which case we can write the equation as

$$\overline{Y}_{112} = \overline{Y}_{...} + \hat{\alpha}_1 + \hat{\beta}_1 + \hat{\gamma}_2 + \widehat{(\alpha\beta)}_{11} + \widehat{(\alpha\gamma)}_{12} + \widehat{(\beta\gamma)}_{12} + \widehat{(\alpha\beta\gamma)}_{112} \tag{9}$$

Expressions for these parameter estimates follow directly from the formulas shown in Tables 8.9 and 8.11. For our data, we have already seen that $\overline{Y}_{112} = 169$, $\overline{Y}_{...} = 184.5$, $\hat{\alpha}_1 = -5.33$, $\hat{\beta}_1 = -10.00$, and $\hat{\gamma}_2 = -8.50$. After some tedious calculations[5] based on the formulas in Tables 8.9 and 8.11, it can be shown that for our data, $\widehat{(\alpha\beta)}_{11} = -0.67$, $\widehat{(\alpha\gamma)}_{12} = 0.67$, $\widehat{(\beta\gamma)}_{12} = 5.00$ and $\widehat{(\alpha\beta\gamma)}_{112} = 3.33$. Substituting these values into Equation 9, we find that

$$169 = 184.50 + (-5.33) + (-10.00) + (-8.50) + (-0.67) + (0.67)$$
$$+ (5.00) + (3.33),$$

which is in fact an equality, as it must be. The point of this equation is to illustrate why the combination of the biofeedback, Drug X, and diet is less effective than might be expected based on their average effects. The parameter estimates we have calculated show that two influences are primarily responsible here. First, the combination of Drug X and diet is 5 points less effective at lowering blood pressure than the average effect of each would suggest. For this reason, it might be said that Drug X and diet interact antagonistically with one another. (If the whole were better than the sum of its parts, we could say that we have a synergistic interaction.) Second, the combination of all three therapies is 3.33 points less effective than their joint (pairwise) effects would suggest.

The previous discussion suggests that it might be wise not to combine Drug X and the diet in the same package. Indeed, if we combine Drug X and biofeedback without the diet, the cell mean is 168, the lowest mean of all (realize, however, that this mean is not statistically significantly lower than all other means). Alternatively, we might combine the diet and either Drug Y or Z with biofeedback, and the resultant sample mean is only slightly higher. An ultimate clinical decision would necessarily depend on additional factors such as possible side effects, costs, problems of compliance, and so forth. Nevertheless, it is important to realize that treatments in combination may behave differently from what would be expected on the basis of their separate effects. As pointed out in Chapter 7, the primary advantage of factorial designs is their ability to detect such patterns.

Tests to Be Performed When the Three-Way Interaction Is Nonsignificant

Although it may seem incredible, we have not yet finished Figure 8.6. In fact, in a sense we are only half finished. The reason is that so far we have only considered what happens when the three-way interaction is statistically significant. Now we must consider what tests to perform when the three-way interaction is nonsignificant.

In the absence of a three-way interaction, all two-way interactions can be interpreted unambiguously. The reason is that the magnitude of each two-way interaction is consistent (within sampling error) at the various levels of the third factor. As a result, we need not consider all three factors simultaneously but instead can focus on pairs of factors. In effect, we have a two-way design. However, there is an additional complication because we essentially have three different two-way designs: $A \times B$, $A \times C$, and $B \times C$. For this reason, the right-hand side of the flowchart in Figure 8.6 looks very much like Figure 7.2 in triplicate. For example, whereas we had only one two-way interaction to test in the two-way design of Chapter 7, we now have three two-way interactions to test in the three-way design. Nevertheless, the right-hand side of Figure 8.6 for the three-way design follows basically the same logic as did the flowchart in Chapter 7. The primary conceptual difference involves testing of main effects.

When are tests of main effects unambiguous? From Figure 8.6, we can see that a main-effect test is interpreted only when the factor in question is involved in no significant two-way interaction and the three-way interaction is nonsignificant. For example, if $A \times B$, $A \times C$, and $A \times B \times C$ are all nonsignificant, the effect of A is consistent at all combinations of B and C, so the A main effect is unambiguous. However, if any interaction involving A is significant, the effect of A is not the same for every combination of B and C, in which case the main effect of A may be misleading.

It may be helpful to explicitly compare the conditions under which a main effect is generally interpreted in the three-way design to those where a main effect would be interpreted in a two-way design. To make the example more concrete, we continue to consider the A main effect. In the two-way design, the A main effect is usually interpreted if and only if the $A \times B$ interaction is nonsignificant. Similarly, in the three-way design, the A main effect is usually interpreted if and only if the $A \times B$, the $A \times C$, and the $A \times B \times C$ interactions are all nonsignificant. Thus, in both designs, the A main effect is interpreted if and only if the A factor interacts with no other effects in the design. In contrast, when A does interact with another factor, in both designs the effect of A is typically examined within individual levels of the other factor.

As Figure 8.6 shows, when significant two-way interactions occur, they are interpreted just as they were in the two-way design. For example, suppose that the $A \times B$ interaction is statistically significant. According to the figure, tests of A within B and of B within A would be performed next. Two points need to be made here. First, there is no requirement that both types of tests be performed. For example, as we mentioned in Chapter 7, for theoretical reasons, only tests of B within A might be of interest in a particular situation. Second, when $A \times B$ is statistically significant, the flowchart says to test A within B_k. You should realize that this generally implies that A would be tested within each and every level of B. In other words, the k subscript in B_k simply refers to an arbitrary level of the B factor.

Figure 8.6 should prove useful as a guideline for interpreting effects in a three-factor design. However, as we mentioned when we introduced the flowchart, it is by no means a complete solution to all data-analysis problems in a three-way design. For example, the flowchart provides no assistance in deciding whether to use a pooled error term such as MS_W for all tests or to use separate error terms. It also provides no assistance in defining a family and choosing an appropriate procedure for maintaining the α_{FW} level at a desired level. The flowchart also assumes that interactions will be followed up by tests of simple effects. However, as we saw in Chapter 7, there are circumstances where interaction contrasts may be more informative than simple effects. That you understand the logic of the principles that underly the flowchart is important. If you not only can use the flowchart but also understand its logic, you need not be a slave to the flowchart. Instead, when exceptions occur in your studies, you can recognize them and act accordingly. Finally, the logic underlying this flowchart also holds for designs with four or more factors. If you understand the principles used to create Figure 8.6, generalizing them to designs with four or more factors should be reasonably straightforward.

Nonorthogonal Designs

So far in this chapter, we have restricted ourselves to equal-n designs. After the discussion of nonorthogonal two-way designs in Chapter 7, it should not surprise you to learn that additional complications also arise in the three-way design when cell sizes are unequal. As in the two-way design, it is extremely important prior to analyzing the data to understand why cell sizes are unequal. Because the issues are the same in a three-way design as in a two-way design, we refer you back to Chapter 7 instead of repeating the discussion here.

In terms of analysis, the same general issues are pertinent in the three-way design as were pertinent in the two-way design. In particular, it is once again true that there are different weights that can be applied when one or more factors are averaged over. As a result, there are again Type I, Type II, and Type III sums of squares. As we pointed out in Chapter 7, Type I sums of squares are generally of little interest, so we restrict our attention here to Type II and Type III sums of squares.

Recall that in the two-way design, the test of the $A \times B$ interaction yielded the same value for Type II and Type III sums of squares. The reason for this equivalence was that the $A \times B$ interaction in the two-way design did not average over any other factors. However, two-way interactions in three-way designs do average over another factor. For example, the $A \times B$ interaction in a three-way design averages over levels of C (as we saw in Table 8.8). Thus, in a nonorthogonal three-way design, both two-way interactions and main effects yield different values for Type II and Type III sums of squares. However, the $A \times B \times C$ interaction in a three-way interaction does not average over any other factors, and as a consequence, Type II and Type III sums of squares for $A \times B \times C$ are identical, even in a nonorthogonal design. In general, then, Type II and Type III sums of squares of the highest order interaction (i.e., the interaction of all factors in the design) are identical to each other. However, tests of lower order interactions (i.e., interactions that do not involve all factors) and tests of main effects differ, depending on whether these tests are based on Type II or Type III sums of squares.

The procedure for obtaining the Type III sum of squares for an effect is straightforward when conceptualized in terms of model comparisons. Regardless of the effect to be tested, the full model for Type III sum of squares is the same full model that we worked with earlier in the chapter, namely a model that includes all possible effects:

$$Y_{ijkl} = \mu + \alpha_j + \beta_k + \gamma_l + (\alpha\beta)_{jk} + (\alpha\gamma)_{jl} + (\beta\gamma)_{kl} + (\alpha\beta\gamma)_{jkl} + \varepsilon_{ijkl} \qquad \text{(2, repeated)}$$

The restricted model simply omits the parameters associated with the effect to be tested. Thus, the restricted models have the same form as those shown in Table 8.10. The only complication that arises in nonorthogonal designs is that the actual calculation of sums of squares is more complicated than they would be with equal n. In particular, the formulas shown in Table 8.11 are not appropriate in nonorthogonal designs. As in the two-way design, a comparison of models based on Type III sums of squares is a test of unweighted means. In other words, all levels of the factor(s) being averaged over are weighted equally.

The Type II sum of squares for an effect can also be found through model comparisons. However, here even the full model omits parameters of a higher order than the effect being tested if the parameters include the effect being tested. To understand what this means, we will look at tests for each of three effects based on Type II sum of squares: the three-way $A \times B \times C$ interaction, a two-way interaction ($A \times B$), and a main effect (A). First, let's consider the three-way interaction. To decide what the full model should be, we must deal with the "order" of the effect to be tested, where order depends on the number of factors involved in the effect. For example, a main effect includes no other factors in the effect and is thus said to be of order zero. A two-way interaction is of the next highest order, namely order one. A three-way interaction is then referred to as a second-order interaction. In a three-way design, there is no higher order effect than the three-way interaction. Thus, when testing the three-way interaction based on Type II sum of squares, there are no parameters of a higher order than the effect being tested to omit from the model. Hence, the full model is again of the form

$$Y_{ijkl} = \mu + \alpha_j + \beta_k + \gamma_l + (\alpha\beta)_{jk} + (\alpha\gamma)_{jl} + (\beta\gamma)_{kl} + (\alpha\beta\gamma)_{jkl} + \varepsilon_{ijkl} \qquad \text{(2, repeated)}$$

The restricted model is found by omitting the parameters associated with the effect being tested, namely $(\alpha\beta\gamma)_{jkl}$. Thus, the restricted model is given by

$$Y_{ijkl} = \mu + \alpha_j + \beta_k + \gamma_l + (\alpha\beta)_{jk} + (\alpha\gamma)_{jl} + (\beta\gamma)_{kl} + \varepsilon_{ijkl}$$

This is the same as the restricted model for Type III sum of squares. Thus, Type II and Type III sums of squares are identical for testing the three-way $A \times B \times C$ interaction in a three-factor design.

How do we find the Type II sum of squares for a two-way interaction such as $A \times B$? Recall that a two-way interaction is a first-order interaction. Parameters associated with second-order effects are therefore omitted from the full model, if they include parameters associated with $A \times B$. The parameters for the second-order effect (i.e., $A \times B \times C$) are $(\alpha\beta\gamma)_{jkl}$, which includes both α and β, so these parameters are omitted from the full model. Thus, the full model for testing $A \times B$ (or $A \times C$, or $B \times C$, for that matter) is given by

$$Y_{ijkl} = \mu + \alpha_j + \beta_k + \gamma_l + (\alpha\beta)_{jk} + (\alpha\gamma)_{jl} + (\beta\gamma)_{kl} + \varepsilon_{ijkl}$$

The restricted model for testing the $A \times B$ interaction omits, in addition, the $(\alpha\beta)_{jk}$ parameters, yielding

$$Y_{ijkl} = \mu + \alpha_j + \beta_k + \gamma_l + (\alpha\gamma)_{jl} + (\beta\gamma)_{kl} + \varepsilon_{ijkl}$$

Notice that the Type II comparison is different from the Type III comparison in that both of the Type II models omit the $(\alpha\beta\gamma)_{jkl}$ parameters and thus assume that the $A \times B \times C$ interaction is zero in the population. As in the two-way design, when the interaction is indeed zero, leaving out the $(\alpha\beta\gamma)_{jkl}$ parameters in both models increases power; however, when the interaction is nonzero, a bias occurs.

Finally, we need to consider the Type II sum of squares for a main effect. We will use the A main effect as an example. The full model here must omit parameters for all higher order effects that include α parameters. The higher order effects here are $A \times B$, $A \times C$, $B \times C$, and $A \times B \times C$. The corresponding parameters are $(\alpha\beta)_{jk}$, $(\alpha\gamma)_{jl}$, $(\beta\gamma)_{kl}$, and $(\alpha\beta\gamma)_{jkl}$, respectively. All these parameters except for $(\beta\gamma)_{kl}$ contain α and are thus omitted from the full model. Thus, the full model for testing the A main effect is given by

$$Y_{ijkl} = \mu + \alpha_j + \beta_k + \gamma_l + (\beta\gamma)_{kl} + \varepsilon_{ijkl}$$

The restricted model constrains each α_j to equal zero and is thus given by

$$Y_{ijkl} = \mu + \beta_k + \gamma_l + (\beta\gamma)_{kl} + \varepsilon_{ijkl}$$

Again, the Type II sum of squares is different from the Type III sum of squares in that the Type II sum of squares assumes certain effects to be zero. Specifically, for testing the A main effect, the Type II sum of squares approach assumes that the $A \times B$, $A \times C$, and $A \times B \times C$ effects are all zero in the population and hence omits them from both the full and the restricted models.[6] Notice that the effects that are omitted here are the ones that Figure 8.6 shows must be nonsignificant in order for the interpretation of the A main effect to be unambiguous. That is, the A effect is consistent at all combinations of B and C if and only if the $A \times B$, $A \times C$, and $A \times B \times C$ effects truly are zero in the population. The difference between Type II and Type III sums of squares is that the calculation of Type II sum of squares assumes that these higher order effects are literally zero, based on a nonsignificant result in the sample. If the effects are indeed zero in the population, tests based on Type II sum of squares are more powerful than tests based on Type III sum of squares. However, if some of the effects are nonzero, tests based on Type III sum of squares are much more easily interpreted than tests based on Type II sum of squares. In this situation, both tests involve the average A effect (for example) at the $b \times c$ different combinations of the B and C factors. The Type III sum of squares test is easy to interpret because (as in the two-way design) it is based on an unweighted average of the $b \times c$ different A effects. Thus, even if there is in fact some interaction in the population that our interaction tests fail to detect, at least the A effect we are testing is an unweighted average of the various effects that A has at the different combinations of B and C. However, the Type II sum of squares in this situation weights these various effects unequally, where the weights are a complicated function of the cell sizes. Because the cell sizes are typically unequal for reasons we are not interested in, tests based on Type II sum of squares are generally uninterpretable if a true population interaction has gone undetected in the sample. As we said in Chapter 7, our general recommendation is to perform tests based on Type III sums of squares. However, some researchers prefer Type II sums of squares, particularly in situations where there are strong theoretical reasons to expect interactions to be zero and empirical tests of the interactions result in p values substantially above .05 (e.g., above .20 or .25).

HIGHER ORDER DESIGNS

Although this chapter has not considered designs with more than three factors, the logic we have developed here extends in a straightforward manner to such designs. For example, suppose we obtain an $A \times B \times C \times D$ interaction in a four-way design. What would it mean? A four-way interaction would imply that each three-way interaction is different at the different levels of the fourth factor. For example, it would mean that the $A \times B \times C$ interaction is not the same at every level of D. As in two-way and three-way designs, there are other equivalent statements of this interaction as well. Here there are three other equivalent statements: $A \times B \times D$ is not the same at every level of C; $A \times C \times D$ is not the same at every level of B; $B \times C \times D$ is not the same at every level of A.

The same logic applies to a five-way interaction, a six-way interaction, or in fact to a n-way interaction, regardless of the value of n. However, a point comes when it is not terribly informative to say that the $A \times B \times C \times D$ interaction is not the same at every level of E. For this reason (and because of sample-size requirements), designs with many factors are uncommon in the behavioral sciences. Nevertheless, it is useful to know that the logic we have developed here generalizes to higher order designs.

Two other pieces of information are useful when working with higher order factorial designs. First, there is a simple formula for the total number of omnibus effects in any factorial design. By *omnibus effects*, we mean main effects and interactions, but not such effects as simple effects or cell mean comparisons. Specifically, in a completely crossed factorial design (i.e., no missing cells) with F factors, the number of effects equals $2^F - 1$. For example, suppose that we have a two-way design, so that $F = 2$. Then the number of effects according

TABLE 8.24
NUMBER OF EFFECTS OF EACH ORDER AND TOTAL NUMBER OF OMNIBUS
EFFECTS IN A COMPLETELY CROSSED FACTORIAL DESIGN

Number of Factors	Main Effects	Two-Way Interactions	Number of Three-Way Interactions	Four-Way Interactions	Five-Way Interactions	Total of Omnibus Effects
2	2	1	—	—	—	3
3	3	3	1	—	—	7
4	4	6	4	1	—	15
5	5	10	10	5	1	31

to the formula is $2^2 - 1$; 2 raised to the second power is 4, and $4 - 1 = 3$, so there are three omnibus effects. Indeed, this is correct because the omnibus effects are A, B, and $A \times B$. As a second example, suppose that we have a three-way design. Then the formula tells us that the number of omnibus effects is seven, which agrees with our finding earlier in the chapter (see Table 8.8).

Second, there is a formula for the number of effects of each "order" as well. Recall that main effects are of order zero, two-way interactions are of order one, and so forth. In a completely crossed factorial design with F factors, the number of effects of order R is given by

$$\frac{F!}{(R+1)!(F-R-1)!} \tag{10}$$

Here the exclamation sign means factorial. To see how the formula works, consider a three-way design, so $F = 3$. We can find the number of main effects by substituting $F = 3$ and $R = 0$ into Equation 10, yielding

$$\frac{3!}{(0+1)!(3-0-1)!}$$

This equals $6/(1)(2)$, or 3. Indeed, we already know that there are three main effects (i.e., effects of order zero) in a three-way design. Similarly, substituting $F = 3$ and $R = 1$ into Equation 10 also produces a value of 3, because there are three 2-way interactions in a three-factor design. Finally, substituting $F = 3$ and $R = 2$ into Equation 10 produces a value of 1 because there is only one three-way interaction in a three-factor design. Table 8.24 provides additional examples of these two formulas for different values of F, that is, for different numbers of factors.

EXERCISES

1. True or False: A statistically significant three-way $A \times B \times C$ interaction implies that none of the two-way interactions can be interpreted unambiguously.

2. True or False: Main effects in a three-factor design can be interpreted unambiguously even if there is a statistically significant three-way interaction as long as none of the two-way interactions are significant.

*3. Consider the hypothetical population cell means shown in Table 8.1. Assuming equal n, find the marginal mean for the drug-present condition. Also find the corresponding marginal mean for the drug-absent condition. Is there a drug main effect in the population?

4. Consider the hypothetical population cell means shown in Table 8.1. Assuming equal n, find the values of the marginal means to be compared to ascertain whether there is a main effect of diet. Is there a diet main effect in the population?

5. Consider the hypothetical population means shown in Table 8.1 for a $2 \times 2 \times 2$ design. Table 8.5 shows these population means for drug and biofeedback combinations, separately by diet. Similarly, Table 8.6 shows these same means for drug and diet combinations, separately by levels of biofeedback.

   a. Construct a table of these means for biofeedback and diet combinations, separately by drug.

   b. Does the table you constructed in part a demonstrate a three-way interaction in the population? How can you tell?

   c. Is the two-way Biofeedback $\times$ Diet interaction the same when drug is present as when it is absent? Which effect addresses this question?

6. Under what conditions can the B main effect in a three-way $A \times B \times C$ design be interpreted unambiguously?

7. Figure 8.7 shows one way to plot the cell means of Table 8.13. However, there are five additional ways these data could be displayed, because we could have separate plots for any of the three factors, and then either of the two remaining factors could be plotted on the x-axis. For example, we might choose to create one plot for the biofeedback-present condition and a second plot when biofeedback is absent. Further, we might choose to place level of diet on the x-axis.

   a. Draw this plot for the cell means shown in Table 8.13.

   b. What features of the data are highlighted more clearly by the plot in part a than by the plot in Figure 8.7?

   c. What features of the data are highlighted more clearly by the plot in Figure 8.7 than by the plot in part a?

*8. In a $2 \times 2 \times 2$ design, a contrast using the following coefficients is applied to the four cells at C_1, that is, at level 1 of factor C:

$$\begin{array}{cccc} A_1B_1 & A_1B_2 & A_2B_1 & A_2B_2 \\ \hline 1 & -1 & -1 & 1 \end{array}$$

The estimated value of ψ at C_1 is -8. The same coefficients applied to the four cell means at C_2 yields an estimated value of ψ at C_2 of $+8$. From this, which of the following is (or are) true?

   a. A contrast assessing the three-way interaction would have an estimated value of zero.

   b. There is some evidence of an AB interaction overall.

   c. There is some evidence of an ABC interaction.

   d. Tests of the simple two-way interactions of A and B at the two levels of C would be significant.

9. Consider the evidence for main effects and interactions indicated by the cell means shown in the plots and duplicated in the tables below. Assume equal n.

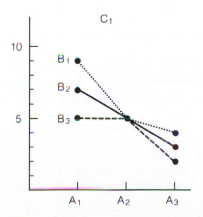 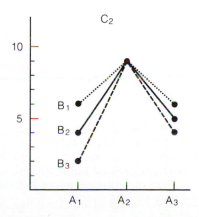

The matrices of cell means plotted above are as follows:

	C_1				C_2		
	A_1	A_2	A_3		A_1	A_2	A_3
B_1	9	5	4	B_1	6	9	6
B_2	7	5	3	B_2	4	9	5
B_3	5	5	2	B_3	2	9	4

a. For which of the effects listed below would the sum of squares be nonzero? In other words, is there some evidence present for each of the following effects?

1. A 5. AC
2. B 6. BC
3. C 7. ABC
4. AB

b. Verbally describe any interactions you believe are present.

*10. Below are the cell means in a three-way factorial design. Assume that there are 10 participants per cell and that $SS_W = 86,400$.

	C_1				C_2		
	B_1	B_2	B_3		B_1	B_2	B_3
A_1	45	55	65	A_1	40	40	70
A_2	55	75	65	A_2	20	30	40

a. Estimate the effect parameters for the main effects of factors A and B.
b. Perform tests of the main effects of factors A and B.
c. Plot the cell means shown above. Is there evidence for a three-way interaction in these data? Support your answer either with a verbal explanation or with numerical evidence.

*11. According to the text, there are three equivalent interpretations of a three-way interaction: (1) the $A \times B$ interaction varies as a function of C, (2) the $A \times C$ interaction varies as a function of B, and (3) the $B \times C$ interaction varies as a function of A. This exercise investigates why these three statements are identical. For simplicity, we restrict ourselves to a $2 \times 2 \times 2$ design.
a. Write the coefficients for a contrast of the eight cell means that would compare $A \times B$ at C_1 to $A \times B$ at C_2. (Hint: The $A \times B$ at C_1 subeffect can be represented as a contrast of four cell means. Let's call this contrast ψ_{c1}. Similarly, the $A \times B$ at C_2 subeffect compares four other cell means and can be written as ψ_{c2}. Then the contrast comparing $A \times B$ at C_1 to $A \times B$ at C_2 is literally given by $\psi_{c1} - \psi_{c2}$, the difference between the contrasts for the subeffects.)
b. Write the coefficients for a contrast of the eight cell means that would compare $A \times C$ at B_1 to $A \times C$ at B_2.
c. Write the coefficients for a contrast of the eight cell means that would compare $B \times C$ at A_1 to $B \times C$ at A_2.
d. How do the contrast coefficients of parts a–c relate to each other? What does this imply about the three equivalent interpretations of a three-way interaction?

*12. A three-factor, between-subjects design, having two levels of factor A, three levels of factor B, and two levels of factor C, has been conceptualized as a one-way design with 12 groups. Assume that you want to use the "special contrasts" option in SPSS MANOVA to assess the following effects: A, B, C, AB, AC, BC, and ABC. Assume that you enter the 12 groups in such a way that the first six groups are at level 1 of A, the last six are at level 2 of A. Within each of these sets of groups, the first two are at level 1 of B, the next two at level 2 of B, and the last two are at level 3 of B. Also, any two successive groups are at different levels of C. The first few lines of contrast coefficients are shown below with labels attached to indicate the effects to which they correspond:

												Effect
1	1	1	1	1	1	1	1	1	1	1	1/	
1	1	1	1	1	1	−1	−1	−1	−1	−1	−1/	A
1	1	0	0	−1	−1	1	1	0	0	−1	−1/	B
0	0	1	1	−1	−1	0	0	1	1	−1	−1/	
1	−1	1	−1	1	−1	1	−1	1	−1	1	−1/	C

a. Add the appropriate additional contrasts to the above that will allow all the desired effects to be tested. Indicate, for each contrast or set of contrasts, the label of the corresponding effect.
b. After completing your analysis, you find that you have a significant three-way interaction. You are interested in assessing the simple AB interactions.

    1. What contrasts would allow you to test AB at C_1 and AB at C_2?
    2. What rows of the original set of contrasts in part a would these new contrasts replace?

13. Which effect(s) in a four-way $A \times B \times C \times D$ nonorthogonal design will have the same value for Type II sums of squares as for Type III sums of squares? Why?

14. Social psychologists during the 1970s and 1980s investigated the generality of the "overjustification effect," which refers to the effect of subjects' receiving greater extrinsic rewards than are justified by their level of effort or performance. The following description is modeled after one of the experiments reported by Crano, W. D., Gorenflo, D. W., & Shackelford, S. L. (1988). Overjustification, assumed consensus, and attitude change: Further investigation of the incentive-aroused ambivalence hypothesis. *Journal of Personality and Social Psychology*, 55, 12–22. The focus of this study concerns students' attitudes toward a recent tuition increase at their university. Through a clever procedure, students were asked to read a prepared speech arguing against the increase but were led to believe that this request was unrelated to the study for which they had been recruited. Participants were randomly assigned to a payment condition. Half of the participants received a $5 payment, whereas the other half were not paid. After reading their speech, half of the participants in each payment condition were asked to read a speech that presented arguments in favor of the increase; the other half received no such countercommunication. The dependent variable to be considered here is a general measure of attitude toward the tuition increase. Higher scores represent more positive attitudes. Finally, a third factor in the design was a subject's initial attitude toward the increase (neutral, negative, or very negative) prior to participating in the study. Consider the following hypothetical (but realistic) cell means:

	Countercommunication Present					
	$5 Payment			**$0 Payment**		
Neutral	*Negative*	*Very Negative*	*Neutral*	*Negative*	*Very Negative*
33.1	31.6	29.3	25.1	23.3	21.1

	Countercommunication Absent					
	$5 Payment			**$0 Payment**		
Neutral	*Negative*	*Very Negative*	*Neutral*	*Negative*	*Very Negative*
30.7	29.3	26.9	26.8	25.3	23.3

Assume that there were 10 participants per cell and that $MS_W = 23.3$.
a. Test the statistical significance of the main effects, two-way interactions, and three-way interaction.

b. Can the main effect of payment be interpreted unambiguously? If not, perform the relevant simple effects tests of payment.

c. Can the main effect of countercommunication be interpreted unambiguously? If not, perform the relevant simple effects tests of countercommunication.

d. Calculate an appropriate measure of association strength for each of the omnibus effects you tested in part a. (Hint: Recall that if an estimated omega-squared value is less than zero, it is usually set equal to zero by convention.)

e. Suppose that a researcher who saw the results of part d claimed that there is strong evidence that countercommunication is unimportant in this paradigm. Use your results from part c together with corresponding confidence intervals to assess the validity of this researcher's claim.

15. In the exercises for Chapters 6 and 7, we considered a study investigating how parent–infant play changes as infants grow older. This exercise uses the same data, but adds the parent's gender as a third factor. Specifically, mothers of four girls and of four boys at each of three ages (7, 10, and 13 months) were videotaped during toy-play interactions with their infants. An equal number of fathers from different families were also observed. The dependent variable to be considered here was the proportion of time parents encouraged pretend play in their children. Suppose the following hypothetical data were obtained:

| | Mothers | | | | | |
| | Girls | | | Boys | | |
7-Month-Olds	10-Month-Olds	13-Month-Olds	7-Month-Olds	10-Month-Olds	13-Month-Olds
.01	.09	.18	.02	.11	.45
.09	.05	.43	.02	.19	.20
.05	.15	.24	.13	.12	.49
.06	.11	.40	.06	.04	.19

| | Fathers | | | | | |
| | Girls | | | Boys | | |
7-Month-Olds	10-Month-Olds	13-Month-Olds	7-Month-Olds	10-Month-Olds	13-Month-Olds
.02	.15	.09	.05	.14	.02
.01	.11	.03	.01	.21	.19
.07	.22	.18	.04	.06	.15
.04	.05	.12	.03	.12	.07

a. Test the statistical significance of the three main effects, the three two-way interactions, and the three-way interaction. Also calculate corresponding measures of association strength for each effect.

b. Plot the cell means in a manner similar to that shown in Figure 8.7. Specifically, draw one plot for girls and a second plot for boys. Place Age on the x-axis for each plot.

c. What effects appear to be present in your plots? Is the visual impression consistent with the results of the significance tests from part a?

d. What additional tests involving the factor of the child's gender should be performed, based on your results from part a? (Hint: You may want to consult Figure 8.6.)

e. According to the flowchart shown in Figure 8.6, what additional tests of effects involving the parent's gender and the child's age might be performed here?

f. Perform any and all appropriate tests of simple effects of parent's gender within levels of the child's age.

g. Find corresponding confidence intervals for each of the effects you tested in part f.

h. Perform any and all appropriate tests of simple effects of the child's age separately for mothers and fathers.

i. Test the linear trend of child's age, separately for mothers and fathers.

j. Find corresponding confidence intervals for each linear trend you tested in part i. In particular, define the slope in terms of a 1-month change in age.

k. Summarize the nature of your findings for these data.

16. During the 1980s, social psychologists renewed their investigation of how participants are influenced by persuasive information. The following study is modeled after an experiment reported by DeBono, K. G., and Harnish, R. J. (1988). Source expertise, source attractiveness, and the processing of persuasive information: A functional approach. *Journal of Personality and Social Psychology*, 55, 541–546. Participants listened to a tape-recorded speech criticizing a university calendar picturing members of the pom-pom squad. All participants listened to the same speaker, but they were randomly assigned either to an expert condition, where they were led to believe that the speaker was a nationally known research psychologist, or to an attractive source condition, where they believed that the speaker was a leader in student government. Within each source condition, participants were randomly assigned to hear one of two versions of the tape, one of which presented strong arguments and the other of which presented weak arguments. The dependent variable was a 7-point Likert scale item (1 = worthless, 7 = valuable) measuring how valuable they thought the calendar was. Finally, participants were classified as either high or low self-monitoring based on their responses to the Self-Monitoring Scale. Consider the following hypothetical data:

High Self-Monitors

Strong Argument		Weak Argument	
Expert Source	Attractive Source	Expert Source	Attractive Source
4	4	3	5
3	4	5	5
4	2	3	7
5	3	2	5
2	5	6	6
5	3	4	4
4	2	4	3
6	3	3	5
3	4	5	6
4	3	3	7
5	2	2	7
4	4	3	6

Low Self-Monitors

Strong Argument		Weak Argument	
Expert Source	Attractive Source	Expert Source	Attractive Source
3	5	5	6
5	4	6	4
5	3	4	4
4	2	7	2
3	4	6	4
2	6	7	5
1	2	5	4
5	4	6	3
3	4	4	4
4	3	6	2
3	4	7	3
4	3	5	4

a. Test the statistical significance of the main effects, the two-way interactions, and the three-way interaction.

b. Is the effect of argument strength (i.e., weak vs. strong) the same when it comes from an expert as from an attractive source?

c. Answer part b for high self-monitoring participants only.

d. Answer part b for low self-monitoring participants only.

e. How can you reconcile the answers you gave in Parts c and d with your answer to part b?

f. Are high self-monitoring participants influenced by argument strength (weak versus strong) if the argument comes from an attractive source?

g. Are high self-monitoring participants influenced by argument strength if the argument comes from an expert source?

h. Are low self-monitoring participants influenced by argument strength if the argument comes from an attractive source?

i. Are low self-monitoring participants influenced by argument strength if the argument comes from an expert source?

j. Which of the following statements provides the most accurate description of the effect of argument strength for these data:

  1. Argument strength has an effect only if it is believed to come from an expert source.
  2. Argument strength has an effect only on high self-monitoring participants who believe the source is an expert.
  3. Argument strength has an effect only on low self-monitoring participants who believe the source is an expert or on high self-monitoring participants who believe the source is attractive.
  4. Argument strength has an effect only on low self-monitoring participants who believe the source is an expert.

17. A counseling psychologist is interested in comparing three types of therapy for modifying snake phobia. However, she does not believe that one type is necessarily best for everyone; instead, the best type may depend on degree (i.e., severity) of phobia. Undergraduate students enrolled in an introductory psychology course are given the Fear Schedule Survey (FSS) to screen out participants showing no fear of snakes. Those displaying some degree of phobia are classified as either mildly or severely phobic on the basis of the FSS. One third of females and one third of males within each level of severity are then randomly assigned to a treatment condition: either systematic desensitization, implosive therapy, or insight therapy. The following data are obtained using the Behavioral Avoidance Test (higher scores indicate less phobia):

	Desensitization			Implosion			Insight		
	Mild	Moderate	Severe	Mild	Moderate	Severe	Mild	Moderate	Severe
Females	10	12	10	15	12	6	13	11	10
	12	9	11	12	10	7	9	7	6
	13	10	9	14	11	5	11	8	8
Males	16	11	12	17	14	10	16	10	11
	14	15	11	18	13	9	12	12	10
	17	13	13	16	12	11	14	14	9

Your task is to analyze these data, to answer any questions you believe would be of theoretical interest. Don't feel compelled to perform an analysis just because it would be possible statistically. Longer is not necessarily better. On the other hand, you probably will not want to stop after testing only main effects and the interaction.

You should describe your findings in a manner consistent with the results section of an American Psychological Association journal. If it seems appropriate, you may want to briefly justify your choice of α level, error term, and so on, but do not let this discussion overshadow what the results mean. Also, you may not want to focus exclusively on significance tests—descriptive statistics may also be useful.

9

Designs With Covariates: ANCOVA and Blocking

The primary goal of the models approach to data analysis is to develop a model that is an adequate representation of the data. Up to now, we have approached this task using as explanatory or predictor variables only those variables that denote group membership. In most situations, such group-membership variables account for a relatively small proportion of the total variance in the dependent variable. The between-group sum of squares typically is less than half of the total sum of squares and frequently is *much* smaller than the within-group sum of squares. This should not be surprising. Although the more extreme early behaviorists may have hoped that they could explain nearly all the variance in behavior by their experimental manipulations, most researchers in the behavioral sciences today expect that preexisting differences among subjects are at least as important a predictor of their scores on the dependent variable as any treatment variable. This chapter considers how best to make use of information you might obtain about the individual differences among subjects that are present at the beginning of your study.

These preexisting differences typically are not the principal focus of your investigation, but might be reflected in background information collected on your subjects at the start of your study. Historically, such variables were labeled *concomitant variables*: literally, variables that come along with the more central parts of the study. The terminology used more often in recent years for referring to such variables is *covariates*, suggesting that they are expected to covary, or correlate, with the dependent variable. In this chapter we use the term covariate interchangeably with concomitant variable to refer to a measure of individual differences among participants.

A correlation would most obviously be expected in the case in which the covariate represents the same conceptual measure as the dependent variable. For example, in a study of the effects of differing instructions on the amount of private speech a young child produces, one might measure the private speech each child produces before and after the experimental manipulation. There is great variation in how much different children talk to themselves; how much each child tends to do this before the manipulation would likely correlate more highly with the postmeasure than would the treatment-group variables. Because the sensitivity of your statistical tests and the corresponding precision of confidence intervals is directly dependent on the proportion of variance in your study that you can account for, to incorporate this continuous variable into your model is clearly desirable. As we tried to anticipate in our discussion in Chapter 3 (see also the tutorial on multiple regression on the data disk), the X variables used as predictors in linear models can be either continuous or discrete variables. We indicate the form of a model with both discrete and continuous variables shortly, but first some preliminary points must be made.

Although it is perhaps easiest to think of the covariate as involving the same instrument or as being the same conceptual measure as the dependent variable, it is not necessary to do so. One could predict a child's private speech after instructions by his or her private speech before instructions, but one might also use a quite different variable such as chronological age or mental age as the covariate. Variables that are on the same scale or expressed in the same units, for example, verbal IQ and performance IQ, are said to be *commensurate*. If one is to compute differences between measures, as is done in a matched-pairs t test, it is necessary that the variables be commensurate.[1] However, for most of the analyses considered in this chapter, the covariate and dependent variables are not required to be commensurate.

A second preliminary point concerns the need to distinguish between using the concomitant variable or covariate in the design of the study as opposed to the analysis. It is possible to use a concomitant variable in the design of the study but not in the analysis, in the analysis but not in the design, or in both the analysis and the design, although not all these options are necessarily desirable. The concomitant variable is used in the design of the study if it is used in the assignment of subjects to groups. The concomitant variable is used in the analysis if it is represented in the models used in analyzing the data. In part, then, the goal may be to equate the groups either experimentally or statistically. To accomplish this "experimentally," one can form the treatment groups in such a way that they are "matched" on the concomitant variable, as long as the concomitant variable scores are available prior to the formation of the treatment groups. The sense in which the groups are matched and the specifics of how the matching can be carried out are described later in the section on blocking. Statistical equating of groups is accomplished by allowing for variation in the covariate both within and between groups in analyzing data. Both experimental and statistical means of controlling for ancillary variables yield advantages.

A related point to the distinction between using the concomitant variable in design as opposed to analysis is the issue of whether the concomitant variable is to be treated as a continuous variable. When the concomitant variable is a continuous variable used to form the groups for the design, it is common practice to ignore at least some of the continuous information in the concomitant variable when the time comes to analyze the data. As we argue subsequently in the chapter, to do so is to throw away information. Alternatively, the concomitant variable can be viewed as a continuous variable throughout. In this situation, the concomitant variable is viewed as varying along with the dependent variable. This is why, as mentioned previously, the concomitant variable in this context is called a *covariate*, and the analysis method that takes into account the relationship between the covariate and the dependent variable is referred to as *analysis of covariance* (ANCOVA). In most ANCOVA studies, the covariate is not considered at the time of forming groups, although as we will see, there could be some advantages in doing so. Rather, ANCOVA is typically viewed as a method of analysis that statistically adjusts for differences on the covariate by including it as a continuous predictor variable in the analysis.

In sum, ANCOVA, like ANOVA, refers to a comparison of models that are special cases of the general linear model. In one sense, the only new wrinkle in ANCOVA is that one of the predictors is a continuous variable. The conceptual problem of interpreting the meaning of an ANCOVA can be difficult, however, particularly in the case in which one has not randomly assigned subjects to groups. Perhaps because of the logical difficulties of statistical adjustment, some prefer to form groups or blocks of subjects that are relatively similar with respect to the covariate. Thus, the covariate in such a blocked design is transformed into an additional factor with discrete levels that is crossed with any other factors included in the design.

This chapter considers the approaches to handling concomitant variables that are represented by both ANCOVA and blocking. We begin with a consideration of analysis methods that treats the concomitant variable as a continuous variable. The primary data-analysis method of ANCOVA is compared with other related approaches, namely the analysis of change scores and the analysis of residuals. Next, we consider methods of analyzing blocked designs and include a discussion of issues that arise when the blocking is carried out after, rather than before, the study is run. Finally, we conclude with a comparison of ANCOVA and blocking approaches.

ANCOVA

The Logic of ANCOVA

The designs in which ANCOVA could be used arise with great regularity in psychological research. The minimal requirements, as far as the design is concerned, are that there be two or more groups and that you have information on some characteristic of your subjects besides the dependent variable. (There are a number of statistical assumptions that are required, of course, for the statistical tests to be valid; we do not concern ourselves with those for the moment.)

The logic of ANCOVA is to address the conditional question of "Would the groups have been different on the postmeasure if they had been equivalent on the covariate?" Thus, one wants to allow for the covariate in essentially the same way that the effects of confounded factors are allowed for in nonorthogonal ANOVA. Put differently, one wants to remove from the unexplained variability and from the treatment effect any variability that is associated with variability in the covariate.

Thus, including a covariate in your model affects your analysis in two ways. First, the within-group variability is reduced by an amount dependent on the strength of the relationship between the dependent variable and the covariate. This reduction is often substantial, particularly when the covariate represents an earlier administration of the same instrument as the dependent variable. In fact, for the sum of squares associated with the covariate (sometimes referred to as the *sum of squares regression*) to be much larger than the sum of squares associated with the treatment effect is not unusual. Thus, the primary impact of entering the covariate into your model is typically a substantial reduction in the unexplained variance and hence a corresponding increase in the power of your analysis to detect treatment effects. Corresponding to this increase in power for statistical tests is an increase in precision for estimating the magnitude of treatment effects. In particular, we see later in the chapter that including a covariate in your model often results in a much narrower confidence interval for the treatment effect than would be obtained in a model without the covariate.

The second possible effect of including a covariate is the adjustment of the estimated magnitude of the treatment effect itself. How large this adjustment is also can depend on how strongly related the dependent variable and the covariate are, but more importantly, the adjustment is affected by how different the experimental groups are on the covariate. If the observed group means on the covariate were all identical, there would be no effect of including a covariate in the model on the magnitude of the estimated treatment effect. In studies in which subjects are randomly assigned to groups, there is reason to expect the group means on the covariate to be similar if not virtually identical; thus, the adjustment in the estimated magnitude of the treatment effect is also correspondingly small. However, in nonrandomized studies or in studies using intact groups such as ethnic or cultural groups, the adjustment in the estimated treatment effect can be substantial. In fact, under certain conditions, which we illustrate shortly, the adjustment can be so dramatic that an effect that would be judged as a significant advantage of Group A over Group B by an ANOVA might be evaluated as a significant advantage of Group B over Group A by ANCOVA. This ability to compensate to some extent for preexisting differences among groups is why ANCOVA is often recommended as a means of addressing the threats to the internal validity that arise in studies with selection differences between groups (e.g., Cook & Campbell, 1979, Chapter 4). Nonetheless, using ANCOVA to equate groups should not be viewed as a substitute for randomization. Even if all the statistical assumptions made by ANCOVA were perfectly met, the equating accomplished by ANCOVA for intact groups is not in the same league as random assignment. When subjects are randomly assigned to groups, you are assured that in the long run—that is, over repeated implementations of a study carried out in the same fashion—there would be no differences between the groups at the start of your study on any dimension. However, ANCOVA, at best, equates the groups on the dimension(s) represented by the particular covariate(s) included in the analysis. There is no assurance that the particular variables chosen represent all, or even the more important, dimensions along which the groups differ. Furthermore, matching groups on one dimension might mean that you are creating differences along a second dimension.

For example, suppose that you want to look at differences between inner-city and suburban school children in their ability to use a particular cognitive strategy in their studying. You might think that it was important to control for potential differences in the IQs of the children so that you would be dealing with two groups of children at approximately the same mental level. This equating of the groups on IQ could be accomplished by forming your groups in such a way that each child in the suburban group would be matched with a child in the inner-city group having approximately the same IQ. As an alternative to such matching, the IQs of children could simply be included as a predictor in your model and an ANCOVA carried out. In either case, the logic of equating the groups is the same. The attempt is to arrive at a "fairer" comparison of inner-city and suburban children by using groups with equal IQs. However, as Meehl (1970a) points out, such systematic matching may result in systematic mismatching. Conceivably, inner-city children may have lower tested IQs but equal motivation to achieve when compared with suburban children; further, IQ and achievement motivation may be positively correlated within each group. By selecting samples of children having a mean IQ that is higher than average for inner-city children but lower than average for suburban children, one might have inadvertently assured that the subpopulations for which your groups represent random samples differ considerably in achievement motivation. That is, inner-city children with above-average IQs may represent a subpopulation of inner-city children who also have high motivation to achieve; conversely, your sample of suburban children who have IQs that are lower than that of suburban children in general may represent a subpopulation of low achievement-motivation suburbanites. The same charge could be leveled at an analysis that covaried IQ, even though the groups represented random samples from the entire populations of inner-city and suburban children. The ANCOVA test for treatment effects can be thought of as an evaluation of the difference between the performance of inner-city and suburban children having IQs that are intermediate between the mean IQs for the two groups. Either method of controlling for IQ, matching or ANCOVA, can result in a comparison of subpopulations that differ from the intact populations in important ways that are relevant to performance on the experimental task.

In sum, although ANCOVA can be used in an effort to make more nearly comparable intact groups that differ in known ways, always remember that the adjustment may well introduce or exaggerate differences along some dimensions while it reduces the differences along other dimensions. The oft-quoted conclusion of Frederic Lord (1967) regarding this quandary bears repeating: "With the data usually available for such studies, there is simply no logical or statistical procedure that can be counted on to make proper allowances for uncontrolled pre-existing differences between groups" (p. 307). Despite this, in randomized studies there is virtually no other design and analysis alternative to ANCOVA that can be as widely and easily used to bring about a legitimate increase in the power of your tests.

Linear Models for ANCOVA

Recall that in Chapter 3, when we first introduced linear models, we indicated the general form of a linear model both verbally and using symbols. Using words, the structure of a linear model is

$$\frac{\text{observed value on}}{\text{dependent variable}} = \frac{\text{sum of effects of}}{\text{allowed-for factors}} + \frac{\text{sum of effects}}{\text{of other factors}}$$

In symbols, we can say the same thing as follows:

$$Y_i = \beta_0 X_{0_i} + \beta_1 X_{1_i} + \beta_2 X_{2_i} + \beta_3 X_{3_i} + \cdots + \beta_p X_{p_i} + \varepsilon_i$$

where Y_i is the score of individual i on the dependent variable, the βs are unknown parameters, and the X terms represent the factors being used to predict performance. Up to now, the X variables have always been either dummy variables indicating group membership or the coefficients for contrasts among selected groups. Thus, all our analyses have involved only discrete predictor variables.

One of the happy advantages of the model-comparison approach is that ANCOVA can be conceptualized as simply a change in form of one of the predictor variables from a discrete to a continuous variable. Older approaches to psychological statistics, which were built around schemes of hand calculations appropriate for desk calculators, frequently encountered real difficulty in trying to present ANCOVA clearly because the computational formulas for ANCOVA are rather messy and hard to code in intuitively meaningful ways. It was easy for the student to miss the logic of ANCOVA by focusing on the calculations involved in following the computational formulas. In contrast, our approach, as usual, emphasizes the model comparison involved in ANCOVA.

To make things concrete, consider the following pre-post design. Assume that you are conducting a training program designed to assist people in losing weight. You solicit a group of volunteers, collect an initial weight measurement for each individual, and randomly assign subjects to either a treatment condition or a waiting-list control. At the end of the training program for the treatment group, you get another weight measurement for each subject. The research question of interest is whether the weight of the subjects receiving the treatment is lower when completing the treatment than the weight of subjects who also volunteered for the program but have not yet received it.

Clearly, in this situation, we would expect that within each group a person's initial weight would be positively correlated with his or her final weight. Thus, the test of the treatment effect could be made more sensitive by including the initial weight in the model.

The test of primary interest in ANCOVA is this test of the treatment effect. In a one-way design, the ANCOVA test of the treatment effect involves the comparison of the following models:

$$\text{Full:} \quad Y_{ij} = \mu + \alpha_j + \beta X_{ij} + \varepsilon_{ij} \tag{1}$$

$$\text{Restricted:} \quad Y_{ij} = \mu + \beta X_{ij} + \varepsilon_{ij} \tag{2}$$

where Y_{ij} is the score of the ith individual in the jth group on the dependent variable, μ is a "grand mean" parameter (but, as we will see, should be conceived as an intercept for a regression line, rather than an estimate of the mean of the Y scores), β is a population regression coefficient, X_{ij} is the score of the ith subject in the jth group on the concomitant variable,[2] and ε_{ij} is the error term for the same subject. As in the general case of one-way ANOVA, these models can be applied to any number of groups and to varying numbers of subjects per group; that is, $j = 1, 2, 3, \ldots, a$ and $i = 1, 2, 3, \ldots, n_j$. We present the formulas as we proceed for this general case but illustrate them using examples of the simplest case of two groups. In terms of the concrete example, X would be the individual's initial weight, Y would be final weight, and β would be directly related to the correlation between these two weights.

Parameter Estimates

Once again, we want to choose the estimates for the parameters of our models in such a way that the fit to the data is as close as possible. ANCOVA models have a major advantage over ANOVA models in attempting to fit the data in that ANCOVA models have the capability of making a different prediction for each individual subject rather than having to make the same prediction for all individuals within a group. This is the case because in ANCOVA the predictions are a function of the score on the covariate X_{ij}, which is uniquely determined for each individual.

Figure 9.1 illustrates this advantage in minimizing errors in ANCOVA. Figure 9.1(a) is relevant to the restricted model for ANOVA, and Figure 9.1(b) is relevant to the restricted

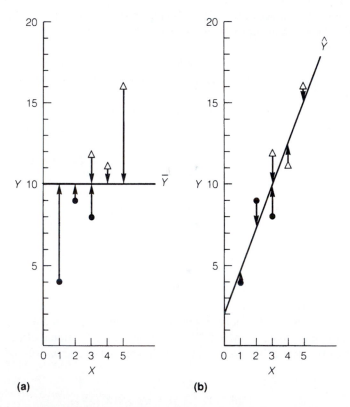

FIG. 9.1. Comparison of errors in (a) ANOVA and (b) ANCOVA restricted models.

TABLE 9.1
DATA FOR COMPARISON OF ANOVA
AND ANCOVA

Subject	Group	X	Y
1	1	1	4
2	1	2	9
3	1	3	8
4	2	3	12
5	2	4	11
6	2	5	16

model for an ANCOVA of the same data. The data represented in each panel are the scores for six subjects.[3] (The numerical values are given in Table 9.1.) These subjects are divided into two groups of three subjects each, but, for the moment, we ignore group membership. This corresponds to the way the data would be represented by the restricted models because they would not include a group-membership parameter.

The restricted model for a two-group ANOVA would make the same prediction for all subjects, namely the grand mean. Thus, the predictions in this model are illustrated by a flat line at $\overline{Y}$, and the errors of prediction are the vertical distances of the data points from this flat line. Rather than picturing the data in a vertical column for each group, the data points are scattered horizontally across the graph with the location being determined by both the X and Y values. However, information on any covariate is ignored by the ANOVA models.

In ANCOVA, in both the restricted and the full models, the predictions are a function of the individuals' X scores. Thus, differential predictions are made for each X value, and in the current example, the predictions of the restricted model would fall along the sloped line shown in Figure 9.1(b). Obviously, the magnitude of the errors, represented again by the length of the vertical lines from the data points to the prediction line, is much less in the ANCOVA case than in the ANOVA situation.

The price paid statistically for this increase in predictive accuracy is a relatively small one, namely a degree of freedom is used to estimate the parameter indicating how steeply sloped the prediction line is. We now move to a consideration of how to estimate this parameter and the other parameters of our ANCOVA models.

Beginning with the ANCOVA restricted model,

$$\text{Restricted:} \quad Y_{ij} = \mu + \beta X_{ij} + \varepsilon_{ij} \qquad \text{(2, repeated)}$$

we must arrive at estimates for μ and β, which for the moment we designate $\hat{\mu}$ and $\hat{\beta}$. Thus, our prediction equation would be

$$\hat{Y}_{ij} = \hat{\mu} + \hat{\beta} X_{ij} \qquad (3)$$

$\hat{\mu}$ is then the value we would predict for Y when $X_{ij} = 0$, which, as can be seen in Figure 9.1(b), is where the line of predictions intersects the Y axis. In ANCOVA, $\hat{\mu}$ is not in general an estimate of the grand mean of the Y scores but is the Y intercept of a regression line. β, however, indicates how many units change in predicted Y scores there should be for each unit change in X. In the simple situation here, once the data are represented in a scatterplot, as in Figure 9.1(b), it is possible to arrive at quite reasonable estimates by inspection. For example, looking at the figure we see that as X increases 4 units, from 1 to 5, Y increases from 4 to 16, or 12 units, suggesting a slope of approximately $12/4 = 3$. Thus, a line with such a slope going through the center of the scatterplot would appear to intersect the Y axis at a Y value of 1 or 2. Although in realistic data-analysis situations you will likely have a computer doing calculations, it is a very good idea to plot your data by computer, or, if that is not available, plot at least a sample of it by hand, to assure that the computer-generated parameter values make sense in light of what your inspection of the data tells you should be reasonable. Many graduate students have been embarrassed by writing theses based on computer-generated summary statistics only to learn later that the results were nonsensical. Frequent pitfalls include giving the computer incorrect values as input (e.g., when a 999 value intended as a code for missing data is treated as a valid observation) or, having entered everything correctly, reading off the wrong number from the screen or printout. Although using a machine that does arithmetic perfectly would seem a foolproof method of analyzing data, the capacity of the human to foul up things is frequently astounding. Try to offset this to some extent by always plotting the raw data for any research study. Especially as the design or analysis becomes more complicated, such as when trying to interpret adjusted means in ANCOVA, a simple graph can prove invaluable in understanding why your computer output must be wrong, or preferably, why it makes perfect sense. In the explanations of ANCOVA that follow, we make extensive use of plots so that you can see what is happening at each step in the analysis.

The statistical criterion used to arrive at "optimal" estimates of the parameters in ANCOVA is, again, the least-squares criterion. In the restricted model, this means choosing the values of $\hat{\mu}$ and $\hat{\beta}$ in such a way that we minimize the sum of squared errors of our predictions:

$$E_R = \sum_j \sum_i e_{ij}^2 = \sum_j \sum_i (Y_{ij} - \hat{Y}_{ij})^2 = \sum_j \sum_i (Y_{ij} - \hat{\mu} - \hat{\beta} X_{ij})^2 \qquad (4)$$

Clearly, E_R will change as a function of what we choose $\hat{\mu}$ and $\hat{\beta}$ to be, with the rate of change in E_R being indicated by what in calculus is called the derivative of the function with respect to $\hat{\mu}$ or $\hat{\beta}$. The only point at which the rate of change of this function will be zero is at its minimal value. Thus, the solution from calculus to this least-squares problem is to set equal to zero the derivatives of the last expression on the right above, and solve for $\hat{\mu}$ and $\hat{\beta}$. Taking derivatives with respect to $\hat{\mu}$ and $\hat{\beta}$ results in the following expressions, respectively, each of which is set equal to zero:

$$2 \sum_j \sum_i (Y_{ij} - \hat{\mu} - \hat{\beta} X_{ij})(-1) = 0 \qquad (5)$$

$$2 \sum_j \sum_i (Y_{ij} - \hat{\mu} - \hat{\beta} X_{ij})(-X_{ij}) = 0$$

These are referred to as the *normal equations*. Solving the first for $\hat{\mu}$ readily yields

$$\hat{\mu} = \overline{Y} - \hat{\beta}\overline{X} = a \qquad (6)$$

We might designate this estimate a, as indicated in Equation 6, the symbol frequently used for the intercept in elementary statistical texts. When we substitute this into the second equation, a little algebraic manipulation yields the least-squares estimate of β:

$$\hat{\beta} = \frac{\sum_j \sum_i (X_{ij} - \overline{X})(Y_{ij} - \overline{Y})}{\sum_j \sum_i (X_{ij} - \overline{X})^2} = b_T \qquad (7)$$

As indicated in Equation 7, we designate this estimated value b_T, because it is the slope when the total sample is treated as one group.

We can illustrate the use of these results by solving for the slope and intercept for the simple data set we have been examining in Figure 9.1 and Table 9.1. We begin with the formula for the slope because Equation 6 requires that we know the slope in order to compute the intercept. First, look closely at Equation 7 to see if you have encountered at least parts of it in different contexts. Note that the definitional formula shown in Equation 7 has a numerator that is identical to the definitional formula for the correlation coefficient, r:

$$r = \frac{\sum_j \sum_i (X_{ij} - \overline{X})(Y_{ij} - \overline{Y})}{\sqrt{\sum_j \sum_i (X_{ij} - \overline{X})^2 \sum_j \sum_i (Y_{ij} - \overline{Y})^2}} \tag{8}$$

Of course, the correlation coefficient is unitless because the XY units in the numerator are canceled by those in the denominator. The regression coefficient however is in "Y over X" units, which is reasonable because a slope indicates how many units in Y the regression line rises or falls for a one-unit increase in X. Realize, however, this means that a regression coefficient of .1 in one study may indicate a stronger relationship than a regression coefficient of 1000 in another study if different variables are involved.

Returning to our numerical example, we first compute deviations from the mean for both X and Y. Then, the sum of the squared deviations in X is computed for the denominator of the slope formula and the sum of the cross-products of deviations is computed for the numerator, as shown in Table 9.2. Thus, the least-squares estimate of b_T is shown to be 2.6, which is slightly smaller than the value we guessed by looking at the extreme values on X and Y. To

TABLE 9.2

CALCULATION OF LEAST-SQUARES ESTIMATES OF SLOPE AND INTERCEPT FOR
THE ANCOVA RESTRICTED MODEL

X	$X - \overline{X}$	Y	$Y - \overline{Y}$	$(X - \overline{X})^2$	$(X - \overline{X})(Y - \overline{Y})$
1	−2	4	−6	4	12
2	−1	9	−1	1	1
3	0	8	−2	0	0
3	0	12	2	0	0
4	1	11	1	1	1
5	2	16	6	4	12
$\sum = 18$		$\sum = 60$		$\sum = 10$	$\sum = 26$
$\overline{X} = 3$		$\overline{Y} = 10$			

Using Equation 7 to compute the slope:

$$b_T = \frac{\sum_j \sum_i (X_{ij} - \overline{X})(Y_{ij} - \overline{Y})}{\sum_j \sum_i (X_{ij} - \overline{X})^2} = \frac{26}{10} = 2.6$$

Using Equation 6 to compute the intercept:

$$a = \overline{Y} - \hat{\beta}\overline{X} = \overline{Y} - b_T\overline{X} = 10 - 2.6(3) = 10 - 7.8 = 2.2$$

The resulting prediction equation:

$$\hat{Y}_{ij} = a + b_T X_{ij} = 2.2 + 2.6 X_{ij}$$

TABLE 9.3

COMPUTATION OF ERROR SUM OF SQUARES ASSOCIATED WITH THE ANCOVA
RESTRICTED MODEL

X	Y	$\hat{Y}$	$Y - \hat{Y}$	$(Y - \hat{Y})^2$
1	4	4.8	−.8	.64
2	9	7.4	1.6	2.56
3	8	10.0	−2.0	4.00
3	12	10.0	2.0	4.00
4	11	12.6	−1.6	2.56
5	16	15.2	.8	.64
				$\sum = 14.40 = E_R$

Predicted values for the ANCOVA restricted model are calculated as follows:

$$
\begin{aligned}
\hat{Y}_{ij} &= 2.2 + 2.6 X_{ij} \\
\hat{Y}_{11} &= 2.2 + 2.6(1) = 2.2 + 2.6 = 4.8 \\
\hat{Y}_{21} &= 2.2 + 2.6(2) = 2.2 + 5.2 = 7.4 \\
\hat{Y}_{31} &= 2.2 + 2.6(3) = 2.2 + 7.8 = 10.0 \\
\hat{Y}_{12} &= 2.2 + 2.6(3) = 2.2 + 7.8 = 10.0 \\
\hat{Y}_{22} &= 2.2 + 2.6(4) = 2.2 + 10.4 = 12.6 \\
\hat{Y}_{32} &= 2.2 + 2.6(5) = 2.2 + 13.0 = 15.2
\end{aligned}
$$

obtain the least-squares estimate of the intercept, we substitute the numerical value we just obtained for the slope into Equation 6. This is done at the bottom of Table 9.2, where we have used b_T rather than $\hat{\beta}$ to denote the estimated value of the slope and have used a rather than $\hat{\mu}$ to denote the estimated intercept parameter. Thus, the prediction equation corresponding to the ANCOVA restricted model is seen to be

$$\hat{Y}_{ij} = 2.2 + 2.6 X_{ij} \tag{9}$$

and we can be certain that these numerical estimates of the slope and intercept parameters result in a smaller sum of squared errors than any other estimates we might try. The computation of the error sum of squares for this restricted model is shown in Table 9.3. Note that the prediction equation given in Equation 9 is in fact the equation for the regression line shown in Figure 9.1(b). Thus, the error sum of squares of 14.40 computed in Table 9.3 corresponds to the sum of squared distances of the observed data points from that line—that is, the sum of the squared lengths of the arrows in Figure 9.1(b).

Now let us move to a consideration of the parameters of the ANCOVA full model:

$$\text{Full:} \quad Y_{ij} = \mu + \alpha_j + \beta X_{ij} + \varepsilon_{ij} \tag{1, repeated}$$

This model, like the restricted model, has a single slope parameter. However, the full model allows for an effect of the treatment variable. We can also use the simple data set of Table 9.1 to illustrate this model and the difference between it and a typical one-way ANOVA model. We assume now that the first three subjects were randomly assigned to Treatment 1 and the next three subjects make up the group randomly assigned to Treatment 2. The data are plotted in this fashion in Figure 9.2; Figure 9.2(a) indicates the predictions of the ANOVA full model, and Figure 9.2(b) indicates the predictions of the ANCOVA full model.

Looking first at Figure 9.2(a), the predictions of the ANOVA full model are represented by two flat lines, one at the sample mean for each group. The predictions of the ANCOVA full model, however, vary again as a function of the individual's score on the covariate X.

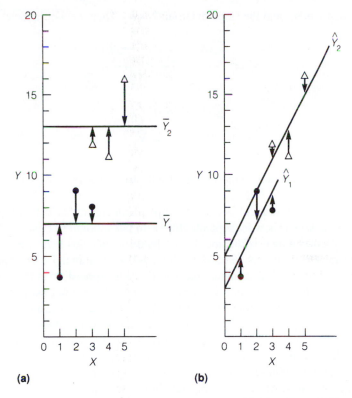

FIG. 9.2.   Comparison of errors in (a) ANOVA and (b) ANCOVA full models.

Once again, the predictions of the ANCOVA full model are closer to the data than those of the ANOVA model. In terms of the graphs, in ANCOVA one is free to tilt the prediction lines in whatever way necessary to best fit the data (as long as the lines for the two groups remain parallel), whereas in ANOVA the prediction lines must be not only parallel but also flat. Thus, the errors of prediction in the ANCOVA model can be no larger than those in ANOVA, and the ANCOVA errors will be smaller if there is any linear relationship between the covariate and the dependent variable. The magnitude of the ANCOVA errors, of course, are the values with the smallest sum of squares that result when the least-squares estimates of the slope and other parameters are inserted in the following:

$$E_F = \sum_j \sum_i e_{ij}^2 = \sum_j \sum_i (Y_{ij} - \hat{Y}_{ij})^2 = \sum_j \sum_i (Y_{ij} - \hat{\mu} - \hat{\alpha}_j - \hat{\beta} X_{ij})^2 \qquad (10)$$

To determine just how steeply to slope the lines to minimize errors, one could view the problem initially as a question of how steep the slope should be in each group separately. In actual practice, we compute a single, pooled estimate of slope directly. However, here we first consider how to compute estimates of the slope separately for each group and how these separate estimates could be pooled to compute a pooled slope. Then, we present the definitional formula that would actually be used for computing the estimate of β in the ANCOVA full model. Considering the groups separately, the methods we developed earlier for determining the least-squares estimates for the restricted model could be applied to each group as if it were the total sample. In general, we could designate the slope for the jth group b_j. So in the two-group case, the slope in Group 1 is b_1, and the slope in Group 2 is b_2. Then we would have

$$b_1 = \frac{\sum_i (X_{i1} - \overline{X}_1)(Y_{i1} - \overline{Y}_1)}{\sum_i (X_{i1} - \overline{X}_1)^2}$$

$$b_2 = \frac{\sum_i (X_{i2} - \overline{X}_2)(Y_{i2} - \overline{Y}_2)}{\sum_i (X_{i2} - \overline{X}_2)^2} \tag{11}$$

Table 9.4 shows the computation of these slopes for the two separate groups. Here, the example was contrived so that $b_1 = b_2 = 2$.

Now the ANCOVA full model has a single slope parameter rather than a separate one for each group. Thus, at issue is how the separate slope estimates should be combined into a single, pooled estimate. Rather than establishing the results using calculus here, we simply state the definitional formulas and attempt to make them plausible by drawing comparisons to things you already know about pooled estimates and about simple regression. In the current data set, because a slope of 2 fits each of the two groups as well as possible, using 2 as the pooled estimate is the only reasonable choice. However, in real data sets there almost certainly will be some variation from one group to the next in the numerical estimate of the slope. The situation is similar to that in ANOVA where one has separate estimates of the population variance—namely the observed variance within each group—and the problem is how to pool these estimates. The solution here, as in the within-group variance case, is to compute a weighted average of the individual group estimates. Also, as in computation of mean square within (cf. Equations 3.61 and 3.63), the weight applied to each separate estimate is the denominator of the formula used to compute that estimate (i.e., $n_j - 1$ for mean square within and $\sum (X_{ij} - \overline{X}_j)^2$ here). Thus, in the two-group case the least-squares estimate of the pooled within-group estimate can be written as

$$\hat{\beta} = \frac{\sum_i (X_{i1} - \overline{X}_1)^2 b_1 + \sum_i (X_{i2} - \overline{X}_2)^2 b_2}{\sum_i (X_{i1} - \overline{X}_1)^2 + \sum_i (X_{i2} - \overline{X}_2)^2} = b_w \tag{12}$$

The weight applied to each slope in the numerator in Equation 12 is inversely proportional to the variance of that slope estimate: the more stable the slope estimate derived for a particular group, the heavier it is weighted. The denominator, as in all weighted averages, is simply the sum of the weights. Also, on the right of Equation 12, we introduce the notation by which we refer to this average or pooled within-group slope, b_w.

Fortunately, as in the case of mean square within, rather than computing a parameter estimate separately for each group and then weighting each by the denominator used in computing the estimate, there is an easier way. We can simply add the numerators for all separate estimates (i.e., add the sums of cross-products of deviations from the group mean) and divide by the sum of the denominators of the separate estimates (i.e., by the sum of the sums of squared deviations around the group means). Using symbols to say the same thing (which is probably clearer here), we have

$$b_w = \frac{\sum_j \sum_i (X_{ij} - \overline{X}_j)(Y_{ij} - \overline{Y}_j)}{\sum_j \sum_i (X_{ij} - \overline{X}_j)^2} \tag{13}$$

TABLE 9.4
CALCULATION OF LEAST-SQUARES ESTIMATES RELEVANT TO THE ANCOVA
FULL MODEL

X	$X - \overline{X}$	Y	$Y - \overline{Y}$	$(X - \overline{X})^2$	$(X - \overline{X})(Y - \overline{Y})$
Group 1					
1	-1	4	-3	1	3
2	0	9	2	0	0
3	1	8	1	1	1
$\sum = 6$		$\sum = 21$		$\sum = 2$	$\sum = 4$
$\overline{X}_1 = 2$		$\overline{Y}_1 = 7$			
Group 2					
3	-1	12	-1	1	1
4	0	11	-2	0	0
5	1	16	3	1	3
$\sum = 12$		$\sum = 39$		$\sum = 2$	$\sum = 4$
$\overline{X}_2 = 4$		$\overline{Y}_1 = 13$			

Computing the slope for each group separately:

$$b_1 = \frac{\sum(X_{i1} - \overline{X}_1)(Y_{i1} - \overline{Y}_1)}{\sum(X_{i1} - \overline{X}_1)^2} = \frac{4}{2} = 2$$

$$b_2 = \frac{\sum(X_{i2} - \overline{X}_2)(Y_{i2} - \overline{Y}_2)}{\sum(X_{i2} - \overline{X}_2)^2} = \frac{4}{2} = 2$$

Using Equation 12 to compute b_W from b_1 and b_2:

$$b_W = \frac{\sum(X_{i1} - \overline{X}_1)^2 b_1 + \sum(X_{i2} - \overline{X}_2)^2 b_2}{\sum(X_{i1} - \overline{X}_1)^2 + \sum(X_{i2} - \overline{X}_2)^2} = \frac{2 \cdot 2 + 2 \cdot 2}{2 + 2} = \frac{8}{4} = 2$$

More typically, Equation 13 would be used to compute b_W directly from the sum of squares
and cross-products within groups:

$$b_W = \frac{\sum\sum(X_{ij} - \overline{X}_j)(Y_{ij} - \overline{Y}_j)}{\sum\sum(X_{ij} - \overline{X}_j)^2} = \frac{4 + 4}{2 + 2} = \frac{8}{4} = 2$$

Using Equations 16 and 17 to compute the intercepts:

$$a_1 = \overline{Y}_1 - b_W\overline{X}_1 = 7 - 2(2) = 7 - 4 = 3$$
$$a_2 = \overline{Y}_2 - b_W\overline{X}_2 = 13 - 2(4) = 13 - 8 = 5$$

Table 9.4 shows computations using this definitional formula for b_W, as well as using the
weighted average of Equation 12.

We must now consider how to estimate the remaining parameters of the ANCOVA full
model. Although it may be surprising, it is easiest to consider the estimates for μ and α at the
same time. If we substitute estimates for the parameters in Equation 1, the prediction for the
full model could be written

$$\hat{Y}_{ij} = \hat{\mu} + \hat{\alpha}_j + \hat{\beta}X_{ij} \tag{14}$$

In the case in which $X = 0$, our predictions could be written

$$\hat{Y}_{ij} = \hat{\mu} + \hat{\alpha}_j \tag{15}$$

Thus, in terms of our hypothetical data set, $\hat{\mu} + \hat{\alpha}_1$ would be the Y value where the prediction line for Group 1 intersects the Y axis, and $\hat{\mu} + \hat{\alpha}_2$ would be the Y intercept for Group 2. Analogous to the bivariate regression case, the prediction line for each group goes through the point corresponding to the mean value of X and the mean value of Y for that group. That is, the regression line for Group 1 minimizes errors by being centered at the point $(\overline{X}_1, \overline{Y}_1)$ and decreases by b_W units for each unit decrease in X. Thus, in going from an X value of $\overline{X}_1$ to an X value of 0, the predicted value drops $b_W \overline{X}_1$ units down from $\overline{Y}_1$. In terms of parameter estimates, this means

$$\hat{\mu} + \hat{\alpha}_1 = \overline{Y}_1 - b_W \overline{X}_1 = a_1 \tag{16}$$

So, as in the restricted model, we can arrive at an estimate of the intercept quite readily once the value of the slope is known, and we denote this intercept by an a, now adding a subscript to designate group number. In the second group in the example, then, we would have

$$\hat{\mu} + \hat{\alpha}_2 = \overline{Y}_2 - b_W \overline{X}_2 = a_2 \tag{17}$$

or, in general,

$$\hat{\mu} + \hat{\alpha}_j = \overline{Y}_j - b_W \overline{X}_j = a_j \tag{18}$$

The bottom of Table 9.4 shows computations for the intercepts of our two-group example.

Comparison of Models

Now we are ready to carry out the model comparison to determine if the ANCOVA full model is a significantly better description of the data than is the ANCOVA restricted model. The form of our F test, of course, is the same general form that we have encountered repeatedly in this book, that is,

$$F = \frac{(E_R - E_F)/(df_R - df_F)}{E_F/df_F}$$

We computed the error sum of squares for the restricted model in Table 9.3. Computation of the corresponding quantity for the full model is carried out in Table 9.5. Thus, the comparison of the adequacy of the model including parameters for a group effect with the model without group parameters boils down here to a comparison of a value of E_F of 12.0 and a value of E_R of 14.4. Naturally, the difference in the simplicity of the models must also be considered. The restricted model for this two-group situation involves the computation of one slope and one intercept parameter. In general, this is the case for one-way ANCOVA designs. Thus, we have

$$df_R = N - 2 \tag{19}$$

in general, which here means that $df_R = 6 - 2 = 4$. For the full model, we would have a different intercept for each group, plus a common slope parameter, so the degrees of freedom, would in general, depend on a, the number of groups in the design. That is, we would estimate $a + 1$ parameters, so

$$df_F = N - (a + 1) = N - a - 1 \tag{20}$$

TABLE 9.5

CALCULATION OF THE ERROR SUM OF SQUARES FOR THE ANCOVA
FULL MODEL

X	Y	$\hat{Y}$	$Y - \hat{Y}$	$(Y - \hat{Y})^2$
Group 1				
1	4	5	-1	1
2	9	7	2	4
3	8	9	-1	1
				$\sum = 6$
Group 2				
3	12	11	1	1
4	11	13	-2	4
5	16	15	1	1
				$\sum = 6$

$E_F = \sum_j \sum_i (Y_{ij} - \hat{Y}_{ij})^2 = 6 + 6 + 12$

Predicted values for the ANCOVA full model are calculated as follows:

$$Y_{ij} = a_j + b_W X_{ij}$$

Group 1:

$$\begin{aligned}
\hat{Y}_{i1} &= a_1 + b_W X_{i1} \\
\hat{Y}_{11} &= 3 + 2(1) = 3 + 2 = 5 \\
\hat{Y}_{21} &= 3 + 2(2) = 3 + 4 = 7 \\
\hat{Y}_{31} &= 3 + 2(3) = 3 + 6 = 9
\end{aligned}$$

Group 2:

$$\begin{aligned}
\hat{Y}_{i2} &= a_2 + b_W X_{i2} \\
\hat{Y}_{12} &= 5 + 2(3) = 5 + 6 = 11 \\
\hat{Y}_{22} &= 5 + 2(4) = 5 + 8 = 13 \\
\hat{Y}_{32} &= 5 + 2(5) = 5 + 10 = 15
\end{aligned}$$

This implies that the ANCOVA test of the treatment effect in an a group case involves an F having $(a - 1)$ and $(N - a - 1)$ degrees of freedom:

$$F = \frac{(E_R - E_F)/[(N - 2) - (N - a - 1)]}{E_F/(N - a - 1)} = \frac{(E_R - E_F)/(a - 1)}{E_F/(N - a - 1)} \tag{21}$$

in general. In our simple two-group case then, $df_F = 6 - 2 - 1 = 3$. Thus, the F test for the group effect, allowing for the covariate, has $4 - 3 = 1$ and 3 degrees of freedom and is computed as follows:

$$F = \frac{(14.4 - 12)/(4 - 3)}{12/3} = \frac{2.4/1}{4} = .6 \tag{22}$$

which clearly is nonsignificant. Thus, we conclude that the model including the X scores but not the group effect adequately accounts for the data.

How does this compare with the result that would have been achieved had we carried out an ANOVA of these data to test for the group effect? Table 9.6 shows computation of the ANOVA, which ignores the covariate. If the covariate had not been considered, we would have concluded that there was a significant group effect because the observed F of 7.714 is larger than the tabled value of 7.71. How can this occur given the greater power that we expect when we use ANCOVA? We address this question in the next section.

TABLE 9.6
COMPUTATIONS FOR ANOVA OF TWO-GROUP DATA

X	Y	$Y - \overline{Y}_j$	$(Y - \overline{Y}_j)^2$
Group 1			
1	4	-3	9
2	9	2	4
3	8	1	1
	$\sum = 21$		$\sum = 14$
	$\overline{Y}_2 = 7$		
Group 2			
3	12	-1	1
4	11	-2	4
5	16	3	9
	$\sum = 39$		$\sum = 14$
	$\overline{Y}_2 = 13$		

$$E_F = \sum_j \sum_i (Y_{ij} - \overline{Y}_j)^2 = 14 + 14 = 28$$

$$E_R - E_F = \sum_j n(\overline{Y}_j - \overline{Y})^2 = 3(7 - 10)^2 + 3(13 - 10)^2 = 2 \cdot 3 \cdot 3^2 = 54$$

$$F = \frac{(E_R - E_F)/(df_R - df_F)}{E_F/df_F} = \frac{54/1}{28/4} = 7.714$$

Two Consequences of Using ANCOVA

Recall that including a covariate in the model results in two consequences: First, the sum of squares of the errors in your models is decreased; second, the sum of squares for the group effect—that is, the difference between E_R and E_F—is adjusted. Because appreciating these two consequences is the essence of understanding ANCOVA, we consider them now in some detail in the context of our numerical example. We can examine both of these effects explicitly here by comparing the ANCOVA and ANOVA sums of squares.

Test of Regression

The first consequence is seen by a comparison of the ANCOVA full model with the ANOVA full model, that is,

$$Y_{ij} = \mu + \alpha_j + \beta X_{ij} + \varepsilon_{ij} \qquad \text{(1, repeated)}$$

and

$$Y_{ij} = \mu + \alpha_j + \varepsilon_{ij} \qquad (23)$$

In fact, the latter could be viewed as a special case of the former where the slope is restricted to zero. That means that the sum of squared errors for the models can be compared in an F test. The test is typically referred to as the test of regression because it reflects the strength of the regression of Y on X. For the current data, the test of regression would yield

$$F = \frac{(28 - 12)/1}{12/3} = \frac{16}{4} = 4$$

which is not close to the critical value for $\alpha = .05$ of 10.1. However, although because of the very few degrees of freedom available in this sample data set this result is not significant, the sum of squared errors has been reduced to less than half of its initial value (i.e., from 28 to 12) by the addition of the covariate. Thus, in fact, smaller effects could be detected by ANCOVA here rather than by ANOVA.

Estimated Conditional Means

However, the particular numerical estimate of the magnitude of the group effect in ANCOVA typically is somewhat different than in ANOVA. This is the second consequence of using ANCOVA. In the ANOVA test of the group effect (see Table 9.6), the addition of the group parameter to the model resulted in a reduction of 54 in the sum of squared errors in the restricted model. In the ANCOVA test of the group effect (see Equation 22), however, adding in the group effect resulted in a reduction of only 2.4 in the sum of squared errors in the restricted model. We can refer to the plots of these data as a way of understanding these results. The plots for the restricted and full models were shown in Figures 9.1 and 9.2, respectively. For ease of comparison, Figure 9.3(a) presents these predictions again for the ANOVA models, and Figure 9.3(b) presents these predictions again for the ANCOVA models. In terms of these plots, the reduction in sum of squares associated with the group effect—that is, the numerator sum of squares for the F test—is related to the distance between the lines in the plot. For ANOVA, the sum of squares for the effect is directly related to the distance between the two lines representing the predictions of the full model. The difference between these

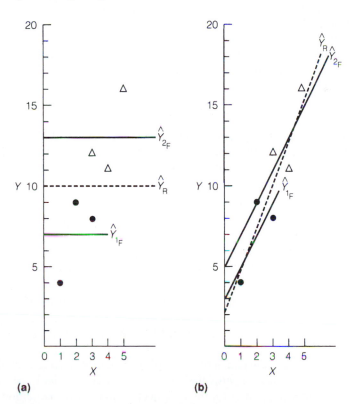

FIG. 9.3.   The difference between the predictions of the full and restricted models for both (a) ANOVA and (b) ANCOVA.

lines of six units corresponds of course to the difference between the two sample means of 13 and 7. For ANCOVA, the prediction lines for the two groups are clearly much closer together. The ANCOVA–full model predictions can be similar in the two groups but still fit the data well because of the prediction lines' steep slope, which reflects the strong regression of Y on X.

To describe the situation somewhat more precisely, the sum of squares for an effect will in general depend on the extent to which the predictions of the full model depart from those of the restricted model. In terms of the plots, the critical feature is how far the predictions made by the full model for the six observations deviate from the corresponding predictions made by the restricted model. That is, how far are the solid lines from the dashed line? In terms of symbols, it can be shown that the numerator sum of squares can be expressed simply in terms of the difference between $\hat{Y}_F$ and $\hat{Y}_R$. As noted in Chapter 3 (see p. 90), it is the case that

$$E_R - E_F = \sum_{\text{all obs}} (\hat{Y}_F - \hat{Y}_R)^2 \tag{24}$$

where the subscript "all obs" just means that the summation is over all observations. Here, because of the steep regression line in the entire sample, the predictions of the restricted model $\hat{Y}_R$ are quite close to those for the full model $\hat{Y}_F$.

Perhaps the clearest perspective on the reduced sum of squares for the group effect in ANCOVA as opposed to ANOVA is provided by returning to the conditional question asked by ANCOVA. ANCOVA asks, What would the group effect have been if the two groups had been at the same mean value on the covariate? Answering this involves examination of the predicted Y values at a particular point on the X scale—namely at $\overline{X}$, the grand mean across all observations on the covariate. These predicted values are typically called adjusted means and are the estimates according to the full model of the expected values on Y for the various groups when $X = \overline{X}$. Because the prediction equation for the full model is

$$\hat{Y}_j = a_j + b_W X_{ij} \tag{25}$$

we could use our numerical values for a_j and b_w and set X_{ij} equal to $\overline{X}$ to get the appropriate predicted values. However, the difference from the observed means is made somewhat clearer if we express $\hat{Y}_F$ in terms of $\overline{Y}_j$. Recall that $a_j = \overline{Y}_j - b_w \overline{X}_j$ (see Equation 18). Substituting this for a_j in Equation 25 and factoring b_w, we obtain

$$\hat{Y}_j = \overline{Y}_j - b_W \overline{X}_j + b_W X_{ij} = \overline{Y}_j - b_W(\overline{X}_j - X_{ij}) \tag{26}$$

Thus, to obtain the predicted value of $\hat{Y}$ at the grand mean on the covariate, we let X_{ij} equal $\overline{X}$ in Equation 26. This gives us the following expression for obtaining "adjusted" means, $\overline{Y}'_j$—that is, the mean Y scores we would have expected to observe in the study, assuming the correctness of our model, if the groups had been equivalent on the covariate

$$\overline{Y}'_j = \overline{Y}_j - b_W(\overline{X}_j - \overline{X}) \tag{27}$$

Although we follow here the convention of calling this an *adjusted mean*, it should be stressed that this is simply an estimate of a particular conditional mean. That is, $\overline{Y}'_j$ is the estimate of the mean of the Y scores in Group j for those subjects who meet the condition of having an X score equal to $\overline{X}$. We could estimate other means as well, for any other X value of interest. However, because in most research projects only one overall indicator of the performance

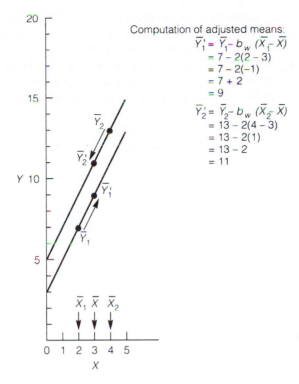

Computation of adjusted means:

$$\bar{Y}_1' = \bar{Y}_1 - b_w \, (\bar{X}_1 - \bar{X})$$
$$= 7 - 2(2 - 3)$$
$$= 7 - 2(-1)$$
$$= 7 + 2$$
$$= 9$$

$$\bar{Y}_2' = \bar{Y}_2 - b_w \, (\bar{X}_2 - \bar{X})$$
$$= 13 - 2(4 - 3)$$
$$= 13 - 2(1)$$
$$= 13 - 2$$
$$= 11$$

FIG. 9.4.   Portrayal and computation of adjusted means as predicted Y scores at the point where the covariate score is $\bar{X}$.

in a treatment condition is of interest, the estimated conditional mean for $X = \bar{X}$ is denoted the adjusted mean. The adjustment in the mean of Y to take into account the deviation of the group's covariate mean from the grand covariate mean is comparable to what happens in nonorthogonal ANOVA when we allow for the effects of other factors (see Chapter 7). Here, we are examining the group effect by estimating the marginal means after removing any variability that could be accounted for by variability among the group means on X.

In the particular numerical example we have been working on, the adjustment for the covariate would change the mean in Group 1 from 7 to 9. In Group 2, the adjusted mean would be 11 as opposed to the observed value of 13. Figure 9.4 shows the simple computations and the relationship between the observed and adjusted means. (The group means are taken from our original computations for the full model in Table 9.4.) Notice carefully the way in which the predicted Y value (or adjusted mean) differs from the observed mean $\bar{Y}_j$ as a function of the relationship between the observed group mean on X, $\bar{X}_j$, and the grand mean on X. For example, in Group 1, the mean X score of 2 is below the grand mean X score of 3. Because there is a positive relationship between X and Y, we would expect that, if Group 1 in general had had higher X scores, their mean Y score would also have been higher. The slope of the regression line, of course, indicates how much higher we should expect the Y score to be for each unit increase in X. In fact, the "adjustment" process can be thought of quite simply but correctly as sliding the mean Y score up or down the regression line as necessary so that you are directly above the grand mean on X. In Group 2, because the observed mean on X was higher than the grand mean and the slope of the line was positive, our predicted Y value for the point $X = \bar{X}$ is lower than $\bar{Y}_2$. This sliding of the expected Y values up or down the regression lines is represented in the figure by the arrows.

In this particular case then, the second consequence of ANCOVA was to reduce substantially the numerator sum of squares in the F test. Because the numerator sum of squares could be affected in different ways, it is important to put this in perspective.

It should be clear from Figure 9.4 that, as we anticipated in our discussion of the logic of ANCOVA, two factors affect how the means are adjusted: (1) the differences between the group means on the covariate and (2) the slope of the regression lines. In fact, there is a multiplicative relationship between these factors, as shown in the computations in the figure, whereby $\overline{X}_j - \overline{X}$ is multiplied by b_w. Thus, if either of these two factors is zero in the population, the adjusted means tend to be very similar to the unadjusted means, and hence the ANCOVA numerator sum of squares would typically be quite similar to the ANOVA numerator sum of squares. In any study in which the covariate is assessed prior to the assignment to groups and then subjects are assigned at random to treatment conditions, we would expect the group means on the covariate to be rather similar. Because this typically happens in laboratory experiments and in analog clinical studies, using ANCOVA in these situations produces numerator sums of squares that are little different from those that would be obtained in ANOVA. In particular, the difference between the adjusted means has the same expected value as the difference between the unadjusted means over replications of the experiment with different participants.

Examples of Adjusted Effects

The current numerical example is actually more representative of what might happen in a nonrandomized study or quasi-experiment, for example, where intact groups are employed. In such a case, adjusted effects can be considerably different than unadjusted effects. Figure 9.5 illustrates several possibilities. In each case, we designate the group that has the higher conditional mean on Y as Group 2. For example, Group 2 might be a treatment that is thought to produce some benefit on the outcome measure relative to the Group 1 (control) condition. The question is, "How do you adjust your estimate of the treatment-control difference for the preexisting differences on the covariate X?" We illustrate different examples of adjustments where the outcome and covariate are positively correlated within groups [Figure 9.5(a, c, and e)] and where the outcome and covariate are negatively correlated within groups [Figure 9.5(b, d, and f)]. In each case, the dependent-variable Y is taken as a direct indicator of how positive the outcome is. Figure 9.5(a) illustrates an outcome like that in the simple numerical examples we have been considering. This is perhaps the most common result of using ANCOVA in quasi-experiments in which one is attempting to control for a specific threat to internal validity. For example, in an aggressive treatment program for problem drinkers, a larger number of individuals may drop out than from an untreated control group. Comparing those completing treatment with the control group may show a large apparent treatment benefit on a dependent measure of number of abstinent days in the 6 months after treatment. A partial control for this differential mortality might be accomplished by covarying a premeasure of compliance that indicated who was likely to complete treatment. Assuming that the mean compliance of those completing treatment ($\overline{X}_2$) is higher than that of the untreated controls ($\overline{X}_1$) and that compliance is positively related to outcome (as indicated by the positive slopes of the within-group regression lines), the adjusted estimate of the treatment effect could be considerably smaller than the unadjusted difference in means, as in Figure 9.5(a). Figure 9.5(b) shows the same type of effect, but for a covariate that is negatively related to outcome. In this example, X might be an indicator of the pretreatment severity of the individual's drinking problem.

Figure 9.5 (c), (d), (e), and (f) illustrate situations in which a more favorable picture of the treatment effect is given by adjusting for a covariate. Figure 9.5(c) illustrates a case in which, although there is a positive relationship between the covariate and the dependent variable within each group, the group with the higher observed mean on the dependent variable actually started

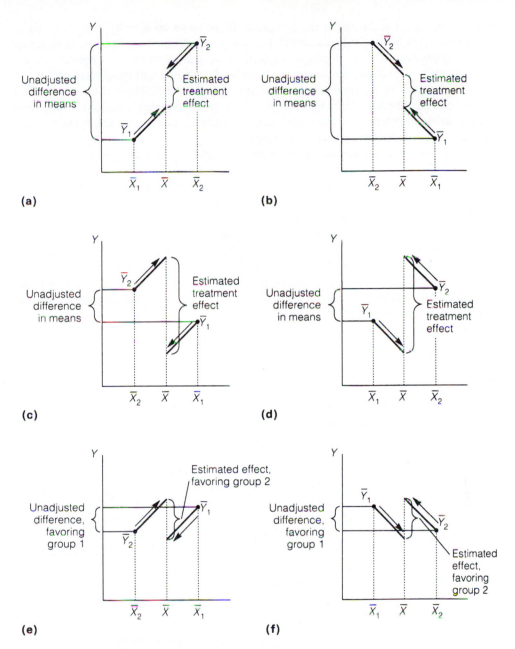

FIG. 9.5. Some possible relationships between unadjusted and adjusted estimates of treatment effect: (a and b) An apparent treatment benefit due primarily to preexisting differences; (c and d) estimate of treatment effect increased by adjusting for preexisting difference; (e and f) an apparent harmful effect of treatment seen as benefit by adjusting for preexisting differences.

with the lower covariate mean. Thus, the treatment effect, reflected in the advantage of $\bar{Y}_2$ over $\bar{Y}_1$, means that the treatment received by Group 2 has more than made up for an initial deficit. This would be the ideal outcome in many social programs such as HeadStart. There, the children selected for special treatment would frequently be lower on some predictor variable such as socioeconomic status (SES) that would be positively related to a dependent variable, such as reading achievement at the end of the first grade. If such a group actually achieved a higher score on the dependent variable, the initial deficit would make the benefit of the treatment all the more impressive. If the two groups had been at the same level on the covariate initially, it is plausible to expect that the treatment group's advantage would have been even larger. This, in fact, would be the implication of covarying SES for the estimated treatment effect, as is illustrated by the adjusted means (the points above $\overline{X}$) in Figure 9.5(c). The same result is shown in Figure 9.5(d) for a covariate, such as number of hours per week spent watching television, that is negatively related to outcome.

If the groups are sufficiently disparate on the covariate and sufficiently close on the unadjusted Y means, even though the group with the higher covariate mean is ahead of the other group on the unadjusted dependent measure, our best guess of the expected results if both groups had been at $\overline{X}$ might be that the group with the lower mean on Y would have had a significant advantage. This situation is illustrated in Figure 9.5(e), and an analogous situation for a negative covariate-dependent variable relationship is shown in Figure 9.5(f). For example, HeadStart children might score lower on reading achievement at the end of the first grade than children who were included in the program; however, if children had all been at the same SES level (or had been subjected to the same number of hours of television viewing), then HeadStart might have shown a significant benefit. ANCOVA with its adjusted means provides some evidence relevant to such conditional assertions.[4]

Summary

To summarize, the primary statistical effect of including a covariate in your model in randomized experiments is typically to bring about a substantial reduction in the unaccounted-for variance. This means you have greater power for the detection of treatment effects. A secondary effect in randomized experiments is that the estimated magnitude of the treatment effect itself can be different in ANCOVA than in ANOVA. In nonrandomized studies, however, this effect of adjusting the treatment effect may be much more important than the reduction in within-group error because of large differences across groups on the covariate. The adjusted treatment means are appropriately thought of as estimates based on the full model of the mean performance that would have been obtained in each treatment group if it had comprised a subpopulation of subjects with a covariate score of $\overline{X}$. Such predictions could actually be made for any X score, either graphically by reading off the Y values on the regression lines directly above that X score or numerically by setting X_{ij} in Equation 26 to the X score of interest. The variability of these estimated Y scores depends on exactly where the X value of interest is. Consideration of the details concerning estimating such variability and of more complex ANCOVA models is postponed until we have dealt with the assumptions underlying the statistical tests in ANCOVA.

Assumptions in ANCOVA

For the statistical tests we have described to be valid, the following minimal assumptions must be met concerning the elements of the ANCOVA model:

$$Y_{ij} = \mu + \alpha_j + \beta X_{ij} + \varepsilon_{ij} \qquad \text{(1, repeated)}$$

1. In the population, the error scores ε_{ij} must be independently and normally distributed.
2. In the population, the error scores ε_{ij} must have an expected value of zero and a constant variance.

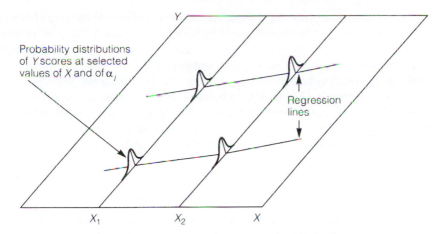

FIG. 9.6.   Conditional Y probability distributions.

Basic Implications

Several aspects of these mathematical assumptions are not obvious. Some of these can be explicitly tested; other aspects lend themselves only to logical analysis. We discuss various components of these assumptions in turn. First, because in the model

$$Y_{ij} = \mu + \alpha_j + \beta X_{ij} + \varepsilon_{ij} \qquad\qquad (1, \text{repeated})$$

all the terms on the right side of the equation are assumed to be fixed (more on this in a moment) except for the error term, if ε_{ij} is normally distributed, then the conditional Y scores must be normally distributed. By "conditional Y scores" we mean the subpopulation of Y scores at a particular combination of values of α_j and X_{ij}. This is illustrated in Figure 9.6 in which the probability distribution of Y is sketched in for selected values of X, separately for each group.

Second, the relationship between Y and X is presumed to be linear. The assumption that the errors have an expected value of zero implies that the expected value of Y may be written as

$$\mathscr{E}(Y_{ij}) = \mathscr{E}(\mu + \alpha_j + \beta X_{ij} + \varepsilon_{ij}) = \mu + \alpha_j + \beta X_{ij} + \mathscr{E}(\varepsilon_{ij})$$
$$= \mu + \alpha_j + \beta X_{ij} \qquad\qquad (28)$$

Thus, the conditional mean of Y is a linear function of X within each group. Tests and generalizations of this feature of the model are considered briefly later in the chapter.

Third, implicit in the statement of the model is the presumption that the separate within-group regression lines have the same slope. For the standard ANCOVA linear model to be appropriate for a data-analysis situation, the slopes of the regression lines in the different groups should be equal within sampling error. In the extension to this chapter, we consider the issue of possible heterogeneity of regression in detail, including how to test for heterogeneity and how to alter your analysis if heterogeneity appears to be present.

Fourth, the fact that the covariate values are assumed to be fixed does not mean that the values of the covariate were decided on before the experiment was run. Rather, the assumption is that statistical inferences are made about the characteristics of the population of hypothetical replications having the same distribution of covariate scores. Thus, statistical inferences can technically be made only to the Y values expected at the particular X values included in the study, which is conventional in regression. The question of whether the covariate is fixed or random is a logical one to be answered not only by consideration of how the values were obtained, but also by consideration of what inferences are of interest (see Rogosa, 1980, p. 308). Because the values of the covariate are often obtained in the same manner as the dependent variable—for example, by administrating the same paper-and-pencil test pre and post—some authors recommend that the covariate be regarded as a random effect (cf. Huitema, 1980, pp. 86, 121). (We discuss random effects in Chapter 10.) In terms of how the standard ANCOVA test of the treatment effect is carried out, it does not matter whether the covariate is regarded as fixed or random (Scheffé, 1959, p. 196). Typically, investigators have been content to make their statistical inferences to the levels of X included in the study and make any extrapolations to other levels on nonstatistical grounds.

Lack of Independence of Treatment and Covariate

Although not technically a requirement, there are other conditions that, when met, make the interpretation of an ANCOVA much more straightforward. The basic desideratum is that the covariate and the treatment be statistically independent. The issue is similar to the desire for orthogonality in factorial designs. When two factors are orthogonal, one can interpret tests of one factor without regard to the other. In a one-way ANCOVA, the covariate can be viewed as a second factor. If the covariate and the treatment are not statistically independent, allowing for the covariate in your model as a rule alters the magnitude of the estimated treatment effect, just as the test for one of two nonorthogonal factors is different when you allow for the other rather than ignore it.

There are two opposite and rather extreme views regarding the role of the independence conditions. As with most extreme views, the best course is to avoid both extremes. One extreme position is to expect ANCOVA to serve as a panacea for problems of nonindependence. The other extreme view is to shun the use of ANCOVA altogether if the groups differ in their mean X scores. Keep each of these positions in mind as we mention how to test for independence and discuss how lack of independence can arise.

How to Test for Lack of Independence.   Because the treatment variable is discrete and the covariate is a continuous variable, one can test for the primary implication of the independence of the two—namely equal means on the covariate across groups—quite simply by performing an ANOVA using the covariate as the dependent variable. Significant dependence is indicated by the rejection of the null hypothesis in this test.

How Lack of Independence Can Arise.   At least four different situations could result in a rejection of the null hypothesis of no relationship between the treatment variable and the covariate. Because interpretations and further methods of analysis differ across the various situations, it is important to distinguish among them. The situations are presented in the order of increasing difficulty of interpretation.

Case 1:   One might have carefully collected scores on the covariate prior to the start of the experiment and randomly assigned subjects to treatment conditions only to find when you begin your data analysis that the treatment groups differ "significantly" on the covariate. This might be termed a *fluke random assignment* or *unhappy randomization*, a term apparently coined by Kenny (1979). In fact, you know that the decision indicated by the ANOVA of the covariate represents a Type I error because, over hypothetical replications of the random-assignment procedure, you are assured that the mean covariate scores will be equal across groups. However, despite this, the problem remains of how to carry out and interpret analyses comparing the groups on the dependent variable when you know that in your sample the groups differ systematically on the covariate. The best solution to this problem is to avoid it entirely by using an assignment procedure that assures equal means on X, not just in the long run but also in your particular study. The advantages of such stratified random assignment have been demonstrated by Maxwell, Delaney, and Dill (1984) and are discussed in greater detail in a subsequent section of Chapter 9 comparing ANCOVA and blocking. Given this modified type of random assignment was not used and you find yourself with markedly different group means on X despite simple random assignment, what can be done?

To answer this question it is helpful to distinguish between the unconditional Type I error rate and the conditional Type I error rate. The unconditional Type I error rate is the probability of falsely rejecting the null hypothesis if the entire experiment were conducted repeatedly, starting each time at the beginning of the study, so that the values of X appearing in each group vary across replications. Thus, the unconditional Type I error rate is based on infinitely many assignments of individuals to groups. As such, either an ANOVA disregarding the covariate or an ANCOVA incorporating the covariate properly maintains the unconditional Type I error because randomization guarantees control of this Type I error rate as long as the necessary statistical assumptions have been met.

The conditional Type I error rate, however, is the probability of falsely rejecting the null hypothesis over multiple replications keeping the specific covariate values that occurred in this particular assignment. In other words, now that we know that the groups differ on X, how likely is it to commit a Type I error conditional on this particular configuration of covariate values? An ANOVA disregarding the covariate typically leads to an inflated conditional Type I error rate even with random assignment. Thus, researchers who believe that it is important to control the conditional Type I error rate need an alternative to ANOVA when groups differ on the covariate. Fortunately, Senn (1989) and Maxwell (1994) show that ANCOVA properly controls the conditional Type I error rate as long as the necessary statistical assumptions have been met even when groups differ significantly on the covariate. Thus, although an ANOVA would be valid for controlling the unconditional Type I error rate, an ANCOVA would be preferred because it controls both the unconditional and the conditional Type I error rate. The reason for preferring ANCOVA, besides the usual one of increased power through reduced error, is that it can adjust for the bad hand dealt you by the random assignment. Readers interested in further details on unconditional and conditional size may want to consult Maxwell, O'Callaghan, and Delaney (1993). On a related topic, a later section of Chapter 9 discusses issues involved in choosing covariates to include in the model in randomized studies.

It is critical here to note that the differences between groups on the covariate scores are being assumed to have arisen despite the fact that, for all values of X, subjects had an equal probability of being in each one of the treatments. Perhaps it is worth noting that certain procedures used to recruit subjects for psychology experiments do not meet this criterion, despite the fact that the reason for the relationship between the treatment conditions and the covariate may not be obvious at all to the experimenter. For example, suppose that in a human-learning experiment you recruit participants for different treatment conditions by posting a sign-up sheet for each that bears only the name of the experiment and the time the session is to be run. If you find that the GPA scores you were planning to use as a covariate differ significantly across the treatment conditions, you cannot be assured that the covariance adjustment is adequate. It may well be that, for whatever reason, experimental sessions at different times may attract students who differ in their GPAs and possibly other characteristics. Allowing participants to distribute themselves across experimental conditions, even though they have minimal information about the conditions, does not constitute random assignment. If the participants distribute themselves across the conditions, your experiment would fall into the fourth cause of nonindependence of treatment and covariate discussed later. Yet if you controlled the assignment to conditions in such a way that participants had an equal probability of being placed in each treatment condition regardless of their X score, ANCOVA can be used knowing that the adjusted estimate of the treatment effect is unbiased regardless of how nonrandom any particular instance of random assignment might appear (see Rubin, 1977).

Case 2: A second situation in which lack of independence between the covariate and the treatment can arise is in using a *biased assignment* procedure. This refers to the situation "where the covariate is used as a measure of the extent to which subjects 'need' some kind of treatment" (Huitema, 1980, p. 140). For example, subjects with a phobia score above a certain value may be assigned to a phobia-treatment condition, whereas subjects with a lower score would be assigned to a different condition such as a waiting-list control, an example of what is known as a *regression discontinuity design* (Shadish, Cook, & Campbell, 2002, provide an excellent chapter on this design). As long as the phobia score is the sole basis of assigning subjects to the treatment conditions, ANCOVA can be used without hesitation to perform a test of the adjusted treatment effect. This yields an unbiased test and an estimated treatment effect that is independent of the difference on the pretest regardless of whether the covariate contains measurement error (Rubin, 1977). Readers are cautioned, however, that implementations of the biased assignment study that permit no overlap between groups in the X scores represented rely heavily on model assumptions, for example, homogeneity of regression (cf. Weisberg, 1979, p. 1153). Rather than having groups that do not overlap in X scores, one could have the probability of assignment to a treatment condition changing as a function of their X score (cf. Huitema, 1980, p. 141). For example, one could divide subjects into thirds on the basis of their X scores, with the lowest third being assigned to the treatment, the highest third being assigned to the control condition, and the middle third being randomly divided between the two conditions. Thus, the probability of assignment to treatment would be 0, 1, or $\frac{1}{2}$.

Case 3: A third and more problematic situation occurs when the treatment affects the covariate. This only occurs, of course, when the covariate is assessed after the onset of treatment. In some cases, it may seem a trivial matter whether the questionnaire requesting information from which you will derive scores on a covariate is passed out to participants before or after the instruction sheet that constitutes the different "treatment" conditions. However, to avoid ambiguity, it is best if at all possible to assess the subjects' covariate scores prior to any differential treatment of subjects taking place. The basic concern is that if the treatments differentially affect the covariate scores, then an ANCOVA of the dependent variable, which equates the groups on the covariate, would in fact remove from the treatment sum of squares part of the treatment effect that you really want included. Suppose that an investigator wants to determine the relative effectiveness of two strategies for coping with pain. Instruction and practice in a single strategy are given in each of 10 sessions, with the dependent measure being the number of seconds the subject tolerated an increasingly painful stimulus. Perhaps the investigator suspects, reasonably enough, that there are individual differences in pain tolerance and attempts to predict variation in the dependent measure by an assessment of pain tolerance taken at the end of the first session. Using such a measure as a covariate in an attempt to maximize the chances of detecting a treatment effect on the dependent variable would be misguided. Presuming the treatments do produce differential effects, that these effects may at least begin to emerge by the end of a single session is altogether reasonable. To covary the first session's pain tolerance is to ask the conditional question, "How different would the expected scores on the dependent measure be if the groups were at the same point on the covariate?" However, the two groups may already differ at the end of the first session because of the treatment effect. If so, it is quite possible that the major effect of covarying Session 1 tolerance would not be a reduction in residual error, but a reduction in the treatment sum of squares by removing part of the effect of interest.

As is often the case, such a usage of ANCOVA would be inappropriate not because the technique produced the wrong answer, but because it was used to answer the wrong question, or more accurately, the question ANCOVA addresses was not understood, and hence its answer was misinterpreted. ANCOVA could, however, shed some light here on a question that would be of interest. That is, one might wonder if the treatment produced an effect in Session 10 over and above what would be predicted on the basis of the effect present at Session 1.

This use of ANCOVA also can frequently be capitalized on to see if a particular variable should be ruled out as a potential mediator of a treatment effect on another variable. A fairly standard example (cf. Myers, 1979, p. 430) of this is an investigation of teaching methods where one method produces higher scores on a common examination but also results in students studying more. It may be of interest then to pursue the question, "Can the effect on examination scores be accounted for by the difference in time spent studying?" If a significant treatment effect on examination scores is still observed when study time is covaried, then one can conclude that the study-time differences are not responsible for the exam-score differences. Note, however, that the converse is not true. That is, if the test of treatment effects were no longer significant when study time was adjusted for, it does not mean that the study-time differences caused the exam-score differences. The different teaching methods may have affected a third variable that was responsible for both the study-time and the exam-score effects. One teaching method may have so captured the students' attention that they picked up more information in the initial teaching session and spent more time studying on their own.

To conclude this consideration of the impact of having the treatment affect the covariate, if one's purpose is, as is usually the case in experimental studies, to simply increase the precision of your analysis of the treatment effect on the dependent variable, then one should avoid using as a covariate a variable that has, or even could have, been affected by the treatment. If, however, one's purpose is to explore whether a particular variable served to mediate the treatment's effects on the dependent variable, then ANCOVA can be used with caution. Part of the need for caution concerns the potential for committing errors of the general form of "correlation implies causation." Another cause for caution is that the adjusted effect must be interpreted by making inferences about whether the treatment effect can be accounted for by (do not read "caused by") the covariate *as measured in the experiment*. As Huitema (1980, p. 108) stresses, frequently investigators' real interest is in the construct (e.g., time spent on task) that is only fallibly measured by the covariate (e.g., time a student reports having studied). Conclusions regarding such underlying constructs, whatever the outcome of the ANCOVA, must be made at least partially on nonstatistical grounds.

Case 4: A fourth and final cause of lack of independence between the covariate and the treatment is that the study is not a true experiment, but a quasi-experiment—that is, subjects are not randomly assigned to treatment conditions. This situation poses the most difficult interpretation problems of all. As we previously considered at length in our discussion of the logic of ANCOVA, there is no way of knowing that the differences on the covariate are the only important ones between groups when differential selection factors are operating.

Although certainly not an equivalent of random assignment, ANCOVA can be helpful nonetheless, and its use could still be recommended though interpretations of the results of the analysis must be made very cautiously. Modifications of ANCOVA to deal with measurement error in the covariate may also be required in the nonequivalent-group case. Consider the extremely complicated problem of differences across racial groups in measured IQ. For example, Jensen (1980, p. 44) reports the difference between Black students' and White students' tested IQ to be approximately 15 points. Despite the wide variation of opinion among psychologists about the validity of a single IQ score for measuring intelligence and despite the even greater controversy concerning the cause of differences between racial groups in tested IQ, a reasonable consensus could be obtained for the proposition that a nontrivial proportion of the variation in IQ of young adults is related to variation in their home environments. Clearly, this is a question that does not lend itself to experimental control, because one cannot ethically carry out the required manipulation. ANCOVA can be used to shed some light on how much of an adjustment in the group differences would be called for. However, to recall our earlier remarks about the correlation–causation fallacy, there is no way of knowing whether experimentally controlling home environments at a standard level would produce (cause) a reduction in the group means of the amount suggested by an ANCOVA. To make the example more concrete, a measure of SES might be used as an indicator of the characteristics of the home environment, which would be relevant to predicting tested IQ. However, two factors besides the correlation-does-not-imply-causation problem virtually assure that a typical ANCOVA would not make exactly the correct adjustment. Both are related to the assumption that the covariate is measured without error. First, the measurement of SES is itself a difficult problem, and it is practically assured that some measurement error would perturb the results—for example, a parent's occupation may be reported erroneously or inappropriately scored as an indicator of SES. We consider how to adjust for measurement error in the next section. Second, the SES measure is of interest as an indicator itself of the underlying construct, quality of home environment. Thus, even if a perfectly reliable measure of SES were obtained, the construct of interest would still be measured imperfectly. Families at the same SES level, for example, might have home environments that differ considerably in features relevant to the measured IQs of children from those homes.

A further problem in using ANCOVA with intact groups, besides that raised by having a fallible covariate, is the possibility that the question addressed by ANCOVA concerns a population of subjects that does not exist. For example, assume that a developmental psychologist conducts a study of the effectiveness of a cognitive-training strategy with a covariate assessing the developmental level of the child. Perhaps the covariate is the numerical score on an assessment procedure designed to assess whether the child is at the stage of concrete processing or at the stage of formal operations. It may actually be the case that the data display all the characteristics implied by the statistical assumptions listed earlier. However, if Piaget is right and the assessment procedure is a valid measure of the developmental stages he hypothesized, the distribution of scores on the covariate should be bimodal. In fact, there should be no subjects midway between the concrete operations mean and the formal operations mean, but that is in effect the point to which ANCOVA is extrapolating to make the treatment comparison. One might still reason in this situation that the test of the constant treatment effect is of interest, because if the ANCOVA model is correct, this would be appropriate for concrete operations and formal operations subjects. However, the typical adjusted means, which are estimated at the grand mean on the covariate, would likely not be of interest, because no such subject exists.

A large body of literature is devoted to the problems of modeling and interpreting nonequivalent group studies. Readers are referred to time-honored discussions by Meehl (1971), Overall and Woodward (1977), Reichardt (1979), and Weisberg (1979). More recent excellent treatments include Little, An, Johanns, and Giordani (2000); Rosenbaum (2002); Shadish, Cook, and Campbell (2002); West, Biesanz, and Pitts (2000); and Winship and Morgan (1999).

Summary Regarding Lack of Independence of Treatment and Covariate. Certainly, we have seen that ANCOVA cannot blithely be applied with the expectation that an appropriate correction for the lack of independence of the treatment and covariate will always be made. Nonetheless, it is also clear that ANCOVA can be used to address data-analysis questions of interest in each of the four cases we have considered. Certainly, Keppel's view that "if there is any possibility that the treatments may have affected the scores on the control variable, the analysis of co-variance is inappropriate" (1982, p. 503) represents an extreme view that would preclude fruitful and legitimate uses of ANCOVA. However, the difficulties of interpretation can be great; particularly in nonequivalent group studies, ambiguities are virtually assured. However, as Huitema argues, to condemn ANCOVA because of these ambiguities is inappropriate: "ANCOVA is innocent; measurement error and nonequivalent group studies are culpable" (Huitema, 1980, p. 115).

Measurement Error in Covariate

What is the consequence of using such a fallible "covariate"? If the study used random assignment, the major effect is simply that the power of the ANCOVA test would be somewhat less than it would have been with a perfectly reliable covariate, but still the power with ANCOVA would likely be greater than that with an ANOVA ignoring the covariate. With a nonrandomized study, however, the problem is considerably more serious than a slight loss of power. In an intact group study, such as the study of racial differences in IQ, the point of using ANCOVA is to attempt to adjust for differences across groups on the covariate. As we have seen—for example, in Figure 9.4—the magnitude of the adjustment in the treatment means depends on how far apart the groups are on the covariate. In fact, if $\mu_{YW} - \mu_{YB}$ is the difference between the mean IQs of Whites and Blacks in the population and $\mu_{XW} - \mu_{XB}$ is the corresponding difference between the two racial groups in quality of home environment relevant to performance on the IQ test, we can then express the difference in the adjusted mean IQ quite simply.

First, however, we must introduce a bit of notation. Let $\sigma^2_{\text{true }X}/\sigma^2_X$ be the proportion of the variation in the observed X scores corresponding to variation in the construct of interest. Let $\beta_{\text{true }X}$ be the population regression coefficient appropriate for predicting the IQ scores from the true values of the covariate construct, and let $\beta_{\text{fallible }X}$ be the population regression coefficient being estimated when the fallible measure is used as the covariate. Then, measurement error causes a reduction in the slope as follows:

$$\beta_{\text{fallible }X} = \beta_{\text{true }X}\left(\frac{\sigma^2_{\text{true }X}}{\sigma^2_X}\right) \tag{29}$$

Thus, whereas we would like to estimate the adjusted population effect

$$\mu_{YW} - \mu_{YB} - \beta_{\text{true }X}(\mu_{XW} - \mu_{XB})$$

we are, with a fallible covariate, actually estimating the following adjusted effect:

$$\mu_{YW} - \mu_{YB} - \beta_{\text{true }X}\left(\frac{\sigma^2_{\text{true }X}}{\sigma^2_X}\right)(\mu_{XW} - \mu_{XB}) \tag{30}$$

Because $\sigma^2_{\text{true }X}/\sigma^2_X$ is always less than 1 unless X is a perfect measure, ANCOVA represents an underadjustment for preexisting differences in the mean values on X. Depending on the pattern of means, this underadjustment can either produce significant ANCOVA F tests when the true adjusted effect is zero or result in failure to detect treatment effects present in the true adjusted effects.

Figure 9.7 illustrates the former situation for our race-differences-in-intelligence example. Assume that the tested IQ for Whites in the population is 108 and for Blacks it is 92. Further assume that the corresponding means on the measure of home environments are 40 for Blacks and 80 for Whites. Finally, assume that with a perfect measure of home environments that

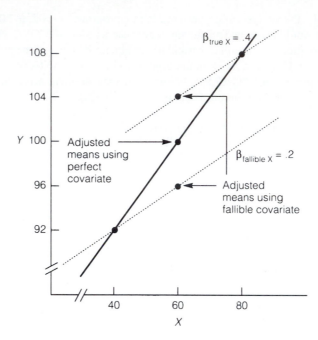

FIG. 9.7. Underadjustment resulting from using a fallible covariate in a nonequivalent-group study.

the regression slope would be .4, but that the proportion of true score variance in our fallible measure is only .5. Whereas a correct adjustment would result in identical mean IQ scores for Blacks and Whites, using a fallible covariate here implies that the observed difference between group means was reduced only half as much as it should have been.

A number of corrections for measurement error in the covariate have been proposed. The basic requirement over and above those for a standard ANCOVA is that you have an estimate of the reliability of the covariate. The interested reader is referred to Huitema (1980, Chapter 14) for references and a computational example of one of the procedures. More recent advances in developing models allowing for measurement errors stress latent variables. This class of models is often referred to as *structural equation modeling*. Numerous excellent textbooks have been written on structural equation modeling, including Bollen (1989), Kaplan (2000), Kenny (1979), Kline (1998), and Raykov and Marcoulides (2000).

Numerical Example

We now introduce a numerical example in order to summarize many of the points we have made so far as well as to motivate the need for measures of effect and/or confidence intervals to supplement significance tests. The data shown in Table 9.7 represent a hypothetical three-group study assessing different interventions for depression. Specifically, suppose 30 depressive individuals have been randomly assigned to one of three conditions: (1) selective serotonin reuptake inhibitor (SSRI) antidepressant medication, (2) placebo, or (3) wait list control. The Beck Depression Inventory (BDI) has been administered to each individual prior to the study, and then later is administered a second time at the end of the study. In essence, the question of interest is whether individuals in some groups change more than do individuals in other groups. Thus, it might seem natural to compute a change score for each person. In fact, we describe this analysis in more detail later in the chapter. However, for now we simply state that ANCOVA

TABLE 9.7
PRETEST AND POSTTEST BECK DEPRESSION SCORES FOR
INDIVIDUALS IN THREE CONDITIONS

	SSRI		Placebo		Wait list	
	Pre	Post	Pre	Post	Pre	Post
	18	12	18	11	15	17
	16	0	16	4	19	25
	16	10	15	19	10	10
	15	9	14	15	29	22
	14	0	20	3	24	23
	20	11	25	14	15	10
	14	2	11	10	9	2
	21	4	25	16	18	10
	25	15	11	10	22	14
	11	10	22	20	13	7
Mean	17.0	7.3	17.7	12.2	17.4	14.0

almost always is superior to analyzing change scores in randomized designs. For this reason, we consider here only the results obtained from applying an ANCOVA to these data.

Before describing the ANCOVA results, we might also comment that it is tempting simply to examine the data for the SSRI group and conclude that SSRI is clearly effective because literally all 10 individuals improved by at least 1 point on the BDI in this condition. However, some or all of this improvement may be attributable to *spontaneous recovery*, which refers to a possible tendency for individuals to improve even in the absence of any intervention, especially when they were selected initially because of their extreme scores. Until we compare the improvement in the SSRI group to that of other groups, we are not justified in making any claims about the influence of SSRI on depression.

Notice that the last line of Table 9.7 shows the pretest and posttest means for each of the three conditions. As expected with random assignment, there are minimal differences in the pretest means of the three groups. However, much larger differences between the groups have emerged for the posttest.

As previous sections of this chapter emphasize, ANCOVA compares adjusted means. Recall that the expression for the adjusted mean $\overline{Y}'_j$ of Group j is given by

$$\overline{Y}'_j = \overline{Y}_j - b_W(\overline{X}_j - \overline{X}) \qquad \text{(27, repeated)}$$

We can compute the adjusted means for our data from the pretest and posttest means shown in Table 9.7 as well as the fact (to be shown in a moment) that here, $b_W = 0.65$. Substituting these values into Equation 27 reveals that the adjusted means for our three groups are equal to 7.5, 12.0, and 14.0, respectively. Although hand calculations are straightforward once b_W has been obtained, adjusted means are also readily available in most statistical packages. For example, Table 9.8 shows adjusted means as calculated by SAS PROC GLM using an LSMEANS command. Notice that rounding the values shown in Table 9.8 to one decimal place produces values that agree with our hand calculations. Most importantly, whichever way we calculate adjusted means, notice that the adjusted means $\overline{Y}'_j$ are very similar to the unadjusted means $\overline{Y}_j$ in these data. This is precisely what we would expect in a randomized study. In the long run, the groups would not differ at the pretest, in which case Equation 27 implies that $\overline{Y}'_j$ and $\overline{Y}_j$ also would not differ in the long run. In any specific sample, however, differences typically exist,

TABLE 9.8

SAS LSMEANS SHOWING ADJUSTED
MEANS FOR TABLE 9.7 DATA

	Least Squares Means	
Group	Post LSMEAN	LSMEAN Number
1	7.5366157	1
2	11.9848948	2
3	13.9784895	3

TABLE 9.9

SAS OUTPUT FOR TABLE 9.7 DATA

The GLM Procedure

Dependent Variable: post

Source	DF	Sum of Squares	Mean Square	F Value	Pr > F
Model	3	553.831929	184.610643	6.35	0.0023
Error	26	756.334738	29.089798		
Corrected Total	29	1310.166667			

R-Square	Coeff. Var.	Root MSE	Post Mean
0.422719	48.29996	5.393496	11.16667

Source	DF	Type I SS	Mean Square	F Value	Pr > F
Group	2	240.4666667	120.2333333	4.13	0.0276
PRE	1	313.3652625	313.3652625	10.77	0.0029

Source	DF	Type III SS	Mean Square	F Value	Pr > F
Group	2	217.1494781	108.5747390	3.73	0.0376
PRE	1	313.3652625	313.3652625	10.77	0.0029

Parameter	Estimate	Standard Error	t Value	Pr > |t|
Intercept	2.771508306 B	3.82268702	0.73	0.4749
Group 1	−6.441873754 B	2.41332649	−2.67	0.0129
Group 2	−1.993594684 B	2.41276578	−0.83	0.4162
Group 3	0.000000000 B	.	.	.
PRE	0.645315615	0.19661520	3.28	0.0029

NOTE: The $X'X$ matrix has been found to be singular, and a generalized inverse was used to solve the normal equations. Terms whose estimates are followed by the letter "B" are not uniquely estimable.

and as we noted earlier in the chapter, using ANCOVA properly controls both unconditional and conditional Type I error rates as long as necessary statistical assumptions are met. Nevertheless, some researchers might be tempted to use the expected equality of unadjusted means and adjusted means as a reason to use ANOVA instead of ANCOVA here. In a later section of this chapter, we see that not only does this strategy fail to control conditional Type I error rate, but it also typically fails to capitalize on the power and precision offered by ANCOVA.

What does ANCOVA tell us about group differences in adjusted means on depression scores in Table 9.7? Table 9.9 shows output from SAS PROC GLM to answer this question. The first significance test included in the SAS output compares the typical ANCOVA full model with our restricted ANOVA model from Chapter 3:

$$\text{Full:} \quad Y_{ij} = \mu + \alpha_j + \beta X_{ij} + \varepsilon_{ij} \qquad \text{(1, repeated)}$$

$$\text{Restricted:} \quad Y_{ij} = \mu + \varepsilon_{ij} \qquad \text{(3.54, repeated)}$$

This model comparison is a simultaneous test of group effects and the covariate. Although it is produced by default in many statistical packages, it is not necessarily directly relevant to our question here, because it does not allow us to assess the intervention effect by itself. Thus, the F value of 6.35 for our data tells us only that we can reject a hypothesis that group effects and the regression coefficient for the covariate are all zero. In other words, this value essentially tells us one of three things is true: (a) some of the α_j parameters do not equal zero, (b) β does not equal zero, or (c) some of the α_j parameters do not equal zero *and* β does not equal zero, but it does not allow us to make an inference about which of these three possibilities is true here. Notice in particular that the statistically significant F value of 6.35 in our example does not necessarily tell us anything about group differences, because the difference between the full and restricted models may (or may not) simply reflect the exclusion of the β parameter from the restricted model. For this reason, we still need to consider a different pair of models to compare.

More pertinent for our purposes is the next section of the output shown in Table 9.9, which shows separate tests of the intervention effect and the covariate. Notice that as of this writing SAS PROC GLM produces both Type I and Type III sums of squares and corresponding tests. As we explained in Chapter 7 when we discussed nonorthogonal designs, we generally recommend interpreting results based on Type III sums of squares. In our particular case here, the Type I sum of squares for Group pertains to unadjusted means, whereas the Type III sum of squares pertains to adjusted means. In particular, the Type III sum of squares for Group is obtained as the difference in the error sum of squares of the following two models:

$$\text{Full:} \quad Y_{ij} = \mu + \alpha_j + \beta X_{ij} + \varepsilon_{ij} \qquad \text{(1, repeated)}$$

$$\text{Restricted:} \quad Y_{ij} = \mu + \beta X_{ij} + \varepsilon_{ij} \qquad \text{(2, repeated)}$$

However, as we said near the beginning of the chapter, this is precisely the model comparison that is typically of primary interest in ANCOVA. In our data, the F value obtained from this comparison equals 3.73, which yields a p value of .0376. Thus, we can conclude that the three groups' population means are not all the same. We would usually want to formulate contrasts of adjusted means to examine which specific groups differ from one another, so we turn to that topic shortly.

The bottom portion of Table 9.9 shows parameter estimates from the full model of Equation 1. Of particular note is the estimated coefficient for "pre," the covariate. Recall that the estimated regression coefficient for the β parameter in the full model of Equation 1 is b_W. It immediately follows from Table 9.9 that b_W in these depression data equals approximately 0.65, which you may recall is the value we used at the beginning of this section when we calculated adjusted means.

Measures of Effect

As in other designs, we often want to supplement significance tests with measures of effect. As we introduced in Chapter 3, we can once again distinguish measures of association strength from effect size measures and choose whichever type is more informative for a specific situation. In general, both types follow the same basic logic we have developed in designs without a covariate.

In addition to choosing between measures of association strength and effect size measures, it is important to consider the conceptual role of the covariate when reporting and interpreting measures of effect in analysis of covariance. Much as we discussed with regard to factorial designs in Chapter 7, we can regard a covariate as either an extrinsic or intrinsic component of the design. In essence, an *extrinsic component* contributes additional variance to the dependent variable over and above what would be considered "natural" variability. An *intrinsic component*, however, simply correlates with some portion of the natural variability. Thus, an extrinsic component is typically a factor manipulated by the experimenter, whereas an intrinsic component is more likely to be a naturally occurring individual difference variable. From this perspective, a covariate is almost always an intrinsic component of the design. As such, we would usually not want to remove variance it may explain in the dependent variable from our conceptualization of total variance. We emphasize this perspective in our presentation, although it is important to understand that calculations and subsequent interpretations would differ if we were to regard the covariate as extrinsic.

As we have seen in previous chapters, one measure of association strength is simply R^2. From Chapter 3, the general form of R^2 is given by

$$R^2 = \frac{E_\text{R} - E_\text{F}}{E_\text{R}} \qquad \text{(3.90, repeated)}$$

The only complication in an ANCOVA design is deciding on appropriate models to serve as the basis for calculating R^2 from Equation 3.90.

One pair of models comes from the full and restricted ANCOVA models themselves:

$$\text{Full:} \quad Y_{ij} = \mu + \alpha_j + \beta X_{ij} + \varepsilon_{ij} \qquad \text{(1, repeated)}$$

$$\text{Restricted:} \quad Y_{ij} = \mu + \beta X_{ij} + \varepsilon_{ij} \qquad \text{(2, repeated)}$$

For example, we can see from Table 9.9 that for our depression data, $E_\text{F} = 756.33$ (see the line labeled "Error" near the top of the table). We can easily calculate E_R by realizing that the value of E_R must equal E_F plus the sum of squares attributable to the group effect. For these data this implies that E_R must equal $756.33 + 217.15$ (i.e., 973.48). Substituting these values into Equation 3.90 reveals that R^2 equals 0.22. We could then conclude that the intervention effect accounts for 22% of the variance in our depression measure. However, notice that the restricted model of Equation 2 includes the covariate as a predictor. As a consequence, the error variance in the model reflects variance in the dependent variable that is not accounted for by the covariate. What this means in our case is that we have really shown that the intervention effect accounts for 22% of the variance in posttest depression once we control for pretest depression. Stated differently, if we considered a subset of individuals all of whom had identical pretest levels of depression, the intervention explains 22% of the variance in their posttest levels of depression. Although this value is correct mathematically, it may not reflect our true intent. In particular, by controlling for pretest in our calculation, we have effectively regarded it as an extrinsic component of the design. Although this is not necessarily wrong, it does mean that our conceptualization of variance in the outcome measure is confined to a subset of individuals who were identical on the pretest, as opposed to being defined variance in terms of everyone in the population regardless of pretest status.

What if we prefer to conceptualize variance in the dependent variable in terms of everyone in the population? In this case, the denominator needs to be based on a model that does not reduce the variance in Y as a function of X. Our usual ANOVA restricted model serves this purpose:

$$\text{Restricted:} \quad Y_{ij} = \mu + \varepsilon_{ij} \qquad \text{(3.54, repeated)}$$

For example, Table 9.9 shows that the sum of squared errors for this model for our depression data is 1310.17 (see the line labeled "Corrected Total"). To assess the extent to which the intervention reduces unexplained variance in the restricted model of Equation 3.54, we need to form a model that allows for group effects. The usual ANOVA full model serves this purpose:

$$\text{Full:} \quad Y_{ij} = \mu + \alpha_j + \varepsilon_{ij} \qquad \text{(3.66, repeated)}$$

The difference in sum of squared errors between these two models is simply the usual ANOVA sum of squares between groups, which in our data equals 240.47 (see the Type I SS for the Group effect). The ratio of 240.47 to 1310.17 is 0.18. Thus, the intervention effect accounts for 18% of the total variance. Of course, it is not surprising that the intervention accounts for less of the total variance than of the variance controlling for the pretest, because the variance controlling for the pretest is necessarily less than the total variance.

As we have seen for previous designs, an R^2 value describes the proportion of variance accounted for in the sample, but is not intended to serve as an estimate of the proportion of variance accounted for in the population. Instead, an omega squared value is generally preferable for this purpose. Following Olejnik and Algina (2000), omega squared for group effects in ANCOVA when the covariate is regarded as intrinsic can be written as

$$\hat{\omega}^2 = \frac{df_{\text{effect}} \, (MS_{\text{effect}} - MS_{\text{error}})}{SS_{\text{total}} + MS_{\text{error}}} \qquad (31)$$

We can calculate omega squared for our depression data using the information shown earlier in Table 9.9. Specifically, $df_{\text{effect}} = 2$, $MS_{\text{effect}} = 108.57$, $MS_{\text{error}} = 29.09$, and $SS_{\text{total}} = 1310.17$, so that the value of omega squared here is 0.12. Thus, we would estimate that the intervention accounts for 12% of the total variance in posttest depression scores in the population.

Standardized means provide an alternative to measures of association strength, especially when we want to compare two specific conditions to one another. Once again, we must decide how best to conceptualize variance, because standardization requires that raw scores be transformed to z scores based on some measure of variance. As before, we generally believe that covariates should be regarded as intrinsic, so this is the approach we illustrate here.

When the covariate is considered to be intrinsic, our conceptualization of error variance should not control for the covariate. Thus, an appropriate estimate of error variance can be derived from a model that includes only a group effect, which is the full ANOVA model

$$\text{Full:} \quad Y_{ij} = \mu + \alpha_j + \varepsilon_{ij} \qquad \text{(3.66, repeated)}$$

Once we know the sum of squared errors and degrees of freedom for this model, it becomes straightforward to determine a standard deviation we can use as the basis for standardization. Of course, one way to find the sum of squared errors is simply to perform an ANOVA on the data. An equivalent approach is to use the information we already have from our ANCOVA. In particular, notice that our ANCOVA results tell us (1) the sum of squared errors for the full ANCOVA model

$$\text{Full:} \quad Y_{ij} = \mu + \alpha_j + \beta X_{ij} + \varepsilon_{ij} \tag{1, repeated}$$

as well as (2) the difference between the sum of squared errors of this full model and a model that omits the covariate, which is simply our full ANOVA model. For example, Table 9.9 shows that the sum of squared errors for the full ANCOVA model equals 756.33. The table also shows that the difference between the sum of squared errors for the full ANCOVA model and a model that omits the covariate (and thus becomes the full ANOVA model) equals 313.37. Thus, the sum of squared errors for the full ANOVA model must be 1069.70 (i.e., 756.33 + 313.37). The degrees of freedom for the full ANOVA model equal $N - a$, which in our data is 27. By dividing the sum of squared errors by the degrees of freedom, we obtain MS_W, which provides an unbiased estimate of error variance (see Equations 3.97 and 3.98 for a reminder). In our data, $MS_W = 39.62$. The corresponding standard deviation is the square root of the variance, or 6.29 here.

Finally, we can obtain standardized differences between adjusted means by dividing the difference between the adjusted means by our estimate of the within-group standard deviation. For example, to compare the adjusted means of two selected groups l and m, we would form

$$\hat{d} = \frac{\overline{Y}'_l - \overline{Y}'_m}{\sqrt{MS_W}} \tag{32}$$

Recall that for our depression data we have already found that the adjusted means are 7.5 for the antidepressant group, 12.0 for the placebo group, and 14.0 for the control group. Now that we know that the square root of MS_W is 6.29, we can calculate standardized mean differences between each pair of groups. For example, $\hat{d}$ comparing antidepressant and control equals 1.03 [i.e., $(14.0 - 7.5)/6.29$], which would be regarded as a very large treatment effect. The $\hat{d}$ value for placebo versus control equals 0.32, which is somewhat larger than Cohen's definition of a small effect.

Comparisons Among Adjusted Group Means

Tests of specific contrasts among the adjusted group means can be developed by considering their variances. Recall the adjusted mean of the jth group, adjusting for the departure of the group's covariate mean from the grand covariate mean, is

$$\overline{Y}'_j = \overline{Y}_j - b_W(\overline{X}_j - \overline{X}) \tag{27, repeated}$$

In a randomized study, this adjusted mean estimates the population mean of the jth group, which we denote μ_j. As we develop in the chapter extension, the variance of this estimator is

$$\sigma^2_{\overline{Y}'_j} = \sigma^2_\varepsilon \left[\frac{1}{n_j} + \frac{(\overline{X}_j - \overline{X})^2}{\sum_j \sum_i (X_{ij} - \overline{X}_j)^2} \right] \tag{33}$$

We can estimate this simply by substituting for σ_ε^2 the observed mean square error for our full model (see Equation 1) and denote this estimator $s_{\bar{Y}_j'}^2$:

$$s_{\bar{Y}_j'}^2 = \frac{E_F}{df_F}\left[\frac{1}{n_j} + \frac{(\bar{X}_j - \bar{X})^2}{\sum_j \sum_i (X_{ij} - \bar{X}_j)^2}\right] \tag{34}$$

When the overall test of the treatment effect is significant in a one-way ANCOVA involving three or more groups, it may be of interest to perform tests of specific pairwise differences between groups. The contrast or difference between adjusted means in two selected groups— for example, Groups l and m—can be expressed as

$$\hat{\psi} = \bar{Y}_l' - \bar{Y}_m' = \bar{Y}_l - b_W(\bar{X}_l - \bar{X}) - [\bar{Y}_m - b_W(\bar{X}_m - \bar{X})]$$
$$= \bar{Y}_l - \bar{Y}_m - b_W(\bar{X}_l - \bar{X}_m) \tag{35}$$

This estimates the difference between the population means μ_l and μ_m and has variance

$$\sigma_{\bar{Y}_j' - \bar{Y}_m'}^2 = \sigma_\varepsilon^2\left[\frac{1}{n_l} + \frac{1}{n_m} + \frac{(\bar{X}_l - \bar{X}_m)^2}{\sum_j \sum_i (X_{ij} - \bar{X}_j)^2}\right] \tag{36}$$

Again, this variance can be estimated simply by substituting our observed mean square for σ_ε^2:

$$s_{\bar{Y}_l' - \bar{Y}_m'}^2 = \frac{E_F}{df_F}\left[\frac{1}{n_l} + \frac{1}{n_m} + \frac{(\bar{X}_l - \bar{X}_m)^2}{\sum_j \sum_i (X_{ij} - \bar{X}_j)^2}\right] \tag{37}$$

Under the standard ANCOVA assumptions, the ratio of the square of the estimated contrast value in Equation 35 to its variance is distributed as an F with 1 and $N - a - 1$ degrees of freedom:

$$F = \frac{(\bar{Y}_l' - \bar{Y}_m')^2}{s_{\bar{Y}_l' - \bar{Y}_m'}^2} \tag{38}$$

(This type of ratio of a squared contrast value to its variance is one of the ways tests of contrasts were developed in Chapter 4. If you need a review, see the discussion of Equation 4.47.)

If C such planned pairwise comparisons among adjusted means are conducted, then, as usual, a Bonferroni adjustment to control the overall α at .05 could be accomplished by requiring the F in Equation 38 to be significant at α/C.

Just like multiple comparisons in one-way ANOVA discussed in Chapter 5, if all possible pairwise comparisons between means are of interest, or if the pairs to be tested are decided on after examining the data, then tests should be carried out by making reference to a studentized range distribution. This can be done in the ANCOVA situation in one of two ways, depending on what is assumed about the concomitant variable. If the X variable is regarded as fixed, as in the one-way ANOVA case, a Tukey test can be performed by comparing the F value computed for each pairwise test using Equation 38 against $q^2/2$, where q is the value in Appendix Table A.4 at the desired α for a groups and $N - a - 1$ denominator degrees of freedom. If, however, the covariate is regarded as a random effect, then the same F value would be compared against a slightly different critical value from the *generalized studentized–range distribution* (Bryant & Paulson, 1976). The critical value is q_{BP}^2, where the value of q_{BP}, the generalized studentized range, is read from Table A.8. Generally, q_{BP} is slightly (less than 5%) larger than the q critical value for the same α level, number of means, and error df.

When tests of complex comparisons involving multiple treatment means are desired, generalizations of the previously discussed expressions for the estimated value and variance of pairwise contrasts can be used. The estimated contrast value in general is just the linear combination of adjusted means of interest:

$$\hat{\psi} = \sum_j c_j \overline{Y}'_j \tag{39}$$

which can be expressed in terms of the observed group means on X and Y:

$$\hat{\psi} = \sum_j c_j [\overline{Y}_j - b_W(\overline{X}_j - \overline{X})] = \sum_j c_j \overline{Y}_j - b_W \sum_j c_j \overline{X}_j \tag{40}$$

The estimated variance of such a contrast can be written (cf. Cochran, 1957; Neter, Wasserman, & Kutner, 1985, p. 873)

$$s_{\hat{\psi}}^2 = \frac{E_F}{df_F} \left[\sum_j \frac{c_j^2}{n_j} + \frac{\left(\sum_j c_j \overline{X}_j \right)^2}{\sum_j \sum_i (X_{ij} - \overline{X}_j)^2} \right] \tag{41}$$

Then, the test statistic

$$F = \frac{\hat{\psi}^2}{s_{\hat{\psi}}^2} \tag{42}$$

is distributed as an F with 1 and $N - a - 1$ degrees of freedom. If multiple complex comparisons are being tested, each may be evaluated either using the Bonferroni method, if the contrasts are planned, or against a Scheffé critical value, if the contrasts are post hoc. The Scheffé critical value for an a-group study would be $(a - 1)F_{(a-1), (N-a-1)}$.

An alternative to testing contrasts is to form confidence intervals for contrasts. As we discussed in Chapter 5, when more than one contrast is of potential interest, we generally recommend the formation of simultaneous confidence intervals. Chapter 5 presented a very general expression for forming such intervals:

$$\text{estimate} \pm (\text{critical value}) (\text{estimated standard error}) \tag{5.12, repeated}$$

For adjusted means, the estimate itself comes from Equation 35 for a pairwise comparison or from Equation 40 for a complex comparison. The critical value is the same as would be used in a significance test and thus depends on the types of comparisons being investigated (e.g., pairwise versus complex, planned versus post hoc). The estimated standard error comes from

TABLE 9.10

SAS OUTPUT FOR SIMULTANEOUS 95% CONFIDENCE
INTERVALS OF PAIRWISE COMPARISONS OF ADJUSTED
MEANS BASED ON TUKEY

| | | Least Squares Means for Effect group | | |
| | | Difference Between Means | Simultaneous 95% Confidence Limits for LSMean(i)-LSMean(j) | |
i	j			
1	2	−4.448279	−10.451703	1.555145
1	3	−6.441874	−12.438734	−0.445013
2	3	−1.993595	− 7.989062	4.001872

the square root of the expression in Equation 37 for pairwise comparisons and from the square root of the expression in Equation 41 for complex comparisons.

Fortunately, we can often rely on statistical packages to form appropriate simultaneous confidence intervals, or at worst to provide all of the intermediate values needed to form the desired intervals. For example, suppose we wanted to create simultaneous 95% confidence intervals for all pairwise comparisons of adjusted means in our three-group depression data. Table 9.10 shows SAS output obtained from an LSMEANS command, which produces the desired intervals based on a Tukey critical value. The intervals shown here imply that we can have 95% confidence in all three of the following statements: (1) SSRI produces BDI scores somewhere between 10.45 points lower and 1.56 points higher than placebo, (2) SSRI produces BDI scores between 12.44 and 0.45 points lower than control, and (3) placebo produces BDI scores between 7.99 points lower and 4.00 points higher than control. Notice that the only interval that fails to contain zero is the second interval, so we can infer that SSRI truly lowers BDI scores as compared to control.

Two other points deserve consideration. First, as of this writing, none of the major statistical packages provide critical values based on the Bryant–Paulson approach. Using this approach requires finding the estimated standard error either from Equation 37 or Equation 41, or deriving the value from computer output. For example, we can infer the estimated standard error of the first contrast from Table 9.10. To see how, first notice that the difference between either limit of the confidence interval and the midpoint of the interval equals 6.00. This value must equal the product of the critical value and the estimated standard error. From Table A.4, we can see that the q value for $\alpha = .05$, 3 groups, and 26 degrees of freedom is approximately 3.52. Now we must realize that the critical value itself is given by $q/\sqrt{2}$, which equals 2.49. It then follows that the estimated standard error must equal 2.41 (i.e., 6.00/2.49). We can now use this value along with the appropriate Bryant–Paulson critical value from Table A.8 to form a new confidence interval. Interpolating for 26 degrees of freedom in this table produces a critical value of 3.59 for 1 covariate. We must remember to divide this value by the square root of 2 and then multiply this result by the estimated standard error (2.49 here) to produce our interval. This produces a value of 6.32, which we now add and subtract from −4.45, which is the difference in adjusted sample means. The result is an interval from −10.77 to 1.87. Notice this interval is somewhat wider than that obtained from Tukey, as would be expected given the difference in critical values.

Second, Westfall, Tobias, Rom, Wolfinger, and Hochberg (1999) discuss the fact that Tukey's method is only approximate when a covariate is included in the model. They recommend an exact simulation-based method for forming confidence intervals. This method is implemented in SAS and is a straightforward option in the LSMEANS statement.

Generalizations of the ANCOVA Model

The basic ANCOVA model we have been discussing throughout the chapter

$$\text{Full:} \quad Y_{ij} = \mu + \alpha_j + \beta X_{ij} + \varepsilon_{ij} \qquad \text{(1, repeated)}$$

can be easily generalized to encompass different relationships and variables. We mention some possible extensions here but do not go into computational details. The logic of the analyses as a way of accommodating to individual differences remains the same. However, the computations are such that you will almost certainly want to use a computer program for the analyses discussed in this section. Fortunately, SAS, and SPSS can easily be used to carry out such analyses.

Multiple Covariates

The ANCOVA model can readily accommodate more than a single predictor. Denoting a second concomitant variable as Z and subscripting the slopes to indicate the associated predictor variable, we would have the full model:

$$Y_{ij} = \mu + \alpha_j + \beta_X X_{ij} + \beta_Z Z_{ij} + \varepsilon_{ij} \qquad (43)$$

As we note in our discussion of multiple regression (see the tutorial on regression on the data disk), the increase in the adequacy of the model resulting from adding variable Z depends not only on the relationship between Z and Y, but also on that between Z and X. Thus, other things being equal, variable Z would contribute more to the predictive accuracy of the model if it were relatively unrelated to X. Although it is the case that adding more covariates almost certainly increases the model's R^2, one rapidly reaches the point of diminishing returns. Because the estimate of the parameters in a model depends on the other terms being estimated, including additional covariates can actually make the estimates of the treatment effects of primary interest less precise. This is particularly true when the study involves relatively few subjects. Most behavioral science studies are sufficiently small that two or three covariates will be the upper limit.

Adjusted means for the model in Equation 43, of course, depend on the group mean on Z as well as X. Specifically,

$$\overline{Y}'_j = \overline{Y}_j - b_{W_x}(\overline{X}_j - \overline{X}) - b_{W_z}(\overline{Z}_j - \overline{Z}) \qquad (44)$$

Kirk (1995, p. 726) provides further computational details.

Nonlinear Relationships

The linear (i.e., straight line) relationship between X and Y, which we have noted is assumed by the basic ANCOVA model (see our discussion of Equation 28), is not a necessary part of covariance analysis (Neter et al., 1996, p. 1017). The general linear model is linear in the parameters, not in the X–Y relationship. That is, the prediction represents some linear (that is, additive) combination or weighted sum of parameter estimates, but, as we noted in Chapter 6, the weights may be such that the relation between X and Y is curvilinear. A tremendous variety of curve forms could be modeled by including combinations of various powers of X in the model. However, in most behavioral science research, the linear relationship between Y and X accounts for the vast majority of the variability in Y that is associated with X. If, for theoretical reasons or because of trends you note in scatterplots of your data, you suspect a nonlinear relationship between the dependent variable and covariate, then this should be examined in your modeling. You may allow for a quadratic relationship simply by including X^2 as well as X in your model, that is,

$$Y_{ij} = \mu + \alpha_j + \beta_L X_{ij} + \beta_Q X_{ij}^2 + \varepsilon_{ij} \tag{45}$$

where we have added subscripts L and Q to our βs to indicate linear and quadratic trends, respectively. In fact, a test for linearity[5] can be carried out by comparing the model in Equation 45 with the basic ANCOVA model in Equation 1. If the test indicates that X^2 significantly enhances adequacy, then it can be retained in your model for testing other effects and contrasts of interest. Little, An, Johanns, and Giordani (2000) provide an especially valuable description of methods for relaxing the linearity assumption in the context of nonrandomized group comparisons.

Multifactor Studies

To this point, we have considered ANCOVA only for single-factor designs. Naturally, ANCOVA can be used in designs involving more than a single factor. For example, we could generalize our basic ANCOVA model having effect parameters α_j and slope parameter β to include the effects γ_k of another factor, say factor C:

$$Y_{ijk} = \mu + \alpha_j + \gamma_k + \alpha\gamma_{jk} + \beta X_{ijk} + \varepsilon_{ijk} \tag{46}$$

where $j = 1, 2, \ldots, a$ levels of factor A, $k = 1, 2, \ldots, c$ levels of factor C, and $i = 1, 2, \ldots, n_{jk}$ subjects in cell jk. Now, besides the adjusted cell means, one will likely be interested in the adjusted marginal means. The adjusted cell means, A marginals and C marginals are, respectively,

$$\overline{Y}'_{jk} = \overline{Y}_{jk} - b_W(\overline{X}_{jk} - \overline{X}_{..})$$
$$\overline{Y}'_{j.} = \overline{Y}_{j.} - b_W(\overline{X}_{j.} - \overline{X}_{..})$$
$$\overline{Y}'_{.k} = \overline{Y}_{.k} - b_W(\overline{X}_{.k} - \overline{X}_{..}) \tag{47}$$

Kirk (1995, p. 733ff.) or Neter, et al. (1996, p. 1028ff.) provide computational details regarding tests and confidence intervals.

Choosing Covariates in Randomized Designs

The most common type of covariate in behavioral research is a pretest. However, we have just seen in the previous section that not only are other types of variables potential covariates, but more generally, the ANCOVA model can easily accommodate more than one covariate. How many covariates to include in a model is a complicated question. The answer depends in part on whether the design is an observational study or a randomized study. In an observational study, the primary role of covariates is to reduce bias. Failing to include relevant covariates in the model leads to biased estimates of treatment effects (see Appendix B Part II for details). Knowing what variables to control for in observational studies usually requires deep understanding of the phenomena being investigated (see such sources as Rosenbaum, 2002, and Shadish, Cook, & Campbell, 2002, for excellent discussions of these complications). However, bias is not an issue in randomized designs (although attrition can create bias even with random assignment, in which case the design may effectively have become an observational study). Instead, the primary purpose of including covariates in a randomized design is to increase power and precision.

Raab, Day, and Sales (2000) provide a thorough evaluation of different strategies for choosing covariates to include in a randomized design. Their single most important conclusion is that variables to be included as covariates in the analysis should be identified based on theory. In other words, decisions about what covariates to include in the model should be made in the design phase of the study instead of waiting until actual data have been obtained. In particular, the alternative of sifting through the data at hand to choose covariates is fraught with peril. For example, one approach with some intuitive appeal would be to measure numerous potential covariates and then see which ones correlate with the outcome variable reasonably well. It might seem logical to include only those variables that exceed some cutoff (e.g., $r = 0.30$) as covariates. Unfortunately, however, this approach cannot be recommended. It runs the risk of underestimating true error variance by capitalizing on chance in selection of covariates, and as a consequence leads to an actual alpha level greater than the nominal value. In other words, adopting this strategy leads to too many Type I errors and confidence intervals that are too narrow. A different data-based strategy also involves sifting through the data, but this approach uses as covariates only those variables for which the treatment groups differ. This strategy has exactly the opposite problem of the first data-based strategy in that it leads to conservative tests and confidence intervals. The bottom line is that data-based strategies are not recommended.

So how should theory guide the choice of covariates? Raab et al. (2000) suggest approaching the answer to this question in two steps. First, some variables may be balanced in the design. This refers to a situation where the experimenter has assigned individuals to groups in a manner that ensures that the groups cannot differ on the variable in question. For example, in our depression example, prior to forming treatment groups, the experimenter might have obtained a pretest score for each of the 30 individuals in the study. These scores could be blocked into 10 sets of 3 each. Random assignment to condition would then occur within each block. Notice that such an approach guarantees that group differences on this variable will be virtually nonexistent. Raab et al. (2000) show that it is generally advantageous to include all such variables that have been balanced in the design as covariates in the model to be used for data analysis. Thus, balanced variables are incorporated in both the design and the analysis.

Whether or not some variables have been balanced in the design, there will often be additional variables that are candidates as covariates. How should a researcher decide which (if any) of these to include as eventual covariates? The answer to this question depends on three factors: (1) the sample size, (2) the number of balanced variables already included in the design and the model, and (3) the extent to which the additional variables correlate with the dependent variable over and above the balanced variables already included in the model. Specifically, Raab et al. (2000) show that for comparing two groups with equal sample sizes, r additional covariates increase power and precision if the following inequality holds:

$$r < R^2(N - b - 2) \tag{48}$$

where R^2 is the population partial R square predicting the dependent variable from the r covariates after having controlled for any balanced predictors, N is total sample size, and b is the number of balanced predictors already included in the model. For example, suppose $N = 50$ and no balanced predictors are included in the model. We believe that our best candidate covariate correlates 0.40 with the outcome variable. Should we include this covariate in the model? Yes, because r here is only 1, which is less than 7.68 [i.e., $(.40^2)(48)$]. Suppose we suspect that this first covariate together with a second covariate would account for 20% of the variance in Y. Should we use a two-covariate model? Once again, the answer is yes, because in this case, 2 is less than 9.6. Following this general logic provides guidelines for selecting an appropriate number of covariates, although it is important not to overestimate the unique contribution of potential covariates in explaining additional variance in the dependent variable. To put this conclusion in perspective, why not include as many covariates as time and money allow? After all, won't each additional covariate explain at least a little bit more of the variance in Y? The catch is that we lose a degree of freedom for each additional covariate (because we must estimate a slope parameter for each covariate we include in the model), so in reality there is a trade-off between explaining more variance and having fewer degrees of freedom. Equation 48 shows the implications of this trade-off in deciding how many covariates would be optimal.

Sample Size Planning and Power Analysis in ANCOVA

The previous section provided some guidelines for choosing an appropriate number of covariates to include in a randomized design. However, generally more important than the number of covariates is the number of subjects. How large should the sample be? Of course, there is not necessarily a single correct answer to this question, but nevertheless, judicious planning leads to informative studies. As mentioned, the primary benefit of including one or more covariates in a randomized design is increased power and precision. In an observational study, however, covariates serve to reduce bias. Because of this distinction, our presentation of power analysis and sample size planning focuses on randomized designs.

You may recall that in Chapter 3 we introduced f as a standardized measure of effect size for ANOVA designs, where f is defined by

$$f = \sigma_m/\sigma_\varepsilon \qquad \text{(3.89, repeated)}$$

Power analysis in ANCOVA designs also relies on f. The only important difference (in a randomized design) is that σ_ε is typically smaller with a covariate. To see why, let's compare full models for ANOVA and ANCOVA. The full model for a one-way ANOVA design is

$$\text{Full:} \quad Y_{ij} = \mu + \alpha_j + \varepsilon_{ij} \qquad \text{(3.66, repeated)}$$

whereas the full model for a one-way ANCOVA is

$$\text{Full:} \quad Y_{ij} = \mu + \alpha_j + \beta X_{ij} + \varepsilon_{ij} \qquad \text{(1, repeated)}$$

Remember that the ratio E_F/df_F provides an unbiased estimate of the error variance σ_ε^2 for a model. Furthermore, we saw earlier in this chapter that one of the two consequences of using ANCOVA is that the sum of squared errors for the full model is decreased. In other words, E_F for the ANCOVA model is smaller than E_F for the ANOVA model to the extent that X correlates with Y (because to the extent that X correlates with Y, X also accounts for variance in Y, leaving less unexplained variance in the model). Thus, a successful covariate reduces unexplained variance. Because σ_ε appears in the denominator of the expression for f, reducing σ_ε increases the effect size. As a consequence, ANCOVA can provide more power than ANOVA for a fixed sample size. Alternatively, ANCOVA can provide the same power as ANOVA while requiring a smaller sample size.

In particular, the key insight here is to realize that we can write the unexplained error variance σ_ε^2 in ANCOVA as

$$\sigma_{\varepsilon(\text{ANCOVA})}^2 = \sigma_{\varepsilon(\text{ANOVA})}^2(1 - \rho^2) \tag{49}$$

where ρ is the population correlation between the covariate X and the dependent variable Y. More generally, when multiple covariates are included in the model, ρ is the population multiple correlation between Y and the set of X variables. Notice that Equation 49 follows from the well-known property that the square of the correlation coefficient reflects the proportion of explained variance.

To understand the practical implications of Equation 49, let's return to an example we introduced in Chapter 3. Consider a randomized three-group design in which our anticipated population means are 400, 450, and 500. We expect the within-group population standard deviation to be 100. This information allows us to calculate our f value of 0.4082, which is very close to Cohen's definition of a large effect size ($f = 0.40$). We saw in Chapter 3 that 21 subjects per group (i.e., a total sample size of 63) would be needed to have a power of .80 to detect group differences in this situation (as usual, this assumes that we have set α at .05).

Now suppose a covariate is available that we anticipate would correlate .50 with the dependent variable. Would we still need a sample size of 63 to obtain a power of .80? To answer this question, we must compute σ_ε for the ANCOVA design. Substituting $\rho = .50$ into Equation 49 along with the ANOVA error variance of 10,000 (i.e., 100^2) reveals that the ANCOVA error variance would be reduced to 7,500, which in turn means that σ_ε would be reduced from 100 to 86.60. As a result, the ANCOVA f value increases from 0.4082 to 0.4713.

Determining an appropriate sample size necessitates using the charts in Appendix Table A.11 (unless we have the benefit of power analysis software). As usual, we must specify:

1. The numerator degrees of freedom
2. The Type I error rate α
3. The denominator degrees of freedom
4. An effect-size parameter ϕ, which reflects the sample size and the magnitude of the effect.

The numerator degrees of freedom in a one-way ANCOVA design is $a - 1$, just as in a one-way ANOVA. In our example, $a - 1 = 2$. We typically set $\alpha = .05$. The denominator degrees of freedom in ANCOVA once again reflect the degrees of freedom of the full model. However, we have to be careful to remember that we must estimate a slope parameter for each covariate in the model, so with p covariates, we have $N - a - p$ denominator degrees of freedom. Finally, ϕ is found as it was in ANOVA, namely,

$$\phi = f\sqrt{n} \tag{3.100, repeated}$$

where f is the standardized effect for ANCOVA and n is the number of subjects per group. As we have seen previously, n affects both ϕ and denominator degrees of freedom, so sample size planning using the Appendix Table A.11 charts must proceed in a trial-and-error fashion. In our particular case, $n = 15$ implies $\phi = 1.83$ and $n = 16$ implies $\phi = 1.89$. With 44 degrees of freedom, $n = 16$ appears to yield a power value just slightly greater than .80.

What have we learned here? Given our anticipated population parameters, an ANOVA would require a total sample size of 63 individuals to produce a power of .80. An ANCOVA based on a covariate expected to correlate .50 with the dependent variable would require a total sample size of only 48 individuals to yield exactly the same power. Thus, ANCOVA allows us to conduct a study with the same power as ANOVA and yet use nearly 25% fewer research participants. When subjects are at a premium (either because each participant literally costs time and money or simply because recruitment itself is time consuming), the potential benefits of ANCOVA can be extremely valuable.

In many situations, we may be at least as interested in the precision with which we can estimate treatment effects as we are in the power to detect an effect. ANCOVA also can be beneficial for increasing precision of estimating treatment group differences in randomized designs. We saw in Chapter 4 that the estimated variance of a contrast in a one-way ANOVA design can be written as

$$\text{estimated Var}\left(\hat{\psi}\right) = \sum_{j=1}^{a} \left(c_j^2/n_j\right)s_j^2 \qquad \text{(4.46, repeated)}$$

With homogeneity of variance, we can use MS_W (which we can also write as E_F/df_F) in place of each separate group's variance estimate, in which case we can rewrite Equation 4.46 as

$$\hat{\sigma}_{\hat{\psi}}^2 = \frac{E_F}{df_F}\left[\sum_j \frac{c_j^2}{n_j}\right] \qquad (50)$$

We saw earlier in this chapter that the comparable expression in ANCOVA is

$$s_{\hat{\psi}}^2 = \frac{E_F}{df_F}\left[\sum_j \frac{c_j^2}{n_j} + \frac{\left(\sum_j c_j \overline{X}_j\right)^2}{\sum_j \sum_i (X_{ij} - \overline{X}_j)^2}\right] \qquad \text{(41, repeated)}$$

At first glance, it might appear that the only difference between Equations 50 and 41 is the extra term in brackets for Equation 41. In reality, we must realize that the values of E_F and df_F will also differ for the two equations because Equation 50 is based on a full ANOVA model, whereas Equation 41 is based on a full ANCOVA model. Because of the difference in models, E_F/df_F under ANCOVA is roughly $(1 - r^2)$ as large as E_F/df_F under ANOVA. For example, if $r = .50$, E_F/df_F for ANCOVA is approximately 75% as large as E_F/df_F for ANOVA. Furthermore, the extra term in brackets for ANCOVA is usually small in a randomized design unless samples are very small. The end result can be seen from the fact that the width of a confidence interval is directly proportional to the square root of the estimated variance of the contrast. Thus, an interval formed with ANCOVA is narrower by a factor of almost $\sqrt{1 - r^2}$ compared to an interval from ANOVA. For example, all other things being equal, if $r = .50$, a confidence interval for a contrast in a randomized design tends to be approximately 87% as wide as the same interval if the covariate is not included in the model. Thus, including one or more covariates in the model to analyze data from a randomized design can substantially increase precision for estimating group differences.

ALTERNATE METHODS OF ANALYZING DESIGNS WITH CONCOMITANT VARIABLES

There are numerous alternative methods of analyzing designs with concomitant variables. None are as flexible or as generally useful as the ANCOVA procedures we have discussed.

However, because of their widespread use in the literature and the fact that some of the methods are preferred over ANCOVA in certain situations, we consider three alternatives, albeit briefly. The three methods are the ANOVA of residuals, the analysis of gain scores, and blocking.

ANOVA of Residuals

ANCOVA is sometimes presented as being strictly equivalent to first regressing the dependent variable on the concomitant variable, then computing a set of residual scores by subtracting the estimates yielded by the regression equation from the observed scores, and finally performing an ANOVA of these residual scores. Although intuitively appealing, it has been shown by Maxwell, Delaney, and Manheimer (1985) that the two methods are not equivalent. Performing an ANOVA of a single set of residuals results in a model comparison in which the parameter estimates used in one of the models are not least-squares estimates for that model. This results in the test statistic not being appropriately distributed. Thus, despite the fact that the method has been used in the literature, performing an ANOVA of a set of residuals is an analysis strategy that should be avoided.

Gain Scores

Earlier in the chapter, we noted that in ANCOVA the dependent variable and the covariate need not be commensurate. In those cases where they are, an analysis of gain scores may be of interest either instead of, or more likely in addition to, an ANCOVA. ANCOVA is, of course, designed for making comparisons across groups. Gain scores, however, can be used either to ask about mean change within a single group or to ask about group differences in change. The unique advantage of analyzing gain scores is that it allows one to ask the question, "Was there significant change from pretreatment to posttreatment within a specific group (or averaging over groups)?" This question frequently is of interest in applied situations. For example, if a variety of clinical treatments are being compared for their effectiveness in helping a group of clients, one often is interested in whether there was significant evidence for improvement both overall and within specific treatment groups. ANCOVA is not suited for addressing such questions because it always asks about differences between groups. Assuming that one has commensurate variables, such as a pretest and posttest on the same clinical instrument, then the question of whether there has been significant change from pretest to posttest is answered by performing what is essentially a matched-pairs t test of the data. The denominator of the test differs somewhat from a matched-pairs t because the error term is based on within-group deviations rather than deviations around the grand mean.

  If X_{ij} is the score on the pretest and Y_{ij} the score on the posttest, one would compute a difference score for each subject, $D_{ij} = Y_{ij} - X_{ij}$. The test for a significant gain would correspond to a comparison of the following models:

$$\begin{aligned} \text{Full:} \quad & D_{ij} = \mu + \varepsilon_{ij} \\ \text{Restricted:} \quad & D_{ij} = 0 + \varepsilon_{ij} \end{aligned} \tag{51}$$

However, the denominator of the test would use the conventional error term for a between-subjects ANOVA on the difference scores, that is, the sum of squared errors associated with the fullest possible model:

$$D_{ij} = \mu_j + \varepsilon_{ij} \tag{52}$$

Although this type of question is often of practical interest, interpretations of change from pretest to posttest must keep in mind possible effects such as history and maturation. In other words, even if significant change is observed, it is usually difficult to infer that this change is literally caused by the treatment. As we pointed out earlier in this book, causal inference is greatly strengthened by random assignment of individuals to conditions. Yet this obviously entails comparing groups to one another instead of observing change within a single group.

One could also carry out a test of whether the mean gain scores differ across groups—that is, a standard one-way ANOVA using D_{ij} as the dependent variable. Both an ANOVA of gain scores and an ANCOVA would address the same general question: Allowing for preexisting differences, are there differences between groups on the posttest? The distinction between the methods has to do with how the adjustment for initial differences is made. We could write the models being compared in an ANOVA of gain scores:

$$\text{Full:} \quad Y_{ij} = \mu + \alpha_j + X_{ij} + \varepsilon_{ij}$$
$$\text{Restricted:} \quad Y_{ij} = \mu + X_{ij} + \varepsilon_{ij} \tag{53}$$

These are identical to the models used in ANCOVA, except that the slope of regression of the postscores on the prescores has been constrained to be 1 in both the full and the restricted models. Because the relationship between the postscores and prescores is almost certainly not perfect, the error scores in these models in general are larger than those in the corresponding ANCOVA models in which the slope estimates can be chosen to minimize error. The result of this in randomized studies is that an ANCOVA typically is more powerful than an ANOVA of gain scores.

It should be stressed here that, although the same general question is being addressed, quite different conclusions might be reached by the two methods in the same study, particularly in nonrandomized studies. When subjects are randomly assigned to conditions, the expected magnitude of the treatment effects is the same in the two analyses. Furthermore, with random assignment, the two analyses are testing exactly the same null hypothesis in the population. For example, consider a two-group design. The analysis comparing mean gain scores is testing a null hypothesis that

$$\mu_{Y_1} - \mu_{X_1} = \mu_{Y_2} - \mu_{X_2} \tag{54}$$

However, random assignment guarantees us that the groups do not differ on the pretest X, so Equation 54 reduces to

$$\mu_{Y_1} = \mu_{Y_2} \tag{55}$$

Equation 55 is the same null hypothesis we would be testing if we ignored the pretest altogether and simply tested posttest mean differences with ANOVA. This is also the same hypothesis we are testing with ANCOVA in a randomized design.

Does this suggest that it really does not matter whether we use ANCOVA, ANOVA on posttest only, or ANOVA on gain scores as long as we have a randomized design? No, it does not suggest this. Although all three methods test the same null hypothesis in a randomized design, the three approaches are not literally equivalent to one another. Keep in mind that we have already seen that ANCOVA typically provides better power and precision than an ANOVA in a randomized design, and the same logic applies when the covariate happens to be a pretest. Similarly, we just suggested that the error of the ANCOVA models tends to be smaller than the error of the ANOVA gain model. For this reason, ANCOVA is also typically more powerful and precise than ANOVA on gain scores in randomized designs.

We can see why ANCOVA is generally better here by comparing error variances. Recall that we showed earlier that the error variance for the ANCOVA model is given by

$$\sigma^2_{\varepsilon(\text{ANCOVA})} = \sigma^2_{\varepsilon(\text{ANOVA})}(1 - \rho^2) \qquad\qquad (49, \text{repeated})$$

It can be shown that when the pretest and posttest have equal variances, the error variance for the gain score analysis is

$$\sigma^2_{\varepsilon(\text{gains})} = 2\sigma^2_{\varepsilon(\text{ANOVA})}(1 - \rho) \qquad\qquad (56)$$

Now it turns out algebraically that $1 - \rho^2$ is always less than $2(1 - \rho)$, so that the ANCOVA error variance is always less than the gain scores error variance (except in the unrealistic case where $\rho = 1$, in which case both error variances equal 0). Thus, ANCOVA provides more power and precision than the gain scores analysis in a randomized design.

Because of smaller errors in ANCOVA, it is possible that an ANOVA of gains might miss the significance level needed for you to reject the hypothesis that all groups gained the same amount; yet, at the same time, an ANCOVA might result in the conclusion that the groups differ significantly in their posttest scores, even though there may be no differences between groups on the pretest. For the sake of completeness, we should acknowledge that the analysis of gain scores does have one advantage over ANCOVA for comparing groups. The ANOVA of gain scores does not require estimating the slope parameter β. Thus, the ANOVA full model has 1 more degree of freedom, which translates into a slightly lower critical value than for ANCOVA. Except for very small sample sizes, this advantage is inconsequential and far outweighed by the smaller error variance of the ANCOVA model.

In summary, with randomized studies, the two methods test exactly the same hypothesis and estimate exactly the same group differences. However, this does not mean that the methods are interchangeable. ANCOVA is almost always preferable because it provides more power and precision. In some situations, variations of the standard pretest–posttest design may provide yet additional power and precision. For example, the next section of this chapter describes blocking, which can be combined with ANCOVA to increase power and precision. As another example, Maxwell (1994) describes how using a posttest that is somewhat longer than the pretest can also often increase power and precision. In a similar vein, Kraemer and Thiemann (1989) describe how collecting additional observations between the pretest and the posttest can also increase power, although in most situations continuing to use the pretest as a covariate results in yet greater power and precision (Venter, Maxwell, & Bolig, 2002).

As usual, things are more complicated without random assignment. In particular, ANCOVA and ANOVA of gain scores do not generally even test the same hypothesis in the absence of random assignment. A famous example of this point was offered by Frederic Lord and has come to be known as *Lord's paradox*. The hypothetical example concerned the interest of a large university "in investigating the effects on the students of the diet provided in the university dining halls and any sex difference in these effects" (Lord, 1967, p. 304). Assume that weights are available for both male and female students eating in the dining halls at the beginning and end of an academic year. Thus, one could perform either an ANOVA of gain scores or an ANCOVA with gender as the between-groups factor. In Lord's example, the mean weight for the group of women students at the end of the year was identical to that at the beginning. Although some individual women had gotten heavier and some lost weight, the

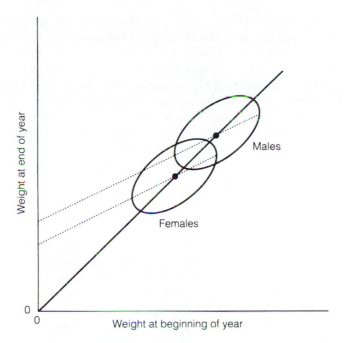

FIG. 9.8.   Scatterplots of initial and final weights for male and female students (after Lord, 1967).

overall distribution of weights was unchanged over the course of the year. The same was true for men. This situation is represented by the scatterplots in Figure 9.8.

An analysis of the gain scores that could be computed here would indicate that there was no change overall and that there was no evidence of a gender difference in amount of change because the mean gain score in each group was zero. However, when an ANCOVA is performed on these data, one obtains a highly significant group effect. The apparent discrepancy between these two analyses constitutes the paradox.

The paradox is fairly easily resolved, however, in the light of our previous discussions of the logic of ANCOVA (see the beginning of this chapter) and of the use of ANCOVA with intact groups (see "Lack of Independence of Treatment and Covariate"). ANCOVA gives a different answer than an ANOVA of gains here because it is addressing a different specific question. Remember the conditional nature of the question being addressed, which is sometimes expressed as: If the groups were equivalent on the premeasure, would we expect there to be a difference on the postmeasure? Here we could phrase the question, "For subpopulations of males and females having identical pretest weights—for example, at the grand mean weight for the two sexes combined—would a difference in mean weight at the end of the year be expected?" For example, if the mean weight of females is 120 pounds and that of males is 160, the grand mean, assuming equal numbers of males and females, is 140 pounds. Males weighing 140 pounds are lighter than the average male and some regression back toward the mean of the whole population of males would be expected over the course of the year. Females weighing 140 similarly would be unusually far above the mean weight for females and would be expected as a group to show some regression downward over the academic year.

The same point is illustrated graphically by the within-group regression lines, which are the dashed lines in Figure 9.8. ANCOVA is asking whether there is any vertical separation between these lines, and clearly there is. In terms of the adjusted means, which would lie on these lines, the adjusted mean for males is higher than that for females. The fly in the ointment, which hopefully can now be seen clearly, is that these adjusted means (or the question addressed by ANCOVA) are not of interest in this situation. We are not interested in whether those males and females who start the year weighing the same weigh the same at the end of the year. Rather, we want to know the change in females as a group and in males as a group, whatever their initial weights happen to be. When the conditional question asked by ANCOVA is not of interest, as may frequently be the case in intact group studies, then the ANOVA of gain scores is to be preferred. The choice between the two analyses should be made in quasi-experiments only after careful consideration of the goals of the analysis. Winship and Morgan (1999) provide an especially good account of the complexities involved in choosing between these approaches for analyzing quasi-experimental data.

Blocking

A method of handling concomitant variables that is relatively common in some research areas is that of blocking, or *stratification* as it is often called. Subjects are sorted into groups or blocks that are relatively homogeneous as far as scores on the concomitant variable are concerned, and then treatments are randomly assigned within each block. The method involves treating the concomitant variable explicitly as a factor having certain discrete levels in the analysis. For example, if the motor skills of an elderly population were being studied by comparing the performance of different groups of subjects on a variety of tasks, the groups might be subdivided into various age categories, for example, 60–69 years, 70–79 years, and 80 and older. Thus, instead of having a single-factor design with a covariate of age, one would use a two-way ANOVA with the factors of task and age.

Such randomized block designs were inherited by psychology from agricultural experimentation where the blocking variable frequently was a discrete variable. For example, cattle from each of various farms might be randomly assigned to one of two diets. The farms then could be used as a blocking factor. (There are some additional complications for the analysis that arise in such a study because farms might be viewed a random factor. This is discussed in Chapter 10.)

In psychology, however, the individual difference variables most commonly used do not take on discrete values naturally, but must be artificially grouped for purposes of analysis. Whenever one treats a continuous variable such as age as a discrete variable, one is throwing away information, and one might suspect there would be a cost in terms of a drop in the precision in the analysis. In fact, there is.

However, it should be noted that blocking typically implies not only an analysis method, but also a method of assigning subjects to conditions in the first place. There are various methods by which the blocks can be formed. These methods attempt to achieve one of two goals. That is, the blocks are formed either (1) so that equal segments of the range of the concomitant variable are included in each block or (2) so that equal proportions of the population fall into each block. The most commonly used method is a variation of the latter procedure. If there are to be b blocks of subjects and a treatments, typically the total number of subjects used in the experiment would be selected to be a multiple of the number of treatment–block combinations—for example, a b n—so that there could be an equal number of subjects per cell. In the simplest case to understand, subjects are first ranked according to their scores on the concomitant variable X. The a n subjects with the highest scores on X would be Block 1, the an subjects with the next highest scores on X would be Block 2, and so on. Within each block, subjects would be randomly assigned to conditions subject to the constraint that there be n subjects from that block placed in each treatment. Of course, in many situations, not all subjects can be ranked at the beginning of the study because some subjects have not yet been identified. Friedman, Furberg, and DeMets (1998) and Matthews (2000) provide especially clear explanations of more complicated strategies that can be used in such situations.[6]

This restricted randomization method assures that the means of the concomitant variable in the different treatment conditions are very similar. This should be obvious because the assignment method assures that equal numbers of subjects from each portion of the X distribution are included in each treatment condition, so the distribution of X is similar across treatments. This fact has favorable implications for the sensitivity of the analysis. The general principle at work, of course, is that of experimental control: the less the influence of random variation, the more apparent a treatment effect of a fixed magnitude becomes. The specifics of how this works here can be seen more clearly by considering what the result would be of forming treatment groups by using a randomized block-assignment procedure and then doing an ANCOVA (which is the procedure we recommend). Recall from our expressions of the error of an adjusted mean (see Equations 33 and 34) that the sensitivity of our analysis is greater the closer the group mean of the covariate is to the grand covariate mean. Because the randomized block-assignment procedures assure that the covariate means are virtually identical across treatments, the adjusted means are less variable and the analysis more sensitive.

With the assignment procedure just discussed, the typical randomized block analysis is a straightforward two-way ANOVA. The fullest possible model would be

$$Y_{ijk} = \mu + \alpha_j + \beta_k + \alpha\beta_{jk} + \varepsilon_{ijk} \tag{57}$$

where α_j refers (as usual) to the effect of treatment j, β_k is the effect associated with the kth block of subjects, $\alpha\beta_{jk}$ is the treatment $\times$ block-interaction effect associated with cell jk, and ε_{ijk} is the population error score for the ith individual in cell jk. Such a design would usually have equal n, so that all effects would be orthogonal.

An example serves to illustrate how the randomized block analysis compares to an ANCOVA. Assume that three blocks of elderly subjects, with six subjects per block, are formed according to age, as mentioned previously. That is, equal numbers of participants from those in their sixties, seventies, and eighties are assigned to three task conditions assessing motor control. The dependent variable is a count of the number of errors made in performing the task. Table 9.11 presents a hypothetical data set[7] showing the ages (X) and error scores (Y), along with a summary table giving cell and marginal means. Although the ages range from 60 to 87, the stratified assignment procedure results in the means on the covariate all being within 1 year of each other. With simple random assignment, however, we would have expected the range of means on the covariate to be more than four times as large.

A randomized block analysis would treat this design as a 3×3, two-way ANOVA. The source table for this analysis is shown in the upper portion of Table 9.12. The most striking thing about this summary of the results is the very large effect of the blocking factor, which here reflects the deterioration of motor control with advancing age. On occasion, the test of the blocking factor is not mentioned in journal article reports of analyses because the effect is obviously expected, as it would be here. However, its importance in increasing the sensitivity of the analysis is clear when one compares the test of the task effect with that in a conventional one-way ANOVA in which information about the age of the subjects is ignored (see middle part of Table 9.12). Although the sum of squares associated with the task effect is identical in the two analyses, the F is less than 1 in a one-way ANOVA but approaches significance in the randomized block analysis when the block main effect and the blocks $\times$ task interaction have been removed from the error term. Notice that the sums of squares for blocks, task $\times$ blocks, and error in the randomized block analysis add up exactly to the sum of squares for error in the one-way ANOVA ($1933.78 + 99.55 + 230.00 = 2263.33$).

TABLE 9.11
DATA ILLUSTRATING A RANDOMIZED BLOCK DESIGN

		Task (Factor A)					
		1		*2*		*3*	
		X	Y	X	Y	X	Y
Block (Factor B)	*1*	60	14	62	10	63	19
		69	24	66	16	67	25
	2	74	16	71	22	73	30
		76	26	78	30	76	36
	3	82	36	83	41	86	44
		85	40	87	47	87	50

Cell and Marginal Means Task

		1		*2*		*3*		*Marginals*	
		X	Y	X	Y	X	Y	X	Y
Block	*1*	64.5	19	64.0	13	65.0	22	64.50	18.00
	2	75.0	21	74.5	26	74.5	33	74.67	26.67
	3	83.5	38	85.0	44	86.5	47	85.00	43.00
	Marginals	74.33	26.00	74.50	27.67	75.33	34.00	74.72	29.22

TABLE 9.12
ALTERNATIVE ANALYSES OF DATA IN TABLE 9.7

Source Table for Randomized Block Analysis

Source	SS	df	MS	F	p
Task (factor A)	213.78	2	106.89	4.18	.052
Blocks (factor B)	1933.78	2	966.89	37.83	.001
Task × blocks (AB)	99.55	4	24.89	.97	.469
Error	230.00	9	25.56		

Source Table for ANOVA

Source	SS	df	MS	F	p
Task	213.78	2	106.89	0.71	.512
Error	2263.33	15	150.89		

Source Table for ANCOVA

Source	SS	df	MS	F	p
Task	152.04	2	76.02	5.25	.020
Within-cell regression	2060.45	1	2060.45	142.20	.001
Error	202.88	14	14.49		

Thus, the randomized block analysis represents a substantial improvement over the one-way analysis in terms of sensitivity. However, the question remains of how the randomized block analysis compares to an ANCOVA. The source table for the ANCOVA is provided at the bottom of Table 9.12.

Although the ANCOVA source table is similar to that for the randomized block analysis, there are differences, and these illustrate the distinctions between the two methods. There are three principal points to be noted.

1. The conventional ANCOVA allows for only the linear relationship between the dependent variable and the covariate, whereas the typical randomized block analysis allows for all possible trends. This means that the direct effect of the concomitant variable will have 1 degree of freedom associated with it in ANCOVA, but $b - 1$ degrees of freedom in randomized blocks, where b equals the number of blocks. In most applications in the behavioral sciences, this proves to be a disadvantage for the randomized block analysis because the linear trend accounts for the lion's share of the explainable variance. Because the sums of squares associated with the concomitant variable typically are about the same in the two analyses, allowing for two, three, or four trends makes the mean square associated with the concomitant variable in the randomized block analysis one-half, one-third, or one-quarter that in the ANCOVA. With three blocks of subjects, as in the current example, the randomized block analysis allows for linear and quadratic trends, and the mean square of 966.89 associated with age is approximately half of the comparable value of 2060.45 in the ANCOVA results.

2. ANCOVA makes use of all the quantitative information in the covariate, whereas the randomized block analysis typically ignores information. Although subjects were grouped into blocks according to age, it is clear from Table 9.7 that there is some heterogeneity of ages remaining within blocks, and this is predictive of the number of errors made. Thus, although only a linear trend is allowed for, more variability in the dependent variable can be predicted by the concomitant variable in ANCOVA (notice the larger sum of squares, 2060.45 vs. 1933.78, in Table 9.12) because of using exact ages rather than decades.

The greater sensitivity of ANCOVA to quantitative information shows up in another way as well, namely by adjusting for the variation among the group means on the covariate. The randomized block analysis, however, is carried out as if the concomitant variable and the task factors were orthogonal. Although the decades of ages are equally represented in each task group, there is some variation among the mean ages for the groups, as seen at the bottom of Table 9.11. Notice also that just as there is a positive relationship between age and errors in each task condition, the group means on the dependent variable have the same rank order as the covariate group means. Thus, when allowance is made for this, the sum of squares for tasks is reduced, here from 213.78 to 152.04. [If the rationale for this is not immediately obvious, reference back to the similar situation in Figures 9.4 and 9.5(a) and the related discussion should clarify things quickly.] The bottom line, as far as use of quantitative information is concerned, is that ANCOVA presents a more accurate picture of the data, both in terms of within-group and between-group adjustments for the exact value of the covariate.

3. Interaction tests can be carried out using either a covariance or a blocking analysis, but ANCOVA interaction tests consume fewer degrees of freedom and permit inferences to be made about the treatment effect at any point on the X dimension. The loss of degrees of freedom in blocking analyses can become critical in designs using relatively few subjects, such as this one. This is particularly true if there is a large number of cells in the design even without the blocking factor or if there is a large number of blocks, because the degrees of freedom available for error is equal to the total number of subjects minus the product of these numbers. [For example, with 18 subjects, 3 task conditions, and 3 blocks, the degrees of freedom for error is $18 - (3 \times 3) = 9$. If there had been 5 task conditions, adding a blocking factor with 3 levels would have required estimation of 15 parameters, so only 3 degrees of freedom would be available for error.] Thus, in multifactor designs, to add a blocking factor with as many levels as one would like may be impossible. If a covariance approach is adopted, however, the

greatest number of parameters required (i.e., allowing for an interaction or heterogeneity of regression) is just twice that which would be needed if the concomitant variable were ignored, rather than b times the same quantity as in the blocking approach. As we develop in the chapter extension, two parameters are required for each cell in the ANCOVA approach when the test of heterogeneity is carried out. However, in this particular example, as one might have expected on the basis of the task × block interaction, there is little evidence for heterogeneity of regression. When the test of heterogeneity of regression is carried out here, one obtains $F(2, 12) = 1.75$, $p > .2$, with the residual error in the full model that allows for a different slope in each cell being $E_F = 157.07$. Because the model assuming homogeneous slopes results in only slightly more error, the conventional ANCOVA, as shown at the bottom of Table 9.12, can be used to carry out the test of the task effect, which is presumably of most interest in this situation.

This comparison of the ANCOVA and blocking tests of the task factor is not atypical. The greater sensitivity to within-group variation on the concomitant variable and the fact that fewer degrees of freedom are consumed by other effects permits ANCOVA to achieve a smaller mean square error and a larger F value for the test of the task factor. Here, the test is significant at the $\alpha = .05$ level in ANCOVA, but just misses significance ($p = .052$) in the block analysis. Although varying statistical decisions about significance across the two tests obtains only for marginal effects, the greater sensitivity of ANCOVA over blocked analyses for the same data is a very general result (see Maxwell, Delaney, & Dill, 1984).

Conclusions Regarding Blocking

Although randomized block analyses address similar questions to ANCOVA and result in greater power than designs ignoring concomitant variables, they generally should be avoided in favor of ANCOVA approaches. However, it is often advantageous to use some form of restricted randomization for the formation of groups instead of relying on simple random assignment to groups. Although groups are formed by this restricted randomization procedure, ANCOVA should be used for the analysis in general because of its greater sensitivity to intragroup and intergroup variations on the covariate. Its use of fewer degrees of freedom is also frequently an important advantage. When scores on the concomitant variable are not available for all subjects in advance, ANCOVA can still be used either with simple random assignment or restricted randomization. Once again, we refer interested readers to such sources as Friedman, Furberg, and DeMets (1998) and Matthews (2000) for additional details regarding various forms of restricted randomization.

There are exceptions when a randomized block analysis might be preferred. One would occur in the admittedly unusual situation in which the relationship between the concomitant variable and the dependent variable was expected to be nonlinear but of unknown form. (If the form of the relationship could be specified, the correct term, for example, X^2 for quadratic or X^3 for cubic trends, could be included, as we have noted, as a covariate in the analysis in addition to X.) A second situation calling for a blocking analysis would be when types of subjects are identified on the basis of profiles that contain some variables for some subjects and different variables for others. Problem drinkers might be those who report drinking over a specified amount, who are reported by a significant other as having behavioral problems resulting from drinking, or who have a physical condition threatened by their drinking. If categories of subjects are identified but cannot be ordered, then obviously ANCOVA could not be used, but we would normally tend to think of this design as simply including an additional factor with discrete levels rather than including a concomitant variable.

EXERCISES

1. In a one-way design with a premeasure, one could test for treatment effects either by using an ANOVA (i.e., ignoring the premeasure) or an ANCOVA. What is the conceptual difference in the question addressed by ANCOVA as opposed to ANOVA?

*2. What do you look for in a covariate? That is, in thinking about the design of a study, what characteristics of a variable would make it a promising covariate? Why?

3. Assume that the covariate in a two-group study is correlated negatively within groups with the dependent variable and that the mean of the covariate is higher in the treatment group than the control. Further assume that the unadjusted mean on the dependent variable in the treatment group is higher than that in the control group. Is the difference between the ANCOVA adjusted means on the dependent variable greater or less than the difference between the unadjusted means on the dependent variable? Why?

*4. Consider the following simple set of data for a two-group study in which prescores and postscores are available for each of five subjects in each of the groups.

Group C		Group T	
Pre	Post	Pre	Post
1	5	5	14
3	8	7	17
3	7	7	16
1	2	5	11
2	3	6	12

  a. In an ANCOVA test of the difference between the groups' postscores adjusting for the prescores, what models are being compared?
  b. Plot the data. As you might suspect on the basis of your plot, an ANOVA of the postscores ignoring the prescores is highly significant, $F(1, 8) = 31.15$. On the basis of your plot, attempt to "intuit" the approximate results of the ANCOVA test of the group effect. That is, would the ANCOVA F be larger or smaller than that for the ANOVA test? Why?
  c. Considering only Group C, determine the regression equation for predicting postscores from prescores. Do the same for Group T. What do your results imply the estimated parameter values for your full model in part a will be?
  d. Using the results of part c, determine the score that the full model would predict for each subject. Use these to determine the errors of prediction and E_F.
  e. Determine the sum of squared errors associated with the restricted model. Some intermediate results that you could use to determine this value easily are that the sum of squares total for the postscores is 254.5 and the correlation between prescores and postscores obtained when all 10 pairs of scores are treated as being in one group is .95905.
  f. Using the results of parts d and e, perform the ANCOVA test of the treatment effect and state your conclusion.

5. An experimenter hoped to increase the precision of his experiment by obtaining information on subjects that could be used as a covariate in an ANCOVA. Because it was inconvenient to collect this information at the start of the experiment, he did so at the completion of the experimental session for each subject, just before debriefing subjects. He had 20 subjects available for a single-factor experiment with four treatment conditions. Subjects were randomly assigned to conditions with the restriction of equal sample sizes in each group. Once all the data were in hand, the experimenter performed three analyses: one the planned ANCOVA, one an ANOVA of the dependent variable, and one an ANOVA of scores on the covariate. The results are as follows:

	ANCOVA Analyses			
Source	SS	df	MS	F
A (adj)	18.65	3	6.22	<1
Within (adj)	128.12	15	8.54	

	ANOVA of Dependent Variable			
Source	SS	df	MS	F
A	112.15	3	37.38	4.05*
Within	147.60	16	9.22	

	ANOVA of Covariate Scores			
Source	SS	df	MS	F
A	27.40	3	9.13	6.01†
Within	24.40	16	1.52	

*$p < .05$
†$p < .01$

a. One test that is not reported is the test of within-group regression of the dependent variable on the covariate. If it is possible to perform such a test given the information shown, carry out and interpret this test of regression that would normally be performed as a part of the ANCOVA. In any case, specify the models being compared in such a test.

b. Based on the experimental design and the above analyses, how do you interpret the results of the ANCOVA? Is ANCOVA appropriate here?

6. You perform an experiment comparing two methods for teaching a particular arithmetic skill. All students participating are randomly assigned to one of the two conditions. Prior to administering the treatments to your two groups of subjects, you have each subject take a pretest that results in scores that are generally in the middle of the range of possible scores on the test. However, on the posttest (which is a parallel form of the pretest), you observe something of a ceiling effect in both groups. You are contemplating whether to perform an analysis of gain scores or an ANCOVA. Which should you use? Why?

7. It is sometimes stated that ANCOVA requires the treatment and covariate to be independent. Some psychologists further state that if they are not independent, then ANCOVA should not be used. Do you agree? Briefly justify your answer.

8. A graduate student is planning a study to investigate the effectiveness of the "keyword" method (a mnemonic strategy) for increasing subjects' ability to remember. A total of 30 subjects are used; specifically, 15 are randomly assigned to her treatment group and 15 to her control group. Her adviser recommends that she block on IQ and then randomly assign to treatments within her blocks.

a. Is this a good idea? Why or why not?

b. Let's suppose that she does block on IQ and has five IQ blocks. Her adviser says that because the blocking factor is of no intrinsic interest (i.e., it simply assures that the groups are comparable), she can simply perform a one-way between-subjects ANOVA to test her treatment effect. Is this good advice? Why or why not?

c. A fellow graduate student has suggested that she analyze her data as a 2 × 5 factorial design. Is this approach better than her adviser's? Why or why not?

d. Are there any other approaches besides her adviser's or the fellow student's that she should consider? Briefly justify your answer.

*9. The primary statistical advantage of including a pretest in a randomized design is to decrease error variance. Suppose we let σ_ε^2 represent the error variance in a posttest-only design. As mentioned in the chapter (see Equations 49 and 56), it can be shown that in a randomized design in which the pretest and posttest have equal variances (often a reasonable assumption), the error variances for ANCOVA and a gain score analysis are

$$\sigma^2_{\varepsilon(\text{ANCOVA})} = \sigma^2_\varepsilon (1 - \rho^2)$$

$$\sigma^2_{\varepsilon(\text{gains})} = \sigma^2_\varepsilon 2(1 - \rho)$$

where ρ is the population correlation within groups between the pretest and the posttest. A graduate student is planning a randomized study in which he anticipates that

$$\mu_1 = 10, \quad \mu_2 = 20, \quad \mu_3 = 30$$

and $\sigma_\varepsilon = 20$ (these figures correspond to a large effect size). He plans to use 10 subjects per group. Find the power the student would have with each approach (posttest only, ANCOVA, and gain scores) in each of the following situations (assuming $\alpha = .05$, and equal variances for the pretest and posttest):

a. $\rho = 0$
b. $\rho = .3$
c. $\rho = .5$
d. $\rho = .7$
e. What overall conclusion(s) do you draw here?
(Hint: Calculate ϕ, as we discussed in Chapter 3. Recall

$$\phi = \frac{\sqrt{\Sigma \alpha_j^2 / a}}{\sigma_\varepsilon / \sqrt{n}}$$

where σ_ε is to be understood as referring to the error standard deviation of the approach being used.)

10. A researcher is planning to compare three groups of 20 individuals each in a randomized study. Suppose that he has included 10 females and 10 males in each of his groups. He is also contemplating whether to include five additional covariates in his model.
    a. Should gender be included in his model? Why or why not?
    b. Suppose he expects the five additional covariates to explain 9% of the variance in the dependent variable, controlling for the effect of gender. Should these five variables be included as covariates? Why or why not?

11. A cognitive psychologist is considering how to select covariates to include in her model in a randomized design. All of the potential covariates have been measured prior to assigning subjects to groups. Which of the following strategies would you recommend to her? Why?
    a. Wait until after assigning subjects to groups, and include as covariates only those variables for which the groups differ significantly at the .05 level.
    b. Decide prior to conducting the study which covariates to include in the model. Include as covariates any and all variables likely to differ between groups.
    c. Decide prior to conducting the study which covariates to include in the model. Include those covariates likely to correlate at least .30 with the dependent variable.
    d. Wait until all data have been collected. Include as covariates all variables that correlate at least .30 with the dependent variable.

12. (To be done by computer.) The chapter talks at some length about the best way to analyze data from a randomized pretest–posttest design. To see how various analytic strategies might compare to one another in a realistic situation, let's return to the data shown in Table 9.7. Recall that Table 9.9 presented ANCOVA results for these data.
    a. Because groups were randomly assigned here, it might seem acceptable to ignore pretest scores in comparing the groups on the posttest. Test to see whether there is a significant difference between groups on the pretest.
    b. Based on your answer to part a, you might decide to proceed to conduct an ANOVA on posttest scores, ignoring pretest scores. How do your results compare to the ANCOVA results shown in Table 9.9? In particular, does the ANOVA yield a statistically significant result at the .05 level?

    c. Another possible approach might be to analyze gain scores. Conduct an ANOVA on gain scores. How do your results compare to the ANCOVA results shown in Table 9.9? In particular, does the ANOVA yield a statistically significant result at the .05 level?

    d. A colleague suggests that your pattern of results implies that ANCOVA appeared superior because it exaggerated the differences between the groups. How would you respond to this colleague's statement?

    e. What do your results comparing the three different approaches suggest about the relative merits of ANCOVA, ANOVA on posttest only, and ANOVA on gain scores for analyzing data from randomized pretest–posttest designs?

13. (To be done by computer.) Problem 12 asks you to compare three different methods of analyzing data from pretest–posttest designs in terms of whether they yield statistically significant results. This problem asks you to compare the confidence intervals obtained from each of the same three methods of analysis. Specifically, assume throughout the problem that simultaneous 95% confidence intervals are of interest for the collection of three pairwise comparisons. Once again, this problem relies on the data shown in Table 9.7 for illustrative purposes.

    a. Because subjects were randomly assigned to groups, you might decide to proceed to form confidence intervals based on an ANOVA on posttest scores, ignoring pretest scores. In other words, you decide to form 95% simultaneous confidence intervals for each pairwise difference in posttest means. How do your intervals compare to the ANCOVA intervals shown in Table 9.10?

    b. Another possible approach might be to analyze gain scores. Form 95% simultaneous confidence intervals for each pairwise difference in gain score means. How do your results compare to the ANCOVA intervals shown in Table 9.10?

    c. A colleague suggests that some of your ANCOVA intervals may have excluded zero when intervals based on the other methods did not because ANCOVA exaggerated the differences between the groups. How would you respond to this colleague's statement?

    d. What do your results comparing the three different approaches suggest about the relative merits of ANCOVA, ANOVA on posttest only, and ANOVA on gain scores for analyzing data from randomized pretest–posttest designs?

EXTENSION: HETEROGENEITY OF REGRESSION

As noted in the chapter, the specification of the traditional ANCOVA model is such that all the separate within-group slopes are presumed to be equal. Of course, it is quite possible that at this point our model is incorrect to a greater or lesser extent. Some textbook authors have treated homogeneity of regression as if it were the most critical statistical assumption in ANCOVA. For example, Kirk (1995, p. 724) speaks of the assumption of homogeneity of regression as "this key assumption." Cohen and Cohen in a similar vein refer to the "crucial [ANCOVA] assumption of equal covariate regression coefficients" (1983, p. 319, but see also fn. 7, p. 320, and p. 381). However, the excellent work of Rogosa (1980) demonstrates the reasonableness of tests of an overall treatment effect in certain situations involving heterogeneous regression slopes. Rogosa proposes that ANCOVA can be used but advises that, in general, one should be using ANCOVA models that allow for heterogeneous regressions. This is because even moderate heterogeneity results in the standard ANCOVA F statistic being inappropriately distributed. We consider Rogosa's suggested procedures after we detail how a test for heterogeneity of regression could be carried out.

TEST FOR HETEROGENEITY OF REGRESSION

As usual, the test involves the comparison of two models with one model being a special case of the other. At issue is whether a model that allows for not only different intercepts but also different slopes across the groups will have significantly less error than a model that constrains the slopes to be equal. Thus, the restricted model for the test of heterogeneity of regression is identical to the full model used in the ANCOVA test of treatment effects. The full model differs only in that the slope parameter is subscripted to indicate that it takes on a different value in each group. That is, we compare

$$\text{Full:} \quad Y_{ij} = \mu + \alpha_j + \beta_j X_{ij} + \varepsilon_{ij} \tag{E.1}$$

$$\text{Restricted:} \quad Y_{ij} = \mu + \alpha_j + \beta X_{ij} + \varepsilon_{ij} \tag{E.2}$$

The estimates of the parameters in the restricted model are, of course, the same here as when this model was considered previously:

$$\hat{\beta} = b_{\mathrm{W}} = \frac{\sum_j \sum_i (X_{ij} - \overline{X}_j)(Y_{ij} - \overline{Y}_j)}{\sum_j \sum_i (X_{ij} - \overline{X}_j)^2} \tag{9.13, repeated}$$

$$\hat{\mu} + \hat{\alpha}_j = a_j = \overline{Y}_j - b_{\mathrm{W}}\overline{X}_j \tag{9.18, repeated}$$

Likewise in the full model, the slope estimate for each group separately is just the sum of cross-products for that group over the sum of squared deviations on the covariate:

$$\hat{\beta}_j = b_j = \frac{\sum_i (X_{ij} - \overline{X}_j)(Y_{ij} - \overline{Y}_j)}{\sum_i (X_{ij} - \overline{X}_j)^2} \tag{E.3}$$

Thus, in each group, the regression line intersects the mean for that group (i.e., the point $\overline{X}_j, \overline{Y}_j$), but it slopes somewhat differently in each group. In any group j, the regression line is at a height of $\overline{Y}_j$ when it is $\overline{X}_j$ units away from the origin along the horizontal axis. Thus the intercept for the jth group is $b_j \times \overline{X}_j$ units below the mean for that group. That is, in the *full model* here, we have

$$\hat{\mu} + \hat{\alpha}_j = a_j = \overline{Y}_j - b_j\overline{X}_j \tag{E.4}$$

A comparison of these two models, of course, involves a comparison of their sum of squared errors. Thus, once again we must examine $E_{\mathrm{R}} - E_{\mathrm{F}}$. For the test of homogeneity of regression, we have

$$E_{\mathrm{R}} - E_{\mathrm{F}} = \sum_j \sum_i (Y_{ij} - \hat{Y}_{ij_{\mathrm{R}}})^2 - \sum_j \sum_i (Y_{ij} - \hat{Y}_{ij_{\mathrm{F}}})^2 \tag{E.5}$$

Now we can write our prediction equations in deviation score form:

$$\hat{Y}_{ij_{\mathrm{R}}} = \overline{Y}_j + b_{\mathrm{W}}(X_{ij} - \overline{X}_j) \text{ and } \hat{Y}_{ij_{\mathrm{F}}} = \overline{Y}_j + b_j(X_{ij} - \overline{X}_j)$$

Thus, the increase in error resulting from assuming homogeneous slopes can be written

$$E_{\mathrm{R}} - E_{\mathrm{F}} = \sum_j \sum_i [Y_{ij} - \overline{Y}_j - b_{\mathrm{W}}(X_{ij} - \overline{X}_j)]^2 - \sum_j \sum_i [Y_{ij} - \overline{Y}_j - b_j(X_{ij} - \overline{X}_j)]^2 \tag{E.6}$$

It turns out[1] that this difference in errors can be written very simply here:

$$E_{\mathrm{R}} - E_{\mathrm{F}} = \sum_j (b_j - b_{\mathrm{W}})^2 \sum_i (X_{ij} - \overline{X}_j)^2 \tag{E.7}$$

That is, the differences of the individual slopes from their weighted average b_{W} are squared, weighted by the denominators of the individual slopes, and summed across groups. (This corresponds exactly to the form of SS_{B} in ANOVA, in which the differences of the individual group means from their weighted average $\overline{Y}$ are squared, weighted by the denominators of the expressions for the cell means n, and summed across groups.)

TABLE 9 E.1
HYPOTHETICAL DATA TO ILLUSTRATE
HETEROGENEITY OF REGRESSION

Subject	Group	X	Y
1	1	1	5
2	1	2	9
3	1	3	7
4	2	3	11
5	2	4	11
6	2	5	17

The test of this difference in the adequacy of the two models would as always follow our general form for the F test, with the degrees of freedom in the numerator being the difference in the number of parameters required by the two models. In the full model here, we would be estimating a intercepts and a slopes, whereas in the restricted model, we require a intercepts and a single slope. Thus, the numerator has $[N - (a + 1)] - [N - 2a]$, or $a - 1$, degrees of freedom.

We can now write the general form of our test of homogeneity of regression for the one-way ANCOVA as follows:

$$
F = \frac{(E_R - E_F)/(df_R - df_F)}{E_F/df_F}
$$

$$
= \frac{\sum_j (b_j - b_W)^2 \sum_i (X_{ij} - \overline{X}_j)^2/(a - 1)}{\sum_j \sum_i [Y_{ij} - \overline{Y}_j - b_j(X_{ij} - \overline{X}_j)]^2/(N - 2a)} \tag{E.8}
$$

We can illustrate this test with the simple two-group numerical example we used at the beginning of Chapter 9 (see Table 9.1), after making some minor modifications in the data so that they reflect some heterogeneity of regression. Table 9E.1 shows the modified data. The data were altered in such a way that the means in both groups are the same as in the original example, as is the pooled within-group slope. However, now the slope in Group 2 is considerably steeper than that in Group 1. Table 9E.2 shows the computations for the pooled slope and intercepts in the typical ANCOVA model. Those for the ANCOVA model modified to allow for heterogeneity of regression, which we might refer to as the *ANCOHET model*, are in Table 9E.3. Figure 9E.1 shows the data together with the prediction lines.

Using the individual error scores computed in the tables, we can obtain the values of E_R and E_F and use the general form of the F test to carry out the test of heterogeneity of regression. From Table 9E.2 we have $E_R = \sum_j \sum_i (Y_{ij} - \hat{Y}_{ij_R})^2 = 8 + 8 = 16$, and from Table 9E.3 we have $E_F = \sum_j \sum_i (Y_{ij} - \hat{Y}_{ij_F})^2 = 6 + 6 = 12$. Thus, we have

$$
F = \frac{(E_R - E_F)/(df_R - df_F)}{(E_F/df_F)} = \frac{(16 - 12)/(3 - 2)}{12/2} = \frac{4/1}{6} = .667
$$

which obviously is not significant. The interested reader will, of course, want to confirm that $E_R - E_F$ here could be obtained by the formula shown in Equation E.7 for the sum of squares for heterogeneity of regression[2]:

$$
E_R - E_F = \sum_j (b_j - b_W)^2 \sum_i (X_{ij} - \overline{X}_j)^2 = (1 - 2)^2 2 + (3 - 2)^2 2 = 2 + 2 = 4
$$

Naturally, a difference in slopes across groups as striking as that shown in Figure 9E.1 would typically be detected as significant in a real study. Here, of course, the example was constructed so that the calculations could readily be followed without even a calculator. However, this means that there is virtually no power to detect an effect because of the very small number of cases. The main point of the

TABLE 9 E.2
SOLUTION FOR THE MODEL ASSUMING HOMOGENEOUS SLOPES

	X	$X - \overline{X}_j$	Y	$Y - \overline{Y}_j$	$(X - \overline{X}_j)^2$	$(X - \overline{X}_j)(Y - \overline{Y}_j)$	$\hat{Y}_R$	$Y - \hat{Y}_R$	$(Y - \hat{Y}_R)^2$
Group 1									
	1	-1	5	-2	1	2	5	0	0
	2	0	9	2	0	0	7	2	4
	3	1	7	0	1	0	9	-2	4
	$\sum = 6$		$\sum = 21$		$\sum = 2$	$\sum = 2$			$\sum = 8$
	$\overline{X}_1 = 4$		$\overline{Y}_1 = 7$						
Group 2									
	3	-1	11	-2	1	2	11	0	0
	4	0	11	-2	0	0	13	-2	4
	5	1	17	4	1	4	15	2	4
	$\sum = 12$		$\sum = 39$		$\sum = 2$	$\sum = 6$			$\sum = 8$
	$\overline{X}_2 = 4$		$\overline{Y}_2 = 13$						

$$b_W = \frac{\sum_j \sum_i (X_{ij} - \overline{X}_j)(Y_{ij} - \overline{Y}_j)}{\sum_j \sum_i (X_{ij} - \overline{X}_j)^2} = \frac{2 + 6}{2 + 2} = \frac{8}{4} = 2$$

$$a_1 = \overline{Y}_1 - b_W \overline{X}_1 = 7 - 2(2) = 3$$

$$a_2 = \overline{Y}_2 - b_W \overline{X}_2 = 12 - 2(4) = 5$$

$$\hat{Y}_{i1_R} = 3 + 2X_{i1}$$

$$\hat{Y}_{i2_R} = 5 + 2X_{i2}$$

TABLE 9 E.3
SOLUTION FOR THE MODEL ALLOWING FOR HETEROGENEOUS SLOPES

	X	$X - \overline{X}_j$	Y	$Y - \overline{Y}_j$	$(X - \overline{X}_j)^2$	$(X - \overline{X}_j)(Y - \overline{Y}_j)$	$\hat{Y}_F$	$Y - \hat{Y}_F$	$(Y - \hat{Y}_F)^2$
Group 1									
	1	-1	5	-2	1	2	6	-1	1
	2	0	9	2	0	0	7	2	4
	3	1	7	0	1	0	8	-1	1
	$\sum = 6$		$\sum = 21$		$\sum = 2$	$\sum = 2$			$\sum = 6$
	$\overline{X}_1 = 4$		$\overline{Y}_1 = 7$						
Group 2									
	3	-1	11	-2	1	2	10	1	1
	4	0	11	-2	0	0	13	-2	4
	5	1	17	4	1	4	16	1	1
	$\sum = 12$		$\sum = 39$		$\sum = 2$	$\sum = 6$			$\sum = 6$
	$\overline{X}_2 = 4$		$\overline{Y}_2 = 13$						

$$b_1 = \frac{\sum_i (X_{i1} - \overline{X}_1)(Y_{i1} - \overline{Y}_1)}{\sum_i (X_{i1} - \overline{X}_1)^2} = \frac{2}{2} = 1 \quad b_2 = \frac{\sum_i (X_{i2} - \overline{X}_2)(Y_{i2} - \overline{Y}_2)}{\sum_i (X_{i2} - \overline{X}_2)^2} = \frac{6}{2} = 3$$

$$a_1 = \overline{Y}_1 - b_1 \overline{X}_1 = 7 - 1(2) = 5 \qquad a_2 = \overline{Y}_2 - b_2 \overline{X}_2 = 13 - 3(4) = 1$$

$$\hat{Y}_{i1_F} = 5 + 1X_{i1}$$

$$\hat{Y}_{i2_F} = 1 + 3X_{i2}$$

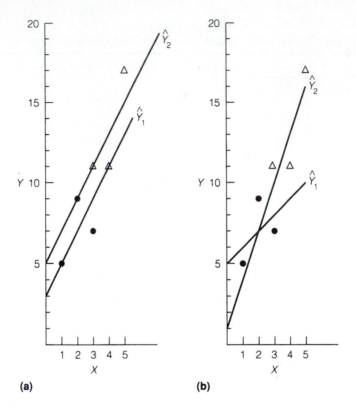

FIG. 9E.1.   Comparison of the predictions of the (a) ANCOVA model assuming homogeneous slopes with those of the (b) ANCOHET model that allows for heterogeneity of regression.

example is simply to illustrate how to calculate the test, but it also raises the issue of what should be done when you have reason to suspect, either on the basis of a scatterplot like that in Figure 9E.1 or on the basis of a test, that there is some evidence for heterogeneity of regression in the population.

ACCOMMODATING HETEROGENEITY OF REGRESSION

Fortunately, a range of techniques exist for modeling this situation effectively. Unfortunately, they have not been widely used because of misconceptions about the meaningfulness of inferences about treatment effects in the presence of heterogeneity of regression and because of the dearth of packaged programs to perform the analyses and of textbook treatments of how such analyses should be interpreted. We move now to a consideration of these techniques based on the ANCOHET model.

An analogy may help to introduce the techniques. In two-way ANOVA, the interest is more often in the main effects of the factors than in their interaction. Nonetheless, we used an error term based on a model that incorporated an interaction parameter so that we would have an unbiased estimate of population variance regardless of the correctness of any decision about the significance of any particular effect. Even more to the point, when evidence for an interaction is obtained, the analysis does not stop, but one usually proceeds to tests of simple main effects. The same strategy can be applied effectively in ANCOVA allowing for heterogeneous slopes.

Rogosa (1980) shows that, if there is heterogeneity of regression in the population, the typical ANCOVA test of treatment effects is not distributed appropriately. An alternative procedure in the presence of mild to moderate heterogeneity is to compute the adjusted treatment sum of squares as in a typical ANCOVA but use as an error term the error associated with the ANCOHET model, just as would be done in ANOVA when the interaction was nonsignificant. (How to make decisions about the extent of heterogeneity is discussed later.) This provides an appropriately distributed test of the hypothesis that there are no treatment effects, at the cost of only $a - 1$ degrees of freedom for error.

To characterize the treatment effect more completely, it is desirable with moderate to pronounced heterogeneity to assess the treatment effect as a function of the value of the covariate. The need for this should be obvious from considering a plot like that in Figure 9E.1(b). There, for low X values, the predicted Y scores in Treatment 1 are higher than those in Treatment 2, whereas the reverse is true for individuals with high X scores. If the traditional ANCOVA model were exactly right, of course, the vertical distance between the population regression lines would be a constant for all values of X. When there is reason to believe this is not the case, one would like to estimate the magnitude of the treatment effect as a function of X and have a way of assessing its significance. Our basic tack is to develop an estimate of the treatment effect somewhat like we did with the difference between adjusted means—that is, the difference between the predicted scores for different conditions at a given value of X—and then derive the variability of this estimated difference. A ratio of the square of the estimated effect to its variance estimate can then be used as a statistical test.

The basic problem involves the estimation of the vertical distance between regression lines. Because this is difficult to envision, let us begin our consideration of this problem by referring to the simple regression situation involving a single group with one predictor and one dependent variable. Besides deriving estimates of the dependent variable in this case using a simple regression equation, we can also relatively easily derive estimates of the variability of our predictions. The variability in the predictions themselves can be illustrated by considering what might happen over repeated samples in which the X values remain fixed across samples. Figure 9E.2 displays the regression lines that might result for three samples of Y values.

Two points about the variability of estimated Y values are suggested by the plot. First, the farther the particular X value is from $\overline{X}$, the more the predicted Y values vary across repeated samplings. Second,

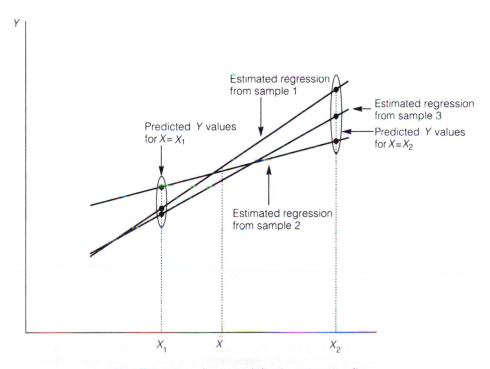

FIG. 9E.2.   Sampling variability in regression lines.

the variation in the predicted Y values is the result of two features of the regression line: the height of the line generally and its slope.

We can see these results more rigorously by considering a deviation form of the regression equation. Let X_p be the particular X value at which we wish to estimate Y, and let the corresponding predicted value $\hat{Y}_p$ be the estimated mean of the conditional probability distribution. Then, in the simple (i.e., two-variable) regression situation, as we develop in the discussion of multiple regression on the data disk (see Equation 2 of Statistical Tutorial 2), we can write

$$\hat{Y}_p = \overline{Y} + b(X_p - \overline{X}) \tag{E.9}$$

Under the assumption that the X values are fixed and that the errors are normally distributed in the population, the variability of $\hat{Y}_p$ can be shown[3] to be decomposable into the following two components:

$$\sigma_{\hat{Y}_p}^2 = \sigma_{\overline{Y}}^2 + (X_p - \overline{X})^2 \sigma_b^2 \tag{E.10}$$

The first component, the variability of $\overline{Y}$, should by now be quite familiar, that is, $\sigma_{\overline{Y}}^2 = \sigma^2/n$. However, we now have the magnitude of the estimate of error depending on the X value as well as the variability in Y. That is, because β is not known but is estimated by a statistic, we expect our slope estimates to vary somewhat from sample to sample as illustrated in Figure 9E.2. How much difference the error in b makes gets larger and larger as X_p moves farther away from $\overline{X}$. This is illustrated in Figure 9E.3.

The variance of our slope statistic itself can be derived fairly easily once we rewrite the definitional formula for the slope in a convenient form, namely

$$b = \sum k_i Y_i \tag{E.11}$$

where the k_i are simple functions[4] of the X values:

$$k_i = \frac{X_i - \overline{X}}{\sum (X_i - \overline{X})^2} \tag{E.12}$$

Now, because the variance of a linear combination of independent random variables is simply the sum of the original variances, each weighted by the square of the original weight, we immediately have the

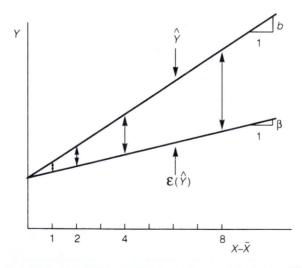

FIG. 9E.3.   When doubling the extent to which X deviates from $\overline{X}$, the extent to which the estimated conditional mean deviates from the true conditional mean also doubles.

following expression for σ_b^2, the variance of the slope estimate b:

$$\sigma_b^2 = \text{Var}(b) = \text{Var}\left(\sum k_i Y_i\right) = \sum k_i^2 \text{ Var}(Y_i) \tag{E.13}$$

where Var is to be read as "the variance of" the expression that follows within parentheses. Making use of the fact that the variances of Y_i are constant and equal to σ^2, then substituting for k_i we obtain

$$\sigma_b^2 = \sigma^2 \sum k_i^2 = \sigma^2 \sum \left[\frac{X_i - \overline{X}}{\sum(X_i - \overline{X})^2}\right]^2$$

$$= \sigma^2 \frac{\sum(X_i - \overline{X})^2}{\left[\sum(X_i - \overline{X})^2\right]^2} = \sigma^2 \frac{1}{\sum(X_i - \overline{X})^2} \tag{E.14}$$

We are now ready to substitute our results into Equation E.10 to obtain the final form of the variability of our estimated conditional mean $\hat{Y}_p$:

$$\sigma_{\hat{Y}_p}^2 = \frac{\sigma^2}{n} + (X_p - \overline{X})^2 \frac{\sigma^2}{\Sigma(X_i - \overline{X})^2}$$

$$= \sigma^2 \left[\frac{1}{n} + \frac{(X_p - \overline{X})^2}{\sum(X_i - \overline{X})^2}\right] \tag{E.15}$$

Thus, we have now derived the variance of the estimated mean Y score for a particular X score X_p in simple regression, and we have shown that it is more variable than the sample mean Y score, and increasingly so as X_p departs more from $\overline{X}$, just as was illustrated by Figures 9E.2 and 9E.3.

A similar but somewhat different result obtains in ANCOVA. The similarity concerns the variance of the estimated mean Y score for a particular X score in a particular group. For $X = X_p$ and group j, we have

$$\hat{Y}_{pj} = \hat{\mu} + \hat{\alpha}_j + \hat{\beta} X_p = \overline{Y}_j - b_W \overline{X}_j + b_W X_p = \overline{Y}_j + b_W (X_p - \overline{X}_j) \tag{E.16}$$

Thus, as in the simple-regression situation, the variance of our estimated conditional mean Y score increases as X_p departs from $\overline{X}_j$:

$$\sigma_{\hat{Y}_{pj}}^2 = \text{Var}(\overline{Y}_j) + \text{Var}[b_W(X_p - \overline{X}_j)] = \frac{\sigma^2}{n_j} + (X_p - \overline{X}_j)^2 \text{ Var}(b_W)$$

$$= \sigma^2 \left[\frac{1}{n_j} + \frac{(X_p - \overline{X}_j)^2}{\sum_j \sum_i (X_{ij} - \overline{X}_j)^2}\right] \tag{E.17}$$

(The intermediate steps of the derivation follow along the same lines as those for Equation E.15.) However, in ANCOVA, interest centers on the predicted scores at the grand mean on X (i.e., the adjusted Y means) and in the vertical distance between them. Letting $X_p = \overline{X}$ in Equation E.16 results in the standard equation for the adjusted means:

$$\hat{Y}_j = \overline{Y}_j + b_W(\overline{X} - \overline{X}_j) = \overline{Y}_j - b_W(\overline{X}_j - \overline{X}) \tag{9.27, repeated}$$

Thus, the square of the standard error of this adjusted mean, following Equation E.17, is

$$\sigma_{\hat{Y}_j}^2 = \sigma^2 \left[\frac{1}{n_j} + \frac{(\overline{X}_j - \overline{X})^2}{\sum_j \sum_i (X_{ij} - \overline{X}_j)^2}\right] \tag{E.18}$$

In one-way designs, the contrasts that are most often of interest are pairwise comparisons between groups. Because interpretation of a treatment effect is considerably more complicated in the case of heterogeneous regressions, where the magnitude of the difference between groups changes continuously as a function of the covariate, it is even more likely that contrasts would focus on only two groups at a time. Thus, for these reasons and for simplicity of development in what immediately follows, we consider only the two-group case. After the tests for this situation have been developed, we suggest a strategy for the general a-group situation. With only two groups, under the assumption of homogeneous slopes, we would be most interested in the difference between the two adjusted means:

$$\hat{Y}_1 - \hat{Y}_2 = \overline{Y}_1 - b_{\mathrm{W}}(\overline{X}_1 - \overline{X}) - [\overline{Y}_2 - b_{\mathrm{W}}(\overline{X}_2 - \overline{X})]$$
$$= (\overline{Y}_1 - \overline{Y}_2) - b_{\mathrm{W}}(\overline{X}_1 - \overline{X}_2) \tag{E.19}$$

Notice that, although the comparison is a comparison of the estimated Y means at $\overline{X}$, $\overline{X}$ does not appear in the final form of Equation E.19. Furthermore, this would be true regardless of the particular value X_p at which we might compute the difference between our estimates of the conditional Y means. Thus, it perhaps should not be surprising that, although it is unlike the simple regression situation, the standard error of this estimated treatment effect does not depend on the value of X at which we estimate it. That is, when homogeneous slopes are assumed, the precision of our estimate of the treatment effect is "maintained for all values of X" (Rogosa, 1980, p. 311), with the variance of our estimate in Equation E19 being

$$\sigma^2_{\hat{Y}_1 - \hat{Y}_2} = \sigma^2 \left[\frac{1}{n_1} + \frac{1}{n_2} + \frac{(\overline{X}_1 - \overline{X}_2)^2}{\sum_j \sum_i (X_{ij} - \overline{X}_j)^2} \right] \tag{E.20}$$

This variance expression is like those for the conditional mean (in Equation E.15) and for the adjusted mean (in Equation E.18) in that there is a component for the variability of the mean estimates and another component for the variability of the slope estimate. Because we now have two independent group means, the variance of their difference is the sum of the variances of each mean separately. For the slope estimate, its variance is simply multiplied by the square of the coefficient $(\overline{X}_1 - \overline{X}_2)$ shown in Equation E.19. We can estimate this variance by replacing σ^2 in Equation E.20 by the mean square error associated with our traditional ANCOVA full model. Denote this mean square error s^2. Thus, $(N - 3)s^2$ would be equal to the residual sum of squares associated with the model using a common, pooled estimate of the slope.

We are now finally ready to return to the problem of estimating the vertical distance between two nonparallel regression lines and determining the variability of that estimate. These results build on those we have just presented for the simple regression situation and for ANCOVA with homogeneous slopes. Recall that our prediction equation for the ANCOHET model can be written (see Equations E.1, E.3, and E.4):

$$\hat{Y}_{ij} = a_j + b_j X_{ij} \tag{E.21}$$

Thus, if we substitute for X_{ij} some particular value of the covariate—for example, X_p—the difference in estimated conditional means for the two groups would be

$$\hat{Y}_{p1} - \hat{Y}_{p2} = a_1 + b_1 X_p - (a_2 + b_2 X_p)$$
$$= a_1 - a_2 + (b_1 - b_2)X_p \tag{E.22}$$

An alternative way of writing this estimated difference, in which we substitute the expressions for our estimated values of the intercepts, makes it easier to understand the variance estimate. That is, we can write the vertical distance between the two regression lines:

$$\hat{Y}_{p1} - \hat{Y}_{p2} = (\overline{Y}_1 - b_1 \overline{X}_1) - (\overline{Y}_2 - b_2 \overline{X}_2) + (b_1 - b_2)X_p$$
$$= \overline{Y}_1 - \overline{Y}_2 + b_1(X_p - \overline{X}_1) - b_2(X_p - \overline{X}_2) \tag{E.23}$$

To determine the variability of this estimate, we must consider not only the sampling error of the Y group means, but also both the variance of our estimate of b_1, which equals $\sigma^2/\sum_i (X_{i1} - \overline{X}_1)^2$, and the variance of our estimate of b_2, $\sigma^2/\sum_i (X_{i2} - \overline{X}_2)^2$. Thus, similar to Equation E.20, but now allowing for heterogeneous slopes, the variability of our estimate of the vertical distance between the lines can be written:

$$\sigma^2_{\hat{Y}_{p1}-\hat{Y}_{p2}} = \sigma^2 \left[\frac{1}{n_1} + \frac{1}{n_2} + \frac{(X_p - \overline{X}_1)^2}{\sum_i (X_{i1} - \overline{X}_1)^2} + \frac{(X_p - \overline{X}_2)^2}{\sum_i (X_{i2} - \overline{X}_2)^2} \right] \qquad (E.24)$$

A comparison with the variance of the estimate of a single mean in regression (Equation E.15) or ANCOVA (Equation E.17) shows that the variance of the distance between two regression lines is simply the sum of the variances of conditional means estimated by each. We can estimate this variance, and thereby move toward carrying out a test of the significance of the difference between the regression lines at any arbitrary value of X, by simply replacing σ^2 in Equation E.24 by the mean square error associated with the model allowing for heterogeneous slopes, which we denote s^2_{het}. In the two-group situation in which we estimate a slope and an intercept for each group, our model would have $N - 4$ degrees of freedom. Thus, a test of the significance of the difference between the two lines—that is, of the treatment effect at an X value X_p—would be carried out as a simple t test with $N - 4$ degrees of freedom. That is,

$$t = \frac{\hat{Y}_{p1} - \hat{Y}_{p2} - 0}{\hat{\sigma}_{\hat{Y}_{p1}-\hat{Y}_{p2}}} \qquad (E.25)$$

where the denominator is

$$\hat{\sigma}_{\hat{Y}_{p1}-\hat{Y}_{p2}} = s_{\text{het}} \left[\frac{1}{n_1} + \frac{1}{n_2} + \frac{(X_p - \overline{X}_1)^2}{\sum_i (X_{i1} - \overline{X}_1)^2} + \frac{(X_p - \overline{X}_2)^2}{\sum_i (X_{i2} - \overline{X}_2)^2} \right]^{1/2} \qquad (E.26)$$

with s_{het} being the square root of s^2_{het}, which, as we suggested previously, is the error E_F for the ANCOHET model (Equation E. 1) divided by $N - 4$.

As can be seen in this expression for the estimated standard error (Equation E.26), the precision of our estimate of the treatment effect decreases the farther the particular point X_p at which we are evaluating it is from the group means of the covariate. This is similar to what we saw in the simple regression situation (Equation E.15 and Figure 9E.3). Thus, if X_p is chosen near the center of the distribution of X scores, the accuracy of our estimation of the treatment effect increases. In fact, it turns out that the accuracy is greatest at a point corresponding to a weighted average of the group means on the covariate (with the weight for each mean being the sum of squares on the covariate in the other group). This point is referred to in the literature as the *center of accuracy*, denoted C_a. Surprisingly, the vertical distance between the two nonparallel regression lines at the center of accuracy corresponds exactly to the estimate of the difference between adjusted means in a typical ANCOVA assuming a common slope. Thus, one can interpret the difference between adjusted means in ANCOVA as the treatment effect for an "average" individual—that is, an individual whose X score is roughly at the center of the distribution of X scores—regardless of whether the regressions are parallel. The difference between the ANCOHET and the ANCOVA tests of this difference is in the error term. The ANCOVA test is perfectly valid only if the assumption of parallelism is exactly met. The ANCOHET test is actually more like the tests commonly used in factorial ANOVA in that it is valid regardless of whether there is an interaction in the population (nonparallelism). The form of the error term for the ANCOHET test of the treatment effect at the center of accuracy reduces to

$$\hat{\sigma}_{\hat{Y}_{Ca1}-\hat{Y}_{Ca2}} = s_{\text{het}} \left[\frac{1}{n_1} + \frac{1}{n_2} + \frac{(\overline{X}_1 - \overline{X}_2)^2}{\sum_j \sum_i (X_{ij} - \overline{X}_j)^2} \right]^{1/2} \qquad (E.27)$$

Let us pause at this point to underscore what the methodology that we have introduced allows us to do. The test of heterogeneity of regression (Equation E.8) permits an initial assessment of the need for allowing for varying slopes. Certainly, if this test is significant, we would proceed in the analysis making use of an ANCOHET model. Also, we may well want to use an ANCOHET model even if the test for heterogeneity of regression is not significant—either because the test approached significance or because we have reason to suspect heterogeneity on other grounds. The formulas presented in Equations E.21–E.27 make it possible to perform what may be thought of as tests of simple main effects. These tests can be made at any point of interest on the X dimension. In the absence of practical reasons for preferring other points, the treatment effect would typically be evaluated at the center of accuracy, a point in between the group means on the covariate at which our estimate of the treatment effect can be made with the greatest accuracy. The calculations for carrying out such a test for the simple data set presented in Tables 9E.1–9E.3 are illustrated in Table 9E.4.

As shown in the table, the test of the treatment effect in the center of the distribution, allowing for heterogeneous slopes, is nonsignificant. Three points regarding the computations are noteworthy. First, if one compares this test with a standard ANCOVA test, the results turn out to be quite similar. The ANCOVA test yields $F(1, 3) = 0.45$, or $t(3) = \sqrt{(0.45)} = .67$, as opposed to the ANCOHET test result of $t(2) = -.63$. Here, our estimate of population error variance s_{het}^2 in the ANCOHET model is actually larger than the corresponding estimate s^2 in the ANCOVA model (6 vs. 5.33). This is so because, with the extremely small n in the current situation, the reduction in error sum of squares resulting from allowing for heterogeneous slopes is more than offset by the loss of a single degree of freedom. Because this is generally not true and because in a pragmatic if not in a conceptual sense the only difference between

TABLE 9 E.4
TEST OF TREATMENT EFFECT AT THE CENTER OF ACCURACY

Means*		ANCOHET Model Estimates*		ANCOVA Model Estimates*	
$\overline{X}_1 = 2$	$\overline{Y}_1 = 7$	$b_1 = 1$	$a_1 = 5$		$a_1 = 3$
$\overline{X}_2 = 4$	$\overline{Y}_2 = 13$	$b_2 = 3$	$a_2 = 1$	$b_W = 2$	$a_2 = 5$
		$E_F = 12$	$df_F = 2$	$E_R = 16$	$df_R = 3$

Computation of Adjusted Treatment Effect in ANCOVA

$$\text{Adjusted Means: } \overline{Y}'_j = \overline{Y}_j - b_W(\overline{X}_j - \overline{X}) \tag{9.27, repeated}$$
$$\text{For group 1: } \overline{Y}'_1 = 7 - 2(2 - 3) = 7 - 2(-1) = 7 + 2 = 9$$
$$\text{For group 2: } \overline{Y}'_2 = 13 - 2(4 - 3) = 13 - 2(1) = 13 - 2 = 11$$
$$\text{Difference between adjusted means: } \overline{Y}'_1 - \overline{Y}'_2 = 9 - 11 = -2$$

Computation of Standard Error of the Estimate of the Treatment Effect at the Center of Accuracy

$$\hat{\sigma}_{\hat{Y}_{Ca1} - \hat{Y}_{Ca2}} = s_{\text{het}} \left[\frac{1}{n_1} + \frac{1}{n_2} + \frac{(\overline{X}_1 - \overline{X}_2)^2}{\sum_j \sum_i (X_{ij} - \overline{X}_j)^2} \right]^{1/2} \tag{E.27, repeated}$$

$$s_{\text{het}}^2 = \frac{E_F}{df_F} = \frac{\sum_j \sum_i (Y_{ij} - \hat{Y}_{ij_F})^2}{N - 4} = \frac{6 + 6}{6 - 4} = \frac{12}{2} = 6 \tag{from Table 9E.3}$$

$$\sum_j \sum_i (X_{ij} - \overline{X}_j)^2 = 2 + 2 = 4$$

$$\hat{\sigma}_{\hat{Y}_{Ca1} - \hat{Y}_{Ca2}} = \sqrt{6} \left[\frac{1}{3} + \frac{1}{3} + \frac{(2 - 4)^2}{4} \right]^{1/2} = \sqrt{6} \left[\frac{2}{3} + \frac{4}{4} \right]^{1/2} = \sqrt{6} \cdot \sqrt{5/3} = \sqrt{30/3} = \sqrt{10}$$

Test of Treatment Effect at Center of Accuracy

$$t = \frac{\hat{Y}_{Ca1} - \hat{Y}_{Ca2}}{\hat{\sigma}_{\hat{Y}_{Ca1} - \hat{Y}_{Ca2}}} = \frac{\overline{Y}'_1 - \overline{Y}'_2}{(10)^{1/2}} = \frac{-2}{3.16} = -0.63, \text{ nonsignificant}$$

*Previous results computed in Tables 9E.1–9E.3.

the two tests is in the estimate of error variance, the ANCOHET test of the treatment effect at the center of accuracy typically yields larger F values than the corresponding ANCOVA test.

Second, it is worth confirming, as we indicated would be the case, that the difference between the ANCOVA adjusted means is exactly equal to the vertical difference between the nonparallel regression lines at the center of accuracy. This is particularly easy to do here because of the location of the center of accuracy in this artificial data set. Because the sums of squares around the covariate group means are identical for the two groups (both equal 2), when these are used as weights to compute the weighted average of the group means that defines the center of accuracy, the resulting value is simply the grand mean on the covariate. The estimated Y values for the nonparallel regression lines corresponding to this $\overline{X}$ value of 3 can be read easily off the plot in Figure 9E.1(b) or the computed $\hat{Y}$ values shown in Table 9E.3. There we determine that in Group 1, the estimated Y value at $X = 3$ is 8, whereas in Group 2, a Y value of 10 is estimated. Although these are different from the corresponding ANCOVA adjusted means of 9 and 11, respectively, the point is that the treatment effect indicated by the difference between the two adjusted means is identical to the treatment effect in the ANCOHET model at the center of accuracy, that is, $9 - 11 = 8 - 10 = -2$.

Third, and finally, we must stress that the significance test just performed is appropriate for the case in which you want to examine the treatment effect only at a single prespecified point on the X dimension. If you want to investigate the treatment effect at multiple points on the X dimension, which you would be prone to do when the covariate is itself a factor of interest rather than just a "nuisance" variable to be controlled statistically, then some modification of these procedures is needed. These are detailed in the next section.

Simultaneous Tests

The reason for needing simultaneous tests is essentially the same as that discussed in Chapter 5, when we introduced multiple-comparison procedures. When performing multiple tests or when performing tests after examining the data, the possibility of Type 1 error increases unless adjustments are made in the tests. The concern in the earlier chapters was because of the variety of contrasts that could be examined in multiple-group studies, but here the concern is with the large number of points on the X dimension at which the treatment effect could be investigated.

Potthoff (1964) extends a procedure known as the Johnson–Neyman technique to handle the problem of controlling α despite the large number of possible X values at which tests could be made. His solution makes use of the Working–Hotelling procedure for establishing confidence bounds around a regression line (see Neter, et al. 1996, p. 156ff.). The solution is in practice a simple one, and is similar to the Scheffé procedure for multiple comparisons in that the only difference from the test developed previously is that a multiple of a value taken from a standard F table is used as the critical value for your test. That is, the square of the observed t value computed using Equation E.25 would be compared not against an F with 1 and $N - 4$ degrees of freedom, but against a somewhat larger critical value. We might, following Neter, et al. (1996, p. 156), refer to this critical value as W^2, where for any desired α this would be computed as

$$W^2 = 2F(2, N - 4) \tag{E.28}$$

This critical value can be used to test the significance of the treatment effect at any number of X values, and the probability of a Type I error being made anywhere in the set of tests is not more than the nominal α level used in selecting the F value. In fact, a common approach to summarizing the results of such tests is to determine regions of significance. That is, one could specify the portion(s) of the X axis at which the treatment effect was significantly different from zero. This information can be most useful in clinical, educational, or other applied settings in which the instrument being used as a covariate in one study is being explored to determine within what ranges of scores assignment to one treatment rather than another would be expected to produce a difference. Such information could be used in planning how future assignment to treatment or instructional options could be carried out to maximize expected outcomes. See Rogosa (1980, 1981) for additional details on regions of significance.

If there are more than two groups in the study and you wish to do multiple pairwise comparisons, the procedures we developed can be used simply by using a Bonferroni procedure to determine the α level for the selection of a critical value of F and hence for W^2 in Equation E.28. Thus, with five contrasts, by using $.05/5 = .01$ as the α level for choosing the F in Equation E.28 you can control α_{EW} for the tests at .05.

Summary Regarding Heterogeneity of Regression

We have now developed how to test for heterogeneity of regression; how to carry out a summary test of the treatment effect at a single, preselected X value, which is valid whether or not there is heterogeneity of regression; and, finally, how to determine at any and all X values of interest whether the treatment effect is significant there. What remains to be done is to specify a set of guidelines indicating when these procedures should be used.

As noted previously, texts frequently treat homogeneity of regression as a necessary assumption for use of ANCOVA. Guidelines regarding the use of ANCOVA in the face of heterogeneity of regression have been drawn from Monte Carlo studies such as those reported and discussed in Glass, Peckham, and Sanders (1972) and Hamilton (1976, 1977). These can now be viewed in a somewhat different light given Rogosa's (1980) analytical results.

It is quite possible to argue that the effects of heterogeneity of regression when present are typically small and in a conservative direction so that one can proceed with a typical ANCOVA without much uneasiness even when you suspect heterogeneity of regression. However, our recommendation is that one should have a bias for using the ANCOHET procedures. The only disadvantage of ANCOHET would be a potential for a slight loss in power if the regressions were perfectly parallel, whereas the advantages are substantial—the possibility of a much more thorough description of your data in those cases in which the treatment effect depends on X.

Admittedly, there are times when a complete conditional analysis is not of interest—for example, differential assignment to conditions in the future may not be practical even if you know how treatment effectiveness varies as a function of X. Nonetheless, as we have shown, ANCOHET could be used to provide a single, overall test of the treatment effect. Such an ANCOHET test is recommended in this situation because (1) given that some evidence for heterogeneity is virtually assured, the overall ANCOHET test is more powerful than the corresponding ANCOVA test of treatment effect; and (2) the models being used in the test are being made sufficiently flexible to represent any population heterogeneity of regression at a very small cost, that is, slight reduction in the denominator degrees of freedom of the test.

In practical terms, one might carry out an ANCOHET analysis if any of a set of preliminary conditions were met. First, if one has reason to expect heterogeneity on the basis of theory or previous empirical work, then use the ANCOHET approach. Second, if heterogeneity is not anticipated but a test for heterogeneity approaches significance—for instance, $p < .2$—then use the ANCOHET approach.

Once one has opted for the ANCOHET approach, the question arises as to whether to test for the treatment effect at a single point or use the simultaneous test procedures to allow for tests to be carried out at several points on the X dimension. Certainly, if the regression lines intersect within the range of X values observed in the study, a simultaneous analysis would be called for. Otherwise, if there is practical or theoretical interest in the treatment effect for various subpopulations identified by X scores, then one would want to carry out the simultaneous analysis. If neither of these conditions are met, then a single overall ANCOHET test of the treatment effect would suffice.

The practical cost of following these recommendations is merely that a few hand calculations may be required because the major computer packages at the moment do not have routines for testing the significance of the treatment effect at arbitrary points on X. Nonetheless, as shown in Table 9E.4, the required tests can be carried out as a simple t test. The predicted Y scores are readily computed as an option in one of the standard computer routines. The standard error used in the denominator of the test can be computed, following Equation E.27 as illustrated in Table 9E.4, with a hand calculator in a few minutes once the within-group regressions have been computed and an ANOVA on the covariate has been performed, so that the means and within-group sum of squares for X are known.

10

Designs with Random or Nested Factors

DESIGNS WITH RANDOM FACTORS

Introduction to Random Effects

To this point, we have considered models appropriate for the situation in which all factors have levels selected because of the interest of the investigator in those particular levels. Such factors are said to be *fixed* because the same, fixed levels would be included in replications of the study. If one were interested in comparing the relative effectiveness of behavior modification and psychoanalytic approaches to treating agoraphobia, for example, then only experiments containing implementations of these two particular approaches would be relevant to the question of interest.

In other experimental situations, the levels included in any one test of a factor are arbitrary, and the concern is with generalizing not to the effects of a few particular levels of a factor, but to a population of levels that the selected levels merely represent. For example, if one wonders about the effects of different high school math teachers in a school district on the math achievement scores of students in their classes, it might not be feasible to include all the math teachers in a study. However, if you randomly select a small group of teachers to participate in your study, you would like to make inferences to the effects of the whole population of teachers in the district, just as you want to make inferences to a population of subjects even though you can only randomly sample a small group for inclusion in your study.

Factors having randomly selected levels are termed *random factors* (see Ch. 2, p.58), and the statistical models appropriate for analyzing experiments based on such factors are termed *random-effects models*. If an experiment contains both random and fixed factors, a *mixed model* is appropriate. The terms involved in the linear model appear the same in all these cases. For example, in a two-factor design, the linear model could be written

$$Y_{ijk} = \mu + \alpha_j + \beta_k + (\alpha\beta)_{jk} + \varepsilon_{ijk}$$

regardless of whether the design involved only fixed effects, only random effects, or a combination of fixed and random effects. However, the assumptions made about the terms in the linear model would differ, and consequently the way the ANOVA should be carried out would also differ across these three cases.

Recall that in the fixed-effects case we must make only a few assumptions about the errors ε_{ijk} in our model in order to get a "valid" F. In particular, we assume that the errors are normally and independently distributed, with each having an expectation of zero and a variance of σ_ε^2 over hypothetical replications of the experiment. Implicitly, we also assume that the levels of the factors are fixed, so that if replications of the experiment are carried out, the same levels of the factors are used. Thus, the values of the effect parameters applicable to the study are the same for each replication. Although, of course, we typically do not know the "true" effect of a factor for the population, we do assume that what we are seeing in any one experiment is that true effect on each individual, perturbed only by random error.

But when the levels included in an experiment, and thus their true effects, are also changing across replications, this has an impact on the variability we should anticipate in the scores on the dependent variable. Referring to our algebraic model above of how the Y scores arise, when we assume some of the other terms besides ε are randomly varying, familiar quantities, like MS_A or MS_B, which assess particular aspects of the variability of the Y scores, have different expected values than in the fixed effects case. That is, such mean squares then reflect the variability induced by including different randomly selected levels of the factors in each replication of the experiment.

In the random-effects case (sometimes referred to as a *variance-components case*), we assume that the levels of a factor included in the experiment are drawn at random from a population of levels. Frequently, it is appropriate to view such independent variables as being not so much "manipulated" as "sampled." Thus, one may sample classrooms, therapists, dosage levels of a drug, or possible orderings of stimuli presented in a study. To examine the effects of such factors, the appropriate model assumes that the corresponding effect parameters in the model—for example, the α_js—randomly vary as well as the ε_{ijk}s. As always, our statistical model must reflect the realities of the experimental situation in order for our analysis to be valid.

However, there will be at times an element of choice, or at least room for debate, in how one defines the "realities of the experimental situation." Perhaps most commonly in psychology, the issue of whether a factor should be a random factor is debatable because the levels of that factor typically represent a convenience sample rather than a true random sample from some population of levels. For example, in a clinical outcome study, you might use a number of clinical psychologists as therapists to administer various treatment modalities. You then would probably want to know whether therapists differ in effectiveness in this situation. The particular therapists included in the study would in all likelihood be those friends or colleagues that you could conveniently get to participate, rather than a sample drawn at random from a large population of therapists.

How you analyze your data in such a situation depends in part at least on what questions are of interest. As one alternative, you may wonder if the effectiveness of your treatments varies across *this particular set* of therapists. In that case, therapists would be treated as a fixed factor, and your inferences would be to the population of hypothetical replications involving the same therapists but different clients. On the other hand, your interest may be in whether these treatments would vary in their impact on clients across therapists *in general*. In that case, therapists should be treated as a random factor. Then, one's inferences would be to the set of hypothetical replications involving different clients on each replication *and* different therapists.

Although one can always offer logical arguments to support extrapolations beyond the particular levels of a factor included in a study, this latter procedure allows such arguments to be buttressed to some extent by statistical evidence. That is, the hypothesis tested in a random-effects design concerns the effects of a population of therapists rather than just those included in the study. The population, however, is often purely hypothetical in that it is, for example, that set of therapists for which the actual therapists in the study represent a simple random sample. Thus, the inference from the results to any real population would still necessarily be made to some extent on nonstatistical grounds. Keeping this in mind, we now present the procedures for testing hypotheses regarding the effects of a population of potential levels of a factor, starting first with the single-factor case and then generalizing to two-factor and mixed designs.

One-Factor Case

Model

Chapter 3 introduced a model for one-way designs in terms of the population means of the a groups. We now use a very similar full model to introduce a one-way random-effects analysis:

$$Y_{ij} = \mu_j + \varepsilon_{ij} \tag{1}$$

where $i = 1, 2, 3, \ldots, n_j$ and $j = 1, 2, 3, \ldots, a$. The terms of the model are the same as in the fixed-effects case (cf. Equation 3.54), but we assume some of the terms have different characteristics. The error scores are still presumed to be normally distributed in the population with mean zero and variance σ_ε^2. However, now we assume that the μ_j, rather than being fixed from one replication to the next, are also independent, normally distributed random variables with mean μ and variance σ_α^2. The α subscript is used because variation in the μ_j reflects the effect of factor A. Finally, the μ_j and the ε_{ij} are assumed to be independent.

The distinction between the two kinds of variability in this model is made clear by portraying them graphically and illustrating their meaning in concrete examples. The μ_j would be sampled from one normal distribution, which has a mean of μ and a standard deviation of σ_α, as shown at the top of Figure 10.1. In the figure, three values of μ_j are indicated, corresponding to three conditions that might conceivably be selected. Each of these values in turn corresponds to the mean of a distribution of Y values. The variances of these three distributions of Y values shown in the lower part of the figure are all assumed to be equal to each other but would in general be different from the value of σ_α^2.

For example, to continue the illustration of therapists as defining the levels of the random factor, the director of a clinic in a large psychology department might wonder how much of the variability in the general severity index his graduate trainees give clients on intake is due to which trainee is doing the rating rather than variability among clients. The μ_j term then is the mean of the general severity rating that would be obtained if the jth clinical graduate student were to evaluate everyone in the population of potential clients, μ is the mean of all such means for the population of graduate trainees, σ_ε is the standard deviation across clients of the ratings given by a particular trainee, and σ_α is the standard deviation of the trainees' individual means around μ.

The desire of investigators to generalize from responses to a convenient set of confederates or materials to all members of a class is pervasive (—e.g., comparing three therapists trained in motivational interviewing with three who were not trained and wanting to generalize to all trained versus untrained therapists, or comparing the male confederates used in a study of social support with female confederates and wanting to make statements about how the genders differ in communicating social support). However, use of appropriate methodology including analyses incorporating random effects is not common in all areas of psychology (cf. Wells & Windschitl, 1999). One reason for perpetutation of incorrect practice besides the additional effort required to carry out a correct analysis might be that treating the random factor as fixed

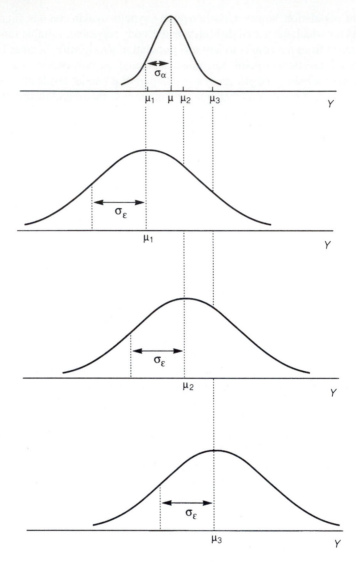

FIG. 10.1. Representation of a full model for a one-way random-effects design.

or ignoring it altogether in multifactor designs can result in some tests being positively biased, as we explain in the next section. Despite this, random-effects models are commendably used with great regularity in certain areas such as language and memory studies. In part because of a very widely cited early article by Herb Clark (1973) and the further work it stimulated (e.g., Forster & Dickinson, 1976; Wike & Church, 1976), a majority of all published papers in at least the *Journal of Memory and Language* make use of tests based on a random effects model (cf. Raaijmakers, Schrijnemakers, & Gremmen, 1999). To illustrate the kind of problem that researchers are trying to address with such analyses, consider that there are a vast number of ways to select words and combine them to illustrate a particular linguistic form. Thus, such "stimulus" or "materials" factors are often treated as random effects. For example, in a study of prose comprehension, of the host of paragraphs that would meet the constraints of a particular study such as length and structure, you might select three for use in your study. Using reading time as the dependent variable, the mean reading time of all possible subjects on a particular passage corresponds to μ_j in the model. The variability of all potential subjects' reading times on a given passage is assumed to be σ_ε^2 for each passage, whereas the variability among all the means for the various passages that might have been included in the study is σ_α^2.

Model Comparisons

In the one-factor mixed-model design, the test of interest, as in the fixed-effects case, asks whether constraining the means of all levels of the factor to be the same significantly increases the lack of fit of the model. Thus, to test factor A, we compare the following models:

$$
\begin{aligned}
\text{Full:} \quad & Y_{ij} = \mu_j + \varepsilon_{ij} \\
\text{Restricted:} \quad & Y_{ij} = \mu + \varepsilon_{ij}
\end{aligned}
\tag{2}
$$

The hypotheses corresponding to these models are expressed somewhat differently than in the fixed-effects case, namely

$$
\begin{aligned}
H_1 &: \sigma_\alpha^2 > 0 \\
H_0 &: \sigma_\alpha^2 = 0
\end{aligned}
\tag{3}
$$

Although the null hypothesis again implies that all the group means are equal and the alternative hypothesis allows for them to vary, as was true in the fixed-effects case, the use of σ^2s instead of μs represents more than just a change in notation. Now one's inferences would be regarding not just the effects of those levels included in the study but regarding the effects of the whole population of levels of the factor from which the selected levels were sampled.

Despite this difference in the nature of the hypotheses, the test for a one-factor design is carried out in exactly the same way as we did in the fixed-effects case. However, there are differences in the expected value of various terms in the analysis. As we show shortly, although these do not affect the analysis in the one-way case, such differences in expected values imply the presence of a random factor typically alters the way the analysis is carried out in more complicated designs.

Expected Values

The expected values of the terms in the F test depend in part on the expected value and variance of the Y scores. Because of the assumptions made about the means and independence of the μ_j and ε_{ij} terms, the expected value and variance of the Y scores, respectively, are

$$
\mathscr{E}(Y_{ij}) = \mu \tag{4}
$$

$$
\text{Var}(Y_{ij}) = \sigma_\alpha^2 + \sigma_\varepsilon^2 \tag{5}
$$

As was true in the fixed-effect case, the error scores computed in the least-squares solution for the full model are simply the deviations from the cell means. Thus, the variance estimate derived from these deviation scores is an unbiased estimate of the population variance of the ε_{ij}. That is,

$$
\mathscr{E}(E_F/df_F) = \mathscr{E}(MS_W) = \sigma_\varepsilon^2 \tag{6}
$$

regardless of whether the null hypothesis is true or false.

The critical expected value in designs involving random factors is that of the numerator of the typical F test, that is, $\mathscr{E}[(E_R - E_F)/(df_R - df_F)]$. In the case of an equal-n design,[1] this expected mean square for the A effect can be written

$$\mathscr{E}(MS_A) = \mathscr{E}\left[\frac{(E_R - E_F)}{(df_R - df_F)}\right] = \sigma_\varepsilon^2 + n\sigma_\alpha^2 \tag{7}$$

Note the relationship between the expected values of the numerator and denominator of the F. Under the null hypothesis, $\sigma_\alpha^2 = 0$ and $\mathscr{E}(MS_A) = \mathscr{E}(MS_W)$. To the extent σ_α^2 is nonzero, the numerator tends to reflect this and be greater than the denominator. Thus, numerator and denominator manifest the desired relation (which we first encountered in Chapter 3, p. 111) of the numerator's expected mean square having only one additional term over those in the denominator, and that additional term corresponding to the effect being tested.

Two-Factor Case

Expected Mean Squares

When we move to designs involving two independent variables, all three conceivable variations on the presence of random factors are possible. That is, if neither factor is random, we have the fixed-effects case; if both are random, it is a random-effects case; and if only one factor is random, the design is said to be mixed.

With such multiple-factor designs, a somewhat counterintuitive result occurs in the impact of the random factor on the expected mean square for the various effects. Specifically, the presence of a random factor causes the term for the interaction of that factor with the other factor in the design to appear in the expression for the expected mean square for the main effect of the *other* factor. Let us see something of how this may occur by considering a simple numerical example.

To expand on the clinical graduate student example introduced earlier in the chapter, assume that each of the trainees is asked to do multiple therapy sessions, some taking a behavioral approach, some taking a psychodynamic approach, and some taking a Rogerian approach. After each session, a faculty supervisor rates the effectiveness of the session on a 7-point scale.

Let us assume that the situation is such that some student therapists earn higher ratings with one clinical modality than another, but that overall there are no differences in the average abilities of the student therapists, nor in the average effectiveness of the various approaches to therapy. To illustrate what we should expect the numerator of the F tests for main effects to equal, consider the means in Table 10.1 to be the population mean ratings for the 18 clinical trainees in a particular program. Each student has a rating for each of the three therapy modes under consideration, reflecting his or her true effectiveness with that method. Note that we are bypassing the error component that would cause variability in individual scores. The numbers presented are to be interpreted as population means, for example, the mean rating that would be obtained if a particular trainee were to use a particular method with all the potential clients. Although we, of course, would not know these values in practice and although the means in the table are clearly more patterned than one would expect in reality, such a set of means illustrates the difficulty that the presence of a random factor introduces into the analysis of factorial designs. The numbers are arranged so that, as indicated by the marginal means, the 18 trainees all have the same average effectiveness scores and the means achieved under the three therapy modes are identical as well. Thus, in the population there is no main effect of either the factor of clinical trainee or therapy mode.

Is this the case if we randomly sample levels of the clinical trainee factor rather than including all 18 graduate students? Results differ depending on which trainees are selected.

TABLE 10.1

EXAMPLE OF THE EFFECTS OF AN INTERACTION IN THE POPULATION BETWEEN A
RANDOM FACTOR AND A FIXED FACTOR

I. Population Means for Three Therapy Modes and for the Entire Population of Trainees

								Clinical Trainee											
Therapy Mode	a	b	c	d	e	f	g	h	i	j	k	l	m	n	o	p	q	r	Mean
Psychodynamic	7	6	5	7	6	5	4	4	4	1	2	3	4	4	4	1	2	3	4
Behavioral	4	4	4	1	2	3	7	6	5	7	6	5	1	2	3	4	4	4	4
Rogerian	1	2	3	4	4	4	1	2	3	4	4	4	7	6	5	7	6	5	4
Mean	4	4	4	4	4	4	4	4	4	4	4	4	4	4	4	4	4	4	4

II. Population Means for Three Therapy Modes and for a Sample of Trainees

	Clinical Trainee			
Therapy Mode	g	k	r	Mean
Psychodynamic	4	2	3	3.00
Behavioral	7	6	4	5.67
Rogerian	1	4	5	3.33
Mean	4	4	4	4.00

If we were to select Students *g*, *k*, and *r*, for example, to serve as the "levels" of the random factor of clinical trainee, the marginal means for the trainees would still be identical, but the marginal means for the fixed factor of therapy mode would differ. That is, there appears to be a main effect of therapy mode. As shown in the lower part of Table 10.1, this particular set of students would make the behavioral approach appear most effective, the Rogerian approach somewhat worse than average, and the psychodynamic approach worst of all.

The reason for this apparent difference across levels of therapy mode when in fact there are no differences overall in the population is, of course, that clinical trainee and therapy mode interact. What the numerical example shows is that the presence of an interaction between a random and a fixed factor does not affect the main effect of the random factor, but it can cause the variability among the means for the fixed factor to increase. Thus, a model comparison assessing the effect of restricting the parameter corresponding to the fixed-effects factor to be zero may suggest that this leads to an increase in error in describing the data when in fact it would not if all levels of the random factor had been included in the study. This implies that our typical *F* test would have a positive bias in testing this effect. That is, the numerator would reflect components other than just error and the effect being tested. The test statistic we have employed previously could be expressed here verbally as the ratio of the following components:

$$\text{"Standard" test for therapy mode} = \frac{\text{Variability due to subjects, therapy mode} \times \text{clinical trainee, and therapy mode}}{\text{Variability due to subjects}}$$

Because we want our test statistic to have a numerator that differs from the denominator only as a result of the effect of the factor being tested, some adjustment of our test statistics is required.

The precise adjustment needed can be seen by examining the expected value of the mean square for each effect, that is, the expected value of the difference in sums of squared errors for the models being compared over the difference in the number of parameters in the two models.

TABLE 10.2
KINDS OF COMPONENTS OF EXPECTED VALUES OF MEAN SQUARES
FOR EFFECTS IN VARIOUS TWO-FACTOR DESIGNS

	Design		
Effect	*Fixed Effects (Factors A and B both fixed)*	*Mixed (Factor A fixed, Factor B random)*	*Random Effects (Factors A and B both random)*
A	Error and A	Error, AB, and A	Error, AB, and A
B	Error and B	Error and B	Error, AB, and B
AB	Error and AB	Error and AB	Error and AB

We present algebraic expressions for these expected values momentarily, but the key point to understand is that having randomly selected levels of a factor affects the kinds of components included in some of these expected value expressions. In the conventional fixed effects design (as shown on the left in Table 10.2), the variability among the means corresponding to any effect reflects only the random errors associated with individual observations and any true difference that effect makes in the population. However, in the mixed design, in which one factor is fixed and the other is random, we have just seen that when there was no main effect of the fixed factor, nonetheless the interaction of the fixed factor with the random factor still caused the marginal means for the levels of the fixed factor to differ. Admittedly, there are typically some differences across levels of the random factor, but the presence of a main effect of the random factor does not affect the apparent evidence for a main effect of the fixed factor. Because the marginal means for the fixed factor are averages across levels of B, their values generally depend on which levels of B are selected. Yet if there were just a main effect of B and no interaction (e.g., some trainees get consistently low ratings and others consistently high), the evidence for an A main effect would not be altered by which levels of B were selected. However, any interaction of the fixed and random factors would intrude on or inflate the variability among the marginal means for the fixed factor. When not just the average rating but the difference between levels of A varies across levels of B, then the differences among the A marginal means depend on which levels of B are selected. This is indicated in the column for the mixed design in Table 10.2, where you see that the mean square for the main effect of A includes components depending on the size of the errors and the AB interaction, as well as the A main effect itself. The general principle is that, when there is a random factor present in a design, any interaction of that factor with another factor affects the mean square for the main effect of the other factor. When both factors are random, the "other" factor is a random factor, regardless of which factor is being considered. Thus the expected mean square for each main effect would include a component reflecting the interaction effect, as shown on the right of Table 10.2.

We now move to a consideration of the algebraic expressions corresponding to these ideas by relating them to the terms of our models. Expressions for the expected mean squares of the effects are shown in Table 10.3 for three types of equal-n, two-factor designs. Although the within-group error is not listed as a separate effect, note that, for all designs, mean square within—that is, E_F divided by df_F—has an expected value of σ_ε^2.

Model Comparisons

The model comparisons involved are the usual ones for a particular effect, regardless of the type of design. For example, the mean square for factor A is derived from a comparison of

TABLE 10.3
EXPECTED VALUES OF NUMERATORS OF THE TEST STATISTIC FOR
INDIVIDUAL EFFECTS IN VARIOUS TWO-FACTOR CROSSED DESIGNS*

	Design		
Effect	Fixed Effects (Factors A and B both fixed)	Mixed (Factor A Fixed, Factor B random)	Random Effects (Factors A and B both random)
A	$\sigma_\varepsilon^2 + bn\theta_\alpha^2$	$\sigma_\varepsilon^2 + n\sigma_{\alpha\beta}^2 + bn\theta_\alpha^2$	$\sigma_\varepsilon^2 + n\sigma_{\alpha\beta}^2 + bn\sigma_\alpha^2$
B	$\sigma_\varepsilon^2 + an\theta_\beta^2$	$\sigma_\varepsilon^2 + an\sigma_\beta^2$	$\sigma_\varepsilon^2 + n\sigma_{\alpha\beta}^2 + an\sigma_\beta^2$
AB	$\sigma_\varepsilon^2 + n\theta_{\alpha\beta}^2$	$\sigma_\varepsilon^2 + n\sigma_{\alpha\beta}^2$	$\sigma_\varepsilon^2 + n\sigma_{\alpha\beta}^2$

*Results are for a design with a levels of factor A, b levels of factor B, and n subjects per cell. Symbols are explained in the text. Values given above are expectations of the form $\mathscr{E}(MS_{\text{effect}}) = \mathscr{E}[(E_R - E_F)/(df_R - df_F)]$, where the restricted model in each case is arrived at by imposing the restriction on the full model that all effect parameters associated with a particular effect are zero.

models:

$$\text{Full:} \quad Y_{ijk} = \mu + \alpha_j + \beta_k + (\alpha\beta)_{jk} + \varepsilon_{ijk}$$
$$\text{Restricted:} \quad Y_{ijk} = \mu + \beta_k + (\alpha\beta)_{jk} + \varepsilon_{ijk} \tag{8}$$

In the equal-n case, we have

$$E_R - E_F = SS_A = \sum_j \sum_k \sum_i e_{ijk,R}^2 - \sum_j \sum_k \sum_i e_{ijk,F}^2$$

$$= \sum_j \sum_k \sum_i \hat{\alpha}_j^2$$

$$= bn \sum_j \hat{\alpha}_j^2 = bn \sum_j (\overline{Y}_{j.} - \overline{Y}_{..})^2 \tag{9}$$

Dividing by the number of independent α_j parameters yields

$$(E_R - E_F)/(df_R - df_F) = \frac{SS_A}{df_A} = MS_A = bn \frac{\sum_j \hat{\alpha}_j^2}{a - 1} \tag{10}$$

Although this mean square is computed in the same way in all three designs, nonetheless its expected value differs depending on what is assumed about the effect parameters, for example, α_j and $(\alpha\beta)_{jk}$, in the particular design.

In the fixed-effects case, the expected mean square is simply the sum of two components, one reflecting the within-cell error variance and the other the extent to which the population marginal means at different levels of factor A differ from each other. Specifically, it can be shown that

$$\mathscr{E}(MS_A) = \mathscr{E}\left(\frac{bn \sum_j \hat{\alpha}_j^2}{a - 1}\right) = \sigma_\varepsilon^2 + bn \frac{\sum_j \alpha_j^2}{a - 1} \tag{11}$$

Because the quantities $\alpha_j = \mu_j - \mu$ represent the entire set of population mean deviations, dividing the sum of their squares by $a - 1$ does not actually yield a variance. Thus, rather than denoting it by a σ^2, we need to use a different symbol, and the conventional one, as shown in Table 10.3, is θ^2 (Greek letter theta squared). (Rather than using a Greek letter, some computer programs as of this printing refer to such expressions involving the sum of the squared effects in a more generic way in the output generated when a random factor is specified or expected mean squares are requested, e.g. simply as a *Quadratic Term* in the SPSS GLM routine or as Q (*effect*) in the SAS GLM procedure.) The value of θ^2 for an effect is defined as the sum of the squared population parameter values for that particular effect divided by the degrees of freedom for the effect. Thus we have

$$\theta_\alpha^2 = \frac{\sum_j \alpha_j^2}{a-1} \qquad \theta_\beta^2 = \frac{\sum_k \beta_k^2}{b-1} \qquad \theta_{\alpha\beta}^2 = \frac{\sum_j \sum_k (\alpha\beta)_{jk}^2}{(a-1)(b-1)} \tag{12}$$

The expected values for the other designs shown in Table 10.3 also deserve comment. The components corresponding to the random effects in these designs are denoted, as discussed previously, by σ^2 terms. For example, the effect of the random factor B is indicated by σ_β^2, because the particular values of β_k included in the study are presumed to be a random sample from a normally distributed population with mean of 0 and variance σ_β^2. The coefficient of each σ^2 term is the number of observations used to compute each marginal or cell mean whose variability it reflects. For example, the marginal mean for each level of factor B is based on *an* scores, whereas the interaction effect depends on the cell means, which are based only on n observations.[2]

Our trainee example illustrates a mixed design, with therapy mode being the fixed factor A and clinical trainee the random factor B. As that example suggested, the mean square for the main effect of the random factor reflects only random error and variability among the various levels of the factor in the population. Note that the interaction effect of a fixed factor and a random factor is a random effect because the particular interaction parameters included in a study depend on which levels of factor B were randomly selected. Thus, the $(\alpha\beta)_{jk}$ terms in our model in this case are also viewed as a random sample from a normally distributed population.

In the mixed-model case, the typical assumption made about the interaction terms in the model is that, like usual interaction parameters, they are restricted to sum to zero. Recall from Chapter 7 that not only do interaction parameters have a grand sum of zero but they also sum to zero within each row and column. In a mixed design, this means that the sum across the infinite number of levels of the random factor is zero for each level of the fixed factor, and that for every possible level of the random factor, the sum across the levels of the fixed factor is zero. This suggests that for the sample of levels of the random factor included in the study, the interaction terms may not sum to zero across that subset of levels of the random factor. However, it is still the case that whatever level of the random factor happens to be included, the interaction terms sum to zero across levels of the fixed factor. That is, if A is the fixed factor, the $(\alpha\beta)_{jk}$ terms are subject to the restriction that

$$\sum_{j=1}^{a} (\alpha\beta)_{jk} = 0 \quad \text{for all } k$$

Thus, this model is sometimes referred to as the *model with restricted interaction effects.* Alternative models are possible and are discussed in Hocking (1973) and are clearly explained in the text by Cobb (1998, p. 571ff.).[3]

Perhaps of most interest in the mixed-design case is the expected mean square for the fixed-effect factor. The $\mathscr{E}(MS_A)$ for this design reflects not only random error associated with individual scores and the magnitude of the effect of factor A in the population, θ_α^2, but also the interaction of the two factors in the population as shown in Table 10.3.

The situation is similar in the random-effects design. However, because the other factor is a random factor regardless of which main effect is being considered, the expected mean square for each main effect includes the interaction of that factor with the other.

Selection of Error Terms

For the fixed-effects design, the appropriate error term or denominator of the test statistic for all effects is, of course, E_F/df_F or MS_W. Mean square within is the correct denominator term because each of the effects in the fixed-effects design differs from MS_W in expected value only by one component, namely, that for the effect under consideration. This is true also for the interaction effect in the mixed and random-effects two-factor designs. Thus, MS_W can be used as the denominator in tests of the AB effect for these designs as well.

However, if we were to use MS_W in the test of the main effect of the fixed factor in the mixed design, we would *not* really be testing simply the main effect of the fixed factor. Rather, we would actually be performing a test of whether there was evidence for a main effect of the fixed factor *or* an interaction. This would be true also for each of the main effects in the random-effects design. The mistaken practice of using MS_W as a means of testing such main effects in mixed or random effect designs leads to F values that, in general, are too large, unless the interaction is exactly zero in the population. Fortunately, we can meet the criterion of having an error term that differs in expected value only by the component associated with the effect being tested by using the mean square for the interaction as the error term in such cases. Table 10.4 shows the error terms for all effects in the different types of two-factor designs we have been considering.

We can summarize rather succinctly the source of the difficulty for the analysis posed by the presence of a random factor and the nature of the solution outlined. The difficulty is that the expected value of the mean square—that is, the expected value of $(E_R - E_F)/(df_R - df_F)$—for an effect includes, besides error variance, not only a component for the population magnitude of that effect but also a component reflecting the magnitude of the interaction of that effect with any random factor.

The solution is to choose an error term that is appropriate for the particular effect being considered. The rules for how to determine such an error term can be stated fairly simply as well, not only for two-factor designs but also for any completely crossed, between-subjects factorial design. Specifically, two rules determine the exact error term for an effect:

TABLE 10.4

ERROR TERMS FOR TESTS OF SPECIFIC EFFECTS IN DIFFERENT TYPES
OF COMPLETELY CROSSED TWO-FACTOR DESIGNS*

		Design			
Fixed Effects (Factors A and B both fixed)		*Mixed (Factor A fixed, Factor B random)*		*Random Effects (Factors A and B both random)*	
Effect	Error Term	Effect	Error Term	Effect	Error Term
A	MS_W	A	MS_{AB}	A	MS_{AB}
B	MS_W	B	MS_W	B	MS_{AB}
AB	MS_W	AB	MS_W	AB	MS_W

*$MS_W = E_F/df_F$, and $MS_{AB} = (E_R - E_F)/(df_R - df_F)$, where the restricted model imposes the restriction on the null model that all $(\alpha\beta)_{jk} = 0$.

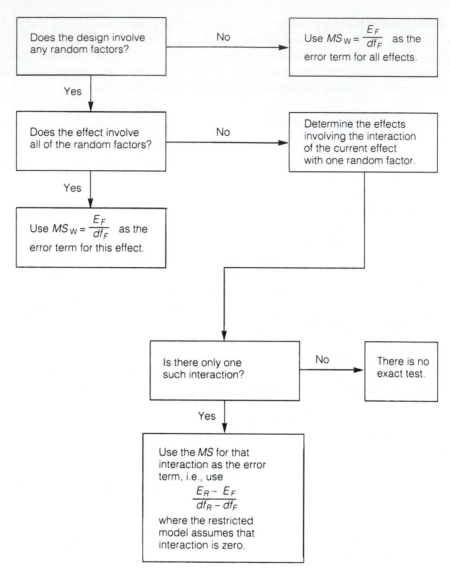

FIG. 10.2. Flowchart to assist in the selection of appropriate denominator terms for tests of effects in completely crossed factorial designs.

1. If there are no random factors in the design or if the effect being tested contains all random factors, then use $MS_W = E_F/df_F$ as the error term.
2. Otherwise, use as the error term the interaction with a random factor of the effect being tested. That is, use as the error term $MS_{\text{interaction}} = (E_R - E_F)/(df_R - df_F)$, where the restriction imposed on the fullest model is that these interaction parameters are zero. If there is more than one random factor besides any included in the current effect, no exact test is possible.

The flowchart in Figure 10.2 summarizes these rules.

Several comments are in order at this point. First, it appears from Figure 10.2 that you can reach a dead end where there is no acceptable error term. This rarely occurs. Note in this regard that, as long as there is only one random factor among those factors crossed with each other in a factorial design, then there is always an exact test. Because use of random independent variables is relatively unusual in the behavioral sciences, for a single experiment to involve multiple random factors is very unusual.

Second, random factors are often not of interest in themselves but are included merely as control factors. The random-factor levels may represent different materials, such as different prose passages in a human memory experiment, which are not at all the main focus of the experiment. Thus, a common approach to analyzing the data in such a situation with multiple random factors is to do a preliminary analysis of the random control factors, particularly to determine if a control factor interacts with any other factors in the experiment. If it does not, then one could decide to ignore this factor entirely in subsequent analyses. Following this strategy frequently allows one to sidestep the problem of multiple random factors not permitting exact tests of certain effects. The primary cost entailed in such a strategy is that the mean square error associated with the full model may be slightly larger than it might have been because the variability due to the random factor has not been removed (see discussion of Alternative Tests following the Numerical Example we present next). This is likely to appear a negligible cost compared to the benefit of being able to carry out exact tests of the effects of interest. Furthermore, the degrees of freedom in the denominator of the F ratio are generally much smaller when an interaction with a random factor is used as the error term instead of mean square within. If the number of levels of the random factor is small, the critical value for the F required to declare significance may be quite large. This is another consideration that might motivate one to perform such a preliminary analysis of the random factor; if there is little evidence for its importance—for example, all effects involving this factor yielding $p > .2$—there is some justification for dropping the factor from the final analysis in order to have tests of the effects of primary interest based on more degrees of freedom (considerations bearing on possibly dropping a random factor based on preliminary tests are discussed in more detail in the next section in the context of a numerical example).

Third, if one concludes that multiple random factors must be retained either because of their inherent interest or because of the presence of evidence that they interact with other factors, it is possible to construct quasi-F ratios in those cases in which there is not an exact test available. The logic in such a case is to take a combination of mean squares for various effects, adding some and subtracting others, so that the linear combination has the desired expected value. The resulting test statistic only approximately follows an F distribution. The interested reader is referred to Chapter 12 for a brief introduction to quasi-F ratios, or to Myers (1979, p. 191ff.) or Kirk (1995, pp. 406–408) for more detailed treatments.

NUMERICAL EXAMPLE

Assume that an educational products firm markets study programs to help high school students prepare for college entrance exams such as the ACT, and wants to compare a new computer-based training program with their standard packet of printed materials. The firm would like to be able to generalize to all American high schools but only has the resources to conduct a study in a few schools. Thus, assume four high schools are selected at random from a listing of all public schools in the country. Volunteers from the junior classes at these schools are solicited to take part in an eight-session after-school study program. Ten students from each school are permitted to take part, and equal numbers from each school are assigned randomly to the two study programs. Designating the type of study program as factor A (a_1 designates

TABLE 10.5
DATA AND ANALYSES FOR ACT TRAINING EXAMPLE

I. Data on Post-Test Simulating ACT

Study Program:		Computer *a1*				Standard *a2*		
School:	School 1	School 2	School 3	School 4	School 1	School 2	School 3	School 4
	b1	*b2*	*b3*	*b4*	*b1*	*b2*	*b3*	*b4*
	28	26	24	20	30	34	31	33
	26	26	24	20	28	31	29	30
	26	25	19	20	28	29	25	28
	23	21	14	18	25	27	21	26
	17	17	14	12	19	24	19	23
$\overline{Y}_{jk}$	24	23	19	18	26	29	25	28
s^2_{jk}	18.5	15.5	25.0	12.0	18.5	14.5	26.0	14.5

Cell and Marginal Means

$\overline{Y}_{jk}$	*b1*	*b2*	*b3*	*b4*	$\overline{Y}_{j.}$
a1	24	23	19	18	21
a2	26	29	25	28	27
$\overline{Y}_{.k}$	25	26	22	23	24

Parameter Estimates

$\widehat{\alpha\beta}_{jk}$	*b1*	*b2*	*b3*	*b4*	$\hat{\alpha}_j$
a1	+2	0	0	−2	−3
a2	−2	0	0	+2	+3
$\hat{\beta}_k$	+1	+2	−2	−1	

II. Computations of Sums of Squares

$$SS_W = \sum_j \sum_k (n-1)s^2_{jk} = 4\sum_j\sum_k s^2_{jk} = 4 \cdot 144.5 = 578$$

$$SS_A = bn \sum_j \hat{\alpha}^2_j = 4 \cdot 5[(-3)^2 + 3^2] = 20(18) = 360$$

$$SS_B = an \sum_k \hat{\beta}^2_k = 2 \cdot 5[1^2 + 2^2 + (-2)^2 + (-1)^2] = 10(10) = 100$$

$$SS_{AB} = n \sum_j \sum_k \widehat{\alpha\beta}^2_{jk} = 5[2^2 + 0^2 + 0^2 + (-2)^2 + (-2)^2 + 0^2 + 0^2 + 2^2] = 5 \cdot 16 = 80$$

III. Source Table

Source	SS	df	MS	F	p	Denom. Term
A	360	1	360.000	13.500	.035	AB
B	100	3	33.333	1.845	.159	Within
AB	80	3	26.667	1.476	.240	Within
Within	578	32	18.063			

the computer-based program and a_2 designates the standard paper-and-pencil program) and the particular school as factor B, assume the data in Table 10.5 are obtained.

In such a situation, factor A would typically be regarded as fixed and factor B as random. The computation of cell and marginal means, as well as the estimates of the parameters of our models, would be carried out the same as always. Results are shown below the data in the table. Similarly, the computation of the sums of squares within and for the A, B, and AB effects could proceed as usual, with sum of squares within being the sum of the variances weighted by one less than the cell size, and the sum of squares for each effect being the sum over all observations of the estimated effect parameters squared, as indicated in part II of Table 10.5. Degrees of freedom associated with these sums of squares are computed in the usual way. The Source Table at the bottom of Table 10.5 indicates how these terms are combined to carry out tests of the two main effects and interactions. The novel aspect of this table is the test of the main effect of factor A, the fixed effect factor of type of study program. As indicated on the right of the table, instead of the denominator of this test being MS_W, it is MS_{AB}, the mean square for the interaction of the fixed and random factors. That is, the observed F value for factor A is computed as $F_A = 360/26.667 = 13.500$. Note that this observed value of the F for the test of factor A is compared with critical values from an F distribution with 1 and 3 degrees of freedom, which is 10.1 for $\alpha = .05$, instead of using an F with 1 and 32 degrees of freedom. Thus, we would conclude here that the mean scores on the simulated ACT are significantly different with the two study programs, with the new computer-based method leading to lower scores.

Alternative Tests and Design Considerations with Random Factors

Not surprisingly, the test of the effect of the fixed factor could turn out quite differently if MS_W were to be used as the error term instead of MS_{AB}. For the data reported in Table 10.5, even though $MS_W = 18.063$ and $MS_{AB} = 26.667$ are not strikingly different, using MS_W as the error term in the test of factor A would yield $F_{obs}(1,32) = 19.931$, $p = .00009$, instead of $F_{obs}(1,3) = 13.500$, $p = .035$, with both the smaller error term and the increased degrees of freedom contributing to the much smaller p value in the test with MS_W. Is such an approach ever justified? The answer is definitely Yes only if factor B may be regarded as a fixed factor. In our example, this might be the case if the interest were restricted to these particular four schools rather than a larger population. Otherwise, there is considerable debate about use of an error term other than MS_{AB}. Some authors (e.g., Green & Tukey, 1960) suggest that one might drop an interaction term from one's model based on preliminary tests. The issues are similar to those discussed in considering using Type II rather than Type III sums of squares in Chapter 7 (cf., p. 334). The difficulty with such approaches is that their legitimacy hinges on the decisions reached in the preliminary tests being correct. For example, although the test of the AB interaction did not approach significance in Table 10.5, $p > .2$, it could nonetheless be the case that there is some AB interaction in the population that we failed to detect. Thus, continuing to use MS_{AB} as the error term regardless of how the test of the AB interaction turns out is the more conservative approach.

Nonetheless, one's knowledge of a particular domain and background information about the factor are also relevant. If one has good reasons for expecting the random factor to have minimal effects, including minimal interaction with the other factor, then that belief coupled with confirming statistical evidence may warrant use of alternative, more powerful tests. This applies both in the case of random crossed factors and in the case of the random nested factors, which we consider shortly. The clear difference in degrees of freedom available for the different tests calls attention to issues experimenters should consider in the design of studies. This is particularly true when experimenters can exert some control over the homogeneity of the levels of the random factor. That is, a benefit in terms of statistical power for detecting effects of interest is an important reason why researchers would do well to devote much time and care to the training of experimenters, confederates, or raters who constitute the levels of the random factor in a design. If at the end of training these assistants are, in fact, so homogeneous that it matters not which one a particular subject encounters, then one may justify using an alternative test. For example, in a two-factor mixed design, if one had reason to expect that there would not be an interaction between the random and fixed factors and this were confirmed by obtaining a p value in a preliminary test of the interaction effect greater than .2, one could drop the $\alpha\beta$ term from one's model. It turns out in such a case that the appropriate mean square for the tests of the main effects of A and B would then be one that used as an error term the mean square resulting from pooling the interaction and within-cell sources. Thus, in our numerical example we would compute

$$MS_{\text{residual}} = \frac{SS_{\text{within}} + SS_{\text{AB}}}{df_{\text{within}} + df_{\text{AB}}} = \frac{578 + 80}{32 + 3} = \frac{658}{35} = 18.80$$

Using this as the error term would yield a considerably different test of the fixed factor, that is $F(1, 35) = 19.149$, $p = .0001$. Alternatively, if one concluded that there were no evidence for either a B effect nor an AB interaction, one could simply rerun one's analysis as a one-factor design. This would yield a test of A with a new error term based on a pooling of the sums of squares for B, AB, and within, and $F(1, 38) = 18.047$, $p = .0001$. Kirk (1995, p. 408ff.) provides a helpful discussion of the issues and additional references to relevant literature if you wish to pursue alternative tests in this situation. Exercise 7 at the end of the current chapter is also relevant.

However, because of the pervasive effects of individual differences among people, it often is not realistic to expect that one can eliminate relevant differences in a few days or weeks of training. In such a case the most practical way of increasing power may be through simply increasing the number of levels of the random factor so that one has a reasonable number of degrees of freedom (e.g., 10 or more) associated with the random effect to be used as the error term.

Follow-up Tests and Confidence Intervals

Follow-up tests of particular contrasts and construction of confidence intervals would proceed as we have discussed previously (e.g., Chapters 5 and 7), with the exception that the mean square for the denominator error term appropriate for the omnibus test of an effect, if different from MS_W, would replace MS_W in formulas for testing subeffects. For example, a confidence interval on a difference between the levels of a fixed factor in a mixed design in which the fixed factor had only two levels as in our ACT example might be written as

$$(\overline{Y}_{1.} - \overline{Y}_{2.}) \pm \sqrt{F_{(.05;1,df_{\text{denom}})}} \sqrt{MS_{\text{denom}}\left(\frac{1}{n_{1+}} + \frac{1}{n_{2+}}\right)}$$

where MS_{denom} refers to the mean square for the AB interaction instead of MS_W, and where the particular ns are as usual the number of observations going into the computation of each of the two means being compared. For the data in Table 10.5, we would have

$$(21 - 27) \pm \sqrt{F_{(.05;1,3)}} \sqrt{MS_{\text{AB}}\left(\tfrac{1}{20} + \tfrac{1}{20}\right)}$$

$$-6 \pm \sqrt{10.1}\sqrt{26.667\left(\tfrac{1}{20} + \tfrac{1}{20}\right)}$$

$$-6 \pm 3.178\sqrt{2.667}$$

$$-6 \pm 3.178(1.633)$$

$$-6 \pm 5.190$$

$$-11.190, \ -.810$$

Consistent with our hypothesis test which found significant evidence for the effect of the training program, the fact that the confidence interval does not include 0 indicates that the computer-based training program leads to lower scores on the ACT than does the paper-and-pencil program, although the magnitude of the deficit could be anywhere from just over 11 points to less than a single point.

When there are more than two levels of a factor, one might want to construct simultaneously confidence intervals around particular contrast estimates such as particular pair-wise differences. In our ACT example, although the school effect was not significant, one might use a Tukey critical value for forming confidence intervals around particular differences of interest in pairs of schools, using an adaptation of the formula in Table 5.8:

$$(\overline{Y}_{.g} - \overline{Y}_{.h}) \pm (q_{.05;b,df_w}/\sqrt{2})\sqrt{MS_W\left(\frac{1}{n_{+g}} + \frac{1}{n_{+h}}\right)}$$

So, for example, the 95% simultaneous confidence interval on the difference in the means for Schools 2 and 3 in our example would be

$$(26 - 22) \pm (q_{.05;4,32}/\sqrt{2})\sqrt{18.063\left(\frac{1}{10} + \frac{1}{10}\right)}$$

$$4 \pm (3.84/\sqrt{2})\sqrt{3.6125}$$

$$4 \pm 2.715(1.901)$$

$$4 \pm 5.161$$

$$-1.161, \quad 9.161$$

Measures of Association Strength

In Chapter 3, we introduced measures of the strength of association between an independent variable and a dependent variable that described effects on a standardized scale of 0 to 1 indicating the proportion of variability explained or accounted for by a factor. Recall, that the sample proportion, R^2, was found to be positively biased as an estimate of the proportion of variance accounted for in the population. Hence we had to adjust or shrink the sample estimate in order to have an unbiased estimate of the population proportion, ω^2 (omega squared). In Chapter 7, we saw how both the sample value and the population estimate could be modified in multifactor designs so they were not inappropriately reduced by the effects of other factors that were extrinsic to the effect of the factor of interest. This yielded the measures of association strength we denoted $R^2_{partial}$ and $\hat{\omega}^2_{partial}$.

The sample values of R^2 and $R^2_{partial}$ can be estimated the same way in crossed designs involving random factors as in the designs considered previously, that is,

$$R^2 = \frac{SS_{effect}}{SS_{Total}} \tag{13}$$

and[4]

$$R^2_{partial} = \frac{SS_{effect}}{SS_W + SS_{effect}} \tag{14}$$

The estimates of population variance accounted for, ω^2, which we previously presented were based on expressions for expected mean squares derived by assuming all factors except subjects were fixed. Because these expected values are affected by the presence of a random factor, we must now introduce a different measure of variance accounted for that is appropriate for random effects.

Intraclass Correlation

The proportion of population variance accounted for by a random effect is referred to as the intraclass correlation,[5] denoted ρ_I. This measure is directly analogous to ω^2 for fixed effects, with both measures estimating

$$\frac{\text{population variance associated with current effect}}{\text{total population variance}}$$

In the case of a design with only a single random factor, the intraclass correlation estimates the ratio

$$\frac{\sigma_\alpha^2}{\sigma_\alpha^2 + \sigma_\varepsilon^2}$$

Given that $\mathcal{E}(MS_W) = \sigma_\varepsilon^2$ and $\mathcal{E}(MS_A) = \sigma_\varepsilon^2 + n\sigma_\alpha^2$ (see Equations 6 and 7), we can estimate σ_α^2 as $\hat{\sigma}_\alpha^2 = (MS_A - MS_W)/n$ and estimate σ_ε^2 as $\hat{\sigma}_\varepsilon^2 = MS_W$, which implies that ρ_I may be estimated as follows:

$$\hat{\rho}_I = \frac{MS_A - MS_W}{MS_A + (n-1)MS_W} \tag{15}$$

In the case of two-factor designs, there is not a single formula in terms of mean squares defining $\hat{\rho}_I$. The form of the expression depends on whether one or both factors are random, as well as on whether the overall proportion or a partial form of ρ_I is being estimated. In any case it is easier to define $\hat{\rho}_I$ in terms of the variance components or the estimates of the σ^2 terms that appear in the expressions for the expected mean squares. It turns out that we may in general define the estimated proportion of variance accounted for in the population by a random effect in a multifactor design as

$$\hat{\rho}_{I:\text{effect}} = \frac{\hat{\sigma}_{\text{effect}}^2}{\hat{\sigma}_{\text{effect}}^2 + \sum \hat{\sigma}_{\text{other effects}}^2 + \hat{\sigma}_{\text{error}}^2} \tag{16}$$

Thus, for the main effects and interaction in a two-factor design we would have

$$\hat{\rho}_{I:A} = \frac{\hat{\sigma}_\alpha^2}{\hat{\sigma}_\alpha^2 + \hat{\sigma}_\beta^2 + \hat{\sigma}_{\alpha\beta}^2 + \hat{\sigma}_\varepsilon^2} \qquad \hat{\rho}_{I:B} = \frac{\hat{\sigma}_\beta^2}{\hat{\sigma}_\alpha^2 + \hat{\sigma}_\beta^2 + \hat{\sigma}_{\alpha\beta}^2 + \hat{\sigma}_\varepsilon^2}$$

$$\hat{\rho}_{I:AB} = \frac{\hat{\sigma}_{\alpha\beta}^2}{\hat{\sigma}_\alpha^2 + \hat{\sigma}_\beta^2 + \hat{\sigma}_{\alpha\beta}^2 + \hat{\sigma}_\varepsilon^2} \tag{17}$$

The variance components are estimated based on the expected values of the mean squares shown in Table 10.3. For example, in the case of a design with two random factors, the estimates of the variance components are

$$\hat{\sigma}_\alpha^2 = \frac{MS_A - MS_{AB}}{bn} \qquad \hat{\sigma}_\beta^2 = \frac{MS_B - MS_{AB}}{an}$$

$$\hat{\sigma}_{\alpha\beta}^2 = \frac{MS_{AB} - MS_W}{n} \qquad \hat{\sigma}_\varepsilon^2 = MS_W \tag{18}$$

Note that because any of the mean squares being subtracted in the above expressions may be larger on occasion than the mean square from which it is subtracted, it is possible that you could get a negative estimate of one of these variance components. Because we know that the true value of any variance is nonnegative, the convention is to set the estimate to zero any time a negative value is obtained. Once obtained, the estimated variance components can be used to compute not only the overall proportions of variance explained via Equation 17 but also the estimates of the *partial* intraclass correlations as follows

$$\hat{\rho}_{I:A,\text{partial}} = \frac{\hat{\sigma}_\alpha^2}{\hat{\sigma}_\alpha^2 + \hat{\sigma}_\varepsilon^2} \qquad \hat{\rho}_{I:B,\text{partial}} = \frac{\hat{\sigma}_\beta^2}{\hat{\sigma}_\beta^2 + \hat{\sigma}_\varepsilon^2}$$

$$\hat{\rho}_{I:AB,\text{partial}} = \frac{\hat{\sigma}_{\alpha\beta}^2}{\hat{\sigma}_{\alpha\beta}^2 + \hat{\sigma}_\varepsilon^2} \tag{19}$$

In the case of a mixed design, in which A is fixed and B is random, the form for the estimate of the proportion of variance accounted for overall would be essentially the same as in (17), but with $\sum \alpha_j^2/a$ substituted for σ_α^2 and $\hat{\omega}^2$ used to designate the measure for the fixed factor. That is,

$$\hat{\omega}_A^2 = \frac{\sum \hat{\alpha}_j^2/a}{\sum \hat{\alpha}_j^2/a + \hat{\sigma}_\beta^2 + \hat{\sigma}_{\alpha\beta}^2 + \hat{\sigma}_\varepsilon^2} \qquad \hat{\rho}_{I:B} = \frac{\hat{\sigma}_\beta^2}{\sum \hat{\alpha}_j^2/a + \hat{\sigma}_\beta^2 + \hat{\sigma}_{\alpha\beta}^2 + \hat{\sigma}_\varepsilon^2}$$

$$\hat{\rho}_{I:AB} = \frac{\hat{\sigma}_{\alpha\beta}^2}{\sum \hat{\alpha}_j^2/a + \hat{\sigma}_\beta^2 + \hat{\sigma}_{\alpha\beta}^2 + \hat{\sigma}_\varepsilon^2} \tag{20}$$

where

$$\frac{\sum \hat{\alpha}_j^2}{a} = \frac{(a-1)}{abn}(MS_A - MS_{AB}) \qquad \hat{\sigma}_\beta^2 = \frac{MS_B - MS_W}{an}$$

$$\hat{\sigma}_{\alpha\beta}^2 = \frac{MS_{AB} - MS_W}{n} \qquad \hat{\sigma}_\varepsilon^2 = MS_W \tag{21}$$

Using these quantities, one can arrive at the estimates for the corresponding partial measures for a mixed design:

$$\hat{\omega}_{A,\text{partial}}^2 = \frac{\sum \hat{\alpha}_j^2/a}{\sum \hat{\alpha}_j^2/a + \hat{\sigma}_\varepsilon^2} \qquad \hat{\rho}_{I:B,\text{partial}} = \frac{\hat{\sigma}_\beta^2}{\hat{\sigma}_\beta^2 + \hat{\sigma}_\varepsilon^2}$$

$$\hat{\rho}_{I:AB,\text{partial}} = \frac{\hat{\sigma}_{\alpha\beta}^2}{\hat{\sigma}_{\alpha\beta}^2 + \hat{\sigma}_\varepsilon^2} \tag{22}$$

Numerical Example

Referring back to the source table for the example of the training program for the ACT (see Table 10.5), we can now readily compute the various measures of association strength for the main effects and interaction in our study. The R^2 measures are just the ratios of the sums of squares for these effects to SS_{Total}, which here is $360 + 100 + 80 + 578 = 1118$. Thus, the R^2 for the effect of the study program factor, for example, is $360/1118 = .322$. The corresponding value of R_{partial}^2 is arrived at, as we indicated in Equation 14, by reducing the denominator of this ratio to just the sum of the SS_A and SS_W, that is, $360/(360 + 578) = 360/938 = .384$. Values of R^2 and of R_{partial}^2 for the other effects are computed similarly and are displayed in the columns of Table 10.6 labelled Sample Values.

The estimates of the overall proportion of population variance accounted for may be computed using the definitions in Equation 20, but we first must estimate the variance components as defined in Equation 21. These variance components may be estimated as follows:

$$\frac{\sum \hat{\alpha}_j^2}{a} = \frac{(a-1)}{abn}(MS_A - MS_{AB}) = \frac{(2-1)}{2 \cdot 4 \cdot 5}(360 - 26.667) = \frac{333.33}{40} = 8.333$$

$$\hat{\sigma}_\beta^2 = \frac{MS_B - MS_W}{an} = \frac{33.333 - 18.063}{2 \cdot 5} = 15.271/10 = 1.527$$

$$\hat{\sigma}_{\alpha\beta}^2 = \frac{MS_{AB} - MS_W}{n} = \frac{26.667 - 18.063}{5} = 8.604/5 = 1.721$$

$$\hat{\sigma}_\varepsilon^2 = MS_W = 18.063$$

Thus, we may compute the proportion of variance we would expect the training program to account for in a population of individuals from various schools as

$$\hat{\omega}_A^2 = \frac{\sum \hat{\alpha}_j^2/a}{\sum \hat{\alpha}_j^2/a + \hat{\sigma}_\beta^2 + \hat{\sigma}_{\alpha\beta}^2 + \hat{\sigma}_\varepsilon^2} = \frac{8.333}{8.333 + 1.527 + 1.721 + 18.063}$$

$$= \frac{8.333}{29.644} = .281$$

Similar substitutions into the formulas for the intraclass correlations in Equation 20 yield estimates of .052 and .058 for the proportion of population variance accounted for by the School factor and the Program by School interaction, respectively.

One could imagine that one could regard the School factor as extrinsic to the Program factor, for example, one might be interested in the difference that the Program might make for the students in one particular school, or for a population of home schoolers for whom the magnitude of the School effect here might be of questionable relevance. The estimates of the partial measures of population variance shown in the rightmost column of Table 10.6 are appropriate for such a situation where the other factors are regarded as extrinsic. For example, computation of the population estimate of the partial effect of the Program factor is carried out following Equation 22:

$$\hat{\omega}_{A,partial}^2 = \frac{\sum \hat{\alpha}_j^2/a}{\sum \hat{\alpha}_j^2/a + \hat{\sigma}_\varepsilon^2} = \frac{8.333}{8.333 + 18.063} = \frac{8.333}{26.396} = .316$$

TABLE 10.6
ESTIMATES OF ASSOCIATION STRENGTH MEASURES FOR ACT TRAINING PROGRAM EXAMPLE

| | Strength of Association Measures | | | |
| | Sample Values | | Population Estimates | |
Effect	R^2	$R^2_{partial}$	Overall	Partial
A (Program, fixed)	.322	.384	$\hat{\omega}_A^2 = .281$	$\hat{\omega}_{A,partial}^2 = .316$
B (School, random)	.089	.148	$\hat{\rho}_{I:B} = .052$	$\hat{\rho}_{I:B,partial} = .078$
AB	.072	.122	$\hat{\rho}_{I:AB} = .058$	$\hat{\rho}_{I:AB,partial} = .087$

Using Statistical Computer Programs to Analyze Designs with Random Factors

As we have seen, the primary impact of having a random factor in a design is that it may alter the way tests of certain effects are carried out. Most statistical computer packages have methods for specifying the error terms against which effects are to be tested. For example, in SPSS, if one uses the MANOVA routine, one can specify error terms for any effect on the syntax command line used to indicate the effects to be tested. The effects to be listed are specified in MANOVA on a DESIGN statement, and each effect may be followed by "VS x" to indicate that x is the denominator error term to be used in testing that effect. Numbers may be used to indicate particular sources of variance that are identified by putting "$= n$" after an effect that is to be used as an error term in testing some other effect. So for our ACT numerical example, the tests of effects appropriate for treating methods as a fixed factor and school as a random factor may be achieved via the syntax lines:

```
MANOVA act by method (1,2) school (1,4)
   /DESIGN = method vs 1, school vs within, method by school = 1
   vs within.
```

As of this writing, one cannot designate particular error terms to be used with SPSS's popular point-and-click programs such as the Univariate General Linear Model. However, appropriate tests can be achieved by pasting the default syntax onto the file in the syntax editor and modifying it by addition of a line asking for a particular test. For example, if one were to designate on the Univariate analysis screen "act" as the dependent variable, and "method" and "school" as fixed effects, the default syntax written to the syntax editor when the Paste button is selected would be

```
UNIANOVA
   act BY method school
   /METHOD = SSTYPE (3)
   /CRITERIA = ALPHA (.05)
   /DESIGN = method school method*school.
```

Although unlike in MANOVA one cannot specify error terms on the UNIANOVA DESIGN statement itself, one can insert a command line immediately before this requesting a different error term than Within be used for testing the Method effect, as follows:

```
/TEST method vs method*school
```

SAS's Proc GLM also uses a "Test" statement to specify the error term (indicated by $E=$) corresponding to particular effects or hypotheses being tested (indicated by $H=$). The independent variables or factors are first designated on a CLASS statement, and effects to be tested are indicated on a MODEL statement. The syntax for our mixed design then might be:

```
proc glm;
   class method school;
   model act = method school method*school;
   test H = method E = method*school;
   run;
```

Determining Power in Designs with Random Factors

Power for designs with random factors has not been as commonly discussed as power for fixed effects designs. This is likely in part because of the fact that somewhat different methods are required with random effects than those appropriate for determining power to detect fixed effects. As Scheffé (1959, p. 226ff.) demonstrated, the power to detect random effects is based on *central F* distributions rather than the noncentral F distributions used for power analyses with fixed effects. This means that the Pearson–Hartley power charts in Appendix A.11 cannot be used. However, power can be computed easily for certain random effects designs using readily available software (cf. O'Brien & Muller, 1993, p. 333).

In general, the distribution used to determine power for random effects is just a multiple of the F distribution that is appropriate when the null hypothesis is true. The multiplier turns out to be the ratio of the expected values of the numerator and denominator terms used to compute the F. That is, when there is a nonzero random effect, distribution of the test statistic is indicated by the following multiple of a standard F:

$$\frac{\text{expected value of } MS_{\text{numerator}}}{\text{expected value of } MS_{\text{denominator}}} \times F_{df_{\text{num}}, df_{\text{denom}}}$$

Consider for example a one-way design in which a levels of a factor are selected randomly from a population of possible levels, with n observations at each of the a levels. From Equations 6 and 7 we can determine that the ratio of the expected values would be

$$\frac{\mathscr{E}(MS_A)}{\mathscr{E}(MS_W)} = \frac{\sigma_\varepsilon^2 + n\sigma_\alpha^2}{\sigma_\varepsilon^2} = 1 + n\frac{\sigma_\alpha^2}{\sigma_\varepsilon^2}$$

The ratio of variances on the right is essentially the square of the effect size measure f (which was defined as the ratio of the standard deviation of the population means for the different levels of the factor to the within-group standard deviation) that we used to determine power in the one-way, fixed-effects designs (see Equation 3.89). However, because this effect size measure must be estimated differently in the random effects case, we denote the ratio $\sigma_\alpha/\sigma_\varepsilon$ as f_{rand} here to remind us of that fact. Using this notation, the ratio of expected mean squares can be expressed simply as $1 + nf_{\text{rand}}^2$.

Sample sizes necessary to achieve a particular level of power to detect a random effect can be determined in a trial-and-error fashion by proposing different values of a, the number of groups, and n, the number of subjects per group. These values determine the critical value of F needed to declare significance at a given α level, and the power of the test is then defined as the probability the observed F will exceed this critical value, i.e.

$$\text{power} = \Pr\{[(1 + nf_{\text{rand}}^2)F] \geq F_{\text{crit}}\}$$

The numerical value of power can be computed easily in either SAS or SPSS. For example, assume one wants to determine the needed sample size for a one-way design in which three levels of a random factor are to be used, tests are to be conducted with a .05 alpha level, and one projects that the standard deviation of the group means in the population is .4 of a within-group standard deviation. To compute power values for several values of n in SPSS, one would first set up a simple data table where each line describes a possible scenario in terms of the size of the study and the size of effect. For example, four variables would be sufficient here as illustrated in the data table below:

a	n	frand	alpha
3	20	.40	.05
3	40	.40	.05
3	60	.40	.05
3	80	.40	.05

Then one can compute the power for each scenario by running the following SPSS syntax file. These commands compute first the value of the ratio of the expected mean squares (denoted "EMSratio"); then the critical value of F (denoted "F_crit" below) resulting from the degrees of freedom implied by the number of groups, a, and the sample size, n, is computed; and finally the resulting power is arrived at by determining the proportion of the appropriate central F distribution (for the specified random effect size) that would be greater than the critical value:

```
compute EMSratio = 1 + n*(frand**2).
compute F_crit = idf.F(1-alpha, a-1, a*n-a).
compute power = 1-cdf.F (F_crit/EMSratio, a-1 , a*n-a).
EXECUTE.
```

These commands would transform the data set to the following:

a	n	frand	alpha	EMSratio	F_crit	power
3	20	.40	.05	4.20	3.16	.48
3	40	.40	.05	7.40	3.07	.66
3	60	.40	.05	10.60	3.05	.75
3	80	.40	.05	13.80	3.03	.80

It may seem surprising with an effect size as large as .4, which we characterized as a large effect size in Chapter 3, that 240 total subjects would be required to achieve a power of .8. There are two reasons for this. First, recall that with random effects the effect size is defined in terms of the variability of the population means over all possible levels of the random factor. In any one study, only a small number (here, three) of these population means are selected, and because the distribution of the variance of this small subset of means is quite positively skewed, most of the time the actual variance among the selected means is less than the mean population variance. The power analysis for random effects must take this into consideration. Second, the power of a random effects design is affected not only by the total number of subjects and the effect size, but also by how many levels of the random factor are used. In situations in which the number of levels of the random factor is discretionary, one can often achieve a higher level of power for a fixed total sample size or achieve the same level of power with a smaller total sample by choosing to use more levels of the random factor. For example, if the 240 total subjects in this scenario had been divided into 8 groups of 30 each, the power would have been .93 instead of .80. Similarly, one could have achieved the same power of .80 arrived at with 240 subjects spread over 3 groups by using 7 groups of 20 each, for only 140 subjects total. Tables showing the optimal number of groups to use for a given projected effect size and total N were developed by Barcikowski (1973) and are presented in abbreviated form in Winer et al. (1991, p. 140). The optimal number of groups can be approximated for a fixed total N by trying different combinations of a and n in SPSS as described previously.

One may wish to estimate the effect size to use in a power analysis from sample data. It is sufficient for most purposes to replace the variance terms in the definition of f_{rand} or in the ratio of expected mean squares by the appropriate estimated variance component. In the case of a one-way random effects design, we saw in the development of the formula for the intraclass correlation for that situation (see Equation 15) that the estimates of the variance terms were $\hat{\sigma}_{\alpha}^2 = (MS_A - MS_W)/n$ and $\hat{\sigma}_{\varepsilon}^2 = MS_W$. This suggests that we could estimate the square of the effect size measure for random effects as follows:

$$\hat{f}_{\text{rand}}^2 = \frac{\hat{\sigma}_{\alpha}^2}{\hat{\sigma}_{\varepsilon}^2} = \frac{MS_A - MS_W}{nMS_W}$$

For example, assume data are available from a three-group pilot study with a random factor which yielded means of 40, 45, and 50 based on 20 subjects per group and found MS_W to be 100. Using standard methods for computing MS_A as $\sum n\hat{\alpha}_j^2/(a - 1)$, we obtain $MS_A = 20(25 + 0 + 25)/2 = 500$, which allows us to compute the square of the estimated effect size as[6]:

$$\hat{f}_{\text{rand}}^2 = \frac{\hat{\sigma}_{\alpha}^2}{\hat{\sigma}_{\varepsilon}^2} = \frac{MS_A - MS_W}{nMS_W} = \frac{500 - 100}{20 \cdot 100} = \frac{400}{2000} = .2$$

Plugging in .4472, the square root of .2, for the value of f_{rand} into an SPSS data set as described previously and trying different values of n, we find that if we restrict our attention to another three-group study, we would need to use 65 subjects per group to achieve a power of .80.

In multifactor designs with both fixed and random factors, including the nested designs we consider later in the chapter, it is possible to arrive at estimates of power for any fixed effects in the design using a slight generalization of the verbal formula we first presented in Chapter 7. There we indicated how the value of ϕ ("phi," the effect parameter used in the Pearson–Hartley power charts based on the noncentral F distribution) could be computed under the assumption that all effects would be tested against MS_{Within}. That was appropriate for fixed effects designs. Now we generalize this to the case in which the error term in the denominator of the F test may be some other mean square, as is the case in designs involving random factors. The more general formulation of ϕ, appropriate for determining the power of fixed effects in such designs, is arrived at simply by replacing the population error variance term, σ_{ε}^2, which was the expected value of MS_{Within}, by the expected value of whatever mean square is appropriate to use as the denominator term for the test of that fixed effect. That is, ϕ may in general be defined as

$$\phi = \sqrt{\frac{\sum_{\text{all obs}} (\text{effect parameter})^2}{(df_{\text{effect}} + 1)\,\mathscr{E}(MS_{\text{denom}})}}$$

To illustrate, if the effect of interest were the fixed factor A in a two-factor mixed design, where the denominator error term used to test A would be MS_{AB}, then the definition of ϕ would be

$$\phi = \sqrt{\frac{\sum_{\text{all obs}} \alpha_j^2}{(df_A + 1)\,\mathscr{E}(MS_{AB})}} = \sqrt{\frac{bn\sum \alpha_j^2/a}{\sigma_{\varepsilon}^2 + n\sigma_{\alpha\beta}^2}}$$

Notice that on the right above we moved the degrees of freedom term into the numerator. This helps to make clear that once the variance components have been estimated, as in Equation 21 for this mixed design, including the component, $\sum \alpha_j^2 / a$, for the fixed effect, the value of ϕ may be readily estimated as

$$\hat{\phi} = \sqrt{\frac{bn \sum \hat{\alpha}_j^2 / a}{\hat{\sigma}_\varepsilon^2 + n \hat{\sigma}_{\alpha\beta}^2}}$$

Power then could be estimated by trying different values of b and n, remembering to use the df appropriate for the interaction term as the denominator df [here $= (a-1)(b-1)$]. If instead of ϕ, one must have the noncentrality parameter λ required by some programs, this may be computed simply from ϕ as $(df_{effect} + 1)\phi^2$. In general, we can define this noncentrality parameter as

$$\lambda = \frac{\sum_{\text{all obs}} (\text{effect parameter})^2}{\mathscr{E}(MS_{denom})}$$

For random effects in multifactor designs, a multiple of the *central F* distribution is used, as we saw for a one-way random effects design. The critical step in being able to compute power is to determine the appropriate multiple to use, which we denoted EMSratio in the SPSS syntax presented previously. The general definition of this multiplier is

$$\text{EMSratio} = \frac{\text{expected value of } MS_{numerator}}{\text{expected value of } MS_{denominator}}$$

Expressions for these expected mean squares for complex designs can be obtained from various sources such as Gaito (1960) or generated using rules explained by Kirk (1994, p. 402ff.) Once you have the expressions for the appropriate mean squares, the estimates of the variance components derived from pilot data can be inserted to arrive at an estimate of EMSratio. Power can then be determined as illustrated previously, again using df appropriate for whatever effects would be in the numerator and denominator of the test.

It should be noted that there are questions regarding the accuracy of these power estimates in *mixed* designs, with the most serious problems concerning the estimates of the power to detect an interaction between a fixed and a random factor (see Koele, 1982; Scheffé, 1959, p. 270ff.; Winer et al., 1991, p. 415). However, what is also clear is that ignoring the presence of a random factor, as some may be tempted to do in an effort to achieve a simpler analysis, can lead to very biased tests and estimates of effects (cf. Murray & Hannan, 1990; Wampold & Serling, 2000). Thus, we believe investigators should be carrying out analyses incorporating the random factors present in their designs, and hope that providing guidance about how to estimate power for such analyses encourages that, even if the power analysis itself is only a rough approximation in mixed designs. Perhaps the most important point to stress is that in designs with random factors, power in general depends on both the number of subjects and the number of levels of the random factor, with the number of levels of the random factor typically being the more critical consideration.

Finally, we remind readers that alternative analysis methods that can accommodate random and nested factors as well as the unequal sample sizes common in field research are presented in Chapters 15 and 16.

DESIGNS WITH NESTED FACTORS

Introduction to Nested Factors

We have opted to discuss random and nested factors in a single chapter. Although they are conceptually distinct, in practice they occur together very often. The conceptual distinctions can be stated simply. Whereas the basic idea of a random factor has to do with how the levels of a factor are selected, the essential idea of a nested factor has to do with how the levels of multiple factors are combined. Also, whereas the basic implication of having a random factor in a design has to do with what error term is appropriate for testing individual effects, the essential implication of having a nested factor in a design has to do with what effects it even makes sense to try to test and interpret in the first place.

A factor is said to be *nested within a second factor* if each level of the first factor occurs in conjunction with only one level of the second factor. Note that nesting in general is not a symmetrical arrangement. Figure 10.3 illustrates a design in which factor B is nested within levels of factor A. Whereas level 1 of factor B occurs in conjunction with only level 1 of factor A, level 1 of factor A occurs in conjunction with both levels 1 and 2 of factor B. As the figure suggests, one way of thinking about nested designs is that they are designs with missing cells.

A factor can also be nested within multiple factors instead of a single factor. A factor is said to be *nested within a combination of other factors* if each of its levels occurs in conjunction with only one combination of levels of the other factors. Figure 10.4 presents the simplest example of this type of design. Factors A and B each have two levels and are crossed with each other so that all possible combinations of levels of these two factors are represented. Factor C is nested within these combinations of levels of factors A and B. Note that there are eight different levels of factor C. If C were to be crossed with A and B, there would be 2 × 2 × 8, or 32, cells in the design. Yet, because of the nesting, we have observations in only eight cells.

That we do not have as many cells as we would in a completely crossed factorial implies that we do not have as many between-cell degrees of freedom and hence that we cannot carry out all the conventional tests of main effects and interactions. Recall that our fullest possible model in terms of means would have one parameter for each of the eight nonvacant cells. Thus, seven independent contrasts, or restrictions, on these eight parameters could be tested. But the conventional test in a three-way design of, say, the main effect of a factor C with eight levels would itself require seven restrictions, which would not leave any available for testing for the effects involving factors A or B.

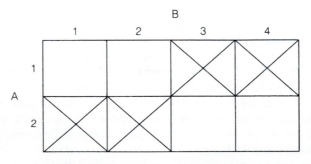

FIG. 10.3.   A simple nested design. Note that factor B is nested within levels of factor A. An × in a cell indicates that no observations are available for that cell.

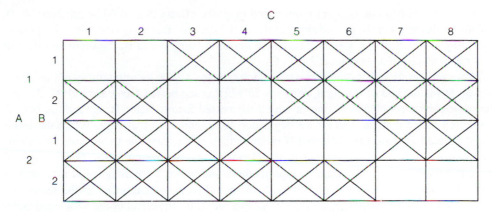

FIG. 10.4.   Nesting within a combination of factors. Note that factor C is nested within combinations of levels of factors A and B, or briefly, within A and B. An × in a cell again indicates the cell is missing.

To determine which effects it makes most sense to test, we return to the simple nested design shown in Figure 10.3 and point out some of the assumptions we make about the nested factor. As indicated in the first half of the chapter, in the behavioral sciences, random factors are sometimes included in a design as a crossed rather than a nested factor. However, if a nested factor is included in a design, it is typically a random factor. Thus, we begin our discussion with the analysis of a two-factor nested design in which the nested factor is random. Second, we assume that the number of levels of the nested factor is held constant across levels of the other factor and that the number of observations per cell is also equal across all cells.[7]

Some reflection on the design shown in Figure 10.3 should convince you that certain of the effects that would be tested in a crossed design cannot be evaluated here. Consider first the interaction between factors A and B. An interaction is indicated by the extent to which the difference between levels 1 and 2 of A at one particular level of factor B is different from that at another selected level of factor B. However, because levels 1 and 2 of factor A do not both occur at any level of B, there is obviously no way in this design to determine the extent to which the difference between them changes across B. A similar statement can be made about the consistency of differences between two levels of the nested factor B. Although multiple levels of B occur at one level of A so that one can compute the difference in their effects at that level of A, levels of B occur in conjunction with only one level of A, so there is nothing to which this difference can be compared. Note that we are not claiming that if levels of B were to be combined with multiple levels of A that there would be no interaction. An interaction may well be present in such a situation. Rather, what is being asserted here is just that we cannot determine whether there is an interaction with this design.

Consider next the main effect of the nested factor. At first glance, it might appear that this may be tested because we could obtain a marginal mean for each level of B and use these to test the restriction that the corresponding population means are all equal. Although such a restriction could be tested, the test would not be simply one of the main effect of B. In the nested design of Figure 10.3, the "marginal" means for B are simply the cell means, because there is only one cell per level of B. Also, the difference between the two levels of B at a_1 and the two levels of B at a_2 may will be affected by the effect of factor A.

What, then, is interpretable? Although the overall main effect of B cannot be assessed, the simple main effect of this nested factor can be assessed within each level of factor A. Tests of these simple main effects could be carried out separately, essentially as one-way ANOVAs.

However, more often one is equally interested in all the effects that could be attributed to B, and thus a single test of the pooled simple effects of the nested factor is performed. (We present an example of such a test shortly.) Thus, the question being asked is, "Is there an effect of factor B at level 1 of A *or* at level 2 of A?"

Now consider the effect of the nonnested factor, factor A. The interpretability of this effect, as well as the method of testing it, depends on whether the nested factor is random. Perhaps the most common situation is one in which the nested factor, factor B, is random, but the nonnested factor is fixed, and so we begin our discussion with that case. When the levels of the nested factor are truly selected at random, then it is reasonable to attribute systematic differences across levels of factor A to the effects of that nonnested factor. For example, if clinical trainees are nested within therapy method, and trainees are assigned at random to a particular method, then over replications there should be no bias induced in the mean of a particular method by the presence of the trainee factor. Thus, the effect of the nonnested factor is interpretable, but consider now how it should be tested. If factor B is random, the population means for the cells within a given level of A vary over replications to the extent that there are simple effects of factor B. If trainees differ from each other, as they certainly will to some extent, then which trainees are selected influences the mean for a given method because it is arrived at by averaging across the trainees using that method. Therefore, even if there were no variability at all among the subjects within a cell nor any effect of factor A (method), we would nonetheless expect the mean of all observations within a particular level of A to vary from one replication to the next because of sampling a different set of levels of B (trainees) to include in that replication. This is very similar to what characterizes the main effect of the fixed factor in a mixed *crossed* design—it can be tested, but one must take into account in the test the fact that the presence of the random factor may influence the apparent effect of the fixed factor. Because the mean square for the fixed, nonnested factor here reflects both population error variance and the effect of the nested random factor, as well as the true effect in the population of the fixed factor, the appropriate error term is the mean square for the simple effects of the random factor because it reflects both of the first two components but not the effect to be tested. This consequence for the expected mean square in the mixed, nested design is shown in the middle of Table 10.7. This table, like Table 10.2 for crossed designs, gives a verbal summary of the different components that appear in the expected mean squares for the different effects in two-factor nested designs.

When both the nested and nonnested factors are random, the same conclusions hold about the interpretability and the kinds of components included in the expected mean squares for the effects. This is indicated on the right side of Table 10.7.

When both the nested and nonnested factors are regarded as fixed, the analysis but not the interpretation is easier. That is, as suggested by the components listed for the fixed design in Table 10.7, because the only component randomly varying over replications is the error

TABLE 10.7

KINDS OF COMPONENTS OF EXPECTED VALUES OF MEAN SQUARES FOR EFFECTS IN SELECTED TWO-FACTOR NESTED DESIGNS (FACTOR B IS NESTED WITHIN LEVELS OF FACTOR A)

	Design		
Effect	*Fixed Effects (Factors A and B both fixed)*	*Mixed (Factor A fixed, Factor B random)*	*Random Effects (Factors A and B both random)*
A	Error and A	Error, B, and A	Error, B, and A
B within A	Error and B	Error and B	Error and B

term associated with individual subjects, the within-cell error is the appropriate error term for testing all effects, because both the nested and nonnested factors reflect only such errors and any true effects of the factor being considered. However, interpretation of the meaning of such a test becomes problematic. If the same, fixed levels of the nested factor were to be used in all replications of the study, one could not know whether the differences across the levels of the nonnested factor were the result of the effects of that factor or the effects of the nested factor. For example, if the same clinical trainees were always paired with a particular therapy method, one would not know if the resulting effects were reflecting the effects of the particular therapists or the method they were using.

To summarize, in a design in which a factor is nested within the levels of a fixed factor, the main effect of the nested factor and its interaction with the other factor cannot be tested. However, the simple main effects of the nested factor can be tested, and the main effect of the nonnested factor can be tested. When the nested factor is random, the appropriate test of the other factor involves using the effect of the nested factor as the denominator term in the test. That is, in designs with nested random factors, their effects intrude on the expected mean squares of the factors within which they are nested. If the nested factor is fixed, interpretation of the test of the nonnested factor is ambiguous.

The impact of nested random factors is something that we have not discussed explicitly in prior chapters. However, it has been implicit in all the F tests we considered in previous chapters. Although it would have been unnecessarily cumbersome to develop tests in this way initially, it is useful now to note that in all of our between-subjects designs we have implicitly been dealing with a random nested factor of subjects. The sampling error resulting from randomly sampling and/or assigning subjects for the groups in a between-subjects design contributed to the variability among the group means. The σ_ε^2 component in the expected mean squares for the effects in a fixed-effects design (see Table 10.3) is there because of a random factor of subjects nested within each of these effects. Some authors—for example, Keppel (1991)— emphasize this by referring to the within-groups source of variance not as error variance but as, for example, S/AB, where the slash notation, which we use as well, indicates that the factor to the left of the slash—in this case, subjects—is nested within combinations of levels of the factors to the right, here factors A and B.

Using B/A to denote the effect of factor B which is nested within levels of A, we show the algebraic expressions for the expected mean squares for examples of two-factor nested designs in Table 10.8. As was the case for the crossed designs discussed earlier in the chapter, we use θ^2 terms to denote the effects of fixed factors and σ^2 terms to denote the effects of

TABLE 10.8

EXPECTED VALUES OF NUMERATORS OF THE TEST STATISTIC FOR EFFECTS IN
SELECTED TWO-FACTOR NESTED DESIGNS (FACTOR B
IS NESTED WITHIN LEVELS OF FACTOR A)

	Design		
Effect	Fixed Effects (Factors A and B both fixed)	Mixed (Factor A fixed, Factor B random)	Random Effects (Factors A and B both random)
A	$\sigma_\varepsilon^2 + bn\theta_\alpha^2$	$\sigma_\varepsilon^2 + n\sigma_\beta^2 + bn\theta_\alpha^2$	$\sigma_\varepsilon^2 + n\sigma_\beta^2 + bn\sigma_\alpha^2$
B within A	$\sigma_\varepsilon^2 + n\theta_\beta^2$	$\sigma_\varepsilon^2 + n\sigma_\beta^2$	$\sigma_\varepsilon^2 + n\sigma_\beta^2$

Note: Results are for a design with a levels of factor A, b different levels of factor B at each level of A, and n subjects per cell. Values given are expectations of the form $\mathscr{E}(MS_{\text{effect}}) = \mathscr{E}[(E_R - E_F)/(df_R - df_F)]$, where the restricted model in each case is arrived at by imposing the restriction on the full model that all effect parameters associated with a particular effect are zero.

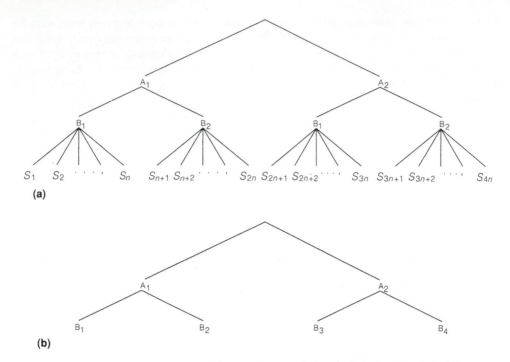

(a)

(b)

FIG. 10.5. Using hierarchical diagrams to represent nested factors. (a) Treating subjects explicitly as a factor nested within combinations of levels of two crossed factors. (b) Factor B nested within levels of factor A. The factor of subjects, which is nested within combinations of levels of A and B, is suppressed.

random factors. We wait to present the precise definitions of these terms until we introduce the models for nested designs in the context of a numerical example, but they are analogous to those presented previously for crossed designs.

One way of schematically representing nested factors that is a useful heuristic for determining the influence of a nested factor on the other effects in the design is the hierarchical diagram shown in Figure 10.5. Figure 10.5(a) shows how what we have treated as a basic two-way crossed design would be represented if subjects were to be treated explicitly as a factor. Nesting is indicated by the fact that the subscripts designating particular subjects are different as one moves from one combination of levels of A and B to another. Although perhaps totally explicit, this seems an unnecessarily complex way of representing a basic 2×2 design. Thus, we do not treat subjects explicitly as a factor until we are forced to do so in Chapters 11 and 12, when we consider repeated measures designs where the subjects factor is crossed with other factors. Figure 10.5(b) presents the hierarchical structure of a basic two-factor nested design, where again the levels of the nested factor are subsumed under the levels of the factor within which it is nested. The variability induced by the nested factor here being a random factor is transmitted upward to all higher levels of the hierarchy, in something of the same fashion that the shaking of the foundations of a physical structure is felt at all higher levels of the structure. This is true both in the upside-down tree structure of Figure 10.5(a), where explicit variability among subjects causes variability among the means of the basic $A \times B$ design, and in Figure 10.5(b), where which levels of factor B are selected at a particular level of factor A would contribute to the variability of the marginal A means over replications.[8]

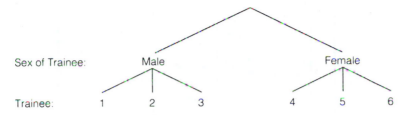

FIG. 10.6. Hierarchical structure of clinical trainee example.

Example

We can expand slightly on the student therapist example of the random-effects section to illustrate a nested design. Assume that the director of the clinic decides to test for a difference across genders in the general severity ratings that graduate students assign to clients. If three male and three female clinical students are randomly selected to participate, and each is randomly assigned four clients with whom to do an intake interview, then we would have a design of the form shown in Figure 10.6 and might obtain data like that shown in Table 10.9. We discuss the analysis of these data as we introduce the relevant model comparisons.

Models and Tests

For this nested design, we could begin by writing our full model in terms of cell means in the same way as we did for a two-way crossed design:

$$\text{Full:} \quad Y_{ijk} = \mu_{jk} + \varepsilon_{ijk} \tag{23}$$

where $j = 1, 2, \ldots, a$ designates levels of factor A; $k = 1, 2, \ldots, b$ designates levels of factor B nested within a level of A; and $i = 1, 2, \ldots, n$ designates subjects in the jkth cell. (Note that we are assuming here that there are an equal number of observations per cell and that the number of levels of the nested factor remains the same across all levels of A.) Although such an approach facilitates thinking about tests of individual contrasts in the cell means, it does not make explicit that the observations are presumed to reflect the effects of two distinct factors. Further, the model does not explicitly suggest the way in which the structure of the design is different than in a crossed design. Thus, one would have to keep in mind that the meaning of the k subscript changes depending on the value of j. For example, as indicated in Table 10.9, level $k = 2$ of the trainee factor refers to a different trainee when $j = 1$ (males) than when $j = 2$ (females). Finally, because the nested factor is often random, we will need to refer to particular effects in designating appropriate error terms, as we did in the other designs earlier in this chapter involving random factors. For these reasons, we prefer to state our models here in terms of the effects of the two factors:

$$Y_{ijk} = \mu + \alpha_j + \beta_{k/j} + \varepsilon_{ijk} \tag{24}$$

Here, the familiar α_j term as usual reflects the effect of being at the jth level of factor A and may be defined as the extent to which the population marginal mean for level j of factor A deviates from the grand mean, that is, $\alpha_j = \mu_j - \mu$. For example, α_1 indicates the extent to which the mean rating given by male trainees differs from the mean rating for the entire population of all possible trainees. The notation, $\beta_{k/j}$, for the effect of the nested factor is new. We need a new approach because, as discussed, it is not possible to assess the main effect of the nested

TABLE 10.9

DATA AND ANALYSES FOR CLINICAL TRAINEE EXAMPLE

I. General Severity Ratings

| | | Male $j=1$ | | | | | | | | Female $j=2$ | | | | | |
| | Trainee 1 $k=1$ | | | Trainee 2 $k=2$ | | | Trainee 3 $k=3$ | | | Trainee 4 $k=1$ | | | Trainee 5 $k=2$ | | | Trainee 6 $k=3$ | |
i	Cl	Rating	i	Cl	Rating	i	Cl	Rating	i	Cl	Rating	i	Cl	Rating	i	Cl	Rating
1	a	49	1	e	42	1	i	42	1	m	53	1	q	44	1	u	58
2	b	40	2	f	48	2	j	46	2	n	59	2	r	54	2	v	63
3	c	31	3	g	52	3	k	50	3	o	63	3	s	54	3	w	67
4	d	40	4	h	58	4	l	54	4	p	69	4	t	64	4	x	72
$\bar{Y}_{jk}$:		40			50			48			61			54			65
$\bar{Y}_{j.}$:					46									60			
$\hat{\beta}_{k/j}$:		−6			+4			+2			+1			−6			+5
$\sum_i (Y_{ijk} - \bar{Y}_{jk})^2$:		162			136			80			136			200			106

II. Test of Simple Effects of Trainee

$$E_F = \sum_j \sum_k \sum_i (Y_{ijk} - \bar{Y}_{jk})^2 = 162 + 136 + 80 + 136 + 200 + 106 = 820 = SS_W$$

$$E_R - E_F = \sum_{\text{all obs}} (\hat{Y}_{jk_F} - \hat{Y}_{jk_R})^2 = \sum_j \sum_k \sum_i \hat{\beta}_{k/j}^2 = \sum_j \sum_k n \hat{\beta}_{k/j}^2 = 4[(-6)^2 + 4^2 + 2^2] + 4[1^2 + (-6)^2 + 5^2]$$

$$= 4(36 + 16 + 4) + 4(1 + 36 + 25) = 4(56) + 4(62) = 224 + 248 = 472 = SS_{B/A}$$

$$F = \frac{(E_R - E_F)/(df_R - df_F)}{E_F/df_F} = \frac{SS_{B/A}/df_{B/A}}{SS_W/df_W} = \frac{472/4}{820/(24-6)} = \frac{118}{820/18} = \frac{118}{45.56} = 2.59, \text{ n.s.}$$

500

III. Test of Main Effect of Gender

$$E_R - E_F = \sum_{\text{all obs}} (\hat{Y}_{jk_F} - \hat{Y}_{jk_R})^2 = \sum_j \sum_k \sum_i \hat{\alpha}_j^2 = bn \sum_j (\bar{Y}_{j.} - \bar{Y})^2$$

$$= 3 \cdot 4[(46 - 53)^2 + (60 - 53)^2] = 1176 = SS_A$$

$$F = \frac{(E_R - E_F)/(df_R - df_F)}{SS_{B/A}/df_{B/A}} = \frac{SS_A/df_A}{472/4} = \frac{1176/1}{118} = 9.97, \, p < .05$$

IV. Source Table

Source	SS	df	MS	F	p	Denom. Term
A (Gender)	1176	1	1176	9.966	.034	B/A
B/A (Trainee within Gender)	472	4	118	2.590	.072	Within
Within	820	18	45.556			

factor nor its interaction with the other factor in this design. Instead, we include a component in the model indicating the simple effect of the kth level of factor B at the jth level of factor A, that is, among all those possible levels of factor B that could have occurred at a given level of factor A, how much difference does being at this particular level of B make? Algebraically, the $\beta_{k/j}$ parameters may be defined as the difference between a population cell mean and the population marginal mean for the level of the nonnested factor where this cell appears, that is,

$$\beta_{k/j} = \mu_{jk} - \mu_{j.}$$

To illustrate, in our example, $\beta_{3/2}$ indicates the extent to which the mean rating that would be given by the third female clinical trainee deviates from the mean for the population of all female trainees.

　To test the effect of the nested factor, given we are asssuming here it is a random factor, is to test the null hypothesis that the variance of the β effects, σ_β^2, is 0. Given our full model stated in terms of effects in (24), we can accomplish this by comparison with a model incorporating the restriction that the simple effects of the nested factor are all 0, or that

$$\beta_{k/j} = 0 \quad \text{for all } j \text{ and } k \tag{25}$$

Because we are using this notation for simple effects for the first time, a few words about the meaning of such restrictions might be helpful. Thinking of A as the row factor and B as the (nested) column factor (as in the schematic diagram in Figure 10.3), Equation 25 is saying that there are no simple effects of the column factor in any row. This is equivalent to asserting in our example that all three population means in row 1 are equal, as are all the population means in row 2:

$$\mu_{11} = \mu_{12} = \mu_{13}$$
$$\mu_{21} = \mu_{22} = \mu_{23} \tag{26}$$

Thus, Equation 25 implies four independent restrictions on the population cell means, two at each level of factor A. We can carry out an omnibus test of these restrictions by comparing the full model with a restricted model from which the β parameters have been eliminated:

$$\text{Restricted:} \quad Y_{ijk} = \mu + \alpha_j + \varepsilon_{ijk} \tag{27}$$

　Least squares estimates of the parameters can be arrived at by substituting observed cell and marginal means for the corresponding population values. In the full model we would have

$$\hat{\alpha}_j = \hat{\mu}_{j.} - \mu = \overline{Y}_{j.} - \overline{Y}$$
$$\hat{\beta}_{k/j} = \hat{\mu}_{jk} - \hat{\mu}_{j.} = \overline{Y}_{jk} - \overline{Y}_{j.} \tag{28}$$

Note that combining the parameter estimates appropriate for the full model yields the cell means

$$\hat{Y}_{jk_F} = \hat{\mu} + \hat{\alpha}_j + \hat{\beta}_{k/j} = \overline{Y} + \overline{Y}_{j.} - \overline{Y} + \overline{Y}_{jk} - \overline{Y}_{j.} = \overline{Y}_{jk}$$

The parameter estimates for the restricted model are the same except that the β parameters are constrained to be 0. When combined, these estimates yield as predictions the marginal means for the nonnested factor

$$\hat{Y}_{jk_R} = \hat{\mu} + \hat{\alpha}_j = \overline{Y} + \overline{Y}_{j.} - \overline{Y} = \overline{Y}_{j.}$$

The sum of squared errors for the full model is thus based on deviations from the cell means and is SS_W, as usual. The difference in the sum of squared errors for the two models can be expressed in terms of the differences in the models' predictions, or as

$$E_R - E_F = \sum_{\text{all obs}} (\hat{Y}_{jk_F} - \hat{Y}_{jk_R})^2 = \sum_j \sum_k \sum_i (\overline{Y}_{jk} - \overline{Y}_{j.})^2$$

Because this difference for each observation is the value of $\hat{\beta}_{k/j}$ (see Equation 28), the numerator SS for our test of the effect of the nested factor, which is denoted $SS_{B/A}$ to indicate B is nested within levels of A, reduces simply to the sum over all observations of the estimated effect parameters squared, that is,

$$SS_{B/A} = \sum_j \sum_k \sum_i \hat{\beta}_{k/j}^2 = \sum_j \sum_k n\hat{\beta}_{k/j}^2$$

Note also that at each level of j one is computing the sum of squared deviations of cell means from an average of the cell means in exactly the same fashion as was done in a one-way ANOVA (see Chapter 3, Equation 56). Thus, the sum of squares for the nested factor can be thought of as the pooling of the sums of squares from multiple one-way ANOVAs. Or, to use the same notation for simple effects we introduced in discussing two-way designs (see Chapter 7, Equation 41), and apply this to the current example in which we have just two levels of A:

$$SS_{B/A} = \sum_{j=1}^{a} SS_{BwA_j} = SS_{BwA_1} + SS_{BwA_2}$$

Solutions for our numerical example are shown below the data in Table 10.9. Sum of squares within, or E_F, of course is just the sum of squared deviations of the individual observations around the cell means. The sum of squares for the effect of the nested factor of Trainee, which is arrived at by squaring the estimates of the simple effect parameters $\beta_{k/j}$ and summing over all observations, can be viewed as the combining of the sum of squares for the simple effect of Trainee among males ($SS_{BwA_1} = 224$) and the sum of squares for the simple effect of Trainee among females ($SS_{BwA_2} = 248$). We will have more to say about degrees of freedom shortly, but for the present it suffices to note that in the full model here, we estimated as many independent parameters as we had cells (i.e., 6), whereas in the restricted model we estimated only as many parameters as we had levels of the gender factor (i.e., 2). Thus, the denominator degrees of freedom is the number of independent observations minus the number of parameters estimated in the full model, or $24 - 6 = 18$, and the numerator degrees of freedom is the difference in the number of parameters required by the two models, or $6 - 2 = 4$. The observed F value of 2.59 obtained using these degrees of freedom and the calculated sums of squares is compared against a critical value of $F(4, 18) = 2.93$, and thus is nonsignificant at $\alpha = .05$.

The test of the main effect of gender is a test of the restriction that $\alpha_j = 0$, or equivalently that the marginal mean for male trainees is the same as that for females, $\mu_{1.} = \mu_{2.}$. We wish to determine the increase in error resulting from imposing such a restriction on the full model.

Thus, the test of the main effect of the nonnested factor compares the models

$$\text{Full:}\quad Y_{ijk} = \mu + \alpha_j + \beta_{k/j} + \varepsilon_{ijk}$$

$$\text{Restricted:}\quad Y_{ijk} = \mu + \beta_{k/j} + \varepsilon_{ijk}$$

(29)

We saw earlier that the predictions for this full model are the cell means. The predictions for the restricted model now differ from the cell means just by the estimated value of the gender effect, $\hat{\alpha}_j$:

$$\hat{Y}_{jk_R} = \hat{\mu} + \hat{\beta}_{k/j} = \overline{Y} + (\overline{Y}_{jk} - \overline{Y}_{j.}) = \overline{Y}_{jk} - (\overline{Y}_{j.} - \overline{Y}) = \overline{Y}_{jk} - \hat{\alpha}_j$$

Thus, the sum of squares for the A main effect reduces to a multiple of the squared estimated effects, as was the case in both one-way and multifactor crossed designs (see, for example, Equation 3.78 or 7.26):

$$E_R - E_F = \sum_{\text{all obs}} (\hat{Y}_{jk_F} - \hat{Y}_{jk_R})^2 = \sum_j \sum_k \sum_i \hat{\alpha}_j^2 = bn \sum_j \hat{\alpha}_j^2$$

The numerator of our test as usual is based on this difference in the errors of our two models over the difference in their degrees of freedom. (The only slight precaution we would offer is that you just need to be careful to use the number of levels per nest for the value of b, not the total number of different levels of factor B included in the design. Thus, although the present example involves 6 different clinical trainees, the value of b is 3, the number of trainees of each gender.) As we argued earlier, however, it is necessary to compare this against something other than mean square within. As Table 10.8 suggests, the mean square for the effect of the random nested factor has the exactly appropriate expected value to allow an isolation of the effect of the factor within which it is nested. Using the mean square for the nested factor as the denominator in the test of the main effect of the nonnested factor is illustrated in part III of Table 10.9. Notice that, although the numerator involves the usual $a - 1$, or $2 - 1 = 1$ degrees of freedom, the denominator term now involves only 4 degrees of freedom; thus, the critical F required to claim significance at the .05 level is $F(1, 4) = 7.71$. In the present test, our observed F exceeds this value, and we conclude, given the pattern of means, that female trainees give significantly higher severity ratings than do male trainees.

It may be disconcerting at first that the test of the fixed factor here is based on so few denominator degrees of freedom and that this would remain unaffected by the number of clients that each trainee rates. However, the question asked at this top level of the hierarchy is one appropriately answered by reference to the variability observed at the next highest level. That is, the question of whether male trainees rate differently from female trainees is appropriately answered by reference to the variability among trainees and by taking into consideration how many trainees were sampled.

Degrees of Freedom

Although it is always the case that one can determine the degrees of freedom associated with an effect by taking the difference between the number of parameters in the two models being compared in a test of that effect, it is convenient to have some simple rules for determining degrees of freedom. We saw in crossed factorial designs (cf., the summary in Table 8.11 for the general three-way A $\times$ B $\times$ C design) that the degrees of freedom for the main effect of a factor is one less than the number of levels of that factor and that the expressions for the degrees of freedom for main effects can simply be multiplied to determine the degrees of freedom for interactions. Thus, in a two-factor crossed design in which factor A has a levels and factor B has b levels, the A and B main effects have $a - 1$ and $b - 1$ degrees of freedom, respectively, and their interaction has $(a - 1)(b - 1)$ degrees of freedom. These three sources exhaust the between-group degrees of freedom in a two-factor design with ab cells, that is,

$$df_A + df_B + df_{AB} = (a - 1) + (b - 1) + (a - 1)(b - 1)$$
$$= a - 1 + b - 1 + ab - a - b + 1$$
$$= ab - 1$$

In a two-factor nested design, for example, B/A, in which there are b levels of the nested factor at each of the a levels of the other factor, we would still have ab groups total and $ab - 1$ between-group degrees of freedom, but these are divided up differently. The main effect of the nonnested factor still has $a - 1$ degrees of freedom as usual. But, the degrees of freedom for the nested factor involve a pooling of degrees of freedom from the simple effects, in the same way that the sums of squares for B/A was the cumulation of the SS for the various simple effects of B. As noted, the B/A effect essentially involves the pooling the results of multiple one-way ANOVAs. In our numerical example, the effect of Trainee within Gender was strictly equivalent to computing first the sum of squares for trainees as in a one-way ANOVA of the differences among the three male trainees, which would have been based on $3 - 1$ or 2 df and then combining it with the comparable sum of squares from a one-way ANOVA of the differences among the three female trainees, which also would have had $3 - 1$ or 2 df. In general, we would have $b - 1$ df for each of the a levels of factor A, and so pooling these results in a total of $a(b - 1)$ degrees of freedom for the B/A effect:

Source	df
B within A_1	$b-1$
B within A_2	$b-1$
B within A_3	$b-1$
$\vdots$	$\vdots$
B within A_a	$b-1$

$$SS_{B/A} = \sum_{j=1}^{a} SS_{BwA_j} \quad df_{B/A} = \sum_{j=1}^{a} (b - 1) = a(b - 1)$$

Thus, in a two-factor nested design, the two effects also exhaust the between-group degrees of freedom[9]

$$df_A + df_{B/A} = (a - 1) + a(b - 1)$$
$$= a - 1 + ab - a$$
$$= ab - 1$$

In general, the simple rule for computing degrees of freedom then is that, for crossed effects, one takes the product of terms equal to 1 less than the number of levels of each factor involved in the effect, but in a nested effect, which we indicate with a slash (e.g., B/A), one still computes a product but without subtracting one from the number of levels for any factor appearing to the right of the slash.

Statistical Assumptions and Related Issues

In introducing Table 10.8, we mentioned that we would give definitions of the terms used in the expected mean squares once we had introduced our models that included nested effects for the first time. The values of the expected mean squares depend on what we assume about the terms in our model. In our full model,

$$Y_{ijk} = \mu + \alpha_j + \beta_{k/j} + \varepsilon_{ijk} \qquad \text{(24, repeated)}$$

when A and B are both assumed to be fixed effects, the α and β terms would be fixed constants over replications. As before, the components of our expected mean squares are functions of the squared effect parameters—summed over all levels of the effect and divided by the degrees of freedom of the effect. For a fixed, nonnested factor A, the component would again be denoted θ_α^2 and be defined as

$$\theta_\alpha^2 = \frac{\sum\limits_j \alpha_j^2}{a - 1}$$

However, for a fixed, nested factor we would have different effects at each level of the nonnested factor, in which case the component would be defined as

$$\theta_\beta^2 = \frac{\sum\limits_j \sum\limits_k \beta_{k/j}^2}{a\,(b - 1)}$$

When a factor is random, the corresponding effect parameters are assumed to be normally distributed with a mean of zero and a variance denoted by a σ^2 term. For a random, nonnested factor, this variance just depends on how much each of the a population marginal means deviate from the grand mean, $\alpha_j = \mu_{j.} - \mu$. For a random nested factor, we actually have a different sets of deviations of population cell means from population marginal means, that is, $\beta_{k/j} = \mu_{jk} - \mu_{j.}$. The novel assumption now encountered for the first time is that these β terms have the same amount of variability at each level of factor A. When we compute and use in our tests a single mean square for estimating the pooled effect of the nested factor, we are implicitly assuming homogeneity of variance, in that we are assuming that the variability among $\beta_{k/j}$ terms is the same at each level of j.

Theoretically, such an assumption of homogeneity of variance could be tested using procedures such as O'Brien's (1981) test described in Chapter 3, with cell means at a given level of factor A replacing individual observations. However, if the number of levels of the nested factor is small, as is often the case, one may have very little power for detecting a difference in the variance estimates that are estimating the different simple effects of the nested factor. Nonetheless, it may be appropriate to carry out an adjusted test of the main effect of the nonnested factor, such as a Welch test, which does not require homogeneity of variance, because the adjustment in degrees of freedom could make a nontrivial difference in the critical value for the test, again because degrees of freedom are small. To illustrate, if the variability in the ratings of female trainees relative to male trainees in the data in Table 10.7 were as large as 100 to 1, O'Brien's test for heterogeneity of variance might not approach significance, for example, $F < 2$ and $p > .25$. Yet if one were to go ahead and use a Welch-adjusted test of the nonnested factor, the denominator df in such a case might be 2 rather than 4 as in the unadjusted test, which would increase the F critical value required to claim significance at $\alpha = .05$ from 7.73 to 18.49.

As mentioned, although the nested factor is typically random, it is not mandatory that it be so. For example, one might carry out a two-factor design, similar to what we have just discussed, in a clinic in which there were only three male and three female psychologists involved in treatment delivery. If one's interest is simply in generalizing to the typical performance of these six individuals, then both the effect of therapist gender and the effect of therapist nested within gender would be treated as fixed. In this case, the expected mean square for the effect of both the nested and the nonnested factor would involve only within-cell error and a term reflecting the true effect in the population of that factor. Thus, as in the fixed-effects designs we considered in previous chapters, MS_W can be used as the denominator term for all effects, assuming homogeneity of variance.

Another consideration in assuming fixed effects is that the analysis can proceed when there are unequal n or unequal numbers of levels of the nested factor in different nests. Although analyses with unequal n, as we saw in Chapter 7, yield different results when carried out with different types of sums of squares, at least some exact tests may be carried out (but see Searle, 1994). However, designs with unequal n involving random effects do not yield exact solutions with standard least squares approaches. In such cases, approximate tests may be constructed, but are not developed here. Fortunately, SPSS can compute these approximate tests. And, as Searle commented in a related context, "the approximations may be of some use. Furthermore, they utilize the relatively easy arithmetic of the analysis of variance method, which is sometimes advantageous in face of the greater complexity of other analyses" (1971, p. 431). We survey some of the more complex approaches that have been developed in recent years in Chapter 16.

Follow-up Tests and Confidence Intervals

When significant effects are found for one of the factors in a nested design, it is often of interest to construct confidence intervals around the differences in means or even around the individual means themselves as well as carrying out follow-up tests of contrasts of interest for factors with more than two levels. It is again the case that the appropriate error term to use in these intervals and tests is the denominator term used in the test of the relevant overall effect. In our clinical trainee example, to construct a confidence interval around the magnitude of the gender difference, one would use the mean square for the random nested factor of trainee to determine the precision of this difference. Thus, we would have

$$(\overline{Y}_{1.} - \overline{Y}_{2.}) \pm \sqrt{F_{(.05;1,df_{\text{denom}})}}\sqrt{MS_{\text{denom}}\left(\frac{1}{n_{1+}} + \frac{1}{n_{2+}}\right)}$$

but now MS_{denom} would be $MS_{B/A}$. Substituting the numerical values from Table 10.9 and using $F_{(.05;1,4)} = 7.71$ yields

$$(46 - 60) \pm \sqrt{7.71}\sqrt{118\left(\frac{1}{12} + \frac{1}{12}\right)}$$

or limits of -26.314 and -1.686 around a point estimate of male trainees having a mean rating 14 points below that of females.

We illustrate a simultaneous follow-up-test procedure by comparing the mean rating of the last two female trainees in our data. Because pairwise follow-up comparisons would likely be performed only within genders, one might define the set of possible comparisons of interest as the 3 pairwise comparisons among male trainees and the 3 pairwise comparisons among female trainees. Because the comparisons of interest are this subset of all possible comparisons among 6 means, this is one time where the Bonferroni adjustment would be preferable to a Tukey adjustment for paired comparisons. The Bonferroni critical F value from Table A.3 for 6 comparisons with 18 df would be 8.78. The confidence interval on the difference in the mean ratings of the last two trainees would thus be

$$(54 - 65) \pm \sqrt{8.78}\sqrt{45.556\left(\tfrac{1}{4} + \tfrac{1}{4}\right)}$$

or -11 ± 14.140, which contains 0, indicating the difference between these two trainees is nonsignificant.

Strength of Association in Nested Designs

Measures of proportion of variance accounted for may be computed for nested designs in similar fashion to other designs. There is some question about which partial measure is most meaningful, but otherwise computations are fairly straightforward.

To illustrate with the Gender effect in our numerical example, the proportion of sum of squares total $(1176 + 472 + 820 = 2468)$ accounted for by this factor in the sample was $R^2 = 1176/2468 = .476$, whereas the conventional assessment of $R^2_{partial}$ would be

$$R^2_{partial} = \frac{SS_A}{SS_A + SS_W} = \frac{1176}{1176 + 820} = \frac{1176}{1996} = .589$$

There is some justification, however, for considering the partial effect of gender relative to the error variability induced by individual trainees, rather than relative to the variability among ratings given individual clients. By this logic, SS_W is replaced by $SS_{B/A}$ in the previous formula, yielding

$$R^2_{partial} = \frac{SS_A}{SS_A + SS_{B/A}} = \frac{1176}{1176 + 472} = \frac{1176}{1648} = .711$$

This is the way in which SPSS assesses the magnitude of this effect, which it now refers to as *partial eta squared*, in its Univariate General Linear Model procedure. If one wants to assess the proportion of the variability among the mean ratings of the individual *trainees* assigning the ratings that is accounted for by their gender, then this is the appropriate measure. One should just keep in mind, however, that this may not be representative of the proportion of variability in the ratings given individual *clients* that is accounted for by the gender of the rater.

The population estimates of variability accounted for again require that one have estimates of the variance components associated with the various effects in the design. The estimates may be derived from the expected mean squares for the specific nested design, and are presented in Table 10.10 for various two-factor designs. For our numerical example, these variance

TABLE 10.10
ESTIMATES OF VARIANCE COMPONENTS FOR TWO-FACTOR DESIGNS WITH NESTING

Effect	A & B both Fixed	A Fixed, B Random	A & B both Random
Error	$\hat{\sigma}_\varepsilon^2 = MS_W$	$\hat{\sigma}_\varepsilon^2 = MS_W$	$\hat{\sigma}_\varepsilon^2 = MS_W$
B/A	$\dfrac{\sum_j \sum_k \hat{\beta}_{k/j}^2}{ab} = \dfrac{(b-1)}{b}\dfrac{(MS_{B/A} - MS_W)}{n}$	$\hat{\sigma}_\beta^2 = \dfrac{MS_{B/A} - MS_W}{bn}$	$\hat{\sigma}_\beta^2 = \dfrac{MS_{B/A} - MS_W}{bn}$
A	$\dfrac{\sum_j \hat{\alpha}_j^2}{a-1} = \dfrac{(a-1)}{a}\dfrac{MS_A - MS_W}{bn}$	$\dfrac{\sum_j \hat{\alpha}_j^2}{a-1} = \dfrac{(a-1)}{a}\dfrac{MS_A - MS_{B/A}}{bn}$	$\hat{\sigma}_\alpha^2 = \dfrac{MS_A - MS_{B/A}}{bn}$

components would be estimated as follows:

$$\frac{\sum \hat{\alpha}_j^2}{a} = \frac{(a-1)}{a}\frac{(MS_A - MS_W)}{bn} = \frac{(2-1)}{2 \cdot 3 \cdot 4}(1176 - 118) = \frac{1058}{24} = 44.083$$

$$\hat{\sigma}_\beta^2 = \frac{MS_{B/A} - MS_W}{n} = \frac{118 - 45.556}{4} = 72.444/4 = 18.111$$

$$\hat{\sigma}_\varepsilon^2 = MS_W = 45.556$$

Thus, the estimate of the overall and partial $\hat{\omega}^2$ values for the effect of the gender factor would be

$$\hat{\omega}_A^2 = \frac{\sum \hat{\alpha}_j^2/a}{\sum \hat{\alpha}_j^2/a + \hat{\sigma}_\beta^2 + \hat{\sigma}_\varepsilon^2} = \frac{44.083}{44.083 + 18.111 + 45.556}$$

$$= \frac{44.083}{107.750} = .409$$

and

$$\hat{\omega}_{A,\text{partial}}^2 = \frac{\sum \hat{\alpha}_j^2/a}{\sum \hat{\alpha}_j^2/a + \hat{\sigma}_\varepsilon^2} = \frac{44.083}{44.083 + 45.556}$$

$$= \frac{44.083}{89.639} = .492$$

As suggested previously, not only tests of other effects, but the estimates of the magnitude of their effects, such as those we have just considered, can also be considerably biased by ignoring nested random factors in one's analysis. Wampold and Serlin (2000) demonstrate that, under plausible scenarios such as where the random nested factor has an intraclass correlation of .3, ignoring the presence of such a factor not only can lead to a three-fold or greater inflation of Type I error rates, but estimates of the strength of association of the fixed nonnested factor such as $\hat{\omega}^2$ can be twice as large as they should be.

Using Statistical Computer Programs to Analyze Nested Designs

You may have noted that it is possible to use the same notation for the levels of a nested design as we used with a crossed factor (see Equation 23). Although it is critical to keep the nesting in mind in deciding which effects to test and, when the nested factor is random, how these effects should be tested, at a superficial level there are similarities to a crossed design as long as the number of levels of the nested factor stays the same across all "nests." In particular, the total number of groups is then the product of the maximum values of the subscripts used to designate levels of the various factors in both crossed and nested designs.

A pragmatic implication of this fact is that one can specify the factors, whether nested or crossed, involved in a problem in the same way in the initial description of a design in most computer programs. For example, as of this writing, the first line of syntax for SPSS's MANOVA procedure could be

```
MANOVA Y BY THERAPY (1, 2), TRAINEE (1, 3)/
```

regardless of whether trainees were nested within or crossed with therapies. The nesting would affect only the list of which effects are to be tested indicated on the DESIGN statement, for example,

```
DESIGN = THERAPY VS 1, TRAINEE WITHIN THERAPY = 1 VS WITHIN/
```

Although perhaps confusing at first glance because WITHIN has two meanings on this line, the first indicating nesting and the second within-cell error, it is clearer once it is recalled that VS is used to indicate the denominator term to be used in testing a particular effect.

Nesting may be indicated using SAS's PROC GLM by using parentheses on the MODEL statement to indicate nesting. For example, in a design with two factors designated "a" and "b," a model statement of the form:

```
model y = a b(a);
```

could be used to request a test of the pooled simple effects of b within a. If the nested factor is random, then the test of factor a would require a "test" statement, which we introduced in our discussion of computer syntax earlier in the chapter. Here one could request that the mean square for the nested random factor be used as the denominator error term in testing the effect of factor a with a line after the model statement of the form

```
test H = a E = b(a);
```

Many programs can also generate expected mean squares, but the model used to generate these may differ from that developed here, at least for mixed designs. This is the case for those generated using SPSS's Variance Components routine or for those generated by SAS either through the RANDOM statement in PROC GLM or through the separate NESTED or VARCOMP procedures.

The expected mean squares, however, are rarely of interest in themselves. Typically, they are of interest only as a means of determining what error term is appropriate as the denominator in the test of a particular effect. This step of consulting tables of expected mean squares, however, can be bypassed entirely in most cases where an exact test of an effect exists, by following a fairly simple set of rules for deciding on an error term. It is to such a set of decision rules that we now turn.

Selection of Error Terms when Nested Factors are Present

The rules stated in the discussion of selection of error terms at the beginning of this chapter, when the concern was with crossed random factors, must be elaborated to accommodate designs

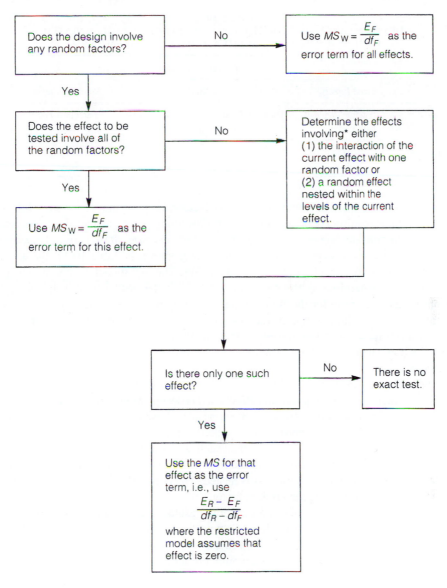

Does the design involve any random factors?

No → Use $MS_W = \dfrac{E_F}{df_F}$ as the error term for all effects.

Yes ↓

Does the effect to be tested involve all of the random factors?

No → Determine the effects involving* either (1) the interaction of the current effect with one random factor or (2) a random effect nested within the levels of the current effect.

Yes ↓

Use $MS_W = \dfrac{E_F}{df_F}$ as the error term for this effect.

Is there only one such effect?

No → There is no exact test.

Yes ↓

Use the MS for that effect as the error term, i.e., use
$$\frac{E_R - E_F}{df_R - df_F}$$
where the restricted model assumes that effect is zero.

* See text for interpretation of these rules in designs that involve both nesting and more than two factors.

FIG. 10.7.   Flowchart to assist in the selection of appropriate denominator terms for tests of effects in crossed or nested designs.

involving nesting. The basic issue with nested designs, as we have seen, is that the variability induced by a random nested factor in a hierarchical design is transmitted up to all higher levels of the hierarchy. Previously we had said that, in mixed or random crossed designs, tests of effects not involving all random factors should use as a denominator term the interaction of that effect with a random factor, assuming there is only one such interaction effect. Now we must place "having a random factor nested under the effect to be tested" on a par with "having an interaction of the effect to be tested with a random factor." This is done in Figure 10.7, a flowchart to help one select the correct error term in nested designs.

TABLE 10.11
DENOMINATOR TERMS FOR TESTING EFFECTS IN TWO-FACTOR NESTED
DESIGNS (FACTOR B IS NESTED WITHIN LEVELS OF FACTOR A)

	Design			
	Fixed Effects	*Mixed*		*Random Effects*
Effect	(Factors A and B both fixed)	(Factor A fixed, Factor B random)	(Factor A random, Factor B fixed)	(Factors A and B both random)
A	MS_W	$MS_{B/A}$	MS_W	$MS_{B/A}$
B/A	MS_W	MS_W	MS_W	MS_W

In the case of nested designs involving only two factors, applying the rules is straightforward. Table 10.11 shows resulting denominator terms for the four possible such designs. We consider these briefly in turn, starting on the left. In the fixed-effects case, MS_W is used because there are no random factors present. In the other three cases shown in Table 10.11, the answer to the first question in the flowchart of Figure 10.7 is Yes. The first mixed design, in which only the nested factor is random, is the most common two-factor nested design. In this case, in determining the error term for the A effect, the answer to the second question of whether the effect involves all random factors in the design is No, and following the rules presented in the flowchart, we determine that the B/A effect qualifies for consideration and eventually for selection as the denominator term. MS_W is used for testing B/A because that effect involves all the random factors.

The second mixed design of Table 10.11 in which the nested factor is fixed is the one most seldom encountered. For both A and B/A effects in this design, MS_W is used as the denominator term because there are no other random effects besides those involved in the specification of these effects. Note that, in answering the flowchart's question, "Does the effect to be tested involve all of the random factors?" for an effect such as "B/A," a factor is said to be involved in the effect to be tested even if it appears to the right of the slash, that is, even if it is merely the factor within which the factor of interest is nested. Thus, in this sense, the B/A effect would here be judged to "involve" A, the random factor.

The final case, in which both factors are random, results in selecting B/A as the denominator term for A because B/A is the one random effect nested within levels of the effect to be tested. In the case of the test of B/A, both random factors are involved in the effect, which leads to the selection of MS_W as the appropriate denominator term.

Complications That Arise in More Complex Designs

In general, regardless of the complexity of a design, the only contributors to the expected mean square of an effect besides the effect itself are interactions with random factors or random nested effects. This general principle leads to the two categories of effects identified in the box on the right of the flowchart in Figure 10.7 that is used to determine potential error terms other than MS_W. In this section, we develop how these criteria are to be interpreted in more complex designs that involve both nesting and more than two factors.

We adopt certain conventions of notation to facilitate our discussion. In working with complex designs, it helps to have a way of designating very briefly which of the factors are random rather than fixed. Thus, in the following discussion, we continue to designate factors by single letters but adopt the convention (cf. Keppel, 1982) of using lowercase letters to designate random factors and capital letters to designate fixed factors. Also, when a factor is nested within combinations of levels of multiple other factors, we use parentheses to explicitly group the factors within which the nesting is occurring. So, for example, we denote a design (like that shown in Figure 10.4) in which factor C is nested within combinations of levels of factors A and B as $C/(A \times B)$, instead of $C/A \times B$, which might be misinterpreted to mean that C is nested within A but crossed with B. If the nested factor is random, the designation would be $c/(A \times B)$.

We are now ready to offer caveats regarding how to interpret both specifications (1) and (2) in the flowchart in order to determine which effects might qualify as a potential error term for testing a particular effect. First, consider what "(1) the interaction of the current effect with one random effect" might mean in the context of different three-factor designs. In a completely crossed $A \times B \times c$ design (that is, where factor c is random and factor A and B are fixed), the interpretation is straightforward: If you want to test the AB interaction, the ABc interaction qualifies as a potential error term. However, in nested designs, where instead of sources corresponding to all possible interactions we have certain nested interactions, specification (1) must be interpreted as having a broader application.

To illustrate, consider a three-factor design where a random factor c is nested in A but crossed with B, a design we could denote as $B \times c/A$. In order to test the AB interaction, Bc/A must be judged, for present purposes, to be an interaction of the effect to be tested with a random factor. Although Bc/A is not strictly speaking an interaction of AB with c, the basic concern is that some interaction with a random effect might intrude on the effect of interest. A few moments reflection reveals that a Bc/A interaction, if present, would indeed influence the means bearing on an AB interaction. Specifically, note that, at each level of A, if there is an interaction in the population between B and c, which levels of c are sampled would affect the magnitude of the B marginal means at that level of A. And, because different levels of c are sampled for each level of A, the B means would be affected differentially across levels of A, thus contributing to the AB interaction.

Before formulating this into a more general rule, we need to point out another aspect of the nested interactions that can occur in higher order designs. In particular, consider now the test of the B main effect in the $B \times c/A$ design. As we just noted, at each level of A, any Bc interaction in the population would cause the marginal means for the levels of B to be affected by which c levels are selected. By the same logic we discussed in the first half of this chapter, the test of the main effect of the fixed factor B appropriately uses the interaction of the fixed factor with a random factor as an error term—the only difference in this nested design is that we can pool or average several simple $B \times c$ interactions to get a more stable estimate of the magnitude of the interaction of the fixed and random factor. So the B effect would also be tested by comparison with the Bc/A effect. To summarize, rule (1) for determining potential error terms might be restated as: "Determine the effects denoting an interaction involving the factor(s) in the current effect and one random factor," but it must be understood that one or more of the factors in the effect to be tested, as well as additional fixed factors, can appear in the potential error term simply as factor(s) within which an interaction with a random factor is nested. (Expressing this search for a potential error term in a very literal way, you are looking for an effect specified by a set of letters that includes all the letters in the effect to be tested plus one additional lowercase letter—extra capital letters on the right of the slash can be ignored, and some of the original letters can be on the right side of the slash, but the new lowercase letter must be on the left side of the slash.)

Now moving to the other category of potential error terms, namely "(2) a random effect nested within the levels of the current effect," we must offer an additional caveat: How this is interpreted in higher order designs depends on the context, that is, on whether other factors in the design are fixed or random. To develop the rationale for this, let us consider four different designs in which a random factor c is nested within combinations of levels of two other factors, at least one of which is fixed, as shown in Table 10.12. Our primary interest is in the error term

TABLE 10.12
SOURCES AND ERROR TERMS FOR FOUR DESIGNS IN WHICH
A RANDOM FACTOR IS NESTED WITHIN COMBINATIONS
OF LEVELS OF TWO OTHER FACTORS

Design	Source	Error Term
1. c/(A × B)	A	c/(AB)
	B	c/(AB)
	AB	c/(AB)
	c/(AB)	Within
2. c/(A × b)	A	Ab
	b	c/(Ab)
	Ab	c/(Ab)
	c/(Ab)	Within
3. c/B/A	A	c/B/A
	B/A	c/B/A
	c/B/A	Within
4. c/b/A	A	b/A
	b/A	c/b/A
	c/b/A	Within

appropriate for testing the fixed, nonnested factor A. In the first case of a c/(A × B) design, in which the other nonnested factor B is also fixed, the only source of random variability besides subjects is the random selection of levels of factor c. Put differently, the fixed levels of B do not inflate the expected mean square of the A effect any more than they do in a two-factor, fixed-effects design. Thus, although c/(AB) is a random factor nested within combinations of levels of both the current fixed factor and another fixed factor, it is the appropriate error term for testing factor A. Similar to what we saw in our consideration of rule (1), extra capital letters to the right of the slash, like the B in c/(AB), can be ignored in determining an appropriate error term.

In the second design of Table 10.12, that is, c/(A × b), the other nonnested factor besides factor A is random. This means that the marginal means for factor A are perturbed both by the presence of random factor c at a lower level of the hierarchy and also by any interaction with random factor b. Once again, the A × b cell means are made more variable by the random selection of levels of c, but now when we consider the A main effect, the random factor b contributes additonal variability over and above that resulting from random selection of levels of c. Thus, in the c/(A × b) design, Ab is the appropriate error term for testing the A effect. So, in interpreting rule (2) as it applies to the test of A for these first two designs, we see that c/(AB) must be considered a random effect nested within the levels of the current effect, whereas c/(Ab) should not be. Stated in more explicit terms, rule (2) must be understood to mean: "Determine the effects involving a random effect nested directly within the levels of the current effect or *within combinations of levels of the current effect and of a fixed factor(s)*."

A similar result obtains in the case of the last two designs in Table 10.12, in which random factor c is nested within levels of one factor, which in turn in nested within levels of another. When the factor in the intermediate level of the hierarchy is fixed, it does not contribute to the expected mean square of factor A, but it does when it is random. Thus, in determining potential error terms for use in a test of A, c/B/A is listed as a random factor nested within levels of the current effect, whereas c/b/A would not be. Stating the expanded rule literally, we are again looking for effects involving the letters used to specify the current effect plus one additional lowercase letter—with the understanding that additional capital letters appearing to the right of any slash can be ignored, but extra lowercase letters on the right of a slash cannot be.

To illustrate these rules with some concrete variations on our previous examples, assume now that samples of therapists (factor t) are drawn randomly from various clinics in a study of the effectiveness of various treatment modalities (M). How to combine such factors in a design is not just an abstract point. Frequently, in applied clinical studies, it is a real concern whether therapists and sites should be crossed with or nested within treatment modalities. The issues are the familiar ones of construct and internal validity, and usually it is a matter of "choosing your poison," because there are no perfect solutions. For example, if, in the interests of construct validity of your treatment modality implementation, you want to use as the therapist for each modality someone who believes that modality to be the most effective approach, then therapists would necessarily be confounded with modalities, which threatens the internal validity of your study. A partial solution in this situation is to have multiple therapists nested within each modality and use, at least in a design in which these were the only two factors, variability among therapists within modalities as an error term for assessing the modality effect. However, you might think it better just to have each therapist provide all treatment modalities to avoid such confoundings of the differences between therapists with modalities. This may be better for internal validity, but now construct validity would likely be threatened, because each therapist is plausibly biased toward a particular modality and the effectiveness of a modality may depend on the proportion of therapists you have in your sample who are biased toward that particular modality. Again in a two-factor design, one would want in such a case to use an indicator of the extent to which a modality's effectiveness depended on the therapist administering it (i.e., the modality × therapist interaction) as the error term for assessing the modality effect. Although the substantive issues may be clear enough to dictate one design rather than another (e.g., in some situations potential carryover effects of delivering one treatment might preclude an individual from administering another fairly), the particular error term appropriate for testing the effect of most interest in a given design is also relevant and can be affected by the presence of a third factor. We consider several possible arrangements of the three factors of therapists, clinic, and modality in Table 10.13.

In the first design, assume the clinics (c) to be included in the study are sampled randomly as well as the therapists (t) within the clinics. A design of this structure might be arrived at

TABLE 10.13
SOURCES AND ERROR TERMS FOR VARIOUS THREE-FACTOR
DESIGNS INVOLVING NESTED FACTORS

Design	Source	Error Term
1. t/(M × c)	M	Mc
	c	t/Mc
	Mc	t/Mc
	t/(Mc)	Within
2. t/(M × C)	M	t/MC
	C	t/MC
	MC	t/MC
	t/(MC)	Within
3. t/c/M	M	c/M
	c/M	t/c/M
	t/c/M	Within
4. M × t/C	C	t/C
	t/C	Within
	M	Mt/C
	MC	Mt/C
	Mt/C	Within

as a result of a decision that equal numbers of therapists from each clinic should be asked to use each of the modalities (M). That is, each therapist, perhaps in the interests of internal validity, is asked to use just one modality, but all modalities are represented at each of the clinics. Thus, modalities would be crossed with clinics, and therapists would be nested within clinic–modality combinations. This structure can be indicated briefly by the notation t/(M × c). Assume that observations are collected on n clients for each therapist in the study. The sources to be tested in such a design are then M, c, Mc, and t/(Mc). The investigator would probably be most interested in the first of these effects, that is, the modality main effect, but could test the others as well. Considering these in reverse order and in light of the flowchart of Figure 10.7, the nested effect of therapists, t/(Mc), involves both the random effects and so could be tested against MS_W. The modality by clinic interaction, Mc, does not involve all the random effects, and so one looks for and finds as an error term a random effect nested within the levels of the Mc effect, namely t/Mc. Similarly, the clinic main effect, c, does not involve all the random factors, and as we explained in the discussion of how rule (2) in the flowchart is to be interpreted, t/Mc, is accepted as the error term for testing c, because it qualifies as a random effect nested within combinations of levels of the current effect (c) and a fixed factor (M). Finally, the effect of most interest, the modality main effect, is evaluated using as an error term its interaction with the random factor of clinics, according to rule (1). The nested random effect, t/(Mc), cannot be used because, given our expanded statement of rule (2), it is not a random effect nested directly within modalities or within combinations of modalities and the levels of a fixed factor. The sources of variability of interest and the corresponding denominator error terms to be used in testing each of these effects is indicated for this design at the top of Table 10.13.

Next, consider what would happen if there were only three clinics to which you wished to generalize, and you include them all in your study so that it can be regarded as a fixed factor. In this second case, therapists (t) would be the only random factor in a three-factor design, t/(M × C), having the same kind of nesting as before. The tests for the three effects other than modality would be carried out similarly to the previous design, with MS_W being used to test the nested effect of therapists and t/(MC) being used to test the clinic main effect and the modality by clinic interaction. However, in the test of treatment modalities, t/(MC) would now be the appropriate denominator term, because therapists are nested within combinations of modality and the additional fixed effect of clinics.

Finally, two other designs are shown in the table as well. In some situations, there is a concern of contamination of an experimental design as a result of communication between groups of subjects who are receiving different treatments. To avoid this, sometimes it is necessary for all subjects in a given locale to receive the same kind of treatment. One way that might be effected in our current example would be for clinics to be nested within modalities. Thus, the third design assumes that all therapists in a clinic use the same modality and that each modality is implemented in multiple clinics, with therapists and clinics both being randomly sampled and, again, n clients being observed per therapist. This means that not only are therapists nested within clinic–modality combinations, but that clinics are nested within modalities—a design structure we may denote t/c/M. Note that in the case of the test of modalities, c/M is the error term of choice because it is the one random effect nested directly within modalities. The nested effect of clinics in this completely hierarchical design would reflect both the random variation induced by sampling clinics as well as that induced by the random factor of therapists lower in the hierarchy. In terms of our expanded rule (2), t/c/M is excluded from consideration as an error term for factor M because its designation includes more than one additional random effect.

The fourth design reflects the situation in which, to avoid a confounding of therapists with modalities, each therapist is asked to use all modalities. Therapists might still be randomly sampled from three fixed clinics. We designate the structure of this design M × t/C. The two nested effects in this design, therapists within clinics and the modality by therapist interaction within clinics, involve all the random factors in the design and so would be tested against MS_w. The clinic main effect does not involve a random factor, but would be tested against the random factor of therapists nested directly within its levels, t/C. The error terms for the modality main effect and modality by clinic interaction would be selected according to the expanded rule (1), with Mt/C, the average of several simple interactions of the fixed factor of modality with the random factor of therapist, in each case qualifying as "an interaction involving the factor(s) in the current effect and one random factor." Applying this rule in terms of the letters involved in the effects, in the test of M, we accept Mt/C as an interaction with M, because the extra capital C to the right of the slash can be ignored, and in the test of MC, we accept Mt/C because the C counts as being involved, even though it is to the right of the slash.

One very important variation on this last design is one in which there is only a single observation in each cell. For example, assume in the M × t/C design that only one client is treated by each therapist–modality combination. You will see in the next two Chapters 11 and 12 that this yields a design of essentially the same structure as a repeated measures design. And thus, the analysis of such repeated measures designs can be approached, at least from one perspective, as the analysis of designs involving a random factor that is crossed with one or more fixed factors and nested within others. The methods developed in this chapter provide the rationale for the traditional approach to the analysis of repeated measures designs, which we take up next.

EXERCISES

1. True or False: In a one-factor design, whether the factor is fixed or random does not affect the way in which the test of that factor is carried out.

2. True or False: In a two-factor mixed design, the test of the effect of the fixed factor is carried out in the same way it would be in a fixed-effects design.

3. True or False: The numerator and denominator of the F statistic should have the same expected value if the null hypothesis is true.

4. True or False: When the null hypothesis is false, the expected values of the numerator and denominator of the F should differ only by the component associated with the effect being tested.

5. True or False: That some of the factors in a design are nested renders uninterpretable certain of the effects that normally would be tested if all of the factors in the design were completely crossed.

6. Explain intuitively why, in a mixed design, the presence in the population of an interaction between a random and a fixed factor inflates the estimate of the main effect of the fixed factor.

*7. Dr. R. U. Normal has obtained data from 45 subjects to compare three methods of therapy: rational–emotive therapy (RET), client-centered therapy (CCT), and behavior modification (BMOD). Three therapists were used; each therapist treated five clients with each method of therapy. Assume the following ratings of the effectiveness of the therapy were obtained.

		Therapist		
		1	*2*	*3*
	RET	40, 42, 36, 35, 37	40, 44, 46, 41, 39	36, 40, 41, 38, 45
Method	*CCT*	42, 39, 38, 44, 42	41, 45, 40, 48, 46	41, 39, 37, 44, 44
	BMOD	48, 44, 43, 48, 47	41, 40, 48, 47, 44	39, 44, 40, 44, 43

a. Dr. Normal analyzed these data as a one-way design, completely ignoring "therapist." What did he find?

b. Dr. I. M. Skewed analyzed these data as a two-way design, treating both factors as fixed. His primary interest was in the method main effect. Was it statistically significant?

c. Dr. Kurtosis also analyzed these data as a two-way design, but she treated the "therapist" factor as random. What did she find? Was the method main effect statistically significant?

d. How do the sums of squares for the method main effect compare in parts a, b, and c?

e. How do the error terms for testing the method main effect compare in parts a, b, and c?

f. Does it seem sensible that Skewed and Kurtosis obtained different results? Why or why not?

8. As a follow-up to Exercise 7, assume Dr. Kurtosis wants to compute measures of effect for these data. Recall that Dr. Kurtosis analyzed these data as a two-factor, mixed design with a fixed factor of Method and a random factor of Therapist.

a. Compute both the sample values and population estimates of percentage of variance accounted for by the two main effects and interaction, reporting both overall and partial measures (see Table 10.6 for an example).

b. Dr. Kurtosis is struck by how different some of the estimates of association strength computed in part a turned out to be. She wonders which of these is the right answer to particular questions. For example, she reasons that therapist characteristics are an unavoidable factor whenever these therapies are delivered, and she wants to know if these three methods of therapy were used with the population of all qualified therapists, what proportion of the variance in the therapy effectiveness ratings would the Methods factor be expected to account for? Which of the measures of association strength computed in part a is the best answer to this question?

c. Dr. Skewed says his primary interest is in the Therapist factor, and that he concludes the Method factor is not really an inherent part of the Therapist effect, reasoning that this Therapist factor would have an effect even if all therapists were using only a single Method. Assuming then that Method is treated as an extrinsic factor (see Chapter 7), which of the measures of association strength is the best estimate of the proportion of variance in therapy effectiveness ratings that the Therapist factor would be expected to account for?

9. For the current exercise, you are to analyze the blood pressure data presented in Table 8.12. However, to adapt things for this chapter, we presume that the fixed factors of biofeedback and diet are crossed with a random factor of research assistant instead of a fixed factor of drug. Thus, assume the data are as follows:

	Biofeedback			No Biofeedback		
	Research Assistant 1	Research Assistant 2	Research Assistant 3	Research Assistant 1	Research Assistant 2	Research Assistant 3
Diet Absent						
170	186	180	173	189	202	
175	194	187	194	194	228	
165	201	199	197	217	190	
180	215	170	190	206	206	
160	219	204	176	199	224	
158	209	194	198	195	204	
Diet Present						
161	164	162	164	171	205	
173	166	184	190	173	199	
157	159	183	169	196	170	
152	182	156	164	199	160	
181	187	180	176	180	179	
190	174	173	175	203	179	

a. Perform an ANOVA on these data, adjusting appropriately for the presence of a random factor of Research Assistant.

b. Compare the results of your tests with those reported in Table 8.14, in which all factors were assumed fixed [compare your results of tests involving the Research Assistant factor with those involving what was called "B (drug)" in Table 8.14]. Which tests are unchanged? Why?

c. Consider how you might characterize the magnitude of the biofeedback effect with these data. Using sample values, what proportion of the variance in this set of data is accounted for by the biofeedback main effect? How does this value compare with the partial version of the proportion of variance accounted for by this factor? In a three-factor design such as this, computation of overall estimated population values of proportion of variance accounted for in general requires estimation of a number of different variance components, but computation of the *partial* estimated population proportion of variance accounted for can be done only with the estimation of the variance components for error and for the effect of interest. As usual, $\hat{\sigma}_\varepsilon^2 = MS_W$, and the expression for the partial population proportion of variance accounted for by factor A in a three-factor design is still (see Equation 22):

$$\hat{\omega}_{A,\text{partial}}^2 = \frac{\sum \hat{\alpha}_j^2 / a}{\sum \hat{\alpha}_j^2 / a + \hat{\sigma}_\varepsilon^2}$$

What is your estimate and interpretation of $\hat{\omega}_{A:\text{ partial}}^2$ for the Biofeedback factor here?

*10. Assume that a master's degree student plans to investigate the effectiveness of listening to different types of tape recordings as a way of helping children cope with the discomfort of dental procedures. In particular, she wants to see whether listening to children's music or to children's stories is more effective, and whether any advantage that does occur is consistent across two procedures: teeth cleaning and filling cavities. There obviously are any number of tape recordings that could be used in the study. She selects three musical and three story tapes for investigation from published lists of children's tapes. She proposes to use a total of 60 children in her study and to randomly assign an equal number of children to each possible combination of a tape and a dental procedure.

One of the student's master's thesis committee members says that he likes her basic design, but he is concerned about the power of the test of the factor of kind of tape. He wants her to run twice as many subjects so that she would have more degrees of freedom in the denominator of her test of this effect; this would result in her being able to claim significance at a lower critical value of F.

a. Describe the design and the appropriate analysis:

(1) Diagram the design and label the basic structure, specifying any nesting

(2) List all testable effects and indicate for each whether it is fixed or random

(3) For each testable effect, indicate its degrees of freedom and the appropriate error term and the degrees of freedom of the error term.

b. On the basis of your answer to part a, suggest how the student should respond (in a positive, constructive manner, of course) to her master's thesis committee member.

11. A management consultant firm has developed a new method of conducting workshops that they believe has a number of advantages over the already established procedure. They want to evaluate the relative effectiveness of the two methods. However, there is one problem: They offer workshops on a wide variety of topics (e.g., on-the-job training, productivity, selection) and do not want to expend a great deal of resources on the evaluation. Therefore, they decide to concentrate on their three most popular workshop categories (topics) and for each category conduct 4 workshops, 2 using the new method and 2 using the old method (resulting in a total of 12 separate workshops). Assume that 11 subjects participate in each workshop.

a. Indicate the structure of the design; then for each effect, determine the appropriate error term. Indicate the degrees of freedom associated with each effect and error term.

b. A critic observes that the critical value of the F test for the methods effect is so large that it will be difficult in this design to achieve significance. Do you agree? Why? If you do agree, what could be done to remedy the problem?

*12. A researcher is interested in comparing two different concept-formation tasks, one involving a disjunctive concept and the other involving a conjunctive concept, under two conditions of informative feedback—either immediate knowledge of results or knowledge of results that is delayed by 10 s. The researcher realizes that concept learning problems differ considerably from each other in difficulty, and so he decides to use a variety of problems selected from those used in previously published research in order to increase the external validity of his study. Four different problems are selected for use in conjunction with each of the two types of concept-formation tasks. Presented below are the mean numbers of errors made before reaching a performance criterion. Each cell mean is based on the performance of the two subjects randomly assigned to that condition.

	Mean Errors to Criterion					
Concept:	*Disjunctive*			*Conjunctive*		
Feedback:	*Immediate*	*Delayed*			*Immediate*	*Delayed*
Problem 1	3	3	Problem 5	1	2
Problem 2	3	5	Problem 6	1	1
Problem 3	2	6	Problem 7	4	5
Problem 4	4	6	Problem 8	0	2

a. Describe the structure of the design, indicating whether factors are crossed or nested, fixed or random. If a factor is nested, indicate the factor(s) within which it is nested.
b. List the effects that can be tested in this design and the appropriate denominator error term for each.
c. Perform an ANOVA to test the effects you listed in part b. Assume that MS_W is 5.0.

13. Assume you are hoping to submit a grant proposal to investigate dose–response relationships in a psychopharmacological study of depression, planning to pursue your work in New Mexico, where psychologists were recently granted prescription privileges. From the range of acceptable dosages of your favorite antidepressant, you select three dosages at random for investigation. Four psychologists are available for the study and you regard them as representative of the pool of psychologists who might eventually be granted prescription privileges. Each psychologist in your pilot study prescribes each of the three dosage levels to five of his or her depressed clients. When scores on a depression scale are gathered at the end of the study and analyzed, the following mean squares are obtained, with the associated degrees of freedom shown in the following table.

Effect	*MS*	*df*
drug	3.0	2
psychologist	2.0	3
drug × psychologist	1.0	6
Within	1.0	48

a. Carry out appropriate tests of both of the main effects and interaction.
b. Using the mean squares given, compute estimates of the variance components associated with the two main effects, the interaction and within-group error.
c. Use the variance components computed in part b to estimate values of the intraclass correlation for each of the effects in the design.
d. Assume in your grant proposal you want to project the sample size required to achieve a particular level of power for detecting an effect of the drug dosage factor. As a first step, how could you express algebraically the ratio of the mean squares for the numerator and denominator terms that would be involved in the test of this factor? How could this ratio be expressed if you were to

substitute the numerical values of your variance components as estimates of the variances in the expected mean squares?

e. (Requires use of the computer.) Assuming you were to continue with a sample of four psychologists in your study, how many subjects would each of these have to treat in order to achieve a power of .80 for detecting the drug effect at an alpha of .05? If you were able to recruit a total of eight psychologists to participate in your study, how many subjects would each need to treat to achieve a power of .80?

III

Model Comparisons
for Designs Involving
Within-Subjects Factors

The method of pairing [a variation of a within-subjects design] . . . illustrates well the way in which an appropriate experimental design is able to reconcile two desiderata, which sometimes appear in conflict. On the one hand we require the utmost uniformity in the . . . material, which is the subject of experiment, in order to increase the sensitiveness of each individual observation, and, on the other, we require to multiply observations so as to demonstrate so far as possible the reliability and consistency of the results.

—SIR RONALD A. FISHER, *DESIGN OF EXPERIMENTS*

11

One-Way Within-Subjects
Designs: Univariate Approach

All the designs we have considered to this point share a common characteristic: there has been a single observed value of the dependent measure for each subject. As a consequence, to test the existence of a treatment effect, we compared scores between different groups of subjects. For this reason, the designs we have encountered so far are often referred to as *between-subjects designs*.

In contrast, this chapter considers designs in which two or more measures are obtained for each subject in the study. Thus, with this type of design, we can test the existence of a treatment effect by comparing the several different scores obtained within a group of subjects. Not surprisingly, a common name given to this type of design is *within-subjects designs*. Another term often used in the psychological literature to describe this design is a *repeated-measures design*, because two or more measures are collected for each subject.

The repeated-measures design constitutes the second major building block of experimental design. Most designs used in psychology represent some combination of the repeated-measures design and the between-subjects design. Thus, this chapter is very important because it sets the stage for most of the more complex designs encountered in psychological research. These more complex designs are discussed in Chapters 12 and 14.

PROTOTYPICAL WITHIN-SUBJECTS DESIGNS

Before considering the data analysis of within-subjects designs, we briefly introduce some typical situations where a repeated-measures design might arise. Specifically, three different types of situations lead to a repeated-measures design.

The first situation is one in which each subject or unit of analysis is observed in *a* different treatment conditions. The same behavioral measure would be used as the dependent variable in each condition. For example, suppose that a physiological psychologist is interested in the differential effects of two drugs. Drug A might be thought to increase aggressive behavior and Drug B to decrease aggressive behavior. Perhaps the population in which the drugs are to be tested is pairs of rhesus monkeys, with a score giving the total number of aggressive behaviors by either monkey during an observation period being a single measure for the pair. (In this case, the pair is the unit of analysis.) Almost certainly there will be pronounced differences between pairs of monkeys in the amount of aggressive behavior that would be observed normally. To prevent these between-pair differences from inflating the error term used to assess the effects of the drugs, the investigator might use a design in which each pair experienced both drugs. Half the pairs of subjects might both be given Drug A and then be observed for the period of time the drug is expected to be active; later, the same pairs of subjects would all receive Drug B and again have their aggressive behavior observed. The other half of subjects would also experience both drugs, but in reverse order. Thus, the same measure of aggressive behavior would be taken twice for each unit. This type of design is frequently referred to as a *crossover design*, especially in medical research, because each subject literally crosses over from one treatment to the other during the course of the experiment. Such a repeated-measures design allows an assessment of the effects of the drugs in which the differences across pairs in average level of aggressiveness would not influence the magnitude of the error estimate at all. This capability of achieving a more sensitive design by preventing individual differences from contributing to the error variance is typically the primary motivation for selecting a within-subjects design.

A second situation that produces a repeated-measures design occurs when scores on each of *a* different tests are collected for each subject. For example, scores on the MMPI Psychasthenia Scale and the MMPI Depression Scale might be obtained for a group of individuals. Repeated-measures ANOVA could be used to test for a difference in the means of these two scales for the population from which this sample was drawn. In general, for the results of such a comparison to be meaningful, the two tests (or subtests) must be comparably scaled. In other words, the comparison of the two MMPI scales is meaningful because both scales were constructed so as to have a mean of 50 and a standard deviation of 10 in the norm group. However, a comparison of the MMPI Schizophrenia Scale and the Wechsler Adult Intelligence Scale (WAIS) for a group of subjects would be meaningless because the tests are not comparably scaled. Although there is nothing in the statistical machinery to prohibit such a comparison, the results would have no psychologically meaningful interpretation.

The third situation to be considered is that some aspect of a subject's behavior may be measured at two or more different times. For example, a developmental psychologist might be interested in how performance on a certain task changes with a child's age. The performance of a group of children might be measured every 6 months from the time a child is 18 months old until he or she is 36 months old. Notice that such a design implies a longitudinal study, whereas the between-subjects design corresponds to a cross-sectional study. We also point out that a not so unusual consequence of longitudinal designs is the problem of missing data. A researcher who plans to measure a group of children every 6 months between the ages of 18 and 36 months is truly fortunate if every child can, in fact, be measured at every time point. In reality, some amount of missing data is likely in such a situation. Statisticians have developed a variety of models for attempting to make valid inferences in the face of missing data. One very useful approach, based on multilevel modeling (also called *hierarchical linear modeling*) is presented in Chapter 15. Another viable approach is multiple imputation, developed largely by Rubin and colleagues (Rubin, 1987; Little & Rubin, 1987). Shadish, Cook, and Campbell (2001) provide an excellent overview of methods for addressing attrition in the context of estimating treatment effects.

A few more words regarding terminology are appropriate here. First, some authors prefer to restrict "repeated measures" to the third situation, in which the same individual is literally measured repeatedly across time. With this terminology, all three situations involve "within-subjects" designs, but only the third is characterized as repeated measures. Our preference is to consider any of the three possibilities to be repeated-measures designs. Second, situations such as the second, in which *a* test scores are compared, are often referred to as *profile analysis*, because a basic goal of the study is to assess the mean profile of subjects' scores on these tests. Finally, the repeated-measures design is closely related to the randomized-block design. In the general case of this design, na subjects are divided into n blocks of a subjects each. Subjects are then assigned (randomly, if possible) to the a treatment conditions within each block. When $a = 2$, the design is often called a *matched-pairs design*. The repeated-measures design can be conceptualized as a randomized-block design where within each block there are a replicates of the same subject.

ADVANTAGES OF WITHIN-SUBJECTS DESIGNS

At this point, we briefly mention two of the advantages of a within-subjects design. First, more information is obtained from each subject in a within-subjects design than in a between-subjects design. This is obviously true, because in the within-subjects design, each subject contributes a scores, whereas in the between-subjects design, each subject contributes only one score on the dependent variable. As a result, the number of subjects needed to reach a certain level of statistical power is often much lower in within-subjects designs than in between-subjects designs. When the cost of obtaining subjects is high (in terms of money, time, or effort), the within-subjects design has a distinct advantage in this regard.

Second, as mentioned previously, because comparisons in the repeated-measures design are made within subjects, variability in individual differences between subjects is removed from the error term. In essence, each subject serves as his or her own control in the within-subjects design, reducing the extraneous error variance. The effect is very similar to that for ANCOVA in a randomized experiment. In both cases, the practical implication is that statistical power can be increased by using each subject as his or her own control.

Notice that the net effect of each advantage of the within-subjects design is to increase power for a fixed number of subjects, or, alternatively, to allow a desired level of power to be reached with fewer subjects than would usually be required in a between-subjects design. In fact, a formula (presented later in this chapter) shows explicitly that both advantages combine to make the within-subjects design more powerful than a corresponding between-subjects design.

We hasten to add that the within-subjects design also possesses a number of potential disadvantages. A full discussion of the choice between repeated-measures and between-subjects designs is premature until procedures for analyzing repeated-measures data have been presented. Thus, we now turn to issues of data analysis. Once this presentation is complete, we return to the issues involved in choosing between the two types of design.

ANALYSIS OF REPEATED-MEASURES DESIGNS WITH TWO LEVELS

The Problem of Correlated Errors

We begin the investigation of how to analyze repeated-measures designs by considering the simplest possible case, namely, the situation in which there are only two levels of the repeated factor. Consider the data displayed in Table 11.1. (Ignore the column labeled e for the moment.) Six subjects have been observed under each of two treatment conditions, yielding 12 scores in all on the dependent variable. How might we determine whether the population mean for Condition 1 differs from the population mean for Condition 2?

First, consider the model we used in Chapter 3 for the one-way between-subjects design:

$$Y_{ij} = \mu + \alpha_j + \varepsilon_{ij} \tag{1}$$

TABLE 11.1
DATA FOR A TWO-LEVEL
REPEATED-MEASURES DESIGN

Subject	Treatment Condition	Y	e
1	1	8	0
	2	10	0
2	1	3	−5
	2	6	−4
3	1	12	4
	2	13	3
4	1	5	−3
	2	9	−1
5	1	7	−1
	2	8	−2
6	1	13	5
	2	14	4

TABLE 11.2
PATTERN OF e_{ij} VALUES
FOR DATA IN TABLE 11.1

Subject	e_{i1}	e_{i2}
1	0	0
2	−5	−4
3	4	3
4	−3	−1
5	−1	−2
6	5	4

where Y_{ij} is the score on the dependent variable for the ith subject in the jth condition, μ is the grand mean parameter, α_j is the effect associated with the jth condition, and ε_{ij} is the error for the ith subject in the jth condition. It turns out that there is a special need here to focus on ε, the error term. Recall from Chapter 3 that the analog in the sample to the population value of ε_{ij} is given by

$$e_{ij} = Y_{ij} - \overline{Y}_j \qquad (2)$$

for a one-way design, where the treatment condition means $\overline{Y}_1$ and $\overline{Y}_2$ are here 8 and 10, respectively. The last column of Table 11.1 displays the values of e_{ij} for these hypothetical data. Careful inspection of these error values shows a striking pattern. As can be seen more clearly from Table 11.2, subjects with positive errors (Y scores above the treatment-condition mean) for Condition 1 also have positive errors (Y scores above the treatment-condition mean) for Condition 2: the same is true of negative errors (scores below the mean). Specifically, the correlation between e_{i1} and e_{i2} can be shown to equal 0.96 here. Although it is conceivable that this correlation is a chance occurrence in the sample and unrepresentative of the population as a whole, it seems more plausible to conclude that a correlation exists in the population.[1] In other words, ε_{i1} and ε_{i2} are likely correlated because a subject who achieves a high score in one condition is also likely to achieve a relatively high score in the other condition. If ε_{i1} and ε_{i2} are indeed correlated, we have a problem. Remember from Chapter 3 that a basic ANOVA assumption is that errors must be independent from one another. However, correlation implies dependence, so this assumption is violated whenever ε_{i1} and ε_{i2} are correlated. Two further points should be made here. First, ε_{i1} and ε_{i2} are correlated in almost *every* repeated-measures study. For most behavioral phenomena, there are systematic individual differences between subjects, creating a correlation between the errors. Second, in general, ANOVA is not robust to violations of the independence assumption. For these reasons, we need to employ different data-analysis procedures for the within-subjects design than we used in the between-subjects design.

Reformulation of Model

There are several ways we might modify the model of Equation 1 to make it appropriate for a within-subjects design. We illustrate the modification that is most straightforward for the special case of a two-level factor. We see later that this modification also provides a foundation for the multivariate approach to be presented in Chapter 13.

Let's reexamine the model represented by Equation 1:

$$Y_{ij} = \mu + \alpha_j + \varepsilon_{ij} \qquad \text{(1, repeated)}$$

We could write this model in two parts as

$$Y_{i1} = \mu + \alpha_1 + \varepsilon_{i1} \qquad (3)$$

for Treatment Condition 1, and as

$$Y_{i2} = \mu + \alpha_2 + \varepsilon_{i2} \qquad (4)$$

for Condition 2. Suppose that we were to subtract Equation 3 from Equation 4. The result would be

$$Y_{i2} - Y_{i1} = \alpha_2 - \alpha_1 + \varepsilon_{i2} - \varepsilon_{i1} \qquad (5)$$

The following substitutions could now be made: D_i for $Y_{i2} - Y_{i1}$, μ for $\alpha_2 - \alpha_1$, and ε_i for $\varepsilon_{i2} - \varepsilon_{i1}$, yielding

$$D_i = \mu + \varepsilon_i \qquad (6)$$

as a new model for the data. D_i represents the difference between the scores obtained in the second and first conditions for the ith subject, μ represents the difference between the effects of the second and first conditions, and ε once again represents error. Notice that the original model of Equation 1 was based on two scores from each subject, whereas the model of Equation 6 requires only one score per subject. As a consequence, each subject contributes only one observation of ε, removing the dependency among the errors in Equation 1.

The null hypothesis of Equation 1 was written

$$H_0 : \alpha_1 = \alpha_2 = 0 \qquad (7)$$

Because μ is defined to be $\alpha_2 - \alpha_1$, the equivalent null hypothesis for Equation 6 is thus

$$H_0 : \mu = 0 \qquad (8)$$

The corresponding restricted model is given by

$$D_i = 0 + \varepsilon_i \tag{9}$$

or just

$$D_i = \varepsilon_i \tag{10}$$

To test the null hypothesis, least-squares estimates can be obtained, and the sum of squared errors compared as before. The procedure is very simple, because the model in Equation 6 contains only one parameter and the model in Equation 9 (or, equivalently, Equation 10) has no parameters. In Equation 6, the least-squares estimate of μ is given by $\overline{D}$, so that

$$E_F = \sum_i (D_i - \overline{D})^2 \tag{11}$$

In Equation 9, each estimated score is zero, yielding

$$E_R = \sum_i (D_i - 0)^2 = \sum_i D_i^2 \tag{12}$$

The difference between E_R and E_F is easier to find if we first rewrite E_F as

$$E_F = \left(\sum D_i^2 \right) - n\overline{D}^2 \tag{13}$$

Then,

$$E_R - E_F = n\overline{D}^2 \tag{14}$$

Recall from previous chapters that the expression for the F test statistic is in general given by

$$F = \frac{(E_R - E_F)/(df_R - df_F)}{E_F/df_F}$$

Making the appropriate substitutions for the problem at hand,

$$F = \frac{n\overline{D}^2/[n - (n - 1)]}{\left[\left(\sum D_i^2 \right) - n\overline{D}^2 \right]/(n - 1)} \tag{15}$$

which reduces to

$$F = \frac{n\overline{D}^2}{s_D^2} \tag{16}$$

where

$$s_D^2 = \frac{\sum D_i^2 - n\overline{D}^2}{n - 1} \tag{17}$$

is the unbiased estimate of the population variance of the D scores. The observed F value must be compared to a critical F with 1 and $n - 1$ degrees of freedom. Because the F has a

TABLE 11.3
CALCULATIONS FOR DATA IN TABLE 11.1

Subject	$Y_1 = score\ in$ Condition 1	$Y_2 = score\ in$ Condition 2	$D = Y_2 - Y_1$	D^2
1	8	10	2	4
2	3	6	3	9
3	12	13	1	1
4	5	9	4	16
5	7	8	1	1
6	13	14	1	1
			$\sum D = 12$	$\sum D^2 = 32$

$$E_F = \sum(D_i - \overline{D})^2$$

$$= (2-2)^2 + (3-2)^2 + (1-2)^2 + (4-2)^2 + (1-2)^2 + (1-2)^2$$

$$= 8$$

Alternatively: $\quad E_F = \left(\sum D_i^2\right) - n\overline{D}^2 = 32 - 6(2)^2 = 32 - 24 = 8$

$$E_R = \sum D_i^2 = 32$$

$$F = \frac{(E_R - E_F)/(df_R - df_F)}{E_F/df_F} = \frac{(32-8)/(6-5)}{8/5} = 15.0$$

Alternatively: $\quad F = \dfrac{n\overline{D}^2}{\left(\sum D_i^2 - n\overline{D}^2\right)/(n-1)} = \dfrac{6(2)^2}{[32 - 6(2)^2]/(6-1)} = \dfrac{24}{8/5} = 15.0$

$F_{.05;\,1,5} = 6.61$, so H_0 is rejected at .05 level.

---

single numerator degree of freedom here, the test could also be written as a t test with $n - 1$ degrees of freedom. Specifically,

$$t = \frac{\sqrt{n}\,\overline{D}}{s_D} \tag{18}$$

or as

$$t = \frac{\overline{D}}{s_D/\sqrt{n}} \tag{19}$$

Equation 19 should look familiar because it is the formula for a dependent t test, as found in most behavioral statistics texts. Thus, with two levels of the repeated factor, the model-comparisons test reduces to the usual dependent t test. Table 11.3 shows step-by-step calculations for testing the null hypothesis for the data in Table 11.1.

ANALYSIS OF WITHIN-SUBJECTS DESIGNS WITH MORE THAN TWO LEVELS

When the repeated factor consists of more than two levels (i.e., when $a > 2$), the analysis becomes considerably more complicated. Once again, the model used previously for between-subjects designs is inappropriate here because errors typically are correlated as a result of systematic individual differences. There are two very different approaches that can be taken to deal with this problem. The approach that we prefer is the multivariate approach and is discussed in detail in Chapters 13 and 14. In brief, the logic of this approach is based on the formation of D variables (i.e., difference scores), as we used for the two-level case. However, in the a-group case, we need to form $a - 1$ D variables. When $a = 2$, we only need one D variable, which makes the resulting analysis quite simple. More generally, with a levels, the analysis is somewhat more complicated.

Instead of presenting the multivariate approach now, we first present an alternate approach, which is more traditional in the psychological literature. This approach, called the *univariate* or *mixed-model approach*, requires a set of restrictive assumptions, which we discuss later in this chapter. Nevertheless, the approach is important for two reasons. First, it continues to be widely used in psychological research. That you are aware of the necessary assumptions is important, so that you can evaluate whether these assumptions have been violated in a particular application of this approach. Second, there are several modifications of this approach that attempt to circumvent the restrictive set of assumptions. For the moment, we simply say that these modifications appear to work reasonably well, so that they constitute a viable alternative to the multivariate approach in some situations.

We present yet another approach based on mixed models in Chapter 15. It turns out that this approach is particularly useful when confronted with missing data, as often happens in longitudinal designs. In this context, we should acknowledge that the choices among these various analytic methods are sometimes complicated, and in fact statisticians continue to develop new methods for analyzing data from within-subjects designs. Readers interested in a thorough review of currently available options are directed to an excellent article by Keselman, Algina, and Kowalchuk (2001).

TRADITIONAL UNIVARIATE (MIXED-MODEL) APPROACH

The traditional view of a repeated-measures design is to regard it as a two-factor design. Specifically, one factor represents the repeated condition (e.g., time, drug, subtest), whereas the second factor represents subjects. The rationale for this conceptualization can be understood by considering the data in Table 11.4. When the data are displayed this way, the design looks very much like other factorial designs we have already encountered.

TABLE 11.4
DATA FOR a-LEVEL REPEATED-MEASURES
DESIGN (WITH $a = 4$)

		Treatment Condition			
		1	*2*	*3*	*4*
	1	8	10	7	5
	2	9	9	8	6
	3	7	5	8	4
	4	9	6	5	7
Subject	*5*	8	7	7	6
	6	5	4	4	3
	7	7	6	5	4
	8	8	8	6	6
	9	9	8	6	5
	10	7	7	4	5

Although the traditional analysis of repeated-measures data proceeds by treating the data in terms of this two-factor design, there are two ways in which the design differs from the typical factorial designs discussed previously. First, there is only one observation per cell of the design. Second, although treatment condition is usually a fixed factor, the subjects factor is a random factor because these particular subjects have been randomly selected from a larger population. Thus, the design is like the mixed designs of Chapter 10 in that there is one fixed factor and one random factor. It should now be obvious that the reason this method of analysis is often called the *mixed-model approach* is because with this conceptualization the effects do indeed follow a mixed model.

Comparison of Full and Restricted Models

An appropriate model for repeated-measures data is given by

$$Y_{ij} = \mu + \alpha_j + \pi_i + (\pi\alpha)_{ij} + \varepsilon_{ij} \tag{20}$$

where Y_{ij} is the score on the dependent variable for the ith subject in the jth condition, μ is the grand mean parameter, α_j is the effect associated with the jth condition, π_i is the effect associated with the ith subject (or *participant*), $(\pi\alpha)_{ij}$ is the effect of the interaction of the ith subject and the jth condition, and ε_{ij} is the error for the ith subject in the jth condition. Notice that this model is identical to the model we used in Chapter 7 for a factorial design.[2] The hypothesis to be tested here is

$$H_0 : \alpha_1 = \alpha_2 = \cdots = \alpha_a = 0$$

so a restricted model is given by

$$Y_{ij} = \mu + \pi_i + (\pi\alpha)_{ij} + \varepsilon_{ij} \tag{21}$$

However, you should recall from our discussion of random-effects models in Chapter 10 that the proper denominator term of the F statistic (i.e., the error term) depends on whether the effect being tested is fixed or random. In our design, there is one fixed factor (condition) and one random factor (subjects). The effect being tested is fixed because it is the main effect of condition. According to Chapter 10, to test a fixed effect when there is one random factor in the model, the appropriate denominator term is obtained by restricting the interaction of the fixed and random factors to zero. This can be accomplished most easily[3] in our design by omitting the $(\pi\alpha)_{ij}$ interaction parameters from Equations 20 and 21; in this case, our models become

$$\text{Full model:} \quad Y_{ij} = \mu + \alpha_j + \pi_i + \varepsilon_{ij} \tag{22}$$

$$\text{Restricted model:} \quad Y_{ij} = \mu + \pi_i + \varepsilon_{ij} \tag{23}$$

At this point, an F test can be obtained from the usual formula:

$$F = \frac{(E_R - E_F)/(df_R - df_F)}{E_F/df_F}$$

A special word is needed for computing the degrees of freedom here. Suppose that n subjects are each observed under a repeated conditions, yielding na scores in all. Then, the degrees of freedom for the two models are

$$df_F = na - (\text{\# independent parameters})$$
$$= na - [1 + (a-1) + (n-1)]$$
$$= na - n - a + 1$$
$$= (n-1)(a-1)$$
$$df_R = na - (\text{\# independent parameters})$$
$$= na - [1 + (n-1)]$$
$$= na - n$$
$$= n(a-1)$$

Notice then that

$$df_R - df_F = n(a-1) - (n-1)(a-1)$$
$$= [n - (n-1)](a-1)$$
$$= a - 1$$

Estimation of Parameters: Numerical Example

To perform the F test, we must calculate E_R and E_F, which necessitates obtaining parameter estimates in each model. To see how parameter estimates are obtained, consider the data displayed in Table 11.5. The data show that 12 subjects have been observed in each of 4 conditions. To make the example easier to discuss, let's suppose that the 12 subjects are children who have been observed at 30, 36, 42, and 48 months of age. In each case, the dependent variable is the child's age-normed general cognitive score on the McCarthy Scales

TABLE 11.5
HYPOTHETICAL McCARTHY DATA FOR 12 CHILDREN

Subject	Age (Months)				Marginal Mean
	30	36	42	48	
1	108	96	110	122	109
2	103	117	127	133	120
3	96	107	106	107	104
4	84	85	92	99	90
5	118	125	125	116	121
6	110	107	96	91	101
7	129	128	123	128	127
8	90	84	101	113	97
9	84	104	100	88	94
10	96	100	103	105	101
11	105	114	105	112	109
12	113	117	132	130	123
Marginal Mean	103	107	110	112	108

of Children's Abilities. Although the test is normed so that the mean score is independent of age for the general population, our 12 children may come from a population in which cognitive abilities are either growing more rapidly or less rapidly than average. Indeed, this is the hypothesis our data allow us to address.[4] In other words, although the sample means suggest that the children's cognitive abilities are growing, a significance test is needed if we want to rule out sampling error as a likely explanation for the observed differences.

The estimation of parameters in the models of Equations 22 and 23 is actually very straight-forward. Because there is an equal number of subjects in each treatment condition (i.e., the design is orthogonal), parameter estimates for Equation 22 are given by

$$\hat{\mu} = \sum_{i=1}^{n}\sum_{j=1}^{a} Y_{ij}/na = \overline{Y}_{..}$$

$$\hat{\alpha}_j = \left(\sum_{i=1}^{n} Y_{ij}/n\right) - \overline{Y}_{..} = \overline{Y}_{.j} - \overline{Y}_{..}$$

$$\hat{\pi}_i = \left(\sum_{j=1}^{a} Y_{ij}/a\right) - \overline{Y}_{..} = \overline{Y}_{i.} - \overline{Y}_{..}$$

and for Equation 23 are given by

$$\hat{\mu} = \sum_{i=1}^{n}\sum_{j=1}^{a} Y_{ij}/na = \overline{Y}_{..}$$

$$\hat{\pi}_i = \left(\sum_{j=1}^{a} Y_{ij}/a\right) - \overline{Y}_{..} = \overline{Y}_{i.} - \overline{Y}_{..}$$

Thus, the parameter estimates simply depend on the marginal means of the data. In particular, notice that $\hat{\mu}$ is just the mean of all scores, whereas $\hat{\alpha}_j$ is the difference between the mean of Condition j (averaged over subjects) and the grand mean, and $\hat{\pi}_i$ is the difference between the mean of Subject i (averaged over conditions) and the grand mean.

To find the sum of squared errors of each model, we must consider $\hat{Y}_{ij}$, the predicted score for Subject i in Condition j. For the full model, we have

$$\begin{aligned}
\hat{Y}_{ij} &= \hat{\mu} + \hat{\alpha}_j + \hat{\pi}_i \\
&= \overline{Y}_{..} + (\overline{Y}_{.j} - \overline{Y}_{..}) + (\overline{Y}_{i.} - \overline{Y}_{..}) \\
&= \overline{Y}_{.j} + \overline{Y}_{i.} - \overline{Y}_{..}
\end{aligned} \tag{24}$$

For the restricted model, the corresponding expression is

$$\begin{aligned}
\hat{Y}_{ij} &= \hat{\mu} + \hat{\pi}_i \\
&= \overline{Y}_{..} + (\overline{Y}_{i.} - \overline{Y}_{..}) \\
&= \overline{Y}_{i.}
\end{aligned} \tag{25}$$

Let's pause for a moment to compare Equations 24 and 25. The difference between these equations, and hence the nature of the restriction being imposed, can be understood most

TABLE 11.6
PREDICTED SCORES FROM THE FULL MODEL FOR
THE DATA OF TABLE 11.5

Subject	Age (Months)			
	30	36	42	48
1	104	108	111	113
2	115	119	122	124
3	99	103	106	108
4	85	89	92	94
5	116	120	123	125
6	96	100	103	105
7	122	126	129	131
8	92	96	99	101
9	89	93	96	98
10	96	100	103	105
11	104	108	111	113
12	118	122	125	127

TABLE 11.7
PREDICTED SCORES FROM THE RESTRICTED
MODEL FOR THE DATA OF TABLE 11.5

Subject	Age (Months)			
	30	36	42	48
1	109	109	109	109
2	120	120	120	120
3	104	104	104	104
4	90	90	90	90
5	121	121	121	121
6	101	101	101	101
7	127	127	127	127
8	97	97	97	97
9	94	94	94	94
10	101	101	101	101
11	109	109	109	109
12	123	123	123	123

easily by comparing Tables 11.6 and 11.7. Table 11.6 presents predicted scores from the full model (based on Equation 24) for the data of Table 11.5. Table 11.7 presents the corresponding scores for the restricted model (based on Equation 25). Table 11.6 shows that the full model allows for differences between both rows and columns. The restricted model, however, allows for differences between rows (i.e., subjects), but the columns of predicted scores are identical (see Table 11.7). Thus, the restricted model regards any differences between the columns (i.e., the conditions) in the actual data (Table 11.5) as simply being the result of sampling error. However, to the extent that the columns do in fact differ from one another, the full model would provide a better fit to the data than would the restricted model.

Once again, to perform a test of the null hypothesis, we must find the sum of squared errors for the two different models. In each case, then, we must calculate

$$\sum_{i=1}^{n} \sum_{j=1}^{a} (Y_{ij} - \hat{Y}_{ij})^2$$

where $\hat{Y}_{ij}$ is the predicted score from the particular model. In other words, we need to square each discrepancy between an actual score and a predicted score and add up these squared discrepancies. Tables 11.8 and 11.9 show the calculations for our data. We now turn to a more general formulation of the sum of squared errors.

TABLE 11.8
DISCREPANCIES BETWEEN ACTUAL SCORES (TABLE 11.5) AND
PREDICTED SCORES OF THE FULL MODEL (TABLE 11.6)

	Age (Months)			
Subject	30	36	42	48
1	4	−12	−1	9
2	−12	−2	5	9
3	−3	4	0	−1
4	−1	−4	0	5
5	2	5	2	−9
6	14	7	−7	−14
7	7	2	−6	−3
8	−2	−12	2	12
9	−5	11	4	−10
10	0	0	0	0
11	1	6	−6	−1
12	−5	−5	7	3
$\sum_{i=1}^{12}(Y_{ij}-\hat{Y}_{ij})^2$	474	584	220	728

$$E_F = \sum_{j=1}^{4}\sum_{i=1}^{12}(Y_{ij}-\hat{Y}_{ij})^2 = 2006$$

TABLE 11.9
DISCREPANCIES BETWEEN ACTUAL SCORES (TABLE 11.5) AND
PREDICTED SCORES OF THE RESTRICTED MODEL (TABLE 11.7)

	Age (Months)			
Subject	30	36	42	48
1	−1	−13	1	13
2	−17	−3	7	13
3	−8	3	2	3
4	−6	−5	2	9
5	−3	4	4	−5
6	9	6	−5	−10
7	2	1	−4	1
8	−7	−13	4	16
9	−10	10	6	−6
10	−5	−1	2	4
11	−4	5	−4	3
12	−10	−6	9	7
$\sum_{i=1}^{12}(Y_{ij}-\hat{Y}_{ij})^2$	774	596	268	920

$$E_R = \sum_{j=1}^{4}\sum_{i=1}^{12}(Y_{ij}-\hat{Y}_{ij})^2 = 2558$$

Making use of the predictions we developed in Equations 24 and 25, we see that the sum of squared errors for the full model equals

$$E_F = \sum_{i=1}^{n} \sum_{j=1}^{a} (Y_{ij} - \hat{Y}_{ij})^2$$

$$= \sum_{i=1}^{n} \sum_{j=1}^{a} [Y_{ij} - (\overline{Y}_{.j} + \overline{Y}_{i.} - \overline{Y}_{..})]^2$$

$$= \sum_{i=1}^{n} \sum_{j=1}^{a} (Y_{ij} - \overline{Y}_{.j} - \overline{Y}_{i.} + \overline{Y}_{..})^2$$

We have seen this formula earlier in a different context. Recall from Chapter 7 that this is the formula for the interaction sum of squares in a two-way factorial design. Thus, the sum of squared errors for the full model can be found simply by calculating the interaction sum of squares. Symbolically, we have

$$E_F = SS_{A \times S} \tag{26}$$

where $SS_{A \times S}$ represents the sum of squares due to the treatment by subject interaction.

In a similar fashion, the sum of squared errors for the restricted model is given by

$$E_R = \sum_{i=1}^{n} \sum_{j=1}^{a} (Y_{ij} - \hat{Y}_{ij})^2 = \sum_{i=1}^{n} \sum_{j=1}^{a} (Y_{ij} - \overline{Y}_{i.})^2$$

This can be rewritten as

$$E_R = \sum_{i=1}^{n} \sum_{j=1}^{a} (Y_{ij} - \overline{Y}_{i.} - \overline{Y}_{.j} + \overline{Y}_{..} + \overline{Y}_{.j} - \overline{Y}_{..})^2$$

which, after some tedious algebra, reduces to

$$E_R = \sum_{i=1}^{n} \sum_{j=1}^{a} (Y_{ij} - \overline{Y}_{.j} - \overline{Y}_{i.} + \overline{Y}_{..})^2 + \sum_{j=1}^{a} n(\overline{Y}_{.j} - \overline{Y}_{..})^2$$

The first expression on the right side of the equality is just $SS_{A \times S}$. The second expression is identical to what we encountered in Chapter 7 for the sum of squares for a main effect in a two-factor design, in this case, SS_A. Thus, we have

$$E_R = SS_{A \times S} + SS_A$$

Obviously, then

$$E_R - E_F = SS_A \tag{27}$$

We can now obtain an F test from the general formula

$$F = \frac{(E_R - E_F)/(df_R - df_F)}{E_F/df_F}$$

which reduces to

$$F = \frac{SS_A/(a-1)}{SS_{A \times S}/(n-1)(a-1)}$$

or

$$F = \frac{MS_A}{MS_{A \times S}} \tag{28}$$

For the data in Table 11.5, we have $E_R = 2558$ (see Table 11.9) and $E_F = 2006$ (see Table 11.8); thus,

$$F = \frac{552/3}{2006/33} = 3.03$$

which for an F distribution with 3 and 33 degrees of freedom implies a p value of .042. Thus, we can reject the null hypothesis that the population means at all four ages are equal.

It might be helpful to consider the formula for the F statistic in Equation 28 more closely. Why should the ratio of MS_A to $MS_{A \times S}$ inform us about whether to reject the null hypothesis? First, this makes intuitive sense, because $MS_{A \times S}$ is an index of the extent to which the A effect varies from subject to subject. Large variability signifies that differences in means are less consistent across individuals. Thus, the ratio of MS_A to $MS_{A \times S}$ reflects the average magnitude of condition differences relative to the inconsistency of those differences. As a consequence, the observed F value would be large to the extent that there were consistent condition differences from subject to subject. Such consistency provides confidence that observed average differences can safely be generalized beyond the particular sample to the population. Inconsistent condition differences, however, create greater doubt about the nature of condition differences beyond the observed data. Second, this F test has the same form as the F test we developed in Chapter 10 for a mixed two-factor design. As Table 10.3 shows, when A is fixed and B is random, $MS_{A \times B}$ is the appropriate error term. In the repeated-measures design, the random factor is subjects, which we have designated by S, so $MS_{A \times S}$ is the proper error term for testing the A effect, as shown in Equation 28.

ASSUMPTIONS IN THE TRADITIONAL UNIVARIATE (MIXED-MODEL) APPROACH

To use the previous approach to analyze repeated-measures data, the data must meet a set of rather restrictive assumptions. Besides the usual assumptions of random sampling from the population, independence of subjects, and normality, there is a homogeneity assumption similar to that required in between-subjects designs. Specifically, for within-subjects designs, there is a *homogeneity of treatment-difference variances* assumption.[5] This means that if we take two treatment levels—for example, l and m—and subtract scores for one level from scores for another level, the resulting score $Y_l - Y_m$ must have the same population variance for every pair of levels. The variance of the difference $Y_l - Y_m$ can be written as

$$\sigma^2_{Y_l - Y_m} = \sigma^2_{Y_l} + \sigma^2_{Y_m} - 2\text{Cov}(Y_l, Y_m) \tag{29}$$

$$= \sigma^2_{Y_l} + \sigma^2_{Y_m} - 2\rho_{lm}\sigma_{Y_l}\sigma_{Y_m} \tag{30}$$

where ρ_{lm} is the population correlation of scores in treatment level l with those in treatment level m.

Homogeneity, Sphericity, and Compound Symmetry

Huynh and Feldt (1970) and Rouanet and Lépine (1970) showed independently that the homogeneity of treatment-difference variances assumption is equivalent to assuming that the population covariance matrix has a certain form. This form, which is called *sphericity* (or interchangeably, *circularity*), can for all practical purposes be defined only with matrix algebra. For this reason, we instead discuss a special case of sphericity, which is known as *compound symmetry*. A covariance matrix is defined to possess compound symmetry if and only if all the variances are equal to each other and all the covariances are equal to each other. However, an equivalent property is that every measure must have the same variance and all correlations between any pair of measures must be equal. Symbolically, we can represent these two conditions as

$$\sigma^2_{Y_l} = \sigma^2_{Y_m} \tag{31}$$

for all l and m and

$$\rho_{lm} = \rho_{jk} \tag{32}$$

for all j, k, l, and m. For simplicity, when Equations 31 and 32 are true, we could use σ^2 to represent the common variance of every measure and use ρ to represent the common correlation between every pair of measures. What does compound symmetry imply about the variances of the differences between treatment levels? From Equation 30, we know that the general form of this variance is given by

$$\sigma^2_{Y_l - Y_m} = \sigma^2_{Y_l} + \sigma^2_{Y_m} - 2\rho_{lm}\sigma_{Y_l}\sigma_{Y_m} \tag{30, repeated}$$

However, when compound symmetry holds, we can replace $\sigma^2_{Y_l}$ and $\sigma^2_{Y_m}$ with σ^2 (and, of course, σ_{Y_l} and σ_{Y_m} with σ) and ρ_{lm} with ρ. As a result, we have

$$\sigma^2_{Y_l - Y_m} = \sigma^2 + \sigma^2 - 2\rho\sigma\sigma = 2\sigma^2(1 - \rho)$$

Notice that the variance of the difference does not depend on the particular levels l and m. Thus, compound symmetry implies that the homogeneity of treatment-difference variances assumption is satisfied. Stated differently, compound symmetry is a sufficient condition for the validity of the mixed-model approach. However, strictly speaking, compound symmetry is technically not a necessary condition, because compound symmetry is a special case of sphericity. As Figure 11.1 shows, matrices that satisfy compound symmetry are a subset of those that satisfy sphericity, and from a technical standpoint, sphericity is the assumption required by the mixed model approach. However, in practice, there are only two related situations in which the distinction between sphericity and compound symmetry is of potential importance. First, when there are only two levels of the repeated factor, there is only one difference between levels, so Equation 30 is always satisfied. Thus, when $a = 2$, the sphericity assumption is always met. However, the population matrix does not necessarily possess compound symmetry because the variance of scores at level 1 may not equal the variance at level 2. Nevertheless, the mixed-model approach is always valid (at least in terms of the homogeneity assumption) when $a = 2$ because sphericity is guaranteed here. Second, we see in Chapter 12 that sphericity can also be satisfied even when compound symmetry does not hold in designs with two or more repeated factors; this distinction is usually only important when at least one of the repeated factors has only two levels. In the single-factor design we are considering

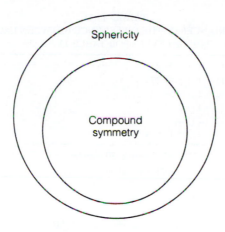

FIG. 11.1. Relationship between compound symmetry and sphericity.

TABLE 11.10
CORRELATIONS BETWEEN MEASURES ON McCARTHY
SCORES OF TABLE 11.5

Age (Months)	Age (Months)			
	30	36	42	48
30	1.000	.795	.696	.599
36	.795	1.000	.760	.466
42	.696	.760	1.000	.853
48	.599	.466	.853	1.000

in this chapter, it would be highly unusual (although theoretically possible) to find a matrix that possesses sphericity but not compound symmetry unless $a = 2$. Thus, for all practical purposes, compound symmetry is a requirement for the mixed-model analysis method in a one-way repeated-measures design any time the repeated factor has more than two levels.

Numerical Example

To develop further understanding of these conditions, it might be helpful to reconsider the data displayed in Table 11.5. Although we obviously cannot compute population variances and correlations for these data, we can compute their sample counterparts. The sample variances (s^2) turn out to be 187.96 for the 30-month scores, 200.51 for the 36-month scores, 177.96 for the 42-month scores, and 217.86 for the 48-month scores. Informal inspection of these four sample variances suggests that the values are rather similar to each other, and any differences between them might simply reflect sampling error. Instead of considering a formal test at this point, let's consider the correlations among the scores. Table 11.10 shows the six correlations among the four variables in the form of a 4×4 matrix. We can see that the values of the sample correlations vary substantially from each other. For example, scores at 36 and 48 months correlate only 0.466, whereas scores at 42 and 48 months correlate 0.853. In general, correlations are highest here for those pairs of measures that are closest together in time, a common finding in the behavioral literature. This pattern of roughly equal variances but substantially different correlations across levels of the within-subjects factor is perhaps the most common result in

TABLE 11.11
VARIANCES OF THE DIFFERENCE BETWEEN EACH
PAIR OF LEVELS FOR TABLE 11.5 DATA*

$\mathrm{Var}(Y_2 - Y_1) = 79.82$
$\mathrm{Var}(Y_3 - Y_2) = 91.27$
$\mathrm{Var}(Y_4 - Y_3) = 59.82$
$\mathrm{Var}(Y_3 - Y_1) = 111.27$
$\mathrm{Var}(Y_4 - Y_2) = 223.64$
$\mathrm{Var}(Y_4 - Y_1) = 163.64$

* Y_1 = McCarthy score at 30 months,
Y_2 = McCarthy score at 36 months,
Y_3 = McCarthy score at 42 months, and
Y_4 = McCarthy score at 48 months.

repeated-measures designs in the behavioral sciences. However, as Table 11.11 shows, this pattern of roughly equal variances but unequal correlations leads to differences in the variances of the differences between the various pairs of levels. Specifically, in accordance with Equation 30, the variance of the difference tends to be smallest when scores from the two levels are highly correlated and tends to be largest when the correlation is low. If this pattern holds in the population as well as in the sample, it represents a violation of the homogeneity of treatment-difference variances required for the validity of the traditional univariate approach to analyzing such designs.

Even though these sample correlations are unequal, such inequalities might simply reflect sampling error. Perhaps the corresponding population correlations are, in fact, equal to one another. More precisely, real interest centers on whether the required treatment-differences homogeneity assumption is met for the population. Mauchly's sphericity test is a procedure for testing the null hypothesis that the homogeneity condition holds in the population. However, we do not present the details of this test, because Keselman, Rogan, Mendoza, and Breen (1980) show that Mauchly's test has little value as a preliminary test prior to the test of mean differences. (Readers desiring more information on Mauchly's test should refer to Keselman et al., 1980, or to Kirk, 1982, p. 260.)

After the discussion of robustness in between-subjects designs, a reasonable guess would be that Mauchly's test is of little value because the mixed-model approach is robust to violations of the homogeneity assumption. However, as McCall and Appelbaum (1973) and others show, the mixed-model approach is not robust to violations of homogeneity. When the assumption is false, the actual probability of a Type I error may be as high as .10 or .15 as compared to a nominal value of .05. Thus, the usual mixed-model ANOVA test is inappropriate unless the homogeneity condition is met.

ADJUSTED UNIVARIATE TESTS

When the homogeneity assumption is false, it is possible to perform an "adjusted test" of the equality of means. Box (1954) derived a measure denoted by ε that indexes how far a population covariance matrix departs from homogeneity. A matrix satisfying the homogeneity assumption always has an ε value of 1.0; any other matrix has an ε value between 0.0 and 1.0, where lower values indicate a more extreme departure from the assumption. He also showed that the ratio of MS_A to $MS_{A \times S}$ (our observed F) approximately follows an F distribution with adjusted degrees of freedom even when homogeneity is false. Specifically, the F distribution which $MS_A/MS_{A \times S}$ approximates has numerator degrees of freedom equal to

$\varepsilon(a - 1)$ and denominator degrees of freedom equal to $\varepsilon(n - 1)(a - 1)$. If ε were known, it would be possible to calculate the observed F as $MS_A/MS_{A \times S}$ and compare it to a new critical F with appropriately adjusted degrees of freedom. However, this result is of limited practical value, because ε is an unknown population parameter. Fortunately, there is a practical alternative; in fact, there are three: the Geisser–Greenhouse lower-bound correction, Geisser and Greenhouse's $\hat{\varepsilon}$ adjustment (which Geisser and Greenhouse suggested for sample data, based on Box's mathematical work), and the Huynh–Feldt $\tilde{\varepsilon}$ adjustment. For each of these three approaches, we briefly describe its underlying theory and then apply it to the data in Table 11.5.

Lower-Bound Adjustment

Geisser and Greenhouse (1958) showed that the lowest possible value for ε in an a-level design equals $1/(a - 1)$. For example, if $a = 2$, $\varepsilon = 1.0$ (Why?); if $a = 3$, ε can be no smaller than .50; if $a = 4$, ε can be no smaller than .33; and so on. Geisser and Greenhouse recommended that a conservative test of the null hypothesis that all means are equal could be obtained by comparing $MS_A/MS_{A \times S}$ to a critical value with 1 and $n - 1$ degrees of freedom. Notice that their lower bound implies that

$$df_{\text{num}} = \varepsilon(a - 1) \geq \left(\frac{1}{a - 1}\right)(a - 1) = 1$$

$$df_{\text{den}} = \varepsilon(n - 1)(a - 1) \geq \left(\frac{1}{a - 1}\right)(n - 1)(a - 1) = n - 1 \qquad (33)$$

In other words, their lower bound for ε together with Box's ε-adjusted degrees of freedom suggests that the smallest possible appropriate degrees of freedom equal 1 for the numerator and $n - 1$ for the denominator. Notice also that this procedure is conservative because smaller degrees of freedom correspond to a larger critical F value. In this sense, the Geisser–Greenhouse lower-bound approach suggests that no matter how badly the homogeneity assumption is violated, the largest possible critical F value needed is one with 1 and $n - 1$ degrees of freedom.

For the data in Table 11.5, the observed F value was 3.03. With the Geisser–Greenhouse lower-bound approach, this F should be compared to a critical value with 1 and 11 (i.e., $12-1$) degrees of freedom. The corresponding critical F is 4.84. Because the observed F is less than the critical F, the null hypothesis cannot be rejected with this approach.

$\hat{\varepsilon}$ Adjustment

Geisser and Greenhouse's $\hat{\varepsilon}$ (pronounced "epsilon hat") approach provides a method for estimating the population value of ε on the basis of observed sample data. The value of $\hat{\varepsilon}$, like that of ε, is always between $1/(a - 1)$ and 1.0. Because the sample value is almost always greater than the theoretical lower bound, the $\hat{\varepsilon}$ adjustment is usually less severe than the lower bound adjustment. Unfortunately, the calculation of $\hat{\varepsilon}$ is extremely tedious, as shown by its computational formula:

$$\hat{\varepsilon} = \frac{a^2(\overline{E}_{jj} - \overline{E}_{..})^2}{(a - 1)\left[\left(\sum\sum E_{jk}^2\right) - \left(2a \sum \overline{E}_{j.}^2\right) + \left(a^2 \overline{E}_{..}^2\right)\right]}$$

where E_{jk} is the element in row j and column k of the sample covariance matrix, $\overline{E}_{jj}$ is the mean of the diagonal entries (variances) in the sample covariance matrix, $\overline{E}_{j.}$ is the mean of the entries in the jth row of the sample covariance matrix, and $\overline{E}_{..}$ is the mean of all entries in the sample covariance matrix. Fortunately, major statistical packages such as SAS and SPSS calculate $\hat{\varepsilon}$ as well as the corresponding adjusted degrees of freedom: $df_{\text{num}} = \hat{\varepsilon}(a - 1)$ and $df_{\text{den}} = \hat{\varepsilon}(n - 1)(a - 1)$.

For the data in Table 11.5, it turns out that the value of $\hat{\varepsilon}$ equals 0.61, indicating a marked departure from the homogeneity condition. Notice, however, that the .61 value still is substantially above the .33 theoretical minimum of the Geisser–Greenhouse approach. For $a = 4$, $n = 12$, and $\hat{\varepsilon} = 0.61$, the resulting degrees of freedom are 1.83 and 20.13. Finding the appropriate critical value is complicated by the presence of fractional degrees of freedom. One can round downward (to 1 and 20 here), interpolate, or find the critical F for the fractional degrees of freedom using a computer program. Taking the latter course (using PROC BETAINV of SAS) shows that the appropriate critical F value is 3.59. Although this value is considerably less than the Geisser–Greenhouse critical value, it is still larger than the observed F of 3.03, so the null hypothesis cannot be rejected with the $\hat{\varepsilon}$ approach. Notice that with most modern statistical packages, there is no need to calculate the critical value because the p value itself is given.

Until the mid-1980s, the lower-bound correction was used much more frequently than the $\hat{\varepsilon}$ adjustment because the value of $\hat{\varepsilon}$ is so tedious to calculate. Now that statistical packages have incorporated calculations of $\hat{\varepsilon}$, the use of the $\hat{\varepsilon}$ adjustment is preferable to the lower-bound correction because the $\hat{\varepsilon}$ adjustment is less conservative. Numerous studies (e.g., Collier, Baker, Mandeville, & Hayes, 1967; Maxwell & Arvey, 1982) found that the $\hat{\varepsilon}$ procedure properly controls Type I error and yet is more powerful than the lower-bound correction. Nevertheless, even the $\hat{\varepsilon}$ procedure tends to be somewhat conservative because $\hat{\varepsilon}$ tends to systematically underestimate ε, particularly when ε is close to 1.0. An intuitive explanation for this underestimation comes from the way in which $\hat{\varepsilon}$ is calculated. In particular, although it is certainly not obvious from the formula, it turns out that $\hat{\varepsilon}$ can equal 1.0 only if all sample treatment-difference variances are exactly equal to each other; otherwise, $\hat{\varepsilon}$ is less than 1.0. However, if the homogeneity assumption is satisfied (so that $\varepsilon = 1.0$), it is the population treatment-difference variances that are all equal. Even in this situation, the sample treatment-difference variances would inevitably be somewhat different from each other, and $\hat{\varepsilon}$ would be less than 1.0. Thus, $\hat{\varepsilon}$ tends to overadjust the degrees of freedom by underestimating ε. Huynh and Feldt (1976) developed another estimate of ε in an attempt to correct the bias in $\hat{\varepsilon}$ for large values of ε.

$\tilde{\varepsilon}$ Adjustment

The Huynh–Feldt $\tilde{\varepsilon}$ procedure (pronounced "epsilon tilde") provides yet a third method of adjustment, which is similar to the Geisser–Greenhouse $\hat{\varepsilon}$ approach in that the population value of ε is once again estimated from sample data. They derived $\tilde{\varepsilon}$ as the ratio of two unbiased estimators, but as they acknowledge, $\tilde{\varepsilon}$ itself is not unbiased. Whereas $\hat{\varepsilon}$ tends to underestimate ε, $\tilde{\varepsilon}$ tends to overestimate ε. In fact, $\tilde{\varepsilon}$ can be greater than 1.0; when this occurs, $\tilde{\varepsilon}$ is set equal to 1.0 because it is known that the population parameter ε can never be larger than 1.0. Once $\hat{\varepsilon}$ has been calculated, it is easy to find the value of $\tilde{\varepsilon}$. In a single-factor design, the relationship is given by

$$\tilde{\varepsilon} = \frac{n(a - 1)\hat{\varepsilon} - 2}{(a - 1)[n - 1 - (a - 1)\hat{\varepsilon}]} \tag{34}$$

Once again, major statistical packages such as SAS and SPSS are capable of calculating $\tilde{\varepsilon}$. It can be shown that $\tilde{\varepsilon} \geq \hat{\varepsilon}$ for any set of data, with equality holding only when $\hat{\varepsilon} = 1/(a - 1)$. Thus, the degrees of freedom for the $\tilde{\varepsilon}$ procedure is always at least as large as the degrees of freedom for the $\hat{\varepsilon}$ procedure. As a result, the critical F for $\tilde{\varepsilon}$ is typically smaller than the critical F for $\hat{\varepsilon}$, leading to more rejections of the null hypothesis. Although this implies an increase in power, it also implies an increase in the Type I error rate. We return to this point in a moment.

For the data in Table 11.5, the value of $\tilde{\varepsilon}$ is 0.72, which is larger than the $\hat{\varepsilon}$ value of 0.61, as it must be. The adjusted degrees of freedom for the Huynh–Feldt approach equal $\tilde{\varepsilon}(a-1)$ for the numerator and $\tilde{\varepsilon}(n-1)(a-1)$ for the denominator. For $a=4, n=12$, and $\tilde{\varepsilon}=0.72$, the resulting degrees of freedom are 2.18 and 23.94. The corresponding critical F value is 3.31. Although this value is less than the critical F for both Geisser and Greenhouse's $\hat{\varepsilon}$ and the lower-bound approaches, it is still larger than the observed F of 3.03, so the null hypothesis cannot be rejected with the $\tilde{\varepsilon}$ approach.

Summary of Four Mixed-Model Approaches

We have now seen four different ways to test the null hypothesis that all means are equal in a within-subjects design. Table 11.12 presents a summary of the four approaches, both in general and in the specific case of the Table 11.5 data. As Table 11.12 shows, all four of the mixed-model approaches use Equation 28 to obtain an observed F value:

$$F = \frac{MS_A}{MS_{A \times S}} \tag{28, repeated}$$

The only difference among the methods concerns the degrees of freedom for the critical F value. As a result, for any set of data, the methods can be ranked in terms of the likelihood of rejecting the null hypothesis in the following order (from most to least likely): unadjusted, $\tilde{\varepsilon}$ adjusted, $\hat{\varepsilon}$ adjusted, and lower-bound adjusted.

How should a researcher choose which approach is best? We can make several general recommendations. First, we believe that the unadjusted mixed-model test should never be used because it is extremely sensitive to the sphericity assumption. As we mentioned earlier, the actual α level can be as high as .10 or .15 for a nominal α level of .05. For a nominal α level of .01, the actual α level can be as high as .06 (Keselman & Rogan, 1980), so even a "highly significant" result with a p value near .01 cannot necessarily be trusted. Despite our recommendation, which simply echoes many earlier recommendations, many behavioral researchers continue to use the unadjusted test. For example, Vasey and Thayer (1987) found that more than 50% of within-subjects studies published in the 1984 and 1985 volumes of *Psychophysiology* reported only the unadjusted test. However, Jennings (1987) describes a new editorial policy begun by *Psychophysiology* in 1987 that requires that all papers with repeated-measures designs must use either one of the adjusted mixed-model tests or the multivariate approach to be described in Chapters 13 and 14. The implementation of adjusted tests in statistical packages is likely to hasten the demise of the unadjusted test, appropriately so in our opinion.

A second general conclusion is that the Greenhouse–Geisser lower-bound correction is overly conservative. This approach was quite useful before $\hat{\varepsilon}$ and $\tilde{\varepsilon}$ adjustments were available in statistical packages, but as we pointed out earlier, the $\hat{\varepsilon}$ adjustment is more powerful than the lower-bound correction and yet still maintains Type I error at or below the nominal value.

Thus, the two viable approaches listed in Table 11.12 are the $\tilde{\varepsilon}$-adjusted and $\hat{\varepsilon}$-adjusted methods. Our general recommendation is to use the $\hat{\varepsilon}$ adjustment because, on occasion, $\tilde{\varepsilon}$ can fail to properly control the Type I error rate. Fortunately, it can be shown from Equation 34 that for large n, the values of $\hat{\varepsilon}$ and $\tilde{\varepsilon}$ are virtually identical, so these two methods usually reach the same conclusion except for small sample sizes. When they do differ, $\hat{\varepsilon}$ is the safer choice because it avoids the potential liberal bias of $\tilde{\varepsilon}$.

TABLE 11.12
SUMMARY OF FOUR MIXED-MODEL APPROACHES

Approach	General Form			Observed F Statistic	Table 11.5 Data		Critical F
	Test Statistic	df for Critical F			df for Critical F		
		Numerator	Denominator		Numerator	Denominator	
Unadjusted	$F = \dfrac{MS_A}{MS_{A \times S}}$	$a - 1$	$(a - 1)(n - 1)$	3.03	3	33	2.90
Huynh–Feldt $\tilde{\varepsilon}$	$F = \dfrac{MS_A}{MS_{A \times S}}$	$\tilde{\varepsilon}(a - 1)$	$\tilde{\varepsilon}(a - 1)(n - 1)$	3.03	2.18	23.94	3.31
Greenhouse–Geisser $\hat{\varepsilon}$ (Box's $\hat{\varepsilon}$)	$F = \dfrac{MS_A}{MS_{A \times S}}$	$\hat{\varepsilon}(a - 1)$	$\hat{\varepsilon}(a - 1)(n - 1)$	3.03	1.83	20.13	3.59
Greenhouse–Geisser lower-bound correction	$F = \dfrac{MS_A}{MS_{A \times S}}$	1	$n - 1$	3.03	1	11	4.84

Recall that earlier in the chapter we mentioned yet another approach for analyzing data from within-subjects designs—the multivariate approach. As Chapters 13 and 14 show, there are some situations in which the multivariate approach is preferable to any of the mixed-model approaches considered in this chapter. Chapters 13 and 14 discuss the relative advantages of the approaches in detail.

MEASURES OF EFFECT

Measures of effect are frequently of interest in within-subjects designs, just as they are in between-subjects designs. We begin our consideration of measures of effect in within-subjects designs by presenting procedures for calculating omega squared. Then we consider standardized effect sizes, which leads naturally to the general topics of individual comparisons and of confidence intervals.

Olejnik and Algina (2000) use previous work by Dodd and Schultz (1973) to provide the following formula for calculating omega squared in one-way within-subjects designs:

$$\hat{\omega}^2 = \frac{(a-1)(MS_A - MS_{A \times S})}{SS_{\text{Total}} + MS_S} \tag{35}$$

Although the numerator terms of Equation 35 are familiar, neither of the denominator terms plays a direct role in the F statistic we have developed in this chapter, so both require some further explanation. Remember that the restricted model we used to derive our F test is of the form

$$\text{Restricted model:} \quad Y_{ij} = \mu + \pi_i + \varepsilon_{ij} \tag{23, repeated}$$

For reasons we discussed earlier in the chapter, notice that the restricted model allows an effect due to subjects. However, in principle, we could consider an even more restricted model of the form

$$\text{Most Restricted model:} \quad Y_{ij} = \mu + \varepsilon_{ij} \tag{36}$$

which simply omits subject effects from the model. You may recognize the model in Equation 36 as the restricted model we encountered in Chapter 3 for between-subjects designs. The sum of squared errors of this most restricted model equals SS_{Total} (just as for the between-subjects design), and the difference between the sum of squared errors of this model and the restricted model that allows for subject effects equals SS_S, that is, the sum of squares due to subjects. Then MS_S, the mean square for subjects, is the sum of squares divided by $n - 1$ (the degrees of freedom for the subjects effect).

Given this background, we can now use Equation 35 to compute omega squared for the McCarthy data in Table 11.5. For these data, we have already seen that $SS_A = 552$, and $SS_{A \times S} = 2006$, which implies that the corresponding mean squares equal 184.00 and 60.79, respectively. We need to find either SS_S or SS_{Total} to complete the calculation. It turns out that $SS_S = 6624$, which then implies that $SS_{\text{Total}} = 9182$ (i.e., the sum of 552, 2006, and 6624). We can now find omega squared for the age effect as

$$\hat{\omega}^2 = \frac{3(184.00 - 60.79)}{9182.00 + (6624.00/11)}$$

which reduces to a value of 0.04. Thus, our best estimate is that the age effect accounts for approximately 4% of the total population variance in McCarthy scores in children between the ages of 30 months and 48 months.

We close this discussion with two miscellaneous points. First, there is a version of partial omega squared for within-subjects designs that excludes systematic differences between subjects from the definition of total population variance. As a consequence, partial omega squared is often much larger than the version we describe here. We have chosen not to present partial omega squared because subject variance is always regarded as a component of the total population variance in between-subjects designs, and it seems advisable not to disregard it in within-subjects designs. Nevertheless, interested readers can learn more about partial omega squared in within-subjects designs from Olejnik and Algina (2000). Second, we focused our presentation on omega squared, but eta squared and epsilon squared can also be defined in within-subjects designs. Once again, Olejnik and Algina (2000) provide details.

An alternative to omega squared or other measures of association strength is provided by measures of effect size. Recall that in between-subjects designs we can calculate a standardized mean difference d as a description of effect size. We can also calculate d in within-subjects designs. The only complication here is that we must decide on an appropriate standard deviation to serve as a basis for a standard scale. The first candidate we might consider would be the square root of $MS_{A \times S}$ because this is the error term for testing within-subjects effects. Although there is nothing literally wrong with this choice, it is not the typical choice and it is also not the choice we recommend. The disadvantage of basing standardized effects on $MS_{A \times S}$ is that a standardized effect defined this way is usually substantially larger than a standardized effect with comparable mean differences in a between-subjects design. Why does this matter? As we mentioned in Chapter 3, a major goal of developing effect size measures is to provide a standard metric that meta-analysts and others can interpret across studies that vary in their dependent variables as well as types of designs. If we were to use the square root of $MS_{A \times S}$ to define an effect size measure in within-subjects designs, we would create a situation where effect sizes would typically be larger in within-subjects designs than in between-subjects designs. Generally preferable would be an effect size measure expected to have the same value in both types of designs.

To arrive at such comparability, we need to remember how we identified an appropriate standard deviation in the one-way between-subjects design. There we used MS_W, which was derived from the error term of our full model

$$Y_{ij} = \mu + \alpha_j + \varepsilon_{ij} \qquad \text{(3.66, repeated)}$$

Notice that the between-subjects model is different from any of the models we consider in this chapter in that it contains an effect for treatment but no effect for subjects. In order to obtain a comparable effect size measure in within-subjects designs, we must base our standard deviation on a model of the same form as the model of Equation 3.66.

Finding the sum of squared errors for this model turns out to be straightforward. Remember that in a within-subjects design, the total sum of squares can be written as

$$SS_{\text{Total}} = SS_A + SS_S + SS_{A \times S} \qquad (37)$$

The model of Equation 3.66 allows only for an effect due to treatments, so any remaining influences appear in the error term. This means that the error term of the model consists of the sum of SS_S and $SS_{A \times S}$. Thus, the desired standard deviation for calculating a standardized effect size should be based on the sum of SS_S and $SS_{A \times S}$. To obtain a standard deviation, we need to divide by degrees of freedom (which gives us a variance estimate) and then take the square root (to convert the variance to a standard deviation). Notice that the SS_S term has $n - 1$ degrees of freedom, whereas the $SS_{A \times S}$ term has $(a - 1)(n - 1)$ degrees of freedom.

Summing $n - 1$ plus $(a - 1)(n - 1)$ yields $a(n - 1)$ as the degrees of freedom for the sum of SS_S and $SS_{A \times S}$. Putting all of this together, we can express our standard deviation estimate as

$$sd = \sqrt{\frac{SS_S + SS_{A \times S}}{a(n - 1)}} \tag{38}$$

In our numerical example of Table 11.5, we saw in our discussion of omega squared that $SS_S = 6624$ and $SS_{A \times S} = 2006$. Substituting these two values along with $a = 4$ and $n = 12$ into Equation 38 yields a value of 14.00 for sd in these data. We can now use this value of 14.00 as the denominator for d, a standardized mean difference. For example, according to Table 11.5, the sample mean McCarthy scores were 103, 107, 110, and 112 at ages 30, 36, 42, and 48 months, respectively. We could now express any desired mean difference as a standardized difference. For example, McCarthy scores at ages 36 and 30 months for these children differ by 0.29 standard deviations [i.e., d for the difference between 36 and 30 months is $(107 - 103)/14.00$]. Similarly, d for the difference between scores at 48 and 30 months is 0.64 [i.e., $(112 - 103)/14.00$]. Thus, by standard conventions, we could say that the difference between scores at 30 and 36 months is on the "small" side (literally $d = 0.20$), whereas the difference between scores at 30 and 48 months is halfway between "medium" ($d = 0.50$) and "large" ($d = 0.80$). More generally, we could calculate a standardized mean difference not just for pairwise comparisons, but for complex comparisons as well, keeping in mind that the sum of the absolute value of contrast coefficients should be 2 when estimating a standardized mean difference.

Before considering this more general topic of contrasts, we mention a few conceptual points about standardized mean differences. First, sd as defined by Equation 38 is exactly equal to square root of the MS_W we would calculate if we were to regard our data as having come from a between-subjects design. Recall from Chapter 3 (see Equation 3.63) that with equal n, MS_W is simply the average within-group variance. If we were to regard the data in Table 11.5 as coming from a between-subjects design, the within-group variances would have values of 188, 200.55, 178, and 218, respectively. Averaging these four values and taking the square root yields 14.00, just as we found for sd from Equation 38. Second, the reason for this equivalence can be understood from Chapter 7. In an equal-n factorial design, the sum of SS_S plus $SS_{A \times S}$ is equal to the sum of squares of S within A, but this is precisely what we call SS_W in a between-subjects design. Third, as in the between-subjects design, it is important to consider the extent to which this average standard deviation is an accurate representation of the individual standard deviations. In other words, heterogeneity of variance can raise questions about the wisdom of averaging the separate variances, in which case it might be preferable to calculate an sd based only on the groups represented in the numerator of d, or even an sd based only on a control condition. Fourth, notice that if we were to use the square root of $MS_{A \times S}$ as the denominator of our standardized mean differences, we would obtain much larger values for our measures of effect. Specifically, the denominator would then be 7.80 (which is the square root of 60.79), only a little more than half the value of 14.00. Thus, standardized effect sizes would be nearly twice as large when defined in terms of the $A \times S$ interaction. However, this definition does not consider systematic individual differences to be relevant in defining a standard metric; because such individual differences often constitute a sizable proportion of the total variance, omitting them inflates measures of effect. Fifth, we can see this even more clearly by realizing that sd as defined by Equation 38 is a weighted average of MS_S and $MS_{A \times S}$. In particular, if we replace the sum of squares expressions in Equation 38 with comparable mean squares multiplied by corresponding degrees of freedom, and rewrite $a(n - 1)$ as the sum of $(n - 1)$

plus $(a-1)(n-1)$, we have

$$sd = \sqrt{\frac{(n-1)MS_S + (a-1)(n-1)MS_{A \times S}}{(n-1)+(a-1)(n-1)}} \tag{39}$$

In most within-subjects designs, MS_S is considerably larger than $MS_{A \times S}$, so even though more weight is given to $MS_{A \times S}$ than to MS_S (whenever there are more than two levels of the factor), nevertheless, sd as defined by Equation 39 is usually considerably larger than $MS_{A \times S}$. Thus, the choice of defining an appropriate metric for reporting and interpreting standardized mean differences in within-subjects designs is likely to make a substantial difference in the apparent magnitude of the effect, which is why we have gone into considerable detail explaining why we believe sd is more appropriate than $MS_{A \times S}$ to use as a yardstick for measuring such effects.

COMPARISONS AMONG INDIVIDUAL MEANS

Individual comparisons of means are usually of interest in within-subjects designs, just as they are in between-subjects designs. The traditional method of testing comparisons in a repeated-measures design involves using the same formula we used in the between-subjects design for finding the sum of squares due to the contrast:

$$E_R - E_F = (\hat{\psi})^2 \bigg/ \sum \left(\frac{c_j^2}{n_j} \right) \tag{4.39, repeated}$$

Because we have equal n in the repeated-measures design, this formula can be rewritten as

$$SS_\psi = \frac{n(\hat{\psi})^2}{\sum c_j^2}$$

Then, in the traditional approach, a test statistic is obtained by dividing the sum of squares for the contrast by the interaction mean square:

$$F = \frac{SS_\psi}{MS_{A \times S}} \tag{40}$$

Appropriate critical values to take into account other comparisons to be tested follow the same logic as we presented in Chapter 5 for between-subjects designs. In particular, Bonferroni's method would simply require comparing the p value corresponding to the F value from Equation 40 to .05/C. A critical value for Tukey's method would be

$$\frac{q_{.05; a, (a-1)(n-1)}^2}{2} \tag{41}$$

whereas for Scheffé's method, the critical value would be

$$(a-1)F_{.05; a-1, (a-1)(n-1)} \tag{42}$$

Although Equations 40–42 constitute the traditional formulas for testing contrasts in repeated-measures designs, we believe that they should not be used because these traditional approaches depend strongly on the sphericity assumption. In fact, tests of comparisons are considerably more sensitive to violations of sphericity than is the main-effect test. Boik (1981) showed that even small departures from sphericity can lead to highly biased tests of comparisons. The problem arises because $MS_{A \times S}$ is an average error term, but the average value is too small for some contrasts and too large for others when sphericity fails to hold. When $MS_{A \times S}$ is too small for a specific contrast, Boik found that the actual error rate for that contrast can reach .70 or more for a nominal α level of .05. When $MS_{A \times S}$ is too large for a specific contrast, the power for testing that contrast can be near .05, even for a moderately strong effect. Thus, using $MS_{A \times S}$ as the error term for testing contrasts can have deleterious effects on both Type I error and power. In addition, using $\hat{\varepsilon}$ or $\tilde{\varepsilon}$ adjustments here is not a satisfactory solution because they fail to address the lack of power problem.

Recall that we encountered a similar situation in Chapters 4 and 5, when we discussed tests of contrasts in between-subjects designs. We saw in these chapters that when the homogeneity of variance assumption is false, using MS_W as an error term for testing all contrasts cannot be recommended. The solution in the between-subjects design was to use a separate variance estimate approach, which allowed each contrast to have its own error term. It turns out that this same strategy can also be used in within-subjects designs. However, we defer a discussion of the separate variance estimate approach in within-subjects designs until Chapters 13 and 14. The reason for this organization of topics is that we will see that the separate variance estimate approach for testing contrasts is consistent with the multivariate approach for testing the condition main effect.

CONFIDENCE INTERVALS FOR COMPARISONS

As usual, confidence intervals can provide a very effective method for interpreting data in within-subjects designs. However, as we have just explained in our brief consideration of testing comparisons, traditional formulas for confidence intervals depend very strongly on the validity of the sphericity assumption. When this assumption is not met, some intervals are too narrow and others are too wide. As a result, some intervals that we believe to provide 95% confidence would, in fact, over repeated samplings contain the true population value much less than 95% of the time. Other intervals would suffer from the exact opposite problem of containing the true population value more than 95% of the time. Although this may not sound so bad, the reason their coverage exceeds 95% is because these intervals are wider than they truly need to be, so we do not achieve as much precision as we otherwise could.

It turns out that the solution to this problem is to use a separate error term for each contrast instead of using $MS_{A \times S}$ as a pooled error term. The use of separate error terms is covered in detail in Chapters 13 and 14, because they are consistent with the multivariate approach to repeated measures. However, because of the importance of this topic, we provide a preview in this chapter.

We present formulas for each of two different ways of forming confidence intervals. The first way depends strongly on the validity of the sphericity assumption, because it uses $MS_{A \times S}$. The second way does not depend on sphericity, because it uses a separate error term for each contrast.

If we could somehow know that the sphericity assumption has been met, we could use $MS_{A \times S}$ as an estimate of error in forming confidence intervals. When sphericity holds, an appropriate confidence interval for any contrast ψ can be found from

$$\hat{\psi} \pm w \sqrt{MS_{A \times S} \sum_{j=1}^{a} \left(c_j^2 / n_j \right)} \tag{43}$$

where w is chosen so as to control the appropriate error rate. For example, as we discuss in Chapter 5, possible choices for w include

$$w = \sqrt{F(.05; 1, \ df_{(a-1)(n-1)})} \qquad \text{for } \alpha_{PC} = .05$$

$$w = \sqrt{F(.05/C; 1, \ df_{(a-1)(n-1)})} \qquad \text{for Bonferroni}$$

$$w = q(.05; a, \ df_{(a-1)(n-1)})/\sqrt{2} \qquad \text{for Tukey}$$

$$w = \sqrt{(a-1)F(.05; a-1, df_{(a-1)(n-1)})} \qquad \text{for Scheffé}$$

The good news is that intervals using these various forms of w can be obtained simply in most standard statistical packages. The bad news is that intervals using Equation 43 depend strongly on the sphericity assumption.

If there is any doubt whatsoever about the validity of the sphericity assumption, intervals should not be calculated using Equation 43. Instead, it becomes important to use a separate error term for each interval instead of the pooled $MS_{A \times S}$ error term. We defer thorough consideration of this topic until Chapter 13. For now, we show only how to form a confidence interval for a pairwise comparison without assuming sphericity. The appropriate formula is given by

$$\hat{\psi} \pm w \sqrt{\frac{\text{Var}(Y_l - Y_m)}{2} \sum_{j=1}^{a} \left(c_j^2/n_j\right)} \tag{44}$$

where $\text{Var}(Y_l - Y_m)$ is the variance of the difference between scores at level l and level m of the repeated factor. Recall that we computed this type of difference for the McCarthy data in Table 11.11. Notice that this term divided by 2 has replaced $MS_{A \times S}$ in Equation 43. Instead of using the pooled error term $MS_{A \times S}$, Equation 44 uses an error term specific to each pairwise comparison. Otherwise, Equations 43 and 44 are identical (although we must realize that the denominator degrees of freedom used for w are now $n-1$ in Equation 44 instead of $(a-1)(n-1)$ as they were for Equation 43).

To see how all this works, we consider two possible pairwise comparisons for the McCarthy data: (1) the difference between means at 42 and 48 months, that is, μ_3 and μ_4; and (2) the difference between means at 30 and 48 months, that is, μ_1 and μ_4. To keep things simple, we assume that we are satisfied to control each per-comparison alpha level at .05. Table 11.13 shows the confidence interval for each of these comparisons, using the pooled error term of Equation 43 and also the separate error term of Equation 44, the latter being computed based on the appropriate difference score variance (see Table 11.11).

The intervals shown in Table 11.13 imply that the difference between means at 42 and 48 months could plausibly be zero, whether we use a pooled or a separate error term. However, we can be reasonably certain that the mean difference between scores at 30 and 48 months is not zero, once again using either type of error term. Notice in particular that the choice of error

TABLE 11.13
CONFIDENCE INTERVALS FOR TWO PAIRWISE
COMPARISONS FOR TABLE 11.5 DATA

	Pooled Error Term	Separate Error Term
$\mu_4 - \mu_3$	2.00 ± 6.48	2.00 ± 4.54
$\mu_4 - \mu_1$	9.00 ± 6.48	9.00 ± 8.78

term does not affect the center of the interval. However, the choice of error term does affect the width of the interval.

The pooled error term based on $MS_{A \times S}$ suggests that the interval width for any pairwise comparison in the McCarthy data is 6.48. In reality, if sphericity is violated, some pairwise comparisons are more variable than others, (see Table 11.11). The intervals based on separate variance estimates shown in Table 11.13 underscore that differences comparing means spaced close together in time are likely to be less variable than those spaced farther apart.

More generally, the pooled error term $MS_{A \times S}$ of Equation 43 assumes that every pairwise difference is estimated with the same precision. In contrast, the separate error term approach of Equation 44 allows some mean differences to be estimated more precisely than others. It can be shown that with a large number of subjects, the *average* interval width of all pairwise comparisons using Equation 44 would be essentially the same as the constant interval width using $MS_{A \times S}$ as in Equation 43. From this perspective, the pooled error term approach provides intervals with the correct average width when we average over all pairwise comparisons, but none of the individual intervals may have an appropriate width. For this reason, we strongly recommend using Equation 44 and procedures to be described in Chapters 13 and 14 to form confidence intervals in within-subjects designs.

OPTIONAL

Confidence Intervals with Pooled and Separate Variances

At this point, you might complain that even though it is clear that the pooled and separate variance error terms produce different intervals, we have failed to provide a compelling argument for preferring the separate variance approach. Although a complete justification is beyond the scope of this book, we take a moment here to illustrate the theoretical grounds for preferring the separate variance approach.

Statisticians often use simulation methods to investigate the performance of different statistical approaches when assumptions may be violated. We illustrate how simulation can reveal the problem with using a pooled error term to form confidence intervals for a contrast when sphericity is violated in a within-subjects design.

Consider a within-subjects design with four levels. We consider two different pairwise comparisons in this design: (1) the mean of level 2 minus the mean of level 1, and (2) the mean of level 4 minus the mean of level 1. We generate random data for 50 subjects in which the population means of levels 1 and 4 equal 50 whereas the population mean of level 2 equals 54. Thus, 95% of intervals we would form for $\mu_2 - \mu_1$ should contain 4, whereas 95% of intervals for $\mu_4 - \mu_1$ should contain 0. We assume normality (technically, multivariate normality) and allow scores at each level to have a standard deviation of 15. However, we do not assume sphericity. Instead, we assume the correlation matrix shown in Table 11.14. Notice in particular that levels 1 and 2 correlate .8 with one another, whereas levels 1 and 4 correlate only .2 with one another.

Figure 11.2 shows confidence intervals formed over 10 replications from this population. (Formal simulation studies usually involve several thousand replications, but our purpose here is simply to illustrate

TABLE 11.14
POPULATION CORRELATION MATRIX
FOR SIMULATED DATA

	Y_1	Y_2	Y_3	Y_4
Y_1	1.0	0.8	0.5	0.2
Y_2	0.8	1.0	0.8	0.5
Y_3	0.5	0.8	1.0	0.8
Y_4	0.2	0.5	0.8	1.0

Confidence Intervals for $\mu_4 - \mu_1$

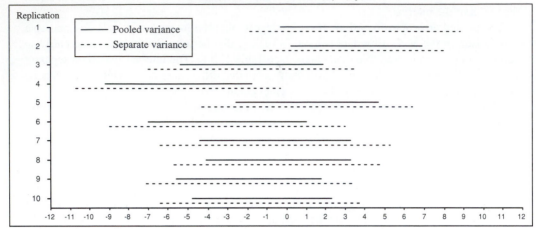

Confidence Intervals for $\mu_2 - \mu_1$

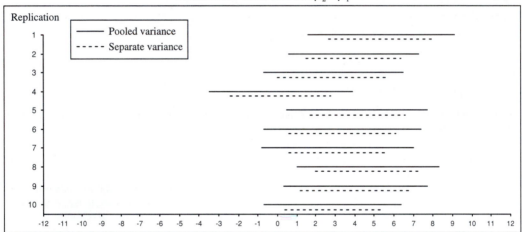

FIG. 11.2.   Confidence intervals over 10 replications for the population mean differences indicated. Solid lines indicate interval widths computed using pooled error terms; dashed lines indicate interval widths computed using separate error terms.

the general pattern of intervals, which is why we display only 10 replications.) This figure contains several important lessons. First, consider the interval for $\mu_4 - \mu_1$. Recall that the population value of this mean difference is 0, so ideally 95% of intervals we form should contain 0. Figure 11.2 shows that 9 of the 10 separate variance intervals do, in fact, contain 0, but that only 8 of the 10 pooled variance intervals contain 0. Although we would need to continue well beyond 10 replications to draw any firm conclusions, if we were to do so, we would discover in the long run that 95% of the separate variance estimates contained 0 whereas a considerably smaller percentage of the pooled variance intervals would contain 0. Thus, the pooled variance approach fails to produce intervals in which we can truly be 95% confident.

Now consider the interval for $\mu_2 - \mu_1$. Ideally, 95% of the intervals for this difference should include the population value of 4. Figure 11.2 shows that both the pooled and the separate variance intervals contain 4 in 9 of the 10 replications. At first glance, this seems to suggest that neither approach is better than the other for this comparison. However, a closer look at Figure 11.2 shows that the two approaches differ dramatically in one respect. Namely, the intervals for the separate variance approach are much narrower than the intervals for the pooled approach. Thus, the separate variance approach provides more precise estimates of the population difference than does the pooled approach for this contrast. Among other things, this translates to a power advantage for the separate variance approach. To see how, consider how many of the 10 intervals for each approach contain 0. Only 2 of the separate variance intervals contain 0. This means that in 8 of the 10 replications, we could reject a null hypothesis (at $\alpha = .05$) that the population means of levels 1 and 2 are equal to one another. To the extent that this pattern maintained itself over a much larger number of replications, we would know that the power of the test equaled .80. Now consider the pooled variance estimate. Examination of Figure 11.2 shows that only 5 of the 10 pooled variance intervals for $\mu_2 - \mu_1$ fail to contain 0. The greater width of the pooled variance intervals has lowered the probability that the interval will be entirely above 0, which means that we have less power and precision with the pooled variance interval than with the pooled variance interval.

To summarize the practical implications of our demonstration, notice that we have identified problems with the pooled variance intervals for both $\mu_4 - \mu_1$ and $\mu_2 - \mu_1$. In the former, the pooled variance intervals tend to be too narrow, so that fewer than 95% of the intervals contain the true population value. In the latter, the pooled variance intervals tend to be too wide, so that we have lost the opportunity for greater power and precision with a narrower interval. In general, when sphericity fails to hold, some pooled variance intervals will be too narrow and others will be too wide, neither of which is desirable. Using separate variance intervals immediately solves this problem, and thus is our recommendation except in cases where there is strong support for the sphericity assumption.

To add theoretical understanding to our practical implications, we briefly describe why some intervals are too narrow and others too wide with the pooled variance approach. Recall from Equation 30 that the variance of the difference $Y_l - Y_m$ between any two levels l and m can be expressed as

$$\sigma^2_{Y_l - Y_m} = \sigma^2_{Y_l} + \sigma^2_{Y_m} - 2\rho_{lm}\sigma_{Y_l}\sigma_{Y_m} \qquad \text{(30, repeated)}$$

We generated our random data from a population where the variance of every level equaled 225. The source of the violation of the sphericity assumption was different correlations between different pairs of levels. In particular, scores at levels 1 and 2 correlate .8 in the population, whereas scores at levels 1 and 4 correlate only .2 in the population. Substituting these values into Equation 30 reveals that the population variance of $Y_2 - Y_1$ is 90, whereas the population variance of $Y_4 - Y_1$ is 360. In other words, the first pairwise comparison is only one-fourth as variable as the second. This difference is reflected in Figure 11.2. Notice that the center of the intervals for $\mu_2 - \mu_1$ varies much less from one replication to the next than does the center of the intervals for $\mu_4 - \mu_1$. That is, the first difference is more stable than is the second. The separate variance intervals reflect this stability. Because the first difference is relatively stable, intervals for this difference can be relatively narrow. In contrast, because the second difference is relatively unstable, intervals for this difference must be much wider. Thus, the widths of the separate variance intervals successfully reflect the relative stabilities of the differences themselves. However, the pooled variance approach requires that every interval within a replication be the same width. As a consequence, some intervals are systematically too narrow and others too wide when sphericity does not hold.

CONSIDERATIONS IN DESIGNING WITHIN-SUBJECTS EXPERIMENTS

As we pointed out at the beginning of the chapter, there are three types of repeated measures designs:

1. Subjects can be observed in different treatment conditions.
2. Scores on different tests (or scales) can be compared.
3. Subjects can be observed longitudinally across time.

The remainder of the chapter deals with the first type of design. In particular, we hope to achieve two goals. First, we discuss some further issues in properly designing this type of study. Second, we compare the relative merits of within-subjects and between-subjects designs for comparing the effects of different treatments.

Order Effects

We will orient our discussion around a hypothetical example we introduced at the beginning of the chapter. Suppose that a physiological psychologist wants to compare the effects of Drugs A and B on aggressiveness in pairs of monkeys. Further suppose that the psychologist has decided to use a repeated-measures design, so that every pair of monkeys will be observed under the influence of both Drug A and Drug B.

How should the study be conducted? One possibility would be to administer Drug A to every pair, observe the subsequent interactions for a period of time, and then administer Drug B to every pair. However, such a design has poor internal validity (see Chapter 1) because it confounds potential drug differences with the possible effects of time. In other words, even if a significant difference between the drugs is obtained, the difference may not have occurred because the drugs truly have a differential effect on aggressiveness. A plausible rival hypothesis is that the monkeys were becoming more or less aggressive (whichever is consistent with the data) across time, independently of differential drug effects. Alternatively, a true difference between the drugs might fail to be detected because time effects might cancel out the real difference in the drugs.

An obvious solution to this problem is to counterbalance the order in which treatments are administered. To counterbalance, we administer Drug A first to half of the monkeys and Drug B first to the other half, with the monkeys being randomly assigned to one half or the other. This type of design is known as a *crossover design* because midway through the study each subject crosses over to the other treatment condition. The logic behind the crossover design is that any main effect of order is controlled for (although not eliminated). As a result, the crossover design possesses much stronger internal validity than does the design where order and treatment condition were confounded.

Differential Carryover Effects

However, even the crossover design is not immune to threats to validity. The greatest threat is the potential presence of a *differential carryover effect*. The general idea of a carryover effect is that the first treatment administered to a subject may continue to have an effect that carries over to the subject's behavior during the second treatment condition. For example, after pairs of monkeys have received Drug A, the nature of their interaction may be altered as a result of Drug A, even when we observe them after administering Drug B. Carryover per se is not necessarily a problem; however, differential carryover is. Differential carryover occurs when the carryover effect of Treatment Condition 1 onto Treatment Condition 2 is different from the carryover effect of Treatment Condition 2 onto Treatment Condition 1. When drugs constitute the treatments, as in our example, this problem is usually handled by incorporating a "wash-out" period between the two drugs. With a long enough time interval between the two administrations, the hope is that any effects of the first drug will have disappeared by the time the second drug is administered.

Although this procedure may successfully eliminate differential carryover effects of drugs (see Fisher & Wallenstein, 1981, for further discussion), even a wash-out period may be insufficient to prevent differential carryover in some behavioral research. For example, suppose

TABLE 11.15
PLAUSIBLE TREATMENT MEANS FOR
STRATEGY INSTRUCTION CROSSOVER STUDY

	Time	
Group	*1*	*2*
Control, then strategy	10	20
Strategy, then control	20	20

that a psychologist wants to investigate the effectiveness of teaching 8-year-old children a "chunking" strategy to improve free-recall performance. We further suppose that the strategy condition is to be compared to a control condition in which no special instructions are given. If a repeated-measures design is used, free-recall performance of one-half of the subjects should first be assessed in the control condition, followed by strategy training, and then a second assessment of performance. The other half of subjects should first receive strategy training and assessment, followed by the control condition and a second assessment. However, there is a problem in this design. If the strategy training is effective, that is, if the children learn how to use chunking to improve their free recall, this effect will likely carry over into the second phase of performance, the control condition. However, when the control condition comes first, it will likely have a much smaller carryover effect. Because the two carryover effects are unequal, we have differential carryover. The specific problem can be understood by examining Table 11.15, which shows a set of means that might plausibly occur in this study. The subjects who receive the control instructions first show a 10-point improvement from strategy instruction. However, the subjects who receive the strategy first show no change whatsoever across the two conditions. As a result, our best guess (assuming equal n) would appear to be that strategy instructions cause a 5-point improvement in scores. However, a more plausible interpretation is that the treatment comparison is confounded by differential carryover, and that, in fact, strategy instruction really improves scores by 10 points.[6] The important point is that the crossover design is a poor choice for answering the question of interest here.

What alternative design might be used instead? One possibility might be to let control precede strategy for all subjects. However, this design would be even worse because, as we have seen, treatment effects and order effects are completely confounded in this design. Another possibility might be to allow a long wash-out period. However, if the strategy instructions truly have the desired effect, there is likely to be some permanent change in the manner in which subjects approach such tasks in the future. Somewhat paradoxically then, if the treatment has the desired effect, no amount of wash-out time may be long enough to eliminate differential carryover. What are we to do then? Probably the best course of action here would be to abandon the within-subjects design entirely. As we discuss momentarily, some types of questions are simply much better suited to between-subjects designs, and questions involving comparisons of different strategies usually fall into this category.

Controlling for Order Effects with More Than Two Levels: Latin Square Designs

Controlling for main effects of order is fairly straightforward with two levels of the repeated factor. However, additional practical complications arise when the repeated factor has more than two levels. To understand why, suppose we want to compare four treatments in a within-subjects design. Following our previous discussion for two levels, to control for order main

TABLE 11.16
A CYCLIC LATIN SQUARE DESIGN
FOR FOUR TREATMENTS*

Subject	Position			
	1	*2*	*3*	*4*
1	A	B	C	D
2	B	C	D	A
3	C	D	A	B
4	D	A	B	C

*A, B, C, and D refer to the four treatment conditions.

effects, we could randomly assign an equal number of subjects to each possible order of the four treatments. However, we would quickly discover that there are 24 possible orders of four treatments, so we need 24 subjects just to represent each order once. In fact, we would probably want to have several subjects per order, necessitating a considerably larger sample. In general, with a treatments to be compared, the number of possible orders is $a!$ (a factorial). For example, when a is 3, there are 6 orders; when a is 4, there are 24 orders; when a is 5, there are 120 orders; and so forth. Thus, administering treatments in all possible orders may not be practical.

There are basically two alternatives to using all possible orders. First, we can randomize the order of treatments for each individual subject. For example, suppose that we now want to compare the effects of four different drugs (A, B, C, and D) on aggressiveness in pairs of monkeys. With this approach, we would randomly choose an order for the first pair, then choose a random order for the second pair, and so forth. By randomizing the order of treatments individually for each subject, we are guaranteed that the order main effect would be controlled for in the long run, that is, the control is probabilistic rather than deterministic.

A second alternative provides a more deterministic control over the order main effect. Table 11.16 displays a possible arrangement for administering treatments. For example, one group of subjects receives the treatments in the order A, B, C, D; a second group receives them in the order B, C, D, A; and so forth. The important feature of this design is that each treatment appears exactly once in each possible sequential position. For example, Treatment A is first for Group 1, second for Group 4, third for Group 3, and fourth for Group 2. Such a design is called a *Latin square*. Its main benefit is that the main effect of position is controlled for because every treatment appears equally often in every position.

Many researchers who use Latin square designs seem to believe that the Latin square shown in Table 11.16 is the only Latin square for four treatment groups. If this were so, there would be a serious problem with Latin square designs. To understand the problem with this particular design, notice that Treatment B always follows immediately after A, C always immediately follows B, D always immediately follows C, and A always immediately follows D. This systematic pattern makes this particular Latin square particularly susceptible to carryover effects.

The specific Latin square shown in Table 11.16 is called a *cyclic square*. A cyclic square of any size (not just 4×4) is obtained by first ordering the treatments alphabetically in row 1. Then, row 2 is formed by moving the first treatment in row 1 to the far right and by shifting all other treatments one position to the left. The same operation is then applied to successive rows. As we have seen, although the cyclic design is popular with many researchers, it is not a good design. Fortunately, there are other Latin squares to consider as alternatives.

Table 11.17 shows three additional Latin squares for the $a = 4$ design, as well as the cyclic square of Table 11.16. Notice that in each square, each treatment appears exactly once in each

TABLE 11.17
STANDARD SQUARES FOR FOUR TREATMENTS

Square 1

	Position			
Subject	*1*	*2*	*3*	*4*
1	A	B	C	D
2	B	C	D	A
3	C	D	A	B
4	D	A	B	C

Square 2

	Position			
Subject	*1*	*2*	*3*	*4*
1	A	B	C	D
2	B	A	D	C
3	C	D	A	B
4	D	C	B	A

Square 3

	Position			
Subject	*1*	*2*	*3*	*4*
1	A	B	C	D
2	B	A	D	C
3	C	D	B	A
4	D	C	A	B

Square 4

	Position			
Subject	*1*	*2*	*3*	*4*
1	A	B	C	D
2	B	D	A	C
3	C	A	D	B
4	D	C	B	A

position. Also notice that both the first row and first column of every square are in the order A, B, C, D. A square where the first row and first column are both in alphabetical order is called a *standard square*. As shown in Table 11.17, there are four standard squares for the $a = 4$ design.

Table 11.17 might seem to suggest that there are a total of four possible Latin squares to choose from when $a = 4$. In fact, there are 576 possible Latin squares when $a = 4$, because it is possible to rearrange the rows and columns of the squares shown in Table 11.17 and still have a Latin square.

How should one of these 576 squares be chosen? The first step is to randomly select one of the standard squares. Then rows and columns are randomly permuted producing a new Latin square. To understand this process, suppose that we have randomly chosen Square 3. Next, to permute the rows, we must randomly order the numbers 1, 2, 3, and 4. Suppose that our random order is 3, 1, 4, 2. We then rewrite Square 3 with row 3 at the top, then row 1, and so forth. Rewriting Square 3 in this way yields

C	D	B	A
A	B	C	D
D	C	A	B
B	A	D	C

Finally, we select another random ordering of the numbers 1, 2, 3, and 4 to permute the columns. Suppose that this time our random ordering is 3, 4, 1, and 2. Rewriting the columns in this order produces

B	A	C	D
C	D	A	B
A	B	D	C
D	C	B	A

Notice that each treatment appears exactly once in each position, meeting the requirements of a Latin square. Further notice that this square improves on the cyclic square of Table 11.16 in that Treatment A no longer always precedes B, B no longer always precedes C, and so forth. In actual research, there would typically be more than four subjects included in the study. When this is so, the square we have just produced should generally be used only for the first four subjects. A second group of four subjects would receive the treatments based on a separately randomly constructed square, as would a third group, and so forth. The use of separate random Latin squares strengthens the validity of the design. Such a design is called a *replicated Latin square design*. Notice that the design requires that the number of subjects must be a multiple of *a*.

An alternative to randomly constructing a square in the aforementioned manner is to use a digram-balanced square, which is a Latin square in which each treatment immediately follows and immediately precedes each other treatment exactly once.[7] An example of such a square for $a = 4$ is

A	B	D	C
B	C	A	D
C	D	B	A
D	A	C	B

Rows of this square can be permuted, but columns cannot be. Digram-balanced squares can be constructed only when *a* is even; when *a* is odd, it is also necessary to construct and use a mirror image of the square. Further details are available in Cochran and Cox (1957), Fleiss (1986), Namboodiri (1972), and Wagenaar (1969).

Two further comments need to be made regarding Latin squares. First, the discussion of analyzing data from Latin squares has been conspicuous because of its absence. In some respects, this absence mirrors current practice, which is often to use a Latin square to design the study but to ignore it in data analysis. Such researchers simply use the procedures we developed earlier in the chapter for analyzing data from one-way within-subjects designs. However, as Fisher pointed out in 1935 (pp. 74–75), and as Gaito echoed in 1961, the data analysis should match the design. The reason we have not discussed data analysis here is that the proper method of analysis depends on issues that are discussed in Chapter 12. Thus, Chapter 12 presents data analysis for the Latin square design. Second, it is important to realize what the

Latin square design does not control for. Although it does control for order main effects, it does not control for persistent differential carryover. Thus, when persistent differential carryover is anticipated, a between-subjects design is once again more appropriate.

RELATIVE ADVANTAGES OF BETWEEN-SUBJECTS AND WITHIN-SUBJECTS DESIGNS

At the beginning of the chapter, we briefly mentioned some advantages of within-subjects designs for comparing the effects of different treatment conditions. We now summarize these advantages as well as possible disadvantages of the within-subjects design.

The first major potential advantage of the within-subjects design is that n subjects generate na data points. For example, if $a = 4$, 10 subjects produce 40 data points. A between-subjects design would require 40 subjects to yield 40 data points. When acquiring enough subjects for a study is difficult, as it often is in behavioral research, the need for fewer subjects in a within-subjects design can be a tremendous advantage. However, if subjects are readily available, but obtaining data in each condition takes a long time, a between-subjects design may actually be preferable.

The second major potential advantage of the within-subjects design is increased power to detect true treatment effects. Because differences between treatments are obtained by comparing scores within each subject, the influence of the subject main effect has been removed from the error term (see the full model of Equation 22). Thus, systematic individual differences do not contribute to the error term, as they do in between-subjects designs. In this regard, the within-subjects design is similar to the analysis of covariance, which we saw in Chapter 9 uses a covariate to control for individual differences between subjects and hence reduces the magnitude of the error term. It is important to understand that this power advantage for the within-subjects design over the between-subjects design (with no covariates) exists even when the within-subjects design includes n subjects and the between-subjects design includes na subjects. To the extent that systematic individual differences between subjects are large, $MS_{A \times S}$ in the within-subjects design will be less than MS_W in the between-subjects design, yielding more power for the within-subjects design.

The implications of the previous paragraph can be made explicit through a formula comparing sample sizes in between-subjects and within-subjects designs. Venter and Maxwell (1999) followed work originated by Senn (1993) to compare three types of designs: between-subjects posttest only, between-subjects pretest–posttest analyzed with ANCOVA, and within-subjects. Specifically, they presented formulas comparing the number of subjects needed in each type of design to achieve equal power (The results presented are approximate in that they do not reflect differences across designs in degrees of freedom; but such differences are of little consequence whenever sample size is at least moderately large, e.g., 20 or more). For example, they showed that in the case of a two-group design, the total number of subjects N_W needed for the within-subjects design is related to N_B, the total number of subjects in the between-subjects design, as follows:

$$N_W = N_B(1 - \rho)/2 \tag{45}$$

where ρ is the population correlation between scores at the two levels of the within-subjects design. Notice that this formula explicitly demonstrates the two power advantages of the within-subjects design. First, the "2" in the denominator of the right side of the equation shows that even when ρ equals zero, the within-subjects design needs only one-half as many

TABLE 11.18
TOTAL SAMPLE SIZE REQUIRED BY VARIOUS DESIGNS TO HAVE POWER
OF .80 FOR DETECTING A MEDIUM DIFFERENCE BETWEEN TWO MEANS

	Type of Design			
	Between-Subjects			
ρ	Posttest Only	Pre–Post ANCOVA	Pre–Post Change	Within-Subjects
0.0	128	128	256	64
0.3	128	117	180	45
0.5	128	96	128	32
0.7	128	66	77	20

subjects as the between-subjects design. Once again, the reason is that each subject in the within-subjects design contributes 2 data points, whereas each subject in the between-subjects design contributes only 1 data point. Second, the $(1 - \rho)$ term in the numerator reflects the benefit of using each subject as his or her own control. To the extent that systematic individual differences exist, ρ is sizable, thus reducing even further the number of subjects needed in the within-subjects design.

Although the within-subjects design clearly has a power advantage over the between-subjects posttest only design, it is less obvious how the within-subjects design compares to a between-subjects design with a pretest. Venter and Maxwell (1999) show that when the pretest–posttest correlation equals the correlation between levels in the within-subjects design, the sample sizes for the two designs are related as follows:

$$N_{\text{W}} = N_{\text{PP}}/[2(1 + \rho)] \tag{46}$$

where N_{PP} is the total number of subjects for the pretest–posttest design analyzed with ANCOVA. The practical implication of Equation 46 is that the within-subjects design also requires fewer subjects than the pretest–posttest design, especially for larger values of ρ.

Table 11.18 provides one perspective on the sample sizes needed in different designs. This table shows the total sample size needed to obtain a power of .80 for detecting a medium effect size in a randomized two-group study as a function of ρ under the aforementioned assumptions. Four designs are considered: between-subjects posttest-only, between-subjects pretest–posttest analyzed with ANCOVA, between-subjects pretest–posttest analyzed with change scores, and within-subjects. We want to draw your attention to three points. First, the within-subjects design clearly requires the fewest subjects, and its advantage is striking when ρ is moderate to large. Second, consistent with the principles we developed in Chapter 9, including a pretest and performing ANCOVA can substantially reduce the subjects needed in a between-subjects design, but only when the pretest–posttest correlation ρ is moderately large. Third, including a pretest but analyzing change scores instead of using ANCOVA can be much worse than ignoring the pretest altogether. For this reason, when a pretest is included in a randomized design, it is almost always preferable to analyze the data with ANCOVA instead of change scores.

We conclude our discussion of power advantages with three final points. First, under compound symmetry, Equation 45 can be generalized to the case of a levels as follows:

$$N_{\text{W}} = N_{\text{B}}(1 - \rho)/a \tag{47}$$

Not surprisingly, the economy of the within-subjects design is even greater here than in the simpler two-level design. Second, although in theory Equation 47 could be used to determine necessary sample size in a within-subjects design, we do not recommend its general use because it relies on compound symmetry. In Chapter 13 we present an alternative formula based on the multivariate approach, but, for the moment, the most relevant method of determining sample size in within-subjects designs comes from Muller and Barton (1989), who derived an approach that does not require sphericity. A detailed description of their method is beyond the scope of this book, but fortunately their approach has recently begun to appear in selected power analysis software. As of this writing, the most complete implementation of their approach is available in Elashoff (2000). Third, Vonesh (1983) compared the power of within-subjects and between-subjects designs for testing individual comparisons. Although his results are complicated by several factors, the general practical implication appears to be that the within-subjects approach is typically more powerful whenever the minimum correlation between measures is at least .25.

The primary potential disadvantage of the within-subjects design is differential carryover, which we have seen biases estimates of treatment effects. For this reason, certain types of independent variables are typically not manipulated in a within-subjects design. Examples of such variables would include strategy training, instructions involving deception, and types of psychotherapy. A common characteristic of these variables is that their effects are likely to persist over time. Although permanent effects do not necessarily lead to differential carryover, in most practical situations they do. Thus, within-subjects designs are usually most appropriate for studying independent variables whose effects are likely to be temporary.

Another issue that must be considered is that within-subjects and between-subjects designs may not be answering the same question, even when the manipulated variables appear to be the same. The reason they may differ is that in the within-subjects design, subjects experience each manipulation in the context of other manipulations. In the between-subjects design, each subject experiences only one manipulation. We are not trying to argue that either situation is better, simply that they are different. For further discussion of this issue, see Greenwald (1976), Grice (1966), Kazdin (1980), Poulton (1975), and Rothstein (1974).

We make two final points in closing this section. First, do not forget that within-subjects designs are also useful for purposes other than comparing manipulated variables. In particular, one of the most frequent uses of within-subjects designs in the behavioral sciences is to study change over time. Chapter 15 provides additional detail about recent statistical developments for analyzing data from longitudinal designs. Second, within-subjects factors are often combined with between-subjects factors in the same design. These designs are discussed in Chapter 12 (mixed-model approach) and in Chapter 14 (multivariate approach).

INTRACLASS CORRELATIONS FOR ASSESSING RELIABILITY

We introduced the intraclass correlation in Chapter 10 as a measure of strength of relationship in designs with a random factor. Intraclass correlations can also be very relevant in within-subjects designs. In particular, intraclass correlations provide measures of reliability when subjects are rated by multiple judges or obtain scores on multiple items of a test or scale. To distinguish this application of intraclass correlation from its use as a measure of effect size, we will use a different notation than in Chapter 10. The current notation will also allow us to distinguish between the variety of cases that arise in estimating reliability.

Our presentation here closely follows Shrout and Fleiss's (1979) classic article on intraclass correlations. To motivate this topic, Table 11.19 duplicates a table from Shrout and Fleiss showing hypothetical data obtained from four judges, each of whom has rated six targets (i.e., subjects). Before proceeding, we need to make three points. First, notice that the structure

TABLE 11.19
RATINGS ON SIX SUBJECTS FROM
FOUR JUDGES

Subject	Judge			
	1	2	3	4
1	9	2	5	8
2	6	1	3	2
3	8	4	6	8
4	7	1	2	6
5	10	5	6	9
6	6	2	4	7

of the data in Table 11.19 is identical to the structure of the McCarthy data in Table 11.5. The only difference is that the within-subjects factor is now judge instead of time. Second, the within-subjects factor might have been item, instead of judge. Third, we could proceed by testing hypotheses and forming estimates about the means of the within-subjects factor. However, in this section our interest is focused on a different aspect of the data. Specifically, we may be interested in knowing to what extent scores obtained for our targets are generalizable over a different set of judges or items. More precisely, how much of the variance between subjects' scores is true variance? This is precisely the definition of reliability in classical test theory (e.g., Crocker & Algina, 1986). Stated differently, reliability is the squared correlation between subjects' observed scores and their (unknown) true scores. If reliability is high, scores we actually observe can be said to be highly correlated with the unknown true scores we would ideally like to measure. Thus, reliability is a crucial component of adequate measurement.

A common way to estimate reliability of measures in the behavioral sciences is to obtain multiple measures of a presumed construct for each subject, either through multiple judges or multiple items. The degree of similarity across judges or items reflects the reliability of the measure. Shrout and Fleiss (1979) describe four types of intraclass correlation that are relevant to the within-subjects design. We briefly describe each, along with an explanation of when each is likely to be the preferred index of reliability.

How reliable are judges' ratings in Table 11.19? The answer depends on how we conceptualize reliability. In particular, Shrout and Fleiss (1979) suggest that we need to consider two issues in order to answer this question for within-subjects data. First, do we want our reliability measure to reflect consistency or agreement? To understand this distinction, consider the hypothetical data shown in Table 11.20. Notice that the rank order of targets is identical for each of the three judges (in fact, not only are the ranks identical, but the scores are also perfectly linearly related to one another in this example). However, in an absolute sense, the ratings provided by Judge 2 are clearly very different from the ratings of the other two judges. Would we want to conclude that reliability is high or low in these data? Shrout and Fleiss (1979) convincingly argue that the answer to this question depends on whether we conceptualize reliability in terms of consistency or agreement. Consistency is relatively low in these data, because the columns of scores do not closely resemble one another. In other words, what score a target is likely to receive depends strongly on which judge provides the rating. However, agreement is high in these data because the relative position of any target in the distribution of scores is identical for each and every judge. So whether reliability is low or high here depends on how we choose to think about reliability. Specifically, do we want mean differences between judges to affect our measure of reliability? If we do, we should use what Shrout and Fleiss refer to as a *Case 2 intraclass correlation*. If we do not want mean differences to affect our measure, we should use a *Case 3 intraclass correlation*.

TABLE 11.20
RATINGS ON FIVE SUBJECTS FROM
THREE JUDGES

		Judge	
Subject	*1*	*2*	*3*
1	9	5	11
2	6	2	8
3	8	4	10
4	7	3	9
5	4	0	6

Shrout and Fleiss (1979) show that the difference between Case 2 and Case 3 intraclass correlations is reflected in different formulas for estimating reliability. Specifically, when the goal is to estimate the reliability of a single judge (more about this in a moment), the respective formulas can be written as ICC(2, 1) for Case 2 and ICC(3, 1) for Case 3. The estimated Case 2 intraclass correlation coefficient is given by

$$ICC(2, 1) = \frac{MS_S - MS_{A \times S}}{MS_S + (a - 1)MS_{A \times S} + a(MS_A - MS_{A \times S})/n} \tag{48}$$

The estimated Case 3 intraclass correlation coefficient is given by

$$ICC(3, 1) = \frac{MS_S - MS_{A \times S}}{MS_S + (a - 1)MS_{A \times S}} \tag{49}$$

From a computational perspective, the only difference between ICC(2, 1) and ICC(3, 1) is the presence or absence of a third term in the denominator. This term reflects the extent to which MS_A is larger than $MS_{A \times S}$, or, in other words, the extent to which the means of the levels of A differ from one another. Keep in mind that in the context of judges or items, the levels of A are literally the individual judges or items. Thus, this term reflects how much the means of different judges or items differ from one another. Comparing Equations 48 and 49 shows that ICC(2, 1) is sensitive to such mean differences, whereas ICC(3, 1) is not. To illustrate this distinction, let's return to the data of Table 11.20.

The values of mean squares for subjects (S), raters (A), and their interaction (A×S) for the Table 11.20 data are as follows:

$$MS_S = 11.10$$
$$MS_A = 46.67$$
$$MS_{A \times S} = 0.00$$

Note that the zero value for $MS_{A \times S}$ reflects the fact that there is literally no interaction in these artificial data. For every subject, the scores from Rater 2 are 4 points lower than those from Rater 1, and the scores from Rater 3 are 2 points higher than those from Rater 1. In real data, we would not expect a mean square to equal zero, but we have chosen to present a simplified example to illustrate the difference in the types of intraclass correlation.

Substituting the three values of the mean squares into Equations 48 and 49 reveals that

$$ICC(2, 1) = 0.28$$
$$ICC(3, 1) = 1.00$$

for these data. Why is ICC(2, 1) so much less than ICC(3, 1) here? The reason is that they answer different questions. Specifically, ICC(2, 1) is a measure of consistency. To what extent are ratings consistent across judges? To understand exactly what this means, suppose we wanted to know which subject is truly highest on the construct of interest. Examining all three columns in Table 11.20 shows that all three judges rate Subject 1 highest. Does this mean that Subject 1 is consistently rated higher than other subjects are rated? Not literally, because, for example, Judge 1 rates everyone but Subject 5 higher than Judge 2 rates Subject 1. Thus, if we were to compare Subject 1 as rated from Judge 2 to other subjects as rated by Judge 1, we would conclude that Subject 1 has a lower score than most of the other subjects. However, ICC(3, 1) is a measure of agreement. In other words, to what extent do the judges agree with one another about the relative position of subjects on the construct of interest? From this perspective, the judges are in perfect agreement with one another, so ICC(3, 1) equals 1.00 for these data. The bottom line is that you must decide whether mean differences between judges should affect your measure of reliability. If the answer is yes, then ICC(2, 1) is appropriate, whereas if the answer is no, then ICC(3, 1) is preferable. We should also note that ICC(2, 1) is usually somewhat lower than ICC(3, 1), but this is not a reason to prefer ICC(3, 1), because although consistency is more difficult to achieve than agreement, consistency may be what is of theoretical interest.

The remainder of this section uses the data of Table 11.19 to motivate our discussion. Using the same methods for these data shows that ICC(2, 1) equals .29 and ICC(3, 1) equals .71 here. Once again, there is a sizable difference because the judges are using different portions of the rating scale (e.g., the ratings of Judge 1 range from 6 to 10, whereas those of Judge 2 range from 1 to 5). If judges were more consistent in using the same range of the rating scale, ICC(2, 1) and ICC(3, 1) would be more similar to one another.

So far we have considered the reliability of a single judge. However, in many situations, the question of real interest involves the reliability of a composite score obtained by averaging over judges or items. For example, in the data of Table 11.19, we might form an average score for each subject by calculating a mean over judges. The reliability of this mean score will always be greater than the reliability of a single judge (assuming the reliability of a single judge is greater than zero), which is precisely why we often prefer to base further analyses on such mean ratings.

Shrout and Fleiss (1979) denote the reliability of ratings obtained from a judges as:

$$ICC(2, a) = \frac{MS_S - MS_{A \times S}}{MS_S + (MS_A - MS_{A \times S})/n} \tag{50}$$

and

$$ICC(3, a) = \frac{MS_S - MS_{A \times S}}{MS_S} \tag{51}$$

for consistency and agreement, respectively. For the sake of clarity, we should acknowledge that Shrout and Fleiss use the letter k to represent the number of judges, so their actual notation is ICC(2, k) and ICC(3, k). In the Table 11.19 data, ICC(2, 4) equals .62 and ICC(3, 4) equals .91. The increases from .29 and .71 reflect the benefit of averaging over individual raters or items.

Shrout and Fleiss (1979) point out that ICC(3, k) is equivalent to Cronbach's (1951) alpha coefficient, one of the most common reliability indices in the behavioral sciences. This index is itself a generalization of the Kuder–Richardson (1937) Formula 20 for dichotomous data.

In closing, Shrout and Fleiss (1979) provide additional formulas for forming confidence intervals for population values of various intraclass correlation coefficients. They also describe tests of significance. Finally, they also describe situations calling for different types of coefficients, such as the choice between measures of consistency and agreement.

EXERCISES

1. Within-subjects designs and ANCOVA are similar in that they both attempt to achieve greater power by doing what?

2. Some experimental factors can be manipulated either between subjects or within subjects.
   a. What are the two principal advantages of using a within-subjects design?
   b. What weakness of within-subjects designs might cause an experimenter to decide against using them in certain areas of research even though conceivably they could be used there?

*3. The following hypothetical data represent level of EEG activity in four locations of the brain among five subjects who were engaged in a mental arithmetic task. The question of interest is whether there is differential level of EEG activity across the four locations.

Subject	Location			
	1	2	3	4
1	3	6	4	5
2	4	7	4	8
3	2	1	1	3
4	4	5	1	5
5	7	6	5	9

   a. Calculate predicted scores for the full model for these data.
   b. Calculate discrepancies between the actual scores and the predicted scores of part a.
   c. Calculate predicted scores for the restricted model for these data.
   d. Calculate discrepancies between the actual scores and the predicted scores of part c.
   e. Use the results of parts b and d to calculate an observed F value for these data. Is there a statistically significant difference among the locations, using an unadjusted test?
   f. Would your answer to part e change if you used the Geisser–Greenhouse lower-bound correction?
   g. How do the results of using the $\hat{\varepsilon}$ adjustment compare to the results you obtained in parts e and f?
   h. How do the results of using the $\tilde{\varepsilon}$ adjustment compare to the results you obtained in parts e and f?

*4. Consider the data shown in Table 11.1 of the text.
   a. Find SS_A and $SS_{A \times S}$ for these data.
   b. Based on your answer to part a, calculate an observed F value for these data.
   c. How does the F value you found in part b compare to the F value reported in Table 11.3 for testing H_0: $\mu_D = 0$?
   d. Is your answer to part c consistent with the assertion that Equation 16 is a special case of Equation 28?

*5. The following data have been collected from five individuals in a one-way within-subjects design with three levels:

Subject	Treatment Condition		
	1	2	3
1	10	12	14
2	2	5	5
3	5	6	10
4	12	15	18
5	16	17	18

a. Calculate SS_A, SS_S, and $SS_{A \times S}$ for these data.

b. Can you reject a null hypothesis that the population means of the three treatment conditions are equal to each other?

c. Suppose that an investigator mistakenly analyzed these data as if they came from a between-subjects design. Find SS_A and SS_W for these data. How do these values compare to the values you calculated in part a?

d. Could you reject a null hypothesis that the population means of the three treatment conditions are equal to each other if the data were analyzed as if they came from a between-subjects design?

e. How do parts a–d demonstrate one of the major potential advantages of a within-subjects design?

*6. Consider the data of Table 11.5.

a. Perform a one-way between-subjects ANOVA on an adjusted dependent variable defined as $Y_{ij} - \overline{Y}_i$. In other words, subtract the row marginal mean from each score prior to performing the ANOVA.

b. How does the F value you obtained in part a compare to the F value obtained from Equation 28 in the text?

c. How do the answers to parts a and b help explain that a one-way within-subjects ANOVA is like a one-way between-subjects ANOVA in which each subject serves as his or her own control?

7. True or False: In a one-way within-subjects design having two levels, the fact that the minimum value of ε is 1.0 indicates that the restrictive assumption of homogeneity of treatment-difference variances made by the univariate approach cannot be violated in such a design.

8. A psychologist has conducted a study involving one within-subjects factor with five levels. The test of the omnibus null hypothesis yields an F value of 4.43, with 4 numerator and 20 denominator degrees of freedom. When a colleague argues that the finding might be misleading if sphericity was violated, the psychologist argues that the finding was "robust" because of the very low p value ($p = .01$).

a. Are you convinced by this argument, or might the low p value plausibly be a result of violating the sphericity assumption?

b. Would your answer change if the psychologist had obtained an F value of 6.80? Why or why not?

*9. Find the theoretical minimum value of ε in each of the following situations:

a. $n = 15$, $a = 3$
b. $n = 12$, $a = 4$
c. $n = 16$, $a = 5$
d. $n = 10$, $a = 2$

10. Find the numerator and denominator degrees of freedom for the critical F using the Geisser–Greenhouse lower-bound correction in each of the following situations:

a. $n = 15$, $a = 3$
b. $n = 12$, $a = 4$
c. $n = 16$, $a = 5$
d. $n = 10$, $a = 2$

*11. Find the critical F value for the unadjusted mixed-model approach and the critical F value for the Geisser–Greenhouse lower-bound correction approach in each of the following situations:

a. $n = 15$, $a = 3$
b. $n = 12$, $a = 4$
c. $n = 16$, $a = 5$
d. $n = 10$, $a = 2$

12. Explain in your own words why $\hat{\varepsilon}$ tends to underestimate ε when the sphericity assumption is valid in the population.

13. According to Table 11.11, the variance of the difference between 48- and 36-month McCarthy scores in the Table 11.5 data is much greater than the difference between 48- and 42-month scores.

a. Calculate the change from 36 to 48 months for each subject.
b. Calculate the variance of the scores you calculated in part a.
c. Calculate the change from 42 to 48 months for each subject.
d. Calculate the variance of the scores you calculated in part c.
e. Is there more variability in change from 36 to 48 months than in change from 42 to 48 months? Does such a pattern seem plausible in actual data? Explain your answer.

14. Consider the following population covariance matrix:

$$\begin{bmatrix} 1.0 & 0.5 & 1.0 & 1.5 \\ 0.5 & 2.0 & 1.5 & 2.0 \\ 1.0 & 1.5 & 3.0 & 2.5 \\ 1.5 & 2.0 & 2.5 & 4.0 \end{bmatrix}$$

Each entry on the diagonal represents a population variance, whereas each off-diagonal element represents a covariance.
a. Does this matrix possess compound symmetry? How can you tell?
b. Is the homogeneity of treatment-difference variances assumption met for these data?
c. How do your answers to parts a and b relate to the relationship between compound symmetry and sphericity shown in Figure 11.1?

15. True or false: Sphericity is an important assumption for hypothesis tests in within-subjects designs, but is of much less concern for forming confidence intervals.

16. An experimenter is planning to conduct a study using a repeated-measures design with four levels, which we label A, B, C, and D. A total of 20 subjects will be included in the study. To control for order effects, one group of 5 subjects will receive the treatments in the order A, B, C, D. A second group of 5 subjects will receive the treatments in the order B, C, D, A. A third group of 5 subjects will receive the treatments in the order C, D, A, B. The final group of 5 subjects will receive the treatments in the order D, A, B, C. Will the proposed design properly control order effects? Why or why not?

17. (To be done by computer.) A developmental psychologist is interested in the role of the sound of a mother's heartbeat in the growth of newborn babies. Fourteen babies were placed in a nursery where they were constantly exposed to a rhythmic heartbeat sound piped in over the PA system. Infants were weighed at the same time of day for four consecutive days, yielding the following data (weight is measured in ounces):

Subject	Day 1	Day 2	Day 3	Day 4
1	96	98	103	104
2	116	116	118	119
3	102	102	101	101
4	112	115	116	118
5	108	110	112	115
6	92	95	96	98
7	120	121	121	123
8	112	111	111	109
9	95	96	98	99
10	114	112	110	109
11	99	100	99	98
12	124	125	127	126
13	100	98	95	94
14	106	107	106	107

a. Test the omnibus null hypothesis that the population mean weight is the same for all 4 days, using the unadjusted mixed-model approach.

b. Would your answer to part a change if you were to use the $\hat{\varepsilon}$ adjustment? (Hint: After finding the answer to part a, you should be able to answer part b without having to calculate $\hat{\varepsilon}$.)

c. Would your answer to part a change if you were to use the $\tilde{\varepsilon}$ adjustment? (Hint: After finding the answer to part a, you should be able to answer part c without having to calculate $\tilde{\varepsilon}$.)

d. How do the results of parts a–c compare to each other?

e. Calculate the value of omega squared for these data. How would you interpret this value?

f. Find the standardized mean difference between weight at Day 1 and weight at Day 4. How would you describe the magnitude of this difference?

g. Is this a good design for assessing the effects of a heartbeat sound on infants' growth? Why or why not? How could the internal validity of the design be strengthened?

18. Psychologists have become increasingly interested in the role of perceived control as it affects individuals' abilities to cope with stress. This exercise is modeled after Bandura, A., Taylor, C. B., Williams, L., Mefford, I. N., & Barchas, J. D. (1985) "Catecholamine secretion as a function of perceived coping self-efficacy." *Journal of Consulting and Clinical Psychology, 53*, 406–414. They hypothesized that perceived coping self-efficacy would mediate the effects of an environmental stressor on hormone secretions indicative of a physiological response to stress. Twelve individuals with phobic dread of spiders served as subjects. They each rated their perceived coping self-efficacy for 18 tasks requiring increasingly threatening interactions with a large spider. Three of the 18 tasks were individually selected for each subject, so as to have one strong, one medium, and one weak self-efficacy task for each subject. Subjects were then individually instructed to perform each of their three tasks in a counterbalanced order. In reality, no subject was able to perform the weak perceived self-efficacy task. The dependent variable to be considered here, level of norepinephrine secretion, was one of several physiological measures obtained from each subject.

Consider the following (hypothetical) data, where higher scores are indicative of greater stress.

Subject	Strong	Medium	Weak
1	.38	.25	.20
2	.36	.41	.37
3	.16	.49	.43
4	.22	.26	.18
5	.17	.27	.24
6	.41	.48	.40
7	.34	.39	.22
8	.19	.25	.34
9	.25	.35	.30
10	.36	.40	.32
11	.24	.33	.29
12	.30	.35	.27

a. Does the mean level of norepinephrine differ according to the strength of perceived self-efficacy? Analyze the data using the unadjusted F test.

b. Would your answer to part a change if you used the Geisser–Greenhouse lower-bound adjusted test?

c. (To be done by computer.) What is the value of $\hat{\varepsilon}$ for these data? Does your answer to part a change with this procedure?

d. Suppose that it was decided post hoc to test two comparisons: strong versus weak, and medium versus the average of strong and weak. Is either of these comparisons statistically significant?

e. Suppose strength of self-efficacy were conceptualized as a quantitative factor with equally spaced levels. How would you label the comparisons tested in part d?

f. Form a confidence interval for the mean difference between strong and weak condition means, assuming sphericity.

    g. Form a confidence interval for the mean difference between strong and weak condition means, without assuming sphericity.

    h. How do your intervals in parts f and g compare to each other?

    i. It seems plausible that subjects might have experienced less stress if they had been allowed to begin with their strong self-efficacy task, then move to the medium task, and finally end with the weak task. Would this design have been preferable to the design that was actually used? Why or why not?

19. (To be done by computer.) Until the 1960s it was believed that infants had little or no pattern vision during the early weeks or even months of their lives. The following study is modeled after an experiment reported by Fantz, R. L. (1963) "Pattern vision in newborn infants." *Science, 140*, 296–297. Fourteen infants under 48 hr old were exposed to a series of targets, presented in a random sequence to each infant. Three of the targets contained black-and-white patterns: a schematic face, concentric circles, and a section of newspaper. The fourth target was an unpatterned white circle. A blue background was provided in all cases to contrast with the target. The dependent measure is the length of gaze (in sec) of an infant at a particular target. The following (hypothetical) data were obtained:

Subject	Face	Circle	Newspaper	White
1	3.1	3.4	1.7	1.8
2	1.3	0.6	0.7	0.5
3	2.1	1.7	1.2	0.7
4	1.5	0.9	0.6	0.4
5	0.9	0.6	0.9	0.8
6	1.6	1.8	0.6	0.8
7	1.8	1.4	0.8	0.6
8	1.4	1.2	0.7	0.5
9	2.7	2.3	1.2	1.1
10	1.5	1.2	0.7	0.6
11	1.4	0.9	1.0	0.5
12	1.6	1.5	0.9	1.0
13	1.3	1.5	1.4	1.6
14	1.3	0.9	1.2	1.4

    a. Test the omnibus null hypothesis for these data using the unadjusted mixed-model approach.

    b. Test the same hypothesis using the $\hat{\varepsilon}$ adjustment.

    c. Test the same hypothesis using the $\tilde{\varepsilon}$ adjustment.

    d. How do the results of parts a–c compare to each other?

20. A psychologist wants to compare a treatment intervention to a control condition. His best guess is that the treatment will produce a medium effect in the population. Furthermore, he suspects that the correlation between scores in the two conditions would be around 0.5.

    a. What total sample size will he need to have a power of .80 in a posttest-only design?

    b. What total sample size will he need to have a power of .80 in a within-subjects design?

    c. What other considerations beyond sample size should influence his ultimate choice of which design is preferable?

21. A developmental psychologist wants to study the role of maternal warmth on infants' emotional development. She has trained graduate students to rate mothers' warmth while watching videotapes of mothers interacting with their infants. Before proceeding to use this measure in later studies, she is interested in the psychometric properties of her measure. She has obtained the following data from three raters, each of whom rated the same 14 mothers on a scale from 1 (least warmth) to 9 (most warmth).

Mother	Rater 1	Rater 2	Rater 3
1	4	6	4
2	7	7	6
3	3	3	5
4	8	9	8
5	2	4	5
6	6	6	6
7	1	3	3
8	8	9	8
9	5	7	4
10	1	4	4
11	9	8	9
12	4	3	7
13	2	4	5
14	6	8	5

a. Calculate a measure of agreement for a single rater.
b. Calculate a measure of consistency for a single rater.
c. When would a measure of agreement be more appropriate and when would a measure of consistency be more appropriate?
d. The psychologist ultimately plans to average ratings from these three raters and use this average as a predictor of later infant development. Which if either of the values you calculated in parts a and b provides an appropriate index of reliability under these conditions? If yet a different index might be more appropriate, calculate it and explain its interpretational advantage.

12

Higher-Order Designs with Within-Subjects Factors: Univariate Approach

This chapter extends the mixed-model methodology developed in Chapter 11 for one-way within-subjects designs to more complicated factorial designs. In this respect, this chapter is related to Chapter 11 just as Chapters 7 and 8 are related to Chapter 3 for between-subjects designs. We will see that the concepts developed in Chapters 7 and 8 for between-subjects factorial designs are applicable for within-subjects factorial designs as well. The only real difference is that the statistical tests must once again take into account the fact that the design involves a within-subjects factor.

There are two rather different ways in which the one-way within-subjects design of Chapter 11 can be generalized. First, there might be a second within-subjects factor included in the design. Although it is possible for one factor to be nested under the other, more frequently these two factors are crossed with one another. For this reason, we focus our attention almost exclusively on the design in which the within-subjects factors are crossed. Second, besides a within-subjects factor, there might also be a between-subjects factor. In other words, one (or more) between-subjects factor could be crossed with one (or more) within-subjects factor in the same design. We discuss these two types of designs separately, beginning with the design where both factors (or more generally, all factors) are within-subjects.

At the outset, we should state that this chapter describes only the mixed-model approach to analyzing both types of designs. However, a set of restrictive assumptions similar to those discussed in Chapter 11 must be met for this approach to be valid. As in the one-way design, $\hat{\varepsilon}$- and $\tilde{\varepsilon}$-adjustment procedures can also be used in factorial designs when the assumptions of the unadjusted approach have not been met. Alternatively, the multivariate approach does not require these restrictive assumptions and thus needs no adjustments. Chapter 14 presents the multivariate approach for factorial within-subjects designs.

DESIGNS WITH TWO WITHIN-SUBJECTS FACTORS

To motivate the analysis of this type of design, we orient our discussion around a specific study in which a two-way within-subjects design might be used. Suppose that a perceptual

TABLE 12.1
HYPOTHETICAL REACTION TIME DATA FOR 2 × 3 PERCEPTUAL EXPERIMENT

Subject	Noise Absent			Noise Present		
	0° Angle	4° Angle	8° Angle	0° Angle	4° Angle	8° Angle
1	420	420	480	480	600	780
2	420	480	480	360	480	600
3	480	480	540	660	780	780
4	420	540	540	480	780	900
5	540	660	540	480	660	720
6	360	420	360	360	480	540
7	480	480	600	540	720	840
8	480	600	660	540	720	900
9	540	600	540	480	720	780
10	480	420	540	540	660	780
Mean	462	510	528	492	660	762

psychologist studying the visual system was interested in determining the extent to which interfering visual stimuli slow the ability to recognize letters. Subjects are brought into a laboratory and seated in front of a tachistoscope. Subjects are told that they will see either the letter T or the letter I displayed on the screen. In some trials, the letter appears by itself, but in other trials, the target letter is embedded in a group of other letters. This variation in the display constitutes the first factor, which is referred to as *noise*. The noise factor has two levels—absent and present. The other factor varied by the experimenter is where in the display the target letter appears. This factor, which is called *angle*, has three levels. The target letter is either shown at the center of the screen (i.e., 0° off-center, where the subject has been instructed to fixate), 4° off-center or 8° off-center (in each case, the deviation from the center varies randomly between left and right). Table 12.1 presents hypothetical data for 10 subjects. As usual, the sample size is kept small to make the calculations easier to follow. The dependent measure is reaction time (latency), measured in milliseconds (ms), required by a subject to identify the correct target letter. Notice that each subject has six scores, one for each combination of the 2 × 3 design. In an actual perceptual experiment, each of these six scores would itself be the mean score for that subject across a number of trials in the particular condition. Although "trials" could be used as a third within-subjects factor in such a situation, more typically trials are simply averaged over to obtain a more stable measure of the individual's performance in each condition.

Omnibus Tests

The questions to be addressed in this factorial design are exactly the same as those discussed in Chapter 7 for two-way between-subjects designs. In any two-way design, the initial questions typically of most interest are the significance of the two main effects and the interaction.[1] In other words, the effects to be tested are the same whether the factors are within or between subjects. However, the reason we cannot immediately finish the chapter here is that, although the effects are the same, the way in which they are tested changes. Thus, our attention throughout the chapter largely is focused on choosing an appropriate error term. We devote somewhat less attention to the rationale for the sequence of tests we choose to perform because the underlying logic is identical to that developed in Chapters 7 and 8 for the between-subjects design. If you feel the need for a reminder, we especially encourage you to look back at Figures 7.2 (p. 308) and 8.6 (p. 362), which present general guidelines for choosing tests to perform in two-way and three-way designs.

The three effects to be tested for the data of Table 12.1 are the main effect of angle (which we designate as A), the main effect of noise (which we designate B), and the interaction of angle and noise. To consider how we might test these effects, recall from Chapter 11 how we analyzed data from a design with only one within-subjects factor. The one-way design was analyzed as a two-factor design, with one factor representing the repeated condition and the second factor representing subjects. Exactly the same approach can be taken in the case of multiple within-subjects factors.

An appropriate full model for the two-way within-subjects design is given by

$$Y_{ijk} = \mu + \alpha_j + \beta_k + \pi_i + (\alpha\beta)_{jk} + (\alpha\pi)_{ji} + (\beta\pi)_{ki} + (\alpha\beta\pi)_{jki} + \varepsilon_{ijk} \qquad (1)$$

where Y_{ijk} is the score on the dependent variable for the ith subject at the jth level of A and kth level of B; μ is the grand mean parameter; α_j is the effect associated with the jth level of A; β_k is the effect associated with the kth level of B; π_i is the effect associated with the ith subject; $(\alpha\beta)_{jk}$ is the effect of the interaction of the jth level of A and the kth level of B; $(\alpha\pi)_{ji}$ is the effect of the interaction of the jth level of A and the ith subject; $(\beta\pi)_{ki}$ is the effect of the interaction of the kth level of B and the ith subject; $(\alpha\beta\pi)_{jki}$ is the effect of the three-way interaction of the jth level of A, the kth level of B, and ith subject; and ε_{ijk} is the error for the ith subject in the jth level of A and kth level of B. This model is identical to the model we used in Chapter 8 for a three-way between-subjects design, except that now the third factor is "subject."

As shown in Equation 1, there are seven effects included in the full model for the two-way within-subjects design. Specifically, there are three main effects (A, B, and S), three two-way interactions (A × B, A × S, and B × S), and one three-way interaction (A × B × S). Recall that this agrees with our discussion in Chapter 8 of three-way between-subjects designs, where we stated that there were seven effects of potential interest.

The magnitude of each of these seven effects can be determined by comparing the full model of Equation 1 to a restricted model that omits the parameters associated with the effect in question. The resulting difference in sum of squared errors represents the sum of squares attributable to that particular effect. As usual with equal n, this difference can be obtained directly from the full model. The sum of squares attributable to an effect equals the sum of squared parameter estimates for that effect in the full model, with the sum being computed across all abn observations. Although it is useful conceptually to realize that these sums of squares can be calculated by using least squares to estimate parameters in the full and the restricted models, there is a simpler alternative in practice. After some tedious algebra similar to that demonstrated in Chapter 7 for the two-way between-subjects design, it is possible to write general expressions for the sum of squares attributable to each effect in the two-way within-subjects design. Table 12.2 shows these sums of squares and corresponding degrees of freedom. Examining Table 12.2 shows that the sum of squares and degrees of freedom for each effect are calculated in exactly the same manner as for any other completely crossed three-way design.[2] As we will see shortly, the only distinguishing feature of the two-way within-subjects design is how error terms are chosen for testing these effects.

As stated earlier, we are interested in testing three effects in this two-way design: the A main effect, the B main effect, and the AB interaction. If this were not a within-subjects design and if all factors were fixed instead of random, mean square within (MS_W) could be used as an error term (i.e., denominator in the F statistic) for testing each effect. However, in the present design, a different error term is needed, just as it was in Chapters 10 and 11; indeed, there is not even a within-cell term that could be used in this design because there is only one observation per cell. As in the previous two chapters, the choice of an error term is dictated by the expected mean squares of the effects in the model.

TABLE 12.2
SUM OF SQUARES AND DEGREES OF FREEDOM FOR EACH EFFECT IN A TWO-WAY
WITHIN-SUBJECTS DESIGN

Effect	General Expression for SS	Specific Expression for SS	df
S	$\sum_{k=1}^{b}\sum_{j=1}^{a}\sum_{i=1}^{n}\hat{\pi}_i^2$	$ab\sum_{i=1}^{n}(\overline{Y}_{i..} - \overline{Y}_{...})^2$	$n-1$
A	$\sum_{k=1}^{b}\sum_{j=1}^{a}\sum_{i=1}^{n}\hat{\alpha}_j^2$	$bn\sum_{j=1}^{a}(\overline{Y}_{.j.} - \overline{Y}_{...})^2$	$a-1$
A × S	$\sum_{k=1}^{b}\sum_{j=1}^{a}\sum_{i=1}^{n}\widehat{(\alpha\pi)}_{ji}^2$	$b\sum_{j=1}^{a}\sum_{i=1}^{n}(\overline{Y}_{ij.} - \overline{Y}_{i..} - \overline{Y}_{.j.} + \overline{Y}_{...})^2$	$(a-1)(n-1)$
B	$\sum_{k=1}^{b}\sum_{j=1}^{a}\sum_{i=1}^{n}\hat{\beta}_k^2$	$an\sum_{k=1}^{b}(\overline{Y}_{..k} - \overline{Y}_{...})^2$	$b-1$
B × S	$\sum_{k=1}^{b}\sum_{j=1}^{a}\sum_{i=1}^{n}\widehat{(\beta\pi)}_{ki}^2$	$a\sum_{k=1}^{b}\sum_{i=1}^{n}(\overline{Y}_{i.k} - \overline{Y}_{i..} - \overline{Y}_{..k} + \overline{Y}_{...})^2$	$(b-1)(n-1)$
A × B	$\sum_{k=1}^{b}\sum_{j=1}^{a}\sum_{i=1}^{n}\widehat{(\alpha\beta)}_{jk}^2$	$n\sum_{j=1}^{a}\sum_{k=1}^{b}(\overline{Y}_{.jk} - \overline{Y}_{.j.} - \overline{Y}_{..k} + \overline{Y}_{...})^2$	$(a-1)(b-1)$
A × B × S	$\sum_{k=1}^{b}\sum_{j=1}^{a}\sum_{i=1}^{n}\widehat{(\alpha\beta\pi)}_{jki}^2$	$\sum_{k=1}^{b}\sum_{j=1}^{a}\sum_{i=1}^{n}(Y_{ijk} - \overline{Y}_{ij.} - \overline{Y}_{i.k} - \overline{Y}_{.jk} + \overline{Y}_{i..} + \overline{Y}_{.j.} + \overline{Y}_{..k} - \overline{Y}_{...})^2$	$(a-1)(b-1)(n-1)$

TABLE 12.3
EXPECTED MEAN SQUARES FOR EACH EFFECT
IN A TWO-WAY WITHIN-SUBJECTS DESIGN*

	Design
Effect	$\mathcal{E}(MS_{\text{effect}})$
S	$\sigma_\varepsilon^2 + ab\sigma_\pi^2$
A	$\sigma_\varepsilon^2 + b\sigma_{\alpha\pi}^2 + nb\theta_\alpha^2$
A × S	$\sigma_\varepsilon^2 + b\sigma_{\alpha\pi}^2$
B	$\sigma_\varepsilon^2 + a\sigma_{\beta\pi}^2 + na\theta_\beta^2$
B × S	$\sigma_\varepsilon^2 + a\sigma_{\beta\pi}^2$
A × B	$\sigma_\varepsilon^2 + \sigma_{\alpha\beta\pi}^2 + n\theta_{\alpha\beta}^2$
A × B × S	$\sigma_\varepsilon^2 + \sigma_{\alpha\beta\pi}^2$

*Results are for a design with a levels of factor A, b levels of factor B, and n subjects. Factors A and B are assumed to be fixed.

Table 12.3 shows the expected mean square associated with each effect, where it is assumed that factors A and B are fixed but S is random. As usual, the error term for an effect should be chosen so that the expected mean square of the effect itself contains only one additional term over those in the denominator and that term should correspond to the effect being tested. Given Table 12.3, it is easy to choose appropriate error terms for the A, B, and AB effects. For example, the expected mean square for the A × S interaction differs from the expected mean square for the A main effect only in that the latter includes an additional term, namely $nb\theta_\alpha^2$. However, this term reflects the A main effect itself and is zero if the null hypothesis is true. Thus, the A × S interaction is an appropriate error term for testing the A main effect. As a result, when the null hypothesis is true, the ratio

$$F = MS_{\mathrm{A}}/MS_{\mathrm{A} \times \mathrm{S}} \qquad (2)$$

is distributed as an F statistic with $(a - 1)$ numerator and $(a - 1)(n - 1)$ denominator degrees of freedom (when requisite assumptions, to be discussed later, are met). Similarly, the B effect is tested by

$$F = MS_{\mathrm{B}}/MS_{\mathrm{B} \times \mathrm{S}} \qquad (3)$$

and the AB effect is tested by

$$F = MS_{\mathrm{A} \times \mathrm{B}}/MS_{\mathrm{A} \times \mathrm{B} \times \mathrm{S}} \qquad (4)$$

A general pattern should be apparent in Equations 2–4. In all three cases, the denominator of the F test is the interaction of subjects with the effect being tested. This pattern exemplifies a general rule that can be used in more complicated designs, as long as all factors are within-subjects and are considered to be fixed rather than random (of course, the subjects factor itself is considered to be random). The general rule in this case is that any effect can be tested by forming a ratio of the mean square of the effect divided by the mean square of the interaction between the subjects factor and the effect:

$$F = MS_{\mathrm{effect}}/MS_{\mathrm{effect} \times \mathrm{S}} \qquad (5)$$

In fact, this general rule follows from the principles developed for designs with random factors because the within-subjects factorial design is a special case of the designs considered in Chapter 10. That Equation 5 is consistent with Chapter 10 can be seen most easily by reconsidering Figure 10.2. According to Figure 10.2, when there is only one random factor in the design, the appropriate denominator term of the F statistic for testing any fixed effect is the interaction of the random factor and the fixed effect being tested. However, this is precisely the form of the F statistic shown in Equation 5.

As we pointed out in Chapter 11, Equation 5 also has a strong intuitive rationale. Recall that an interaction between two factors is an index of the extent to which a main effect of one factor is not consistent across levels of the other factor. Thus, $MS_{\mathrm{effect} \times \mathrm{S}}$ is an index of the extent to which the "effect" in question is inconsistent from one subject to another. Because $MS_{\mathrm{effect} \times \mathrm{S}}$ is in the denominator of the F statistic, larger values of $MS_{\mathrm{effect} \times \mathrm{S}}$ (i.e., less consistency of the effect from one subject to another) lead to smaller F values. Thus, the numerator of the F statistic of Equation 5 (i.e., MS_{effect}) is an index of the average size of the effect (i.e., averaging over subjects), whereas the denominator is an index of the inconsistency of the effect across subjects.

Numerical Example

At this point, it is appropriate to reconsider the data shown in Table 12.1. Table 12.4 shows the cell means and marginal means for these data. Table 12.5 presents the corresponding ANOVA table for these data. The sums of squares are obtained by applying the formulas of Table 12.2, and the appropriate error term for each effect is chosen in accordance with the principles discussed regarding Table 12.3. The p values of Table 12.5 show that both main effects and the interaction are statistically significant at the .05 level. As with the other designs we have considered previously, significant omnibus effects are typically pursued with further tests.

TABLE 12.4
CELL MEANS AND MARGINAL MEANS FOR TABLE 12.1 DATA

		Noise (B)		
		Absent	Present	Marginal Means
	0° Angle	462	492	477
Angle (A)	4° Angle	510	660	585
	8° Angle	528	762	645
	Marginal Means	500	638	569

TABLE 12.5
ANOVA TABLE FOR DATA IN TABLE 12.1

Source	SS	df	MS	F	p
A	289,920	2	144,960	40.72	.0001
A × S	64,080	18	3,560		
B	285,660	1	285,660	33.77	.0003
B × S	76,140	9	8,460		
A × B	105,120	2	52,560	45.31	.0001
A × B × S	20,880	18	1,160		

Before considering these other tests, we pause momentarily to point out that, as usual, we may want to supplement hypothesis tests with measures of effect. As we described in Chapter 7, there are a variety of such measures in a factorial design. Consistent with the logic we developed in Chapter 7, we generally believe that the value of omega squared we calculate for a main effect in a factorial design should be identical to the value we would have obtained for that effect in a single-factor design. Yet another issue, which we originally dealt with in Chapter 11, is the extent to which we want our effect size measure to be similar to what we would have obtained in a between-subjects design. The measure we have chosen to present partials out other effects in the design except for the subjects effect, and thus produces results similar to what we would expect for this effect by itself in a between-subjects design. The resulting formula is given by

$$\hat{\omega}^2 = \frac{df_{effect}\,(MS_{effect} - MS_{effect \times S})}{SS_{effect} + SS_{effect \times S} + SS_S + MS_S} \tag{6}$$

For our reaction time data, the omega squared values for A, B, and AB can be computed directly from Table 12.5 with the additional piece of information not shown in the table that SS_S equals 292,140, and thus MS_S equals 32,460. Substituting into Equation 6 reveals that the omega squared values for A, B, and AB are given by .42, .40, and .23, respectively. Two points are worth emphasizing here. First, the omega squared values suggest that all three effects are sizable in our data. Second, we might be tempted to conclude from the F values shown in Table 12.5 that the interaction effect is larger than either main effect. However, the interaction actually has a smaller omega squared value than either of the main effects. The explanation for this apparent contradiction is that the denominator of the F test depends only on $MS_{effect \times S}$, whereas the denominator of omega squared involves SS_S. In our data, the interaction is large relative to its interaction with subjects, but is not so large in an absolute sense, as we can see by realizing that the mean square interaction value of 52,560 is substantially smaller than the mean square of either of the main effects. Thus, we should not rely exclusively on F values to judge the relative importance of effects in within-subjects designs.

Readers interested in other measures of association strength in within-subjects designs can find additional information in Olejnik and Algina (2000). As an aside, we should point out that our Equation 6 is different from any of their formulas because they assume that either all effects or no effects will be partialled, whereas our formula partials all other effects except for the subjects main effect. As a consequence, omega squared values computed using our formula tend to be larger than values computed from their total variance formulas, but smaller than those from their partial variance formulas.

The nature of follow-up tests to be performed in the two-way within-subjects design is the same as in the two-way between-subjects design discussed in Chapter 7; as was true for the omnibus tests, the only difference is what source is used as the denominator of the F test.

Further Investigation of Main Effects

The meaning to be attached to significant effects in the two-way within-subjects design is the same as in the two-way between-subjects design. For example, consider the statistically significant main effects found for both A (angle) and B (noise) in our numerical example. The statistically significant main effect for A implies that the three marginal means for A whose sample values are 477, 585, and 645 (see Table 12.4) are not all equal to each other in the population.[3] Similarly, the statistically significant B effect implies that the population marginal mean for noise absent is different from the population marginal mean for noise present. Notice that no further tests are necessary for interpreting the noise effect because it has only two levels. However, specific comparisons would typically be performed on the angle factor, to better understand the precise nature of the angle main effect.

There are two different approaches for testing contrasts (regardless of whether the contrasts are comparisons of marginal means, comparisons of cell means, or interaction contrasts) in the two-way within-subjects design, just as there have been in previous designs. As before, the distinction between the two approaches is whether to use a pooled error term or a separate error term for each contrast. To illustrate both approaches, we assume that we are testing a comparison involving marginal means of the A factor, which we designate A_{comp}. An F statistic based on a pooled error term is given by

$$F = SS_{A_{comp}}/MS_{A \times S} \tag{7}$$

Alternatively, the F ratio based on a separate error term is given by

$$F = SS_{A_{comp}}/MS_{A_{comp} \times S} \tag{8}$$

Notice that Equations 7 and 8 both follow the basic logic of Equation 5. However, Equation 7 uses the same error term for testing every contrast of A marginal means, whereas Equation 8 uses a separate error term for each contrast.

To see how Equations 7 and 8 work in practice, let's return to the marginal means shown in Table 12.4. Because angle is a quantitative factor, we might want to perform a trend analysis, much as we discussed in Chapter 6 for between-subjects designs. Specifically, suppose we decide to test the quadratic trend for the angle marginal means. From Appendix Table A.10, the contrast coefficients for a quadratic trend with three levels are 1, −2, and 1. In general, the sum of squares for a contrast of the A marginal means equals

$$SS_\psi = nb(\hat{\psi})^2 \bigg/ \sum_{j=1}^{a} c_j^2 \tag{9}$$

where $\hat{\psi}$ is the sample value of the contrast and c_j is the contrast coefficient for level j. Notice that b appears in Equation 9 because we are comparing A marginal means, each of which is based on nb individual scores. For our data,

$$\hat{\psi} = 477 - 2(585) + 645 = -48$$

Thus, the quadratic sum of squares equals

$$SS_\psi = (10)(2)(-48)^2/6 = 7680$$

The F value for the quadratic trend using Equation 7 is given by

$$F = 7680/3560 = 2.16$$

with 1 and 18 degrees of freedom. It turns out that $MS_{A_{comp} \times S} = 2880$ for the quadratic trend, so the F value for Equation 8 equals

$$F = 7680/2880 = 2.67$$

with 1 and 9 degrees of freedom. Thus, the quadratic trend for angle is nonsignificant, whether the error term of Equation 7 or Equation 8 is used. It should be stressed that it is possible in some circumstances for Equations 7 and 8 to yield very different results from one another.

We defer a complete theoretical comparison of the two tests until Chapters 13 and 14. However, we state now that the F statistic in Equation 7 is valid only when a homogeneity assumption like that discussed in Chapter 11 is met. Equation 8, however, uses a separate error term for each comparison, which makes the homogeneity assumption unnecessary. The distinction between Equations 7 and 8 should seem somewhat familiar, because we discussed a similar problem for testing comparisons in between-subjects designs. In both types of designs, the use of pooled error terms (as in Equation 7) is not robust to violations of homogeneity assumptions. As a consequence, in most within-subjects designs, in which the homogeneity assumption is likely to be violated, using Equation 8 is generally preferred to Equation 7. However, as we will see in Chapter 13, the use of a separate error term as exemplified by Equation 8 is more compatible with the multivariate approach to repeated measures designs than the mixed-model approach. Specifically, Chapter 13 points out that a significant main effect when tested with the multivariate approach implies the existence of at least one contrast that would be declared significant by Equation 8 with a critical value chosen to maintain the α_{FW} level appropriately. Similarly, a nonsignificant multivariate A main effect implies that no such contrast exists. Because this one-to-one correspondence holds, the multivariate main-effect test is said to be *coherent* with the use of Equation 8 for tests of comparisons. However, the mixed-model omnibus test turns out to be coherent with Equation 7 but not with Equation 8. If the homogeneity assumption is met, this poses no problems, because Equation 7 is appropriate when homogeneity holds. Equation 8 is also appropriate when homogeneity holds. However, F tests based on Equation 8 are somewhat less powerful than those based on Equation 7 when the homogeneity assumption is met because of the larger denominator degrees of freedom with the pooled error term. If homogeneity is violated, the separate error term of Equation 8 is generally more appropriate, but its results are not necessarily consistent with the mixed-model main-effect test. Indeed, as we discuss in Chapters 13 and 14, this is one of the primary reasons that we generally prefer the multivariate approach over the mixed-model approach to repeated measures.

Further Investigation of an Interaction—Simple Effects

As in between-subjects factorial designs, the most frequent method of interpreting a statistically significant interaction is to perform tests of simple effects. In our numerical example, we found a significant angle × noise interaction. To better understand this interaction, a logical next step would be to test the angle effect at each noise level individually, as well as to test the noise effect at each individual level of angle. Notice that, in either case, we have effectively reduced the two-factor design to a one-factor design. For this reason, we can find the numerator sum of squares for the F statistic by treating the data as if they came from a single-factor design. For example, consider the effect of angle when noise is absent (i.e., the effect of A within B_1). As usual, in a one-way design, the sum of squares for an effect is given by

$$SS_{effect} = n \sum_{j=1}^{a} (\overline{Y}_j - \overline{Y}_.)^2$$

where $\overline{Y}_j$ indicates the means of the individual levels and $\overline{Y}_.$ is the grand mean of these means (notice that $\overline{Y}_.$ here is not the grand mean of all the means in the design, but only of the three means when noise is absent). For our data, the relevant means are shown in Table 12.4: $\overline{Y}_1 = 462$, $\overline{Y}_2 = 510$, $\overline{Y}_3 = 528$, and $\overline{Y}_. = 500$. Hence, the sum of squares due to angle when noise is absent is given by

$$SS_{effect} = 10[(462 - 500)^2 + (510 - 500)^2 + (528 - 500)^2] = 23,280$$

The question of an appropriate error term now arises. The logic of Equation 5 would suggest using the interaction of subjects and the A-within-B_1 effect as the error term, and indeed this is appropriate. However, it is simpler computationally and conceptually to realize that this interaction term is just the interaction of subjects and angle for the noise-absent data. In other words, this error term is literally identical to the mixed-model error term in the one-way design where angle is the only factor, because scores under the noise-present condition are completely disregarded. For the data in Table 12.1, the error sum of squares equals 41,520. Taking a ratio of the corresponding mean squares results in

$$F = \frac{23,280/2}{41,520/18} = 5.05$$

which with 2 numerator and 18 denominator degrees of freedom corresponds to a p value of .018. To reiterate, this is exactly the same result that would be obtained from conducting a one-way within-subjects analysis of the angle effect for the data obtained in the noise-absent condition only. Because we have effectively performed a one-way mixed-model analysis, the assumptions required for the simple-effects test are the same as those discussed in Chapter 11. In particular, the homogeneity assumption discussed there is required, although ε adjustments (discussed later in this chapter) can be performed when the assumption is violated. Table 12.6 presents the F values, degrees of freedom, and p values for all the simple-effects tests that might be of interest for the data in Table 12.1. All the simple effects are significant at the .05 level, except for the effect of noise at an angle of zero degrees. As we discussed in Chapter 7 for the two-way design, some investigators might use a Bonferroni adjustment to control the α_{FW} level for each effect. In this case, tests of A within B would need to be significant at the .05/b level (.025 in our example), and tests of B within A would need to be significant at the .05/a level (.017 in our example). In our particular data, the results are the same with the Bonferroni adjustment as without.

TABLE 12.6
SIMPLE-EFFECTS TESTS FOR THE DATA IN TABLE 12.1

Effect*	Numerator df	Denominator df	F	p
AwB_1	2	18	5.05	.018
AwB_2	2	18	77.02	.001
BwA_1	1	9	1.55	.244
BwA_2	1	9	19.74	.002
BwA_3	1	9	125.59	.001

*A = angle, B = noise

Notice that the effects of angle at a fixed level of noise have 2 numerator degrees of freedom (see Table 12.6) because the angle factor has three levels. As usual, we would typically test specific comparisons of the angle factor, both for noise absent and for noise present, because both angle simple effects were statistically significant. As already stated, we defer detailed discussion of comparisons until Chapters 13 and 14. However, notice that comparisons conducted as a follow-up to a significant simple-effects test are in essence comparisons in a one-way within-subjects design. As a consequence, either Equation 7 or Equation 8 can be used, although as before, Equation 8 is generally to be preferred because it requires fewer assumptions.

Interaction Contrasts

We should also mention that interaction contrasts provide an alternative method for investigating an interaction, just as they did in the between-subjects design. In a two-way within-subjects design, if the A factor has a levels and the B factor has b levels, the A × B interaction has $(a - 1)(b - 1)$ numerator degrees of freedom (see Table 12.2). The sum of squares for a given component in the within-subjects design is found in just the same manner as in the between-subjects design. Specifically, the component can be represented as a contrast among the ab means in the design. To illustrate this in some detail, suppose that we want to test whether the difference between reaction times for 0° and 8° angles is the same when noise is present as when noise is absent. From Table 12.4, we see that the mean difference in reaction time between 0° and 8° is 270 ms when noise is present, but only 66 ms when noise is absent. The sum of squares attributable to this contrast can be calculated as

$$SS_\psi = n(\hat{\psi})^2 \bigg/ \sum_{j=1}^{ab} c_j^2 \qquad (10)$$

where $\hat{\psi}$ is the sample value of the contrast and c_j is the contrast coefficient for level j.[4] Notice that Equation 10 regards the data as coming from a one-way design with ab levels [$ab = (3)(2) = 6$ in our example] because we are no longer explicitly considering the factorial structure of the data in our calculations. For the data in Table 12.4, $\hat{\psi} = 204$ (i.e., $270 - 66$), $n = 10$, and $\sum_{j=1}^{ab} c_j^2 = 4$ (notice that the AB_{11} and AB_{32} cells receive weights of $+1$ and the AB_{31} and AB_{12} cells receive weights of -1, whereas the AB_{21} and AB_{22} cells receive weights of 0). Thus, the sum of squares for this interaction contrast equals 104,040.

Recall from Equations 7 and 8 that either of two error terms might be used to test a comparison of marginal means. A similar choice exists for testing the significance of an interaction contrast. An F test analogous to Equation 7 for testing an interaction contrast is

$$F = SS_{A_{comp} \times B_{comp}}/MS_{A \times B \times S} \tag{11}$$

whereas an F test analogous to Equation 8 is

$$F = SS_{A_{comp} \times B_{comp}}/MS_{A_{comp} \times B_{comp} \times S} \tag{12}$$

The same issues we discussed in comparing Equations 7 and 8 are also relevant for choosing between Equations 11 and 12. Consistent with our earlier preference for Equation 8, we generally prefer Equation 12 because it does not assume homogeneity. However, Equation 12, like Equation 8, is more compatible with the multivariate approach described in Chapters 13 and 14 than with the mixed-model approach of this chapter.

For the data in Table 12.1, Equations 11 and 12 yield very similar results. From Table 12.5, we know that $MS_{A \times B \times S}$ equals 1160 for these data; thus, using Equation 11 yields

$$F = 104,040/1160 = 89.69$$

with 1 and 18 degrees of freedom. It turns out that $MS_{A_{comp} \times B_{comp} \times S} = 1240$, so the F for Equation 12 equals

$$F = 104,040/1240 = 83.90$$

with 1 and 9 degrees of freedom. Obviously, this interaction contrast is highly significant regardless of which error term is used. Thus, the difference in reaction time between 0° and 8° angles is different when noise is present than when it is absent. Specifically, from the means in Table 12.4, we can see that the mean difference in reaction time between 0° and 8° angle conditions is larger when noise is present than when it is absent. Alternatively, an equivalent statement is that the noise effect is larger in the 8° angle condition than in the 0° angle condition.

Statistical Packages and Pooled Error Terms Versus Separate Error Terms

Although the differences in the F values we obtained with pooled and separate error terms were negligible, other effects in these data might show large differences between the two approaches. In general, the two approaches can lead to quite different conclusions. As we discuss at some length in Chapter 4 (and briefly in subsequent chapters), when homogeneity is violated, the pooled error term test is too liberal for some contrasts and too conservative for others. For this reason, we generally prefer the use of a separate error term, especially with within-subjects designs, in which homogeneity is likely to be violated. Unfortunately, when analyses are performed by statistical packages, insufficient documentation may be provided to ascertain which type of error term is being used. However, it is simple to determine which type has been used by examining denominator degrees of freedom. Tests of comparisons using a separate error term have $n - 1$ denominator degrees of freedom in within-subjects designs. However, tests based on Equation 7 would have $(a - 1)(n - 1)$ denominator degrees of freedom [or $(b - 1)(n - 1)$ df for the comparisons involving the B factor], and tests based on the pooled error term of Equation 11 would have $(a - 1)(b - 1)(n - 1)$ denominator degrees of freedom. Thus, the denominator degrees of freedom shown in the printout for the F test reveal which type of error term has been used.

Assumptions

The mixed-model approach to analyzing data from factorial within-subjects designs requires similar assumptions to those presented in Chapter 11 for one-way within-subjects designs. In particular, there is once again a homogeneity assumption that must be met if the mixed-model F tests are to be valid.

Recall from Chapter 11 that the homogeneity assumption is equivalent to a sphericity assumption for the covariance matrix. Although the assumption actually pertains to the covariance matrix, it is usually much easier to interpret correlations than covariances, so at times we discuss the assumption in terms of correlations.

In the one-way design, the validity of the homogeneity assumption can be examined by considering an $a \times a$ covariance matrix, where a is the number of levels of the within-subjects factor. A similar approach is relevant when there are multiple within-subjects factors, except now there is a different matrix for each within-subjects effect. To clarify this point, consider the data of Table 12.1. If these data came from a one-way design with six levels, we would form a 6×6 covariance matrix to consider the extent to which the homogeneity assumption has been met. In fact, however, the data came from a 3×2 factorial design. As a consequence, we did not test a null hypothesis that all levels have the same population mean. Instead, we performed three omnibus tests: the A main effect, the B main effect, and the AB interaction. Because these three tests we perform in the factorial design are different from the tests we would have performed if the data came from a one-way design with six levels, the covariance matrices that must be examined for homogeneity are also different.

In fact, we must consider a different covariance matrix for each effect to be tested. Thus, there is one covariance matrix for the A main effect, a second for the B main effect, and a third for the AB interaction. The homogeneity assumption can be satisfied for any one of these matrices but not the others, so we must consider each one individually. It should also be noted that yet other matrices are of interest when other tests are performed, such as simple-effects tests. We consider the relevant covariance matrices for each of the three omnibus tests to be performed.

To understand the nature of the covariance matrix corresponding to the A main effect, it is necessary to recall the meaning of the main effect. Remember that a main effect involves differences between marginal means, where these means have been calculated by averaging across any other factors in the design. For example, we saw in Table 12.4 that the A marginal means for our sample are 477, 585, and 645. One way to conceptualize the test of the A main effect is to regard not just the means but also the scores for the individual subjects as averaged over the other factors in the design. Table 12.7 presents such scores for the A effect for the data in Table 12.1. Notice that each score for a given subject is simply that subject's mean response time for that angle, where the mean is the average of the noise-absent and the noise-present scores. It can be shown that performing a one-way mixed-model ANOVA on the data in Table 12.7 yields an F value of 40.72, which is exactly the value we reported in Table 12.5 for the A main effect in the factorial design.[5] Because the F values are identical (as they always would be, for any data), they must require the same assumptions. However, we already know from Chapter 11 what assumptions are required for the F statistic calculated from the data in Table 12.7 to be valid. Specifically, the three levels of A shown in Table 12.7 must obey the homogeneity of treatment-difference variances assumption.

Table 12.8 presents the covariance matrix for the data shown in Table 12.7. To simplify interpretations, correlations between the variables are also shown and are discussed momentarily. Notice that the covariance matrix has three rows and three columns because the A factor in our design has three levels. We can see from Table 12.8 that the correlations between scores in different angle conditions are very similar to each other. However, the variances are rather

TABLE 12.7
MEAN REACTION TIMES FOR EACH SUBJECT FOR EACH
LEVEL OF THE ANGLE FACTOR, AVERAGING OVER NOISE

Subject	0° Angle	4° Angle	8° Angle
1	450	510	630
2	390	480	540
3	570	630	660
4	450	660	720
5	510	660	630
6	360	450	450
7	510	600	720
8	510	660	780
9	510	660	660
10	510	540	660
Mean	477	585	645

TABLE 12.8
COVARIANCES AND CORRELATIONS BETWEEN THE
THREE ANGLE SCORES SHOWN IN TABLE 12.7*

	0° Angle	4° Angle	8° Angle
0° Angle	4090	.75	.72
4° Angle	3950	6850	.79
8° Angle	4350	6150	8850

*Variances appear on the diagonal, covariances appear below
the diagonal, and correlations appear above the diagonal.

different, with more variability in scores in the 8° condition than in the 0° condition. As discussed in Chapter 11, Mauchly's test of sphericity could be performed to ascertain whether the homogeneity assumption has been met for the A main effect. However, as pointed out in Chapter 11, it is generally preferable to modify the degrees of freedom of the critical value with an ε-adjustment procedure, instead of performing Mauchly's test. We consider ε adjustments after we discuss the homogeneity assumption for the B main effect and the AB interaction.

As we stated earlier, a different covariance matrix is relevant for the B main effect because the B effect averages over levels of A, whereas the A effect averages over levels of B. Table 12.9 presents each subject's mean score for noise absent and for noise present, where the mean is the average of the three angle scores at that particular level of noise. Once again, a one-way mixed-model ANOVA on the data of Table 12.9 yields an F value of 33.77, identical to the value reported in Table 12.5 for the B main effect in the factorial design. For this F statistic to be valid, the two levels of B shown in Table 12.9 must obey the homogeneity of treatment-difference variances assumption.

Table 12.10 presents the covariance matrix and the correlation for the data shown in Table 12.9. The matrix has two rows and two columns because the B factor has two levels. It is important to realize that with only two levels of the factor, there is only one correlation coefficient, so inequality of correlations is not a concern here as it was for the A factor (which has three levels and hence three correlation coefficients). Although Table 12.10 shows that scores are considerably more variable when noise is present than when noise is absent, this disparity is also not of concern when the factor has only two levels. The reason is that the assumption we discussed in detail in Chapter 11 requires that the variance of the difference

TABLE 12.9
MEAN REACTION TIME FOR EACH
SUBJECT FOR EACH LEVEL OF THE NOISE
FACTOR, AVERAGING OVER ANGLE

Subject	Noise Absent	Noise Present
1	440	620
2	460	480
3	500	740
4	500	720
5	580	620
6	380	460
7	520	700
8	580	720
9	560	660
10	480	660
Mean	500	638

TABLE 12.10
COVARIANCE MATRIX AND CORRELATION COEFFICIENT
FOR THE TWO NOISE SCORES SHOWN IN TABLE 12.9*

	Noise Absent	Noise Present
Noise Absent	4088.89	.64
Noise Present	4000.00	9551.11

*Variances appear on the diagonal, the covariance appears below the diagonal, and the correlation appears above the diagonal.

scores formed from any two levels of the factor must be a constant. However, when the factor only has two levels, there is only one such difference, so that the assumption is automatically met for any set of data. Thus, the F test presented for the B main effect in Table 12.5 is necessarily valid, because B has only two levels (as usual, we must also assume normality, but this is a less important assumption for Type I error). Notice that it is not necessary that scores at the two levels of B be equally variable, because the assumption pertains to difference scores formed from the two levels. Although the mixed-model approach being discussed here generally produces a different F value from the multivariate approach of Chapters 13 and 14, we will see in Chapter 14 that the multivariate approach also yields an F value of 33.77 (with 1 and 9 degrees of freedom) for the B main effect for the data in Table 12.1.

Finally, yet a third covariance matrix is relevant for the AB interaction because this effect does not average over either A or B. Instead, the interaction assesses whether the B difference is the same at each level of A. Table 12.11 presents scores that address this question. For each subject, a given score represents the noise effect (i.e., reaction time when noise is present minus reaction time when noise is absent) at a particular level of the angle factor. It can be shown that a one-way mixed-model ANOVA on the data of Table 12.11 yields an F value of 45.31, identical to the value reported in Table 12.5 for the AB interaction. For this F statistic to be valid, the three levels of A shown in Table 12.11 must obey the homogeneity of treatment-difference variances assumption. Be careful to notice that, although there were also three levels of A in Table 12.7, the scores themselves are completely different, so the homogeneity assumption might be met for one of the effects but not the other.

TABLE 12.11
NOISE EFFECT ON REACTION TIME FOR EACH SUBJECT
AT EACH LEVEL OF ANGLE*

Subject	0° Angle	4° Angle	8° Angle
1	60	180	300
2	−60	0	120
3	180	300	240
4	60	240	360
5	−60	0	180
6	0	60	180
7	60	240	240
8	60	120	240
9	−60	120	240
10	60	240	240
Mean	30	150	234

* Each score is the difference between a subject's reaction time when
noise is present minus the reaction time when noise is absent.

TABLE 12.12
COVARIANCES AND CORRELATIONS BETWEEN THE
THREE ANGLE SCORES SHOWN IN TABLE 12.11*

	0° Angle	4° Angle	8° Angle
0° Angle	5800	.86	.52
4° Angle	7000	11400	.71
8° Angle	2600	5000	4360

*Variances appear on the diagonal, covariances appear below
the diagonal, and correlations appear above the diagonal.

Table 12.12 presents covariances and correlations for the data shown in Table 12.11. We can see from Table 12.12 that both the correlations and the variances are rather different from each other. Once again, although Mauchly's test could be performed, ε adjustments are generally preferable.

To this point, we have seen that the extent to which the homogeneity assumption has been met may differ from one effect to another. Before considering ε adjustments, we should mention one other approach that is sometimes used to analyze data from factorial within-subjects designs. This approach uses the same error term to test all effects, unlike the approach we have presented (which uses $MS_{A \times S}$ to test A, $MS_{B \times S}$ to test B, and $MS_{A \times B \times S}$ to test AB). This error term is obtained as

$$MS_{error} = (SS_{A \times S} + SS_{B \times S} + SS_{A \times B \times S})/(df_{A \times S} + df_{B \times S} + df_{A \times B \times S}) \qquad (13)$$

As Equation 13 shows, MS_{error} is a weighted average of $MS_{A \times S}$, $MS_{B \times S}$, and $MS_{A \times B \times S}$. For the data in Table 12.1, MS_{error} equals 3580. F ratios are calculated in this approach by using MS_{error} as the denominator for all tests. For our data, this approach yields $F = 40.49$ for the A main effects, $F = 79.79$ for the B main effect, and $F = 14.68$ for the AB interaction. Each of these F ratios would now have 45 denominator degrees of freedom, instead of the 9 or 18 associated with the approach presented in Table 12.5. Indeed, the only potential advantage of using MS_{error} for all tests is that the denominator degrees of freedom are increased, leading to a lower critical value and hence somewhat higher power. However, this potential advantage comes at a high cost, because the required homogeneity assumption is now even stricter. For an F statistic formed from MS_{error} to be valid, the entire $ab \times ab$ (6×6 in our example) matrix must obey the homogeneity assumption. In essence, this implies that not only do the individual matrices of Tables 12.8, 12.10, and 12.12 possess homogeneity, but also that $MS_{A\times S}$, $MS_{B\times S}$, and $MS_{A\times B\times S}$ differ from each other only as the result of sampling error. We believe that such a strong assumption is unlikely to be met in most applications and thus recommend against the general use of MS_{error} as an error term in factorial within-subjects designs.

Adjusted Univariate Tests

We presented three adjusted univariate test procedures in Chapter 11: the Geisser–Greenhouse lower-bound correction, Box's $\hat{\varepsilon}$ adjustment (also called the Geisser–Greenhouse $\hat{\varepsilon}$ adjustment), and the Huynh–Feldt $\tilde{\varepsilon}$ adjustment. All three approaches can also be used for factorial within-subjects designs. As in the one-way design, each involves an adjustment of the numerator and denominator degrees of freedom of the critical value against which the observed value is judged. Notice that the adjustment is applied only to the critical value; the observed value is not adjusted in any of the three approaches.

Each effect being tested in a factorial within-subjects design is subject to a different adjustment because, as we have seen, effects may differ in the extent to which the homogeneity assumption has been satisfied. In particular, for the data of Table 12.1, the adjustment for the A main effect is based on the covariance matrix in Table 12.8, the adjustment for the B main effect is based on the matrix in Table 12.10, and the adjustment for the interaction is based on the matrix in Table 12.12. As a consequence, there are three potentially different $\hat{\varepsilon}$ values and three potentially different $\tilde{\varepsilon}$ values.

As we discussed in Chapter 11, calculation of $\hat{\varepsilon}$ or $\tilde{\varepsilon}$ by hand is extremely tedious. Fortunately, most major statistical packages such as SAS and SPSS now calculate both $\hat{\varepsilon}$ and $\tilde{\varepsilon}$ for factorial as well as one-way within-subjects designs. The computations of $\hat{\varepsilon}$ and $\tilde{\varepsilon}$ are based on the same formulas as we presented in Chapter 11 for the one-way design:

$$\hat{\varepsilon} = \frac{r^2(\overline{E}_{jj} - \overline{E}_{..})^2}{(r-1)\left[\left(\sum_{k=1}^{r}\sum_{j=1}^{r} E_{jk}^2\right) - \left(2r\sum_{j=1}^{r}\overline{E}_{j.}^2\right) + \left(r^2\overline{E}_{..}^2\right)\right]}$$

$$\tilde{\varepsilon} = \frac{n(r-1)\hat{\varepsilon} - 2}{(r-1)[n-1-(r-1)\hat{\varepsilon}]}$$

Three comments must be made here. First, E_{jk} is the element in row j and column k of the covariance matrix for the effect being tested. Notice that to use these formulas for our data, the correlations shown above the diagonal in Tables 12.8, 12.10, and 12.12 must be replaced by the corresponding covariances, which is simple to do because each matrix is symmetric (i.e., the element in row j and column k is identical to the element in row k and column j). Second, the r in these formulas indicates the number of rows of the covariance matrix. In Chapter 11, r was always equal to a, so we wrote the formula in terms of a. Now, however, r can assume different values for different effects. Third, we have presented these formulas not so much because we expect you to calculate $\hat{\varepsilon}$ and $\tilde{\varepsilon}$ by hand, but instead primarily to show you explicitly that the underlying logic behind $\hat{\varepsilon}$ and $\tilde{\varepsilon}$ adjustments in factorial within-subjects designs is identical to the logic we developed in Chapter 11 for the one-way design. The only

TABLE 12.13
RESULTS OF APPLYING ADJUSTED UNIVARIATE PROCEDURES TO DATA
IN TABLE 12.1

Effect	Procedure	Numerator df	Denominator df	Critical Value*	p Value
A	Unadjusted	2	18	3.55	.0001
	Huynh–Feldt $\tilde{\varepsilon}$	2	18	3.55	.0001
	Greenhouse–Geisser $\hat{\varepsilon}$ (Box's $\hat{\varepsilon}$)	1.92	17.31	3.62	.0001
	Geisser–Greenhouse lower-bound correction	1	9	5.12	.0001
B	Unadjusted	1	9	5.12	.0003
	Huynh–Feldt $\tilde{\varepsilon}$	1	9	5.12	.0003
	Greenhouse–Geisser $\hat{\varepsilon}$ (Box's $\hat{\varepsilon}$)	1	9	5.12	.0003
	Geisser–Greenhouse lower-bound correction	1	9	5.12	.0003
AB	Unadjusted	2	18	3.55	.0001
	Huynh–Feldt $\tilde{\varepsilon}$	2	18	3.55	.0001
	Greenhouse–Geisser $\hat{\varepsilon}$ (Box's $\hat{\varepsilon}$)	1.81	16.27	3.73	.0001
	Geisser–Greenhouse lower-bound correction	1	9	5.12	.0001

* Critical value for $\alpha = .05$.

real change here is that it is necessary to identify the covariance matrix that corresponds to the effect being tested.[6] For our purposes, it is sufficient to report that the value of $\hat{\varepsilon}$ for the A main effect equals 0.96 as calculated from the covariance matrix in Table 12.8. The corresponding $\tilde{\varepsilon}$ value equals 1.21, but because this exceeds 1.00, it is shrunk back to 1.00. For the B main effect, $\hat{\varepsilon}$ can be calculated from the covariance matrix in Table 12.10 to equal 1.00. However, $\hat{\varepsilon}$ always equals 1.00 when the factor has only two levels because, as we have already seen, homogeneity is guaranteed to hold. Also, $\tilde{\varepsilon}$ is set equal to 1.00 when the factor has only two levels, as B does. Finally, $\hat{\varepsilon}$ for the AB interaction equals 0.90 based on the covariance matrix in Table 12.12. The corresponding $\tilde{\varepsilon}$ value equals 1.11, which is again shrunk back to 1.00.

Table 12.13 summarizes the effects of the various adjustment procedures for the data in Table 12.1. The adjustments have little effect here for two reasons. First, the observed F values are quite large, so that there is substantial evidence that the effects being tested are nonzero. Second, the covariance matrices do not depart substantially from homogeneity. Even if they did, however, the results for the Geisser–Greenhouse lower-bound procedure in Table 12.13 show that all three effects are still easily statistically significant at the .05 level.

We must stress that the various procedures do not always agree as nicely as they do in Table 12.13. Particularly when some factors have many levels, results may diverge considerably because the theoretical minimum values for $\hat{\varepsilon}$ and $\tilde{\varepsilon}$ become very small as the number of levels increases.

It is also important to remember that $\hat{\varepsilon}$ and $\tilde{\varepsilon}$ values are different for different effects. For example, although ε necessarily equals 1.0 for a B main effect with two levels, ε could be as low as 0.5 for an A main effect with three levels, even in the same data set. Also, $\hat{\varepsilon}$ and $\tilde{\varepsilon}$ values must be calculated for other effects that might be tested, such as simple effects. For example, for the data in Table 12.1, it can be shown that the $\hat{\varepsilon}$ value for the simple effect of angle when noise is present equals 0.78. Notice that this value is considerably less than any of the values for the A main effect, the B main effect, or the AB interaction. Thus, it is usually necessary in factorial within-subjects designs to consider the extent to which homogeneity has been violated separately for every effect to be tested.

Confidence Intervals

As usual, we may want to supplement hypothesis tests with confidence intervals. Unfortunately, as we discussed and showed in Chapter 11, confidence intervals based on the traditional mixed-model approach of Chapters 11 and 12 are extremely sensitive to violations of the sphericity assumption. For this reason, we defer any detailed consideration of confidence intervals for factorial within-subjects designs until Chapter 14, where we see that the multivariate approach provides a method of testing hypotheses and forming confidence intervals that does not require sphericity.

If we could somehow know that the sphericity assumption has been met (for example, when a factor has only two levels), we could use $MS_{\text{effect} \times S}$ as an estimate of error in forming confidence intervals. When sphericity holds, an appropriate confidence interval for any contrast ψ can be found from

$$\hat{\psi} \pm w \sqrt{MS_{\text{effect} \times S} \sum_{j=1}^{a} \left(c_j^2 / n_j \right)} \qquad (14)$$

where w is chosen so as to control the appropriate error rate. For example, as we discussed in Chapter 5, possible choices for w include

$$w = \sqrt{F(.05; 1, df_{\text{effect} \times S})} \qquad \text{for } \alpha_{\text{PC}} = .05$$
$$w = \sqrt{F(.05/C; 1, df_{\text{effect} \times S})} \qquad \text{for Bonferroni}$$
$$w = q(.05; a, df_{\text{effect} \times S}) / \sqrt{2} \qquad \text{for Tukey}$$
$$w = \sqrt{(df_{\text{effect}}) F(.05; df_{\text{effect}}, df_{\text{effect} \times S})} \qquad \text{for Scheffé}$$

Quasi-*F* Ratios

So far in this chapter, we have assumed that both A and B are fixed-effects factors. In some situations, however, it might make sense to regard one of the factors as random, as we discussed in Chapter 10. Although it would also be possible to have two random factors (in addition to subjects), such designs are very unusual in practice, so we restrict our attention to designs in which one factor is fixed but the other is random. We consider two different types of within-subjects designs in which one factor is fixed and the other is random. As usual, we continue to regard the subjects factor as random.

We begin consideration of the first type of design with an example. Suppose that a developmental psychologist is interested in comparing fathers' responsivity to infant cues when the mothers are present versus when they are absent. Infants, mothers, and fathers are brought into a laboratory room designed to mimic a living room in the natural environment. For one-half of all families, all three family members are brought into the room initially. After a fixed period of time, the experimenter asks the mother to leave the room. For the other half of families, only the infant and father initially enter the room. After a fixed period of time, the mother also enters. Although sequence effects might be of interest themselves in this study, they are ignored for our purposes here.[7] A score for each father's responsivity to the infant is obtained from multiple trained observers using a Likert Rating Scale (e.g., each father might be rated

TABLE 12.14
EXPECTED MEAN SQUARES FOR EACH EFFECT
IN A TWO-WAY WITHIN-SUBJECTS DESIGN
WHEN THE B FACTOR IS RANDOM

Effect	$\mathscr{E}(MS_{effect})$
S	$\sigma_\varepsilon^2 + \sigma_{\alpha\beta\pi}^2 + a\sigma_{\beta\pi}^2 + ab\sigma_\pi^2$
A	$\sigma_\varepsilon^2 + \sigma_{\alpha\beta\pi}^2 + n\sigma_{\alpha\beta}^2 + b\sigma_{\alpha\pi}^2 + nb\theta_\alpha^2$
A × S	$\sigma_\varepsilon^2 + \sigma_{\alpha\beta\pi}^2 + b\sigma_{\alpha\pi}^2$
B	$\sigma_\varepsilon^2 + a\sigma_{\beta\pi}^2 + na\sigma_\beta^2$
B × S	$\sigma_\varepsilon^2 + a\sigma_{\beta\pi}^2$
A × B	$\sigma_\varepsilon^2 + \sigma_{\alpha\beta\pi}^2 + n\sigma_{\alpha\beta}^2$
A × B × S	$\sigma_\varepsilon^2 + \sigma_{\alpha\beta\pi}^2$

from 1 to 7 by each observer). Although there might be some advantages to having different observers (i.e., raters) in the different conditions, we assume here that the same observers are used in both conditions. Thus, the design is a two-way within-subjects factorial design, exactly like the design we have considered to this point. For example, we could let A represent the condition factor (mother present versus absent), let B represent the observer factor, and let S represent the subject (i.e., family) factor, in which case we have an A × B × S design.

Unlike our previous discussion of this design, however, we might regard B as a random effects factor because we would presumably want to generalize our results beyond the specific observers included in the study. As we noted in Chapter 10, some researchers would disagree, primarily because it is unlikely that our particular observers have been randomly sampled from some larger population of observers. In any event, we proceed as if observer were a random factor. Sums of squares and degrees of freedom can still be calculated as shown in Table 12.2. However, the expected mean squares shown in Table 12.3 are no longer correct because B is a random factor. Table 12.14 presents the expected mean squares for each effect when the B factor is random. These expected mean squares show that the ratio $MS_A/MS_{A\times S}$ is, in general, no longer an appropriate F statistic for testing the A main effect, that is, the effect of the mother being present or absent. Notice that, as we have seen before, it is the fixed effect whose test of significance is changed when the other factor is now regarded as random. It turns out that no single effect is an appropriate error term for testing A. Instead, we must resort to a quasi-F ratio of the form

$$F' = \frac{MS_A + MS_{A\times B\times S}}{MS_{A\times S} + MS_{A\times B}} \tag{15}$$

(The notation F' denotes a quasi-F.) The rationale for this ratio is that the expected value of the numerator now contains only one additional term ($nb\theta_\alpha^2$) not contained in the expected value of the denominator. Because this term corresponds to the effect to be tested, the ratio is an appropriate statistic. However, the ratio is only approximately distributed as an F, even when all assumptions hold. Also, calculation of degrees of freedom for a critical F value is very tedious. The interested reader is referred to Kirk (1995, p. 407ff.) or Myers (1979, p. 191ff.) for details. We should mention one other point regarding this design. The use of a quasi-F test here would necessitate having a large number of observers, if power to detect a meaningful A effect is to be adequate. It is much more typical in studies using observers (i.e., raters) to use a relatively small number of raters and to test the A effect by forming the ratio of MS_A to $MS_{A\times S}$ as if B were fixed. However, this approach can be defended even if B is random if there is sufficient theoretical rationale to believe that $\sigma^2_{\alpha\beta}$ equals zero, because then under the null hypothesis $\mathscr{E}(MS_A)$ equals $\mathscr{E}(MS_{A\times S})$, even when B is random. In particular, if raters are sufficiently trained so that interrater agreement is very high, $\sigma^2_{\alpha\beta}$ will be zero or practically zero because it reflects the extent to which raters disagree (i.e., are inconsistent) across levels of A. Thus, sufficient training of raters may justify testing A as if B were fixed, even if the investigator wants to generalize findings across raters. Intuitively, if raters can be trained so well that they always agree with each other, then any results that are obtained with one rater would be obtained with other raters as well.[8]

We now consider a second type of within-subjects design in which one factor is fixed and the other is random. Santa, Miller, and Shaw (1979) give an example of a social psychologist who is interested in the effects of gender bias in advertising. Subjects read and evaluate a set of job advertisements, one-third of which are biased for females, one-third of which are biased for males, and one-third of which are neutral. An experimenter would probably want to include several advertisements within each of these classes to be certain that any effects claimed to be the result of bias were not in fact really produced by other specific characteristics of the particular advertisements. This design differs from our previous design because advertisement is now nested under the bias factor instead of being crossed with it. When the advertisement factor is regarded as fixed, usual F tests are appropriate (provided other mixed-model assumptions have been met). However, when the factor is regarded as random, once again, a quasi-F ratio is necessary. The interested reader is referred to Santa, Miller, and Shaw (1979) for additional information.

ONE WITHIN-SUBJECTS FACTOR AND ONE BETWEEN-SUBJECTS FACTOR IN THE SAME DESIGN

A second way in which the one-way design of Chapter 11 can be generalized is to have one within-subjects factor and one between-subjects factor. This type of design is common in the behavioral sciences because it provides a compromise between a design in which all factors are within-subjects and a design in which all factors are between-subjects. Such a compromise often proves to be extremely useful because it offers the economy of subjects of the within-subjects design while it is less susceptible to problems of differential carryover or an excessive number of trials for each subject that might occur with a completely within-subjects design. This design is also naturally suited for studying different groups of subjects across time in a longitudinal fashion. Notice that the samples might be from naturally occurring populations, such as females and males, or they might be the result of the experimenter's manipulation, such as treatment and control. In any event, the important point for our purposes is that this design is used often in the behavioral sciences, so a thorough understanding of data analysis appropriate for this design is essential.

To motivate such analyses, we consider a variation of the example we discussed earlier for the two-way within-subjects factorial design. Suppose that a perceptual psychologist is interested in age differences in task performance, where the task is similar to that described earlier. Specifically, the researcher is interested in determining whether older adults respond more slowly than do younger adults. Although age might be regarded as a continuous variable, we assume that the researcher is interested in comparing individuals who are approximately 20 years old with individuals who are at least 60. For example, young subjects might consist of college students, and older subjects might consist of college faculty over the age of 60.[9] To simplify the resultant design somewhat, we assume that the noise factor is no longer of interest but that the angle factor still is. Thus, the design to be used has two factors—age and angle. Given the nature of these two factors, it seems natural for age to be between-subjects and angle to be within-subjects. To see why, let's consider two other alternatives, the first of which is for both factors to be between-subjects. The primary disadvantage of this design is that it would require many more subjects because each subject would contribute scores at only one level of angle. In most research settings, subjects are at a premium, so there is a distinct advantage to gathering as much data as would be meaningful from each subject.[10] The second alternative is for both factors to be within-subjects. However, it is impractical to use age as a within-subjects factor unless the age range to be studied is small (typically no more than a few months or at most a few years, as it might be for studying children, because developmental changes are usually most rapid at younger ages). In our perceptual example, the age difference of interest compares subjects who are approximately 20 years of age with subjects who are at least 60. It hardly seems practical to wait 40 years to see how the 20 year olds develop. Thus, for practical reasons, age needs to be a between-subjects factor here. However, we said that angle should probably be a within-subjects factor, in which case we end up with a design where one factor is between-subjects and the other is within-subjects.

Before proceeding with our example, a word about terminology may be helpful. This type of design is often called a *split-plot design*, which is a holdover from its uses in agricultural research. The design is also sometimes called a *mixed design* because it mixes between-subjects and within-subjects factors. However, in the statistical literature, the term *mixed design* is usually used for any design that has both random- and fixed-effect factors, regardless of whether they are between-subjects or within-subjects.

As usual, to make our discussion of data analysis more concrete, we consider a set of hypothetical data. Table 12.15 presents data for 10 older subjects. Once again, the dependent measure is reaction time. Notice that each subject has three scores, one for each level of the angle factor. We use the data presented in Table 12.7 to represent the reaction times of the young subjects. Notice that Table 12.7 presented data as a function of the angle factor alone because scores were averaged over the noise factor. Thus, we have data for 20 subjects in all—the 10 younger subjects whose scores are shown in Table 12.7 and the 10 older subjects whose scores are shown in Table 12.15.

Omnibus Tests

Notice that once again we have a two-factor design. As we discussed earlier, the effects to be tested are the same whether the factors are within- or between-subjects. Thus, we typically are interested in testing the two main effects and the interaction. The sums of squares for these

TABLE 12.15
REACTION TIME FOR EACH OLDER SUBJECT
FOR EACH LEVEL OF THE ANGLE FACTOR

Subject	0° Angle	4° Angle	8° Angle
1	420	570	690
2	600	720	810
3	450	540	690
4	630	660	780
5	420	570	780
6	600	780	870
7	630	690	870
8	480	570	720
9	690	750	900
10	510	690	810
Mean	543	654	792

effects are calculated just as for other two-way designs. However, the error terms to be used in significance tests must once again take into account whether the effect being tested is within- or between-subjects.

The three effects to be tested in our example are the main effect of age (which we designate as A), the main effect of angle (which we now designate as B, instead of A), and the interaction of age and angle. Because there is a within-subjects factor in the design (viz., angle), "subjects" are once again included as a factor in the design and as an effect in the full model for the data.

An Appropriate Full Model

An appropriate full model for this design is given by

$$Y_{ijk} = \mu + \alpha_j + \beta_k + \pi_{i/j} + (\alpha\beta)_{jk} + (\beta\pi)_{ki/j} + \varepsilon_{ijk} \tag{16}$$

where Y_{ijk} is the score on the dependent variable for the ith subject at the jth level of A and kth level of B, μ is the grand mean parameter, α_j is the effect associated with the jth level of A, β_k is the effect associated with the kth level of B, $\pi_{i/j}$ is the effect associated with the ith subject in the jth level of A, $(\alpha\beta)_{jk}$ is the effect of the interaction of the jth level of A and the kth level of B, $(\beta\pi)_{ki/j}$ is the effect of the interaction of the kth level of B and the ith subject in the jth level of A, and ε_{ijk} is the error for the ith subject in the jth level of A and kth level of B. As in Chapter 10, i/j notation indicates that subjects (indexed by i) are nested within levels of A (indexed by j).

How is this model different from the model we used for the two-way within-subjects factorial design, that is, the model in which both factors (A and B) were within-subjects? That model was written as

$$Y_{ijk} = \mu + \alpha_j + \beta_k + \pi_i + (\alpha\beta)_{jk} + (\alpha\pi)_{ji} + (\beta\pi)_{ki} + (\alpha\beta\pi)_{jki} + \varepsilon_{ijk} \tag{1, repeated}$$

Comparing Equations 1 and 16 reveals a difference in the way that the subjects effect is represented. In Equation 1, subjects appears as an effect in four terms: π_i, $(\alpha\pi)_{ji}$, $(\beta\pi)_{ki}$, and $(\alpha\beta\pi)_{jki}$. However, in Equation 16, subjects appears as an effect in only two terms: $\pi_{i/j}$ and $(\beta\pi)_{ki/j}$.

To begin to understand why the models treat subjects differently, let's consider the $(\alpha\pi)_{ji}$ term of Equation 1. Remember that this term represents the interaction of subjects and the A factor and thus reflects the extent to which the A effect is different from one subject to another. There is no $(\alpha\pi)_{ji}$ term in Equation 16 because subjects are not crossed with the A factor in the split-plot design. Instead, each subject appears in only one level of A, so it is impossible with this design to ascertain the extent to which the A effect is different from one individual subject to another. For instance, in our specific example, we cannot determine the extent to which age and subject interact—that is, some subjects age differently from others—because each subject is either old or young. Because we have a cross-sectional rather than a longitudinal design, this issue cannot be addressed in our design. Statistically speaking, the subjects factor is nested under the age factor instead of being crossed with it. The $\pi_{i/j}$ term in Equation 16 represents the nested effect of subjects within an age group. Recall from Chapter 10 that such a nested effect takes the place of a main effect and an interaction in a factorial design. This is exactly what has happened here, because $\pi_{i/j}$ in Equation 16 has taken the place of $\pi_i + (\alpha\pi)_{ji}$ in Equation 1. A similar argument shows that $(\beta\pi)_{ki/j}$ in Equation 16 has taken the place of $(\beta\pi)_{ki} + (\alpha\beta\pi)_{jki}$ in Equation 1. To summarize, the model of Equation 16 differs from the model of Equation 1 because the subjects factor is no longer crossed with the A factor, the between-subjects factor. Instead, the subjects factor is nested under A. As a consequence, the single $\pi_{i/j}$ term replaces the main effect and interaction terms that appeared in Equation 1. For this reason, there are now only five effects included in the full model for the split-plot design.

Before proceeding, be certain you understand why the $(\beta\pi)_{ki/j}$ term does appear in the model, although it represents the interaction of subjects with the B factor (angle, in our example). The reason is that the subjects factor is completely crossed with the B factor; each subject has a score at each and every level of B, so it is possible to determine the extent to which the B effect varies from one subject to another. Thus, an interaction term for the S and B factors appears in the model because these two factors are crossed, but an interaction term for S and A does not appear because S is nested under A instead of being crossed with A.

Restricted Models

The magnitude of each of the five effects in Equation 16 can be determined by comparing the full model of Equation 16 to a restricted model that omits the parameters associated with the effect in question. The resulting difference in sum of squared errors represents the sum of squares attributable to that particular effect. Table 12.16 shows sums of squares and degrees of freedom for each effect in the model. The S/A and B × S/A notation, which we introduced in Chapter 10, serves as a reminder that the S effect is nested under A. Thus, the S/A notation corresponds to the $\pi_{i/j}$ effect term in Equation 16, whereas B × S/A corresponds to the $(\beta\pi)_{ki/j}$ term.

Comparing the specific expressions for sums of squares in Table 12.16 with those for the two-way within-subjects design, shown in Table 12.2, is instructive. Notice that the sums of squares for the three effects to be tested (i.e., A, B, and A × B) are identical in the two cases. The differences occur in the remaining terms, which, as we see momentarily, are the error terms. For example, Table 12.16 shows that $SS_{S/A}$ is calculated by squaring the difference between each subject's average score (averaging over levels of B) and the average of all scores in that group, summing these squared differences across groups, and multiplying the result by b, the number of levels of B. This calculation is similar to that for SS_S in Table 12.2, except that in the two-way within-subjects design, an average score can be calculated for each subject averaging over both A and B. Such a calculation is impossible in the split-plot design because each subject appears at only one level of A. Comparing Tables 12.16 and 12.2 also shows that the relationship between $SS_{B \times S/A}$ and $SS_{B \times S}$ follows the same pattern as the aforementioned relationship between $SS_{S/A}$ and SS_S.

TABLE 12.16
SUMS OF SQUARES AND DEGREES OF FREEDOM FOR EACH EFFECT IN
A SPLIT-PLOT DESIGN

Effect	General Expression for SS	Specific Expression for SS	df
A	$\sum_{k=1}^{b}\sum_{j=1}^{a}\sum_{i=1}^{n}\hat{\alpha}_j^2$	$bn\sum_{j=1}^{a}(\overline{Y}_{.j.} - \overline{Y}_{...})^2$	$a - 1$
S/A	$\sum_{k=1}^{b}\sum_{j=1}^{a}\sum_{i=1}^{n}\hat{\pi}_{i/j}^2$	$b\sum_{j=1}^{a}\sum_{i=1}^{n}(\overline{Y}_{ij.} - \overline{Y}_{.j.})^2$	$N - a$
B	$\sum_{k=1}^{b}\sum_{j=1}^{a}\sum_{i=1}^{n}\hat{\beta}_k^2$	$an\sum_{k=1}^{b}(\overline{Y}_{..k} - \overline{Y}_{...})^2$	$b - 1$
A × B	$\sum_{k=1}^{b}\sum_{j=1}^{a}\sum_{i=1}^{n}\widehat{(\alpha\beta)}_{jk}^2$	$n\sum_{j=1}^{a}\sum_{k=1}^{b}(\overline{Y}_{.jk} - \overline{Y}_{.j.} - \overline{Y}_{..k} + \overline{Y}_{...})^2$	$(a-1)(b-1)$
B × S/A	$\sum_{k=1}^{b}\sum_{j=1}^{a}\sum_{i=1}^{n}\widehat{(\beta\pi)}_{ki/j}^2$	$\sum_{k=1}^{b}\sum_{j=1}^{a}\sum_{i=1}^{n}(Y_{ijk} - \overline{Y}_{ij.} - \overline{Y}_{.jk} + \overline{Y}_{.j.})^2$	$(N-a)(b-1)$

TABLE 12.17
EXPECTED MEAN SQUARES FOR EACH
EFFECT IN A SPLIT-PLOT DESIGN*

Effect	$\mathscr{E}(MS_{effect})$
A	$\sigma_\varepsilon^2 + b\sigma_\pi^2 + nb\theta_\alpha^2$
S/A	$\sigma_\varepsilon^2 + b\sigma_\pi^2$
B	$\sigma_\varepsilon^2 + \sigma_{\beta\pi}^2 + na\theta_\beta^2$
A × B	$\sigma_\varepsilon^2 + \sigma_{\beta\pi}^2 + na\theta_{\alpha\beta}^2$
B × S/A	$\sigma_\varepsilon^2 + \sigma_{\beta\pi}^2$

*Results are for a design with a levels of factor A, b levels of factor B, and n subjects. Factors A and B are assumed to be fixed.

Error Terms

Table 12.17 shows the expected mean square associated with each effect, where it is assumed that factors A and B are fixed but S is random. From the general principles we developed earlier for choosing an error term, it should be obvious how to test the A, B, and AB effects of interest here. The respective F tests are given by

$$F = MS_A/MS_{S/A} \tag{17}$$

$$F = MS_B/MS_{B\times S/A} \tag{18}$$

$$F = MS_{A\times B}/MS_{B\times S/A} \tag{19}$$

As usual, for these tests to be valid, statistical assumptions must be considered. We discuss this topic later in the chapter.

At this point, it may be helpful to develop an intuitive understanding of the error terms used in Equations 17–19. First, consider the F test of Equation 17 for the main effect of the between-subjects factor. Recall that a main effect represents a difference among marginal means, where all other factors in the design have been averaged over. For the data of Tables 12.7 and 12.15, we could calculate an average (i.e., mean) score for each subject, averaging over the three levels of angle. Notice that the resulting data fit a one-way between-subjects design; the within-subjects factor in the original design has been eliminated because we averaged over it. Analyzing these data in a one-way between-subjects design would yield exactly the same F value as is obtained from Equation 17. We see later in the chapter that this equivalence has important implications for the assumptions underlying the F test of the between-subjects main effect.

Second, consider the F test of the within-subjects main effect, shown in Equation 18. The error term used for this test, $MS_{B\times S/A}$, is very similar to the error term we developed earlier for designs in which all factors are within-subjects. Recall that in the completely within-subjects design, an appropriate error term for testing any effect given by $MS_{effect\times S}$, that is, the mean square interaction of the effect and subjects. In the split-plot design, $MS_{B\times S/A}$ is the mean square interaction of the B effect and subjects nested within A. How does $MS_{B\times S/A}$ relate to $MS_{effect\times S}$ of the completely within-subjects design? It can be shown that $MS_{B\times S/A}$ is a weighted average (i.e., a weighted mean) of the a different $MS_{B\times S}$ values that could be calculated at each separate level of A. Specifically, with two levels of A, as in our example, it can be shown that

$$MS_{B\times S/A} = \frac{(n_1 - 1)MS_{B\times S/A_1} + (n_2 - 1)MS_{B\times S/A_2}}{(n_1 - 1) + (n_2 - 1)} \tag{20}$$

whereas in the general case of a levels of A, the equation is given by

$$MS_{B \times S/A} = \frac{\sum(n_j - 1)MS_{B \times S/A_j}}{\sum(n_j - 1)} \tag{21}$$

Equations 20 and 21 show that $MS_{B \times S/A}$ is a weighted average of the separate $MS_{B \times S/A_j}$ terms, with weights proportional to $n_j - 1$, the degrees of freedom for S/A_j. From Equations 20 and 21, you should be able to understand the rationale for using $MS_{B \times S/A}$ as an error term for testing the B main effect. In essence, we know from Chapter 11 that $MS_{B \times S/A_j}$ is an appropriate error term for testing B at the jth level of A (if homogeneity assumptions are met) because this is simply a one-way within-subjects design given we are ignoring all other levels of A. The rationale for averaging the separate $MS_{B \times S/A_j}$ terms across the levels of A is based on an assumption that separate $MS_{B \times S/A_j}$ values differ from one another only as the result of sampling error. As a result, it is important to notice that using $MS_{B \times S/A}$ as an error term is based on two logically distinct assumptions. The first assumption is that $MS_{B \times S/A_j}$ is an appropriate error term for level j of the A factor. The second assumption is that the a separate $MS_{B \times S/A_j}$ terms are all estimates of a single common population value. As we discuss later in the chapter, it is possible either for both assumptions to be met, or one but not the other, or for both to be violated. However, the basic point for the moment is that $MS_{B \times S/A}$ has the same meaning in a split-plot design as $MS_{effect \times S}$ has in completely within-subjects designs.

Third, we need to consider the F test for the interaction of the between- and within-subjects factors, shown in Equation 19. Notice that the error term for this test, $MS_{B \times S/A}$, is the same as the error term for the within-subjects main effect. Because we are testing the A $\times$ B interaction, the logic of the $MS_{effect \times S}$ error term might suggest $MS_{A \times B \times S}$ as an appropriate error term here. However, there is no A $\times$ B $\times$ S term in the split-plot design because A and S are not crossed. Instead, the appropriate error term is given by $MS_{B \times S/A}$, as shown in Equation 19. The error term for the A $\times$ B interaction is the same as the error term for the B main effect because we are still interested in the separate B effects at each level of A. However, as we saw in Chapter 7 when we first discussed interactions, instead of averaging these separate effects to obtain the B main effect, the A $\times$ B interaction compares these separate effects to each other. Nevertheless, in both cases the error term is the same. The most important point to notice here is that the interaction of the between-subjects factor with the within-subjects factor is analyzed using a within-subjects source of variance as an error term.

It should also be pointed out that the three F tests shown in Equations 17–19 are consistent with the principles we developed in Chapter 10. That this is true can be seen by reconsidering Figure 10.7.

Numerical Example

Now that we have developed the omnibus tests for the split-plot design, let's reconsider the data of Tables 12.7 and 12.15. Table 12.18 displays the cell means and the marginal means

TABLE 12.18
CELL MEANS AND MARGINAL MEANS FOR DATA OF TABLES 12.7 AND 12.15

		Angle (Within-Subjects)			
		0°	4°	8°	
Age (Between-Subjects)	Young	477	585	645	569
	Old	543	654	792	663
		510	619.5	718.5	

TABLE 12.19
ANOVA TABLE FOR DATA IN TABLES 12.7 (YOUNG SUBJECTS) AND
12.15 (OLD SUBJECTS)

Source	SS	df	MS	F	p
A	132,540	1	132,540	7.28	.0147
S/A	327,900	18	18,217		
B	435,090	2	217,545	143.91	.0001
A × B	21,090	2	10,545	6.98	.0028
B × S/A	54,420	36	1,512		

for our data. Table 12.19 presents the corresponding ANOVA table. The sums of squares are obtained by applying the formulas of Table 12.16, and the appropriate error term is chosen according to Equations 17–19. The p values of Table 12.19 show that both main effects and the interaction are statistically significant at the .05 level. As usual, we may want to supplement these tests with measures of effect. As we mentioned earlier in the chapter, there are a variety of possible measures. Our preference is once again to partial all effects except subjects. In this case, omega squared for A (the between-subjects factor) is the same as it would be if we were simply to average over B, producing a single-factor between-subjects design. Similarly, omega squared for B is comparable to the value we would obtain in a single-factor design involving only B. In so doing, we are regarding both A and B as extrinsic factors, so different approaches are needed with intrinsic factors. Interested readers are referred to Olejnik and Algina (2000) for additional reading, although as was true earlier in the chapter, our specific formulation is different from any of the formulas they present for this design. Given our conceptualization, omega squared for the main effect of the between-subjects factor A can be computed as

$$\hat{\omega}_A^2 = \frac{SS_A - (a-1)MS_{S/A}}{SS_A + SS_{S/A} + MS_{S/A}} \tag{22}$$

The comparable expressions for the within-subjects effects B and AB are

$$\hat{\omega}_B^2 = \frac{(b-1)(MS_B - MS_{B \times S/A})}{SS_B + SS_{B \times S/A} + SS_{S/A} + MS_{S/A}} \tag{23}$$

and

$$\hat{\omega}_{AB}^2 = \frac{(a-1)(b-1)(MS_{AB} - MS_{B \times S/A})}{SS_{AB} + SS_{B \times S/A} + SS_{S/A} + MS_{S/A}} \tag{24}$$

In our data, the numerical values of omega squared are .25 for the age main effect, .52 for the angle main effect, and .04 for the interaction of age and angle. Thus, the age and angle main effects account for considerably more variance than does the interaction. Even so, the interaction may be the effect of most theoretical interest.

As in other designs, significant omnibus effects are typically pursued with further tests. The nature of follow-up tests to be performed in the split-plot design is the same as in the two-way between-subjects design of Chapter 7 and the two-way within-subjects design discussed earlier in this chapter. In other words, the nature of the questions is the same as in the other two-way factorial designs. The only difference is, once again, what source is used as the denominator of the F test.

Further Investigation of Main Effects

Between-Subjects Factor

The meaning of a main effect in a split-plot design is the same as in the other two-way factorial designs we have already discussed. For example, consider the statistically significant main effect we found for age, the between-subjects factor in our numerical example. As usual, the statistically significant A main effect implies that the two marginal means are different from one another in the population. From Table 12.18, the sample marginal mean for young subjects is 569 (notice that this is the mean of 477, 585, and 645 because we are averaging over B), and the sample marginal mean for old subjects is 663 (which is the mean of 543, 654, and 792). Thus, the p value of .0147 for the A main effect means that a difference as large as we observed in our sample (i.e., 569 vs. 663) would occur in only 1.47 of every 100 experiments if the null hypothesis were true. For this reason, we can reject the null hypothesis at the .05 level. Because there are only two levels of A, it is unnecessary to perform further tests to ascertain which specific levels of A are different from one another. However, in cases where A has more than two levels and the A main effect is statistically significant, multiple-comparisons procedures would typically be used.

We already know how to use multiple-comparisons procedures for pursuing the meaning of a significant between-subjects main effect in a split-plot design. By performing the between-subjects main effect test, we are averaging over the within-subjects factor and effectively eliminating it from the design. As we discussed earlier, the between-subjects main effect F test in the split-plot design is identical to the F test that would occur if each subject's mean score were used as the dependent variable in a purely between-subjects design. The same relationship holds for individual comparisons as well, so that contrasts of the marginal means for the A factor can be tested simply by averaging each subject's scores across the within-subjects factor and performing between-subjects contrasts of the resulting scores. As a result, the principles developed in Chapters 4 and 5 apply with no modifications whatsoever to tests of the between-subjects marginal means in a split-plot design.

Within-Subjects Factor

In our numerical example, we also obtained a statistically significant main effect for angle, the within-subjects factor. Because the angle factor has three levels, we might want to test comparisons among these levels, to better understand the nature of the angle main effect.[11] As we have seen in previous designs, there are two basic approaches for testing a within-subjects comparison in a split-plot design. One approach uses a pooled error term, whereas the other approach uses a separate error term for each contrast. Before seeing the formulas for the F tests of the two approaches, recall that, in our notation, B represents the within-subjects factor (angle in the numerical example) and A represents the between-subjects factor (age in the numerical example). The first approach for testing a within-subjects comparison in a split-plot design is to form an F ratio given by

$$F = SS_{B_{comp}}/MS_{B \times S/A} \tag{25}$$

The second approach forms the F ratio as

$$F = SS_{B_{comp}}/MS_{B_{comp} \times S/A} \tag{26}$$

Obviously, the only difference between these two approaches involves the choice of error term. Notice that the F test of Equation 25 uses the same error term for all contrasts, whereas the

F test of Equation 26 uses a separate error term for each specific contrast. If you look back at Equations 7 and 8, you should see that Equation 25 is the split-plot equivalent of Equation 7 and Equation 26 is the split-plot equivalent of Equation 8. (Notice that Equations 7 and 8 test a comparison of A marginal means because A was a within-subjects factor in that design, whereas Equations 25 and 26 test a comparison of B marginal means because we have used B to represent the within-subjects factor in the split-plot design. However, Equations 7 and 8 could be rewritten by replacing A with B to make them look more like Equations 25 and 26.)

The choice between Equations 25 and 26 involves the same issues as the choice between Equations 7 and 8. Specifically, Equation 25 is valid only if a homogeneity assumption like that discussed in Chapter 11 is met. When the assumption is violated, using Equation 25 can be very misleading, because the F test using a single common error term is not robust when homogeneity fails to hold. As a consequence, in most split-plot designs, in which the homogeneity assumption is likely to be violated, using Equation 26 is generally preferred over Equation 25. However, Equation 26 turns out to be more compatible with the multivariate approach to repeated measures than the mixed-model approach. For this reason, we defer further consideration of the choice of error terms until Chapters 13 and 14.

To see how Equations 25 and 26 work in practice, let's test the quadratic trend for the marginal means of the angle factor. As shown in Table 12.18, the sample angle marginal means are 510, 619.5, and 718.5. The contrast coefficients for a quadratic trend among three levels are 1, -2, and 1 (see Appendix Table A.10). The sum of squares for the contrast equals

$$SS_{B_{comp}} = \frac{na(\hat{\psi})^2}{\sum_{k=1}^{b} c_k^2} \tag{27}$$

where $\hat{\psi}$ is the sample value of the contrast and c_k is the contrast coefficient for level k. Notice that a appears in Equation 27 because we are comparing B marginal means, each of which is based on na individual scores. (With unequal n, na would simply be replaced by N, the total number of subjects in the sample.) For our data,

$$\hat{\psi} = 510 - 2(619.5) + 718.5 = -10.5$$

Thus, the quadratic sum of squares equals

$$SS_{B_{quad}} = (10)(2)(-10.5)^2/6 = 367.5$$

The F value for the quadratic trend using Equation 25 is given by

$$F = 367.5/1512 = 0.24$$

with 1 and 36 degrees of freedom. It turns out that $MS_{B_{quad} \times S/A} = 1160.83$, so the F value using Equation 26 equals

$$F = 367.5/1160.83 = 0.32$$

with 1 and 18 degrees of freedom. For these data, the quadratic trend for angle is nonsignificant even with α_{PC} set at .05, whether the error term of Equation 25 or 26 is used. However, we should emphasize again that in many circumstances Equation 26 may yield a very different result from Equation 25.

Further Investigation of an Interaction—Simple Effects

As in other factorial designs, the most typical method of interpreting a statistically significant interaction in a split-plot design is to perform tests of simple effects. In our numerical example, we found a significant age × angle interaction, which might be pursued by testing the angle effect within each level of age, as well as testing the age effect within each level of angle. We need to discuss both types of simple-effects tests because in one case (angle within age) we effectively have a one-way within-subjects design; whereas in the other case (age within angle) we effectively have a one-way between-subjects design.

Within-Subjects Effects at a Fixed Level of Between-Subjects Factor

We begin by considering the simple effect of angle (the within-subjects factor) at a fixed level of age (the between-subjects factor). For example, consider the effect of angle for young subjects. The question is, are the three sample means of 477 (for 0°), 585 (for 4°), and 645 (for 8°) shown in Table 12.18 significantly different from each other? Looking at the layout of these means in Table 12.18 should convince you that, in effect, we have a one-way within-subjects design, because we are no longer considering the older subjects whose inclusion was responsible for the between-subjects factor. As usual, in a one-way design, the sum of squares for an effect is given by

$$SS_{\text{effect}} = n \sum_{j=1}^{a} (\overline{Y}_j - \overline{Y}_.)^2$$

where $\overline{Y}_j$ indicates the means of the individual levels and $\overline{Y}_.$ is the grand mean of these means. For the sake of comparison, notice that in our original notation (see Table 12.16), the sum of squares for the effect of B at A_1 could be written as

$$SS_{\text{B at } A_1} = n \sum_{k=1}^{b} (\overline{Y}_{.1k} - \overline{Y}_{.1.})^2$$

Substituting the sample means of 477, 585, and 645 together with $n = 10$ (because we are only using the data from young subjects) yields

$$SS_{\text{B at } A_1} = 144{,}960$$

We must now consider the choice of an error term, that is, a denominator against which to test $SS_{\text{B at } A_1}$. Recall that we calculated $SS_{\text{B at } A_1}$ by realizing that, in effect, we have a one-way within-subjects design when we investigate the B effect at a fixed level of A. Following this logic, it would seem reasonable to use the same error term that would be used in a one-way within-subjects design, namely the mean square interaction of the effect with subjects (as usual, the validity of this error term rests on a homogeneity assumption to be discussed later). Because we are considering only young subjects, this interaction would be B × S for subjects at the A_1 level of the A factor. We previously designated this interaction as $MS_{\text{B} \times \text{S}/A_1}$ (you may want to refer back to Equation 20 for a reminder of this notation). For our data (in Table 12.7, for young subjects), the value of $MS_{\text{B} \times \text{S}/A_1}$ equals 1780. An F test for testing the effect of B at A_1 can be obtained from

$$F = MS_{\text{B at } A_1} / MS_{\text{B} \times \text{S}/A_1} \tag{28}$$

Because $SS_{\text{B at A}_1}$ equals 144,960 and B has three levels,

$$MS_{\text{B at A}_1} = 144{,}960/2 = 72{,}480$$

Thus, the F value for the simple effect of angle for young subjects equals

$$F = 72{,}480/1780 = 40.72$$

which is significant at the .05 level (or at the .025 level, if we decided to divide α by the number of simple effects tests of the angle factor, which is one approach we discussed in Chapter 7).

We might now perform comparisons of the mean angle levels for young subjects, but before considering that possibility, we must consider an alternate error term that might be used instead of $MS_{\text{B}\times\text{S/A}_1}$. Recall from Equation 20 that $MS_{\text{B}\times\text{S/A}}$ is an average of $MS_{\text{B}\times\text{S/A}_1}$ and $MS_{\text{B}\times\text{S/A}_2}$ when A has two levels, as it does in our example. The assumption made in using $MS_{\text{B}\times\text{S/A}}$ as an error term for omnibus tests of B and A $\times$ B is that $MS_{\text{B}\times\text{S/A}_1}$ and $MS_{\text{B}\times\text{S/A}_2}$ differ from one another only because of sampling error. If this assumption is true, $MS_{\text{B}\times\text{S/A}}$ provides a better estimate of the common population variance than either $MS_{\text{B}\times\text{S/A}_1}$ or $MS_{\text{B}\times\text{S/A}_2}$ by themselves because $MS_{\text{B}\times\text{S/A}}$ is based on more subjects. The superiority of the estimate is translated into increased degrees of freedom, and as a result, increased statistical power. However, as we explained in our Chapter 7 discussion of simple-effects tests in factorial between-subjects designs, simple-effects tests are not robust to violations of this assumption. When the assumption is violated, simple-effects F tests tend to be too large for some levels of A and too small for others. Which error term should be preferred? With large samples (e.g., when the degrees of freedom for $MS_{\text{B}\times\text{S/A}_j}$ exceeds 50 as an arbitrary but reasonable guideline), using a separate error term of the form $MS_{\text{B}\times\text{S/A}_j}$ is preferable because the additional degrees of freedom afforded by $MS_{\text{B}\times\text{S/A}}$ has literally almost no effect. However, with small samples, the choice is more difficult because the power advantage of using $MS_{\text{B}\times\text{S/A}}$ can be substantial if the assumption is met. Also, the assumption is often true (or true for all practical purposes) in many behavioral applications, especially when the between-groups factor reflects a manipulation on the part of the experimenter rather than preexisting intact groups. As of this writing, the major statistical packages (e.g., SAS, SPSS) use $MS_{\text{B}\times\text{S/A}}$ as the error term in their split-plot analysis of variance procedures. However, it is obviously simple (no pun intended) to use $MS_{\text{B}\times\text{S/A}_j}$ as the error term, by literally ignoring all other groups.[12] For our numerical example, the simple effect of angle for the young subjects remains statistically significant if we use $MS_{\text{B}\times\text{S/A}}$ as the error term, because the F value we obtain equals $72{,}480/1512 = 47.95$.

As we stated earlier, because the simple effect of angle is statistically significant for young subjects, we would typically test specific comparisons of the angle factor for young subjects. Notice that these comparisons are in effect comparisons in a one-way within-subjects design. As a consequence, an error term specific to that individual comparison (as in Equation 8) is generally preferred.

So far, we have considered only one side of the possible simple-effects tests to be performed in a split-plot design, namely, the effect of the within-subjects factor at a fixed level of the between-subjects factor. In many research situations, however, we may be just as interested in the simple-effects test of the between-subjects factor at a fixed level of the within-subjects factor.

Between-Subjects Effects at a Fixed Level of Within-Subjects Factor

In our numerical example, we would almost certainly be interested in testing the age effect at each level of angle (assuming that we are interested in simple-effects tests in the first place). For example, let's consider the effect of age in the $0°$ angle condition. The question is, Are the two sample means of 477 (for young subjects) and 543 (for old subjects) as shown in Table 12.18 significantly different from one another? Looking at the layout of means in Table 12.18 should convince you that for this question we have in effect a one-way between-subjects design because we are no longer considering multiple levels of angle, which was the within-subjects factor. The sum of squares for an effect in a one-way design is easy to calculate. If we let $\overline{Y}_1 = 477$ and $\overline{Y}_2 = 543$, then

$$SS_{\text{effect}} = \sum_{j=1}^{a} n_j (\overline{Y}_j - \overline{Y}_.)^2$$

where n_j is the number of subjects on which $\overline{Y}_j$ is based and $\overline{Y}_.$ is the grand mean of these means. For the sake of completeness, notice that in our original notation (see Table 12.16), the sum of squares for the effect of A at B_1 could be written as

$$SS_{\text{A at B}_1} = \sum_{j=1}^{a} n_j (\overline{Y}_{.j1} - \overline{Y}_{..1})^2$$

Substituting the sample means of 477 and 543 into either formula together with $n_1 = 10$, $n_2 = 10$, and a grand mean of 510 yields

$$SS_{\text{A at B}_1} = 21{,}780$$

Notice that because there are only two levels of A in our example, the degrees of freedom for the A effect (either the A main effect or the simple effect of A at a fixed level of B) equals 1. Hence,

$$MS_{\text{A at B}_1} = SS_{\text{A at B}_1}/1 = 21{,}780$$

As usual, we must now consider the choice of an appropriate error term. Recall that we calculated $SS_{\text{A at B}_1}$ by realizing that in effect we have a one-way between-subjects design when we investigate the A effect at a fixed level of B. Following this logic, it seems natural to use the same error term that would be used in a one-way between-subjects design, namely MS_W. Because we are only considering scores in the $0°$ angle condition, we could designate this mean square within as $MS_{\text{S/A at B}_1}$. (Notice that we might also write this term as $MS_{\text{W at B}_1}$. However, the S/A notation is probably better, because it reminds us that subjects are nested under A, the between-subjects factor.) It is easy to calculate $MS_{\text{S/A at B}_1}$, the mean square within age groups for the $0°$ angle scores, using the formulas developed in Chapter 3 for a one-way between-subjects design. For our data,

$$MS_{\text{S/A at B}_1} = 6890$$

Thus, the F value for the simple effect of A (age) at B_1 ($0°$ angle) is given by

$$F = MS_{\text{A at B}_1}/MS_{\text{S/A at B}_1}$$
$$= 21{,}780/6890$$
$$= 3.16 \tag{29}$$

In general, there are $a - 1$ numerator and $N - a$ denominator degrees of freedom associated with this F value. In our specific case, the degrees of freedom equal 1 and 18; the corresponding p value is .092, so the effect is nonsignificant even without any possible adjustments of the α level for tests of A that might also be performed at B_2 and B_3.

Once again, there is an alternate error term that might be used here. Notice that in the approach we have developed so far, a separate error term is used for each simple-effects test of the between-subjects factor. Specifically, $MS_{\text{S/A at } B_k}$ is used to test the simple effect of A at the kth level of B. However, an alternate procedure would be to use a pooled error term obtained from the average of all b $MS_{\text{S/A at } B_k}$ separate error terms. The formula for this error term, which is traditionally referred to as $MSWCELL$ (which is not the same as $MS_{\text{S/A}}$), is

$$MSWCELL = \sum_{k=1}^{b} MS_{\text{S/A at } B_k}/b \tag{30}$$

You may wonder why $MSWCELL$ is an unweighted average, unlike other pooled error terms, which have been weighted averages. In fact, $MSWCELL$ is a weighted average, but the weights are all equal because there must be the same number of subjects at each level of B. Thus, in this case (i.e., equal weights), the weighted average simplifies to an unweighted average. It can be shown that an equivalent computational form for $MSWCELL$ is given by[13]

$$MSWCELL = (SS_{\text{S/A}} + SS_{\text{B} \times \text{S/A}})/b(N - a) \tag{31}$$

which is usually more convenient than Equation 30 for calculating $MSWCELL$ in a split-plot design.

As usual, the potential advantage of $MSWCELL$ over $MS_{\text{S/A at } B_k}$ is an increase in degrees of freedom, which implies a lower critical value and hence more power if the homogeneity assumption is met. However, when the assumption is violated, typically all simple-effects tests are biased, with some yielding F values that systematically tend to be too small and others yielding F values that systematically tend to be too large. As of this writing, the major statistical packages (e.g., SAS and SPSS) use $MS_{\text{S/A at } B_k}$ instead of $MSWCELL$ as the error term for testing simple effects of the between-subjects factor at a fixed level of the within-subjects factor.[14] At first glance, this seems inconsistent, because all three packages use a pooled error term for testing effects of the within-subjects factor at a fixed level of the between-subjects factor. In neither case are the resulting tests with a pooled error term robust to violation of assumptions, so robustness cannot be the explanation for using a pooled error term for one test but a separate error term for the other. Instead, the rationale for this difference is that one assumption is often more likely to be violated than the other in behavioral research. We stated earlier that the various $MS_{\text{B} \times \text{S/A}_j}$ terms often estimate the same population variance, especially when the levels of A represent groups formed by the experimenter. Thus, a pooled error term is often justified for testing B effects within levels of A. For testing A effects within levels of B, the assumption required for a pooled error term is that the various $MS_{\text{S/A at } B_k}$ terms all estimate the same population variance. Although this assumption is undoubtedly valid in some behavioral applications of the split-plot design, in many behavioral studies the assumption is likely to be false. It is especially likely that the assumption will fail to hold when the within-subjects factor is time, as it often is in split-plot designs, because scores often become more variable with the passage of time. In any event, the test using $MS_{\text{S/A at } B_k}$ always requires fewer assumptions than the test using MSWCELL, so for this reason we tend to prefer it, unless the degrees of freedom for $MS_{\text{S/A at } B_k}$ is small, and there is a strong theoretical reason to believe that scores will be equally variable within groups (i.e., levels of A) for the different levels of the within-subjects factor (B).

In our particular data, the choice between $MS_{S/A \text{ at } B_1}$ and $MSWCELL$ as the error term for testing the age difference in the 0° angle condition turns out to make no practical difference. From Equation 31 and Table 12.19, $MSWCELL$ equals 7080 for our data. Using this error term for the age effect at 0° produces an F value of 3.08, which with 1 and 54 degrees of freedom is still nonsignificant at the .05 level.

In general, when statistically significant simple effects of A are found at a fixed level of B, further tests are performed to isolate the nature of the A effect. Of course, such tests are unnecessary when A has only two levels, as it does in our example. However, when A has three or more levels, specific comparisons can be tested by regarding the data as representing a one-way between-subjects design. Thus, the principles we developed in Chapters 4 and 5 can be applied in this situation.

Interaction Contrasts

As in other factorial designs, another approach to probing a statistically significant interaction is to test interaction contrasts. The sum of squares attributable to an interaction contrast can be found most easily by conceptualizing the contrast as a comparison among the ab means in the design. To illustrate this procedure in some detail, we make use of our numerical example.

Recall that earlier in the chapter we found that the quadratic trend for angle was nonsignificant for our data. However, this does not preclude the possibility that the quadratic trend for angle differs as a function of age. In other words, the quadratic trend for angle might be different for young subjects as compared to old subjects. Before proceeding, you may want to convince yourself that this is indeed possible in our data, despite the nonsignificant quadratic trend for angle. (Hint: Look at Table 12.18. Which means are involved in testing whether the quadratic trend differs as a function of age? Were the same means used in obtaining the nonsignificant quadratic trend for angle?) Recall that because the angle factor has three levels, the coefficients for the quadratic trend are 1, −2, and 1 (see Appendix Table A.10). From Table 12.18, we can see that the value of the angle quadratic trend for young subjects equals −48. For old subjects, the value of the angle quadratic trend is 27. We want to test the difference between these two values, so the value of the contrast to be tested equals 75 [i.e., 27 − (−48)]. It should be noted that subtracting 27 from −48 and obtaining a value of −75 would ultimately yield the same sum of squares. Also, notice that in terms of the six cell means shown in Table 12.18, our interaction contrast has coefficients (reading across the rows, from left to right) of −1, 2, −1, 1, −2, and 1. Thus, we are giving negative weights to the contrast coefficients that were initially 1, −2, and 1 in the first row because what we are interested in is the value of the quadratic trend for old subjects minus the value of the quadratic trend for young subjects. We can then find the sum of squares for the interaction contrast from

$$SS_\psi = n(\hat{\psi})^2 \bigg/ \sum_{j=1}^{ab} c_j^2$$

where $\hat{\psi}$ is the sample value of the contrast and c_j is the contrast coefficient for cell j. Notice that j ranges from 1 to 6 in our example, and from 1 to ab in general, because we are simply conceptualizing the data in terms of six cell means at this point. For the data in Table 12.18, we have $\hat{\psi} = 75$, $n = 10$, and $\sum_{j=1}^{ab} c_j^2 = 12$ (recall that the six coefficients equaled −1, 2,

$-1, 1, -2$, and 1). Thus, the sum of squares for the interaction contrast is given by

$$SS_\psi = 10(75)^2/12 = 4687.5$$

As usual, the next problem is determining an error term, and several possibilities arise. Because the interaction contrast represents 1 of the $(a-1)(b-1)$ degrees of freedom of the omnibus $A \times B$ interaction, one approach is to use the error term that was used for the interaction, namely, $MS_{B \times S/A}$. The equation for this F test would be

$$F = SS_{A_{comp} \times B_{comp}}/MS_{B \times S/A} \tag{32}$$

For our data, this F test yields a value of $4687.5/1512 = 3.101$, with 1 and 54 degrees of freedom for the age difference in the angle quadratic trend. This F value would not allow us to reject the null hypothesis at the .05 level, even without a possible adjustment of the α level for any other contrasts we might also test.[15]

Using $MS_{B \times S/A}$, a pooled error term, for testing interaction contrasts has the usual pros and cons. If requisite assumptions are met, degrees of freedom are maximal, so power is somewhat higher than with a separate error term. However, the F test of Equation 32 is not robust to violations of homogeneity. In particular, two homogeneity assumptions are required, one across levels of A and the other across levels of B. The necessity of this assumption can perhaps be made clearest by realizing that in our 2×3 design, $MS_{B \times S/A}$ is an unweighted average of four components[16]:

$$MS_{B \times S/A} = (MS_{B_{linear} \times S/A_1} + MS_{B_{linear} \times S/A_2} + MS_{B_{quad} \times S/A_1} + MS_{B_{quad} \times S/A_2})/4 \tag{33}$$

In our example, the values of these four components turn out to be $MS_{B_{linear} \times S/A_1} = 2120.00$, $MS_{B_{linear} \times S/A_2} = 1605.00$, $MS_{B_{quad} \times S/A_1} = 1440.00$, and $MS_{B_{quad} \times S/A_2} = 881.67$. It is easily verified that the average of these four values is 1511.67, which has been rounded off to 1512 throughout the chapter for simplicity.

It might be argued that, because we are testing only the quadratic trend of angle, our error term should be based on this specific component of the angle effect. Because the interaction contrast involves both A_1 and A_2 (remember that we are literally comparing the quadratic trend at A_1 vs. the trend at A_2), a possible error term would be given by the average of $MS_{B_{quad} \times S/A_1}$ and $MS_{B_{quad} \times S/A_2}$: $MS_{B_{quad} \times S/A} = (MS_{B_{quad} \times S/A_1} + MS_{B_{quad} \times S/A_2})/2$, which equals 1160.83 for our data. The general form of this F test is given by

$$F = SS_{A_{comp} \times B_{comp}}/MS_{B_{comp} \times S/A} \tag{34}$$

In our data, the F value equals $4687.5/1160.83 = 4.038$, with 1 and 18 degrees of freedom. The corresponding p value without any adjustment for multiple tests equals .0597, so this approach also fails to find significance at the .05 level.

Although using Equation 34 instead of Equation 32 results in fewer degrees of freedom, the advantage of Equation 34 is that it does not require a homogeneity assumption across the levels of B. As we have stated on several occasions, such an assumption fails to hold in many behavioral applications, so Equation 34 is generally preferred to Equation 32. However, Equation 34 is more consistent with the multivariate approach to repeated measures, so we wait until Chapters 13 and 14 for a detailed discussion of the use of separate error terms for testing contrasts in within-subjects designs. Finally, we should mention that there are two possible versions of Equation 34. One approach uses all levels of the A factor to calculate $MS_{B_{comp} \times S/A}$,

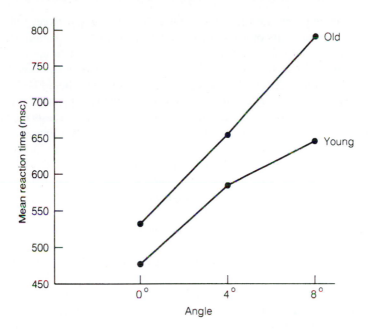

FIG. 12.1.   Plot of reaction times for old and young subjects as a function of angle.

whereas the other uses only those levels of A that are explicitly involved in the interaction contrast. The former has more degrees of freedom than the latter, but also requires homogeneity across levels of A. Notice that this choice is not an issue in our example because there are only two levels of the A factor, and both are naturally involved in the interaction contrast.

Finally, Figure 12.1 helps to clarify the nature of the age × angle interaction. There is some indication that the shape of younger subjects' mean reaction time might involve an inverted-U quadratic component, whereas the plot for older subjects suggests a U-shaped trend. That the test of the age by quadratic trend of angle interaction contrast was nonsignificant means that this difference cannot be regarded as conclusive, so another study might be conducted with a larger number of subjects to further investigate this issue. Also, the figure clearly shows the age main effect and the angle main effect. Also, recall from Table 12.19 that the interaction is statistically significant. The plot of cell means suggests that the age groups differ most in the 8° angle condition. This issue could be pursued by testing an appropriate interaction contrast. Alternatively, the simple effect of age at each level of angle could be tested, although this would not address the specific question of whether the age difference is larger at 8° than at 0° or 4° .

Assumptions

As we have seen, the split-plot design is a combination of between-subjects and within-subjects designs. Not surprisingly, the statistical assumptions required in the split-plot design are also a combination of between- and within-subjects assumptions. We now discuss these assumptions for omnibus tests, as well as follow-up tests of simple effects and interaction contrasts.

We learned earlier that the F test of the between-subjects main effect (denoted A) in the split-plot design is identical to an F test that could be conducted as a one-way between-subjects test on the mean score for each subject, averaging over levels of the within-subjects factor. Thus, the assumptions are the same as those for a one-way between-subjects design, namely normality, homogeneity of variance, and independence of observations (i.e., subjects). The practical importance of these assumptions for testing the A main effect in a split-plot design is exactly the same as their importance in a one-way between-subjects design, which we discussed in Chapter 3. As usual, scores for different subjects should be independent of each other, or serious biases may result. Violations of normality typically have little impact on the F test, although, as Chapter 3's Extension notes, more powerful tests may be available for nonnormal data. Finally, with equal n, the F test is generally robust to violations of homogeneity of variance. With unequal n, the test is not robust, and modifications discussed in the Chapter 3 Extension are preferable when heterogeneity of variance obtains. Be certain you understand to what scores these assumptions apply. They are assumptions that refer to the mean score calculated for each subject, averaging over levels of the within-subjects factor. The assumptions do not necessarily have to hold for the original scores themselves, although if they do hold for the original scores, it can be shown that they must also hold for the mean scores as well.

The required statistical assumptions for testing the B and A × B effects are rather different from those required for testing the A effect. Notice that B and A × B are both within-subjects effects and that both use $MS_{B \times S/A}$ as the denominator of their F tests (see Equations 18 and 19). Besides the usual assumptions of normality and of independence of subjects, the mixed-model F tests of the B and A × B effects also require two other assumptions. First, it is assumed that within each level of A (the between-subjects factor), the levels of B display the homogeneity of treatment-difference variances property discussed in Chapter 11. Recall that the rationale for using $MS_{B \times S/A}$ as an error term was based partially on the fact that $MS_{B \times S/A_j}$ would be an appropriate error term for testing B effects at the jth level of A, if homogeneity is valid. Also, remember that this homogeneity assumption holds if and only if the population covariance matrix of the data possesses sphericity. The second required assumption is that these a covariance matrices, each of which is calculated at an individual level of A, must be identical to one another in the population.[17] It is important to realize that these two assumptions are logically separate from one another, in the sense that it is entirely possible for either to hold when the other is false. The most important practical aspect of these assumptions is that the B and A × B mixed-model tests are not robust to violations of the homogeneity of treatment-difference variances assumption. This should not be surprising because other within-subjects tests discussed earlier in this chapter and in Chapter 11 have also depended heavily on this assumption. The significance tests are robust to the second assumption, as long as sample sizes are equal. However, as sample sizes depart from equality, the tests become less robust. In general, however, the crucial assumption is that the covariance matrix corresponding to the B effect must exhibit sphericity. When the assumption is not met, there is a systematic tendency for the actual rate of Type I errors to exceed its nominal value. As we said before, this assumption is likely to be violated in many behavioral applications. For this reason, it is often appropriate to consider either ε-adjusted tests, to be discussed momentarily, or a multivariate approach to analyzing split-plot data, to be discussed in Chapter 14.

As we have discussed throughout the chapter, the necessary assumptions required for follow-up tests depend strongly on the nature of the error term chosen for conducting these tests. Table 12.20 summarizes the available choices for each type of test and indicates which assumptions are required, as well as whether the test tends to be robust to violations of that assumption. As Table 12.20 shows, most of the within-subjects tests we discuss in this chapter are sensitive to the assumption that the covariance matrix of the repeated factor possesses sphericity. When this assumption is false, there are two alternatives to the mixed-model tests we have discussed: ε-adjusted tests and multivariate tests. We discuss ε-adjusted tests next

TABLE 12.20
ASSUMPTIONS AND ROBUSTNESS PROPERTIES OF OMNIBUS AND FOLLOW-UP
TESTS IN SPLIT-PLOT DESIGNS

Test	Error Term*	Assumptions			
		Equality of Levels of A		Spherical Covariance Matrix	
		Required?	Robust?	Required?	Robust?
A	$MS_{S/A}$ (17)	Yes[†]	Yes[‡]	No	—
A_{comp}	$MS_{S/A}$	Yes[†]	No	No	—
B	$MS_{B \times S/A}$ (18)	Yes[§]	Yes[‡]	Yes	No
B_{comp} ⎫	$MS_{B \times S/A}$ (25)	Yes[§]	Yes[‡]	Yes	No
⎬ or					
⎭	$MS_{B_{comp} \times S/A}$ (26)	Yes[§]	Yes[‡]	No	—
A × B	$MS_{B \times S/A}$ (19)	Yes[§]	Yes[‡]	Yes	No
⎫	$MS_{B \times S/A}$	Yes[§]	Yes[†]	Yes	No
B at A_j ⎬ or					
⎭	$MS_{B \times S/A_j}$ (28)	No	—	Yes	No
⎫	$MSWCELL$	Yes[‖]	Yes[‡]	Yes[#]	No
A at B_k ⎬ or					
⎭	$MS_{S/A \text{ at } B_k}$ (29)	Yes[‖]	Yes[†]	No	—
$A_{comp} \times B_{comp}$	$MS_{B \times S/A}$ (32)	Yes[§]	No	Yes	No
	or				
	$MS_{B_{comp} \times S/A}$ (34)	Yes[§]	No	No	—

*The numbers in parentheses after the error term show the equation number for testing this effect.
[†]The assumption is that mean scores averaged over levels of B must be equally variable.
[‡]Robust with equal n. With unequal n, not generally robust.
[§]The assumption is that the population covariance matrices must be identical at every level of A.
[‖]The assumption is that scores at this level of B must be equally variable for all levels of A.
[#]The assumption is that scores must be equally variable for all levels of B.

and multivariate tests in Chapter 14. It is also important to note that comparisons involving different levels of a within-subjects factor are especially sensitive to violations of sphericity, as we discussed in Chapter 11. Adjusted tests do not solve this problem, but the multivariate approach does, which is why we defer consideration of confidence intervals for this design until Chapter 14.

Adjusted Univariate Tests

As in the other designs we have encountered, three adjusted univariate test procedures are available in split-plot designs: the Geisser–Greenhouse lower-bound correction, Box's $\hat{\varepsilon}$ adjustment (also called the Greenhouse–Geisser $\hat{\varepsilon}$ adjustment), and the Huynh–Feldt $\tilde{\varepsilon}$ adjustment. As before, each involves an adjustment of the numerator and denominator degrees of freedom of the critical value against which the observed value is judged. In all three procedures, the adjustment is applied only to the critical value, with no adjustment whatsoever of the observed value of the test statistic.

At the outset, it is important to realize that there is no need to consider adjusted tests for effects involving only A, because these tests do not require sphericity (see Table 12.20). Thus, only within-subjects effects might be adjusted by one of these three approaches.

Although there are two omnibus within-subjects effects in the split-plot design (e.g., the B main effect and the A × B interaction), notice that both of these effects use $MS_{B \times S/A}$ as the error term. As a consequence, the $\hat{\varepsilon}$ value for B equals the $\hat{\varepsilon}$ value for A × B; the same equality holds for $\tilde{\varepsilon}$. Indeed, we will see in Chapters 13 and 14 that $\hat{\varepsilon}$ and $\tilde{\varepsilon}$ can be regarded as indices of the extent to which the individual $MS_{B_{comp} \times S/A}$ components of $MS_{B \times S/A}$ are providing independent (i.e., uncorrelated) estimates of a common population parameter. The important point for our purposes is that because B and A $\times$ B are both based on $MS_{B \times S/A}$, we do not need a different adjustment factor for each within-subjects effect, as we did with two within-subjects factors. To emphasize the distinction, remember that when A and B are both within-subjects factors, there were three different error terms: $MS_{A \times S}$ for testing A, $MS_{B \times S}$ for testing B, and $MS_{A \times B \times S}$ for testing A $\times$ B. Because there are three error terms, there are three values of $\hat{\varepsilon}$ and three values of $\tilde{\varepsilon}$. In the split-plot design with one within-subjects factor, there is one error term (i.e., $MS_{B \times S/A}$), and hence one value of $\hat{\varepsilon}$ and one value of $\tilde{\varepsilon}$. In addition, this single value of $\hat{\varepsilon}$ and the single value of $\tilde{\varepsilon}$ are also appropriate for testing simple effects of B at fixed levels of A and for testing interaction contrasts, if $MS_{B \times S/A}$ is used as the error term. Of course, if $MS_{B \times S/A_j}$ is used as the error term for testing B at A_j, we calculate $\hat{\varepsilon}$ and $\tilde{\varepsilon}$ values using only the data from the jth level of A. Similarly, if $MS_{B_{comp} \times S/A}$ is used as the error term for testing an interaction contrast, no $\hat{\varepsilon}$ or $\tilde{\varepsilon}$ adjustment is necessary because sphericity is not required for the F test to be valid with this separate error term.

Calculating $\hat{\varepsilon}$ or $\tilde{\varepsilon}$ by hand is again tedious. Most major statistical packages (e.g., SAS and SPSS) calculate both $\hat{\varepsilon}$ and $\tilde{\varepsilon}$ for split-plot designs. For our numerical example, it turns out that $\hat{\varepsilon} = 0.94$ and $\tilde{\varepsilon} = 1.10$. Because $\tilde{\varepsilon}$ exceeds 1.00, it is shrunk back to 1.00. Because $\tilde{\varepsilon}$ in its shrunken form equals 1.00, using $\tilde{\varepsilon}$ here is literally equivalent to performing unadjusted tests. In addition, $\hat{\varepsilon}$ is so close to 1.00 that $\hat{\varepsilon}$-adjusted tests are for all practical purposes equivalent to unadjusted tests. However, as we have cautioned before, in many behavioral research studies, $\hat{\varepsilon}$ and $\tilde{\varepsilon}$ would be much lower than they are here, in which case their use may have a dramatic impact on the statistical significance of one's findings.

MORE COMPLEX DESIGNS

Designs with Additional Factors

In the real world of research, of course, designs are not necessarily restricted to two factors. Although the analysis of more complex designs is necessarily more complicated than what we have discussed in this chapter, the same logic applies. Thus, if you understand the principles we developed in Chapters 7 and 8 for between-subjects factorial designs and in this chapter for within-subjects factorial designs, you should be able to analyze more complex designs without a great deal of added difficulty.

Besides our abstract assurances, it might be helpful to explicate a few general rules. We assume that all factors except S (subjects) are regarded as fixed-effects factors.[18] In this case, any effect that involves only between-subjects factors can be analyzed using MS_W as the error term. As usual, MS_W would be calculated by first averaging scores across the levels of all within-subjects factors to obtain a single score for each subject. As we saw in Table 12.16, MS_W for the complex design would then equal MS_W from the resulting one-way between-subjects design multiplied by the number of scores on which the average for each subject was obtained (b in Table 12.16). Notice that there will be $N - a$ denominator degrees of freedom for the F statistic, where N is the total number of subjects and a is the total number of groups (i.e., truly distinct groups of subjects). Knowing the degrees of freedom provides at least a partial check of one's results, especially if they are obtained from a computer program. Of course, as Table 12.20 shows, a homogeneity assumption is required in order for MS_W to produce a test statistic whose distribution is exactly an F random variable; however, the test is robust with equal n. As a second rule, tests involving only between-subjects effects at a fixed level of a within-subjects factor should generally use MS_W calculated just at the fixed level as an error term. Notice that this rule corresponds to using $MS_{S/A \text{ at } B_k}$ as the error term for testing A at B_k in a split-plot design with one between- and one within-subjects factor.

Naturally, tests involving a within-subjects factor require a different error term. As a third rule, tests of effects involving a within-subjects factor should use the mean square interaction of the effect itself by subjects within groups as the error term. Notice that this rule holds whether the effect to be tested also includes one or more between-subjects factors. Also notice that this rule is a straightforward generalization of Equation 5:

$$F = MS_{\text{effect}}/MS_{\text{effect} \times S} \qquad \text{(5, repeated)}$$

This third rule tells us that any effect involving a within-subjects factor can be tested as

$$F = MS_{\text{effect}}/MS_{\text{effect} \times S \text{ within groups}}$$

As a partial check of one's results, the denominator degrees of freedom here should equal $N - a$ times the numerator degrees of freedom (where N and a are as defined in the previous paragraph). Thus, significance tests in more complex designs really are straightforward generalizations of the tests we have developed. Readers who are interested in additional information should consult the excellent articles by Hertzog and Rovine (1985) and O'Brien and Kaiser (1985).

However, in more complex within-subjects designs—just as in the within-subjects designs we have discussed in detail—we must once again concern ourselves with the homogeneity of treatment-differences variances assumption. As in simpler designs, this assumption can equivalently be stated as a requirement that the covariance matrix for the effect to be tested must exhibit sphericity. When this assumption fails to hold, as it often will in many behavioral applications, the unadjusted mixed-model F test is not robust. As usual, there are two alternatives: ε-adjusted tests or a multivariate approach. The logic of the ε-adjusted tests is identical to what we have seen already in Chapter 11 and this chapter. Chapters 13 and 14 consider the multivariate approach, beginning with a simple one-way within-subjects design and then moving to more complex designs.

Latin Square Designs

The design considerations we discussed in Chapter 11 are also pertinent in factorial within-subjects designs. In particular, when the repeated factor represents a treatment manipulation, order effects must again be considered. The general issues to be considered remain the same as in Chapter 11, so we do not repeat the discussion here. Instead, we want to return to our previous discussion of the Latin square design, which you may recall provides a method for controlling order effects.

Although we discussed design principles for Latin squares at some length, we did not discuss analysis in Chapter 11. The reason we postponed analysis considerations until now is that Latin square designs involve two within-subjects factors, and thus the analysis builds on principles we have developed in this chapter. In general, the two within-subjects factors are treatment condition and time period (i.e., sequential position in the order of treatment administration).

We approach the analysis of data from Latin square designs through an example we began in Chapter 11. Specifically, suppose that we are interested in comparing the effects of three drugs (A, B, and C) on aggressiveness in monkeys. To control for possible order effects, we use a Latin square design. Specifically, we suppose that six subjects are available (as we discussed

TABLE 12.21
HYPOTHETICAL AGGRESSIVENESS SCORES FROM
REPLICATED LATIN SQUARE DESIGN

			Time	
	Subject	*1*	*2*	*3*
	1	9(B)	3(C)	6(A)
Square 1	2	18(A)	6(B)	12(C)
	3	12(C)	15(A)	5(B)
	4	14(C)	8(B)	11(A)
Square 2	5	17(A)	9(C)	9(B)
	6	7(B)	7(A)	7(C)

in Chapter 11, a subject is actually a pair of monkeys in this design). Following the design principles outlined at the end of Chapter 11, we use a replicated Latin square design with two randomly constituted squares. Subjects are then randomly assigned to rows of the squares.

Table 12.21 presents hypothetical outcome data from this study. The dependent measure can be thought of as the number of aggressive behaviors engaged in during a fixed time period. Notice that each score is a function of three possible influences: subject, time period, and treatment condition (which here is drug, with three levels, either A, B, or C). Following this logic, a full model for the data can be written as

$$Y_{ijk} = \mu + \alpha_j + \beta_k + \pi_i + \varepsilon_{ijk} \tag{35}$$

where Y_{ijk} is the score on the dependent variable for the ith subject at the jth level of A (treatment) and kth level of B (time), μ is the grand mean parameter, α_j is the effect associated with the jth level of A (treatment), β_k is the effect associated with the kth level of B (time), π_i is the effect associated with the ith subject or participant, and ε_{ijk} is the error term for the ith subject in the jth level of A and kth level of B. Notice that there are two within-subjects factors in the model, treatment condition and time, in addition to the subjects factor. However, the full model for the Latin square design is a main-effects model, that is, a model with no interactions. In general, interactions are not estimated with this design, because not all possible combinations of levels of the factors (or combinations of values of i, j, and k) are observed.

The null hypothesis to be tested is that the effects of all treatments are equal to each other. Symbolically, the null hypothesis can be written as

$$H_0 : \alpha_1 = \alpha_2 = \cdots = \alpha_a$$

As usual, a side restriction is imposed that the α_j parameters must sum to zero, that is, $\sum_{j=1}^{a} \alpha_j = 0$. However, this implies that when the null hypothesis is true, every α_j parameter equals zero. As a consequence, the null hypothesis leads to a restricted model of the form

$$Y_{ijk} = \mu + \beta_k + \pi_i + \varepsilon_{ijk} \tag{36}$$

As usual, the test of the treatment effect is obtained by using an F statistic to compare the full and restricted models:

$$F = \frac{(E_R - E_F)/(df_R - df_F)}{E_F/df_F}$$

As in previous designs, the sums of squared errors of the two models are given by

$$E_F = \sum_{k=1}^{a} \sum_{j=1}^{a} \sum_{i=1}^{n} [Y_{ijk} - \hat{Y}_{ijk}(F)]^2 \qquad (37)$$

$$E_R = \sum_{k=1}^{a} \sum_{j=1}^{a} \sum_{i=1}^{n} [Y_{ijk} - \hat{Y}_{ijk}(R)]^2 \qquad (38)$$

where for these models

$$\hat{Y}_{ijk}(F) = \hat{\mu} + \hat{\alpha}_j + \hat{\beta}_k + \hat{\pi}_i \qquad (39)$$

$$\hat{Y}_{ijk}(R) = \hat{\mu} + \hat{\beta}_k + \hat{\pi}_i \qquad (40)$$

Least squares parameter estimates in both models are obtained from the relevant marginal means (note that the grand mean is based on a total of only na scores):

$$\hat{\mu} = \sum_{k=1}^{a} \sum_{j=1}^{a} \sum_{i=1}^{n} Y_{ijk}/na$$

$$\hat{\alpha}_j = \overline{Y}_{.j.} - \overline{Y}_{...}$$

$$\hat{\beta}_k = \overline{Y}_{..k} - \overline{Y}_{...}$$

$$\hat{\pi}_i = \overline{Y}_{i..} - \overline{Y}_{...}$$

Let's now see how we can apply these formulas to our numerical example. Table 12.22 shows the marginal means and parameter estimates for the observed data. Notice that the treatment marginal means show that aggressiveness is highest for drug A and least for drug B.

TABLE 12.22
MARGINAL MEANS AND PARAMETER ESTIMATES
FOR TABLE 12.21 DATA

	Marginal Means	Parameter Estimate
Subject		
1	$\overline{Y}_{1..} = 6.00$	$\hat{\pi}_1 = -3.72$
2	$\overline{Y}_{2..} = 12.00$	$\hat{\pi}_2 = 2.28$
3	$\overline{Y}_{3..} = 10.67$	$\hat{\pi}_3 = 0.94$
4	$\overline{Y}_{4..} = 11.00$	$\hat{\pi}_4 = 1.28$
5	$\overline{Y}_{5..} = 11.67$	$\hat{\pi}_5 = 1.94$
6	$\overline{Y}_{6..} = 7.00$	$\hat{\pi}_6 = -2.72$
Condition		
1 (A)	$\overline{Y}_{.1.} = 12.33$	$\hat{\alpha}_1 = 2.61$
2 (B)	$\overline{Y}_{.2.} = 7.33$	$\hat{\alpha}_2 = -2.39$
3 (C)	$\overline{Y}_{.3.} = 9.50$	$\hat{\alpha}_3 = -0.22$
Time		
1	$\overline{Y}_{..1} = 12.83$	$\hat{\beta}_1 = 3.11$
2	$\overline{Y}_{..2} = 8.00$	$\hat{\beta}_2 = -1.72$
3	$\overline{Y}_{..3} = 8.33$	$\hat{\beta}_3 = -1.39$
Grand Mean	$\overline{Y}_{...} = 9.72$	$\hat{\mu} = 9.72$

TABLE 12.23
PREDICTED SCORES AND ERRORS FOR FULL AND RESTRICTED MODELS

Subject	Treatment	Time	Y_{ijk}	$\hat{Y}_{ijk}(F)$	$Y_{ijk} - \hat{Y}_{ijk}(F)$	$\hat{Y}_{ijk}(R)$	$Y_{ijk} - \hat{Y}_{ijk}(R)$
1	2	1	9	6.72	2.28	9.11	−0.11
1	3	2	3	4.06	−1.06	4.28	−1.28
1	1	3	6	7.22	−1.22	4.61	1.39
2	1	1	18	17.72	0.28	15.11	2.89
2	2	2	6	7.89	−1.89	10.28	−4.28
2	3	3	12	10.39	1.61	10.61	1.39
3	3	1	12	13.56	−1.56	13.78	−1.78
3	1	2	15	11.56	3.44	8.94	6.06
3	2	3	5	6.89	−1.89	9.28	−4.28
4	3	1	14	13.89	0.11	14.11	−0.11
4	2	2	8	6.89	1.11	9.28	−1.28
4	1	3	11	12.22	−1.22	9.61	1.39
5	1	1	17	17.39	−0.39	14.78	2.22
5	3	2	9	9.72	−0.72	9.44	−0.94
5	2	3	9	7.89	1.11	10.28	−1.28
6	2	1	7	7.72	−0.72	10.11	−3.11
6	1	2	7	7.89	−0.89	5.28	1.72
6	3	3	7	5.39	1.61	5.61	1.39

However, a significance test is needed to assess the generalizability of this pattern beyond the sample. Table 12.23 presents the predicted scores for the full model (from Equation 39) and for the restricted model (from Equation 40) for each observed score on the dependent variable. The sum of squared errors for the full model for these data is given by

$$E_F = \sum_{k=1}^{a} \sum_{j=1}^{a} \sum_{i=1}^{n} [Y_{ijk} - \hat{Y}_{ijk}(F)]^2 = 40.44$$

Similarly, the sum of squared errors for the restricted model equals[19]

$$E_R = \sum_{k=1}^{a} \sum_{j=1}^{a} \sum_{i=1}^{n} [Y_{ijk} - \hat{Y}_{ijk}(R)]^2 = 115.88$$

Thus, the sum of squares attributable to the treatment effect, $E_R - E_F$, equals 75.44. Alternatively, $E_R - E_F$ can be found directly from the formula

$$E_R - E_F = SS_{\text{effect}} = n \sum_{j=1}^{a} (\overline{Y}_{.j.} - \overline{Y}_{...})^2$$

Notice that the n term appears in the formula because each marginal mean $\overline{Y}_{.j.}$ is based on n observations. For our data, this formula yields

$$SS_{\text{effect}} = n \sum_{j=1}^{a} (\overline{Y}_{.j.} - \overline{Y}_{...})^2$$

$$= 6[(12.33 - 9.72)^2 + (7.33 - 9.72)^2 + (9.50 - 9.72)^2]$$

$$= 75.44$$

This value is the same (within rounding error) as our previous value.

The final step in obtaining an observed F value is to calculate the degrees of freedom for the two models. In both cases, the degrees of freedom equal the number of observations (i.e., scores) minus the number of independent parameters. The number of observations here is na, because each of the n subjects is observed in each of the a conditions. The full model has one μ parameter, $a - 1$ independent α parameters, $a - 1$ independent β parameters, and $n - 1$ independent π parameters. Thus, the degrees of freedom for the full model equals

$$df_F = na - (1 + a - 1 + a - 1 + n - 1)$$
$$= na - 2a - n + 2$$
$$= (n - 2)(a - 1) \tag{41}$$

The restricted model has one μ parameter, $a - 1$ independent β parameters, and $n - 1$ independent π parameters. Thus, its degrees of freedom are given by

$$df_R = na - (1 + a - 1 + n - 1)$$
$$= na - 1 - n + 1$$
$$= (n - 1)(a - 1) \tag{42}$$

The difference in the degrees of freedom of the two models equals

$$df_R - df_F = (n - 1)(a - 1) - (n - 2)(a - 1) = a - 1 \tag{43}$$

which is just the number of independent parameters that were restricted to equal zero according to the null hypothesis.

The form of the F statistic for testing treatment effects in a replicated Latin square design can be obtained by substituting degrees of freedom from Equations 41 and 43 into the general expression for the F statistic:

$$F = \frac{(E_R - E_F)/(df_R - df_F)}{E_F/df_F} = \frac{(E_R - E_F)/(a - 1)}{E_F/(n - 2)(a - 1)}$$

For our numerical example, we know that $E_R - E_F = 75.44$ and $E_F = 40.44$. Substituting these values yields

$$F = \frac{75.44/(3 - 1)}{40.44/(6 - 2)(3 - 1)} = 7.46$$

With 2 numerator and 8 denominator degrees of freedom, the corresponding p value is .01. Thus, we can reject the null hypothesis that the three drugs have equal effects on aggressiveness.

We end our discussion of the Latin square design by reiterating a point we made in Chapter 11, namely that the analysis should match the design. Many researchers who use Latin square designs fail to analyze their data accordingly, and instead use the analysis procedures of Chapter 11. However, the resultant analysis is almost inevitably conservative and consequently not as powerful as it might be (see Exercise 20 for an illustration of this point). Thus, replicated Latin square designs should be analyzed using the procedures we developed in this chapter, which explicitly take into account the nature of the design itself.

EXERCISES

1. True or False: The denominator of the F statistic for testing a within-subjects effect can be conceptualized as an index of the extent to which the effect is inconsistent from subject to subject.

2. True or False: The primary difference between data analysis in factorial between-subjects designs and factorial within-subjects designs is that the meaning of a significant interaction is different.

3. True or False: The between-subjects main effect F test in the split-plot design is identical to the F test that would occur if each subject's mean score were used as the dependent variable in a purely between-subjects design.

4. True or False: The necessary statistical assumptions for testing between-subjects effects in a split-plot design are identical to those required for testing within-subjects effects in the design.

5. True or False: Using a separate error term for testing contrasts involving a within-subjects effect is more consistent with the mixed-model approach than with the multivariate approach to repeated measures.

*6. Consider a design that uses two factors (in addition to subjects), factor A with three levels and factor B with four levels, both of which are manipulated within subjects. Eleven subjects participate in the study and serve in all conditions. You decide to take the univariate approach to analyzing this design. Specify the effects to be tested in this design, the associated error terms, and degrees of freedom for each. You are aware that in the univariate approach to repeated measures you need to perform adjusted tests of certain effects in order to account for possible violation of the assumption of sphericity. Thus, also indicate for each tested effect the lower bound of ε for that effect. Express your results in the form of a table with the following headings:

Testable Effects		Error Term		
Source	df	Source	df	Lower Bound of ε

7. What does it mean to say that the A main effect in a two-way A × B within-subjects design averages over levels of B? To address this question, consider the data shown in Table 12.1 for a 3 × 2 design, in which angle has three levels and noise has two levels. In what sense does the angle main effect average over levels of noise? Table 12.7 presents the mean reaction time for each subject for each level of the angle factor, averaging over the two levels of noise.
   a. Is there a statistically significant angle main effect for the data shown in Table 12.7?
   b. How does the F value you obtained in part a compare to the F value for the angle main effect in the 3 × 2 design (see Table 12.5)?
   c. Based on your answer to part b, what does it mean to say that the A main effect in a two-way A × B within-subjects design averages over levels of B?

*8. A psychologist used a microcomputer statistical package to analyze data from a two-way 3 × 4 within-subjects design with 15 subjects (we call the factor with three levels A and the factor with four levels B). For each of the following effects, what should the value of the denominator degrees of freedom be, if the computer program has used a separate error term for testing contrasts?
   a. a comparison of the marginal means of A
   b. a comparison of the marginal means of B
   c. an interaction contrast
   d. a comparison of the first two levels of A within the third level of B.

9. Kosslyn describes a program of research investigating processes involved in the formation of a visual image [Kosslyn, S. M. (1988). "Aspects of a cognitive neuroscience of mental imagery." *Science*, 240, 1621–1626]. In one condition of one study, subjects were shown an uppercase letter superimposed on a grid. They were then shown a blank grid and a lowercase letter. Their task was to decide whether the corresponding uppercase letter would occupy one or two specific cells of the grid. In a second condition of this study, the task was the same, but the internal lines of the grid were eliminated and only the brackets at the four corners were presented. Perceptual theory suggests that

when grid lines are present, subjects use a categorical representation of how line segments in letters are connected. However, when only brackets are present, subjects use a coordinate representation to arrange the parts of the stimulus letter. In both conditions, the stimulus was presented to the right visual field half of the time (and hence seen first in the left cerebral hemisphere) and to the left visual field on remaining trials (and hence seen first in the right cerebral hemisphere). The primary dependent variable of interest was response time (in milliseconds) averaged over a number of trials. The following hypothetical data assume that each of 10 subjects has been assessed in both the grids condition and the brackets condition:

	Grids Condition		Brackets Condition	
Subject	Left Hemisphere	Right Hemisphere	Left Hemisphere	Right Hemisphere
1	1600	1670	1690	1690
2	1420	1590	1580	1590
3	1670	1730	1790	1800
4	1430	1560	1550	1460
5	1550	1510	1570	1590
6	1520	1600	1680	1600
7	1610	1730	1780	1670
8	1600	1710	1670	1710
9	1680	1720	1800	1710
10	1570	1500	1610	1520

a. Perform a test of the condition main effect, the hemisphere main effect, and the condition × hemisphere interaction.

b. Calculate omega squared values for each of the effects you tested in part a. How do these values inform your interpretation of the results from part a?

c. Based on your answers to part a, would it be appropriate to perform simple-effects tests here? If so, test effects of condition within hemisphere and hemisphere within condition.

d. Form a 95% confidence interval for the condition effect within the left hemisphere. Form a comparable interval within the right hemisphere.

e. Do your results support Kosslyn's contention that two different classes of processes are used to form mental images? In particular, do your results support the statement that some of the processes used to arrange parts of images are more efficient in the left hemisphere, whereas for other processes, the right hemisphere is more efficient?

f. Is the sphericity assumption required for your analyses here? Why or why not?

g. Should you consider using either the $\hat{\varepsilon}$ adjustment for the $\tilde{\varepsilon}$ adjustment here? Why or why not?

10. Suppose that a perceptual psychologist wants to compare younger and older adults on the perceptual tasks described in Chapter 12. As described in the chapter, angle is a within-subjects factor. Suppose that the experimenter obtains reaction times for all subjects first in the 0° angle condition, second in the 4° angle condition, and finally in the 8° angle condition. Further suppose that the resultant cell means have the same pattern as those shown in Table 12.18. Could the psychologist unambiguously assert on the basis of such results that age differences are larger for larger angles? If not, what alternate hypothesis might you propose to explain this pattern of results?

11. A psychologist has collected data for 15 females and 15 males on an eight-item Fear of Statistics Scale (FSS) in order to investigate whether a gender difference exists. Her data analysis consists of a t test for the two groups, using the sum over the eight items as the dependent variable for each subject. However, a colleague argues that her analysis method throws away data and hence loses power. The colleague suggests that she use a split-plot design, with gender as a between-subjects factor and item as a within-subjects factor. (Hint: Items here can be thought of as levels of a fixed factor.).

a. Will the colleague's approach result in higher statistical power for assessing a gender difference on the FSS than the t test?

b. Explain (briefly) the reason for your answer in part a.

*12. Assume that you are a reader on a master's thesis committee. A student has carried out a study of the effects of mood on recall for different kinds of material. Each subject from a total sample of 40 was randomly assigned to either a depressed mood-induction condition or a neutral-mood condition. Following the mood induction, each subject was given a list of verbal tasks to solve, some of which were easy and some of which were difficult. The hypothesis motivating the study was that on a test of incidental recall of the verbal tasks, the decrement in performance exhibited by the depressed subjects would be greater on the difficult items than on the easy items. The following source table was included in the thesis:

Source	SS	df	MS	F
Mood	360	1	360	7.2
Difficulty	160	1	160	3.2
Mood × difficulty	160	1	160	3.2
Within	3800	76	50	

a. What is wrong with this analysis?
b. If the analysis were to be done correctly, what sources, error terms, and degrees of freedom would be used?
c. Can you determine the sum of squares for any of the effects in the correct analysis?

*13. What is the meaning of the main effect of the between-subjects factor in a split-plot design? To address this question, consider the data shown in Tables 12.7 and 12.15. Table 12.19 shows that the F value for the main effect of the between-subjects factor (age) for these data is 7.28.
a. For each subject in Tables 12.7 and 12.15, calculate a mean reaction time score by averaging over the three levels of angle.
b. Perform a one-way ANOVA on the mean scores you calculated in part a.
c. How does the F value you obtained in part b compare to the F value for the age main effect in the split-plot design?
d. Is your answer to part c consistent with the fact that according to Table 12.20, the test of the between-subjects main effect in a split-plot design does not require the sphericity assumption? Why or why not?

*14. According to Exercise 13, the main effect of the between-subjects factor in a split-plot design can be tested by simply collapsing over levels of the within-subjects factor and then performing a one-way between-subjects ANOVA. Does an analogous result apply for the main effect of the within-subjects factor? In particular, can the main effect of the within-subjects factor be tested by simply ignoring the between-subjects factor and then performing a one-way within-subjects ANOVA? To address this question, we once again consider the data shown in Tables 12.7 and 12.15.
a. Suppose that you were to ignore the between-subjects factor of age. Then, these data could be regarded as coming from a one-way within-subjects design. Perform a one-way ANOVA on the data for these 20 subjects.
b. How does the F value you obtained in part a compare to the F value reported in Table 12.19 for the within-subjects main effect (designated as B in the table)?
c. To explore why the two F values you compared in part b are not identical, we consider the numerator and the denominator of the F statistic separately. How does the sum of squares for the within-subjects main effect you calculated in part a compare to the value reported in Table 12.19?
d. How does the error sum of squares you calculated in part a compare to the value reported in Table 12.19? Is the difference between these two values equal to any sum of squares shown in Table 12.19?
e. Are the denominator degrees of freedom for the test you performed in part a the same as the denominator degrees of freedom for B × S/A, as shown in Table 12.19? Is the difference between these values equal to the degrees of freedom for any of the other sources shown in Table 12.19?

f. Can the F value for the within-subjects main effect in a split-plot design be obtained by simply ignoring the between-subjects factor and then performing a one-way within-subjects ANOVA? If not, briefly explain why this approach fails to produce the same F value.

*15. For each of the following follow-up tests in a split-plot design, state whether the test requires an assumption of sphericity, if the designated error term is chosen as described below:

a. Test of B_{comp}, using $MS_{B \times S/A}$ as the error term

b. Test of B_{comp}, using $MS_{B_{comp} \times S/A}$ as the error term

c. Test of B at A_j, using $MS_{B \times S/A_j}$ as the error term

d. Test of $A_{comp} \times B_{comp}$, using $MS_{B_{comp} \times S/A}$ as the error term

e. Test of $A_{comp} \times B_{comp}$, using $MS_{B \times S/A}$ as the error term

f. Test of A_{comp}, using $MS_{S/A}$ as the error term

16. For each of the following follow-up tests in a split-plot design, state whether the designated error term is more consistent with the mixed-model or the multivariate approach to repeated measures:

a. Test of B_{comp}, using $MS_{B \times S/A}$ as the error term

b. Test of B_{comp}, using $MS_{B_{comp} \times S/A}$ as the error term

c. Test of B at A_j, using $MS_{B \times S/A_j}$ as the error term

d. Test of $A_{comp} \times B_{comp}$, using $MS_{B_{comp} \times S/A}$ as the error term

e. Test of $A_{comp} \times B_{comp}$, using $MS_{B \times S/A}$ as the error term

17. Exercise 17 in Chapter 11 introduced hypothetical data obtained by a developmental psychologist interested in the role of the sound of a mother's heartbeat in the growth of newborn babies. This exercise uses the same data, but now we assume that half of the infants were assigned to a control group. Specifically, seven babies were randomly assigned to a condition in which they were exposed to a rhythmic heartbeat sound piped in over the PA system. The other seven babies were placed in an identical nursery, but without the heartbeat sound. Infants were weighed at the same time of day for four consecutive days, yielding the following data (weight is measured in ounces):

	Heartbeat Group			
Subject	Day 1	Day 2	Day 3	Day 4
1	96	98	103	104
2	116	116	118	119
3	102	102	101	101
4	112	115	116	118
5	108	110	112	115
6	92	95	96	98
7	120	121	121	123
	Control Group			
1	112	111	111	109
2	95	96	98	99
3	114	112	110	109
4	99	100	99	98
5	124	125	127	126
6	100	98	95	94
7	106	107	106	107

a. Test the group main effect, the day main effect, and the group $\times$ day interaction.

b. Calculate the value of omega squared for each of these effects.

c. Write one or two sentences interpreting the meaning of the results you obtained in parts a and b.

d. (To be done by computer.) Repeat part a using the $\hat{\varepsilon}$ adjustment. To which effects is this adjustment applied?

e. (To be done by computer.) Repeat part a using the $\tilde{\varepsilon}$ adjustment. To which effects is this adjustment applied?

f. Explain why this two-group design is superior to the design described for these data in Chapter 11, where we assumed that all 14 infants were exposed to the heartbeat sound.

g. Although the two-group design is a great improvement over the one-group design described earlier for these data, might there still be some plausible threats to the validity of a conclusion that exposure to heartbeat sounds affects infants' growth?

18. DeCasper and Fifer conducted a study to investigate the extent to which newborn infants are able to discriminate their mother's voice from the voice of another woman, a process which could influence the formation of the mother–infant bond [DeCasper, A. J., & Fifer, W. P. (1980). "Of human bonding: Newborns prefer their mothers' voices." *Science, 208*, 1174–1176]. The subjects were 10 newborns younger than 3 days of age. Baseline measures of each infant's sucking activity on a nonnutritive nipple were obtained for 5 min. Of particular interest was the *median interburst interval* (IBI), defined as the elapsed time between the end of one burst of sucking and the beginning of the next. A *burst* was defined as a series of individual sucks separated from one another by no more than 2 s. After baseline measures had been obtained, five infants were randomly assigned to a condition in which IBIs greater than or equal to their individual baseline median would produce a tape recording of their own mother's voice. Bursts terminating intervals less than their baseline median produced a recording of the voice of one of the other nine mothers. The other five infants were assigned to a reversed condition. For them, bursts shorter than their median produced the mother's voice, and bursts longer than the median produced the nonmaternal voice. Two measures were obtained for each infant: median IBI during baseline and median IBI over a 20-min period with differential vocal feedback. The following data (IBIs in seconds) approximate the actual data obtained in the study.

Group 1 (Larger IBI Produced Maternal Voice)

Subject	Baseline IBI	Feedback IBI
1	4.4	6.4
2	1.0	1.9
3	3.4	5.2
4	3.3	3.3
5	4.5	4.0

Group 2 (Smaller IBI Produced Maternal Voice)

Subject	Baseline IBI	Feedback IBI
1	5.8	1.8
2	4.3	1.9
3	3.7	2.5
4	3.4	1.7
5	3.8	3.0

a. Perform tests of the group main effect, the baseline versus feedback main effect, and the group × baseline versus feedback interaction.

b. Which of the three effects in part a is of the greatest theoretical importance? How would you interpret the results you obtained in part a for this effect?

c. Is the sphericity assumption necessary for any of the effects you tested in part a? Why or why not?

d. Might the pattern of results obtained here reflect the fact that shorter (or longer) IBIs were easier to produce after baseline, instead of infants' expressing a preference for their own mother's voice?

19. Jemmott, J. B., Borysenko, J. Z., Borysenko, M., McClelland, D. C., Chapman, R., Meyer, D., and Benson, H. (1983) report a study investigating the effect of academic stress on immune function ("Academic stress, power motivation, and decrease in secretion rate of salivary secretory

immunoglobulin A." *The Lancet, 1*, 1400–1402). Immune function was measured five times during the academic year: an initial low-stress period, three high-stress periods coinciding with major exams, and a final low-stress period. Forty-seven first-year dental students served as subjects. Each subject was identified as belonging to one of three personality types on the basis of responses to the Thematic Apperception Test, which was administered prior to the assessment of immune function. The three groups were an inhibited power syndrome (IPS) group, a relaxed affiliative syndrome (RAS) group, and a residual or control (C) group, which consisted of subjects who failed to fit the criteria for either of the other two groups. The dependent measure was the rate of secretion of salivary secretory immunoglobulin A (s-IgA), obtained at each of the five time points. Higher values of s-IgA secretion rate (measured as mg s-IgA/min) reflect stronger functioning of the immune system. Consider the following hypothetical (but realistic) data:

			IPS Group		
Subject	*Sept.*	*Nov.*	*Apr.*	*June*	*July*
1	.21	.20	.21	.19	.16
2	.19	.20	.16	.14	.13
3	.25	.16	.16	.16	.13
4	.11	.09	.10	.10	.14
5	.19	.13	.15	.11	.11
6	.18	.16	.16	.17	.10
7	.21	.18	.15	.18	.08
8	.16	.12	.14	.11	.18
9	.20	.14	.11	.13	.11

			RAS Group		
Subject	*Sept.*	*Nov.*	*Apr.*	*June*	*July*
1	.28	.28	.25	.29	.29
2	.22	.18	.16	.21	.25
3	.30	.27	.26	.26	.29
4	.24	.23	.24	.23	.23
5	.26	.22	.23	.19	.17
6	.27	.22	.20	.22	.24
7	.32	.25	.24	.21	.23
8	.20	.19	.21	.27	.28
9	.21	.22	.20	.19	.20
10	.33	.28	.25	.28	.27
11	.23	.18	.19	.24	.28
12	.17	.12	.15	.14	.12
13	.20	.17	.14	.18	.19
14	.22	.23	.19	.24	.22
15	.24	.22	.22	.22	.21

			C Group		
Subject	*Sept.*	*Nov.*	*Apr.*	*June*	*July*
1	.14	.12	.09	.17	.19
2	.25	.18	.15	.16	.26
3	.22	.21	.14	.16	.19
4	.17	.12	.10	.12	.15
5	.17	.15	.12	.12	.14
6	.14	.12	.11	.12	.20

(Continued)

			C Group		
Subject	Sept.	Nov.	Apr.	June	July
7	.17	.12	.12	.09	.14
8	.20	.14	.16	.12	.15
9	.25	.24	.20	.13	.17
10	.15	.07	.05	.13	.15
11	.19	.12	.14	.15	.18
12	.23	.17	.20	.19	.27
13	.20	.19	.18	.16	.21
14	.20	.19	.19	.16	.24
15	.24	.16	.20	.20	.21
16	.15	.09	.12	.12	.20
17	.15	.16	.12	.09	.17
18	.18	.18	.17	.16	.21
19	.23	.22	.20	.15	.21
20	.22	.18	.14	.12	.18
21	.15	.15	.13	.17	.16
22	.22	.14	.16	.17	.24
23	.22	.14	.14	.16	.15

a. Test the statistical significance of the group main effect, the time main effect, and the group × time interaction. Use the unadjusted mixed-model approach.
b. Calculate the value of omega squared for each of the effects you tested in part a. How do these values add to your interpretation of the hypothesis tests you conducted in part a?
c. (To be done by computer.) Repeat part a using the $\hat{\varepsilon}$ adjustment.
d. (To be done by computer.) Repeat part a using the $\tilde{\varepsilon}$ adjustment.
e. Test the group effect at each individual time point.

*20. Both Chapters 11 and 12 state that researchers often fail to analyze their data as a Latin square design, even when they have expended great efforts to create such a design. To better understand issues involved in analyzing such data, reconsider the data shown in Table 12.21. What if these data were analyzed ignoring the time factor? How would the results compare to the results reported in the chapter?
a. Perform a one-way within-subjects ANOVA on the subject × drug data shown in Table 12.21. Ignore the presence of the time factor. (Hint: Be certain to reorder the columns of the table, so that the columns correspond to the three drugs, instead of the three time points.)
b. How does the F value you obtained in part a compare to the F value of 7.46 reported in the chapter?
c. How does the sum of squares for the drug effect you found in part a compare to the value of 75.44 reported in the chapter?
d. How does the denominator sum of squares you found in part a compare to the value of 40.44 reported in the chapter?
e. The sum of squares attributable to the time main effect for these data is 87.44. How is this relevant to the two values compared in part d?
f. How does the answer to part e help explain why it is often important to use a Latin square analysis to analyze data from Latin square designs?

21. A cognitive psychologist was interested in the effects of different difficulty manipulations on subjects' recall of brief text passages. Each of three different difficulty manipulations was believed to induce a different type of processing of the written material. The three difficulty manipulations of interest here were letter deletion, sentence scrambling, and a control condition [suggested by McDaniel, M. A., Einstein, G. O., Dunay, P. K., & Cobb, R. E. (1986) "Encoding difficulty and memory: Toward a unifying theory." *Journal of Memory and Language, 25*, 645–656]. Suppose that a within-subjects design is chosen and that three different passages are to be used as stimuli.

Each subject in the study reads all three passages. However, in one passage, letters have been deleted. In a second passage, sentences have been scrambled. The third passage serves as a control. The following design has been used for the 12 subjects in the study (LD indicates letter deletion, SS indicates sentence scrambling, and C indicates control).

Subject	Passage 1		Passage 2		Passage 3	
1	LD	(55)	SS	(38)	C	(54)
2	SS	(43)	C	(36)	LD	(39)
3	C	(49)	LD	(42)	SS	(39)
4	SS	(40)	C	(38)	LD	(42)
5	C	(61)	LD	(46)	SS	(45)
6	LD	(41)	SS	(26)	C	(40)
7	C	(53)	LD	(39)	SS	(43)
8	SS	(47)	C	(39)	LD	(41)
9	LD	(33)	SS	(36)	C	(36)
10	LD	(52)	SS	(36)	C	(51)
11	C	(53)	LD	(45)	SS	(42)
12	SS	(51)	C	(43)	LD	(47)

The numbers in parentheses represent recall scores for each subject in the designated condition.

a. What type of design has the cognitive psychologist used here?

b. Test whether the three difficulty manipulations have a differential effect on recall.

c. Suppose that the psychologist were to analyze these data without controlling for any differences between passages. Would a statistically significant difference among the difficulty manipulations be obtained?

d. Why are the F values in parts b and c different? Which approach provides a better test of the differences among the difficulty manipulations? Why?

13

One-Way Within-Subjects Designs: Multivariate Approach

Chapters 11 and 12 presented the mixed-model, or univariate, approach for analyzing data from within-subjects designs. Traditionally, this approach has been the most frequently used method for analyzing repeated measures data in psychology, but research during the 1970s and 1980s pointed out the limitations of this approach. In particular, evidence accumulated that the mixed-model approach is quite sensitive to violations of the sphericity assumption required by the covariance matrix. Although the ε adjustments discussed in Chapters 11 and 12 provide one potential solution to this problem, our belief is that this solution is usually less useful than yet another solution, namely the multivariate approach. We defer our justification for this statement until later in the chapter. Once we explain the logic of the multivariate approach, we are able to discuss why it is generally preferable to the ε adjusted mixed-model approach. For the moment, however, we simply state that the multivariate approach requires no assumption of sphericity, can be substantially more powerful than the mixed-model approach (although under some circumstances, it can be also be substantially less powerful), is straightforward to use with statistical packages, and leads naturally to appropriate tests of specific individual comparisons.

Our general outline in this chapter parallels the development of the mixed-model approach in Chapter 11. First, we briefly review analysis of repeated-measures designs with two levels. Second, we consider designs with three levels. Third, we consider designs with more than three levels. Although we see eventually that the basic formulas are the same in all three cases, the logic underlying these formulas is easiest to understand when the $a = 2$ and $a = 3$ cases are considered as special cases of the more general design.

A BRIEF REVIEW OF ANALYSIS FOR DESIGNS WITH TWO LEVELS

Recall that Chapter 11 began with a description of analysis procedures for repeated measures designs with two levels. Our intention here is to review these procedures briefly to form the foundation for the multivariate approach with more than two levels. If you find our presentation here too succinct, you may want to return to the beginning of Chapter 11 for additional details.

TABLE 13.1
DATA FOR TWO-LEVEL DESIGN

Subject	Time 1 (Y_1)	Time 2 (Y_2)	$D = Y_2 - Y_1$
1	2	3	1
2	4	7	3
3	6	8	2
4	8	9	1
5	10	13	3
Mean	6	8	2

You may be surprised that we recommend returning to the mixed-model approach of Chapter 11 for more detail because the multivariate approach of this chapter is a competitor of the mixed-model approach. The reason for our recommendation is that in the special case of designs with two levels, the mixed-model and multivariate approaches are exactly identical. Nevertheless, we believe that the transition to the multivariate approach with more than two levels is made easier by beginning our discussion in this chapter with a review of the two-level case. Once we consider the more general multivariate approach, we see why the two approaches are equivalent in this special case.

To motivate our discussion, consider the data in Table 13.1. As usual, in our hypothetical examples, the sample size has been kept small to facilitate your working through our calculations, to convince yourself that you understand the necessary computations.

The null hypothesis to be tested here is that the population means of Time 1 and Time 2 are equal to one another. Recall from Chapter 11 that in order to test this hypothesis we formed a difference score for each subject. The multivariate approach also requires that we form a difference score. The right-most column of Table 13.1 shows such a difference score, Time 2 score minus Time 1 score, for each subject. The full model for the difference score is given by

$$D_i = \mu + \varepsilon_i \tag{1}$$

where D_i is the difference score for the ith subject, μ represents the difference between the effects of Time 2 and Time 1, and ε represents error. The null hypothesis that the population means of Time 1 and Time 2 are equal is equivalent to the hypothesis that the difference scores have a population mean of zero. Thus, this hypothesis implies that μ in Equation 1 equals zero, which leads to a restricted model given by

$$D_i = 0 + \varepsilon_i \tag{2}$$

or just

$$D_i = \varepsilon_i \tag{3}$$

The error sum of squares for the full and restricted models are

$$E_F = \sum_{i=1}^{n}(D_i - \overline{D})^2 \tag{4}$$

$$E_R = \sum_{i=1}^{n} D_i^2 \tag{5}$$

Recall that the expression for the F-test statistic is in general given by

$$F = \frac{(E_R - E_F)/(df_R - df_F)}{E_F/df_F}$$

After substituting from Equations 4 and 5 and performing some simple algebra, the F statistic for comparing the full model of Equation 1 with the restricted model of Equation 3 equals

$$F = n\overline{D}^2/s_D^2 \tag{6}$$

For the data of Table 13.1, it can be shown that $\overline{D} = 2$ and $s_D^2 = 1$. Because $n = 5$, it follows that the observed value of the F statistic is 20. The observed F is compared to a critical F with 1 and $n - 1$ degrees of freedom. For $\alpha = .05$, the critical F with 1 and 4 degrees of freedom is 7.71 (see Appendix Table A.2). Thus, we can reject the null hypothesis that μ equals zero at the .05 level because the observed F exceeds the critical F. In terms of models, a model restricting the mean score to be equal to zero fits the data significantly less well than a model that allows the mean to be freely estimated. Thus, we can conclude that the population means of Time 1 and Time 2 are not equal to one another.

MULTIVARIATE ANALYSIS OF WITHIN-SUBJECTS DESIGNS WITH THREE LEVELS

Next we consider designs with three levels. Although we could at this point consider the general case of three or more levels, we momentarily postpone the "or more" part because the formulas to be developed are simpler in the three-level case. Once we develop this case, we see that the formulas for more than three levels are straightforward generalizations of the formulas for three levels.

Table 13.2 presents hypothetical data for a three-level design. The null hypothesis to be tested is that the population means of scores at all three time points are equal to each other. It is obvious from visual inspection of the data in Table 13.2 that scores tend to increase over time. However, we must conduct a formal test to ascertain whether this apparent difference is statistically significant.

Need for Multiple D Variables

The logic behind the multivariate approach for three levels is based on the formation of D variables (i.e., difference scores), as in the two-level case. However, a single difference

TABLE 13.2
DATA FOR THREE-LEVEL DESIGN

Subject	Time 1 (Y_1)	Time 2 (Y_2)	Time 3 (Y_3)
1	2	3	5
2	4	7	9
3	6	8	8
4	8	9	8
5	10	13	15
6	3	4	9
7	6	9	8
8	9	11	10
Mean	6	8	9

TABLE 13.3
DIFFERENCE SCORES FOR DATA OF TABLE 13.2

Subject	$D_1 = Y_2 - Y_1$	$D_2 = Y_3 - Y_2$
1	1	2
2	3	2
3	2	0
4	1	-1
5	3	2
6	1	5
7	3	-1
8	2	-1
Mean	2	1

score cannot be used to explain all the possible patterns of mean differences that could occur among the three levels, as was possible in the two-level case. In other words, with only two levels, the only difference that can even potentially occur is that the two levels are simply different. This difference is completely captured by a single difference score contrasting the two levels. However, with three or more levels, an infinite pattern of mean differences could potentially occur. Although it is possible to formulate planned comparisons, it is highly unlikely that any single planned comparison by itself explains completely the pattern of mean differences that occurs in the data.[1]

With three levels, we can completely explain any possible pattern of mean differences by forming two D variables, that is, two difference scores. As we saw in Chapter 4 for between-subjects designs, three levels implies 2 degrees of freedom, which corresponds to two independent comparisons. The particular difference scores we choose do not matter for testing the omnibus null hypothesis, as long as the two comparisons underlying the difference scores are linearly independent (see the discussion in Chapter 4 for more details on linear independence). We have more to say about the irrelevance of the specific difference scores later in the chapter.

Returning to the data of Table 13.2, we must form two difference scores to test the null hypothesis that all three time periods have the same population mean. Table 13.3 displays the scores for a particular pair of difference scores D_1 and D_2, where $D_1 = $ Time 2 $-$ Time 1, and $D_2 = $ Time 3 $-$ Time 2. The question now becomes how to test whether the population means of D_1 and D_2 both equal zero, because both equal zero if and only if all three time periods have equal means.

We now have a multivariate problem because we have two scores (D_1 and D_2) for each subject. Notice that in the two-level case, we were able to simplify our design to a univariate problem because there we could form a single D variable. However, in the three-level design, we have two D variables for each subject. In addition, it is quite possible that these two D variables correlate with one another, both in the sample and in the population. As we see later in the chapter, the multivariate approach is sensitive to such a possible correlation in a manner that a univariate approach is not.

Full and Restricted Models

The multivariate test that both D variables have population means of zero can be conceptualized in terms of model comparisons, very much like a univariate test. Specifically, we can write full and restricted models for both D_1 and D_2. The full model for D_1 is given by

$$D_{1i} = \mu_1 + \varepsilon_{1i} \tag{7}$$

where D_{1i} is the score of the ith subject on D_1, μ_1 is the population mean of D_1, and ε_{1i} reflects the error for the ith subject. Because, according to the null hypothesis, D_1 has a population mean of zero, the restricted model is obtained by restricting μ_1 of Equation 7 to equal zero, in which case the restricted model for D_1 is given by

$$D_{1i} = 0 + \varepsilon_{1i} \tag{8}$$

or simply

$$D_{1i} = \varepsilon_{1i} \tag{9}$$

By similar reasoning, the corresponding full and restricted models for D_2 are given by

$$D_{2i} = \mu_2 + \varepsilon_{2i} \tag{10}$$

$$D_{2i} = \varepsilon_{2i} \tag{11}$$

respectively. Least-squares estimates are readily obtained because each full model has only one parameter and each restricted model has none. In Equation 7, the least-squares estimate of μ_1 is $\overline{D}_1$, and in Equation 10, the least-squares estimate of μ_2 is $\overline{D}_2$. In each case, the error for a particular subject is that subject's score minus the predicted score, so in each full model an error for a subject is that subject's deviation from the mean on a D variable. Notice that the restricted models of Equations 9 and 11 predict every subject's score to be zero, so here an error for a subject is simply that subject's score on the D variable in question.

The notion of errors here can probably be conceptualized most easily by returning to the D variables of Table 13.3. Table 13.4 shows the corresponding errors for full and restricted models for both D_1 and D_2. The e_1 column shows errors for D_1, and the e_2 column shows errors for D_2. The e_1^2 and e_2^2 columns show squared errors, which not surprisingly play an important role here. The meaning of the $(e_1)(e_2)$ columns is explained in a moment.

Just as in the univariate case, the sum of squared errors is important for judging the adequacy of a model. This sum of squared errors can be calculated for each variable individually (i.e., D_1 or D_2) simply by summing the e^2 scores across subjects for the individual variable and the specific model. Thus, for D_1, Table 13.4 shows that $E_F = 6$ and $E_R = 38$. For D_2, the figures are $E_F = 32$ and $E_R = 40$. The general expressions for these sums of squared errors are the

TABLE 13.4
ERRORS FOR FULL AND RESTRICTED MODELS FOR D_1 AND D_2 VARIABLES
OF TABLE 13.3

Subject	Full Model					Restricted Model				
	e_1	e_2	e_1^2	e_2^2	$(e_1)(e_2)$	e_1	e_2	e_1^2	e_2^2	$(e_1)(e_2)$
1	−1	1	1	1	−1	1	2	1	4	2
2	1	1	1	1	1	3	2	9	4	6
3	0	−1	0	1	0	2	0	4	0	0
4	−1	−2	1	4	2	1	−1	1	1	−1
5	1	1	1	1	1	3	2	9	4	6
6	−1	4	1	16	−4	1	5	1	25	5
7	1	−2	1	4	−2	3	−1	9	1	−3
8	0	−2	0	4	0	2	−1	4	1	−2
Sum	0	0	6	32	−3	16	8	38	40	13

same as in the univariate case with only a single D variable. Specifically, for the full model we have

$$E_F(D_1) = \sum_{i=1}^{n}(D_{1i} - \overline{D}_1)^2 = \sum_{i=1}^{n} e_{1i}^2(F) \qquad (12)$$

for D_1, and

$$E_F(D_2) = \sum_{i=1}^{n}(D_{2i} - \overline{D}_2)^2 = \sum_{i=1}^{n} e_{2i}^2(F) \qquad (13)$$

for D_2. For the restricted model, the corresponding expressions are

$$E_R(D_1) = \sum_{i=1}^{n} D_{1i}^2 = \sum_{i=1}^{n} e_{1i}^2(R) \qquad (14)$$

$$E_R(D_2) = \sum_{i=1}^{n} D_{2i}^2 = \sum_{i=1}^{n} e_{2i}^2(R) \qquad (15)$$

The Relationship Between D_1 and D_2

Although the usual F statistic for comparing models could be used to test the null hypothesis for either D_1 or D_2 individually, our goal is to test a null hypothesis that both D_1 and D_2 have population means of zero. The multivariate test that accomplishes this goal not only considers the sum of squared errors for D_1 and D_2 individually, but also uses the relationship between D_1 and D_2. This relationship can be captured for a model by multiplying each subject's e_1 score times his or her e_2 score for that model. At this point, we must see how this multiplication process reflects the relationship between the variables, as well as find out how this term can be incorporated into a test statistic.

We first consider what meaning can be attached to the product of e_1 and e_2 for each subject. Specifically, we examine $\sum_{i=1}^{n} e_{1i}e_{2i}$ first for the full model and then for the restricted model. It turns out that $\sum_{i=1}^{n} e_{1i}(F)e_{2i}(F)$, which is called a *sum of cross-products* for the full model, is closely related to the correlation between D_1 and D_2. Recall that the formula for the correlation is of the form

$$r_{D_1 D_2} = \frac{\sum_{i=1}^{n}(D_{1i} - \overline{D}_1)(D_{2i} - \overline{D}_2)}{\sqrt{\sum_{i=1}^{n}(D_{1i} - \overline{D}_1)^2 \sum_{i=1}^{n}(D_{2i} - \overline{D}_2)^2}}$$

However, we can simplify this expression by realizing that

$$e_{1i}(F) = D_{1i} - \overline{D}_1 \qquad \text{and} \qquad e_{2i}(F) = D_{2i} - \overline{D}_2$$

Making these substitutions yields

$$r_{D_1 D_2} = \frac{\sum\limits_{i=1}^{n} e_{1i}(F) \, e_{2i}(F)}{\sqrt{\sum\limits_{i=1}^{n} e_{1i}^2(F) \sum\limits_{i=1}^{n} e_{2i}^2(F)}}$$

This expression can be further simplified by substituting from Equations 12 and 13:

$$r_{D_1 D_2} = \frac{\sum\limits_{i=1}^{n} e_{1i}(F) \, e_{2i}(F)}{\sqrt{E_F(D_1) E_F(D_2)}}$$

Rearranging terms, we have

$$\sum_{i=1}^{n} e_{1i}(F) \, e_{2i}(F) = r_{D_1 D_2} \sqrt{E_F(D_1) E_F(D_2)} \tag{16}$$

The point of all of this algebra is that the cross-product term $\sum_{i=1}^{n} e_{1i}(F) e_{2i}(F)$ is a function of the correlation between D_1 and D_2 and the sum of squared errors for D_1 and D_2 in the full model. Thus, as stated earlier, the cross-product term provides information about the strength of relationship of D_1 and D_2. Table 13.4 shows that the sum of cross-products for D_1 and D_2 in the full model for our data equals -3. This corresponds to a correlation coefficient of -0.217, so D_1 and D_2 are slightly negatively related in our data.

What is the meaning of the restricted model sum of cross-products, represented by $\sum_{i=1}^{n} e_{1i}(R) \, e_{2i}(R)$? Recall that an error in the restricted model is simply the score on the D variable itself. Thus, the restricted model sum of cross-products is simply $\sum_{i=1}^{n} D_{1i} D_{2i}$, the sum of the products of the two D variables. After some straightforward algebra, it can be shown that

$$\sum_{i=1}^{n} D_{1i} D_{2i} = \sum_{i=1}^{n} (D_{1i} - \overline{D}_1)(D_{2i} - \overline{D}_2) + n \overline{D}_1 \overline{D}_2$$

so that

$$\sum_{i=1}^{n} e_{1i}(R) \, e_{2i}(R) = \sum_{i=1}^{n} e_{1i}(F) \, e_{2i}(F) + n \overline{D}_1 \overline{D}_2$$

This equation shows that the restricted model sum of cross-products equals the full model sum of cross-products plus the product of sample size times $\overline{D}_1$ times $\overline{D}_2$. Thus, the restricted model sum of cross-products also reflects the degree of relationship between D_1 and D_2, but does so in a manner that also reflects the means of $\overline{D}_1$ and $\overline{D}_2$.

Matrix Formulation and Determinants

Now that we have an indication that the sum of cross-products reflects the degree of relationship between the variables, we must address the question of how this quantity can be incorporated into a test statistic. Notice that we have three indices for each model: two sum-of-squared-error terms (one for D_1 and one for D_2) and one sum-of-cross-products term. Multivariate analysis of variance (MANOVA) compares these three indices for the full model to the three indices for the restricted model through matrices. A matrix is simply a rectangular array of numbers. We construct one matrix for the full model and a second matrix for the restricted model.

To simplify our notation, we let $E_{11}(F)$ and $E_{22}(F)$ represent the sum of squared errors for the full model for D_1 and D_2, respectively. The sum of cross-products for the full model is written as $E_{12}(F)$. The same notation is used for the restricted model, except that the F in parentheses will be replaced by R.

Given this notation, the matrix for the full model is written as

$$\mathbf{E(F)} = \begin{bmatrix} E_{11}(F) & E_{12}(F) \\ E_{12}(F) & E_{22}(F) \end{bmatrix} \tag{17}$$

Similarly, the matrix for the restricted model is written as

$$\mathbf{E(R)} = \begin{bmatrix} E_{11}(R) & E_{12}(R) \\ E_{12}(R) & E_{22}(R) \end{bmatrix} \tag{18}$$

The task now is to somehow compare these two matrices. The concept of a *determinant* allows us to accomplish this task. The determinant of a matrix is an ordinary number, which distills the multivariate information in a matrix into a single piece of information. Determinants play an important role in multivariate statistics because the determinant can reflect the "generalized variance" of more than one variable. We view the determinant as a useful tool, without dwelling on its mathematical foundation. Readers who are interested in learning more about determinants should consult such references as Green and Carroll (1976) or Namboodiri (1984).

Notice that $\mathbf{E(F)}$ and $\mathbf{E(R)}$, the matrices of Equations 17 and 18, have two rows and two columns. Such a matrix is referred to as a 2×2 matrix. The determinant in this case is defined as the difference between the product of the two numbers on the major diagonal of the matrix minus the product of the two numbers off the diagonal. To indicate the determinant of a matrix, vertical lines are placed on either side of the letter representing the matrix.[2] Thus, for the determinant of $\mathbf{E(F)}$ we have

$$|\mathbf{E(F)}| = E_{11}(F)E_{22}(F) - [E_{12}(F)]^2$$

Similarly, the determinant of $\mathbf{E(R)}$ is given by

$$|\mathbf{E(R)}| = E_{11}(R)E_{22}(R) - [E_{12}(R)]^2$$

Before seeing how these determinants can be incorporated into a significance test, it might be helpful to provide some intuitive meaning for the determinant. Notice that the determinant of the matrix for the full model is

$$|\mathbf{E(F)}| = E_{11}(F)E_{22}(F) - [E_{12}(F)]^2$$

Substituting from Equation 16 for $E_{12}(F)$ yields

$$|\mathbf{E(F)}| = E_{11}(F)E_{22}(F) - r_{D_1 D_2}^2 E_{11}(F)E_{22}(F)$$

Collecting terms, we have

$$|\mathbf{E(F)}| = E_{11}(F)E_{22}(F)(1 - r_{D_1 D_2}^2) \tag{19}$$

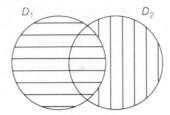

FIG. 13.1. Venn diagram representation of sums of squared Errors for D_1 and D_2.

For purposes of interpretation, we place brackets around the two right-most terms:

$$|\mathbf{E(F)}| = E_{11}(F)\left[E_{22}(F)\left(1 - r_{D_1 D_2}^2\right)\right]$$

The meaning of $E_{11}(F)$ should be clear. It equals the sum of squared errors in the full model for D_1, and hence reflects the extent to which the full model fails to completely explain scores on D_1. What about the term in brackets? It reflects the sum of squares in D_2 that neither the full model nor scores on D_1 can explain because $1 - r_{D_1 D_2}^2$ is the proportion of D_2 sum of squares left unexplained by D_1. Thus, the term in brackets reflects the sum of squares unique to D_2 (as opposed to shared with D_1) that the full model has not explained. In this manner, the determinant reflects simultaneously the extent to which the full model fails to explain scores on D_1 and D_2 together. A similar argument could be applied to the determinant for the restricted model.

That you understand what the determinant has accomplished here is important because we continue to use determinants throughout this and the next chapter. Thus, we detour momentarily to present another perspective on the determinant. The Venn diagram in Figure 13.1 provides a conceptual picture of the full model sum of squared errors for two variables, D_1 and D_2. Specifically, the circle on the left represents $E_{11}(F)$, the sum of squared errors for the full model on D_1. Similarly, the circle on the right represents $E_{22}(F)$, the sum of squared errors for the full model on D_2. The determinant $|\mathbf{E(F)}|$ provides an index of how large the two circles taken together are. The specific way in which the determinant reflects such an index is shown by the horizontal and vertical stripes in Figure 13.1. The horizontal stripes depict the area that corresponds to $E_{11}(F)$. From Equation 19, the determinant equals the product of $E_{11}(F)$ and a term of the form $[E_{22}(F)(1 - r_{D_1 D_2}^2)]$. The vertical stripes represent this second term because they depict the portion of D_2 that is uncorrelated with D_1. In other words, the vertical stripes represent that portion of $E_{22}(F)$ that is unique to D_2, in that the vertical stripes exclude the overlap between D_1 and D_2. However, the area of overlap has already been represented by $E_{11}(F)$. Notice that if we were simply to multiply $E_{11}(F)$ by $E_{22}(F)$, our index of error would count the area of overlap twice. However, the determinant avoids this problem by multiplying $E_{11}(F)$ by the portion of $E_{22}(F)$ that is unique to D_2, as represented by the vertical stripes in Figure 13. 1.

Test Statistic

The determinants of the full and restricted models form an F-test statistic in the following manner:

$$F = \frac{(|\mathbf{E(R)}| - |\mathbf{E(F)}|)/(df_R - df_F)}{|\mathbf{E(F)}| / df_F} \tag{20}$$

where df_R and df_F refer to the degrees of freedom for the restricted and full models, respectively. As usual, the degrees of freedom for a model equal the number of observations (sample size) minus the number of estimated parameters. When the within-subjects factor has three levels, there are two D variables, so there are two parameters estimated in the full model (μ_1 for D_1 and μ_2 for D_2). Thus, the degrees of freedom for the full model equals $n - 2$. There are no parameters to be estimated in the restricted model, so its degrees of freedom equals n. With a three-level factor, then, Equation 20 becomes

$$F = \frac{(|\mathbf{E}(\mathbf{R})| - |\mathbf{E}(\mathbf{F})|)/2}{|\mathbf{E}(\mathbf{F})|/(n-2)} \tag{21}$$

We now see how this formula can be applied to our data. From Table 13.4 and Equations 17 and 18, the error matrices for the full and restricted models are given by

$$\mathbf{E}(\mathbf{F}) = \begin{bmatrix} 6 & -3 \\ -3 & 32 \end{bmatrix}$$

$$\mathbf{E}(\mathbf{R}) = \begin{bmatrix} 38 & 13 \\ 13 & 40 \end{bmatrix}$$

The determinant of $\mathbf{E}(\mathbf{F})$ equals

$$|\mathbf{E}(\mathbf{F})| = 6(32) - (-3)^2 = 183$$

Similarly, the determinant of $\mathbf{E}(\mathbf{R})$ is

$$|\mathbf{E}(\mathbf{R})| = 38(40) - (13)^2 = 1351$$

Substituting these values into Equation 21 yields

$$F = \frac{(1351 - 183)/2}{183/(8-2)} = 19.148$$

The p value associated with the F ratio is .0032; we can conclude that the population means of the three time periods are significantly different from each other at the .05 level.

MULTIVARIATE ANALYSIS OF WITHIN-SUBJECTS DESIGNS WITH a LEVELS

So far we have seen how to analyze data from within-subjects designs when the design consists of a single factor with either two or three levels. We now see that the same logic can be used regardless of the number of levels—that is, for a factor with a levels, where a is any number greater than or equal to 2.

Forming D Variables

In the general case of a levels of the repeated factor, it is necessary to form $a - 1$ D variables. The null hypothesis that all a levels of the repeated factor have equal population means is equivalent to a null hypothesis that all $a - 1$ D variables have population means of zero. As in the case of two or three levels, this hypothesis can be tested by comparing full and restricted models. In general, there are $a - 1$ full models and $a - 1$ corresponding restricted models because there must be both a full and a restricted model for each of the $a - 1$ D variables. Sums of squared errors are found for these models using least squares according to formulas shown in Equations 12–15. Because there are $a - 1$ D variables, there are $a - 1$ sums of squared errors for full models and $a - 1$ corresponding sums of squared errors for restricted models.

Recall that when there are two D variables it is also necessary to compute a sum-of-cross-products term, once using the errors of the full model and then again using the errors of the restricted model. In the general case of $a - 1$ D variables, comparable sums of cross-products must be calculated for every pair of D variables. For example, if $a = 4$, there are three D variables. Then sums of cross-products must be calculated for variables D_1 and D_2, D_1 and D_3, and D_2 and D_3, both for the errors of the full model and the errors of the restricted model. In general, then, it can be shown that it is necessary to calculate $(a - 1)(a - 2)/2$ sums of cross-products both for the full model and the restricted model.[3]

The sums of squared errors and sums of cross-products are once again represented in matrix form. With $a - 1$ D variables, the matrix has $a - 1$ rows and $a - 1$ columns. To show the form of this matrix, let $E_{ii}(F)$ and $E_{ii}(R)$ be the error sum of squares for D_i for the full and restricted models, respectively. Similarly, let $E_{ij}(F)$ and $E_{ij}(R)$ be the sum of cross-products of D_i and D_j for the full and restricted models, respectively. Then the general form of the matrix for the full model is

$$
\begin{bmatrix}
E_{11}(F) & E_{12}(F) & E_{13}(F) & \cdots & E_{1(a-1)}(F) \\
E_{12}(F) & E_{22}(F) & E_{23}(F) & \cdots & E_{2(a-1)}(F) \\
E_{13}(F) & E_{23}(F) & E_{33}(F) & \cdots & E_{3(a-1)}(F) \\
\vdots & \vdots & \vdots & & \vdots \\
E_{1(a-1)}(F) & E_{2(a-1)}(F) & E_{3(a-1)}(F) & & E_{(a-1)(a-1)}(F)
\end{bmatrix}
$$

Similarly, for the restricted model, the matrix is given by

$$
\begin{bmatrix}
E_{11}(R) & E_{12}(R) & E_{13}(R) & \cdots & E_{1(a-1)}(R) \\
E_{12}(R) & E_{22}(R) & E_{23}(R) & \cdots & E_{2(a-1)}(R) \\
E_{13}(R) & E_{23}(R) & E_{33}(R) & \cdots & E_{3(a-1)}(R) \\
\vdots & \vdots & \vdots & & \vdots \\
E_{1(a-1)}(R) & E_{2(a-1)}(R) & E_{3(a-1)}(R) & & E_{(a-1)(a-1)}(R)
\end{bmatrix}
$$

Once again, the determinants of these two matrices are used to form an F statistic. We do not attempt to describe how to find the determinant of an $(a - 1)$ by $(a - 1)$ matrix because we assume that such computations are left to a computer program. What is important for our purposes is to realize that the conceptual meaning of the determinant in the $a - 1 \times a - 1$ case is the same as it was for a 2×2 matrix. Namely, the determinant once again reflects simultaneously the extent to which a model fails to explain scores on the set of D variables collectively. Readers interested in further details are referred to such books as Graybill (1969), Green and Carroll (1976), Namboodiri (1984), and Searle (1966).

Test Statistic

After the determinants of $\mathbf{E(F)}$ and $\mathbf{E(R)}$ have been calculated, the calculation of the F statistic is straightforward. Equation 20, which was presented for a three-level factor, also is appropriate when the factor has a levels:

$$F = \frac{(|\mathbf{E(R)}| - |\mathbf{E(F)}|)/(df_R - df_F)}{|\mathbf{E(F)}|\, df_F} \qquad \text{(20, repeated)}$$

This formula can be made more explicit by specifying df_R and df_F in the general case of a levels. As before, there are no parameters to be estimated in the restricted models, so $df_R = n$. Because there are $a - 1$ D variables, there are $a - 1$ parameters to be estimated in the full models (i.e., μ_1 for D_1, μ_2 for D_2, and so forth up to μ_{a-1} for D_{a-1}). Thus, $df_F = n - (a - 1) = n - a + 1$. The general form of the F statistic is given by

$$F = \frac{(|\mathbf{E(R)}| - |\mathbf{E(F)}|)/(a - 1)}{|\mathbf{E(F)}|\, /(n - a + 1)} \qquad (22)$$

This observed F value is compared to a critical F value with $a - 1$ and $n - a + 1$ degrees of freedom.

In case you may not have noticed, there is a remarkable similarity between Equation 20 and the equation for an F statistic in the univariate problems that we have discussed in Chapters 3–12. The form of the univariate F statistic we have seen repeatedly is given by

$$F = \frac{(E_R - E_F)/(df_R - df_F)}{E_F/df_F}$$

Equation 20 has exactly the same form, except that the univariate sum-of-squared-error terms are replaced by the corresponding determinant of the sum-of-squares and cross-products matrix

$$F = \frac{(|\mathbf{E(R)}| - |\mathbf{E(F)}|)/(df_R - df_F)}{|\mathbf{E(F)}|\, /df_F} \qquad \text{(20, repeated)}$$

This similarity should convince you of the flexibility and power of approaching hypothesis tests through model comparisons. The same underlying logic applies to the multivariate tests here as it does to univariate tests.

Numerical Example

At this point, a numerical example involving more than two D variables may help solidify your understanding of the multivariate approach to repeated measures. Table 13.5 presents the hypothetical McCarthy IQ scores for 12 subjects that originally appeared as Table 11.5 in Chapter 11. Because $a = 4$ here (i.e., there are four levels of the repeated factor), it is necessary to define three D variables. Table 13.6 presents scores for the 12 subjects on the following three D variables: $D_1 = Y_2 - Y_1$, $D_2 = Y_3 - Y_2$, and $D_3 = Y_4 - Y_3$, where Y_1, Y_2, Y_3, and Y_4 represent IQ scores at 30, 36, 42, and 48 months, respectively. Table 13.7 presents the errors for the full model for D_1, D_2, and D_3. Recall that a subject's error for the full model is the subject's deviation from the mean of the D variable. Table 13.7 also shows the squared-errors and cross-products scores for the full model. Table 13.8 presents the comparable data for the restricted model. Recall that a subject's error for the restricted model is simply the subject's

TABLE 13.5
HYPOTHETICAL McCARTHY DATA FOR 12 CHILDREN

Subject	Age (Months)			
	30	36	42	48
1	108	96	110	122
2	103	117	127	133
3	96	107	106	107
4	84	85	92	99
5	118	125	125	116
6	110	107	96	91
7	129	128	123	128
8	90	84	101	113
9	84	104	100	88
10	96	100	103	105
11	105	114	105	112
12	113	117	132	130

TABLE 13.6
DIFFERENCE SCORES FOR DATA OF TABLE 13.5

Subject	$D_1 = Y_2 - Y_1$	$D_2 = Y_3 - Y_2$	$D_3 = Y_4 - Y_3$
1	−12	14	12
2	14	10	6
3	11	−1	1
4	1	7	7
5	7	0	−9
6	−3	−11	−5
7	−1	−5	5
8	−6	17	12
9	20	−4	−12
10	4	3	2
11	9	−9	7
12	4	15	−2
Mean	4	3	2

score on the D variable. The sums of squared errors and cross-products must be placed in matrix form. From Table 13.7, the matrix for the full model is

$$\mathbf{E(F)} = \begin{bmatrix} 878 & -329 & -440 \\ -329 & 1004 & 399 \\ -440 & 399 & 658 \end{bmatrix}$$

From the Table 13.8, the matrix for the restricted model is

$$\mathbf{E(R)} = \begin{bmatrix} 1070 & -185 & -344 \\ -185 & 1112 & 471 \\ -344 & 471 & 706 \end{bmatrix}$$

It can be shown that the determinant for the matrix of the full model equals 290,177,920 (i.e., two hundred ninety million, one hundred seventy-seven thousand, nine hundred twenty),

TABLE 13.7
ERRORS FOR THE FULL MODEL FOR D_1, D_2, AND D_3 VARIABLES OF TABLE 13.6

Subject	e_1	e_2	e_3	e_1^2	e_2^2	e_3^2	$(e_1)(e_2)$	$(e_1)(e_3)$	$(e_2)(e_3)$
1	−16	11	10	256	121	100	−176	−160	110
2	10	7	4	100	49	16	70	40	28
3	7	−4	−1	49	16	1	−28	−7	4
4	−3	4	5	9	16	25	−12	−15	20
5	3	−3	−11	9	9	121	−9	−33	33
6	−7	−14	−7	49	196	49	98	49	98
7	−5	−8	3	25	64	9	40	−15	−24
8	−10	14	10	100	196	100	−140	100	140
9	16	−7	−14	256	49	196	−112	−224	98
10	0	0	0	0	0	0	0	0	0
11	5	−12	5	25	144	25	−60	25	−60
12	0	12	−4	0	144	16	0	0	−48
Sum	0	0	0	878	1004	658	−329	−440	399

TABLE 13.8
ERRORS FOR THE RESTRICTED MODEL FOR D_1, D_2, AND D_3 VARIABLES
OF TABLE 13.6

Subject	e_1	e_2	e_3	e_1^2	e_2^2	e_3^2	$(e_1)(e_2)$	$(e_1)(e_3)$	$(e_2)(e_3)$
1	−12	14	12	144	196	144	−168	−144	168
2	14	10	6	196	100	36	140	84	60
3	11	−1	1	121	1	1	−11	11	−1
4	1	7	7	1	49	49	7	7	49
5	7	0	−9	49	0	81	0	−63	0
6	−3	−11	−5	9	121	25	33	15	55
7	−1	−5	5	1	25	25	5	−5	−25
8	−6	17	12	36	289	144	−102	−72	204
9	20	−4	−12	400	16	144	−80	−240	48
10	4	3	2	16	9	4	12	8	6
11	9	−9	7	81	81	49	−81	63	−63
12	4	15	−2	16	225	4	60	−8	−30
Sum	48	36	24	1070	1112	706	−185	−344	471

whereas the determinant for the restricted model equals 506,853,568 (five hundred six million, eight hundred fifty-three thousand, five hundred sixty-eight).[4] To find the value of the F statistic, we must also realize that $df_F = 9$ and $df_R = 12$. Substituting these values into the formula for the F statistic, we arrive at

$$F = \frac{(506{,}853{,}568 - 290{,}177{,}920)/(12 - 9)}{290{,}177{,}920/9}$$

which reduces to an F value of 2.2401. With 3 numerator and 9 denominator degrees of freedom, the associated p value is 0.1525. Thus, the mean differences are nonsignificant at the .05 level. Recall from Chapter 11 that this is the same conclusion we reached from the $\hat{\varepsilon}$- and $\tilde{\varepsilon}$-adjusted mixed-model tests, but that the unadjusted mixed-model test produced a significant result at the .05 level. A general comparison of the various approaches is presented at the end of this chapter.

MEASURES OF EFFECT

Measures of effect are frequently of interest in within-subjects designs, just as they are in between-subjects designs. We begin our consideration of measures of effect in within-subjects designs by presenting procedures for calculating omega squared. Then we consider standard-ized effect sizes. After a section on determining sample size, we then consider the general topics of individual comparisons and of confidence intervals.

We have seen that there are two fundamentally different approaches for testing effects in within-subjects designs: the mixed-model approach of Chapter 11 and the multivariate approach of this chapter. Each of these approaches also provides a basis for computing omega squared as measure of association strength. Surprisingly, although we generally recommend the multivariate approach of this chapter for testing effects, we nevertheless recommend that omega squared be calculated based on the mixed-model of Chapter 11.

We (1) briefly summarize the same version of omega squared we originally presented in Chapter 11, (2) present a version of omega squared based on the multivariate approach, and (3) explain why we generally prefer the mixed-model version of omega squared to the multivariate version.

Olejnik and Algina (2000) use previous work by Dodd and Schultz (1973) to provide the following formula for calculating omega squared in one-way within-subjects designs:

$$\hat{\omega}^2 = \frac{(a-1)(MS_A - MS_{A \times S})}{SS_{Total} + MS_S} \qquad \text{(11.35, repeated)}$$

Pages 547–550 of Chapter 11 provide a full description of the components of omega squared. Here we simply state that we can find each of these components from the mixed-model ap-proach. We saw in Chapter 11 that the value of omega squared for the McCarthy data of Table 13.5 is 0.04. Thus, our best guess is that age accounts for approximately 4% of the total population variance in McCarthy scores in children between the ages of 30 and 48.

Olejnik and Algina (2000) also provide a formula for omega squared in within-subjects designs based on the multivariate approach:

$$\omega^2_{multi} = 1 - \frac{n\Lambda}{df_{error} + \Lambda} \qquad (23)$$

where Λ is known as *Wilks's lambda* after Samuel Wilks, who developed its use in multivariate statistics. We say more about Wilks's lambda in Chapter 14, but for now it suffices to say that lambda is the ratio of the determinant of the full model to the determinant of the restricted model:

$$\Lambda = \frac{|\mathbf{E(F)}|}{|\mathbf{E(R)}|} \qquad (24)$$

Most standard statistical packages such as SAS and SPSS provide the value of Wilks's lambda directly, so it is not necessary to know the values of the determinants themselves, although most packages also provide these as well. We can complete our calculation of omega squared by realizing that df_{error} is the same as df_F, which in general is given by $n - a + 1$ in the single-factor within-subjects design.

For example, we can compute the multivariate version of omega squared for the McCarthy data by realizing that $n = 12$, $df_{error} = 9$, and Λ can be found to equal 0.5725 either directly from a statistical package or by taking the ratio of 290,177,920 to 506,853,568 (recall that we found these values for the determinants of the full and restricted models when we calculated an F value for testing the omnibus null hypothesis). Substituting these values into Equations 23 and 24 reveals that the value of the multivariate version of omega squared for the McCarthy data is 0.28. Thus, our best guess from a multivariate perspective is that age accounts for approximately 28% of the total population variance in McCarthy scores in children between the ages of 30 and 48.

Notice that our value of the multivariate omega squared is approximately seven times larger than our value of the mixed-model omega squared for the same data. At first glance, this might seem to be another advantage of the multivariate approach, because after all we would certainly like to account for as much variance as possible. In reality, however, the appreciably larger value for the multivariate omega squared reflects not an advantage, but instead a different way of conceptualizing total variance. In particular, variance attributable to systematic individual differences between people is excluded from total variance in the multivariate conceptualization.

As a consequence, the multivariate omega squared does not have the same interpretation as the mixed-model omega squared, and the fact that the multivariate omega squared is almost always much larger than the mixed-model omega squared does not suggest that we should prefer multivariate omega squared. We would not go so far as to say that the multivariate omega squared is wrong, but instead that it provides a correct answer to a question that usually is not the question we really want answered. We believe that variability due to subjects should ordinarily be included in our conceptualization of total variance, in which case the mixed-model version of omega squared is to be preferred.

An alternative to omega squared or other measures of association strength is provided by measures of effect size. Recall that in between-subjects designs we can calculate a standardized mean difference d as a description of effect size. We can also calculate d in within-subjects designs. The only complication here is that we must decide on an appropriate standard deviation to serve as a basis for a standard scale. As we discussed in Chapter 11, we generally recommend conceptualizing d in within-subjects designs so as to achieve comparability with d in between-subjects designs. As we described in some detail in Chapter 11, we can accomplish this goal by defining a standard deviation as

$$sd = \sqrt{\frac{SS_S + SS_{A \times S}}{a(n-1)}} \qquad \text{(11.38, repeated)}$$

We can then define and calculate a standardized mean difference by taking any mean difference (pairwise or complex as long as the sum of absolute values of coefficients is two) and dividing it by sd as shown in Equation 11.38. You may want to look back at Chapter 11 for an illustration in the McCarthy data.

CHOOSING AN APPROPRIATE SAMPLE SIZE

Calculating statistical power and choosing an appropriate sample size is more complicated in within-subjects designs than in between-subjects designs. The additional complication is that effect size in repeated-measures designs depends not only on population means and population variances, but also on population covariances. Although the mathematics necessary to calculate power is relatively straightforward, in practice it is difficult to specify accurate values of all parameters that influence power. Instead of attempting to provide a thorough theoretical presentation of power in within-subjects designs, we present some general guidelines for choosing an appropriate sample size to guarantee sufficient power when using the multivariate approach to analyze repeated-measures data.

Tables 13.9–13.11 present sample sizes to achieve a power of .50, .80, and .95, respectively, for $\alpha = .05$. As the tables show, the necessary sample size depends on the number of levels of the repeated factor, minimum degree of correlation between scores at these levels, and

TABLE 13.9
MINIMUM SAMPLE SIZE NEEDED TO ACHIEVE POWER OF .50 WITH $\alpha = .05$

Number of Levels	Minimum Correlation	Design*	0.25	0.50	0.75	1.00	1.25	1.50
2	—	CRD	124	32	15	9	7	5
	0	RMD	125	33	16	10	7	6
	.1		113	30	15	9	7	6
	.2		101	27	13	9	7	5
	.3		88	24	12	8	6	5
	.4		76	21	11	7	6	5
	.5		64	18	9	6	5	4
	.6		52	15	8	6	5	4
	.7		39	12	7	5	4	4
	.8		27	9	5	4	4	3
	.9		15	6	4	3	3	3
3	—	CRD	160	41	19	11	8	6
	0	RMD	162	43	21	14	10	8
	.1		146	39	19	13	9	8
	.2		130	35	18	12	9	7
	.3		115	31	16	11	8	7
	.4		99	27	14	10	8	6
	.5		83	23	12	9	7	6
	.6		67	19	11	8	6	6
	.7		51	16	9	7	6	5
	.8		35	12	7	6	5	5
	.9		19	8	6	5	4	4
4	—	CRD	186	48	22	13	9	7
	0	RMD	189	51	25	16	12	10
	.1		170	46	23	15	11	9
	.2		152	41	21	14	11	9
	.3		133	37	19	13	10	8
	.4		115	32	17	12	9	8
	.5		97	28	15	10	8	7
	.6		78	23	13	9	8	7
	.7		60	18	11	8	7	6
	.8		41	14	9	7	6	6
	.9		23	9	7	6	5	5
5	—	CRD	207	53	24	14	10	7
	0	RMD	211	57	28	18	14	11
	.1		190	52	26	17	13	11
	.2		170	46	24	16	12	10
	.3		149	41	21	15	11	10
	.4		129	36	19	13	11	9
	.5		108	31	17	12	10	9
	.6		87	26	15	11	9	8
	.7		67	21	12	10	8	7
	.8		46	16	10	8	7	7
	.9		26	11	8	7	7	6

TABLE 13.9
(Continued)

Number of Levels	Minimum Correlation	Design*	0.25	0.50	0.75	1.00	1.25	1.50
					d			
6	—	CRD	225	57	26	15	10	8
	0	RMD	230	62	31	20	15	13
	.1		207	56	29	19	15	12
	.2		185	51	26	18	14	12
	.3		163	45	24	16	13	11
	.4		140	40	21	15	12	10
	.5		118	34	19	14	11	10
	.6		96	29	16	12	10	9
	.7		73	23	14	11	9	9
	.8		51	18	12	9	9	8
	.9		29	12	9	8	8	7

*CRD: completely randomized design; RMD: repeated-measures design.

TABLE 13.10
MINIMUM SAMPLE SIZE NEEDED TO ACHIEVE POWER OF .80 WITH = .05

Number of Levels	Minimum Correlation	Design*	0.25	0.50	0.75	1.00	1.25	1.50
					d			
2	—	CRD	253	64	29	17	12	9
	0	RMD	254	65	30	18	13	10
	.1		228	59	28	17	12	9
	.2		203	53	25	15	11	8
	.3		178	46	22	14	10	8
	.4		153	40	19	12	9	7
	.5		128	34	16	10	8	6
	.6		103	28	14	9	7	6
	.7		78	21	11	7	6	5
	.8		53	15	8	6	5	4
	.9		28	9	6	4	4	3
3	—	CRD	310	79	36	21	14	10
	0	RMD	312	81	38	23	16	12
	.1		281	73	34	21	15	11
	.2		250	65	31	19	14	11
	.3		219	58	28	17	12	10
	.4		188	50	24	15	11	9
	.5		158	42	21	13	10	8
	.6		127	34	17	11	9	7
	.7		96	27	14	10	8	6
	.8		65	19	11	8	6	6
	.9		34	11	7	6	5	5
4	—	CRD	350	89	40	23	15	11
	0	RMD	353	92	43	26	19	14
	.1		318	83	39	24	17	13
	.2		284	74	36	22	16	13
	.3		249	66	32	20	15	12
	.4		214	57	28	18	13	11
	.5		179	48	24	16	12	10
	.6		144	39	20	13	10	9
	.7		109	31	16	11	9	8
	.8		74	22	13	9	8	7
	.9		39	13	9	7	6	6

TABLE 13.10
(Continued)

Number of Levels	Minimum Correlation	Design*	d					
			0.25	0.50	0.75	1.00	1.25	1.50
5	—	CRD	383	97	44	25	17	12
	0	RMD	387	101	48	29	21	16
	.1		349	91	44	27	19	15
	.2		311	82	39	25	18	14
	.3		273	72	35	22	16	13
	.4		234	63	31	20	15	12
	.5		196	53	27	18	13	11
	.6		158	44	23	15	12	10
	.7		120	34	18	13	10	9
	.8		82	25	14	11	9	8
	.9		44	15	10	8	8	7
6	—	CRD	412	104	47	27	18	13
	0	RMD	417	109	52	32	23	18
	.1		375	98	47	29	21	17
	.2		334	88	43	27	20	16
	.3		293	78	38	24	18	15
	.4		252	68	34	22	16	14
	.5		211	58	29	19	15	12
	.6		170	47	25	17	13	11
	.7		129	37	20	14	12	10
	.8		88	27	16	12	10	9
	.9		47	17	11	10	9	8

*CRD: completely randomized design; RMD: repeated-measures design.

TABLE 13.11
MINIMUM SAMPLE SIZE NEEDED TO ACHIEVE POWER OF .95 WITH = .05

Number of Levels	Minimum Correlation	Design*	d					
			0.25	0.50	0.75	1.00	1.25	1.50
2	—	CRD	417	105	48	27	18	13
	0	RMD	418	106	49	28	19	14
	.1		377	96	44	26	18	13
	.2		335	86	39	23	16	12
	.3		294	75	35	21	14	11
	.4		252	65	30	18	13	10
	.5		210	54	26	16	11	8
	.6		169	44	21	13	9	7
	.7		127	34	16	10	8	6
	.8		86	23	12	8	6	5
	.9		44	13	7	5	5	4
3	—	CRD	496	125	56	32	21	15
	0	RMD	498	127	58	35	23	17
	.1		448	115	53	31	21	16
	.2		399	102	48	28	20	15
	.3		349	90	42	25	18	13
	.4		300	78	37	22	16	12
	.5		251	65	31	19	14	11
	.6		201	53	26	16	12	9
	.7		152	41	20	13	10	8
	.8		102	28	15	10	8	7
	.9		53	16	9	7	6	5

TABLE 13.11
(Continued)

Number of Levels	Minimum Correlation	Design*	d 0.25	0.50	0.75	1.00	1.25	1.50
4	—	CRD	551	139	63	36	23	17
	0	RMD	554	142	66	39	27	20
	.1		499	128	59	35	24	18
	.2		444	114	53	32	22	17
	.3		389	101	47	29	20	16
	.4		334	87	41	25	18	14
	.5		279	73	35	22	16	13
	.6		224	59	29	18	14	11
	.7		169	46	23	15	12	10
	.8		114	32	17	12	9	8
	.9		59	18	11	9	7	7
5	—	CRD	596	150	67	39	25	18
	0	RMD	600	154	71	43	29	22
	.1		540	139	65	39	27	21
	.2		481	124	58	35	25	19
	.3		421	109	52	32	22	17
	.4		362	94	45	28	20	16
	.5		302	80	38	24	18	14
	.6		243	65	32	21	15	13
	.7		184	50	25	17	13	11
	.8		124	35	19	13	11	9
	.9		65	21	13	10	9	8
6	—	CRD	634	160	72	41	27	19
	0	RMD	639	164	77	46	32	24
	.1		576	149	69	42	29	22
	.2		512	133	62	38	27	21
	.3		449	117	55	34	24	19
	.4		386	101	48	30	22	17
	.5		323	85	41	26	19	16
	.6		259	69	35	22	17	14
	.7		196	54	28	19	14	12
	.8		133	38	21	15	12	11
	.9		69	22	14	11	10	9

*CRD: completely randomized design; RMD: repeated-measures design.

the anticipated effect size. We first illustrate how to use these tables. Then we discuss the underlying theory and practical implications to be drawn from the theory.

Suppose that we are planning a four-group within-subjects study. We plan to use the multivariate approach to analyze our data and we use an α level of .05. How many subjects do we need? The answer depends on three factors: the power we desire, the anticipated effect size, and the correlation between scores at each level. Let's suppose for the moment that we are willing to have a power of .50. Given this choice, there is a 50% chance that we will detect a true effect of the anticipated magnitude. Table 13.9 provides sample sizes for a power value of .50. To use the table, we must next specify d, which is defined to be

$$d = \frac{\mu_{max} - \mu_{min}}{\sigma}$$

where it is assumed that every level of the factor has a common population standard deviation

σ. Suppose that we want to detect a true effect if d is as large as 0.75, that is, if there is a three-quarters standard deviation difference between the largest and the smallest mean. Finally, we must specify the smallest correlation we anticipate among the levels of the factor. In other words, with four levels of the factor, there are six correlations to consider: ρ_{12}, ρ_{13}, ρ_{14}, ρ_{23}, ρ_{24}, and ρ_{34}. The smallest value among these six correlations must be specified. Suppose we decide that the minimum correlation is likely to be .4. From Table 13.9, with four levels of the factor, a d value of 0.75, and a minimum correlation of .4, 17 subjects are needed to obtain a power of .50.

If a power of .80 were desired for the same number of levels, d, and correlation, Table 13.10 shows that 28 subjects would be needed. Similarly, from Table 13.11, 41 subjects would be needed to achieve a power of .95. Thus, the number of subjects to include in the study depends greatly on the desired power. Comparing sample sizes across different values of d and across different values of the minimum correlation shows that the necessary sample size can also vary greatly as a function of these factors. Because the needed sample size depends on these three factors (desired power, d, and correlation) even for a fixed number of levels, it is impossible to state a general rule such as, "20 subjects should be used in a four-level repeated-measures design." Instead, researchers should specify particular values for these three factors and pick a sample size accordingly. When it is difficult to anticipate precise values of d and minimum correlation in advance, it may be wise to specify a range of possible values. For example, with four levels, suppose that a power of .80 is desired, but d could be anywhere between 0.75 and 1.00 and the minimum correlation could be anywhere between .3 and .5. From Table 13.10, the necessary sample size ranges from 32 (for $d = 0.75$, correlation = .3) to 16 (for $d = 1.00$, correlation = .5). Thus, somewhere between 16 and 32 subjects should be included in the study. The exact number of subjects ultimately chosen should depend on factors such as the availability of subjects and the costs (in terms of time and effort, as well as money) of including additional subjects. In real-world research, there is no single "correct" value for the number of subjects needed in a study. However, Tables 13.9–13.11 provide researchers with guidelines for choosing reasonable sample sizes in repeated-measures designs.

The values in Tables 13.9–13.11 are based on mathematical results derived by Vonesh and Schork (1986). They show that the noncentrality parameter δ^2 of the F statistic in the multivariate approach to repeated measures is greater than or equal to $nd^2/2(1 - \rho_{min})$, where ρ_{min} is the minimum correlation. This formulation assumes that each level of the repeated factor has the same population variance, but population correlations are allowed to differ, as often is the case in repeated-measures designs. The values shown in Tables 13.9–13.11 were obtained by using a noncentrality parameter value of $\delta^2 = nd^2/2(1 - \rho_{min})$ in the noncentral F distribution. As Vonesh and Schork (1986) show, this value is a minimum value, so the actual power obtained from using the sample sizes shown in Tables 13.9–13.11 is at least as large as the stated power for the specific values of d and ρ_{min}. The actual power may be greater than the stated power for either of two reasons. First, the sample-size tables assume that the population means of all levels except μ_{max} and μ_{min} equal the grand mean. To the extent that this is false and other group means also differ from the grand mean, power is increased. Second, the tables assume that ρ_{min} is the correlation between the levels represented by μ_{max} and μ_{min}. However, the actual power is somewhat larger for other patterns of mean differences and correlations. The practical consequence of these two points is that Tables 13.9–13.11 provide a lower bound for the power obtained for particular values of d and ρ_{min}. In other words, the sample sizes shown in Tables 13.9–13.11 guarantee that the resultant power is at least as large as .50, .80, and .95, respectively.

Before leaving our discussion of these sample-size tables, we should draw your attention to some patterns in the tables. First, notice that the required number of subjects generally increases as the number of levels increases. Thus, it typically takes more subjects to compare a larger number of levels. Second, the number of subjects increases for corresponding entries as we move from Table 13.9 to Table 13.10 to Table 13.11. To increase power, all other things being equal, the number of subjects must be increased. Third, as d increases, the number of subjects decreases. Larger effects can be detected with fewer subjects. Fourth, as ρ_{min} increases, the number of subjects decreases. Higher correlations are indicative of greater consistency in subjects' relative scores across treatments; greater consistency makes effects easier to detect. Indeed, such consistency is the reason that the repeated-measures design is often more powerful than the between-subjects design, which leads to our final point.

Each CRD row in Tables 13.9–13.11 shows the number of subjects needed in a *completely randomized design* (hence, CRD), which is another term for a between-subjects design. Two important points must be made comparing the CRD sample-size values to the RMD (repeated-measures design) values. First, let's compare the CRD sample size to an RMD sample size for a fixed value of d, number of levels, and desired power. Typically, the sample size needed for the CRD is less than the sample size needed for the RMD when the correlation is zero because the CRD has larger denominator degrees of freedom. However, in most cases, if the correlation is even as large as .1 or .2, the RMD sample size is less than the CRD sample size. Second, it is important to realize that the CRD values shown here are the number of subjects per level. Because each subject appears in only one level (i.e., group), the total number of subjects needed for the study is the tabled value times the number of levels. In the RMD, however, every subject appears in every level, so the tabled value itself is the total number of subjects needed for the study. To ensure that this point is clear, consider this example. Suppose that we want a power of .80 in a four-level study. We anticipate an effect size of $d = 1.00$. In the RMD, the minimum correlation is expected to be .4. From Table 13.10, 18 subjects are needed for the RMD. The corresponding entry for the between-subjects design is 23, which means 23 subjects per group. Thus, the total number of subjects needed in the between-subjects design is 92 (4×23). Thus, a power of .8 can be obtained with 18 subjects in the RMD, but requires a total of 92 subjects in the between-subjects design. This illustration should provide some insight into the popularity of repeated-measures designs in the behavioral sciences, in which subjects are often a precious commodity. Nevertheless, it would be a serious mistake to infer that repeated-measures designs are always preferable to between-subjects designs. As we discuss near the end of Chapter 11, certain types of questions can only be accurately addressed with between-subjects designs.

CHOICE OF D VARIABLES

We have now seen how to analyze data from a one-way repeated-measures design using the multivariate approach. At this point, we need to consider how we should choose the $a - 1$ D variables from the original a variables. We demonstrate empirically that the choice of D variables is irrelevant for testing the omnibus null hypothesis. Although we do not provide a mathematical proof, it can be shown that the only requirement is that the contrasts underlying the D variables must be linearly independent (again, see Chapter 4). Of course, strictly speaking, another requirement is that the sum of coefficients for each individual contrast must sum to zero.

To show that the particular choice of D variables is irrelevant, let's return to the three-level data of Table 13.2. (Although we can make the same point with the four-level data of Table 13.5, we work with the smaller three-level data set for computational simplicity.) Recall that the way we analyzed these data was to form two D variables: $D_1 = $ Time 2$-$ Time 1,

TABLE 13.12
LINEAR AND QUADRATIC D VARIABLES FOR DATA
OF TABLE 13.2

Subject	$D_1 = Linear$	$D_2 = Quadratic$
1	3	−1
2	5	1
3	2	2
4	0	2
5	5	1
6	6	−4
7	2	4
8	1	3
Mean	3	1

and $D_2 =$ Time 3− Time 2. Using these two D variables, we obtained an observed F value of 19.148 ($p = .0032$); we concluded that the population means of the three time periods are not all equal.

What would have happened if we had chosen a different pair of D variables? For example, because the repeated factor here is time, which is quantitative in nature, we might have formed D variables to represent the linear and quadratic trends much as we discussed in Chapter 6 for between-subjects designs. When $a = 3$, the coefficients for these trends are $−1, 0, 1$ for linear and $−1, 2, −1$ for quadratic (see Appendix Table A.10). If we let Y_1, Y_2, and Y_3 represent the original variables for Time 1, Time 2, and Time 3, respectively, we can write our new pair of D variables as $D_1 = Y_3 − Y_1$ and $D_2 = 2Y_2 − Y_1 − Y_3$. Table 13.12 shows the scores for our eight subjects on these two D variables. As usual, we now must calculate sum-of-squared-errors and sum-of-cross-product terms for the full and restricted models. As before, the full models are $D_{1i} = \mu_1 + \varepsilon_{1i}$ and $D_{2i} = \mu_2 + \varepsilon_{2i}$. Least-squares estimates are $\overline{D}_1$ for μ_1 and $\overline{D}_2$ for μ_2; thus, the error for a particular subject is the subject's deviation from the mean on the particular D variable. As before, the restricted models imply that μ_1 and μ_2 both equal zero, so the restricted models predict every subject's score on both D_1 and D_2 to be zero. Thus, the error for a subject is simply that subject's score on the particular D variable.

Table 13.13 presents the errors for the full model and for the restricted model. From this table, the matrix of sum of squares and cross-products for the full model is

$$\mathbf{E(F)} = \begin{bmatrix} 32 & −26 \\ −26 & 44 \end{bmatrix}$$

The matrix for the restricted model is

$$\mathbf{E(R)} = \begin{bmatrix} 104 & −2 \\ −2 & 52 \end{bmatrix}$$

It follows that the two determinants are given by

$$|\mathbf{E(F)}| = 32(44) − (−26)^2 = 732$$

and

$$|\mathbf{E(R)}| = 104(52) − (−2)^2 = 5404$$

TABLE 13.13
ERRORS FOR FULL AND RESTRICTED MODELS FOR D_1 AND D_2 VARIABLES
OF TABLE 13.12

Subject	Full Model					Restricted Model				
	e_1	e_2	e_1^2	e_2^2	$(e_1)(e_2)$	e_1	e_2	e_1^2	e_2^2	$(e_1)(e_2)$
1	0	−2	0	4	0	3	−1	9	1	−3
2	2	0	4	0	0	5	1	25	1	5
3	−1	1	1	1	−1	2	2	4	4	4
4	−3	1	9	1	−3	0	2	0	4	0
5	2	0	4	0	0	5	1	25	1	5
6	3	−5	9	25	−15	6	−4	36	16	−24
7	−1	3	1	9	−3	2	4	4	16	8
8	−2	2	4	4	−4	1	3	1	9	3
Sum	0	0	32	44	−26	24	8	104	52	−2

Equation 21 provides the formula for the F statistic with two D variables:

$$F = \frac{(|\mathbf{E(R)}| - |\mathbf{E(F)}|)/2}{|\mathbf{E(F)}|/(n-2)} \qquad \text{(21, repeated)}$$

Substituting the appropriate values into this equation yields

$$F = \frac{(5404 - 732)/2}{732/(8-2)} = 19.148$$

However, this is precisely the F value we obtained earlier with our other choice of D variables. Thus, as claimed, the same F value occurs regardless of the choice of coefficients used to define the D variables.

Although our empirical demonstration by no means carries the weight of a mathematical proof, such a proof is beyond the scope of this book. The interested reader is referred to Bock (1975), Harris (1985), Morrison (1976), or Timm (1975) for a more mathematical description. These books also provide a more technical presentation of "linear independence" than the intuitive "redundancy" explanation in Chapter 4.

TESTS OF INDIVIDUAL CONTRASTS

Although we have just seen that the particular choice of D variables is irrelevant for testing the omnibus null hypothesis, different D variables provide different information about which individual means differ from one another. As in between-subjects designs, a significant omnibus F value simply implies that a true difference exists somewhere among the means. To pinpoint the precise nature of this difference, it is necessary to test individual contrasts.

As we mentioned briefly in Chapters 11 and 12, there are two rather different approaches for testing contrasts in repeated-measures designs. Not surprisingly, one of these is based on the logic of the mixed-model approach to the omnibus test, whereas the other is based on the multivariate approach. Our presentation focuses on the multivariate-based approach. After providing a brief overview of the mixed-model approach as well, we explain why we strongly prefer the multivariate approach.

Remember from our discussion of contrasts in between-subjects designs that testing a contrast involves two issues: calculating an observed value of the test statistic and determining an appropriate critical value. Calculating the observed value of the test statistic is simplified because it does not matter what other contrasts (if any) are also being tested. The protection required for performing multiple tests is obtained through the critical value. Thus, we can begin our consideration of testing contrasts in within-subjects designs by learning how to calculate the observed value of the test statistic. One we have accomplished this goal, we can consider the determination of an appropriate critical value.

To make calculation of the observed value of the test statistic more concrete, let's consider a specific problem. Suppose that we are interested in testing a null hypothesis that the linear trend is zero in the population for the data of Table 13.2. The first step in finding the value of the test statistic is to form the corresponding D variable. When $a = 3$, we have already seen that the coefficients of the linear trend are $-1, 0$, and 1, so the appropriate D variable is simply

$$D = Y_3 - Y_1$$

Table 13.12, which we used earlier to demonstrate the irrelevance of the choice of D variables for the omnibus null hypothesis, presents scores on the linear D variable for each of the eight subjects. The null hypothesis to be tested is that this D variable has a population mean of zero. This hypothesis can be tested by comparing a full model and a restricted model:

$$\text{Full:} \quad D_i = \mu + \varepsilon_i$$

$$\text{Restricted:} \quad D_i = 0 + \varepsilon_i$$

The least-squares estimate for μ will be $\overline{D}$, so errors for both models can be calculated very easily. In fact, we already calculated errors for both models when we performed the omnibus test. As shown in Table 13.13, we found that $E_F = 32$ and $E_R = 104$ for the linear variable. To determine whether this difference is statistically significant, we can use our usual formula

$$F = \frac{(E_R - E_F)/(df_R - df_F)}{E_F/df_F}$$

Notice that E_R and E_F are numbers instead of matrices because now our hypothesis pertains to only a single D variable. As a result, we are performing a univariate test. Also, notice that the restricted model has no parameters, so $df_R = n$. The full model has one parameter, so $df_F = n - 1$. Making these substitutions, the general expression for testing an individual contrast is given by

$$F = \frac{(E_R - E_F)/1}{E_F/(n - 1)} \tag{25}$$

which obviously simplifies to

$$F = \frac{E_R - E_F}{E_F/(n - 1)} \tag{26}$$

For our data, the F value then equals

$$F = \frac{104 - 32}{32/(8 - 1)} = 15.75$$

Before considering whether this value of 15.75 is statistically significant, we must make several additional points. First, when we performed the omnibus test for these data, we compared two matrices. The matrix for the full model was given by

$$\begin{bmatrix} 32 & -26 \\ -26 & 44 \end{bmatrix}$$

whereas the matrix for the restricted model was

$$\begin{bmatrix} 104 & -2 \\ -2 & 52 \end{bmatrix}$$

Notice that the numbers in the first row and first column of the two matrices are 32 and 104, which are the two sum of squared errors we compared to test the contrast. Thus, the test of the contrast makes use of part of the same data used in the multivariate test of the omnibus hypothesis. As stated previously, the omnibus hypothesis tests whether both D_1 and D_2 have means of zero, whereas the test of a contrast looks at a single variable individually. The test of the contrast is thus a univariate test of the specific D variable, and for this reason is often labeled as a *univariate test* in computer printouts. Second, although we presented an example of how to find the value of the F statistic for testing a linear trend, the same approach is appropriate for testing any contrast. All that is required is to form the D variable whose coefficients correspond to the contrast of interest and calculate E_F and E_R for the resultant variable. Third, hand calculations can be simplified even further here, because there is only a single D variable. As shown earlier in the chapter, for a single D variable, the formula for the F statistic simplifies to

$$F = n\overline{D}^2/s_D^2 \qquad\qquad (6, \text{repeated})$$

Thus, this form of the F can also be used for testing individual contrasts.

OPTIONAL

Quantitative Repeated Factors

A fourth point is pertinent when the repeated factor is quantitative, such as time or dosage level. There is a special meaning that can be attached to a subject's linear D score because each subject's linear D score is proportional to the slope of that subject's least-squares regression line when the score is regressed on the quantitative predictor variable. To illustrate this point, we again consider the data of Table 13.2. Let's suppose that the three time periods represented here are 12 months, 24 months, and 36 months. What would happen if we performed a regression analysis of the three scores for subject 1? There are 3 X values: 12, 24, and 36. There are three corresponding Y values: 2, 3, and 5. The slope of a least-squares regression line is given by

$$b = \frac{\sum(X - \overline{X})(Y - \overline{Y})}{\sum(X - \overline{X})^2}$$

Substituting the three X and Y pairs into this formula results in a value of $b = 0.125$. Thus, the best-fitting regression line (in the sense of least squares) suggests that this subject's score increases by one-eighth of a point every month. Table 13.14 shows the slope of the least-squares regression line for each of the eight subjects, as well as the score on the linear D variable, reproduced from Table 13.12. There is a striking

TABLE 13.14
VALUES OF THE SLOPE OF THE LEAST-SQUARES
REGRESSION LINE AND OF THE LINEAR D
VARIABLE FOR DATA OF TABLE 13.2

Subject	Slope	Linear D
1	0.125	3
2	0.208	5
3	0.083	2
4	0.000	0
5	0.208	5
6	0.250	6
7	0.083	2
8	0.042	1

relationship between the numbers in the two columns of Table 13.14. Every subject's score on D is 24 times his or her slope.[5] In general, it can be shown that the slope for the ith subject, b_i, is related to the subject's D score, D_i, by the following formula:

$$b_i = D_i / h \sum_{j=1}^{a} c_j^2$$

The value of h expresses the relationship between the units of the time factor (expressed as deviations from the mean) and the values of the coefficients. Specifically, the two sets of numbers are necessarily proportional to one another, and h is the constant of proportionality. In our example, the units of the factor are 12, 24, and 36. Expressed as deviations from the mean, they become -12, 0, and 12 (because 24 is the mean of 12, 24, and 36). The coefficients for D are -1, 0, and 1. Thus, $h = 12$ because the units of the factor are uniformly 12 times larger than the coefficients. Notice also that the sum of squared coefficients $\sum_{j=1}^{a} c_j^2$ equals 2, so we have

$$b_i = D_i / 24$$

in agreement with Table 13.14. We elaborate on this point because repeated-measures designs often involve time as a within-subjects factor. Our illustration, which holds for any value of a, shows an interesting way in which the test of a linear trend across time can be conceptualized. In effect, such a test asks whether the average (i.e., mean) subject has scores whose straight-line slope across time equals zero. There is sometimes also a practical advantage to viewing the test of the linear trend from this perspective. If data are missing (presumably at random) for some mixture of subjects at varying time points, it is still possible to calculate a regression slope for each subject (as long as at least two observations are available for the subject). These slopes can then be used as D variables in a repeated-measures analysis.[6]

MULTIPLE-COMPARISON PROCEDURES: DETERMINATION OF CRITICAL VALUES

We have now seen how to conduct the first step in testing a contrast, namely the calculation of the observed value of the test statistic. We are now ready to discuss the second step, the determination of an appropriate critical value.

If it is deemed appropriate to use a per-comparison alpha level, determining the appropriate critical value is trivial. Recall that the F statistic for testing an individual comparison is

$$F = \frac{(E_R - E_F)/1}{E_F/(n-1)} \qquad \text{(25, repeated)}$$

As this expression shows, the F statistic has 1 numerator and $n-1$ denominator degrees of freedom. No adjustment is needed to use the desired per-comparison alpha level.

As an illustration, we discovered that the observed F value for a linear trend in the data of Table 13.2 equals 15.75. If we decide to use a per-comparison alpha level of .05, Appendix Table A.2 of the F distribution shows that the critical F equals 5.59 for 1 numerator and 7 denominator degrees of freedom (remember that there were eight subjects in the data set). Thus, we can reject a null hypothesis of no linear trend at the .05 level. In other words, there is a statistically significant linear trend.

Planned Comparisons

If the familywise alpha level for a set of planned comparisons is to be maintained at .05, an adjustment in the critical value is necessary. As we discussed in Chapter 5 for the between-subjects design, the Bonferroni approach is again applicable. Instead of using a per-comparison alpha level of .05, a per-comparison level of $.05/C$ is used, where C is the total number of planned comparisons. Of course, .05 is used if it is the desired familywise alpha level, as it usually is; otherwise, any other desired familywise level is divided by C. The easiest way to implement the Bonferroni approach is to obtain the p value for the individual contrast from a computer program. The resultant p value can then be compared to $.05/C$. For example, the p value associated with the F value of 15.75 for the linear trend in Table 13.2 is .0057. Suppose that we were testing both the linear and quadratic trends and wanted to maintain familywise alpha at .05. The linear trend is still statistically significant because the observed p value of .0057 is smaller than .025, which we use as the critical p value because it is .05/2. In summary, tests of planned comparisons in repeated-measures designs are based on the same logic and follow the same procedures as in the between-subjects design.

Pairwise Comparisons

In the between-subjects design, we advocate the use of Tukey's WSD to maintain familywise alpha at the desired level of testing all pairwise comparisons. However, our recommendation in the within-subjects design is to use the Bonferroni approach. This approach should be used regardless of whether the researcher planned to test all pairwise comparisons or only made this decision after examining the data.

The procedure for using the Bonferroni approach to test pairwise comparisons is the same as for the general case of planned comparisons. Namely, the observed p value is compared to $.05/C$, where .05 (or some other value, if desired) is the familywise alpha level and C is the number of contrasts potentially being tested. In the case of pairwise contrasts, $C = a(a-1)/2$ because this is the formula for the number of distinct pairs with a levels.

It may seem odd that Tukey's WSD is not being recommended for testing pairwise comparisons in repeated-measures designs. The recommendation is based on Maxwell (1980), who showed that Tukey's approach here does not always successfully maintain α_{FW} at the desired level. In essence, the reason for this failure is that the homogeneity of variance assumption required by the WSD is violated unless the sphericity assumption required by the mixed-model repeated-measures approach is met. The Bonferroni procedure does not require this assumption, and hence maintains α_{FW} at the desired level.

Post Hoc Complex Comparisons

As in the between-subjects design, occasions arise in within-subjects designs in which the investigator decides after examining the data to test one or more complex comparisons. For example, consider the data in Table 13.2 again. Although it seems reasonable to test planned linear and quadratic trends for these data, suppose for the moment that the repeated factor were qualitative instead of quantitative. In this case, it might be decided post hoc to test the difference between the first level and the average of the other two, because levels 2 and 3 have similar means. The appropriate D variable would be

$$D = Y_1 - \frac{1}{2}(Y_2 + Y_3)$$

where Y_1, Y_2, and Y_3 refer to Time 1, Time 2, and Time 3, respectively. Using either Equation 6 or 26, we would obtain an observed F value of 31.818. The appropriate critical value comes from a multivariate extension of Scheffé's method developed by Roy and Bose. The formula for the critical value (CV) is given by

$$\text{CV} = \frac{(n-1)(a-1)F_{\alpha_{FW}; a-1, n-a+1}}{(n-a+1)} \tag{27}$$

where α_{FW} is the familywise alpha level and $F_{\alpha_{FW}; a-1, n-a+1}$ is the critical value for an F with $a-1$ numerator and $n-a+1$ denominator degrees of freedom. For our data, $a = 3$ and $n = 8$, so the CV of Equation 27 becomes CV $= (8-1)(3-1)(5.14)/(8-3+1) = 11.99$. Thus, the mean of D is significantly different from zero. Even after having looked at the data, we can conclude that the population mean of level 1 is different from the average of the means for levels 2 and 3.

The rationale for the Roy–Bose critical value in Equation 27 is exactly the same as in the between-subjects design. Specifically, recall that in the between-subjects design, the omnibus F test is significant if and only if there exists some contrast that is significant using Scheffé's method. This same coherence also holds in the within-subjects design.

After observing the data, it is always possible to find a contrast whose observed F value is $(n-1)(a-1)/(n-a+1)$ times larger than the observed omnibus F value. No other contrast can have a larger observed F value. For convenience, let's label the D variable associated with this largest observed F as D_{max}. We know that the observed F value for D_{max}, which we label F_{max}, equals

$$F_{max} = \frac{(n-1)(a-1)F_{omnibus}}{(n-a+1)}$$

When does F_{max} exceed the Roy–Bose critical value of Equation 27? It does if and only if

$$(n-1)(a-1)F_{omnibus}/(n-a+1) > (n-1)(a-1)F_{\alpha_{FW}; a-1, n-a+1}/(n-a+1)$$

However, this inequality obviously holds if and only if

$$F_{omnibus} > F_{\alpha_{FW}; a-1, n-a+1}$$

which is equivalent to a rejection of the omnibus null hypothesis. Thus, it is possible to obtain significance for at least one contrast using the Roy–Bose critical value if and only if the omnibus test is significant.

OPTIONAL

Finding D_{max}

Finding the coefficients of the D_{max} variable is more difficult than in the between-subjects design. In the between-subjects design, the optimal coefficients depend only on the sample means; however, in the within-subjects design, the optimal coefficients depend not only on the sample means but also on the interrelationships among the variables. It is necessary to use matrix algebra to incorporate these interrelationships into the calculation of the optimal coefficients. For this reason, we provide only a brief overview.

Let's return to the D variables of Table 13.3, which were obtained from the data in Table 13.2. When a multivariate analysis is performed, it is possible to obtain raw discriminant weights, which convey information about the relative weights to be assigned to variables so as to maximize an effect. For our data, the weight for D_1 is 1.08448, and the weight for D_2 is 0.19424. Thus, D_1 is more influential than D_2 in rejecting the null hypothesis. However, our real interest is to find weights for the original Y variables. We can accomplish this through matrix multiplication. The discriminant weights must be written as a column vector, which we label $\mathbf{w}$. For our data, we have

$$\mathbf{w} = \begin{bmatrix} 1.08448 \\ 0.19424 \end{bmatrix}$$

Next, the coefficients used to derive the D variables from the original Y variables must be written in matrix form; we denote the matrix $\mathbf{T}$. Each column corresponds to a D variable and each row to a Y variable. Recall that D_1 in Table 13.3 was defined as $D_1 = Y_2 - Y_1$. This implies that the first column of $\mathbf{T}$ has elements -1, 1, and 0. Similarly, D_2 was defined as $D_2 = Y_3 - Y_2$, so the second column of $\mathbf{T}$ has elements 0, -1, and 1. Combining the two columns yields

$$\mathbf{T} = \begin{bmatrix} -1 & 0 \\ 1 & -1 \\ 0 & 1 \end{bmatrix}$$

The coefficients for the maximum contrast (or optimal subeffect, as it is sometimes called) are obtained by multiplying $\mathbf{T}$ by $\mathbf{w}$. Specifically, if we let $\mathbf{v}$ be the vector of optimal weights, then $\mathbf{v} = \mathbf{Tw}$. For our data,

$$\mathbf{v} = \begin{bmatrix} -1 & 0 \\ 1 & -1 \\ 0 & 1 \end{bmatrix} \begin{bmatrix} 1.08448 \\ 0.19424 \end{bmatrix}$$

which results in

$$\mathbf{v} = \begin{bmatrix} -1.08448 \\ 0.89024 \\ 0.19424 \end{bmatrix}$$

Thus, the optimal D variable is

$$D_{max} = -1.08448Y_1 + 0.89024Y_2 + 0.19424Y_3$$

Several points must be made here. First, notice that the sum of the coefficients for D_{max} equals zero, as it must if the contrast is to be meaningful. Second, it can be shown that the observed F value for testing a null hypothesis that the population mean of D_{max} is zero equals 44.678. Recall that the omnibus observed F value for these data was 19.148. Thus, within rounding error, it is the case that

$$F_{max} = \frac{(n-1)(a-1)F_{omnibus}}{(n-a+1)}$$

because

$$44.678 = \frac{(8-1)(3-1)(19.148)}{(8-3+1)}$$

Third, notice that the optimal coefficients do not closely match the pattern of mean differences for Y_1, Y_2, and Y_3. As we saw in Table 13.2, the means of Y_1, Y_2, and Y_3 are 6, 8, and 9, respectively. Such a pattern would seem to suggest that the optimal contrast might weight the first and third levels most heavily. In fact, however, the optimal contrast is essentially a comparison of levels 1 and 2, with relatively little weight placed on the third level. The coefficients do not closely match the mean differences here because the optimal coefficients depend on the relationships among the variables and the standard deviations of the variables, as well as on the means. For our data, the correlation between Y_1 and Y_2 is much higher ($r = .966$) than either the correlation of Y_1 and Y_3 ($r = .719$) or Y_2 and Y_3 ($r = .772$). The standard deviations of the three variables are roughly the same. Because Y_1 and Y_2 are so highly correlated, the $Y_2 - Y_1$ difference score has a small variance. Another look at Equation 6 for testing a contrast shows that, all other things being equal, a small variance implies a large F value:

$$F = n\overline{D}^2/s_D^2 \qquad \text{(6, repeated)}$$

Thus, even though $Y_3 - Y_1$ has a larger mean than does $Y_2 - Y_1$, the F value for $Y_2 - Y_1$ is larger than the F value for $Y_3 - Y_1$ because the variance of $Y_2 - Y_1$ is so much smaller than the variance of $Y_3 - Y_1$.

We emphasize that rarely if ever would a researcher interpret the D_{max} variable itself. In our example, it is difficult to describe the psychological importance of $-1.08448Y_1 + 0.89024Y_2 + 0.19424Y_3$. However, the coefficients of D_{max} serve as a suggestion for more easily interpreted and hence more meaningful coefficients that might also prove to be significant. In our example, a natural choice would seem to be $D = Y_2 - Y_1$, which yields an F value of 37.3333 and hence easily exceeds the Roy–Bose critical value of 11.99.

■

CONFIDENCE INTERVALS FOR CONTRASTS

As in other designs, it is often useful to supplement hypothesis tests with confidence intervals for specific contrasts. You may recall a very general expression we provided in Chapter 5 for a confidence interval:

$$\text{estimate} \pm (\text{critical value}) (\text{estimated standard error}) \qquad \text{(5.12, repeated)}$$

We can continue to use this expression in within-subjects designs. Just as a single D variable provides a direct mechanism for testing a hypothesis about a contrast, a single D variable also provides a direct mechanism for forming a confidence interval. Specifically, the expression for a confidence interval in a within-subjects design can be expressed as

$$\overline{D} \pm w\sqrt{\hat{s}_D^2/n} \tag{28}$$

where $\overline{D}$ is the sample mean of the D variable, w is a critical value from the appropriate distribution (more on this in a moment), $\hat{s}_D$ is the standard deviation of the D variable, and n is sample size. This formula is in fact a special case of the usual formula given for finding the confidence interval for the mean in a single-sample design, because $\hat{s}_D/\sqrt{n}$ is the standard error of $\overline{D}$. The only thing that makes our situation different from that of a typical introductory statistics presentation is that the variable of interest here (i.e., D) is itself a difference score. Once we realize that, everything else follows from the usual procedure for forming a confidence interval for a single mean.

Computing the mean of D and the standard error of $\overline{D}$ is straightforward even by hand but especially with a statistical package. In a practical sense, all that remains is to determine the appropriate value of w. As usual, the choice of w depends on how we intend to control the error rate. As we discussed in our previous section on hypothesis testing, the most likely choices in a within-subjects design are

$$w = \sqrt{F_{.05;\,1,n-1}} \qquad\qquad\qquad \text{for } \alpha_{\text{PC}} = .05$$

$$w = \sqrt{F_{.05/C;\,1,n-1}} \qquad\qquad\quad \text{for Bonferroni}$$

$$w = \sqrt{(n-1)(a-1)F_{.05;\,a-1,\,n-a+1}/(n-a+1)} \quad \text{for Roy–Bose}$$

Let's consider a few examples of how we might form confidence intervals in the McCarthy IQ data. First, suppose we wanted to form a 95% confidence interval for the population difference in means at 30 months and 36 months. Because we represented this difference with our D_1 variable earlier in the chapter, we can rely on values we have already calculated to compute much of what we need to form our confidence interval. For example, Table 13.6 showed us that the sample mean difference of IQ at 36 months minus IQ at 30 months equals 4.00 in our data. Thus, $\overline{D}$ equals 4.00. Similarly, Table 13.7 showed that the sum of squared errors for D_1 in the full model equal 878. It follows that the variance for D_1 equals 878/11 (i.e., divided by $n-1$), which equals 79.82. The corresponding standard deviation of D_1 thus equals 8.93 (i.e., the square root of 79.82). Before we rush to substitute this value into our confidence interval, we must be clear that 8.93 is the value of the standard deviation of D, and eventually we must find the standard deviation of $\overline{D}$. We can find the standard deviation of the mean simply by dividing 8.93 by the square root of n, which gives us a value of 2.58 for our data. All that remains is to determine the appropriate critical value. Suppose that this contrast represents a single planned comparison, so that we are comfortable setting alpha at .05 for this specific comparison. In this case, the critical value is the square root of the critical F value (at .05) with 1 numerator and 11 denominator degrees of freedom. Appendix Table A.2 shows that the critical F itself equals 4.84, so the square root equals 2.20. Substituting all of the values into the formula for a confidence interval yields an interval given by

$$4.00 \pm (2.20)(2.58)$$

which then simplifies to

$$4.00 \pm 5.68$$

TABLE 13.15
SAS OUTPUT OF CONFIDENCE INTERVALS FOR SEVERAL CONTRASTS
IN McCARTHY DATA

Parameter	Estimate	Standard Error	t Value	Pr > |t|	95% Confidence Limits	
36 minus 30	4.00000000	2.57905315	1.55	0.1492	−1.67645771	9.67645771
42 minus 36	3.00000000	2.75790874	1.09	0.3000	−3.07011620	9.07011620
48 minus 42	2.00000000	2.23267743	0.90	0.3895	−2.91408988	6.91408988
48 minus 30	9.00000000	3.69274473	2.44	0.0330	0.87232365	17.12767635
Mean linear trend	0.50000000	0.22307916	2.24	0.0466	0.00900609	0.99099391

Thus, we can be 95% confident that the population mean IQ score at 36 months is somewhere between 1.68 points lower and 9.68 points higher than the population mean at 30 months. Notice also that the interval contains zero, so we cannot reject the hypothesis that the population means at these two ages are equal to each other.

Table 13.15 provides lines of output from SAS showing confidence intervals for several different contrasts of possible interest. We discuss several aspects of this table. First, notice that the confidence interval labeled as the difference between the 36 month and 30 month means is identical to the interval we just calculated. Thus, once we understand how to do the calculations and interpret them, we can rely on statistical packages such as SAS and SPSS to do the actual computations on our data. Second, suppose we decided that we wanted to form a confidence interval for the mean differences between each pair of adjacent waves of data in our design. In other words, we might want to consider three possible differences: 36 minus 30 months, 42 minus 36 months, and 48 minus 42 months. The table shows that we can use SAS (or similar packages) to form such intervals simply by creating each appropriate D variable and then forming a confidence interval for the mean of that variable. However, suppose we decided that we should regard these three differences as a single family and control alpha at .05 for this family. Assuming we planned to form these three intervals prior to data collection, we must then use an adjusted critical value based on the Bonferroni method. Appendix Table A.3 shows that the new critical F value would be 7.95 instead of our previous value of 4.84. As of this writing, neither SAS nor SPSS provides a direct way of incorporating this critical value into an analysis, so it is necessary to do a few calculations by hand. However, we can still rely on our computer output for much of what we need. For example, consider a Bonferroni-adjusted interval for the mean difference between 36 and 30 months. We know from the output that the sample mean difference is 4.00, and we also know that the estimated standard error of this difference is 2.58. The only remaining number we need to form a confidence interval is the critical value, which is the square root of 7.95. Substituting these values into our expression for a confidence interval yields

$$4.00 \pm (2.82)(2.58)$$

which simplifies to

$$4.00 \pm 7.27$$

Notice how this interval compares to the interval we constructed when we regarded this contrast as a single planned comparison. Both intervals are centered at 4.00, but this new interval is roughly 25% wider than the original interval because we now want 95% confidence for all three intervals simultaneously. A post hoc interval based on the Roy–Bose method turns out to be even larger, as it typically does unless the number of planned comparisons becomes very large.

It is interesting to note that even without controlling alpha for multiple tests, all three of the intervals comparing adjacent means contain zero. Thus, it is plausible that there is no population difference between means at 30 and 36 months, 36 and 42 months, and 42 and 48 months. Of course, this then seems to imply that the population means may be equal for all four ages. Although this interpretation is consistent with the nonsignificant omnibus test for these data, it may well be the case that neither an examination of adjacent means nor an omnibus test provides the most powerful test of possible mean differences over age levels. Because age is a quantitative factor, we may prefer to examine polynomial trends in the data. For example, suppose we had a theoretical reason to focus our attention on the linear trend. We might then decide to form a confidence interval for the linear trend, regarding it as a single planned comparison. The linear trend is often of special interest because when the true relationship is either linear or quadratic, the linear trend can be interpreted as the average rate of change during the time interval. For example, in the McCarthy data, the linear trend would represent the average rate of change in IQ scores between 30 and 48 months. We can estimate this value by forming a D variable. As usual, scaling of coefficients for a contrast (i.e., for the D variable) cannot be ignored when our goal is to form a confidence interval instead of simply testing a hypothesis. To understand this point, let's consider the coefficients given in Appendix Table A.10 for a linear trend in a design with four levels as in the McCarthy data. The table shows that the coefficients are -3, -1, 1, and 3. These coefficients are perfectly fine for conducting a hypothesis test, but may not tell us what we want to know in a confidence interval. Recall that we could multiply all four coefficients by any constant without changing the value of an observed F statistic. However, both the center and the width of a confidence interval depend on the exact coefficients we choose. Thus, we must scale the contrast in meaningful units. To do so, we must define our D variable accordingly. In our optional section on quantitative factors earlier in the chapter, we showed that the formula for the least-squares slope estimate can be written as

$$b = \frac{\sum (X - \overline{X})(Y - \overline{Y})}{\sum (X - \overline{X})^2}$$

where Y represents a subject's score on a given level of the dependent variable and X represents the value of the level itself. In the McCarthy data, the values of X are 30, 36, 42, and 48. (Notice this corresponds to scaling age in months. We could just as easily scale X as 2.5, 3.0, 3.5, and 4.0, which then corresponds to measuring age in years.) We can use this expression to form a confidence interval for the population mean slope. With X values of 30, 36, 42, and 48, the value of each deviation score (i.e, the difference between each X and the mean of X) becomes -9, -3, 3, and 9. The sum of squared deviations equals 180 [i.e., $(-9)^2 + (-3)^2 + (3)^2 + (9)^2$]. In order to form a confidence interval for the population slope, we must create a D variable using coefficients of $-9/180$, $-3/180$, $3/180$, and $9/180$. Once we form this D variable, we can proceed to form an interval as usual.

The last line of Table 13.15 shows SAS output providing a confidence interval for the population mean slope using this approach. The sample mean slope is 0.50. This tells us that the 12 children in our sample experienced an average increase of one-half IQ point each month between 30 and 48 months of age. Could this simply reflect sampling error, or can we infer that it reflects something real? The output shows that a 95% confidence interval has a lower limit of 0.009 and an upper limit of 0.991. Thus, we can be 95% confident that the true rate of change is somewhere between roughly .01 and 1.00 IQ units per month. Because zero is not included in this interval, we can infer that the population mean rate of change is positive. However, even though the interval does not contain zero, it is still quite wide, reflecting considerable uncertainty about the precise average rate of change. The culprit here is the small sample size. Obtaining a more precise estimate here would mean obtaining a larger (but ideally still random) sample of children.

All the methods for testing contrasts and forming confidence intervals that we have presented in this chapter are based on the multivariate approach to repeated measures, in that the test of a contrast uses a portion of the information used by the multivariate approach. However, as we discussed in Chapters 11 and 12, it is also possible to test contrasts using a mixed-model approach. As we see shortly, mixed-model tests of contrasts rely heavily on the sphericity assumption. Before we can see why this is true, we must consider in more detail the relationship between the mixed-model approach and the multivariate approach.

THE RELATIONSHIP BETWEEN THE MULTIVARIATE APPROACH AND THE MIXED-MODEL APPROACH

Given our presentation to this point, the multivariate and mixed-model approaches to analyzing repeated-measures data probably seem entirely different. After all, in the multivariate approach, we calculate determinants of matrices obtained from D variables, whereas the mixed-model approach makes no use of determinants or even matrices. In the mixed-model approach, the F statistic is simply calculated as

$$F = MS_A/MS_{A \times S} \qquad \text{(11.28, repeated)}$$

On the surface, this bears little resemblance to the multivariate formula, except insofar as we have seen that both formulas come from comparing models using least squares.

Orthonormal Contrasts

The purpose of this section is to develop an explicit connection between the multivariate and mixed-model approaches. To accomplish this goal, it is useful to work with orthonormal contrasts, which are contrasts that possess two properties. First, a set of orthonormal contrasts must be orthogonal. Second, the coefficients of each individual contrast must be normalized. This means that the sum-of-squared coefficients must equal 1.0.

We continue working with the data from Table 13.2 to make our theoretical points easier to follow. What would happen if we used orthonormal contrasts to create our two D variables? To answer this question, we need two orthonormal contrasts. We can simplify our task by realizing that the linear and quadratic D variables we formed earlier (see Table 13.12) were obtained from orthogonal contrasts. Recall that the D variables we used were

$$D_1 = Y_3 - Y_1 \qquad \text{and} \qquad D_2 = 2Y_2 - Y_1 - Y_3$$

To make the coefficients more explicit, the variables can be rewritten as

$$D_1 = (-1)Y_1 + (0)Y_2 + (1)Y_3$$
$$D_2 = (-1)Y_1 + (2)Y_2 + (-1)Y_3$$

We can verify that the contrasts are indeed orthogonal because the sum of products of the coefficients equals zero:

$$(-1)(-1) + (0)(2) + (1)(-1) = 0$$

However, these contrasts are not yet normalized because the sum-of-squared coefficients is two for the linear trend and six for the quadratic trend. Normalizing the coefficients is quite simple. All we must do is to divide each nonnormalized coefficient by the square root of the sum-of-squared coefficients for that particular contrast. For example, because the sum-of-squared coefficients for the linear trend is 2, we must divide each nonnormalized coefficient by $\sqrt{2}$. If we let D_1^* represent the resulting (normalized) variable, we have

$$D_1^* = (-0.70711)Y_1 + (0)Y_2 + (0.70711)Y_3$$

Notice that the coefficients for D^* are proportional to the coefficients for D, but the sum-of-squared coefficients for D^* equals 1.0 (within rounding error), so that D^* is a normalized contrast. Following the same logic for the quadratic trend yields

$$D_2^* = (-0.40825)Y_1 + (0.81650)Y_2 + (-0.40825)Y_3$$

Suppose that we performed a multivariate analysis of D_1^* and D_2^* instead of D_1 and D_2. Would the results be different? Although we could duplicate the procedures used to obtain Tables 13.12 and 13.13 to answer this question, we instead take a shortcut. It should be apparent that D_1^* and D_1 are closely related, as are D_2^* and D_2. In particular,

$$D_1^* = 0.70711 D_1 \qquad \text{and} \qquad D_2^* = 0.40825 D_2$$

As these equations show, D_1^* and D_2^* are really the same variables as D_1 and D_2—they are simply measured on a different metric. We can take advantage of this fact by realizing as a result that for any given subject

$$(D_{1i}^*)^2 = (0.70711 D_{1i})^2 = 0.5000 D_{1i}^2 \tag{29}$$

$$(D_{2i}^*)^2 = (0.40825 D_{2i})^2 = 0.1667 D_{2i}^2 \tag{30}$$

$$D_{1i}^* D_{2i}^* = (0.70711 D_{1i})(0.40825 D_{2i}) = 0.2887 D_{1i} D_{2i} \tag{31}$$

Because these equalities hold for each individual subject, they must also hold for the sums of squares and sums of cross-products, which are the numbers ultimately needed for performing a test. Recall that from Table 13.13 we found error matrices for the full and restricted models:

$$\mathbf{E(F)} = \begin{bmatrix} 32 & -26 \\ -26 & 44 \end{bmatrix}$$

$$\mathbf{E(R)} = \begin{bmatrix} 104 & -2 \\ -2 & 52 \end{bmatrix}$$

We must now realize (see Table 13.13) that 32 and 104 are sums of D_1^2 terms, 44 and 52 are sums of D_2^2 terms, and -26 and -2 are sums of $D_1 D_2$ terms. From Equation 29, the sum of the $(D_1^*)^2$ terms for the full model is related to the sum of the D_1^2 terms in the following manner:

$$\sum_{i=1}^{n}(D_{1i}^*)^2 = \sum_{i=1}^{n}\left(0.5000D_{1i}^2\right) = 0.5000\sum_{i=1}^{n}D_{1i}^2$$

$$= 0.5000(32) = 16$$

Thus, for the normalized linear trend, the sum of squared errors for the full model is 16. Similarly, the restricted model sum of squared errors for the normalized linear trend is

$$\sum_{i=1}^{n}(D_{1i}^*)^2 = 0.5000(104) = 52$$

The same logic holds for the sum of squared errors for the quadratic trend and for the sum of cross-products. Specifically, from Equation 30, the sums of $(D_2^*)^2$ terms must be 7.3333 and 8.6667, again for the full and restricted models. Finally, from Equation 31, the sum of $D_1^*D_2^*$ terms for the two models must be -7.5055 and -0.5774. Arranging these new numbers in matrix form and letting $\mathbf{E}^*(\mathbf{F})$ and $\mathbf{E}^*(\mathbf{R})$ represent the full and restricted matrices for the normalized D variables yields

$$\mathbf{E}^*(\mathbf{F}) = \begin{bmatrix} 16.0000 & -7.5055 \\ -7.5055 & 7.3333 \end{bmatrix}$$

$$\mathbf{E}^*(\mathbf{R}) = \begin{bmatrix} 52.0000 & -0.5774 \\ -0.5774 & 8.6667 \end{bmatrix}$$

The F statistic for the omnibus test is given by Equation 20:

$$F = \frac{(|\mathbf{E}(\mathbf{R})| - |\mathbf{E}(\mathbf{F})|)/(df_R - df_F)}{|\mathbf{E}(\mathbf{F})|/df_F} \qquad \text{(20, repeated)}$$

The determinant of $\mathbf{E}(\mathbf{F})$ is

$$|\mathbf{E}(\mathbf{F})| = (16)(7.3333) - (-7.5055)^2 = 61.0000$$

and the determinant of $\mathbf{E}(\mathbf{R})$ is

$$|\mathbf{E}(\mathbf{R})| = (52)(8.6667) - (-0.5774)^2 = 450.3333$$

Substituting these values into Equation 20 (along with $df_F = 6$ and $df_R = 8$) yields an observed F value of 19.148. Not surprisingly, this is exactly the same F value we obtained earlier for the omnibus test without normalizing the trend variables. As we stated then, the choice of D variables is irrelevant for the omnibus multivariate test. However, the matrices that result from orthonormal variables have some special properties, which is why we have gone to all the trouble of normalizing the variables. It is to these properties that we now turn.

Comparison of the Two Approaches

To compare the $\mathbf{E}^*(\mathbf{F})$ and $\mathbf{E}^*(\mathbf{R})$ matrices of the multivariate approach to results from the mixed-model approach, we first need to see what the mixed-model results are for these data.

TABLE 13.16
MIXED-MODEL ANALYSIS OF THE DATA IN TABLE 13.2

Source	SS	df	MS	F	p
Time	37.3333	2	18.6667	11.2	.0015
Subjects × time	23.3333	14	1.6667		

Table 13.16 shows the ANOVA table that is produced by a mixed-model analysis of the data in Table 13.2. Although it is apparent that the mixed-model approach agrees with the multivariate approach that the null hypothesis should be rejected for these data, we want to focus our attention on another similarity between the two approaches.

From Table 13.16, the sum of squares for the subjects by time interaction is 23.3333. Recall from Chapter 11 that this interaction sum of squares is also the error sum of squares for the full model in the mixed-model approach. Does this value have an analog in the multivariate approach? At first, the answer would seem to be no, because there is an entire matrix of errors for the full model in the multivariate approach. Before reaching this conclusion, however, let's look closely at the full matrix for our data:

$$\mathbf{E}^*(\mathbf{F}) = \begin{bmatrix} 16.0000 & -7.5055 \\ -7.5055 & 7.3333 \end{bmatrix}$$

You may have noticed that the sum of the two diagonal elements of $\mathbf{E}^*(\mathbf{F})$ (i.e., 16.0000 and 7.3333) equals the sum of squared errors (23.3333) for the full model in the mixed-model approach. Such an equality always holds when the D variables have been formed through orthonormal contrasts.[7] We discuss later why the mixed-model approach does not make use of information in the off-diagonal elements of the error matrix. Before pursuing this issue, however, we explore whether there is a similar equality for the restricted models of the two approaches.

From Table 13.16, the sum of squares for the time main effect is 37.3333. Recall from Chapter 11 that the main-effect sum of squares is the difference between the sum of squared errors of the full model and the restricted model in the mixed-model approach. Once again, this value can easily be reproduced from the multivariate approach. The matrix for the restricted model for our data is

$$\mathbf{E}^*(\mathbf{R}) = \begin{bmatrix} 52.0000 & -0.5774 \\ -0.5774 & 8.6667 \end{bmatrix}$$

The sum of the diagonal elements (i.e., 52.0000 and 8.6667) is 60.6667. Subtracting the sum of the diagonal elements of $\mathbf{E}^*(\mathbf{F})$ from the sum of the diagonal elements of $\mathbf{E}^*(\mathbf{R})$ yields $60.6667 - 23.3333 = 37.3333$, which equals the sum of squares for the main effect in the mixed model.

This same relationship between the multivariate and the mixed models holds as long as the contrasts defining the D variables are orthonormal. To formalize the relationship, it is helpful to know that the sum of the diagonal elements of a square matrix is called the *trace* of the matrix. The expression $tr(\mathbf{A})$ is used to indicate the trace of a matrix $\mathbf{A}$. With this knowledge, the formula for the mixed-model F can be written in terms of the multivariate matrices as

$$F = \frac{\{tr(\mathbf{E}^*(\mathbf{R})) - tr(\mathbf{E}^*(\mathbf{F}))\}/(a-1)}{tr(\mathbf{E}^*(\mathbf{F}))/(n-1)(a-1)} \qquad (32)$$

where the asterisk (*) is a reminder that the matrices must have been formed from orthonormal contrasts. Taking another look at the formula for the multivariate F shows that it differs from the mixed-model F in two respects:

$$F = \frac{(|\mathbf{E}(\mathbf{R})| - |\mathbf{E}(\mathbf{F})|)/(a-1)}{|\mathbf{E}(\mathbf{F})|/(n-a+1)} \qquad \text{(22, repeated)}$$

First and most important, the multivariate approach is based on the determinants of matrices, whereas the mixed-model approach is based on traces of matrices. The practical implication of this difference is that the determinant is a function of all elements of the matrix, whereas the trace obviously depends only on the diagonal elements. As a result, the multivariate approach is sensitive to relationships among the D variables, whereas the mixed-model approach is not. Second, the mixed-model approach has larger denominator degrees of freedom than does the multivariate approach.

It is important to emphasize that Equation 32 produces the correct mixed-model F value only when the D variables are orthonormal. This requirement has not only theoretical but also practical implications. As of this writing, the SPSS MANOVA procedure can produce both the mixed-model F test and the multivariate F test in a single MANOVA statement. The mixed-model F is invoked by an AVERF command.[8] For the AVERF to be correct, MANOVA creates an orthonormal set of contrasts, even if the user has specified a set of nonorthogonal contrasts. In other words, in this situation, MANOVA does not use the D variables that the user has specified. As a result, the univariate tests printed out by the program are misleading because they do not correspond to the D variables that were input by the user. Because of this possible confusion, it is always wise to request that the statistical package print the relationship between the original Y variables and the new D variables. This is accomplished in SPSS MANOVA by specifying PRINT = TRANSFORM. Although neither SPSS GLM nor SAS procedures suffer from this particular point of potential confusion, this example should serve as a warning to individuals who assume that they can obtain correct information from statistical packages without having to learn any statistical theory.

At this point, we are ready to consider why the mixed-model approach, unlike the multivariate approach, ignores the off-diagonal elements of the error matrices. The basic distinction between the two approaches is that the mixed-model approach requires an assumption of sphericity. Recall from Chapter 11 that sphericity is a property exhibited by certain specific forms of the covariance matrix for the Y variables. Huynh and Feldt (1970) and Rouanet and Lépine (1970) showed independently that the population covariance matrix of the Y variables possesses sphericity if and only if the population $\mathbf{E}^*(\mathbf{F})$ matrix of an orthonormal set of D variables possesses two properties: the off-diagonal elements all equal zero, and every diagonal element is the same. Because both of these properties are important, we discuss each in some detail.

If the mixed-model assumption of sphericity has been met, the population values of the off-diagonal elements of $\mathbf{E}^*(\mathbf{F})$ are all zero. Of course, sample values differ somewhat from zero, but any such discrepancies reflect nothing more than sampling error if the sphericity assumption is satisfied. In this case, there is no reason whatsoever to incorporate information from the off-diagonal elements into a test statistic because there is literally no information in these values. They simply reflect random fluctuations around zero. However, if the sphericity assumption is not met, the off-diagonal population elements of $\mathbf{E}^*(\mathbf{F})$ are not generally zero. In this case, these elements do contain useful information. The multivariate approach makes use of this information, whereas the mixed-model approach ignores these values and thus implicitly assumes incorrectly that they reflect only random fluctuations. Thus, in summary, when sphericity holds, the multivariate test is suboptimal because it includes random and irrelevant information (i.e., noise) in its decision. However, when sphericity fails to hold, the mixed-model test is suboptimal because it fails to include relevant information in its decision. Although it may be overly simplistic, in a sense our general preference for the multivariate test is based on the belief that incorporating irrelevant information is a less serious error than failing to incorporate relevant information. As we see shortly, this intuitive view translates into statistical considerations of Type I and Type II error rates that ultimately form the basis for our preference.

If the sphericity assumption holds, it is also the case that all diagonal elements of the population $\mathbf{E}^*(\mathbf{F})$ matrix are equal to each other. In essence, this is a homogeneity of variance assumption. That this is so can be seen by recalling that a diagonal element of $\mathbf{E}^*(\mathbf{F})$ is simply a sum-of-squared deviations from the mean. If each element is divided by n (in the population) or $n-1$ (in the sample), the result is a variance. Thus, requiring equal diagonal elements of $\mathbf{E}^*(\mathbf{F})$ is equivalent to requiring equality of variances of each D^* variable. In symbols, the assumption is that $\sigma_{D_1^*}^2 = \sigma_{D_2^*}^2 = \cdots = \sigma_{D_{a-1}^*}^2$. Of course, even if such an equality holds in the population, the corresponding sample variances (e.g., $s_{D_1^*}^2, s_{D_2^*}^2$) differ at least slightly from each other because of sampling error.

OPTIONAL

Reconceptualization of ε in Terms of E*(F)

We saw in the previous section that one difference between the multivariate approach and the mixed-model approach is that the multivariate approach is based on all elements of the $\mathbf{E}^*(\mathbf{F})$ matrix, whereas the mixed-model approach uses only the diagonal elements of $\mathbf{E}^*(\mathbf{F})$. When homogeneity holds, only the diagonal elements are relevant; but when homogeneity does not hold, it is a mistake to ignore the off-diagonal elements of the $\mathbf{E}^*(\mathbf{F})$ matrix.

One perspective on understanding how the ε-adjusted tests improve on the unadjusted mixed-model test is to realize that the ε-adjusted tests incorporate information about the off-diagonal elements of the $\mathbf{E}^*(\mathbf{F})$ matrix into their calculation. Huynh (1978) showed that $\hat{\varepsilon}$ can be calculated from the elements of the $\mathbf{E}^*(\mathbf{F})$ matrix in the following manner:

$$\hat{\varepsilon} = \frac{\left(\sum_{i=1}^{a-1} E_{ii}^*(\mathbf{F})\right)^2}{(a-1)\sum_{i=1}^{a-1}\sum_{j=1}^{a-1}(E_{ij}^*(\mathbf{F}))^2} \tag{33}$$

where $E_{ij}^*(\mathbf{F})$ refers to the element in row i and column j of the $\mathbf{E}^*(\mathbf{F})$ matrix. Before proceeding to discuss the theoretical implications of this formula, it may be helpful to demonstrate its use on the data from Table 13.2. We saw in the previous section that $\mathbf{E}^*(\mathbf{F})$ for these data is given by

$$\mathbf{E}^*(\mathbf{F}) = \begin{bmatrix} 16.0000 & -7.5055 \\ -7.5055 & 7.3333 \end{bmatrix}$$

It then follows that the numerator of $\hat{\varepsilon}$ equals

$$\left(\sum_{i=1}^{a-1} E_{ii}^*(F)\right)^2 = (16.0000 + 7.3333)^2 = (23.3333)^2 = 544.4429$$

Similarly, the denominator of $\hat{\varepsilon}$ equals

$$(a-1)\sum_{i=1}^{a-1}\sum_{j=1}^{a-1}(E_{ij}^*(F))^2 = (3-1)[(16.0000)^2 + (-7.5055)^2 + (-7.5055)^2 + (7.3333)^2]$$

$$= 844.8847$$

Thus, the value of $\hat{\varepsilon}$ for these data is

$$\hat{\varepsilon} = \frac{544.4429}{844.8847} = 0.64444$$

If we wanted, we could now use Equation 11.34 to find the corresponding value of $\tilde{\varepsilon}$:

$$\tilde{\varepsilon} = \frac{n(a-1)\hat{\varepsilon} - 2}{(a-1)[n-1-(a-1)\hat{\varepsilon}]} \qquad\qquad \text{(11.34, repeated)}$$

which for our data yields $\tilde{\varepsilon} = 0.7276$.

What does Equation 33 for calculating $\hat{\varepsilon}$ from the $E^*(F)$ matrix reveal about the nature of the $\hat{\varepsilon}$ adjustment? First, notice that the adjusted test, unlike the unadjusted mixed-model test, incorporates information about the off-diagonal elements of $E^*(F)$ into the test. Because the off-diagonal elements are squared and appear only in the denominator of the expression for $\hat{\varepsilon}$ (see Equation 33), larger off-diagonal elements of $E^*(F)$ (either positive or negative) lead to lower values of $\hat{\varepsilon}$. This should seem reasonable, because remember that when homogeneity holds, the off-diagonal elements deviate from zero only because of sampling error. In this case, the off-diagonal elements should have values close to zero, minimizing their influence in the denominator. However, when homogeneity is not met, the off-diagonal elements may be nonzero even in the population. In this case, the off-diagonal elements may deviate appreciably from zero, causing $\hat{\varepsilon}$ to be much less than 1.0. Thus, if homogeneity is violated, $\hat{\varepsilon}$ tends to compensate for the violation by reducing the degrees of freedom of the critical value.

Second, we saw in the previous section that if homogeneity holds, the diagonal elements of the population $E^*(F)$ matrix are equal to each other. Although it may not be immediately obvious from Equation 33, $\hat{\varepsilon}$ is also sensitive to the degree of inequality of the diagonal elements of $E^*(F)$. This point can be understood most easily by comparing two hypothetical $E^*(F)$ matrices, both of which have off-diagonal elements of zero. Let's first consider such an $E^*(F)$ matrix that also has equal diagonal elements. For example, $E^*(F)$ might equal

$$E^*(F) = \begin{bmatrix} 9 & 0 \\ 0 & 9 \end{bmatrix}$$

From Equation 33, $\hat{\varepsilon}$ for this matrix equals

$$\hat{\varepsilon} = \frac{(9+9)^2}{(3-1)(9^2 + 0^2 + 0^2 + 9^2)} = \frac{324}{2(81+81)} = 1.0$$

Of course, we would expect $\hat{\varepsilon}$ to equal 1.0 when the homogeneity assumption is perfectly satisfied, as it is here. Now, however, let's consider another $E^*(F)$ matrix, which again has off-diagonal elements of zero, but this time has unequal diagonal elements. For example, $E^*(F)$ might equal

$$E^*(F) = \begin{bmatrix} 15 & 0 \\ 0 & 3 \end{bmatrix}$$

From Equation 33, $\hat{\varepsilon}$ for this matrix equals

$$\hat{\varepsilon} = \frac{(15+3)^2}{(3-1)(15^2 + 0^2 + 0^2 + 3^2)} = \frac{324}{468} = 0.6923$$

Thus, unequal diagonal elements of $\mathbf{E}^*(\mathbf{F})$ lower the value of $\hat{\varepsilon}$.

Using the $\hat{\varepsilon}$ adjustment (or $\tilde{\varepsilon}$) allows the mixed-model F test to be sensitive to the entire $\mathbf{E}^*(\mathbf{F})$ matrix, removing a typical inadequacy of the unadjusted mixed-model test. When homogeneity holds, off-diagonal elements of $\mathbf{E}^*(\mathbf{F})$ are near zero, and the diagonal elements are nearly equal to each other. As a result, $\hat{\varepsilon}$ (and $\tilde{\varepsilon}$) are close to 1.0, and the degrees of freedom for the critical value of the adjusted test are close to those of the unadjusted test. However, when homogeneity does not hold, off-diagonal elements of $\mathbf{E}^*(\mathbf{F})$ are farther from zero, and/or the diagonal elements vary from each other in value. As a result, $\hat{\varepsilon}$ (and $\tilde{\varepsilon}$) may be substantially less than 1.0, lowering the degrees of freedom for the critical value of the adjusted test. The corresponding increase in the critical value itself prevents the increase in Type I errors that would occur with the unadjusted mixed-model test.

■

MULTIVARIATE AND MIXED-MODEL APPROACHES FOR TESTING CONTRASTS

Although the homogeneity of variance of D^* variables is an assumption required for the mixed-model omnibus test, its validity is even more important for testing contrasts. Recall from our discussion of homogeneity of variance in between-subjects designs that the omnibus test there is rather robust to violations of this assumption (with equal n, which we have in the repeated-measures design) but that tests of contrasts are not robust. In the between-subjects design, when homogeneity fails, it is necessary to use an error term specific to each contrast. The same logic applies in the within-subjects design. Furthermore, the multivariate approach uses a specific error term, but the mixed-model approach does not.

We should state that throughout the remainder of this chapter, when we refer to the mixed-model approach for testing contrasts, we mean the use of a pooled error term. In the one-way within-subjects design, this is an error term of the form $MS_{A \times S}$, to be used for testing any contrast of interest. As we mentioned in Chapters 11 and 12, it is also possible to use a separate (or, specific) error term. In the one-way within-subjects design, this is an error term of the form $MS_{A_{comp} \times S}$, whose value changes depending on the particular comparison being tested.

Before comparing the use of pooled and separate error terms in detail, we must explain why we equate the use of a pooled error term with the mixed-model approach and the use of a separate error term with the multivariate approach. If planned comparisons are tested, using a pooled error term parallels the mixed-model approach for the omnibus test because both assume sphericity. The use of a separate error term parallels the multivariate approach for the omnibus test because neither assumes sphericity. In fact, the observed F value obtained using a separate error term is literally identical to the F value that is obtained from Equation 6 for testing a contrast with the multivariate approach.

When post hoc tests are conducted, there is an even stronger connection between the mixed-model approach and the pooled error term, and between the multivariate approach and the separate error term. The mixed-model omnibus test is statistically significant if and only if a statistically significant comparison can be found using a pooled error term and a critical value (CV) of the form

$$CV = (a - 1)F_{.05; a-1, (a-1)(n-1)} \tag{11.42, repeated}$$

However, the multivariate omnibus test is statistically significant if and only if a statistically significant comparison can be found using a separate error term and a CV of the form

$$CV = (n-1)(a-1)F_{\alpha_{FW}; a-1, n-a+1}/(n-a+1) \qquad \text{(27, repeated)}$$

Thus, using a pooled error term is compatible with the mixed-model approach, and using a separate error term is compatible with the multivariate approach.

Despite this compatibility, testing the omnibus hypothesis with the mixed-model approach and testing comparisons using a separate error term is sometimes recommended. The problem with this combination is that inconsistencies may arise. For example, it is possible to obtain a statistically significant omnibus test, but then be able to find no significant contrasts, because none exists with a separate error term (when compared to the appropriate post hoc CV, as given in Equation 27). It is also possible for the omnibus test to be nonsignificant, yet a significant post hoc comparison could have been found using a separate error term. As a consequence, if a separate error term is used for testing contrasts, there is no purpose to performing a mixed-model omnibus test. However, the multivariate test would be useful because it informs us as to whether any significant contrasts exist, using a separate error term.

Thus, to reiterate, in our terminology, the mixed-model approach to testing a contrast refers to the use of a pooled error term, and the multivariate approach to testing a contrast refers to the use of a separate error term.

Numerical Example

To make the presentation of the multivariate and mixed-model approaches more concrete, let's reconsider the data of Table 13.2. How would the multivariate and mixed-model approaches differ in the way that the linear trend (for example) would be tested? To begin to answer the question, let's take another look at the $\mathbf{E}^*(\mathbf{F})$ and $\mathbf{E}^*(\mathbf{R})$ matrices for the normalized linear and quadratic trends for our data:

$$\mathbf{E}^*(\mathbf{F}) = \begin{bmatrix} 16.000 & -7.5055 \\ -7.5055 & 7.3333 \end{bmatrix}$$

$$\mathbf{E}^*(\mathbf{R}) = \begin{bmatrix} 52.0000 & -0.5774 \\ -0.5774 & 8.6667 \end{bmatrix}$$

For ease of discussion, we again let $E_{ij}^*(\mathbf{F})$ and $E_{ij}^*(\mathbf{R})$ refer to the element in row i and column j of the full and restricted error matrices, respectively. We have already seen that the multivariate approach to testing an individual contrast consists simply of treating the relevant D variable as a single variable, at which point a univariate test is conducted. In terms of symbols,

$$\text{multi } F = \frac{E_{11}^*(\mathbf{R}) - E_{11}^*(\mathbf{F})}{E_{11}^*(\mathbf{F})/(n-1)} \qquad (34)$$

is the expression for testing D_1 in the multivariate approach. For our data, $E_{11}^*(\mathbf{F}) = 16$ and $E_{11}^*(\mathbf{R}) = 52$, so the F value is $(52 - 16)/[16/(8 - 1)] = 15.75$. The mixed-model approach uses the same numerator but a different denominator. The mixed-model approach assumes homogeneity of variance, which means that the two diagonal elements of $\mathbf{E}^*(\mathbf{F})$ [i.e., $E_{11}^*(\mathbf{F})$ and $E_{22}^*(\mathbf{F})$] should be equal except for sampling error. Based on this assumption, the average of $E_{11}^*(\mathbf{F})$ and $E_{22}^*(\mathbf{F})$ is a better estimate of the population variance than either term is by itself. Thus, instead of using $E_{11}^*(F)$ in the denominator, the mixed-model approach uses $(E_{11}^*(F) + E_{22}^*(F))/2$. In general, there are $a - 1$ such terms, so we would have

$$(E_{11}^*(F) + E_{22}^*(F) + \cdots + E_{(a-1)(a-1)}^*(F))/(a - 1)$$

We can simplify this expression by realizing that the sum of E^* elements here is simply the sum of the diagonal elements of $\mathbf{E}^*(\mathbf{F})$, which is the trace of $\mathbf{E}^*(\mathbf{F})$ and is written as $tr(\mathbf{E}^*(\mathbf{F}))$. Thus, the formula for the mixed-model F test of the D_1 contrast can be obtained by substituting $tr(\mathbf{E}^*(\mathbf{F}))/(a - 1)$ for $E_{11}^*(F)$ in the denominator of the multivariate approach of Equation 34. The result of this substitution yields

$$\text{mixed } F = \frac{E_{11}^*(R) - E_{11}^*(F)}{tr(\mathbf{E}^*(\mathbf{F}))/(a - 1)(n - 1)} \tag{35}$$

For our data, $E_{11}^*(R) = 52$, $E_{11}^*(F) = 16$, and $tr(\mathbf{E}^*(\mathbf{F})) = 23.3333$, so the observed mixed-model F for the linear trend is

$$F = \frac{52 - 16}{23.3333/(3 - 1)(8 - 1)} = 21.6$$

Notice that the mixed-model value of 21.6 is nearly 40% larger than the multivariate F value of 15.75. Before discussing whether this increase is a real improvement, it is useful to consider the F statistics of Equations 34 and 35 from another perspective.

The Difference in Error Terms

Recall that we showed that the trace of $\mathbf{E}^*(\mathbf{F})$ is equal to the mixed-model error sum of squares for its full model. However, this error sum of squares is also $SS_{A \times S}$, the sum of squares for the interaction of the factor (A) and subjects (S). Hence, Equation 35 can be rewritten as:

$$\text{mixed } F = \frac{E_{11}^*(R) - E_{11}^*(F)}{SS_{A \times S}/(a - 1)(n - 1)}$$

Because the term $(a - 1)(n - 1)$ represents the interaction degrees of freedom, the expression can be simplified to

$$\text{mixed } F = \frac{E_{11}^*(R) - E_{11}^*(F)}{MS_{A \times S}} \tag{36}$$

Thus, the mixed-model approach uses $MS_{A \times S}$, the same error term as used in the omnibus test, for testing all contrasts.

The multivariate approach, however, uses $E_{11}^*(F)/n - 1$ as the error term, that is, as the denominator of the F. Remember that $E_{11}^*(F)$ is simply the sum of squared deviations from the mean for D_1. Dividing this quantity by $n - 1$ results in a variance, namely $s_{D_1^*}^2$, the variance of the D_1^* variable. Also, we saw earlier in the chapter that the difference in sum of squared errors of the restricted and full models—that is, $E_{11}^*(R) - E_{11}^*(F)$—equals $n(\overline{D}_1^*)^2$. Thus, Equation 34 for the multivariate approach to testing a contrast can be rewritten as

$$\text{multi } F = \frac{n(\overline{D}_1^*)^2}{s_{D_1^*}^2} \tag{37}$$

In fact, this formula (which is really the same as Equation 6) can be used regardless of whether the contrast coefficients for the D_1 variable are normalized. However, we have written the equation in its normalized form to facilitate comparison with the mixed-model equation. Following the same logic for the mixed-model approach, the trace of $\mathbf{E}^*(\mathbf{F})$ is the sum of $a - 1$ sums of squared deviations from their respective means. Dividing by $n - 1$ results in $a - 1$ variances, one for each D^* variable. Thus, Equation 35 can be written as

$$\text{mixed } F = \frac{n(\overline{D_1^*})^2}{\left(s_{D_1^*}^2 + s_{D_2^*}^2 + \cdots + s_{D_{a-1}^*}^2 \right) / (a - 1)}$$

To simplify our notation, let's let $\overline{s}_{D^*}^2$ represent the mean variance of the $a - 1 D^*$ variables. Then the F statistic for the mixed-model approach to testing a contrast is

$$\text{mixed } F = \frac{n(\overline{D_1^*})^2}{\overline{s}_{D^*}^2} \tag{38}$$

Comparing Equations 37 and 38 shows quite obviously that there is only one difference between the multivariate and the mixed-model approaches to testing a contrast. The multivariate approach uses an error term specific to the particular contrast being tested, whereas the mixed-model approach uses a pooled error term based on the average variance of the $a - 1$ orthonormal variables. Which approach is better? Intuition would suggest that the multivariate approach is better if the population variances are unequal, whereas the mixed-model approach is better if the population variances are equal. In this case, intuition is correct, which leads to three further questions. If the variances are equal, to what extent is the mixed-model approach superior to the multivariate approach? If they are unequal, to what extent is the multivariate approach better? Finally, how likely is it that population variances are equal?

Which Error Term Is Better?

If the homogeneity of variance assumption is valid for the $a - 1$ orthonormal D variables, the mixed-model approach is superior to the multivariate approach for testing contrasts. As comparing Equations 37 and 38 shows, the mixed-model approach uses a pooled (i.e., average) variance in the denominator, whereas the multivariate approach does not. If homogeneity holds, the long-run expected values of the two denominators are equal. As a result, the observed value of the F statistic for the two approaches differs only because of sampling error. In the long run, both approaches yield the same average observed F value.[9] However, in a particular sample, the mixed-model estimate of the population variance is likely better than the estimate of the multivariate approach because the mixed-model estimate is based on additional data. This advantage is reflected in the denominator degrees of freedom, which equal $(n - 1)(a - 1)$ for the mixed-model approach but only $n - 1$ for the multivariate approach. As a consequence of the increased degrees of freedom, the mixed-model critical value is always at least slightly less than the critical value of the multivariate approach, regardless of whether the comparison is planned or post hoc. For example, for the data of Table 13.2, where $n = 8$ and $a = 3$, an α_{PC} of .05 would imply a critical F value of 5.59 for the multivariate approach and 4.60 for the mixed-model approach. If the sample size were larger, the difference would be smaller. For example, if $n = 21$ and $a = 3$, an α_{PC} of .05 implies critical F values of 4.35 and 4.08 for the multivariate and mixed-model approaches, respectively. Of course, all other things being equal, a lower critical value is preferable because it implies greater statistical power. However, the difference in power is generally not very large, unless the sample size is quite small. For example, even when n is only 8, if we assume that $a = 3$, $\alpha_{PC} = .05$, and $\phi = 2.1$, the power of the multivariate approach is 0.72, whereas the power of the mixed-model approach is 0.79. As expected, for larger sample sizes, the difference in power is even smaller. In the preceding example, if n were 21 instead of 8, the power of the multivariate approach would be 0.81, whereas the power of the mixed-model approach would be 0.83. It should be realized that the relative power differences generally increase when α_{PC} is effectively lowered (either because of multiple planned comparisons or because of post hoc adjustments). Nevertheless, the power advantage of the mixed-model approach for testing contrasts is typically small even when the homogeneity of variance assumption is met.

If the homogeneity of variance assumption fails to hold for the $a - 1$ orthonormal D^* variables, the mixed-model approach to testing contrasts encounters serious difficulties. As in the between-subjects design, tests of some contrasts are overly conservative (implying lowered power), whereas tests of other contrasts are too liberal (i.e., too many Type I errors are made) if homogeneity fails. Boik (1981) showed that departures from nominal values can be severe for some contrasts even when the ε value for the covariance matrix indicates only a slight departure from sphericity. Two examples from the data in Table 13.2 illustrate the extent of differences between the two approaches. First, consider a test of the linear trend. We found earlier that $E_{11}^*(R) - E_{11}^*(F) = 36$ for the linear trend and that $E_{11}^*(F) = 16$ for this variable individually. We applied Equations 34 and 35 to these data and discovered that the observed F value of the multivariate approach is 15.75 and that the F value of the mixed-model approach is 21.6. Although the larger F value might at first seem to be better because it is more significant, further thought reveals that the F value can be larger for only one of two reasons: either the F is larger because of random sampling error or the homogeneity assumption has been violated. The former explanation is not really an advantage because random error is obviously just as likely to produce a smaller F as it is a larger F. However, if the homogeneity assumption has been violated, the mixed-model approach uses an inappropriate error term. As a result of using an error term that is too small, the Type I error rate exceeds .05, perhaps even doubling or tripling it. Thus, in neither case is this larger observed F value an advantage. As a second example, consider testing the difference between the means of Time 1 and Time 2. This difference can be tested by constructing a D variable of the form $D = Y_2 - Y_1$, which we considered in Tables 13.3 and 13.4. In nonnormalized form, we found that $E_{11}(F) = 6$ and $E_{11}(R) = 38$. Although we could immediately write the F of the multivariate approach as

$$F = \frac{38 - 6}{6/(8 - 1)}$$

we instead consider the comparable sums of squared errors for the normalized D variable because these values are required by the mixed-model approach. Because the sum of squared coefficients for the D variable, as constructed above, equals 2, the normalized sums of squares are one-half of the previously discussed values. Thus, $E_{11}^*(F) = 3$, and $E_{11}^*(R) = 19$. As a result, the F of the multivariate approach is given by

$$F = \frac{19 - 3}{3/(8 - 1)} = 37.3333$$

The mixed-model approach has the same numerator but uses $MS_{A \times S}$ as the denominator. As Table 13.16 shows, $MS_{A \times S} = 1.6667$ for the data. Thus, the F value of the mixed-model approach equals

$$F = \frac{19 - 3}{1.6667} = 9.6$$

Thus, the observed F of the mixed-model approach is only slightly more than one-quarter as large as the F of the multivariate approach. This calculation demonstrates vividly that the multivariate approach is not always conservative (in the sense of a lower F value) just because it does not take the gamble of assuming homogeneity. If homogeneity fails, there are by mathematical necessity some contrasts whose observed F value tends to be less with the mixed-model approach than with the multivariate approach. Tests of such contrasts are too conservative with the mixed-model approach, and power is lowered. However, there are also other contrasts for which the mixed-model approach yields too many rejections of the null hypothesis, that is, too many Type I errors. It should also be noted that ε adjustments used for the omnibus mixed-model approach are of questionable benefit for testing contrasts. The effect of either an $\hat{\varepsilon}$ or an $\tilde{\varepsilon}$ adjustment is to increase the critical value for all contrasts because the denominator degrees of freedom are lowered from $(n - 1)(a - 1)$ to either $\hat{\varepsilon}(n - 1)(a - 1)$ or $\tilde{\varepsilon}(n - 1)(a - 1)$. However, the observed F value would be unchanged. In particular, the error term would still be $MS_{A \times S}$ for all contrasts. Although using the larger critical value that results from ε adjustment tends to prevent excessive Type I errors for some contrasts, it also makes tests of other contrasts even more conservative than they would have been without the adjustment. In essence, ε adjustments are of limited value for testing contrasts because they always lower the probability of a rejection, as compared to an unadjusted test using $MS_{A \times S}$ as the error term. However, as the multivariate approach shows, the problem with using $MS_{A \times S}$ as the error term for testing all contrasts is that it is sometimes too small and at other times too large. The multivariate approach solves this problem by sometimes using a denominator larger than $MS_{A \times S}$ and at other times using a denominator smaller than $MS_{A \times S}$. No such solution is available with the mixed-model approach, adjusted or unadjusted, because $MS_{A \times S}$ is still used as the error term for testing all contrasts. In summary, tests of contrasts conducted from the mixed-model formulas are not robust to violations of the homogeneity of variance assumption.

This lack of robustness leads to our third question: How likely is it that the assumption of equal population variances is valid? The assumption of equal variances for $a - 1$ orthonormal D^* variables is met if the covariance matrix of the a original variables possesses sphericity. As was discussed in Chapter 11, this assumption is equivalent to an assumption of homogeneity of treatment-difference variances. For all practical purposes, in a single-factor repeated-measures design, this assumption implies that all population correlations between the a original variables must be equal and all a original variables must have the same variance. Such a requirement is very restrictive, and unlikely to be satisfied in practice. For example, in many applications, the repeated factor is time. Observations obtained closer in time almost inevitably correlate more highly than those separated further in time. When this happens, the homogeneity assumption is violated. However, when the repeated factor represents some dimension other than time, it is more likely that the homogeneity assumption might be at least approximately true. Even so, as we mentioned previously, Boik (1981) showed that even small departures from the assumption can drastically affect the Type I and Type II error rates for testing certain individual contrasts. Thus, the mixed-model approach for testing contrasts should be avoided, unless clear evidence is available to indicate that the homogeneity assumption has been met. As mentioned in Chapter 11, Mauchly's test is a procedure for testing the null hypothesis that the homogeneity condition holds in the population.

However, as O'Brien and Kaiser (1985) point out, Mauchly's test is adversely affected by nonnormality, tending to accept the homogeneity assumption too often for short-tailed distributions and to reject too often for heavy-tailed distributions. As Huynh and Mandeville (1979) show, these tendencies become even more pronounced for larger sample sizes, so large n is no protection. Of course, with small n, the test might fail to reject the assumption simply because of low power resulting from an insufficient sample size. In summary, there are few circumstances in which researchers can be even relatively certain that their data satisfy the homogeneity assumption required by the mixed-model approach. In the absence of such assurance, mixed-model tests of certain individual contrasts may be severely distorted. As a consequence, our recommendation is that contrasts in repeated-measures designs routinely be tested using the multivariate approach with a separate error term specific to each individual contrast.

A GENERAL COMPARISON OF THE MULTIVARIATE AND MIXED-MODEL APPROACHES

We have presented in some detail two rather different approaches for analyzing data from repeated-measures designs: the multivariate approach and the mixed-model approach. Of course, in some respects the situation is even more complicated, because there are several possible methods for adjusting degrees of freedom in the mixed-model approach. The purpose of this section is to summarize the advantages and disadvantages of each approach. As often happens in statistics, if we had enough prior knowledge about certain characteristics of the population, it would be immediately apparent which approach would be superior for our data. However, the amount and type of information required to make a choice that we would know to be optimal is rarely if ever available in the behavioral sciences. As a consequence, we must consider the relative costs of using a less than optimal approach as well as the likelihood that requisite assumptions of the two approaches are met.

Assumptions

A fundamental difference between the two approaches is that they require different statistical assumptions. As stressed repeatedly throughout our discussion, the basic difference in assumptions is that the mixed-model approach makes an assumption of homogeneity that is not required by the multivariate approach. We have seen that this assumption can be expressed in any of four equivalent ways. First, the assumption can be stated as a homogeneity of population treatment-difference variances; this form of the assumption was emphasized in Chapter 11. Second, an equivalent expression of the assumption is that the variables in a set of $a - 1$ orthonormal D^* contrast variables must be uncorrelated and have equal variances in the population. Third, in terms of matrices, the assumption requires that the error matrix for the full model for any set of $a - 1$ orthonormal D^* variables must have a certain restrictive form in the population. Specifically, the off-diagonal elements must equal zero (corresponding to a correlation coefficient of zero), and the diagonal elements must be a common value (corresponding to equal variances). The fourth form of the expression is not theoretically necessary for the mixed-model approach to be valid. However, in the single-factor repeated-measures design, the three forms of stating the assumption imply for all practical purposes that two conditions are both true of the original Y variables. First, the population correlation between any pair of variables is a constant. Second, every variable has the same population variance. Stating the assumption in this form makes it clear that this assumption required by the mixed-model approach is unlikely to be met in most repeated-measures designs. Thus, the multivariate approach is preferable to the mixed-model approach in that the assumptions required by the mixed-model approach are more restrictive and less likely to be satisfied in practice.[10]

Although the multivariate approach is generally superior to the mixed-model approach with respect to assumptions, there are other dimensions that must also be considered. In particular, we compare the two approaches along three additional dimensions: tests of contrasts, Type I error rates for the omnibus tests, and Type II error rates for the omnibus tests.

Tests of Contrasts

The most persuasive argument for the multivariate approach is that it is "the natural generalization of the use of the specific type of error term for contrasts with 1 degree of freedom" (O'Brien & Kaiser, 1985, p. 319). The mixed-model approach, however, is consistent with the use of a pooled (average) error term. We have seen that the use of such an average error term can be extremely misleading in the absence of homogeneity. If contrasts are to be tested with a specific error term, as we think they should be, then it seems appropriate to adopt a consistent approach for the omnibus test. As we said earlier in the chapter, a significant contrast exists using a specific error term and an appropriate critical value (given by Equation 27) if and only if the omnibus test is significant with the multivariate approach. In general, there is no relationship between tests of contrasts with a specific error term and the omnibus test of the mixed-model approach, either adjusted or unadjusted. Consistency between the omnibus test and tests of contrasts, which only the multivariate approach provides, is the primary reason we recommend it as the better approach. The only exception occurs when n is very small relative to a, which is a problem we discuss in terms of Type II error rates.

Type I Error Rates

Before we compare the approaches with respect to Type II error, we first consider Type I error. When the homogeneity assumption is not satisfied, the use of the unadjusted mixed-model approach cannot be recommended because its actual Type I error rate can reach double or triple the nominal α level. In other words, when α is set at .05, the mixed-model analysis may reject the null hypothesis 10% or even 15% of the time despite the fact that the null hypothesis is true. Two alternatives are available: an ε adjustment of the degrees of freedom in the mixed-model approach or the multivariate approach. There are theoretical reasons to prefer the multivariate alternative, because when multivariate normality holds, its actual α level is guaranteed mathematically to be equal to the desired nominal α level. The ε-adjustment procedures, however, are only approximate. There is no guarantee that the actual α level will remain at the nominal value. Nevertheless, numerous empirical studies (see Maxwell & Arvey, 1982, for a review) have demonstrated that the ε-adjustment procedures (particularly $\hat{\varepsilon}$) maintain the actual α near the nominal value across a wide range of conditions. Thus, in theory, Type I error rate considerations favor the multivariate approach. However empirical evidence suggests that the ε-adjusted mixed-model approaches represent a viable alternative with respect to Type I error.

Type II Error Rates

The situation with respect to Type II error is extremely complicated. Before considering the complexities, we remind you that the discussion of Type II error is also in reality a discussion of power, because the statistical power of a test equals 1.0 minus the probability of a Type II error. If it were known that all assumptions of the mixed-model approach were met, it would provide the most powerful method of analysis for repeated-measures data. For this reason (and because the actual α level would equal the nominal α level), the mixed-model analysis would be superior to any other alternative. However, this superiority is limited in practice because the homogeneity assumption is unlikely to be satisfied. When the homogeneity assumption fails to hold, neither approach is uniformly more powerful than the other. Power comparisons are exceedingly complicated here, because the relative power of the mixed-model and multivariate approaches depends on the population means, the population covariance matrix, and the relationship of mean differences to covariances. (Exercises 14 and 15 at the end of the chapter illustrate this point in some detail.) For some parameter values, the mixed-model approach is more powerful, but for other parameter values, the multivariate approach is more powerful. Anticipating these parameter values correctly is very difficult in practice, except perhaps when pilot data are available or when very similar studies have already appeared in the literature. In situations in which parameter values can be anticipated with some accuracy, it is possible to choose between the multivariate and mixed-model approaches on the basis of a power analysis. In other words, a researcher can use procedures developed by Muller and Barton (1989), such as implemented in Elashoff (2000), to calculate the expected power of the mixed-model approach. Similar calculations can then be performed for the multivariate approach as described by such sources as Algina and Keselman (1997), Davidson (1972), and Vonesh and Schork (1986). Such parallel analyses can reveal which approach is likely to yield more power for a fixed sample size for a presumed pattern of means and covariances. Although we hope we have made clear that power is not the only consideration in choosing an approach, nevertheless, such planning may be very worthwhile when suitable prior estimates of population parameters are available.

Unfortunately, however, it is not unusual that prior estimates of population parameters are not available, or at least choosing between the two approaches based on any such estimates may seem ill-advised. This does not make power analysis any less relevant, but it does make it more complicated. Because this is such a complex topic, we must refer the interested reader to two excellent articles for details. Davidson (1972) provides an insightful comparison of the relative power of the multivariate and mixed-model tests. Algina and Keselman (1997) update and expand Davidson's earlier paper by considering a broad array of possible population configurations. We cannot go into all the nuances of what Davidson (1972) and Algina and Keselman (1997) found, but we can state some of their general conclusions.

One additional crucial factor influences the relative power of the mixed-model and multivariate approaches. Knowledge concerning this influence, unlike the population means and covariances, is available to the researcher, and in fact is even at least partially under his or her control. This additional influence is sample size. Not surprisingly, larger samples tend to produce greater power for both the mixed-model and the multivariate approaches. What is less intuitive but more important for our purposes is that sample size also influences the relative power of the two approaches. All other things being equal, the multivariate test is relatively less powerful than the mixed-model test as n decreases. Notice that this statement does not stipulate which test is more powerful than the other. Instead, it implies that if the multivariate test has a power advantage for a certain pattern of population means and covariances, the magnitude of the advantage tends to decrease for smaller n and increase for larger n. (In fact, for very small n, the power advantage of the multivariate approach may not just decrease, but may actually become a disadvantage, even when the pattern of means and covariances is otherwise favorable to the multivariate approach.) However, if the mixed-model test is more powerful for a particular pattern of population means and covariances, its advantage tends to be largest for small n. The practical implication of these results is that the multivariate test may lack power relative to the mixed-model test when n is small, especially if a is large. Unfortunately, there is no magical dividing line between "small" and "large," so it is impossible to state a precise rule for when n necessarily favors the mixed-model approach. In fact, such a rule is literally impossible, because the power of both approaches depends not only on n but also the population means and covariances. It is theoretically possible for the multivariate test to be more powerful than the mixed-model test even for very small n, if the means and covariances happen to relate in a manner that strongly favors the multivariate approach. Nevertheless, the multivariate approach is inadvisable for small n.

When a researcher lacks sufficient information to have confidence in a formal comparison of the two approaches, Algina and Keselman (1997) provide general guidelines for choosing between the two approaches. Specifically, they recommend the multivariate test if (1) $a \leq 4$, $\varepsilon \leq 0.90$, and $n \geq a + 15$ as well as when (2) $5 \leq a \leq 8$, $\varepsilon \leq 0.85$, and $n \geq a + 30$. When these conditions are not met, they recommend an adjusted mixed-model approach. Notice that the multivariate test tends to be preferable for moderately large samples when sphericity is violated. Also notice that they do not provide suggestions for more than eight levels, because they did not simulate such situations in their study. Of course, it may be difficult to anticipate prior to collecting data the likely value of ε and choosing between the approaches based on the observed value of ε in the sample may be problematic, but the general relevance of ε is clear. Algina and Keselman caution that even when their conditions are met, there is no guarantee that the multivariate approach is more powerful. Similarly, when the conditions are not met, it could be the case that the multivariate approach is actually more powerful. However, the relative power of the two approaches is likely to be more similar as one nears the boundaries of Algina and Keselman's (1997) conditions, so their guidelines are especially useful for delineating situations in which one approach tends to be more powerful than the other, as well as situations in which the two approaches tend to be similar in power.

Several related issues remain to be discussed. First, Tables 13.9–13.11 should be used as guidelines for choosing a sample size with the multivariate approach. However, circumstances beyond an investigator's control may preclude obtaining the recommended sample size. What if this sample size cannot be obtained, and at the same time, n is less than $a + 15$? Although one could proceed with the multivariate test and hope for the best, our advice would be to formulate a small number of planned comparisons, if at all possible. Although these tests may not be very powerful either for small n, they are likely more powerful than either multivariate or mixed-model omnibus tests. It should also be recognized that one way to perform planned comparisons is to "plan" to test all pairwise comparisons. Although such an approach may be rather atheoretical, it nevertheless avoids some of the difficulties of the omnibus multivariate test. When the researcher has no specific planned comparisons in mind, another alternative may be to reduce a by averaging scores over trials, for example, until the multivariate test is advisable. If neither of these options is feasible, the mixed-model test of the omnibus hypothesis can be performed. Second, why is the size of n relative to a so important for the multivariate approach? The answer to this question is contained in the denominator degrees of freedom. Recall that they equal $n - a + 1$ for the multivariate approach because $a - 1$ parameters have been estimated, one for each of the $a - 1$ D variables. As we discussed previously, lower denominator degrees of freedom imply a higher critical F value, and hence less power. If n is only slightly larger than a, the denominator degrees of freedom may be so small that power is quite low. In fact, it is important to note that the multivariate approach requires that n be at least as large as a. If n is less than a, the denominator degrees of freedom would be zero or negative, which is impossible. As a consequence, the multivariate approach is literally impossible mathematically if n is less than a.[11] For situations such as these, testing planned comparisons or using the mixed-model approach are the only alternatives. Third, it may seem puzzling that when homogeneity fails to hold the mixed-model approach commits too many Type I errors, yet may be less powerful than the multivariate approach.

Although this may seem to contradict the fact that Type I and Type II errors are inversely related, in reality there is no contradiction, because the two tests are based on different test statistics. The technical explanation is that the multivariate test has a steeper power curve (or *operating characteristic curve*, as it is sometimes called) in some situations. In case the technical explanation is less than completely satisfactory, a more intuitive analogy may help. Suppose that we were to compare the multivariate approach to a rather strange approach to testing the null hypothesis that simply involves tossing a fair six-sided die. If we obtain a 1 on our toss, we reject the null hypothesis; otherwise, we do not. You should be able to convince yourself that $\alpha = 1/6$ for this approach; thus, it commits too many Type I errors. Nevertheless, its power is only $1/6$, no matter how false the null hypothesis is. Thus, the multivariate test is more powerful than tossing the die, for reasonable alternative hypotheses. The test obtained by tossing a die has a higher Type I error rate but less power than the multivariate test. Because the test based on tossing a die fails to consider information in the data, its power curve is literally flat, making it insensitive to departures from the null hypothesis. We should immediately add that we are not implying that the mixed-model approach is analogous to tossing a die. It is a viable alternative that in some circumstances may be preferable to the multivariate approach. Our point is simply to show that it is possible for a test to make more Type I errors than another test, and yet the first test can be less powerful than the second.

Summary

Power considerations do not uniformly favor either approach over the other. Our recommendation can best be summarized by quoting from Davidson (1972): "Provided that n exceeds k [the number of levels of the repeated factor] by a few, the modified univariate test ranges, with respect to power, from somewhat better to much worse than the multivariate test" (p. 451), and "among theoretically possible cases, the multivariate test is usually somewhat more powerful provided that n exceeds k by a few" (p. 452). Thus, our general recommendation based on power is that the multivariate approach should be used as long as n is chosen appropriately. However, Algina and Keselman (1997) show that especially when n is small, certain combinations of means and covariances can make the multivariate test noticeably less powerful than the adjusted mixed-model test. Even so, Algina and Keselman found that for a substantial majority of different configurations of means and covariances, "the multivariate test was more sensitive than the adjusted degrees of freedom tests" (1997, p. 212). Thus, considerations of both Type I and Type II error rates give a slight edge, in our opinion, to the multivariate approach over the ε-adjusted mixed-model approaches.

Table 13.17 summarizes the issues involved in choosing between the multivariate and mixed-model approaches. As we said, our general preference is for the multivariate approach, although as Table 13.17 shows, the choice involves a number of complex issues.

There is yet one other reason to prefer the multivariate approach to the mixed-model approach. In many respects, the logic underlying the multivariate approach generalizes more easily to complex factorial designs than does the logic of the mixed-model approach. As we discuss in Chapter 12, using the mixed-model approach in factorial designs sometimes involves complicated problems of choosing an appropriate error term or determining an appropriate ε

TABLE 13.17
SUMMARY OF COMPARISON BETWEEN THE MULTIVARIATE AND
MIXED-MODEL APPROACHES

Assumptions
1. The mixed-model approach requires an assumption of homogeneity (or, sphericity), which is unlikely to be met in many behavioral studies.
2. The multivariate approach requires no such homogeneity assumption. It does assume multivariate normality, whereas the mixed-model approach assumes only univariate normality. However, violations of either normality assumption are generally regarded as less serious than violations of sphericity.

Tests of Contrasts
1. The multivariate approach is consistent with the use of specific error terms for testing contrasts.
2. The mixed-model approach is consistent with the use of a pooled (i.e., average) error term for testing contrasts. However, a pooled error term can lead to very misleading results when the homogeneity assumption is violated, even if the violation is slight.

Type I Error Rate
1. The Type I error rate of the multivariate approach is exact, assuming that its assumptions have been met.
2. When the homogeneity assumption is not satisfied, the Type I error rate of the unadjusted mixed-model test may be double or triple the nominal value. The ε-adjusted tests provide much better control, but they are only approximate, even when necessary assumptions have been met.

Type II Error Rate (Power)
1. When homogeneity holds, the mixed-model test is more powerful than the multivariate test.
2. When homogeneity fails to hold, neither test is uniformly more powerful than the other. For moderate sample sizes, the multivariate test ranges from somewhat less powerful to much more powerful than the mixed-model test. For small sample sizes, the multivariate test is inadvisable and may even be mathematically impossible.

adjustment of the degrees of freedom. As we see in Chapter 14, neither of these complications arises in applying the multivariate approach to factorial designs.

EXERCISES

1. True or False: The multivariate approach to a one-way repeated measures design with a levels requires that $a - 1$ D variables be formed.

2. True or False: The determinant of a matrix is itself another matrix.

3. True or False: The denominator "degrees of freedom" of the omnibus F statistic in the multivariate approach to repeated measures is always less than the corresponding degrees of freedom in the mixed-model approach.

4. True or False: A psychologist is planning a study with three levels of a repeated factor. Anticipated population parameters are $\mu_1 = 40, \mu_2 = 45, \mu_3 = 50, \sigma_1 = \sigma_2 = \sigma_3 = 10, \rho_{12} = .7, \rho_{13} = .5$, and $\rho_{23} = .7$. The multivariate approach with 13 subjects guarantees statistical power of at least .80.

5. True or False: It is possible to obtain statistical significance for at least one contrast using a separate variance approach and the Roy–Bose critical value if and only if the omnibus test is significant with the multivariate approach.

6. True or False: Although a stringent homogeneity assumption is required for the mixed-model omnibus test in a repeated measures design, no such assumption is needed for testing contrasts with the mixed-model approach (i.e., using a pooled error term).

*7. (To be done by hand.) The following data represent level of EEG activity in four locations of the brain among five subjects who were engaged in a mental arithmetic task. The question of interest is whether there is differential level of EEG activity across the four locations.

		Location		
Subject	1	2	3	4
1	3	6	4	5
2	4	7	4	8
3	2	1	1	3
4	4	5	1	5
5	7	6	5	9

Although in actual practice, the multivariate approach would not be advisable with such a small sample size, this exercise uses the multivariate approach for pedagogical purposes.

a. Calculate three D variables for each subject: $D_1 = $ Location 2 − Location 1, $D_2 = $ Location 3 − Location 1, and $D_3 = $ Location 4 − Location 1.

b. Calculate the errors of the full model for each subject on each D variable in part a. (Also calculate squared errors and cross-product errors for each subject.)

c. Repeat part b for the restricted model.

d. From your results in parts b and c, calculate $|E(F)|$ and $|E(R)|$.

e. Should we reject a null hypothesis that the population means for the four locations are equal to each other? Show your work.

f. What meaning can be attached to the determinants you calculated in part d? To explore this question, let's first consider $|E(F)|$: How does $|E(F)|$ relate to the sums of squares for errors in the full model?

   (1) Find the sum of squared errors for e_1.

   (2) Find the unexplained (i.e., residual) sum of squares for e_2, when e_2 is predicted from e_1. (Hint: $r^2_{e_1 e_2} = .4$)

   (3) Find the unexplained (i.e., residual) sum of squares for e_3, where e_3 is predicted from both e_1 and e_2. (Hint: $R^2_{e_3.e_1,e_2} = .402778$)

   (4) How do the values in (1)–(3) relate to $|E(F)|$? What does this imply about how you might interpret $|E(F)|$?

   (5) The same type of relationship holds for $|E(R)|$, except that it is necessary to work with uncorrected sums of squares (i.e., regression equations without an intercept term). For our data, these uncorrected sums of squares have the following values: uncorrected SS for $e_1 = 21$; uncorrected residual SS for e_2 predicted from $e_1 = 14.57143$; uncorrected residual SS for e_3 predicted from e_1 and $e_2 = 9.09804$. Verify that the type of relationship you found for $|E(F)|$ also holds for $|E(R)|$.

g. Suppose that we had planned to test a single comparison involving Locations 1 and 4. Would this contrast be statistically significant for our data? Show your work.

*8. (Can be done by calculator or computer.) The following $E(F)$ and $E(R)$ matrices have been obtained for 12 subjects:

$$E(F) = \begin{bmatrix} 1584 & 528 \\ 528 & 704 \end{bmatrix}$$

$$E(R) = \begin{bmatrix} 2784 & 1248 \\ 1248 & 1136 \end{bmatrix}$$

a. Should the omnibus null hypothesis be rejected using the multivariate approach?

b. Let's suppose that these matrices were obtained from a set of orthonormal contrasts. Can the omnibus null hypothesis be rejected using the unadjusted mixed-model approach?

c. Suppose that the D_1 variable in the matrices represents a linear trend. Can the null hypothesis of no linear trend be rejected using an α_{PC} of .05?

9. (To be done by computer.)
   a. Reanalyze the data in Table 13.5 by using the multivariate approach to perform a simultaneous test of the linear, quadratic, and cubic trends. How does your obtained F compare to the F value reported in the chapter?
   b. Suppose that we planned to test only the linear trend for these data. Would the trend be statistically significant?
   c. Suppose that we chose to test the linear trend only after examining the data. Would the statistical significance of the trend remain the same as in part b?
   d. Explain how you could have used your answer to part a to answer part c without having to perform any further calculations after the omnibus test.
   e. The least-squares estimated slopes of a simple linear regression of IQ on age for the 12 subjects shown in Table 13.5 are as follows: 0.933, 1.667, 0.533, 0.867, −0.100, −1.133, −0.133, 1.433, 0.133, 0.500, 0.200, and 1.100. Test whether these scores come from a population with a nonzero mean. How does your result compare to your answer to part b?
   f. The mixed-model approach would use $MS_{A \times S}$ as the error term for testing the linear trend. How does the resultant F value compare to the F value you obtained using a separate error term? Which error term is better here? Why?

10. (To be done by computer.) Until the 1960s, it was believed that infants had little or no pattern vision during the early weeks or even months of their lives. The following study is modeled after an experiment reported by Fantz, R. L. (1963) "Pattern vision in newborn infants." *Science, 140,* 294–297. Fourteen infants under 48 hours old were exposed to a series of targets, presented in a random sequence to each infant. Three of the targets contained black-and-white patterns: a schematic face, concentric circles, and a section of newspaper. The fourth target was an unpatterned white circle. A blue background was provided in all cases to contrast with the target. The dependent measure is the length of gaze (in seconds) of an infant at a particular target. The following (hypothetical) data were obtained:

Subject	Face	Circle	Newspaper	White
1	3.1	3.4	1.7	1.8
2	1.3	0.6	0.7	0.5
3	2.1	1.7	1.2	0.7
4	1.5	0.9	0.6	0.4
5	0.9	0.6	0.9	0.8
6	1.6	1.8	0.6	0.8
7	1.8	1.4	0.8	0.6
8	1.4	1.2	0.7	0.5
9	2.7	2.3	1.2	1.1
10	1.5	1.2	0.7	0.6
11	1.4	0.9	1.0	0.5
12	1.6	1.5	0.9	1.0
13	1.3	1.5	1.4	1.6
14	1.3	0.9	1.2	1.4

   a. Test the omnibus null hypothesis of no mean difference among the targets.
   b. (Optional.) Find the coefficients of D_{max} from your analysis in part a. How would you interpret this contrast?
   c. Suppose that instead of performing the omnibus test, you had decided to perform all pairwise comparisons. What would you find?
   d. As yet another alternative, formulate a theoretically meaningful set of three orthogonal contrasts. Test each contrast, maintaining your α_{FW} at .05.

11. This problem uses a subset of the data from Exercise 10. Suppose that this study had been conducted by obtaining data only in the "Face" and "Newspaper" conditions. In other words, use only the data from these two conditions in answering the remainder of this question.

a. Calculate the value of omega squared for these data based on Equation 11.35.
b. Calculate the value of omega squared for these data based on Equation 13.23.
c. In the special case of two levels of the within-subjects factor, the multivariate omega squared shown in Equation 13.23 can be written as

$$\hat{\omega}^2_{multi} = \frac{(n-1)\,SS_A}{(n-1)\,SS_A + nSS_{A \times S}}$$

Verify that this form of omega squared produces the same numerical value you calculated in part b for these data.
d. Compare the expression shown in part c to the expression shown in Equation 11.35. What role if any does SS_S play in each expression, and what does this imply about the role played by systematic individual differences in determining a definition of total variance?
e. How does your answer to part d explain why omega squared as calculated from Equation 13.23 is larger than omega squared as calculated from Equation 11.35 for these data? Which expression do you believe is more meaningful here? Why?

12. This problem uses the data from Exercise 10.
a. Form simultaneous 95% confidence intervals for the set of all pairwise comparisons. Interpret your results.
b. How do the results of part a compare to the results of part c in Exercise 10?
c. Part d of Exercise 10 asked you to test a theoretically meaningful set of three orthogonal contrasts, maintaining at α_{FW} .05. Your task now is to form 95% simultaneous confidence intervals for these same contrasts. Interpret your results.

13. (To be done by computer.) A developmental psychologist is interested in the role of the sound of a mother's heartbeat in the growth of newborn babies. Fourteen babies were placed in a nursery where they were constantly exposed to a rhythmic heartbeat sound piped in over the PA system. Infants were weighed at the same time of day for 4 consecutive days, yielding the following data (weight is measured in ounces):

Subject	Day 1	Day 2	Day 3	Day 4
1	96	98	103	104
2	116	116	118	119
3	102	102	101	101
4	112	115	116	118
5	108	110	112	115
6	92	95	96	98
7	120	121	121	123
8	112	111	111	109
9	95	96	98	99
10	114	112	110	109
11	99	100	99	98
12	124	125	127	126
13	100	98	95	94
14	106	107	106	107

a. Test the omnibus null hypothesis that the population mean weight is the same for all 4 days.
b. Suppose that you had planned to test only the linear trend. What would your results show?
c. Form a 95% confidence interval for the population slope, regressing weight (in ounces) on age (in days). What is the relationship between your interval and the test you conducted in part b?
d. Suppose instead of planning to test the linear trend that you had planned to test differences from one day to the next (i.e., differences between adjacent days). Perform these tests, and maintain α_{FW} at .05.
e. Form 95% simultaneous confidence intervals for the differences you tested in part d. What is the relationship between your intervals and the tests you conducted in part d?

f. Is this a good design for assessing the effects of a heartbeat sound on infants' growth? Why or why not? How could the internal validity of the design be strengthened?

*14. (To be done by computer.) Consider the following data obtained for 13 subjects.

Subject	Time 1	Time 2	Time 3
1	2	4	7
2	6	5	4
3	4	7	5
4	5	7	4
5	3	3	3
6	1	1	6
7	7	12	8
8	4	5	3
9	3	5	8
10	3	6	1
11	5	8	2
12	2	7	8
13	7	8	6

a. Test the omnibus null hypothesis using the multivariate approach.
b. Test the omnibus null hypothesis using the mixed-model approach. Although in actual practice, you might want to adjust the degrees of freedom, you need consider only the unadjusted test here.
c. How can you explain the results for parts a and b if the multivariate test is conservative and the mixed-model test is liberal? Is the multivariate test really conservative? Is the mixed-model test necessarily more powerful than the multivariate test?

15. (To be done by computer.) This exercise continues to use the data from Exercise 14 with the following changes:

The Time 3 scores of four subjects are different. Subject 1 has a score of 6, Subject 10 has a score of 4, Subject 11 has a score of 3, and Subject 12 has a score of 5.
A constant value of 0.4227 is to be added to each subject's Time 1 score. (Hint: This is easy to do with most statistical packages. For example, in SPSS, use a COMPUTE statement; in SAS, use an assignment statement after an INPUT in the DATA step.)
A constant value of 1.5773 is to be subtracted from each subject's Time 2 score.
A constant value of 1.1547 is to be added to each subject's Time 3 score, after first altering the four scores as described above.

a. Test the omnibus null hypothesis using the multivariate approach.
b. Test the omnibus null hypothesis using the mixed-model approach.
c. Based on your answers to parts a and b, is it possible for the mixed-model approach, even after an appropriate adjustment (using $\hat{\varepsilon}$ or $\tilde{\varepsilon}$) and even when $n \geq a + 10$, to yield significance when the multivariate approach does not?
For further reading, Davidson (1972) discusses types of data for which the multivariate test is more powerful (as exemplified by Exercise 14) and other types of data for which the mixed-model test is more powerful (as exemplified by Exercise 15).

*16. (To be done by computer or by hand.) We saw in Exercise 14 that the multivariate test was statistically significant, but the mixed-model test was nonsignificant for these data. Does a contrast exist that would be significant if tested post hoc using a separate error term? It can be shown that D_{max} for these data is given by: $D_{max} = .56$ Time $1 - .54$ Time $2 - .02$ Time 3.
a. Test this contrast for significance using an appropriate post hoc critical value.
b. How would you interpret this contrast?
c. Is the mixed-model omnibus test necessarily a valid indicator of whether it is fruitless to search for a statistically significant post hoc contrast using a separate error term? Why or why not?

17. (To be done by computer or by hand.) We saw in Exercise 15 that the multivariate test is now nonsignificant whereas the mixed-model test is significant. Does a contrast exist that would be significant if tested post hoc using a separate error term? It can be shown that D_{max} for these data is given by $D_{max} = -.30$ Time $1 - .10$ Time $2 + .40$ Time 3.
   a. Test this contrast for significance using an appropriate post hoc critical value.
   b. Does a significant mixed-model omnibus test necessarily imply that a contrast can be found that is significant if tested post hoc using a separate error term? Justify your answer.

18. A psychologist reports that she calculated a mixed-model F value of 5.73 for her repeated-measures data. With 1 numerator and 19 denominator degrees of freedom, the result was significant at the .05 level. Should she have used the multivariate approach? Why or why not?

19. A psychologist has used the multivariate approach to analyze his repeated-measures data for 25 subjects. He reports an F value of 2.97, with 4 and 19 degrees of freedom. Should we trust his assertion that the null hypothesis should be rejected, or should we question his claim? Why?

20. Repeated-measures data with six levels have been collected for five subjects. Should the multivariate approach be used to analyze these data? Why or why not?

21. True or false: The mixed-model approach of Chapter 11 for analyzing data from within-subjects designs has probably remained more popular than the multivariate approach of this chapter because it is more likely to produce statistically significant results.

22. The chapter points out that some statistical packages create orthonormal D variables, even if the user has requested a nonorthogonal set. The following data allow you to determine whether your favorite program allows you to test nonorthogonal contrasts within the multivariate approach. Consider the following data for five hypothetical subjects:

Subject	Condition 1	Condition 2	Condition 3
1	2	4	5
2	3	3	4
3	4	5	4
4	3	1	5
5	5	4	6
Mean	3.4	3.4	4.8

   a. Ask the computer program to create the following $2\ D$ variables: $D_1 =$ Condition $2-$ Condition 1, and $D_2 =$ Condition $3-$ Condition 2. Obtain univariate tests of D_1 and D_2 within the repeated-measures program.
   b. Test D_1 in part a by hand.
   c. Explain why you obtained the F value that resulted in part b.
   d. Did the computer program yield the same answer as you obtained in part b? If so, the computer allows you to test nonorthogonal contrasts. If not, the program probably orthonormalizes its D variables. Remember that most programs print the transformation matrix being used to obtain D variables. (Of course, if your answer is different from the computer's, you may also want to check your arithmetic!)

14

Higher Order Designs With Within-Subjects Factors: The Multivariate Approach

This chapter extends the multivariate methodology developed in Chapter 13 for one-way within-subjects designs to more complicated factorial designs. As such, the methods to be developed in this chapter are an alternative to the mixed-model approach to factorial within-subjects designs discussed in Chapter 12.

The general outline in this chapter parallels the development of the mixed-model approach in Chapter 12. First, we consider two-way factorial designs where both factors are within-subjects. Second, we consider two-way designs where one factor is between-subjects and the other is within-subjects. Third, we briefly compare the multivariate and mixed-model approaches for these two types of designs.

You should recall from Chapter 13 that the multivariate approach to the one-way within-subjects design requires the formation of $a - 1$ D variables (where a is the number of levels of the repeated factor). We will see in this chapter that the same logic also works in much more complicated designs. The only real complication turns out to be choosing the particular D variables to correspond to the hypotheses of interest. We begin with a design where both within-subjects factors have only two levels, because it is easiest to comprehend the formation of D variables when each factor has only two levels. Once we have considered this special case in some detail, we consider the more general $a \times b$ design.

TWO WITHIN-SUBJECTS FACTORS, EACH WITH TWO LEVELS

To consider this design and analysis in detail, we orient our discussion around a specific study where a two-way within-subjects design might be used. The example and corresponding data to be used here are the same as we used in Chapter 12, except that for the moment we will only consider two levels of each factor. Nevertheless, we will once again describe the study in some detail, because some readers may not have read Chapter 12 if they are focusing on the multivariate approach to repeated measures instead of the mixed-model approach. Readers who did read Chapter 12 may nevertheless benefit from a brief review of the perceptual study originally introduced in Chapter 12.

TABLE 14.1
HYPOTHETICAL REACTION TIME DATA FOR A 2 × 2 PERCEPTUAL EXPERIMENT

Subject	Y_1 Noise Absent, 0° angle	Y_2 Noise Absent, 8° angle	Y_3 Noise Present, 0° angle	Y_4 Noise Present, 8° angle
1	420	480	480	780
2	420	480	360	600
3	480	540	660	780
4	420	540	480	900
5	540	540	480	720
6	360	360	360	540
7	480	600	540	840
8	480	660	540	900
9	540	540	480	780
10	480	540	540	780
Mean	462	528	492	762

Suppose that a perceptual psychologist studying the visual system was interested in determining the extent to which interfering visual stimuli slow the ability to recognize letters. Participants are brought into a laboratory and seated in front of a tachistoscope. They are told that they will see either the letter T or the letter I displayed on the screen. In some trials, the letter appears by itself, but in other trials the target letter is embedded in a group of other letters. This variation in the display constitutes the first factor, which is referred to as noise. The noise factor has two levels—absent and present. The other factor varied by the experimenter is where in the display the target letter appears. This factor, which is called angle, also has two levels. The target letter is either shown at the center of the screen (where the participant has been told to fixate), or 8° off center (with the deviation from the center randomly varying between left and right). Table 14.1 presents hypothetical data for 10 participants. As usual, the sample size is kept small to minimize the computational burden. The dependent measure is reaction time (or latency) measured in milliseconds. Each participant has four scores, one for each combination of the 2 × 2 design. In an actual perceptual experiment, each of these four scores would itself be the mean score for that individual across a number of trials in the particular condition.

The statistical questions to be addressed in this factorial design are precisely the same as those discussed in Chapter 7 for between-subjects factorial designs. In any two-way design, the questions typically of most interest are the significance of the two main effects and the interaction.[1] The effects to be tested are the same regardless of whether the factors are within- or between-subjects. Although the nature of the effects is the same, the way in which they are tested changes.

The three effects to be tested here are the main effect of angle (which we designate A), the main effect of noise (which we designate B), and the interaction of angle and noise. If we were interested in testing all three of these effects simultaneously, we could proceed along the lines of Chapter 13 by forming three D variables to be subjected to a multivariate test. However, because of our 2 × 2 design, we typically want a test of each effect considered separately. To conduct these tests, we still form D variables as in Chapter 13, but instead of testing all D variables simultaneously, we test each one individually. The only new aspect of the procedure is choosing how to form the D variables; in a sense, this is also not new because it follows the logic we developed in Chapter 7 for the meaning of main effects and interactions.

TABLE 14.2
CELL MEANS AND MARGINAL MEANS
FOR DATA IN TABLE 14.1

		Angle		
		0°	8°	
Noise	Absent	462	528	495
	Present	492	762	627
		477	645	561

TABLE 14.3
DIFFERENCE SCORES FOR DATA OF TABLE 14.1

Subject	D_1	D_2	D_3
1	180	180	240
2	150	30	180
3	90	210	60
4	270	210	300
5	120	60	240
6	90	90	180
7	210	150	180
8	270	150	180
9	150	90	300
10	150	150	180
Mean	168	132	204

Formation of Main-Effect D Variables

To see how D variables are formed in a 2×2 within-subjects design, we first consider the angle main effect. As always, a main effect involves a comparison of marginal means, averaging over the other factor(s) in the design. As Table 14.2 shows, for our data the angle main effect compares the marginal mean of 477 (the average of 462 and 492) with the marginal mean of 645 (the average of 528 and 762). Of course, 477 and 645 are both averages of cell means. However, we could also average scores for each participant individually because the noise factor we need to average over is a within-subjects factor. For example, participant 1's average 0° score is 450, whereas his or her average 8° score is 630. This particular participant's reaction time averages 180 msec longer (630 vs. 450) for the 8° angle condition than for the 0° angle condition. If the other 9 participants' data show a similar pattern, we would infer that there is indeed a main effect due to angle. The first column of Table 14.3 (labeled D_1) shows these scores for all 10 participants. Indeed, all 10 participants have an average 8° reaction time that is slower than their average 0° reaction time. Such consistency strongly supports the existence of an angle main effect. Nevertheless, it is important to develop the procedure for testing a main effect in the 2×2 design formally.

We will see that the basic logic of the hypothesis test in the two-way design is identical to the logic we used in Chapter 13 for the one-way design. The only new concept here is the creation of appropriate D variables. To understand how D variables are formed, let's consider how the D_1 scores in Table 14.3 were obtained. Recall that we averaged over the other factor (noise) and then found the difference between the average 8° score and the average 0° score for each participant. To represent this procedure in symbols, we will define the four original variables as follows:

$$Y_1 = \text{noise absent, } 0° \text{angle reaction time}$$
$$Y_2 = \text{noise absent, } 8° \text{angle reaction time}$$
$$Y_3 = \text{noise present, } 0° \text{angle reaction time}$$
$$Y_4 = \text{noise present, } 8° \text{angle reaction time}$$

Given this notation, D_{1i} is defined to be

$$D_{1i} = .5(Y_{2i} + Y_{4i}) - .5(Y_{1i} + Y_{3i}) \tag{1}$$

for the ith subject. Notice that D_{1i} is just the difference between the average $8°$ score and the average $0°$ score for participant i.

The null hypothesis for the angle main effect is that the population marginal means for the $0°$ and the $8°$ conditions are equal to one another. However, this is equivalent to stating that the difference in population marginal means equals zero. Thus, if the null hypothesis is true, the population mean of the D_1 variable will equal zero. As usual, we can test a null hypothesis that μ_1, the population mean of D_1, equals zero by comparing full and restricted models. The full model for the difference score allows μ_1 to be nonzero and is given by

$$D_{1i} = \mu_1 + \varepsilon_{1i} \tag{2}$$

The null hypothesis stipulates that $\mu_1 = 0$, which leads to a restricted model of the form

$$D_{1i} = 0 + \varepsilon_{1i} \tag{3}$$

or just

$$D_{1i} = \varepsilon_{1i} \tag{4}$$

As in the one-way design with two levels we considered at the beginning of Chapter 13, the error sums of squares for the full and restricted models are

$$E_F = \sum_{i=1}^{n}(D_{1i} - \overline{D}_1)^2 \tag{5}$$

$$E_R = \sum_{i=1}^{n} D_{1i}^2 \tag{6}$$

As usual, the general expression for the F statistic is given by

$$F = \frac{(E_R - E_F)/(df_R - df_F)}{E_F/df_F} \tag{7}$$

As we saw in Chapter 13, after substituting from Equations 5 and 6 and performing some simple algebra, the F statistic of Equation 7 can be simplified in this particular case to

$$F = n\overline{D}_1^2/s_{D_1}^2 \tag{8}$$

From Table 14.3, $n = 10$, $\overline{D}_1 = 168$, and $s_{D_1}^2$ can be shown to equal 4,240. The value of the F statistic then equals 66.57. The observed F is compared to a critical F with 1 and $n - 1$ df. For $\alpha = .05$, the critical F with 1 and 9 df is 5.12; thus, our observed F is easily significant at the .05 level, agreeing with our intuitive view of the D_1 scores in Table 14.3. Notice that, although we are taking the multivariate approach here, the test we performed is just a univariate test because the angle effect can be captured with a single D variable. We will consider the implications of the multivariate approach yielding a univariate test after we have considered the noise main effect and the angle $\times$ noise interaction.

The main effect for noise can be tested in exactly the same manner we tested the angle main effect. The only change is that the difference score we form now must reflect the noise effect instead of the angle effect. Specifically, we now want to average over the levels of angle and find the difference between the average score when noise is present and the average score when noise is absent. Thus, letting D_2 represent this noise effect, we have

$$D_{2i} = .5(Y_{3i} + Y_{4i}) - .5(Y_{1i} + Y_{2i}) \tag{9}$$

Table 14.3 shows the D_{2i} scores for our 10 participants. The test of significance is once again obtained by applying Equation 8 (using D_2 instead of D_1), which yields an F value of 45.37 for our data, which like the angle main effect is highly statistically significant.

Formation of Interaction D Variables

The final omnibus test is the angle $\times$ noise interaction. How can we obtain a D variable to represent the interaction? Recall that an interaction means that the effect of one factor (say, angle) is different at different levels of the other factor (here, noise). Thus, a measure of the magnitude of an interaction effect could be found by taking the difference between the angle effect when noise is present and the angle effect when noise is absent. To illustrate this idea, let's again consider the data for participant 1. We can see from Table 14.1 that when noise was present this individual responded 300 ms slower in the 8° condition than in the 0° condition. Thus, for this individual, the angle effect was 300 ms when noise was present. On the other hand, when noise was absent, this individual responded only 60 ms slower in the 8° condition than in the 0° condition. Thus, for this individual, the angle effect was 60 ms when noise is absent. The difference between these two angle effects represents the magnitude of interaction. For this individual, the difference between the two angle effects was 240 (300 ms − 60 ms). At least for this individual, the angle effect was stronger when noise was present than when it was absent. The D_3 column of Table 14.3 shows these scores for all 10 participants, and it is apparent that everyone in the sample showed a somewhat larger angle effect when noise was present than when noise was absent.

At this point, we need to consider more closely how D_3 scores were obtained. In symbols, D_3 can be written as

$$D_{3i} = (Y_{4i} - Y_{3i}) - (Y_{2i} - Y_{1i}) \tag{10}$$

Notice that $Y_{4i} - Y_{3i}$ is the angle effect (8° score minus 0° score) when noise is present. Similarly, $Y_{2i} - Y_{1i}$ is the angle effect (also 8° score minus 0° score) when noise is absent. Thus, D_{3i} is indeed the difference between the two angle effects. If the interaction null hypothesis is true, the population difference between the two angle effects equals zero. This hypothesis can be tested by once again applying Equation 8 (using D_3 instead of D_1), which yields an F value of 83.90 for our data, which again is highly statistically significant.

Two further points must be made regarding the D_3 variable. First, we defined D_3 as the difference between two angle effects, namely the angle effect when noise was present minus the angle effect when noise was absent. However, our D_3 scores can also be conceptualized as the difference between two noise effects. To see why, notice from Equation 10 that D_3 can be rewritten as

$$D_{3i} = Y_{4i} - Y_{3i} - Y_{2i} + Y_{1i} \tag{11}$$

However, if we rearrange terms, the expression in Equation 11 is equivalent to

$$D_{3i} = (Y_{4i} - Y_{2i}) - (Y_{3i} - Y_{1i})$$

But $Y_{4i} - Y_{2i}$ is the noise effect for the 8° angle condition, and $Y_{3i} - Y_{1i}$ is the noise effect for the 0° angle condition. Thus, D_3 can be thought of as either the difference between angle effects or the difference between noise effects. This equality follows from our initial discussion of the meaning of an interaction back in Chapter 7 on between-subjects factorial designs. Recall that we showed in Chapter 7 that an $A \times B$ interaction can be interpreted as implying that differences between levels of A vary at different levels of B or, equivalently, that differences between levels of B vary at different levels of A. Second, seeing how the proper coefficients for D_3 can be obtained from the coefficients for D_1 and D_2 will be useful when either or both factors have more than two levels. Recall that D_{1i} was defined as

$$D_{1i} = .5(Y_{2i} + Y_{4i}) - .5(Y_{1i} + Y_{3i}) \tag{1, repeated}$$

It will be helpful to consider the coefficients for Y_{1i}, Y_{2i}, Y_{3i}, and Y_{4i} in that order, so we can rewrite D_{1i} as

$$D_{1i} = -.5Y_{1i} + .5Y_{2i} - .5Y_{3i} + .5Y_{4i}$$

To simplify our task a bit, we could replace all 0.5 values by 1.0 (in effect, doubling all the D_{1i} scores[2]), yielding

$$D_{1i} = -1Y_{1i} + 1Y_{2i} - 1Y_{3i} + 1Y_{4i} \tag{12}$$

Following the same procedure for D_{2i}, we can write D_{2i} as

$$D_{2i} = -1Y_{1i} - 1Y_{2i} + 1Y_{3i} + 1Y_{4i} \tag{13}$$

Finally, from Equation 11, we can write D_{3i} as

$$D_{3i} = 1Y_{1i} - 1Y_{2i} - 1Y_{3i} + 1Y_{4i}$$

The coefficients for D_{3i}, the interaction difference score, are related to the coefficients of D_{1i} and D_{2i}, the two main-effect difference scores, by a simple rule. For example, to obtain the Y_{1i} coefficient for D_{3i}, we can multiply the Y_{1i} coefficient for D_{1i} (i.e., -1) times the Y_{1i} coefficient for D_{2i} (i.e., -1). Sure enough, -1 times -1 equals 1, the Y_{1i} coefficient for the D_{3i} variable. The same rule works for Y_{2i}, Y_{3i}, and Y_{4i}. Although the theory behind this principle is too advanced for our purposes (it involves something called Kronecker or direct products of matrices, which are described in such multivariate statistics textbooks as Bock, 1975, and Finn, 1974), the principle itself provides a handy rule for generating interaction difference variables from main-effect difference variables. As we said, we will see later that this rule is especially useful when one or both factors have more than two levels.

Relationship to the Mixed-Model Approach

Although we could now consider simple-effects tests (the only potential follow-up tests in a 2×2 design—why?), we postpone consideration of all follow-up tests until we discuss the general $a \times b$ design. However, there is one further theoretical point that must be made, which applies only to the specific case of a 2×2 design. As we stated earlier, although by forming D variables we are following the principles of the multivariate approach to repeated measures, all our tests turn out to be univariate tests—that is, each of our three tests (angle main effect, noise main effect, and Angle × Noise interaction) turn out to involve a single D variable. The tests are all univariate because when both factors have only two levels, all three effects to be tested (A, B, and $A \times B$) have only 1 numerator degree of freedom. The same F value that is produced by the multivariate approach is also produced by the mixed-model approach in a 2×2 design, provided that the mixed-model approach uses an error term of the form $MS_{\text{effect} \times S}$. The degrees of freedom are equivalent as well; thus, the multivariate and mixed-model approaches are literally identical to one another if all factors have only two levels. If this equivalence seems odd to you, remember from Chapter 12 that the sphericity assumption required in the mixed-model approach is necessarily satisfied for testing an effect with only 1 numerator degree of freedom. Thus, when all factors have only two levels, there is no need to debate the merits of the multivariate and mixed-model approaches. However, when some factors have more than two levels, the equivalence fails to hold, and relative merits must be considered. It is to the more general two-way within-subjects design that we now turn our attention.

MULTIVARIATE ANALYSIS OF TWO-WAY $a \times b$ WITHIN-SUBJECTS DESIGNS

Although the principles we have just developed for the 2×2 within-subjects design can also be applied to the more general $a \times b$ within-subjects design, the analysis of the $a \times b$ design is more complicated than the analysis of the 2×2, for two reasons. First, creation of appropriate D (difference) variables is slightly more complicated. As we will see, when a factor has more than two levels, not surprisingly, more than one D variable must be formed. Second, because more than one D variable must be formed for each effect, the resulting tests are truly multivariate. As a consequence, we must once again concern ourselves with determinants of matrices, as we did in Chapter 13, for one-way designs.

To motivate our discussion of analyzing the $a \times b$ within-subjects design, we continue with the perceptual experiment example we have been considering. So far in this chapter, we have considered only a 2×2 version of this example because we omitted the 4° angle condition we originally included in Chapter 12. At this point, we reinstate this condition, so that we have a 2×3 design, just as we did in Chapter 12. Table 14.4 presents data for the 2×3 design. These data are identical to those presented in Table 12.1, to facilitate comparing results from the multivariate approach to those of the mixed-model approach.

Formation of Main-Effect D Variables

We assume that we are interested in testing the statistical significance of the two main effects and the interaction. As usual, the first step in the multivariate approach is to form D variables that correspond to the effects to be tested.

We begin by considering the angle main effect. Because the angle factor has three levels, we have to form two D variables, just as we did in Chapter 13. Notice that the number of levels of the other factor (i.e., noise) has no effect on the number of D variables we need because each subject's angle-effect scores simply average across all levels of the noise factor. As usual, if we are only concerned with the omnibus main effect for angle, we can choose any two comparisons we want to represent the angle main effect.[3] However, because the angle factor is quantitative, we will form the two D variables to represent the linear and quadratic trends of angle, much as we did in Chapter 6 for between-subjects factors. With three levels, the coefficients for the linear trend are -1, 0, and 1, whereas those for the quadratic trend are 1, -2, and 1 (see Appendix Table A.10). To apply these coefficients to our data in order to obtain scores on the linear and quadratic D variables, we must remember that because we are testing the angle main effect we have to average over the other factor in the design (i.e., noise). For example, the linear coefficients of -1, 0, and 1 need to be applied individually for each participant to that participant's average $0°$, $4°$, and $8°$ condition scores, respectively, where we have averaged over noise. Let's consider participant 1 (see Table 14.4). His or her average response time is 450 in the $0°$ condition, 510 in the $4°$ condition, and 630 in the $8°$ condition. Applying the coefficients of -1, 0, and 1 yields a value of 180 (notice that this value is simply the difference between the average $8°$ score and the average $0°$ score). It will be helpful to represent what we have done algebraically in symbols. We represent the six original scores as follows:

$$Y_1 = \text{noise absent, } 0° \text{angle reaction time}$$

$$Y_2 = \text{noise absent, } 4° \text{angle reaction time}$$

$$Y_3 = \text{noise absent, } 8° \text{angle reaction time}$$

$$Y_4 = \text{noise present, } 0° \text{angle reaction time}$$

$$Y_5 = \text{noise present, } 4° \text{angle reaction time}$$

$$Y_6 = \text{noise present, } 8° \text{angle reaction time}$$

Given this notation, we find participant 1's linear trend for angle by first averaging over levels of noise and then taking the difference between the $8°$ average score and the $0°$ average score.

TABLE 14.4
HYPOTHETICAL REACTION TIME DATA FOR A 2 × 3 PERCEPTUAL EXPERIMENT

| Subject | Noise Absent | | | Noise Present | | |
	0° Angle	4° Angle	8° Angle	0° Angle	4° Angle	8° Angle
1	420	420	480	480	600	780
2	420	480	480	360	480	600
3	480	480	540	660	780	780
4	420	540	540	480	780	900
5	540	660	540	480	660	720
6	360	420	360	360	480	540
7	480	480	600	540	720	840
8	480	600	660	540	720	900
9	540	600	540	480	720	780
10	480	420	540	540	660	780
Mean	462	510	528	492	660	762

TABLE 14.5
DIFFERENCE SCORES FOR DATA OF TABLE 14.4

Subject	D_1	D_2	D_3	D_4	D_5
1	180	60	180	240	0
2	150	−30	20	180	60
3	90	−30	240	60	−180
4	270	−150	220	300	−60
5	120	−180	40	240	120
6	90	−90	80	180	60
7	210	30	180	180	−180
8	270	−30	140	180	60
9	150	−150	100	300	−60
10	150	90	180	180	−180
Mean	168	−48	138	204	−36

In terms of symbols, if we let D_{1i} represent the linear trend for angle, we have

$$D_{1i} = -1[.5(Y_{1i} + Y_{4i})] + 0[.5(Y_{2i} + Y_{5i})] + 1[.5(Y_{3i} + Y_{6i})] \qquad (14)$$

Notice that each term in brackets is an average reaction time for a particular level of the angle factor. For example, $.5(Y_{1i} + Y_{4i})$ is the average score for participant i in the 0° angle condition. Further notice that Equation 14 then applies the linear coefficients of -1, 0, and 1 to these average scores. Table 14.5 presents the D_1 scores for all 10 participants. Following the same logic, if we let D_{2i} represent the quadratic trend for angle, we have

$$D_{2i} = 1[.5(Y_{1i} + Y_{4i})] - 2[.5(Y_{2i} + Y_{5i})] + 1[.5(Y_{3i} + Y_{6i})] \qquad (15)$$

Table 14.5 also presents the D_2 scores for all 10 participants. To test the statistical significance of the angle main effect, we must test a null hypothesis that both D_1 and D_2 have population means of zero. We will see momentarily that this test is performed exactly as it was in Chapter 13. However, before considering this test, we will first finish our discussion of the formation of D variables.

The other main effect to be tested is the noise main effect. Not surprisingly, the way in which we form D variables for this main effect is exactly the same way in which we formed D variables for the angle main effect. Of course, now we average over angle, whereas before we averaged over noise. Notice that after we average over angle, we only have two scores for each participant—an average reaction time when noise is present and an average reaction time when noise is absent. The reason we have only two scores is because the noise factor has only two levels. As a result, we need to form only one D variable, which is simply defined as the difference between the average score when noise is present and the average score when noise is absent. In terms of symbols, if we let D_{3i} represent this difference score for the noise main effect, we have

$$D_{3i} = \left[\tfrac{1}{3}(Y_{4i} + Y_{5i} + Y_{6i})\right] - \left[\tfrac{1}{3}(Y_{1i} + Y_{2i} + Y_{3i})\right] \qquad (16)$$

Notice that each term in brackets is an average score calculated over the levels of the angle factor. D_{3i} is simply the difference between the average score when noise is present (i.e., Y_{4i} through Y_{6i}) and the average score when noise is absent (Y_{1i} through Y_{3i}). Table 14.5 presents the D_3 scores for all 10 participants.

Formation of Interaction D Variables

The final effect to be tested is the interaction of angle and noise. Although it would be fairly easy to develop the coefficients for the D variables intuitively in our rather simple 2×3 design, it is probably better to get some practice using the algorithm we developed in our discussion of the 2×2 design. Once we have obtained the coefficients, we will then develop an intuitive explanation of them.

Recall that to use the algorithm for generating interaction D variables, we must already have formed the main-effect D variables. In our case, we have three such D variables:

$$D_{1i} = -1[.5(Y_{1i} + Y_{4i})] + 0[.5(Y_{2i} + Y_{5i})] + 1[.5(Y_{3i} + Y_{6i})] \quad \text{(14, repeated)}$$

$$D_{2i} = 1[.5(Y_{1i} + Y_{4i})] - 2[.5(Y_{2i} + Y_{5i})] + 1[.5(Y_{3i} + Y_{6i})] \quad \text{(15, repeated)}$$

$$D_{3i} = \left[\tfrac{1}{3}(Y_{4i} + Y_{5i} + Y_{6i})\right] - \left[\tfrac{1}{3}(Y_{1i} + Y_{2i} + Y_{3i})\right] \quad \text{(16, repeated)}$$

Remember that D_1 and D_2 represent the angle main effect, whereas D_3 represents the noise main effect. The algorithm is easier to use if we first rewrite the D variables so that the Y variables appear in order from Y_1 to Y_6 on the right-hand side of each equation. Reordering the Y variables and carrying out the appropriate multiplication in Equations 14 through 16 yields

$$D_{1i} = -.5Y_{1i} + 0Y_{2i} + .5Y_{3i} - .5Y_{4i} + 0Y_{5i} + .5Y_{6i} \quad (17)$$

$$D_{2i} = .5Y_{1i} - 1Y_{2i} + .5Y_{3i} + .5Y_{4i} - 1Y_{5i} + .5Y_{6i} \quad (18)$$

$$D_{3i} = -\tfrac{1}{3}Y_{1i} - \tfrac{1}{3}Y_{2i} - \tfrac{1}{3}Y_{3i} + \tfrac{1}{3}Y_{4i} + \tfrac{1}{3}Y_{5i} + \tfrac{1}{3}Y_{6i} \quad (19)$$

Finally, we are less prone to mistakes if we express all coefficients for D_1, D_2, and D_3 as integers (i.e., whole numbers). We can accomplish this goal by multiplying the coefficients of D_1 by 2, D_2 by 2, and D_3 by 3, yielding

$$D_{1i} = -1Y_{1i} + 0Y_{2i} + 1Y_{3i} - 1Y_{4i} + 0Y_{5i} + 1Y_{6i} \quad (20)$$

$$D_{2i} = 1Y_{1i} - 2Y_{2i} + 1Y_{3i} + 1Y_{4i} - 2Y_{5i} + 1Y_{6i} \quad (21)$$

$$D_{3i} = -1Y_{1i} - 1Y_{2i} - 1Y_{3i} + 1Y_{4i} + 1Y_{5i} + 1Y_{6i} \quad (22)$$

Now that we have written the D variables in this form, creation of the interaction D variables will be easier. Recall that in the 2×2 design, we obtained each coefficient of the interaction D variable by multiplying the corresponding coefficients of the two main-effect D variables. Our situation is now more complicated because we have more than two main-effect D variables. Instead, we have a total of three: D_1 and D_2 for the angle effect and D_3 for the noise effect. In this situation, it turns out that we will create two interaction D variables. One comes from the product of D_1 and D_3 coefficients, and the other comes from the product of D_2 and D_3 coefficients. Carrying out this multiplication of coefficients of D_1 and D_3 yields

$$D_{4i} = 1Y_{1i} + 0Y_{2i} - 1Y_{3i} - 1Y_{4i} + 0Y_{5i} + 1Y_{6i} \quad (23)$$

Similarly, multiplying the coefficients of D_2 and D_3 produces

$$D_{5i} = -1Y_{1i} + 2Y_{2i} - 1Y_{3i} + 1Y_{4i} - 2Y_{5i} + 1Y_{6i} \quad (24)$$

Notice that in each case the sum of the coefficients equals zero; it can be shown that this must happen if the algorithm is applied correctly and is thus a useful check on one's arithmetic. The last two columns of Table 14.5 present scores on D_4 and D_5; do not worry if the numbers themselves do not mean much to you at this point.

As promised, we now develop an intuitive explanation of D_4 and D_5, beginning with D_4. Remember that D_4 was obtained by multiplying the coefficients of D_1, the linear angle variable, by the coefficients of D_3, the noise-effect variable. We can best understand the meaning of D_4 by rewriting Equation 23 in the following form:

$$D_{4i} = (-1Y_{4i} + 0Y_{5i} + 1Y_{6i}) - (-1Y_{1i} + 0Y_{2i} + 1Y_{3i}) \tag{25}$$

(You may want to convince yourself that Equation 25 is equivalent to Equation 23 by carrying out the subtraction in Equation 25.) The term in the first set of parentheses $(-1Y_{4i} + 0Y_{5i} + 1Y_{6i})$ is the linear trend for angle when noise is present. Similarly, the term in the second set of parentheses $(-1Y_{1i} + 0Y_{2i} + 1Y_{3i})$ is the linear trend for angle when noise is absent. Because the second set is subtracted from the first set, D_4 is the difference between the linear trend for angle when noise is present versus the linear trend when noise is absent. The fact that all 10 participants have positive D_4 scores (see Table 14.5) implies that for every participant, the linear effect of angle is stronger when noise is present than when it is absent. Thus, D_4 represents one component (i.e., 1 df) of the angle × noise interaction; namely the interaction of noise with the linear trend for angle. Also, remember how we derived the coefficients for D_4. We multiplied the coefficients of D_1, the linear trend for the angle main effect, by the coefficients of D_3, the noise main effect. As we have just seen, the resultant coefficients produce a D variable that represents the interaction of D_1 and D_3, the two variables whose coefficients we multiplied. This correspondence turns out to be a general consequence of using our algorithm, which is one reason it proves to be so useful. A similar meaning can be attached to D_5. We can rewrite Equation 24 as

$$D_{5i} = (1Y_{4i} - 2Y_{5i} + 1Y_{6i}) - (1Y_{1i} - 2Y_{2i} + 1Y_{3i}) \tag{26}$$

The term in the first set of parentheses is the quadratic trend for angle when noise is present, whereas the term in the second set of parentheses is the quadratic trend for angle when noise is absent. Because we are again taking the difference between the two sets, D_5 represents the interaction of noise with the quadratic trend for angle.

It is important to realize that D_4 and D_5 together collectively represent the interaction of angle and noise. In the general case of an $a \times b$ design, the interaction would have $(a - 1)(b - 1)$ df. In our example, $a = 3$ and $b = 2$, so the interaction has 2 df. The D_4 variable accounts for 1 df, and D_5 accounts for the other. Testing the two variables simultaneously in a multivariate test then constitutes a test of the interaction effect as a whole.

Before considering these multivariate tests, it is necessary to consider how the algorithm for constructing interaction D variables works when both factors have more than two levels. Recall that we originally illustrated the algorithm for a 2×2 design and then moved on to a 3×2 design. In each case, we multiplied the coefficients of variable(s) representing the A main effect by the coefficients of variable(s) representing the B main effect. In the general $a \times b$ design, there are $a - 1$ D variables for the A main effect and $b - 1$ D variables for the B main effect. The algorithm requires that the coefficients of each of the $a - 1$ variables be multiplied by the coefficients of each of the $b - 1$ variables, producing $(a - 1)(b - 1)$ D variables as a result. Not coincidentally, $(a - 1)(b - 1)$ is the number of degrees of freedom for the interaction. As in our examples, each individual interaction D variable accounts for 1 df. The collection of $(a - 1)(b - 1)$ interaction D variables accounts for the omnibus $A \times B$ interaction.

Omnibus Tests—Multivariate Significance Tests

Now that we have learned how to form D variables in a two-way within-subjects design, we are in a position to see how these variables are used to perform F tests. Because we want to test three distinct hypotheses (viz., A main effect, B main effect, and $A \times B$ interaction), we must perform three F tests. Each test is based on the principles we developed in Chapter 13. In fact, each test is a straightforward application of Chapter 13 formulas with no modifications whatsoever. The only difference from Chapter 13 is that, instead of performing one simultaneous test of all our variables, as we did in Chapter 13, we perform three tests here, each on a subset of our variables.

Let's begin by considering the A main effect. In general, we would have $a - 1$ D variables to represent this effect. The null hypothesis for the A main effect is equivalent to a null hypothesis that all $a - 1$ of these D variables have population means equal to zero. We can test this hypothesis just as we did in Chapter 13 by comparing a full model of the form

$$D_{vi} = \mu_v + \varepsilon_{vi}$$

to a restricted model of the form

$$D_{vi} = 0 + \varepsilon_{vi}$$

for each variable v. (*Note*: v is used here as an arbitrary placeholder to represent variable number v, reminding us that we will have as many pairs of full and restricted models as we have variables). Sums of squared errors and sums of cross-products are calculated just as they were in Chapter 13, once for the errors of the full model and once for the errors of the restricted model. As a result, we end up with two matrices: $\mathbf{E(F)}$ for the full model and $\mathbf{E(R)}$ for the restricted model. In general, each matrix is square, with $a - 1$ rows and $a - 1$ columns, because we are testing the A main effect. The determinants of these two matrices can be used to compute an F statistic just as they were with Equation 13.20:

$$F = \frac{(|\mathbf{E(R)}| - |\mathbf{E(F)}|)/(df_R - df_F)}{|\mathbf{E(F)}|/df_F} \tag{27}$$

For the A main effect, $a - 1$ parameters have been estimated in the full model; thus, $df_F = n - (a - 1) = n - a + 1$. No parameters have been estimated in the restricted model; thus, $df_R = n$. As a consequence, the F statistic for testing the A main effect is given by

$$F = \frac{(|\mathbf{E(R)}| - |\mathbf{E(F)}|)/(a - 1)}{|\mathbf{E(F)}|/(n - a + 1)} \tag{28}$$

where $\mathbf{E(R)}$ and $\mathbf{E(F)}$ are the error matrices for the A main-effect D variables.

For the data in Table 14.4, we can compute $\mathbf{E(F)}$ and $\mathbf{E(R)}$ matrices for the D_1 and D_2 variables shown in Table 14.5. We will not go through the steps of these calculations because they are identical to the steps we showed in detail in Chapter 13. For this reason, we simply state that the error matrices for the full and restricted models for D_1 and D_2 are given by

$$\mathbf{E(F)} = \begin{bmatrix} 38,160 & 3,240 \\ 3,240 & 77,760 \end{bmatrix}$$

$$\mathbf{E(R)} = \begin{bmatrix} 320,400 & -77,400 \\ -77,400 & 100,800 \end{bmatrix}$$

The determinant of $\mathbf{E(F)}$ equals 2,956,824,000, and the determinant of $\mathbf{E(R)}$ equals 26,305,560,000. Substituting these values along with $n = 10$ and $a = 3$ into Equation 28 produces an F value of 31.59. With 2 and 8 df, the associated p value is .0002; thus, we can conclude that there is an angle main effect, using the .05 level of statistical significance.

Tests of the other two effects proceed in the same fashion. The only new wrinkle here is that because the noise factor has only two levels, there is only one D variable (D_3) to represent the noise main effect. Nevertheless, Equation 27 can still be used because the determinant of a matrix with only one row and one column is defined to be equal to the single number that constitutes this matrix. For our data

$$\mathbf{E(F)} = [50,760] \qquad \text{and} \qquad \mathbf{E(R)} = [241,200]$$

Substituting these values into Equation 27 produces an F value of 33.77, which implies a statistically significant noise main effect. In general, the F statistic for testing the B main effect would be given by

$$F = \frac{(|\mathbf{E(R)}| - |\mathbf{E(F)}|)/(b - 1)}{|\mathbf{E(F)}|/(n - b + 1)} \tag{29}$$

where $\mathbf{E(R)}$ and $\mathbf{E(F)}$ are the error matrices for the B main-effect D variables.

The test of the interaction also follows the same logic and differs only in that matrices are formed for the interaction D variables (D_4, and D_5 in our data). In general, there are $(a - 1)(b - 1)$ such variables. The null hypothesis that there is no interaction is equivalent to a null hypothesis that all $(a - 1)(b - 1)$ of these D variables have population means equal to zero. This should seem reasonable because each individual interaction D variable accounts for 1 df of the overall interaction. By testing all $(a - 1)(b - 1)$ interaction D variables simultaneously, we are therefore testing the overall $A \times B$ interaction. Once again, we use Equation 27 to perform this test. The specific form of the F statistic for testing the $A \times B$ interaction is given by

$$F = \frac{(|\mathbf{E(R)}| - |\mathbf{E(F)}|)/(a - 1)(b - 1)}{|\mathbf{E(F)}|/n - [(a - 1)(b - 1)]} \tag{30}$$

where $\mathbf{E(R)}$ and $\mathbf{E(F)}$ are the error matrices for the interaction D variables. For our data, the value of the observed F equals 44.91, which with 2 and 8 df has an associated p value less than .001. Thus, the angle $\times$ noise interaction is significant at the .05 level, as were the angle main effect and the noise main effect.

MEASURES OF EFFECT

As we discussed in Chapter 11, measures of effect can be obtained either from a multivariate or a mixed-model perspective. Even though we generally recommend the multivariate approach for hypothesis testing, as we explained in Chapter 11 we prefer the mixed-model formulation of omega squared because it can treat individual differences between subjects just as they are treated in between-subjects designs. For that reason, we recommend exactly the same form of omega squared that we introduced in Chapter 12 for the two-way within-subjects design. Specifically, you may recall that the formula for omega squared in this design is given by

$$\hat{\omega}^2 = \frac{df_{\text{effect}} \, (MS_{\text{effect}} - MS_{\text{effect} \times \text{S}})}{SS_{\text{effect}} + SS_{\text{effect} \times \text{S}} + SS_{\text{S}} + MS_{\text{S}}} \tag{12.6, repeated}$$

As we stated in Chapter 12, for our reaction time data, the omega squared values for A, B, and AB can be computed directly from Table 12.5, with the additional piece of information not shown in the table that SS_S equals 292,140 and thus MS_S equals 32,460. Substituting into Equation 12.6 reveals that the omega squared values for A, B, and AB are given by .42, .40, and .23, respectively. We should also point out that none of these sum of squares or mean square terms are directly involved in the multivariate test; nevertheless, most statistical packages will provide values of these terms as an option within the multivariate approach. Also, interested readers are once again directed toward Olejnik and Algina (2000) for other possible measures of association strength in this design.

Further Investigation of Main Effects

As usual, when statistically significant main effects are obtained, we may want to test comparisons of the marginal means. As we have discussed in earlier chapters, when the interaction is statistically significant, we should at the very least qualify our interpretation of the marginal means by making it explicit that they represent averages whose individual components differ to differing extents across the other factor. We proceed with comparing marginal means in our numerical example primarily for pedagogical reasons; although depending on the precise purpose of the study, the marginal means might or might not truly be of interest, given the statistically significant interaction.

In our numerical example, statistically significant main effects were obtained both for noise and for angle. Because the noise factor has only two levels, no further tests are necessary for interpreting the nature of the noise main effect. On the other hand, the angle factor has three levels; thus, specific comparisons are likely to be useful for further understanding the angle effect.

As always, two things must be determined to test a comparison: an observed value and a critical value. The observed value of the test statistic for the multivariate approach to testing a main-effect comparison turns out to be extremely simple. All that must be done is to form a D variable whose coefficients correspond to the comparison to be tested. Then the significance test is a test of the null hypothesis that the population mean of this D variable equals zero. The formula for the observed value of the F statistic is just the same as it was in Chapter 13:

$$F = n\overline{D}^2/s_D^2 \qquad \text{(13.6, repeated)}$$

For example, suppose that we want to test the quadratic trend for the angle marginal means in our numerical example. The first step is to form an appropriate D variable. In fact, we have already performed this step, because we earlier chose D_2 to represent the quadratic trend of angle. Recall that D_2 was defined as

$$D_{2i} = 1[.5(Y_{1i} + Y_{4i})] - 2[.5(Y_{2i} + Y_{5i})] + 1[.5(Y_{3i} + Y_{6i})] \qquad \text{(15, repeated)}$$

Next, we must compute $\overline{D}_2$ and $s_{D_2}^2$ to use Equation 13.6. From Table 14.5, $\overline{D}_2 = -48$. Also from Table 14.5, we can show that $s_{D_2}^2 = 8,640$. Substituting these values along with $n = 10$ into Equation 13.6 yields

$$F = 10(-48)^2/8,640 = 2.67$$

as the observed F value for the quadratic trend of angle. It turns out that we have seen this observed F value before. We obtained an F of 2.67 for the quadratic angle trend in the mixed-model approach of Chapter 12 when we used a separate error term (Equation 12.8 instead of 12.7). We will have more to say about how the multivariate and mixed-model approaches compare when we have finished our discussion of follow-up tests.

To judge the statistical significance of this observed F value, we must compare it to a critical value. The possible procedures are exactly the same here as they were in Chapter 13. The only difference is a possible change in notation. In Chapter 13, there was only one factor, with a levels. In this chapter, the a is replaced by b if we are testing comparisons of the B marginal means. No other changes are necessary, because when we are comparing marginal means we have averaged over the other factor, effectively converting the two-way design into a one-way design for the purposes of the test.

The choice of an appropriate critical value depends on what other contrasts, if any, are being tested. One option is to set α_{PC} at a desired figure, in which case the critical F value is simply read from the F table with 1 numerator and $n - 1$ denominator degrees of freedom. If a set of C planned comparisons is to be tested, α_{PC} for each contrast is adjusted to be equal to $.05/C$, using the Bonferroni technique. As we discussed in Chapter 13, the Bonferroni procedure is also appropriate for testing pairwise comparisons of marginal means in a two-way within-subjects design. Finally, for testing post hoc complex comparisons, the appropriate critical value comes from the multivariate extension of Scheffé's method developed by Roy and Bose. The formula is the same as that given in Equation 13.27, except that b replaces a when B marginal means are being compared. Thus, for tests involving comparisons of the A marginal means, the critical value (CV) is

$$CV = (n - 1)(a - 1)F_{\alpha_{FW}; a-1, n-a+1}/(n - a + 1) \tag{31}$$

Similarly, for tests involving comparisons of the B marginal means, the CV is

$$CV = (n - 1)(b - 1)F_{\alpha_{FW}; b-1, n-b+1}/(n - b + 1) \tag{32}$$

For our numerical example, the observed F value of 2.67 is nonsignificant, even using an α_{PC} of .05, because with 1 and 9 df the critical F at the .05 level equals 5.12. Of course, if additional contrasts were also being tested, the appropriate critical value would be even larger; thus, the quadratic trend for angle would remain nonsignificant.

Further Investigation of an Interaction—Simple Effects

As in other factorial designs, the most frequent approach for interpreting a statistically significant interaction in a two-way within-subjects design is to perform tests of simple effects. In our numerical example, we obtained a significant angle × noise interaction. A logical next step would be to test the angle effect at each noise level individually, as well as to test the noise effect at each individual level of angle.

As usual in the multivariate approach to repeated measures, the key to testing simple effects is to form appropriate D variables. To see how D variables are created, let's first consider the simple effect of noise at individual levels of angle. A D variable to test the effect of noise in the $0°$ angle condition would be given by $D_{6i} = Y_{4i} - Y_{1i}$, where Y_{4i} is a participant's reaction time when noise is present in the $0°$ angle condition and Y_{1i} is the same participant's reaction time when noise is absent in the $0°$ angle condition. We have labeled this simple-effect D variable D_6, because we have already formed five other D variables. (Be certain you understand that there is nothing special about the six designation here. We have used it simply to avoid confusion with the other five variables we have already formed.) Also notice that a single D variable suffices for testing the simple effect of noise in the $0°$ angle condition, because noise has only two levels. As usual, an observed F can be computed from Equation 27

$$F = \frac{(|\mathbf{E(R)}| - |\mathbf{E(F)}|)/(df_R - df_F)}{|\mathbf{E(F)}|/df_F}$$

(27, repeated)

which simplifies to Equation 13.6 in the case of a single D variable:

$$F = n\overline{D}^2/s_D^2$$

(13.6, repeated)

Using either formula yields an F value of 1.55 for the noise effect in the $0°$ angle condition in our data. This F value is nonsignificant at the .05 level, even without a possible adjustment of the alpha level for any other simple-effects tests to be performed. Not suprisingly, this F value is precisely the same value that would be obtained if a one-way within-subjects analysis were performed using only the data from the $0°$ angle condition. Be certain to understand that in most situations, we would also want to test the noise effect at the $4°$ and $8°$ angle conditions. Appropriate D variables for these two tests would be given by

$$D_{7i} = Y_{5i} - Y_{2i} \quad \text{and} \quad D_{8i} = Y_{6i} - Y_{3i}$$

respectively. For our data, both of these effects are considerably stronger than the noise effect in the $0°$ angle condition. The F values for noise at $4°$ and noise at $8°$ are 19.74 and 125.59, respectively. Thus, the data suggest that the effect of noise intensifies as the angle increases. We will see momentarily that interaction contrasts provide a more explicit method for testing this hypothesis.

Before we consider interaction contrasts, we should not forget that we would probably want to test the simple effect of angle at each noise level. The procedure is the same as we just saw for testing noise within levels of angle; the only difference is in the particular D variables we form. For example, let's consider the simple effect of angle when noise is absent. Because the angle factor has three levels, we must form two D variables to represent the angle effect. The particular choice of variables does not matter; thus, we continue to use linear and quadratic variables as our specific choice, just as we did earlier with D_1 and D_2. Indeed, the only change from D_1 and D_2 now that we are interested in simple effects is that we no longer want to average across levels of noise, as we did earlier (see Equations 14 and 15). Instead, we want to consider only one level of noise at a time. Thus, two appropriate D variables for testing the simple effect of angle when noise is absent are

$$D_{9i} = -1Y_{1i} + 0Y_{2i} + 1Y_{3i}$$
$$D_{10i} = 1Y_{1i} - 2Y_{2i} + 1Y_{3i}$$

Testing these two D variables simultaneously with Equation 27 provides a test of the simple effect of angle when noise is absent. For our data, the observed F value is 7.24, which with 2 and 8 df corresponds to a p value of .016. Similarly, the simple effect of angle when noise is present can be tested by forming two other D variables:

$$D_{11i} = -1Y_{4i} + 0Y_{5i} + 1Y_{6i}$$
$$D_{12i} = 1Y_{4i} - 2Y_{5i} + 1Y_{6i}$$

Applying Equation 27 to these two D variables produces an observed F value of 45.07, which with 2 and 8 df corresponds to a p value of .001. As was the case for the simple effect of noise, these two F values for the simple effect of angle (7.24 and 45.07) are exactly the same values that would be obtained if one-way multivariate within-subjects analyses were performed using only the data from the relevant noise condition.

Yet one more set of tests would probably be conducted here, because we obtained statistically significant simple effects for angle, which has three levels. All that we know so far is that angle has some kind of effect on reaction time, both when noise is absent and when it is present. To determine the nature of the angle effect, we need to test comparisons of individual cell means, within levels of the noise factor. Performing these tests is very straightforward with the multivariate approach. We begin by considering the angle effect when noise is absent. To test comparisons here, all we have to do is to test D_9 and D_{10} individually, instead of testing them simultaneously as we did to obtain our F value of 7.24. Because we are now testing D variables individually, Equation 27 again simplifies to Equation 13.6:

$$F = n\overline{D}^2/s_D^2 \qquad\qquad (13.6, \text{repeated})$$

For our data, the F value for D_9 is 12.24, whereas the F value for D_{10} is 0.53. Each has 1 and 9 (i.e., $n - 1$) df. Of course, we have to choose an appropriate critical value in accordance with whatever other contrasts we may also be testing. In particular, D_9 and D_{10} might not exhaust all contrasts of the angle factor we want to test, in which case more D variables would be formed and Equation 13.6 would be applied to them as well. A similar procedure would be used for probing the nature of the angle effect when noise is present.

Interaction Contrasts

As in other factorial designs, interaction contrasts provide an alternative to simple effects for investigating an interaction. As we pointed out in discussing the omnibus interaction test, in general there are $(a - 1)(b - 1)$ D variables that collectively represent the $A \times B$ interaction. Each individual D interaction variable represents a single degree of freedom of the $A \times B$ interaction and can be tested using Equation 13.6:

$$F = n\overline{D}^2/s_D^2 \qquad\qquad (13.6, \text{repeated})$$

Thus, the mechanics of the test are no different from the mechanics of other multivariate tests in repeated-measures designs. The only difference from other tests is the interpretation of the D variables.

This meaning can best be understood by returning to our numerical example. Recall from our earlier discussion of the omnibus interaction test that D_4 and D_5 collectively represent the omnibus interaction. The D_4 variable by itself represents the interaction of noise with the linear trend of angle. That is, D_4 represents the extent to which the linear trend for angle when noise is present is different from the linear trend for angle when noise is absent. The D_5 variable has a similar interpretation, except that it represents the interaction of noise with the quadratic trend for angle. Applying Equation 13.6 to our data yields an F value of 83.90 for D_4 and an F value of 1.00 for D_5. Each F has 1 numerator and 9 (i.e., $n - 1$) denominator degrees of freedom.

As usual, the appropriate critical value against which to compare these observed F values depends on what other contrasts might be tested. At one extreme, we might use an α_{PC} of .05, in which case we would simply read the critical value from the F table. For our data, the critical value equals 5.12. Alternatively, if we planned to test C interaction contrasts, we would divide α_{FW} (typically .05) by C. Notice that C would often equal $(a - 1)(b - 1)$, because this is the number of degrees of freedom for the interaction; however, there is no reason that C must equal $(a - 1)(b - 1)$. Instead, C might be smaller than $(a - 1)(b - 1)$. For example, C would equal 1 if, before conducting the study, we could pinpoint a single interaction contrast to test. Of course, we would have to resist the possible temptation to test a few other "planned" contrasts after looking at the data. Alternatively, C could be larger than $(a - 1)(b - 1)$. Just as we might plan to test more than $a - 1$ contrasts in a one-way design with a levels, we could also test more than $(a - 1)(b - 1)$ interaction contrasts. At some point, as C gets larger, the Bonferroni approach becomes less powerful than using a post hoc method. The appropriate critical value for post hoc tests of interaction contrasts again comes from the multivariate extension of Scheffé's method developed by Roy and Bose. This critical value for interaction contrasts is given by

$$\text{CV} = (n - 1)(a - 1)(b - 1)F_{\alpha_{FW};(a-1)(b-1),n-[(a-1)(b-1)]}/(n - [(a - 1)(b - 1)]) \qquad (33)$$

Notice that Equation 33 has the same general form as Equations 31 and 32. In fact, a more general expression of which all three equations (31, 32, and 33) are special cases is given by

$$\text{CV} = (n - 1)(df_{\text{effect}})F_{\alpha_{FW};df_{\text{effect}},n-df_{\text{effect}}}/(n - df_{\text{effect}}) \qquad (34)$$

Finally, we should state that for our data, the test of D_4 is statistically significant even if tested post hoc, whereas the test of D_5 would be nonsignificant even if tested with an α_{PC} of .05. Thus, the noise by linear trend of angle variable appears to reflect an important component of the interaction. As Table 14.5 shows, the noise effect becomes stronger as the angle deviates from $0°$. In addition, the form of this strengthening appears to be linear.[4] In other words, the noise effect seems to grow stronger in direct proportion to the extent to which the level of the angle condition differs from $0°$.

CONFIDENCE INTERVALS FOR CONTRASTS

We have just seen how to perform tests of contrasts of marginal means (for main effects), as well as simple effects and interaction contrasts (for interactions). As usual, we may want to supplement these tests with confidence intervals. Fortunately, the procedure for forming confidence intervals in the two-way within-subjects design follows exactly the same logic we developed in Chapter 13 for the one-way within-subjects design.

Recall that the formula we provided in Chapter 13 for a confidence interval for a contrast in the one-way within-subjects design was given by

$$\overline{D} \pm w\sqrt{\hat{s}_D^2/n} \qquad (13.28, \text{ repeated})$$

Exactly the same formula applies in a two-way within-subjects design. There are only two differences in two-way designs. First, as we have already seen in this chapter, the coefficients we use to form a D variable need to reflect the structure of the two-way design. Second, once we have determined the coefficients that represent the effect of interest, the remaining steps are exactly the same as those for the one-way design, except that the value of w also needs to reflect the structure of the two-way design.

Forming confidence intervals using Equation 13.28 in the two-way within-subjects design is especially straightforward with statistical packages. In fact, all that we need is a package that provides the standard error of a mean, because, as we discussed in Chapter 13, the term under the square root in Equation 13.28 is simply the standard error of the mean of our D variable. In addition, w is the square root of whatever critical value is appropriate (depending on whether this interval is for a single planned comparison, one of C planned comparisons, or was chosen post hoc). In other words, we could rewrite Equation 13.28 as

$$\overline{D} \pm (\sqrt{\text{CV}})(se_{\overline{D}}) \tag{35}$$

where CV is the critical value (such as shown in Equations 31 through 34) and $se_{\overline{D}}$ is the estimated standard error of the mean of D.

Many packages (such as SAS and SPSS) will complete the entire task by also including w in the calculation as long as we are willing to regard this interval as a single planned interval with no need to control for multiple intervals. Notice that some packages also allow the user to specify a confidence level other than 95%, in which case Bonferroni-adjusted intervals can be formed by defining the confidence level (CL, in percentage terms, as opposed to a proportion) to be

$$\text{CL} = 100 - \frac{5}{C} \tag{36}$$

where as usual C is the number of planned comparisons. Forming intervals based on the Roy–Bose critical value will usually require calculating intervals by hand, because most packages will not automatically calculate an interval based on Equations 31 through 34. However, even here values for the mean of D and its standard error can be copied directly from computer output, so all that remains to be done by hand is to multiply the standard error by the Roy–Bose critical value.

For example, Table 14.6 shows a portion of SPSS output providing the mean, standard error, and 95% confidence intervals for four contrasts of possible interest in our reaction time data. As an aside, we should note that as of this writing, SPSS reports not only the mean, its standard error, and a confidence interval, but also other statistics (such as median, trimmed mean, maximum, minimum, skewness, and kurtosis), but we have chosen not to show them here in the interest of brevity. In all four cases, 95% confidence pertains to a single comparison, not a collection of comparisons.

The first variable shown in the table is the same D_1 variable shown previously in Table 14.5. As such, D_1 is the difference for each participant between reaction time for the 8^0 angle condition minus the 0^0 angle condition, averaging over the noise condition. In other words, D_1 represents a contrast of the angle marginal means. Table 14.6 shows us that the sample estimate for the mean of D_1 is 168.00, which is identical to the mean value shown earlier in Table 14.5, as it must be. Table 14.6 further shows that the standard error for the mean of D_1 equals 20.59, which then yields a 95% confidence interval for the population difference between marginal means between 121.42 and 214.58.

The other variables in Table 14.6 reflect other types of effects. Specifically, D_9 has the same definition and meaning as earlier in the chapter in that it represents the difference between the 8^0 angle condition and the 0^0 angle condition when noise is absent. D_{11} is the same contrast between angles, but when noise is present. Finally, the variable labeled as NA_NP08 is an interaction contrast. Namely, it is literally $D_{11} - D_9$. Notice that the mean value of NA_NP08 is exactly equal to the difference in the means of D_{11} and D_9.

TABLE 14.6
CONFIDENCE INTERVALS FOR FOUR CONTRASTS IN REACTION TIME
DATA

Descriptives		Statistic	Std. Error
D_1	Mean	168.0000	20.5913
	95% confidence interval for mean		Lower bound 121.4193
			Upper bound 214.5807
D_9	Mean	66.0000	18.8680
	95% confidence interval for mean		Lower bound 23.3177
			Upper bound 108.6823
D_{11}	Mean	270.0000	27.2029
	95% confidence interval for mean		Lower bound 208.4627
			Upper bound 331.5373
NA_NP08	Mean	204.0000	22.2711
	95% confidence interval for mean		Lower bound 153.6194
			Upper bound 254.3806

Implicit in Table 14.6 is the important point that forming confidence intervals for contrasts in the two-way within-subjects design always involves Equation 35 regardless of the type of effect. Whether the effect is a comparison of marginal means, of simple effects means, or of an interaction contrast, Equation 35 can be used. The only possible difference among these types of contrasts occurs when it is deemed necessary to invoke familywise control of the alpha level, in which case a critical value appropriate to the type of effect must be used.

OPTIONAL

The Relationship Between the Multivariate and the Mixed-Model Approaches

The multivariate and mixed-model approaches to analyzing data from two-way within-subjects designs relate to one another in a very similar manner to the way they are related for analyzing data from one-way designs, which we discussed in Chapter 13. To make the relationship between the two methods explicit, it is again necessary to work with orthonormal contrasts. Recall that orthonormal contrasts must be orthogonal and that the sum of squared coefficients for an orthonormalized contrast equals 1.0.

To develop the relationship between the two approaches, we again consider the data in Table 14.4. Recall that we formed five D variables to test the two main effects and the interaction. When we expressed the coefficients of these variables as integers, the equations for the five D variables were as follows:

$$D_{1i} = -1Y_{1i} + 0Y_{2i} + 1Y_{3i} - 1Y_{4i} + 0Y_{5i} + 1Y_{6i} \qquad \text{(20, repeated)}$$

$$D_{2i} = 1Y_{1i} - 2Y_{2i} + 1Y_{3i} + 1Y_{4i} - 2Y_{5i} + 1Y_{6i} \qquad \text{(21, repeated)}$$

$$D_{3i} = -1Y_{1i} - 1Y_{2i} - 1Y_{3i} + 1Y_{4i} + 1Y_{5i} + 1Y_{6i} \qquad \text{(22, repeated)}$$

$$D_{4i} = 1Y_{1i} + 0Y_{2i} - 1Y_{3i} - 1Y_{4i} + 0Y_{5i} + 1Y_{6i} \qquad \text{(23, repeated)}$$

$$D_{5i} = -1Y_{1i} + 2Y_{2i} - 1Y_{3i} + 1Y_{4i} - 2Y_{5i} + 1Y_{6i} \qquad \text{(24, repeated)}$$

It can be shown that these contrasts are all orthogonal to each other; that is, they form an orthogonal set.[5] Thus, all that remains to be done is to normalize the coefficients of each contrast. As in Chapter 13, this is accomplished by dividing each nonnormalized coefficient by the square root of the sum of squared coefficients for that particular contrast. For example, because the sum of squared coefficients for D_1 is 4, we need to divide each nonnormalized coefficient by 2 (the square root of 4). Carrying out this process

TABLE 14.7
$E^*(F)$ AND $E^*(R)$ MATRICES FOR A MAIN EFFECT, B MAIN
EFFECT, AND A × B INTERACTION

Effect	$E^*(F)$	$E^*(R)$
A	$\begin{bmatrix} 38{,}160.0 & -1{,}870.6 \\ -1{,}870.6 & 25{,}920.0 \end{bmatrix}$	$\begin{bmatrix} 320{,}400.0 & -44{,}686.9 \\ -44{,}686.9 & 33{,}600.0 \end{bmatrix}$
B	$[76{,}140]$	$[361{,}800]$
A×B	$\begin{bmatrix} 11{,}160.0 & 3{,}325.5 \\ 3{,}325.5 & 9{,}720.0 \end{bmatrix}$	$\begin{bmatrix} 115{,}200.0 & -7{,}274.6 \\ -7{,}274.6 & 10{,}800.0 \end{bmatrix}$

for all five D variables results in the following orthonormal set of D^* variables:

$$D^*_{1i} = -.5Y_{1i} + 0Y_{2i} + .5Y_{3i} - .5Y_{4i} + 0Y_{5i} + .5Y_{6i}$$

$$D^*_{2i} = .2887Y_{1i} - .5774Y_{2i} + .2887Y_{3i} + .2887Y_{4i} - .5774Y_{5i} + .2887Y_{6i}$$

$$D^*_{3i} = -.4082Y_{1i} - .4082Y_{2i} - .4082Y_{3i} + .4082Y_{4i} + .4082Y_{5i} + .4082Y_{6i}$$

$$D^*_{4i} = .5Y_{1i} + 0Y_{2i} - .5Y_{3i} - .5Y_{4i} + 0Y_{5i} + .5Y_{6i}$$

$$D^*_{5i} = -.2887Y_{1i} + .5774Y_{2i} - .2887Y_{3i} + .2887Y_{4i} - .5774Y_{5i} + .2887Y_{6i}$$

Remember that D^*_1 and D^*_2 represent the angle main effect, D^*_3 represents the noise main effect, and D^*_4 and D^*_5 represent the interaction. For each test, there is a full matrix, denoted $E^*(F)$, and a restricted matrix, denoted $E^*(R)$. Computation of these matrices follows the same principles used in Chapter 13, so we do not bother with computational details here. Instead, we simply refer you to Table 14.7, which presents three $E^*(F)$ and three $E^*(R)$ matrices, one for each of the three effects being tested.

Comparing Table 14.7 to Table 12.5 shows that the same relationship holds here between the sum of the diagonal elements of an E^* matrix in the multivariate approach and a sum-of-squares term in the mixed-model approach. For example, the sum of the two diagonal elements of $E^*(F)$ for the A main effect equals 64,080, which is equal to $SS_{A \times S}$ in the mixed-model approach. The sum of the two diagonal elements of $E^*(R)$ for the A main effect equals 354,000. Subtracting 64,080 from 354,000 yields 289,920, which is the value of SS_A in the mixed-model approach. The same type of equality holds for the B and the $A \times B$ effects. As a result, the mixed-model F for an effect can again be written in terms of the multivariate matrices as

$$F = \frac{\{tr(E^*(R)) - tr(E^*(F))\}/df_{\text{effect}}}{tr(E^*(F))/(n-1)df_{\text{effect}}} \tag{37}$$

where $tr(E^*(R))$ and $tr(E^*(F))$ denote the trace (i.e., sum of diagonal elements) of the restricted and full matrices for the effect being tested. Notice that Equation 37 is a straightforward generalization of Equation 13.32, which we developed for a one-way within-subjects design:

$$F = \frac{(tr(E^*(R)) - tr(E^*(F)))/(a-1)}{tr(E^*(F))/(n-1)(a-1)} \tag{13.32, repeated}$$

As in the one-way design, the mixed-model F test differs from the multivariate F test because the mixed-model F test is based on an assumption of sphericity. If the sphericity assumption is met, the population values of the off-diagonal elements of an $E^*(F)$ matrix are all zero. In addition, if sphericity holds, the population values of the diagonal elements of $E^*(F)$ are all equal to one another; thus, the sample mean of these values (i.e., $tr(E^*(F))/df_{\text{effect}}$) is a good estimate of the single underlying population value. As we discussed in Chapter 12, sphericity may be met for some effects and yet fail for other effects, even in the same study. For example, the sphericity assumption is necessarily true for the B effect in our study because the B factor has only two levels. As a result, we only needed to form one D variable to capture the B main effect, and there are no off-diagonal elements in $\mathbf{E}^*(\mathbf{F})$ for the B main effect (see Table 14.7). Also, there is only one diagonal element of $\mathbf{E}^*(\mathbf{F})$; thus, equality of all diagonal elements need not be a concern. Not only is there no need to assume sphericity for the B effect here, but the mixed-model and multivariate approaches yielded exactly the same F value for the B main effect in our data. With both approaches, the F value was 33.77, with 1 and 9 df. Such an equality always occurs for all single degree of freedom effects, as long as $MS_{\text{effect} \times S}$ is used as the error term in the mixed-model approach.

It is also important to realize that the test of the B main effect in our example is valid even if compound symmetry fails to hold for the 6×6 matrix that would result from correlating scores in the six different conditions. Recall that compound symmetry requires that all correlations be equal to one another in the population. However, we have just argued that the sphericity assumption is always met for an effect with only 1 df (as long as $MS_{\text{effect} \times S}$ is used as the error term), so sphericity and compound symmetry are different assumptions. It can be shown that compound symmetry implies sphericity—that is, if the compound symmetry assumption is met, the sphericity assumption is also met. However, the reverse is not always true, because it is possible for sphericity to hold in the absence of compound symmetry.

■

Multivariate and Mixed-Model Approaches for Testing Contrasts

The relationship between the multivariate and mixed-model approaches for testing contrasts in the two-way within-subjects design is much the same as the relationship in the one-way design. For the same reasons as we discussed in Chapter 13, we recommend testing a contrast with an error term that corresponds specifically to that contrast. The formula for the F test of a contrast is given by

$$F = n\overline{D}^2/s_D^2 \qquad \text{(13.6, repeated)}$$

Notice that this formula for the F test is appropriate for testing both planned and post hoc comparisons.

The purpose of this section is to compare the mixed-model and multivariate approaches to testing contrasts in a two-way within-subjects design. As we discussed in Chapter 12, either of two error terms might be used for testing a within-subjects comparison. One approach uses a pooled error term (see, for example, Equations 12.7 and 12.11), whereas the second approach uses a separate error term (see, for example, Equations 12.8 and 12.12). As we have stated before, our preference is strongly in favor of the separate error term, because it does not assume sphericity. The pooled error term, on the other hand, does assume sphericity, and F tests using the pooled error term are not robust to violations of sphericity.

If planned comparisons are tested, there is no need to perform an omnibus test. In this circumstance, it is not really meaningful to talk in terms of the multivariate or mixed-model approach because these are two approaches for conducting the omnibus test. Nevertheless, using a pooled error term for testing planned comparisons closely parallels the mixed-model approach to conducting the omnibus test, because both assume sphericity. Using a separate error term, on the other hand, parallels the multivariate approach because neither assumes sphericity. When comparisons are tested in a post hoc fashion, there is an even stronger connection. The omnibus test is statistically significant with the mixed-model approach if and only if a statistically significant comparison can be found using a *pooled* error term and a critical value of the form

$$CV = (df_{\text{effect}})F_{\alpha_{\text{FW}}; df_{\text{effect}}, df_{\text{effect} \times S}}$$

where df_{effect} refers to the omnibus effect (for example, the A main effect). On the other hand, the omnibus test is statistically significant with the multivariate approach if and only if a statistically significant comparison can be found using a separate error term and a critical value of the form

$$CV = (n-1)(df_{\text{effect}})F_{\alpha_{\text{FW}}; df_{\text{effect}}, n - df_{\text{effect}}}/(n - df_{\text{effect}}) \qquad \text{(34, repeated)}$$

Thus, the use of a pooled error term is compatible with the mixed-model approach, and the use of a separate error term is compatible with the multivariate approach, just as was true in Chapter 13 for the one-way design. Once again, this is a major reason for preferring the multivariate approach to repeated measures.

Comparison of the Multivariate and Mixed-Model Approaches

The advantages and disadvantages of the multivariate and mixed-model approaches in the two-way within-subjects design are essentially the same as in the one-way design. Instead of repeating their relative merits here, we refer you to our earlier extended discussion of this issue at the end of Chapter 13. As before, our general recommendation is to use the multivariate approach unless sample sizes are very small. For a rough rule of thumb, for testing any within-subjects effect with the multivariate approach, n should probably exceed the degrees of freedom for the effect by at least 10 to 20 or more.

ONE WITHIN-SUBJECTS FACTOR AND ONE BETWEEN-SUBJECTS FACTOR IN THE SAME DESIGN

A second type of factorial design with a within-subjects factor is the split-plot design, which contains a between-subjects factor as well as a within-subjects factor. Chapter 12 discussed several reasons for the importance of this design in the behavioral sciences.

We begin our discussion of this design by considering the same example that we analyzed in Chapter 12. Recall that in the example a perceptual psychologist is interested in age differences in reaction time on a perceptual task. As in Chapter 12, age is a between-subjects factor with two levels (young and old). The other factor in the design, angle, has three levels (0°, 4°, and 8°), which represent the position of the stimulus item in the participant's visual field. As in Chapter 12, angle is a within-subjects factor.

Split-Plot Design With Two Levels of the Repeated Factor

To simplify our initial consideration of the multivariate approach to split-plot designs, we begin with an example where the within-subjects factor has only two levels. The formulas we develop here serve primarily to illustrate the logic that can also be applied when the repeated factor has more than two levels. Table 14.8 presents the same data that we analyzed in Chapter 12 for 10

TABLE 14.8
REACTION TIME DATA FOR YOUNG
AND OLD SUBJECTS IN THE 0° AND
8° ANGLE CONDITIONS

Young Subjects	0°	8°
1	450	630
2	390	540
3	570	660
4	450	720
5	510	630
6	360	450
7	510	720
8	510	780
9	510	660
10	510	660
Mean	477	645
Old Subjects	**0°**	**8°**
1	420	690
2	600	810
3	450	690
4	630	780
5	420	780
6	600	870
7	630	870
8	480	720
9	690	900
10	510	810
Mean	543	792

young participants and 10 old participants, except that for the moment we are only analyzing data from the 0° and 8° conditions of the angle factor.[6]

In any two-factor design, the effects to be tested are typically the two main effects and the two-way interaction. In our example, then, we test the main effect of age (which we will designate as A), the main effect of angle (which we designate as B), and the interaction of age and angle.

Main Effect of Between-Subjects Factor

As usual, the multivariate approach to this within-subjects design requires that we create new transformed variables (e.g., D variables) to perform significance tests. To understand the nature of these variables in a split-plot design, we begin by considering the main effect of age, the between-subjects factor. As always, a main effect involves a comparison of marginal means, averaging over the other factor(s) in the design. For our data, we need to average over the angle factor. We can accomplish this quite easily for each subject, simply by averaging each participant's 0° score with his or her 8° score. To formalize this notion, we let

$$Y_{1ij} = 0° \text{ angle reaction time} \quad \text{and} \quad Y_{2ij} = 8° \text{ angle reaction time}$$

for participant i in group j. Then, the average score for this individual is simply given by

$$M_{ij} = (Y_{1ij} + Y_{2ij})/2 \tag{38}$$

The designation of M will be used here to remind us that we are computing a mean score for each participant. Notice that this M variable is similar to the D variables we have encountered previously in that both M and D are new, transformed variables that are linear combinations of the original Y variables. However, the M variable differs from these D variables in that D variables involve differences among the Ys, whereas M does not. Indeed, the coefficients assigned to the Ys have always summed to zero for all our D variables, but they obviously do not sum to zero for M. Whereas the D variables can be thought of as contrasts among the Y variables, the M variable is an average of all the Ys instead of a difference between them.

Table 14.9 presents the M scores for the 20 participants whose Y scores were shown in Table 14.8. (Table 14.9 also shows D scores. Although you can probably guess how they were calculated, do not worry about them for the moment.) Now that we have calculated M scores for each participant, the test of the age main effect is straightforward. The sample marginal mean on M for the young participants is 561 (see Table 14.9), which is simply the average reaction time for younger participants, where we have averaged over the $0°$ and $8°$ angle conditions. Notice that 561 is the average of 477 and 645, which were shown in Table 14.8 to be the mean reaction times for younger participants in the $0°$ and $8°$ angle conditions, respectively. Similarly, the value of the sample mean on M for the older participants, 667.5, is the average of 543 and 792, the $0°$ and $8°$ angle means for older participants. The test of the age main effect is simply a test of whether the two sample means on M are statistically significantly different from one another. We can answer this question by performing a one-way between-subjects ANOVA, using the M score for each participant as the dependent variable. Thus, this test is a

TABLE 14.9
M AND D SCORES FOR THE DATA
IN TABLE 14.8

Young Subjects	M	D
1	540	180
2	465	150
3	615	90
4	585	270
5	570	120
6	405	90
7	615	210
8	645	270
9	585	150
10	585	150
Mean	561	168

Old Subjects	M	D
1	555	270
2	705	210
3	570	240
4	705	150
5	600	360
6	735	270
7	750	240
8	600	240
9	795	210
10	660	300
Mean	667.5	249

straightforward application of the principles we developed in Chapter 3. Specifically, we can compare a full model to a restricted model, using the same models we used in Chapter 3. We write the full model as

$$M_{ij} = \mu + \alpha_j + \varepsilon_{ij} \tag{39}$$

where M_{ij} is the mean score on Y_1 and Y_2 for participant i in Group j, μ is the grand mean parameter for M, α_j is the effect of the jth level of A (the between-subjects factor) on M, and ε_{ij} is the error associated with participant i in Group j. As usual, the effect parameters α_j are defined so that $\alpha_j = \mu_j - \mu$, where μ_j is the population mean on the M variable for Group j and μ is the grand mean, defined as $\mu = \sum \mu_j / a$. The null hypothesis to be tested for the A main effect implies that the α_j parameters all equal zero, leading to a restricted model given by

$$M_{ij} = \mu + \varepsilon_{ij} \tag{40}$$

The full and restricted models are compared using least-squares estimates of the parameters in each model, which yields our usual F test:

$$F = \frac{(E_R - E_F)/(df_R - df_F)}{E_F/df_F}$$

Because we are performing a one-way between-subjects ANOVA with M as the dependent variable, we can simplify the expression for the F statistic just as we did in Chapter 3:

$$F = \frac{\sum\limits_{j=1}^{a} n_j (\overline{M}_j - \overline{M})^2/(a-1)}{\sum\limits_{j=1}^{a} \sum\limits_{i=1}^{n_j} (M_{ij} - \overline{M}_j)^2/(N-a)} \tag{41}$$

where $\overline{M}_j$ and $\overline{M}$ are the mean for the jth group and the grand mean, respectively, and N is the total number of participants summed over the levels of the between-subjects factor. In our example, $N = 20$, because $n_1 = 10$ and $n_2 = 10$. We also have $\overline{M}_1 = 561$, $\overline{M}_2 = 667.5$, $\overline{M} = 614.25$, and $\sum_{j=1}^{a} \sum_{i=1}^{n_j} (M_{ij} - \overline{M}_j)^2 = 110{,}452.5$ (see Table 14.9). Substituting these values into Equation 41 yields an F value of 9.24 with 1 and 18 df. The corresponding p value is .007; thus, the age main effect is statistically significant at the .05 level. We postpone a more general discussion of the between-subjects main effect until we consider a design with more than two levels of the within-subjects factor.

Within-Subjects Effects

Notice that the age main effect here is a between-subjects effect, because it averages over the within-subjects factor. The other two effects yet to be tested, the angle main effect and the age × angle interaction, are within-subjects effects, because both involve the difference between scores in the 0° angle condition and the 8° angle condition. Indeed, consistent with the multivariate approach to repeated measures, both of these effects are tested by forming D variables. A single D variable is sufficient to represent the angle effect in our example, because angle has only two levels:

$$D_{ij} = Y_{2ij} - Y_{1ij} \tag{42}$$

where Y_{2ij} is the $8°$ angle reaction time and Y_{1ij} is the $0°$ angle reaction time for participant i in Group j. (We could just as easily have defined D_{ij} to be $Y_{1ij} - Y_{2ij}$. The F values would be identical either way.) The right-most column of Table 14.9 shows the D scores calculated from Table 14.8 for our 20 participants.

Before proceeding with a formal test, let's pause momentarily to think intuitively about what the D scores in Table 14.9 mean. One striking characteristic of these D scores is that all 20 participants have a positive D value. This is important, because it means that every participant's reaction time was longer in the $8°$ angle condition than in the $0°$ angle condition, which strongly suggests the presence of an angle main effect. As always, the main effect averages over the other factor(s) in the design. Thus, the angle main effect should average over the two age groups instead of comparing them. The angle main-effects test should be a test of whether the average D score differs significantly from zero, when we average over both age groups. The other effect to be tested is the age $\times$ angle interaction. Unlike the angle main effect, the interaction does involve a comparison of the age groups, because the interaction is a measure of whether the angle effect differs for the different age groups. It is important to realize that the D score we have calculated is a measure of the angle effect for each participant. To the extent that these D scores tend to be larger for some age groups than for others, an interaction is indicated. We can see from Table 14.9 that in our example the angle effect tends to be larger for older participants than for younger ones. At this point, you should have some intuitive feeling that the D scores are useful for answering two questions. First, the average of all the D scores seems related to the angle main effect. Second, the difference between the D scores for older and younger participants seems related to the age $\times$ angle interaction. We now show how formal tests can be developed from these relationships.

Notice from Table 14.9 that we have a one-way between-subjects design for the D variable, just as we had for the M variable. As a result, we can again write a full model of the form

$$D_{ij} = \mu + \alpha_j + \varepsilon_{ij} \tag{43}$$

where D_{ij} is the difference between Y_2 and Y_1 for participant i in Group j, μ is the grand mean parameter for D, α_j is the effect of the jth level of A (the between-subjects factor) on D, and ε_{ij} is the error associated with participant i in Group j. It is extremely important to realize that the μ and α_j terms of Equation 43 generally have different values from the μ and α_j terms of Equation 39, because in one case the dependent variable is D, whereas in the other case it is M. In other words, the two equations have the same form because both are full models for one-way between-subjects designs; however, the numerical values of the parameters and the parameter estimates will generally differ in the two equations, because the dependent variables are different. The parameters in Equation 43 are defined in the usual manner, so that $\alpha_j = \mu_j - \mu$, where μ_j is the population mean on the D variable for Group j, and μ is the grand mean on the D variable. We define the grand mean μ to be $\mu = \sum_{j=1}^{a} \mu_j / a$. However, an alternate definition might be used with unequal n, where μ could be defined as $\mu = \sum_{j=1}^{a} n_j \mu_j / N$. The distinction is that the first definition yields an unweighted mean and the second yields a weighted mean. Of course, with equal n, the two definitions are equivalent.[7]

Test of the Interaction

Recall from our intuitive discussion that we need to perform two tests on the D variable. The angle main effect is a test of the average value of D, averaging over A. The age $\times$ angle interaction is a test of whether the average D value differs at different levels of A. We consider both of these tests, beginning with the interaction. If there is no interaction in the population, then the two age groups should show the same mean effect for angle. Recall that D represents the angle effect. Thus, if there is no interaction, the two age groups should show no mean difference on D. In other words, if the null hypothesis is true that there is no interaction, the α_j parameters all equal zero. An appropriate restricted model is given by

$$D_{ij} = \mu + \varepsilon_{ij} \tag{44}$$

The F test from Chapter 3 can be used to compare the full model of Equation 43 to the restricted model of Equation 44. Analogous to the F test on the M variable (Equation 41), the F test for the interaction is given by[8]

$$F = \frac{\sum\limits_{j=1}^{a} n_j (\overline{D}_j - \overline{D})^2 / (a-1)}{\sum\limits_{j=1}^{a} \sum\limits_{i=1}^{n_j} (D_{ij} - \overline{D}_j)^2 / (N-a)} \tag{45}$$

Substituting the values from Table 14.9 along with $\overline{D} = 208.5$ and $\sum \sum (D_{ij} - \overline{D}_j)^2 = 67,050$ into Equation 45 yields an F value of 8.81, with 1 and 18 df. The corresponding p value is .008; thus, the age × angle interaction is statistically significant at the .05 level. From Table 14.9, we can see that the angle effect is stronger for older participants ($\overline{D}_2 = 249$), than for younger participants ($\overline{D}_1 = 168$). We postpone a discussion of follow-up tests for the interaction until we consider a design with more than two levels of the within-subjects factor.

Within-Subjects Main Effect

The one remaining omnibus effect to be tested is the within-subjects main effect, that is, the angle main effect in our example. We argued earlier that an angle main effect would be reflected in the average D score, averaging over age groups. Specifically, the grand mean of D should be statistically different from zero if there is an angle main effect. On the other hand, if there is no angle main effect in the population, then the population grand mean of D equals zero. The population grand mean of D is represented by μ in the full model of Equation 43. Thus, if the null hypothesis is true that there is no angle main effect, μ equals zero. An appropriate restricted model is given by

$$D_{ij} = \alpha_j + \varepsilon_{ij} \tag{46}$$

Our task at this point is to compare this restricted model of Equation 46 to the full model of Equation 43. We already know that the full model is equivalent to a cell means model; thus, the full model predicts each participant's score to be the mean score of that participant's group, that is, $\hat{D}_{ij}(F) = \overline{D}_j$. As a result, the sum of squared errors for the full model equals

$$E_F = \sum_{j=1}^{a} \sum_{i=1}^{n_j} [D_{ij} - \hat{D}_{ij}(F)]^2$$

$$= \sum_{j=1}^{a} \sum_{i=1}^{n_j} (D_{ij} - \overline{D}_j)^2 \tag{47}$$

We must now consider the sum of squared errors for the restricted model of Equation 46, which is a model unlike any other we have considered previously in this book, because it has no grand mean term. For this reason, we consider the sum of squared errors for this model in considerable detail. It is crucial to remember that the α_j parameters are not independent of one another. Recall that α_j is defined as $\alpha_j = \mu_j - \mu$. As a result

$$\sum_{j=1}^{a} \alpha_j = \sum_{j=1}^{a}(\mu_j - \mu) = \sum_{j=1}^{a}\mu_j - \sum_{j=1}^{a}\mu = \sum_{j=1}^{a}\mu_j - a\mu$$

However, $\mu = \sum_{j=1}^{a}\mu_j/a$, so

$$\sum_{j=1}^{a} \alpha_j = \sum_{j=1}^{a}\mu_j - a\left(\sum_{j=1}^{a}\mu_j/a\right)$$

$$= \sum_{j=1}^{a}\mu_j - \sum_{j=1}^{a}\mu_j = 0$$

Thus, the individual α_j values are constrained to sum to zero.[9] In the case of two levels of A, such as in our example, it follows that $\alpha_2 = -\alpha_1$. In general, the implication is that we have only $a-1$ independent α_j parameters. This is all relevant, because we must find the least-squares estimates of the α_j parameters in Equation 46. Because the α_j parameters are constrained to sum to zero, it is necessary to use constrained least squares to obtain parameter estimates. Because this approach is too advanced for our level, we simply state without proof that the constrained least-squares estimator for α_j in Equation 46 turns out to be $\hat{\alpha}_j = \overline{D}_j - \overline{D}$.[10]

Notice that the sum of these parameter estimates, that is, $\sum_{j=1}^{a}\hat{\alpha}_j$ is guaranteed to obey the constraint of summing to zero. For example, in our data, we know that $\overline{D}_1 = 168$ and $\overline{D}_2 = 249$ from Table 14.9. Thus, $\overline{D} = 208.5$, and the values of the parameter estimates are

$$\hat{\alpha}_1 = 168 - 208.5 = -40.5$$

$$\hat{\alpha}_2 = 249 - 208.5 = 40.5$$

It can be shown that any other pair of values that sums to zero results in a larger sum of squares than the values of -40.5 and 40.5. In general, the restricted model of Equation 46 predicts each participant's score to be equal to $\hat{\alpha}_j$, that is

$$\hat{D}_{ij}(R) = \hat{\alpha}_j = \overline{D}_j - \overline{D}$$

As a result, the sum of squared errors for the restricted model equals

$$E_R = \sum_{j=1}^{a}\sum_{i=1}^{n_j}[D_{ij} - \hat{D}_{ij}(R)]^2$$

$$= \sum_{j=1}^{a}\sum_{i=1}^{n_j}[D_{ij} - (\overline{D}_j - \overline{D})]^2$$

To obtain a more workable form of E_R, it is helpful to rewrite E_R as

$$E_R = \sum_{j=1}^{a}\sum_{i=1}^{n_j}[(D_{ij} - \overline{D}_j) + \overline{D}]^2$$

Expanding the square of this expression, we get

$$E_R = \sum_{j=1}^{a} \sum_{i=1}^{n_j} (D_{ij} - \overline{D}_j)^2 + 2\sum_{j=1}^{a} \sum_{i=1}^{n_j} (D_{ij} - \overline{D}_j)\overline{D} + \sum_{j=1}^{a} \sum_{i=1}^{n_j} \overline{D}^2$$

However, this expression can be simplified in two ways. First, the middle term equals zero, because $\overline{D}$ is a constant and can be factored out. We are then left with each participant's deviation from the group mean, which equals zero within each group. Second, the far right term equals $N\overline{D}^2$, where N is total sample size. This follows because $\overline{D}^2$ is a constant for every participant. Thus, we can rewrite E_R as

$$E_R = \sum_{j=1}^{a} \sum_{i=1}^{n_j} (D_{ij} - \overline{D}_j)^2 + N\overline{D}^2$$

However, from Equation 47, we know that

$$\sum_{j=1}^{a} \sum_{i=1}^{n_j} (D_{ij} - \overline{D}_j)^2 = E_F$$

so that

$$E_R = E_F + N\overline{D}^2$$

which means that the difference in the error sums of squares of the restricted and full models is given by

$$E_R - E_F = N\overline{D}^2 \tag{48}$$

To be certain that you don't miss the forest because of the trees, what all of the preceding algebra has shown is that the sum of squares for the angle main effect equals $N\overline{D}^2$. For our data, $N = 20$ and $\overline{D} = 208.5$, so the sum of squares for the angle main effect equals 869,445. This expression for the sum of squares of the within-subjects main effect should seem reasonable to you even if you had trouble understanding the algebraic derivation. Notice that $\overline{D}^2$ is large anytime $\overline{D}$ differs substantially from zero, either positively or negatively. However, we argued earlier that it is just such a departure of $\overline{D}$ from zero that indicates an angle main effect. The presence of N in the formula should also seem reasonable, because $\overline{D}$, the difference in the marginal means of the within-subjects factor, is based on N participants.

Now that we have found the expression for the difference in the sum of squared errors of the restricted and full models, we can easily write the expression for the F test of the angle main effect. Recall that the general form of the F statistic is given by

$$F = \frac{(E_R - E_F)/(df_R - df_F)}{E_F/df_F}$$

From Equation 48, we know that

$$E_R - E_F = N\overline{D}^2$$

From Equation 47, we know that

$$E_F = \sum_{j=1}^{a} \sum_{i=1}^{n_j} (D_{ij} - \overline{D}_j)^2$$

All that remains is to determine the degrees of freedom of the two models. As we showed earlier, in general, the restricted model has $a - 1$ independent parameters, so its degrees of freedom equal $N - (a - 1)$, or $N - a + 1$. The full model has a parameters, so its degrees of freedom equal $N - a$. Of course, then, $df_R - df_F = 1$. This is logical, because the restricted model has one fewer parameter (namely, μ) than the full model. Thus, the F statistic for the within-subjects main effect equals

$$F = \frac{N\overline{D}^2}{\sum\limits_{j=1}^{a} \sum\limits_{i=1}^{n_j} (D_{ij} - \overline{D}_j)^2 / (N - a)} \tag{49}$$

with 1 and $N - a$ degrees of freedom.[11] For our data, the observed value of the F statistic equals 233.41, with 1 and 18 df, which is obviously highly statistically significant. As we suspected from a visual inspection of the D scores in Table 14.9, participants responded significantly more slowly in the $8°$ angle condition than in the $0°$ angle condition. One final point will be helpful to us later when we consider split-plot designs with more than two levels of the within-subjects factor. Notice that the denominator terms of Equations 45 and 49 are identical. This means that the error term for the interaction test is identical to the error term for the within-subjects main-effects test. The reason for this equivalence is that both tests use the model shown in Equation 43 as the full model, and the full model comprises the denominator of the F test. As you may recall, this equivalence also parallels an equivalence of error terms in the mixed-model approach, where $MS_{B \times S/A}$ was used as the error term for testing both the B and $A \times B$ effects.

Summary

Thus, Equations 41, 45, and 49 provide F tests for the multivariate approach to the between-subjects main effect, the interaction, and the within-subjects main effect, respectively, in a split-plot design where the repeated factor has only two levels. Although these equations have some intrinsic merit, they are useful primarily as building blocks for split-plot designs where the repeated factor has more than two levels. The reasons these equations are not especially interesting in and of themselves is that when the repeated factor has only two levels, the F tests of the multivariate approach are equivalent to those of the mixed-model approach. Thus, when the repeated factor has only two levels, Equation 12.17 is equivalent to Equation 14.41, Equation 12.18 is equivalent to Equation 14.49, and Equation 12.19 is equivalent to Equation 14.45. The reason for this equivalence is that, as we have seen before, when the repeated factor has only two levels, the sphericity assumption is necessarily satisfied. However, when the repeated factor has three or more levels, sphericity may or may not hold. Whether it does or does not, the multivariate and mixed-model approaches are no longer equivalent. Although Equations 45 and 49 no longer apply when the repeated factor has three or more levels, the logic behind the comparison of models is still relevant. The only complication (admittedly, not a minor one) is that we need more than one D variable, requiring us again to formulate matrices in order to arrive at F tests.

General $a \times b$ Split-Plot Design

Although the principles developed in the previous section for the split-plot design with two levels of the repeated factor can also be applied when the repeated factor has more than two levels, the actual analysis is more complicated. We saw that when the repeated factor has two levels, we form two new variables. One of these variables, which we designate M, is a participant's mean score and is used to test the between-subjects main effect. The other variable, which we designate D, is the difference between the participant's two original scores and is used to test the two within-subjects effects (i.e., the within-subjects main effect and the two-way interaction). Although we have two variables (M and D), the multivariate approach can be carried out with univariate tests when there are only two levels of the repeated factor, because we do not test M and D simultaneously. However, when the repeated factor has more than two levels, the within-subjects tests of the multivariate approach are truly multivariate. The reason is that it is necessary to form more than one D variable and to test these multiple D variables simultaneously, much as we did in Chapter 13 and earlier in this chapter.

To make our discussion of analyzing the $a \times b$ split-plot design easier to follow, we continue with our perceptual experiment. So far in our discussion of the multivariate approach to the split-plot design, we have considered the data in Table 14.8, which omitted the 4° angle condition. At this point, we reinstate the 4° condition so that we have a 2 × 3 design, where it is the repeated factor that has three levels. Table 14.10 presents data for the 2 × 3 design. These data are identical to those analyzed in Chapter 12 (see Tables 12.7 and 12.15) to facilitate comparisons of the multivariate approach and the mixed-model approach.

TABLE 14.10
REACTION TIME DATA FOR YOUNG AND OLD
SUBJECTS IN THREE ANGLE CONDITIONS

Young Subjects	0°	4°	8°
1	450	510	630
2	390	480	540
3	570	630	660
4	450	660	720
5	510	660	630
6	360	450	450
7	510	600	720
8	510	660	780
9	510	660	660
10	510	540	660
Mean	477	585	645

Old Subjects	0°	4°	8°
1	420	570	690
2	600	720	810
3	450	540	690
4	630	660	780
5	420	570	780
6	600	780	870
7	630	690	870
8	480	570	720
9	690	750	900
10	510	690	810
Mean	543	654	792

Between-Subjects Main Effect

We will assume that we are interested in testing the two main effects and the interaction. As usual, the first step in the multivariate approach to the $a \times b$ split-plot design is to create new, transformed variables. As in the design we considered earlier with only two levels of the repeated factor, we begin by computing a variable to represent each participant's mean score across the levels of the within-subjects factor. We adopt the following notation:

$$Y_{1ij} = 0° \text{ angle reaction time}$$

$$Y_{2ij} = 4° \text{ angle reaction time}$$

$$Y_{3ij} = 8° \text{ angle reaction time}$$

for participant i in Group j. For our data, each participant's mean score is simply calculated as

$$M_{ij} = (Y_{1ij} + Y_{2ij} + Y_{3ij})/3$$

Regardless of the number of levels of the within-subjects factor or of the between-subjects factor, only one M variable is formed. With b levels of the within-subjects factor, the formula for M is

$$M_{ij} = \sum_{k=1}^{b} Y_{kij}/b \tag{50}$$

where Y_{kij} designates the score for participant i in Group j at level k of the repeated factor. Indeed, only one M variable is formed even if there is more than one within-subjects factor and/or more than one between-subjects factor. After all, a participant's average score can always be represented by one number, namely, the mean of all of his or her scores. More technically, M is used to test between-subjects effects, which by their very nature average over all within-subjects factors. Thus, in any design with one or more between-subjects factors and one or more within-subjects factors, we always form one M variable, which represents each participant's mean score averaged over every score for that participant.[12]

Table 14.11 presents the M score for each of the 20 participants whose Y scores were shown in Table 14.10. (Table 14.11 also presents scores on D_1 and D_2, to be discussed later.) We can test the age main effect by performing a one-way between-subjects ANOVA with M as the dependent variable. The equation for the observed F value is the same as it was when the repeated factor (i.e., angle) had only two levels:

$$F = \frac{\sum_{j=1}^{a} n_j(\overline{M}_j - \overline{M})^2/(a-1)}{\sum_{j=1}^{a} \sum_{i=1}^{n_j} (M_{ij} - \overline{M}_j)^2/(N-a)} \tag{41, repeated}$$

Substituting the values from Table 14.11 into Equation 41 yields an F value of 7.28 with 1 and 18 df. The corresponding p value is .0147; thus, the age main effect is statistically significant at the .05 level.

Before considering the other two effects to be tested, we want to compare the F value we obtained here with the F value we obtained in Chapter 12 using the mixed-model approach for these same data. Looking back at Table 12.19 shows that the mixed-model approach also

TABLE 14.11
M, D_1, AND D_2 SCORES FOR THE DATA IN TABLE 14.9

Young Subjects	M	D_1	D_2
1	530	180	60
2	470	150	−30
3	620	90	−30
4	610	270	−150
5	600	120	−180
6	420	90	−90
7	610	210	30
8	650	270	−30
9	610	150	−150
10	570	150	90
Mean	$\overline{M}_1 = 569$	$\overline{D}_{11} = 168$	$\overline{D}_{21} = -48$

Old Subjects	M	D_1	D_2
1	560	270	−30
2	710	210	−30
3	560	240	60
4	690	150	90
5	590	360	60
6	750	270	−90
7	730	240	120
8	590	240	60
9	780	210	90
10	670	300	−60
Mean	$\overline{M}_2 = 663$	$\overline{D}_{12} = 249$	$\overline{D}_{22} = 27$

yielded an F value of 7.28 with 1 and 18 df for the age main effect. The multivariate and mixed-model approaches are equivalent here, because the age main effect is a between-subjects effect. To test this effect, we have averaged over the within-subjects factor, leaving us with a between-subjects design. The multivariate and mixed model approaches differ only in tests involving the within-subjects effect (i.e., tests involving angle). Notice that this equivalence is also consistent with our discussion of assumptions in Chapter 12, because we stated there that the sphericity assumption is not required for testing the between-subjects main effect. Thus, it is unnecessary to choose between the multivariate and mixed-model approaches for testing between-subjects effects in split-plot designs, because they always yield equivalent results for these effects.

Within-Subjects Effects

Not surprisingly, the multivariate approach does not yield the same results as the mixed-model approach for testing the within-subjects main effect or the interaction when the repeated factor has more than two levels. To test within-subjects effects with the multivariate approach, it is necessary to form D variables. As usual, if the repeated factor has b levels, $b - 1$ D variables must be created. In our example, angle has three levels, so we must form two D variables. The choice of the two variables does not matter for the omnibus test (you may recall our demonstration of this fact in Chapter 13). However, it is convenient to form D variables to represent specific comparisons we may wish to test of the repeated factor. Because the angle factor in our example is quantitative, we choose D_1 and D_2 to represent the linear and quadratic trends for angle, respectively. With three levels, from Appendix Table A.10, the coefficients of the linear trend are -1, 0, and 1, and those of the quadratic trend are 1, -2, and 1. Thus, in terms of our original Y variables, D_1 and D_2 are defined as

$$D_{1ij} = -1Y_{1ij} + 0Y_{2ij} + 1Y_{3ij}$$

$$D_{2ij} = 1Y_{1ij} - 2Y_{2ij} + 1Y_{3ij}$$

where Y_{1ij}, Y_{2ij}, and Y_{3ij} are the $0°$, $4°$, and $8°$ angle reaction times, respectively, for participant i in Group j. Notice that D_{1ij} could be rewritten simply as the difference between the $8°$ and the $0°$ scores for each participant: $D_{1ij} = Y_{3ij} - Y_{1ij}$. Table 14.11 presents D_1 and D_2 scores for each of our 20 participants.

The tests of the angle main effect and the age $\times$ angle interaction proceed much as they did when the angle factor had only two levels. The only difference is that we now have two D variables to be analyzed simultaneously, whereas before we had only one D variable. As a result, we must consider full and restricted matrices for our data, instead of just full and restricted sums of squared errors. Recall that when we had only one D variable, we formed a full model of the form

$$D_{ij} = \mu + \alpha_j + \varepsilon_{ij} \tag{43, repeated}$$

With two D variables, we need one full model for D_1 and a second full model for D_2. These full models are given by

$$D_{1ij} = \mu_1 + \alpha_{1j} + \varepsilon_{1ij} \tag{51}$$

$$D_{2ij} = \mu_2 + \alpha_{2j} + \varepsilon_{2ij} \tag{52}$$

Notice that μ_1 is the grand mean parameter for D_1, and μ_2 is the grand mean parameter for D_2. Similarly, α_{1j} and α_{2j} are the between-subjects effect parameters for D_1 and D_2, respectively. Do not let the extra subscript 1 or 2 in Equation 51 and 52 (as compared to Equation 43) confuse you. For example, μ_1 has the same meaning for D_1 as μ had for D. We simply need the 1 subscript to distinguish the grand mean of D_1 from the grand mean of D_2. As when the repeated factor had two levels, we generally prefer to define μ_1 and μ_2 as unweighted means if sample sizes are unequal. Be certain to understand that if the repeated factor had b levels, we would have $b - 1$ full models, one for each of the $b - 1$ D variables we would have formed.

Within-Subjects Main Effect

We need to consider two restricted models for D_1 and D_2, one that allows us to test the interaction and the other that allows us to test the within-subjects main effect. Let's consider the within-subjects main effect first. The null hypothesis for this effect states that the grand means of all the b original Y variables are equal to each other. However, this is equivalent to stating that the grand means of all the $b - 1$ D variables equal zero. In our example, where $b = 3$, we have two restricted models, one for D_1 and another for D_2. The restricted models for testing this hypothesis are given by

$$D_{1ij} = \alpha_{1j} + \varepsilon_{1ij} \tag{53}$$

$$D_{2ij} = \alpha_{2j} + \varepsilon_{2ij} \tag{54}$$

The next step is to obtain least-squares estimates of parameters, both in the full models and in the restricted models. We can then calculate errors for D_1 and D_2 for each participant and compare the magnitude of errors for the full model to those of the restricted model. We present these steps in considerable detail to show that, although the nature of the models is different, the procedure for testing the within-subjects main effect follows the principles we have used throughout Chapter 13 and this chapter. That we have two variables for each participant has no effect on parameter estimation. In particular, the formulas we use here are identical to those we developed earlier for a single D variable (i.e., Equations 47 and 48), except that we must include a subscript to designate the particular D variable. As before, the predicted score for each participant from the full model is the mean score of that participant's group. This follows because the full models in Equations 51 and 52 are cell means models. As a result, we have

$$\hat{D}_{1ij}(F) = \overline{D}_{1j}$$

$$\hat{D}_{2ij}(F) = \overline{D}_{2j}$$

Thus, the errors for participant i in Group j are given by the differences between the participant's actual scores (D_{1ij} and D_{2ij}) and the predicted scores:

$$e_{1ij}(F) = D_{1ij} - \overline{D}_{1j}$$

$$e_{2ij}(F) = D_{2ij} - \overline{D}_{2j}$$

As we have done previously in this chapter and in Chapter 13, we use the sums of e_1^2, e_2^2, and $(e_1)(e_2)$ to construct a matrix for the full model. Recall that we let $E_{11}(F)$ and $E_{22}(F)$ denote the sum of squared errors for the full model for D_1 and D_2, respectively. Similarly, we let $E_{12}(F)$ denote the sum of cross-products for the full model. In general, with two D variables, we would form a matrix for the full model of the form

$$\mathbf{E(F)} = \begin{bmatrix} E_{11}(F) & E_{12}(F) \\ E_{12}(F) & E_{22}(F) \end{bmatrix}$$

For our data, if we were to compute each participant's error scores and then calculate sums of squared errors and cross products, we would see that the matrix for the full model is given by

$$\mathbf{E(F)} = \begin{bmatrix} 67,050 & -9,090 \\ -9,090 & 125,370 \end{bmatrix}$$

We must also obtain least-squares estimates for the parameters in the restricted models of Equations 53 and 54. Once again, the formulas we use are identical to those we developed for a single D variable. The predicted scores from the restricted models are

$$\hat{D}_{1ij}(R) = \overline{D}_{1j} - \overline{D}_1$$

$$\hat{D}_{2ij}(R) = \overline{D}_{2j} - \overline{D}_2$$

The errors for participant i in Group j are thus given by

$$e_{1ij}(R) = D_{1ij} - (\overline{D}_{1j} - \overline{D}_1) = D_{1ij} - \overline{D}_{1j} + \overline{D}_1$$

$$e_{2ij}(R) = D_{2ij} - (\overline{D}_{2j} - \overline{D}_2) = D_{2ij} - \overline{D}_{2j} + \overline{D}_2$$

If we were to compare each participant's errors from the full and restricted models, we would see that the $e_1(F)$ and $e_1(R)$ errors differ only in that every participant's $e_1(R)$ score is 208.5 ms larger than his or her $e_1(F)$ score. The e_2 scores show a similar pattern, except that the $e_2(R)$ scores are 10.5 msec less than the $e_2(F)$ scores. Not coincidentally, 208.5 is the sample grand mean of D_1, and -10.5 is the sample grand mean of D_2. The errors of the restricted models differ from the errors of the full model to the extent that the sample grand means of the D variables differ from zero. Thus, if the null hypothesis is true, the sample grand means differ from zero entirely due to sampling error, and the errors of the restricted model should be similar to those of the full model. On the other hand, if the null hypothesis is false, the errors of the restricted model are likely to be appreciably greater than those of the full model. In general, with two D variables, we can form a matrix for the restricted model of the form

$$\mathbf{E(R)} = \begin{bmatrix} E_{11}(R) & E_{12}(R) \\ E_{12}(R) & E_{22}(R) \end{bmatrix}$$

For our data, it turns out that the matrix for the restricted model is given by

$$\mathbf{E(R)} = \begin{bmatrix} 936,495 & -52,875 \\ -52,875 & 127,575 \end{bmatrix}$$

Before proceeding with a formal comparison of the $\mathbf{E(F)}$ and $\mathbf{E(R)}$ matrices to test the within-subjects main effect, it is useful to see how the individual elements of $\mathbf{E(R)}$ relate to the elements of $\mathbf{E(F)}$. You may recall that when we had a single D variable, we showed that

$$E_R = E_F + N\overline{D}^2$$

The same relationship holds here, so

$$E_{11}(R) = E_{11}(F) + N\overline{D}_1^2$$
$$E_{22}(R) = E_{22}(F) + N\overline{D}_2^2$$

Similarly, it turns out that

$$E_{12}(R) = E_{12}(F) + N\overline{D}_1\overline{D}_2$$

These relationships can be verified for our data by recalling that $\overline{D}_1 = 208.5$ and $\overline{D}_2 = -10.5$. Thus, as was true for the errors of individual participants, the full and restricted matrices differ from one another to the extent that $\overline{D}_1$ and/or $\overline{D}_2$ differ from zero.

We are now in a position to consider how to compare the $\mathbf{E(F)}$ and $\mathbf{E(R)}$ matrices to arrive at an F test of the within-subjects main effect. As before, these matrices are compared by calculating the determinant of each matrix. In the general case of an $a \times b$ split-plot design, the test statistic is given by

$$F = \frac{(|\mathbf{E(R)}| - |\mathbf{E(F)}|)/(b-1)}{|\mathbf{E(F)}|/(N-a-b+2)} \tag{55}$$

This F statistic has $b - 1$ numerator and $N - a - b + 2$ denominator degrees of freedom, where N refers as usual to the total sample size, summed across all levels of the A factor.[13] The values of the determinants of the full and restricted matrices for our numerical example are rather imposing numbers, because the individual elements of $\mathbf{E(F)}$ and $\mathbf{E(R)}$ are themselves large numbers. Nonetheless, with the help of a computer or a calculator that displays a large number of digits, it can be shown that the determinants for our data equal

$$|\mathbf{E(F)}| = 8{,}323{,}430{,}400$$

$$|\mathbf{E(R)}| = 116{,}677{,}584{,}000$$

Substituting these two values as well as $a = 2$, $b = 3$, and $N = 20$ into Equation 55 yields an F value of 110.65 with 2 and 17 df. The corresponding p value is less than .0001, so there is a highly statistically significant angle effect for our data.

Test of the Interaction

The remaining omnibus effect to be tested is the interaction. As always, this test involves a comparison of full and restricted models. Recall that the full models we used for testing the within-subjects main effect were given by

$$D_{1ij} = \mu_1 + \alpha_{1j} + \varepsilon_{1ij} \qquad \text{(51, repeated)}$$
$$D_{2ij} = \mu_2 + \alpha_{2j} + \varepsilon_{2ij} \qquad \text{(52, repeated)}$$

These same full models are also used for testing the interaction of the between- and within-subjects factors. We must now determine the restricted models that are implied by the interaction null hypothesis. The null hypothesis for the interaction states that the differences between the means of the levels of the within-subjects factor are a constant for every level of the between-subjects factor. In other words, if the null hypothesis is true, there are no group differences on the within-subjects differences. However, this absence of group differences implies that all α_j parameters equal zero. The appropriate restricted models are thus given by

$$D_{1ij} = \mu_1 + \varepsilon_{1ij} \qquad \text{(56)}$$
$$D_{2ij} = \mu_2 + \varepsilon_{2ij} \qquad \text{(57)}$$

The next step is to obtain least-squares estimates of parameters. Notice that we only have to perform this step for the restricted models, because the full models for the interaction are identical to the full models for the within-subjects main effect. The least-squares estimates of the μ_1 and μ_2 parameters in Equations 56 and 57 are the sample grand means $\overline{D}_1$ and $\overline{D}_2$, respectively.[14] Thus, the restricted models simply predict each participant's score on a D variable to equal the grand mean of that variable:

$$\hat{D}_{1ij}(R) = \overline{D}_1 \qquad \text{and} \qquad \hat{D}_{2ij}(R) = \overline{D}_2$$

As a result, the errors for participant i in Group j are given by

$$e_{1ij}(R) = D_{1ij} - \overline{D}_1 \qquad \text{and} \qquad e_{2ij}(R) = D_{2ij} - \overline{D}_2$$

In general, with two D variables, we would form a matrix for the restricted model of the form

$$\mathbf{E(R)} = \begin{bmatrix} E_{11}(R) & E_{12}(R) \\ E_{12}(R) & E_{22}(R) \end{bmatrix}$$

For our data, calculating sums of squared errors and cross-products yields a matrix for the restricted model given by

$$E(R) = \begin{bmatrix} 99{,}855 & 21{,}285 \\ 21{,}285 & 153{,}495 \end{bmatrix}$$

Be sure to understand that this matrix has different values from the matrix for the restricted model corresponding to the main effect test, because the individual errors for each participant are different in the two restricted models. For example, the error for participant i in Group j for the D_1 variable is given by

$$e_{1ij}(R) = D_{1ij} - \overline{D}_{1j} + \overline{D}_1$$

for testing the within-subjects main effect but is given by

$$e_{1ij}(R) = D_{1ij} - \overline{D}_1$$

for testing the interaction. Because each participant's error in the restricted model for testing the interaction will typically be different from that same participant's error in the restricted model for testing the main effect, the matrices we obtain for the two different restricted models will typically be different from one another.

Before considering the formal test to compare $E(R)$ and $E(F)$, it may be instructive to see how the individual elements of the $E(R)$ and $E(F)$ matrices are related. When we compare the full and restricted models for D_1 (Equations 51 and 56, respectively), we are simply performing a one-way between-subjects ANOVA. We learned in Chapter 3 that the formula for the between-group sum of squares can be written as

$$SS_B = \sum_{j=1}^{a} n_j (\overline{Y}_j - \overline{Y})^2$$

where Y is the dependent variable. The same relationship holds here, so that

$$E_{11}(R) = E_{11}(F) + \sum_{j=1}^{a} n_j (\overline{D}_{1j} - \overline{D}_1)^2$$

Similarly

$$E_{22}(R) = E_{22}(F) + \sum_{j=1}^{a} n_j (\overline{D}_{2j} - \overline{D}_2)^2$$

It can also be shown that

$$E_{12}(R) = E_{12}(F) + \sum_{j=1}^{a} n_j (\overline{D}_{1j} - \overline{D}_1)(\overline{D}_{2j} - \overline{D}_2)$$

These relationships can be verified for our data by recalling that $n_1 = n_2 = 10$, $\overline{D}_{11} = 168$, $\overline{D}_{12} = 249$, $\overline{D}_1 = 208.5$, $\overline{D}_{21} = -48$, $\overline{D}_{22} = 27$, and $\overline{D}_2 = -10.5$ (see Table 14.11 for these figures). Of course, the three formulas given above would save us a lot of work if we were computing quantities by hand, because we would not have to compute errors for each participant individually for both the full and the restricted models. However, we typically rely on a computer to perform calculations, so our primary purpose for giving you these formulas is to show how the elements of the restricted matrix differ from the elements of the full matrix. Specifically, the elements differ to the extent that different groups have different sample means on the D variables. However, this is just an index of the extent to which there is an interaction in the sample, which is precisely what we want to test in the population.

We are now ready to consider how to compare the $\mathbf{E(F)}$ and $\mathbf{E(R)}$ matrices to arrive at an F test of the interaction. For reasons that are too advanced to discuss in this book, the procedure to be used is different when there are only two levels of the between-subjects factor (i.e., $a = 2$) than when there are more than two levels (i.e., $a > 2$).[15] We begin with the special case where $a = 2$, both because it is simpler and because $a = 2$ in our numerical example. Once we have presented the F test in this special case, we consider the more general case where $a \geq 2$.

In the special case of a $2 \times b$ split-plot design (i.e., two levels of the between-subjects factor and b levels of the within-subjects factor), we can proceed with an F test of the same general form that we used for testing the within-subjects main effect. With a $2 \times b$ split-plot design, the test statistic for the interaction is given by

$$F = \frac{(|\mathbf{E(R)}| - |\mathbf{E(F)}|)/(a-1)(b-1)}{|\mathbf{E(F)}|/(N-a-b+2)} \tag{58}$$

Because this formula is applicable only when $a = 2$, it can be simplified to

$$F = \frac{(|\mathbf{E(R)}| - |\mathbf{E(F)}|)/(b-1)}{|\mathbf{E(F)}|/(N-b)} \tag{59}$$

The F statistic for the interaction in the $2 \times b$ split-plot design has $b - 1$ numerator degrees of freedom and $N - b$ denominator degrees of freedom. For our data, we have already seen that $|\mathbf{E(F)}| = 8,323,430,400$, because the $\mathbf{E(F)}$ matrix for the interaction is identical to $\mathbf{E(F)}$ for the within-subjects main effect. The determinant of the restricted matrix for the interaction can be shown to be $|\mathbf{E(R)}| = 14,874,192,000$. Substituting these two values, as well as $b = 3$ and $N = 20$, into Equation 59 yields an F value of 6.69 with 2 and 17 df. The corresponding p value is .0072, so the age $\times$ angle interaction is statistically significant at the .05 level.

When the between-subjects factor has more than two levels, a different formula is needed for the F test. Notice that when this factor has only two levels, we have performed a multivariate extension of the t test. However, when the factor has more than two levels, neither a multivariate t test nor a univariate t test is applicable. In a sense, this is why Equations 58 and 59 are no longer applicable. In fact, however, there is a more technical explanation requiring knowledge of matrix algebra. Instead of attempting to explain the reason, we simply describe how the test must be modified.[16]

Even when $a > 2$, $\mathbf{E(F)}$ and $\mathbf{E(R)}$ matrices are formed in exactly the same manner as when $a = 2$. However, the way in which $\mathbf{E(F)}$ and $\mathbf{E(R)}$ are incorporated into a test statistic is somewhat different. In fact, when $a > 2$, four different multivariate test statistics are available. The test statistics are Wilks's lambda, the Pillai–Bartlett trace, Roy's greatest characteristic root, and the Hotelling–Lawley trace. Although for many data sets all four test statistics are likely to reach the same conclusion regarding statistical significance, such agreement is by no means guaranteed. In addition, without more theoretical information regarding the population than is usually available, it is generally impossible to state which test statistic is best. As a result, statisticians are not in complete agreement as to which test is best in practice. We will restrict our discussion to Wilks's lambda and the Pillai–Bartlett trace. Wilks's lambda is historically the most widely used of the four statistics and generalizes most easily from the foundation we have developed, because it is the only statistic of the four that is based on determinants. We have chosen to present the Pillai–Bartlett trace because there is some evidence suggesting that it is the most robust of the four statistics.

Before we consider Wilks's lambda, it will be helpful to rewrite Equation 58 for the F test when $a = 2$. Recall that this equation was

$$F = \frac{(|\mathbf{E(R)}| - |\mathbf{E(F)}|)/(a - 1)(b - 1)}{|\mathbf{E(F)}|/(N - a - b + 2)} \qquad \text{(58, repeated)}$$

We can rewrite the portion of this equation involving the determinants of the $\mathbf{E(R)}$ and $\mathbf{E(F)}$ matrices (i.e., the part omitting degrees of freedom terms) as follows:

$$\frac{|\mathbf{E(R)}| - |\mathbf{E(F)}|}{|\mathbf{E(F)}|} = \frac{|\mathbf{E(R)}|}{|\mathbf{E(F)}|} - \frac{|\mathbf{E(F)}|}{|\mathbf{E(F)}|} = \frac{|\mathbf{E(R)}|}{|\mathbf{E(F)}|} - 1 \qquad (60)$$

Wilks's lambda, about which we discuss more momentarily, is denoted Λ and is defined as

$$\Lambda = \frac{|\mathbf{E(F)}|}{|\mathbf{E(R)}|} \qquad (61)$$

Notice then that $|\mathbf{E(R)}|$ divided by $|\mathbf{E(F)}|$ (as in Equation 60) is the reciprocal of Λ, that is

$$\frac{|\mathbf{E(R)}|}{|\mathbf{E(F)}|} = \frac{1}{\Lambda}$$

Making this substitution into Equation 60 yields

$$\frac{|\mathbf{E(R)}| - |\mathbf{E(F)}|}{|\mathbf{E(F)}|} = \frac{1}{\Lambda} - 1$$

which can be rewritten as

$$\frac{|\mathbf{E(R)}| - |\mathbf{E(F)}|}{|\mathbf{E(F)}|} = \frac{1}{\Lambda} - 1$$

$$= \frac{1}{\Lambda} - \frac{\Lambda}{\Lambda}$$

$$= \frac{1 - \Lambda}{\Lambda}$$

Now, if we substitute this result into Equation 58, we have a new form for the F test when $a = 2$

$$F = \frac{(1 - \Lambda)/(a - 1)(b - 1)}{\Lambda/(N - a - b + 2)} \qquad (62)$$

where Λ is defined as before, namely

$$\Lambda = \frac{|\mathbf{E(F)}|}{|\mathbf{E(R)}|} \qquad \text{(61, repeated)}$$

Equation 62 is an entirely legitimate equation for testing the interaction when $a = 2$; indeed, we have just derived it algebraically from Equation 58, so the two equations produce identical F values when $a = 2$. Although for this reason Equation 62 is of no practical value when

$a = 2$, it is nevertheless useful, because it will make clearer the rationale for the form of the F test when $a > 2$.

When a ≥ 2, the F test based on Wilks's lambda is given by

$$F = \frac{(1 - \sqrt[q]{\Lambda})/(a - 1)(b - 1)}{\sqrt[q]{\Lambda}/[mq - .5(a - 1)(b - 1) + 1]} \tag{63}$$

This F statistic has $(a - 1)(b - 1)$ numerator degrees of freedom and $mq - .5(a - 1)(b - 1) + 1$ denominator degrees of freedom (m and q are defined momentarily). Before explaining this admittedly ominous formula, we should hasten to tell you that most multivariate analysis of variance (MANOVA) computer packages calculate this F value for you. Nevertheless, it is useful to consider this F statistic piece by piece to better understand it.

First, notice that just like Equation 62, this F test is based on Λ, the ratio of $|\mathbf{E(F)}|$ to $|\mathbf{E(R)}|$. However, Equation 63, unlike Equation 62, requires that we calculate the qth root of Λ (as we said, q is defined momentarily). Nevertheless, the basic idea is the same. If the errors of the restricted model are similar in magnitude to those of the full model, $|\mathbf{E(R)}|$ will be only slightly larger than $|\mathbf{E(F)}|$. As a result, Λ—which, remember, equals $|\mathbf{E(F)}|$ divided by $|\mathbf{E(R)}|$—will be only slightly less than 1. Regardless of the value of q, $1 - \sqrt[q]{\Lambda}$ and $\sqrt[q]{\Lambda}$ will both be close to 1.0, so the F value will be relatively small. On the other hand, if the restricted model provides a much worse explanation of the data than does the full model, $|\mathbf{E(R)}|$ will be much larger than $|\mathbf{E(F)}|$. As a consequence, Λ will be much less than 1. However, as Λ decreases, the term $(1 - \sqrt[q]{\Lambda})/\sqrt[q]{\Lambda}$ increases, so the F value will be relatively large.

Second, it is necessary to define m and q in Equation 63. The respective formulas are

$$m = N - .5(a + b + 1)$$

$$q = \sqrt{\frac{(a - 1)^2(b - 1)^2 - 4}{(a - 1)^2 + (b - 1)^2 - 5}}$$

When $(a - 1)^2 + (b - 1)^2 = 5$, q is defined to equal 1.

Third, this form of the multivariate F test is called Rao's approximation, because it was developed by a statistician named Rao who proved that the sampling distribution of the statistic defined in Equation 63 approximates the F distribution. However, the statistic is distributed exactly as an F (provided the usual statistical assumptions are met) if $a = 2$ or $a = 3$ (regardless of the value of b), or if $b = 2$ or $b = 3$ (regardless of the value of a). The formulas given in Table 14.12 for $a = 2$ agree with Equation 59, which we developed earlier for the special case of $a = 2$. Also, the formulas in Table 14.12 for $b = 2$ can be shown to be equivalent to Equation 45, which we developed earlier for testing the interaction when $b = 2$. Thus, all other formulas we have developed for the multivariate test of the interaction in the split-plot design are special cases of Equation 63.

Fourth, we should point out a few facts regarding the degrees of freedom of this F test. First, notice that the numerator degrees of freedom always equal $(a - 1)(b - 1)$, which is exactly what we would expect for the interaction of two factors with a and b levels. Second, the denominator degrees of freedom are often different from what we have become accustomed to, because of the way in which the test statistic in Equation 63 approximates the F distribution. For example, as Table 14.12 shows, the denominator degrees of freedom can exceed N, the total sample size. Also, in larger designs, the degrees of freedom for the denominator can be fractional (i.e., not a whole number). Because most computer programs provide p values, this poses no practical problems, although it has been known to arouse suspicion in unsuspecting dissertation committee members and journal reviewers.

TABLE 14.12

VALUES OF a AND b FOR WHICH WILKS'S LAMBDA TEST OF THE
INTERACTION IS DISTRIBUTED EXACTLY AS AN F RATIO

			df	
a	b	Formula for F	Numerator	Denominator
2	Any	$\dfrac{(1-\Lambda)/(b-1)}{\Lambda/(N-b)}$	$b-1$	$N-b$
3	Any	$\dfrac{(1-\sqrt{\Lambda})/(b-1)}{\sqrt{\Lambda}/(N-b-1)}$	$2(b-1)$	$2(N-b-1)$
Any	2	$\dfrac{(1-\Lambda)/(a-1)}{\Lambda/(N-a)}$	$a-1$	$N-a$
Any	3	$\dfrac{(1-\sqrt{\Lambda})/(a-1)}{\sqrt{\Lambda}/(N-a-1)}$	$2(a-1)$	$2(N-a-1)$

Keep in mind that the foregoing discussion has been restricted to one of four possible test criteria, namely, Wilks's lambda. We now present a brief introduction to the Pillai–Bartlett trace statistic. As we said earlier, the Pillai–Bartlett trace is also based on the $\mathbf{E(F)}$ and $\mathbf{E(R)}$ matrices. However, the information in these matrices is converted into an F test differently than Wilks's lambda. Once $\mathbf{E(F)}$ and $\mathbf{E(R)}$ matrices have been obtained, the next step in computing the Pillai–Bartlett trace is to subtract the $\mathbf{E(F)}$ matrix from the $\mathbf{E(R)}$ matrix. The resultant matrix, denoted $\mathbf{H}$, is called the hypothesis sum of squares and cross-product matrix, and is defined as $\mathbf{H} = \mathbf{E(R)} - \mathbf{E(F)}$. The $\mathbf{E(R)}$ matrix is usually denoted $\mathbf{T}$ and is called the total sum of squares and cross-product matrix. The next step requires that the $\mathbf{H}$ matrix be multiplied by the inverse of $\mathbf{T}$. If you are unfamiliar with matrix algebra, this operation is analogous to division with ordinary numbers. In a sense, then, we are dividing $\mathbf{H}$ by $\mathbf{T}$; however, the result is a $(b-1) \times (b-1)$ matrix instead of a single number.[17] Instead of attempting to explain these matrix operations here, we simply state that the result of multiplying $\mathbf{H}$ by the inverse of $\mathbf{T}$ yields the following matrix for testing the interaction for the data in Table 14.10:

$$\begin{bmatrix} .2951 & .1570 \\ .2732 & .1453 \end{bmatrix}$$

The Pillai–Bartlett trace, usually denoted V, is simply the sum of the diagonal elements of this matrix (recall that the sum of diagonal elements is called the trace of a square matrix). For our data, then, $V = 0.4404$. An approximate F test based on V is obtained from the following equation:

$$F = \frac{(N-a-b+s+1)V}{l(s-V)} \tag{64}$$

where $s =$ the smaller of $a-1$ and $b-1$, and $l =$ the larger of $a-1$ and $b-1$. The degrees of freedom for the F equal $(a-1)(b-1)$ for the numerator and $s(N-a-b+s+1)$ for the denominator. Recall that in our numerical example, $a=2$ and $b=3$. Thus, $s=1$ and $l=2$, so that the F statistic for the Pillai–Bartlett trace for our data is given by

$$F = \frac{(20-2-3+1+1)(0.4404)}{2(1-0.4404)} = 6.69$$

with $(2 - 1)(3 - 1) = 2$ numerator degrees of freedom and $1(20 - 2 - 3 + 1 + 1) = 17$ denominator degrees of freedom.

You may have noticed that this F value of 6.69 with 2 and 17 df for the Pillai–Bartlett trace is identical to the F value we obtained using Equation 59, which is a special case of Wilks's lambda. Although the Pillai–Bartlett trace and Wilks's lambda tests are generally different from one another, it can be shown that they are equivalent in the special case where s, the smaller of $a - 1$ and $b - 1$, equals 1. Thus, if $a = 2$ or $b = 2$ (or both), then Wilks's lambda and the Pillai–Bartlett trace produce exactly the same results. Indeed, the reason we obtained the same F value and degrees of freedom with the two tests is because $a = 2$ in our example. It can also be shown that when $s = 1$, the other two tests we mentioned (Roy's greatest characteristic root and the Hotelling–Lawley trace) also yield exactly the same result as both Wilks's lambda and the Pillai-Bartlett trace. Thus, when $s = 1$, all four tests necessarily agree precisely; when $s > 1$, in general, all four tests disagree to some extent, although in practice the tests are often quite similar.[18]

At this point it is appropriate to explain why we did not raise the distinction among these four tests in Chapter 13 or in the first half of this chapter. Notice that in both these earlier sections of the book, we were testing effects that involved only within-subjects factors, whereas now we are considering the interaction of a within-subjects factor with a between-subjects factor. In all earlier cases, $s = 1$, so that all four tests produce identical results. Thus, we had no need to distinguish among the four tests, although many MANOVA computer programs nevertheless report all four F tests even when $s = 1$.

Remember that for the interaction in a split-plot design, we defined s as the smaller of $a - 1$ and $b - 1$. More generally, $s =$ the smaller of df_{effect} and p, where p is the number of dependent variables. The df_{effect} term refers to the degrees of freedom per variable for the effect being tested. In other words, df_{effect} equals the difference in the number of parameters in the full and restricted models for a single variable. Until we considered the test of the interaction in a split-plot design, our tests of within-subjects effects could always be represented as a comparison of models of the form

$$D_i = \mu + \varepsilon_i \text{ (full model)}$$

$$D_i = \varepsilon_i \text{ (restricted model)}$$

The difference in the number of parameters equals one for each variable, so $df_{effect} = 1$. As a result, $s = 1$ regardless of the number of levels of the within-subjects factor. Hence, all four tests always yield identical F values for testing any purely within-subjects effect. Only effects that involve both between- and within-subjects factors ever yield different F values for the four different multivariate test statistics.

MEASURES OF EFFECT

As we have seen earlier in this chapter as well as in Chapter 13, omega squared can be derived from either the multivariate or mixed-model perspective. As we explained in detail in Chapter 13, although we generally recommend the multivariate approach for testing within-subjects effects, we prefer the mixed-model formulation of omega squared, because it regards individual differences between subjects as a source of total variance, just as in betweeen-subjects designs. Thus, our recommended formulation for omega squared in split-plot designs is identical to the approach we presented in Chapter 12.

Specifically, our recommended formulas for omega squared for the split-plot design are as follows. For the main effect of the between-subjects factor A, omega squared can be computed as

$$\hat{\omega}_A^2 = \frac{SS_A - (a-1)MS_{S/A}}{SS_A + SS_{S/A} + MS_{S/A}} \qquad \text{(12.22, repeated)}$$

The comparable expression for the within-subjects effects B and AB are

$$\hat{\omega}_B^2 = \frac{(b-1)(MS_B - MS_{B \times S/A})}{SS_B + SS_{B \times S/A} + SS_{S/A} + MS_{S/A}} \qquad \text{(12.23, repeated)}$$

and

$$\hat{\omega}_{AB}^2 = \frac{(a-1)(b-1)(MS_{AB} - MS_{B \times S/A})}{SS_{AB} + SS_{B \times S/A} + SS_{S/A} + MS_{S/A}} \qquad \text{(12.24, repeated)}$$

Even though some of the components of Equations 12.22 through 12.24 are not directly involved in calculating the multivariate test statistic, most statistical packages will provide values for these components as an option in the multivariate approach to repeated measures. In our data, the numerical values of omega squared are .25 for the age main effect, .52 for the angle main effect, and .04 for the interaction of age and angle. Thus, the age and angle main effects account for considerably more variance than does the interaction. Even so, as we noted in Chapter 12, the interaction may be the effect of most theoretical interest. While omega squared and similar indices can help us ascertain the numerical size of effects, they are no substitute for a thorough understanding of the subject matter.

Further Investigation of Main Effects

As we discussed in Chapter 12, we do not need to introduce any new procedures for pursuing the meaning of a significant between-subjects main effect in a split-plot design. Comparisons of the marginal means of the between-subjects factor can be tested simply by averaging each participant's scores across the within-subjects factor and performing between-subjects contrasts of the resulting scores. As a result, the principles we developed in Chapters 4–6 can be directly applied to comparisons of between-subjects marginal means in a split-plot design.

Comparisons of within-subjects marginal means in a split-plot design are tested in much the same manner as in totally within-subjects designs. Specifically, a D variable is formed whose coefficients correspond to the comparison to be tested. As in other within-subjects designs, the null hypothesis is that the population mean of this D variable equals zero. However, the split-plot design is different from totally within-subjects designs, because it includes a between-subjects factor whose effect must be taken into account. As we saw earlier in the chapter, an appropriate full model for a D variable in a split-plot design is given by

$$D_{ij} = \mu + \alpha_j + \varepsilon_{ij} \qquad \text{(43, repeated)}$$

The restricted model for testing that the grand mean of D equals zero in the population can be written as

$$D_{ij} = \alpha_j + \varepsilon_{ij} \qquad \text{(46, repeated)}$$

Earlier in the chapter, we derived the F statistic for comparing these two models:

$$F = \frac{N\overline{D}^2}{\sum\limits_{j=1}^{a}\sum\limits_{i=1}^{n_j}(D_{ij} - \overline{D}_j)^2/(N - a)} \qquad \text{(49, repeated)}$$

This F statistic has 1 numerator and $N - a$ denominator degrees of freedom.

If the particular D variable to be tested was one of the D variables formed to perform the multivariate test, the numerator and denominator values for the F statistic in Equation 49 are readily available from the appropriate diagonal elements of the $\mathbf{E(F)}$ and $\mathbf{E(R)}$ matrices. To illustrate this point, suppose that we want to test the statistical significance of the quadratic trend for the marginal means of the angle factor in our numerical example. Recall that our D_2 variable was chosen to represent this quadratic trend:

$$D_{2ij} = 1Y_{1ij} - 2Y_{2ij} + 1Y_{3ij}$$

Remember that the D_1 variable represents the linear trend for angle. When we considered D_1 and D_2 simultaneously, we calculated the following $\mathbf{E(F)}$ and $\mathbf{E(R)}$ matrices:

$$\mathbf{E(F)} = \begin{bmatrix} 67{,}050 & -9{,}090 \\ -9{,}090 & 125{,}370 \end{bmatrix}$$

$$\mathbf{E(R)} = \begin{bmatrix} 936{,}495 & -52{,}875 \\ -52{,}875 & 127{,}575 \end{bmatrix}$$

As usual, $\mathbf{E(F)}$ corresponds to the full model of Equation 43, and $\mathbf{E(R)}$ corresponds to the restricted model of Equation 46. We do not need to compare the entire matrices at this point, because we are only interested in the D_2 variable. For this specific variable, the error sums of squares for the full and restricted models are given by the values in the second row and second column of the $\mathbf{E(F)}$ and $\mathbf{E(R)}$ matrices, respectively. Thus, in our example, $E_F = 125{,}370$, and $E_R = 127{,}575$ for the quadratic trend. We can substitute these values into Equation 49 by realizing that

$$E_F = \sum\limits_{j=1}^{a}\sum\limits_{i=1}^{n_j}(D_{ij} - \overline{D}_j)^2 \qquad \text{(47, repeated)}$$

$$E_R - E_F = N\overline{D}^2 \qquad \text{(48, repeated)}$$

For our data, we have

$$\sum\limits_{j=1}^{a}\sum\limits_{i=1}^{n_j}(D_{ij} - \overline{D}_j)^2 = 125{,}370$$

and

$$N\overline{D}^2 = 2{,}205$$

Substituting these values along with $N = 20$ and $a = 2$ into Equation 49 yields an F value of 0.32 with 1 and 18 df. As in other cases we have seen, this F value is identical to the F value we obtained for the quadratic angle trend in the mixed-model approach of Chapter 12 when we used a separate error term (Equation 12.26 instead of 12.25). As we discuss in more detail later in the chapter, once again the multivariate approach is compatible with the use of a separate error term, whereas the mixed-model approach is compatible with the use of a pooled error term.

To judge the statistical significance of a contrast, we must, of course, compare the observed F value to an appropriate critical value. The choice of an appropriate critical value depends, as usual, on what other contrasts are being tested. One possibility is to set α_{PC} at a desired figure, in which case the critical F value is simply read from the F table with 1 numerator and $N - a$ denominator degrees of freedom. If a set of C planned comparisons is to be tested, α_{PC} for each contrast can be adjusted to equal $.05/C$, using the Bonferroni technique. As we discussed in Chapter 13, the Bonferroni method is also appropriate for testing pairwise comparisons of within-subjects marginal means in a split-plot design. Finally, for testing post hoc complex comparisons, the appropriate critical value comes from the multivariate extension of Scheffé's method developed by Roy and Bose. The formula follows from the same logic we used to arrive at Equation 13.27. Remembering that A denotes the between-subjects factor and B the within-subjects factor in a split-plot design, the appropriate critical value for testing complex contrasts among the levels of B is given by

$$CV = (N - a)(b - 1)F_{\alpha_{FW}; b-1, N-a-b+2}/(N - a - b + 2) \tag{65}$$

For our numerical example, the observed F value of 0.32 is nonsignificant even using an α_{PC} of .05 because, with 1 and 18 df, the critical F at the .05 level equals 4.41. Of course, if additional contrasts were being tested, the appropriate critical value would be even larger, so the quadratic trend for angle would remain nonsignificant. For example, if the quadratic trend were tested as a post hoc complex comparison, the .05 critical value would be calculated from Equation 65 as follows:

$$CV = (20 - 2)(3 - 1)(3.59)/(20 - 2 - 3 + 2) = 7.60$$

a value which is appreciably larger than 4.41, the critical value for an α_{PC} of .05.

We should also point out that using a statistical package for performing the multivariate test of the within-subjects main effect also simplifies testing contrasts of the marginal means. The reason is that such programs typically report univariate as well as multivariate tests. These univariate tests are simply the tests of the individual D variables that collectively represent the omnibus effect, which is tested by the multivariate test. For the angle effect in our example, most multivariate computer programs (e.g., SAS and SPSS) report not only that the observed F for the multivariate test of the angle main effect equals 110.65, but also that the univariate F value for D_1 (the linear trend) equals 233.41, and that the F value for D_2 (the quadratic trend) equals 0.32. Of course, D_1 and D_2 must be chosen to reflect the contrasts to be tested, and as we discussed in Chapter 13, this can be problematic with some computer programs if the D variables of interest are nonorthogonal. Also, be certain you understand that the univariate tests we are referring to here are different from the univariate F test of the mixed-model approach. Although the mixed-model approach does produce a univariate F test, it is still an omnibus test of the main effect. On the other hand, the univariate tests of individual D variables are tests of specific contrasts of the marginal means of the within-subjects factor.

Further Investigation of an Interaction—Simple Effects

As in most factorial designs, the most typical method of interpreting a statistically significant interaction in a split-plot design is to perform tests of simple effects. In our numerical example, we found a significant age × angle interaction, which we could pursue by testing the age effect within each level of angle, as well as the angle effect within each level of age. As we pointed out in Chapter 12, we need to consider how to perform both types of simple-effects tests, because in one case (age within angle) we effectively have a one-way between-subjects design, whereas in the other case (angle within age) we effectively have a one-way within-subjects design.

Between-Subjects Effects at a Fixed Level of Within-Subjects Factor

We begin by considering the simple effect of age (the between-subjects factor) at a fixed level of angle (the within-subjects factor), which we would almost certainly be interested in testing in our example because it tells us whether younger participants differ significantly from older participants at various specific levels of angle. It is important to notice that we no longer have a within-subjects factor in this design, because we are considering only one level of the within-subjects factor. As a result, we are only interested in one score per participant, and we can simply perform a one-way between-subjects ANOVA on this variable. The analysis proceeds in exactly the same manner as we discussed in Chapter 12. Not surprisingly, then, the mixed-model and multivariate approaches are identical for testing the simple effect of A (the between-subjects factor) at a fixed level of B (the within-subjects factor). The two approaches are identical simply because (as we pointed out a moment ago) we effectively eliminate the within-subjects factor from the design when we focus our attention on a single level of the within-subjects factor:

Three further points need to be made here. First, recall from Chapter 12 that we discussed two possible error terms for simple-effects tests of A within levels of B. We stated a general preference in Chapter 12 for using $MS_{S/A \, at \, B_k}$ as an error term instead of MSWCELL (as defined in Equation 12.30), because the use of separate error terms of the form $MS_{S/A \, at \, B_k}$ does not require sphericity. If a researcher is using the multivariate approach we are discussing in this chapter, it seems sensible to use $MS_{S/A \, at \, B_k}$ as the error term for testing simple effects of A within B, because neither the omnibus multivariate test nor the simple-effects test using this error term assumes sphericity. As we mentioned in Chapter 12, the major statistical packages such as SAS and SPSS all use $MS_{S/A \, at \, B_k}$ as the error term instead of MSWCELL.

Second, notice that the test that results from using $MS_{S/A \, at \, B_k}$ as the error term is literally identical to performing a one-way between-subjects univariate ANOVA on an individual Y variable. Is important not to confuse this univariate test with the univariate test we perform to test comparisons of the within-subjects marginal means. Remember that Y denotes one of our original variables. In this sense, a Y variable is very different from a D variable. Indeed, a D variable is a transformed variable that we create as some specific linear combination of the original Y variables. Thus, the simple effect of A at a particular level of B is tested by performing a one-way between-subjects univariate ANOVA on an original Y variable. Comparisons of within-subjects marginal means are univariate tests also, but they are performed on D variables instead of Y variables.

The third point is that when statistically significant simple effects of A are found at a fixed level of B, further tests are typically conducted to isolate the nature of the effect. Of course, such tests are unnecessary when A has only two levels, as it does in our example. However, when A has three or more levels, specific comparisons can be tested at a fixed level of B by regarding the data as a one-way between-subjects design. Thus, the principles we developed in Chapters 4 through 6 can be used to test comparisons among individual cell means within a fixed level of the within-subjects factor.

Within-Subjects Effects at a Fixed Level of Between-Subjects Factor

We frequently will also want to test the simple effect of the within-subjects factor at fixed levels of the between-subject factor. For example, we might want to test the significance of the angle effect separately for younger participants and for older participants. To illustrate this procedure, we arbitrarily focus on the angle effect for younger participants (the test for older participants would follow exactly the same logic). The question of interest here is, Are the sample means of 477,585, and 645 (see Table 14.10) significantly different from each other? In effect, we have a one-way within-subjects design, because we are no longer considering the older participants, whose previous inclusion was responsible for the between-subjects factor. Recall from our discussion of simple effects of B within A in Chapter 12 that either of two error terms might be used in the mixed-model approach. Two different error terms are also available in the multivariate approach, although they are not the same as the two terms in the mixed-model approach. In fact, the two "error terms" in the multivariate approach are really error matrices, unlike the mixed-model approach, where the choice was between two mean square terms.

We begin by considering the error matrix that results from performing a one-way within-subjects multivariate analysis of the data for younger participants, literally ignoring the data for older participants. To conduct this test, we simply use the principles we developed in Chapter 13. Specifically, we begin by forming $b - 1$ D variables. In our example, we would form two D variables, because the angle factor has three levels. As usual, the particular choice of D variables does not matter for testing the simple effect. Nevertheless, it will be convenient to let D_1 be the linear trend and D_2 the quadratic trend for angle, because we may want to test these specific comparisons in a later analysis. As we discussed in detail in Chapter 13, full and restricted models are developed for D_1 and D_2, leading to an error score for each participant on each variable for each model. The full and restricted models are compared through a full matrix $\mathbf{E(F)}$ and a restricted matrix $\mathbf{E(R)}$. We do not go through the steps of these calculations, because they are identical to the steps we showed in detail in Chapter 13. Instead, we simply state that the error matrices for the full and restricted models for D_1 and D_2 for younger participants are given by

$$\mathbf{E(F)}_1 = \begin{bmatrix} 38,160 & 3,240 \\ 3,240 & 77,760 \end{bmatrix}$$

$$\mathbf{E(R)}_1 = \begin{bmatrix} 320,400 & -77,400 \\ -77,400 & 100,800 \end{bmatrix}$$

The 1 subscript that appears in $\mathbf{E(F)}_1$ and $\mathbf{E(R)}_1$ is used as a reminder that these matrices are based on the data from A_1, that is, the first level of the A factor. In general, for testing the effect of B at A_j, we would represent these matrices as $\mathbf{E(F)}_j$ and $\mathbf{E(R)}_j$.

An F test is obtained by comparing the determinants of these two matrices. The equation we developed in Chapter 13 for the one-way design was

$$F = \frac{(|\mathbf{E(R)}| - |\mathbf{E(F)}|)/(a-1)}{|\mathbf{E(F)}|/(n-a+1)} \qquad \text{(13.22, repeated)}$$

where there was a single group of n participants with a levels of the repeated factor. A corresponding equation for testing the simple effect of B at A_j in the split-plot design is given by

$$F = \frac{(|\mathbf{E(R)}_j| - |\mathbf{E(F)}_j|)/(b-1)}{|\mathbf{E(F)}_j|/(n_j-b+1)} \qquad (66)$$

where there are n_j subjects at level j of the A factor and there are b levels of the within-subjects factor. In our example, the determinant of $\mathbf{E(F)}_j$ equals 2,956,824,000, and the determinant of $\mathbf{E(R)}_j$ equals 26,305,560,000. Substituting these values along with $n_1 = 10$ and $b = 3$ into Equation 66 yields an F value of 31.59. In general, there would be $b-1$ numerator and $n_j - b + 1$ denominator degrees of freedom associated with this F statistic. With 2 and 8 df, as in our example, the associated p value is .0002, so we can conclude that there is a statistically significant angle effect for younger participants, using the .05 level of significance.

An alternate error matrix might also be used to test the simple effect of B at a fixed level of A. The $\mathbf{E(F)}$ matrix we used earlier in the chapter for testing both the angle main effect and the age $\times$ angle interaction was

$$\mathbf{E(F)} = \begin{bmatrix} 67{,}050 & -9{,}090 \\ -9{,}090 & 125{,}370 \end{bmatrix}$$

This error matrix is the sum of $\mathbf{E(F)}_1$ and $\mathbf{E(F)}_2$, that is, the full-model error matrices for younger and older participants separately. In other words, we could form a linear D_1 variable and a quadratic D_2 variable for older participants, just as we have already done for younger participants. If we then fit a full model to the data for older participants, completely disregarding the data for younger participants, the error matrix for the full model is

$$\mathbf{E(F)}_2 = \begin{bmatrix} 28{,}890 & -12{,}330 \\ -12{,}330 & 47{,}610 \end{bmatrix}$$

where the 2 subscript designates the second level of A, that is, older participants. The $\mathbf{E(F)}$ matrix we found earlier relates to the $\mathbf{E(F)}_1$ and $\mathbf{E(F)}_2$ matrices in the following manner: Each element of $\mathbf{E(F)}$ equals the sum of the corresponding elements of $\mathbf{E(F)}_1$ and $\mathbf{E(F)}_2$. For example, $67{,}050 = 38{,}160 + 28{,}890$, and the same form of equality holds for the other three elements as well. Matrix addition is performed by adding corresponding elements in just this fashion; thus, we can say that the sum of the $\mathbf{E(F)}_1$ and $\mathbf{E(F)}_2$ matrices equals $\mathbf{E(F)}$.

When a homogeneity assumption (to be discussed momentarily) is met, a more powerful test of the angle effect for younger participants can be performed by basing the error term on the data from older participants as well as younger participants. Specifically, we can use $\mathbf{E(F)}$ as the error term for testing B within A_j, just as we used $\mathbf{E(F)}$ for testing the B main effect and the $A \times B$ interaction. Recall that the degrees of freedom associated with $\mathbf{E(F)}$ equal $N - a - b + 2$ (see Equation 55). The form of the F statistic is somewhat more complicated than what we have previously encountered, because the error matrix for the full model is computed from all participants, whereas the matrices reflecting the magnitude of the within-subjects simple effect are computed on only a subset of the participants. As a result, the F statistic for testing the simple effect of B at A_j with an error term based on all participants is given by

$$F = \frac{(|E(F) + E(R)_j - E(F)_j| - |E(F)|)/(b-1)}{|E(F)|/(N-a-b+2)} \tag{67}$$

The somewhat unusual looking term $|E(F) + E(R)_j - E(F)_j|$ requires that we find the determinant of the matrix that results from adding corresponding elements of $E(F)$ and $E(R)_j$ and then subtracting corresponding elements of $E(F)_j$.[19] To compute this determinant for our data, it is helpful to recall that we have previously computed the following matrices:

$$E(F) = \begin{bmatrix} 67,050 & -9,090 \\ -9,090 & 125,370 \end{bmatrix}$$

$$E(R)_1 = \begin{bmatrix} 320,400 & -77,400 \\ -77,400 & 100,800 \end{bmatrix}$$

$$E(F)_1 = \begin{bmatrix} 38,160 & 3,240 \\ 3,240 & 77,760 \end{bmatrix}$$

Adding corresponding elements of $E(F)$ and $E(R)_1$ produces a matrix given by

$$\begin{bmatrix} 387,450 & -86,490 \\ -86,490 & 226,170 \end{bmatrix}$$

We must now subtract corresponding elements of $E(F)_1$, yielding

$$\begin{bmatrix} 349,290 & -89,730 \\ -89,730 & 148,410 \end{bmatrix}$$

The determinant of this matrix equals

$$|E(F) + E(R)_1 E(F)_1| = (349,290)(148,410) - (-89,730)^2 = 43,786,656,000$$

We previously found that $|E(F)| = 8,323,430,400$. Substituting these values along with $N = 20$, $a = 2$, and $b = 3$ into Equation 67 yields an F value of 36.22. In general, there are $b-1$ numerator and $N-a-b+2$ denominator degrees of freedom associated with this F statistic. With 2 and 17 df, as in our example, the associated p value is .0001, so the F test using $E(F)$ as an error term concurs with the F test using $E(F)_j$, indicating that there is a statistically significant angle effect for younger participants.

Choosing between $E(F)$ and $E(F)_j$ as an appropriate error term involves the usual considerations of choosing between a pooled and a separate error term. To see why, we need to examine the relationship between $E(F)$ and the separate $E(F)_j$ matrices more closely. When the A factor has a levels, $\mathbf{E}(\mathbf{F})$ is equal to the sum of all a $\mathbf{E}(\mathbf{F})_j$ matrices, that is,

$$\mathbf{E}(\mathbf{F}) = \sum_{j=1}^{a} \mathbf{E}(\mathbf{F})_j$$

The meaning of this equality is clarified by realizing that each $\mathbf{E}(\mathbf{F})_j$ sum of squares and cross-products matrix is itself equal to $(n_j - 1)$ times the covariance matrix for the D variables at level j of A. If we let S_j represent this sample covariance matrix, it follows that

$$\mathbf{E}(\mathbf{F}) = \sum_{j=1}^{a} (n_j - 1) S_j$$

Thus, $\mathbf{E}(\mathbf{F})$ is a weighted sum of the separate covariance matrices. When the underlying population covariance matrices are identical to each other for each level of A, $\mathbf{E}(\mathbf{F})$ provides a more stable measure of error than does any separate $\mathbf{E}(\mathbf{F})_j$ matrix by itself. This advantage is reflected in the fact that the F statistic using $\mathbf{E}(\mathbf{F})$ has more denominator degrees of freedom $(N - a - b + 2)$ than does the F statistic using $\mathbf{E}(\mathbf{F})_j$ (which has $n_j - b + 1$ denominator degrees of freedom). When the assumption is met, the critical value is less when $\mathbf{E}(\mathbf{F})$ is used as the error term, so statistical power is increased. However, when the assumption is false, both Type I and Type II error rates may be distorted in either direction (i.e., either too liberal or too conservative). As we discussed in earlier chapters, the simple-effects F test based on a pooled error term is not robust to violations of homogeneity assumptions even with equal n.[20]

What should a researcher do in practice? As usual, the choice between a pooled and a separate error term is not always straightforward. In theory, one solution might be to perform a test of the assumption that the a covariance matrices for the D variables all equal each other in the population. Indeed, such a test is available, and it is called Box's M test. However, Box's M test depends very strongly on an assumption of normality and is not robust to violations of this assumption (Olson, 1974). Thus, Box's M test is generally of little practical value for choosing between pooled and separate error terms. When samples are sufficiently large (perhaps 40 or so, per level of A), a separate error term is preferable because the additional degrees of freedom afforded by the pooled error term will in all likelihood be inconsequential. However, when samples are small, the choice is more difficult and should probably be based on the researcher's theoretical beliefs as to whether different groups of participants are likely to display different variances and covariances. We should add that as of this writing most statistical packages such as SAS and SPSS use a pooled error term by default. However, as we pointed out in Chapter 12, it is simple to perform tests using a separate error term. For example, in SAS these tests can be obtained by using PROC SORT and BY commands; in SPSS, the corresponding commands are SORT CASES and SPLIT FILE.

Cell Mean Comparisons

In our particular numerical example, the pooled and separate error terms yield very similar results. Because with either error term we obtained a significant angle effect for younger participants, we would probably want to conduct yet one more series of tests to ascertain the precise nature of the angle effect for younger participants. As usual, contrasts among the levels of the within-subjects factor are tested in the multivariate approach by forming an appropriate D variable. For example, suppose that we decide to test the quadratic trend for younger participants. Because we are focusing our attention on one level of A, this test is essentially a straightforward application of the principles we developed in Chapter 13 for testing contrasts in one-way within-subjects designs. The only reason we qualified the preceding sentence by stating the test is essentially a straightforward application is that there is again a choice of error terms. If we decide to test the simple effect using the $\mathbf{E(F)}_j$ matrix, it then makes sense to use only the data from the jth level of A for testing contrasts at that level. If, on the other hand, we use the pooled $\mathbf{E(F)}$ matrix for the simple-effects test, it is reasonable to continue using an error term that pools over the levels of A for testing contrasts of B at A_j. Because either approach may be preferable to the other, depending on the likely validity of the homogeneity assumption, we illustrate both approaches.

First, let's assume that we used the separate $\mathbf{E(F)}_j$ matrix to test the simple effect of B at A_j. In this situation, the F statistic for testing a contrast among the levels of B at A_j follows directly from Chapter 13, except that we need to change the notation to reflect the fact that the test is being performed within a level of A. In Chapter 13, the F statistic for testing a contrast was given by

$$F = \frac{n\overline{D}^2}{s_D^2} \qquad \text{(13.6, repeated)}$$

In a split-plot design, we simply need to add one subscript to represent the particular D variable to be tested and a second subscript to indicate that all calculations are performed at level j of the A factor. For example, the F statistic for testing D_2 can be written as

$$F = \frac{n_j\overline{D}_{2j}^2}{s_{D_{2j}}^2} \qquad (68)$$

For our data, $n_1 = 10$, $\overline{D}_{21} = -48$ (see Table 14.11), and $s_{D_{21}}^2 = 8{,}640$. Substituting these values into Equation 68 yields an F value of 2.67. This F statistic has 1 numerator and $n_j - 1$ denominator degrees of freedom (thus, 1 and 9 in our example); we postpone consideration of a critical value for the moment.

If the particular D variable to be tested was one of the D variables formed to perform the multivariate test, the numerator and denominator values for the F statistic in Equation 68 are readily available from the appropriate diagonal elements of the $\mathbf{E(F)}_j$ and $\mathbf{E(R)}_j$ matrices. For the quadratic angle trend for younger participants, the values of these diagonal elements are 77,760 for $\mathbf{E(F)}_1$ and 100,800 for $\mathbf{E(R)}_1$. The difference in these two values—that is, the diagonal element of $\mathbf{E(R)}_j$ minus the diagonal element of $\mathbf{E(F)}_j$—equals $n_j\overline{D}_{2j}^2$, the numerator of the F. The denominator of the F—that is, $s_{D_{2j}}^2$—is obtained by dividing the diagonal element of $\mathbf{E(F)}_j$ by $n_j - 1$. For our data, the difference in values equals 23,040. The denominator equals 8,640, producing an F value of 2.67, as we have already seen.

Second, we might have used the pooled $\mathbf{E(F)}$ matrix to test the simple effect of B at A_j. To pool across levels of A for testing a contrast of B at A_j, we simply modify Equation 68 so that the denominator is the variance of D_2 averaged over the levels of A

$$F = \frac{n_j\overline{D}_{2j}^2}{s_{D_{2p}}^2} \qquad (69)$$

where the p subscript is a reminder that the variance estimate of D_2 has been pooled over levels of A. Recall that such a pooled variance is also referred to as a mean square for participants within A, so that $s_{D_{2p}}^2$ is simply mean square within for the D_2 variable. For our data, $s_{D_{2p}}^2$ is the (unweighted) average of $s_{D_{11}}^2$ which equals 8,640, and $s_{D_{22}}^2$, which equals 5,290.[21] Thus, the pooled estimate equals 6,965. The resultant F value obtained from substituting this value along with $n_1 = 10$ and $\overline{D}_{21} = -48$ into Equation 69 is 3.31. In general, this F statistic has 1 numerator and $N - a$ denominator degrees of freedom.

Once again, if the particular D variable to be tested was one of the D variables formed to conduct the multivariate test, the numerator and denominator values for the F statistic in Equation 69 are readily available from the appropriate diagonal elements of the $\mathbf{E(F)}_j$, $\mathbf{E(R)}_j$, and $\mathbf{E(F)}$ matrices. In particular, because the numerator of Equation 69 is identical to the numerator of Equation 68, this quantity is again equal to the appropriate diagonal element of $\mathbf{E(R)}_j$ minus the corresponding diagonal element of $\mathbf{E(F)}_j$. The only difference between Equations 68 and 69 is that the denominator of Equation 68 was based on $\mathbf{E(F)}_j$, but the denominator of Equation 69 is based on $\mathbf{E(F)}$. Specifically, $s^2_{D_{2p}}$ is obtained by dividing the appropriate diagonal element of $\mathbf{E(F)}$ by $N - a$. For the quadratic angle effect, the appropriate element of $\mathbf{E(F)}$ appears in the second row and second column and has a value of 125,370. Dividing 125,370 by 18 (i.e., $20 - 2$) produces a denominator equal to 6,965, which as we saw earlier is indeed $s^2_{D_{2p}}$.

The choice of an appropriate critical value against which to compare the observed F value of either Equation 68 or Equation 69 depends as always on what other contrasts, if any, are being tested. If a per-comparison alpha level is desired, the critical F value is simply read from the F table with 1 numerator and $n_j - 1$ denominator degrees of freedom for Equation 68 and with 1 numerator and $N - a$ denominator degrees of freedom for Equation 69. If a set of C planned comparisons is to be tested, α_{PC} for each contrast is simply adjusted to equal α_{FW}/C, using the Bonferroni procedure. The Bonferroni technique is also appropriate for testing pairwise comparisons. Finally, for testing complex comparisons, the appropriate critical value once again comes from the multivariate extension of Scheffé's method developed by Roy and Bose. When the separate error term $s^2_{D_{2j}}$ of Equation 68 has been used, the appropriate critical value is given by

$$\text{CV} = (n_j - 1)(b - 1)F_{\alpha_{FW}; b-1, n_j-b+1}/(n_j - b + 1) \tag{70}$$

When the pooled error term $s^2_{D_{2p}}$ of Equation 69 has been used, the critical value equals

$$\text{CV} = (N - a)(b - 1)F_{\alpha_{FW}; b-1, N-a-b+2}/(N - a - b + 2) \tag{71}$$

One final comment must be made here. As we discussed in Chapter 7, α_{FW} for the tests in the preceding paragraph could be set in either of two ways. First, we might consider each individual level of A to constitute a separate family, in which case we would typically set α_{FW} equal to .05. In our example, we might regard questions of the angle effect for younger participants as answering a distinct theoretical question from the angle effect for older participants, justifying our treating each age group as a separate family. Second, we might regard the a separate levels of A collectively as representing a single family. In this case, α_{FW} in the preceding paragraph would typically equal $.05/a$, because we would want to keep the Type I error rate for all tests to be performed within a level of A at $.05/a$.

Interaction Contrasts

As usual, another approach for interpreting a statistically significant interaction is to test interaction contrasts. Because the omnibus interaction F statistic has $(a - 1)(b - 1)$ numerator degrees of freedom, it may be of interest to isolate one or more single degree of freedom interaction contrasts that are contributing to the omnibus interaction.

The procedure for testing an interaction contrast in a split-plot design follows rather directly from the procedure used to test the omnibus interaction. Recall that the omnibus interaction was tested by comparing the a levels of A on the $b - 1$ D variables simultaneously through a multivariate test. An interaction contrast is tested similarly, but there are two differences. First, instead of an omnibus comparison of all of the levels of A, a specific contrast of the levels of A is chosen. Second, instead of testing for a group difference on all $b - 1$ D variables, one D variable is selected to represent a contrast among the levels of B. Because there is only a single dependent variable in the test of an interaction contrast, the within-subjects factor is effectively eliminated, and there is no need for a multivariate test. Thus, the principles of Chapter 4 can be applied to test a specific between-group comparison on the particular D variable of interest. The sum of squares for the contrast equals

$$SS_\psi = (\hat{\psi})^2 \Big/ \sum_{j=1}^{a} (c_j^2/n_j) \tag{72}$$

where $\hat{\psi} = \sum_{j=1}^{a} c_j \overline{D}_j$. An error term is provided by mean square within for the D variable, which we previously denoted $s_{D_p}^2$, but which we will now write as $MS_{S/A(D)}$, because of its greater similarity to the notation we used in Chapter 4. The F statistic for testing an interaction contrast is then given by

$$F = SS_\psi / MS_{S/A(D)} \tag{73}$$

We can rewrite this F statistic in another form by substituting from Equation 72 for SS_ψ, yielding

$$F = \frac{(\hat{\psi})^2}{MS_{S/A(D)} \sum_{j=1}^{a} (c_j^2/n_j)} \tag{74}$$

which (except for the notation of $MS_{S/A(D)}$) is identical to Equation 4.41. Again, the reason for this equivalence is that we are simply testing a specific between-group comparison, exactly as we did in Chapter 4. The only difference is that the dependent variable for this test is now a D variable, which we calculated as a contrast of the levels of the within-subjects factor.

To illustrate the procedure for testing an interaction contrast, suppose that we want to test whether the quadratic trend for younger participants is different from the quadratic trend for older participants. From Table 14.11, we know that $\overline{D}_{21} = -48$ and $\overline{D}_{22} = 27$, where $\overline{D}_{21}$ is the mean quadratic score for younger participants and $\overline{D}_{22}$ is the mean quadratic score for older participants. We can then define the interaction contrast as

$$\hat{\psi} = \overline{D}_{21} - \overline{D}_{22}$$
$$= -48 - 27 = -75$$

Earlier we found that mean square within for the quadratic D variable equals 6,965 in our data, so $MS_{S/A(D)} = 6{,}965$. Substituting these values along with $n_1 = n_2 = 10$, $c_1 = 1$, and $c_2 = -1$ into Equation 74 results in an observed F value of 4.04. In general, this F statistic has 1 numerator and $N - a$ denominator degrees of freedom. In our example, then, the degrees of freedom are 1 and 18, resulting in a p value of .0597 without any adjustment for the possibility of multiple tests. We should point out that these are exactly the same F and p values we obtained when we used a separate error term in Chapter 12 (as in Equation 12.34) for testing an interaction contrast. However, this approach is consistent with the multivariate omnibus interaction test instead of the mixed-model test, because an appropriate critical value for post hoc tests is obtained from the multivariate approach.

As always, the choice of a critical value depends on what other contrasts are being tested. If a set of planned comparisons is tested, α_{PC} for each contrast can simply be adjusted to equal α_{FW}/C, using the Bonferroni method. For post hoc comparisons, an appropriate critical value comes from the multivariate extension of Scheffé's method developed by Roy and Bose. When A has only two levels (as in our example), this critical value is given by

$$CV = (N - a)(a - 1)(b - 1)F_{\alpha_{FW};(a-1)(b-1),N-a-b+2}/(N - a - b + 2) \qquad (75)$$

Because Equation 75 is only appropriate for the situation where A has two levels, we can substitute $a = 2$ into Equation 75 to get

$$CV = (N - 2)(b - 1)F_{\alpha_{FW};b-1,N-b}/(N - b) \qquad (76)$$

When a is greater than two, the critical value is more complicated because s is greater than one. Finding the value of the appropriate post hoc critical value then requires the use of tables of Roy's greatest characteristic root. Such tables are available in Harris (1985). See Harris (1985) or O'Brien and Kaiser (1985) for further details.

Notice that when $a = 2$ (as in our example), the test of an interaction contrast is identical to an ANOVA on an appropriately chosen D variable. Thus, in effect, we are comparing a full model of the form

$$D_{ij} = \mu + \alpha_j + \varepsilon_{ij}$$

to a restricted model of the form

$$D_{ij} = \mu + \varepsilon_{ij}$$

The distinction between an interaction contrast and a contrast of marginal means is sometimes difficult to grasp. For example, we tested an interaction contrast that examined whether the quadratic angle trend for older participants differs from the quadratic angle trend for younger participants. Earlier in the chapter, we had tested the significance of a quadratic trend for the marginal means of the angle factor. The test of marginal means uses the same full model as the interaction contrast, namely, a model of the form

$$D_{ij} = \mu + \alpha_j + \varepsilon_{ij}$$

However, the restricted model is different. The restricted model for the test of marginal means is given by

$$D_{ij} = \alpha_j + \varepsilon_{ij}$$

Thus, the test of marginal means asks whether the D variable has a population mean of zero, averaging over groups. The interaction contrast, on the other hand, asks whether the two groups have different population means on D. Thus, the interaction contrast compares the two groups, whereas the test of marginal means averages over groups.

CONFIDENCE INTERVALS FOR CONTRASTS

We have now seen how to perform a variety of tests using the multivariate approach in a split-plot design. As usual, we may want to supplement these tests with confidence intervals. The logic behind forming confidence intervals in split-plot designs follows the same general principles we have seen in other designs. The only new complication here is that we must determine how to form an appropriate dependent variable for our interval. However, this turns out to be exactly the same issue we have already addressed in our recent discussion of hypothesis testing.

In all cases, the general form of a confidence interval in a split-plot design is the same as in other designs, namely

$$\hat{\psi} \pm (\sqrt{CV})(se_{\hat{\psi}}) \tag{77}$$

where $\hat{\psi}$ is the estimated value of the contrast, CV is an appropriate critical value, and se is the estimated standard error of the contrast. There are basically only two further complications. First, the contrast may be based on any of three types of variables, M, D, or Y (i.e., a specific level of the within-subjects factor). The calculation of the standard error differs depending on which type of variable is relevant for the contrast. Second, as in other designs, statistical packages will sometimes provide an appropriate value for CV, but at other times intervals have to be calculated by hand, making use of $\hat{\psi}$ and se values from computer output.

Notice that we could form a confidence interval for a wide variety of types of effects, such as: (1) a contrast among levels of the marginal mean of the between-subjects factor, (2) a contrast among levels of the marginal mean of the within-subjects factor, (3) a contrast among levels of the within-subjects factor at a specific level of the between-subjects factor, (4) a contrast among levels of the between-subjects factor at a specific level of the within-subjects factor, (5) an interaction contrast. As usual, which of these types of intervals we should choose to form in any given study may depend in part on which omnibus effects are statistically significant, but even more so on what effects are of theoretical or practical importance given the purpose of the study.

For pedagogical purposes, we will use data from our reaction time study to illustrate an example of each of the five types of confidence intervals we described in the previous paragraph. It is important to understand that we are not suggesting that this is the "correct" set of confidence intervals to form in this study. Instead, we simply want to illustrate the formation and interpretation of each type of interval.

Table 14.13 shows SAS output for five confidence intervals in our reaction time data. As usual, each interval is centered at a mean difference. The width of each interval comes from multiplying a critical value (or in some cases, the square root of a critical value) by the estimated standard error of the contrast. Especially in complex designs, most current statistical packages do not directly accommodate the great variety of possible multiple comparisons procedures. Thus, as we have seen for other designs, it is typically necessary to perform a few hand calculations when adjusting for multiple tests. In particular, the intervals shown in the SAS output of Table 14.13 implicitly assume that we have chosen a per-comparison alpha level of .05 for each contrast. However, because SAS provides a standard error for each contrast, it is straightforward to adjust the width of an interval for multiple comparisons if we so desire.

In particular, notice that when the dependent variable is either M or Y, we effectively have a between-subjects design. Any contrast based on M or Y necessarily compares levels of the between-subjects factors to one another. As such, the multiple comparison procedures

TABLE 14.13

CONFIDENCE INTERVALS FOR FIVE CONTRASTS IN SPLIT-PLOT DESIGN

(1) *Levels of Between-Subjects Marginal Means*

Parameter	Estimate	Standard Error	t Value	Pr > |t|	95% Confidence Limits	
Age diff in marginal mean	94.0000000	34.8488801	2.70	0.0147	20.7852197	167.2147803

(2) *Levels of Within-Subjects Marginal Means*

Parameter	Estimate	Standard Error	t Value	Pr > |t|	95% Confidence Limits	
Mean quadratic trend	5.25000000	9.33072880	0.56	0.5806	−14.35313379	24.85313379

(3) *Levels of Within-Subjects Factor at a Specific Level of Between-Subjects Factor*

Parameter	Estimate	Standard Error	t Value	Pr > |t|	95% Confidence Limits	
Quad for young	24.0000000	13.1956432	1.82	0.0856	−3.7230177	51.7230177

(4) *Levels of Between-Subjects Factor at a Specific Level of Within-Subjects Factor*

Parameter	Estimate	Standard Error	t Value	Pr > |t|	95% Confidence Limits	
Mean age diff. at 8	147.000000	38.0657326	3.86	0.0011	67.026863	226.973137

(5) *Interaction Contrast*

Parameter	Estimate	Standard Error	t Value	Pr > |t|	95% Confidence Limits	
Age diff. in linear trend	81.0000000	27.2946881	2.97	0.0082	23.6559881	138.3440119

described in Chapter 5 are appropriate for this type of contrast in a split-plot design. Contrasts based on D require one of three approaches. First, no adjustment needs to be made to the critical value when alpha is to be maintained only for this specific comparison. Second, a Bonferroni correction is necessary when all comparisons have been planned (including the possibility of testing all pairwise comparisons). It is often possible to implement this correction in statistical packages simply by specifying a confidence interval other than 95% (recall Equation 14.36 from earlier in the chapter). Third, when complex post hoc comparisons are of interest, it is necessary to use a Roy-Bose correction. Appropriate critical values are shown in Equation 65 for comparisons of marginal means of the within-subjects factor, in Equations 70 and 71 for comparisons of within-subject levels within a specific level of the between-subjects factor, and in Equation 76 for interaction contrasts (but recall that this equation applies only when $a = 2$; otherwise, as we mentioned earlier, special tables are required).

Before proceeding to discuss each of the intervals shown in Table 14.13, we will mention that forming such intervals can sometimes be confusing, even when we have a statistical package at our disposal. Fortunately, there are two simple ways to increase the likelihood that the interval provided by a statistical package is in fact the interval we intend. First, we can compare the t statistic shown for the contrast with an F statistic we may have obtained from a hypothesis testing framework. Assuming that the same error term applies to both, we should see that the square of the t value equals the F value. Such equality is necessary but not sufficient, in part because the scaling of coefficients is important for confidence intervals. Thus, our contrast coefficients might be off by a constant of proportionality, and yet we would still see that the square of the t value equals the F value. Second, we can also compare the estimate of the contrast (i.e., the center of the interval) to the sample mean difference in our data. We should be able to verify that the estimated value of the contrast is indeed the intended linear combination of cell means. If so, we do not need to worry about the contrast coefficients being off by a constant of proportionality. On the other hand, if the estimated mean difference from a computer output is (for example) twice the mean difference we calculate by hand, this strongly suggests that we need to rethink the scaling of our contrast coefficients. We will illustrate both of these verification checks while discussing the results shown in Table 14.13.

Let's begin with the first confidence interval shown in the table. This interval reflects the age difference in marginal means, averaging over the within-subjects angle factor. According to the table, the best estimate of the corresponding difference in the population is 94 points. This makes sense, because doing a little arithmetic on the data in Table 14.10 reveals that the average reaction time for older participants is 663, whereas the average for younger participants is 569. The difference between 663 and 569 is 94, confirming that the contrast shown in the table correctly reflects the intended contrast. Further, the t value of 2.70 when squared equals 7.29, which agrees within rounding error with the value of 7.28 we found when we tested the age main effect in these data. Thus, having reassured ourselves that the contrast has been properly formulated, we can now proceed to interpret what it means. Our best guess is that the population mean difference between older and younger participants' reaction times averaging over the levels of angle is 94 ms. We can be 95% confident that the true population difference is between 20.79 and 167.21 ms. Notice that zero is not included in the interval, consistent with the statistically significant effect for the age main effect. Further understand that how much more informative the confidence interval is than the hypothesis test ultimately hinges on our ability to interpret the limits of 20.79 and 167.21. On the one hand, we might judge even the smallest difference of 20.79 to be enormous, in which case we have learned quite a bit from the interval. Or, on the other hand, if we judge 167.21 to be trivially small, we now know from the interval that even though the age difference is statistically significant, it may not be important. Yet another possible interpretation is that the interval is so wide that we may feel unable to judge the importance of the age difference. Such a result would suggest that we needed a larger sample. Finally, notice that especially when the units of the dependent variable are arbitrary, we may have difficulty deciding which of these descriptions fits our data, which then suggests that the confidence interval in this case may not provide any helpful information beyond the hypothesis test. Finally, we simply want to point out that this confidence interval comes from applying the principles of Chapter 4 to our M variable. In particular, we showed in Chapter 4 that a confidence interval can be formed as

$$\hat{\psi} \pm \sqrt{F_{\alpha;1,N-a}} \sqrt{MS_W \sum_{j=1}^{a} \left(c_j^2 / n_j\right)} \qquad \text{(4.48, repeated)}$$

Equation 4.48 also applies to the split-plot design whenever we are forming a contrast of levels of the between-subjects factor, as we are here. The contrast of marginal means of the age factor requires that we form an M variable for each participant. Once we have done so, functionally we have a single-factor between-subjects design, which is why we can use Equation 4.48 as long as we remember that all calculations using this equation are based on M as the dependent variable.

The second interval shown in Table 14.13 illustrates a comparison of levels of marginal means of a within-subjects factor. Specifically, the contrast of presumed interest here is the quadratic trend of marginal means of the angle factor, which we would examine by forming a quadratic D variable for each participant. The SAS output tells us that the estimated value of this contrast is 5.25. We can see where this value comes from by realizing that the marginal means of the angle factor equal 510, 619.5, and 718.5 for the 0°, 4°, and 8° conditions, respectively. If we choose to operationalize our quadratic trend with coefficients of -0.5, 1.0, and -0.5 for the three conditions, the resultant estimated value of the contrast is indeed 5.25. Table 14.13 reveals that the 95% confidence interval for the corresponding population mean runs from -14.35 to 24.85. Notice that this interval contains zero, consistent as it must be with the nonsignificant t value of 0.56, which itself is consistent (within rounding error) with the F value of 0.32 we reported earlier for the quadratic trend of angle marginal means.

The third interval shown in Table 14.13 also involves the quadratic trend for the angle factor. However, instead of examining the marginal means, this new contrast examines the quadratic angle effect only for younger participants. Thus, instead of being based on the marginal means for angle, this contrast represents a cell means comparison we might pursue as a followup to an interaction. As in the second comparison, we would again form a quadratic D for each participant, but our estimate of the mean of this D would now be based only on younger participants. As we described in our earlier discussion of testing effects of B at A_j, the standard error and also the critical value might either be based on only the younger participants or we could use all participants if we believe homogeneity of variance to hold here. Both approaches can easily be implemented in statistical packages such as SAS. In the particular case of Table 14.13, we have chosen to present the interval where all participants are used to find an estimated standard error. The table shows us that the estimated value of the contrast in the reaction time data is 24, which, we can verify from Table 14.10, corresponds to contrast coefficients of -0.5, 1.0, and -0.5, as in our second contrast of the previous paragraph. The 95% confidence interval has a lower limit of -3.72 and an upper limit of 51.72. Once again, this interval also contains zero, which is consistent with the observed t value of 1.82, which itself is consistent with the F value of 3.31 we reported for this effect earlier in the chapter.

The fourth interval represents another cell mean comparison, which we might investigate as a follow-up to an interaction. This time, however, the contrast compares levels of the between-subjects factor at a fixed level of the within-subjects factor. As the table shows, the contrast compares mean reaction times of younger and older participants in the 8° angle condition. As such, scores in the 0° and 4° conditions are irrelevant here, so effectively we have a single-factor between-subjects design. For this reason, we could directly use any of the equations we originally developed in Chapters 4 and 5 for this design. It is apparent that the estimated value of 147 shown in Table 14.13 is simply the difference between the mean values of 792 and 645 we saw earlier in Table 14.10. The SAS output further tells us that with 95% confidence, we can assert that the population age difference in reaction times under the 8° angle condition is at least 67.03 msec and at most 226.97 ms. Notice in particular that this interval does not contain zero, consistent with a statistically significant simple effect of age in the 8° angle condition (with no attempt to control the alpha level for other tests we might also regard as belonging to the same family).

The fifth interval illustrates an interaction contrast. Specifically, it addresses the question of whether the linear trend for the angle factor is the same for younger participants as for older participants. To answer this question, we would first form a linear D variable for each and every participant. In this case with three levels, our contrast can be defined as the difference between a person's score in the 8° angle condition minus his or her score in the 0° angle condition (notice that we could divide this difference by 8 if we wanted to interpret the slope as the change in reaction time for every increase of 1°). You may recall that the D_1 variable shown in

Table 14.11 is precisely this D variable. Our contrast reflects the difference between the mean of this D variable for older participants as compared to the mean for younger participants. The estimate shown in Table 14.13 is thus the difference between the mean D_1 of 249 for older participants and the mean D_1 of 168 for younger participants (the values of 249 and 168 come from Table 14.11). The SAS output further shows that the 95% confidence interval stretches from 23.66 to 138.34. Notice that the interval is entirely above zero. Thus, we can conclude with 95% confidence that increasing the angle from zero degrees to 8° has a larger effect on the mean reaction time of older participants than younger participants. The difference in the effect could be as small as 23.66 ms or as large as 138.34 ms. As always, the ultimate interpretation of these values depends much less on statistics than on knowledge of the subject matter.

OPTIONAL

The Relationship Between the Multivariate and the Mixed-Model Approaches

The multivariate and mixed-model approaches for analyzing data from a split-plot design relate to one another as they do for other designs. As before, we do not provide a mathematical proof of this relationship, but instead demonstrate it empirically for our data.

An appropriate reminder at this point is that the multivariate and mixed-model approaches yield identical results for testing between-subjects effects. In essence, if there is only one score per participant entered into a particular test of significance, the two approaches produce equivalent results. Thus, our comparison of the two approaches concerns itself with the main effect of the within-subjects factor and with the interaction between the two factors.

Recall that we formed two D variables in our example to perform the multivariate test. The first D variable represented the linear trend for angle and was defined as

$$D_{1ij} = -1Y_{1ij} + 0Y_{2ij} + 1Y_{3ij}$$

The second D variable, which represented the quadratic trend for angle, was defined as

$$D_{2ij} = 1Y_{1ij} - 2Y_{2ij} + 1Y_{3ij}$$

To compare the two approaches, we must normalize the coefficients of these contrast variables. Notice that the linear and quadratic trends are already orthogonal to one another, so we need not worry further about this requirement. As usual, each nonnormalized coefficient must be divided by the square root of the sum of squared coefficients for that particular contrast. Carrying out this process for the linear and quadratic trend variables yields

$$D_{1ij}^* = -.7071Y_{1ij} + 0Y_{2ij} + .7071Y_{3ij}$$
$$D_{2ij}^* = .4082Y_{1ij} - .8164Y_{2ij} + .4082Y_{3ij}$$

We could now perform the multivariate test on D_1^* and D_2^* by calculating a full matrix $\mathbf{E}^*(\mathbf{F})$ and two restricted matrices $\mathbf{E}^*(\mathbf{R})$, one for the B main effect and one for the $A \times B$ interaction. Although such a procedure would produce the desired results, it is much simpler to work directly from the matrices we already calculated for the nonnormalized D_1 and D_2 variables. Earlier in the chapter, we found that the full and restricted matrices for D_1 and D_2 were given by

$$\mathbf{E(F)} = \begin{bmatrix} 67{,}050 & -9{,}090 \\ -9{,}090 & 125{,}370 \end{bmatrix}$$

$$\mathbf{E_B(R)} = \begin{bmatrix} 936{,}495 & -52{,}875 \\ -52{,}875 & 127{,}575 \end{bmatrix}$$

$$\mathbf{E_{A \times B}(R)} = \begin{bmatrix} 99{,}855 & 21{,}285 \\ 21{,}285 & 153{,}495 \end{bmatrix}$$

where $\mathbf{E_B(R)}$ is the restricted matrix for the B main effect and $\mathbf{E_{A \times B}(R)}$ is the restricted matrix for the $A \times B$ interaction. We can compute the $\mathbf{E^*}$ matrices for the normalized variables by realizing that for each participant

$$D_{1ij}^* = .7071 D_{1ij}$$
$$D_{2ij}^* = .4082 D_{2ij}$$

As a result

$$(D_{1ij}^*)^2 = .5(D_{1ij})^2$$
$$(D_{2ij}^*)^2 = .1667(D_{2ij})^2$$
$$D_{1ij}^* D_{2ij}^* = .2887 D_{1ij} D_{2ij}$$

It then follows that the row 1, column 1 element of each $\mathbf{E^*}$ matrix equals .5 times the corresponding element of each $\mathbf{E}$ matrix. Similarly, the row 2, column 2 element of each $\mathbf{E^*}$ matrix equals .1667 times the corresponding element of each $\mathbf{E}$ matrix. Finally, the row 1, column 2 and row 2, column 1 elements of each $\mathbf{E^*}$ matrix equal .2887 times the corresponding elements of each $\mathbf{E}$ matrix. Carrying out the necessary multiplication results in the following $\mathbf{E^*}$ matrices:

$$\mathbf{E^*(F)} = \begin{bmatrix} 33{,}525.00 & -2{,}624.06 \\ -2{,}624.06 & 20{,}895.00 \end{bmatrix}$$

$$\mathbf{E_B^*(R)} = \begin{bmatrix} 468{,}247.50 & -15{,}263.70 \\ -15{,}263.70 & 21{,}262.50 \end{bmatrix}$$

$$\mathbf{E_{A \times B}^*(R)} = \begin{bmatrix} 49{,}927.50 & 6{,}144.45 \\ 6{,}144.45 & 25{,}582.50 \end{bmatrix}$$

We can now consider the relationship between these $\mathbf{E^*}$ matrices and three sums of squares in the mixed-model approach: $SS_{B \times S/A}$, SS_B, and $SS_{A \times B}$. The sum of the two diagonal elements of $\mathbf{E^*(F)}$ equals 54,420, which we saw in Chapter 12 is $SS_{B \times S/A}$ for our data. Remembering that the sum of the diagonal elements of a matrix is its trace, which is abbreviated tr, enables us to write

$$SS_{B \times S/A} = tr(\mathbf{E^*(F)})$$

The relationships involving SS_B and $SS_{A \times B}$ are similarly given by

$$SS_B = tr(\mathbf{E_B^*(R)}) - tr(\mathbf{E^*(F)})$$
$$SS_{A \times B} = tr(\mathbf{E_{A \times B}^*(R)}) - tr(\mathbf{E^*(F)})$$

As a result, the mixed-model F tests for B and $A \times B$ can be written as

$$F = \frac{\{tr(\mathbf{E}_\mathbf{B}^*(\mathbf{R})) - tr(\mathbf{E}^*(\mathbf{F}))\}/(b - 1)}{tr(\mathbf{E}^*(\mathbf{F}))/(N - a)(b - 1)} \tag{78}$$

for the B main effect, and

$$F = \frac{\{tr(\mathbf{E}_{\mathbf{A} \times \mathbf{B}}^*(\mathbf{R})) - tr(\mathbf{E}^*(\mathbf{F}))\}/(a - 1)(b - 1)}{tr(\mathbf{E}^*(\mathbf{F}))/(N - a)(b - 1)} \tag{79}$$

for the $A \times B$ interaction.

The practical implication of Equations 78 and 79 is that once again the multivariate approach is sensitive to all elements of the $\mathbf{E}^*$ matrices, whereas the mixed-model approach ignores the off-diagonal elements. The reason, as before, is that if the sphericity assumption required by the mixed-model approach is met, the population values of the off-diagonal elements of the $\mathbf{E}^*(\mathbf{F})$ matrix are all zero. In addition, if sphericity holds, the population values of the diagonal elements of $\mathbf{E}^*(\mathbf{F})$ are all equal to one another so that the sample mean of these values—that is, $tr(\mathbf{E}^*(\mathbf{F}))/(b - 1)$—is a good estimate of the single underlying population value. However, if sphericity fails to hold, the mixed-model approach suffers from an inflated Type I error rate, unless ε adjustments are applied to the degrees of freedom of the critical value.

Also notice that the trace of the $\mathbf{E}^*(\mathbf{F})$ matrix forms the denominator sum of squares for testing both the B main effect and the $A \times B$ interaction. For this reason, the sphericity assumption is either met for both effects or it fails for both. When there is only one within-subjects factor, there is only one matrix for which the sphericity assumption is an issue. If, however, there were a second within-subjects factor in the design, we would need to consider additional matrices, just as we did earlier in the chapter for factorial within-subjects designs.

ASSUMPTIONS OF THE MULTIVARIATE APPROACH

Although the multivariate approach does not require that the sphericity assumption of the mixed-model approach be valid, the multivariate approach nevertheless shares several assumptions in common with the mixed-model approach. For example, because these two approaches produce identical F tests for between-subjects effects, it follows that their assumptions are also identical. Recall that between-subjects effects are tested by performing a between-subjects ANOVA on an M variable, where M is simply a variable that averages over the levels of the within-subjects factor(s). As we discussed in Chapter 12, the necessary assumptions are thus the same as those for a between-subjects design, namely, normality, homogeneity of variance, and independence of the M scores. The detailed discussion of these assumptions in Chapter 3 is equally pertinent to the split-plot design.

The assumptions for testing the B and $A \times B$ effects are rather different from those required for testing the A main effect, because B and $A \times B$ are both within-subjects effects. Before discussing the assumptions of the multivariate approach, it is helpful to recall the assumptions of the mixed-model approach. Besides the usual assumptions of normality and independence, the mixed-model approach requires two other assumptions, which together are called multisample sphericity. First, the mixed-model approach assumes sphericity of the population covariance matrix for each level of the A factor. Second, it assumes that the population covariance matrix at one level of A is identical to the population covariance matrix at every other level of A. As we have emphasized previously, the multivariate approach does not require the sphericity assumption. However, it shares the assumption with the mixed-model approach that all a population covariance matrices are identical to each other. The multivariate tests tend to be robust to this homogeneity of covariance matrix assumption, as long as sample sizes are equal. As we stated earlier in the chapter, there is some evidence (Olson, 1976) that the Pillai–Bartlett trace test statistic is the most robust of the four multivariate test statistics when $a > 2$. Of course, when $a = 2$, all four multivariate test statistics are equivalent. As usual, when sample sizes depart from equality, the tests become less robust. In any case, when heterogeneity is suspected, Lix and Keselman (1995) provide a very readable account of an approach that does not require the homogeneity of covariance matrix assumption. As of this writing, the approach they describe has not been implemented in any of the major statistical packages, but Lix and Keselman (1995) provide SAS code that greatly simplifies the application of their approach to data analysis. Finally, as we pointed out in Chapter 13, the multivariate approach also assumes multivariate normality and independence of observations.

MULTIVARIATE AND MIXED-MODEL APPROACHES FOR TESTING WITHIN-SUBJECTS CONTRASTS

We saw earlier in the chapter that the multivariate approach for testing within-subjects contrasts involves the formation of an appropriate D variable. When a univariate test is conducted on this variable, no assumption of sphericity is required. We also saw that the use of a separate error term, which was one of the methods we discussed in Chapter 12, produces identical results to the multivariate approach. The use of a pooled error term, which was the other method we discussed in Chapter 12, may yield very different results, because this approach depends strongly on the validity of the sphericity assumption. For this reason, we recommend using a separate error term for each contrast. However, as in other designs, the use of a separate error term is more consistent with the multivariate approach than with the mixed-model approach for analyzing split-plot data.

If a separate error term is to be used and if an omnibus test is desired, it makes sense to use the multivariate approach for performing the omnibus test. This omnibus test is statistically significant with the multivariate approach if and only if a statistically significant contrast can be found using a separate error term and an appropriate critical value, such as those given by Equations 65, 70, 71, 75, and 76. Thus, if the multivariate test is statistically significant, specific contrasts are worth testing; if the multivariate test is not significant, there is no reason to test specific contrasts, because none can be significant with a separate error term. What if the mixed-model approach were used instead to perform the omnibus test? It is entirely possible for the mixed-model approach to yield a nonsignificant omnibus F test, and yet a specific statistically significant contrast exists when tested with the separate error term, even using an appropriate post hoc critical value. The reverse can also happen. That is, the mixed-model omnibus test can be statistically significant, and yet no significant specific contrast exists when tested with a separate error term and an appropriate critical value. Thus, the mixed-model test fails to provide an unambiguous signal to the researcher as to whether post hoc tests should be conducted (unless we are willing to use a pooled error term). The multivariate approach, on the other hand, does provide this information, which is one reason we prefer it in general.[22]

Of course, another viable option is to test planned contrasts, using a separate error term for each contrast. With this approach, to perform an omnibus test is unnecessary, so the distinction between the mixed-model and multivariate approaches is largely irrelevant. Notice, however, that the choice of error term is still relevant for testing planned contrasts. Not surprisingly, we continue to recommend the use of a separate error term for each contrast.

Comparison of the Multivariate and Mixed-Model Approaches

The advantages and disadvantages of the multivariate and mixed-model approaches in the split-plot design are essentially the same as in completely within-subjects designs. For this reason, we refer you to our earlier extended discussion at the end of Chapter 13 for more information. As before, our general recommendation is to use the multivariate approach unless sample sizes are very small. A rough rule of thumb for a minimum sample size required with the multivariate approach can be stated in terms of the between-subjects and within-subjects degrees of freedom. The between-subjects degrees of freedom will equal the number of participants on which the error matrix for the full model is based, minus the number of groups formed by these participants. For example, if the error matrix for the full model is based on all participants in a split-plot design, the between-subjects degrees of freedom will equal $N - a$. On the other hand, if only participants at level j are used to form the error matrix for the full model, the between-subjects degrees of freedom will equal $n_j - 1$. The within-subjects degrees of freedom will equal the number of D variables involved in a particular test. The rough rule of thumb can now be stated: The between-subjects degrees of freedom should probably exceed the within-subjects degrees of freedom by at least 10 to 20 if the multivariate approach is to be used.

OPTIONAL

More Complex Designs

We have focused our attention in this chapter on designs with two factors. However, both the logic and the procedural details we have developed generalize to higher-order designs. For example, the tests to be conducted in a three-way design with one or more repeated factors would be the same as those discussed in Chapter 8 for between-subjects designs. In particular, the flowchart shown in Figure 8.6 can still be used as a general guideline for choosing what effects to test. However, as in two-way repeated-measures designs, the form of the F test must take into account the lack of independence that arises from having more than one score per participant.

To illustrate how tests are conducted in higher-order repeated measures designs, we consider a four-way $A \times B \times E \times F$ design. (We do not designate the design as $A \times B \times C \times D$, because D continues to designate a "difference" variable.) We assume that factors A and B are between-subjects factors and that E and F are within-subjects factors. As usual, the number of levels of the factors is designated as a, b, e, and f for A, B, E, and F, respectively. We further assume that all factors are completely crossed. This implies that data are obtained for $a \times b$ distinct groups of participants, where each participant contributes $e \times f$ scores.

Table 8.24 shows that there are 15 omnibus effects to be tested in a four-way design: four main effects (viz., A, B, E, and F), six two-way interactions (viz., $A \times B$, $A \times E$, $A \times F$, $B \times E$, $B \times F$, and $E \times F$), four three-way interactions (viz., $A \times B \times E$, $A \times B \times F$, $A \times E \times F$, and $B \times E \times F$), and one four-way interaction (viz., $A \times B \times E \times F$). Interpretation of results would typically begin by considering the significance of the four-way interaction, then the three-way interactions, and so forth. We do not attempt to describe interpretations here, because they are fundamentally the same in repeated measures designs as in between-subjects designs. Instead, our focus is on what models to compare and what variables to form in order to test each effect of interest, because these are the issues that change in a repeated measures design.

We begin by considering the transformed variables that must be formed in the $A \times B \times E \times F$ design. After seeing how these variables are formed, we present full and restricted models to be compared. In the process, we will see that each of the 15 effects of interest can be tested by choosing an appropriate set of transformed variables (or, in some cases, a single transformed variable) and then comparing appropriate full and restricted models for this set of variables.

Each participant contributes $e \times f$ scores to the data, because there are e levels of E and f levels of F, where E and F are the two repeated factors. We continue to refer to these original variables as Y variables. As in the designs we considered earlier in the chapter, the multivariate approach requires that these $e \times f$ original Y variables be transformed into a new set of variables. It is helpful to state at the outset that these new, transformed variables can be conceptualized best as constituting four types of variables. First, as in our earlier designs, a mean variable M can be calculated for each participant. Following the same logic as in the other designs of this chapter, a participant's score on M is literally the mean of the participant's scores on the original $e \times f$ Y variables.

The other three types of variables follow directly from the procedures we developed at the beginning of the chapter for designs with two repeated factors. In particular, transformed variables are formed for the $A \times B \times E \times F$ design just as they were at the beginning of the chapter when there were no between-subjects factors. The presence (or absence) of between-subjects factors has no effect on how transformed D variables are defined. Thus, the second type of variable is a set of $e - 1$ variables, each of which represents a contrast of the levels of E averaged over F. Each variable is a difference variable or a D variable in our abbreviated notation. For clarity, we refer to this set of variables as the D_E set, where the E subscript serves as a reminder that these variables reflect differences among the levels of the E factor. Specifically, the set of $e - 1$ D_E variables collectively represents average differences among the e levels of the E factor, where the average is computed over levels of F, the other within-subjects factor. Notice that scores on each of the $e - 1$ D_E variables would be computed just as they were at the beginning of the chapter in the design that had two repeated factors but no between-subjects factors. Similarly, the third type of variable is a set of $f - 1$ D variables, each of which represents a contrast of the levels of F averaged over E. We designate this set of variables as D_F. Finally, the fourth type of variable is a set of $(e - 1)(f - 1)$ D variables, each of which represents a component of the $E \times F$ interaction. This set is designated $D_{E \times F}$.

To summarize, the original $e \times f$ Y variables are transformed into four new sets of variables:

1. One M variable
2. $e - 1$ D_E variables
3. $f - 1$ D_F variables
4. $(e - 1)(f - 1)$ $D_{E \times F}$ variables.

The total number of transformed variables equals $1 + (e - 1) + (f - 1) + (e - 1)(f - 1)$. However, expanding the final term of this expression yields $1 + (e - 1) + (f - 1) + ef - f - e + 1$, which is equivalent to $ef + e - e + f - f + 1 - 1 - 1 + 1$, which reduces to ef. Thus, the total number of transformed variables equals the total number of original variables. A typical reaction to this statement might be, So why did we bother to transform the variables in the first place? The answer is that the sets of transformed variables explicitly contain information about the effects we want to test. Although the same information exists in the original variables, the form of the original variables does not permit us to test the effects of interest directly.

Transforming the original variables enables us to represent within-subjects effects. However, we also need a mechanism for incorporating between-subjects effects into our analyses. This is accomplished by forming a full model whose parameters correspond to the between-subjects effects in the design. For example, when we had only one between-subjects factor (and one within-subjects factor), we formed a full model of the form

$$M_{ij} = \mu + \alpha_j + \varepsilon_{ij} \qquad \text{(39, repeated)}$$

for the M variable and a model of the form

$$D_{ij} = \mu + \alpha_j + \varepsilon_{ij} \qquad\qquad\qquad (43, \text{ repeated})$$

for each D variable. The important point to notice here is that the full models have the same form for M and as for D. In both cases, the model corresponds to the between-subjects design, because there was one between-subjects factor. For this reason, the model has the same form as the models we introduced in Chapter 3.

Our current four-way $A \times B \times E \times F$ design has two between-subjects factors, so the appropriate full model now needs to include additional parameters to reflect the A main effect, the B main effect, and the $A \times B$ interaction. As a result, the full model has the same form as the full model we developed in Chapter 7 for two-way between-subjects designs. Specifically, in the four-way design, we will have a full model of the form

$$M_{ijk} = \mu + \alpha_j + \beta_k + (\alpha\beta)_{jk} + \varepsilon_{ijk}$$

for the M variable and a model of the form

$$D_{ijk} = \mu + \alpha_j + \beta_k + (\alpha\beta)_{jk} + \varepsilon_{ijk}$$

for each of the D variables. As in Chapter 7, μ is a grand mean parameter, α_j is an effect associated with the jth level of A, β_k is an effect associated with the kth level of B, and $\alpha\beta_{jk}$ is a parameter for the $A \times B$ interaction. When M is the dependent variable, the full model allows for A main effects, B main effects, and $A \times B$ interaction effects on each participant's mean score, averaged over levels of the repeated factors. Similarly, the full model for the dependent variable D allows for A, B, and $A \times B$ effects to exert themselves on differences among the levels of the repeated factors. The various combinations of restricted models and dependent variables together allow us to test the effects of interest.

Table 14.14 shows the type of dependent variable and the type of restriction to employ to test each omnibus effect in the $A \times B \times E \times F$ design. To ensure that the table is clear, we consider how to test a few specific effects. First, let's consider the A main effect. According to the table, this effect is tested using M as the dependent variable. Thus, the full model is

$$M_{ijk} = \mu + \alpha_j + \beta_k + (\alpha\beta)_{jk} + \varepsilon_{ijk}$$

The restriction imposed on this model is that all α_j parameters equal zero, which leads to a restricted model of the form

$$M_{ijk} = \mu + \beta_k + (\alpha\beta)_{jk} + \varepsilon_{ijk}$$

The F test comparing these models is conducted exactly as we described in Chapter 7. Although we hope that this brief description clarifies how to perform the test of the A main effect, even more important is to understand why such a procedure produces a test of the A main effect. The crucial point here is to remember that the M variable has averaged over the E and F factors. Thus, the model comparison we have performed effectively compares A marginal means, averaging over all other factors in the design, which is just the definition of a main effect.

Second, let's consider the $A \times E$ interaction. Table 14.14 shows that this effect is tested using the set of D_E variables as dependent variables. There are $e - 1$ variables in this set, necessitating a multivariate analysis whenever $e \geq 3$, that is, whenever the E factor has three or more levels. For each variable in the set, an appropriate full model is given by

$$D_{ijk} = \mu + \alpha_j + \beta_k + (\alpha\beta)_{jk} + \varepsilon_{ijk}$$

TABLE 14.14

TESTS OF OMNIBUS EFFECTS IN AN A × B × E × F DESIGN

Between-Subjects Effects—Full Model: $M_{ijk} = \mu + \alpha_j + \beta_k + (\alpha\beta)_{jk} + \varepsilon_{ijk}$

Effect	Type of Dependent Variable	Number of Dependent Variables	Restricted Parameters	df_{num}	df_{den}
A	M	1	$H_0: \alpha_j = 0$	$a-1$	$N-ab$
B	M	1	$H_0: \beta_k = 0$	$b-1$	$N-ab$
A×B	M	1	$H_0: \alpha\beta_{jk} = 0$	$(a-1)(b-1)$	$N-ab$

Within-Subjects Effects—Full Model: $D_{ijk} = \mu + \alpha_j + \beta_k + (\alpha\beta)_{jz} + \varepsilon_{ijk}$

Effect	Type of Dependent Variable	Number of Dependent Variables	Restricted Parameters	df_{num}	df_{den}
E	D_E	$e-1$	$H_0: \mu = 0$	$e-1$	$N-ab-e+2$
F	D_F	$f-1$	$H_0: \mu = 0$	$f-1$	$N-ab-f+2$
E×F	$D_{E×F}$	$(e-1)(f-1)$	$H_0: \mu = 0$	$(e-1)(f-1)$	$N-ab-(e-1)(f-1)+1$
A×E	D_E	$e-1$	$H_0: \alpha_j = 0$	$(a-1)(e-1)$	Rao*
B×E	D_E	$e-1$	$H_0: \beta_k = 0$	$(b-1)(e-1)$	Rao*
A×B×E	D_E	$e-1$	$H_0: (\alpha\beta)_{jk} = 0$	$(a-1)(b-1)(e-1)$	Rao*
A×F	D_F	$f-1$	$H_0: \alpha_j = 0$	$(a-1)(f-1)$	Rao*
B×F	D_F	$f-1$	$H_0: \beta_k = 0$	$(b-1)(f-1)$	Rao*
A×B×F	D_F	$f-1$	$H_0: (\alpha\beta)_{jk} = 0$	$(a-1)(b-1)(f-1)$	Rao*
A×E×F	$D_{E×F}$	$(e-1)(f-1)$	$H_0: \alpha_j = 0$	$(a-1)(e-1)(f-1)$	Rao*
B×E×F	$D_{E×F}$	$(e-1)(f-1)$	$H_0: \beta_k = 0$	$(b-1)(e-1)(f-1)$	Rao*
A×B×E×F	$D_{E×F}$	$(e-1)(f-1)$	$H_0: (\alpha\beta)_{jk} = 0$	$(a-1)(b-1)(e-1)(f-1)$	Rao*

* When Rao's F approximation is used, denominator degrees of freedom equal $df_{den} = mq - .5pd_H + 1$, where

$$m = N - ab + d_H - .5(p + d_H + 1)$$

$$q = \sqrt{\frac{(pd_H)^2 - 4}{p^2 + d_H^2 - 5}} \quad \text{where } q = 1 \text{ if } p^2 + d_H^2 = 5$$

p = number of dependent variables

d_H = number of independent restricted parameters (per dependent variable)

The restriction imposed on this model is that all α_j parameters equal zero, which leads to a restricted model of the form

$$D_{ijk} = \mu + \beta_k + (\alpha\beta)_{jk} + \varepsilon_{ijk}$$

Errors for each participant must be calculated for both the full and restricted models. Sums of squared errors and sums of cross-products can then be put in matrix form, and an F statistic can be calculated. In general, as Table 14.14 shows, the numerator degrees of freedom equal $(a - 1)(e - 1)$, whereas the denominator degrees of freedom come from Rao's approximation (if Wilks's lambda is chosen as the test statistic). All of this discussion leads to what is in many respects the crucial question: Why does testing a null hypothesis that all α_j parameters equal zero test the $A \times E$ interaction? As in our discussion of the A main effect, the crucial point is to remember the nature of the dependent variable(s). The variables used to test the $A \times E$ interaction are the D_E difference variables, which collectively represent differences among levels of E, averaged over F. Testing whether the α_j parameters equal zero asks, Is there an A effect on the differences among levels of E? However, the presence of such an effect implies that the E differences vary at different levels of A, which means that A and E interact. Also notice that the other two factors in the design have been averaged over, as required for a two-way interaction in a four-way design. Specifically, F has been averaged over, because the variables in the D_E set are defined to average over F. The B factor has also been averaged over, because of the meaning of the α_j parameters in the full model. Thus, testing for an A effect on the set of D_E variables provides a test of the $A \times E$ interaction.

The other tests in Table 14.14 are based on the same underlying logic. In addition, follow-up tests could be performed by varying the nature of the models being compared, by varying the definitions of the transformed variables, or both. Fortunately, if the logic is understood, the mechanics can be handled easily with available statistical packages.

We have now presented procedures for using the multivariate approach in a variety of repeated-measures designs. It may be helpful to summarize a general procedure that can be employed for any combination of between-subjects and within-subjects factors. The general procedure can be conceptualized in terms of three steps:

1. Form an M variable and D variables that correspond to the within-subjects effects to be tested. Scores are calculated for every participant on each variable, irrespective of any between-subjects factors.
2. Form a full model whose parameters correspond to between-subjects effects, irrespective of any within-subjects factors.
3. Calculate an F statistic by comparing the full model of Step 2 to an appropriate restricted model, using sets of variables from Step 1 as dependent variables.

Table 14.15 provides general rules for calculating degrees of freedom for the multivariate approach to analyzing data from split-plot designs. Our purpose in presenting this table might be unclear, because whatever computer program you are using will undoubtedly calculate degrees of freedom for you. However, calculating degrees of freedom by hand and checking them against the computer printout is frequently a good idea. Although it is unlikely that a "bug" in the computer program has caused it to calculate degrees of freedom incorrectly, it is not so unlikely that the computer program may have provided the right answer to the wrong question. In other words, in complex designs, it is all too easy to think that a particular p value on the printout establishes the statistical significance of a certain effect, whereas in fact the instructions given to the program caused it to test an entirely different effect. Although checking degrees of freedom does not guarantee accuracy, it does provide some additional assurance that the correct effect has been tested.

A few additional remarks may clarify some of the entries in Table 14.15. First, the numerator degrees of freedom for an effect are the same as in other designs. For example, the d_H entry for the numerator degrees of freedom of a between-subjects effect equals the number of independent restricted

TABLE 14.15

GENERAL RULES FOR DEGREES OF FREEDOM
IN SPLIT-PLOT DESIGNS

Type of Effect	df_{num} [†]	df_{den} [‡]
Between	d_H	$N - g$
Within*	p	$N - g - p + 1$
Between × within	pd_H	$mq - .5pd_H + 1$

*"Within" means any within-subjects effect that averages over levels of the between-subjects factor(s).

[†] d_H is the number of independent restricted parameters (per dependent variable). For a given variable, d_H equals $df_R - df_F$. p is the number of dependent variables.

[‡] N is total sample size. g is the number of groups (or between-subjects cells) in the design. m is defined as $m = N - g + d_H - .5(p + d_H + 1)$. q is defined as

$$q = \sqrt{\frac{(pd_H)^2 - 4}{p^2 + d_H^2 - 5}} \quad \text{where } q = 1 \text{ if } p^2 + d_H^2 = 5$$

parameters, which is equivalent to $df_R - df_F$, as in earlier designs. This formula is appropriate regardless of the number of between-subjects factors in the model and applies to any type of between-subjects effect (e.g., main effect, interaction, simple effect, etc.). Similarly, the numerator degrees of freedom for any purely within-subjects effect (i.e., one which averages over levels of any between-subjects factors) equal the number of dependent variables. Finally, numerator degrees of freedom for effects involving between × within interactions equal the product of the respective degrees of freedom. Thus, for all types of effects, the numerator degrees of freedom in a split-plot design follow the same rules as in other designs.

Denominator degrees of freedom are straightforward, except for between × within interactions. For example, denominator degrees of freedom for between-subjects effects are the same as they would be if there were no within-subjects factors in the design. Denominator degrees of freedom for purely within-subjects effects are also easily calculated, as shown in Table 14.15. It is also worth pointing out that all four multivariate test statistics yield the same result for purely within-subjects effects. As the table shows, denominator degrees of freedom are considerably more complicated for effects involving between × within interactions. We should also add that the formula shown in the table is for Rao's approximation to Wilks's lambda. In general, the four multivariate test statistics differ at least slightly from each other for tests of between × within interactions. The only situation where the tests necessarily are identical is when $s = 1$. The s parameter equals the smaller of p and d_H, so unless $p = 1$ or $d_H = 1$, the four test statistics are not identical.

The analysis of data from higher-order repeated measures designs can obviously become quite complicated. The technical complications should not cause you to lose sight of the underlying logic. Remember the three-step process that can be applied no matter how complicated the design:

1. Variables are transformed to represent within-subjects effects.
2. A full model whose parameters correspond to between-subjects effects is formed.
3. The full model of Step 2 is compared to a restricted model, using sets of variables from Step 1.

Understanding the logic behind these three steps should enable you to analyze and interpret data from higher-order repeated measures designs. For readers interested in further specific details, several good sources are available. We particularly recommend Hand and Taylor (1987), Hertzog and Rovine (1985), and O'Brien and Kaiser (1985).

EXERCISES

1. True or False: Although the multivariate approach to repeated measures generally yields different results than the univariate (mixed-model) approach for testing omnibus effects, the two approaches are identical for testing contrasts.

2. True or False: The multivariate approach and the mixed-model approach to repeated measures in split-plot designs always yield identical F values for tests of between-subjects effects.

3. True or False: A major difference between data analysis in factorial between-subjects designs and split-plot designs is that the meaning of a significant interaction is different.

4. True or False: There are four different multivariate test statistics that can be used for testing an interaction in a split-plot design where both factors have more than two levels.

*5. A psychologist has conducted a study with a two-way 3×4 within-subjects design. We designate the three-level factor as A and the four-level factor as B.
    a. List the omnibus effects to be tested in this design.
    b. How many D variables will be needed to test each of the effects in part a?
    c. Assume that 20 participants have been used in the study. Find the numerator and denominator degrees of freedom for each of the effects in part a.

6. Table 14.1 presents data for a two-way 2×2 within-subjects design. The F values obtained with the multivariate approach are 66.57 for the angle main effect, 45.37 for the noise main effect, and 83.90 for the angle × noise interaction. Analyze these same data using the mixed-model approach of Chapter 12. How do your results compare to those obtained with the multivariate approach? Why?

7. The chapter states that the difference variables D_4 of Equations 23 and 25 are equivalent to one another. The interaction contrast of Equation 23 was obtained by applying the algorithm for generating an interaction difference variable:

$$D_{4i} = 1Y_{1i} + 0Y_{2i} - 1Y_{3i} - 1Y_{4i} + 0Y_{5i} + 1Y_{6i} \tag{23}$$

Equation 25 was written as

$$D_{4i} = (-1Y_{4i} + 0Y_{5i} + 1Y_{6i}) - (-1Y_{1i} + 0Y_{2i} + 1Y_{3i}) \tag{25}$$

    a. How would you interpret the effect represented by the D_4 variable of Equation 25?
    b. Carry out the subtraction in Equation 25. Are the coefficients of Equation 25 equivalent to those of Equation 23?

*8. Suppose that 20 participants have participated in a 3×4 two-way within-subjects design. We represent the factor with three levels as A and the factor with four levels as B.
    a. Suppose that all pairwise comparisons of A marginal means are to be tested. Find the numerical value of the critical value (CV) that should be used to maintain α_{FW} at .05.
    b. How would your answer to part a change if post hoc complex comparisons were also to be tested?
    c. Suppose that an interaction contrast were to be tested post hoc. Find the numerical value of the CV that should be used to maintain α_{FW} at .05.

*9. A graduate student has used a two-way 2×4 within-subjects design for his thesis. Fifteen individuals served as participants. His most interesting result was a statistically significant A main effect. According to the computer program he used (which uses the mixed-model approach), the F value for this effect was 5.61 with 1 numerator and 98 denominator degrees of freedom. His thesis adviser has asked him to reanalyze his data using the multivariate approach. Will he necessarily obtain the same result once again for the A main effect? Explain your answer.

10. Kosslyn describes a program of research investigating processes involved in the formation of a visual image, Kosslyn, S. M. (1988). Aspects of a cognitive neuroscience of mental imagery. *Science, 240*, 1621–1626. In one condition of one study, participants were shown an uppercase letter superimposed on a grid. They were then shown a blank grid and a lowercase letter. Their

task was to decide whether the corresponding uppercase letter would occupy one or two specific cells of the grid. In a second condition of this study, the task was the same, but the internal lines of the grid were eliminated and only the brackets at the four corners were presented. Perceptual theory suggests that when grid lines are present, participants use a categorical representation of how line segments in letters are connected. However, when only brackets are present, participants use a coordinate representation to arrange the parts of the stimulus letter. In both conditions, the stimulus was presented to the right visual field half of the time (and hence seen first in the left cerebral hemisphere) and to the left visual field on remaining trials (and hence seen first in the right cerebral hemisphere). The primary dependent variable of interest was response time (in milliseconds) averaged over a number of trials. The following hypothetical data assume that each of 10 participants has been assessed in both the grids condition and the brackets condition:

	Grids Condition		Brackets Condition	
Subject	Left Hemisphere	Right Hemisphere	Left Hemisphere	Right Hemisphere
1	1,600	1,670	1,690	1,690
2	1,420	1,590	1,580	1,590
3	1,670	1,730	1,790	1,800
4	1,430	1,560	1,550	1,460
5	1,550	1,510	1,570	1,590
6	1,520	1,600	1,680	1,600
7	1,610	1,730	1,780	1,670
8	1,600	1,710	1,670	1,710
9	1,680	1,720	1,800	1,710
10	1,570	1,500	1,610	1,520

a. Perform a test of the condition main effect, the hemisphere main effect, and the condition × hemisphere interaction.

b. Calculate omega squared values for each of the effects you tested in part a. How do these values inform your interpretation of the results from part a?

c. Based on your answers to part a, would it be appropriate to perform simple-effects tests here? If so, test effects of condition within hemisphere and hemisphere within condition.

d. Form a 95% confidence interval for the condition effect within the left hemisphere. Form a comparable interval within the right hemisphere. How would you interpret these intervals?

e. Form a 95% confidence interval for the difference between the condition effect within the left hemisphere and the condition effect within the right hemisphere. How would you interpret this interval?

f. To what extent can you use your results in parts a through e to support Kosslyn's contention that two different classes of processes are used to form mental images? In particular, do your results support the statement that some of the processes used to arrange parts of images are more efficient in the left hemisphere, whereas for other processes, the right hemisphere is more efficient?

g. Is the sphericity assumption required for your analyses here? Why or why not?

*11. Under what conditions will the mixed-model and multivariate approaches necessarily yield the same results for testing the following effects in an $A \times B$ split-plot design (A is between, B is within)?

a. A main effect

b. B main effect

c. $A \times B$ interaction

12. Assume that the multivariate approach is being used to analyze a between × within design. The test of whether the grand means are zero for the transformed variables that represent contrasts among the levels of the within-subjects factor is a test of which omnibus effect?

*13. Consider the following cell means in a 3×2 split-plot design:

	B	
	1	*2*
A *1*	10	12
2	16	20
3	16	16

Twenty participants were observed at each level of A, the between-subjects factor. Two transformed dependent variables were formed for each participant: $M_i = (Y_{1i} + Y_{2i})/2$ and $D_i = Y_{2i} - Y_{1i}$. The within-cell standard deviations for M were $s_1 = 4$, $s_2 = 6$, and $s_3 = 5$. The corresponding values for D were $s_1 = 6$, $s_2 = 4$, and $s_3 = 4$.

a. Test the statistical significance of the A main effect.
b. Test the statistical significance of the B main effect.
c. Test the statistical significance of the $A \times B$ interaction.

14. Harter et al. (1998) report a study investigating various aspects of "voice" in adolescent female and male high school students. Harter, S. (1998). Level of voice among female and male high school students: Relational context, support, and gender orientation. *Developmental Psychology, 34*, 892–901. "Voice" refers to the extent to which adolescents are able to overcome some possible tendency to suppress opinions. This exercise is modeled after data collected by Harter et al. (1998) but uses a simplified design with many fewer participants than the actual study (which had a sample size over 300). Suppose that two scales have been administered to 15 female ninth graders and to 15 male ninth graders (females' scores should be assumed to be independent of males' scores). One of these scales measures voice with female friends, whereas the other scale measures voice with male friends. Each scale consists of 10 items, scored from 1 to 4, where higher scores reflect greater levels of voice. Each individual's scale score is his or her average score across the 10 items on the scale. Consider the following hypothetical (but realistic) data:

Females		Males	
Male Friend	*Female Friend*	*Male Friend*	*Female Friend*
2.50	3.10	3.40	3.10
3.40	3.60	3.10	2.20
3.30	3.70	2.50	2.10
2.10	2.00	3.30	3.40
3.00	3.90	3.50	3.20
2.70	3.00	3.00	2.60
3.60	3.50	2.80	3.40
3.20	3.90	2.80	2.90
2.90	2.60	3.10	2.90
3.00	3.30	3.00	2.50
3.10	3.60	3.00	2.30
3.00	3.40	3.00	3.20
2.50	3.20	2.40	2.20
2.40	3.00	2.50	2.40
2.50	3.10	2.30	2.10

a. Perform tests of (1) the main effect of gender of the respondent, (2) the main effect of gender of the friend, and (3) the interaction of gender of respondent and gender of the friend.
b. The investigator who collected these data gave them to her research assistant to be analyzed. However, the research assistant conceptualized the design differently. In particular, instead of regarding the within-subjects factor as representing gender of the friend, he thought of this factor

in terms of whether the friend was the same gender or the opposite gender as the respondent. Thus, the data for the research assistant have the following structure:

Females		Males	
Same Gender	Opposite Gender	Same Gender	Opposite Gender
3.10	2.50	3.40	3.10
3.60	3.40	3.10	2.20
3.70	3.30	2.50	2.10
2.00	2.10	3.30	3.40
3.90	3.00	3.50	3.20
3.00	2.70	3.00	2.60
3.50	3.60	2.80	3.40
3.90	3.20	2.80	2.90
2.60	2.90	3.10	2.90
3.30	3.00	3.00	2.50
3.60	3.10	3.00	2.30
3.40	3.00	3.00	3.20
3.20	2.50	2.40	2.20
3.00	2.40	2.50	2.40
3.10	2.50	2.30	2.10

Perform tests of three effects for these data: (1) main effect of gender of the respondent, (2) main effect of same versus opposite gender of the friend, and (3) interaction between gender of respondent and same versus opposite gender of the friend.

c. What is the relationship between the F values you obtained in part a and the F values you obtained in part b?

d. To understand why the relationships you identified in part c occur here, we will consider the full and restricted models in each part. Let's start with the full model for the between-subjects main effect, which we could write as $M_{ij} = \mu + \alpha_j + \varepsilon_{ij}$. How does the M variable in your part a analysis compare to the M variable in the part b analysis? What does this imply about the relationship between the tests of the between-subjects main effects in the two analyses?

e. Continuing part d, let's now consider the full model for the within-subjects tests. We could write this model as $D_{ij} = \mu + \alpha_j + \varepsilon_{ij}$. In both parts a and b, we test the within-subjects main effect by restricting μ to be zero. Similarly, in both parts a and b, we test the interaction by restricting all α_j parameters to be zero. If we used the same restrictions in both parts a and b, why were the answers not identical for the same tests? The answer is revealed in the D variable. How does the D variable of part a compare to the D variable of part b? How does this explain the pattern of results you identified in part c?

15. Exercise 18 at the end of Chapter 12 described a study that investigated the extent to which newborn infants are able to discriminate their mother's voice from the voice of another woman. Five infants in the first condition could produce a tape recording of their own mother's voice by increasing the interval between bursts of sucking on a nonnutritive nipple relative to their baseline rate of sucking; otherwise, they heard a recording of the voice of one of the other mothers whose infant was a participant in the study. Five other infants in the second condition could produce a tape recording of their own mother's voice by decreasing the interval between bursts of sucking; otherwise, they also heard a nonmaternal voice. The following data (IBIs in seconds) approximate the actual data obtained in the study:

Group 1 (Larger IBI-Produced Maternal Voice)		
Participant	Baseline IBI	Feedback IBI
1	4.4	6.4
2	1.0	1.9
3	3.4	5.2
4	3.3	3.3
5	4.5	4.0

Group 1 (Smaller IBI-Produced Maternal Voice)		
1	5.8	1.8
2	4.3	1.9
3	3.7	2.5
4	3.4	1.7
5	3.8	3.0

a. Perform tests of the group main effect, the baseline versus feedback main effect, and the group × baseline versus Feedback interaction.

b. A graduate student has reconceptualized these data. For each participant, she calculated a score reflecting that infant's preference for the maternal voice. Specifically, for Group 1: Maternal Preference = Feedback − Baseline; and for Group 2 participants: Maternal Preference = Baseline − Feedback. Notice that with this definition, higher positive difference scores in both groups reflect greater preference for the mother's voice. Given this definition, the data from this study can be conceptualized as follows:

Group 1	
Participant	Maternal Preference
1	2.0
2	0.9
3	1.8
4	0.0
5	−0.5

Group 2	
1	4.0
2	2.4
3	1.2
4	1.7
5	0.8

A model for these data can be written as $Y_{ij} = \mu + \alpha_j + \varepsilon_{ij}$, where Y_{ij} is the maternal preference score for the ith participant in the jth group. Test a null hypothesis that the grand mean parameter equals zero for these data.

c. Is the F value you obtained in part b equal to any of the F values you obtained in part a? What is the meaning of the test you have conducted here?

d. Test a null hypothesis that the α_j parameters equal zero for the maternal preference scores.

e. Is the F value you obtained in part d equal to any of the F values you obtained in part a? What is the meaning of the test you have conducted here?

16. A graduate student has conducted a study using a 3 × 4 split-plot design. Which of the four multivariate test statistics would you recommend that he use for testing the within-subjects main effect? Why?

17. The student in Exercise 16 reports that he obtained an F value of 3.22 with 6 and 80 df for one of his effects. His adviser can't believe that he is so trusting of computer printouts. After all, he had only 15 participants in each of his three groups. His adviser tells him that she certainly would have expected him to know that degrees of freedom cannot be larger than the number of participants. He is uncertain what to do next and turns to you for assistance.
    a. Is it possible that his computer printout is correct, that is, that he really has 6 and 80 df? Justify your answer.
    b. If the printout is correct, which effect is being tested?
    c. Which test statistic was used?
    d. What would the degrees of freedom be for the Pillai–Bartlett test statistic?
    e. From the available information, can you provide the observed F for the Pillai–Bartlett test? Why or why not?

*18. The same student in Exercises 16 and 17 has decided to test the following post hoc contrast: the average of levels 1 and 2 of B versus the average of levels 3 and 4 of B, within the first level of A where A is the between-subjects factor. Using a pooled error term (i.e., pooled across levels of A), he obtained an observed F value of 4.13 for this contrast. Is the contrast statistically significant, if he wants to maintain his alpha level at .05 for the family of all possible comparisons that could be conducted within the first level of A? Justify your answer.

19. A psychologist has used a $2 \times 3 \times 3$ design, where the first factor (A) is between-subjects and the other two factors (B and C) are within-subjects. The psychologist plans to use the multivariate approach to analyze her data.
    a. How many M variables will she need to define?
    b. How many D variables will she need to define?
    c. So far, she has defined the following four variables:

B_1C_1	B_1C_2	B_1C_3	B_2C_1	B_2C_2	B_2C_3	B_3C_1	B_3C_2	B_3C_3
1	−1	0	1	−1	0	1	−1	0
1	1	−2	1	1	−2	1	1	−2
1	1	1	−1	−1	−1	0	0	0
1	1	1	1	1	1	−2	−2	−2

What effect(s) can she test with the first pair of variables?
    d. What effect(s) can she test with the second pair of variables?
    e. Define additional variables that will enable her to test the remaining omnibus effects of interest.

*20. A researcher has conducted a study using a $3 \times 2 \times 4$ design. The first two factors are between-subjects, and the third factor is within-subjects. Ten participants were obtained for each of the between-subjects cells. Wilks's lambda is chosen as the multivariate test statistic.
    a. How many dependent variables will be needed to test the three-way interaction?
    b. Write both the full model and the restricted model for one of the dependent variables used in part a to test the three-way interaction.
    c. How many numerator degrees of freedom are there for the F test of the three-way interaction?
    d. What will the value of the denominator degrees of freedom be equal to, for the three-way interaction?

21. Exercise 17 at the end of Chapter 11 introduced hypothetical data obtained by a developmental psychologist interested in the role of the sound of a mother's heartbeat in the growth of newborn babies. This exercise uses the same data, but now we assume that half of the infants were assigned to a control group. Specifically, 7 babies were randomly assigned to a condition where they were exposed to a rhythmic heartbeat sound piped in over the PA system. The other 7 babies were placed in an identical nursery, but without the heartbeat sound. Infants were weighed at the same time of day for 4 consecutive days, yielding the following data (weight is measured in ounces):

		Heartbeat Group		
Participant	*Day 1*	*Day 2*	*Day 3*	*Day 4*
1	96	98	103	104
2	116	116	118	119
3	102	102	101	101
4	112	115	116	118
5	108	110	112	115
6	92	95	96	98
7	120	121	121	123

		Control Group		
Participant	*Day 1*	*Day 2*	*Day 3*	*Day 4*
1	112	111	111	109
2	95	96	98	99
3	114	112	110	109
4	99	100	99	98
5	124	125	127	126
6	100	98	95	94
7	106	107	106	107

Despite the rather small sample size, use the multivariate approach throughout this problem to analyze these data.

a. Test the group main effect, the day main effect, and the group × day interaction.

b. Calculate the value of omega squared for each of the effects you tested in part a.

c. Write one or two sentences interpreting the meaning of the results you obtained in parts a and b. (Hint: A plot of the cell means may aid in your interpretation.)

d. Is the linear trend for days different in the heartbeat condition from the control condition? Treat this question as a single planned comparison.

e. Form a 95% confidence interval for the difference in the slopes of the heartbeat group and the control group. How is your interval related to the test you conducted in part d? How would you interpret your interval?

f. Test the linear trend within each group for significance. Use an error term pooled over the two groups.

g. Form a 95% confidence interval for the linear trend within each group (using a pooled error term, as in part f). How are your intervals related to the tests you conducted in part f? How would you interpret your intervals?

h. Another way to view these data might be to test the simple effect of condition at each day. Perform these tests, using an a level of .05 for each test. Do your results seem consistent with the results you obtained in parts d and f? How can you explain this pattern of results?

i. Yet another way to analyze these data might be to investigate the change across adjacent days. Suppose that we wanted to answer three questions:
   (1) Is there a group difference in the change from Day 1 to Day 2?
   (2) Is there a group difference in the change from Day 2 to Day 3?
   (3) Is there a group difference in the change from Day 3 to Day 4?
   Treat these questions as planned comparisons and perform tests of the three questions maintaining α_{FW} at .05.

j. How might confidence intervals help explain the pattern of results you obtained in parts h and i? To explore this possibility, begin by forming a 95% confidence interval for the simple effect of condition at each day. You may use 95% for each individual interval. Now also form intervals corresponding to the tests you conducted in part i. Specifically, form simultaneous 95% confidence intervals for the group differences in change for adjacent days. Finally, consider two aspects of how the intervals corresponding to part h compare to those corresponding to part i. First, which intervals tend to be centered farthest from zero? Second, which intervals tend to be narrowest? Why are some intervals narrower than others? How does this help explain the pattern of results you obtained in parts h and i?

    k. Suppose that after looking at the data, a researcher decided to consider the following contrast of the time factor: $-3(Day\ 1) - 1(Day\ 2) + 1(Day\ 3) + 3(Day\ 4)$. Would the two groups differ significantly on this contrast, maintaining α_{FW} at .05?

    l. Explain why this two-group design is superior to the design described for these data in Chapter 11, where we assumed that all 14 infants were exposed to the heartbeat sound.

    m. Although the two-group design is a great improvement over the one-group design described earlier for these data, might there still be some plausible threats to the validity of a conclusion that exposure to heartbeat sounds affects infants' growth?

22. Jemmott et al. (1983) report a study investigating the effect of academic stress on immune function. Jemmott et al. (1983). Academic stress, power, motivation, and decrease in secretion rate of salivary secretory immunoglobulin A. *The Lancet, 1*, 1400–1402. Immune function was measured five times during the academic year: an initial low-stress period, three high-stress periods coinciding with major exams, and a final low-stress period. Forty-seven first-year dental students served as participants. Each was identified as belonging to one of three personality types on the basis of responses to the Thematic Apperception Test, which was administered prior to the assessment of immune function. The three groups were an inhibited power syndrome (IPS) group, a relaxed affiliative syndrome (RAS) group, and a residual or control (C) group, which consisted of those who failed to fit the criteria for either of the other two groups. The dependent measure was the rate of secretion of salivary secretory immunoglobulin A (s-IgA), obtained at each of the five time points. Higher values of s-IgA secretion rate (measured as mg s-IgA/min) reflect stronger functioning of the immune system. Consider the following hypothetical (but realistic) data:

IPS Group

Participant	September	November	April	June	July
1	.21	.20	.21	.19	.16
2	.19	.20	.16	.14	.13
3	.25	.16	.16	.16	.13
4	.11	.09	.10	.10	.14
5	.19	.13	.15	.11	.11
6	.18	.16	.16	.17	.10
7	.21	.18	.15	.18	.08
8	.16	.12	.14	.11	.18
9	.20	.14	.11	.13	.11

RAS Group

Participant	September	November	April	June	July
1	.28	.28	.25	.29	.29
2	.22	.18	.16	.21	.25
3	.30	.27	.26	.26	.29
4	.24	.23	.24	.23	.23
5	.26	.22	.23	.19	.17
6	.27	.22	.20	.22	.24
7	.32	.25	.24	.21	.23
8	.20	.19	.21	.27	.28
9	.21	.22	.20	.19	.20
10	.33	.28	.25	.28	.27
11	.23	.18	.19	.24	.28
12	.17	.12	.15	.14	.12
13	.20	.17	.14	.18	.19
14	.22	.23	.19	.24	.22
15	.24	.22	.22	.22	.21

(Continued)

		C Group			
Participant	September	November	April	June	July
1	.14	.12	.09	.17	.19
2	.25	.18	.15	.16	.26
3	.22	.21	.14	.16	.19
4	.17	.12	.10	.12	.15
5	.17	.15	.12	.12	.14
6	.14	.12	.11	.12	.20
7	.17	.12	.12	.09	.14
8	.20	.14	.16	.12	.15
9	.25	.24	.20	.13	.17
10	.15	.07	.05	.13	.15
11	.19	.12	.14	.15	.18
12	.23	.17	.20	.19	.27
13	.20	.19	.18	.16	.21
14	.20	.19	.19	.16	.24
15	.24	.16	.20	.20	.21
16	.15	.09	.12	.12	.20
17	.15	.16	.12	.09	.17
18	.18	.18	.17	.16	.21
19	.23	.22	.20	.15	.21
20	.22	.18	.14	.12	.18
21	.15	.15	.13	.17	.16
22	.22	.14	.16	.17	.24
23	.22	.14	.14	.16	.15

a. Test the statistical significance of the group main effect, the time main effect, and the group × time interaction.

b. Calculate the value of omega squared for each effect you tested in part a.

c. Test the group effect at each individual time point. Use an alpha level of .05 for each test.

d. Perform pairwise comparisons of the groups at each individual time point. Maintain α_{FW} at .05 for each time point.

e. Form simultaneous 95% confidence intervals for each pairwise comparison of groups at each individual time point. Maintain confidence at 95% for each time point. How are your intervals related to the tests you conducted in part d? How would you interpret your intervals?

f. September and July were perceived to be low-stress periods by these students; they perceived November, April, and June to be high-stress periods. Is the difference between the groups the same for the average of the low-stress periods as it is for the average of the high-stress periods? Use an alpha level of .05 for this test.

g. Perform pairwise comparisons of the groups to ascertain which specific groups are different from each other in part f. Maintain α_{FW} at .05.

h. Form simultaneous 95% confidence intervals for all pairwise comparisons of group differences between the average of the low-stress periods and the average of the high-stress periods. How are your intervals related to the tests you conducted in part g? How would you interpret your intervals?

i. Another question of potential interest concerns immune recovery from June to July. Do the groups change equally from June to July? Use an alpha level of .05 for this test.

j. Test the statistical significance of the change from June to July for each group individually, to determine which groups demonstrate a recovery of the immune system. With an alpha level of .05 for each group, how would you interpret your results?

k. Form a 95% confidence interval for the change from June to July for each group individually. How are your intervals related to the tests you conducted in part j? How would you interpret your intervals?

IV

Alternative Analysis Strategies

Multilevel analysis has developed a great deal over this 10 year period. In the social and behavioral sciences the technique caught on like wildfire, and many applications have been published. In some areas, HLM has become the norm for good data analysis, and the basic software packages have been generalized and perfected. Perhaps even more importantly, mixed models (of which multilevel models are an important special case) have become very dominant in statistics.
—JAN DE LEEUW, *SERIES EDITOR'S INTRODUCTION TO THE SECOND EDITION OF HIERARCHICAL LINEAR MODELS,* 2002

15

An Introduction to Multilevel Models for Within-Subjects Designs

Chapters 10 through 12 discussed designs with random factors, with a special focus on within-subjects designs. Chapters 13 and 14 provided a multivariate alternative for analyzing data from within-subjects designs. Chapters 15 and 16 present yet additional methods for analyzing data from designs that include one or more random factors. In general, the methods of these two chapters can be useful whenever scores are potentially correlated with one another. When might we expect scores to be correlated? One typical example is in within-subjects designs, where we obtain more than one score from each individual. Scores from the same person are usually more similar to one another than scores from different people, in which case scores will correlate with one another. Scores can also be correlated even when we obtain only a single score from each person. A typical example is when individuals are organized into clusters, such as classrooms, factories, or communities. Once again, scores within a cluster are usually more similar to one another than are scores between clusters, leading to a pattern of correlations among the scores. This chapter focuses on the first situation, where multiple scores are obtained from each individual. The next chapter presents the second situation, where scores are clustered, as in a nested design.

The last decade has seen a tremendous growth in the development of models for correlated data. These models are variously referred to as multilevel models, hierarchical linear models, mixed models, and random coefficients models. One reason for the diversity of names is that theoretical development as well as applications of these models has occurred in a wide array of disciplines, including statistics, biostatistics, psychology, and education. Not surprisingly, somewhat different terminology has developed across disciplines, reflecting in part the somewhat distinct uses each discipline has typically made of the methods. Nevertheless, there is a common core to the methods, and that is what we intend to present in these two chapters.

ADVANTAGES OF NEW METHODS

Within-Subjects Designs

Why have these new methods received so much attention? One reason is that they allow a variety of choices for modeling correlations in the data. In this respect, the methods could be thought of as playing a similar role to the multivariate approach to within-subjects designs presented in Chapters 13 and 14. However, as we will see, these new methods provide a much greater range of options for modeling correlations, so they are more generally applicable than the multivariate approach.

A second reason is that the methods often provide a viable approach for handling missing data, or more generally an unequal number of observations. Missing data is obviously a pervasive problem in longitudinal research, which is a major reason these new methods have received so much attention for repeated measures designs. Recall that the multivariate approach of Chapters 13 and 14 requires that each individual have complete data; anyone with even a single omitted score must be omitted from the analysis. Not only does this omission lower power, but it also can create biased estimates of mean differences unless very strong assumptions are met for the pattern of missing data. The new methods of this chapter, in contrast, allow all of the available data to be used and require a less stringent assumption about the pattern of missing data. In fact, these new methods do not even require that any two individuals be measured at the same time point. For example, not only may some individuals be measured only once, some twice, others three times, and so forth, but the precise times of measurement can differ from individual to individual. In a treatment outcome study, one person might be assessed at 7 days, 14 days, and 21 days, whereas another person might be assessed at 6 days, 13 days, and 24 days. The methods of Chapters 11 through 14 would be forced to ignore these differences and regard both individuals as having been assessed at "Time 1," "Time 2," and "Time 3." However, the methods of this chapter would allow the precise times of measurement to be incorporated into the statistical model.

A third reason for the popularity of these new methods is that they accommodate both categorical and continuous predictor variables. In this respect, they offer some of the same advantages as analysis of covariance (ANCOVA) models we presented in Chapter 9. For example, a developmental psychologist interested in language development might include a measure of the mother's vocabulary as a predictor in a model of the child's vocabulary development measured over time. Notice that the mother's vocabulary would probably be measured at only a fixed point in time, in which case it is called a time-invariant covariate. However, mixed models also allow time-varying covariates to be included. For example, at each time point where the child's vocabulary is measured, the investigator might also obtain a measure of the extent to which the mother has spoken to the child. This variable would then become a time-varying covariate in the model.

Overview of Remainder of Chapter

Hopefully, even this very brief introduction has convinced you that mixed models can be useful for analyzing data in a variety of designs. At this point we feel compelled to qualify our enthusiasm with a note of caution. In part because these methods are so flexible, a single book chapter cannot hope to cover them in sufficient depth and breadth. Indeed, a number of excellent books have been written on these methods, and even most of these book-length treatments do not attempt to be exhaustive, but instead focus on the use of these methods for one type of design. Thus, just as the title of our chapter suggests, our presentation is at best an introduction to these methods. We hope that this chapter will accomplish two goals: (1) to illustrate the importance of these methods in behavioral research and (2) to establish a conceptual framework for further study of these methods. At the end of the chapter, we recommend sources for additional reading for those individuals who have been persuaded that they should use these methods in their research.

WITHIN-SUBJECTS DESIGNS

Various Types of Within-Subjects Designs

We have seen in Chapters 11 through 14 that that there are several varieties of within-subjects designs. For example, each and every individual might be assessed under multiple conditions, in which case the goal is typically to determine the effects of the various treatments. Another example that we will consider to fall into this same category occurs when each of several family members is measured on a common scale. For example, a child, a mother, and a father might all be assessed on their perception of some aspect of family functioning. Although it may seem odd to consider each family member as a "condition," this is effectively the same type of design. Alternatively, each individual research participant may be assessed at multiple points in time, but no one changes condition over time, in which case the goal is typically to determine the pattern of any change that has occurred over time. Notice that in this case there may also be an interest in treatment effects (or other correlates of change), but each person would then be assigned to one and only one condition, so condition would constitute a between-subjects factor. Yet a third type of within-subjects design occurs when each person has been assessed on multiple subscales of a test.

The methods we will present here apply to all three of these broad types of within-subjects designs. However, our presentation will emphasize the use of mixed models for analyzing data from longitudinal designs. We have chosen this focus for two reasons. First, as we have already mentioned, mixed models are especially important when confronted with missing data. Longitudinal designs are clearly more fraught with problems of missing data than are the other types of within-subjects designs. Second, mixed models provide a variety of ways to model correlations among observations. Such correlations frequently display certain characteristic types of patterns in longitudinal designs, making them prime candidates for mixed model analysis.

We should also stress that the majority of our attention will focus on the application of these methods to a very simple example of a longitudinal design. Specifically, we will emphasize the development of these methods for the single-factor designs we introduced in Chapters 11 and 13. However, it is important to realize from the outset that the methods we present in this chapter can easily be extended to more complicated designs, such as the factorial designs of Chapters 12 and 14. We have chosen to focus on the simpler design in order to develop the basic principles with the fewest possible distractions. However, after having done so, a section of the chapter will briefly describe extensions of these new methods to more complicated designs.

Models for Longitudinal Data

We will begin our consideration of mixed models for analyzing longitudinal data by returning to a reconsideration of the mixed-model ANOVA approach we presented in Chapter 11. Although we could instead immediately begin with a presentation of the newer methods, we believe it is important to establish a bridge between the approaches. You might find it odd that we feel compelled to establish a bridge when the general viewpoint we expressed in Chapters 11 through 14 was that the mixed-model approach is severely limited by its reliance on the assumption of sphericity. However, we will see in this chapter that the new methods, even though they build from the mixed-model ANOVA approach, do not necessarily require an assumption of sphericity. Instead, they can often avoid this assumption by allowing more realistic models to be developed. The only real drawback of our strategy is that it defers a

TABLE 15.1
HYPOTHETICAL McCARTHY DATA FOR 12 CHILDREN

| Subject | Age (Months) | | | | Marginal Mean |
	30	36	42	48	
1	108	96	110	122	109
2	103	117	127	133	120
3	96	107	106	107	104
4	84	85	92	99	90
5	118	125	125	116	121
6	110	107	96	91	101
7	129	128	123	128	127
8	90	84	101	113	97
9	84	104	100	88	94
10	96	100	103	105	101
11	105	114	105	112	109
12	113	117	132	130	123
Marginal Mean	103	107	110	112	108

presentation of how the new methods are advantageous. However, once we have explored the connections between the methods, we will be in a position to explain the advantages of the new methods.

Review of the ANOVA Mixed-Model Approach

We will begin by reviewing our Chapter 11 presentation of the ANOVA mixed-model approach to within-subjects designs. Specifically, we will once again use the hypothetical McCarthy data originally shown in Table 11.5 to motivate our presentation. For convenience, these data are repeated in Table 15.1. Notice that data have been obtained at four ages for 12 children. We will presume at least initially that the null hypothesis we wish to test is that the population mean McCarthy score is the same at all four ages. We saw in Chapter 11 that one way to test this hypothesis is to compare the following full and restricted models:

| Full model: | $Y_{ij} = \mu + \alpha_j + \pi_i + \varepsilon_{ij}$ | (11.22, repeated) |
| Restricted model: | $Y_{ij} = \mu + \pi_i + \varepsilon_{ij}$ | (11.23, repeated) |

As we saw in Chapter 11, the resultant F statistic reduces to

$$F = \frac{MS_A}{MS_{A \times S}}$$

(11.28, repeated)

which for the data of Table 15.1 leads to an F value of 3.03, which with 3 and 33 degrees of freedom implies a p value of .042. Thus, we would reject the null hypothesis at the .05 level with this method of analysis.

There is one key point in understanding the justification for Equation 11.28, and how this approach relates to the new methods of this chapter. In particular, we need to consider how we dealt with the fact that the subjects effect (represented by π_i) is a random effect. Notice that we obtained parameter estimates as usual through least squares, and we obtained sums of squared errors for our models as usual. Only at the very last step of the process did we take into account the fact that the subjects effect is random. As we discussed at some length in

Chapter 10, random effects often lead to different expected mean squares, and thus the need for a different error term than would have been appropriate in the absence of any random effects. In this case, we have assumed that the subjects effect is random, which is why its interaction with age (i.e., $MS_{A \times S}$) is the appropriate error term (recall that "*error term*" here simply refers to the denominator of the F statistic).

The description we have just encountered is typical of the manner in which ANOVA addresses data from designs with random factors. In general, the ANOVA approach to random effects basically estimates parameters and calculates sums of squares without regard to whether effects are fixed or random. Only after having performed these initial calculations do any distinctions between fixed and random effects come under consideration. Such distinctions are taken into account by calculating expected mean squares and determining appropriate error terms using the logic we developed in Chapter 10.

The ANOVA approach generally works fine as long as all sample sizes are equal. (Of course, as we discussed in Chapter 11, this approach is very sensitive to the assumption of sphericity; later in the chapter we will show how more realistic models can avoid this assumption.) However, unequal sample sizes (such as occur due to missing data in longitudinal designs) become problematic. One reason for understanding the problem created by unequal sample size is to remember from Chapter 7 the difficulties that emerge in unequal n designs. For example, we saw in Chapter 7 that there is no unique expression for the sum of squares of a main effect in a factorial design with unequal n. As you might imagine, this creates serious difficulties for analyzing data involving random effects, because the choice of an error term relies on being able to identify expected mean squares. If there is not even a clear way of determining the sum of squares, efforts to express expected mean squares become even more problematic. From the perspective of mathematical statistics, even when estimators can be derived using the ANOVA approach, they no longer are guaranteed to have certain desirable statistical properties when sample sizes are unequal, such as when data are missing. Readers interested in further details comparing maximum likelihood and ANOVA are referred to McCulloch and Searle (2001).

RANDOM EFFECTS MODELS

Maximum Likelihood Approach

The new alternatives that have largely developed in the 1990s take a fundamentally different approach. Instead of waiting until the final step of calculating a test statistic to take random effects into account, these new methods distinguish between fixed and random factors at the very beginning of model formulation. This alternative approach offers two important advantages. First, unequal n (such as occurs with missing data) does not present the insurmountable difficulties it does for the ANOVA approach. Second, it is much easier to specify complex models that include multiple random effects. We will see momentarily that this often provides the researcher with the ability to formulate and test a much more realistic model than would be feasible with the ANOVA approach.

It is important to acknowledge one drawback of the alternative approach. Because fixed and random effects are distinguished from the beginning of the process, it is no longer appropriate to use least squares to estimate parameters. Instead, it is necessary to use maximum likelihood estimation.[1] A full description of maximum likelihood estimation could fill an entire book by itself. Further, it often becomes mathematically complex. Worse yet, in some situations, it is impossible to write a formula for maximum likelihood estimates. Instead, estimates sometimes must be determined through an iterative procedure. Fortunately, the calculations themselves can be left to computer programs. Of course, the availability of programs for performing calculations hardly guarantees that the methods have been used appropriately and interpreted wisely.

OPTIONAL

An Example of Maximum Likelihood Estimation

Our approach toward maximum likelihood estimation will largely be illustrative. Consideration of maximum likelihood methods in mixed models of this chapter and Chapter 16 requires considerable background in matrix algebra and mathematical statistics. Readers with such backgrounds can consult McCulloch and Searle (2001) for a detailed explanation of maximum likelihood methods for mixed models.

Even though it is beyond the scope of this book to provide a thorough presentation of maximum likelihood estimation for mixed models, it is possible to provide a flavor of how maximum likelihood estimation works in much simpler situations.

We will illustrate maximum likelihood estimation in a much simpler context than mixed models. In particular, suppose we have observed scores for four individuals on some measure of interest. Specifically, the four scores we have observed are 3.0, 4.1, 4.3, and 4.6. We will assume that these four scores constitute a random sample from some unknown population. Based on this limited information, what is our best guess of the population mean of the distribution from which these scores have been sampled? Some natural choices for our guess would be the sample mean or the sample median. But which of these should we choose, or why not consider other possible guesses? Maximum likelihood estimation provides a rigorous method of estimating parameters, and thus can resolve the ambiguity about what estimate might be best. Further, mathematical statisticians have proven that maximum likelihood estimators have certain desirable properties across broad conditions, such as being asymptotically efficient (i.e, precise) and asymptotically unbiased, which guarantees that maximum likelihood estimators will be more accurate than other estimators when sample size is sufficiently large. Of course, in our case, we have only four observations, so we have no guarantee of benefitting from these properties, but we have chosen to keep the sample size small for the sake of simplicity.

So how should we estimate the population mean based on observed scores of 3.0, 4.1, 4.3, and 4.6? The basic idea of maximum likelihood estimation is that we should choose an estimated value for the population mean that makes the data we have observed most likely. For example, it would seem less likely to obtain these four scores if the population mean were 10 than if the population mean were a value somewhere closer to 3, 4, or 5. According to the principles of maximum likelihood, we should calculate how likely these four scores would be for a variety of possible population means and then choose as our estimate whatever value makes the observed data most likely.

To determine what estimate makes the data most likely, we must consider the likelihood function. The likelihood function for n randomly sampled observations can be written as

$$L(x_1, x_2, \ldots, x_n; \theta)$$

where θ is the parameter to be estimated. When observations are sampled randomly and independently, the likelihood becomes

$$L(x_1, x_2, \ldots, x_n; \theta) = f(x_1; \theta) f(x_2, \theta) \ldots f(x_n; \theta)$$

where f denotes the density function (i.e., probability distribution) in the population.

Implicit in the formula for the likelihood function is the fact that calculating the likelihood of the observed data requires that we specify a distribution for the data. In other words, we cannot proceed until we specify a particular choice for the probability distribution f. In our case, we will assume a normal distribution. We do so largely because mixed models also assume normality. However, it is important to realize that the estimator we derive for the normal distribution would not necessarily continue to be the estimator if we were to specify some different distribution for our data.

The density function f for a normal distribution can be written as

$$f(x) = \frac{1}{\sqrt{2\pi\sigma^2}} e^{-\frac{(x-\mu)^2}{2\sigma^2}}$$

where μ is the population mean and σ is the population standard deviation. To minimize the mathematical details of our remaining work, we will further assume that we know that the population standard deviation equals 1.0. In other words, we will proceed as if we knew that our four scores come from a normal distribution with a standard deviation of 1.0, in which case all that remains to be estimated is the mean of the population distribution. It turns out that our estimator would be the same in this case (i.e., for the normal distribution) regardless of the value of σ, but the mathematics would be more complicated if we were to acknowledge that we do not really know the population standard deviation.

Making use of the density function for the normal distribution (where $\sigma = 1$), we can now write the likelihood function for four observations as

$$L(x_1, x_2, x_3, x_4; \mu) = \left(\frac{1}{\sqrt{2\pi}}\right)^4 e^{-\frac{(x_1-\mu)^2}{2}} e^{-\frac{(x_2-\mu)^2}{2}} e^{-\frac{(x_3-\mu)^2}{2}} e^{-\frac{(x_4-\mu)^2}{2}}$$

Given our observed values of 3.0, 4.1, 4.3, and 4.6, we can replace each x in the expression above with its corresponding observed value. Doing so yields a likelihood function of the form

$$\left(\frac{1}{\sqrt{2\pi}}\right)^4 e^{\frac{-(3.0-\mu)^2}{2}} e^{\frac{-(4.1-\mu)^2}{2}} e^{\frac{-(4.3-\mu)^2}{2}} e^{\frac{-(4.6-\mu)^2}{2}}$$

Even with our simplifications, this likelihood function may still seem intimidating. However, notice that we have reached a point where everything in the function is a constant except for μ. As a consequence, the value of the likelihood function now depends only on μ. Thus, we could substitute various values of μ into the likelihood function, calculate the value of the function, and in the process eventually see what value maximizes the function.

Of course, calculating the likelihood function for every possible value of μ would quickly become rather tedious (especially because in theory there are an infinite number of possible values of μ). Nevertheless, it is straightforward to graph the likelihood as a function of μ. Figure 15.1 shows this graph, where values on the x-axis represent different choices for μ, and the y-axis shows the resultant value of the likelihood function. This graph shows that choosing μ to equal a value near 4.0 maximizes the likelihood function. As our estimate of μ departs from 4.0 (either positively or negatively), the likelihood

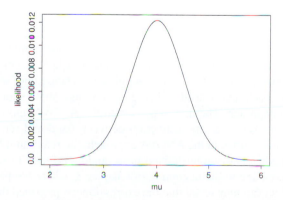

FIG. 15.1. Graph of likelihood of sample data as a function of μ in a normal distribution.

declines. Thus, this graph strongly suggests that the value of μ that makes our observed data most likely is 4.0.

In this particular case, we can confirm that the value of 4.0 is indeed the maximum likelihood estimate for these data. The reason is that we can use calculus to find the maximum of the likelihood function. Differentiating the logarithm of the likelihood function (which turns out to be much easier than finding the derivative of the likelihood function itself) and setting the derivative equal to zero ultimately reduces to

$$\sum_{i=1}^{n} (x_i - \mu) = 0$$

Solving this expression for μ leads to

$$\hat{\mu} = \frac{\sum_{i=1}^{n} x_i}{n}$$

which simply shows that the maximum likelihood estimator of the population mean of a normal distribution is the sample mean. In our data, the sample mean is 4.0, so this is our maximum likelihood estimate. The data we observed are more likely to have occurred if the population mean is 4.0 than if the mean were any other value, so we choose 4.0 as our estimate. More generally, this derivation suggests one reason that the sample mean is used so frequently as an estimator in applied statistics. If we are willing to assume normality, the sample mean is the maximum likelihood estimator of the population mean. As such, we know that many desirable properties are associated with the sample mean as an estimator. Nevertheless, in general it is important to realize that these desirable properties may hold only if the normality assumption is true, so when normality is questionable, better estimators may exist.

Exactly the same idea as we have illustrated here is at work when we use maximum likelihood estimation in mixed models. However, the mathematics becomes much more complex than in our simple example of estimating the population mean of a normal distribution. In general, it is impossible to use calculus to derive equations for estimating parameters, so numerical methods must be used to find parameter estimates that maximize the likelihood. In this sense, using maximum likelihood estimation for mixed models is akin to the idea behind Figure 15.1, where we calculated the likelihood for a variety of possible values of μ and then chose as our estimate of μ the value that led to the highest likelihood. Once again, readers seeking a more detailed mathematical explanation are advised to consult McCulloch and Searle (2001). ∎

Comparison of ANOVA and Maximum Likelihood Models

Instead of attempting to provide additional technical details of maximum likelihood estimation, we will attempt to give readers an intuitive understanding of how it works in mixed models by returning to the data shown in Table 15.1. Suppose we decided not to analyze these data with the ANOVA approach, but instead gathered our courage and decided to embark on the maximum likelihood approach. The first step, as with the ANOVA approach, is to specify a full model for the data. Whereas any distinction between fixed and random effects may at least temporarily be disregarded in the ANOVA approach, the maximum likelihood approach requires that we immediately distinguish fixed from random effects. To see what this means, let's return all the way back to the beginning of Chapter 3, where we presented the general form of a linear model. You may recall that the expression we provided there was

$$Y_i = \beta_0 X_{0i} + \beta_1 X_{1i} + \beta_2 X_{2i} + \beta_3 X_{3i} + \cdots + \beta_p X_{pi} + \varepsilon_i \qquad \text{(3.1, repeated)}$$

We now need to be clear that Equation 3.1 should be regarded as the form of the general linear model, where we are implicitly assuming that all factors are fixed. In contrast, the general linear mixed model that forms the basis for maximum likelihood estimation explicitly indicates the possible presence of both fixed and random effects in the model. Although the notation for this model is less universal than that of the purely fixed effects model, one popular notational scheme uses the letter Z to designate random effects. Just as a distinction is made between fixed predictor variables X and random predictor variables Z, a similar distinction is made between the parameters (i.e, coefficients) associated with each type of variable. We continue to use β to represent the parameter associated with a fixed effect. However, we will now use u to represent the parameter associated with a random effect. One immediate drawback of this notation is that it is critical to distinguish u (literally, the letter u) as a parameter associated with a random effect from μ (the Greek letter mu) as a parameter associated with a fixed effect. Despite this potential confusion, we adopt this notation because it appears to be in the process of becoming standard notation in the literature. Thus, a model with three fixed effects (not counting the intercept β_0) and one random effect could be written as

$$Y_i = \beta_0 X_{0i} + \beta_1 X_{1i} + \beta_2 X_{2i} + \beta_3 X_{3i} + u_i Z_i + \varepsilon_i \tag{1}$$

More generally, a model could have p fixed effects and q random effects, in which case it could be written as

$$Y_i = \beta_0 X_{0i} + \beta_1 X_{1i} + \beta_2 X_{2i} + \cdots + \beta_p X_{pi} + u_{1i} Z_{1i} + u_{2i} Z_{2i} + \cdots + u_{qi} Z_{qi} + \varepsilon_i \tag{2}$$

The models shown in Equations 1 and 2 make explicit the conceptual distinction between fixed effects and random effects. In particular, one aspect of the difference between the fixed effect parameters and the random effect parameters is crucially important in understanding the mixed model. Notice that each fixed effect parameter, as represented by a β, has one and only one subscript. In contrast, each random effect parameter, as represented by a u, has two subscripts. The inclusion of the i subscript here denotes the fact that the value of each u varies from person to person. Indeed, this is precisely what makes the effect random instead of fixed. Thus, the β parameters are included in the mixed model to represent those effects that we believe are constant over participants, whereas the u parameters are included to represent effects that we believe vary from participant to participant. Although this distinction may seem rather abstract at the moment, we make it now because it provides a valuable framework for the remainder of the chapter. The distinction should become clearer as we introduce specific examples of random effects, but we encourage you to think about these specific examples in this broader framework. One final point of clarification may be helpful before we proceed. Notice that a fixed effect can often be regarded as a population mean, where differences between individuals have been averaged over, eliminating the need for an i subscript. For example, a fixed effect parameter, say β_1, might reflect the population mean slope of scores over time on Y. Suppose some individuals' scores increase over time, but others decrease. If the average slope across all individuals is zero, it then follows that β_1 would equal zero. On the other hand, if increases dominate, β_1 would be greater than zero. Thus, by testing hypotheses about β_1 as well as forming a confidence interval for β_1, we can answer questions about average patterns of change in our data. Suppose that β_1 indeed equals zero in a particular situation. Does this imply that no one is changing? Not necessarily, because it could be the case that some individuals' scores increase dramatically, but their increases are offset by other individuals whose scores are decreasing. Individual differences are represented by random effects in the model. For example, u_i might represent the deviation of individual i's slope from the population mean slope β_1. If no one is truly changing, each person's value of u_i would be zero. On the other hand, even if β_1 is zero, some individuals may have positive values of u_i whereas other individuals have negative values of u_i. What is the difference between the first situation where no one is changing and the second situation where individuals are changing differently from one another? In the first situation, the variance of u_i is zero, whereas in the second situation the variance of u_i is not zero. Thus, just as we saw when we dealt with random effects in Chapter 10, questions about random effects typically are addressed by considering the variances of those effects. We will also see that when we have more than one random effect in a model we may be interested in the covariances, which tell us whether the effects are correlated with one another.

At first glance, the models shown in Equations 1 and 2 may look very different from any models we have previously discussed. However, from one perspective, they differ from certain previous models only in that they make explicit the distinction between fixed and random effects. For example, consider how the model shown in Equation 1 compares to the ANOVA full model we used in Chapter 11:

$$Y_i = \beta_0 X_{0i} + \beta_1 X_{1i} + \beta_2 X_{2i} + \beta_3 X_{3i} + u_i Z_i + \varepsilon_i \qquad \text{(1, repeated)}$$
$$Y_{ij} = \mu + \alpha_j + \pi_i + \varepsilon_{ij} \qquad \text{(11.22, repeated)}$$

Although these models look very different on the surface, there is in fact a very close correspondence between them. The ANOVA model shown in Equation 11.22 uses μ and α_j to represent fixed effects associated with multiple time points in the design; the mixed model simply uses indicator variables to represent these same effects. For example, with scores observed at four time points as in the McCarthy example, we would need to code three indicator variables to represent possible effects of time, just as shown in Equation 1. Thus, the fixed portions of Equation 1 and Equation 11.22 are mathematically equivalent despite their visual difference.

Although the two models provide equivalent representations of any fixed effects, their representation of random effects is different, and this difference becomes the crucial distinction between the ANOVA approach and the maximum likelihood approach. As Equation 11.22 shows, the ANOVA model stipulates the presence of effects due to persons (i.e., "subject" effects). Under this scenario, we proceed by estimating each π_i parameter, just as we do for each α_j parameter. Thus, nothing in the estimation process distinguishes parameters representing random effects from parameters representing fixed effects. Only after parameters have been estimated does the ANOVA approach acknowledge the presence of random effects by calculating expected mean squares and determining appropriate error terms.

The maximum likelihood approach treats random effects differently. In this approach, random effects are distinguished from fixed effects prior to parameter estimation. In fact, the actual random effects parameters are defined differently in this approach than in the ANOVA approach. In the maximum likelihood approach, the random effect to be estimated in Equation 1 is the variance of u, that is, the variance of the effect associated with individuals. (Be careful once again to distinguish u, which corresponds to a random effect and hence can be described in terms of a population variance, from μ, which is a fixed population parameter and thus can be described in terms of its specific value as opposed to a variance.) You may recall from Chapter 10 that even in the simplest single-factor design, when the factor is random the null hypothesis to be tested is whether the variance of the treatment effects equals zero. Remember that this is a different null hypothesis than the one we test with a fixed factor, where the question is whether the effect of each level included in the design is zero. The maximum likelihood approach acknowledges from the beginning that the focus of interest with a random factor is the variance associated with this factor, and thus this variance becomes the parameter to be estimated. The ANOVA approach, on the other hand, begins by acting as if the factor were fixed, estimates the effect for each individual person, and only after obtaining these estimates uses them as a springboard to estimate the variance associated with the person effect.

We will see momentarily that in some situations these two approaches converge on the same result. However, in general, they can produce different results. The advantage of the maximum likelihood approach is that it directly provides an estimate of the parameter of ultimate interest, the variance associated with the random effect(s). The ANOVA approach estimates this parameter only indirectly, by first calculating the effect of each specific level of the random factor. It turns out that in a balanced design ("balanced" in this context means that everyone is measured at the same time points and that there is no missing data), this approach works just fine, but when the design is unbalanced, the ANOVA approach becomes problematic, and the maximum likelihood approach becomes necessary.

One other way in which the ANOVA and maximum likelihood approaches differ is the way in which they implement the normality assumption (or, more generally, any type of distributional assumption). The ANOVA approach uses least squares to estimate parameters. Although least squares is known to have certain desirable properties when data are normally distributed, there is nothing in the least squares estimation process itself that directly relies on normality. The maximum likelihood approach, on the other hand, requires a distributional assumption from the start. This approach requires an explicit assumption that the random effect parameter u (in the model shown in Equation 1) is normally distributed. Thus, we are assuming that if we could observe the entire population of individuals, their effects would follow a normal distribution. Notice that this is a different normality assumption from the one placed on the error term, which is a further assumption of the maximum likelihood approach. Armed with these two types of normality assumptions, the maximum likelihood approach proceeds to estimate the parameters of the general linear mixed model.

Numerical Example

Our numerical example may help to illustrate some of the abstract points we have developed regarding the maximum likelihood approach and how it compares to the ANOVA approach. We will reconsider the McCarthy data shown in Table 15.1. Suppose we were to use the maximum likelihood approach as exemplified in Equation 1 to analyze these data. What would we find, and how would it compare with the ANOVA approach?

Before considering the maximum likelihood analysis, Table 15.2 provides a context for interpreting the maximum likelihood results by first summarizing the results of the ANOVA approach when applied to these data. In particular, Table 15.2 is an excerpt of the output from SAS PROC GLM for these data. To set the stage for comparing this output with the maximum likelihood output, we wish to call your attention to three aspects of Table 15.2. First, notice the test of the omnibus null hypothesis. The table confirms the result we saw earlier in Chapter 11, that this hypothesis would be rejected based on an F statistic of 3.03, with 3 numerator and 33 denominator degrees of freedom, yielding a p value of .0432. Second, notice that the PROC GLM implementation of the ANOVA approach has provided estimates of the time effects. Because of the manner in which GLM parameterizes models (see Appendix B for more details), the estimate of the effect of the last level of time is fixed at zero. The other three estimates then represent deviations of each other level from the last level. In these data, these estimates are −9, −5, and −2. These values are simply the mean difference between Time 4 and each of the other times. For example, the value of −9 is simply the difference between the mean at Time 1 (103, as shown in Table 15.1) and the mean at Time 4 (112). Third, the ANOVA approach has provided similar estimates of each effect associated with persons. For example, participant 1 has a mean of 109, which is 14 points lower than the mean for participant 12, which is why

TABLE 15.2
ANOVA ANALYSIS OF TABLE 15.1 DATA

The GLM Procedure

Dependent Variable: iq

Source	DF	Sum of Squares	Mean Square	F Value	Pr > F
Model	14	7176.000000	512.571429	8.43	<.0001
Error	33	2006.000000	60.787879		
Corrected Total	47	9182.000000			

	R-Square	Coeff Var	Root MSE	iq Mean
	0.781529	7.219128	7.796658	108.0000

Source	DF	Type 3 SS	Mean Square	F Value	Pr > F
id	11	6624.000000	602.181818	9.91	<.0001
timecat	3	552.000000	184.000000	3.03	0.0432

Parameter		Estimate	Standard Error	t Value	Pr > |t|
Intercept		127.0000000 B	4.35846442	29.14	<.0001
id	1	−14.0000000 B	5.51306987	−2.54	0.0160
id	2	−3.0000000 B	5.51306987	−0.54	0.5900
id	3	−19.0000000 B	5.51306987	−3.45	0.0016
id	4	−33.0000000 B	5.51306987	−5.99	<.0001
id	5	−2.0000000 B	5.51306987	−0.36	0.7191
id	6	−22.0000000 B	5.51306987	−3.99	0.0003
id	7	4.0000000 B	5.51306987	0.73	0.4732
id	8	−26.0000000 B	5.51306987	−4.72	<.0001
id	9	−29.0000000 B	5.51306987	−5.26	<.0001
id	10	−22.0000000 B	5.51306987	−3.99	0.0003
id	11	−14.0000000 B	5.51306987	−2.54	0.0160
id	12	0.0000000 B	.	.	.
timecat	0	−9.0000000 B	3.18297237	−2.83	0.0079
timecat	1	−5.0000000 B	3.18297237	−1.57	0.1258
timecat	2	−2.0000000 B	3.18297237	−0.63	0.5341
timecat	3	0.0000000 B	.	.	.

the parameter estimate associated with "id 1" is −14. Pay particular attention to the fact that there is nothing in these parameter estimates to distinguish random from fixed effects.

Before considering the output from the maximum likelihood approach, we will take a momentary detour to briefly introduce an example of how one might implement this procedure in statistical software. Our general emphasis throughout this book is on concepts instead of software, largely because software often undergoes frequent revisions, leading to obsolete examples of input syntax. However, in this case we have chosen to make a small exception, primarily because at the time of this writing, the maximum likelihood method is not well-known and involves either unique procedures in such packages as SAS or entire stand-alone programs such as HLM (Raudenbush, Bryk, Cheong, & Congdon, 2000) and MLWiN (Rasbash et al., 2000). In addition, we should explain that we have chosen to illustrate input and output from SAS, not necessarily because we believe it is always the best software for conducting these analyses, but primarily because it is likely to be more widely available than any of the special purpose software.

We will organize much of this chapter around various ways in which PROC MIXED in SAS can be used to analyze longitudinal data. To begin, let's consider how to analyze the McCarthy data using the model shown in Equation 1. Although the syntax we present here is correct at the time of this writing, certain details may change in the coming years. Even so, we assume that the general concepts showing the relationship between Equation 1 and syntax will be helpful despite any specific changes that may be implemented in the program. Because we will relate the syntax to the model, we will repeat Equation 1 here for easy reference:

$$Y_i = \beta_0 X_{0i} + \beta_1 X_{1i} + \beta_2 X_{2i} + \beta_3 X_{3i} + u_i Z_i + \varepsilon_i \qquad \text{(1, repeated)}$$

To fit this model to the McCarthy data, we obviously must have an appropriate input data set. An example of the SAS code to create such a data set is:

```
data new;
    input id timecat iq;
    cards;
[48 lines of data follow, 1 for each combination of subject and time]
```

For our purposes, what is important to understand here is that the data file has 48 rows and three columns. (Users who are familiar with SAS will recognize that the semicolon that appears at the end of each line is required to separate the commands from one another.) Each column corresponds to a variable in the data file. Specifically, "id" simply designates each individual. For example, with 12 participants, we would typically code each person uniquely as 1 to 12. The variable "timecat" indicates whether the score on each line was obtained at 30, 36, 42, or 48 months. We will have more to say about coding this variable later in the chapter. Finally, the variable "iq" is the McCarthy score obtained for a specific child at a specific time point.

Having created an appropriate input data set, the following four lines of SAS code fit the model of Equation 15.1 to the McCarthy data:

```
proc mixed;
    class timecat;
    model iq=timecat / s;
    random int/subject=id;
```

The first line simply invokes the PROC MIXED procedure. The second line indicates that "timecat" is a categorical (i.e, class) variable. In other words, "timecat" is a single variable in the data file, but the "class" command tells SAS to create three indicator variables to represent the effect of time (see Appendix B for more details on how SAS creates indicator variables). The heart of PROC MIXED is in the next two statements. The model statement begins by listing the name of the dependent variable to the left of the equals sign. In our data file, we chose to label this variable as "iq." To the right of the equals sign we must include all fixed effects in the model. As we can see from Equation 1, the only fixed effects here are the indicator variables corresponding to time, which is why "timecat" is the only variable listed to the right of the equals sign. The remainder of this line (i.e., the slash and the "s" that follows it) are optional. Asking for the "s" option provides parameter estimates of the fixed effects (SAS calls these estimates solutions, which explains why we designate this option as "s"). Also, we should point out that PROC MIXED includes an intercept in the fixed portion of the model by default. In other words, unless we explicitly tell the program to omit the intercept, it will automatically include β_0 in the model and will provide an estimate of this parameter, even though we have not literally included an X_{0i} variable in our data file.

TABLE 15.3
MAXIMUM LIKELIHOOD ANALYSIS OF TABLE 15.1 DATA

The Mixed Procedure

Solution for Fixed Effects

Effect	timecat	Estimate	Standard Error	DF	t Value	Pr > |t|
Intercept		112.00	4.0429	18.1	27.70	<.0001
timecat	0	−9.0000	3.1830	33	−2.83	0.0079
timecat	1	−5.0000	3.1830	33	−1.57	0.1258
timecat	2	−2.0000	3.1830	33	−0.63	0.5341
timecat	3	0	.	.	.	.

Type 3 Tests of Fixed Effects

Effect	Num DF	Den DF	F Value	Pr > F
timecat	3	33	3.03	0.0432

Covariance Parameter Estimates

Cov Parm	Subject	Estimate
Intercept	id	135.35
Residual		60.7879

If we ran the model as described so far without the RANDOM statement, PROC MIXED would fit a model of the form

$$Y_i = \beta_0 X_{0i} + \beta_1 X_{1i} + \beta_2 X_{2i} + \beta_3 X_{3i} + \varepsilon_i \tag{3}$$

However, this is not the model we want, because it fails to include the random effects term. We instruct SAS to include any random effects with a separate RANDOM statement, as shown on the last line of the syntax above. In our case, we want to include a single random effect, which SAS labels as each participant's intercept. We will see later in the chapter why SAS uses this label, but for the moment at a practical level, you simply need to realize that "intercept" is not literally a variable in the data set. Finally, to the right of the slash, we tell SAS that each participant is potentially allowed to have his or her own individual value for the random intercept term. The actual participant identifier in the data set is labeled as "*id*," which is the reason "*id*" appears to the right of the equals sign.

Table 15.3 shows an excerpt of the output from SAS PROC MIXED, which uses the maximum likelihood approach to analyze these data. First, notice that this output contains separate sections for the fixed portion of the model and the random portion (labeled "Covariance Parameter Estimates"). This separation reflects the fact that the maximum likelihood approach distinguishes fixed and random effects from the outset. Second, notice that the parameter estimates for the fixed effects shown here are identical to the estimates shown for the ANOVA approach in Table 15.2. In fact, not only are the two sets of estimates identical, but so are the standard errors, *t* values, and *p* values. Third, the maximum likelihood approach also provides a test of the omnibus null hypothesis. The *F* value of 3.03 with 3 numerator and 33 denominator degrees of freedom, along with the *p* value of .0432, probably seem very familiar by now. Fourth, Table 15.3 shows two values for the random portion of the model. The value of 60.7879, listed as "Residual," is the same (within rounding error) as the value of 60.787879, listed as "Error" in Table 15.2. The two approaches have agreed on the error variance, that is, the variance of ε in the model. However, the maximum likelihood approach has also yielded a direct estimate of the subject variance, as shown by the value of 135.35, listed as "Intercept." No such direct estimate was obtained from the ANOVA approach, because its partitioning of sums of squares did not attempt to take into account the random nature of the subjects factor. Instead, the variance due to subjects is implicit in the ANOVA approach.[2]

At this point, it may seem as if the only advantage of the maximum likelihood approach is that it provides a direct estimate of the subject variance. (And footnote 2 shows that even that advantage is largely illusory, because the ANOVA approach yields the same value for these data, with only minor additional calculations.) However, we have purposely chosen this simple example of the maximum likelihood approach not to show off its advantages, but instead to show its direct connection to the ANOVA approach when every individual is measured at the same time point and no data are missing. In this very simple case, the two approaches can be regarded as identical. However, even when the data are so well behaved, as in this example, there can be significant advantages to the maximum likelihood approach. To begin to see how, we need to remind ourselves that the analysis we have performed here relies strongly on the sphericity assumption, which is almost certainly likely to be violated in longitudinal data. Further, whether we have used the ANOVA approach or the maximum likelihood approach, our F test is not robust to violations of this assumption.

Before you despair completely, there is some good news. The maximum likelihood approach even with balanced data offers us two related advantages over the ANOVA approach. First, we will see momentarily that it provides another perspective on the sphericity assumption. In particular, we will see how the way we have specified the random portion of our model forces us to assume sphericity. This new perspective leads to a second advantage of this approach. Namely, we will see that by specifying the random portion of the model differently, we can relax the sphericity assumption. In so doing, we are likely to obtain a more realistic model and more accurate tests and confidence intervals.

Implicit in the previous paragraph is the fact that how we formulate the random effects portion of a model often affects our interpretation of the fixed effects parameters. In particular, different variations of random effects can have sizable influences on the estimated standard errors of the fixed effects and thus on confidence intervals and hypothesis tests involving the fixed effects. One clear example of this phenomenon occurs when we omit a random effect entirely. For example, if we were to analyze the McCarthy data omitting Z_i from the model shown in Equation 1, the resultant F value for the time main effect becomes 0.94, considerably less than the previous value of 3.03 we obtained with Z_i included in the model. (Exercise 13 at the end of this chapter asks you to verify this new value of 0.94.) It is not a coincidence that 0.94 is also the F value we would obtain if we were to treat the McCarthy data as if they came from a between-subjects design instead of a within-subjects design. By omitting Z_i or any other random effect from the model, we are effectively assuming that all scores are uncorrelated with one another, as they should be in a purely between-subjects design, which is why both of these approaches yield an F value of 0.94. Notice that failing to allow for the actual correlation in the data has produced a very conservative test. Although this direction of bias is not infrequent when we fail to correctly model the correlations in the data, it is also not inevitable. As we have seen, including Z_i avoids this conservative bias but frequently overcompensates, because the resultant F statistic becomes too liberal (i.e., we make too many Type I errors) when correlations do not meet the sphericity assumption. Thus, failing to model the correlation structure appropriately can also produce tests whose true Type I error rates exceed .05 and whose true confidence levels are below the desired nominal level. Thus, in general, how a researcher chooses to model random effects has consequences not only for interpreting these random effects but also for interpreting the fixed effects.

We will also see later in this chapter that random effects can be of interest in and of themselves, because they provide information about individual differences. Especially when more than one random effect is included in a model, we are often interested in questions of how these effects relate to one another. However, as we have just discussed, even in the somewhat unusual situation where a researcher has absolutely no interest in individual differences, specification of random effects in the model is nevertheless important because of the possible influence on inferences regarding fixed effects.

A Closer Look at the Random Effects Model

The model we have used so far to analyze the McCarthy data is given by

$$Y_i = \beta_0 X_{0i} + \beta_1 X_{1i} + \beta_2 X_{2i} + \beta_3 X_{3i} + u_i Z_i + \varepsilon_i \qquad \text{(1, repeated)}$$

We will see shortly that there are a variety of other ways in which we might express both the fixed and the random portions of this model. Initially, we will focus our attention on the random portion; subsequently, we will consider the fixed portion. Notice that the model depicted in Equation 1 specifies a single random effect, namely, the effect of subjects. But exactly what does it mean to say that subjects have an effect? We will consider the answer to this question in the context of a longitudinal design, just like that of the McCarthy data.

The primary justification for including the random effect term Z_i in Equation 1 is that it allows individuals to differ from one another. Without this term in the model, we would be implicitly assuming the complete absence of individual differences. Such a strong assumption is rarely likely to be true, which is why we include Z_i in the model. However, what may be less obvious at this point is that the inclusion of Z_i as a single random effect also implies a specific type of difference between individuals. To understand what is implied here, suppose for a moment that we could know the population value of the mean at each time point. In particular, as in the McCarthy example, suppose we have four time points, and that the population means over time are 101, 104, 106, and 106, respectively. If we were to exclude Z_i from our model, we would be assuming that each and every individual's scores are in fact equal to 101, 104, 106, and 106, except for error. Under this model, the only reason any individual ever scores higher than the mean or lower than the mean at any time point is because of error. By implication, someone whose score is 120 at Time 1 should be no more likely to score above 104 at Time 2 than someone whose Time 1 score is 90. In most situations, this assumption is implausible, because there will typically be systematic individual differences between people that manifest themselves across occasions. The likely consequence of imposing this assumption on our analysis even when it is false is that the errors in the model will be correlated with one another, violating a crucial assumption, as we discussed in Chapter 3.

Including Z_i provides at least a partial solution. On a positive note, including Z_i now allows some individuals to score higher than others. For example, a specific person (labeled A, so we can refer to them later) might be expected to score 111, 114, 116, and 116 instead of 101, 104, 106, and 106. A different person (Person B) might be expected to score lower than average, such as 97, 100, 102, and 102. Including the random effect in the model allows for true differences between individuals. However, as these two examples begin to show, there is still a rather strong assumption about the way in which individuals differ from one another. In particular, by including Z_i as the single random effect in our model, we are implicitly assuming that individual differences between participants remain constant over time. For example, notice that Person A in our example above always scores 14 points higher than Person B at every time point. According to our model, this is the only pattern of difference that should occur for any two individuals. Any deviations from this pattern are assumed to be random error, and thus are captured by ε_i, the error term of the model. However, if systematic deviations occur, the error terms will likely correlate with one another, leading to problems in testing hypotheses and forming confidence intervals.

Graphical Representation of Longitudinal Data

Before considering other possible models for the McCarthy data, it may be useful to consider the models we have already fit to the data from a different perspective. Graphical representations are often helpful for understanding data, and longitudinal data are certainly no exception to this rule. We will first present a graph of the data shown in Table 15.1. Then we will consider how our full and restricted models relate to this graph. Later in the chapter we will return to a graphical representation of additional models that we will develop.

Figure 15.2 presents a *trajectory plot* of the McCarthy scores shown in Table 15.1. The x-axis represents the age of assessment and thus ranges from 30 to 48 months for these data. The y-axis represents the McCarthy score. The figure contains a collection of 12 trajectories, one for each participant. Each individual trajectory consists of three line segments, one from 30 to 36 months, a second from 36 to 42 months, and a third from 42 to 48 months. For example, notice that toward the upper left corner of the graph one individual appears to have a score of approximately 130 at 30 months. Looking at Table 15.1 shows us that participant 7 had a score of 129 at 30 months. We can verify that the line that begins near 130 does in fact represent the scores of participant 7 by seeing from Table 15.1 that this child proceeded to score 128 at 36 months, 123 at 42 months, and 128 at 48 months. Following this line in Figure 15.2 shows that the segment from 30 to 36 months is essentially flat, then there is a

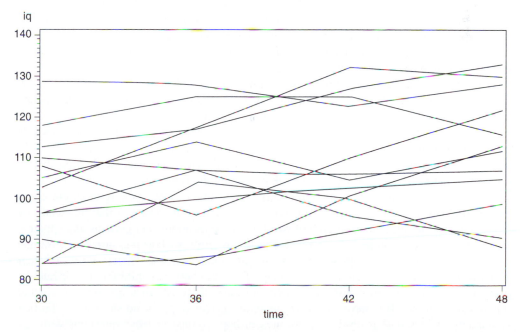

FIG. 15.2. Trajectory plots of McCarthy scores from 15.1.

small decline from 36 to 42 months, which is followed by a comparable increase from 42 to 48 months. To be certain that you understand this figure, notice that two children achieved scores of 84 at 30 months. One child, participant 4, scored somewhat higher at each subsequent test occasion. The other child's trajectory was much less steady, rising to 104 at 36 months, falling slightly to 100 at 42 months, and then falling even more to 88 at 42 months. You should be able to identify each of these participants in Figure 15.2. We need to issue one word of caution about the figure. Line segments are used to connect adjacent scores, so we can follow the trajectory of each participant. However, the data clearly do not provide information about the nature of change during times where no measurement took place. As a result, we have no empirical justification for connecting adjacent points with straight lines, but it is conventional to use them in this context, with the understanding that they serve as a visual aid.

Trajectory plots can provide an essential supplement to the numerical information we obtain using PROC MIXED and other similar software. In particular, the goal of PROC MIXED can be thought of as identifying patterns in the trajectory plot. What types of patterns might exist in a plot such as that shown in Figure 15.2? The answer relates back to our discussion of fixed and random effects. For example, it might be the case that the average score tends to increase over time. Thus, one possible pattern would be a tendency for trajectories to slope upward as we move forward in time (from left to right). Of course, other average patterns could also exist. Perhaps scores initially increase but then begin to decrease. Such a pattern might reflect a quadratic trend. Such average effects, whether they be linear, quadratic, or of some other form, would be fixed effects because they reflect population averages. However, another type of pattern might exist in the data. Irrespective of whether scores tend to increase or decrease on average, it might be the case that some individuals show a different rate of increase than do others. Your first reaction to this statement might be to think that of course such differences must always exist. However, the real question is whether any such differences that appear in the figure represent actual population differences or are instead merely a reflection of such influences as measurement error. By now you should realize that this is precisely why we use inferential statistics, typically either to test a hypothesis or form a confidence interval, or both. Thus, the graphical representation and the formal output from PROC MIXED should go hand in hand and supplement one another.

Different readers may have different views of what patterns if any emerge from Figure 15.2. However, our guess is that many readers may shrug their shoulders and lament the fact that no patterns whatsoever seem to emerge. Keep in mind that if clear patterns pop out from visual representations of data, there is likely to be less need for statistical inference. The other side of the coin is that even if patterns do not literally pop out, that does not mean that all hope is lost. Inferential statistical procedures may detect patterns that are not necessarily immediately obvious to the naked eye. Ideally, an interplay between the two approaches can prove to be beneficial, as each approach helps to inform the other. In any case, looking more closely at Figure 15.2 suggests some tendency for scores to slope upward. The fact that this tendency is not universal implies either or both of two further explanations: (1) Perhaps any apparent tendency for scores to increase is simply a reflection of error, such as measurement error and sampling error; and (2) perhaps scores of some individuals increase whereas scores of other individuals decrease, reflecting true individual differences between children in their rates of growth. If children do truly vary in their growth rates, there is still a question of whether the average child tends to have a positive slope, a negative slope, or no slope at all. Further examination of the data is needed before we can hope to answer these questions with any degree of conviction. In particular, we believe that models beyond those we have considered so far are necessary to probe these questions.

Graphical Representation of the Random Intercept Model

Before considering possible alternative models for longitudinal data, it is important to consider our random intercept model from a graphical perspective. As we have discussed, including a random intercept term Z_i in the model allows individuals to differ systematically from one another. However, the nature of that difference is assumed to follow a very specific form. We can depict the role of the random intercept effect graphically. Remember that the model with a random intercept term can be written as

$$Y_i = \beta_0 X_{0i} + \beta_1 X_{1i} + \beta_2 X_{2i} + \beta_3 X_{3i} + u_i Z_i + \varepsilon_i \qquad \text{(1, repeated)}$$

Table 15.3 showed the result of fitting this model to the McCarthy data. In particular, not only did Table 15.3 show the value of estimated parameters, but it also showed the result of comparing this model to a restricted model where β_1, β_2, and β_3 are hypothesized to equal zero. We will now see how we can develop a graphical representation of this model comparison.

As we have discussed, the model shown in Equation 1 allows for two types of effects: (1) average differences between time points and (2) consistent differences between participants. Figure 15.3 shows how these effects can be represented graphically. Specifically, Figure 15.3 depicts the predicted scores for each of our 12 participants at each of the four time points, based on the random intercept model of Equation 1. [Predicted trajectories for only 10 participants actually appear in the figure, because two pairs of participants have the same marginal means (see Table 15.1), and thus these pairs of participants have the same estimated participant effect parameters.]

We wish to call your attention to two salient characteristics of Figure 15.3. First, notice that the average predicted score increases over time. This is consistent, as it must be, with

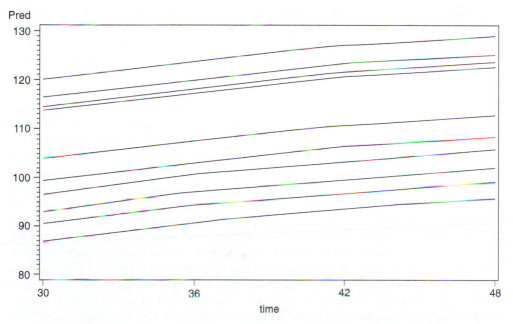

FIG. 15.3. Fitted trajectory plots of McCarthy scores based on random intercept model.

the fixed effects solution we saw in Table 15.3. According to this model, the population mean increases over time. As an aside, it is important to point out that the form of this increase is not literally linear. Although they may look linear at first glance, the changes shown in the figure are in fact slightly nonlinear. Each line shows a change of 4 points between 30 and 36 months, a change of 3 points between 36 and 42 months, and a change of 2 points between 42 and 48 months. We should hasten to acknowledge that the departure from nonlinearity may turn out to be nonsignificant here (so we may conclude that any nonlinearity in Figure 15.3 simply reflects measurement error or sampling error). Nevertheless, the important point at the moment is that our model allows a nonlinear pattern to emerge, to the extent that a nonlinear pattern exists in the data.

Second, even more striking than the tendency for scores to increase is the fact that all the lines shown in Figure 15.3 are parallel to one another. It is essential to realize that the predicted scores from the random intercept model will always possess this property. In other words, whether or not the actual trajectories (as in Figure 15.2) appear parallel to one another, the trajectories presumed by the model will necessarily be parallel. The reason, as we discussed earlier, is that including a single random effect in the model allows individuals to differ in only a single way, and in this case that single way is in their intercept parameter. Thus, Figure 15.3 shows a collection of line segments, which differ from one another only in their intercepts. In other words, our model assumes that the only true pattern of individual differences in the actual data of Figure 15.2 can be explained as a difference in intercepts, as shown in Figure 15.3. We will return to the implications of this assumption momentarily, and later in the chapter we will present a model that allows for other types of differences between participants.

How would Figure 15.3 change if we were to omit the random intercept effect from our model? We should omit this effect if we believe that all differences between individuals as shown in the observed trajectories of Figure 15.2 reflect nothing more than measurement error and sampling error. In this case, there would be no true individual differences between participants whatsoever. In this scenario, a graphical representation would consist of a single trajectory, whose values would be 103, 107, 110, and 112 at the four time points. Under this model we would be assuming that everyone would have these same four scores (or, more precisely, the actual population values) if it were not for measurement error and sampling error. The random intercept model, on the other hand, is more flexible than this in that it allows a unique intercept for the trajectory of each individual.

How can we interpret the F test of the fixed effects in our model? For example, how can we interpret the F value of 3.03 and corresponding p value of .0432 in the McCarthy data? Once again, a graphical representation may provide a valuable perspective. Figure 15.3 shows the predicted scores from the random intercept model of Equation 1. Notice that this is the full model, because it includes the fixed effects in the model. Figure 15.3 shows that as a consequence, the full model allows average scores to differ from one another across time.

Figure 15.4 shows predicted scores from the corresponding restricted model for the McCarthy data. The only difference between this figure and Figure 15.3 is that each trajectory is now a flat line. According to the restricted model, trajectories will be flat because the null hypothesis implies that scores do not change over time. Thus, the only reason we might observe trajectories that are not flat is measurement error or sampling error according to this model. The F test of fixed effects thus can be thought of in terms of a comparison of Figure 15.3 with Figure 15.4. Of course, the data must enter the picture somehow, so a more complete way of phrasing the graphical interpretation is that the test of fixed effects asks whether the predictions shown in Figure 15.3 fit the data of Figure 15.2 significantly better than the predictions shown in Figure 15.4. In the McCarthy data, the answer is yes, the predictions of Figure 15.3 are significantly better. Thus, from this perspective, we can reject a null hypothesis

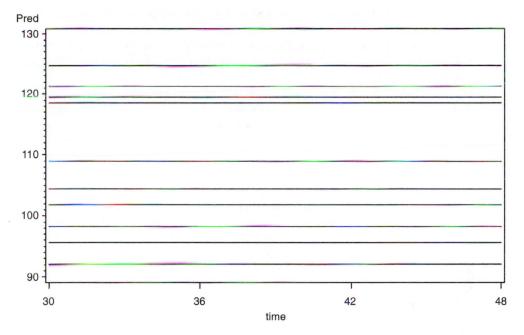

FIG. 15.4. Fitted trajectory plots of McCarthy scores based on random intercept model restricted to allow no mean differences over time.

that the population means follow a flat trajectory such as that shown in Figure 15.4. Instead, we have evidence beyond a reasonable doubt that the trajectories are not flat, in accordance with Figure 15.3.

You might be perfectly content to stop at this point, but we feel compelled to raise a potential problem. What if neither Figure 15.3 nor Figure 15.4 is a very accurate representation of the data? If the random intercept model is the correct model, Figure 15.3 should represent all systematic patterns displayed in Figure 15.2 of the actual data. Stated differently, any possible pattern in the actual data that is not reflected in Figure 15.3 is presumed by the random intercept model to have resulted from measurement error or sampling error, and thus not to reflect a true effect. However, Figure 15.2 suggests at least the possibility that participants' trajectories may not be parallel. Although it could turn out that departures from parallelism result from purely random sources (such as measurement error), it may not be wise to make this assumption without considering other alternatives. Unfortunately, that is exactly what we would be doing if we were to stop at this point.

In many situations the pattern displayed in Figure 15.3 is almost certain to be too restrictive. Notice that the pattern allows individuals to have different starting points in the study, but assumes that any change that takes place is a constant for everyone. However, in reality, if change is indeed occurring, it seems much more likely that some individuals will change more rapidly than others.

At this point it is helpful to conceptualize the growth patterns shown in Figure 15.3 in geometric terms. For example, if we think in terms of trend analysis, there are four possible components to change with four time points: an intercept, a linear trend, a quadratic trend, and a cubic trend. Figure 15.3 allows individuals to have different intercepts from one another, but assumes the absence of differences in linear, quadratic, and cubic trends. In other words, the model depicted in this figure assumes that there is no true variation in these trends. If this assumption is correct, we can omit such variation from our model. Notice that this is precisely what we did in the model shown in Equation 1. This model contains only a single random effect, which we can now see is an intercept term. This model allows individuals to have different starting points, but assumes the complete absence of any systematic differences between individuals in change over time.

We have established that the Equation 1 model will often be unrealistic. Not surprisingly, there is a statistical price to pay for this lack of realism. Figure 15.3 is a visual representation of compound symmetry, which you may recall from Chapter 11 is a special case of the sphericity assumption that we argued is often problematic in within-subjects designs. Remember that the sphericity assumption pertains to the covariance matrix of scores at the various time points. In particular, Figure 15.3 corresponds to two types of patterns in the covariance matrix. First, notice from the figure that the spread in scores at any one time point is identical to the spread at any other time point. This is a consequence of the parallelism between lines. Second, the correlation between scores at any pair of time points will be a constant, according to the pattern displayed in the figure. In fact, the only reason this correlation does not equal 1.00 is because of the presence of random error (as reflected by ε_i) in the data.

What is the point of all this? We now have another way of thinking about the sphericity assumption we initially considered in Chapter 11. For longitudinal data, assuming sphericity can be thought of as assuming that different individuals have different intercepts (i.e., different starting points), but that their patterns of change over time do not differ. Of course, this is a very strong assumption, which simply provides another perspective on why the sphericity assumption is likely to be violated in longitudinal data.

Fortunately, there is yet another benefit to conceptualizing the sphericity assumption from this perspective. As we pointed out, the model shown in Equation 1 implicitly assumes that any linear, quadratic, and cubic effects are constant from person to person, that is, that they have zero variance and thus are not included as random effects in the model. However, if we believe that this assumption is likely to be false, we can simply revise our model to include one or more additional random effects. Recall from Equation 2 that the general form of the mixed linear model allows for the possibility of multiple random effects:

$$Y_i = \beta_0 X_{0i} + \beta_1 X_{1i} + \beta_2 X_{2i} + \cdots + \beta_p X_{pi} + u_{1i} Z_{1i} + u_{2i} Z_{2i} + \cdots + u_{qi} Z_{qi} + \varepsilon_i$$

$$(2, \text{repeated})$$

For example, we might believe that individuals are likely to differ not only in their intercepts, but also in their linear trends, that is, their slopes. We could accommodate such an assumption in Equation 2 by including two random effects, one for the intercept and one for the slope. The resultant model would then have the form

$$Y_i = \beta_0 X_{0i} + \beta_1 X_{1i} + \beta_2 X_{2i} + \cdots + \beta_p X_{pi} + u_{1i} Z_{1i} + u_{2i} Z_{2i} + \varepsilon_i \qquad (4)$$

As with the first model we considered for the McCarthy data (i.e., the model shown in Equation 1), maximum likelihood can be used to estimate the parameters of the model shown in Equation 4. Once again, the maximum likelihood approach makes a distinction between the fixed effect parameters (as before, the β parameters) and the random effect parameters (u_{1i} and u_{2i}). There are several additional wrinkles we must consider here.

Coding Random Effects Predictor Variables

First, we need to consider the coding of the two random effects predictor variables Z_1 and Z_2. Recall that Z_{1i} represents the intercept of the growth trajectory for Individual i. This intercept is coded just as it typically is in a linear model. Specifically, each time point is assigned a value of 1 for each individual. As is true in multiple regression (see Appendix B for more details), mixed model software typically uses this coding method by default, so it is usually not necessary to include Z_{1i} as a separate variable in the data file. Whereas Z_{1i} represents each individual's intercept, Z_{2i} represents the linear component of the growth trajectory for Individual i. Unlike Z_{1i}, the linear term Z_{2i} is generally not generated automatically by mixed model software, so it usually needs to be included explicitly as a variable in the data file.

Coding of the linear Z_{2i} variable is not complicated, but does involve one nuance. For example, consider the McCarthy data. Recall that the four time points correspond to 30, 36, 42, and 48 months of each child's age. Thus, the intuitive way of coding Z_{2i} is to use values of 30, 36, 42, and 48. Although this is perfectly acceptable, it is not the only choice. One possible limitation of this approach is that the intercept term Z_{1i} becomes the McCarthy score at an age of 0 months. However, the researcher might be more interested in conceptualizing the intercept as the initial time point of actual observations. This redefinition can be accomplished easily, by redefining Z_{2i} as 0, 6, 12, and 18 at the four time points. Notice that with this method of coding, an Z_{2i} value of 0 corresponds to a child's actual age of 30 months. The general principle to keep in mind here is that the intercept represents the expected value of the trajectory when the predictor variable has a value of 0. Thus, one frequent choice is to code Z_{2i} so that its initial value for each individual equals 0. However, the ultimate choice depends on how the investigator would like to interpret the intercept. As a consequence, there are a variety of options available. For example, in the McCarthy data, another choice would be to scale Z_{2i} as -9, -3, 3, and 9. This method of scaling produces an intercept that represents a child's estimated McCarthy score at an age of 39 months, so the intercept now can be interpreted as a child's average score during the period of observation. Notice that this method of coding is proportional to the orthogonal polynomial coefficients shown in Appendix Table A.10. Yet another option that might sometimes be useful would be to code Z_{2i} as -18, -12, -6, and 0. Now the intercept corresponds to the child's estimated McCarthy score at 48 months, the end of the observation period. This method of coding would then allow examination of individual differences at the end of the study, as reflected by u_1.

Two further points need to be made here. First, notice that the coding choice for Z_{2i} affects the interpretation of the random intercept term. Ironically, however, the choice does not affect the interpretation of the linear component itself. Thus, if interest were to focus exclusively on the linear component of change, by and large it does not matter which of these coding methods is used. In fact, the range of options is yet wider, because we could also use such choices as 0, 0.5, 1.0, and 1.5 or -0.75, -0.25, 0.25, and 0.75. Notice that we have simply changed the metric of time, which now corresponds to years instead of months. As long as we keep in mind the metric we have chosen, it makes no difference whether we choose to scale time in months, years, or any other measure. Second, notice that Z_{2i} contains an i subscript. Thus, the model requires us to code this variable for each individual. Often this coding will be the same for each individual. For example, in the McCarthy data, every individual is measured at identical times of 30, 36, 42, and 48 months, so the four values of Z_{2i} are the same for every individual, and in this respect, the values of Z_{2i} are the same for every value of i. When this condition holds, we say that the design is balanced. However, as we have hinted earlier, in some situations this condition may not hold. For example, some individuals may be missing observations at certain time points, so they have no score on the dependent variable to correspond with a specific value of Z_{2i}. A major benefit of the maximum likelihood approach is that parameters can be estimated, confidence intervals formed, and hypotheses tested even though certain individuals are missing some data. The method is able to proceed because of the i subscript on Z_{2i}, which allows the values of time to vary from person to person. In fact, as we have said earlier, there is no requirement that any two individuals be measured at the same time points. For example, in many research situations, it would be very impractical to begin measuring each participant at precisely the same age. Instead, it is more likely that one child might be measured at 30, 35, 41, and 48 months, whereas a second child might be measured at 29, 37, 40, and 46 months. Or, a gerontological researcher is unlikely to design a longitudinal study so that all participants are 65 years old at the beginning of data collection. As a result, the age at which individuals are measured will vary from person to person. By allowing an i subscript on Z_{2i}, the model can accommodate such patterns of observation with no special difficulties.

Random Effects Parameters

We have seen that the maximum likelihood approach distinguishes random effects parameters from fixed effects parameters at the outset of model formulation. Recall that when we had a single random effect in our model, this approach yields a direct estimate of the variance due to subjects (in the McCarthy data, the numerical value of this variance estimate was 135.35). We can now realize that this estimate can be thought of as an estimate of the variance across subjects in the intercepts of their individual trajectories.

Interpretation follows the same logic but becomes slightly more complicated when more than one random effect is included in the model. One obvious complication is that we now must also consider the variance of additional random effects. In particular, when a random linear trend is included, its variance becomes another parameter to be estimated. Less obvious perhaps is that we must also consider whether the two random effects are correlated with one another. For example, individuals with higher than average intercepts might also tend to have higher than average slopes, in which case there would be a positive correlation between u_1 and u_2, the random intercept and the random slope. This would be a case where "the rich get richer," because individuals starting out higher would increase their advantage over those who started out lower. However, notice that high scores are not necessarily better—perhaps individuals who were initially most depressed tend to become yet more depressed at a faster pace than those who were initially lower on depression. Alternatively, individuals with higher than average intercepts could tend to have lower than average slopes, in which case there would be a negative correlation between u_1 and u_2. This would be an example of a compensatory phenomenon, where those initially below average were in the process of catching up (or even surpassing) those with higher initial scores. Of course, yet another possibility is that u_1 and u_2 may be uncorrelated. Initial status and rate of change may be independent of one another.

Three issues associated with interpretation of random effects are worth further discussion. First, as we have just seen in the special case of two random effects, whenever the model includes multiple random effects, we need to consider not only the variance of each random effect, but also the correlations among the effects. To understand this point in more detail, recall that we expressed the general form of the mixed linear model as

$$Y_i = \beta_0 X_{0i} + \beta_1 X_{1i} + \beta_2 X_{2i} + \cdots + \beta_p X_{pi} + u_{1i} Z_{1i} + u_{2i} Z_{2i} + \cdots + u_{qi} Z_{qi} + \varepsilon_i$$

$$(2, \text{repeated})$$

implying that in general the model contains q random effects. With q random effects, there are a total of $q(q + 1)/2$ random parameters to be estimated. We can conceptualize this total as consisting of two parts: q variances and $q(q - 1)/2$ correlations. Alternatively, we can think of these parameters in terms of a $q \times q$ covariance matrix. In either case, we typically rely on maximum likelihood to estimate all of these parameters, although there are occasionally situations where we might, for example, stipulate that all of the correlations are fixed equal to zero, in which case only the variances would be estimated (this is sometimes referred to as a variance components model). It is important to realize that these parameters are not simply nuisances in the model. Although our primary attention often pertains to the fixed effects in the model, nevertheless, the random effects parameters can also be informative. For example, it may be quite interesting to learn whether the correlation between intercept and slope is positive, negative, or zero.

Second, it is also important to realize that the interpretation of the random effects parameters often depends on how we have chosen to code the corresponding variables. For example, in the case of a random intercept and a random slope, how we might interpret the correlation between u_1 and u_2 will depend on how we coded Z_{1i} and Z_{2i}. The reason is that as we discussed earlier, the meaning of the random intercept u_1 depends on how we chose to code the random slope Z_{2i}. For example, in the McCarthy data, suppose we chose to code Z_{2i} as 0, 6, 12, and 18, and found a correlation of 0.12 between the intercept and the slope. We could legitimately interpret this as suggesting a very small positive correlation (essentially equal to zero) between initial status at 30 months of age and rate of change from 30 months to 48 months. However, suppose that we had instead chosen to code Z_{2i} as -9, -3, 3, and 9. There is no reason to expect that the correlation between the intercept and the slope will still equal 0.12, because the meaning of the intercept is different in the model with this new coding. In general, the correlation will now equal some different value, because it represents the correlation between the average score during this interval and the rate of change during this interval. If our interest lies exclusively in the fixed effects, it will not matter which way we code Z_{2i}, because parameter estimates, confidence intervals, and hypothesis tests for the fixed effects will be the same regardless of which way we choose to code the random effects. However, if we are also interested in learning about the pattern of individual differences, we must be careful to code the random effects variables in a manner that will correspond to our desired interpretation.

Third, it is also important to realize that in theory any pattern of relationships among the random effects could be accompanied by any pattern of parameter values for the fixed effects. For example, suppose that the fixed effects reveal that scores tend to increase over time. In other words, suppose that the data show convincingly that the population mean is increasing over time. This pattern does not necessarily tell us anything about the random effects parameters. For example, suppose we have two random effects in our model, an intercept and a slope. Further suppose we have coded the slope variable so that a zero corresponds to initial status at the beginning of the study. The fact that the mean score is increasing tells us nothing in and of itself about individual differences between participants. For example, it could be the case that individuals with higher than average values at the beginning of the study change most rapidly, in which case u_1 and u_2 would correlate positively. However, it is also possible that individuals with higher than average values at the beginning of the study will change least rapidly, in which case u_1 and u_2 would correlate negatively. Estimates for the fixed effects only tell us about the pattern of scores for the average person, but they are silent with respect to the existence of possible patterns of individual differences in the data. The practical point is that random effects parameters convey a different type of information from fixed effects parameters. Depending on the investigator's goals, one type may be of much greater interest than the other, or both may be of equal interest.

Numerical Example

After all of this conceptual development about incorporating a second random effect in the model, it is finally time to see how this works in practice. Once again, we will begin by briefly illustrating current syntax for SAS PROC MIXED. We will assume that an appropriate input data set has already been created. There is no need to modify the data set that would have been created to fit a single random intercept effect to the data. However, for reasons that we will explain momentarily, it is necessary to have two versions of the time variable, one of which is categorical and the other of which is continuous. Telling SAS to create a duplicate of the time variable also provides an opportunity to make a decision about the scaling of this variable, in particular how we want to define the zero point of the scale. For example, we might decide that we want the random intercept variable to represent initial status at 30 months, the first time point of the study. You may recall that we showed the following set of commands for the "data" step when we fit only the random intercept term in the model:

```
data new;
   input id timecat iq;
   cards;
[48 lines of data follow, 1 for each combination of subject and time]
```

We can modify these commands simply by adding one new line (between the "input" line and the "cards" line) that scales time so that the original score of 30 is transformed to a new score of 0:

```
time=timecat −30;
```

We now have two variables to represent time. We will instruct PROC MIXED to consider "timecat" as a categorical (i.e., "class") variable, in which case it will construct three indicator variables to represent the four levels of time.[3] Because we will not include a "class" statement for "time," PROC MIXED will regard it as a continuous variable, which we can then use to represent the linear component of time, thus allowing participants to display systematic individual differences in their average rate of change. The following four lines of SAS code fit the model of Equation 4 to the McCarthy data:

```
proc mixed covtest cl;
   class timecat;
   model iq=timecat/s;
   random int time/subject=id type=un;
```

Several points need to be made before proceeding. First, notice that with one minor exception, the first three lines here are identical to the syntax we showed earlier for fitting a single random effect to the data. For reasons we will explain below, we have chosen to add "covtest" and "cl" to the first line. We could also have included these commands in the program for a single random effect, but they become more relevant here. Otherwise, in both SAS programs, the fixed portion of the model presumes four levels of time as a categorical variable, so the second and third lines of the two programs are identical to one another. Later in the chapter we will consider a model where different fixed effects are specified, which will necessitate changing these two lines. Second, the "random" line of this program is similar to, but not exactly the same as, the "random" line of the earlier program. In particular, there are two differences:

TABLE 15.4
MAXIMUM LIKELIHOOD ANALYSIS OF TABLE 15.1 DATA, ALLOWING RANDOM
SLOPE AS WELL AS RANDOM INTERCEPT

The Mixed Procedure

Solution for Fixed Effects

Effect	timecat	Estimate	Standard Error	DF	t Value	Pr > |t|
Intercept		112.00	4.2312	11	26.47	<.0001
timecat	0	−9.0000	4.0924	22	−2.20	0.0387
timecat	1	−5.0000	3.3030	22	−1.51	0.1443
timecat	2	−2.0000	2.7216	22	−0.73	0.4702
timecat	3	0	.	.	.	.

Type 3 Tests of Fixed Effects

Effect	Num DF	Den DF	F Value	Pr > F
timecat	3	22	1.78	0.1801

Covariance Parameter Estimates

Cov Parm	Subject	Estimate	Standard Error	Z Value	Pr Z	Alpha	Lower	Upper
UN(1,1)	id	168.02	83.1941	2.02	0.0217	0.05	77.1275	606.50
UN(2,1)	id	−3.2421	3.6387	−0.89	0.3729	0.05	−10.3739	3.8896
UN(2,2)	id	0.3892	0.2622	1.48	0.0689	0.05	0.1448	2.7800
Residual		37.4364	11.2875	3.32	0.0005	0.05	22.3922	74.9933

(1) The variable "time" has been added to "int" as a random effect and (2) "type=un" has been added as an option to the right of the slash. The inclusion of "time" as a random effect simply instructs SAS that we now have two random effects in our model. Thus, participants are allowed to display systematic individual differences in both slope and intercept parameters. Specifying "type=un" as an option tells SAS that the covariance matrix of the random effects is unstructured, which simply means that we are allowing the slope and intercept to correlate with one another. As an alternative, we could specify "type=vc" if we wanted SAS to fit a model constraining the slope and intercept to be uncorrelated, but we would typically not want to impose such a constraint without strong prior theoretical justification. In general, notice that we can include or exclude specific random effects from our model easily, by modifying the RANDOM statement in PROC MIXED.

Table 15.4 shows an excerpt of the output from SAS PROC MIXED when the model with random slopes and intercepts is fit to the McCarthy data. As usual, we will highlight several aspects of the table, with special attention to how the results shown here compare to those shown previously in Tables 15.2 and 15.3. We will begin by considering information about the fixed effects in the model. First, notice that the parameter estimates for the fixed effects shown in Table 15.4 are identical to the estimates shown previously in Tables 15.2 and 15.3. Such equivalence will always occur with a balanced design (as long as the same fixed effects are specified in every model), but will not generally hold when the data are unbalanced. Second, although the point estimates are identical, the standard errors, t values, and p values are different than they were previously. As we have discussed, different formulations of random effects lead to different estimated standard errors, thus producing different confidence intervals and significance tests. Third, specifying random intercept and slope parameters leads to an F value of 1.78 with 3 numerator and 22 denominator degrees of freedom, which leads to a p value of .18 for the omnibus null hypothesis that population means do not change over time.[4] Notice that the value of 1.78 is appreciably less than the value of 3.03 we obtained when we assumed the intercept was the only random effect that needed to be included in our model. In particular, the main effect of time is no longer statistically significant at the .05 level when we assume both slope and intercept to be random effects. We will return to further consideration of this discrepancy after we discuss the random effects portion of the table.

Table 15.4 also provides information about the random effects in our model. Because we have two Z variables in our model, there are a total of four covariance parameter estimates: (1) the variance of u_1, which in our case is an intercept parameter, (2) the variance of u_2, in our case a slope parameter, (3) the covariance of u_1 with u_2, and (4) the error variance, that is, the variance of ε in the model. The table shows that the estimated values for these parameters are 168.02, 0.3892, -3.2421, and 37.4364, respectively. Often, the parameter of most interest is the covariance between the intercept and the slope, so for now we will concentrate on that parameter. Later we will consider a different model for these data, where the variances as well as the covariance take on a special meaning. Thus, we will defer full interpretation of the variance parameters until we develop this later model. To enhance interpretation of the covariance, it is useful to convert it to a correlation, which we can do by dividing -3.2421 by the square root of the product of 168.02 and 0.3892, which gives us a value of -0.40. (Alternatively, as of this writing, specifying "gcorr" as another option on the "random" line provides this value directly.) This value suggests a moderate to strong negative correlation between initial status and rate of change. Thus, there is some evidence to suggest that individuals whose scores are lower at 30 months are likely to experience larger gains between 30 and 48 months than are those individuals whose scores are higher at 30 months.[5] However, before making too much of this finding, we need to realize that it is plausible that the population value of this correlation is in fact zero. Notice in Table 15.4 that the z value for this estimate is -0.89, which yields a p value of 0.3729. Thus, this correlation fails to reach statistical significance at the .05 level. Further notice that the distinct possibility that the population correlation may be positive is reflected in the 95% confidence interval for the covariance, which ranges from -10.3739 to 3.8896. The problem here is that with only 12 participants, we are unable to determine a precise estimate of the true correlation between initial status and rate of change. If this were a major goal of the study, a considerably larger sample size would have been needed.

Graphical Representation of a Model with Random Slope and Intercept

We have seen that a major potential benefit of including a random slope as well as a random intercept in a model is that this combination imposes a less severe assumption than sphericity about the covariance matrix. We will now illustrate this benefit graphically.

Figure 15.5 shows the predicted trajectories for the McCarthy data based on the random intercept and slope model of Equation 4. Of particular interest is to compare this figure with Figure 15.3, which you may recall showed corresponding predictions for the full model that allowed only a random intercept effect. The obvious difference between the graphs is that the trajectories shown in Figure 15.5 show different rates of change for different children. Indeed, such differences are exactly what the random slope effect allows the model to allow for. To the extent that individuals truly differ in their rates of change, Figure 15.5 will be a better representation than Figure 15.3 of the data in Figure 15.2, in which case inferences (such as significance tests and confidence intervals) should be based on a model that includes a random slope as well as a random intercept.

It is also worth pointing out two ways in which Figure 15.5 is not different from Figure 15.3. First, although one may have to look closely, once again the trajectories shown in Figure 15.5

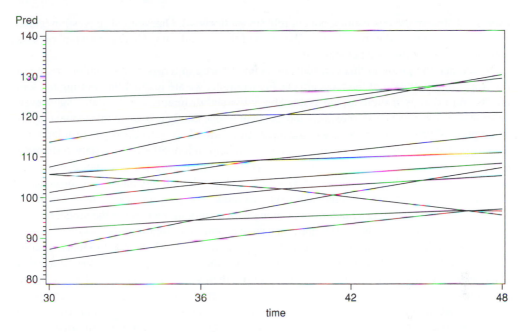

FIG. 15.5. Fitted trajectory plots of McCarthy scores based on random intercept and slope model.

are not straight lines. In a moment, we will consider yet another model for the data that
imposes an assumption of linearity on the trajectories. Second, it is interesting to consider
what the average predicted score would be at each time point in Figure 15.5. As it turns out,
the averages of the predicted scores would be 103, 107, 110, and 112 for 30, 36, 42, and 48
months, respectively. You may remember that these are exactly the same four averages that
occur for the predicted scores in Figure 15.3. Notice also that these values are consistent with
the parameter estimates we found in Table 15.3, which were identical to the estimates we found
in Table 15.2, where the only random effect was the intercept. Thus, Figures 15.3 and 15.5
depict the same average changes between time points, but they differ in terms of how they
conceptualize the form of individual change that produces these averages.

Further Consideration of Competing Models

In this chapter we have now considered three full models for the McCarthy data. All three of
these models specify identical fixed effects, namely, that each time point is allowed to have
its own population mean. However, the models differ in their specification of random effects.
The first model we considered allows for a random intercept. We then briefly considered a
model that allowed no random effects. Finally, we considered a model that allows a random
intercept and a random slope. We have seen that even though the specification of fixed effects
was identical for these three models, we do not reach the same interpretation of the fixed effects
in these three models. Allowing a random intercept yielded an F value of 3.03, which was
statistically significant at the .05 level. Allowing no random effects yielded an F value of 0.94,
nonsignificant at the .05 level. Allowing a random slope as well as a random intercept yielded
an F value of 1.78, once again nonsignificant at the .05 level.

Obviously, how we ultimately interpret changes over time in mean McCarthy scores will
depend on which random effects model we choose to base our interpretation on. Unfortunately,

choosing between models is often not entirely straightforward. Our general suggestion is that such choices often need to rely on a combination of theory and data. There are several reasons that the choice is generally not automatic.

Notice that the problem that confronts us can be viewed in terms of assumptions required for proper interpretation of the fixed effects. For example, we are justified in omitting random effects entirely only if there are no systematic individual differences in the data whatsoever, and that as a consequence all scores are independent of one another. If we fit this model but our assumption is wrong, inferences regarding fixed effects are likely to be distorted. Similarly, we are justified in including a random intercept but no other random effects if the only systematic difference between people is in their initial status, in which case the covariance matrix of scores will exhibit sphericity. However, as we discussed at length in Chapters 11 through 14, if our assumption is incorrect, inferences from this model can be quite erroneous. We will see momentarily that including a random slope along with a random intercept in the model relaxes the sphericity assumption but still requires a less stringent assumption of its own.

In general, then, we continue to confront the problem of possibly needing to make a set of assumptions in order to address questions of theoretical interest. One persistent dilemma is that in theory we could begin with a test of the assumptions themselves. For example, it is possible to test whether the variances and/or covariances of various random effects are zero. For example, look once again at the section of Table 15.4 labeled "Covariance Parameter Estimates." The column headed "Pr Z" gives the p value associated with a test of each random effect in the model. For the McCarthy data, the only random effect that is statistically significant at the .05 level is the intercept. Thus, we might interpret the nonsignificant results for the slope and the covariance between the slope and the intercept as proof that the random slope term can be dropped from the model. If we follow this path, we could then reject the null hypothesis for the fixed effects at the .05 level, and thus conclude that mean McCarthy scores are changing over time.

Although the aforementioned strategy has some appeal, it also has some serious problems. Most important is that when samples are small, the power to detect effects is likely to be low, so true effects may well go undetected. In this case, we are susceptible to dropping effects from the model that should have been included, but we are given a false sense of confidence because of the nonsignificant test of the assumption. One remedy for this problem is to use a different alpha level for the test. For example, instead of using an alpha level of .05, we might choose to use an alpha level of .25, so that less evidence is required against the null hypothesis before we are prepared to reject it. Notice that with this less stringent alpha level, we would now conclude that the random slope effect is needed in our model for the McCarthy data. On the other hand, with very large samples, power may be so high that even trivial effects are judged statistically significant and are thus included in the model when they are not truly needed. Yet one further issue here is a more technical complication. The z values provided by PROC MIXED are somewhat problematic for tests of variances[6] (but tests of covariances avoid this problem), and further, our question really involves both the random slope itself as well as its covariance with the random intercept. Verbeke (1997) discusses this problem in some detail and suggests a possible solution.

How should we proceed given all of these complications? In longitudinal studies in the behavioral sciences, we suspect that individuals (be they humans or not) will typically differ in their rate of change. Thus, most often there will probably be strong theoretical reasons to allow for a random slope effect in the model. However, especially where theoretical expectations may be less clear, the data themselves can help resolve the question of whether a random slope is needed. In addition to examining growth trajectories of individual participants (such as in Figure 15.2 and ensuing figures, for example), significance tests can be used to guide this decision as long as the complications of the previous paragraph are kept in mind. Following this logic, our conclusion in the McCarthy data would be to conclude that the random slope effect (and its covariance with the intercept) should be retained in the model.

Additional Models Deserving Consideration

Of the three full models we have considered so far for the McCarthy data, our judgment is that the most appropriate model includes three indicator variables for the fixed effects (thus making this a "cell means" model, because each time point is allowed to have its own population mean) and two Z variables for the random effects (namely, a random intercept and a random slope). Suppose we were to think about the indicators for the fixed effects in terms of trends, which seems natural when the factor is quantitative, as it is here. From this perspective, our fixed model includes linear, quadratic, and cubic effects. Notice that in contrast, the random effects portion of the model allows for only a random slope component. The fact that the model does not include random effects for the quadratic or cubic trends implies that we consider them not to vary systematically across participants. By including quadratic and cubic effects in the fixed portion of the model, we are allowing the population means of these trends to be nonzero. However, by excluding them from the random effects portion of the model, we are assuming that whatever the mean value is for each trend, it is also the value of the trend for each individual in the population. At first glance, this may sound contradictory. It is not, because it is certainly possible mathematically that every participant could have the same nonzero value of the quadratic or cubic trend. In most behavioral data, however, it seems more likely that if the trend exists at all, participants are likely to show some systematic variability around the population mean. When this is true, a nonzero mean will be accompanied by a random effect with nonzero variance. Indeed, we might expect that the only time a random effect would have no variance is when the corresponding trend simply has no effect whatsoever. For example, children's growth on a particular measure might truly be linear, so that quadratic and cubic effects are simply nonexistent, not just on average but literally for each individual child. In this case, the population mean of each nonlinear trend would be zero, and the variance of each nonlinear trend would also be zero.

Let us consider the possible implications of the previous paragraph for the McCarthy data. Although our full model of three indicator variables and two Z variables is not mathematically wrong, we nevertheless might want to consider other models with a closer correspondence between the fixed and random effects. We obviously have two choices. One option would be to include additional random effects in the model. Alternatively, we could exclude certain fixed effects from the model. Although neither of these approaches is necessarily the "right" one, we will focus our attention on the second choice. However, before proceeding to illustrate it, we want to mention that readers should feel generally prepared already for embarking on the first approach. We have seen how to add a random linear effect to the model. Adding a random quadratic effect to the model follows the same basic logic. Of course, after having fit such a model, the researcher is once again confronted with the problem of choosing the best model for the data. The logic we developed for comparing competing models with and without a random slope effect continues to hold, although as the number of models under consideration increases, choosing a "best" model not surprisingly becomes increasingly more difficult.

Suppose we have decided to focus our attention on a model that includes a random intercept effect and a random slope effect (we will assume throughout our discussion that we have also chosen to include the covariance between these effects in our model, although the general logic that follows would still be applicable even if we were to omit the covariance). In this context, our primary goal is to investigate the polynomial trends of the fixed effects. We could potentially proceed in either of two ways. One possibility would follow from our decision to omit higher order trends (i.e., trends beyond the linear trend) from the random effects portion of the model. We might then decide a priori to include only a linear trend in the fixed effects portion of the model. The other option is to allow the full model to contain all possible trends, but to test each for significance expecting that all higher order trends may turn out to be nonsignificant. At this point we will illustrate the second approach, although we will eventually come back to further consideration of the first approach.

To illustrate the investigation of fixed trend effects, we will once again consider the Mc-Carthy data. Recall that our goal is to examine all possible fixed trend effects in a model that includes random intercept and slope effects. As usual, we will use SAS PROC MIXED to illustrate these analyses. The following command lines allow us to investigate the fixed trend effects:

```
proc mixed;
   class timecat;
   model iq=timecat / s ddfm=satterth;
   random int time/ subject=id type=un;
   contrast 'time main effect' timecat 1 −1 0 0, timecat 0 1 −1 0, timecat 0 0 1 −1;
   contrast 'time linear' timecat −3 −1 1 3;
   contrast 'time quad' timecat 1 −1 −1 1;
   contrast 'time cubic' timecat −1 3 −3 1;
```

With the exception of the new "contrast" lines, these commands are virtually identical to commands we have already seen. The only real change occurs in the "model" line, where we see a new option, namely, "ddfm=satterth." (The alert reader may notice that another difference from the most recent syntax we provided is that the "proc mixed" line does not contain "covtest" or "cl." We have chosen not to show them here, because their presence would simply result in duplicating output we have already seen.) This option instructs PROC MIXED to replace the default containment method of calculating degrees of freedom with an option based on theory developed by a statistician named Satterthwaite. We have chosen to illustrate this option here because it may be especially useful for tests of contrasts. The final four "contrast" lines instruct PROC MIXED to test (1) the time main effect, (2) the linear trend of time, (3) the quadratic trend of time, and (4) the cubic trend of time, respectively. Of course, we have already tested the main effect, but we have included it here to see how it can also be tested through a simultaneous test of $a − 1$ contrasts.

Table 15.5 shows an excerpt of the output that results from issuing these commands to PROC MIXED. The top part of the table shows that parameter estimates and estimated standard errors are the same as in Table 15.4, which they must be because the underlying models are identical to one another. The only difference between the values in the top parts of the table is that the t values and p values are slightly different, because of the different method that has been used to calculate degrees of freedom. Similarly, the "Type 3 Tests of Fixed Effects" of Tables 15.4 and 15.5 are virtually identical. Once again, the only difference is in denominator degrees of freedom, which results in a small difference in the corresponding p values.

The part of Table 15.5 of special interest is the section labeled "Contrasts." As we have already said, we did not really need to use a "contrast" statement to test the time main effect, but we have included it here simply to confirm that testing three polynomial trends simultaneously yields the same observed F value of 1.78 we have already seen. The remaining lines under

TABLE 15.5
MAXIMUM LIKELIHOOD CONTRAST ANALYSIS OF TABLE 15.1 DATA,
ALLOWING RANDOM SLOPE AS WELL AS RANDOM INTERCEPT

The Mixed Procedure

Solution for Fixed Effects

Effect	timecat	Estimate	Standard Error	DF	t Value	Pr > |t|
Intercept		112.00	4.2312	12.2	26.47	<.0001
timecat	0	−9.0000	4.0924	11.9	−2.20	0.0485
timecat	1	−5.0000	3.3030	22.4	−1.51	0.1440
timecat	2	−2.0000	2.7216	31.8	−0.73	0.4678
timecat	3	0	.	.	.	.

Type 3 Tests of Fixed Effects

Effect	Num DF	Den DF	F Value	Pr > F
timecat	3	19.4	1.78	0.1841

Contrasts

Label	Num DF	Den DF	F Value	Pr > F
time main effect	3	17.2	1.78	0.1885
time linear	1	11	5.02	0.0466
time quad	1	22	0.32	0.5770
time cubic	1	22	0.00	1.0000

"Contrast" provide us with new information about the McCarthy data. First, notice that the test of the linear trend is statistically significant (using a per-comparison alpha level of .05), as shown by an observed F value of 5.02, which with 1 numerator and 11 denominator degrees of freedom yields a p value of .0466. Neither the quadratic nor the cubic trends are statistically significant here.

We want to pause momentarily to make five related points. First, the F values and p values obtained for the fixed effect trends will, like the omnibus test, depend on how we decide to specify random effects in our model. For example, we would obtain different results if we included only a random intercept in our model. Second, if you happen to have a photographic memory and also happen to have worked Exercise 9 in Chapter 13, you may realize that you have already seen an F value of 5.02 and a p value of .0466 for the McCarthy data. These are precisely the values we would obtain if we tested the linear trend using the separate variance approach described in Chapter 13. Third, the F and p values shown for the quadratic and cubic trends in Table 15.5 will generally not be the same as those calculated in Exercise 9 of Chapter 13 (actually, for these data, the cubic trends are the same, because the numerator of the F ratio turns out to be exactly zero in these artificial data). Instead, when quadratic and cubic random effects are not included in the model, the error term used to test their corresponding fixed effects is a pooled average of the two effects. Fourth, if you were to omit the random slope effect from the model and test the linear trend, you would find an observed F value of 8.88, which with 3 numerator and 33 denominator degrees of freedom would yield a p value of .0054. This value turns out to be exactly the same as obtained in part f of Exercise 9 in Chapter 13, which asks you to test the linear trend using a pooled error term as described in Chapter 11. Fifth, after having seen this pattern of results, you will probably not be surprised to hear that there is a close relationship between the specification of random effects and corresponding error terms for testing fixed effects. In fact, we developed this principle back in Chapter 10. How we test an effect often depends on whether we regard the effect as fixed or random. Here we are seeing that using a pooled error term (as in Chapters 11 and 12) to test an effect is consistent with regarding that effect as fixed. On the other hand, using a separate error term (as in Chapters 13 and 14) is consistent with regarding that effect as random. Of course, the nice thing about using PROC MIXED or similar software to perform these tests is that it automatically chooses the proper error term, as long as we have been careful to specify the random effects we want to include in our model.[7]

We mentioned that if we have sufficient a priori theoretical reasons to expect only a linear trend among population means, an alternative full model would simply include only a linear trend among the fixed effects. Notice that all of the full models we have considered to this point for the McCarthy data allow each level of time to have its own population mean. In this respect, until now, all of our full models have been "cell means" models. However, as we initially suggested all the way back in Chapter 4, there are times where theory justifies the formation of planned comparisons, in which case our full model may contain only those effects we plan to test (see Appendix B for further discussion of formulation of full models). Following this logic, we could effectively omit quadratic and cubic trends from both the fixed and the random portions of the model. From another perspective, we might decide to fit a more parsimonious model to our data after having discovered that the quadratic and cubic fixed effects were nonsignificant. Of course, in this approach, we need to be sensitive to the possibility that we may have had insufficient power to detect these effects, especially if the sample size is as small as in our McCarthy data example. In any case, whether we planned to test the linear trend for theoretical reasons or chose to fit a more parsimonious model based on exploration of the data (or made this decision based on a combination of theory and data), we could write our full model simply as

$$Y_i = \beta_0 X_{0i} + \beta_1 X_{1i} + u_{1i} Z_{1i} + u_{2i} Z_{2i} + \varepsilon_i \tag{5}$$

The model includes two fixed effects and two random effects. In both cases, one effect is an intercept and the other is a slope. Specifically, β_0 is the population mean of the intercept, and u_{1i} represents the deviation from this mean for Individual i. Similarly, β_1 is the population mean slope, and u_{2i} is once again the deviation of Individual i from this mean. This formulation of a full model has an attractive feature we previously mentioned. Namely, this model assumes that those effects for which individuals may differ from one another are exactly the same effects whose average value may be different from zero. You should understand that this type of model is by no means restricted to intercepts and slopes. For example, we could easily include a fixed quadratic variable and a random quadratic variable in the model if we so desired. The distinguishing characteristic is that each fixed effect corresponds precisely to a random effect. Language can be confusing here. For example, suppose we include both a fixed linear effect and a random linear effect in a particular model. In this case, we would typically say that the linear effect is random, even though the model also allows this random effect to have a mean different from zero. Thus, saying that an effect is random does not preclude including a corresponding fixed effect in the same model. We typically would say that the linear effect is fixed in a model if we have included no random linear effect in the model. In general, models where each fixed effect is accompanied by a corresponding random effect are frequently referred to as "growth curve models." There is an entire literature on this type of model, one of whose most interesting features is that it forms a linkage between mixed models and structural equation (i.e., "LISREL") models. The interested reader is referred to Willett and Sayer (1994) for an introduction to this linkage.

TABLE 15.6

MAXIMUM LIKELIHOOD GROWTH CURVE ANALYSIS OF TABLE 15.1 DATA,
ALLOWING RANDOM SLOPE AS WELL AS RANDOM INTERCEPT

The Mixed Procedure

Solution for Fixed Effects

Effect	Estimate	Standard Error	DF	t Value	Pr > |t|
Intercept	103.50	4.0231	11	25.73	<.0001
time	0.5000	0.2231	11	2.24	0.0466

Type 3 Tests of Fixed Effects

Effect	Num DF	Den DF	F Value	Pr > F
time	1	11	5.02	0.0466

Covariance Parameter Estimates

Cov Parm	Subject	Estimate	Standard Error	Z Value	Pr Z	Alpha	Lower	Upper
UN(1,1)	id	169.85	83.1163	2.04	0.0205	0.05	78.5431	601.15
UN(2,1)	id	−3.3731	3.6296	−0.93	0.3527	0.05	−10.4870	3.7408
UN(2,2)	id	0.4037	0.2607	1.55	0.0607	0.05	0.1550	2.5632
Residual		34.8167	10.0507	3.46	0.0003	0.05	21.2275	67.3808

We can use PROC MIXED rather easily to fit the model shown in Equation 5 to the McCarthy data. An example of SAS code to accomplish this goal is given by

```
proc mixed covtest cl;
    model iq=time / s;
    random int time/ subject=id type=un gcorr;
```

The first and third lines are identical to command lines we have seen previously. Only the second line is different, because only the fixed effects portion of the model has been altered. Specifically, we now want to include the planned linear trend of time as a fixed effect, instead of including time as a categorical variable with four levels. This code sets up exactly this model, because "time" is not a "class" variable, in which case SAS interprets "time" as a continuous variable and includes its linear effect in the model.

Table 15.6 shows an excerpt of the output that results from applying this code to the McCarthy data. Not surprisingly, the significance test of the fixed linear effect is identical to the test of the linear trend contrast we saw in Table 15.5. Thus, it might seem that nothing at all is different about this new model formulation. However, comparing the models shown in Equations 4 and 5 reminds us that the fixed effect parameters are different in these two models. This difference is reflected in the "Solution for Fixed Effects" portion of Tables 15.5 and 15.6. Table 15.5 presents effects comparing all four time points to one another,[8] whereas Table 15.6 presents effects based on the intercept and slope parameters of the model shown in Equation 5. In particular, as we mentioned earlier, β_0 in the Equation 5 model is the population mean value of initial status (assuming we have coded time so that the value of zero corresponds to the first wave of observation). Similarly, β_1 is the population mean value of the slope of individuals' change in the dependent variable over time.

The potential advantage of the growth curve model is that the parameters of the model often directly correspond to our questions about change. For example, if we believe that each individual's change over time follows a straight line (except for errors, such as errors of measurement, and other nonsystematic distortions), we can use the information presented in Table 15.6 to better understand the nature of the change process. The table implies that our best guess about the population mean McCarthy score at 30 months is 103.50. Notice that this value is close to, but yet not identical to, the observed sample mean at 30 months, which was 103.00. Both estimates are based on models, but the two models are different from each other. The value of 103.00 is derived from a model that allows each time point to have its own population mean. In this case, the sample mean is the best estimate of the population mean. The value of 103.50, on the other hand, is derived from a model that stipulates that each individual's growth follows a straight line. If this more restricted model is in fact the true model for the population (or at least very close to the true model), our estimate of 103.50 will be more precise than our estimate of 103.00. On the other hand, if this model is not at all the true model, our estimate of 103.50 may be biased. Thus, in general, we cannot be certain which estimate is preferable. However, we will assume here that the straight line model has both theoretical and empirical support, and proceed to interpret its parameters.

Table 15.6 also shows us that the estimated value of the population mean slope parameter β_1 equals 0.50. Thus, our best guess is that the average child in this population gains 0.50 points per month on the dependent variable between the ages of 30 and 48 months. Of course, we need to realize that our estimated slope of 0.50 contains uncertainty. We can quantify this uncertainty through the estimated standard error shown in Table 15.6. For example, we might form a 95% confidence interval. The center of this interval will be the estimated value of the parameter. The endpoints will extend in each direction by an amount equal to the product of the estimated standard error times the appropriate critical value. We must find the critical t value for $\alpha = .05$ (two-tailed) and 11 df, which Appendix Table A.1 shows is 2.20. Carrying out the arithmetic shows us that the 95% confidence interval for the slope runs from 0.01 to 0.99. Notice that zero is not included in this interval, which is consistent with the p value below .05 in Table 15.6. However, the confidence interval underscores the high degree of uncertainty in our estimated rate of change. Although our best guess is that this rate equals 0.50 points per month, the confidence interval suggests that the population rate could be as low as 0.01 or as high as 0.99. Of course, the primary reason for such an imprecise confidence interval is probably the small sample size, although we will mention later in the chapter some aspects of the design itself that influence power and precision.

We have seen that one advantage of the growth curve model is that its parameters are often directly interpretable in terms of a plausible model of change. In particular, this model is based on a view that individuals may differ from one another in certain trends and that these differences then also manifest themselves across individuals as trends whose averages may differ from zero. This direct interpretation frequently also leads to further advantages in describing the data. In general, we can think of this description as similar to the typical need to describe effect size or magnitude of effect in other situations we have considered in the book. Although there are many different ways one might choose to describe the nature of change over time, we will illustrate two complementary graphs that we believe are often helpful in conveying a feel for model fit over and above the presentation of tables of numbers.

Graphical Representation of a Growth Curve Model

Figure 15.6 presents predicted trajectories for the McCarthy data based on the growth curve model of Equation 5. The trajectories shown here differ from any of those we have seen previously for full models in that each and every trajectory is assumed to be linear. In other

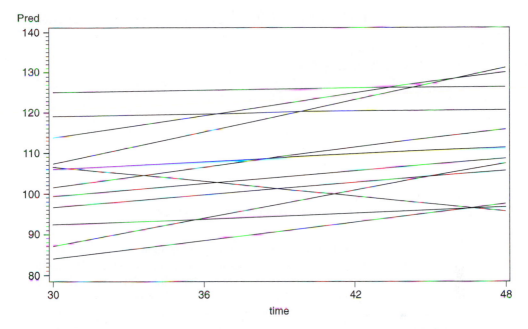

FIG. 15.6.   Fitted trajectory plots of McCarthy scores based on growth curve model.

words, each individual's change over time is assumed to be characterized in terms of two parameters, an intercept and a slope. Further, the figure shows that the model allows each individual to have his or her own value of both parameters.

Comparing Figure 15.6 to Figure 15.5 shows that they are very similar to one another. The only difference is that the trajectories in Figure 15.6 are literally straight lines, whereas those in Figure 15.5 are allowed to deviate from linearity. In the McCarthy data, however, these deviations are so small that even the trajectories of Figure 15.5 appear to be virtually linear. Notice that the small departures from linearity were confirmed in the contrast analyses shown in Table 15.5.

The growth curve model assumes that we can characterize change over time entirely through knowledge of each person's intercept and slope. Under this assumption, a different type of graphical representation from any we have so far encountered is frequently informative. If all of our model assumptions are correct, both the intercept and the slope have normal distributions (in fact, together they are assumed to have a bivariate normal distribution). We can use this assumption along with our parameter estimates to make interesting inferences about the population. The approach we will illustrate is equally applicable for either the intercept or the slope (or to both if we take a multivariate approach), but we will focus our attention on the slope, because often we are literally interested in change.

Assuming that individuals' slopes are in fact normally distributed, two parameters completely capture all of the information in the distribution: the mean and the standard deviation (or, equivalently, the mean and the variance). Notice from Table 15.6 that our best estimate of the population mean of the slope for the McCarthy data is 0.50. We can find our best estimate of the population variance of the slope in the "Estimate" column of "Covariance Parameter Estimates." The table shows that the estimated variance of the slope is 0.4037, which implies that the standard deviation is 0.64. Thus, our best estimate of the population distribution

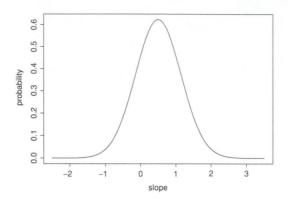

FIG. 15.7. Estimated population distribution of slopes based on growth curve model.

of individuals' slopes is a normal distribution with a mean of 0.50 and a standard deviation of 0.64. Such a summary can provide a very illuminating description of change. For example, Figure 15.7 provides a graphical representation of this distribution. This visual representation obviously provides a succinct description of patterns of change our model suggests for McCarthy scores in the population from which we have drawn our random sample. Depending on the situation, we might supplement such a figure with further numerical calculations. One statistic that might be of particular interest is our estimate of the percentage of children whose scores are increasing. More formally, we could state this as the proportion of scores greater than zero in a normal distribution with a mean of 0.50 and a standard deviation of 0.64. A raw score of 0 in this distribution translates into a z score of -0.78, and by consulting a table of the normal distribution we learn that 78% of scores lie above a z score of -0.78 (notice that the correspondence of the percentage with the z score is a coincidence and not a reflection of some general equality). Thus, our best estimate is that 78% of children in this population will show some increase in scores between the ages of 30 and 48 months, whereas 22% will show a decline. Notice further that the average child is expected to show an increase of 0.50 points per month, equivalent to a gain of 9 points between 30 and 48 months. Of course, there are yet other ways we could characterize rate of growth from these data. Our point is to give you a flavor of the possibilities, but the precise choices depend on what types of statements are of greatest theoretical and practical interest in the researcher's specific situation.

Design Considerations

The primary focus of this chapter is on data analysis. However, we take a brief detour at this moment to point out a special design issue in growth curve modeling. Issues of longitudinal design involve a host of various issues, most of which we cannot even touch on in this presentation. Nevertheless, we believe it is important to highlight one specific issue that can prove to be crucial in growth curve modeling.

Suppose we have decided a priori to perform a growth curve analysis of data we plan to collect. In other words, the model to be fit to the data will have the same number of fixed and random trend effects. In the simplest case, we might fit just a fixed and random slope, but more generally we might contemplate including higher order trends in the model as well. For example, suppose we are especially interested in examining fixed and random quadratic effects in the data we plan to collect.

The critical point we need to make here is that the number of time points in the design needs to be large enough to allow investigation of the effects of possible interest. For example, it should be obvious that if our design has only two time points, we will not be able to examine possible quadratic effects, because a straight line will necessarily suffice to explain change between two time points. Notice that we are not saying that the true pattern of change in this instance is necessarily linear, but instead that the design would not allow us to assess the need to add nonlinear trends to our model.

Less obvious is that when random as well as fixed trends are included in the model, we generally need two more time points than the order of the highest trend. For example, consider a purely linear model. At first glance, two time points would seem sufficient for fitting this model to data, but our rule suggests we need three time points. We can understand the reason for needing three time points by remembering that the inclusion of a random slope (as well as random intercept) in the model allows each individual to have his or her own regression line. If we have only two time points, each person's regression line will fit his or her observed data perfectly, in which case we cannot separate the true effect of slope differences from actual error. In order to obtain a separate estimate of the error in the model, we need to have a third data point for each participant.[9]

This same basic logic holds if we contemplate fitting a model with higher order trends. For example, a model with fixed and random intercept, linear, and quadratic terms would necessarily provide a perfect explanation of every individual's data for three time points. Thus, if the research question calls for a quadratic model, the design should have at least four time points, unless the researcher is willing to assume that the quadratic effect is entirely fixed, that is, every individual has the same value of the quadratic effect, in which case the variance of the quadratic effect is zero. Thus, in general, a model with linear fixed and random effects requires three time points, a model with quadratic fixed and random effects requires four time points, a model with cubic fixed and random effects requires five time points, and so forth.

It is essential to understand that the aforementioned requirements stipulate the mathematical minimum number of time points. This does not necessarily mean that a design with three time points is sufficient for modeling random slopes, because the requirements have not taken statistical power and precision into account. As of this writing, power analysis for mixed models is just beginning to receive serious consideration from statisticians, so it is difficult to provide definitive guidelines. Most of the work to date in this area is based on a model that assumes that all effects beyond the slope and the intercept are nonexistent. In this case, two aspects of the design can have a strong influence on power. First, power increases as the number of time points in the design increases. Second, the duration of the study has an even greater influence on power than the number of time points. As long as the assumed model is true (or at least approximately true), lengthening the duration of the study often has a sizable effect on power and precision. For example, in the hypothetical McCarthy study we have discussed throughout this chapter, if change is truly linear, power would have been much less if the study had been designed to assess children at 30, 31, 32, and 33 months of age instead of 30, 36, 42, and 48 months of age. The greater power and precision that come from extending the duration of the study frequently presents a trade-off between power and the patience of the researcher. We do not presume that we can offer rules for resolving this trade-off, but we believe it is essential for researchers to understand the nature of the trade-off. Equally essential is to realize that this trade-off occurs under the assumption that the growth curve model is the correct model, and further, that the form of growth is linear. In some situations, the growth curve model may not be the correct model, or even if it is, growth may not be linear. When these assumptions no longer hold, rules and guidelines for study design may be different. Readers are referred to Willett (1989); Willett, Singer, and Martin (1998); Overall (1996); and Maxwell (1998) for examples of methodological studies that have addressed these general issues.

AN ALTERNATIVE TO THE RANDOM
EFFECTS MODEL

As we pointed out earlier, the models we have considered so far in this chapter are extensions of the mixed models we presented in Chapters 11 and 12. It turns out that the maximum likelihood approach also provides extensions to the multivariate models we presented in Chapters 13 and 14. We now turn our attention toward these extensions of the multivariate models. Once again, our presentation is intended to concentrate on concepts. We will use SAS PROC MIXED to illustrate these concepts and will largely forego any attempt to provide mathematical details. We should also note that we will focus on applications of these extensions to longitudinal data, for much the same reason that this was our focus for random effects models. However, it is important to realize that the concepts we develop here for the extensions may also prove to be useful when the within-subjects factor represents an effect other than time, such as experimental condition.

We mentioned earlier in the chapter that there are two potentially distinct reasons for formulating a random effects model. First, in some situations theoretical considerations lead to a model based on individual random effects, such as random slopes and intercepts. In these circumstances, a researcher may be as interested in what can be learned about the random effects as in learning about the fixed effects. Second, in other situations there is little or no direct interest in the random effects themselves. The interest lies almost exclusively in the fixed effects, but random effects are included in the model so as to accommodate likely correlations that will occur from measuring the same individual multiple times. Especially in this second type of situation, an alternative to the random effects model exists. In fact, we have already seen one such alternative, namely, the multivariate approach of Chapters 13 and 14.

The multivariate approach to repeated measures is like the random effects model in that both are able to accommodate correlated data. However, they differ in their basic philosophy. The random effects model does not directly model any correlational structure, but instead specifies certain random effects. The specification of these effects then implies (or induces, it is sometimes said) a corresponding correlational structure. The multivariate approach, on the other hand, directly specifies a correlational structure for the data. In fact, as we saw in Chapters 13 and 14, the multivariate approach includes a parameter for each observed covariance, so no assumptions need be made about the pattern of variances or correlations over time (keep in mind, however, that the multivariate approach does assume that whatever the pattern is, it is equal across levels of any between-subjects factors).

The point of view we espoused in Chapters 13 and 14 was that the multivariate approach has much to recommend it, precisely because it makes no assumptions about variances or correlations over time. We have not changed our minds since the last two chapters, but at this point it is important to delve into some possible limitations of the multivariate approach. First and most obvious is that the multivariate approach requires complete data. Any individual who is missing one or more observations must be excluded from the analysis. Although this may not pose a serious problem when the within-subjects factor is an experimental manipulation, it frequently becomes a problem when the within-subjects factor is time. In any event, missing data not only lower power and decrease precision, but also can create biased parameter estimates. Second, even when no data are missing, a possible disadvantage of the multivariate approach is that it requires a separate estimate for each variance and correlation. For example, with a levels of the within-subjects factor, a total of $a(a + 1)/2$ such parameters must be estimated. Of these, a are variances, and $a(a - 1)/2$ are correlations. The necessity to estimate parameters separately can be costly in terms of power, especially when a is large or sample size is small.

We will see momentarily that extensions to the multivariate approach allow a compromise, where variances and correlations may be allowed to differ, but without necessarily specifying a unique value for each.

These extensions, like the random effects models we have considered earlier in the chapter, are based on maximum likelihood. As usual, a full model is formed and compared to a restricted model. However, neither the full model nor the restricted model contains random effects parameters. Instead, new parameters are introduced to model the correlations among observations directly. The general form of these models looks identical to the form we have presented for the general linear fixed effects model:

$$Y_i = \beta_0 X_{0i} + \beta_1 X_{1i} + \beta_2 X_{2i} + \beta_3 X_{3i} + \cdots + \beta_p X_{pi} + \varepsilon_i \qquad \text{(3.1, repeated)}$$

Often the X variables in Equation 3.1 will all be indicator variables, in which case we could write the model more simply. For example, if the design has only a single within-subjects factor, we could write the full model as

$$\text{Full model:} \quad Y_{ij} = \mu + \alpha_j + \varepsilon_{ij} \qquad (6)$$

or equivalently, as

$$\text{Full model:} \quad Y_{ij} = \mu_j + \varepsilon_{ij} \qquad (7)$$

In either case, the full model would be compared to a restricted model of the form

$$\text{Restricted model:} \quad Y_{ij} = \mu + \varepsilon_{ij} \qquad (8)$$

So far these models appear identical to the between-subjects models we developed in Chapters 3 through 9. You may recall that an important assumption of those models was that the errors must all be uncorrelated with one another. Such an assumption is unlikely to be valid in within-subjects designs, so we must almost always include additional model parameters to allow for some type of correlations in within-subjects designs.

The maximum likelihood approach is based on the models shown in Equations 3.1, 6, 7, and 8, where those models are understood also to include additional parameters that specify the correlational structure for the errors of the model. In other words, we will now explicitly acknowledge that in a within-subjects design with a levels, the errors of the model are likely to correlate with one another. (For a reminder that shows the presence of such correlations, you may want to look back at "The Problem of Correlated Errors" section near the beginning of Chapter 11). Specifically, with a levels, there will be a total of $a(a-1)/2$ correlations. Further, whereas in a between-subjects design we often assume by default that the errors are equally variable, we may want to allow errors to have different variances at different levels of a within-subjects factor.

To make our discussion a little less abstract, we will return to the McCarthy data. Suppose we were to fit a full model of the form of Equations 3.1, 6, or 7 to these data. Regardless of how we write the model, what is important for our purposes here is that the model will include a separate parameter for each time of measurement. The predicted scores will simply be the sample means, which as we have seen are 103, 107, 110, and 112 for these data. Table 15.7 shows the errors obtained from fitting the full model to the data. Notice that each value in the table is simply the difference between the original score shown in Table 15.1 and the corresponding sample mean.

TABLE 15.7
ERRORS FROM FITTING FIXED CELL
MEANS MODEL TO TABLE 15.1 DATA

	Age (Months)			
Subject	30	36	42	48
1	5	−11	0	10
2	0	10	17	21
3	−7	0	−4	−5
4	−19	−22	−18	−13
5	15	18	15	4
6	7	0	−14	−21
7	26	21	13	16
8	−13	−23	−9	1
9	−19	−3	−10	−24
10	−7	−7	−7	−7
11	2	7	−5	0
12	10	10	22	18

TABLE 15.8
COVARIANCE MATRIX FOR ERRORS SHOWN IN TABLE 15.7

	Age (Months)			
Age (Months)	30	36	42	48
30	188.00	154.36	127.36	121.18
36	154.36	200.55	143.64	97.45
42	127.36	143.64	178.00	168.09
48	121.18	97.45	168.09	218.00

No further complications would ensue if the errors shown in Table 15.7 obeyed two properties: (1) each column of scores is equally variable, and (2) scores in any pair of columns are uncorrelated with one another. Not surprisingly, at least the latter of these properties is unlikely to hold in within-subjects designs (it is more likely although by no means guaranteed that the errors may be equally variable). Even a casual glance at Table 15.7 suggests that scores in one column are in reality related to scores in other columns. For example, participants with negative errors in one column (such as participants 3, 4, 8, 9, and 10) appear likely to have negative errors in other columns as well. Correspondingly, participants with positive errors in one column (such as participants 2, 5, 7, and 12) tend to have positive errors in other columns as well.

More formally, Table 15.8 shows the 4×4 covariance matrix based on the errors of Table 15.7. In order to use the full models of Equations 3.1, 6, and 7 with no further consideration, we would have to assume that (1) any discrepancies in the four diagonal values (i.e., 188.00, 200.55, 178.00, and 218.00) reflect sampling error, and (2) all remaining values (i.e., all values not on the diagonal of the matrix) would be exactly zero except for any influence of sampling error. Although we might be able to garner support for the first assumption, the second appears blatantly false. Notice that the off-diagonal covariance terms would be zero only if there were no systematic differences of any type between individuals, because the covariance between any pair of errors is exactly equal here to the covariance between the same pair of original scores as shown in Table 15.1.[10] However, the trajectories we saw earlier in

TABLE 15.9
CORRELATION MATRIX FOR ERRORS
SHOWN IN TABLE 15.7

	Age (Months)			
Age (Months)	30	36	42	48
30	1.000	.795	.696	.599
36	.795	1.000	.760	.466
42	.696	.760	1.000	.853
48	.599	.466	.853	1.000

Figure 15.2 strongly suggest that children have different trajectories, producing relationships between scores measured at different points in time. Table 15.9 shows these relationships expressed as correlations. No new information is contained in the correlations, because they can be calculated directly from the covariances shown in Table 15.8. Nevertheless, we present them here for two reasons: (1) They provide a more intuitive feel for the pattern of relationships between scores across time than do the covariances, and (2) one of the methods we will consider momentarily is easier to understand in terms of correlations than in terms of covariances.

The point of all this is actually rather simple. We must introduce a mechanism for allowing the errors of our full model to correlate with one another. We have already seen that one way of accomplishing this goal is to specify random effects, such as random intercepts and slopes. By allowing different participants to have different trajectories, we are indirectly allowing scores to correlate over time. Although specifying random effects is one way of allowing for correlations, at this point we want to consider a more direct alternative, where we directly specify the type of covariance structure we believe to be appropriate for our data. This proves to be very straightforward with the appropriate software (once we have decided what type of structure to specify—we will come back to further consideration of this decision shortly). For example, SAS PROC MIXED provides a "repeated" statement that allows direct specification of a certain structure for the covariances of the errors in a model. Thus, combining a "repeated" statement with a "model" statement accommodates correlated errors in the fixed effects specified by the "model" statement. We will consider several examples of "repeated" statements for the McCarthy data. At the risk of being repetitive, we will mention that the same input data set is used here as was used by the random effects models. Thus, the data steps in our case are given by

```
data new;
    input id timecat iq;
    cards;
[48 lines of data follow, 1 for each combination of subject and time]
```

These data definition lines are followed by syntax for PROC MIXED. The precise form of that syntax is determined by what type of structure we wish to specify for the covariance matrix. The most general possibility, as it turns out, is not to constrain the structure, but instead let it be determined entirely by the data (hopefully this sounds familiar—we will return to this possibility momentarily). In general, then, with a levels of the within-subjects factor, we would specify $a(a + 1)/2$ parameters for the covariance matrix.

The following four lines of PROC MIXED code specify a "cell means" model for fixed effects and an unconstrained model for correlated errors:

```
proc mixed;
   class timecat;
   model iq=timecat / s;
   repeated/ subject=id type=un hlm hlps rcorr;
```

Notice that the first three lines are identical to lines we have seen earlier when we specified a random effects model analysis of these data. Thus, the only difference in the commands is that a "repeated" statement has replaced the "random" statement we used earlier. As with the random statement, the presence of "subject=id" simply informs the program that the variable "id" designates the participants for whom we expect data to be correlated. The "type" option allows us to specify the precise structure we want to fit to the errors of the model. Specifying "un" means that we want to fit an "unstructured" matrix to the errors. In other words, by specifying "type=un" we are not imposing any specific type of structure on the data. Instead, we are allowing a separate parameter for each and every one of the $a(a + 1)/2$ elements of the covariance matrix. The "rcorr" option simply prints the estimated value of each of these $a(a + 1)/2$ elements as a correlation (specifying "r" prints each element of the covariance matrix, but we have chosen to show "rcorr" here because the correlations are usually more easily interpreted than the covariances). We will defer discussion of the final options listed here, "hlm," and "hlps," until we consider interpretation of the output from the model.

Table 15.10 shows an excerpt of the output produced by these command lines. As usual, near the top of the table are estimates of the fixed effects. As before, the estimates from this model are identical to those we have seen for all other equivalent fixed full models, although keep in mind that such equalities will generally not occur except in the special case of a balanced design such as we have here. Further notice that the standard errors of the estimates are somewhat different from those we have seen for other models, because we are now specifying a different error structure for the data.

The next section of the table shows three tests of the omnibus null hypothesis. Is there evidence in these data that population mean McCarthy scores change over time? Or, stated another way, how do the following pair of models compare to one another

$$\text{Full model:} \quad Y_{ij} = \mu_j + \varepsilon_{ij} \qquad\qquad (7, \text{repeated})$$
$$\text{Restricted model:} \quad Y_{ij} = \mu + \varepsilon_{ij} \qquad\qquad (8, \text{repeated})$$

where μ_j is the population mean at Time j. Also, we should keep in mind that we have allowed the error terms ε_{ij} to correlate in an unstructured manner. The first of the three tests shown in the table is (as of this writing) the default for PROC MIXED, and yields an F value of 2.74 for the model comparison. With 3 numerator and 11 denominator degrees of freedom, the associated p value is .0941, so we cannot reject the null hypothesis at the .05 level. The second and third tests are identical to each other here (because we have balanced data), and appear on the printout because we specified "hlm" and "hlps" options on the "repeated" line and (by the way, the acronym "hlm" here derives not from "hierarchical linear modeling," but instead from the first initials of the three statisticians on whose work this test statistic is based). In the special case of an unstructured covariance matrix, PROC MIXED is able to perform a more accurate calculation of the denominator degrees of freedom than is generally available through the default method. Notice that the denominator degrees of freedom for the Hotelling–Lawley–McKeon and Hotelling–Lawley–Pillai–Samson Statistics equal 9 instead of 11. This discrepancy also explains the difference in the F values themselves, because the F value of 2.74 obtained with the default method is simply 11/9 times the value of 2.24 obtained from both of the other methods. The bottom line is that with an unstructured covariance matrix,

TABLE 15.10
MAXIMUM LIKELIHOOD ANALYSIS OF TABLE 15.1 DATA, ALLOWING
UNSTRUCTURED COVARIANCE MATRIX

The Mixed Procedure

Solution for Fixed Effects

Effect	timecat	Estimate	Standard Error	DF	t Value	Pr > |t|
Intercept		112.00	4.2622	11	26.28	<.0001
timecat	0	−9.0000	3.6927	11	−2.44	0.0330
timecat	1	−5.0000	4.3170	11	−1.16	0.2713
timecat	2	−2.0000	2.2327	11	−0.90	0.3895
timecat	3	0	.	.	.	.

Type 3 Tests of Fixed Effects

Effect	Num DF	Den DF	F Value	Pr > F
timecat	3	11	2.74	0.0941

Type 3 Hotelling–Lawley–McKeon Statistics

Effect	Num DF	Den DF	F Value	Pr > F
timecat	3	9	2.24	0.1528

Type 3 Hotelling–Lawley–Pillai–Samson

Statistics

Effect	Num DF	Den DF	F Value	Pr > F
timecat	3	9	2.24	0.1528

Covariance Parameter Estimates

Cov Parm	Subject	Estimate
UN(1,1)	id	188.00
UN(2,1)	id	154.36
UN(2,2)	id	200.55
UN(3,1)	id	127.36
UN(3,2)	id	143.64
UN(3,3)	id	178.00
UN(4,1)	id	121.18
UN(4,2)	id	97.45
UN(4,3)	id	168.09
UN(4,4)	id	218.00

Estimated R Correlation Matrix for Subject 1

Row	Col1	Col2	Col3	Col4
1	1.0000	0.7950	0.6962	0.5986
2	0.7950	1.0000	0.7602	0.4661
3	0.6962	0.7602	1.0000	0.8533
4	0.5986	0.4661	0.8533	1.0000

the tests obtained with the "hlm" and "hlps" options are likely to be more accurate than the default test, so we will focus our interpretation on these methods.

The F values obtained with the Hotelling–Lawley–McKeon and Hotelling–Lawley–Pillai–Samson approaches both equal 2.24. With 3 numerator and 9 denominator degrees of freedom, the corresponding p value is .1528. Thus, under the assumption of an unstructured covariance matrix for the errors, we are unable to reject the null hypothesis at the .05 level. There are three further issues we need to consider at this point: (1) What are the covariance estimates from this model? (2) What are the estimated correlations from this model? (3) Have we seen an F value of 2.24 and a p value of .1528 somewhere else for these data?

We will begin by considering the covariance estimates for the model, which appear near the bottom of Table 15.10. Ten values appear here, one for each element of the 4×4 covariance matrix. Comparison of these 10 values quickly reveals that they are identical to the values we saw in Table 15.8 for the covariance matrix of the errors from Table 15.7. Indeed, this is precisely what it means to have specified an "unstructured" covariance matrix for the errors. Instead of imposing some theoretical structure on the errors, we have allowed each element of the matrix to be represented by its own parameter, which is why each of the 10 sample values is perfectly duplicated by the model estimate. The good news is that we have perfectly represented the 10 elements of the covariance matrix. Thus, we can be assured in this sense that our test of fixed effects has in fact accommodated the correlated nature of our data. However, the bad news is that it took us 10 parameters to create this perfect representation. Perhaps we could do essentially as well with fewer parameters. We will return to this possibility shortly, but for now we will address our other remaining questions.

The last section of Table 15.10 displays estimated correlations from our model. Given that we just saw that the estimated covariances from our model are identical to the sample covariances in the data, it may not surprise you to learn that the exact same relationship holds for correlations as well. In particular, the correlations shown in Table 15.10 are identical (within rounding error) to the correlations we saw earlier in Table 15.9. Once again, this equivalence will always hold when we specify an unstructured covariance matrix, as we have done in our SAS syntax.

Have we seen an F value of 2.24 and a p value of .1528 for these data somewhere else? You can probably guess that we have, or else we would not have raised the question. But where? The answer is back in Chapter 13. The multivariate approach to repeated measures of the McCarthy data yielded the same F and p values as we have obtained by specifying an unstructured covariance matrix in PROC MIXED.[11] We need to deal with three related issues at this point: (1) Why are the F and p values the same here? (2) Will the F and p values always be the same? (3) Are there any advantages to the PROC MIXED approach, and if so, what are they?

First, the F and p values are the same here because in both cases we have allowed the covariance matrix of the errors to be completely unstructured. Both approaches have devoted 10 parameters to the 10 distinct elements of the 4×4 covariance matrix. In other words, neither approach has imposed a specific structure on the errors, but instead both have allowed each separate aspect of the error covariance matrix to be estimated by its own parameter.

Second, the two approaches will produce identical F and p values if and only if we have balanced data. Recall that "balanced" means that every participant is observed at the same time points, and no data are missing. If either of these conditions is not met, the two approaches will generally differ from one another. Specifically, when participants are measured at different times or if data are missing (whether or not participants are measured at the same times), parameter estimates, standard errors, confidence intervals, and hypothesis tests will generally be different for the two approaches.

Third, the maximum likelihood mixed model approach can have important advantages over the multivariate approach of Chapters 13 and 14 when data are missing. Longitudinal studies often suffer from missing data, especially when the design is stretched over a period of months or even years. A serious limitation of the multivariate approach to repeated measures is that it requires complete data from every participant. Any individual who is missing even a single score must be discarded from the analysis. This obviously lowers statistical power and precision by lowering the sample size. Further, results can be biased unless data are missing completely at random, which essentially means that factors responsible for missingness are entirely unrelated to the dependent variable. Fortunately, the maximum likelihood mixed model offers advantages over the multivariate approach in both respects. This advantage accrues because the mixed model does not require complete data. Instead, as many observations as are available for any individual are entered into the analysis. For example, when $a = 4$, some individuals may have been observed at only 1, 2, or 3 occasions. Their scores are simply entered into the analysis along with individuals without missing data. Thus, the mixed model will typically provide greater power and precision than the multivariate approach when some data are missing. The mixed model approach also requires a less stringent assumption about missingness than does the multivariate approach. Specifically, the mixed model approach assumes that all factors that contribute to missingness are captured by observed scores. We will say more later in the chapter about this assumption, often called "missing at random" as opposed to "missing completely at random."

In summary, specifying an unstructured covariance matrix for the errors in a mixed model analysis of within-subjects data is closely related to the multivariate approach to within-subjects data we presented in Chapters 13 and 14. In particular, the mixed model analysis can be regarded as an extension of the multivariate approach. When all participants are measured at the same time points and no data are missing, the two approaches are mathematically equivalent. However, the mixed model analysis is more general than the multivariate approach in that it accommodates missing data without having to exclude all participants for whom complete data are not available. Thus, the mixed model approach is especially useful for studies with missing data. This advantage applies not just in longitudinal designs, but also in other types of within-subjects designs that may be susceptible to missing data.

Additional Covariance Matrix Structures

More generally, the mixed model approach can be useful even when no data are missing. The reason is that the mixed model approach allows you to consider error covariance matrix structures beyond an unstructured form. In fact, PROC MIXED allows you to choose from over two dozen possible forms of the covariance matrix. We make no attempt to provide complete coverage of these choices here, but instead will illustrate two alternatives to the unstructured specification. Readers who are interested in learning about the range of possible choices are advised to consult SAS documentation.

You may recall that we specified an unstructured covariance matrix in PROC MIXED through the TYPE option in the REPEATED command. We can specify a different structure simply by replacing *un* with a different key word. We will illustrate two alternatives here: "cs" for compound symmetry, and "ar(1)" for an autoregressive structure.

Suppose we had a theoretical basis for expecting the population covariance matrix of residuals to exhibit compound symmetry. Recall that a covariance matrix possesses compound symmetry when: (1) all variances equal a common value and (2) all covariances equal a common value. We can use PROC MIXED to fit a model to our data where we constrain the covariance matrix for the errors of the model to display compound symmetry. In the case of a

TABLE 15.11

MAXIMUM LIKELIHOOD ANALYSIS OF TABLE 15.1 DATA, SPECIFYING
COMPOUND SYMMETRY STRUCTURE

The Mixed Procedure

Solution for Fixed Effects

Effect	timecat	Estimate	Standard Error	DF	t Value	Pr > |t|
Intercept		112.00	4.0429	11	27.70	<.0001
timecat	0	−9.0000	3.1830	33	−2.83	0.0079
timecat	1	−5.0000	3.1830	33	−1.57	0.1258
timecat	2	−2.0000	3.1830	33	−0.63	0.5341
timecat	3	0	.	.	.	.

Type 3 Tests of Fixed Effects

Effect	Num DF	Den DF	F Value	Pr > F
timecat	3	33	3.03	0.0432

Covariance Parameter Estimates

Cov Parm	Subject	Estimate
CS	id	135.35
Residual		60.7879

Estimated R Correlation Matrix for Subject 1

Row	Col1	Col2	Col3	Col4
1	1.0000	0.6901	0.6901	0.6901
2	0.6901	1.0000	0.6901	0.6901
3	0.6901	0.6901	1.0000	0.6901
4	0.6901	0.6901	0.6901	1.0000

single factor design, we are still comparing the following pair of models:

$$\text{Full model:} \quad Y_{ij} = \mu_j + \varepsilon_{ij} \qquad \text{(7, repeated)}$$
$$\text{Restricted model:} \quad Y_{ij} = \mu + \varepsilon_{ij} \qquad \text{(8, repeated)}$$

However, we are now conducting a comparison of these models under an assumption that the errors of the full model can be described in terms of a covariance matrix that obeys compound symmetry. We can incorporate this assumption in PROC MIXED by replacing the previous REPEATED statement with a slightly different REPEATED statement:

repeated/subject=id type=cs rcorr;

Here, not surprisingly, the "cs" designation for "type" implies compound symmetry.

Table 15.11 shows an excerpt of the output produced by using PROC MIXED to fit a model with compound symmetry to the McCarthy data. Notice that the model comparison under an assumption of compound symmetry yields an F value of 3.03, which implies a p value of .0432. This pair of F and p values may sound familiar by now. In fact, more generally, this entire table is literally identical (except for one minor change in notation) to a table we have already seen. Specifically, if you go back through the previous tables in this chapter, you will discover that Table 15.11 is indistinguishable from Table 15.3. The reason for this equivalence is that, as we discussed at length earlier in the chapter, a model with a single random intercept term imposes compound symmetry on the covariance matrix. Thus, there are two seemingly different but ultimately equivalent ways of imposing compound symmetry: (1) directly on the matrix itself, as with the "repeated" statement in PROC MIXED, or (2) indirectly, by specifying a single random intercept effect, as with a "random" statement in PROC MIXED. The end result is the same either way. As an aside, notice that by specifying "rcorr" in our syntax, the output as shown in Table 15.11 also provides the estimated correlation matrix from our model. The table shows that our model estimates the correlation between any two time points to equal 0.69. The reason every correlation is estimated to be the same value is that we have imposed a compound symmetry structure on our data.

Of course, we have maintained a view that the compound symmetry structure is likely to be implausible in most longitudinal research in the behavioral sciences. For example, the correlations we saw earlier in Table 15.9 suggest a pattern rather different from that imposed by the compound symmetry assumption. In other words, the actual correlations shown in Table 15.9 appear systematically different from the Table 15.11 correlations estimated by the compound symmetry model for these data. Nevertheless, it may represent a more reasonable assumption in other types of within-subjects designs, such as designs where levels represent different treatment manipulations. Partly for this reason and partly for purely pedagogical reasons, we will consider one more aspect of the compound symmetry model. In particular, we want to call your attention to the relationship between the covariance matrix shown in Table 15.8 and the covariance parameter estimates produced by the compound symmetry model. Suppose we were to suspend our skepticism and assume that compound symmetry is truly a correct assumption for our McCarthy data. If the assumption is true, two things are necessarily true in the population: (1) all diagonal elements of the covariance matrix equal one another and (2) all off-diagonal elements of the covariance matrix equal one another. Thus, we should be able to describe the population covariance matrix with only 2 parameters, as opposed to the 10 parameters of the unrestricted model. Of course, when we look at the elements of the matrix shown in Table 15.8, each value is different from any other value. However, it is possible that these differences merely reflect sampling error. If we were to observe a larger sample, perhaps all of the diagonal elements would converge toward a single common value, whereas at the same time all of the off-diagonal elements would also converge toward their own common value. Based on the data we have obtained from only 12 participants, what would be our best guess of these two common values? A reasonable guess would be the sample mean of the values we have actually observed, and indeed this turns out to be precisely what happens in the model that imposes compound symmetry on the data. For example, the mean of the four diagonal elements (188.00, 200.55, 178.00, and 218.00) shown in Table 15.8 is 196.14. The corresponding mean for the off-diagonal elements is 135.35.

Two points are pertinent here. First, how do these means of 196.14 and 135.35 compare to values we obtained imposing compound symmetry on the data? Notice in Table 15.11 that the parameter estimate attributed to participants is 135.35. This value is the estimated covariance between scores, which results in this model from the fact that we have allowed each participant to have his or her own intercept. In addition, the sum of 135.35 and 60.7879 equals 196.14, which is the mean diagonal element in the covariance matrix.[12] Thus, the residual in the model is the variance attributable to error over and above the variance that results from individual differences between participants. Second, it is important to reiterate that the compound symmetry model assumes that only two parameters are necessary to explain the pattern of variances and covariances in the covariance matrix. If this assumption is valid, power and precision are enhanced, because we have reduced the number of parameters we must estimate. However, if the assumption is false, we have emphasized earlier in this chapter as well as in Chapters 11 through 14 that we cannot trust interpretation of hypothesis tests and confidence intervals in this model, because they are not robust to violations of this assumption.

We have now seen how we can impose compound symmetry on the error covariance matrix of our model. However, this structure typically is not plausible in longitudinal data, because it assumes equal correlations for all pairs of time points. In most longitudinal data, pairs closer together in time will tend to correlate more highly than pairs farther apart in time. There are a variety of ways of specifying this general type of structure in mixed model analysis. We have chosen to illustrate what is arguably the most popular example here, an autoregressive model, which assumes that an individual's score at any given time point depends entirely on his or her score at previous times plus a random error component. Specifically, we will consider a first-order autoregressive model, which assumes that a person's score at any time point depends only on their score at the immediately prior time point plus error. In contrast, a second-order autoregressive model would assume that scores at any time point depend only on scores at the two immediately prior time points plus error. We should also mention that the autoregressive model we consider here assumes that variances are equal over time, but variations of the model are available that allow variances to change over time. Complete consideration of autoregressive models is beyond the scope of our presentation, but Campbell and Kenny (1999) provide an excellent and very readable presentation of these methods.

Suppose yet again that we wish to test a null hypothesis that population mean McCarthy scores are equal over time. As before, we can conceptualize this test as a comparison of

$$\text{Full model:} \quad Y_{ij} = \mu_j + \varepsilon_{ij} \qquad\qquad (7, \text{repeated})$$
$$\text{Restricted model:} \quad Y_{ij} = \mu + \varepsilon_{ij} \qquad\qquad (8, \text{repeated})$$

where μ_j is the population mean at Time j. However, we now want to compare these models under an assumption that the errors of the full model follow an autoregressive structure. We can perform this test using PROC MIXED once again with a slightly different REPEATED statement:

```
repeated/subject=id type=ar(1) rcorr;
```

Where, not surprisingly, the "ar(1)" designation for "type" implies a first-order autoregressive structure.

Table 15.12 shows an excerpt of the output produced by using PROC MIXED to fit a first-order autoregressive model to the McCarthy data. Because this is a balanced data set, the estimates for the fixed effects are once again identical to those we have seen several times before, but as has also happened each time, the standard errors are now different. Of most interest, the model comparison has yielded an F value of 1.80, which implies a p value of 0.17. Thus, for these data the autoregressive model agrees with the unstructured model (but disagrees with the compound symmetry model) that the null hypothesis should not be rejected at the .05 level. Notice that the estimate of the autoregressive parameter is .81 (i.e., .8064, rounded to two decimal places). Our best estimate from the model is that scores from any pair of adjacent time points should correlate .81, scores separated by two time points should correlate .65 (i.e., .8064 squared), and scores separated by three time points should correlate .52 (i.e., .8064 cubed). Notice that these are indeed the estimated values of the correlations (within rounding error) shown in Table 15.12 as a result of the "rcorr" option in our syntax. Thus, this model assumes that the departures from these values shown in the actual data (see Table 15.9) reflect sampling error. Notice that these estimates conflict with those implicit in the compound symmetry model, which would assume a common correlation for any pair of scores. In particular, for the McCarthy data, the compound symmetry model estimates this common correlation to be .69, as we saw in Table 15.11.

TABLE 15.12
MAXIMUM LIKELIHOOD ANALYSIS OF TABLE 15.1 DATA, SPECIFYING
AUTOREGRESSIVE STRUCTURE

The Mixed Procedure

Solution for Fixed Effects

Effect	timecat	Estimate	Standard Error	DF	t Value	Pr > |t|
Intercept		112.00	4.0768	11	27.47	<.0001
timecat	0	−9.0000	3.9761	33	−2.26	0.0303
timecat	1	−5.0000	3.4095	33	−1.47	0.1520
timecat	2	−2.0000	2.5368	33	−0.79	0.4361
timecat	3	0	.	.	.	.

Type 3 Tests of Fixed Effects

Effect	Num DF	Den DF	F Value	Pr > F
timecat	3	33	1.80	0.1656

Covariance Parameter Estimates

Cov Parm	Subject	Estimate
AR(1)	id	0.8064
Residual		199.45

Estimated R Correlation Matrix for Subject 1

Row	Col1	Col2	Col3	Col4
1	1.0000	0.8064	0.6503	0.5244
2	0.8064	1.0000	0.8064	0.6503
3	0.6503	0.8064	1.0000	0.8064
4	0.5244	0.6503	0.8064	1.0000

TABLE 15.13
MAXIMUM LIKELIHOOD ANALYSES OF LINEAR TREND FOR TABLE
15.1 DATA FOR VARIOUS MODELS

Model	Label	Num DF	Den DF	F Value	Pr > F
Random intercept	time linear	1	33	8.88	0.0054
Random intercept and slope	time linear	1	11	5.02	0.0466
Unstructured	time linear	1	11	5.02	0.0466
Compound symmetry	time linear	1	33	8.88	0.0054
Autoregressive	time linear	1	33	5.00	0.0322

Tests of Contrasts

We have now considered three error structures we might specify for testing our omnibus null hypothesis that population mean McCarthy scores are equal across time. However, just as we discussed for random effects models, individual contrasts may be of interest. In particular, trend analyses are often of interest in longitudinal designs, whether we choose to analyze data from these designs through random effects or through directly modeling the structure of the covariance matrix. In any case, we can use PROC MIXED to obtain tests of contrasts by adding appropriate command lines to those we have already shown. The following four lines provide separate tests of (1) the omnibus hypothesis, (2) the linear trend, (3) the quadratic trend, and (4) the cubic trend:

contrast 'time main effect' timecat 1 −1 0 0, timecat 0 1 −1 0, timecat 0 0 1 −1;
contrast 'time linear' timecat −3 −1 1 3;
contrast 'time quad' timecat 1 −1 −1 1;
contrast 'time cubic' timecat −1 3 −3 1;

These command lines are the same for models with any form of REPEATED or RANDOM statement in PROC MIXED.

Table 15.13 shows the result of testing the linear trend in the McCarthy data under the various models we have considered. For simplicity, we have chosen to display results only for the linear trend. Also note that the table includes results for the random effects models we considered as well as for the three versions of models that directly specify the covariance structure. It is instantly apparent that all of the approaches agree that the linear trend is statistically significant at the .05 (per comparison) level for these data. Possible adjustment for multiple comparisons could eliminate such complete agreement. Even without such adjustment, although this unanimity is reassuring, it is by no means guaranteed to occur in general, even with balanced data. However, there are some patterns in the table that reflect more general equalities. Notice that the random intercept model and the compound symmetry model produce equal F and p values, as would be expected now that we have seen that the two models are mathematically equivalent to one another. As we discussed in Chapter 13, the F and p values for these models assume that the variance of the linear trend equals the variance of all other trends (properly normalized), under which case a pooled error term is justified. However, this is a strong assumption that may be untenable in longitudinal designs, resulting in potential problems because the test is not robust. Notice also that the random intercept and slope model produces the same F and p values as the unstructured model, because both of these approaches base their test of the linear trend on a separate variance estimate. Thus, these methods avoid the assumption that all trends are equally variable. Finally, the autoregressive model is different from all of the other models, although for these data its results are very similar to those of the unstructured and random intercept and slope model.

Overview of Broader Model Comparison

Until now we have at most briefly alluded to the issue of how to choose from among multiple models for our data. The number of possible models can quickly become overwhelming. Just thinking of the fixed effects portion of the model, we might have a parameters (one for each level of the factor), or only one grand mean parameter, or we might allow for one or more trends. To make matters worse, we almost certainly need to acknowledge that we have different ways of modeling the correlations we expect to find in our data. We might allow for one or more random effects, or we might model the covariance structure directly, such as by specifying an unstructured matrix or an autoregressive model. How can we avoid paralysis and proceed to make inferences about our data in which we can have some confidence?

As you might guess, this is a very complicated problem. We would like to be able to tell you that there is a single correct answer to this issue, but in reality this is not the case. In fact, this is an area of active statistical research, so by the time you are reading this book, additional progress may have been made. In any case, we hope to provide some general guidelines that will enable readers to make informed and reasonable decisions about their data.

We will simplify our dilemma from the start by restricting our attention to the omnibus test. The logic we develop here can then be applied to tests of contrasts, if so desired. We have considered five full models for the McCarthy data. Each of these models contains four fixed effect parameters, one for each time point, but the models differ in how they attempt to explain the correlations of scores over time. Ideally, all of these models would reach the same conclusion about whether a restricted model with only one fixed effect parameter provides an adequate explanation of the data. In reality, although that level of agreement is possible, it was not reached with the McCarthy data, so whether we ultimately decide to reject the null hypothesis depends on which model we use as the basis for our decision. Specifically, the random intercept model and the compound symmetry model agree (as they must) in implying that the null hypothesis should be rejected at the .05 level. The other three models, that is, the model with random intercept and slope, the unrestricted model, and the autoregressive model produced tests that failed to reach statistical significance at the .05 level.

Thus, we have conflicting evidence about the plausibility of the null hypothesis. Which full model should we base our conclusion on? We have argued on theoretical grounds that the random intercept model (and hence also the compound symmetry model) should generally not be relied on for longitudinal data. In this case, then, we could base our conclusion on any of the other three models and fail to reject. (Notice, however, that our decision might change if we were to base our conclusion on a planned comparison test of the linear trend.) But what if these models disagreed with one another, as they might for some other data set? In some situations, theoretical considerations might motivate the choice of models, but in other circumstances insufficient theory may be available to guide this choice.

How might we choose from among the models empirically? Your first thought might well be something along the lines of performing a model comparison test. After all, isn't that what this book is all about? Although this idea is often a good one, it will not work in this particular case. To perform a model comparison, we must begin with a full model and impose a null hypothesis to produce a restricted model, which has a subset of the parameters of the full model. However, some pairs of models we have developed here differ in more than one way from each other, so it is not the case that one model is a more restricted version of the other. Models where neither is a simplification of the other are called "non-nested models." Thus, the model comparison approach does not completely solve our problem of needing to compare non-nested models.

Statisticians have developed an alternative method of comparing non-nested models. This alternative is based on "information criteria." Although information criteria are unfortunately not perfect (more on their limitations in a moment), they at least provide some empirical basis for model selection. The basic idea of an information criterion is simply to adjust some index of overall model fit for the number of parameters required to obtain that fit. In other words, one theme of this book involves the search for parsimonious models, because we know that we can always improve the fit of a model to a set of data simply by adding more parameters to the model. However, this improvement may reflect capitalization on chance instead of a better representation of the actual data in the population. Information criteria simply provide one approach for assessing adequacy of model fit while taking into account the complexity of the model.

PROC MIXED provides three information criteria by default: Akaike's Information Criterion (AIC), a finite-sample corrected version of AIC (labeled as AICC), and Schwarz's Bayesian Information Criterion (BIC). Each criterion provides a measure of how well the model fits the data, taking into account the number of parameters in the model. The essential difference between the Akaike criteria and the BIC is that the BIC imposes a heavier penalty for additional parameters. In other words, the BIC rewards parsimony more than does the AIC or the AICC.[13]

TABLE 15.14
INFORMATION CRITERIA COMPARING VARIOUS
MODELS FOR TABLE 15.1 DATA
(SMALLER VALUES ARE BETTER)

	AIC	AICC	BIC
Random intercept	344.8	345.0	345.7
Random intercept and slope	344.4	345.4	346.3
Unstructured	345.1	351.8	350.0
Compound symmetry	344.8	345.0	345.7
Autoregressive	337.1	337.4	338.1

Table 15.14 presents all three criteria for the five full models we have developed for testing the omnibus null hypothesis in the McCarthy data. Smaller values are preferable, or stated another way, models with the lowest values of an information index are best. (Prior to Version 8.1, PROC MIXED reported these values in a different but ultimately equivalent way, which required interpreting negative values of each criterion, and as a consequence preferring models with the smallest absolute value of a criterion.) Thus, according to all three criteria, the best of these five models for the McCarthy data is the autoregressive model. To consider what this means, let's focus on the autoregressive model and the unstructured model. Although the autoregressive model by necessity cannot provide as good a fit in the sample as the unstructured model, it requires considerably fewer parameters. In these data, the parsimony gained by the autoregressive model outweighs the slightly better fit the unstructured model obtains in the sample. Thus, the information indices imply that it is reasonable to infer that there is in fact a structure to the population covariance matrix, and furthermore, that structure appears to follow an autoregressive form. Based on the values shown in Table 15.14, we would have some justification for proceeding to interpret our fixed effects based on the autoregressive model.

Before concluding this section, we will make two additional comments. First, notice that the random intercept and compound symmetry models produced equal values of the AIC as well as the SBC. By now, the equality between these two models should come as no surprise, because we have seen that they are in fact simply two different ways of expressing the same model. Second, we mentioned that information criteria are not perfect. Keselman, Algina, Kowalchuk, and Wolfinger (1998) have shown that information criteria can sometimes fail to identify the true model at an alarming rate. They conducted simulations where the true population model was known, and examined how often the true model would be judged best among a collection of competing models in a sample. Their results suggest that information criteria should not be relied on to the exclusion of theory, and that, unfortunately, model selection probably cannot be automated so easily as simply programming the computer to identify the model with the best value of the information criteria.

COMPLEX DESIGNS

Our focus throughout this chapter has been to establish a conceptual foundation for maximum likelihood analysis of longitudinal data. As such, we have taken a very simple data structure and have shown how the new methods of this chapter extend historical methods of Chapters 11 through 14. However, we would be remiss if we did not provide at least a preview of how these new methods can also be applied to more complex data sets.

Factorial Fixed Effects

The McCarthy data set is especially simple because it contains only a single within-subjects factor. In this respect, it represents a prototypic design from either Chapter 11 or 13. However, in many situations, there is at least one more factor, leading to factorial designs, such as those we present in Chapters 12 and 14. For example, whereas the McCarthy data of Table 15.1 pertained to a single sample of 12 children, more generally we might incorporate a between-subjects factor in the design. Examples of such between-subjects factors would be gender or treatment condition. Fortunately, such additional factors can easily be included in a mixed model analysis. Suppose that we were to consider a variation of the McCarthy data set, where children had been randomly assigned to either a treatment or a control condition, and then assessed at four time points subsequent to the treatment manipulation. The logic we have developed throughout this chapter would also apply to this new design. The only new complication is that we would almost certainly be interested in assessing not just a time main effect, but also a treatment main effect and a time × treatment interaction. As usual, several multilevel software programs can perform the appropriate analyses, but we will use PROC MIXED to illustrate how straightforward it is to include these additional effects. Only two changes are needed to any of the programs we used earlier in the chapter for the McCarthy data. Regardless of whether a RANDOM or REPEATED statement is being used to model correlations in the data, the two changes are: (1) include treatment as a "class" variable and (2) include the treatment main effect and the treatment by time interaction in the MODEL statement. Thus, the new MODEL statement would look something like:

```
model iq=timecat trtmnt timecat*trtmnt/s;
```

where "trtmnt" is the variable name designating treatment condition. This command will produce F tests and other relevant information about the time main effect, the treatment main effect, and the time by treatment interaction based on whatever correlation structure is imposed by a RANDOM or REPEATED statement. Of course, further analyses might examine comparisons, such as trend effects of time, as well as individual comparisons of specific levels of treatment, if this between-subjects factor had more than two levels.

One specific type of between-subjects factor of special interest occurs when longitudinal data are available on two or more cohorts of individuals. Such a design is called a cohort-sequential design or an accelerated design, and offers among its advantages the ability to study development over a wide age range without requiring that the study itself last as long as the difference between the youngest and oldest age in the design. For example, consider a design with three cohorts. At the beginning of the study, suppose one set of individuals is 6 years old, another is 8 years old, and a third set is 10 years old. Further suppose that the study lasts 3 years. The advantage of the accelerated design is that data are now available for children ranging in age from 6 to 13 years of age, although the study itself required only 3 years of data collection. The maximum likelihood approach to longitudinal data lends itself particularly well to analysis of data from accelerated designs. Readers interested in further discussion as well as an illustration are advised to consult Raudenbush and Chan (1993).

Yet another possibility is that a design might include more than one within-subjects factor. This type of design is probably less likely to be analyzed with the methods of this chapter, because it is usually less likely that one of the multiple within-subjects factors is time. Instead, it is more likely that the multiple factors represent different treatment combinations. Nevertheless, the methods of this chapter are still applicable. Once again, effects of multiple factors can be assessed simply by including them in the MODEL statement. However, there is one additional complication with more than one within-subjects factor, namely, that the covariance matrix increases in dimension, because it becomes necessary to represent correlations between all levels of all factors. Arguably, the simplest solution is to specify an unstructured matrix, which then corresponds to the approach we developed in Chapter 14. The primary advantage of using the methods of this chapter instead of the multivariate approach of Chapter 14 is that the methods of this chapter would allow participants with missing data to be included in the analysis, unlike the multivariate approach. It is also possible to specify alternatives to the unstructured form, especially through an option in PROC MIXED involving a Kronecker product. Discussion of this possibility is beyond the scope of this chapter, but the interested reader is referred to Galecki (1994) for further information.

Multiple Variables Measured Over Time

Another possible extension of the simple design we have considered in this chapter is that more than one variable can be measured over time. For example, a developmental psychologist might measure both anxiety and depression on a group of children at four points in time. How should such data be analyzed? The answer obviously depends on the theoretical and/or practical questions to be answered. In general, however, the analysis is likely to proceed along either of two lines. The distinction between these two lines hinges largely on whether both variables are regarded as dependent variables or one variable is viewed as a predictor of the other.

In some situations, both variables are regarded as dependent variables, in which case the design is a multivariate extension of the designs we have considered in the chapter. One potential benefit of this design is that it can provide information about the relationship between trajectories for the multiple variables. For example, an investigator might want to assess the extent to which average rate of change in depression is related to average rate of change in anxiety. Full discussion of this approach is well beyond the scope of this chapter, but PROC MIXED facilitates such analyses through the Kronecker product option available for specifying correlations among random effects. MacCallum, Kim, Malarkey, and Kiecolt-Glaser (1997) provides an excellent example of this type of analysis for readers desiring more information.

Alternatively, one variable may be regarded as a predictor of the other. For example, a researcher's primary interest may be to understand changes in depression over time. However, the researcher may believe that changes in depression partly reflect changes in anxiety. In such a case, anxiety can be included as a predictor of depression. Because anxiety is presumed to change over time, it is called a time-varying covariate, as opposed to a time-invariant covariate (or time-invariant predictor), such as gender. In its simplest form, a time-varying covariate can be incorporated in the analysis simply by including it in the model, just as would be done with a time-invariant predictor. However, the situation becomes somewhat more complicated, in that a time-varying covariate may be regarded as a random effect, because it is possible that the regression parameter relating depression and anxiety (in our example) varies across participants. Readers interested in more information about this type of design are advised to consult Bryk and Raudenbush (1992) or Snijders and Bosker (1999).

UNBALANCED DESIGNS

We have periodically alluded to unbalanced designs throughout this chapter, but the actual data we analyzed came from a balanced data set. As we have mentioned, unbalanced data occur in either or both of two situations: (1) missing data or (2) not all participants measured at the same time points. From a purely practical standpoint, we could regard the first of these as a special case of the second, but even so it is useful to consider missing data as a separate issue in its own right.

A major advantage of the maximum likelihood approach of this chapter over the ANOVA methods of Chapters 11 and 12 and over the multivariate methods of Chapters 13 and 14 is that these new methods can easily accommodate missing data. For example, consider the various sets of PROC MIXED commands we applied to the McCarthy data. How would we need to modify our syntax if some scores had been missing? The answer may come as a pleasant surprise: "not at all!" The only difference is that the input data set would no longer have 48 lines (recall that the complete data set has 48 lines, because each of the 12 participants is measured four times). Instead, the input data set would simply have as many lines as there were nonmissing scores. Alternatively, the data set itself might still have 48 lines, but some IQ scores would be designated as missing, so the number of lines of data available to be modeled would be fewer than 48. In either case, PROC MIXED would base its analysis on as many individual lines as had nonmissing IQ scores. The crucial advantage over traditional methods is that individuals with fewer than four scores are not automatically excluded from the analysis.

Including all possible data in the analysis frequently provides two advantages. First, statistical power and precision are improved. In the worst case scenario, if every person is missing at least one score, traditional methods are forced to reduce the sample size to zero, in which case power and precision are a moot point. Even in much less extreme situations, power and precision are enhanced by using as much of the data as possible. Of course, better yet would be to have no missing data. In effect, procedures such as PROC MIXED take into account how much information is available from each participant and proceed to weight each participant accordingly. For example, a participant observed at only 30 and 36 months would receive less weight in the analysis than one observed at 30, 36, and 42 months, who in turn would receive less weight than someone observed at all four time points. By being able to calculate appropriate weights for different patterns of observed data, the maximum likelihood analysis can proceed without having to omit participants with less than complete data.

Second, results obtained by maximum likelihood analysis are valid under a less restrictive set of assumptions than those required by the traditional methods. Specifically, traditional methods require that any data that are missing be "missing completely at random" (MCAR). This means that whatever causes missing data to occur must be completely random insofar as these causes must be unrelated to any variables measured in the study. How might this assumption be violated? Consider our example of assessing McCarthy scores over time. Suppose that unbeknownst to us, individuals with lower scores at Time 1 are at increased risk of dropping out of the study. What will happen if we were to test a null hypothesis that population means are equal over time using the multivariate approach of Chapter 13? The first thing to realize is that we will only be able to use data from individuals who were tested at all four time points. However, unbeknownst to us, we will tend to exclude individuals whose Time 1 scores were low. What effect will this have on our hypothesis? To answer this question, remember from Table 15.4 that we saw a negative relationship between the slope and intercept parameters in the full data set. To the extent that this negative correlation holds in the population, by leaving out individuals with low Time 1 scores we are also leaving out individuals who will tend to have above average slopes. Thus, the individuals with complete data will tend to have below average slopes, biasing the multivariate analysis we perform on them. Under this scenario, our results are biased toward finding a decline in McCarthy scores over time. Arguably the most important point of all here is that we were able to figure out the direction of the bias, because we made use of information about that subset of individuals who failed to provide us with complete data. In particular, notice that if we simply performed the multivariate analysis and hoped for the best, we would have no way to know that our result is likely biased.

Maximum likelihood analysis improves on this problem by using all available data. As a result, instead of requiring that missingness be completely at random, we need to make a less stringent assumption that data are "missing at random" (MAR). This distinction is fairly subtle and not helped by the similarity statisticians have chosen to adopt for the two conditions. The basic distinction is that data can be MAR and yet still be related to variables included in the study. The key assumption is that once we take these measured variables into account, any further causes of missingness must be random. For example, suppose individuals with low Time 1 scores are more likely to drop out. If all other causes of attrition are unrelated to variables measured in the study, the data satisfy the MAR condition, even though we have just seen that they fail to satisfy the MCAR condition. In this case, maximum likelihood analyses such as those of PROC MIXED, HLM, and MLWin provide unbiased parameter estimates. How might we fail to satisfy the MAR assumption? Suppose that missingness depends not only on the Time 1 score, but also on the level of cognitive stimulation provided in the home environment. Further suppose that cognitive stimulation affects scores at later time points. Unless we have measured cognitive stimulation and include it in our model, we will have failed to satisfy the MAR assumption. Without being able to rely on this assumption, we are no longer assured that our parameter estimates are unbiased even when we use maximum likelihood, although it may be plausible that estimates will still be superior to those obtained from methods that require full data. Of course, the problem in the real world is that we rarely know precisely what factors have contributed to attrition. In part for this reason, it is useful to include (within reasonable limits) variables that may be related to attrition in the model even if some of these variables are of no direct theoretical interest. Including such variables in the model and using maximum likelihood approaches to analyze the resulting data at least minimizes the distortions produced by missing data.

CONCLUSION

Before proceeding to the next chapter on nested designs, we will make two final comments. First, recall that we presented several graphical methods in Chapter 3 for assessing the validity of assumptions. Such methods continue to be important in mixed models, but space constraints prevent us from presenting them here. Interested readers are referred to Bryk and Raudenbush (1992), whose book devotes an entire chapter to this topic. Second, readers who are interested in additional information about PROC MIXED are directed toward Singer (1998) and Verbeke and Molenberghs (2000).

EXERCISES

1. Can the specification of the random portion of the model affect the interpretation of the fixed effects? Explain your answer.

2. Briefly explain in your own words the general relationship between a trajectory plot and the fixed and random portions of a mixed model for longitudinal data.

3. Suppose the only random effect we specify is an intercept. What property are we implicitly assuming if we conceptualize the data in terms of a trajectory plot?

4. How are the following related to one another: (1) parallel trajectories, (2) a model whose only random effect is an intercept term, and (3) the statistical assumption of sphericity?

5. Would it be possible to analyze a data set and find that scores are declining over time and yet a random intercept is positively correlated with a random slope?

6. Could one ever justify fitting a model with linear, quadratic, and cubic fixed effects (along with a fixed intercept term, as included by default in most software packages) but only intercept and linear random effects? Why or why not?

7. How can we use the results of a mixed model analysis to estimate the percentage of individuals whose scores are increasing over time?

8. Suppose we intend to fit a model with fixed and random intercept and linear effects to a set of data. What is the minimum number of time points we must have? Briefly explain why.

9. Suppose we intend to fit a model with fixed and random intercept, linear, and quadratic effects to a set of data. What is the minimum number of time points we must have? Briefly explain why.

10. Does a random effects model specify a correlational structure for longitudinal data? Explain your answer.

11. Why not just always use the multivariate approach to repeated measures, as described in Chapters 13 and 14, because it does not constrain the form of the covariance matrix?

12. Does specifying an unstructured covariance matrix for the McCarthy data as shown in Table 15.1 produce the same test of fixed effects as the multivariate approach of Chapter 13? When will this type of correspondence hold?

13. (To be done by computer.) What would it mean to eliminate all random effects from a mixed model analysis of longitudinal data? To consider the answer to this question, we will reexamine the McCarthy data shown in Table 15.1.
   a. Use SAS PROC MIXED or similar multilevel modeling software to fit a model that allows each time point to have its own unique population mean but omits any random effects from the model. Is there a statistically significant difference in means at different ages?
   b. Suppose we were to regard these data as a between-subjects design, in which case there would be four distinct groups of 12 children each. Analyze the data as if this were the true structure of the data. Is there a statistically significant difference in means at different ages?
   c. How do your results in parts a and b compare to one another? Why? What does this tell you about the role of including random effects in models for longitudinal data?
   d. The chapter showed a variety of graphs depicting different models for the McCarthy data. What would a graph corresponding to the model in part a look like?
   e. Does the type of graph (and thus this type of model) you described in part d seem plausible for most longitudinal data in the behavioral and social sciences? Why or why not?

14. (To be done by computer.) Analyses of the McCarthy data (shown in Table 15.1) in the text coded age in months. Specifically, these analyses usually coded time as 0, 6, 12, and 18. Suppose we were to conceptualize age in terms of years instead of months.
   a. Fit a model allowing each time point to have its own unique population mean. Also include a random intercept and a random slope in the model, where the coding of the slope variable is in years instead of months. Allow the random intercept and slope to be correlated with one another. How do your results compare to those reported in the chapter?
   b. Fit a growth curve model presuming a straight-line model for the means along with random intercept and slope effects (where once again, the random effects are allowed to correlate). Code the slope variable in terms of years instead of months. How do your results compare to those reported in the chapter?
   c. Based on your results in parts a and b, what appears to be the effect of coding age in years instead of months?

15. (To be done by computer.) Analyses of the McCarthy data (shown in Table 15.1) in the text concentrated on results where age is coded such that a value of zero corresponds to an age of 30 months.

Suppose we were to conceptualize the zero point differently. Fit a growth curve model presuming a straight-line model for the means along with random intercept and slope effects (where the random intercept and random slope are allowed to correlate with one another). Code the slope variable in months so that a score of zero corresponds to the middle of the observation period from 30 to 48 months.

a. How does your estimate of the mean slope compare to that reported in Table 15.6?

b. How does your estimate of the mean intercept (averaging over individuals' separate intercepts) compare to that reported in Table 15.6?

c. Are your estimates of covariances for the random effects identical to those shown in Table 15.6? Why or why not?

d. What do parts a, b, and c tell you about the effects of coding the zero point for time in longitudinal mixed models?

16. (To be done by computer.) A developmental psychologist is interested in the role of the sound of a mother's heartbeat in the growth of newborn babies. Fourteen babies were placed in a nursery where they were constantly exposed to a rhythmic heartbeat sound piped in over the PA system. Infants were weighed at the same time of day for four consecutive days, yielding the following data (weight is measured in ounces):

Subject	Day 1	Day 2	Day 3	Day 4
1	96	98	103	104
2	116	116	118	119
3	102	102	101	101
4	112	115	116	118
5	108	110	112	115
6	92	95	96	98
7	120	121	121	123
8	112	111	111	109
9	95	96	98	99
10	114	112	110	109
11	99	100	99	98
12	124	125	127	126
13	100	98	95	94
14	106	107	106	107

a. Fit a model allowing each day to have its own mean, but allowing only a random intercept term. How does the F value you obtain for a test of mean differences among days compare to the F value of 1.84 we obtained using the unadjusted univariate approach to repeated measures in Chapter 11? (See Exercise 17, part a, in Chapter 11.)

b. Explain the relationship between the analysis you conducted in part a and the unadjusted univariate approach to repeated measures, as described in Chapter 11.

c. Fit a model once again allowing each day to have its own mean, but allowing random intercept and slope terms (where the intercept and slope are allowed to correlate with one another). How does the evidence for a mean difference among days compare to the analysis you performed in part a? Is there any reason to expect that these two types of analyses will often compare to one another in this way for longitudinal data?

d. Fit a mixed model with no random effects, but instead specifying an unstructured covariance matrix. How does the F value you obtain for a test of mean differences among days compare to the F value of 0.81 we obtained for these data using the multivariate approach to repeated measures in Chapter 13? (See Exercise 13, part a, in Chapter 13.)

e. How might you decide which of the models you have investigated in parts a, c, and d might provide the best answer to the question of whether infants' mean weights are changing over these 4 days? Explain your answer.

f. Fit a growth curve model where each infant's trajectory over days is presumed to follow a straight line. Allow each infant to have his or her own intercept and slope, and allow the intercept and slope to correlate with one another. Does your analysis suggest that mean weight is changing over days? What is your best estimate of the percentage of infants whose weights are increasing over days?

17. Exercise 16 presented hypothetical data obtained by a developmental psychologist interested in the role of the sound of a mother's heartbeat in the growth of newborn babies. This exercise uses the same data, but now we assume that half of the infants were assigned to a control group. Specifically, 7 babies were randomly assigned to a condition where they were exposed to a rhythmic heartbeat sound piped in over the PA system. The other 7 babies were placed in an identical nursery but without the heartbeat sound. Infants were weighed at the same time of day for 4 consecutive days, yielding the following data (weight is measured in ounces):

	Heartbeat Group			
Subject	*Day 1*	*Day 2*	*Day 3*	*Day 4*
1	96	98	103	104
2	116	116	118	119
3	102	102	101	101
4	112	115	116	118
5	108	110	112	115
6	92	95	96	98
7	120	121	121	123

	Control Group			
Subject	*Day 1*	*Day 2*	*Day 3*	*Day 4*
1	112	111	111	109
2	95	96	98	99
3	114	112	110	109
4	99	100	99	98
5	124	125	127	126
6	100	98	95	94
7	106	107	106	107

There are many different models we might potentially fit to these data. Of course, the specific models we investigate should ideally be driven largely by the researcher's theory and corresponding questions of interest. We will simply explore a few examples of models that might be of theoretical interest in a study like this.

a. Fit a model where each group is allowed to have its own mean for each day. Include random intercept and slope effects. Do these data suggest that the time effect is different for the treatment group as compared to the control group? What does this suggest about the effectiveness of the heartbeat intervention?

b. Fit a growth curve model where each infant in each group is allowed to have her or his own intercept and slope. Allow the intercept and slope to correlate with one another. Do the data suggest that treatment group infants tend to have different rates of growth from control group infants? Justify your answer.

18. A developmental psychologist is interested in measuring adolescent's state anxiety levels during the first 3 months of middle school. To address this question, he obtains a random sample of 24 students and measures each student's state anxiety at the beginning of September, October, and November. (For the purposes of this question, you may regard these measurements as equally spaced.) Suppose the following data are obtained:

	Month		
Subject	September	October	November
1	50	48	42
2	50	48	42
3	50	48	58
4	50	48	58
5	50	52	42
6	50	52	42
7	50	52	58
8	50	52	58
9	48	42	33
10	48	42	33
11	48	42	51
12	48	42	51
13	48	48	33
14	48	48	33
15	48	48	51
16	48	48	51
17	46	36	24
18	46	36	24
19	46	36	44
20	46	36	44
21	46	44	24
22	46	44	24
23	46	44	44
24	46	44	44

Even a glance at these data shows some unusual patterns. Most obvious is that there appears to be a clone of each person. (Notice that the data for participant 2 are identical to the data for participant 1, and the same is true for each remaining pair of participants.) We have intentionally created these data to have certain visible patterns, because we will use these data to further develop your understanding of how mixed models handle missing data. As such, we have developed a simplistic data set to make certain concepts easier to follow. As you work the various parts of this problem, you should think about the extent to which the results illustrated here would or would not continue to hold in more complex situations. We will initially assume that no data are missing, but then assume that certain individuals could not be assessed in November and see what impact this missing data has on our analysis.

a. Find the sample mean anxiety score for each month. What do your results suggest about the relationship between anxiety and month?

b. Create as a new variable the difference between each individual's score in November and that individual's score in September. Test to see whether this new variable has a mean different from 0 in the population. How would you interpret the result of this test for these data?

c. Use the multivariate approach to repeated measures to test the linear trend of age in these data. How do your results here compare to those you obtained in part b? Would this relationship always hold?

d. Fit a growth curve model where each individual is allowed to have his or her own intercept and slope. Allow the intercept and slope to correlate with one another. Do the data suggest that the population mean slope is different from zero? How do your results here compare to those you obtained in parts b and c?

The remaining parts of this problem are based on a revised data set. Assume that all individuals were assessed in September and October, but that individuals with even subject numbers were not observed in November. In other words, data are missing in November for participants 2, 4, 6, 8, 10, 12, 14, 16, 18, 20, 22, and 24.

e. As in part a, find the sample mean anxiety score for each month, but now do so only for those 12 individuals for whom complete data are available. What do your results suggest about the relationship between anxiety and month?

f. Create as a new variable the difference between each individual's score in November and that individual's score in September. Use the 12 individuals for whom complete data are available to test whether this new variable has a mean different from 0 in the population. How would you interpret the result of this test for these data?

g. Use the multivariate approach to repeated measures to test the linear trend of age in these data (i.e., the data where 12 individuals are missing a score in November). How do your results here compare to those you obtained in part f? Would this relationship always hold?

h. Fit a growth curve model to these data (where once again only 12 individuals were assessed in November). Allow each individual to have his or her own intercept and slope. Allow the intercept and slope to correlate with one another. Do the data suggest that the population mean slope is different from zero? How do your results here compare to those you obtained in parts f and g?

i. Why are your answers to parts f, g, and h not all the same? In particular, do the methods differ in their estimates of the effect of month on anxiety, or do they differ only in the precision with which this estimate is obtained? (Hint: Form a confidence interval for the slope relating month to anxiety, using each of the approaches in parts f, g, and h. How do these intervals compare to one another?)

j. How could you characterize the pattern of missing data here? Would you state that data appear to be missing completely at random (MCAR)? Or do data appear to be missing at random (MAR), but not completely at random? (Hint: Is missingness in November related to scores at earlier ages? Pretending that we could know all scores in the complete data set, does it appear that those individuals who were not observed in November would have scored differently from those who were observed?)

k. What implications does this distinction between MCAR and MAR have for how the various methods of analysis will compare to one another?

l. If data are missing completely at random, can you expect any of the methods to provide parameter estimates that are not biased by the absence of data? Relate your answer to the pattern of results you obtained in the earlier parts of this problem.

19. A gerontologist wonders whether scores on a cognitive ability test tend to decline with age in the general population. To answer this question, she obtains a random sample of 24 individuals, each of whom is 70 years old at the beginning of the study. Each individual is administered the test at the age of 70, then again at the age of 72 and finally a third time at the age of 74. Suppose the following data are obtained:

	Age		
Subject	70	72	74
1	100	110	121
2	100	90	81
3	100	110	120
4	100	90	80
5	100	110	119
6	100	90	79
7	100	110	125
8	100	90	85
9	100	110	120
10	100	90	80
11	100	110	115
12	100	90	75
13	100	110	123
14	100	90	84
15	100	110	120
16	100	90	80
17	100	110	117
18	100	90	76

(Continued)

Subject	Age		
	70	72	74
19	100	110	122
20	100	90	83
21	100	110	120
22	100	90	80
23	100	110	118
24	100	90	77

Even a glance at these data shows some unusual patterns. Most obvious is that each individual obtained a score of 100 at the age of 70. We have intentionally created these data to have certain visible patterns, because we will use these data to further develop your understanding of how mixed models handle missing data. As such, we have developed a simplistic data set to make certain concepts easier to follow. As you work the various parts of this problem, you should think about the extent to which the results illustrated here would or would not continue to hold in more complex situations. We will initially assume that no data are missing, but then assume that certain individuals could not be assessed at the age of 74 and see what impact this missing data has on our analysis.

a. Find the sample mean ability at each age. What do your results suggest about the relationship between ability and age between 70 and 74?

b. Create as a new variable the difference between each individual's score at age 74 and that individual's score at age 70. Test to see whether this new variable has a mean different from 0 in the population. How would you interpret the result of this test for these data?

c. Use the multivariate approach to repeated measures to test the linear trend of age in these data. How do your results here compare to those you obtained in part b? Would this relationship always hold?

d. Fit a growth curve model where each individual is allowed to have his or her own intercept and slope. Allow the intercept and slope to correlate with one another. Do the data suggest that the population mean slope is different from zero? How do your results here compare to those you obtained in parts b and c?

The remaining parts of this problem are based on a revised data set. Assume that all individuals were assessed at ages 70 and 72, but the following eight individuals were not assessed at age 74: participants 2, 6, 8, 12, 14, 18, 20, and 24.

e. As in part a, find the sample mean ability at each age, but now do so only for those 16 individuals for whom complete data are available. What do your results suggest about the relationship between ability and age between 70 and 74? Do your results here agree with those you found in part a? Why or why not?

f. Create as a new variable the difference between each individual's score at age 74 and that individual's score at age 70. Use the 16 individuals for whom complete data are available to test whether this new variable has a mean different from zero in the population. How would you interpret the result of this test for these data? Do your results agree with those you found in part b? Why or why not?

g. Use the multivariate approach to repeated measures to test the linear trend of age in these data (i.e., the data where 8 individuals are missing a score at age 74). How do your results here compare to those you obtained in part f? Would this relationship always hold?

h. Fit a growth curve model to these data (where once again only 16 individuals were assessed at age 74). Allow each individual to have his or her own intercept and slope. Allow the intercept and slope to correlate with one another. Do the data suggest that the population mean slope is different from zero? How do your results here compare to those you obtained in parts f and g?

i. How does missing data impact the various methods of analyzing these data? Which if any methods give the same answer when data are missing as when data are present?

j. How could you characterize the pattern of missing data here? Would you state that data appear to be missing completely at random (MCAR)? Or do data appear to be missing at random (MAR), but not completely at random? (Hint: Is missingness at age 74 related to scores at earlier ages?

Pretending that we could know all scores in the complete data set, does it appear that those individuals who were not observed at age 74 would have scored differently from those who were observed? Would you change your answer to the previous question if you took into account each person's score at age 72? For example, among those who scored 90 at age 72, is there a difference in the means of those persons who were observed at age 74 and those who were not?)

k. What implications does this distinction between MCAR and MAR have for how the various methods of analysis will compare to one another?

l. If data are missing at random but not completely at random, can you expect any of the methods to provide parameter estimates that are not biased by the absence of data? Relate your answer to the pattern of results you obtained in the earlier parts of this problem.

16

An Introduction to Multilevel Hierarchical Mixed Models: Nested Designs

The previous chapter showed how multilevel mixed models extend analysis of variance (ANOVA) models for the analysis of longitudinal data. This chapter presents the analogous extension for nested designs. Recall that Chapter 10 demonstrated how ANOVA model comparisons can be used to test hypotheses in nested designs. A special focus of the chapter pertained to situations where the nested factor constituted a random effects factor. This chapter continues this same emphasis but considers a new method for analyzing such data. As you might anticipate, this method is the same maximum likelihood approach we developed in Chapter 15 (in particular, as we explained in Chapter 15, we will once again use what is technically known as restricted maximum likelihood). The only difference is that instead of applying maximum likelihood to longitudinal data, as we did in the previous chapter, we will now apply it to nested designs.

Our first goal is to preview the relationship between the maximum likelihood method of this chapter and the ANOVA approach of Chapter 10. Just as occurred in the previous chapter for longitudinal data, we will see in this chapter that there are special cases where the maximum likelihood and ANOVA approaches are equivalent to one another when analyzing data from nested designs. Specifically, when cell sizes are equal the two approaches yield identical results. Thus, researchers fortunate enough to have sufficient control to ensure equal sample sizes can continue to rely on the ANOVA models we presented in Chapter 10. However, even when researchers are able to assign units to treatment conditions at random, cell sizes often end up being unequal in nested designs. For example, suppose an educational psychologist has randomly assigned 10 classrooms to either of two forms of instruction: 5 classrooms receive a novel form of instruction; the other 5 classrooms receive a standard form of instruction. The outcome measure is obtained for each student within each of the classrooms. The methods of Chapter 10 would require the same number of students in each classroom, whereas the new methods to be presented here allow the number of students to differ from one classroom to another. Clearly, in much research involving nested data structures, sample sizes will be unequal, in which case the methods of this chapter become essential.

Another major advantage of the maximum likelihood approach is that it can easily accommodate complex data structures such as those that include additional predictor variables of interest. For example, the educational psychologist we have been considering might be able to measure each child's pretest ability. As we have discussed in Chapter 9, this pretest might be used as a covariate in the model. Further, the psychologist might also measure one or more aspects of the teachers, and these variables might also be candidates for inclusion as covariates in the model. However, we will see later in this chapter that it is important to distinguish variables measured at the student level from those measured at the teacher level. More generally, our model should take into account the proper level of the nested design for each variable in the model. We will see that the maximum likelihood approach provides a natural method for taking the proper data structure into account.

Thus, the ANOVA models of Chapter 10 are perfectly appropriate for analyzing data from simple designs with equal sample sizes. However, investigators who have unequal sample sizes or who wish to include additional variables in a model will generally need to use the maximum likelihood approach of this chapter. As in Chapter 15, we feel the need to issue something of a disclaimer before proceeding. Entire books have been written on the application of maximum likelihood analysis to data from nested designs. Once again, our purpose here is to establish a conceptual foundation, so readers can bridge the gap between standard ANOVA approaches and these more modern maximum likelihood approaches.

REVIEW OF THE ANOVA APPROACH

We will begin by reviewing our Chapter 10 presentation of the ANOVA mixed-model approach to nested designs. Specifically, we will once again use the hypothetical clinical trainee data originally shown in Table 10.9 to motivate our presentation. For convenience, these data are repeated in Table 16.1. As brief background, the goal of the study here is to examine the extent to which female and male clinical psychology graduate student trainees may assign different severity ratings to clients at initial intake. Three female and 3 male graduate students are randomly selected to participate and each is randomly assigned four clients with whom to do an intake interview, after which each clinical trainee assigns a severity rating to each client, producing the data shown in Table 16.1.

TABLE 16.1
GENERAL SEVERITY RATINGS OF CLIENTS
SEEN BY CLINICAL TRAINEES

Male Trainees		
Trainee 1	*Trainee 2*	*Trainee 3*
49	42	42
40	48	46
31	52	50
40	58	54
Female Trainees		
Trainee 1	*Trainee 2*	*Trainee 3*
53	44	58
59	54	63
63	54	67
69	64	72

Notice that we have a nested design because each individual trainee is either male or female. Specifically, then, we could say that the trainee factor is nested under the gender factor. Following the usual convention, we would let A represent the gender factor and B the trainee factor, in which case B is nested within A. Further, we should regard the trainee factor as a random factor, because (1) trainees were selected at random and (2) we wish to generalize our inference about any effect of gender beyond the 6 specific trainees included in the design. Under these circumstances, we saw in Chapter 10 that the ANOVA analysis of these data can still be conceptualized in terms of model comparisons. The numerator sum of squares for the gender effect SS_A is obtained from the difference between the sums of squared errors of the following two models:

$$\text{Full:} \quad Y_{ijk} = \mu + \alpha_j + \beta_{k/j} + \varepsilon_{ijk}$$
$$\text{Restricted:} \quad Y_{ijk} = \mu + \beta_{k/j} + \varepsilon_{ijk}$$

(10.29, repeated)

If the trainee factor were fixed, the appropriate denominator error term for the F test would simply be mean square within. However, we saw in Chapter 10 that when the trainee factor is random as it is here, the appropriate error term is the mean square of the nested effect, that is, the mean square of trainees within gender, $MS_{B/A}$. Specifically, Table 10.8 showed that MS_A and $MS_{B/A}$ have the same expected value in this design when the null hypothesis of no A effect is true. It is for this reason that $MS_{B/A}$ is the appropriate error term for testing the A effect here.

When a random factor B is nested within A, the F test for the effect of factor A is given by

$$F = \frac{MS_A}{MS_{B/A}}$$

(1)

which for the data of Table 16.1 leads to an F value of 9.97. With 1 numerator and 4 denominator degrees of freedom, the corresponding p value is .0343. Thus, we would reject the null hypothesis at the .05 level with the ANOVA approach. Of course, a full interpretation should rely on more than just the F and p values, and at the very least consider the mean difference. In this sample, female trainees assigned severity ratings 14 points higher on average than male trainees. Our hypothesis test tells us that a difference this large is unlikely to have occurred if the null hypothesis were true. You may want to make a mental note of the F value, p value, and degrees of freedom we obtained here, because we will want to compare these results to those obtained from the maximum likelihood approach momentarily.

We want to emphasize two important points before proceeding to consider the maximum likelihood analysis of these data. First, notice that the ANOVA approach estimates parameters and calculates sums of squared errors in the same way regardless of whether factors are fixed or random. It is only after having found sums of squares for various models that the ANOVA approach then takes into account whether factors are fixed or random, and specifies an appropriate error term on that basis. In other words, SS_A would equal 1,176 for our data even if trainee (the B factor) were fixed instead of random. Similarly, $MS_{B/A}$ would still equal 118 even if trainee were fixed. Of course, if trainee were random, we would eventually choose a different error term for testing the gender effect, but the models themselves would be no different if trainee were fixed instead of random. We emphasize this point because we will see that the maximum likelihood approach models random effects differently from fixed effects from the very beginning of model formation.

Second, notice that the model comparison we used to calculate SS_A relied on the fact that we had an equal n design. Even more importantly, we also relied on an equal n design in justifying

$MS_{B/A}$ as the appropriate error term, because the expected mean square expressions shown in Table 10.8 assume equal n. With unequal n, as we discussed in Chapter 7, there is no single correct expression for these mean squares, which not surprisingly creates a serious problem for the ANOVA approach.[1] Because the maximum likelihood approach uses a different model formulation, it does not encounter this difficulty, making it the method of choice when sample sizes are unequal.

MAXIMUM LIKELIHOOD ANALYSIS MODELS FOR THE SIMPLE NESTED DESIGN

Just as we discussed in Chapter 15, a fundamental difference between ANOVA and maximum likelihood analysis of data from nested designs is that ANOVA waits until the final step of calculating a test statistic before taking random factors into account. The maximum likelihood approach, on the other hand, distinguishes between fixed and random factors at the very beginning of model formulation. As it was in Chapter 15, our approach in this chapter is to provide a conceptual introduction to the maximum likelihood method for analyzing data with random factors.

As usual, our conceptual introduction begins with consideration of an appropriate full model for our data. Unlike the ANOVA approach, where the model itself need not distinguish fixed from random factors, the maximum likelihood approach requires that we immediately acknowledge this distinction in our model. When all factors are fixed, we can represent the general linear model as

$$Y_i = \beta_0 X_{0i} + \beta_1 X_{1i} + \beta_2 X_{2i} + \beta_3 X_{3i} + \cdots + \beta_p X_{pi} + \varepsilon_i \qquad \text{(3.1, repeated)}$$

The general linear mixed model that forms the basis for the maximum likelihood analysis of data from nested designs explicitly includes random effects as separate variables in the model. As we mentioned in the previous chapter, a common notational system represents predictors associated with random effects by the letter Z. Although we continue to use β to represent a parameter associated with a fixed effect, we will use u to represent the parameter associated with a random effect. In general, a model with p fixed effects and q random effects would then be written as

$$Y_i = \beta_0 X_{0i} + \beta_1 X_{1i} + \beta_2 X_{2i} + \cdots + \beta_p X_{pi} + u_{1i} Z_{1i} + u_{2i} Z_{2i} + \cdots + u_{qi} Z_{qi} + \varepsilon_i$$
$$\text{(15.2, repeated)}$$

As was true in Chapter 15, it is important to notice that the random effect parameters, unlike the fixed effect parameters, have two subscripts. By definition, fixed effects are assumed to be constant for all observations. Random effects, in contrast, potentially vary in the population.

It may be helpful to consider how the general form of the linear mixed model would apply to our clinical trainee data. In this straightforward example of a nested design, the model could be simplified to

$$Y_i = \beta_0 X_{0i} + \beta_1 X_{1i} + u_{1i} Z_{1i} + \varepsilon_i \qquad (2)$$

where Y_i represents the severity rating for Client i, X_{0i} is an intercept term (typically included by default), X_{1i} is an indicator variable designating whether Client i was seen by a female or a male trainee, Z_{1i} is a random effect variable associated with the specific trainee who saw Client i, and ε_i is as usual an error term to account for all remaining effects not otherwise already included in the model.[2]

The model for the trainee data contains four parameters to be estimated. Two of the parameters reflect fixed effects. As written in Equation 2, one of these parameters is a grand mean parameter, whereas the other is the mean difference between female and male trainees. Appendix B discusses other possible ways of parameterizing the model, but in any case the two model parameters eventually end up representing some aspect of the two population means, namely, the mean severity rating given by females and the mean rating given by males. The other two parameters reflect random effects. As usual, one of these parameters is error variance, that is, the variance of ε_i in the model. The second random effects parameter is also a variance, namely, the variance of trainees' ratings within gender. In terms of the model shown in Equation 2, this parameter is the variance of u_{1i}. There are no additional parameters to be estimated, because we assume that the correlation (or covariance) between ε_i and u_{1i} equals zero.

As we discussed in Chapter 15, a fundamental difference between the model shown in Equation 2 and the models used by the ANOVA approach to nested designs pertains to the distinction between random and fixed effects. Notice that the model used by maximum likelihood analysis, that is, the model shown in Equation 2, distinguishes the random effect of trainees from the fixed effect of gender. As a result, the underlying parameter to be estimated is also different. The ANOVA approach estimates an effect for each trainee as well as an effect for gender. Only after having estimated each of these effects is there any realization that one factor is random while the other is fixed. However, the maximum likelihood approach treats the random effect differently from the fixed effect from the outset. Instead of estimating an effect for each trainee, this approach directly estimates the variance of the trainee effect. In other words, instead of beginning with an estimate of each individual u_i, the maximum likelihood approach instead estimates the variance of u_i. Although this may seem to be a subtle distinction, it can end up having important consequences. On the one hand, directly estimating the variance of u_i proves to be much more complicated mathematically, but it also turns out to be a much more general approach that accommodates unequal sample sizes as well as more complex data structures.

One other way in which the maximum likelihood approach differs from the ANOVA approach is the way in which it implements the normality assumption. As we discussed in Chapter 15, even though the ANOVA approach assumes normality when performing significance tests, using least squares to estimate parameters does not in and of itself assume normality. The maximum likelihood approach, on the other hand, relies on normality from the outset. Not only is the error term ε_i assumed to follow a normal distribution, but so is the random effect u_{1i}. For example, in the clinical trainee data, we are assuming that if we could observe an entire population of trainees, we would discover that the distribution of trainees' severity ratings would follow a normal distribution within each gender.

The variances of the random effects are sometimes of intrinsic interest themselves. For example, we might want to estimate what proportion of observed variance in test scores can be attributed to differences between schools and what proportion can be attributed to differences within schools. In fact, to answer this question in its simplest form, we might not even include a fixed effect in the design, because a one-way design where schools constitute levels of a single random factor might suffice to answer our question. In the behavioral sciences, however, the design will more often include at least one fixed effect. When this is the case, we can as usual conceptualize a hypothesis test in terms of a model comparison. For example, to test the gender effect in the trainee data, we could compare the following pair of models:

$$\text{Full:} \quad Y_i = \beta_0 X_{0i} + \beta_1 X_{1i} + u_{1i} Z_{1i} + \varepsilon_i \tag{3}$$

$$\text{Restricted:} \quad Y_i = \beta_0 X_{0i} + u_{1i} Z_{1i} + \varepsilon_i \tag{4}$$

The obvious difference between these models is that the X_{1i} variable no longer appears in the restricted model. The reason for its absence is that β_1 has been set equal to zero, because β_1 is the mean difference between female and male raters, which is zero according to the null hypothesis. Unfortunately, it is not possible to write a simple expression for the test statistic that results from comparing these two models. In general, the maximum likelihood approach involves an iterative procedure, where parameter estimates and model fit are determined through successive approximations. Thus, there is in general no way to write a formula for the F statistic that emerges from the model comparison. Of course, we should also acknowledge that a thorough analysis of any data necessarily involves more than simply obtaining an F statistic or a p value. As usual, researchers should also be mindful of such issues as model diagnostics to assess plausibility of assumptions (much as we illustrated in Chapter 3, for the single-factor between-subjects design), as well as additional perspectives (such as confidence intervals and measures of effect size) to supplement significance tests.

Numerical Example—Equal n

Having provided a theoretical introduction to the maximum likelihood analysis of nested data, it is now useful to put this theory into action. What would this approach have to say about the data shown earlier in Table 16.1? Recall that the purpose of the study that produced these data was to compare mean severity ratings given at initial intake by female and male clinical trainees. The data come from a study where 3 female and 3 male clinical trainees have been randomly selected to perform intake evaluations on clients. In our specific design, each trainee rates the severity of four clients. We saw in Chapter 10 and reiterated earlier in this chapter that the ANOVA test of the gender difference yields an F value of 9.97. With 1 numerator and 4 denominator degrees of freedom, the corresponding p value is .0343, so we can reject the null hypothesis. According to the ANOVA approach, the data provide evidence beyond a reasonable doubt that female and male clinical trainees differ in their mean severity ratings. In particular, we can conclude that the female population mean is larger than the male population mean.

What would the maximum likelihood approach reveal about these data? To answer this question, we will provide a brief introduction to the use of SAS PROC MIXED for analyzing data from nested designs.[3] As we mentioned in Chapter 15, even though our main emphasis in this book is on concepts, we have chosen to organize much of our presentation of the maximum likelihood approach to nested designs around PROC MIXED. We have chosen to do so not only because the software for these analyses is less familiar than ANOVA software, but also because the calculations themselves are very complex and provide no real insight into the concepts. Nevertheless, readers should understand that our intent in this chapter is to use PROC MIXED as a vehicle for discussing concepts, so readers who intend to use PROC MIXED or other software on their data are advised to consult additional sources such as Bryk and Raudenbush (1992) and Kreft and de Leeuw (1998) for more thorough descriptions. Finally, keep in mind that the syntax we present here is correct as of this writing, but may undergo modifications in the coming years. Even so, the concepts underlying the syntax should remain relevant.

Recall that our full mixed model for the client trainee data is

$$\text{Full:} \quad Y_i = \beta_0 X_{0i} + \beta_1 X_{1i} + u_{1i} Z_{1i} + \varepsilon_i \qquad (3, \text{repeated})$$

To fit this model to our data, we obviously must have an appropriate input data set. An example of the SAS code to create such a data set is given by the following lines:

```
data new;
input trainee gender severity;
cards;
[24 lines of data follow, 1 for each client]
```

The data file has 24 rows and 3 columns. (Users who are familiar with SAS will recognize that the semicolon that appears at the end of each line is included to separate the commands from one another.) Each row represents the data for a specific client, and each column corresponds to a variable in the data file. Specifically, "trainee" designates which individual female or male trainee conducted the intake and is coded 1, 2, or 3. Notice that although there are a total of 6 trainees, there are only 3 trainees within each gender, so the combination of the trainee variable and the gender variable uniquely identify each trainee.[4] The gender variable obviously distinguishes female trainees from male trainees, so a client whose intake was conducted by a female receives one value on this variable, whereas a client whose intake was conducted by a male receives a different value. The precise values do not matter, because we will designate "gender" as a "class" variable in the actual analysis. Finally, the third variable is the severity score assigned by the trainee to this client.

Before jumping immediately into the maximum likelihood analysis of these data, it is important to take a look at the scores themselves. Although a full examination of the data would ideally include several graphical and diagnostic approaches as originally presented in Chapter 3, we will confine ourselves here simply to a consideration of the pattern of means. Given our goal of comparing female and male trainee mean severity scores, we need to see the mean severity score for each individual trainee if we are to put an eventual significance test in the proper context. The following lines of SAS syntax produce the output shown in Table 16.2:

```
proc means mean;
    by gender;
    class trainee;
    types ( ) trainee;
    var severity;
```

The first line invokes the "proc means" procedure and asks for the mean of the variable "severity" as denoted by the "var" statement in the last line. The "by gender" statement produces separate descriptive information for females and for males. The "class" and "types" statement produce means for each trainee within gender, as well as the mean averaging over trainees within a gender.

Table 16.2 shows that the mean severity rating of the 12 clients seen by males was 46, whereas the mean of the 12 clients seen by females was 60. Although it might be tempting simply to perform a t test of the difference between these two means, such an analysis will tend to produce too many Type I errors in a nested design with a random factor such as trainee. For this reason, it is important to examine the mean severity ratings given by the individual trainees. The table shows that the 3 male trainees assigned mean severity ratings of 40, 50, and 48. The 3 female

TABLE 16.2
MEAN SEVERITY RATINGS FOR FEMALE AND MALE TRAINEES

--gender=1--

The MEANS Procedure
Analysis Variable: Severity

N Obs	Mean
12	46.0000000

--gender=1--

Analysis Variable: Severity

Trainee	N Obs	Mean
1	4	40.0000000
2	4	50.0000000
3	4	48.0000000

--gender=2--

The MEANS Procedure
Analysis Variable: Severity

N Obs	Mean
12	60.0000000

--gender=2--

Analysis Variable: Severity

Trainee	N Obs	Mean
1	4	61.0000000
2	4	54.0000000
3	4	65.0000000

trainees assigned mean severity ratings of 61, 54, and 65. At this point, we want to preview what is arguably the most important point of this entire chapter, which is now that we have calculated these summary statistics for each trainee, we can think of our null hypothesis as if we had a sample size of 6 and each of these new scores was the dependent variable for one of the 6 participants. For example, suppose we decided to test the difference between severity ratings given by female and male trainees simply by performing a t test comparing the three scores of 40, 50, and 48 to the three scores of 61, 54, and 65. It would turn out that in this special case where we have equal sample sizes, the p value from this t test would be exactly the same as the p value we will eventually obtain using the maximum likelihood analysis of PROC MIXED. If this equality holds, why not simply always perform the t test? The easy answer to this question is that this type of equality holds only for equal sample sizes in very simple designs. Otherwise, we need to use the maximum likelihood approach. However, even when the maximum likelihood approach is called for, such as in much more complex designs, conceptually we still will calculate some sort of summary measure at the lowest level of the design, and then use this summary measure to make comparisons at a higher level of the design. Thus, it is very useful to grasp the logic of this approach in preparation for more complex designs.

Having created an appropriate input data set and examined descriptive statistics, there are two different ways to fit the model of Equation 3 to the data. We will begin with the approach that may seem more intuitive and discuss each line in some detail. Then we will present an alternative way of formulating the model and briefly describe how it relates to the first formulation. Arguably, the more natural way of fitting the model to the data is given by the five following lines:

```
proc mixed;
    class trainee gender;
    model severity = gender / s;
    random trainee(gender) / subject = trainee(gender);
    estimate 'gender' gender 1 −1;
```

The first line simply invokes the MIXED procedure. The second line specifies that both "trainee" and "gender" should be regarded as class (i.e., categorical) variables. For example, although "trainee" is a single variable in the file, the "class" command tells SAS to create indicator variables to represent the effect of trainee (see Appendix B for more details on how SAS creates indicator variables). The model statement describes the dependent variable and all fixed effects. The name of the dependent variable ("severity" in our example) appears to the left of the equals sign, whereas all fixed effects appear to the right. In our example, "gender" is the only fixed effect. The remainder of the line (i.e., the slash and the *s* that follows it) are optional and requests parameter estimates for the fixed effects. As an aside, we should also note that PROC MIXED includes an intercept in the fixed portion of the model by default, so β_0 is automatically estimated unless we specifically request that it be omitted from the model. We know from our discussion earlier in the chapter that the maximum likelihood method explicitly includes random effects in the model, so it is not surprising that we need to include a "random" command in our syntax. Immediately after the word *random* we list all random effects in the model. In our case, the only random effect is that of trainees within gender. The continuation of this line to the right of the slash tells PROC MIXED that each trainee is presumed to have some potential effect. In other words, the random effect occurs at the level of the individual trainee, not at the level of gender or client. The fifth line (i.e., the "estimate" line) is optional, but is included here because it provides an estimate of the difference between female and male trainees' severity ratings, as we will see when we examine the output produced by these commands.

As we mentioned, there is a second, slightly different way of fitting the same model of Equation 3 to the client trainee data. This way differs from the first way only in that the "random" line is written differently. Specifically, the "random" line of the first way is replaced by the following "random" line:

```
random int/ subject = trainee(gender);
```

The letters *int* immediately after "random" tell PROC MIXED that each participant has his or her own random intercept term. After the slash, we see that a participant in this context is a trainee, so this command tells PROC MIXED to include a random intercept term in the model for each trainee. Including such an intercept here simply means that each trainee's scores are allowed to have their own mean. However, this is exactly the same as saying that there is potentially an effect associated with each trainee, so although this statement looks very different from the first "random" statement, they are in fact identical in this context. In our view,

TABLE 16.3
MAXIMUM LIKELIHOOD ANALYSIS OF TABLE 16.1 DATA

The Mixed Procedure

Solution for Fixed Effects

Effect	Gender	Estimate	Standard Error	DF	t Value	Pr > |t|
Intercept		60.0000	3.1358	4	19.13	< .0001
gender	1	−14.0000	4.4347	4	−3.16	0.0343
gender	2	0	.	.	.	.

Type 3 Tests of Fixed Effects

Effect	Num DF	Den DF	F Value	Pr > F
Gender	1	4	9.97	0.0343

Estimates

Label	Estimate	Standard Error	DF	t Value	Pr > |t|
gender	−14.0000	4.4347	4	−3.16	0.0343

Covariance Parameter Estimates

Cov Parm	Subject	Estimate
Intercept	trainee (gender)	18.1111
Residual		45.5556

specifying the random effect as "trainee(gender)" has the advantage that it is more intuitive and follows more closely with the thinking behind the ANOVA formulation of Chapter 10. However, we will see later in the chapter that specifying the random effect as "int" has the advantage that it generalizes easily to more complex types of designs. For the moment, the choice does not matter, because the results are identical either way. For users of PROC MIXED who might prefer to specify the effect as "int," it is important to point out that it is not necessary to include a variable named "int" in the data file. Instead, "int" is a special keyword in SAS, which tells PROC MIXED to create an intercept variable for each participant, so that the data file itself does not have to include such a variable.

Table 16.3 presents an excerpt of the output produced by PROC MIXED for analyzing the clinical trainee data with the maximum likelihood approach. First, notice that the output contains separate sections for the fixed portion of the model and the random portion (labeled "Covariance Parameter Estimates"), just as it did when we used PROC MIXED to analyze longitudinal data. This separation reflects the fact that the maximum likelihood approach distinguishes fixed and random effects from the outset and provides variance (and, where applicable, covariance) estimates of random effect parameters instead of separately estimating effects of individual trainees.[5]

Having realized that the output distinguishes fixed and random effects from one another, we will discuss each in turn, beginning with the fixed effects. The section of the output labeled "Solution for Fixed Effects" shows parameter estimates, standard errors, degrees of freedom, t values, and p values for each fixed effect parameter in the model. Because of the way in which SAS parameterizes models with categorical (i.e., "class") variables (see Appendix B for more details), the intercept in this model is simply the mean severity rating given by female trainees. In particular, the sample mean severity rating for the 3 female trainees is 60, as confirmed by the "Estimate" column value for the "Intercept" row of the table. Of more interest here is the estimate for gender, which is −14.00. This value is simply the difference between the mean severity rating assigned by male trainees (which was 46) and the mean rating assigned by female trainees (which as we already said was 60). Thus, our single best guess is that the mean severity rating in a population of male trainees would be 14 points lower than the population mean for female trainees. This difference is statistically significant, as shown by the p value of .0343.

Because we have only two levels of gender, the other sections pertaining to fixed effects (namely, "Type 3 Tests of Fixed Effects" and "Estimates") largely duplicate the information that appears in the "Solution for Fixed Effects" section. If gender were to have had more than two levels, these two sections can be especially useful for interpreting the test of the omnibus null hypothesis and specific contrasts of interest, respectively. Even though the information they convey here is largely redundant with that of the first section, we will nevertheless use these two sections to make two additional important points.

First, we might be interested in forming a confidence interval for the difference between the mean of the male severity ratings and the mean of the female severity ratings. We can use the estimated value of -14.00 along with its standard error of 4.4347 to obtain the desired interval. For example, suppose we want a 95% confidence interval for this difference. Appendix Table A.1 shows that the critical t value for 4 degrees of freedom and an area of .025 in each tail of the distribution is 2.78. Thus, the endpoints of the confidence interval will be located 12.33 units away from the center of the interval (notice that 12.33 is simply the product of 4.4347 multiplied times 2.78). Thus, the interval itself ranges from -26.33 to -1.67. We can be 95% confident that the population severity rating for male trainees is between 1.67 and 26.33 units lower than the population mean severity rating for female trainees. Notice that the interval does not contain zero, making it consistent with the statistically significant result we obtained when we saw that the data enabled us to reject the null hypothesis. But also notice that this interval is quite wide, primarily because our design included so few trainees and clients.

Second, the F value of 9.97 and p value of .0343 shown in Table 16.3 for the gender effect may look familiar by now. You may recall that these are exactly the same values we obtained when we used an ANOVA to analyze these data. We can understand if your first reaction is to wonder why we have done all of this additional work if the end result is the same as we could have obtained more easily with an ANOVA. However, the point here is that the maximum likelihood approach is a generalization of the ANOVA approach. In the special case where all cell sizes are equal, the two approaches yield identical tests of fixed effects. In our data, each and every trainee rated four clients, producing an equal n design, which is why the two approaches provided the same test of the gender effect. If cell sizes had been unequal here, the ANOVA approach would not have been applicable (i.e., expected mean squares do not naturally lead to an appropriate F statistic), and we would have needed to use the maximum likelihood approach. We chose to begin the chapter with an equal n design in order to demonstrate the equivalence of the two approaches in this special case. Very shortly, we will consider an unequal n design, as well as more complex designs, in an attempt to demonstrate the unique merits of the maximum likelihood approach.

The output in Table 16.3 also provides information about the random effects in the model, as shown in the section titled "Covariance Parameter Estimates." The specific covariance parameters will depend on the design and the specification of random effects in the design. Recall that in the simple nested design, there are two variance components: (1) σ_ε^2, the variance of ε_i, and (2) σ_u^2, the variance of u_i. The first of these variances represents variability between clients within a trainee, whereas the second represents variability between trainees within gender. In some models (especially longitudinal models), random effects might be allowed to correlate with one another, in which case a covariance parameter would also be estimated. However, we have assumed that ε_i, and u_i are uncorrelated with one another, so no covariance parameter estimate appears in this output.

How should we interpret the covariance parameter estimates shown in Table 16.3? We will begin with the "Residual" estimate, because we need to understand it before we can interpret the "Intercept" estimate. The "Residual" estimate is the estimated residual variance in the model, which is simply an estimate of σ_ε^2, the variance of ε_i. The variance unaccounted for in the Equation 3 model is variance due to client. Thus, the value of 45.5556 shown in Table 16.3 is the estimated variance in severity ratings due to clients or, more specifically, due to clients within trainees. Notice that this value is precisely the same as MS_W for these data in the ANOVA analysis of Chapter 10. This equality will always occur in equal n nested designs such as we have here. We will now turn our attention to the "Intercept" estimate. We have already said that this represents the estimated variance between trainees within gender. But exactly what does that mean, and how should we think about this variance as compared to the variance due to clients? In order to answer this question, we must first be sure we understand the rationale behind the estimate itself. Thus, we will spend a moment developing the rationale for the procedure whereby this estimate is obtained. Suppose we knew the sample mean severity ratings for each of our trainees. How might we use this information to estimate the variance between trainees within gender? The sample means for the 3 female trainees are 61, 54, and 65 (see Table 16.2), and the sample means for the 3 male trainees are 40, 50, and 48 (also shown in Table 16.2). We can calculate the variance of each set of three scores by summing the squared deviations from the mean and dividing by two (i.e., the number of scores minus one). Doing so yields a value of 31 for females and a value of 28 for males. Assuming these two values of 31 and 28 are somewhat different simply due to sampling error, we can average them, yielding a value of 29.50 for our hypothetical data. At first glance, it might seem natural to conclude that the best estimate of the variance between trainees within gender is 29.50. However, taking a peek at Table 16.3 shows this is not the value produced by PROC MIXED. Why not? To answer this question, suppose for a moment that there were in fact no true differences among female trainees and also no true differences among male trainees in the population. In other words, if each trainee were to provide severity ratings on a population of clients, we would discover that each and every population mean for females is the same and each and every population mean for males is the same. (The mean for females might, however, be different from the mean for males; more on this in a moment.) The key insight here is that even if this equality were true, we would nevertheless observe some differences in sample means from trainee to trainee, especially when each trainee has rated only four clients, as in our data. As a result, the value of 29.50 we calculated reflects two possible sources of variance: (1) variance between female trainees and between male trainees, but also (2) variance between clients. Thus, the value of 29.50 probably overestimates the actual variance we are attempting to estimate, which is the variance between trainees within gender. Fortunately, it turns out to be straightforward to correct this bias. Table 10.8 provides the following expected mean square in an equal n nested design when factor A is fixed and factor B is nested

$$E(MS_{B/A}) = \sigma_\varepsilon^2 + n\sigma_\beta^2 \tag{5}$$

where σ_β^2 in the notation of Chapter 10 is identical to σ_u^2 in the notation of the current chapter (i.e., both σ_β^2 and σ_u^2 represent the variance of trainees within gender). Because MS_W provides an unbiased estimate of σ_ε^2, we can substitute it into Equation 5 along with the sample value of $MS_{B/A}$ to obtain an unbiased estimate of the variance due to female and male trainees. Specifically, in an equal n design, this variance is estimated as

$$\hat{\sigma}_\beta^2 = \frac{MS_{B/A} - MS_W}{n} \tag{6}$$

Looking back at Table 10.9 reminds us that when we analyzed these data in Chapter 10, we found that $MS_{B/A} = 118$ and $MS_W = 45.5556$. Indeed, in our data, substituting $MS_{B/A} = 118$, $MS_W = 45.5556$, and $n = 4$ into Equation 6 yields a value of 18.1111 for the estimated variance due to trainees within gender. After all of this, do not fail to notice that we have managed to duplicate the value shown in the PROC MIXED output of Table 16.3.

Four final comments are in order here. First, notice that because the random effects due to clients and to trainees within gender are presumed to be uncorrelated, their variances are additive. Thus, our best estimate of the total variance of scores within gender of trainee is 63.6667 (this is simply the sum of 45.5556 and 18.1111). We can now say that our best estimate is that 28% (i.e., 18.1111 divided by 63.6667) of this variance is due to trainee, whereas the remaining 72% is due to client. Thus, clients account for more variability than do trainees. Even so, the fact that our best single estimate is that trainees account for as much as one fourth of the variance in severity ratings might be judged to be of both practical and scientific importance. Second, notice that differences between trainees would account for a higher percentage of variance if we were to look at variance across all trainees regardless of gender, instead of focusing on the variance due to trainee within gender. Neither of these is necessarily right and the other wrong, but instead they are simply two different questions. Third, notice in Equation 6 that the numerator for estimating the variance due to trainees within gender involves subtracting MS_W from $MS_{B/A}$. Because of sampling error, it is possible for MS_W to exceed $MS_{B/A}$ in a sample, in which case the estimated variance is negative. However, the population variance cannot be negative, so when the estimated variance from Equation 6 is negative, we know that the estimate must be too small. Different software packages handle this situation differently. For example, some report the negative value, whereas others set the value equal to zero. In either case, this result usually indicates one or more of the following: (1) sample sizes (not just participants but also number of levels of the nested factor) are too small to obtain a precise estimate of the variance, (2) the true population variance is very close to zero, (3) one or more assumptions of the model may be incorrect. Fourth, this type of variance partitioning can be very important for answering certain types of questions. For example, we mentioned earlier that studies of school effectiveness may examine the relative magnitude of the variance between schools to the variance within schools. Or, the variance could be partitioned yet further to the variance within classrooms within schools, the variance between classrooms within schools, and the variance between schools. Or, in a different research domain, an investigator may be interested in comparing the variance of some characteristic within twins to the variance between twins, in order to calculate a heritability coefficient.

Numerical Example—Unequal n

We have now seen that the maximum likelihood approach to analyzing data from a simple nested design exactly reproduces the ANOVA approach when all cell sizes are equal. On the one hand, this equivalence is reassuring, because it implies that we can regard the ANOVA approach as a special case of the maximum likelihood approach. Thus, when cell sizes are equal, we can use either approach to analyze our data. Further, the concepts developed from the ANOVA framework continue to apply in the maximum likelihood approach. On the other hand, one could make a compelling argument that there is no need to learn about the maximum likelihood approach if the data to be analyzed come from a simple nested design with equal n. Thus, if the time we have already devoted to the maximum likelihood approach in this chapter is to be useful, we need to examine it in other types of designs.

The remainder of this chapter will describe the maximum likelihood approach in situations where the ANOVA approach is not feasible. Specifically, we will begin by continuing to look at a simple nested design, but now one where sample sizes are no longer equal to one another. After seeing that this presents few complications for the maximum likelihood approach (except computational complications, which we will leave up to the statistical software), we will then consider more complex types of designs. We hope to convince you that the concepts we have developed for implementing the maximum likelihood approach to the simple nested design generalize with minimal complications to more complex designs.

We will orient our presentation of the unequal n nested design around another hypothetical data set. Suppose an educational psychologist has developed an intervention to teach inductive reasoning skills to school children. She decides to test the efficacy of her intervention by conducting a randomized design. Three classrooms of students are randomly assigned to the treatment condition, and 3 other classrooms are assigned to the control.

Before considering the data and ensuing analysis, we want to take a moment to make a few additional comments about the design itself. First, the analysis would proceed in exactly the same manner if this were not an experimental study with random assignment. However, the ability to reach a conclusion about the causal influence of the treatment would almost certainly be compromised. Second, we have chosen to illustrate a design where the number of classrooms is the same in the two conditions. However, the analysis would proceed in exactly the same manner if there were different numbers of classrooms in the two conditions.[6] Third, we have also chosen to illustrate a design with only two treatment conditions. Once again, the only difference in an analysis with more than two levels would be a distinction between the omnibus test and tests of individual contrasts. Fourth, power considerations would almost always suggest more than three classrooms per condition as well as more students per classroom than in our hypothetical data set. As usual, we have chosen to present a smaller data set than would be optimal for reasons of simplicity. In any case, once again the concepts we illustrate here apply in studies with larger sample sizes. Fifth, we are assuming in this example that each classroom is taught by a different teacher. The design and therefore the analysis would be different if, for example, each teacher taught two of the classrooms included in the study. Fifth, we have taken the typical textbook writer's license to describe the alternative to the treatment simply as the control condition. However, it is important to realize that the value of the study may depend greatly on the extent to which the actual definition and implementation of the control condition leads to construct validity of cause. Of course, we have been equally vague in describing the dependent measure, which becomes important in considerations of construct validity of effect.

Table 16.4 shows hypothetical data collected from 29 children who participated in the study assessing the effectiveness of the intervention to increase inductive reasoning skills. We want to call your attention to several aspects of the data. First, the 15 children with condition values of 0 received the control, whereas the 14 children with condition values of 1 received the treatment. Second, 4 of the children in the control condition were students in control Classroom 1, 6 of them were students in control Classroom 2, and 5 were students in control Classroom 3. Along similar lines, 3 of the children in the treatment condition were students in treatment Classroom 1, 5 were students in treatment Classroom 2, and 6 were students in treatment Classroom 3. It is essential to understand that there are a total of six classrooms here; we have coded classroom from 1 to 3 for control as well as treatment, because we will indicate to PROC MIXED that classroom is nested under treatment. Third, scores on the dependent variable appear in the rightmost column under the variable label "induct."

So far in our description, the only difference between the inductive reasoning data in Table 16.4 and the previous clinical trainee severity data in Table 16.1 is that the new data set fails to maintain equal sample sizes. As we would typically expect, some classrooms are larger

TABLE 16.4
DATA FROM THE INDUCTIVE REASONING STUDY

Obs	Room	Cond	Cog	Skill	Induct
1	1	0	46	4	21
2	1	0	52	4	26
3	1	0	60	4	33
4	1	0	44	4	22
5	2	0	46	6	18
6	2	0	48	6	25
7	2	0	50	6	26
8	2	0	54	6	24
9	2	0	50	6	21
10	2	0	48	6	25
11	3	0	52	9	35
12	3	0	50	9	28
13	3	0	46	9	32
14	3	0	50	9	36
15	3	0	58	9	38
16	1	1	42	5	26
17	1	1	46	5	34
18	1	1	50	5	27
19	2	1	52	8	38
20	2	1	54	8	44
21	2	1	46	8	34
22	2	1	56	8	45
23	2	1	48	8	38
24	3	1	42	7	31
25	3	1	46	7	41
26	3	1	44	7	34
27	3	1	52	7	35
28	3	1	56	7	38
29	3	1	54	7	46

than others. (Of course, in reality, few classrooms are as small as those shown in these data, but the important methodological point is simply that the sample sizes are different from one another.) However, the data from the inductive reasoning study are also different in that two additional columns appear in Table 16.4 that had no counterpart in the clinical trainee data. The variable labeled "cog" in Table 16.4 represents cognitive ability scores that have been obtained for each student sometime prior to assigning classrooms to treatment conditions. The variable labeled "skill" represents a global measure of each teacher's teaching skill, once again assessed prior to assigning classrooms to treatment conditions. Notice that these two variables are similar in that we could consider both to be covariates, and in that respect the concepts of Chapter 9 become relevant here. As an aside, a study with a nested design might also include additional predictors such as these two even if random assignment were absent from the design. Of course, the interpretation associated with these variables would then differ, but the statistical analysis would follow the same general logic. Even though these two variables share the characteristic of being covariates in common, there is another sense in which they are very different from one another. Specifically, cognitive ability is a characteristic of the individual student, but teaching skill is a characteristic of the classroom. Notice that cognitive ability scores typically change from every line to the next, whereas teaching skill scores are grouped according to classroom. One of the goals of the remainder of this chapter is to explain how these two types of variables can be included in models for nested data and how to interpret ensuing analyses.

TABLE 16.5
TABLE 16.5
MEAN SCORES FOR THE INDUCTIVE REASONING STUDY BY CLASSROOM

--cond=0---

The MEANS Procedure

N Obs	Variable	Mean
15	induct	27.33
	cog	50.27
	skill	6.47

--cond=0---

Room	N Obs	Variable	Mean
1	4	induct	25.50
		cog	50.50
		skill	4.00
2	6	induct	23.17
		cog	49.33
		skill	6.00
3	5	induct	33.80
		cog	51.20
		skill	9.00

--cond=1---

The MEANS Procedure

N Obs	Variable	Mean
14	induct	36.50
	cog	49.14
	skill	6.93

--cond=1---

Room	N Obs	Variable	Mean
1	3	induct	29.00
		cog	46.00
		skill	5.00
2	5	induct	39.80
		cog	51.20
		skill	8.00
3	6	induct	37.50
		cog	49.00
		skill	7.00

Before entering the realm of hypothesis testing, it is helpful to establish a context for forthcoming analyses by considering mean scores on inductive reasoning, cognitive ability, and teaching skill. Table 16.5 presents means for these three variables separately for the control and treatment conditions. In addition to presenting the means averaging over classrooms, means are presented within each classroom. For example, the mean inductive reasoning score for the

15 students in the control condition was 27.33, whereas the mean score for the 14 students in the treatment condition was 36.50. Although this difference is promising, we know that it is important to consider the means of the individual classrooms. The table shows that these means are 25.50, 23.17, and 33.80 for the control classrooms, and 29.00, 39.80, and 37.50 for the treatment classrooms. If there had been the same number of students in each classroom, we could simply perform a t test comparing the mean of the first three scores (25.50, 23.17, and 33.80) to the mean of the last three scores (29.00, 39.80, and 37.50). However, the presence of unequal sample sizes here necessitates the maximum likelihood approach. Nevertheless, we will see shortly that we can think of the maximum likelihood approach in terms of this t test of six scores, so you may want to keep this perspective in mind as you continue to read.

It is also interesting to note that there is at least some suggestion that both cognitive ability and teaching skill may be related to inductive reasoning. Although the pattern of means shown in Table 16.5 is not completely consistent, there is some tendency for all three variables to covary positively. Even so, it is important to realize that the data in this table only describe how these variables relate to one another between classrooms. In other words, the table provides no information about how inductive reasoning and cognitive ability (for example) may relate to one another within classrooms. It is conceivable that students with lower cognitive ability scores could have higher inductive reasoning scores within individual classrooms, while classrooms with lower mean cognitive ability scores might also tend to have lower mean inductive reasoning scores. Thus, it is important to keep in mind the level of analysis when describing relationships among variables in nested designs.

We will begin by illustrating analysis of the data without considering cognitive ability or teaching skill measures. Thus, the design is a two factor design, where a random classroom factor is nested under a fixed treatment condition factor. In this respect, this design is identical to the clinical trainee severity design. However, unlike the clinical trainee example, sample sizes in the inductive reasoning example are unequal. For this reason, we do not begin by showing results from the ANOVA approach, which is unable to handle unequal sample sizes. Instead, we must rely on the maximum likelihood approach in this situation.

Whether the sample sizes are equal or unequal, the same full model is compared to the same restricted model in order to test the null hypothesis that the fixed factor has no effect in the population:

$$\text{Full:} \quad Y_i = \beta_0 X_{0i} + \beta_1 X_{1i} + u_{1i} Z_{1i} + \varepsilon_i \qquad \text{(3, repeated)}$$
$$\text{Restricted:} \quad Y_i = \beta_0 X_{0i} + u_{1i} Z_{1i} + \varepsilon_i \qquad \text{(4, repeated)}$$

Because the models are the same whether or not sample sizes are equal, the input to SAS PROC MIXED is unchanged except for obvious changes in variable names:

```
proc mixed;
    class room cond;
    model induct = cond / s;
    random int / subject = room(cond);
    estimate 'condition' cond −1 1;
```

Not surprisingly, the output shown in Table 16.6 has the same general form as did the Table 16.3 output for the equal n example. Instead of repeating our former interpretation of this form of output, we will simply point out that the data collected here do not allow us to reject the null hypothesis that the educational intervention has no effect. Correspondingly, we could form a confidence interval for the difference between the population means of the treatment and

TABLE 16.6
TABLE 16.6
MAXIMUM LIKELIHOOD ANALYSIS OF INDUCTIVE REASONING DATA

The Mixed Procedure

Solution for Fixed Effects

Effect	Cond	Estimate	Standard Error	DF	t Value	Pr > |t|
Intercept		35.6261	3.2294	4	11.03	0.0004
cond	0	−8.1485	4.5483	4	−1.79	0.1477
cond	1	0	.	.	.	.

Type 3 Tests of Fixed Effects

Effect	Num DF	Den DF	F Value	Pr > F
cond	1	4	3.21	0.1477

Estimates

Label	Estimate	Standard Error	DF	t Value	Pr > |t|
condition	8.1485	4.5483	4	1.79	0.1477

Covariance Parameter Estimates

Cov Parm	Subject	Estimate
Intercept	room (cond)	26.6270
Residual		20.2551

control groups. To do so, we can take the estimated standard error of 4.5483 as shown in Table 16.6 and multiply it by a critical t value of 2.78 with 4 degrees of freedom (and $\alpha = .05$, two-tailed). Adding and subtracting the resultant product of 12.6443 to the estimated effect of 8.1485 (as shown in Table 16.6) yields a 95% confidence interval for the treatment effect stretching from −4.50 to 20.79. We have to be careful to realize here that our "estimate" command was coded to represent the mean of the treatment group minus the mean of our control group, so the interval tells us that the treatment could be as beneficial as 20.79 units on average or as detrimental as 4.50 units on average. Even so, the interval contains zero, so we cannot reject the null hypothesis, which is another way of saying that the data do not allow us to be certain beyond a reasonable doubt of the direction of any effect the treatment may have on inductive reasoning scores. Of course, if this were an actual study, the flaw in this design is the small number of classrooms and students, which explains why the confidence interval is so wide and does not permit us to reach an informed conclusion about the treatment effect.

MAXIMUM LIKELIHOOD ANALYSIS MODELS FOR COMPLEX NESTED DESIGNS

An important virtue of the maximum likelihood method for analyzing data from nested designs is that the same models can be used whether sample sizes are equal or unequal. The actual calculations become more arduous with unequal n, but modern software largely makes this problem transparent to the user, so he or she can concentrate on the concepts and associated interpretation of results.

Another important benefit of the maximum likelihood method is that it can accommodate more complex designs in a fairly straightforward fashion. Although we cannot hope to cover every conceivable extension of a simple nested design, we have chosen to present two types of extensions that we believe may be most important for behavioral scientists. We will use the "teacher skill" variable to illustrate one of these extensions and the "cognitive ability" variable to illustrate the other.

Recall from Table 16.4 that in addition to measuring each student's inductive reasoning ability at the end of the study, there is also a measure of each teacher's teaching skill as measured sometime prior to the implementation of the intervention. We will now consider what additional questions we might answer with this variable and how to include it in our statistical model. It seems plausible that more skilled teachers might elicit higher inductive reasoning scores from their students, regardless of whether their classroom was assigned to the treatment or control condition. From this perspective, some portion of σ_ε^2, the unexplained (or residual) variance in our original Equation 3 model may in fact be attributable to teaching skill. Thus, there are at least two reasons to consider including teaching skill as a variable in the full mixed model: (1) It may be interesting to assess the extent to which teaching skill correlates with students' inductive reasoning scores and (2) as we described in Chapter 9, including teaching skills as a covariate in the model may reduce unexplained variance and thus increase power and precision of the estimated treatment effect.[7]

Recall from Table 16.4 that we also have measure of each student's cognitive ability, as assessed sometime prior to the implementation of the intervention. As we just discussed for teachers' teaching skill, it seems plausible that students with higher cognitive abilities might obtain higher scores on the inductive reasoning measure. To the extent such a correlation exists, we may have another opportunity to reduce some of the error variance in our original Equation 3 model. In addition, we may also be interested in assessing the extent to which students' cognitive ability scores and inductive reasoning scores correlate with one another. Yet another possible question of interest is whether the relationship between inductive reasoning and cognitive ability is the same in the treatment condition as in the control condition. Thus, for a variety of reasons, we might want to include cognitive ability as a variable in our model.

Having developed some motives for including teaching skill and cognitive ability in our model, we must consider how each type of variable can be included. On the one hand, it sounds as if they may play similar roles here, because both may explain some additional variance. Despite this similarity, however, you may have noticed a fundamental difference between the two variables. The first, teaching skill, is a characteristic of a teacher and is thus measured at the level of the classroom. Cognitive ability, on the other hand, is a characteristic of the student and is thus measured at the student level. We will see in the next two sections of the chapter that this distinction becomes important in how we include these variables in our model. In particular, remember that the maximum likelihood-based model distinguishes fixed effects (the X variables) from random effects (the Z variables) in the initial model formulation, so we must decide whether to include any additional variables as fixed or random, or perhaps even both. Although it might be possible to present rules for such decisions without going through the formality of presenting the underlying statistical models, we believe it is important to present the models in order to have a more thorough understanding. Thus, much of our presentation of the maximum likelihood approach for more complex designs will focus on a conceptual understanding of the models for these designs.

Hierarchical Representation of the Model for a Simple Nested Design

Before considering models for complex designs, we will hope to gain some momentum by briefly returning to models for the simple nested design. In particular, until now we have written the model for this design in terms of one equation. Writing the model this way generally works fine for simple cases, such as two-factor nested designs with no additional variables. However, in more complex designs, it is often helpful to write the model in hierarchical form. Instead of writing the model in terms of a single equation, hierarchical form expresses the model by writing a series of equations, each one of which describes a specific level of data. For example, in the two-way nested design where data are obtained on students whose classrooms are nested under treatment condition, we can write one equation at the level of individual students and a second equation at the level of classrooms. By convention, the equation at the lowest level of the hierarchy is referred to as a level 1 equation. Not surprisingly, the equation at the next level is the level 2 equation, and so forth. We say "and so forth" because complex data structures may have three, four, or even more levels, although we will only consider two levels in this chapter. In our example, then, we will write a level 1 equation at the student level and a level 2 equation at the classroom level.

Let's begin by considering the equation for the student-level inductive reasoning data in Table 16.4. We need to begin by acknowledging that an individual student's inductive reasoning score may depend in part on which classroom the student is in. In other words, scores may tend to be higher in some classrooms than in others, and we would like our model to allow for this possibility. (You may immediately wonder why some classrooms might be different from others. If you thought of this question, you are on the right track, but for reasons that should become clear soon, we will defer this question for the moment.) The most common way of modeling this possibility is to allow each classroom to have its own mean. For example, we could write such a model as

$$Y_i = \mu_i + \varepsilon_i \tag{7}$$

Notice that this model looks very much like one of our earliest models in Chapter 3 for a single-factor design. In fact, the models would be identical except that only a single subscript is used here to designate Individual i without including a second subscript to represent the participant's group.[8] Thus, the model represented by Equation 7 is intended to be exactly the same as the model we first encountered in Chapter 3. The only difference is in notation. We have chosen to deviate from the notation used in Chapter 3 in order to be consistent with the notation used for PROC MIXED, but in any case the important point is to realize that Equation 7 simply says that a student's score may depend on the student's classroom, and each classroom may have a different population mean value on inductive reasoning.

We are now ready to address the question of why classrooms might differ from one another. Certainly, in our example, one possible reason is assignment to treatment condition. Ideally, we hope that classrooms that have received the treatment will have higher scores than those that have not. Suppose we let X_{1i} be an indicator variable to designate whether an individual student i was exposed to the treatment. We can now write a second equation for the classroom-level data:

$$\mu_i = \beta_0 + \beta_1 X_{1i} + u_i \tag{8}$$

This model stipulates that a classroom's mean level of performance μ_i can be expressed as the sum of three components: (1) some baseline value, β_0 which in general is the intercept parameter, (2) a variable X_1, which in our case represents treatment condition, and (3) unexplained differences among classrooms, as represented by u_i. Before proceeding, we must point out that it is necessary to distinguish μ_i from u_i. The Greek parameter μ_i represents the mean score on Y, whereas the ordinary letter u_i is a type of error term, or residual term, which reflects the sources of all influences on the μ_i mean values beyond those included in the model. In other words, omitting u_i would be the same as saying that classroom means are identical to one another once we control for X_{1i}. Although it would be possible to form such a model, we would probably not want to make such a strong assumption at the beginning of an analysis. We will see shortly that the inclusion of u_i plays a pivotal role in the random effects portion of our model.

Examination of Equations 7 and 8 suggests one possible analysis strategy. We could use the data for each classroom to estimate the mean Y score for that classroom. Specifically, we could simply calculate the mean inductive reasoning score for each of the six classrooms separately to obtain an estimate of the μ_i parameter in Equation 7 for each classroom. We saw earlier (in Table 16.5) that the values of these six sample means are 25.50, 23.17, 33.80, 29.00, 39.80, and 37.50 in our data. We could now use these values as dependent variables for Equation 8. In other words, we could now fit the model shown in Equation 8 to these six scores. You may realize that we have already alluded to this analysis strategy. We pointed out earlier in the chapter that in a simple nested design with equal sample sizes, this approach is equivalent to the maximum likelihood analysis of PROC MIXED. However, with unequal sample sizes such as we have here, the two approaches are no longer equivalent to one another. Even so, the two-step strategy provides a useful way of conceptualizing the maximum likelihood approach. Conceptually, the maximum likelihood analysis follows the general logic of estimating the level 1 μ_i parameters in Equation 7 and then using these estimates as dependent variables in the level 2 model. Literally analyzing the data using least-squares through this two-step process would fail to take into account the fact that we have better estimates for larger classrooms than for smaller classrooms. The maximum likelihood approach, on the other hand, does take the differences in sample size into account. Of course, when sample sizes are equal, no differences need to be taken into account, which is why the two approaches become equivalent in this special case. Even when the two approaches are not equivalent, it is often helpful to think about the likelihood analysis in terms of the two-step strategy.

This way of thinking becomes especially useful in more complex designs, so throughout the remainder of the chapter you may want to keep in mind the two-step strategy. To establish a somewhat broader perspective to prepare you for more complex designs, we will briefly summarize the logic of the two-step conceptualization. In the first step, we estimate one or more parameters for each classroom (or, more generally, for each level of the nested factor). So far this parameter has always been a mean, but we will see that in more complex designs, our level 1 model may contain other types of parameters, such as a slope and an intercept. In the second step, the parameter estimates from the first step become dependent variables in a level 2 model.

We will now turn our attention back to the details of the maximum likelihood approach. Remember that we have now written two equations. Equation 7 represents student-level data, whereas Equation 8 represents classroom-level data. Writing these equations separately can be very useful to help understand the structure of a data set. In fact, some statistical software (e.g, HLM) for analyzing data from nested designs relies on writing exactly these types of equations for each hierarchical level of the design. However, PROC MIXED requires the specification of a single equation. We can easily combine Equations 7 and 8 into a single equation by substituting Equation 8 into Equation 7. More precisely, we can take the expression we have for μ_i in Equation 8 and substitute it into Equation 7. Making this substitution yields a single equation that can be written as

$$Y_i = \beta_0 + \beta_1 X_{1i} + u_i + \varepsilon_i \tag{9}$$

Equation 9 bears a striking resemblance to the full model we used for these data:

$$\text{Full:} \quad Y_i = \beta_0 X_{0i} + \beta_1 X_{1i} + u_{1i} Z_{1i} + \varepsilon_i \tag{3, repeated}$$

In fact, the models are equivalent to one another, because the only difference between them is notational. Equation 3 looks different from Equation 9, because it includes X_{0i} and Z_{1i} neither of which appear in Equation 9. However, remember that both X_{0i} and Z_{1i} are intercept terms (i.e., X_{0i} is a fixed effect intercept and Z_{1i} is a random effect intercept), and an intercept by definition equals 1 for each participant. Thus, we could simplify Equation 3 by substituting 1 for both X_{0i} and Z_{1i} in which case we would obtain Equation 9.

Let's pause for a moment to consider what we have accomplished so far. We have just seen that there are two equivalent ways of writing full models for a simple two-factor nested design. One option is to write the model as a single equation, such as Equation 3. Facility in this approach is necessary for using software such as PROC MIXED. The other option is to write several equations, one for each level of the data. This approach is necessary for using other software such as HLM. For our purposes, arguably the most important point of all is that it is possible to translate between the two approaches. This becomes especially important in complex designs, where it is frequently much clearer how to write a separate model for each level of the data, because PROC MIXED requires rewriting the resultant multiple equations as a single equation. We have seen that this translation is trivial for a simple two-factor nested design with no additional variables. We are now prepared to tackle the more difficult translation problems that emerge with additional variables.

Models With Additional Level 2 Variables

We will begin by considering how we can incorporate the teaching skills variable into our full model. Although it is possible to figure out how to incorporate it directly into the single equation form of Equation 3, we will instead consider the multiple equations form of Equations 7 and 8. From this perspective, the first question we must answer is whether teaching skills should be included in the model of Equation 7 or the model of Equation 8. Keep in mind that the distinction between these models is that Equation 7 is a student-level model, whereas Equation 8 is a classroom-level model. The teaching skills variable is a characteristic of the teacher, which means that it is a classroom-level variable and should therefore be included in the classroom-level model of Equation 8. Having reached this determination, all that is necessary is to rewrite the model with the addition of this new variable

$$\mu_i = \beta_0 + \beta_1 X_{1i} + \beta_2 X_{2i} + u_i \tag{10}$$

where X_{2i} is teaching skill. Correspondingly, β_2 is a slope parameter. Specifically, β_2 is the slope of the population regression line regressing μ_i on X_{2i} when X_{1i} is held constant. In words, the parameter is the slope of the regression line relating the mean inductive reasoning score in a classroom to the teacher's rated teaching skill, when we control for condition. This is exactly the same type of analysis of covariance model we presented in Chapter 9. The only difference is that the parameters of Equation 10 are classroom-level parameters instead of subject-level parameters. In a moment, we will consider the implications of this difference for interpreting the analysis of our inductive reasoning data, but first we need to see how to modify our PROC MIXED syntax to accommodate the additional variable of teaching skill.

To write the command lines for PROC MIXED, we must express our full model in terms of a single equation. Once again, this proves to be straightforward, as all we have to do is to substitute the Equation 10 expression for μ_i into Equation 7 (recall that the addition of the teaching skills variable into the model has not affected the student-level model of Equation 7).

Making this substitution yields a single equation of the form

$$Y_i = \beta_0 + \beta_1 X_{1i} + \beta_2 X_{2i} + u_i + \varepsilon_i \tag{11}$$

This full model has three fixed parameters, β_0, β_1, and β_2. Two random effects are included, implying two variance components, σ_u^2 and σ_ε^2. Keep in mind that PROC MIXED, like most similar software, includes the fixed intercept β_0 and the random residual σ_ε^2 as parameters by default, so all that remains to be specified is two fixed effects and one random effect. The resulting syntax is virtually identical to the syntax we used prior to including teaching skill in the model. Specifically, the new syntax is

```
proc mixed;
    class room cond;
    model induct = cond skill/ s;
    random int / subject = room(cond);
    estimate 'condition' cond −1 1;
```

Notice that the "model" statement specifies two fixed effects. The first fixed effect corresponds to condition and will yield an estimate of the β_1 parameter in the model shown in Equation 11. The second fixed effect corresponds to teaching skill and will yield an estimate of the β_2 parameter in the Equation 11 model. The "random" statement is identical to the random statement we specified prior to including teaching skills as a variable in the model.

Before seeing the output associated with these command lines, we want to point out an important implication of the syntax we have developed here. We have seen that adding teaching skills as a level 2 predictor resulted in a modification of the "model" statement in PROC MIXED but no change in the "random" statement. More generally, adding predictor variables to the highest level of the hierarchy changes the nature of fixed effects in the model but has no influence on the specification of random effects. This is an example of the sort of rule we alluded to earlier that when carefully applied can be used as a shortcut for specifying fixed and random effects. Even armed with such shortcuts, however, our advice based on personal experience is that fewer mistakes are generally made by working through the development of appropriate models methodically instead of hoping to save time by using shortcuts.

Table 16.7 presents an excerpt of the output produced by PROC MIXED for analyzing the inductive reasoning data with teaching skills included as a level 2 predictor variable. Several aspects of this table deserve mention. First, notice that the overall format of the output is virtually identical to the format seen earlier in Table 16.6 before we included teaching skills as an additional level 2 predictor. The only difference in appearance is that the new table contains an additional line for "skill" as a fixed effect. We will say more in a moment about how the actual numerical estimates shown in Table 16.7 compare to those in Table 16.6, but first we will focus on the new results themselves.

Table 16.7 shows that teaching skill has a statistically significant relationship with inductive reasoning scores ($p = .0089$). To understand what this means, think back to Equation 10, where we first wrote a full model including teaching skill as a predictor:

$$\mu_i = \beta_0 + \beta_1 X_{1i} + \beta_2 X_{2i} + u_i \tag{10, repeated}$$

According to Table 16.5, the best estimate of β_2 is that it equals 2.31. Remember that when we introduced this model, we said that the β_2 parameter is the slope of the regression line relating the mean inductive reasoning score in a classroom to the teacher's rated teaching skill,

TABLE 16.7

ANALYSIS OF INDUCTIVE REASONING DATA ADDING TEACHING SKILL AS A
LEVEL 2 PREDICTOR

The Mixed Procedure

Solution for Fixed Effects

Effect	Cond	Estimate	Standard Error	DF	t Value	Pr > |t|
Intercept		20.2521	5.8197	3	3.48	0.0401
cond	0	−7.5687	2.7161	3	−2.79	0.0686
cond	1	0	.	.	.	.
skill		2.3092	0.8085	23	2.86	0.0089

Type 3 Tests of Fixed Effects

Effect	Num DF	Den DF	F Value	Pr > F
cond	1	3	7.77	0.0686
skill	1	23	8.16	0.0089

Estimates

Label	Estimate	Standard Error	df	t Value	Pr > |t|
condition	7.5687	2.7161	3	2.79	0.0686

Covariance Parameter Estimates

Cov Parm	Subject	Estimate
Intercept	room (cond)	6.5704
Residual		20.2747

when we control for condition. So, a value of 2.31 for this parameter implies that associated with a change of 1 point in teaching skill is a 2.31 point increase in mean inductive reasoning score. Notice that this statement pertains to a classroom-level effect, not a student-level effect. Of course, we must also keep in mind that we have not randomly assigned levels of teaching skill, so we cannot justify a causal influence here. There may be other variables that happen to correlate with teaching skill that are the true causal agents affecting inductive reasoning.

Also notice from Table 16.7 that the effect of condition is not quite statistically significant at the .05 level. For example, a 95% confidence interval would contain zero, because it would stretch from −1.07 to 16.21. Based on this interval, we can be 95% confident that the treatment could be as beneficial as 16.21 points or as detrimental as 1.07 points, which implies that we cannot rule out the possibility that the treatment has (essentially) no effect whatsoever.

Even though this interval contains zero, it is substantially narrower than the comparable interval we calculated for the treatment effect in a model that did not include teaching skill. Recall from our earlier discussion that the 95% confidence interval for the treatment effect stretched from −4.50 to 20.79. By including teaching skill in the model, we have reduced the width of the confidence interval for the treatment effect by 32%. Of course, the magnitude of this reduction will in general depend on the strength of the relationship between the dependent variable and the covariate, so there is no guarantee that including a covariate will produce such a sizable decline in the width of the interval. Notice that in these data the center of the interval was not very different in the two analyses. Before including teaching skill in the model, the center of the interval was 8.15, whereas the center became 7.57 after including it. The reason the center changed relatively little is because classrooms were randomly assigned to condition, so we know that X_{1i} and X_{2i} (see Equation 10) must be uncorrelated in the population. Any correlation in the sample reflects sampling error, which is then responsible for a slight shift in the center of the confidence interval from sample to sample. Of course, if we had not randomly assigned classrooms to condition, X_{1i} and X_{2i} could correlate substantially, both in the population and in a sample, in which case the center of the interval could change dramatically. Notice also that the denominator degrees of freedom for the condition effect have been reduced from 4 to 3 by adding teaching skill in the model. These degrees of freedom are so small because they depend on the number of classrooms, not the number of students. Unless we have been able to sample a large number of classrooms, it is unwise (and perhaps mathematically impossible) to include very many level 2 predictors in the model.

We have seen that including teaching skill as a level 2 predictor narrowed the confidence interval for the condition effect in these data. This should not seem surprising, because Table 16.7 tells us that teaching skill is significantly related to inductive reasoning, and we know because of random assignment that teaching skill does not correlate with the condition effect, at least in the population. The "Covariance Parameter Estimates" section of the output provides another view of why the confidence interval is narrower when we add teaching skill to the model. Comparing the variance of the intercepts in Tables 16.6 and 16.7 shows that the variance is much smaller when teaching skill is included in the model. To understand what this means, it is helpful to rewrite the two different level 2 equations, the first of which does not include teaching skill and the second of which does:

$$\mu_i = \beta_0 + \beta_1 X_{1i} + u_i \qquad\qquad (8, \text{repeated})$$
$$\mu_i = \beta_0 + \beta_1 X_{1i} + \beta_2 X_{2i} + u_i \qquad\qquad (10, \text{repeated})$$

In each case, the variance of the random intercept parameter shown in Tables 16.6 and 16.7 reflects the variance of the residual term in the model, that is, the variance of u_i. Table 16.6 tells us that with only condition included in the model, the residual variance is 26.63. Table 16.7 tells us that adding teaching skill to the model reduces the error variance to 6.57. The fact that we have been able to reduce the error variance in the model explains why the confidence interval is narrower. Further, we can calculate a squared semipartial correlation coefficient for teaching skill by subtracting 6.57 from 26.63 and dividing the difference by 26.63. The result, 0.75, tells us that teaching skill accounts for 75% of the between-classroom variance in inductive reasoning scores. Notice that if we want, we could also calculate a squared semipartial correlation coefficient for condition by fitting a model to the data that includes teaching skill as a level 2 predictor but omits condition from the model. We should hasten to add that there may be several reasons the value for teaching skill is larger than what we are often accustomed to seeing in behavioral research. First, it is important to realize that the denominator of this ratio is based on the variance of scores between classrooms, not between individual students. Notice that we calculated our R^2 value based on Equations 8 and 10, which are level 2 equations, which in this example means that they are classroom-level equations. Teaching skill may explain quite a bit of the variance between classrooms, but the variance between classrooms could be much smaller than the variance between students (notice that Table 16.6 shows this not to be the case for these data, but it might be true in many actual data sets). Second, the estimated R^2 may be subject to considerable sampling error unless we have been able to sample a sizable number of level 2 units, in this case classrooms. Because the estimate is based on Equations 8 and 10, the effective sample size here is only six classrooms. Third, even if the estimated R^2 value were to be close to the population value, we have to remember that we have not randomly assigned levels of teaching skill, so we cannot claim that teaching skill is responsible for 75% of the variance in inductive reasoning scores in any causal sense. Fourth, notice that the other variance estimate in the "Covariance Parameter Estimates" section of the output has not changed much at all from Table 16.4 to Table 16.5. The variance labeled "Residual" is the residual variance in the level 1 equation. However, whether or not we included teaching skill in the model the level 1 equation remained the same and was based on Equation 7:

$$Y_i = \mu_i + \varepsilon_i \qquad\qquad\text{(7, repeated)}$$

Because both analyses assume the same level 1 model, it is not surprising that the estimated variance of ε_i in the two analyses is virtually identical. Finally, we should alert you that Snijders and Bosker (1994, 1999) have demonstrated that alternate definitions of R^2 can be more meaningful in multilevel models than the standard definition of R^2.

Remember that from one perspective, the teaching skill variable functions as a covariate in this randomized design. Some might regard its inclusion here as a failure because the treatment effect remained nonsignificant. However, we would maintain that there were two benefits of including it. First, remember that although the confidence interval for the treatment effect still included zero, it was considerably narrower when we included teaching skill in the model than when we did not. The difference in the widths of the two intervals would probably have been even larger if there had not been so few classrooms, because we pay a higher price for losing a degree of freedom by including an additional variable when the number of classrooms is small. It seems likely that statistical power has been increased by including teaching skill in the model, even though we failed to reach statistical significance in this particular sample.[9] Second, by including teaching skill in the model, we learned that teachers whose skill is rated higher have students who score higher on inductive reasoning. Notice that in general we might also include yet one additional term involving teaching skill, namely, the interaction of teaching skill and condition. We save this illustration for an exercise at the end of the chapter.

Models with Additional Level 1 Variables

We have now seen an example of a mixed linear model with teaching skill as an additional level 2 variable, so we are now prepared to begin our presentation of a comparable model that includes an additional level 1 predictor. Recall that until now we have implicitly assumed that each individual student's inductive reasoning score depends entirely on the classroom in which the student is placed. Of course, when we say "entirely," we mean that we are willing to regard any other influences as constituting error in our model formulation. This conceptualization becomes clear when we look once more at Equation 7:

$$Y_i = \mu_i + \varepsilon_i \qquad\qquad\text{(7, repeated)}$$

As we discussed previously, this model stipulates that the dependent variable is allowed to differ from classroom to classroom, but all remaining influences are relegated to the error term ε_i. Notice in particular that this model assigns all differences among students' inductive reasoning scores within a classroom to the error term. In this respect, the model is a typical analysis of variance model. However, just as in analysis of covariance, we may believe that we can measure one or more variables for each student that will account for some of the variability in inductive reasoning scores. For example, in our data set, you may recall from Table 16.4 that we have a measure of each child's cognitive ability. To the extent that we expect cognitive ability to correlate with inductive reasoning, we may benefit from including it as a predictor in our model. Specifically, including this variable has the potential not only to reduce error variance, but also to open up additional questions of possible theoretical interest.

Including cognitive ability in our mixed model differs from including teaching skill in the model, because cognitive ability is a student characteristic, whereas teaching skill is a classroom characteristic. Thus, cognitive ability is measured at level 1, whereas teaching skill is measured at level 2. Remember that including teaching skill caused us to modify our level 2 equation, as we can see by comparing Equations 8 and 10. However, we did not modify the level 1 equation when we added teaching skill to the model, as Equation 7 remained the operative level 1 equation.

Deciding to include cognitive ability in the model requires the modification of the level 1 equation, because we need to acknowledge that we now want our model to allow each student's inductive reasoning score to depend not just on the student's classroom but also on the student's cognitive ability. We can represent this conceptualization with the following level 1 equation

$$Y_i = \mu_i + \beta_i X_{1i} + \varepsilon_i \tag{12}$$

where Y_i is the score on the dependent variable for participant i and X_{1i} is the score on the predictor variable (in our example, cognitive ability) for participant i. Notice that this new level 1 model differs from our previous level 1 model of Equation 7 in the appearance of X_{1i} along with its associated β_i parameter.

Before considering the corresponding level 2 model and then how to put the two levels together into a single model, we need to spend some time developing an understanding of the new model we have just created in Equation 12. In particular, we need to know how to interpret the parameters of this model, namely, μ_i and β_i. The meaning of these parameters becomes clearer when we compare Equation 12 to the full model we presented for analysis of covariance in Chapter 9:

$$\text{Full:} \quad Y_{ij} = \mu + \alpha_j + \beta X_{ij} + \varepsilon_{ij} \tag{9.1, repeated}$$

Our new Equation 12 differs from the analysis of covariance full model of Equation 9.1 in three ways: (1) the notation for subscripts is different, as we have pointed out earlier in this chapter, (2) Equation 12 expresses each classroom's intercept as μ_i, whereas Equation 9.1 expresses each intercept as the sum of a grand mean intercept and a deviation (i.e., as $\mu + \alpha_j$), and (3) the model in Equation 12 allows each classroom to have its own slope as well as its own intercept, unlike the model in Equation 9.1, which constrains the slopes to be equal to one another. Of these three differences, the first two are simply matters of notation and are thus of no real consequence. The third difference, however, proves to be important, as we will see momentarily.[10]

The important point to be learned here is that Equation 12 specifies a specific form for the relationship between the two student-level variables Y_i and X_{1i} (be sure you understand that the two student-level variables in our example are inductive reasoning and cognitive ability). First, the model specifies a linear relationship between Y_i and X_{1i}. We know that a straight line is determined by two parameters, a slope and an intercept, which leads to the next two points. Second, the model allows the intercept to differ from classroom to classroom. Third, the model also allows the slope to differ from classroom to classroom.

What all of this means is that the level 1 model specifies a straight-line relationship between inductive reasoning and cognitive ability in our example. What is crucial to understand here is that this straight-line relationship is a within-class relationship. In other words, the idea here is that we might focus our attention on one specific classroom, say Classroom 1 in the control condition. According to the model, there should be a straight-line relationship between students' inductive reasoning scores and their cognitive ability scores within this classroom.

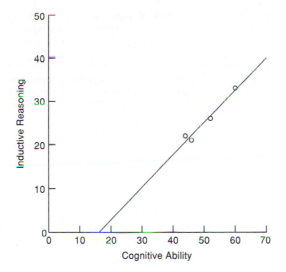

FIG. 16.1.   Scatterplot of inductive reasoning and cognitive ability scores for students in the first classroom of the control condition.

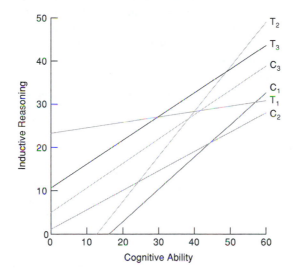

FIG. 16.2.   Regression lines relating inductive reasoning and cognitive ability scores within each of 6 classrooms.

The nature of this straight-line relationship is captured by the intercept and the slope of the line for this classroom. Figure 16.1 shows a scatterplot of the actual inductive reasoning and cognitive ability data for the first classroom in the control condition, along with the estimated regression line calculated from least squares. For these 4 students, the slope of the line is 0.74 and the intercept is −11.97. Of course, in an actual study we would strongly prefer to have many more students per classroom (and probably more classrooms per treatment condition), but even the small sample sizes we have here allow us to demonstrate the concepts of importance.

We could proceed to calculate a least-squares regression line for each of the other classrooms. Figure 16.2 shows the resultant estimated lines, including the line we have already found for the first classroom in the control condition. Table 16.8 presents the numerical values of the slope

TABLE 16.8
SLOPE AND INTERCEPT OF REGRESSION LINE
RELATING INDUCTIVE REASONING AND COGNITIVE
ABILITY FOR EACH CLASSROOM

Condition	Classroom	Slope	Intercept
Control	1	0.74	−11.97
	2	0.45	1.14
	3	0.56	5.00
Treatment	1	0.12	23.25
	2	1.03	−13.19
	3	0.55	10.64

and intercept estimates obtained within each classroom. What can we make of these values? In particular, what interpretation can we place on differences between classrooms, especially those in different treatment conditions? As soon as we begin to consider differences between classrooms, we are entering the realm of level 2 models.

If the slope and intercept estimates shown in Table 16.8 were estimated equally well for all classrooms, we could proceed with a two-step strategy where these scores simply become dependent variables to be modeled in a level 2 model. Although this conceptualization is helpful here, the actual analysis needs to take into account that some of the slopes and intercepts of Table 16.8 are estimated more precisely than others.[11] As we have seen, this is once again where the maximum likelihood approach becomes necessary.

The logic from this point forward proceeds much as it did when we considered teaching skill as an additional level 2 predictor. However, there is one major difference here, where we now have cognitive ability as an additional level 1 predictor. Because we have an additional level 1 predictor in our model, we now have two level 1 parameters in our model, namely, an intercept as well as a slope, as shown in Equation 12:

$$Y_i = \mu_i + \beta_i X_{1i} + \varepsilon_i \qquad \text{(12, repeated)}$$

Notice that before we included cognitive ability as a level 1 predictor, each classroom was characterized by its mean inductive reasoning score, because this was the only level 1 parameter. However, we now have the capability to characterize each classroom in two ways: (1) the slope of the regression line relating inductive reasoning and cognitive ability in the classroom and (2) the intercept of this regression line.

Notice that the treatment effect might manifest itself in terms of the slope, the intercept, or both. For example, although Figure 16.2 and Table 16.8 do not reveal any obvious treatment effect on the slope in our data, it could be the case more generally that the treatment has either increased or decreased the slope relating the level 1 predictor to the level 1 outcome for individuals. For example, one goal of an intervention might be to lessen the dependence of the outcome measure on the predictor. In our example, we might hope to be able to teach inductive reasoning in a manner that makes it less dependent on a student's general cognitive ability. Even if such an effect is not an explicit goal, it is usually wise to investigate the extent to which slope differences have occurred.

Whether or not classrooms (or, more generally, level 2 units) differ in slope, they may or may not differ in intercept. For our data, visual inspection of Figure 16.2 and Table 16.8 leaves open the question of whether the treatment has had any effect on a classroom's intercepts. However, looking at the figure does reveal one shortcoming of the intercept as we have defined it. Notice that the intercept of a regression line represents the mean value of the dependent variable when

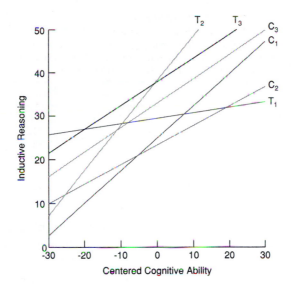

FIG. 16.3.   Regression lines relating inductive reasoning and centered cognitive ability scores within each of 6 classrooms.

the predictor takes on a value of zero. In our case, then, the intercept tells us the mean value of inductive reasoning when cognitive ability equals zero. This presents a major problem, because the distribution of cognitive ability scores in Table 16.4 and Figure 16.2 suggests that a cognitive ability score of zero is "off the scale." Thus, it is almost certainly meaningless to estimate what a classroom's mean inductive reasoning score would be for students whose cognitive ability scores equal zero. The best way to solve this problem is usually to "center" the predictor variable. Centering is accomplished by subtracting the mean score on the predictor from each individual's score. In our data, the mean cognitive ability score is 49.72, so we can calculate a new centered cognitive ability score for each person simply by subtracting 49.72 from their original score. Analyses based on this new centered version of cognitive ability lead to a much more interpretable intercept. Specifically, the intercept now represents the mean inductive reasoning score for students with a cognitive ability score of 49.72. All further analyses in this chapter are based on this centered version of cognitive ability.

Before proceeding with the analysis of our data, we pause for a moment to emphasize the role of centering. We do so because centering often takes on special importance in nested designs with additional level 1 predictor variables. Figure 16.3 repeats the scatterplot of Figure 16.2. The only difference is that the new figure depicts the relationship between inductive reasoning scores and centered cognitive ability scores. Two things are important to notice: (1) centering cognitive ability has not affected the slopes of the six regression lines, but (2) centering has affected the intercepts. If we were interested only in the slopes of the regression lines, it would not matter whether we chose to center the predictor. However, if we are also interested in the intercept, centering clearly can matter. Because the the meaning of the intercept has changed, so have the numerical values of the intercept for each classroom, so that inferences about classroom differences on the intercept may be very different if we center than if we do not. Table 16.9 presents the values of the slope and intercept of the regression line for each of the six classrooms after centering cognitive ability. It is instructive to compare the values in Table 16.9 to those in Table 16.8 before centering cognitive ability. First, notice as claimed that the slope is unaffected by centering cognitive ability. Second, notice that the value of the intercept is often very different after centering than before centering. Classrooms with the steepest slopes,

TABLE 16.9
SLOPE AND INTERCEPT OF REGRESSION LINE
RELATING INDUCTIVE REASONING AND COGNITIVE
ABILITY FOR EACH CLASSROOM USING CENTERED
COGNITIVE ABILITY SCORES

Condition	Classroom	Slope	Intercept
Control	1	0.74	24.92
	2	0.45	23.34
	3	0.56	32.97
Treatment	1	0.12	29.47
	2	1.03	38.27
	3	0.55	37.90

such as Classroom 2 in the Treatment condition, show the greatest change in intercept. Because the effect of centering depends on the slope and the slope itself may differ from classroom to classroom, intercept differences after centering may differ greatly from intercept differences prior to centering. In the inductive reasoning data, centering produces a clearer difference between the intercepts of the treatment and control groups.

We need to make one final point regarding centering. As it turns out, there is more than one way to center a variable in a nested design. For example, we subtracted 49.72 from each person's cognitive ability score because we said that was the mean for cognitive ability. Indeed, this is the mean, but notice specifically that it is the grand mean of cognitive ability, where we have averaged over all 29 individuals in the study. An alternative method for centering the data would be to use each classroom's own mean to center the data for that classroom. This alternative changes the meaning of the intercept yet again. In fact, with this method of centering, each classroom's intercept simply becomes its mean on the dependent variable (inductive reasoning, in our example) with no adjustment for the predictor. Although there are some occasions where this form of centering is useful, they are probably less frequent than those calling for centering with the grand mean. Readers interested in learning more about various choices of centering are advised to read the excellent discussions provided by Kreft and de Leeuw (1998) and Kreft, de Leeuw, and Aiken (1995).

Having completed our discussion of centering, we are ready to return to consideration of level 1 and level 2 models. Recall that the level 1 model for the inductive reasoning data allows each classroom to have its own slope and intercept for the regression line relating inductive reasoning to cognitive ability. Specifically, the level 1 equation can be written as

$$Y_i = \mu_i + \beta_i X_{1i} + \varepsilon_i \qquad \text{(12, repeated)}$$

We now need to develop a level 2 formulation that will let us compare classrooms to one another. One key point here is that because the model in Equation 12 characterizes each classroom in terms of both an intercept and a slope, we have the opportunity to compare classrooms along both of these dimensions. Another way of saying this is that the level 1 model has two parameters, μ_i and β_i, so each of these parameters becomes a dependent variable in a level 2 model. At a conceptual level, we could ask two questions about the estimated classroom parameters shown in Table 16.9: (1) Is there a treatment effect on the slope and (2) is there a treatment effect on the intercept? If all estimates were equally precise (which is unlikely even with equal n, as discussed in Footnote 11), we could simply perform two t tests on these data, one for the intercept and one for the slope. In general, however, the maximum likelihood approach is preferable, because it takes differential precision of estimates into account. Even so, it is useful to realize that the idea behind the maximum likelihood approach is essentially that of performing two t tests on these data.

In order to use maximum likelihood, we need to form appropriate level 2 models. The reason we said "models" in a plural form is because we need one model for the intercept and another model for the slope. Before writing this pair of models, let's refresh our memories about what we did before we incorporated cognitive ability as a level 1 predictor in our model. The simplest formulation we began with was to allow each classroom to have its own mean inductive reasoning score, as indicated by our original level 1 model:

$$Y_i = \mu_i + \varepsilon_i \qquad \text{(7, repeated)}$$

We then wrote a level 2 model with X_{1i} as an indicator variable distinguishing whether a classroom belonged to the treatment or control condition:

$$\mu_i = \beta_0 + \beta_1 X_{1i} + u_i \qquad \text{(8, repeated)}$$

Inferences about β_1 in this level 2 model allowed us to make inferences about the magnitude of the treatment effect on mean classroom inductive reasoning scores.

The same logic allows us to formulate two level 2 models to interpret the parameters of the level 1 model shown in Equation 12, which includes both an intercept and a slope parameter:

$$Y_i = \mu_i + \beta_i X_{1i} + \varepsilon_i \qquad \text{(12, repeated)}$$

Before proceeding, be sure to notice that X_{1i} has a different meaning in Equation 12 than it did in Equation 8, because X_{1i} now represents cognitive ability score instead of treatment group membership. Because we have already used X_{1i} to represent cognitive ability, we will now use X_{2i} as an indicator variable representing treatment group membership, in which case the following pair of models specify a possible treatment effect on the intercept as well as a possible treatment effect on the slope:

$$\mu_i = \beta_0 + \beta_2 X_{2i} + u_{0i} \qquad (13)$$

$$\beta_i = \beta_1 + \beta_3 X_{2i} + u_{1i} \qquad (14)$$

The model in Equation 13 implies that a classroom's intercept μ_i (after centering) can be expressed as the sum of three components: (1) some baseline value, β_0, which is an intercept parameter, (2) a variable X_{2i}, which in our example represents treatment condition, multiplied by an unknown parameter β_2, and (3) unexplained differences among classroom intercepts, as represented by u_{0i}. The model in Equation 14 shows the same type of sum of three components for the slope. Three further points are worth making. First, notice that the parameters of the model for the slope are different from the parameters of the model for the intercept, so, for example, the treatment effect on the slope is allowed to be completely different from the treatment effect on the intercept. Second, in our example, X_{2i} is an indicator variable, but more generally it could be a continuous variable. For example, instead of assessing a possible treatment effect, we could let X_{2i} be teaching skill and examine the effect of teaching skill on the relationship between inductive reasoning and cognitive ability (an exercise at the end of the chapter provides precisely this opportunity). Or, we could leave X_{2i} as an indicator variable representing treatment condition and add X_{3i} as an additional predictor to add teaching skill to the model. Third, there is no mathematical reason that the form of the model for the intercept needs to be identical to the form of the model for the slope. For example, the intercept could be modeled as a function of treatment condition while simultaneously modeling the slope as a function of teaching skill. However, there are often interpretational advantages of using the same predictors for the slope as for the intercept, unless there are compelling theoretical reasons to do otherwise.

As we know, PROC MIXED requires that the specification of a single equation. As before, we can develop a single equation by substituting from the level 2 equation into the level 1 equation. In other words, we can substitute from Equations 13 and 14 into Equation 12. Making this substitution and rearranging terms yields a model of the form

$$Y_i = \beta_0 + \beta_1 X_{1i} + \beta_2 X_{2i} + \beta_3 X_{1i} X_{2i} + u_{0i} + u_{1i} X_{1i} + \varepsilon_i \qquad (15)$$

Although this equation may at first seem foreboding, it is actually rather straightforward when we consider it piece by piece and keep in mind what each X variable represents in our example. It also frequently proves useful to refer back to the separate level 1 and level 2 model formulations of Equations 12, 13, and 14 to understand the parameters of the model written as a single equation like that of Equation 15.

The full model of Equation 15 has four fixed parameters, $\beta_0, \beta_1, \beta_2$, and β_3. We can see from Equation 13 that β_0 is an intercept of intercepts. Its meaning and value depend on how both X_{1i} and X_{2i} are coded, but in most cases β_0 is of little direct interest regardless of the coding method. The β_1 parameter is also an intercept, as we can see from Equation 14, but unlike β_0, β_1 is an intercept of the slope. This often makes it much more interesting than β_0, because we are often interested in assessing the average slope. The precise meaning of β_1 will depend on how any indicator variables in the level 2 model are coded, but in general the parameter represents a mean level of the slope, either within a specific level of a categorical variable or averaging over levels, depending once again on coding choices. Similarly, β_2 is usually of interest because as we can see most clearly in Equation 13, it reflects the treatment effect on classroom intercepts. Similarly, β_3 is also usually of interest, because Equation 14 shows that it reflects the treatment effect on classroom slopes. Equation 15 shows that an equivalent way of thinking about β_3 is that it reflects an interaction between cognitive ability and treatment group. If the treatment affects the slope of the line relating inductive reasoning to cognitive ability, the difference between treatment and control classrooms in inductive reasoning scores will vary as a function of cognitive ability, which is exactly what it means to say that there is an interaction.

The Equation 15 model includes three random effects, u_{0i}, u_{1i}, and ε_i. From Equation 13, we can see that u_{0i} reflects true unexplained differences between classroom intercepts. Similarly, u_{1i} reflects true unexplained differences between classroom slopes. Finally, ε_i reflects unexplained differences between individual students. These three random effects imply three variance components to be estimated, namely, $\sigma_{u_0}^2, \sigma_{u_1}^2$ and σ_ε^2. More often than not, we will also want to include the covariance between u_{0i} and u_{1i} as another parameter to be estimated. Including this parameter allows unexplained differences in classroom intercepts to correlate with unexplained differences in classroom slopes. Perhaps classrooms with higher than expected intercepts tend to have steeper (or shallower) slopes than expected. Including this covariance parameter in the model allows the investigation of such possibilities.

We are now prepared to write the PROC MIXED syntax for our model. Remember that PROC MIXED, like most similar software, includes the fixed intercept β_0 and the random residual variance σ_ε^2 as parameters by default, so we do not need to include them in the command lines. We do, however, have to specify the three remaining fixed effects, the two remaining random variances, and the random covariance. Here is the set of command lines we need, followed by a brief explanation of the lines that are different from those we have seen before:

```
proc mixed;
    class room cond;
    model induct = cond cog cond*cog / s;
    random int cog/ subject = room(cond) type = un;
    estimate 'condition' cond −1 1;
```

The first two lines and the last line are exactly the same as lines we have used throughout the chapter. However, both the "model" line and the "random" line are somewhat different from those we have previously encountered. The model line specifies three fixed effects, namely, "cond," "cog," and "cond*cog." Notice that these are exactly the variables associated with β_1, β_2, and β_3, respectively, in Equation 15 (where the "*" notation in SAS indicates a product term, that is, the product of two variables multiplied together). Thus, as usual, the "model" line specifies the variables that reflect fixed effects in the model. The "random" line indicates the presence of two random effects, one associated with "int" and the other with "cog." Notice that these two effects correspond to the random effects shown in Equation 15, keeping in mind that σ_ε^2 is included in the model by default. Specifically, "int" is implicitly the variable associated with the random effect u_{0i} in Equation 15, because the apparent absence of any variable in the model actually indicates that the variable simply has a constant value of 1. Similarly, "cog" is the variable associated with the random effect u_{1i} in Equation 15. Finally, the inclusion of "type = un" as an option to the right of the slash on the "random" line allows the random effects u_{0i} and u_{1i} to correlate with one another.

Table 16.10 presents an excerpt of the output produced by using PROC MIXED to fit the model shown in Equation 15 to the inductive reasoning data. The top portion of the table, labeled as "Solution for Fixed Effects," displays estimates of the fixed effects parameters in the model. Recall that Equation 15 has four such parameters, namely β_0, β_1, β_2, and β_3. Correspondingly, Table 16.10 shows four nonzero estimates, one for each parameter in the model. We will provide at least a brief discussion of the interpretation of each of these parameters. In many situations, we might very well ignore the intercept β_0 entirely except simply to make sure it looks reasonable. However, we will devote more attention to it here than we might in an actual analysis, largely because it provides a nice mechanism for solidifying some of the logic of the maximum likelihood approach.

The intercept β_0 represents the estimated mean value of Y (inductive reasoning) when all X variables in the model take on a value of zero. In this example, because of the way in which PROC MIXED codes indicator variables (see Appendix B) and because we have centered the cognitive ability variable, the intercept represents the mean value of inductive reasoning in the treatment group for students with a cognitive ability score of 49.72. Thus, our best estimate of this mean is 35.97. Notice that this value is close to the number we would obtain if we simply averaged the three intercept values shown in Table 16.9 for the treatment classrooms. This simple average would equal 35.21. We can understand why the estimate produced by PROC MIXED is slightly larger than this simple average by realizing that the second and third treatment classrooms, which have larger values of the intercept than the first treatment classroom, also have more students, and thus receive more weight than the first classroom in the maximum likelihood analysis. The point we want to underscore here is that the estimate of β_0, and indeed the estimates of all the parameters shown in Table 16.10, are closely related to the estimates shown in Table 16.9. Indeed, if the estimates shown in Table 16.9 were equally precise, we could duplicate the results of the maximum likelihood approach very easily from the data provided in Table 16.9. However, even if sample sizes are equal, these estimates will

TABLE 16.10
ANALYSIS OF INDUCTIVE REASONING DATA ADDING COGNITIVE ABILITY
AS A LEVEL 1 PREDICTOR

The Mixed Procedure

Solution for Fixed Effects

Effect	Cond	Estimate	Standard Error	DF	t Value	Pr > |t|
Intercept		35.9713	2.8042	4	12.83	0.0002
cond	0	−8.9866	3.9487	4	−2.28	0.0852
cond	1	0	.	.	.	.
cog		0.5906	0.2017	4	2.93	0.0429
cog*cond	0	0.09048	0.2870	4	0.32	0.7683
cog*cond	1	0	.	.	.	.

Type 3 Tests of Fixed Effects

Effect	Num DF	Den DF	F Value	Pr > F
cond	1	4	5.18	0.0852
cog	1	4	19.63	0.0114
cog*cond	1	4	0.10	0.7683

Estimates

Label	Estimate	Standard Error	df	t Value	Pr > |t|
condition	8.9866	3.9487	4	2.28	0.0852

Covariance Parameter Estimates

Cov Parm	Subject	Estimate
UN(1, 1)	room(cond)	20.7332
UN(2, 1)	room(cond)	0.7246
UN(2, 2)	room(cond)	2.61E-18
Residual		11.8050

typically not be equally precise (see Footnote 11), which is why the maximum likelihood analysis is preferable.

Of much more interest are the parameters that reflect relationships between inductive reasoning and treatment, as well as inductive reasoning and cognitive ability. Still focusing our attention on the "Solution for Fixed Effects" portion of Table 16.10 for the moment, we can see that the estimated value of "cond" is −8.99. This represents the estimated difference between the control group mean and the treatment group mean on inductive reasoning when other predictors take on a value of zero. Notice that this is simply another way of saying that "cond" represents the β_2 parameter, which we have already seen reflects the treatment effect on classroom intercepts. Because we have centered cognitive ability, the value of −8.99 can be interpreted as the estimated difference between control and treatment means at an average value of cognitive ability. Because we have included a class statement in our model and coded control children as 0 and treatment children as 1, this value of −8.99 is an estimate of the control group population mean minus the treatment group population mean (see Appendix B for more detail on coding class variables). In other words, we could say that our best estimate of the main effect of the treatment is that the control group scores 8.99 points lower than the treatment group. A more natural way to make the same statement would be to say that our best estimate is that the treatment group scores on average 8.99 points higher than the control group, which, notice, is close to the values we have seen in Tables 16.6 and 16.7 before considering cognitive ability, just as we would expect when classrooms have been randomly assigned to treatment conditions. Also notice that the value of -8.99 is close to the difference between the simple unweighted average of the three control intercepts and the three treatment intercepts we saw earlier in Table 16.9.

The table also shows that the estimated value of the "cog" parameter is 0.59. Notice that this corresponds to the β_1 parameter in our model, which means that it is the slope of the regression line relating inductive reasoning and cognitive ability. More specifically, it is the slope when all other predictor variables take on a value of zero. Because of the way PROC MIXED has coded "cond," this implies that the value of 0.59 is the estimated slope of the line in the treatment condition. It is especially important to notice that even though the effect looks like a main effect because PROC MIXED labels it as "cog," it should not be interpreted as a main effect of cognitive ability. Instead, it is more properly the effect of cognitive ability when "cond" equals zero, so that "cog" is actually a simple effect instead of a main effect. Once again, the maximum likelihood estimate of 0.59 is close to the estimate we would obtain simply by averaging the appropriate values in Table 16.9. In this case, a simple unweighted average of the three treatment condition slopes would yield a value of 0.57.

Finally, the table shows that the estimated "cog*cond" parameter has a value of 0.09. This means that the slope of the line relating inductive reasoning and cognitive ability is 0.09 steeper for the control group than for the treatment group. In other words, the estimated slope of this line for the control group is 0.68. As before, this value is reasonably similar to the simple averaged value of 0.58 based on the three control group slopes shown in Table 16.9. It may seem puzzling that the maximum likelihood estimate is higher than the simple average when close examination of the values in Table 16.9 shows that the highest slope of 0.74 comes from the classroom with the fewest students. However, the precision of the slope estimate depends not just on the sample size but also on the heterogeneity of the sample. It turns out that the students in the first control classroom are much more heterogeneous than the students in either of the other two control classrooms, so that the slope estimate in the first control classroom is actually considerably more precise than the estimates in the other two control classrooms, suggesting that the first classroom should receive the most weight, which thus explains why the maximum likelihood estimate is larger than the unweighted average.[12]

The next section of the output shown in Table 16.10 provides "Type 3 Tests of Fixed Effects." Specifically, this section displays tests of main effects and interactions as stipulated in our mixed model. This information is often at least as informative as the "Solution" section, even though some information is often duplicated in the two sections. The "Type 3 Tests" section potentially conveys unique information for either or both of two reasons. First, in general, some of the effects contained in the "Solution" section are main effects and interactions, whereas others are simple effects. Thus, to the extent that one is interested in testing all main effects and interactions contained in the model, the "Type 3 Tests of Fixed Effects" section is most relevant. Second, if some categorical variables had more than two levels, we would also want to look in the "Type 3 Tests" section to obtain tests corresponding to omnibus effects of these factors.

As was true in our previous analyses of these data, the test of the condition main effect is not quite statistically significant at the .05 level. However, notice that by including cognitive ability in the model, the p value for the condition main effect has been reduced from the value of .1477 in Table 16.6 to a value of .0852 shown here. We will say more in a moment about why including cognitive ability appears to have increased the power of the test of the condition effect. The test of cognitive ability is statistically significant at the .05 level, as shown by the p value of .0114. Thus, we can infer that there is some relationship between students' cognitive ability and their inductive reasoning scores within classrooms. Notice that the p value of .0114 is different from the p value shown in the "Solution" section of the output because as we discussed, the parameter being tested in the "Solution" section was the simple effect of cognitive ability only for the treatment classrooms. The p value of .0114, on the other hand, is a test of the relationship between cognitive ability and inductive reasoning for control as well as treatment classrooms, in the sense that to the extent the relationship differs in the two treatment conditions, the test shown here averages over the two conditions, making it a test of a main effect. Finally, the interaction of cognitive ability and treatment condition is nonsignificant, suggesting that the relationship of cognitive ability to inductive reasoning may be the same in treatment classrooms as in control classrooms. In other words, it is plausible that the differences between the three control slopes in Table 16.9 and the three treatment slopes also shown in Table 16.9 simply reflect sampling error. From this perspective, if we were to obtain a population of control and treatment classrooms, we might well discover that the population slopes of the two types of classrooms were identical to one another. Of course, we must hasten to add that we may have had very low power to detect slope differences in our study. Table 16.10 reminds us that these tests are based on only 4 denominator degrees of freedom, because we had a total of only six classrooms. To make matters worse, the number of students in each classroom was also small, so the individual slope estimates for each classroom may not be very precise. Although we have little evidence that the treatment has affected the relationship between cognitive ability and inductive reasoning, the design of our study may have offered limited opportunities to discover such an effect even if it existed in the population.

The next section of the output is labeled "Estimates" and appears because we included an optional "estimate" line in our input commands. Because we have only two levels of the condition factor, the information contained in this section simply duplicates information we have already seen. The only difference is that we have requested an estimate of the treatment mean minus the control mean, whereas earlier estimates were in the opposite direction (i.e., control minus treatment). In general, however, if the factor had more than two levels, we could use the "Estimate" section of the output to obtain information about specific contrasts. Information contained here can be useful either for hypothesis testing or for forming confidence intervals. For example, in our data, we could form a 95% confidence interval using the critical t value of 2.78 for 4 degrees of freedom (see Appendix Table A.1) along with the estimated effect of 8.99 and the estimated standard error of 3.9487. The resultant confidence interval ranges from -1.99 to 19.97. Thus, we can be 95% confident that the effect of the treatment is somewhere between a benefit of 20 points and a harm of 2 points. Notice that the interval contains zero, which is consistent with the failure to reject the null hypothesis at the .05 level. Notice also that the interval is narrower than the very first interval we calculated before including cognitive skill or teaching ability in the model, because that interval ranged from -4.50 to 20.79. Even though including cognitive ability in the model has increased precision, the interval remains distressingly wide, because we have so few classrooms and so few students per classroom.

The final section of the output is labeled "Covariance Parameter Estimates." Although covariance parameter estimates are often of less interest than the fixed effects, we would be remiss if we were to overlook them entirely. Recall that the Equation 15 model contains three random effects, u_{0i}, u_{1i}, and ε_i. The table shows the estimated variance of each of these effects, as well as the covariance between the unexplained portion of the intercept u_{0i} and the unexplained portion of the slope u_{1i}. For example, the parameter labeled as "UN(1,1)" is the element in the first row and first column of the unrestricted covariance matrix. Because "int" was the first random effect we specified, "UN(1,1)" refers to the unexplained variance of the intercept u_{0i}. The table shows us that the estimated unexplained variance of this parameter is 20.73.

Next is the parameter labeled as "UN(2,1)," which is the parameter in the second row and first column of the covariance matrix. We can tell that this parameter does not appear on the diagonal of the matrix, because its row and column designations differ from one another. This tells us that this parameter is a covariance instead of a variance. Specifically, it represents the covariance between the second random effect u_{1i} and the first random effect u_{0i}. In other words, this parameter reflects the covariance between the unexplained component of the intercept and the unexplained component of the slope. The fact that the value shown in the table is positive implies that there is some tendency for higher intercepts to be associated with higher slopes. More precisely, we need to realize that this covariance is between the unexplained portions of the intercept and the slope, and what remains unexplained in our model is any variability within condition. Thus, we can say that there is some positive relationship between classroom intercepts and classroom slopes within condition, such that classrooms with higher average inductive reasoning scores also tend to have higher slopes relating inductive reasoning and cognitive ability. Referring back to Table 16.9 shows that this general tendency manifests itself to some extent in the simple intercepts and slopes calculated within each classroom. We need to make two further points. First, if this relationship were a primary focus of the study, we would probably want to transform the covariance to a correlation, because the numerical value of the correlation would probably be more meaningful. Most mixed model software provides a mechanism for calculating such correlations. Second, if there were sufficient interest in this covariance, we would probably also want to test its statistical significance and perhaps form a confidence interval for the corresponding population parameter. Once again, this option is often available in mixed model software.[13]

The next covariance parameter is labeled as "UN(2,2)," which means that it is the parameter in row 2 and column 2 of the unrestricted covariance matrix. As such, it is the variance of the second random effect, which in our case is the unexplained portion of the slope u_{1i}. The table shows that the estimated value of the unexplained variance of the slope is 2.61E-18. The program has printed this number is scientific notation, because it is so small. The "E-18" indicates that the decimal point must be moved to the left 18 digits in order to obtain the actual value, which would then be written as .00000000000000000261. This number is obviously zero for all practical purposes. Is it plausible that condition explains all of the variance in the slope parameter, so that the unexplained variance equals zero? This seems unlikely, especially when we see from Table 16.9 that slopes appear to differ from classroom to classroom within each condition. Why then would we obtain an estimated unexplained variance of zero? We can understand the answer by remembering that the observed variance in slopes as shown in Table 16.9 consists of two additive sources: true differences between classrooms and sampling error. In these data, the sampling error is so large that it suggests that there is no remaining true variance between classrooms. Although the precise formula no longer applies in this complex design, the idea is much the same as we saw in Equation 6 near the beginning of the chapter:

$$\hat{\sigma}_{\beta}^2 = \frac{MS_{B/A} - MS_W}{n} \qquad \text{(6, repeated)}$$

In general, the variance of the slope can be thought of as being calculated similarly as a difference between the observed variance in slopes and an independent estimate of sampling error. However, as we pointed out in our discussion of Equation 6, the estimate of sampling error (i.e., MS_W in Equation 6) occasionally turns out to be larger than the observed variance itself ($MS_{B/A}$ in Equation 6). When this occurs, the resultant estimate is usually set equal to zero, which is what PROC MIXED has done in our example. As we mentioned in our discussion surrounding Equation 6, such occurrences usually reflect some combination of three factors: (1) sample sizes (both number of classrooms, as well as number of students per classroom) are too small to obtain precise estimates; (2) the true variance is close to zero; and (3) one or more assumptions of the model may be incorrect. The lesson to be learned in our example is almost certainly that our sample size was simply too small to allow us to estimate this variance parameter with any reasonable degree of precision.

The final estimate shown in the covariance parameter section is the residual variance σ_ε^2. Keep in mind that this parameter represents the unexplained variance of the level 1 equation given by Equation 12:

$$Y_i = \mu_i + \beta_i X_{1i} + \varepsilon_i \qquad \text{(12, repeated)}$$

Thus, σ_ε^2 is an indication of the extent to which individual students' inductive reasoning scores within a classroom cannot be predicted from their cognitive ability. Table 16.10 shows that the estimated variance in our data equals 11.80. The most interesting perspective on this value comes from comparing it to the residual variances we obtained in our earlier analyses of these data. Looking back at Table 16.6 shows that the residual variance in our original analysis was 20.26, whereas Table 16.7 shows that the residual variance in the analysis that included teaching skill was 20.27. Why is the new value shown in Table 16.10 so different from the values obtained in the two previous analyses? The answer comes from remembering that in both of these earlier analyses, the level 1 equation specified that each student's inductive reasoning score depended entirely on the student's classroom:

$$Y_i = \mu_i + \varepsilon_i \qquad \text{(7, repeated)}$$

In this model, all differences between students' inductive reasoning scores within classrooms are attributed to the error ε_i and thus contribute to the residual variance σ_ε^2. However, we know that students with higher cognitive ability scores tend to have higher inductive reasoning scores (according to our data), so including cognitive ability as a predictor of inductive reasoning in our model reduces the unexplained variance. Thus, the residual variance in Equation 12 is substantially less than the residual variance in Equation 7. By including cognitive ability in the model, we obtained two benefits: (1) we learned about the relationship between cognitive ability and inductive reasoning, and (2) we increased the precision of the estimated condition effect. Of course, if we had not randomly assigned classrooms to conditions, we might still want to include cognitive ability in our model, but the nature of our inferences would differ in a nonrandomized design.

We have now seen that including cognitive ability in the model offers certain potential benefits. Earlier in the chapter we saw that including teaching skill in the model also offers potential benefits. You might wonder whether it would be even better to construct a model including both variables. We would agree that this is an interesting question, so we have left the exploration of it as an exercise at the end of the chapter. In any event, remember that cognitive ability was a level 1 predictor in our example. As such, it provides an opportunity to gain a greater understanding of individual students. Teaching skill, on the other hand, was a level 2 predictor. As such, it provides an opportunity to gain a greater understanding of why some teachers are more effective than others. Implicit in these statements is perhaps the greatest benefit of multilevel mixed models, namely, that they allow researchers to study phenomena at different levels simultaneously, thus taking into account the context in which individual behavior occurs. As a result, these models provide one approach for combining the perspectives of experimental and correlational psychology, as Cronbach (1957) maintained was necessary in order for psychology to establish itself as a true science of human thought and behavior.

EXERCISES

1. An educational psychologist wants to compare reading achievement scores of children in five experimental classrooms to scores in five standard classrooms. Under what if any conditions will a multilevel analysis of reading scores yield the same basic conclusions as an analysis of variance (as described in Chapter 10)? Explain your answer.

2. An organizational psychologist decides to compare average worker productivity of 20 workers in an assembly plant stressing principles of statistical quality control to the average productivity of 20 workers in a different plant that places no emphasis on statistical quality control.
   a. When would it be reasonable to regard "plant" as a fixed effect and when would it be preferable to regard "plant" as a random effect?
   b. Suppose the psychologist has decided that "plant" should be regarded as a random effect. Is this a good design to assess the average effect of statistical quality control on average worker productivity (i.e., comparing one plant with statistical quality control to one plant without statistical quality control)? Why or why not?
   c. A colleague of the organizational psychologist suggests that the design could be improved by increasing the sample size, that is, by assessing the productivity of more than 20 workers at each plant. Do you agree? Explain your answer.

3. Why might a researcher choose to analyze data using multilevel models instead of analysis of variance even if all sample sizes are equal?

4. Does the maximum likelihood analysis of data from nested designs require a normality assumption? If so, describe exactly what is assumed to be normal.

5. Table 16.1 presents severity ratings for 12 clients rated by a female trainee and 12 clients rated by a male trainee. Assuming that a researcher's specific interest is in evaluating whether female and male trainees tend to provide different mean severity ratings, the most straightforward analysis would seem to be a t test comparing the 12 females' scores with the 12 males' scores.
   a. Perform a t test comparing the 12 females' scores to the 12 males' scores. Is the result statistically significant?
   b. How does your result in part a compare to a multilevel analysis of these data?
   c. Form a 95% confidence interval for the mean difference in females' and males' severity ratings based on your analysis in part a.
   d. Form a 95% confidence interval for the mean difference in females' and males' severity ratings based on a multilevel analysis of the data.
   e. How do your results in parts c and d compare to one another? Explain the basis of any difference you observe.
   f. Is the t test approach of parts a and c a good way for the researcher to answer the question of interest here? Why or why not?

6. Suppose a health psychologist has conducted a study to assess the effects of a lifestyle intervention on hypertension. Groups of workers at an industrial plant are randomly assigned to either a treatment or control condition. Specifically, five groups of approximately 20 workers each are assigned to the treatment condition, and five other groups of approximately 20 workers each are assigned to the control condition.
   a. Write an appropriate level 1 model for this design.
   b. Write an appropriate level 2 model for this design.
   c. Write a single equation that combines your level 1 and level 2 models.
   d. In what sense can you think of the maximum likelihood method as a two-step process? Briefly describe each of these two steps for this design.

7. Consider the inductive reasoning data shown in Table 16.4. The chapter presents a level 1 model where each classroom has its own mean value of inductive reasoning, accompanied by a level 2 model where this mean is explained as a function of condition and the teacher's teaching skill. Yet another possibility not examined in the chapter is that there may be an interaction between condition and teaching skill.

Test the statistical significance of this interaction in these data and interpret your results. (Hint: Your test of the interaction between condition and skill will not depend on whether you center skill, but as described in Appendix B, what SAS prints for the condition effect is really the simple effect of condition when skill equals zero. To make this effect interpretable, it is necessary to code skill so that a value of zero is meaningful. In these data, this can be accomplished by subtracting 6.7 from each teacher's skill level, because 6.7 is approximately the grand mean of the skill variable.)

8. One of the analyses of the inductive reasoning data presented in the chapter considers a level 1 model of the form

$$Y_i = \mu_i + \beta_i X_{1i} + \varepsilon_i$$

where X_{1i} represents the score on a cognitive ability measure for Student i. The meaning of the μ_i depends on how the X variable is coded.

a. Suppose scores on X range from 30 to 70. How would you interpret the meaning of the μ_i parameter in the level 1 model if X is not recoded?

b. Suppose once again that scores on X range from 30 to 70. Unlike part a, however, now suppose that X is recoded by subtracting the grand mean on X from each individual student's X score. How would you now interpret the meaning of the μ_i parameter in the level 1 model?

c. Suppose that instead of subtracting the grand mean on X from each student's score, each classroom's own mean was subtracted from scores for students in that classroom. How would you now interpret the meaning of the μ_i parameter in the level 1 model?

d. How would the different methods of coding X in parts a through c affect your interpretation of the β_i parameter in the level 1 model?

9. Some of the analyses of the inductive reasoning data presented in the chapter include each student's cognitive ability in the model, whereas other analyses include each teacher's teaching skill in the model, but the chapter never presents analyses including both cognitive ability and teaching skill in the model. The purpose of this exercise is to explore models that include both of these variables simultaneously.

a. Write an appropriate level 1 model that includes each student's cognitive ability as well as each student's classroom as predictors of each student's inductive reasoning score.

b. Write an appropriate level 2 model predicting level 1 parameters from condition and teaching skill. Assume that classroom intercepts as well as classroom slopes are random effects. (See the hint at the end of Exercise 7 for more information about coding the skill variable.)

c. Write a single equation that combines the level 1 model from part a with the level 2 model from part b.

d. Use SAS PROC MIXED (or similar mixed model software) to fit the model in part c to the inductive reasoning data. To facilitate interpretation of the intercept term, center cognitive ability around its grand mean. Interpret the results you obtain by describing what effects appear to influence inductive reasoning scores.

e. Notice that parts a through d have resulted in tests of various main effects and interactions associated with three effects: condition, cognitive ability, and teaching skill. Based on our discussion of factorial designs in Chapter 8 (see especially Table 8.21), we could potentially consider three main effects, three two-way interactions, and one three-way interaction among these effects. Which of these seven potential effects did you actually test in part d?

f. How would you need to modify your models to test all seven effects implied in part e?

g. Although sample size (especially number of classrooms) is almost certainly too small here to provide meaningful results for a three-way interaction, nevertheless for pedagogical purposes modify your model as described in part f, and test all seven effects for the inductive reasoning data. Interpret your results.

Appendix A

Statistical Tables

TABLE A.1
CRITICAL VALUES OF *t* DISTRIBUTION

df	α_1: .05 α_2: .10	.025 .05	.0125 .025	.0083 .0167	.00625 .0125	.005 .01
1	6.31	12.71	25.45	38.19	50.92	63.66
2	2.92	4.30	6.21	7.65	8.86	9.92
3	2.35	3.18	4.18	4.86	5.39	5.84
4	2.13	2.78	3.50	3.96	4.31	4.60
5	2.02	2.57	3.16	3.53	3.81	4.03
6	1.94	2.45	2.97	3.29	3.52	3.71
7	1.89	2.36	2.84	3.13	3.34	3.50
8	1.86	2.31	2.75	3.02	3.21	3.36
9	1.83	2.26	2.69	2.93	3.11	3.25
10	1.81	2.23	2.63	2.87	3.04	3.17
11	1.80	2.20	2.59	2.82	2.98	3.11
12	1.78	2.18	2.56	2.78	2.93	3.05
13	1.77	2.16	2.53	2.75	2.90	3.01
14	1.76	2.14	2.51	2.72	2.86	2.98
15	1.75	2.13	2.49	2.69	2.84	2.95
16	1.75	2.12	2.47	2.67	2.81	2.92
17	1.74	2.11	2.46	2.65	2.79	2.90
18	1.73	2.10	2.45	2.64	2.77	2.88
19	1.73	2.09	2.43	2.63	2.76	2.86
20	1.72	2.09	2.42	2.61	2.74	2.85
22	1.72	2.07	2.41	2.59	2.72	2.82
24	1.71	2.06	2.39	2.57	2.70	2.80
26	1.71	2.06	2.38	2.56	2.68	2.78
28	1.70	2.05	2.37	2.55	2.67	2.76
30	1.70	2.04	2.36	2.54	2.66	2.75
32	1.69	2.04	2.35	2.53	2.65	2.74
34	1.69	2.03	2.35	2.52	2.64	2.73
36	1.69	2.03	2.34	2.51	2.63	2.72
38	1.69	2.02	2.33	2.50	2.62	2.71
40	1.68	2.02	2.33	2.50	2.62	2.70
45	1.68	2.01	2.32	2.49	2.60	2.69
50	1.68	2.01	2.31	2.48	2.59	2.68
55	1.67	2.00	2.30	2.47	2.58	2.67
60	1.67	2.00	2.30	2.46	2.58	2.66
70	1.67	1.99	2.29	2.45	2.56	2.65
80	1.66	1.99	2.28	2.45	2.56	2.64
90	1.66	1.99	2.28	2.44	2.55	2.63
100	1.66	1.98	2.28	2.43	2.54	2.63
120	1.66	1.98	2.27	2.43	2.54	2.62
140	1.66	1.98	2.27	2.42	2.53	2.61
160	1.65	1.97	2.26	2.42	2.53	2.61
180	1.65	1.97	2.26	2.42	2.52	2.60
200	1.65	1.97	2.26	2.41	2.52	2.60
∞	1.645	1.96	2.24	2.39	2.50	2.58

Note: α_1 and α_2 represent alpha levels for one-tailed and two-tailed tests, respectively. These critical values were computed using the TINV function of SAS, except for the values corresponding to infinite degrees of freedom, which were computed using the CINV function of SAS.

TABLE A.2
CRITICAL VALUES OF F DISTRIBUTION

df for Denom.	α	1	2	3	4	5	6	7	8	9	10	12	15	20	24	30	40	60	∞
1	.25	5.83	7.50	8.20	8.58	8.82	8.98	9.10	9.19	9.26	9.32	9.41	9.49	9.58	9.63	9.67	9.71	9.76	9.85
	.10	39.9	49.5	53.6	55.8	57.2	58.2	58.9	59.4	59.9	60.2	60.7	61.2	61.7	62.0	62.3	62.5	62.8	63.3
	.05	161	200	216	225	230	234	237	239	240	242	244	246	248	249	250	251	252	254
	.025	648	800	864	900	922	937	948	957	963	969	977	985	993	997	1001	1006	1010	1018
	.01	4052	5000	5403	5625	5764	5859	5928	5982	6022	6056	6106	6157	6209	6235	6261	6287	6313	6366
	.001	4053*	5000*	5404*	5625*	5764*	5859*	5929*	5981*	6023*	6056*	6107*	6158*	6209*	6235*	6261*	6287*	6313*	6366*
2	.25	2.57	3.00	3.15	3.23	3.28	3.31	3.34	3.35	3.37	3.38	3.39	3.41	3.43	3.43	3.44	3.45	3.46	3.48
	.10	8.53	9.00	9.16	9.24	9.29	9.33	9.35	9.37	9.38	9.39	9.41	9.42	9.44	9.45	9.46	9.47	9.47	9.49
	.05	18.5	19.0	19.2	19.3	19.3	19.3	19.4	19.4	19.4	19.4	19.4	19.4	19.5	19.5	19.5	19.5	19.5	19.5
	.025	38.5	39.0	39.2	39.3	39.3	39.3	39.4	39.4	39.4	39.4	39.4	39.4	39.5	39.5	39.5	39.5	39.5	39.5
	.01	98.5	99.0	99.2	99.3	99.3	99.3	99.4	99.4	99.4	99.4	99.4	99.4	99.5	99.5	99.5	99.5	99.5	99.5
	.001	999	999	999	999	999	999	999	999	999	999	999	999	999	1000	1000	1000	1000	1000
3	.25	2.02	2.28	2.36	2.39	2.41	2.42	2.43	2.44	2.44	2.44	2.45	2.46	2.46	2.46	2.47	2.47	2.47	2.47
	.10	5.54	5.46	5.39	5.34	5.31	5.28	5.27	5.25	5.24	5.23	5.22	5.20	5.18	5.18	5.17	5.16	5.15	5.13
	.05	10.1	9.55	9.28	9.12	9.01	8.94	8.89	8.85	8.81	8.79	8.74	8.70	8.66	8.64	8.62	8.59	8.57	8.53
	.025	17.4	16.0	15.4	15.1	14.9	14.7	14.6	14.5	14.5	14.4	14.3	14.2	14.2	14.1	14.1	14.0	14.0	13.9
	.01	34.1	30.8	29.5	28.7	28.2	27.9	27.7	27.5	27.4	27.2	27.0	26.9	26.7	26.6	26.5	26.4	26.3	26.1
	.001	167	148	141	137	135	133	132	131	130	129	128	127	126	126	125	125	124	124
4	.25	1.81	2.00	2.05	2.06	2.07	2.08	2.08	2.08	2.08	2.08	2.08	2.08	2.08	2.08	2.08	2.08	2.08	2.08
	.10	4.54	4.32	4.19	4.11	4.05	4.01	3.98	3.95	3.94	3.92	3.90	3.87	3.84	3.83	3.82	3.80	3.79	3.76
	.05	7.71	6.94	6.59	6.39	6.26	6.16	6.09	6.04	6.00	5.96	5.91	5.86	5.80	5.77	5.75	5.72	5.69	5.63
	.025	12.2	10.6	9.98	9.60	9.36	9.20	9.07	8.98	8.90	8.84	8.75	8.66	8.56	8.51	8.46	8.41	8.36	8.26
	.01	21.2	18.0	16.7	16.0	15.5	15.2	15.0	14.8	14.7	14.6	14.4	14.2	14.0	13.9	13.8	13.8	13.6	13.5
	.001	74.1	61.2	56.2	53.4	51.7	50.5	49.7	49.0	48.5	48.0	47.4	46.8	46.1	45.8	45.4	45.1	44.8	44.0

*These values must be multiplied by 100.

(continued)

TABLE A.2
(Continued)

df for Numerator

df for Denom.	α	1	2	3	4	5	6	7	8	9	10	12	15	20	24	30	40	60	∞
	.25	1.69	1.85	1.88	1.89	1.89	1.89	1.89	1.89	1.89	1.89	1.89	1.89	1.88	1.88	1.88	1.88	1.87	1.87
	.10	4.06	3.78	3.62	3.52	3.45	3.40	3.37	3.34	3.32	3.30	3.27	3.24	3.21	3.19	3.17	3.16	3.14	3.10
5	.05	**6.61**	**5.79**	**5.41**	**5.19**	**5.05**	**4.95**	**4.88**	**4.82**	**4.77**	**4.74**	**4.68**	**4.62**	**4.56**	**4.53**	**4.50**	**4.46**	**4.43**	**4.36**
	.025	10.0	8.43	7.76	7.39	7.15	6.98	6.85	6.76	6.68	6.62	6.52	6.43	6.33	6.28	6.23	6.18	6.12	6.02
	.01	**16.3**	**13.3**	**12.1**	**11.4**	**11.0**	**10.7**	**10.5**	**10.3**	**10.2**	**10.0**	**9.89**	**9.72**	**9.55**	**9.47**	**9.38**	**9.29**	**9.20**	**9.02**
	.001	47.2	37.1	33.2	31.1	29.8	28.8	28.2	27.6	27.2	26.9	26.4	25.9	25.4	25.1	24.9	24.6	24.3	23.8
	.25	1.62	1.76	1.78	1.79	1.79	1.78	1.78	1.78	1.77	1.77	1.77	1.76	1.76	1.75	1.75	1.75	1.74	1.74
	.10	3.78	3.46	3.29	3.18	3.11	3.05	3.01	2.98	2.96	2.94	2.90	2.87	2.84	2.82	2.80	2.78	2.76	2.72
6	.05	**5.99**	**5.14**	**4.76**	**4.53**	**4.39**	**4.28**	**4.21**	**4.15**	**4.10**	**4.06**	**4.00**	**3.94**	**3.87**	**3.84**	**3.81**	**3.77**	**3.74**	**3.67**
	.025	8.81	7.26	6.60	6.23	5.99	5.82	5.70	5.60	5.52	5.46	5.37	5.27	5.17	5.12	5.07	5.01	4.96	4.85
	.01	**13.8**	**10.9**	**9.78**	**9.15**	**8.75**	**8.47**	**8.26**	**8.10**	**7.98**	**7.87**	**7.72**	**7.56**	**7.40**	**7.31**	**7.23**	**7.14**	**7.06**	**6.88**
	.001	35.5	27.0	23.7	21.9	20.8	20.0	19.5	19.0	18.7	18.4	18.0	17.6	17.1	16.9	16.7	16.4	16.2,	15.8
	.25	1.57	1.70	1.72	1.72	1.71	1.71	1.70	1.70	1.69	1.69	1.68	1.68	1.67	1.67	1.66	1.66	1.65	1.65
	.10	3.59	3.26	3.07	2.96	2.88	2.83	2.78	2.75	2.72	2.70	2.67	2.63	2.59	2.58	2.56	2.54	2.51	2.47
7	.05	**5.59**	**4.74**	**4.35**	**4.12**	**3.97**	**3.87**	**3.79**	**3.73**	**3.68**	**3.64**	**3.57**	**3.51**	**3.44**	**3.41**	**3.38**	**3.34**	**3.30**	**3.23**
	.025	8.07	6.54	5.89	5.52	5.29	5.12	4.99	4.90	4.82	4.76	4.67	4.57	4.47	4.42	4.36	4.31	4.25	4.14
	.01	**12.2**	**9.55**	**8.45**	**7.85**	**7.46**	**7.19**	**6.99**	**6.84**	**6.72**	**6.62**	**6.47**	**6.31**	**6.16**	**6.07**	**5.99**	**5.91**	**5.82**	**5.65**
	.001	29.2	21.7	18.8	17.2	16.2	15.5	15.0	14.6	14.3	14.1	13.7	13.3	12.9	12.7	12.5	12.3	12.1	11.7
	.25	1.54	1.66	1.67	1.66	1.66	1.65	1.64	1.64	1.63	1.63	1.62	1.62	1.61	1.60	1.60	1.59	1.59	1.58
	.10	3.46	3.11	2.92	2.81	2.73	2.67	2.62	2.59	2.56	2.54	2.50	2.46	2.42	2.40	2.38	2.36	2.34	2.29
8	.05	**5.32**	**4.46**	**4.07**	**3.84**	**3.69**	**3.58**	**3.50**	**3.44**	**3.39**	**3.35**	**3.28**	**3.22**	**3.15**	**3.12**	**3.08**	**3.04**	**3.01**	**2.93**
	.025	7.57	6.06	5.42	5.05	4.82	4.65	4.53	4.43	4.36	4.30	4.20	4.10	4.00	3.95	3.89	3.84	3.78	3.67
	.01	**11.3**	**8.65**	**7.59**	**7.01**	**6.63**	**6.37**	**6.18**	**6.03**	**5.91**	**5.81**	**5.67**	**5.52**	**5.36**	**5.28**	**5.20**	**5.12**	**5.03**	**4.86**
	.001	25.4	18.5	15.8	14.4	13.5	12.9	12.4	12.0	11.8	11.5	11.2	10.8	10.5	10.3	10.1	9.92	9.73	9.33

	α	1	2	3	4	5	6	7	8	9	10	12	15	20	24	30	40	60	∞
9	.25	1.51	1.62	1.63	1.63	1.62	1.61	1.60	1.60	1.59	1.59	1.58	1.57	1.56	1.56	1.55	1.54	1.54	1.53
	.10	3.36	3.01	2.81	2.69	2.61	2.55	2.51	2.47	2.44	2.42	2.38	2.34	2.30	2.28	2.25	2.23	2.21	2.16
	.05	5.12	4.26	3.86	3.63	3.48	3.37	3.29	3.23	3.18	3.14	3.07	3.01	2.94	2.90	2.86	2.83	2.79	2.71
	.025	7.21	5.71	5.08	4.72	4.48	4.32	4.20	4.10	4.03	3.96	3.87	3.77	3.67	3.61	3.56	3.51	3.45	3.33
	.01	10.6	8.02	6.99	6.42	6.06	5.80	5.61	5.47	5.35	5.26	5.11	4.96	4.81	4.73	4.65	4.57	4.48	4.31
	.001	22.9	16.4	13.9	12.6	11.7	11.1	10.7	10.4	10.1	9.89	9.57	9.24	8.90	8.72	8.55	8.37	8.19	7.81
10	.25	1.49	1.60	1.60	1.59	1.59	1.58	1.57	1.56	1.56	1.55	1.54	1.53	1.52	1.52	1.51	1.51	1.50	1.48
	.10	3.29	2.92	2.73	2.61	2.52	2.46	2.41	2.38	2.35	2.32	2.28	2.24	2.20	2.18	2.16	2.13	2.11	2.06
	.05	4.96	4.10	3.71	3.48	3.33	3.22	3.14	3.07	3.02	2.98	2.91	2.85	2.77	2.74	2.70	2.66	2.62	2.54
	.025	6.94	5.46	4.83	4.47	4.24	4.07	3.95	3.85	3.78	3.72	3.62	3.52	3.42	3.37	3.31	3.26	3.20	3.08
	.01	10.0	7.56	6.55	5.99	5.64	5.39	5.20	5.06	4.94	4.85	4.71	4.56	4.41	4.33	4.25	4.17	4.08	3.91
	.001	21.0	14.9	12.6	11.3	10.5	9.92	9.52	9.20	8.96	8.75	8.45	8.13	7.80	7.64	7.47	7.30	7.12	6.76
11	.25	1.47	1.58	1.58	1.57	1.56	1.55	1.54	1.53	1.53	1.52	1.51	1.50	1.49	1.49	1.48	1.47	1.47	1.45
	.10	3.23	2.86	2.66	2.54	2.45	2.39	2.34	2.30	2.27	2.25	2.21	2.17	2.12	2.10	2.08	2.05	2.03	1.97
	.05	4.84	3.98	3.59	3.36	3.20	3.09	3.01	2.95	2.90	2.85	2.79	2.72	2.65	2.61	2.57	2.53	2.49	2.40
	.025	6.72	5.26	4.63	4.28	4.04	3.88	3.76	3.66	3.59	3.53	3.43	3.33	3.23	3.17	3.12	3.06	3.00	2.88
	.01	9.65	7.21	6.22	5.67	5.32	5.07	4.89	4.74	4.63	4.54	4.40	4.25	4.10	4.02	3.94	3.86	3.78	3.60
	.001	19.7	13.8	11.6	10.4	9.58	9.05	8.66	8.35	8.12	7.92	7.63	7.32	7.01	6.85	6.68	6.52	6.35	6.00
12	.25	1.46	1.56	1.56	1.55	1.54	1.53	1.52	1.51	1.51	1.50	1.49	1.48	1.47	1.46	1.45	1.45	1.44	1.42
	.10	3.18	2.81	2.61	2.48	2.39	2.33	2.28	2.24	2.21	2.19	2.15	2.10	2.06	2.04	2.01	1.99	1.96	1.90
	.05	4.75	3.89	3.49	3.26	3.11	3.00	2.91	2.85	2.80	2.75	2.69	2.62	2.54	2.51	2.47	2.43	2.38	2.30
	.025	6.55	5.10	4.47	4.12	3.89	3.73	3.61	3.51	3.44	3.37	3.28	3.18	3.07	3.02	2.96	2.91	2.85	2.72
	.01	9.33	6.93	5.95	5.41	5.06	4.82	4.64	4.50	4.39	4.30	4.16	4.01	3.86	3.78	3.70	3.62	3.54	3.36
	.001	18.6	13.0	10.8	9.63	8.89	8.38	8.00	7.71	7.48	7.29	7.00	6.71	6.40	6.25	6.09	5.93	5.76	5.42
13	.25	1.45	1.55	1.55	1.53	1.52	1.51	1.50	1.49	1.49	1.48	1.47	1.46	1.45	1.44	1.43	1.42	1.42	1.40
	.10	3.14	2.76	2.56	2.43	2.35	2.28	2.23	2.20	2.16	2.14	2.10	2.05	2.01	1.98	1.96	1.93	1.90	1.85
	.05	4.67	3.81	3.41	3.18	3.03	2.92	2.83	2.77	2.71	2.67	2.60	2.53	2.46	2.42	2.38	2.34	2.30	2.21
	.025	6.41	4.97	4.35	4.00	3.77	3.60	3.48	3.39	3.31	3.25	3.15	3.05	2.95	2.89	2.84	2.78	2.72	2.60
	.01	9.07	6.70	5.74	5.21	4.86	4.62	4.44	4.30	4.19	4.10	3.96	3.82	3.66	3.59	3.51	3.43	3.34	3.17
	.001	17.8	12.3	10.2	9.07	8.35	7.86	7.49	7.21	6.98	6.80	6.52	6.23	5.93	5.78	5.63	5.47	5.30	4.97

(continued)

TABLE A.2
(Continued)

									df for Numerator										
df for Denom.	α	1	2	3	4	5	6	7	8	9	10	12	15	20	24	30	40	60	∞
14	.25	1.44	1.53	1.53	1.52	1.51	1.50	1.49	1.48	1.47	1.46	1.45	1.44	1.43	1.42	1.41	1.41	1.40	1.38
	.10	3.10	2.73	2.52	2.39	2.31	2.24	2.19	2.15	2.12	2.10	2.05	2.01	1.96	1.94	1.91	1.89	1.86	1.80
	.05	4.60	3.74	3.34	3.11	2.96	2.85	2.76	2.70	2.65	2.60	2.53	2.46	2.39	2.35	2.31	2.27	2.22	2.13
	.025	6.30	4.86	4.24	3.89	3.66	3.50	3.38	3.29	3.21	3.15	3.05	2.95	2.84	2.79	2.73	2.67	2.61	2.49
	.01	8.86	6.51	5.56	5.04	4.69	4.46	4.28	4.14	4.03	3.94	3.80	3.66	3.51	3.43	3.35	3.27	3.18	3.00
	.001	17.1	11.8	9.73	8.62	7.92	7.43	7.08	6.80	6.58	6.40	6.13	5.85	5.56	5.41	5.25	5.10	4.94	4.60
15	.25	1.43	1.52	1.52	1.51	1.49	1.48	1.47	1.46	1.46	1.45	1.44	1.43	1.41	1.41	1.40	1.39	1.38	1.36
	.10	3.07	2.70	2.49	2.36	2.27	2.21	2.16	2.12	2.09	2.06	2.02	1.97	1.92	1.90	1.87	1.85	1.82	1.76
	.05	4.54	3.68	3.29	3.06	2.90	2.79	2.71	2.64	2.59	2.54	2.48	2.40	2.33	2.29	2.25	2.20	2.16	2.07
	.025	6.20	4.77	4.15	3.80	3.58	3.41	3.29	3.20	3.12	3.06	2.96	2.86	2.76	2.70	2.64	2.59	2.52	2.40
	.01	8.68	6.36	5.42	4.89	4.56	4.32	4.14	4.00	3.89	3.80	3.67	3.52	3.37	3.29	3.21	3.13	3.05	2.87
	.001	16.6	11.3	9.34	8.25	7.57	7.09	6.74	6.47	6.26	6.08	5.81	5.54	5.25	5.10	4.95	4.80	4.64	4.31
16	.25	1.42	1.51	1.51	1.50	1.48	1.47	1.46	1.45	1.44	1.44	1.43	1.41	1.40	1.39	1.38	1.37	1.36	1.34
	.10	3.05	2.67	2.46	2.33	2.24	2.18	2.13	2.09	2.06	2.03	1.99	1.94	1.89	1.87	1.84	1.81	1.78	1.72
	.05	4.49	3.63	3.24	3.01	2.85	2.74	2.66	2.59	2.54	2.49	2.42	2.35	2.28	2.24	2.19	2.15	2.11	2.01
	.025	6.12	4.69	4.08	3.73	3.50	3.34	3.22	3.12	3.05	2.99	2.89	2.79	2.68	2.63	2.57	2.51	2.45	2.32
	.01	8.53	6.23	5.29	4.77	4.44	4.20	4.03	3.89	3.78	3.69	3.55	3.41	3.26	3.18	3.10	3.02	2.93	2.75
	.001	16.1	11.0	9.00	7.94	7.27	6.81	6.46	6.19	5.98	5.81	5.55	5.27	4.99	4.85	4.70	4.54	4.39	4.06
17	.25	1.42	1.51	1.50	1.49	1.47	1.46	1.45	1.44	1.43	1.43	1.41	1.40	1.39	1.38	1.37	1.36	1.35	1.33
	.10	3.03	2.64	2.44	2.31	2.22	2.15	2.10	2.06	2.03	2.00	1.96	1.91	1.86	1.84	1.81	1.78	1.75	1.69
	.05	4.45	3.59	3.20	2.96	2.81	2.70	2.61	2.55	2.49	2.45	2.38	2.31	2.23	2.19	2.15	2.10	2.06	1.96
	.025	6.04	4.62	4.01	3.66	3.44	3.28	3.16	3.06	2.98	2.92	2.82	2.72	2.62	2.56	2.50	2.44	2.38	2.25
	.01	8.40	6.11	5.18	4.67	4.34	4.10	3.93	3.79	3.68	3.59	3.46	3.31	3.16	3.08	3.00	2.92	2.83	2.65
	.001	15.7	10.7	8.73	7.68	7.02	6.56	6.22	5.96	5.75	5.58	5.32	5.05	4.78	4.63	4.48	4.33	4.18	3.85

	α	1	2	3	4	5	6	7	8	9	10	12	15	20	24	30	40	60	∞
18	.25	1.41	1.50	1.49	1.48	1.46	1.45	1.44	1.43	1.42	1.42	1.40	1.39	1.38	1.37	1.36	1.35	1.34	1.32
	.10	3.01	2.62	2.42	2.29	2.20	2.13	2.08	2.04	2.00	1.98	1.93	1.89	1.84	1.81	1.78	1.75	1.72	1.66
	.05	4.41	3.55	3.16	2.93	2.77	2.66	2.58	2.51	2.46	2.41	2.34	2.27	2.19	2.15	2.11	2.06	2.02	1.92
	.025	5.98	4.56	3.95	3.61	3.38	3.22	3.10	3.01	2.93	2.87	2.77	2.67	2.56	2.50	2.44	2.38	2.32	2.19
	.01	8.29	6.01	5.09	4.58	4.25	4.01	3.84	3.71	3.60	3.51	3.37	3.23	3.08	3.00	2.92	2.84	2.75	2.57
	.001	15.4	10.4	8.49	7.46	6.81	6.35	6.02	5.76	5.56	5.39	5.13	4.87	4.59	4.45	4.30	4.15	4.00	3.67
19	.25	1.41	1.49	1.49	1.47	1.46	1.44	1.43	1.42	1.41	1.41	1.40	1.38	1.37	1.36	1.35	1.34	1.33	1.30
	.10	2.99	2.61	2.40	2.27	2.18	2.11	2.06	2.02	1.98	1.96	1.91	1.86	1.81	1.79	1.76	1.73	1.70	1.63
	.05	4.38	3.52	3.13	2.90	2.74	2.63	2.54	2.48	2.42	2.38	2.31	2.23	2.16	2.11	2.07	2.03	1.98	1.88
	.025	5.92	4.51	3.90	3.56	3.33	3.17	3.05	2.96	2.88	2.82	2.72	2.62	2.51	2.45	2.39	2.33	2.27	2.13
	.01	8.18	5.93	5.01	4.50	4.17	3.94	3.77	3.63	3.52	3.43	3.30	3.15	3.00	2.92	2.84	2.76	2.67	2.49
	.001	15.1	10.2	8.28	7.26	6.62	6.18	5.85	5.59	5.39	5.22	4.97	4.70	4.43	4.29	4.14	3.99	3.84	3.51
20	.25	1.40	1.49	1.48	1.47	1.45	1.44	1.43	1.42	1.41	1.40	1.39	1.37	1.36	1.35	1.34	1.33	1.32	1.29
	.10	2.97	2.59	2.38	2.25	2.16	2.09	2.04	2.00	1.96	1.94	1.89	1.84	1.79	1.77	1.74	1.71	1.68	1.61
	.05	4.35	3.49	3.10	2.87	2.71	2.60	2.51	2.45	2.39	2.35	2.28	2.20	2.12	2.08	2.04	1.99	1.95	1.84
	.025	5.87	4.46	3.86	3.51	3.29	3.13	3.01	2.91	2.84	2.77	2.68	2.57	2.46	2.41	2.35	2.29	2.22	2.09
	.01	8.10	5.85	4.94	4.43	4.10	3.87	3.70	3.56	3.46	3.37	3.23	3.09	2.94	2.86	2.78	2.69	2.61	2.42
	.001	14.8	9.95	8.10	7.10	6.46	6.02	5.69	5.44	5.24	5.08	4.82	4.56	4.29	4.15	4.00	3.86	3.70	3.38
22	.25	1.40	1.48	1.47	1.45	1.44	1.42	1.41	1.40	1.39	1.39	1.37	1.36	1.34	1.33	1.32	1.31	1.30	1.28
	.10	2.95	2.56	2.35	2.22	2.13	2.06	2.01	1.97	1.93	1.90	1.86	1.81	1.76	1.73	1.70	1.67	1.64	1.57
	.05	4.30	3.44	3.05	2.82	2.66	2.55	2.46	2.40	2.34	2.30	2.23	2.15	2.07	2.03	1.98	1.94	1.89	1.78
	.025	5.79	4.38	3.78	3.44	3.22	3.05	2.93	2.84	2.76	2.70	2.60	2.50	2.39	2.33	2.27	2.21	2.14	2.00
	.01	7.95	5.72	4.82	4.31	3.99	3.76	3.59	3.45	3.35	3.26	3.12	2.98	2.83	2.75	2.67	2.58	2.50	2.31
	.001	14.4	9.61	7.80	6.81	6.19	5.76	5.44	5.19	4.99	4.83	4.58	4.33	4.06	3.92	3.78	3.63	3.48	3.15
24	.25	1.39	1.47	1.46	1.44	1.43	1.41	1.40	1.39	1.38	1.38	1.36	1.35	1.33	1.32	1.31	1.30	1.29	1.26
	.10	2.93	2.54	2.33	2.19	2.10	2.04	1.98	1.94	1.91	1.88	1.83	1.78	1.73	1.70	1.67	1.64	1.61	1.53
	.05	4.26	3.40	3.01	2.78	2.62	2.51	2.42	2.36	2.30	2.25	2.18	2.11	2.03	1.98	1.94	1.89	1.84	1.73
	.025	5.72	4.32	3.72	3.38	3.15	2.99	2.87	2.78	2.70	2.64	2.54	2.44	2.33	2.27	2.21	2.15	2.08	1.94
	.01	7.82	5.61	4.72	4.22	3.90	3.67	3.50	3.36	3.26	3.17	3.03	2.89	2.74	2.66	2.58	2.49	2.40	2.21
	.001	14.0	9.34	7.55	6.59	5.98	5.55	5.23	4.99	4.80	4.64	4.39	4.14	3.87	3.74	3.59	3.45	3.29	2.97

(continued)

TABLE A.2
(Continued)

df for Numerator

df for Denom.	α	1	2	3	4	5	6	7	8	9	10	12	15	20	24	30	40	60	∞
26	.25	1.38	1.46	1.45	1.44	1.42	1.41	1.39	1.38	1.37	1.37	1.35	1.34	1.32	1.31	1.30	1.29	1.28	1.25
	.10	2.91	2.52	2.31	2.17	2.08	2.01	1.96	1.92	1.88	1.86	1.81	1.76	1.71	1.68	1.65	1.61	1.58	1.50
	.05	**4.23**	**3.37**	**2.98**	**2.74**	**2.59**	**2.47**	**2.39**	**2.32**	**2.27**	**2.22**	**2.15**	**2.07**	**1.99**	**1.95**	**1.90**	**1.85**	**1.80**	**1.69**
	.025	5.66	4.27	3.67	3.33	3.10	2.94	2.82	2.73	2.65	2.59	2.49	2.39	2.28	2.22	2.16	2.09	2.03	1.88
	.01	**7.72**	**5.53**	**4.64**	**4.14**	**3.82**	**3.59**	**3.42**	**3.29**	**3.18**	**3.09**	**2.96**	**2.81**	**2.66**	**2.58**	**2.50**	**2.42**	**2.33**	**2.13**
	.001	13.7	9.12	7.36	6.41	5.80	5.38	5.07	4.83	4.64	4.48	4.24	3.99	3.72	3.59	3.44	3.30	3.15	2.82
28	.25	1.38	1.46	1.45	1.43	1.41	1.40	1.39	1.38	1.37	1.36	1.34	1.33	1.31	1.30	1.29	1.28	1.27	1.24
	.10	2.89	2.50	2.29	2.16	2.06	2.00	1.94	1.90	1.87	1.84	1.79	1.74	1.69	1.66	1.63	1.59	1.56	1.48
	.05	**4.20**	**3.34**	**2.95**	**2.71**	**2.56**	**2.45**	**2.36**	**2.29**	**2.24**	**2.19**	**2.12**	**2.04**	**1.96**	**1.91**	**1.87**	**1.82**	**1.77**	**1.65**
	.025	5.61	4.22	3.63	3.29	3.06	2.90	2.78	2.69	2.61	2.55	2.45	2.34	2.23	2.17	2.11	2.05	1.98	1.83
	.01	**7.64**	**5.45**	**4.57**	**4.07**	**3.75**	**3.53**	**3.36**	**3.23**	**3.12**	**3.03**	**2.90**	**2.75**	**2.60**	**2.52**	**2.44**	**2.35**	**2.26**	**2.06**
	.001	13.5	8.93	7.19	6.25	5.66	5.24	4.93	4.69	4.50	4.35	4.11	3.86	3.60	3.46	3.32	3.18	3.02	2.69
30	.25	1.38	1.45	1.44	1.42	1.41	1.39	1.38	1.37	1.36	1.35	1.34	1.32	1.30	1.29	1.28	1.27	1.26	1.23
	.10	2.88	2.49	2.28	2.14	2.05	1.98	1.93	1.88	1.85	1.82	1.77	1.72	1.67	1.64	1.61	1.57	1.54	1.46
	.05	**4.17**	**3.32**	**2.92**	**2.69**	**2.53**	**2.42**	**2.33**	**2.27**	**2.21**	**2.16**	**2.09**	**2.01**	**1.93**	**1.89**	**1.84**	**1.79**	**1.74**	**1.62**
	.025	5.57	4.18	3.59	3.25	3.03	2.87	2.75	2.65	2.57	2.51	2.41	2.31	2.20	2.14	2.07	2.01	1.94	1.79
	.01	**7.56**	**5.39**	**4.51**	**4.02**	**3.70**	**3.47**	**3.30**	**3.17**	**3.07**	**2.98**	**2.84**	**2.70**	**2.55**	**2.47**	**2.39**	**2.30**	**2.21**	**2.01**
	.001	13.3	8.77	7.05	6.12	5.53	5.12	4.82	4.58	4.39	4.24	4.00	3.75	3.49	3.36	3.22	3.07	2.92	2.59
40	.25	1.36	1.44	1.42	1.40	1.39	1.37	1.36	1.35	1.34	1.33	1.31	1.30	1.28	1.26	1.25	1.24	1.22	1.19
	.10	2.84	2.44	2.23	2.09	2.00	1.93	1.87	1.83	1.79	1.76	1.71	1.66	1.61	1.57	1.54	1.51	1.47	1.38
	.05	**4.08**	**3.23**	**2.84**	**2.61**	**2.45**	**2.34**	**2.25**	**2.18**	**2.12**	**2.08**	**2.00**	**1.92**	**1.84**	**1.79**	**1.74**	**1.69**	**1.64**	**1.51**
	.025	5.42	4.05	3.46	3.13	2.90	2.74	2.62	2.53	2.45	2.39	2.29	2.18	2.07	2.01	1.94	1.88	1.80	1.64
	.01	**7.31**	**5.18**	**4.31**	**3.83**	**3.51**	**3.29**	**3.12**	**2.99**	**2.89**	**2.80**	**2.66**	**2.52**	**2.37**	**2.29**	**2.20**	**2.11**	**2.02**	**1.80**
	.001	12.6	8.25	6.60	5.70	5.13	4.73	4.44	4.21	4.02	3.87	3.64	3.40	3.15	3.01	2.87	2.73	2.57	2.23

	α	1	2	3	4	5	6	7	8	9	10	12	15	20	24	30	40	60	∞
60	.25	1.35	1.42	1.41	1.38	1.37	1.35	1.33	1.32	1.31	1.30	1.29	1.27	1.25	1.24	1.22	1.21	1.19	1.15
	.10	2.79	2.39	2.18	2.04	1.95	1.87	1.82	1.77	1.74	1.71	1.66	1.60	1.54	1.51	1.48	1.44	1.40	1.29
	.05	4.00	3.15	2.76	2.53	2.37	2.25	2.17	2.10	2.04	1.99	1.92	1.84	1.75	1.70	1.65	1.59	1.53	1.39
	.025	5.29	3.93	3.34	3.01	2.79	2.63	2.51	2.41	2.33	2.27	2.17	2.06	1.94	1.88	1.82	1.74	1.67	1.48
	.01	7.08	4.98	4.13	3.65	3.34	3.12	2.95	2.82	2.72	2.63	2.50	2.35	2.20	2.12	2.03	1.94	1.84	1.60
	.001	12.0	7.76	6.17	5.31	4.76	4.37	4.09	3.87	3.69	3.54	3.31	3.08	2.83	2.69	2.55	2.41	2.25	1.89
120	.25	1.34	1.40	1.39	1.37	1.35	1.33	1.31	1.30	1.29	1.28	1.26	1.24	1.22	1.21	1.19	1.18	1.16	1.10
	.10	2.75	2.35	2.13	1.99	1.90	1.82	1.77	1.72	1.68	1.65	1.60	1.55	1.48	1.45	1.41	1.37	1.32	1.19
	.05	3.92	3.07	2.68	2.45	2.29	2.17	2.09	2.02	1.96	1.91	1.83	1.75	1.66	1.61	1.55	1.50	1.43	1.25
	.025	5.15	3.80	3.23	2.89	2.67	2.52	2.39	2.30	2.22	2.16	2.05	1.94	1.82	1.76	1.69	1.61	1.53	1.31
	.01	6.85	4.79	3.95	3.48	3.17	2.96	2.79	2.66	2.56	2.47	2.34	2.19	2.03	1.95	1.86	1.76	1.66	1.38
	.001	11.4	7.32	5.79	4.95	4.42	4.04	3.77	3.55	3.38	3.24	3.02	2.78	2.53	2.40	2.26	2.11	1.95	1.54
∞	.25	1.32	1.39	1.37	1.35	1.33	1.31	1.29	1.28	1.27	1.25	1.24	1.22	1.19	1.18	1.16	1.14	1.12	1.00
	.10	2.71	2.30	2.08	1.94	1.85	1.77	1.72	1.67	1.63	1.60	1.55	1.49	1.42	1.38	1.34	1.30	1.24	1.00
	.05	3.84	3.00	2.60	2.37	2.21	2.10	2.01	1.94	1.88	1.83	1.75	1.67	1.57	1.52	1.46	1.39	1.32	1.00
	.025	5.02	3.69	3.12	2.79	2.57	2.41	2.29	2.19	2.11	2.05	1.94	1.83	1.71	1.64	1.57	1.48	1.39	1.00
	.01	6.63	4.61	3.78	3.32	3.02	2.80	2.64	2.51	2.41	2.32	2.18	2.04	1.88	1.79	1.70	1.59	1.47	1.00
	.001	10.8	6.91	5.42	4.62	4.10	3.74	3.47	3.27	3.10	2.96	2.74	2.51	2.27	2.13	1.99	1.84	1.66	1.00

This table is abridged from Table 18 in E. S. Pearson and H. O. Hartley (Eds.), *Biometrika tables for statisticians* (3rd ed., Vol. 1), Cambridge University Press, New York, 1970, by permission of the *Biometrika* Trustees.

TABLE A.3
CRITICAL VALUES OF BONFERRONI F DISTRIBUTION WITH 1 NUMERATOR DEGREE OF FREEDOM AND A FAMILYWISE ALPHA LEVEL OF .05

$C =$ Number of Comparisons

Denominator df	1	2	3	4	5	6	7	8	9	10
1	161.45	647.79	1458.36	2593.16	4052.18	5835.43	7942.91	10374.62	13130.56	16210.72
2	18.51	38.51	58.50	78.50	98.50	118.50	138.50	158.50	178.50	198.50
3	10.13	17.44	23.59	29.07	34.12	38.83	43.29	47.54	51.62	55.55
4	7.71	12.22	15.69	18.62	21.20	23.53	25.68	27.68	29.56	31.33
5	6.61	10.01	12.49	14.52	16.26	17.80	19.20	20.48	21.67	22.78
6	5.99	8.81	10.81	12.40	13.75	14.92	15.98	16.93	17.82	18.63
7	5.59	8.07	9.78	11.12	12.25	13.22	14.08	14.86	15.58	16.24
8	5.32	7.57	9.09	10.28	11.26	12.10	12.85	13.52	14.13	14.69
9	5.12	7.21	8.60	9.68	10.56	11.32	11.98	12.58	13.12	13.61
10	4.96	6.94	8.24	9.23	10.04	10.74	11.34	11.89	12.38	12.83
11	4.84	6.72	7.95	8.89	9.65	10.29	10.86	11.36	11.81	12.23
12	4.75	6.55	7.73	8.61	9.33	9.94	10.47	10.94	11.37	11.75
13	4.67	6.41	7.54	8.39	9.07	9.65	10.16	10.60	11.01	11.37
14	4.60	6.30	7.39	8.20	8.86	9.42	9.90	10.33	10.71	11.06
15	4.54	6.20	7.26	8.05	8.68	9.22	9.68	10.09	10.46	10.80
16	4.49	6.12	7.15	7.91	8.53	9.05	9.50	9.90	10.25	10.58
17	4.45	6.04	7.05	7.80	8.40	8.90	9.34	9.73	10.07	10.38
18	4.41	5.98	6.97	7.70	8.29	8.78	9.20	9.58	9.91	10.22
19	4.38	5.92	6.89	7.61	8.18	8.67	9.08	9.45	9.78	10.07
20	4.35	5.87	6.83	7.53	8.10	8.57	8.97	9.33	9.65	9.94
22	4.30	5.79	6.71	7.40	7.95	8.40	8.79	9.14	9.45	9.73
24	4.26	5.72	6.62	7.29	7.82	8.27	8.65	8.98	9.28	9.55
26	4.23	5.66	6.55	7.20	7.72	8.15	8.53	8.85	9.14	9.41
28	4.20	5.61	6.48	7.13	7.64	8.06	8.42	8.74	9.03	9.28
30	4.17	5.57	6.43	7.06	7.56	7.98	8.34	8.65	8.93	9.18

$C = Number\ of\ Comparisons$

Denominator df	1	2	3	4	5	6	7	8	9	10
32	4.15	5.53	6.38	7.01	7.50	7.91	8.26	8.57	8.84	9.09
34	4.13	5.50	6.34	6.96	7.44	7.85	8.19	8.50	8.77	9.01
36	4.11	5.47	6.31	6.91	7.40	7.80	8.14	8.44	8.70	8.94
38	4.10	5.45	6.27	6.88	7.35	7.75	8.09	8.38	8.64	8.88
40	4.08	5.42	6.24	6.84	7.31	7.71	8.04	8.33	8.59	8.83
45	4.06	5.38	6.18	6.77	7.23	7.62	7.94	8.23	8.49	8.71
50	4.03	5.34	6.14	6.71	7.17	7.55	7.87	8.15	8.40	8.63
55	4.02	5.31	6.10	6.67	7.12	7.49	7.81	8.09	8.33	8.55
60	4.00	5.29	6.07	6.63	7.08	7.44	7.76	8.03	8.28	8.49
70	3.98	5.25	6.02	6.57	7.01	7.37	7.68	7.95	8.19	8.40
80	3.96	5.22	5.98	6.53	6.96	7.32	7.62	7.89	8.12	8.33
90	3.95	5.20	5.95	6.50	6.93	7.28	7.58	7.84	8.07	8.28
100	3.94	5.18	5.93	6.47	6.90	7.25	7.54	7.80	8.03	8.24
120	3.92	5.15	5.90	6.43	6.85	7.20	7.49	7.75	7.97	8.18
140	3.91	5.13	5.87	6.40	6.82	7.16	7.45	7.71	7.93	8.14
160	3.90	5.12	5.85	6.38	6.80	7.14	7.43	7.68	7.90	8.10
180	3.89	5.11	5.84	6.37	6.78	7.12	7.41	7.66	7.88	8.08
200	3.89	5.10	5.83	6.35	6.76	7.10	7.39	7.64	7.86	8.06
∞	3.84	5.02	5.73	6.24	6.63	6.96	7.24	7.48	7.69	7.88

Note: These critical values were computed using the FINV function of SAS, except for the values corresponding to infinite denominator degrees of freedom, which were computed using the CINV function of SAS.

TABLE A.4
CRITICAL VALUES OF STUDENTIZED RANGE DISTRIBUTION

r = number of means (Tukey test) or number of steps between ordered means (Newman–Keuls test)

df_{error}	α_{FW}	2	3	4	5	6	7	8	9	10	11	12	13	14	15	16	17	18	19	20	α_{FW}	df_{error}
5	.05	3.64	4.60	5.22	5.67	6.03	6.33	6.58	6.80	6.99	7.17	7.32	7.47	7.60	7.72	7.83	7.93	8.03	8.12	8.21	.05	5
	.01	5.70	6.98	7.80	8.42	8.91	9.32	9.67	9.97	10.24	10.48	10.70	10.89	11.08	11.24	11.40	11.55	11.68	11.81	11.93	.01	
6	.05	3.46	4.34	4.90	5.30	5.63	5.90	6.12	6.32	6.49	6.65	6.79	6.92	7.03	7.14	7.24	7.34	7.43	7.51	7.59	.05	6
	.01	5.24	6.33	7.03	7.56	7.97	8.32	8.61	8.87	9.10	9.30	9.48	9.65	9.81	9.95	10.08	10.21	10.32	10.43	10.54	.01	
7	.05	3.34	4.16	4.68	5.06	5.36	5.61	5.82	6.00	6.16	6.30	6.43	6.55	6.66	6.76	6.85	6.94	7.02	7.10	7.17	.05	7
	.01	4.95	5.92	6.54	7.01	7.37	7.68	7.94	8.17	8.37	8.55	8.71	8.86	9.00	9.12	9.24	9.35	9.46	9.55	9.65	.01	
8	.05	3.26	4.04	4.53	4.89	5.17	5.40	5.60	5.77	5.92	6.05	6.18	6.29	6.39	6.48	6.57	6.65	6.73	6.80	6.87	.05	8
	.01	4.75	5.64	6.20	6.62	6.96	7.24	7.47	7.68	7.86	8.03	8.18	8.31	8.44	8.55	8.66	8.76	8.85	8.94	9.03	.01	
9	.05	3.20	3.95	4.41	4.76	5.02	5.24	5.43	5.59	5.74	5.87	5.98	6.09	6.19	6.28	6.36	6.44	6.51	6.58	6.64	.05	9
	.01	4.60	5.43	5.96	6.35	6.66	6.91	7.13	7.33	7.49	7.65	7.78	7.91	8.03	8.13	8.23	8.33	8.41	8.49	8.57	.01	
10	.05	3.15	3.88	4.33	4.65	4.91	5.12	5.30	5.46	5.60	5.72	5.83	5.93	6.03	6.11	6.19	6.27	6.34	6.40	6.47	.05	10
	.01	4.48	5.27	5.77	6.14	6.43	6.67	6.87	7.05	7.21	7.36	7.49	7.60	7.71	7.81	7.91	7.99	8.08	8.15	8.23	.01	
11	.05	3.11	3.82	4.26	4.57	4.82	5.03	5.20	5.35	5.49	5.61	5.71	5.81	5.90	5.98	6.06	6.13	6.20	6.27	6.33	.05	11
	.01	4.39	5.15	5.62	5.97	6.25	6.48	6.67	6.84	6.99	7.13	7.25	7.36	7.46	7.56	7.65	7.73	7.81	7.88	7.95	.01	
12	.05	3.08	3.77	4.20	4.51	4.75	4.95	5.12	5.27	5.39	5.51	5.61	5.71	5.80	5.88	5.95	6.02	6.09	6.15	6.21	.05	12
	.01	4.32	5.05	5.50	5.84	6.10	6.32	6.51	6.67	6.81	6.94	7.06	7.17	7.26	7.36	7.44	7.52	7.59	7.66	7.73	.01	
13	.05	3.06	3.73	4.15	4.45	4.69	4.88	5.05	5.19	5.32	5.43	5.53	5.63	5.71	5.79	5.86	5.93	5.99	6.05	6.11	.05	13
	.01	4.26	4.96	5.40	5.73	5.98	6.19	6.37	6.53	6.67	6.79	6.90	7.01	7.10	7.19	7.27	7.35	7.42	7.48	7.55	.01	
14	.05	3.03	3.70	4.11	4.41	4.64	4.83	4.99	5.13	5.25	5.36	5.46	5.55	5.64	5.71	5.79	5.85	5.91	5.97	6.03	.05	14
	.01	4.21	4.89	5.32	5.63	5.88	6.08	6.26	6.41	6.54	6.66	6.77	6.87	6.96	7.05	7.13	7.20	7.27	7.33	7.39	.01	
15	.05	3.01	3.67	4.08	4.37	4.59	4.78	4.94	5.08	5.20	5.31	5.40	5.49	5.57	5.65	5.72	5.78	5.85	5.90	5.96	.05	15
	.01	4.17	4.84	5.25	5.56	5.80	5.99	6.16	6.31	6.44	6.55	6.66	6.76	6.84	6.93	7.00	7.07	7.14	7.20	7.26	.01	
16	.05	3.00	3.65	4.05	4.33	4.56	4.74	4.90	5.03	5.15	5.26	5.35	5.44	5.52	5.59	5.66	5.73	5.79	5.84	5.90	.05	16
	.01	4.13	4.79	5.19	5.49	5.72	5.92	6.08	6.22	6.35	6.46	6.56	6.66	6.74	8.82	6.90	6.97	7.03	7.09	7.15	.01	

r = number of means (Tukey test) or number of steps between ordered means (Newman–Keuls test)

df_{error}	α_{FW}	2	3	4	5	6	7	8	9	10	11	12	13	14	15	16	17	18	19	20	α_{FW}	df_{error}
17	.05	2.98	3.63	4.02	4.30	4.52	4.70	4.86	4.99	5.11	5.21	5.31	5.39	5.47	5.54	5.61	5.67	5.73	5.79	5.84	.05	17
	.01	4.10	4.74	5.14	5.43	5.66	5.85	6.01	6.15	6.27	6.38	6.48	6.57	6.66	6.73	6.81	6.87	6.94	7.00	7.05	.01	
18	.05	2.97	3.61	4.00	4.28	4.49	4.67	4.82	4.96	5.07	5.17	5.27	5.35	5.43	5.50	5.57	5.63	5.69	5.74	5.79	.05	18
	.01	4.07	4.70	5.09	5.38	5.60	5.79	5.94	6.08	6.20	6.31	6.41	6.50	6.58	6.65	6.73	6.79	6.85	6.91	6.97	.01	
19	.05	2.96	3.59	3.98	4.25	4.47	4.65	4.79	4.92	5.04	5.14	5.23	5.31	5.39	5.46	5.53	5.59	5.65	5.70	5.75	.05	19
	.01	4.05	4.67	5.05	5.33	5.55	5.73	5.89	6.02	6.14	6.25	6.34	6.43	6.51	6.58	6.65	6.72	6.78	6.84	6.89	.01	
20	.05	2.95	3.58	3.96	4.23	4.45	4.62	4.77	4.90	5.01	5.11	5.20	5.28	5.36	5.43	5.49	5.55	5.61	5.66	5.71	.05	20
	.01	4.02	4.64	5.02	5.29	5.51	5.69	5.84	5.97	6.09	6.19	6.28	6.37	6.45	6.52	6.59	6.65	6.71	6.77	6.82	.01	
24	.05	2.92	3.53	3.90	4.17	4.37	4.54	4.68	4.81	4.92	5.01	5.10	5.18	5.25	5.32	5.38	5.44	5.49	5.55	5.59	.05	24
	.01	3.96	4.55	4.91	5.17	5.37	5.54	5.69	5.81	5.92	6.02	6.11	6.19	6.26	6.33	6.39	6.45	6.51	6.56	6.61	.01	
30	.05	2.89	3.49	3.85	4.10	4.30	4.46	4.60	4.72	4.82	4.92	5.00	5.08	5.15	5.21	5.27	5.33	5.38	5.43	5.47	.05	30
	.01	3.89	4.45	4.80	5.05	5.24	5.40	5.54	5.65	5.76	5.85	5.93	6.01	6.08	6.14	6.20	6.26	6.31	6.36	6.41	.01	
40	.05	2.86	3.44	3.79	4.04	4.23	4.39	4.52	4.63	4.73	4.82	4.90	4.98	5.04	5.11	5.16	5.22	5.27	5.31	5.36	.05	40
	.01	3.82	4.37	4.70	4.93	5.11	5.26	5.39	5.50	5.60	5.69	5.76	5.83	5.90	5.96	6.02	6.07	6.12	6.16	6.21	.01	
60	.05	2.83	3.40	3.74	3.98	4.16	4.31	4.44	4.55	4.65	4.73	4.81	4.88	4.94	5.00	5.06	5.11	5.15	5.20	5.24	.05	60
	.01	3.76	4.28	4.59	4.82	4.99	5.13	5.25	5.36	5.45	5.53	5.60	5.67	5.73	5.78	5.84	5.89	5.93	5.97	6.01	.01	
120	.05	2.80	3.36	3.68	3.92	4.10	4.24	4.36	4.47	4.56	4.64	4.71	4.78	4.84	4.90	4.95	5.00	5.04	5.09	5.13	.05	120
	.01	3.70	4.20	4.50	4.71	4.87	5.01	5.12	5.21	5.30	5.37	5.44	5.50	5.56	5.61	5.66	5.71	5.75	5.79	5.83	.01	
∞	.05	2.77	3.31	3.63	3.86	4.03	4.17	4.29	4.39	4.47	4.55	4.62	4.68	4.74	4.80	4.85	4.89	4.93	4.97	5.01	.05	∞
	.01	3.64	4.12	4.40	4.60	4.76	4.88	4.99	5.08	5.16	5.23	5.29	5.35	5.40	5.45	5.49	5.54	5.57	5.61	5.65	.01	

This table is abridged from Table 29 in E. S. Pearson and H. O. Hartley (Eds.), *Biometrika tables for statisticians* (3rd ed., Vol. 1), Cambridge University Press, New York, 1970, by permission of the *Biometrika* Trustees.

TABLE A.5
CRITICAL VALUES OF STUDENTIZED MAXIMUM
MODULUS DISTRIBUTION

	$\alpha = 0.10$			
	Number of Groups			
df	3	4	5	6
2	4.38	5.30	5.96	6.45
3	3.37	4.01	4.47	4.82
4	2.98	3.51	3.89	4.18
5	2.77	3.24	3.58	3.84
6	2.64	3.07	3.38	3.62
7	2.56	2.96	3.25	3.48
8	2.49	2.88	3.16	3.37
9	2.45	2.82	3.09	3.29
10	2.41	2.77	3.03	3.23
11	2.38	2.73	2.98	3.18
12	2.36	2.70	2.95	3.14
13	2.34	2.67	2.91	3.10
14	2.32	2.65	2.89	3.07
15	2.31	2.63	2.87	3.04
16	2.29	2.62	2.85	3.02
17	2.28	2.60	2.83	3.00
18	2.27	2.59	2.81	2.99
19	2.26	2.58	2.80	2.97
20	2.26	2.57	2.79	2.96
21	2.25	2.56	2.78	2.94
22	2.24	2.55	2.77	2.93
23	2.24	2.54	2.76	2.92
24	2.23	2.53	2.75	2.91
25	2.23	2.53	2.74	2.90
26	2.22	2.52	2.73	2.89
27	2.22	2.52	2.73	2.89
28	2.21	2.51	2.72	2.88
29	2.21	2.51	2.71	2.87
30	2.21	2.50	2.71	2.87
35	2.19	2.48	2.69	2.84
40	2.18	2.47	2.67	2.82
45	2.18	2.46	2.66	2.81
50	2.17	2.45	2.65	2.80
60	2.16	2.44	2.63	2.78
80	2.15	2.42	2.61	2.76
100	2.14	2.41	2.60	2.75
120	2.14	2.41	2.60	2.74
200	2.13	2.40	2.58	2.72
∞	2.11	2.38	2.56	2.70

TABLE A.5
(Continued)

$\alpha = 0.05$

	Number of Groups			
df	3	4	5	6
2	6.34	7.65	8.57	9.28
3	4.43	5.23	5.81	6.26
4	3.74	4.37	4.82	5.17
5	3.40	3.93	4.31	4.61
6	3.19	3.66	4.01	4.28
7	3.06	3.49	3.80	4.05
8	2.96	3.36	3.66	3.89
9	2.89	3.27	3.55	3.77
10	2.83	3.20	3.47	3.68
11	2.78	3.14	3.40	3.60
12	2.75	3.09	3.35	3.54
13	2.72	3.06	3.30	3.49
14	2.69	3.02	3.26	3.45
15	2.67	2.99	3.23	3.41
16	2.65	2.97	3.20	3.38
17	2.63	2.95	3.17	3.35
18	2.62	2.93	3.15	3.32
19	2.61	2.91	3.13	3.30
20	2.59	2.90	3.11	3.28
21	2.58	2.88	3.10	3.26
22	2.57	2.87	3.08	3.25
23	2.57	2.86	3.07	3.23
24	2.56	2.85	3.06	3.22
25	2.55	2.84	3.05	3.21
26	2.54	2.83	3.04	3.20
27	2.54	2.83	3.03	3.19
28	2.53	2.82	3.02	3.18
29	2.53	2.81	3.01	3.17
30	2.52	2.80	3.00	3.16
35	2.50	2.78	2.97	3.13
40	2.49	2.76	2.95	3.10
45	2.48	2.75	2.93	3.08
50	2.47	2.73	2.92	3.06
60	2.45	2.72	2.90	3.04
80	2.44	2.69	2.87	3.01
100	2.43	2.68	2.86	3.00
120	2.42	2.67	2.85	2.98
200	2.41	2.66	2.83	2.96
∞	2.39	2.63	2.80	2.93

(continued)

TABLE A.5
(Continued)

$\alpha = 0.01$

df	Number of Groups			
	3	4	5	6
2	14.44	17.35	19.43	21.02
3	7.91	9.28	10.27	11.03
4	5.99	6.90	7.57	8.09
5	5.11	5.81	6.33	6.74
6	4.61	5.20	5.64	5.99
7	4.30	4.81	5.20	5.50
8	4.08	4.55	4.89	5.17
9	3.92	4.35	4.67	4.92
10	3.80	4.20	4.50	4.74
11	3.71	4.09	4.37	4.59
12	3.63	4.00	4.26	4.48
13	3.57	3.92	4.18	4.38
14	3.52	3.85	4.10	4.30
15	3.47	3.80	4.04	4.23
16	3.43	3.75	3.99	4.17
17	3.40	3.71	3.94	4.12
18	3.37	3.68	3.90	4.07
19	3.35	3.65	3.86	4.03
20	3.32	3.62	3.83	4.00
21	3.30	3.59	3.80	3.97
22	3.28	3.57	3.78	3.94
23	3.27	3.55	3.75	3.91
24	3.25	3.53	3.73	3.89
25	3.24	3.51	3.71	3.87
26	3.23	3.50	3.70	3.85
27	3.21	3.48	3.68	3.83
28	3.20	3.47	3.66	3.81
29	3.19	3.46	3.65	3.80
30	3.18	3.45	3.64	3.78
35	3.15	3.40	3.58	3.73
40	3.12	3.37	3.54	3.68
45	3.10	3.34	3.51	3.65
50	3.08	3.32	3.49	3.62
60	3.06	3.29	3.46	3.59
80	3.02	3.25	3.41	3.54
100	3.01	3.23	3.39	3.51
120	2.99	3.21	3.37	3.49
200	2.97	3.19	3.34	3.46
∞	2.93	3.14	3.29	3.40

Source: Computed by C. W. Dunnett. Abridged from Table 7 in Y. Hochberg and A. C. Tamhane, *Multiple Comparisons Procedures*. Used with permission of John Wiley & Sons, Inc.

TABLE A.6
CRITICAL VALUES OF DUNNETT'S TWO-TAILED TEST FOR COMPARING
TREATMENTS TO A CONTROL

Error df	α	Number of Treatment Means, Including Control (a)								
		2	3	4	5	6	7	8	9	10
5	.05	2.57	3.03	3.29	3.48	3.62	3.73	3.82	3.90	3.97
	.01	4.03	4.63	4.98	5.22	5.41	5.56	5.69	5.80	5.89
6	.05	2.45	2.86	3.10	3.26	3.39	3.49	3.57	3.64	3.71
	.01	3.71	4.21	4.51	4.71	4.87	5.00	5.10	5.20	5.28
7	.05	2.36	2.75	2.97	3.12	3.24	3.33	3.41	3.47	3.53
	.01	3.50	3.95	4.21	4.39	4.53	4.64	4.74	4.82	4.89
8	.05	2.31	2.67	2.88	3.02	3.13	3.22	3.29	3.35	3.41
	.01	3.36	3.77	4.00	4.17	4.29	4.40	4.48	4.56	4.62
9	.05	2.26	2.61	2.81	2.95	3.05	3.14	3.20	3.26	3.32
	.01	3.25	3.63	3.85	4.01	4.12	4.22	4.30	4.37	4.43
10	.05	2.23	2.57	2.76	2.89	2.99	3.07	3.14	3.19	3.24
	.01	3.17	3.53	3.74	3.88	3.99	4.08	4.16	4.22	4.28
11	.05	2.20	2.53	2.72	2.84	2.94	3.02	3.08	3.14	3.19
	.01	3.11	3.45	3.65	3.79	3.89	3.98	4.05	4.11	4.16
12	.05	2.18	2.50	2.68	2.81	2.90	2.98	3.04	3.09	3.14
	.01	3.05	3.39	3.58	3.71	3.81	3.89	3.96	4.02	4.07
13	.05	2.16	2.48	2.65	2.78	2.87	2.94	3.00	3.06	3.10
	.01	3.01	3.33	3.52	3.65	3.74	3.82	3.89	3.94	3.99
14	.05	2.14	2.46	2.63	2.75	2.84	2.91	2.97	3.02	3.07
	.01	2.98	3.29	3.47	3.59	3.69	3.76	3.83	3.88	3.93
15	.05	2.13	2.44	2.61	2.73	2.82	2.89	2.95	3.00	3.04
	.01	2.95	3.25	3.43	3.55	3.64	3.71	3.78	3.83	3.88
16	.05	2.12	2.42	2.59	2.71	2.80	2.87	2.92	2.97	3.02
	.01	2.92	3.22	3.39	3.51	3.60	3.67	3.73	3.78	3.83
17	.05	2.11	2.41	2.58	2.69	2.78	2.85	2.90	2.95	3.00
	.01	2.90	3.19	3.36	3.47	3.56	3.63	3.69	3.74	3.79
18	.05	2.10	2.40	2.56	2.68	2.76	2.83	2.89	2.94	2.98
	.01	2.88	3.17	3.33	3.44	3.53	3.60	3.66	3.71	3.75
19	.05	2.09	2.39	2.55	2.66	2.75	2.81	2.87	2.92	2.96
	.01	2.86	3.15	3.31	3.42	3.50	3.57	3.63	3.68	3.72
20	.05	2.09	2.38	2.54	2.65	2.73	2.80	2.86	2.90	2.95
	.01	2.85	3.13	3.29	3.40	3.48	3.55	3.60	3.65	3.69
24	.05	2.06	2.35	2.51	2.61	2.70	2.76	2.81	2.86	2.90
	.01	2.80	3.07	3.22	3.32	3.40	3.47	3.52	3.57	3.61
30	.05	2.04	2.32	2.47	2.58	2.66	2.72	2.77	2.82	2.86
	.01	2.75	3.01	3.15	3.25	3.33	3.39	3.44	3.49	3.52
40	.05	2.02	2.29	2.44	2.54	2.62	2.68	2.73	2.77	2.81
	.01	2.70	2.95	3.09	3.19	3.26	3.32	3.37	3.41	3.44

(continued)

TABLE A.6
(Continued)

Error df	α	Number of Treatment Means, Including Control (a)								
		2	3	4	5	6	7	8	9	10
60	.05	2.00	2.27	2.41	2.51	2.58	2.64	2.69	2.73	2.77
	.01	2.66	2.90	3.03	3.12	3.19	3.25	3.29	3.33	3.37
120	.05	1.98	2.24	2.38	2.47	2.55	2.60	2.65	2.69	2.73
	.01	2.62	2.85	2.97	3.06	3.12	3.18	3.22	3.26	3.29
∞	.05	1.96	2.21	2.35	2.44	2.51	2.57	2.61	2.65	2.69
	.01	2.58	2.79	2.92	3.00	3.06	3.11	3.15	3.19	3.22

Table reproduced from New tables for multiple comparisons with a control, *Biometrics*, 1964, *20*, 482–491, with permission of the author, C. W. Dunnett, and the editor.

TABLE A.7
CRITICAL VALUES OF DUNNETT'S ONE-TAILED TEST FOR COMPARING
TREATMENTS TO A CONTROL

Error df	α	Number of Treatment Means, Including Control (a)								
		2	3	4	5	6	7	8	9	10
5	.05	2.02	2.44	2.68	2.85	2.98	3.08	3.16	3.24	3.30
	.01	3.37	3.90	4.21	4.43	4.60	4.73	4.85	4.94	5.03
6	.05	1.94	2.34	2.56	2.71	2.83	2.92	3.00	3.07	3.12
	.01	3.14	3.61	3.88	4.07	4.21	4.33	4.43	4.51	4.59
7	.05	1.89	2.27	2.48	2.62	2.73	2.82	2.89	2.95	3.01
	.01	3.00	3.42	3.66	3.83	3.96	4.07	4.15	4.23	4.30
8	.05	1.86	2.22	2.42	2.55	2.66	2.74	2.81	2.87	2.92
	.01	2.90	3.29	3.51	3.67	3.79	3.88	3.96	4.03	4.09
9	.05	1.83	2.18	2.37	2.50	2.60	2.68	2.75	2.81	2.86
	.01	2.82	3.19	3.40	3.55	3.66	3.75	3.82	3.89	3.94
10	.05	1.81	2.15	2.34	2.47	2.56	2.64	2.70	2.76	2.81
	.01	2.76	3.11	3.31	3.45	3.56	3.64	3.71	3.78	3.83
11	.05	1.80	2.13	2.31	2.44	2.53	2.60	2.67	2.72	2.77
	.01	2.72	3.06	3.25	3.38	3.48	3.56	3.63	3.69	3.74
12	.05	1.78	2.11	2.29	2.41	2.50	2.58	2.64	2.69	2.74
	.01	2.68	3.01	3.19	3.32	3.42	3.50	3.56	3.62	3.67
13	.05	1.77	2.09	2.27	2.39	2.48	2.55	2.61	2.66	2.71
	.01	2.65	2.97	3.15	3.27	3.37	3.44	3.51	3.56	3.61
14	.05	1.76	2.08	2.25	2.37	2.46	2.53	2.59	2.64	2.69
	.01	2.62	2.94	3.11	3.23	3.32	3.40	3.46	3.51	3.56
15	.05	1.75	2.07	2.24	2.36	2.44	2.51	2.57	2.62	2.67
	.01	2.60	2.91	3.08	3.20	3.29	3.36	3.42	3.47	3.52

TABLE A.7
(Continued)

Error df	α	Number of Treatment Means, Including Control (a)								
		2	3	4	5	6	7	8	9	10
16	.05	1.75	2.06	2.23	2.34	2.43	2.50	2.56	2.61	2.65
	.01	2.58	2.88	3.05	3.17	3.26	3.33	3.39	3.44	3.48
17	.05	1.74	2.05	2.22	2.33	2.42	2.49	2.54	2.59	2.64
	.01	2.57	2.86	3.03	3.14	3.23	3.30	3.36	3.41	3.45
18	.05	1.73	2.05	2.21	2.32	2.41	2.48	2.53	2.58	2.62
	.01	2.55	2.84	3.01	3.12	3.21	3.27	3.33	3.38	3.42
19	.05	1.73	2.03	2.20	2.31	2.40	2.47	2.52	2.57	2.61
	.01	2.54	2.83	2.99	3.10	3.18	3.25	3.31	3.36	3.40
20	.05	1.72	2.03	2.19	2.30	2.39	2.46	2.51	2.56	2.60
	.01	2.53	2.81	2.97	3.08	3.17	3.23	3.29	3.34	3.38
24	.05	1.71	2.01	2.17	2.28	2.36	2.43	2.48	2.53	2.57
	.01	2.49	2.77	2.92	3.03	3.11	3.17	3.22	3.27	3.31
30	.05	1.70	1.99	2.15	2.25	2.33	2.40	2.45	2.50	2.54
	.01	2.46	2.72	2.87	2.97	3.05	3.11	3.16	3.21	3.24
40	.05	1.68	1.97	2.13	2.23	2.31	2.37	2.42	2.47	2.51
	.01	2.42	2.68	2.82	2.92	2.99	3.05	3.10	3.14	3.18
60	.05	1.67	1.95	2.10	2.21	2.28	2.35	2.39	2.44	2.48
	.01	2.39	2.64	2.78	2.87	2.94	3.00	3.04	3.08	3.12
120	.05	1.66	1.93	2.08	2.18	2.26	2.32	2.37	2.41	2.45
	.01	2.36	2.60	2.73	2.82	2.89	2.94	2.99	3.03	3.06
∞	.05	1.64	1.92	2.06	2.16	2.23	2.29	2.34	2.38	2.42
	.01	2.33	2.56	2.68	2.77	2.84	2.89	2.93	2.97	3.00

Table reproduced from A multiple comparison procedure for comparing several treatments with a control, *Journal of the American Statistical Association*, 1955, *50*, 1096–1121, with permission of the author, C. W. Dunnett, and the editor.

TABLE A.8
CRITICAL VALUES OF BRYANT–PAULSON GENERALIZED STUDENTIZED RANGE

Error df	Number of Covariates	α	— Number of Means (a)										
			2	3	4	5	6	7	8	10	12	16	20
3	1	.05	5.42	7.18	8.32	9.17	9.84	10.39	10.86	11.62	12.22	13.14	13.83
		.01	10.28	13.32	15.32	16.80	17.98	18.95	19.77	21.12	22.19	23.82	25.05
	2	.05	6.21	8.27	9.60	10.59	11.37	12.01	12.56	13.44	14.15	15.22	16.02
		.01	11.97	15.56	17.91	19.66	21.05	22.19	23.16	24.75	26.01	27.93	29.38
	3	.05	6.92	9.23	10.73	11.84	12.72	13.44	14.06	15.05	15.84	17.05	17.95
		.01	13.45	17.51	20.17	22.15	23.72	25.01	26.11	27.90	29.32	31.50	33.13
4	1	.05	4.51	5.84	6.69	7.32	7.82	8.23	8.58	9.15	9.61	10.30	10.82
		.01	7.68	9.64	10.93	11.89	12.65	13.28	13.82	14.70	15.40	16.48	17.29
	2	.05	5.04	6.54	7.51	8.23	8.80	9.26	9.66	10.31	10.83	11.61	12.21
		.01	8.69	10.95	12.43	13.54	14.41	15.14	15.76	16.77	17.58	18.81	19.74
	3	.05	5.51	7.18	8.25	9.05	9.67	10.19	10.63	11.35	11.92	12.79	13.45
		.01	9.59	12.11	13.77	15.00	15.98	16.79	17.47	18.60	19.50	20.87	21.91
5	1	.05	4.06	5.17	5.88	6.40	6.82	7.16	7.45	7.93	8.30	8.88	9.32
		.01	6.49	7.99	8.97	9.70	10.28	10.76	11.17	11.84	12.38	13.20	13.83
	2	.05	4.45	5.68	6.48	7.06	7.52	7.90	8.23	8.76	9.18	9.83	10.31
		.01	7.20	8.89	9.99	10.81	11.47	12.01	12.47	13.23	13.84	14.77	15.47
	3	.05	4.81	6.16	7.02	7.66	8.17	8.58	8.94	9.52	9.98	10.69	11.22
		.01	7.83	9.70	10.92	11.82	12.54	13.14	13.65	14.48	15.15	16.17	16.95
6	1	.05	3.79	4.78	5.40	5.86	6.23	6.53	6.78	7.20	7.53	8.04	8.43
		.01	5.83	7.08	7.88	8.48	8.96	9.36	9.70	10.25	10.70	11.38	11.90
	2	.05	4.10	5.18	5.87	6.37	6.77	7.10	7.38	7.84	8.21	8.77	9.20
		.01	6.36	7.75	8.64	9.31	9.85	10.29	10.66	11.28	11.77	12.54	13.11
	3	.05	4.38	5.55	6.30	6.84	7.28	7.64	7.94	8.44	8.83	9.44	9.90
		.01	6.85	8.36	9.34	10.07	10.65	11.13	11.54	12.22	12.75	13.59	14.21

df		α											
7	1	.05	7.84	7.49	7.03	6.72	6.34	6.11	5.84	5.51	5.09	4.52	3.62
		.01	10.69	10.24	9.64	9.26	8.77	8.48	8.14	7.72	7.20	6.50	5.41
	2	.05	8.46	8.08	7.57	7.24	6.83	6.58	6.28	5.92	5.47	4.85	3.87
		.01	11.64	11.14	10.49	10.06	9.53	9.21	8.83	8.37	7.80	7.03	5.84
	3	.05	9.03	8.63	8.08	7.73	7.29	7.01	6.70	6.31	5.82	5.16	4.11
		.01	12.51	11.97	11.26	10.80	10.23	9.88	9.47	8.98	8.36	7.52	6.23
8	1	.05	7.43	7.10	6.67	6.39	6.03	5.82	5.57	5.26	4.87	4.34	3.49
		.01	9.87	9.46	8.92	8.58	8.15	7.88	7.58	7.20	6.74	6.11	5.12
	2	.05	7.94	7.59	7.12	6.82	6.44	6.21	5.94	5.61	5.19	4.61	3.70
		.01	10.63	10.19	9.61	9.23	8.76	8.48	8.14	7.74	7.23	6.54	5.48
	3	.05	8.42	8.05	7.55	7.23	6.83	6.58	6.29	5.93	5.49	4.88	3.91
		.01	11.34	10.87	10.24	9.84	9.33	9.03	8.67	8.23	7.69	6.95	5.81
10	1	.05	6.87	6.58	6.19	5.94	5.63	5.43	5.21	4.93	4.58	4.10	3.32
		.01	8.82	8.47	8.01	7.72	7.35	7.13	6.86	6.55	6.15	5.61	4.76
	2	.05	7.26	6.95	6.54	6.27	5.93	5.73	5.49	5.19	4.82	4.31	3.49
		.01	9.36	8.99	8.50	8.19	7.79	7.55	7.27	6.93	6.51	5.93	5.02
	3	.05	7.62	7.29	6.86	6.58	6.22	6.01	5.75	5.44	5.05	4.51	3.65
		.01	9.88	9.48	8.96	8.63	8.21	7.96	7.66	7.30	6.84	6.23	5.27
12	1	.05	6.53	6.26	5.90	5.67	5.37	5.19	4.98	4.73	4.40	3.95	3.22
		.01	8.18	7.87	7.46	7.20	6.87	6.67	6.43	6.15	5.79	5.31	4.54
	2	.05	6.83	6.55	6.17	5.92	5.62	5.43	5.20	4.93	4.59	4.12	3.35
		.01	8.60	8.27	7.84	7.56	7.21	7.00	6.75	6.45	6.07	5.56	4.74
	3	.05	7.12	6.82	6.43	6.17	5.85	5.65	5.42	5.14	4.78	4.28	3.48
		.01	9.00	8.65	8.20	7.90	7.54	7.31	7.05	6.74	6.34	5.80	4.94
14	1	.05	6.29	6.03	5.70	5.48	5.20	5.03	4.83	4.59	4.28	3.85	3.15
		.01	7.75	7.47	7.09	6.85	6.55	6.36	6.15	5.89	5.56	5.11	4.39
	2	.05	6.54	6.27	5.92	5.69	5.40	5.22	5.01	4.76	4.44	3.99	3.26
		.01	8.09	7.79	7.40	7.14	6.82	6.63	6.40	6.13	5.78	5.31	4.56
	3	.05	6.78	6.50	6.13	5.89	5.59	5.41	5.19	4.93	4.59	4.13	3.37
		.01	8.41	8.10	7.69	7.42	7.09	6.89	6.65	6.36	6.00	5.51	4.72

(continued)

TABLE A.8
(Continued)

Error df	Number of Covariates	α	Number of Means (a) 2	3	4	5	6	7	8	10	12	16	20
16	1	.05	3.10	3.77	4.19	4.49	4.72	4.91	5.07	5.34	5.55	5.87	6.12
		.01	4.28	4.96	5.39	5.70	5.95	6.15	6.32	6.60	6.83	7.18	7.45
	2	.05	3.19	3.90	4.32	4.63	4.88	5.07	5.24	5.52	5.74	6.07	6.33
		.01	4.42	5.14	5.58	5.90	6.16	6.37	6.55	6.85	7.08	7.45	7.73
	3	.05	3.29	4.01	4.46	4.78	5.03	5.23	5.41	5.69	5.92	6.27	6.53
		.01	4.56	5.30	5.76	6.10	6.37	6.59	6.77	7.08	7.33	7.71	8.00
18	1	.05	3.06	3.72	4.12	4.41	4.63	4.82	4.98	5.23	5.44	5.75	5.98
		.01	4.20	4.86	5.26	5.56	5.79	5.99	6.15	6.42	6.63	6.96	7.22
	2	.05	3.14	3.82	4.24	4.54	4.77	4.96	5.13	5.39	5.60	5.92	6.17
		.01	4.32	5.00	5.43	5.73	5.98	6.18	6.35	6.63	6.85	7.19	7.46
	3	.05	3.23	3.93	4.35	4.66	4.90	5.10	5.27	5.54	5.76	6.09	6.34
		.01	4.44	5.15	5.59	5.90	6.16	6.36	6.54	6.83	7.06	7.42	7.69
20	1	.05	3.03	3.67	4.07	4.35	4.57	4.75	4.90	5.15	5.35	5.65	5.88
		.01	4.14	4.77	5.17	5.45	5.68	5.86	6.02	6.27	6.48	6.80	7.04
	2	.05	3.10	3.77	4.17	4.46	4.69	4.88	5.03	5.29	5.49	5.81	6.04
		.01	4.25	4.90	5.31	5.60	5.84	6.03	6.19	6.46	6.67	7.00	7.25
	3	.05	3.18	3.86	4.28	4.57	4.81	5.00	5.16	5.42	5.63	5.96	6.20
		.01	4.35	5.03	5.45	5.75	5.99	6.19	6.36	6.63	6.85	7.19	7.45
24	1	.05	2.98	3.61	3.99	4.26	4.47	4.65	4.79	5.03	5.22	5.51	5.73
		.01	4.05	4.65	5.02	5.29	5.50	5.68	5.83	6.07	6.26	6.56	6.78
	2	.05	3.04	3.69	4.08	4.35	4.57	4.75	4.90	5.14	5.34	5.63	5.86
		.01	4.14	4.76	5.14	5.42	5.63	5.81	5.96	6.21	6.41	6.71	6.95
	3	.05	3.11	3.76	4.16	4.44	4.67	4.85	5.00	5.25	5.45	5.75	5.98
		.01	4.22	4.86	5.25	5.54	5.76	5.94	6.10	6.35	6.55	6.87	7.11

30	1	.05	2.94	3.55	3.91	4.18	4.38	4.54	4.69	4.91	5.09	5.37	5.58
		.01	3.96	4.54	4.89	5.14	5.34	5.50	5.64	5.87	6.05	6.32	6.53
	2	.05	2.99	3.61	3.98	4.25	4.46	4.62	4.77	5.00	5.18	5.46	5.68
		.01	4.03	4.62	4.98	5.24	5.44	5.61	5.75	5.98	6.16	6.44	6.66
	3	.05	3.04	3.67	4.05	4.32	4.53	4.70	4.85	5.08	5.27	5.56	5.78
		.01	4.10	4.70	5.06	5.33	5.54	5.71	5.85	6.08	6.27	6.56	6.78
40	1	.05	2.89	3.49	3.84	4.09	4.29	4.45	4.58	4.80	4.97	5.23	5.43
		.01	3.88	4.43	4.76	5.00	5.19	5.34	5.47	5.68	5.85	6.10	6.30
	2	.05	2.93	3.53	3.89	4.15	4.34	4.50	4.64	4.86	5.04	5.30	5.50
		.01	3.93	4.48	4.82	5.07	5.26	5.41	5.54	5.76	5.93	6.19	6.38
	3	.05	2.97	3.57	3.94	4.20	4.40	4.56	4.70	4.92	5.10	5.37	5.57
		.01	3.98	4.54	4.88	5.13	5.32	5.48	5.61	5.83	6.00	6.27	6.47
60	1	.05	2.85	3.43	3.77	4.01	4.20	4.35	4.48	4.69	4.85	5.10	5.29
		.01	3.79	4.32	4.64	4.86	5.04	5.18	5.30	5.50	5.65	5.89	6.07
	2	.05	2.88	3.46	3.80	4.05	4.24	4.39	4.52	4.73	4.89	5.14	5.33
		.01	3.83	4.36	4.68	4.90	5.08	5.22	5.35	5.54	5.70	5.94	6.12
	3	.05	2.90	3.49	3.83	4.08	4.27	4.43	4.56	4.77	4.93	5.19	5.38
		.01	3.86	4.39	4.72	4.95	5.12	5.27	5.39	5.59	5.75	6.00	6.18
120	1	.05	2.81	3.37	3.70	3.93	4.11	4.26	4.38	4.58	4.73	4.97	5.15
		.01	3.72	4.22	4.52	4.73	4.89	5.03	5.14	5.32	5.47	5.69	5.85
	2	.05	2.82	3.38	3.72	3.95	4.13	4.28	4.40	4.60	4.75	4.99	5.17
		.01	3.73	4.24	4.54	4.75	4.91	5.05	5.16	5.35	5.49	5.71	5.88
	3	.05	2.84	3.40	3.73	3.97	4.15	4.30	4.42	4.62	4.77	5.01	5.19
		.01	3.75	4.25	4.55	4.77	4.94	5.07	5.18	5.37	5.51	5.74	5.90

Table reproduced from An extension of Tukey's method of multiple comparisons to experimental designs with random concomitant variables. *Biometrika*, 1976, *63*, 631–638, with permission of the editor.

TABLE A.9
CRITICAL VALUES OF CHI-SQUARE DISTRIBUTION

df	.10	.05	.025	.01	.005	.001
1	2.71	3.84	5.02	6.63	7.88	10.83
2	4.61	5.99	7.38	9.21	10.60	13.82
3	6.25	7.81	9.35	11.34	12.84	16.27
4	7.78	9.49	11.14	13.28	14.86	18.47
5	9.24	11.07	12.83	15.09	16.75	20.51
6	10.64	12.59	14.45	16.81	18.55	22.46
7	12.02	14.07	16.01	18.48	20.28	24.32
8	13.36	15.51	17.53	20.09	21.95	26.12
9	14.68	16.92	19.02	21.67	23.59	27.88
10	15.99	18.31	20.48	23.21	25.19	29.59
11	17.28	19.68	21.92	24.72	26.76	31.26
12	18.55	21.03	23.34	26.22	28.30	32.91
13	19.81	22.36	24.74	27.69	29.82	34.53
14	21.06	23.68	26.12	29.14	31.32	36.12
15	22.31	25.00	27.49	30.58	32.80	37.70
16	23.54	26.30	28.85	32.00	34.27	39.25
17	24.77	27.59	30.19	33.41	35.72	40.79
18	25.99	28.87	31.53	34.81	37.16	42.31
19	27.20	30.14	32.85	36.19	38.58	43.82
20	28.41	31.41	34.17	37.57	40.00	45.31
21	29.62	32.67	35.48	38.93	41.40	46.80
22	30.81	33.92	36.78	40.29	42.80	48.27
23	32.01	35.17	38.08	41.64	44.18	49.73
24	33.20	36.42	39.36	42.98	45.56	51.18
25	34.38	37.65	40.65	44.31	46.93	52.62
26	35.56	38.89	41.92	45.64	48.29	54.05
27	36.74	40.11	43.19	46.96	49.64	55.48
28	37.92	41.34	44.46	48.28	50.99	56.89
29	39.09	42.56	45.72	49.59	52.34	58.30
30	40.26	43.77	46.98	50.89	53.67	59.70

Note: These critical values were computed using the CINV function of SAS.

TABLE A.10
COEFFICIENTS OF ORTHOGONAL POLYNOMIALS

Number of Levels	Polynominal	Coefficients								$\sum(c_i)^2$
3	Linear	-1	0	1						2
	Quadratic	1	-2	1						6
4	Linear	-3	-1	1	3					20
	Quadratic	1	-1	-1	1					4
	Cubic	-1	3	-3	1					20
5	Linear	-2	-1	0	1	2				10
	Quadratic	2	-1	-2	-1	2				14
	Cubic	-1	2	0	-2	1				10
	Quartic	1	-4	6	-4	1				70
6	Linear	-5	-3	-1	1	3	5			70
	Quadratic	5	-1	-4	-4	-1	5			84
	Cubic	-5	7	4	-4	-7	5			180
	Quartic	1	-3	2	2	-3	1			28
	Quintic	-1	5	-10	10	-5	1			252
7	Linear	-3	-2	-1	0	1	2	3		28
	Quadratic	5	0	-3	-4	-3	0	5		84
	Cubic	-1	1	1	0	-1	-1	1		6
	Quartic	3	-7	1	6	1	-7	3		154
	Quintic	-1	4	-5	0	5	-4	1		84
8	Linear	-7	-5	-3	-1	1	3	5	7	168
	Quadratic	7	1	-3	-5	-5	-3	1	7	168
	Cubic	-7	5	7	3	-3	-7	-5	7	264
	Quartic	7	-13	-3	9	9	-3	-13	7	616
	Quintic	-7	23	-17	-15	15	17	-23	7	2,184

TABLE A.10
(Continued)

Number of Levels	Polynominal	Coefficients										$\sum(c_j)^2$
9	Linear	−4	−3	−2	−1	0	1	2	3	4		60
	Quadratic	28	7	−8	−17	−20	−17	−8	7	28		2,772
	Cubic	−14	7	13	9	0	−9	−13	−7	14		990
	Quartic	14	−21	−11	9	18	9	−11	−21	14		2,002
	Quintic	−4	11	−4	−9	0	9	4	−11	4		468
10	Linear	−9	−7	−5	−3	−1	1	3	5	7	9	330
	Quadratic	6	2	−1	−3	−4	−4	−3	−1	2	6	132
	Cubic	−42	14	35	31	12	−12	−31	−35	−14	42	8,580
	Quartic	18	−22	−17	3	18	18	3	−17	−22	18	2,860
	Quintic	−6	14	−1	−11	−6	6	11	1	−14	6	780

This table is abridged from Table 47 in E. S. Pearson and H. O. Hartley (Eds.), *Biometrika tables for statisticians* (3rd ed., Vol. 1), Cambridge University Press, New York, 1970, by permission of the *Biometrika* Trustees.

TABLE A.11

PEARSON–HARTLEY POWER CHARTS

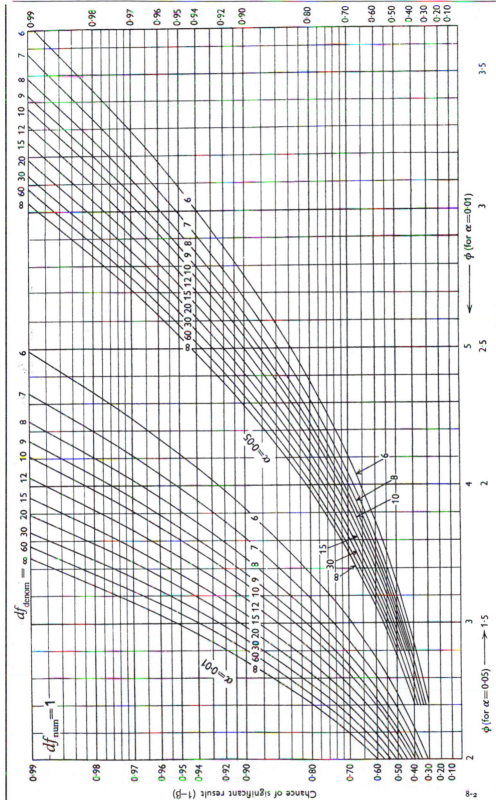

Reproduced with permission from E. S. Pearson and H. O. Hartley, Charts of the power function for analysis of variance tests, derived from the non-central *F*-distribution, *Biometrika*, 1951, *38*, 112–130

(*continued*)

TABLE A.11
(Continued)

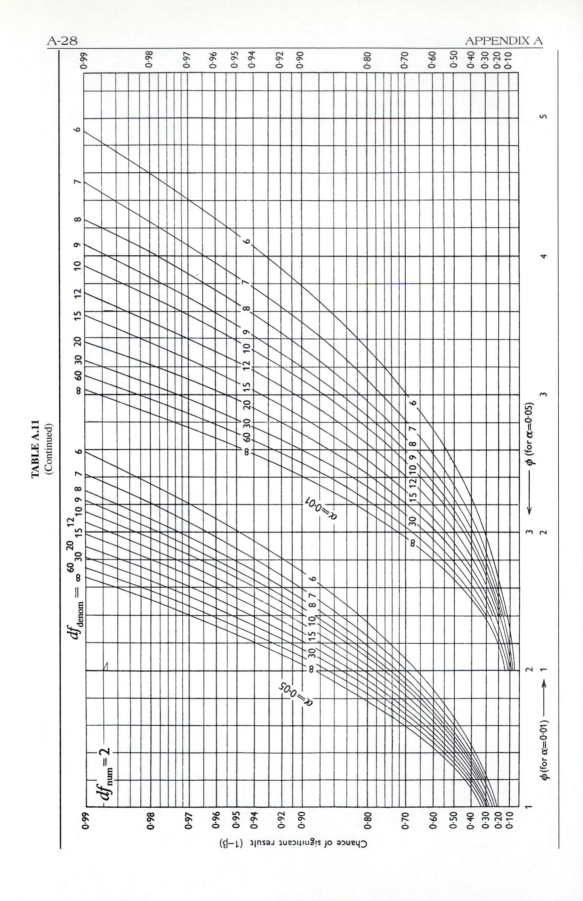

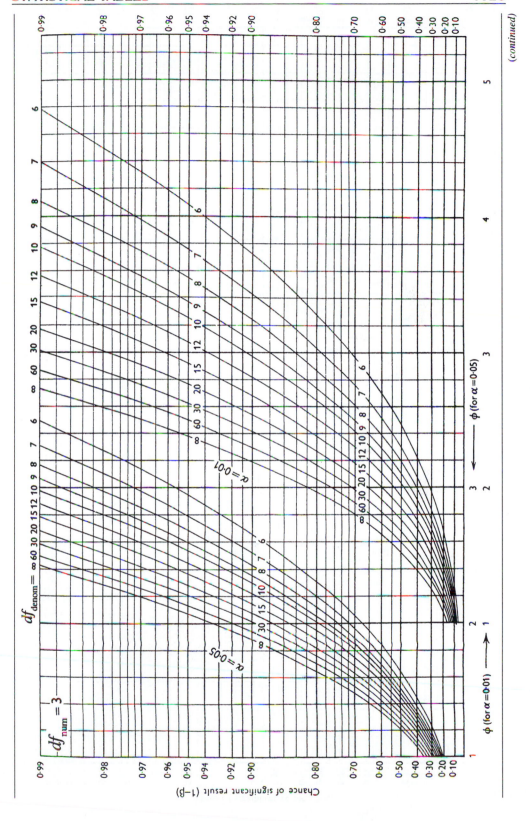

(continued)

TABLE A.11
(Continued)

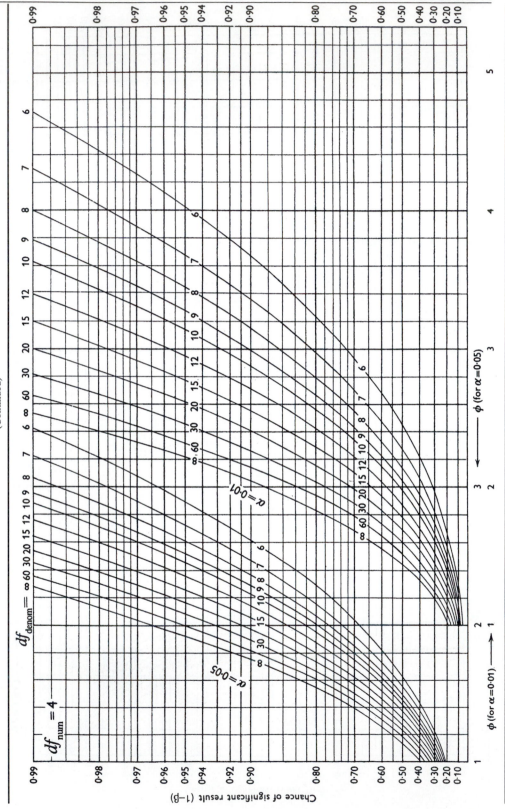

Appendix B

Part I

Linear Models: The Relation Between ANOVA and Regression

There is a close relation between the regression models presented in such standard regression textbooks as Cohen, Cohen, West, and Aiken (2002); Darlington (1990); Judd and McClelland (1989); and Pedhazur (1997) and the ANOVA models we present in this book. We touch upon this relation in the tutorial on regression, but that tutorial is intended primarily as a brief primer on multiple regression for readers who have not already encountered it previously. This appendix, on the other hand, is intended primarily for readers who already have considerable background in regression but who are interested in developing a deeper understanding of the relationship between ANOVA and regression. Specifically, our purpose in this appendix is threefold: (1) to illustrate some examples of the relation between regression and ANOVA, (2) to explain the place of regression models and ANOVA models in a broader methodological framework, and (3) to explain why we have chosen to focus primarily on ANOVA models in this book, although ANOVA is often regarded as a special case of regression.

THE RELATION BETWEEN REGRESSION AND ANOVA MODELS

Statistical models are usually defined in terms of parameters, which specify the form of relationship between variables. It is often the case that two models can be written in different forms with parameters that appear to be different from one another and yet the two models are in fact equivalent to one another. We shall take "equivalent" to mean that even though the specific parameter estimates of the two models may not necessarily be the same, the sum of squared errors of the two models will always be equal to one another.

Single-Factor Between-Subjects Design

For example, consider how to write a full model for the single-factor between-subjects design of Chapter 3. One possible model is the following cell means model:

$$Y_{ij} = \mu_j + \varepsilon_{ij} \qquad \text{(3.54, repeated)}$$

However, Chapter 3 also presents the effects model as an alternative full model:

$$Y_{ij} = \mu + \alpha_j + \varepsilon_{ij} \qquad\qquad (3.66, \text{repeated})$$

Chapter 3 shows that even though these two models have different forms, their sum of squared errors E_F will always equal one another. This equivalence holds even though the effects model has one more parameter than the cell means model, because both models have a independent parameters (it is not the case however throughout the realm of statistical models that any two models having the same number of parameters will necessarily be equivalent models).

Just as it is possible to write more than one ANOVA model to represent the data and yet discover that the two models are equivalent, there is also an entire collection of regression models that are also equivalent to these ANOVA models. To consider some examples of such equivalent models, we will begin with the general form of a linear model for one dependent variable, which Chapter 3 shows can be written as:

$$Y_i = \beta_0 X_{0i} + \beta_1 X_{1i} + \beta_2 X_{2i} + \beta_3 X_{3i} + \cdots + \beta_p X_{pi} + \varepsilon_i \qquad\qquad (3.1, \text{repeated})$$

Let's consider the relationship between this general regression model and the ANOVA effects model:

$$Y_{ij} = \mu + \alpha_j + \varepsilon_{ij} \qquad\qquad (3.66, \text{repeated})$$

To develop the relationship between these two models, we will start with the simplest case of two groups. Notice that we could write the ANOVA effects model in this case as

$$\text{For Group 1:} \quad Y_{i1} = \mu + \alpha_1 + \varepsilon_{i1} \qquad\qquad (1)$$

$$\text{For Group 2:} \quad Y_{i2} = \mu + \alpha_2 + \varepsilon_{i2} \qquad\qquad (2)$$

We can mimic this same result using regression analysis with three X variables:

$$Y_i = \beta_0 X_{0i} + \beta_1 X_{1i} + \beta_2 X_{2i} + \varepsilon_i \qquad\qquad (3)$$

where we define the X variables in the following way:

$$X_{0i} = 1 \text{ for all individuals}$$

$$X_{1i} = 1 \text{ for individuals in Group 1 and 0 for individuals in Group 2}$$

$$X_{2i} = 1 \text{ for individuals in Group 2 and 0 for individuals in Group 1}$$

Notice that with this definition of our 3 X variables, we can write our regression model from Equation 3 as

$$\text{For Group 1:} \quad Y_i = \beta_0(1) + \beta_1(1) + \beta_2(0) + \varepsilon_i \qquad\qquad (4)$$

$$\text{For Group 2:} \quad Y_i = \beta_0(1) + \beta_1(0) + \beta_2(1) + \varepsilon_i \qquad\qquad (5)$$

Simplifying Equations 4 and 5 yields

$$\text{For Group 1:} \quad Y_i = \beta_0 + \beta_1 + \varepsilon_i \qquad\qquad (6)$$

$$\text{For Group 2:} \quad Y_i = \beta_0 + \beta_2 + \varepsilon_i \qquad\qquad (7)$$

Notice that Equation 6 is identical to Equation 1, where $\beta_0 = \mu$ and $\beta_1 = \alpha_1$. Similarly, Equation 7 is identical to Equation 2, where $\beta_0 = \mu$ and $\beta_2 = \alpha_2$. In other words, by defining X variables in regression this way, we obtain a regression model whose parameters are identical to those of the ANOVA effects model.

This relationship between the ANOVA effects model and regression holds not just for two groups, but more generally for a groups. In this more general case, we continue to define $a + 1$ X variables. The general formulation is to define X variables according to the following rule:

$$X_{0i} = 1 \text{ for all individuals}$$

$$X_{ji} = 1 \text{ for individuals in Group } j \text{ and 0 for all other individuals}$$

Notice that the X_0 variable, which we will refer to as a "unit variable" (because it assumes a constant value of 1 for all subjects), allows for a grand mean. There are then a additional X variables, one for each group.

If it were not for one complication, it might be possible to end this appendix immediately. However, as we mentioned briefly in Chapter 3, there is a difficulty in working with either the ANOVA effects model or the comparable regression model. The problem is that we have $a + 1$ parameters, but only a groups. To understand why this is a problem, let's return to our simple example of only 2 groups. We will formulate the problem in terms of the regression models of Equations 6 and 7, but keep in mind that these two equations are formally identical to Equations 1 and 2, so ultimately we must deal with the problem we about to identify regardless of whether we adopt an ANOVA or a regression approach to the data.

Equations 6 and 7 stipulate that scores on Y can be explained in terms of 3 parameters: β_0, β_1, and β_2. Specifically, our model specifies that (1) the mean Y score in Group 1 can be expressed as $\beta_0 + \beta_1$ and (2) the mean Y score in Group 2 can be expressed as $\beta_0 + \beta_2$. We can write these two statements more formally as

$$\mu_1 = \beta_0 + \beta_1 \tag{8}$$

$$\mu_2 = \beta_0 + \beta_2 \tag{9}$$

The problem is that we are allowing ourselves three parameters to explain two population means. Even if the two means are different, we will never need as many as three parameters to reproduce the population means. To see why, suppose that $\mu_1 = 40$ and $\mu_2 = 60$. What are the proper values of β_0, β_1, and β_2? It turns out that there are infinitely many possible values of these three parameters, all of which succeed perfectly in reproducing the population means. We don't have space to list all of the possibilities (listing them all would require an infinite number of pages!), but here are some examples:

$$\beta_0 = 50, \beta_1 = -10, \text{ and } \beta_2 = 10$$

$$\beta_0 = 0, \beta_1 = 40, \text{ and } \beta_2 = 60$$

$$\beta_0 = 60, \beta_1 = -20, \text{ and } \beta_2 = 0$$

$$\beta_0 = 100, \beta_1 = -60, \text{ and } \beta_2 = -40$$

Although these four possiblities may look very different from one another, they all share an important property. Namely, in all four cases, the sum of β_0 and β_1 equals 40 and the sum of β_0 and β_2 equals 60. Thus, all four sets of parameter values imply the correct population means of our two groups. The problem is that we have more parameters than we need. With two groups, we need only two parameters, not three. The problem is essentially the same with more than two groups. In general, with a groups, our effects model has $a + 1$ parameters, but we need only a parameters. Also notice that on a practical note, we have considered the problem in terms of population parameters, but we must confront the exact same problem in a sample. For example, if we have two sample means of 40 and 60, we still do not need three parameter estimates to explain these two values. The same four sets of values shown above when used as parameter estimates would all perfectly reproduce the sample means of 40 and 60, so it would be impossible to identify unique values for $\hat{\beta}_0$, $\hat{\beta}_1$, and $\hat{\beta}_2$. If we cannot find unique values for these parameter estimates, it becomes impossible to interpret the meaning behind the parameters. Without being able to interpret the parameter estimates, we cannot hope to understand what properties of our data are reflected in these parameters. Thus, we must find some way to get around this problem.

To solve this problem, we need to obtain unique values for parameters (and in a sample, unique values for parameter estimates). The solution is to reduce the number of parameters by 1. The way we do this is by establishing a "side condition," as we mentioned in Chapter 3. It turns out that there are a variety of possible side conditions we might impose. Which one we choose does not affect the overall fit of the model, but does affect the meaning of the specific parameters of the model. To explore how this works, we will consider three different side conditions we might impose on our parameters. As we will explain later, each of these three types of side conditions has its own advantages and disadvantages, so there is some value in becoming familiar with all three. As before, we will continue to examine these side conditions from the perspective of regression analysis, in particular the β parameters of the regression model.

Reference Cell Model.
The first side condition we will consider is to constrain β_a, the parameter associated with the last group, to be zero. Intuitively, the idea is that we need to reduce the number of parameters by 1, so why not simply eliminate the last parameter. Stated differently, we have $a + 1$ X variables in our model, but we need only a variables, so it seems reasonable to drop the final variable. It turns out that this is exactly what we are doing when we constrain β_a to equal zero.

To understand what is happening here, let's reconsider the simple case of two groups. Recall from Equations 8 and 9 that in the case of two groups, we can express the relationship between cell means and regression parameters as

$$\mu_1 = \beta_0 + \beta_1 \qquad \text{(8, repeated)}$$

$$\mu_2 = \beta_0 + \beta_2 \qquad \text{(9, repeated)}$$

However, we will now impose our constraint that the parameter associated with the last group equals zero. In the case of two groups, our constraint would be that $\beta_2 = 0$, because $a = 2$. Thus, we can simplify Equations 8 and 9 as

$$\mu_1 = \beta_0 + \beta_1 \qquad (10)$$

$$\mu_2 = \beta_0 \qquad (11)$$

Equations 10 and 11 show us that we now have unique values and thus unique interpretations for β_0 and β_1, the two parameters in our model. Namely, Equation 11 says that β_0 is the population mean of Group 2. Notice that we have to be careful here to realize that the intercept of our regression analysis does not represent the grand mean, but instead represents the mean of Group 2. This happens because in general the intercept is the population value of Y when all X variables equal 0, and in this case X_1 (our only predictor variable with two groups) is zero for individuals in Group 2. The meaning of β_1 becomes clear if we rewrite Equation 10 as

$$\beta_1 = \mu_1 - \beta_0 \qquad (12)$$

Because we know from Equation 11 that $\mu_2 = \beta_0$, we can further rewrite Equation 12 as

$$\beta_1 = \mu_1 - \mu_2 \qquad (13)$$

Equation 13 reveals one of the advantages of this particular side condition, namely that β_1, the parameter associated with our X_1 predictor, represents the difference between the population means of Groups 1 and 2. This is especially convenient because if we want to test a null hypothesis that $\mu_1 = \mu_2$, we can simply test a null hypothesis that $\beta_1 = 0$ in our regression model. Similarly, if we want to form a confidence interval for $\mu_1 - \mu_2$, we can form a confidence interval for β_1 using regression analysis.

Another advantage of this choice of side condition is that it is trivial to implement. By saying that β_a equals zero, we are effectively omitting X_a as a predictor in our model. To see why, let's look again at Equation 3 for two groups:

$$Y_i = \beta_0 X_{0i} + \beta_1 X_{1i} + \beta_2 X_{2i} + \varepsilon_i \qquad \text{(3, repeated)}$$

Imposing the side condition that $\beta_2 = 0$ (recall that β_a is the same as β_2 when $a = 2$) implies that we can write the model as

$$Y_i = \beta_0 X_{0i} + \beta_1 X_{1i} + (0)X_{2i} + \varepsilon_i \qquad (14)$$

which further simplifies to

$$Y_i = \beta_0 + \beta_1 X_{1i} + \varepsilon_i \qquad (15)$$

because X_{2i} drops out when multiplied by zero (notice also that X_{0i} has disappeared in Equation 15 because we have substituted 1 for X_{0i} knowing that $X_{0i} = 1$ for all individuals). Notice that the only difference between Equation 15 and Equation 3 is that the X_2 variable has been omitted from Equation 15. Thus, in a practical sense we can impose the side condition that $\beta_2 = 0$ by omitting X_2 from our model. In other words, we fit a regression model where we intentionally omit the variable representing Group 2. Instead of including two predictor variables in our regression model, when we have two groups, we include only one predictor (although keep in mind that we have also included the unit variable X_0 in our model).

What about the more general case of a groups? Exactly the same logic holds here as well. We simply omit X_a as a predictor. As a consequence, β_0, the intercept term in the model, becomes equal to the population mean of the final group, i.e,

$$\beta_0 = \mu_a \qquad (16)$$

In addition, the β parameter associated with a given predictor variable becomes equal to the difference between the population mean of that group and Group a. In symbols,

$$\beta_j = \mu_j - \mu_a \tag{17}$$

Notice then that each β_j parameter compares one of the first $a - 1$ group means to the mean of the last group. For this reason, the model resulting from this side condition is often referred to as a "reference cell" model where Group a is the reference group against which all other groups are compared. In some situations, such as when one group is a control group and all other groups are experimental groups, the parameters have a very natural interpretation. However, in other situations, it may seem artificial to single out one group and compare it to all of the others. Even so, it turns out that this specific side condition offers additional advantages, which is why it forms the basis of the approach used by many general linear model routines, such as the parameterization resulting from a CLASS statement in SAS PROC GLM and SAS PROC MIXED. We will return to this issue later in the appendix. We should also mention that this method of coding variables to represent group membership is often referred to in the literature as "dummy coding."

One additional point regarding the reference cell model will prove to be helpful for understanding its extension to factorial designs. Remember that the regression intercept β_0 in this model equals μ_a. Implicitly, this leads to a new definition of μ in ANOVA notation. Instead of automatically interpreting μ as the grand mean averaged over all groups, μ effectively becomes μ_a, the mean of group a, in the reference cell model. As usual, we can still define an effect for group j to be of the form

$$\alpha_j = \mu_j - \mu$$

However, the meaning of an "effect" from this perspective is clearly different than it is the ANOVA effects model. In the reference cell model, the effect of group j is the mean difference between it and group a, not the mean difference between group j and the grand mean. This definition has two important implications. First, the effect of group a is now necessarily equal to zero. Notice that this is literally the constraint we have imposed on the effect parameters in order to reduce the number of parameters to be estimated from $a + 1$ to a. Second, the sum of the effects typically no longer equals zero. Both of these points will become important when we examine the reference cell model for a factorial design.

Cell Means Model.

The second side condition we will consider is to constrain β_0 to equal zero. In a moment we will describe how to operationalize this constraint, but first we will examine its meaning in the context of two groups. Recall from Equations 8 and 9 that we can express the relationship between cell means and regression parameters as

$$\mu_1 = \beta_0 + \beta_1 \tag{8, repeated}$$

$$\mu_2 = \beta_0 + \beta_2 \tag{9, repeated}$$

However, if we impose a constraint that $\beta_0 = 0$, we can simplify these equations as

$$\mu_1 = \beta_1 \tag{18}$$

$$\mu_2 = \beta_2 \tag{19}$$

Notice that with this constraint in place, each of the remaining β parameters simply becomes equal to a population mean. In the more general case of a groups, there would be a β parameters, each of which would equal a population mean. For this reason, we say that imposing a side condition where $\beta_0 = 0$ results in a "cell means" model.

Using the cell means model from a regression perspective requires us to constrain β_0 to equal zero. The simplest way to do this is to realize that by saying that β_0 equals zero, we are effectively omitting X_0 as a predictor in our model. To see why, let's look again at Equation 3:

$$Y_i = \beta_0 X_{0i} + \beta_1 X_{1i} + \beta_2 X_{2i} + \varepsilon_i \tag{3, repeated}$$

Imposing the side condition that $\beta_0 = 0$ implies that we can write the model as

$$Y_i = (0)X_{0i} + \beta_1 X_{1i} + \beta_2 X_{2i} + \varepsilon_i \tag{20}$$

which further simplifies to

$$Y_i = \beta_1 X_{1i} + \beta_2 X_{2i} + \varepsilon_i \tag{21}$$

Notice that the only difference between Equation 21 and Equation 3 is that the X_0 variable has been omitted from Equation 21. Thus, in a practical sense we can impose the side condition that $\beta_0 = 0$ by omitting X_0 from our model. In other words, we fit a regression model where we intentionally omit the intercept term. Although this may seem odd, most regression routines in standard statistical packages provide omission of the intercept term as an option.

An advantage of the cell means model is that each parameter of the model has a clear interpretation. We can directly interpret any given β_j as the population mean of Group j. When applied to sample data, estimated regression coefficients, β_j, are simply sample means Y_j for Group j. Despite this ease of interpretation, the cell means model suffers from two disadvantages when viewed from a regression perspective. First, although each individual parameter has a clear interpretation, it can be tedious to examine differences among parameters. In other words, our usual questions are not literally about single population means, but instead about differences between population means. To answer these questions in the cell means model, we must form differences of parameters, whereas other choices of side conditions result in parameters that are already expressed as mean differences. This is not an insurmountable difficulty, but essentially requires the availability of a regression program that allows tests and confidence intervals for linear combinations of regression coefficients. Second, as a minor point, we have already noted that the cell means formulation requires that we omit the intercept term from our model. This also is not insurmountable, but it is unconventional, so it requires care in implementing.

Effects Model.   The third side condition we will consider is already familiar from Chapter 3. You may recall that the side condition we imposed there was that the sum of effects added across all groups equal zero, which we can write in symbols as

$$\sum_{j=1}^{a} \alpha_j = 0 \tag{3.67, repeated}$$

We can rewrite this side condition in a notation for regression by remembering that each regression coefficient β_j equals a corresponding ANOVA effect α_j (as we saw in our comparison of Equations 1 and 6 as well as Equations 2 and 7). With this substitution, Equation 3.67 becomes

$$\sum_{j=1}^{a} \beta_j = 0 \tag{22}$$

To understand this third type of side condition, let's begin with the two-group case. Recall from Equations 8 and 9 that in the special case of two groups, we can express the relationship between cell means and regression parameters as

$$\mu_1 = \beta_0 + \beta_1 \tag{8, repeated}$$

$$\mu_2 = \beta_0 + \beta_2 \tag{9, repeated}$$

However, we will now impose our constraint that the sum of the β_j parameters equals zero. In the case of two groups, our constraint would be

$$\beta_1 + \beta_2 = 0 \tag{23}$$

which we can rewrite as

$$\beta_2 = -\beta_1 \tag{24}$$

By substituting $-\beta_1$ for β_2, we can simplify Equations 8 and 9 as

$$\mu_1 = \beta_0 + \beta_1 \tag{25}$$

$$\mu_2 = \beta_0 - \beta_1 \tag{26}$$

We now need to consider the interpretation of our two parameters (i.e., β_0 and β_1) in this formulation. We will begin with β_0. Suppose we were to add together Equations 25 and 26. The result would be

$$\mu_1 + \mu_2 = 2\beta_0 \tag{27}$$

which we can simply rewrite as

$$\beta_0 = (\mu_1 + \mu_2)/2 \tag{28}$$

The right side of Equation 28 is just the grand mean in the population, which we have previously designated as μ. Thus, we can express Equation 28 as

$$\beta_0 = \mu \tag{29}$$

which in words means that with this side condition, we can interpret β_0 in our regression model as the grand mean μ from an ANOVA perspective.

   Notice that the only remaining parameter in our model is β_1. How can we interpret it? To answer this question, we can rewrite Equation 25 as

$$\beta_1 = \mu_1 - \beta_0 \tag{30}$$

Because we now know from Equation 29 that $\beta_0 = \mu$, we can substitute μ for β_0 in Equation 30, yielding

$$\beta_1 = \mu_1 - \mu \tag{31}$$

This reveals that we can interpret β_1 as the difference between the population mean of Group 1 and the population grand mean. In other words, β_1 is literally the "effect" associated with Group 1, where we understand that "effect" refers to a deviation from the grand mean. Rewriting Equation 26 shows us that we can also use β_1 to find the "effect" associated with Group 2 because

$$-\beta_1 = \mu_2 - \mu \tag{32}$$

so that by changing the sign of β_1 we obtain the "effect" of Group 2, i.e., the deviation of the population mean of Group 2 from the grand mean. Most importantly, Equations 29 and 31 show us that we now have unique values and thus unique interpretations for β_0 and β_1, the two parameters in our model. Furthermore, Equation 31 reveals one of the advantages of this particular side condition, namely that the β_1 parameter has a straightforward interpretation as the "effect" associated with Group 1. In a moment, we will extend this side condition to the general case of a groups, but first let's see how to implement this side condition in a regression model for 2 groups.

   To see how to operationalize this third form of side condition in regression analysis with two groups, let's return to Equation 3:

$$Y_i = \beta_0 X_{0i} + \beta_1 X_{1i} + \beta_2 X_{2i} + \varepsilon_i \tag{3, repeated}$$

Imposing the side condition that $\beta_2 = -\beta_1$ (from Equation 24) allows us to express Equation 3 as

$$Y_i = \beta_0 X_{0i} + \beta_1 X_{1i} - \beta_1 X_{2i} + \varepsilon_i \tag{33}$$

which we can then rewrite as

$$Y_i = \beta_0 X_{0i} + \beta_1(X_{1i} - X_{2i}) + \varepsilon_i \tag{34}$$

Implicit in Equation 34 is that we have redefined the predictor variable to be included in our model. Instead of including X_1 and X_2 as two separate predictor variables, Equation 34 tells us that we now should include a single predictor variable where the score for an individual on this new variable is literally the difference between that individual's score on our original X_1 and our original X_2. To figure out what this means, we need to return to the way we defined our original X variables. Remember that we originally defined our X variables in the following way:

$$X_{0i} = 1 \text{ for all individuals}$$

$$X_{1i} = 1 \text{ for individuals in Group 1 and 0 for individuals in Group 2}$$

$$X_{2i} = 1 \text{ for individuals in Group 2 and 0 for individuals in Group 1}$$

According to Equation 34, we should continue to include in our model an X_0 variable coded as 1 for each individual. However, instead of separate X_1 and X_2 variables, we should form a single predictor created as X_1 minus X_2. Now, here is the key point from a practical perspective. Notice that a predictor defined in this way will have the following property:

$$X_{1i} - X_{2i} = 1 - 0 \text{ for individuals in Group 1}$$

$$X_{1i} - X_{2i} = 0 - 1 \text{ for individuals in Group 2}$$

In words, we need to code our single predictor so that it has a value of 1 for individuals in Group 1 but a value of -1 for individuals in Group 2. Using this method of coding imposes a constraint on our original parameters so that the sum of the ANOVA "effects" equals zero.

We are now ready to generalize this third type of side condition to the case of a groups. The same logic continues to apply in the more general case, but the details become slightly more complicated. Recall that with a groups, we can write our constraint as

$$\sum_{j=1}^{a} \beta_j = 0 \tag{3.67, repeated}$$

In general, we know that

$$\mu_j = \beta_0 + \beta_j \tag{35}$$

To understand the meaning of the β_0 parameter in our regression model, we can sum both sides of Equation 35 across groups, which results in

$$\sum_{j=1}^{a} \mu_j = a\beta_0 + \sum_{j=1}^{a} \beta_j \tag{36}$$

It immediately follows from Equation 3.67 that Equation 36 simplifies to

$$\sum_{j=1}^{a} \mu_j = a\beta_0 \tag{37}$$

which we can rewrite as

$$\beta_0 = \frac{\sum_{j=1}^{a} \mu_j}{a} = \mu \tag{38}$$

Thus, the β_0 parameter in our regression model is the population grand mean. To interpret the remaining parameters in the regression model, we can simply substitute μ for β_0 in Equation 35, and move β_j to the left side of the equation, yielding

$$\beta_j = \mu_j - \mu \tag{39}$$

which shows that the remaining β_j parameters are ANOVA "effect" parameters.

To understand how we need to code our predictor variables in the general case of a groups, recall that the general form of a linear model is given by

$$Y_i = \beta_0 X_{0i} + \beta_1 X_{1i} + \beta_2 X_{2i} + \beta_3 X_{3i} + \cdots + \beta_p X_{pi} + \varepsilon_i \qquad \text{(3.1, repeated)}$$

When we have a groups, we will have a predictors plus X_0, so we can rewrite Equation 3.1 as

$$Y_i = \beta_0 X_{0i} + \beta_1 X_{1i} + \beta_2 X_{2i} + \beta_3 X_{3i} + \cdots + \beta_a X_{ai} + \varepsilon_i \qquad (40)$$

However, we know from Equation 3.67 that

$$\beta_a = -\sum_{j=1}^{a-1} \beta_j$$

which means that we can express Equation 40 as

$$Y_i = \beta_0 X_{0i} + \beta_1 X_{1i} + \beta_2 X_{2i} + \beta_3 X_{3i} + \cdots - \left(\sum \beta_j\right) X_{ai} + \varepsilon_i \qquad (41)$$

We can now rewrite Equation 41 as

$$Y_i = \beta_0 X_{0i} + \beta_1 (X_{1i} - X_{ai}) + \beta_2 (X_{2i} - X_{ai}) + \beta_3 (X_{3i} - X_{ai}) + \cdots + \beta_{a-1} (X_{a-1i} - X_{ai}) + \varepsilon_i$$

$$(42)$$

Equation 42 reveals two important points: (1) our regression model now contains $a - 1$ predictors along with an intercept term, and (2) each predictor is an original predictor minus X_a.

To understand the practical implications of this second point, let's consider the coding of $X_{1i} - X_{ai}$ for individuals in each group. This predictor will have the following property:

$$X_{1i} - X_{ai} = 1 - 0 \text{ for individuals in Group 1}$$

$$X_{1i} - X_{2i} = 0 - 0 \text{ for individuals in Group 2 through } a - 1$$

$$X_{1i} - X_{ai} = 0 - 1 \text{ for individuals in Group a}$$

In words, we need to code our new predictor so that it has a value of 1 for individuals in Group 1, a value of 0 for individuals in all other groups except the last group, and a value of -1 for individuals in the last group. More generally, we could say that we need to code predictor variable X_j so that individuals in Group j receive a value of 1, individuals in Group a receive a value of -1, and individuals in all other groups receive a score of 0. This method of coding ensures us that the resulting regression parameters will reflect ANOVA "effect" parameters.

Numerical Example

At this point it may be helpful to provide a numerical example to illustrate the theoretical developments we have presented. Table B.1 reproduces the data originally shown in the tutorial on regression. The sample size in this example is smaller than should be used in an actual study, but it allows ease of calculation and interpretation. Table B.2 illustrates the three different coding methods we have presented. For example, consider the reference cell model. It contains a unit variable, where each individual receives a score of 1. The remaining $a - 1$ predictor variables are all scored either zero or one. In particular, a "1" appears on variable X_j if and only if an individual belongs to Group j. Finally, notice that we have included only $a - 1$ predictor variables (not counting the unit variable), because we have omitted the predictor for the final group. Next, consider the cell means model. Notice that it does not contain a unit variable. Otherwise, the coding is identical to that for the reference cell model except that here we also include a predictor for the final group. The final third of the table illustrates coding for the effects model. Notice that like the reference cell model, here we include a unit variable. In fact, the only difference from the reference cell model is that in the effects model, the individuals in the final group receive a value of -1 on every predictor variable (except of course they receive a score of 1 on the unit variable, by definition).

TABLE B.1
DATA TO ILLUSTRATE REGRESSION
APPROACH TO ANOVA

Group			
1	*2*	*3*	*4*
11	13	15	17
13	15	17	19

TABLE B.2
THREE CODING SCHEMES FOR TABLE B.1 DATA

Reference Cell Model

Group	Y	X_0	X_1	X_2	X_3
1	11	1	1	0	0
1	13	1	1	0	0
2	13	1	0	1	0
2	15	1	0	1	0
3	15	1	0	0	1
3	17	1	0	0	1
4	17	1	0	0	0
4	19	1	0	0	0

Cell Means Model

Group	Y	X_1	X_2	X_3	X_4
1	11	1	0	0	0
1	13	1	0	0	0
2	13	0	1	0	0
2	15	0	1	0	0
3	15	0	0	1	0
3	17	0	0	1	0
4	17	0	0	0	1
4	19	0	0	0	1

Effects Model

Group	Y	X_0	X_1	X_2	X_3
1	11	1	1	0	0
1	13	1	1	0	0
2	13	1	0	1	0
2	15	1	0	1	0
3	15	1	0	0	1
3	17	1	0	0	1
4	17	1	−1	−1	−1
4	19	1	−1	−1	−1

Table B.3 summarizes parameter estimates and sums of squared errors for the various ANOVA and regression models. We encourage readers to duplicate these results, especially for those with access to ANOVA and regression procedures in statistical packages.

Several points illustrated in Table B.3 deserve special mention. First, notice that all six of these models are equivalent to one another in the sense that the sum of squared errors for each of these full models equals 8. Second, the reason for this equivalence is revealed in the column entitled "Predicted Cell Means." Each and every one of these models ultimately results in the same predicted score for any individual. In other words, regardless of how the model is formulated, the predicted score for someone in Group 1 will be 12, the predicted score for someone in Group 2 is 14, and so forth. Because the models all make the same predictions, they are equivalent to one another. Third, notice that the specific parameter estimates are not necessarily equal to one another. Although for any given ANOVA model there is always a regression model that has the same parameter estimates, the estimates of the effects model, cell means model, and reference cell model are different from one another. These differences reflect the fact that the meaning of specific parameters depends on the specific way in which we have chosen to formulate the model. However, there are certain patterns in the parameter estimates that manifest themselves across all these models. For example, consider the

TABLE B.3
PARAMETER ESTIMATES AND SUM OF SQUARED ERRORS FOR VARIOUS ANOVA AND
REGRESSION MODELS

ANOVA Models	E_F	Parameter Estimates	Predicted Cell Means
Effects	8	$\hat{\mu} = 15, \hat{\alpha}_1 = -3, \hat{\alpha}_2 = -1, \hat{\alpha}_3 = 1$	$\hat{Y}_1 = 12, \hat{Y}_2 = 14, \hat{Y}_3 = 16, \hat{Y}_4 = 18$
Cell Means	8	$\hat{\mu} = 12, \hat{\mu}_2 = 14, \hat{\mu}_3 = 16, \hat{\mu}_4 = 18$	$\hat{Y}_1 = 12, \hat{Y}_2 = 14, \hat{Y}_3 = 16, \hat{Y}_4 = 18$
Reference Cell	8	$\hat{\mu} = 18, \hat{\alpha}_1 = -6, \hat{\alpha}_2 = -4, \hat{\alpha}_3 = -2$	$\hat{Y}_1 = 12, \hat{Y}_2 = 14, \hat{Y}_3 = 16, \hat{Y}_4 = 18$
Regression Models			
Effects	8	$\hat{\beta}_0 = 15, \hat{\beta}_1 = -3, \hat{\beta}_2 = -1, \hat{\beta}_3 = 1$	$\hat{Y}_1 = 12, \hat{Y}_2 = 14, \hat{Y}_3 = 16, \hat{Y}_4 = 18$
Cell Means	8	$\hat{\beta}_1 = 12, \hat{\beta}_2 = 14, \hat{\beta}_3 = 16, \hat{\beta}_4 = 18$	$\hat{Y}_1 = 12, \hat{Y}_2 = 14, \hat{Y}_3 = 16, \hat{Y}_4 = 18$
Reference Cell	8	$\hat{\beta}_0 = 18, \hat{\beta}_1 = -6, \hat{\beta}_2 = -4, \hat{\beta}_3 = -2$	$\hat{Y}_1 = 12, \hat{Y}_2 = 14, \hat{Y}_3 = 16, \hat{Y}_4 = 18$

difference between the parameter estimate associated with Group 1 and the corresponding estimate associated with Group 2. In all six cases, the difference between these two parameter estimates is -2. Such a difference is called an "estimable function" and is meaningful because its value and interpretation remain the same regardless of how we chose to parameterize the model. We will say more about estimable functions later, but for now we will simply say that any contrast of the means (or correspondingly, of the effects) whose coefficients sum to zero will necessarily be an estimable function. Thus, when we are interested in estimating and testing differences among group means, such as by formulating contrasts, we will eventually reach the same conclusion regardless of how we originally parameterized the model. Fourth, it is extremely important to realize that the numerical values of the coded predictor variables do not in general directly represent contrast coefficients. For example, consider X_1 for effects coding as shown in Table B.2. The values of this variable are 1 for Group 1, 0 for Group 2, 0 for Group 3, and -1 for Group 4. A naive interpretation would be that this variable reflects the difference between the means of Groups 1 and 4 (i.e., that β_1 equals $\mu_1 - \mu_4$). However, we have already seen that the actual meaning of this variable is that it indicates the "effect" of Group 1, so that in reality it reflects the difference between the mean of Group 1 and the grand mean. In other words, this variable corresponds to a contrast that compares Group 1 to the average of all (other) groups, which we could represent as a contrast with coefficients of 1, $-1/3$, $-1/3$, and $-1/3$ for Groups 1, 2, 3, and 4, respectively. Notice that there is no direct relationship between the X values of 1, 0, 0 -1 and the coefficients of the contrast represented by this variable. This lack of a direct relationship opens the door for possible confusion and misinterpretation, so we now feel the need to consider the topic of contrasts in some additional detail.

Contrasts in Single-Factor Between-Subjects Designs

So far we have verified that regression can duplicate ANOVA for the omnibus null hypothesis in a single-factor between-subjects design. This next section investigates the connection between ANOVA and regression for contrasts. Specifically, we will see that although the connection is sometimes more difficult to operationalize, once again it is possible to form regression models that are equivalent to ANOVA models for testing contrasts. Our emphasis here is on hypothesis testing, but the results also apply to confidence intervals.

Two fundamentally different but ultimately equivalent approaches exist to test contrasts with regression models. The first of these approaches involves coding predictors so as to obtain tests of specific contrasts directly as tests of specific regression coefficients. The second approach relies not on coding, but instead expresses any contrast of interest as a specific linear combination of the regression coefficients. We will briefly illustrate each of these approaches, and will touch upon some of the complexities that can arise, especially in the first approach.

We will begin by considering how appropriate coding of predictor variables can be used in regression to test contrasts of interest. You may be surprised to learn that various regression books suggest different strategies for testing contrasts. In part, this variety reflects the impressive flexibility of the regression model, but it may also reflect a tradeoff between simplicity and generality. Authors are faced with a choice of either presenting simple approaches that are often but not always appropriate, or else presenting more complicated approaches that are always appropriate.

We have chosen to present one approach for pairwise comparisons and a second approach for complex comparisons. In principle, the approach we describe for complex comparisons could also be used for pairwise comparisons, so it fulfills the criterion of generality but does so at the expense of increased complexity. As such, we should stress that the choice between these two approaches and yet other possibilities described in other sources is ultimately a subjective decision.

We will continue to use the data from Table B.1 to illustrate contrasts. Recall that we have equal n in this example. Certain methods of testing contrasts work fine with equal n, but produce erroneous results with unequal n. In order to demonstrate that the approaches we present here produce accurate results with unequal n, we have chosen to modify the data shown in Table B.1 In particular, we will suppose now that there are a total of 4 observations in the first group.

For simplicity, we will assume that these four individuals have scores of 11, 11, 13, and 13. Notice that the sample mean for the first group is still 12, as it was for the original data. For future reference, we will refer to this unequal n version of our data as our "augmented" data set to distinguish it from our original equal n example.

Pairwise Contrasts via Coding

Suppose a researcher wants to use the augmented data set to test whether groups 1 and 2 have equal population means. From an ANOVA perspective, Equation 4.20 shows that the sum of squares for this contrast equals 5.33. The value of MS_W is 1.67, so from Equation 4.26 the F statistic for this contrast equals 3.20.

How can we obtain the correct F statistic for this contrast using regression? There is more than one way to accomplish this goal, but the method we will present relies on reference cell coding. Specifically, we can compare groups 1 and 2 simply by making either group the reference cell in our coding scheme. The top portion of Table B.4 shows a coding scheme where we have chosen Group 1 as our reference group. The middle portion of Table B.4 shows an excerpt from the output using PROC REG to analyze our data with the aforementioned coding scheme. Notice that the estimated coefficient for X_1 is 2.0, which is simply the difference between the sample means for Groups 1 and 2. The t value for this coefficient is 1.79, which is the square root of our earlier F value of 3.20. As further corroboration, the bottom of Table B.4 shows output from PROC GLM, where we have used an ESTIMATE command to estimate $\mu_2 - \mu_1$. The estimated value is 2.0, which is simply the difference in sample means, and the corresponding t value is 1.79, once again confirming that the regression analysis produced the desired result. Thus, even with unequal n, we can use the reference cell coding method to compare Groups 1 and 2.

What if we also wanted to compare additional pairs of groups? The output from our regression analysis shows that we already have information about the comparisons of Groups 1 and 3 as well as Groups 1 and 4. However, just as obvious is that we have learned nothing of direct interest about any of the pairwise differences that do not involve Group 1. Unfortunately, we cannot simply do one regression analysis with all $a(a-1)/2$ predictor variables (except in the uninteresting case where $a = 2$), because that would give us more than $a - 1$ predictors in one equation. Instead, what we must do is to cycle through $a - 1$ choices of which group is used as the reference group. If a is very large, this is clearly a tedious process, which is one reason in practice there are obvious advantages to using software that does not require us to code our own predictor variables for a regression analysis.

TABLE B.4
PAIRWISE CONTRASTS VIA CODING

		Reference Cell Coding for Augmented Data			
Group	$\underline{Y}$	$\underline{X}_0$	$\underline{X}_1$	$\underline{X}_2$	$\underline{X}_3$
1	11	1	0	0	0
1	11	1	0	0	0
1	13	1	0	0	0
1	13	1	0	0	0
2	13	1	1	0	0
2	15	1	1	0	0
3	15	1	0	1	0
3	17	1	0	1	0
4	17	1	0	0	1
4	19	1	0	0	1

Output From SAS PROC REG
Parameter Estimates

Variable	DF	Parameter Estimate	Standard Error	t Value	Pr> $|t|$
Intercept	1	12.00000	0.64550	18.59	<.0001
x1	1	2.00000	1.11803	1.79	0.1238
x2	1	4.00000	1.11803	3.58	0.0117
x3	1	6.00000	1.11803	5.37	0.0017

Output from SAS PROC GLM for Comparing First Two Groups

Parameter	Estimate	Standard Error	t Value	Pr > $|t|$
mu1 vs mu2	2.00000000	1.11803399	1.79	0.1238

Complex Contrasts via Coding.   Suppose a researcher wants to consider a complex comparison. For example, suppose he or she wants to use the augmented data set to test the difference between the mean of Group 4 and the average of the other three groups. Once again, there is more than one way to do this in regression, but we will present a general approach that works with either equal or unequal n.

We will describe this approach in terms of 4 steps:

1. Write the contrast to be tested in terms of its coefficients, as in Chapter 4. For example, in our case the coefficients would be $-1/3, -1/3, -1/3$, and 1 for Groups 1, 2, 3, and 4, respectively.
2. Create $a - 2$ additional contrasts orthogonal to the contrast of interest. Whenever $a > 3$, there are multiple sets of orthogonal contrasts. A simple pair in our case would be one contrast with coefficients of $-1, 1, 0$, and 0 and another contrast with coefficients of $-1, -1, 2$, and 0. Even if only one contrast is of ultimate interest, it is necessary to include $a - 1$ predictors in the regression analysis, especially with unequal n.
3. Each contrast becomes a predictor variable in the regression analysis. For example, scores on X_1 are based on the coefficients of the first contrast, scores on X_2 are based on the coefficients of the second contrast, and so forth. In particular, consider scores on X_1. Each member of Group 1 is assigned a score on X_1 equal to the coefficient for Group 1 in the first contrast. In our example, this score would be $-1/3$. Similarly, each member of Group 2 is assigned a score on X_1 equal to the coefficient for Group 2 in the first contrast. In our example, this score is once again $-1/3$. This process proceeds until scores have been assigned for each individual on each predictor variable.
4. One more step is necessary if we want our regression coefficients to be interpretable as differences in means. To do so, we need to consider two values: (1) the value of our negative coefficient and (2) the value of the positive coefficient (our approach presumes that every group receiving a negative coefficient has the same value for that coefficient, and the same is true for the positive coefficients, although the absolute value of the negative and positive coefficients can be different). We need to scale each predictor variable so that the difference between the negative score and the positive score equals 1. For example, so far our values for X_1 are $-1/3, -1/3, -1/3$, and 1. The difference between the negative value of $-1/3$ and the positive value of 1 is 4/3. Thus, we need to divide each value by 4/3 (i.e., multiply by 3/4). Doing so yields our final codes for X_1: $-1/4, -1/4, -1/4$, and 3/4 for individuals in Groups 1, 2, 3, and 4, respectively. We need to make three additional points. First, the reason we need to rescale in this way in order to interpret each coefficient as a mean difference is that a regression coefficient depicts the change in Y divided by the change in X. If we code X so that its change is 1, then the coefficient will simply reflect the change in Y. Here, the change in X is simply the difference between the negative value and the positive value, so we need to scale our predictors so that this difference is 1. Second, this algorithm for rescaling works only if there at are most 3 distinct values of coefficients: a single negative value applied to one or more groups, a single positive value applied to one or more groups, and a value of 0 applied to one or more groups. A counterexample would be coefficients of $1/3, 2/3, -1$, and 0. Rescaling weighted averages such as this requires more complex methods beyond the scope of this appendix. Third, keep in mind that rescaling is unnecessary if you only want to test hypotheses. Rescaling becomes relevant only when you want to estimate values of mean differences, often in conjunction with confidence intervals.

The top portion of Table B.5 shows the end result of applying these four steps to our augmented data. The middle of the table shows an excerpt of the output from the corresponding regression analysis. Notice that the estimated value for the contrast of interest is 4.0, as reflected by the estimated value for the coefficient associated with X_1. We can tell this is exactly what it should be by realizing that the mean of Group 4 is 18, while the average of the means of the other three groups is 14 (namely, the unweighted average of 12, 14, and 16; a different approach is needed in the less typical case where we want a weighted average). The t value for the contrast equals 3.88, which implies a p value of 0.0082. Notice that the regression results for X_3 here agree exactly with what we saw earlier for the comparison of Groups 1 and 2. Finally, the bottom portion of the table shows an excerpt of results obtained from PROC GLM. As before, this output confirms the results we obtained using regression analysis.

A Good Idea Gone Bad.   Let's return to our example where the only question of interest is a comparison of Groups 1 and 2. A simple method of coding suggests itself for a regression approach to this question. It seems natural to create a predictor variable coded as follows:

$$X_{1i} = \begin{cases} 1 & \text{if the individual belongs to Group 1} \\ -1 & \text{if the individual belongs to Group 2} \\ 0 & \text{otherwise} \end{cases}$$

TABLE B.5
COMPLEX CONTRASTS VIA CODING

		Complex Contrast Coding For Augmented Data			
Group	Y	X_0	X_1	X_2	X_3
1	11	1	−1/4	−1/3	−1/2
1	11	1	−1/4	−1/3	−1/2
1	13	1	−1/4	−1/3	−1/2
1	13	1	−1/4	−1/3	−1/2
2	13	1	−1/4	−1/3	1/2
2	15	1	−1/4	−1/3	1/2
3	15	1	−1/4	2/3	0
3	17	1	−1/4	2/3	0
4	17	1	3/4	0	0
4	19	1	3/4	0	0

Output From SAS PROC REG
Parameter Estimates

Variable	DF	Parameter Estimate	Standard Error	t Value	Pr> $|t|$	Type I SS	Type II SS
Intercept	1	15.00000	0.42696	35.13	<.0001	2073.60000	2057.14286
x1	1	4.00000	1.03190	3.88	0.0082	32.40000	25.04348
x2	1	3.00000	1.07044	2.80	0.0311	16.66667	13.09091
x3	1	2.00000	1.11803	1.79	0.1238	5.33333	5.33333

Output From SAS PROC GLM

Parameter	Estimate	Standard Error	t Value	Pr > $|t|$
4 vs other three	4.00000000	1.03189865	3.88	0.0082

Because we are interested only in the contrast of Groups 1 and 2, we could form a regression model that uses only X_1 as a predictor. Will this yield the same conclusion about the difference between the means of Groups 1 and 2 as the more complicated model that includes all three coded predictors?

As long as we have equal n, things are fairly straightforward. It turns out that this single predictor variable accounts for a sum of squares equal to 4 in the equal n version of our data (i.e., the original data shown in Table B.1), just as in the ANOVA approach. Furthermore, the estimated coefficient for X_1 is −1, just as we would hope when the sample mean of the first group is 12, the sample mean of the second group is 14, and the two groups have been coded as 1 and −1, respectively. However, one immediate complication arises here because we must consider the nature of our full model. The ANOVA full model for these data has 4 parameters, and allows each group to have its own mean. However, if we consider the regression model with only X_1 to be the full regression model, we will not obtain the same result we did in ANOVA. Specifically, for these data, the ANOVA full model has a sum of squared errors of 8 and degrees of freedom of 4. The regression model with only X_1 as a predictor, on the other hand, has a sum of squared errors of 44 and degrees of freedom of 7. As a consequence, the F statistic for regression here equals 0.64, considerably smaller than the ANOVA value of 2.00. However, regression can duplicate the ANOVA value of 2.00 by reformulating the full model as one that contains all four parameters. One way of accomplishing this goal is to form two separate regression models, one of which uses only X_1 as a predictor and the other of which uses $a − 1$ predictors, such as in the effects or reference cell full models. Alternatively, a single analysis with $a−1$ predictors can be undertaken as long as the additional $a − 2$ predictors form an orthogonal set with the X_1 predictor of interest. The choice between these two approaches is a matter of convenience and personal preference because both will yield the desired F value of 2.00 for these data.

Both regression alternatives are somewhat cumbersome, but still relatively straightforward. Unfortunately, however, things become more complicated when sample sizes are unequal. For example, let's now see what happens in our augmented data set with unequal n. Recall that we have seen earlier from Equation 4.26 that the F statistic for this contrast equals 3.20. Now suppose that we use the same natural coding we used previously to compare groups 1 and 2. In the augmented data, the sum of squares accounted for by X_1 equals 13.83, more than twice as large as the value obtained from ANOVA (the interested reader is encouraged to verify the value of 13.83, either by hand or more likely by the regression procedure in a statistical package). The corresponding F value in the regression analysis is 8.30, based on the correct MS_W value of 1.67. In addition, the estimated coefficient for X_1 is no longer -1.00, but instead has become -1.57 even though all four sample means are the same in the augmented data as they were in the original data.

Five points must be stressed here. First, the regression approach has produced an incorrect estimate of the mean difference, an incorrect sum of squares for the contrast, and an incorrect F value, and thus an incorrect test of the desired contrast. The problem is that the simple method of coding that works fine when sample sizes are equal does not test the contrast it might appear intuitively to test when sample sizes are unequal. Instead, the X_1 variable can be shown to be testing an entirely different hypothesis. In particular, by simplifying the general expression for a slope in simple regression, it can be shown that the coefficient for X_1 will be given by

$$\hat{\beta}_1 = \frac{n_1(\overline{Y}_1 - \overline{Y}) - n_2(\overline{Y}_2 - \overline{Y})}{n_1(1 - ((n_1 - n_2)/N))^2 + n_2(1 + ((n_1 + n_2)/N))^2 + (n_3 + n_4)((n_1 - n_2)/n)^2}$$

Substituting $n_1 = 4, n_2 = n_3 = n_4 = 2, \overline{Y}_1 = 12$, and $\overline{Y}_2 = 14$ into this expression for $\hat{\beta}_1$ yields a value of -1.57, just as we obtained in our regression analysis. In this sense, regressing Y on X_1 by itself produces the right answer to the wrong question. Although it may not be obvious, with equal sample sizes, the expression for $\hat{\beta}_1$ given above simplifies greatly to become equal to $(\overline{Y}_1 - \overline{Y}_2)/2$, which then yields the desired result. So this simple approach works fine with equal n, but does not truly test the difference between Groups 1 and 2 with unequal n. Second, it would be a mistake to infer that there is some inherent problem here with regression. Instead, the problem arises from a mistaken belief that the simple method of coding will test the hypothesis of interest. As we have already pointed out, there is not necessarily a direct relationship between the values of a coded variable and the coefficients of a contrast being tested by that variable. Third, regression can be used to test the correct hypothesis, but this necessitates a fundamentally different approach from simply regressing Y on X_1. The most important point is that in general it is necessary to regress Y on an entire set of $a - 1$ predictors (plus the unit variable) in order to obtain the correct test of the desired contrast, even though this may be the only contrast of interest. In fact, for pairwise comparisons, we can always rely on the reference cell model, where we simply define the reference cell to be one of the two groups to be compared. Or more generally, we can use the method presented earlier in the appendix for complex contrasts. Yet other possible options are described in such sources as Cohen, Cohen, West, and Aiken (2002); Darlington (1990); Pedhazur (1997); and Serlin and Levin (1985).

Contrasts via Linear Combinations of Regression Coefficients.

We have just seen that creating appropriate X variables to test contrasts of interest through regression is often tedious at best and can produce erroneous results at worst. In fact, in our judgment, this is one of the main limitations of adopting a regression approach for teaching and learning analysis of variance. However, there is yet another approach that avoids these problems. Instead of attempting to identify appropriate coding methods, this alternative approach relies on forming linear combinations of the parameters of the model. Although this approach may be slightly less intuitive than directly coding contrast variables, it has the advantage of being much more general in that it produces correct values even when sample sizes are unequal and/or contrasts are nonorthogonal. Because of its generality, this approach has been implemented in the general linear model procedure of many popular statistical packages, such as SAS and SPSS.

Most packages that include the capability of forming linear combinations of the parameters are based on the reference cell model, so that is the approach we will illustrate here. The key to understanding how this approach works is to recall the relationship between population means and regression parameters. Recall that this relationship can be written as:

$$\beta_0 = \mu_a \text{ for group } a$$
$$\beta_j = \mu_j - \mu_a \text{ for each group } j$$

Notice that the regression parameter β_a for the final group is necessarily zero, so it need not (indeed, cannot) be estimated from the data. Now consider how this approach goes about testing a pairwise contrast of the difference between the first two means. What needs to be done here is to express μ_1 and μ_2 in terms of the betas, i.e., the regression parameters. Notice that we can accomplish this goal by substituting β_0 for μ_a in the bottom equation and then placing μ_j on the left side of the equation, yielding

$$\mu_j = \beta_0 + \beta_j \text{ for each group } j,$$

We can now rewrite our contrast μ_1 minus μ_2 in terms of the betas as

$$\mu_1 - \mu_2 = (\beta_0 + \beta_1) - (\beta_0 + \beta_2)$$

The β_0 term obviously drops out of this expression, which can then be written more simply as

$$\mu_1 - \mu_2 = \beta_1 - \beta_2$$

What have we accomplished with all of this? We have learned that we can test our pairwise contrast by using the regression model to test whether β_1 and β_2 are equal to one another. We can also form a confidence interval for the mean difference $\mu_1 - \mu_2$ by forming a confidence interval for $\beta_1 - \beta_2$. The same logic applies to any other contrast, pairwise or complex.

This approach has a very important advantage over the direct coding method, namely, that it is completely general. It provides correct answers with equal or unequal sample sizes, pairwise or complex contrasts, and with orthogonal or nonorthogonal sets of contrasts. In theory, the only disadvantage is that it necessitates finding the relationship between the ANOVA parameters μ_j and the regression parameters β_j. In practice, however, this work is often done by the statistical package behind the scenes. For example, the general linear model procedures in SAS and SPSS allow you to specify your hypothesis of interest in terms of ANOVA parameters. The computer program then translates the hypothesis into the regression formulation, and performs the appropriate analysis.

The only serious disadvantage of this approach is that it requires specifying the standard error of the linear combination of regression parameters. The bad news is that the general form of this specification involves matrix algebra. The good news is that SAS, SPSS, and other packages perform these calculations for you, so computational burden need not be an issue.

Numerical Example

We have already used a numerical example to illustrate complications that can emerge in attempting to use direct coding of predictor variables to test contrasts. Thus, in this section we will briefly illustrate how testing linear combinations of parameters in the reference cell model circumvents these difficulties.

We will return to the augmented data set we introduced earlier in this appendix. Table B.6 shows an excerpt of the output from PROC GLM in SAS. The top portion of Table B.6 shows parameter estimates and corresponding information from the reference cell model (as of this writing, this output is obtained from PROC GLM by specifying SOLUTION as a desired option). Several points are especially noteworthy. First, the intercept β_0 is estimated to be 18, because as we discussed, the intercept in the reference cell model represents the mean of the final group, and the sample mean for the fourth group here is in fact 18 (i.e., $\overline{Y}_4 = 18$). Second, notice that β_1 is estimated to be -6, which is simply the difference between the sample mean of the first group ($\overline{Y}_1 = 12$) and the sample mean of the fourth group. Third, the estimates for β_2 and β_3 follow the same logic. Fourth, the estimate for β_4 is zero, because that is the constraint imposed by the reference cell model. Fifth, each estimate is accompanied by its standard error, t-statistic, p-value, and confidence interval. Sixth, the program includes a warning that serves as a reminder that the estimates obtained here reflect a specific choice of constraints we have placed on the parameters.

The next portion of Table B.6 shows the result of including a CONTRAST statement in the command syntax. Specifically, this output results from requesting a contrast of the first two groups. As you may recall, we previously calculated the sum of squares for this contrast using Equation 4.20, and obtained a value of 5.33, in agreement with the value shown in the table. We also found that the observed F value for this contrast is 3.20, once again agreeing with the value shown in the table. While this may not seem like a big deal, keep in mind that obtaining these values with direct coding necessitated tedious creation of $a - 1$ coded predictor variables. As we have stated, however, forming linear combinations of regression coefficients allows SAS PROC GLM and similar programs to duplicate the results we presented in Chapter 4 and elsewhere in the book.

The final portion of Table B.6 shows the result of including an ESTIMATE statement in the command syntax, once again for comparing the first two groups. The information provided by ESTIMATE largely duplicates information obtained from CONTRAST. However, ESTIMATE offers an advantage in that it expresses results in terms of a confidence interval unlike CONTRAST.

Two-Way Between-Subjects Factorial Designs

As in single-factor designs, models for factorial designs can be expressed in terms of either ANOVA or regression, and in terms of effects, cell means, or a reference cell. While the logic we have developed for the single-factor design

TABLE B.6
OUTPUT FROM SAS PROC GLM FOR AUGMENTED DATA SET

The GLM Procedure

Dependent Variable: Y

Parameter	Estimate	Standard Error	t Value	Pr > $|t|$	95% Confidence	Interval
Intercept	18.00000000 B	0.91287093	19.72	<.0001	15.76628530	20.23371470
group 1	−6.00000000 B	1.11803399	−5.37	0.0017	−8.73573062	−3.26426938
group 2	−4.00000000 B	1.29099445	−3.10	0.0212	−7.15894962	−0.84105038
group 3	−2.00000000 B	1.29099445	−1.55	0.1723	−5.15894962	1.15894962
group 4	0.00000000 B	.	.	.	.	.

Note. The X'X matrix has been found to be singular, and a generalized inverse was used to solve the normal equations. Terms whose estimates are followed by the letter 'B' are not uniquely estimable.

Contrast	DF	Contrast SS	Mean Square	F Value	Pr > F
mu1 vs. mu2	1	5.33333333	5.33333333	3.20	0.1238

Parameter	Estimate	Standard Error	t Value	Pr > $|t|$	95% Confidence	Interval
mu1 vs. mu2	−2.00000000	1.11803399	−1.79	0.1238	−4.73573062	0.73573062

TABLE B.7
CELL MEANS AND MARGINAL MEANS FOR 2 × 3 DESIGN

		B(Drug)			
		1(X)	2(Y)	3(Z)	Marginal Means
A(Biofeedback)	1(Present)	168	204	189	187
	2(Absent)	188	200	209	199
	Marginal Means	**178**	**202**	**199**	**193**

extends to factorial designs, the issues become more complicated. Thorough consideration of these complications is beyond the scope of this book.

Instead of attempting to present a variety of models for the two-way design and discussing their interrelationships, we have chosen to focus on a demonstration of the reference cell model in this design. We have chosen this model because as we have already mentioned, it often underlies linear models procedures in current statistical software packages. Our presentation here is intentionally less detailed in the single-factor design, and is intended simply to give readers a general sense for how concepts we developed in the single-factor design can be extended to the factorial design.

We will focus our attention on how the reference cell model can be written as a regression model in order to analyze the data shown in Table 7.9 of the body of the text. As a reminder, the data in this table represented scores for 36 individuals who had received various combinations of Biofeedback and drug therapy for treatment of hypertension. The resultant design was 2 × 3, with two levels of Biofeedback (present or absent) and three types of drugs. For convenience, the cell means and marginal means for these data are reproduced here as Table B.7.

The regression approach based on a reference cell model requires appropriate coding of predictor variables. While any specific cell could serve as the reference cell, we will illustrate the typical default of allowing the final cell in the design to serve as the reference cell. In this 2 × 3 design, this "final" cell will be the cell in row 2 and column 3. Thus, we will need predictors to distinguish other rows and columns from row 2 and column 3. In theory, there are many different ways we could parameterize such a model and if we are clever enough we could figure out how to form linear combinations of these parameters to test whatever types of effects we decide to test, but we will proceed to illustrate how predictors are typically coded so as to set the stage to test effects of interest in factorial designs, such as main effects, interactions, and simple effects.

At the outset we need to remember that the reference cell model includes an intercept term equal to one for every individual. As usual we will represent this predictor variable as X_0, which reminds us that this term is already included in the regression model by default, so we need not actively create this variable ourselves. Before attempting to define additional predictor variables, it may be helpful to anticipate how many predictors we will need to include in our full model. The full model should include a parameter for each population mean, so in a 2 × 3 design we should have a total of 6 parameters. The intercept counts as one of these parameters, so in our case, we should define 5 additional X variables. The general form of the regression model here can thus be written as

$$Y_i = \beta_0 + \beta_1 X_{1i} + \beta_2 X_{2i} + \beta_3 X_{3i} + \beta_4 X_{4i} + \beta_5 X_{5i} + \varepsilon_i$$

where X_1 through X_5 are coded so as to represent differences among the groups. With 2 rows and 3 columns, 1 of these variables will typically reflect a type of row difference, 2 will reflect a type of column difference, and the remaining 2 will reflect the interaction.

We can now proceed to define a predictor that will represent a type of row effect (we will see shortly exactly what type of row effect this variable represents). Specifically, we can define X_1 as follows:

$$X_{1i} = \begin{cases} 1 & \text{if the individual belongs to row 1(i.e., biofeedback present)} \\ 0 & \text{otherwise} \end{cases}$$

Similar logic applies for the columns, except that with 3 columns, we need to create 2 predictors to represent column differences. A typical choice would be:

$$X_{2i} = \begin{cases} 1 & \text{if the individual belongs to column 1(i.e., drug X)} \\ 0 & \text{otherwise} \end{cases}$$

and

$$X_{3i} = \begin{cases} 1 & \text{if the individual belongs to column 2(i.e., drug Y)} \\ 0 & \text{otherwise} \end{cases}$$

The final two predictors then represent the interaction. Each interaction predictor is the product of a row predictor with a column predictor. Because there is one row predictor and there are two column predictors, there will be two interaction predictors. Notice that in general there will be $a-1$ row variables and $b-1$ predictor variables. Thus, $(a-1)(b-1)$ interaction variables will result from multiplying each row variable by each column variable, just as we would expect because $(a-1)(b-1)$ is the numerator degrees of freedom for the interaction effect in the two-way design. In our specific 2×3 design, the predictors are defined as follows:

$$X_{4i} = \begin{cases} 1 & \text{if the individual belongs to row 1 and column 1(i.e., the} \\ & \text{combination of biofeedback present and drug X)} \\ 0 & \text{otherwise} \end{cases}$$

and

$$X_{5i} = \begin{cases} 1 & \text{if the individual belongs to row 1 and column 2(i.e., the} \\ & \text{combination of biofeedback present and drug Y)} \\ 0 & \text{otherwise} \end{cases}$$

Table B.8 shows the result of regressing Y on these five X variables for these 36 individuals, as obtained from PROC REG in SAS. In particular, the table shows each parameter estimate, as well as corresponding standard errors, t values, and p values. As we will see in more detail shortly, we have to be very careful not to misinterpret these parameter estimates. For example, it would be tempting to assume that X_1 represents the row main effect, in which case we might infer that the p value for the row main effect in these data is .0059. In reality, however, X_1 does not represent the main effect of the row factor, but instead the simple effect of row within the third column. We can understand this by returning to our coding scheme. Notice that individuals in the row 2, column 3 cell (i.e., the combination of biofeedback absent and drug Z) have been assigned a score of 0 on all 5 X variables. Thus, the regression model for scores in this specific cell simplifies to

$$Y_i = \beta_0 + \varepsilon_i$$

TABLE B.8

REGRESSION ANALYSIS OF DATA FROM 2 × 3 FACTORIAL DESIGN

Variable	DF	Parameter Estimate	Standard Error	t Value	Pr > |t|
Intercept	1	209.00000	4.77144	43.80	<.0001
x1	1	−20.00000	6.74784	−2.96	0.0059
x2	1	−21.00000	6.74784	−3.11	0.0041
x3	1	−9.00000	6.74784	−1.33	0.1923
x4	1	0	9.54289	0.00	1.0000
x5	1	24.00000	9.54289	2.51	0.0175

Similarly, individuals in row 1, column 3 (i.e., the combination of biofeedback present and drug Z) have been assigned a score of 0 on all variables except for X_1, where they have received a score of 1. Thus, the regression model for scores in this specific cell simplifies to

$$Y_i = \beta_0 + \beta_1 + \varepsilon_i$$

Comparing these two equations shows us that β_1 represents the difference between scores in these two cells. We can now see that the difference between these two cells is simply the simple effect of row in the third column. Indeed, the parameter estimate of −20 shown in Table B.8 equals the difference between the sample means shown in Table B.7. Namely, the value of −20 equals 189 minus 209, as it must. Thus, although we coded X_1 so that all individuals in row 1 received a score of 1 and all individuals in row 2 received a score of 0, β_1 does not represent the row main effect. Instead, β_1 represents the simple effect of row in the third column. One way of understanding this is to realize that the five X variables we have created are correlated, even with equal n. Thus, β_1 reflects the relationship between Y and X_1 when the remaining predictor variables are "held constant." What it means to hold the remaining predictors constant here turns out to correspond to the simple effects test. The other regression coefficients also must be interpreted in this light. While this is no problem whatsoever mathematically, it does show once again that intuitive interpretations of regression parameters may be incorrect.

We can immediately see that the parameters in the regression model do not necessarily have the meaning we might naively assume them to have. As a consequence, interpreting the output shown in Table B.8 is not as straightforward as one might hope. While we could proceed to explain the proper interpretation of each parameter estimate, we will instead take a different approach. Although we could use PROC REG or a similar regression procedure to calculate estimates such as those shown in Table B.8, and then test hypotheses of interest by forming appropriate linear combinations, the availability of GLM procedures in SAS, SPSS, and other packages provides a simpler alternative. At this moment we can well imagine that you may be asking why we have bothered to introduce the confusion surrounding estimates from regression if we are really going to use GLM all along. However, keep in mind that the purpose of this section is to explain the relationship between regression and ANOVA models. Even though the practical import of our discussion may be to convince you always to use GLM and to avoid the complications of interpreting REG, nevertheless it is useful to understand how they are related to one another. Of course, we do not mean to imply that GLM avoids all potential problems of misinterpretation among uninformed researchers. For example, GLM does not automatically center continuous variables, so when continuous and categorical variables are allowed to interact with one another, what appears to be a main effect may in actuality be a simple effect of the categorical variable conditional on a value of 0 for the continuous variable (see West, Aiken, and Krull, 1996, for more on this topic).

Our plan at this point is to reconsider this factorial design from the perspective of GLM. We will illustrate a few tests one might perform using GLM, and then consider how to duplicate these tests using REG. We want to stress that from a purely practical perspective, we could simply use GLM and stop. There is no need to use REG here at all. However, because a major purpose of this appendix is to show the relationship between ANOVA and regression, we will perform a few selected tests both ways.

In particular, we will use both GLM and REG to perform three tests: (1) the row main effect, (2) the simple row effect within the first column, and (3) the interaction contrast within the first two columns. We have chosen these three tests simply because they provide a variety of types of effects one might wish to test. We do not mean to imply in any fashion that they are necessarily the tests that we would really perform on these data—a description of how we might choose a meaningful set of tests was presented in Chapter 7 when we originally presented these data. Also we should be clear that although all of the effects we have chosen to test here are single degree of freedom effects, the same logic applies to multiple degree of freedom tests.

We will begin by considering how to test these three effects in GLM. We can use ESTIMATE and/or CONTRAST to perform these tests. We have chosen to illustrate ESTIMATE because it also provides an estimate of the contrast, which we can then compare to the table of cell means shown in Table B.7. To provide the proper commands to GLM, we must return to the ANOVA formulation of the model. In the case of a two-way between-subjects design, we can write the model as

$$Y_{ijk} = \mu + \alpha_j + \beta_k + (\alpha\beta)_{jk} + \varepsilon_{ijk} \qquad\qquad \text{(7.6, repeated)}$$

To use ESTIMATE or CONTRAST, we need to write the corresponding model for each specific cell mean of the design. In the case of a 2 × 3 design, this yields six equations, one for each cell mean:

$$\mu_{11} = \mu + \alpha_1 + \beta_1 + (\alpha\beta)_{11}$$
$$\mu_{12} = \mu + \alpha_1 + \beta_2 + (\alpha\beta)_{12}$$
$$\mu_{13} = \mu + \alpha_1 + \beta_3 + (\alpha\beta)_{13}$$
$$\mu_{21} = \mu + \alpha_2 + \beta_1 + (\alpha\beta)_{21}$$
$$\mu_{22} = \mu + \alpha_2 + \beta_2 + (\alpha\beta)_{22}$$
$$\mu_{23} = \mu + \alpha_2 + \beta_3 + (\alpha\beta)_{23}$$

The next step is to express the effect of interest in terms of the population cell means. For example, the row main effect compares the average of the three cells in the first row to the average of the three cells in the second row:

$$1/3(\mu_{11} + \mu_{12} + \mu_{13}) - 1/3(\mu_{21} + \mu_{22} + \mu_{23})$$

We now must re-express this linear combination in terms of the ANOVA effect parameters. Substituting from the six previous equations and simplifying yields

$$\alpha_1 - \alpha_2 + 1/3(\alpha\beta)_{11} + 1/3(\alpha\beta)_{12} + 1/3(\alpha\beta)_{13} - 1/3(\alpha\beta)_{21} - 1/3(\alpha\beta)_{22} - 1/3(\alpha\beta)_{23}$$

The final step of the process is to write the appropriate syntax to tell the computer program to estimate this linear combination. As of this writing, the appropriate syntax to estimate this effect in PROC GLM of SAS would have the general form

estimate 'row1 vs. row2' row 1 –1 row*column 1/3 1/3 1/3 –1/3 –1/3 –1/3;

In certain cases such as this one, users are allowed to omit the interaction effects, because SAS will automatically include them when the user has not done so him or herself.

Instead of belaboring the point by deriving similar expressions for the other two effects of interest, the top portion of Table B.9 shows the end results of writing these questions in terms of ANOVA model parameters. The middle of Table B.9 shows the equivalent SAS syntax. The bottom of Table B.9 shows output from PROC GLM for estimating these three contrasts in our data.

Two goals yet remain. First, we will briefly verify that the results shown in Table B.9 are correct. Second, we still need to return to our regression model so we can see how to duplicate these results using regression.

We can easily verify that the results shown in Table B.9 are correct. First, consider the row main effect. Notice that the estimated value of the contrast is -12. Returning to Table B.7 shows that the difference between the row marginal means is indeed -12, because the marginal mean for the first row is 187 and the marginal mean for the second row is 199. In addition, squaring the t value of -3.08 shown in Table B.9 yields a value of 9.49, which is the F value reported for the row main effect in Chapter 7 (see page 263). Second, consider the simple row effect within the first column. The estimated value of the contrast, -20, equals the difference between 168 and 188 from Table B.7. Once again, squaring the t value of -2.96 shown in Table B.9 yields a value of 8.76, which is the same (except for rounding error) as the F value reported for the simple effect in Chapter 7 (see page 302). Finally, consider the interaction contrast within the first two columns. The estimated value of the contrast, -24, equals $(168 + 200)$minus$(188 + 204)$ from Table B.7. As it must, squaring the t value of -2.51 shown in Table B.9 yields a value of 6.30, which once again agrees (within rounding error) with the F value reported for this interaction contrast in Chapter 7 (see page 309).

Our final challenge is to see how these tests we have just performed using PROC GLM can be duplicated in PROC REG. How did PROC GLM test our contrasts, and how does this relate to PROC REG? Unbeknownst to the user, PROC GLM has created the reference cell model we used to perform our regression analysis. Specifying the SOLUTION option in GLM produces the same estimates, standard errors, t values, and p values shown in Table B.8 for the analysis we conducted using PROC REG. However, PROC GLM has an extremely useful advantage over

TABLE B.9
ESTIMATES USING PROC GLM

Effects in terms of model parameters
(1) Row main effect
$$\alpha_1 - \alpha_2 + 1/3(\alpha\beta)_{11} + 1/3(\alpha\beta)_{12} + 1/3(\alpha\beta)_{13} - 1/3(\alpha\beta)_{21} - 1/3(\alpha\beta)_{22} - 1/3(\alpha\beta)_{23}$$
(2) Simple effect of row within first column
$$\alpha_1 - \alpha_2 + (\alpha\beta)_{11} - (\alpha\beta)_{12}$$
(3) Interaction contrast within first two columns
$$(\alpha\beta)_{11} - (\alpha\beta)_{12} - (\alpha\beta)_{21} + (\alpha\beta)_{22}$$

Corresponding SAS PROC GLM Syntax
(1) Row main effect
   estimate 'row1 vs. row2' row 1 −1 row*column 1/3 1/3 1/3 −1/3 −1/3 −1/3;
(2) Simple effect of row within first column
   estimate 'mu11 vs. mu21' row 1 −1 row*column 1 0 0 −1 0 0;
(3) Interaction contrast within first two columns
   estimate 'interaction contrast' row*columns 1 −1 0 −1 1 0;

SAS Output for Data in Table B.4

Parameter	Estimate	Standard Error	t Value	Pr > $|t|$	95% Confidence	Interval
row1 vs. row2	−12.0000000	3.89586676	−3.08	0.0044	−19.9564214	−4.0435786
mu11 vs. mu21	−20.0000000	6.74783916	−2.96	0.0059	−33.7809261	−6.2190739
interaction contrast	−24.0000000	9.54288566	−2.51	0.0175	−43.4891725	−4.5108275

PROC REG from the user's perspective. PROC GLM, unlike PROC REG, allows the user to specify questions of interest in terms of the ANOVA model parameters. However, PROC REG is unaware of any concept of ANOVA model parameters, and requires the user to specify all questions of interest in terms of X_1 through X_5, the predictors we created as indicator codes. In reality, PROC GLM has created these same five predictors, but it does much of the work for the user by translating between the ANOVA effects and the regression parameters.

To understand how PROC GLM does this translation, we will once again consider the same three contrasts we estimated using GLM. However, now we will see how we can estimate and test these contrasts directly using PROC REG. The key here is to realize the relationship between the regression parameters and the ANOVA parameters. At the outset it is crucial to consider the constraints we have placed on parameters by adopting the reference cell approach. For example, consider α_1 and α_2, the effect parameters for the first and second row, respectively. It seems most natural to think of these parameters in terms of the ANOVA effects model, in which case we impose the constraint that α_1 and α_2 must sum to zero. However, we must remember that the constraint in the reference cell model is different. Recall that in our discussion of reference cell coding in the one-way model, we saw that the effect for the final group is set equal to zero. Similarly, in the two-way model, instead of constraining α_1 and α_2 to sum to zero, the reference cell model sets α_2 equal to zero. More generally, instead of imposing any constraints about sums, the reference cell model simply sets an appropriate number of parameters equal to zero.

The top portion of Table B.10 shows the resulting correspondence between ANOVA parameters and regression parameters using reference cell coding for our 2×3 design. We must remember that the meaning of the specific ANOVA parameters is contingent on the constraints we have imposed. For example, the meaning (and therefore the value) of α_1 in the reference cell model will generally be different from the meaning and the value of α_1 in the effects model, even though the same symbol appears in both models. Before abandoning all hope, however, there are certain types of effects whose meaning and value do not depend on our choice of constraint. These effects are called estimable functions, and include such effects as main effects, interactions, marginal mean comparisons, simple effects, interaction contrasts, and cell mean comparisons. All three contrasts we estimated using GLM are examples of estimable functions. Further discussion of estimable functions is beyond the scope of our presentation (for further details, see Green, et al. (1999) or Littell, Freund, and Spector, 1991), so we will simply see how we can use the correspondence shown in the top portion of Table B.10 to estimate and test the three contrasts in which we are interested.

To use our regression model to estimate and test contrasts of interest, we must write each contrast in terms of the parameters of the model, i.e., in terms of β_1 through β_5. This proves to be straightforward once we have written the contrast in terms of ANOVA model parameters, as in Table B.9. For example, consider the row main effect. We saw that this effect can be written in terms of ANOVA model parameters as

$$\alpha_1 - \alpha_2 + 1/3(\alpha\beta)_{11} + 1/3(\alpha\beta)_{12} + 1/3(\alpha\beta)_{13} - 1/3(\alpha\beta)_{21} - 1/3(\alpha\beta)_{22} - 1/3(\alpha\beta)_{23}$$

TABLE B.10
REGRESSION MODEL PARAMETERS AND CORRESPONDING REGRESSION ANALYSIS OF
TABLE B.4 DATA

Relationship of ANOVA and Regression Parameters

ANOVA	Regression
μ	β_0
α_1	β_1
α_2	0
β_1	β_2
β_2	β_3
β_3	0
$(\alpha\beta)_{11}$	β_4
$(\alpha\beta)_{12}$	β_5
$(\alpha\beta)_{13}$	0
$(\alpha\beta)_{21}$	0
$(\alpha\beta)_{22}$	0
$(\alpha\beta)_{23}$	0

Re-expression of contrasts in terms of regression parameters

(1) Row main effect

ANOVA: $\alpha_1 - \alpha_2 + 1/3(\alpha\beta)_{11} + 1/3(\alpha\beta)_{12} + 1/3(\alpha\beta)_{13} - 1/3(\alpha\beta)_{21} - 1/3(\alpha\beta)_{22} - 1/3(\alpha\beta)_{23}$

Regression: $\beta_1 + 1/3\beta_4 + 1/3\beta_5$

(2) Simple effect of row within first column

ANOVA: $\alpha_1 - \alpha_2 + (\alpha\beta)_{11} - (\alpha\beta)_{12}$

Regression: $\beta_1 + \beta_4$

(3) Interaction contrast within first two columns

ANOVA: $(\alpha\beta)_{11} - (\alpha\beta)_{12} - (\alpha\beta)_{21} + (\alpha\beta)_{22}$

Regression: $\beta_4 - \beta_5$

Output from PROC REG

(1) Row main effect

Source	DF	Mean Square	F Value	Pr > F
Numerator	1	1296.00000	9.49	0.0044
Denominator	30	136.60000		

(2) Simple effect of row within first column

Source	DF	Mean Square	F Value	Pr > F
Numerator	1	1200.00000	8.78	0.0059
Denominator	30	136.60000		

(3) Interaction contrast within first two columns

Source	DF	Mean Square	F Value	Pr > F
Numerator	1	864.00000	6.33	0.0175
Denominator	30	136.60000		

All that remains now is to rewrite this linear combination in terms of the regression model parameters. The top portion of Table B.10 allows us to make a simple substitution, yielding

$$\beta_1 - 0 + 1/3\beta_4 + 1/3\beta_5 + 0 - 0 - 0 - 0$$

which can obviously be written more simply as

$$\beta_1 + 1/3\beta_4 + 1/3\beta_5$$

What this tells us is that we can use our regression model to estimate and test the row main effect by estimating and testing this admittedly rather strange looking linear combination of regression parameters. The middle of Table B.10

shows the corresponding expressions for the row simple effect in the first column and for the interaction contrast in the first two columns. The bottom of Table B.10 shows the result of testing each of these three linear combinations of regression parameters using the TEST option of PROC REG in SAS. That the regression results are in fact equivalent to the results shown earlier in Table B.9 using GLM can be seen most easily by comparing the three p-values of the two approaches. Of course, the squared t-values shown in Table B.9 are also equal (within rounding error) to the F values shown in Table B.10.

The equivalence of results in Tables B.9 and B.10 illustrates how it is possible to use regression models with reference cell coding to duplicate results obtained from ANOVA models in two-way factorial designs. Similar logic extends this relationship to more complex designs.

THE RELATION OF ANOVA AND REGRESSION TO OTHER STATISTICAL MODELS

The fact that regression can (1) literally duplicate the ANOVA effects model, and (2) literally duplicate the ANOVA cell means model, and (3) can also include continuous predictor variables makes it an extremely flexible and valuable statistical method. Indeed, if these ANOVA models are special cases of the regression model, it seems reasonable to ask why the majority of this book formulates models in terms of ANOVA parameters instead of regression parameters. We will answer this question in two ways: (1) by considering where ANOVA and regression fit into a broader structure of statistical methods, and (2) by introducing some examples where we believe that the ANOVA formulation has important advantages.

Researchers who understand the relationship between ANOVA and regression can benefit by formulating models that best address their scientific questions instead of forcing their questions to fit a model that may not really be appropriate. Thus, we wholeheartedly endorse books that emphasize the relationship between ANOVA and regression throughout their presentation. Nevertheless, we have chosen not to follow this route, and believe that the reader deserves some explanation for our choice to emphasize ANOVA models.

From one perspective, our choice can be understood in terms of levels of generality. For example, we believe that a major strength of the model comparison approach we employ throughout the book is that the concept of comparing a full model to a restricted model plays a central role in many other types of statistical models. However, a case could be made that our approach is narrow because it focuses so heavily on ANOVA models. Why not present data analysis from a broader perspective, such as regression analysis?

Although there are some advantages associated with presenting material in its most general form, there are frequently associated disadvantages. For example, one issue that must be confronted is how general one should be. Although the regression model provides considerable flexibility, it is hardly the most general statistical model one might contemplate. Instead, the regression model can itself be regarded as a special case of a number of other models.

Figure B.1 provides a graphical depiction of the relationships among some common statistical models. Models nearer the top of the figure are more general than models nearer the bottom. Specifically, when two models are connected with a line, the model at the bottom is a special case of the model at the top. Thus, for example, ANOVA is depicted as a special case of MRA, multiple regression analysis. Multiple regression models are more general than ANOVA models in that they can include not only categorical (i.e., nominal, or "class") predictor variables but also continuous predictors. Similarly, ANOVA is a special case of MANOVA, because ANOVA models allow only a single dependent variable, while MANOVA allows one or more dependent variables. Chapters 13 and 14 illustrate one use of MANOVA as a method for analyzing data from repeated measures designs. Notice that multiple regression analysis and MANOVA are shown on the same level of the figure, and neither is directly connected to the other. These two models are shown this way because neither is a special case of the other. MANOVA is not a special case of regression because regression (with the exception of multivariate multiple regression) allows only one dependent variable. However, regression is also not a special case of MANOVA because MANOVA allows only categorical predictors.

Both regression and MANOVA can be thought of as special cases of the General Linear Model (GLM), which is sometimes called the multivariate general linear model. This model extends MANOVA by allowing continuous as well as categorical predictors. In this sense it is like regression. However, the general linear model is more general than regression in that it allows multiple dependent variables. Yet one other distinction is sometimes made between GLM and regression. For example, Darlington (1990) describes the ability to create a set of indicator variables automatically with a single command as a fundamental difference between general linear model computer programs and regression computer programs.

The general linear model can itself be extended in any of several ways. For example, the generalized linear model (GLIM) extends the general linear model by allowing the dependent variable to take on a distributional form other than normality. This flexibility makes GLIM especially useful for modeling data such as proportions and counts.

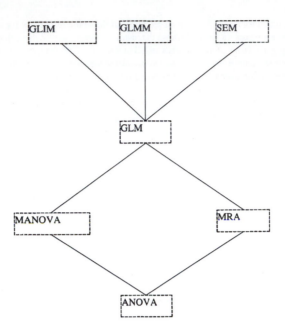

FIG. B.1.   The Relation of ANOVA and Regression to Other Statistical Models

The general linear mixed model (GLMM) provides yet another example of an extension to the general linear model. The GLMM expands the general linear model by allowing predictors to be random as well as fixed. Chapters 15 and 16 provide an introduction to some examples of this type of model. The final model shown in the figure is the structural equation model (SEM), commonly also known as LISREL, the computer package that helped popularize these methods. Structural equation models expand on the general linear model in two ways. First, structural equation models allow relationships to be examined for latent as well as manifest variables. Latent variables, as the name implies, are variables that are not directly observed; instead, manifest variables are included in the model as imperfect manifestations of presumed underlying latent variables. Even without directly measuring latent variables, it is possible to study their relationships under certain conditions and assumptions. In this respect, latent variables are much like factors in traditional factor analysis. Second, structural equation models also allow a variable to serve as both an independent variable and a dependent variable. For example, a child's eagerness to learn might be dependent (at least in part) on certain parental characteristics, while at the same time the child's eagerness to learn has some influence on the child's academic progress. This set of relationships could not be directly examined in the general linear model, because eagerness would need to be either an X variable or a Y variable in the model. However, structural equation modeling allows eagerness to serve as an X variable in one equation and as a Y variable in another equation.

ANOVA "VERSUS" REGRESSION MODELS

Some individuals have suggested that ANOVA should always be conceptualized in terms of regression because ANOVA is simply a special case of regression. However, if the fact that ANOVA is a special case of regression is reason enough by itself to suggest that ANOVA should always be thought of in terms of regression, it would seem to follow logically that we should not stop at the level of regression. As Figure B.1 shows, regression is itself simply a special case of yet other methods. Thus, this logic would seem to imply that both ANOVA and regression should always be thought of in terms of the general linear model, or perhaps in yet higher terms such as structural equation modeling.

Our goal in this book is to present concepts in such a way that they are generally applicable. For example, our basic philosophy of comparing models is applicable throughout the hierarchy shown in Figure B.1. Even though specific test statistics may take on different forms, the ideas remain much the same. Nevertheless, we have chosen to present these ideas primarily in the context of ANOVA models. We made this choice for several related reasons. First, the analysis of data from certain types of designs is much more natural in the ANOVA framework. For example, Chapters 10, 11, and 12 (along with Chapters 15 and 16) show that designs with random effects usually require consideration of multiple error terms, which does not fit easily in the regression framework. Similarly, the multivariate approach to repeated measures presented in Chapters 13 and 14 cannot be accommodated in (univariate) multiple regression. Even in purely between-subjects designs with only fixed effects, we would suggest that more attention needs to be paid to assumptions underlying pooled error terms, especially when forming confidence intervals or testing hypotheses for contrasts. Consideration of separate error terms is much clearer from the perspective of ANOVA instead of regression. Second, from a purely practical perspective it is much easier to test differences in group means using GLM procedures in statistical packages than using regression procedures. As Darlington (1990) points out, a distinguishing characteristic of GLM procedures is that they allow the user to specify questions of interest in terms of ANOVA effect parameters. Thus, researchers will almost certainly rely on an ANOVA conceptualization in using statistical packages to analyze their data. While in theory regression could be used to obtain the same results, we have seen that exclusive reliance on regression can become confusing and tedious even in rather simple designs. Third, ANOVA models provide the most natural and convenient way of thinking about group differences. If your questions are about means, it seems sensible that the parameters of your model should themselves be means, or perhaps differences in means. While parameters of other models such as regression models may also be means or mean differences, the precise meaning of such parameters is often much less clear than in ANOVA models. Fourth, in a similar vein, ANOVA models directly reflect the fact that an investigator's questions pertain to multiple populations. Regression models, on the other hand, do not necessarily reflect multiple populations. Instead, they reflect the relationship between a dependent variable and one or more independent variables in a single population. Of course, we can code indicator variables so as to represent different populations, but even here the method itself addresses the extent to which these indicator variables are related to the dependent variable. Nowhere in the model itself is there a direct expression that multiple populations exist. Fifth, although we believe that ANOVA formulations offer significant advantages, nevertheless it is crucial that researchers not force all of their questions into an ANOVA framework. For example, as numerous authors including ourselves (e.g., Cohen, 1983; Maxwell & Delaney, 1993; Vargha, Rudas, Delaney, & Maxwell, 1996) have shown, artificially categorizing a continuous variable can badly distort the true nature of relationships between variables. Contrary to conventional wisdom, results based on artificial dichotomies are not necessarily conservative. Instead, categorizing continuous variables can sometimes create spurious findings and inflate Type I error rates dramatically, so researchers cannot rely on an excuse that they simply opted for a more conservative way of analyzing their data when they categorized a continuous variable. Thus, with rare exceptions continuous variables should be modeled in their continuous forms, necessitating an extension beyond ANOVA to ANCOVA or the general linear model. However, even here we would suggest that any categorical predictors are best understood in terms of ANOVA parameters, not regression coefficients. The end result is that researchers need to be flexible and able to formulate models that truly reflect their hypotheses and data structures, instead of always attempting to force every analysis into the same model or computerized procedure. Sixth, in summary we agree with the view espoused by Mallows and Tukey (1982) that ANOVA should not be regarded as "simply" a special case of regression. They stated that "It is sometimes said that 'analysis of variance is just a form of regression'. The common occurrence of ANOVAS with several distinct error terms and the absence of both theory and technology for regressions involving two or more error terms makes the failure of this statement, at least with today's notion of regression, quite clear."

Part II

A Brief Primer of Principles of Formulating and Comparing Models

This book approaches questions of designing experiments and analyzing data from the perspective of building and comparing models. As such, much of the emphasis pertains to using sample data to make inferences about the population. In this respect, the goal of data analysis is typically to decide whether the inclusion of certain effects in a statistical model significantly improves the model. However, this begs the question of what effects are considered as possible candidates for inclusion in the first place. The answer to this question inevitably hinges much more on knowledge of the subject area than on statistics. Nevertheless, there are certain statistical principles of model formulation that can help guide a researcher's thought processes about choosing potential effects to include in a model. The purpose of this appendix is to provide a brief introduction to these general principles. We approach these principles through consideration of the consequences of mistakenly excluding relevant variables or including irrelevant variables. In a very general sense, as a researcher contemplates possible candidate effects (i.e., predictor variables) to include in a model, is it better statistically to think small or large? Is leaving out relevant effects more or less problematic than including irrelevant effects? From a narrower statistical perspective, should our full model contain only the effects of specific theoretical interest, or might there be advantages to including additional effects even if we are not directly interested in them? Even though we should emphasize that data analysis should be driven primarily by research questions (and not the other way around), nevertheless we believe that an understanding of the principles we present in this appendix may lead to more informed choices of how best to formulate and build models, which in turn will lead to better answers to theoretical and practical questions in behavioral science research.

Our intent in writing this appendix is to present the material in such a way that it can be read at any point after Chapter 3. Reading this appendix immediately after Chapter 3 can ideally provide a framework for understanding how and why more complex models are developed throughout the remainder of the book. Alternatively, reading this appendix after having read all of Chapters 1 through 16 can ideally provide a synthesis and closure for the "big picture" inherent throughout the book and thus allow readers to be certain they see the "forest amidst the trees." We leave this choice to the discretion of instructors, students, and other readers.

FORMULATING MODELS

We saw near the beginning of Chapter 3 that the general form of a statistical model can be expressed as

$$
\begin{array}{ccc}
\text{observed value} & \text{sum of effects} & \text{sum of effects} \\
\text{on dependent} & = \text{of "allowed-for"} + & \text{of other} \\
\text{variable} & \text{factors} & \text{factors}
\end{array}
$$

This is sometimes written more succinctly as

$$\text{data} = \text{fit} + \text{error}$$

or as

$$\text{observed} = \text{predicted} + \text{error}$$

Regardless of which way we express the general idea of a statistical model, we must decide what effects to include in the model, and what other effects to exclude. By implication, any effects not explicitly included in the model become components of the error term. [1] At first glance, it might seem that the proper approach would be to include "everything" in our model, because it seems natural that to believe that "error" must be bad, so we should do as much as possible to avoid error in our model. While this perspective is not entirely wrong, it is not necessarily entirely right either. The first problem with this mindset is that we typically do not know what "everything" even means. If we already knew with certainty all of the effects that truly influence our dependent variable, we would probably not need to conduct a study. In reality, there is an immediate risk that we may end up including some effects that unbeknownst to us are unnecessary and at the same time no matter how diligent we are, we will probably omit some other effects that are truly relevant. A second problem is yet more practical. Namely, even if we could identify all relevant effects, it would usually be impractical to measure all of them and include them in a single study.

A natural alternative to including "everything" in the model might be to include only the X variables of specific research interest. For example, we might be able to express our hypothesis in terms of a single X variable (say X_1) and Y. It would seem reasonable in this situation to think of a very simple model, namely a model that included only X_1 as a predictor of Y. In fact, in this situation it may seem rather unnecessary even to think in terms of a model. Instead, why not see whether X_1 and Y are in fact related. However, we will see later in the appendix that even in this seemingly simple situation, there may be reasons to think in terms of models, and that doing so will sometimes reveal reasons for including other X variables in our model whether or not they are a central part of our research question.

The main purpose of this appendix is to consider several related questions: (1) How can we decide whether a variable is relevant for including in a statistical model? (2) What are the consequences of omitting a relevant variable? (3) What are the consequences of including an irrelevant variable?

RELEVANCE OF PREDICTOR VARIABLES

To understand whether a particular effect is relevant, it is helpful to return to our basic model formulation from Chapter 3. There we saw that we can write the general case of the univariate general linear model with p predictor variables (not counting the intercept) as

$$Y_i = \beta_0 X_{0_i} + \beta_1 X_{1_i} + \beta_2 X_{2_i} + \beta_3 X_{3_i} + \cdots + \beta_p X_{p_i} + \varepsilon_i \qquad \text{(3.1, repeated)}$$

Before proceeding, we will mention a word about notation. This appendix discusses model formulation in terms of X variables and corresponding β coefficients. However, the principles we present here also apply if we write our model in terms of effect parameters such as

$$Y_{ij} = \mu + \alpha_j + \varepsilon_{ij} \qquad \text{(3.66, repeated)}$$

Appendix B, Part I describes the relationship between these two formulations in more detail, but for our purposes here it suffices to say that we can think of an effect in terms of one or more X variables.

At least in principle, it is straightforward to state whether any particular variable is relevant to the model shown in Equation 3.1. Specifically, any variable with a nonzero population β coefficient is part of the "fit" of the model. By implication, any variable with a zero β coefficient is not really part of the "fit" and thus belongs in the error term of the model. Thus, if our goal is to build a complete model for Y, we should in principle include all X variables with

---

[1] More technically, it could be said that the part of any excluded effect that does not correlate with effects already included in the model becomes a component of the error term.

nonzero β coefficients and exclude all X variables with zero β coefficients. [2] We could debate how well this describes the typical goal of a research program, but for our purposes here it is important to be sure we understand at least in principle what determines whether a population β coefficient is zero or nonzero.

For example, how would we determine whether β_1 in the model shown in Equation 3.1 is zero or nonzero? Although in practice we might use sample data in an attempt to answer this question, for the moment we will concentrate on understanding what it means to say that the population value itself is zero. To arrive at this understanding, we need to consider an alternative model for Y, namely a model that omits X_1. We could write such a model as

$$Y_i = \beta_0 X_{0_i} + \beta_2 X_{2_i} + \beta_3 X_{3_i} + \cdots + \beta_p X_{p_i} + \varepsilon_i \tag{43}$$

This model could be used to obtain a predicted Y score for every individual i. We will denote these predicted scores from this model as $\hat{Y}_i(-1)$. The -1 term in parentheses serves as a reminder that we have omitted X_1 from our model. Notice that we could write the error in prediction for individual i from this model as $Y_i - \hat{Y}_i(-1)$. We can then state that the population value of β_1 is zero if and only if X_1 and the error $Y_i - \hat{Y}_i(-1)$ are uncorrelated in the population. In other words, if X_1 does not improve the prediction of Y after we use the remaining $p - 1$ X variables as predictors, then the β coefficient for X_1 is zero, and X_1 is irrelevant to the model. On the other hand, if X_1 does improve the prediction of Y after we use the remaining $p - 1$ X variables as predictors, then the β coefficient for X_1 is nonzero, and X_1 is relevant to the model.

In many situations it is natural to think of the correlation between X_1 and the error $Y_i - \hat{Y}_i(-1)$ in terms of the correlation between X_1 and Y itself. From a practical perspective, it often seems plausible that variables that correlate with the error $Y_i - \hat{Y}_i(-1)$ will also correlate with Y, and vice versa. While this may frequently be true in behavioral science data, it is not a mathematical necessity. For example, X_1 and Y could be highly correlated with one another, and yet after we predict Y from the other X variables, the relationship between Y and X_1 has vanished in the sense that $Y_i - \hat{Y}_i(-1)$ and X_1 are uncorrelated. To understand how this might happen, suppose we are interested in understanding differences among reading ability in elementary school children. It is a virtual certainty that among all elementary school children, taller children read better than younger children. Thus, if we let Y represent reading ability and X_1 represent height, Y and X_1 are undoubtedly correlated. But the fact that this correlation is nonzero does not necessarily mean that we should include height in our model of reading ability, because the correlation does not necessarily imply that the β coefficient for height predicting reading ability is nonzero. To see why, suppose we have also measured age, which we will denote as X_2. Once we predict Y from X_2, the subsequent errors will in all likelihood be uncorrelated with height. Thus, even though height and reading ability are correlated, height does not improve the prediction of reading ability after we remove the predictability of age. Thus, in this scenario, β_1 is zero even though the correlation between X_1 and Y is nonzero, and we would not need to include X_1 in the model despite its correlation with Y. It turns out that the opposite pattern is also possible. In other words, it is possible that X_1 and Y are uncorrelated, and yet a relationship emerges between $Y_i - \hat{Y}_i(-1)$ and X_1. In this situation, X_1 is said to be a suppressor variable. Thus, from a mathematical perspective, we cannot judge the relevance of a predictor in a model simply on the basis of its correlation with the dependent variable. Even so, in some situations contemplating likely correlates of Y may be a useful way to assemble candidate X variables for inclusion in a model.

Of course, if we have measured Y as well as all p of the X variables, we can use sample data to test whether we need to include X_1 in our model (for example, we could test whether the regression coefficient is statistically significant). But the purpose of our discussion here is more subtle. How should we decide whether to measure X_1 in the first place? What variables are candidates for inclusion in our statistical model? It is unlikely that we can measure "everything" and then pick and choose once we have obtained our data, and even if we could measure "everything" picking and choosing is typically not straightforward because of such complications as performing multiple tests (discussed at length in Chapter 5) and concerns about inappropriate levels of statistical power.

So how do we decide what variables to measure in our study? Should we measure X_1 or should we forgo it? If there were a simple answer to this question, science could presumably follow a simple recipe. In reality, there is no simple answer. However, there are a variety of reasons we might decide to measure a specific variable. Most obvious of these is that this variable is the center of our research attention. In fact, maybe all we care about is whether X_1 and Y are related to one another. Do we really need to worry about measuring any other variables besides X_1 and Y?

---

[2]It is tempting to assume that an effect that correlates with Y should have a non-zero regression coefficient. However, we will see momentarily that this is not necessarily true. An effect can correlate with Y and yet still have a regression coefficient of zero. Similarly, it might seem that an effect with a nonzero regression coefficient must correlate with Y. However, as we describe later in this appendix, it is possible for a predictor variable to have a nonzero regression coefficient even though the variable fails to correlate with Y. Thus, in principle, identifying effects with nonzero regression coefficients involves more than identifying variables that can be expected to correlate with Y.

CONSEQUENCES OF OMITTING
A RELEVANT PREDICTOR

Suppose for simplicity that our research question involves only Y and X_1. When, if ever, should we include other predictor variables in our model? If all other potential predictor variables would have β coefficients of zero, there would be no additional relevant predictors. We will consider the role of such predictor variables in the next section. Here we will instead consider the possibility that one or more other X variables in addition to X_1 might have nonzero β coefficients in the population model for Y. Does the existence of such additional X variables imply that they should not only be measured but also included in our statistical model and ensuing data analysis? We will see that the answer to this question depends in no small part on how one interprets the word "should" in the question of whether these additional variables should be included.

To begin to answer this question, we will consider the simplest case of only one additional X variable, which we will denote as X_2. The principles we illustrate in this simple case generalize in a straightforward fashion to the more complicated case of multiple X variables. Suppose we are planning a study investigating the relationship between X_1 and Y. Further suppose we suspect that both X_1 and X_2 may be relevant predictors (as defined in the previous section) in a model of the form:

$$Y_i = \beta_0 X_{0_i} + \beta_1 X_{1_i} + \beta_2 X_{2_i} + \varepsilon_i \tag{44}$$

What are the consequences of omitting X_2 from this model? In other words, what are the consequences of assessing the relationship between X_1 and Y in a model that does not include X_2, such as

$$Y_i = \beta_0 X_{0_i} + \beta_1 X_{1_i} + \varepsilon_i \tag{45}$$

How important is it to include X_2 in our model? Might there be reasons to exclude X_2 even though we suspect that its regression coefficient is nonzero? All of these questions fall under a general study of specification error, which refers to the problem (typically unknown to the researcher) whereby the model is not correctly specified. What are the consequences of specification error?

We will consider the answers to these questions according to two criteria. First, does omitting X_2 affect the value we will expect to observe for $\hat{\beta}_1$? In other words, does omitting X_2 tend to produce an estimate of β_1 that is either systematically too small or too large, or on average is our estimate still likely to be correct? Second, does omitting X_2 affect how precisely we can estimate β_1? For example, if we were to form a confidence interval for β_1, will be the width of the interval tend to be different if we omit X_2 instead of including it in our model? If so, statistical power will also be affected, so we will say more about this as well momentarily.

In order to explore the effects of excluding X_2 on our two criteria, we need to develop expressions for a regression coefficient and its confidence interval. Although it is possible to write an expression for an estimated regression coefficient in the general case of p predictors, we will keep things simple by considering only 1 or 2 predictor variables. First, if X_1 is the only predictor as in Equation 45, the estimated regression coefficient for X_1 can be written as

$$\hat{\beta}_1 = r_{Y1} \frac{s_Y}{s_{X_1}} \tag{46}$$

where r_{Y1} is the correlation between Y and X_1, and s_Y and s_X are the standard deviations of Y and X, respectively. When both X_1 and X_2 are included in the model, the estimated regression coefficient for X_1 becomes

$$\hat{\beta}_{1\cdot2} = \left(\frac{r_{Y1} - r_{Y2}r_{12}}{1 - r_{12}^2}\right)\left(\frac{s_Y}{s_{X_1}}\right) \tag{47}$$

where the 1.2 subscript for $\hat{\beta}_1$ emphasizes that this is the coefficient for X_1 with X_2 also included in the model. The other new terms in Equation 47 that did not appear in Equation 46 are r_{Y2}, which is the correlation between Y and X_2, and r_{12}, which is the correlation between X_1 and X_2.

Of special interest to us in the remainder of this appendix will be the extent to which the regression coefficient for X_1 excluding X_2 is different from the regression coefficient for X_1 including X_2. However, this is simply the difference between $\hat{\beta}_1$ in Equation 46 and $\hat{\beta}_{1\cdot2}$ in Equation 47. After some algebraic manipulation, we can write this difference as

$$\hat{\beta}_{1\cdot2} - \hat{\beta}_1 = \left(r_{12}\frac{S_Y}{S_{X_1}}\right)\left(\frac{r_{Y1}r_{12} - r_{Y2}}{1 - r_{12}^2}\right) \tag{48}$$

We can simplify this expression yet further because the term in the second set of parentheses turns out to be closely related to $\hat{\beta}_{2\cdot1}$. In particular, the formula for the regression coefficient for X_2 when X_1 is in the model is just the same as the formula for the regression coefficient for X_1 when X_2 is in the model, except we need to reverse all subscripts for X_1 and X_2. Incorporating this modification into Equation E.5, we can write $\hat{\beta}_{2\cdot1}$ as

$$\hat{\beta}_{2\cdot1} = \left(\frac{r_{Y2} - r_{Y_1}r_{12}}{1 - r_{12}^2}\right)\left(\frac{S_Y}{S_{X_2}}\right) \tag{49}$$

Substituting from Equation 49 into Equation 48 and performing a bit of algebraic manipulation allows us to rewrite the expression for the difference between regression coefficients as

$$\hat{\beta}_{1\cdot2} - \hat{\beta}_1 = \left(-r_{12}\hat{\beta}_{2\cdot1}\right)\left(\frac{S_{X_2}}{S_{X_1}}\right) \tag{50}$$

We will examine Equation 50 and its implications in a moment. In particular, we will often be interested in finding conditions under which we might expect the difference between the two coefficients for X_1 to equal zero. Before pursuing this question, however, we will first develop some necessary information on confidence intervals.

A general expression for a confidence interval can be written as

$$\text{estimate} \pm (\text{critical value})(\text{standard error})$$

In the specific case of a regression coefficient, we can rewrite this expression as

$$\hat{\beta}_1 \pm \left(t_{.05;N-p-1}\right)\sqrt{\frac{SS_Y\left(1 - R_{Y\cdot X_1,X_2,\cdots X_p}^2\right)}{SS_{X_1}\left(N - p - 1\right)\left(1 - R_{X_1\cdot X_2,X_3,\cdots X_p}^2\right)}} \tag{51}$$

In the general case of p predictor variables, the critical value comes from a t distribution with $N - p - 1$ degrees of freedom. The standard error of $\hat{\beta}_1$ depends on 5 values: (1) the sum of squares of Y, (2) the sum of squares of X_1, (3) the proportion of variance in Y explained by the p predictor variables, (4) the proportion of variance in X_1 explained by the remaining $p - 1$ predictor variables, and (5) the degrees of freedom.

Now we are ready to return to our questions of how omitting X_2 will affect our conclusions about X_1. Implicit in Equation 50 is the fact that the effect of excluding X_2 depends in part on whether X_1 and X_2 are correlated with one another. We will begin with the case where the two predictor variables are correlated, and then consider what is different if they are not correlated.

Correlated Predictors

When the population correlation between X_1 and X_2 is nonzero, excluding a relevant X_2 variable from our model leads to a biased estimate of the regression coefficient for X_1. To see why, return to Equation 50. If both r_{12} and $\hat{\beta}_{2\cdot1}$ are nonzero, the coefficient for X_1 when X_2 is included in the model will be different from the coefficient for X_1 when X_2 is omitted. The same principle extends from a sample to the population. Thus, when the true model for Y includes X_2, and X_2 correlates with X_1, we need to include X_2 in the model in order to obtain an unbiased estimate of the true population regression coefficient for X_1. Otherwise, even in a very large sample, our estimated value of β_1 is likely to be inaccurate. More generally, this principle applies to the case of p predictor variables. If we hope to obtain an unbiased estimate of the true population regression coefficient for X_1, we must include in the model all variables that correlate with X_1 and also have nonzero regression coefficients in the model for Y. This illustrates the difficulties facing researchers who are unable to assign individuals to groups at random, because the number of variables possibly impacting Y and correlated with X_1 sometimes seems virtually boundless in the behavioral and social sciences.

In this case, excluding X_2 from the model also influences the width of the confidence interval we might form for β_1. However, the width of the interval usually becomes a secondary consideration when the center of the interval is likely to be inaccurate because of bias in the estimation of β_1. For this reason, we will not pursue considerations of width further in this case.

Examples

Chapter 9 contains an extensive discussion of the role of a covariate in adjusting group differences in the absence of random assignment to groups. For example, Figure 9.4 and the accompanying verbal description explain why adjusted differences which arise by including the covariate in the model may be different from unadjusted differences obtained when the covariate is not included in the model. Specifically, in accordance with Equation 50, adjusted differences will differ from unadjusted differences to the extent that both: (a) the covariate is related to the dependent variable, and (b) groups have different means on the covariate (because this implies that the covariate is correlated with group membership). Another example of this general principle occurs in Chapter 7, where we discuss unequal n designs with more than one factor. In so-called nonorthogonal designs, the variables representing the main effects and interaction are correlated with one another. To the extent that main effects and an interaction are non-null, the estimates we obtain for an effect will depend on what other effects we include in our model. In particular, Chapter 7 presents three types of sums of squares (literally Type I, Type II, and Type III) of possible relevance in factorial designs. Each of these types of sums of squares corresponds to a specific question, and we may get different answers to these questions even with the same data in an unequal n factorial design.

Uncorrelated Predictors

When the population correlation between and X_2 is zero, excluding a relevant X_2 variable from our model does not affect the expected value of $\hat{\beta}_1$. Notice that this is a very different outcome from the previous situation we discussed, where X_1 and X_2 were correlated. To see why the outcome is so different now, return to Equation 50. If r_{12} is zero, the coefficient for X_1 when X_2 is included in the model will be equal to the coefficient for X_1 when X_2 is omitted, even if $\hat{\beta}_{2\cdot 1}$ is nonzero. Of course, in a sample r_{12} will typically not be exactly zero even if ρ_{12} does equal zero. However, when ρ_{12} equals zero, the long-run average value of $\hat{\beta}_1$ will equal the long-run average value of $\hat{\beta}_{1\cdot 2}$. Said another way, in a very large sample, $\hat{\beta}_1$ and $\hat{\beta}_{1\cdot 2}$ will essentially be equal to one another. On average, we will tend to obtain the correct value for the regression coefficient for X_1 even if we leave X_2 out of our model. Thus, although the true model for Y includes X_2, if X_2 does not correlate with X_1, we do not need to include X_2 in the model in order to obtain an unbiased estimate of the true population regression coefficient for X_1.

When can we be reasonably certain that some potential predictor X_2 will not correlate with our predictor variable of interest X_1? The one situation where we can typically develop a strong theoretical argument that X_2 will not correlate with X_1 is when we have formed experimental groups through random assignment, and X_1 represents membership in the groups we have formed. From this perspective, the primary benefit of random assignment is that it ensures (in a probabilistic sense) that no other X variables can correlate with X_1. Thus, the beauty of random assignment is that in this respect it relieves us of the responsibility to identify additional predictor variables to include in our model in order to obtain an unbiased estimate of the regression coefficient for our predictor of main theoretical interest. At least in the long run, we can expect to obtain the same estimated effect of X_1 on Y regardless of whether we include other predictors in the model whenever we have randomly assigned individuals to levels of X_1.

The previous discussion might seem to imply that it makes no difference whatsoever whether we include X_2 or exclude X_2 in our model when X_2 is uncorrelated with Y. Although this is true in the long run, it is not necessarily true in general. To begin to understand why, you need to realize that so far our focus has been on the average value we would expect to obtain for $\hat{\beta}_1$. Suppose, however, that one approach might yield values for $\hat{\beta}_1$ that range from 2 to 12 from sample to sample, while a second approach yields values that range from 6 to 8. Clearly we would prefer to use the second approach to estimate the population value of β_1. Although both approaches appear to produce an average value of 7, the second approach is preferable because estimates vary less from sample to sample, and thus any given sample is likely to provide a more precise estimate of the population parameter. Another way of thinking about this is that the second approach will provide narrower confidence intervals than the first approach.

What does this have to do with including or excluding X_2 from our model? We can compare the likely width of confidence interval estimates for the regression coefficient for X_1 in the model with X_2 versus the model without X_2. If there are reasons to expect one of these intervals to be narrower than the other, that will provide grounds for preferring one model over the other. To make this comparison, we need to return to Equation 51. When X_1 is the only predictor variable in the model, we can write this equation more simply as

$$\hat{\beta}_1 \pm \left(t_{.05;N-2}\right)\sqrt{\frac{SS_Y\left(1-r_{Y1}^2\right)}{SS_{X_1}\left(N-2\right)}} \tag{52}$$

Similarly, when X_2 is included in the model, Equation 51 becomes

$$\hat{\beta}_{1\cdot2} \pm (t_{.05;N-3}) \sqrt{\frac{SS_Y \left(1 - R^2_{Y\cdot X_1, X_2}\right)}{SS_{X_1} (N-3) \left(1 - r^2_{12}\right)}} \tag{53}$$

We can use Equations 52 and 53 to see that the ratio of the width of the confidence interval excluding X_2 to the width including X_2 will be given by

$$\frac{t_{.05;N-2}}{t_{.05;N-3}} \sqrt{\frac{(N-3) \left(1 - r^2_{Y1}\right)}{(N-2) \left(1 - R^2_{Y\cdot X_1, X_2}\right)}} \sqrt{1 - r^2_{12}} \tag{54}$$

What does Equation 54 tell us about the widths of the two confidence intervals? The first term, i.e., the ratio of critical t values, will always be smaller than 1.0, but will be very close to 1.0 unless N is very small. For example, even if the total sample size N is only 20, the ratio of critical t values is between 0.99 and 1.00. For larger values of N, the ratio is even closer to 1.0. Thus, there is a slight advantage for the interval excluding X_2, but the advantage will be of no practical value unless N is very small. Now let's jump to the third term (we will consider the second term in a moment). The third term will tend to be very close to 1.0 with random assignment. In fact, when X_1 and X_2 represent two manipulated factors, it will usually be the case that their correlation is exactly zero. Now let's consider the second term. How will the numerator compare to the denominator? There is a potential trade-off here. The $N-3$ portion of the numerator will be smaller than the $N-2$ portion of the denominator, so this part of the ratio is less than 1.0. However, to the extent that X_2 is a relevant predictor of Y, the multiple correlation predicting Y from both X_1 and X_2 will be larger than the correlation predicting Y from X_1 alone. Thus, this portion of the denominator will tend to be smaller than the comparable portion of the numerator, which means that the ratio will exceed 1.0. Thus, one portion of the ratio will be less than 1.0, while another portion will tend to be greater than 1.0. What can we say about the ratio as a whole? After some algebraic manipulation, it is possible to show that the middle term in Equation 54 will be less than 1.0 if and only if

$$\frac{r^2_{Y2}}{\left(1 - R^2_{Y\cdot12}\right) / (N-3)} < 1 \tag{55}$$

We can simplify this by realizing that the left side of the inequality is identical to the observed F value comparing a model with both X_1 and X_2 as predictors to a model with only X_1 as a predictor, when X_1 and X_2 are uncorrelated. Thus, letting F_{β_2} denote this F statistic, we can say that the middle term of Equation 54 will be less than 1 if and only if

$$F_{\beta_2} < 1 \tag{56}$$

In other words, when X_1 and X_2 are uncorrelated and N is large enough (say 20 or more) so that the ratio of critical t values is essentially 1, excluding X_2 will yield a more precise interval than including X_2 if and only if the F statistic associated with X_2 is less than 1. To see why this matters, we need to realize that if the population coefficient for X_2 is zero, we would expect the F value for X_2 to exceed 1 half the time and be less than 1 the other half of the time. However, to the extent that the coefficient for X_2 is nonzero, its F statistic will tend to be larger than 1, in which case including it in our model will lead to a more precise interval for β_1.

So where does all of this leave us? Consider an example where the correlation between Y and X_1 is 0.40, the correlation between Y and X_2 is 0.50, and X_1 and X_2 are uncorrelated. It follows that the squared multiple correlation predicting Y from both X_1 and X_2 then equals 0.41, in which case the second term in Equation 54 will equal 1.19 if the total sample size is large enough that the square root of the ratio of $N-3$ to $N-2$ can be assumed to essentially equal 1.0. This means that in this scenario a confidence interval formed for β_1 without including X_2 in the model will tend to be approximately 20% wider than an interval formed while including X_2 in the model. Thus, even though X_2 is unrelated to X_1, including it in the model improves our ability to estimate the coefficient for X_1 precisely. Including X_2 helps us because X_2 improves the predictability of Y, and thus reduces error variance in the model.

There are two practical implications of this discussion.:

1. When X_2 is uncorrelated with X_1, we do not need to include it in our model in order to obtain an unbiased estimate of the regression coefficient for X_1.

2. When X_2 is uncorrelated with X_1, including X_2 in the model can increase the precision with which we estimate the coefficient for X_1 to the extent that X_2 correlates with Y.

    So although we do not have to include X_2 in our model, there nevertheless may be definite advantages to doing so. From the perspective of hypothesis testing, a narrower confidence interval leads to increased statistical power, so we could say that including X_2 in our model in this scenario increases the power of our test for X_1.

Examples

A classic example of this situation occurs in Chapter 9, where including a covariate in the model for Y can sometimes greatly increase the power to detect a treatment effect (represented by X_1) when we have randomly assigned individuals to groups. Notice that as long as we have random assignment, we do not need to include the covariate in our model in order to obtain an unbiased estimate of the treatment effect. For this reason, many researchers would overlook the option to add the covariate to the model. However, to the extent that the covariate is related to the dependent variable, failing to include it in the model misses an opportunity to explain additional variance and thus increasing power for detecting a treatment effect while also increasing precision to estimate the magnitude of the effect. Another example occurs in the within-subjects designs we present in Chapters 11 through 14 where we (explicitly or implicitly) include a parameter for each subject in the model. For example, the full model we present in Chapter 11 for a single-factor within-subjects design is

$$Y_{ij} = \mu + \alpha_j + \pi_i + \varepsilon_{ij} \qquad (11.22, \text{ repeated})$$

where π_i is an effect associated with person (i.e., subject) i. Notice how this model is different from the corresponding full model we developed for a single-factor between-subjects design:

$$Y_{ij} = \mu + \alpha_j + \varepsilon_{ij} \qquad (3.66, \text{ repeated})$$

The only difference between these models is that the model for within-subjects designs includes extra predictors to reflect potential differences between individual subjects. As long as there are no missing data, variables representing group differences will be uncorrelated with variables representing subject effects. Thus, we could omit the subject variables and still obtain an unbiased estimate of group differences. However, to the extent that the subject variables are predictive of Y (i.e., there are systematic individual differences between subjects), including these extra predictors will (as shown in Equations 54 and 56) increase the precision of our estimated group differences. Indeed, this is precisely why for a fixed number of data points, within-subjects designs are usually more powerful than between-subjects designs.

CONSEQUENCES OF INCLUDING AN IRRELEVANT PREDICTOR

The implication of the previous section might seem to be to include everything in the "kitchen sink" in our model. After all, it seems there can be advantages to including an additional predictor whether or not it is correlated with X_1, the predictor we have presumed to be of particular theoretical interest. However, you need to realize that the previous section assumed throughout that the additional predictor X_2 was a relevant predictor. In other words, we assumed in all of the previous section that the regression coefficient for predicting Y from X_2 was nonzero. In actual research practice, however, we will typically not know before we collect data whether our X_2 variable is in fact a relevant predictor. Suppose we thought that X_2 would be relevant, but unbeknownst to us, in reality X_2 is irrelevant? In other words, suppose we thought that X_2 had a nonzero regression coefficient, but in actuality the population value of the regression coefficient for X_2 is zero. Remember that an "irrelevant" predictor is one whose population regression coefficient equals zero. What are the consequences of including an irrelevant predictor variable in our model?

As we did in our consideration of a relevant X_2 variable, we will consider the effects of including an irrelevant predictor for two separate scenarios. First, we will consider a situation where the irrelevant predictor correlates with X_1. Second, we will consider a scenario where X_2 does not correlate with X_1. Fortunately, in both cases we will be able to rely upon many of the formulas we developed in the previous section.

Correlated Predictors

Suppose that X_2 is correlated with X_1, but that the regression coefficient for X_2 predicting Y is zero with both X_1 and X_2 in the model. Will our estimated coefficient for X_1 still be unbiased? The answer to this question follows immediately from reconsideration of Equation 50:

$$\hat{\beta}_{1\cdot2} - \hat{\beta}_1 = (-r_{12}\hat{\beta}_{2\cdot1})\left(\frac{s_{X_2}}{s_{X_1}}\right) \qquad \text{(50, repeated)}$$

When X_2 is an irrelevant predictor, we would expect its regression coefficient $\hat{\beta}_{2\cdot1}$ to equal zero, which means that we would expect the difference between $\hat{\beta}_{1\cdot2}$ and $\hat{\beta}_1$ to equal zero. Thus, the estimated regression coefficient for X_1 will be unbiased regardless of whether we include X_2 in our model.

In the long run, it does not matter whether we include an irrelevant correlated predictor in our model. However, what about the possible effects in any particular sample? To address this question, we need to consider the confidence interval for the regression coefficient of X_1. Recall from Equation 54 that the ratio of the width of the confidence interval excluding X_2 to the width including X_2 will be given by

$$\frac{t_{.05;N-2}}{t_{.05;N-3}}\sqrt{\frac{(N-3)\left(1-r_{Y1}^2\right)}{(N-2)\left(1-R_{Y\cdot X_1,X_2}^2\right)}}\sqrt{1-r_{12}^2} \qquad \text{(54, repeated)}$$

Once again, the ratio of critical t values can be thought of as equal to 1.0 except in very small samples. In this case, it turns out that we would expect the second term to be close to 1.0 as well. The reason is that now X_2 does not add to the predictability of Y. However, the third term will not equal 1.0 to the extent that X_1 and X_2 are correlated. For example, suppose X_1 and X_2 correlate 0.50 with one another. In this case, the third term equals 0.87, which means that the confidence interval for β_1 excluding X_2 will be 87% as wide as the interval we would obtain if we included X_2. Or, equivalently, by including X_2 in the model, we have increased the likely width of our confidence interval by 15% (i.e., 100 times the reciprocal of 0.87). Thus, if we could realize that X_2 is irrelevant, we should exclude it from our model, because its inclusion decreases the precision with which we can estimate the regression coefficient for X_1.

Example

It might seem difficult to come up with an example of a situation where we would include an irrelevant predictor. Of course, if we could know with certainty that a predictor is in fact irrelevant, we would exclude it. The problem is that in reality we typically cannot know whether a predictor is truly irrelevant. And keep in mind that omitting a relevant predictor that is correlated with X_1 yields a biased estimate of β_1. For this reason, we may prefer to include some predictor X_2 in our model if it correlates with X_1, even if there is some reasonable chance that X_2 may be irrelevant. Indeed, this is exactly the logic in unequal n factorial designs in Chapter 7. Specifically, the Type II sum of squares for a main effect is calculated by omitting the interaction from the model. This is unquestionably the best approach if the interaction (which we can think of here as X_2) is truly irrelevant in the population. In an unequal n design, the predictor representing the interaction will typically correlate with the predictor representing a main effect, so we can increase precision by excluding the interaction from our model when it is irrelevant. However, the rub here is that in so doing we are running a risk that we have in fact excluded a relevant correlated predictor from our model, in which case we saw in the previous section that our estimate of the main effect will be biased. Most statisticians have come to believe that it is generally preferable to sacrifice some precision in order to assure an unbiased estimate, in which case the interaction term would be included in the model. However, if there is strong evidence (perhaps based on a combination of data and theory) that the interaction is truly zero, greater power and precision can be obtained for the main effect by excluding the interaction term from the model.

Uncorrelated Predictors

Suppose that X_2 is uncorrelated with X_1, and that the population regression coefficient for X_2 predicting Y is zero with both X_1 and X_2 in the model. Notice in this case that X_2 is unrelated to any other variables in the system. As such, X_2 is literally random noise. Fortunately, this is precisely what the error term of the model is designed to accommodate. As such, the likely intuition that it should not make much difference whether we include or exclude X_2 in this case is basically correct. Even here, however, there is a theoretical difference, and that theoretical difference can become a practical difference when we realize that in actual research the number of such irrelevant variables we may be contemplating could be much larger than 1.

We can immediately see from Equation 50 that omitting an irrelevant uncorrelated predictor does not bias our estimate of the regression coefficient of X_1. Once again, in the long run or in very large samples, it will not matter whether we include or exclude this type of X_2 in our model.

Including or excluding X_2 in the model does have some effect on the precision with which we can estimate X_1, but the effect is typically quite small. Notice that we would expect the second term in Equation 54 to be essentially 1.0 and the third term to be essentially 0.0 when X_2 correlates with neither Y nor X_1. In particular, based on Equation 56, we can conclude that half the time the second term will be larger and half the time the second term will be smaller if we include X_2. Thus, the only systematic effect of including or excluding X_2 manifests itself in the critical value. As we have already seen, this effect can be ignored unless sample size is very small or unless the number of additional variables we might include becomes large. Not surprisingly, it is preferable to exclude variables that have nothing to do with either Y or X_1, but their inclusion causes little harm when the number of such variables is small relative to sample size.

SUMMARY

It is hardly a surprise to learn that relevant predictors should be included in a model and that irrelevant predictors should be excluded. However, understanding the principles behind this conclusion may be less intuitive. In particular, understanding the consequences of mistakenly excluding a relevant predictor as compared to including an irrelevant predictor may be useful in guiding decisions about what variables to measure and include in a statistical model.

Table B.11 provides a summary of the principles we have developed in this appendix. Implicit in the table is the suggestion that in general it is most important to include variables that are likely to have nonzero coefficients and to correlate with other variables of interest. On the other hand, the variables most important to exclude are those that are correlated with variables of interest but whose coefficients are zero. Of course, in practice, the difficulty with this distinction is that it is typically difficult to know whether the coefficient for a predictor is truly zero or nonzero until we have included it in the model, at least provisionally. Even then, the decision may not be obvious, especially if statistical power may be lacking.

Another implication of the table is the enormous benefit of random assignment to treatments. When our goal is to assess the effect of a variable whose levels are determined by random assignment, we know (probabilistically) that we are in the second row of Table B.11. However, the consequences of mistakenly excluding or including a variable are usually much less in the second row of the table than in the first row. Thus, random assignment offers a degree of protection rarely available in nonrandomized studies.

Finally, we will close with six additional points. First, it is important to realize that X_2^2 is not the same variable as X_2. In other words, at least in theory, it may not be enough to include X_2 in our model because it may relate nonlinearly to Y. For example, in order to obtain an unbiased estimate of β_1, it may be necessary to include both X_2 and X_2^2 in the model. Obviously this can create sizable complications, because even if we are so insightful as to know all of the relevant variables, our work is still not finished because we also have to know how each of them relates to Y. Second, a related type of effect is an interaction effect, initially described in Chapter 7. An interaction effect can be thought of as the product of two or more variables with one another, such as $X_1 X_2$. Notice from this perspective that X_2^2 could be conceptualized as X_2 interacting with itself. In fact, consistent with the idea of an interaction we develop in Chapter 7, an effect due to X_2^2 suggests that the effect of X_2 on Y changes depending on the value of X_2

TABLE B.11
EFFECTS OF EXCLUDING A RELEVANT VARIABLE OR INCLUDING
AN IRRELEVANT VARIABLE

	Excluding a Relevant X	Including an Irrelevant X
Correlated with X_1, predictor of theoretical interest	Biased estimate of β_1	Unbiased estimate of β_1 but estimate is less precise than if irrelevant X were excluded
Uncorrelated with X_1, predictor of theoretical interest	Unbiased estimate of β_1 but estimate is less precise than if relevant X were included	Unbiased estimate of β_1 Estimate is slightly less precise than if irrelevant X were excluded

itself. Readers interested in further similarities between $X_1 X_2$ and X_2^2 and subsequent implications for interpreting interactions and higher-order trends are advised to read Lubinski and Humphreys's (1990) excellent article as well as MacCallum and Mar's (1995) follow-up. Third, it is also important to realize that an observed score on X_2 will frequently be different from the corresponding true score on X_2. To the extent that Y depends on the true score of X_2, but we include an imperfectly measured version of X_2 in our model, we have not completely succeeded in including the truly relevant predictor (Figure 9.7 and the accompanying discussion in Chapter 9 provides an illustration of this problem in the context of analysis of covariance). Structural equation modeling (also referred to as latent variable modeling) provides a viable solution to this dilemma. Many books and articles have been written on this topic. Good introductions are available in such sources as Bollen (1989), Kaplan (2000), and Raykov and Marcoulides (2000). Fourth, we need to point out an additional complication when X_2, the variable we may mistakenly exclude, represents a random effects factor. As we discuss at some length in Chapter 10, the presence of a random effects factor often implies the need for an error term that takes this factor into account, even if our statistical test or interval pertains to a different factor (i.e., predictor) in the model. Thus, omitting relevant random effects factors can have especially unfortunate consequences. Fifth, we have described the goals of model building and the consequences of misspecifying models. These principles are exemplified at various points throughout the body of the text. However, our focus is primarily on the inclusion or exclusion of design factors, especially in randomized studies. As we have seen, issues of including or excluding predictors are often less complex in randomized designs. A broader discussion emphasizing observational studies lacking random assignment is a highly complex topic requiring a book unto itself. Fortunately, we can highly recommend Harrell (2001) for readers who are interested in such a book-length treatment. Sixth, this entire appendix could be thought of as exemplifying the role of parsimony in building statistical models for data. In this respect, it seems fitting to close with a quote from Einstein: "Everything should be made as simple as possible, but not simpler."

Appendix C

Notes

CHAPTER 1

1. A more complete rendering of this statement in Einstein's own words is as follows:

   > The very fact that the totality of our sense experiences is such that by means of thinking (operations with concepts, and the creation and use of definite functional relations between them, and the coordination of sense experiences to these concepts) it can be put in order, this fact is one which leaves us in awe, but which we shall never understand. One may say "the eternal mystery of the world is its comprehensibility." It is one of the great realizations of Immanuel Kant that the setting up of a real external world would be senseless without this comprehensibility.
   >
   > In speaking here concerning "comprehensibility," the expression is used in its most modest sense. It implies: the production of some sort of order among sense impressions, this order being produced by the creation of general concepts, relations between these concepts, and by relations between these concepts and sense experience, these relations being determined in any possible manner. It is in this sense that the world of our sense experiences is comprehensible. The fact that it is comprehensible is a miracle. (Einstein, 1936, p. 351)

2. As noted in the preface, we will be presuming some knowledge of elementary statistics in this book. If you need a review of methods such as the *t* test, see the first statistical tutorial, Review of Basic Statistics, on the data disk.
3. We are for the moment setting aside considerations bearing on the validity of the statistical conclusions which will be the focus of our concern later in this chapter and repeatedly at other points. For now, suffice it to say that there are vagaries (cf. Schmidt, 1996) as well as clear benefits (cf. Wainer, 1999) in the binary accept–reject logic of testing statistical hypotheses. But in any event, such binary decisions fit well with the logic of Popperian falsificationism.
4. The helpful role of meta-analysis (e.g., Schmidt, 1992) in offsetting the decision-making errors in individual studies is not to be denied, and is one reason why we will be covering measures of effect size as well as statistical testing procedures throughout the current volume.
5. A major distinction among experimental designs is whether the same individuals are assessed only once or repeatedly in a given study. This is the distinction between Parts II and III of this book. Perhaps not surprisingly given that psychologists, educators, and others tend to be concerned with change, most behavioral science studies involve repeated measurements of the same units.
6. Huck and Sandler (1979) have an excellent (and fun) book, which is organized somewhat like a series of mysteries, that is designed for practicing your skills at this.
7. Shadish et al. (2002) have extended the notion of construct validity to include the problems of correctly naming or identifying not only the independent and dependent variables, but also the units and settings. While naming the units is an obvious concern when the focus of an investigation is on an individual difference variable, such as a diagnostic category in a clinical population, we prefer to treat such cases as a construct validity issue of the

"independent" variable whose presumed effects or sequelae the investigator hopes to assess. Similarly, while characteristics of the setting could be regarded as representative of a larger category or kind of setting, and problems of the meaning of "setting constructs" be addressed, we believe that the meaning of the independent and dependent variable constructs should be of primary concern. Thus, we will here continue to treat such issues of generalizing beyond the setting of the current study to other locales or environments only as a problem of external validity per Cook and Campbell (1979).

CHAPTER 2

1. A discrete probability distribution is one with a countable (and typically a small finite) number of possible outcomes. An example would be the (flat) distribution of the probabilities of the six outcomes that can occur when you roll a (fair) die.

2. In attempting to formulate the probability of various outcomes, most students when faced with the tea tasting problem begin searching their memories for a familiar discrete probability distribution. Most graduate students in the behavioral sciences have studied the binomial distribution, and so it is frequently suggested as the method of analysis. Whether it is appropriate depends again on how the experiment was run. The binomial distribution arises from a series of independent trials. If the subject were told there were four of each kind of cups, the successive judgments would clearly not be independent because once four cups had been classified as being of one kind, the remaining ones would have to be put into the other category to have any hope of the set of judgments being correct. If the subject were not told there were four cups of each kind, in order to make use of a binomial with probability of success equal to .5, it would be necessary to hypothesize not only that the lady had no discrimination ability but also that she had no bias for responding in favor of one cup over another. Thus, it is not clear that the binomial would be appropriate if the number of cups of each kind were determined in advance, regardless of what the subject was told. If, on the other hand, the subject understood that you determined what kind of cup each successive cup would be by the toss of a fair coin, the binomial could be used. However, in this situation, both experimenter and subject should realize that it is possible that all eight cups might be of a single kind, thus potentially allowing no comparison across kinds of cups.

3. The noncentral hypergeometric can be defined in terms of the odds ratio thought to characterize the true probability of success for the two rows. For a table with fixed marginal frequencies of $R, N - R, n$ and $N - n$ as shown in the table below

r	$n - r$	n
$R - r$	$(N - R) - (n - r)$	$N - n$
R	$N - R$	N

the probability of a particular outcome can be written in terms of the probability of the frequency in the first row and column, f_{11}, taking on a particular value, r. The power of a test can then be determined by summing the probabilities of the outcomes that are in the rejection region, with the probability of each particular outcome being computed according to the noncentral hypergeometric distribution as follows:

$$Pr(f_{11} = r) = \frac{{}_R C_r \; {}_{N-R} C_{n-r} \; \theta^r}{\sum\limits_{i=r\min}^{r\max} {}_R C_i \; {}_{N-R} C_{n-i} \; \theta^i}$$

where θ is the odds ratio of the hypothesized true probabilities of success in the two rows and r min and r max are the minimum and maximum possible values of r. In the case where the marginal frequencies are equal r can range from 0 to n. When the marginal frequencies differ, the range may be restricted (specifically, r max will be the smaller of R and n, and $r$min will be the larger of 0 and $n - (N - r)$).

To illustrate the computation of power, if in the tea-tasting example the probability of classifying a cup as tea first were really .9 for tea-first cups and .3 for milk-first cups, then we would have an odds ratio of:

$$\theta = \frac{p_1/(1 - p_1)}{p_2/(1 - p_2)} = \frac{.9/(1 - .9)}{.3/(1 - .3)} = \frac{9/1}{3/7} = 21$$

Because with four cups of each kind the only persuasive evidence of discrimination ability would be if all cups were correctly classified, the power of such a test could be computed as:

$$Pr\,(f_{11} = 4) = \frac{{}_4C_4\,{}_4C_0\,\theta^4}{\sum\limits_{i=0}^{4} {}_4C_i\,{}_4C_{4-i}\,\theta^i}$$

$$= \frac{1\cdot 1\cdot 21^4}{\sum\limits_{i=0}^{4} {}_4C_i\,{}_4C_{4-i}\,21^i}$$

$$= \frac{194{,}481}{1 + 4\cdot 4\cdot 21 + 6\cdot 6\cdot 21^2 + 4\cdot 4\cdot 21^3 + 1\cdot 1\cdot 21^4}$$

$$= \frac{194{,}481}{1 + 336 + 15{,}876 + 148{,}176 + 194{,}481}$$

$$= \frac{194{,}481}{358{,}870} = .542$$

If more than one outcome could have led to rejection of the null hypothesis, the probabilities of those values of f_{11} occurring would be computed similarly and cumulated to determine the power.

4. Some authors following Berkson (1978) reject the idea of doing Fisher's exact tests, arguing that the marginal totals provide relevant information. While this is sometimes certainly the case, it is not always true (cf. Kempthorne, 1979), such as when both row and column marginals are constrained by the experimenter as in Fisher's tea-tasting example. What can be confusing is that some power analysis programs such as Power and Precision (www.PowerAndPrecision.com) provide an option labeled "Power computation: Fisher's exact test" but in fact compute power assuming the two rows reflect two independent binomial distributions. For example, with data as in the tea-tasting example, the power to detect a difference between population proportions of .9 and .3 is determined by the Power and Precision program as:

$$\text{power} = ({}_4C_4 \cdot 9^4 \cdot 1^0) \cdot ({}_4C_0 \cdot 3^0 \cdot 7^4) = (.6561)(.2401) = .1575$$

clearly different from the value of .542 computed with the noncentral hypergeometric appropriate for the case where the subject was required to give 4 responses of each kind. Other programs (e.g., UnifyPow; see O'Brien, 1998) use approximations to the conditional probability of the noncentral hypergeometric appropriate for Fisher's exact, but with the warning that the approximation may not be very accurate with small sample sizes (cf. O'Brien & Muller, 1993, p. 336).

5. That is, a histogram showing the relative frequency of scores would be low in the middle range and high at either end; hence the distribution looks somewhat like a U. In the current data, there are more scores below 0 and more scores greater than 8 than there are between 0 and 8.

6. The corrected value of t is slightly smaller, 2.046, and in fact is exceeded by .038 of the t distribution.

7. Just how cumbersome may be surprising. For example, if a total of 30 observations are to be assigned in equal numbers to the groups in a study, with two groups over 150 million assignments are possible, and with three groups over 3 trillion assignments are possible. Although the number of calculations for a complete specification of the distribution of a test statistic is clearly prohibitive in general, interest in randomization methods is increasing because of recent developments making such tests more practical. These developments include the design of computational algorithms and computer programs that take random samples from the distribution (for example, Edgington, 1995, pp. 50–51, 68ff; Green, 1977), algebraic simplifications (Gabriel & Hall, 1983), and approximations (Gabriel & Hsu, 1983). At the present writing, the computational methods are still being developed for various designs, and programs for even simple situations are not widely available. Thus, although the logic of randomization testing is important for what we are about, the specific procedures for more complex designs are not considered in subsequent chapters.

8. Students in the behavioral sciences are often familiar with the central limit theorem for explaining why group means can be expected to be normally distributed. However, here we are considering the application of the theorem in the way conceived by its originator, Laplace (Stigler, 1986, p. 143), and that is to view an individual observation or even the error in an individual observation as a composite or summation of the effects of a number of variables.

CHAPTER 3

1. You should note that although the values of ε_i are not known in advance, it is only the βs that are the parameters, or the basic descriptive summaries of the population of Y scores. The parameters are estimated and then the error scores can be determined simply by seeing to what extent the combination of parameters specified by the model deviates from the observed value of the dependent variable. Thus, in one technical sense, the values of ε_i are not part of our model but serve to indicate to what extent our "real" model (consisting only of the weighted sum of parameters) fails to fit the data (see Finn, 1974, p. 6). However, for simplicity, we typically refer to the weighted parameters together with the associated error scores as our model. When used in this way, our model is a complete specification of the data values exactly, and competing models differ in how much of the variance in Y must be accounted for by the ε component of the model.

2. The steps in the derivation are as follows: Beginning with $\sum e_i^2 = \sum (Y_i - \mu_0)^2$, we add and subtract $\overline{Y}$ to each error, group terms, and expand:

$$\sum (Y_i - \mu_0)^2 = \sum (Y_i - \overline{Y} + \overline{Y} - \mu_0)^2$$
$$= \sum (Y_i - \overline{Y})^2 + \sum 2(\overline{Y} - \mu_0)(Y_i - \overline{Y}) + \sum (\overline{Y} - \mu_0)^2$$

The middle term again goes to zero, that is,

$$\sum 2(Y_i - \overline{Y})(\overline{Y} - \mu_0) = 2(\overline{Y} - \mu_0)\sum (Y_i - \overline{Y}) = 0$$

Thus, we have

$$\sum (Y_i - \mu_0)^2 = \sum (Y_i - \overline{Y})^2 + n(\overline{Y} - \mu_0)^2$$

3. The notion of sums of squared errors is pervasive in statistics. Most often these quantities are denoted SS, for sum of squares, or SSE, for sum of squared errors; the models to which these sums of squares correspond might be indicated parenthetically, for example, $SSE(F)$ and $SSE(R)$ for the sum of squared errors associated with the full and restricted models, respectively (cf. Neter, Kutner, Nachtsheim, & Wasserman, 1996, p. 79). Although we use SS notation for making connections with other approaches, it has been our experience that communication is facilitated, particularly for students in the behavioral sciences, by keeping the notation as simple as possible. Thus, we have chosen to denote sum of squared errors, the most commonly used term in our formulas, by a single capital E and indicate the model that generated the errors by a single capital letter subscript, either F for the full model or R for the restricted model. Because a lower case e is almost universally used to designate the error of prediction for an individual observation, it should be an easy transition to think of E as denoting a summary measure of these individual errors. We are attempting to minimize the "symbol shock" of beginning students by having it understood, rather than always explicit, that the way the individual errors are summarized is to square each one and sum the squared values over all individuals in the study.

4. Dividing the denominator of a fraction by $(n - 1)$ is equivalent to multiplying the fraction by $(n - 1)$. In fact, test statistics generally may be viewed as the product of (1) an index, like our PIE, of the size of the effect observed and (2) an index, like $(n - 1)$, of the size of the study. We discuss this perspective in greater detail near the end of the chapter when we consider alternative measures of effects.

5. Once again we make use of the technique of adding zero—that is, $-\overline{Y}_j + \overline{Y}_j$—to the terms used in computing E_R to simplify the numerator of the F statistic:

$$E_R = \sum_j \sum_i (Y_{ij} - \overline{Y})^2 = \sum_j \sum_i (Y_{ij} - \overline{Y}_j + \overline{Y}_j - \overline{Y})^2$$

Grouping terms and expanding, we obtain

$$E_R = \sum_j \sum_i [(Y_{ij} - \overline{Y}_j) + (\overline{Y}_j - \overline{Y})]^2$$
$$= \sum_j \sum_i (Y_{ij} - \overline{Y}_j)^2 + \sum_j \sum_i (\overline{Y}_j - \overline{Y})^2 + 2\sum_j \sum_i (Y_{ij} - \overline{Y}_j)(\overline{Y}_j - \overline{Y})$$

But because the sum of the deviations from the mean in any group equals zero [i.e., $\sum_i (Y_{ij} - \overline{Y}_j) = 0$], the last, cross-product term above always is zero and can be ignored, that is,

$$2\sum_j \sum_i (Y_{ij} - \overline{Y}_j)(\overline{Y}_j - \overline{Y}) = 2\sum_j (\overline{Y}_j - \overline{Y})\sum_i (Y_{ij} - \overline{Y}_j)$$

$$= 2\sum_j (\overline{Y}_j - \overline{Y}) \cdot 0 = 0$$

Thus, $E_R = \sum_j \sum_i (Y_{ij} - \overline{Y}_j)^2 + \sum_j \sum_i (\overline{Y}_j - \overline{Y})^2$.

6. The model-comparison perspective can be translated into SS_{Between} and SS_{Within}, but remember that it is more general than these concepts. One can impose other restrictions on the values of the population group means besides constraining all to be equal. In such a case, for example, E_R may no longer be equal to SS_{Total}. The appropriate model depends on the question of interest, and the theoretical background of a research project may dictate other models. Our general formulation in terms of E_R and E_F still applies although the traditional formulation would not. We consider such a situation in the next section.

7. Twenty subjects were run in each condition. To simplify the calculations for illustrative purposes here, only 10 scores are presented per group. The first 8 are the scores of the first 8 subjects run in each condition. The last two scores were selected from the remaining scores so that the mean of the subsample would equal the mean, rounded to the nearest integer, of all 20 subjects' scores.

8. The conventional grand mean, which is used as an estimate of μ in the restricted model, can be thought of as a weighted average of the group means, where the weights are the sizes of the groups. That is, because $\overline{Y}_j = (\sum_i Y_{ij})/n_j$, we have $\sum_i Y_{ij} = n_j \overline{Y}_j$, which when substituted in the definition of the grand mean $\overline{Y} = (\sum_j \sum_i Y_{ij})/(\sum_j n_j)$ yields $\overline{Y} = (\sum_j n_j \overline{Y}_j)/(\sum_j n_j)$. When the sample sizes are all equal—that is, all $n_j = n$—then this grand mean is seen to be the same as an unweighted average of the group means, that is, $\overline{Y} = (\sum_j n \overline{Y}_j)/(\sum_j n) = (n \sum_j \overline{Y}_j)/na = (\sum_j \overline{Y}_j)/a = \overline{Y}_u$. However, in the unequal-n case, the conventional grand mean will be "pulled" in the direction of the means from the larger groups. We consider the difference between weighted and unweighted means in much greater detail in the context of factorial designs in Chapter 7.

9. On this point, we find ourselves in agreement with Howard Wainer (1999):

> To be perfectly honest, I am a little at a loss to understand fully the vehemence and vindictiveness that have recently greeted NHT [null hypothesis significance testing]. These criticism seem to focus primarily on the misuse of NHT. This focus on the technique rather than on those who misuse it seems to be misplaced. (Don't ask me to be consistent here, because I find the National Rifle Association's similar defense of handguns completely specious.) (p. 212)

10. Abelson's (1995) delightful volume suggests using the MAGIC criteria for evaluating research, where the acronym stands for magnitude of effect, articulation (roughly the clarity, detail and balance in the presentation of one's findings), generality, interestingness and credibility. Statistical tests bear on the credibility of a claim, particularly for novel findings, and on their generality (see Greenwald et al., 1996, on how p values relate to the probability of a successful replication).

11. Two technical points can be made on the basis of his work. First, $\hat{d}$ is positively biased as an estimator of d—that is, the sample value of $\hat{d}$ tends to be somewhat larger than the true parameter. However, if df_F is greater than 10, the expected value of $\hat{d}$ will be less than 10 percent larger than d (Hedges, 1981, p. 113). Second, error of measurement in the dependent variable tends to make S larger than it should be and thus, when present, tends to make $\hat{d}$ smaller. However, if the reliability is greater than .80, error of measurement tends to deflate the expected value of $\hat{d}$ by less than 10 percent (Hedges, 1981, p. 120). Because these two effects are in most situations small and tend to offset each other, $\hat{d}$ may for practical purposes generally be regarded as an essentially unbiased estimator of d.

12. You can shorten this process somewhat, once you have an idea what range of df_{denom} values are plausible, by choosing one of the curves in that range, determining what value of ϕ would yield the desired power, and then solving Equation 3.100 for n.

Alternatively, you may be able to dispense with the use of the power charts entirely even if you do not have specialized power analysis software, because the recent inclusion of noncentral distribution functions in standard packages has made the process of iteration to the sample size needed for a desired power value even easier. For example, in SPSS one could accomplish the iteration process by setting up a small data set where each line reflects a different scenario of values describing the size of the planned study and the size of the anticipated effect. To carry out the power computations for the situation described in the text, a small data set could be set up where the values remain constant for variable "a" (i.e., the number of groups) and for variable "*feffect*" (i.e., the effect size measure f, defined in Equation 3.89), but where the values of the variable "*n*" (i.e., the proposed number of subjects per group) vary, as indicated in the table below:

a	n	feffect
3	10	.4082
3	20	.4082
3	21	.4082
3	25	.4082

Then one can compute the power for each scenario by running the following syntax file. These commands compute first the value of the noncentrality parameter lambda (λ) (denoted "nclambda" below); then the critical value of F (denoted "F_crit" below) resulting from the degrees of freedom implied by the number of groups, a, and the sample size, n, is computed; and finally the resulting power is arrived at by determining the proportion of the noncentral F distribution (with the appropriate degrees of freedom and noncentrality parameter) that would be greater than the critical value:

```
compute nclambda = a*n*(feffect**2).
compute F_crit = idf.F (.95, a - 1, a*n - a).
compute power = 1 - ncdf.F (F_crit, a - 1, a*n - a, nclambda).
EXECUTE.
```

These commands would transform the data set to the following:

a	n	feffect	nclambda	f_crit	power
3	10	.4082	5.00	3.35	.46
3	20	.4082	10.00	3.16	.79
3	21	.4082	10.50	3.15	.81
3	25	.4082	12.50	3.12	.88

Although of course the first time you set up your lines of data you may not know that $n = 21$ should be included, inspection of the power values resulting from a range of values of n allows you to quickly home in on the minimal sample size needed to achieve a power of .8.

13. You may have occasion to use a program for power analysis that requires a specification of mean values which you are trying to project on the basis of pilot data. Values that appropriately adjust for the sampling error in the pilot data can be easily arrived at. The key is to reduce the observed values of the effect parameters by multiplication by a fraction which depends on the value of the F statistic obtained in an ANOVA of the pilot data. Specifically, each alpha value, where $\hat{\alpha}_j = \overline{Y}_j - \overline{Y}$, is adjusted by multiplication by $\sqrt{\frac{F-1}{F}}$:

$$\hat{\alpha}_{j\mathrm{adj}} = \hat{\alpha}_j \sqrt{\frac{F-1}{F}}$$

Then, the estimated value of the mean for the jth group is arrived at by adding this adjusted alpha value to the observed grand mean:

$$\hat{\mu}_j = \overline{Y} + \hat{\alpha}_{j\mathrm{adj}}$$

The result of this adjustment is that the value of f computed from these means will be equal to the value of f_{adj}, as desired.

CHAPTER 3 EXTENSION

1. Wilcox, Charlin, and Thompson's (1986) results suggest that Type I error rates are more likely to be excessive as the number of groups increases. For example, with equal *ns* as small as 11, the Type I error rate of the *t* test remains close to .05, even when the population standard deviations have a 4 : 1 ratio. However, the Type I error rate for a four-group ANOVA with equal *ns* of 11 was .109 when the population standard deviation of one group was four times larger than the standard deviation of the other groups. Even for equal *ns* of 50, the

Type I error rate for ANOVA was .088 in this situation. Thus, for more than two groups, wide disparities in population standard deviations can make the usual ANOVA excessively liberal, even with equal n.

2. SPSS provides the value of the test statistic, degrees of freedom, and p value for both tests.

3. Strictly speaking, MS_B and MS_W are both unbiased estimators of the same population variance if homogeneity holds and the null hypothesis is true. The further assumptions of normality and independence guarantee that the ratio of MS_B and MS_W follows an F distribution.

4. Monte Carlo studies by necessity investigate power differences only under a limited set of conditions. Nevertheless, the value of .03 would seem to be a reasonable figure for most practical situations. The single exception is likely to be where n is very small, in which case F might enjoy a larger advantage over F^*.

5. Cleveland (1985, pp. 135–143) presents two graphical techniques that are especially appropriate for judging whether the data conform to a shift hypothesis when comparing the distributions of two groups. The percentile comparison graph is obtained by plotting the percentiles of one distribution against the corresponding percentiles of the other distribution. If a shift of location describes the difference between the groups, the resultant plot should resemble a straight line. The Tukey sum-difference graph plots sums of corresponding percentiles against differences of corresponding percentiles and should resemble a flat straight line when the shift hypothesis holds. Cleveland argues that comparing means may be misleading when the percentile comparison graph is curved (or the Tukey sum-difference graph is not flat). Indeed, in such a situation, any single value (e.g., mean or median) may hide important characteristics of the difference between the two distributions. Darlington's (1973) ordinal dominance curve methodology provides an interesting alternative in this situation.

6. When population distributions have different shapes, alternative methods have been developed for testing differences between population medians. For further information, see Fligner and Rust (1982) or Wilcox and Charlin (1986).

7. Although the general consensus among statisticians is that the F test is robust to violations of nonnormality, there are some dissenters to this view. For an example, the interested reader should consult Bradley (1978), who provides a very readable set of arguments for why he believes that the robustness of parametric tests has been oversold.

8. As stated earlier, Tomarken and Serlin only sampled from normal populations. Clinch and Keselman (1982) found F^* to be somewhat more robust than W when sampling from nonnormal populations.

9. Relative efficiency as sample sizes approach infinity is referred to as *asymptotic relative efficiency*, which is often abbreviated ARE. Although ARE is a useful concept, the relative efficiency of two tests in small samples may differ considerably from the ARE. In particular, one limitation of the Kruskal–Wallis test is that it is typically impossible to establish a critical value that will set $\alpha = .05$, even when all assumptions have been met. Especially with small sample sizes, α may have to be set considerably below .05, which inevitably results in a loss of power. In such a situation, the relative efficiency of the nonparametric test suffers relative to the parametric test.

10. The sample median is always a median-unbiased estimator of the population median for random sampling. When the population distribution is symmetric, its mean and median are identical. Although the sample mean and sample median are generally different, both are unbiased estimators of the population mean of a symmetric distribution.

11. To simplify even further, we show Huber's estimator with a fixed tuning constant set equal to 1.0. See Hoaglin, Mosteller, and Tukey (1983), Huber (1981), or Wu (1985) for more details.

12. The median can be defined in more than one way when some scores are tied. We have chosen the simplest definition here, which simply ignores the presence of ties, and defines the median to equal the value of the middle observation.

13. Hoaglin, Mosteller, and Tukey (1983) show that M estimators can be thought of as weighted averages of the observations. Specific members of the class differ in terms of how they weight the observations. For example, the mean weights each observation equally, whereas Huber's M estimator weights observation near the center of the data more heavily than observations at the extremes.

CHAPTER 4

1. For later developments in the chapter, it is helpful to note that because

$$\frac{n_1 n_2}{n_1 + n_2} = \frac{1}{\left(\dfrac{1}{n_1} + \dfrac{1}{n_2}\right)}$$

an equivalent form of Equation 27 is

$$F = \frac{(\overline{Y}_1 - \overline{Y}_2)^2}{MS_{\mathrm{W}} \left(\dfrac{1}{n_1} + \dfrac{1}{n_2} \right)}$$

This makes sense because we know that each mean $\overline{Y}_j$ has a sampling variance of σ^2/n_j and that the variance of the difference of two independent random variables is equal to the sum of their individual variances.

2. Of course, the model can be written explicitly. It is just cumbersome (and somewhat confusing) in such a case. The interested reader can demonstrate that the null hypothesis model could be expressed here as

$$Y_{i1} = \mu_1 + \varepsilon_{i1}$$
$$Y_{i2} = \mu_2 + \varepsilon_{i2}$$
$$Y_{i3} = \mu_3 + \varepsilon_{i3}$$
$$Y_{i4} = \tfrac{1}{3}\mu_1 + \tfrac{1}{3}\mu_2 + \tfrac{1}{3}\mu_3 + \varepsilon_{i4}$$

However, if one persists in this approach, one must remember that because each μ_j appears in the model expression for more than one group, the estimate of μ_j here does not depend solely on the observations in the jth group. Thus, for reasons of clarity, the approach taken in the text is preferred here.

3. Strictly speaking, the mathematics also allows hypotheses of the form $H_o : \psi = k$ to be tested, where k is any constant. In other words, k need not equal zero. However, in actual applications, behavioral scientists rarely if ever test a hypothesis other than that ψ equals zero.

4. Lunneborg and Abbott (1983, p. 197) show that a matrix expression for constrained least-squares estimates $_c\mathbf{b}$ is given by

$$_c\mathbf{b} = \mathbf{b} - (\mathbf{X}'\mathbf{X})^{-1}\mathbf{C}[\mathbf{C}'(\mathbf{X}'\mathbf{X})^{-1}\mathbf{C}]^{-1}\mathbf{C}'\mathbf{b}$$

After some tedious algebra, this matrix expression can be written in the following scalar form in the case of an individual contrast:

$$\hat{\mu}_j = \overline{Y}_j - \left(1 \Big/ \sum_{j=1}^{a} \left(c_j^2 \big/ n_j \right) \right) \left(\frac{c_j}{n_j} \right) (\hat{\psi})$$

5. The pooled variance approach also provides an unbiased estimate if sample sizes are equal, and the contrast coefficients for all a groups equal either 1 or -1. In this case, the weights for both approaches simplify to $w_j = 1/a$, so that each group receives an equal weight in deriving a variance estimate.

6. A similar expression applies in the case of unequal sample sizes.

7. The accuracy of this statement depends on the validity of the homogeneity of variance assumption. As we have seen previously, if this assumption is questionable, it may be wise to replace MS_{W} with the expression shown in Equation 42.

8. The alert reader may realize that the strength of association measures we have presented in this chapter are purely descriptive. In other words, they simply reflect the degree of association found in the sample. You may recall that Chapter 3 pointed out that such measures tend to overestimate the degree of association expected in a population, and for that reason Chapter 3 also presented omega squared and adjusted (or shrunken) R^2 as possible alternatives. By and large, methodologists have focused on purely descriptive measures for contrasts and for more complex designs, so that has been our focus in this chapter.

9. Note that linearly independent does not mean statistically independent. This is in contrast to the terminology used in describing variables where it is conventional to say that one variable can have varying degrees of dependence on another, but statistical independence is an absolute property, not a matter of degree. In the present context, linearly dependent is the absolute characteristic meaning one contrast is totally redundant with one or more others, whereas two contrasts can be linearly independent and yet have some degree of relationship. This variation in usage of dependent and independent is perhaps unfortunate but is standard in the statistical literature. With contrasts, the concept of orthogonality, to be introduced shortly, is used to define contrasts that are unrelated. A more detailed exposition of these concepts can be found in Rodgers, Nicewander, and Toothaker (1984).

10. Strictly speaking, for $\hat{\psi}_1$ and $\hat{\psi}_2$ to be statistically independent, the normality assumption must be met. Otherwise, it can only be said that $\hat{\psi}_1$ and $\hat{\psi}_2$ are uncorrelated. Further discussion of the relationship between correlation and independence can be found in Wilcox (1996, p. 301) or Neter et al. (1996, pp. 83, 1318).

CHAPTER 5

1. The Expected Number of Errors per Experiment (ENEPE) is often referred to as the Error Rate per Experiment (ERPE). In fact, the first edition of our book used ERPE instead of ENEPE. However, in this edition we have chosen the term "Expected Number of Errors per Experiment" because we believe it more accurately describes the appropriate concept.

2. Bonferroni-adjusted confidence intervals for the pairwise contrasts can be obtained directly with both SAS and SPSS as long as we are willing to assume homogeneity. We have chosen to show hand calculations here for the sake of consistency, but in practice some work can be saved by relying on SAS or SPSS for the first three intervals shown in Table 5.5.

3. Tukey actually developed several multiple-comparisons procedures, which at times has resulted in confusing labels for the various techniques. The particular method we describe is referred to as Tukey's WSD (for Wholly Significant Difference), Tukey's HSD (for Honestly Significant Difference), or Tukey's T Procedure. As we will see later, the "wholly" and "honestly" terms serve to distinguish Tukey's method from Fisher's LSD (Least Significant Difference), which does not always properly control the α_{EW} level. Also, when we discuss within-subject designs (i.e., repeated measures designs) in Chapters 11–14, we will see that the Bonferroni approach is better than Tukey's technique for testing pairwise comparisons of within-subject means.

4. Tukey originally developed a more general formula that allowed for tests of complex comparisons and pairwise comparisons, but Scheffé's procedure is more powerful for testing complex comparisons.

5. For our purposes, it suffices to state that the studentized maximum modulus distribution is similar in concept to the studentized range distribution. Readers seeking a more mathematical treatment are referred to Dunnett (1980) and to Hochberg and Tamhane (1987).

6. In most published tables of the studentized maximum modulus distribution, the columns refer to the number of comparisons being tested. We have chosen to present the columns in terms of the number of groups because we only discuss the distribution in the context of performing all pairwise comparisons.

7. Notice also that while we can assert that combination therapy is better than drug therapy, it is plausible that combination therapy is no better than diet and biofeedback while at the same time drug therapy is no worse than diet and biofeedback. In other words, we seem to have concluded that μ_1 and μ_4 differ from one another but neither is different from μ_2 and μ_3. A moment's reflection should convince you that if μ_1 and μ_4 differ from one another, they cannot both equal μ_2 (much less both μ_2 and μ_3). The explanation for this predicament is that there is more statistical power for detecting the difference between the largest and smallest population means than for intermediate means. There is no logical contradiction as long as we remember that a nonsignificant statistical test does not imply that the null hypothesis is exactly true. Another way of explaining this pattern of results is to rely on confidence intervals. For example, Table 5.7 shows us that the interval for $\mu_4 - \mu_2$ overlaps the interval for $\mu_1 - \mu_2$ (in particular, both intervals contain zero), but the mere fact that the intervals overlap does not imply that μ_4 equals μ_1.

8. Suppose that we define a contrast to have coefficients given by $c_j = n_j(\overline{Y}_j - \overline{Y})$. The sum of squares for this contrast will equal

$$SS_\psi = (\hat{\psi})^2 \Big/ \sum_{j=1}^{a} c_j^2/n_j$$

However, $\hat{\psi}$ is defined to be

$$\hat{\psi} = \sum_{j=1}^{a} c_j \overline{Y}_j = \sum_{j=1}^{a} n_j(\overline{Y}_j - \overline{Y})\overline{Y}_j$$

Substituting for $\hat{\psi}$ and c_j in the expression for SS_ψ yields

$$SS_\psi = \left[\sum_{j=1}^{a} n_j(\overline{Y}_j - \overline{Y})\overline{Y}_j \right]^2 \Big/ \left[\sum_{j=1}^{a} n_j^2(\overline{Y}_j - \overline{Y})^2/n_j \right]$$

which immediately reduces to

$$SS_\psi = \left[\sum_{j=1}^{a} n_j(\overline{Y}_j - \overline{Y})\overline{Y}_j\right]^2 \bigg/ \sum_{j=1}^{a} n_j(\overline{Y}_j - \overline{Y})^2$$

It can be shown through some simple algebra that

$$\sum_{j=1}^{a} n_j(\overline{Y}_j - \overline{Y})\overline{Y}_j = \sum_{j=1}^{a} n_j(\overline{Y}_j - \overline{Y})^2$$

Making this substitution into the numerator of SS_ψ, we have

$$SS_\psi = \left[\sum_{j=1}^{a} n_j(\overline{Y}_j - \overline{Y})^2\right]^2 \bigg/ \sum_{j=1}^{a} n_j(\overline{Y}_j - \overline{Y})^2$$

$$= \sum_{j=1}^{a} n_j(\overline{Y}_j - \overline{Y})^2$$

$$= SS_B$$

9. See Hochberg and Tamhane (1987) for a review of these studies. However, Kaiser and Bowden (1983) found that the Brown–Forsythe procedure can in some situations produce too many Type I errors. They propose multiplying the Brown–Forsythe critical value by the term $(1 + (a - 2)/df)$, where df is the denominator degrees of freedom.

CHAPTER 6

1. To see that $\sum_{j=1}^{a} c_j \sum_{i=1}^{n_j}(Y_{ij} - \overline{Y})$ can be reduced to $\sum_{j=1}^{a} c_j n_j \overline{Y}_j$, notice that the term $\sum_{i=1}^{n_j}(Y_{ij} - \overline{Y})$ can be simplified as follows:

$$\sum_{i=1}^{n_j}(Y_{ij} - \overline{Y}) = \sum_{i=1}^{n_j} Y_{ij} - \sum_{i=1}^{n_j} \overline{Y}$$

$$= n_j \overline{Y}_j - n_j \overline{Y}$$

Substituting this expression into the numerator of $\hat{\beta}_1$ results in the following new expression for the numerator:

$$\sum_{j=1}^{a} c_j \sum_{i=1}^{n_j}(Y_{ij} - \overline{Y}) = \sum_{j=1}^{a} c_j(n_j \overline{Y}_j - n_j \overline{Y})$$

$$= \sum_{j=1}^{a} c_j n_j \overline{Y}_j - \sum_{j=1}^{a} c_j n_j \overline{Y}$$

$$= \sum_{j=1}^{a} c_j n_j \overline{Y}_j - \left(\overline{Y}\sum_{j=1}^{a} c_j n_j\right)$$

However, $\sum_{j=1}^{a} c_j n_j = 0$ because c_j is defined to be $X_j - \overline{X}$ and

$$\sum_{j=1}^{a} n_j(X_j - \overline{X}) = 0$$

2. See Morrison (1983, p. 10).

3. The expression we show here differs from the expression we developed in Chapter 4 only in that the new expression reflects the rescaling of coefficients necessary to convert from $\hat{\psi}$ to $\hat{\beta}_1$. Specifically, Equation 7 shows that this rescaling involves dividing each coefficient of $\hat{\psi}$ by $\sum c_j^2$ in order to represent the estimated slope. However, this newly scaled contrast has a different standard error from the original $\hat{\psi}$. In order to calculate the new standard error, we must divide the original standard error by the common divisor $\sum c_j^2$. Notice that this is precisely the additional term that appears in Equation 12.

4. The least squares estimate of 2.3 is simply a weighted average of the sample differences of 4, 2, and 1. In other words, the logic behind the estimated slope here suggests that the slope of the "best" straight line is just an average of the slopes of the individual line segments. For example, with equal n and equal spacing of one unit on X and with four levels of the quantitative factor, the estimated slope is given by

$$\hat{\beta}_1 = -.3\overline{Y}_1 - .1\overline{Y}_2 + .1\overline{Y}_3 + .3\overline{Y}_4.$$

If we let $d_1 = \overline{Y}_2 - \overline{Y}_1, d_2 = \overline{Y}_3 - \overline{Y}_2$, and $d_3 = \overline{Y}_4 - \overline{Y}_3$ represent the differences between mean scores on adjacent levels of the factor, the estimated slope turns out to be

$$\hat{\beta}_1 = .3d_1 + .4d_2 + .3d_3$$

which is just a weighted average of the three d terms. This conceptualization is also helpful for understanding the meaning of the estimated value of the slope in the presence of significant nonlinear trends. From this perspective, the slope estimate is a weighted average of the individual slopes between adjacent levels of the factor.

5. We could multiply all coefficients by -1, which would not change the meaning of the contrast but would produce an inverted Ushape, instead of a U-shaped curve.

6. Alternatively, we can arrive at these same predicted values by using the following equation:

$$\hat{Y}_{ij} = \overline{Y} + \left[\frac{\hat{\psi}_{\text{linear}}}{\sum\limits_{j=1}^{a} c_{j(\text{linear})}^2} \right] c_{j(\text{linear})}$$

where the $c_{j(\text{linear})}$ coefficients come from Appendix Table A.10. For our data, $\hat{\psi}_{\text{linear}} = 23$ and $\sum_{j=1}^{a} c_{j(\text{linear})}^2 = 20$ from earlier calculations shown in Table 6.2. Also, $\overline{Y} = 6.25$. Substituting these values into the equation above yields

$$\hat{Y}_{ij} = 6.25 + (23/20)c_{j(\text{linear})}$$

To get predicted scores, $c_{j(\text{linear})}$ values from Appendix Table A.10 are simply substituted into the equation. For our data, the following values are obtained: $\hat{Y}_{i1} = 2.8$, $\hat{Y}_{i2} = 5.1$, $\hat{Y}_{i3} = 7.4$, and $\hat{Y}_{i4} = 9.7$. It is easily verified that these predicted scores are identical to those obtained from using the equation of the best-fitting straight line,

$$\hat{Y}_{ij} = 0.50 + 2.3X_j$$

A similar approach can be used to obtain predicted values from models including nonlinear as well as linear terms.

7. Because of rounding error, substituting values of Time into Equation 4 produces values that are not exactly equal to 2, 6, 8, and 9. However, with sufficient precision, the predicted scores are exactly 2, 6, 8 and 9.

8. This approach must be distinguished from an "unweighted means" analysis, where the sum of squares attributable to a contrast is based on the harmonic mean of sample sizes. The use of the harmonic mean to calculate sum of squares here is not recommended.

CHAPTER 7

1. It might seem that mathematical rather than substantive considerations are dictating how we analyze these data. This would be unfortunate because in general it is preferable to formulate substantive hypotheses, which

can be translated into statistical hypotheses. Only then does data analysis become a consideration (although as we stated in Chapter 2, all these steps, including how the data will eventually be analyzed, should be thought through prior to executing the study). However, for pedagogical purposes, it is helpful here to begin with the mathematics in order to develop an appreciation of the meaning behind the "missing" sum of squares.

2. We briefly discuss the importance of the distinction between disordinal and ordinal interactions later in the chapter. For further reading, see Cronbach and Snow (1977, p. 93), Lubin (1962), and Wilcox (1987b, pp. 208, 220–224).

3. In fact, there are some mathematical advantages to the form of the model shown in Equation 5. However, matrix algebra is required to take advantage of this formulation. Because we generally want to avoid matrix algebra in our presentation if at all possible, the model formulation of Equation 6 will be useful to us. Advanced readers are advised to consult Timm and Carlson (1975) for an exposition of ANOVA based on cell means models, such as the one shown in Equation 5.

4. For example, we could represent the interaction as γ_{jk}, in which case Equation 6 would be written as

$$Y_{ijk} = \mu + \alpha_j + \beta_k + \gamma_{jk} + \varepsilon_{ijk}$$

This form of the model would be perfectly acceptable, but we might have difficulty reminding ourselves that γ_{jk} represented the A × B interaction. The confusion would likely increase in three-way designs (to be covered in Chapter 8), where we have to distinguish four interactions from one another: A × B, A × C, B × C, and A × B × C. As we will see in Chapter 8, the $(\alpha\beta)_{jk}$ form of notation provides mnemonic labels for the various interactions in this design.

5. As stated, these effects are obviously average effects across columns. The effect of row j may or may not be the same within each column, depending on whether the factors do not or do interact. The interpretation of marginal means in the presence of an interaction is sometimes problematic. We will discuss this issue later in the chapter.

6. For technical reasons that are beyond the scope of this book, it is actually preferable to regard the constraint that $\sum_{j=1}^{a} \alpha_j = 0$ as the reason α_j equals the difference $\mu_j - \mu$. In other words, the constraint results in the meaning, instead of the meaning leading to the constraint, as we have presented it.

7. We do not prove that these estimates are least-squares estimates. Instead, we simply provide an intuitive justification by reminding you that the sample mean is a least-squares estimator of a population mean.

8. As discussed in Chapter 5, the definition of a family is somewhat arbitrary, just as is the decision to set α at .05 in the first place. However, it generally seems reasonable to perform three tests with an α of .05 for each test in the factorial design because of the logical structure created by crossing two factors with one another. Of course, we could reduce Type I errors by choosing α_{EW} instead of α_{FW} to equal .05. However, in doing so, we would inevitably reduce the power to detect true effects. As we said in Chapter 5, ultimately these issues boil down to a trade-off between Type I and Type II errors.

9. As discussed in Chapter 5, we would typically want to use Tukey's WSD to control α_{FW} if we are testing all pairwise comparisons or if we decided to test this particular pairwise comparison after having examined the data.

10. The marginal means are particularly misleading when the interaction is disordinal but can also be regarded as misleading even for an ordinal interaction. For example, consider the following cell means in a 2 × 2 design: $\overline{Y}_{11} = 50$, $\overline{Y}_{12} = 66$, $\overline{Y}_{21} = 80$, and $\overline{Y}_{22} = 74$, where as usual the first subscript refers to levels of A and the second subscript refers to levels of B. The marginal means for A are $\overline{Y}_{1.} = 58$ and $\overline{Y}_{2.} = 77$, implying that A_2 is 19 points "better" (on the average) than A_1. For these data, it is true that A_2 is better than A_1 regardless of the level of B, but the difference is 30 points at B_1 and only 8 points at B_2. When A_2 is consistently better (or worse) than A_1 regardless of B, the interaction is ordinal for the A factor. In this situation, the marginal means at least maintain the correct rank ordering of cell means. However, even here, it may be misleading to say that A_2 is 19 points better than A_1. What happens if we consider the marginal means for B? They are $\overline{Y}_{.1} = 65$ and $\overline{Y}_{.2} = 70$, so B_2 is 5 points better (on the average) than B_1. However, at the second level of A, B_2 is actually 6 points worse than B_1. The average value of 5 comes from the average of -6 and $+16$. This inconsistency in the sign of the simple effects of B at specific levels of A implies a disordinal interaction for the B factor. The marginal mean difference of $+5$ in favor of B_2 is especially misleading here, even though $+5$ is the average advantage of B_2 over B_1, just as $+19$ was the average advantage of A_2 over A_1.

11. Notice, however, that the questions being addressed are not literally the same. For example, Dr. Multiple's test of biofeedback effects averages over the three types of drugs. Dr. Single's test is more likely to assess the biofeedback effect in the presence of a single drug because the one-factor design by definition does not include type of drug as a factor.

12. Some individuals would argue that a significance test is not needed here because we are studying the entire population. In other words, the sample is the population, so we do not need a significance test to tell us whether

there is a "true" difference. However, as Beaton (1978), Freedman and Lane (1983), and McCabe (1980) argue, a randomization test could be used in this type of situation to assess how unusual the observed salary difference is, if in fact salaries have been randomly assigned without regard to an employee's gender. As discussed in Chapter 2, ANOVA significance levels usually closely approximate significance levels from randomization tests. Thus, the ANOVA may be quite useful to help us decide whether a particular pay disparity simply reflects natural variation or is truly gender-related.

13. Another method for taking educational attainment into account is analysis of covariance. As we will see in Chapter 9, analysis of covariance is most appropriate when the variable to be taken into account is continuous rather than discrete.

14. The harmonic mean can be thought of as an "effective" sample size. This concept can be illustrated most easily in the case of two groups, whose means (i.e., arithmetic means) are to be compared. For example, suppose we have a sample of 10 observations in group 1 and 40 observations in group 2. The variance of the difference in sample means $\overline{Y}_1 - \overline{Y}_2$ is given by

$$\text{Var}(\overline{Y}_1 - \overline{Y}_2) = \frac{\sigma_1^2}{n_1} + \frac{\sigma_2^2}{n_2}$$

With homogeneity of variance, this expression becomes

$$\text{Var}(\overline{Y}_1 - \overline{Y}_2) = \sigma^2 \left(\frac{1}{n_1} + \frac{1}{n_2} \right)$$

Substituting $n_1 = 10$ and $n_2 = 40$, we find that

$$\text{Var}(\overline{Y}_1 - \overline{Y}_2) = \sigma^2 \left(\frac{1}{10} + \frac{1}{40} \right) = 0.125\sigma^2.$$

Are samples of sizes 10 and 40 as good as two samples each of size 25? After all, 25 is the "average" (i.e., arithmetic mean) of 10 and 40. However, the variance of $\overline{Y}_1 - \overline{Y}_2$ for $n_1 = n_2 = 25$ equals

$$\text{Var}(\overline{Y}_1 - \overline{Y}_2) = \sigma^2 \left(\frac{1}{25} + \frac{1}{25} \right) = 0.080\sigma^2$$

so two samples of size 25 provide a more precise estimate of $\overline{Y}_1 - \overline{Y}_2$ than do samples of sizes 10 and 40. Thus, the "effective" n of $n_1 = 10$ and $n_2 = 40$ is something less than 25. To find out how much less, we can use the harmonic mean of 10 and 40:

$$\tilde{n} = 2/(1/10 + 1/40) = 16$$

Now, the variance of $\overline{Y}_1 - \overline{Y}_2$ for $n_1 = n_2 = 16$ equals

$$\text{Var}(\overline{Y}_1 - \overline{Y}_2) = \sigma^2 \left(\frac{1}{16} + \frac{1}{16} \right) = 0.125\sigma^2,$$

which equals the variance of $\overline{Y}_1 - \overline{Y}_2$ for samples of 10 and 40. Thus, two samples of size 10 and 40 provide the same precision as equal size samples of 16. In this sense, the harmonic mean of sample sizes can be thought of as an "effective" sample size.

15. We could just as easily have used coefficients of 1, 1, −1, and −1, instead of .5, .5, −.5, and −.5. As we saw in Chapter 4, multiplying each coefficient by a constant does not change the sum of squares for the contrast. We have chosen to use coefficients of .5 and −.5 here because the value of this contrast equals the difference in the row marginal means:

$$\begin{aligned} \psi &= .5\mu_{11} + .5\mu_{12} - .5\mu_{21} - .5\mu_{22} \\ &= .5(\mu_{11} + \mu_{12}) - .5(\mu_{21} + \mu_{22}) \\ &= \mu_{1.} - \mu_{2.} \end{aligned}$$

Thus, this choice of coefficients makes the numerical value of the contrast easy to interpret.

16. In reality, Type I sums of squares are calculated in a hierarchical (i.e., sequential) manner, whereby effects are added to the model one at a time. We are assuming here that the A main effect is the first term to be entered into the model.

17. There is also a Type IV sum of squares, but it is identical to Type III, unless one or more cells in the design are missing, that is, unless there are no observations in one or more cells.

18. The reason for these peculiar looking weights is actually very straightforward. The weight for $\overline{Y}_{11} - \overline{Y}_{21}$, namely $n_{11}n_{21}/n_{+1}$, is half the harmonic mean of n_{11} and n_{21}. Similarly, the weight for $\overline{Y}_{12} - \overline{Y}_{22}$, namely $n_{12}n_{22}/n_{+2}$, is half the harmonic mean of n_{12} and n_{22}. Thus, the columns are weighted in proportion to the harmonic mean of the sample sizes in the columns, which implies that each column is being weighted by its "effective" sample size (see Note 14). In this manner, the most precise estimates receive the most weight.

19. Alternatively, models can be formulated in terms of multiple regression. Dummy variables can be created to represent group membership. The regression model for the full model of Equation 6 has $ab - 1$ predictor variables, while the restricted model has $a + b - 2$ predictors (excluding the intercept, in both cases). The difference in error sums of squares then equals

$$E_R - E_F = SS_{total}\left(R^2_{Full} - R^2_{Restricted}\right),$$

where R^2_{Full} and $R^2_{Restricted}$ are the squared multiple correlations for the full and restricted models, respectively. For additional details, see Cohen and Cohen (1983, pp. 335–345); Kirk (1982, pp. 401–422); Kleinbaum, Kupper, and Muller (1988, pp. 457–473); and Pedhazur (1982, pp. 371–387).

20. This statement is true for the Type I sum of squares when the interaction term is the last term to enter the model in the hierarchical sequence, as it usually is.

21. Searle (1987, p. 90) actually writes $E_R - E_F$ as

$$SS_A = \sum_i w_i \left(\overline{Y}_{i.(U)} - \sum_i w_i \overline{Y}_{i.(U)} \Big/ \sum_i w_i\right)^2$$

where

$$1/w_i = (1/b^2)\sum_j (1/n_{ij})$$

However, simple algebra shows that this expression is equivalent to our Equation 68.

22. Remember that a "Type II error" is failing to reject a null hypothesis when it is false. Thus, the meaning of "Type II" here is unrelated to the meaning of "Type II" as applied to sums of squares. Instead, remember that Type II error is related to power. Specifically, power equals 1.0 minus the probability of a Type II error. Thus, the problem here can be thought of as failing to detect the interaction because of insufficient power.

23. However, there is almost always an even greater advantage to forming the blocks prior to assigning subjects to treatments. Both forms of blocking are discussed in greater detail in Chapter 9.

24. For example, "Type II" marginal means can be found easily using PROC GLM in SAS. The MODEL statement should include both main effects, but not the interaction term. The MODEL statement is then followed by an LSMEANS statement that also includes only the main effects.

CHAPTER 8

1. As in the two-way design of Chapter 7, there are also abc independent parameters in the full model of the form given by Equation 2. Although the total number of parameters in this form of the model exceeds abc, they are not all independent of each other. It can be demonstrated just as we did in Chapter 7 that certain constraints must apply to these parameters, reducing the number of independent parameters to abc.

2. Strictly speaking, although this is a logical inference to apply to the population, tests of simple interaction effects of biofeedback × drug within each level of the diet factor could be nonsignificant, both for diet absent and for diet present. Such an occurrence is analogous to finding omnibus significance in a one-way design, yet failing to detect any pairwise differences between groups. For further discussion of this general point, see Levin and Marascuilo (1972).

3. In reality, we might want to test either the effect of biofeedback at each level of the drug factor or the drug effect at each level of biofeedback. In some situations, only one of these two effects will be of theoretical interest, and only it should be tested. However, because the biofeedback and drug factors have been found to interact here, it is important to realize that we would generally want to interpret simple effects instead of main effects, regardless of whether we decide to test both of the effects or only one effect.

4. In fact, as discussed in Chapter 5, if we were interested solely in pairwise comparisons, it would be unnecessary to perform the omnibus test of drug differences first. Instead, we could simply use Tukey's WSD to control the α_{FW} level and skip the omnibus test entirely.

5. These estimates are calculated in the following manner:

$$\widehat{(\alpha\beta)}_{11} = \overline{Y}_{11.} - \overline{Y}_{1..} - \overline{Y}_{.1.} + \overline{Y}_{...}$$
$$= 168.50 - 179.17 - 174.50 + 184.50$$
$$= 0.67$$

$$\widehat{(\alpha\gamma)}_{12} = Y_{1.2} - \overline{Y}_{1..} - \overline{Y}_{..2} + \overline{Y}_{...}$$
$$= 171.33 - 179.17 - 176.00 + 184.50$$
$$= 0.67$$

$$\widehat{(\beta\gamma)}_{12} = Y_{.12} - \overline{Y}_{.1.} - \overline{Y}_{..2} + \overline{Y}_{...}$$
$$= 171.00 - 174.50 - 176.00 + 184.50$$
$$= 5.00$$

$$\widehat{(\alpha\beta\gamma)}_{112} = Y_{112} - \overline{Y}_{11.} - \overline{Y}_{1.2} - \overline{Y}_{.12} + \overline{Y}_{1..} + \overline{Y}_{.1.} + \overline{Y}_{..2} - \overline{Y}_{...}$$
$$= 169.00 - 168.50 - 171.33 - 171.00 + 179.17 + 174.50 + 176.00 - 184.50$$
$$= 3.33$$

6. It might also be assumed that all higher-order effects are zero, whether or not they involve A. In this example, then, the B × C interaction might also be omitted from both the full and the restricted models. For further discussion of what effects to omit from both models, see Appelbaum and Cramer (1974).

CHAPTER 9

1. The question is sometimes raised if one can make different variables commensurate by transforming them to z scores. Doing so would result in both variables being in standard deviation units, and so the new variables would be commensurate by our definition. However, if your interest is in determining if a group of subjects is at the same level on the two measures, as in a matched-pairs t test, transforming to z scores is pointless because you can know in advance that the mean z score must be zero (for both variables). What is useful in some situations is to express two variables in terms of standard deviations away from the mean of a normative group. For example, in a study of brain-damaged patients, one might express their performance on two different measures—for example, finger tapping and grip strength—in terms of z-score units away from the mean of normal adults, and then do a matched-pairs t to determine on which test the extent of impairment is greater.

2. Most texts use deviation scores on the covariate $X_{ij} - \overline{X}$, rather than X_{ij}, in their models. The principal results in ANCOVA in terms of significance tests and the estimates of α_j and β are identical whether raw or deviation score forms of X are used. Using deviation scores has the advantage of resulting in μ being the grand mean on the dependent variable, as in the other models we have treated, instead of the intercept of a regression line (in the restricted model) or the mean of the intercepts of the regression lines (in the full model). However, we prefer to use the raw-score form of X to underscore that ANCOVA and its extensions involve the comparison of regression lines and that an estimate of performance under a particular treatment can be made at any point on the X dimension. This becomes more important when we generalize the model to allow for heterogeneous regressions (see the chapter extension).

3. This is clearly a smaller data set than you would want to use ANCOVA on in practice. However, because the computations are somewhat more involved than previous techniques we have considered, we use a miniscule data set with simple numerical solutions so that the logic of the procedure will not be obscured by messy arithmetic.

4. We are rather guarded about what you can conclude from an ANCOVA in such a quasi-experimental situation because of the implicit causal model underlying the conditional assertion you would be tempted to make–for example, "if the SES of HeadStart children were increased, then their reading achievement will increase." It may be that the causal variable related to SES is the number of books in the home and parental attitude toward reading. If one were to increase SES without affecting these other variables, then reading achievement might not change. See the illuminating discussion of this problem by Meehl (1971) and also our other cautions below, for example, "Lack of Independence of the Treatment and Covariate."

5. Although the conclusion that $\beta_Q = 0$ does not necessarily eliminate all possibility of nonlinearity (because higher-order trends could be present even though a quadratic trend is not), for most practical purposes such a test suffices.

6. Perhaps a few words are in order about how this restricted randomization method might be implemented in practice and how it is related to some other similar procedures. To begin, it is useful to adopt terminology that has largely arisen in the clinical trials literature of medical research, where a distinction is made between "blocking" and "stratification." As Matthews (2000) states, blocking in this literature usually refers specifically to methods of controlling group size. In other words, blocking guarantees that the number of subjects in a treatment group will exactly equal the number in a control group, assuming that is our goal. Stratification, on the other hand, refers to methods for controlling group composition. By stratifying on a comcomitant variable when subjects are assigned to condition, a researcher can influence the extent to which treatment and control groups are composed of individuals of comparable ages. This distinction between blocking and stratification points out that they address somewhat different goals, and in fact we can incorporate either or both into an assignment plan.

While we have touted the benefits of random assignment to conditions, particularly in Chapter 2, it should be acknowledged that simple random assignment can lead to rather unbalanced assignments to conditions, particularly when small numbers of subjects are involved. In designs that do not involve blocking, usually the number of subjects to be assigned to conditions will be sufficiently large that the chances of a clear imbalance in numbers of subjects in each condition are not great. For example, if there were two treatment conditions and a simple random assignment procedure such as flipping a coin were used, the chances that 2/3 or more of the subjects would end up in either condition is only about .12 when the total N is 27, but it increases to .51 when N is 9, and it is certain to occur if N is only 3. When one is making assignments within a homogeneous block of subjects, as in a randomized block or stratified design, the numbers can be quite small because assignments are made separately within each category of subjects. Each block then can be thought of as a separate experiment. To illustrate the difficulties that can arise, Efron (1971) describes an actual experiment using simple random assignment in a test of a treatment of Hodgkin's disease, where in one block 7 subjects were assigned to the treatment and 2 to the control, clearly an undesirable degree of inequality of sample sizes.

The simplest way of assuring a balanced design is just to alternate treatments; for example, the first subject might be assigned to treatment A, the next to treatment B, the third to A, the fourth to B, etc. One of the many difficulties of such a rule is that the experimenter may be tempted to bias the experiment by accepting or excluding potential subjects based on the knowledge of what the next treatment assignment will be, so as to have more promising subjects go into the treatment condition the experimenter hopes to validate. The restricted randomization procedure discussed in the text sidesteps this problem to some extent, but not entirely. For example, if there were 8 subjects in each block and 2 conditions, one would choose 4 at random for condition 1 with the remainder going to condition 2, with each of the $_8C_4$ combinations being equally likely to be assigned to each condition. Only when one got close to the last subject in a block would assignments be determined.

The procedure described in the text and elaborated above is sometimes referred to as a permuted block design (Matts & Lachin, 1988). In a case involving $a > 2$ treatment conditions, the simplest approach would be to have each block consist of only a subjects, and assignments then would be made by randomly choosing one of the $a!$ possible permutations of the numbers 1 through a as the assignments to use for each block of subjects. Such assignment procedures are adequate for most randomized block designs. Computerized routines such as Proc Plan in SAS can be used to generate the permutations of treatment assignments for each block. One of the attractive features of this permuted block assignment strategy is that it can readily be extended to several control or blocking factors. Within each combination of levels of these control factors, assignments are made in the fashion described to assure that each block of a successive subjects within that category has one subject assigned to each condition.

In situations where there is concern about the fact that the assignment of the last subject within a block could be determined and experimenters who are not blind to past assignments of subjects to conditions might try to bias entry of succeeding subjects based on knowing which treatment the next subject will be assigned to, one might opt for one of a class of "biased coin" assignment procedures (Efron, 1971). In the biased coin approach, which is easiest to conceptualize when assignments are being made to either a treatment or a control condition, each subject's assignment is decided by the flip of a coin, but whenever the numbers of subjects assigned so far to the two conditions differ, the coin is biased in favor of whichever condition has had fewer subjects assigned to it to date.

A variation on the biased coin procedure that has been gaining in popularity in the addictions literature is known as urn randomization (Stout, Wirtz, Carbonari, & Del Boca, 1994; Wei, 1977). This is something of a compromise between a regular biased coin procedure and a permuted block design. In the urn randomization method, the probability of assignments to conditions are continually updated with each successive subject's assignment. The regular biased coin keeps the probability of assignment to a condition fixed at say 2/3 whenever that condition has fewer subjects, whether the imbalance across conditions in subjects assigned to date is 17 vs. 18, or 0 vs. 2. In the urn randomization procedure, the extent of bias in the urns used to make assignments reflects the extent of imbalance to date in the assignments. Because of the need to continually track all assignments, this procedure is harder to implement than others, and requires either special software or specially trained staff (cf. Stout et al., 1994).

Permuted block procedures are fine for most randomized block designs. In special circumstances, such as when one wants no assignments to be deterministic or when there are a larger number of control factors than can be accomodated in a permuted blocks design without having many categories with very few subjects, options like the urn randomization procedure may be worth the additional trouble. Friedman, Furberg, and DeMets (1998) and Matthews (2000) describe yet another method known as minimization that is especially well suited for addressing the simultaneous goals of blocking and stratification in the presence of multiple concomitant variables.

7. A reviewer notes that these rather contrived data suggest an unrealistically consistent deterioration of motor control with age. (We readily agree that people, particularly professors, do not pass on so predictably!) However, such data allow us to illustrate the statistical loss of sensitivity associated with blocking. Admittedly this effect may be somewhat less pronounced when blocking is used with more realistic data.

CHAPTER 9: EXTENSION

1. Both E_R and E_F can be viewed as binomials of the form $(p - q)^2$. When these are expanded the p^2 terms are the same for E_R and E_F and so drop out. The cross-product terms, which are of the form $-2pq$, as frequently is the case in expressions for sums of squares, can be rewritten and shown to be a multiple of the final term, that is, $-2pq = -2q^2$. Thus, the difference between E_R and E_F can be expressed as the difference between the q^2 terms, and Equation E.7 is one way of writing this difference.

2. With real data, one would also certainly want to analyze the data by computer. Fortunately, most computer packages can carry out such a test of heterogeneity of regression as a test of an interaction between a factor and a covariate, though it may not be immediately obvious how to do so in some "point and click" versions of programs. For example, in the current version of SPSS, to test for heterogeneity of regression in the Univariate version of the General Linear Model analysis procedure, in addition to specifying Y as the dependent variable, Group as the fixed factor, and X as the covariate on the main screen, one would need to be specific about the particular model to test. This is done by clicking the "Model" button and then choosing "Custom" under "Specify Model." To specify the group as an effect to be tested, one would click on "group(F)" under "Factors & Covariates" and then click ▸ to make it appear in the Model box, and to specify the test of the covariate one would similarly highlight "$x(C)$" and then click ▸ to have this also listed in the model box. To get the critical test of heterogeneity of regression, one needs to simultaneously highlight both "group(F)" and "$x(C)$" by holding down the Ctrl key and clicking each of these terms. The default option of "Interaction" should be showing in the Build Terms box, and if not should be selected from the pull down menu. Clicking ▸ should make "group*x" appear in the Model box. Alternatively one could specify the test by entering the following commands in the syntax window:

```
UNIANOVA
    y BY group WITH x
    /METHOD = SSTYPE(3)
    /INTERCEPT = INCLUDE
    /PRINT = DESCRIPTIVE PARAMETER
    /CRITERIA = ALPHA(.05)
    /DESIGN = group x group*x.
```

If one is using a program that does not permit one to test such interactions of a discrete variable (group) and a continuous variable (x), it is possible to get carry out the test of heterogeneity of regression indirectly by taking the SS error from a standard ANCOVA to use as the value of E_R and then compute E_F as the sum of the separate SS residual values obtained by doing a regression of the dependent variable on the covariate separately within each group. While this latter procedure involves a few hand calculations, it has the advantage of making the different regression equations obvious (such as those shown at the bottom of Table 9E.3), with the varying values of the estimates of the slopes being of most interest.

3. The proof makes use of the fact that both $\overline{Y}$ and b can be expressed as linear combinations of the Y_i and that the covariance of $\overline{Y}$ and b can be shown to be zero.

4. This is a legitimate rewriting of the definitional formula for the slope because $\sum(X_i - \overline{X})(Y_i + \overline{Y}) = \sum(X_i - \overline{X})Y_i$. This in turn is true because $\sum(X_i - \overline{X})(Y_i - \overline{Y}) = \sum(X_i - \overline{X})Y_i - \sum(X_i - \overline{X})\overline{Y}$, but $\sum(X_i - \overline{X})\overline{Y} = \overline{Y}\sum(X_i - \overline{X}) = 0$ because the sum of the deviations from the mean must equal zero. Thus, we have

$$b = \frac{\sum(X_i - \overline{X})Y_i}{\sum(X_i - \overline{X})^2}$$

which may be rewritten

$$b = \sum \frac{X_i - \overline{X}}{\sum(X_i - \overline{X})^2} Y_i$$

CHAPTER 10

1. The only difference in the one-way case with unequal n is that the multiplier of σ_α^2 will be somewhat less than the mean of the n_js. In general, in a one-way random-effects design, $\mathscr{E}(MS_\alpha) = \mathscr{E}[(E_R - E_F)/(df_R - df_F)] = \sigma_\varepsilon^2 + n'\sigma_\alpha^2$, where $n' = [1/(a-1)][\sum n_i - (\sum n_i^2/\sum n_i)]$. If all $n_j = n$, then $n' = n$, else $0 < n' < \overline{n}$.

2. The precise values of the coefficients can differ slightly from those given for specific effects under certain assumptions but this will not really concern us. The values given are correct for the situation where the size of the population of levels for the random effect is assumed to be infinitely large. This is the usual case. In the situation where there is a known finite number of levels of the random factor, the exact multiplier of particular variance components can include a correction factor that is inversely related to the proportion of the possible levels included in the actual study. To illustrate, in the hypothetical example where a sample of 3 clinical trainees out of a population of 18 was included in a study, the correction factor is $1 - 3/18 = 5/6$. However, even in this situation the correction factor is used only to adjust the multiplier of the interaction component when it appears in the expression for the expected mean square for some other effect. So in the clinical trainee example the expected mean square for the main effect of the fixed factor would actually include a $\sigma_{\alpha\beta}^2$ term with a coefficient of $(5/6)n$ instead of n. For details, see Kirk (1995, pp. 402–405). But this technicality does not affect the decision about which term should be used as the denominator error term, which is our primary concern.

3. In fact, both SPSS and SAS generate $\mathscr{E}(MS)$ for the mixed design case based on a different set of assumptions, referred to as the "unrestricted model for mixed interaction terms". That is, their approach does *not* require the restriction (or what we have referred to as elsewhere in the text as a side condition, cf. Chapter 3) that the interaction effects add to 0 across the levels of the fixed factor. Such an approach avoids the mathematical complication of the random interaction terms tending to be negatively correlated. That is, in our approach, which is the one historically used in standard sources in psychology (such as Kirk, 1995) and elsewhere (e.g., Neter, Wasserman, & Kutner, 1985), the fact that interaction effects must sum to zero means that if you know some are positive this implies that others will be negative and vice versa. For example, in our clinical trainee example, if we know the interaction effects for trainee g are 0 and $+3$ for the Psychodynamic and Behavioral conditions, then that for the Rogerian condition must be -3, whereas for trainee r the fact that the first two interaction effects are nonnegative means the last has to be negative.

   The basic problem with the unrestricted approach is that avoiding the negatively correlated interaction terms is purchased at the cost of a considerable loss of meaning of the test of the main effect of the random factor. Not requiring the interaction effects to sum to zero across levels of the fixed factor implies that the particular random interaction effects selected in any study will affect the marginal means for the random factor as well as those for the fixed factor. The theoretical implication of this unrestricted approach is that the expected mean square for the random factor will include a term for the interaction as well as for the error and the random factor, e.g. the expected mean square for the trainee factor would include components for trainee, error *and* interaction. The practical implication of this approach is that the test of the main effect of the random factor would need to use the mean square for interaction as the denominator error term.

We reject the unrestricted approach however because the null hypothesis being tested in the test of the random factor in such an approach is no longer that the true marginal means are equal across the levels of the random factor. Referring again to our example, if the interaction effects don't even have to sum to zero across the three methods for a particular trainee, then the true trainee effects could be zero yet the marginal mean for different trainees might differ–one trainee might have a high marginal mean because all her interaction effects were positive and another trainee's marginal mean might be quite low because he had all negative interaction "effects." This flies in the face not only of the meaning of an interaction but of the very idea of any effect as a departure from some baseline value. Throughout this book, effects are treated like any set of deviations from a mean, which are required to sum to zero when all such effects are considered.

We want a conclusion of no main effect of a random factor to mean that the population marginal means for the levels of that factor are equal. If one takes the default tests that SPSS gives you when you specify one factor fixed and one factor random, this standard meaning of the null hypothesis no longer applies to the test of the random factor in a mixed design. For an extended discussion of the issues involved and a clearly developed numerical example, see Cobb (1997, pp. 371–381).

4. As we noted in Ch. 3, R^2 is sometimes called "eta squared" and not surprisingly partial R^2 is sometimes called "partial eta squared." SPSS has an option in its Univariate version of the General Linear Model for users to request estimates of effect size, which in version 10 were labeled "Eta Squared" and in version 11 were labeled "Partial Eta Squared." Despite the varying labels, they were computed identically, but in two-factor designs with a random factor present, they are computed differently than we are recommending. In particular, SPSS computes a partial eta squared by including in the denominator not MS_W but the mean square used in the denominator to test the current effect. So, for example, in the current example with the ACT training program, because the test of Method uses the Method by School interaction as its error term, the mean square for this interaction is used by SPSS in computing its partial eta squared. This is in essence ignoring the variability associated with the individuals taking the test. We will argue later that the School factor might for some purposes be regarded as extrinsic to the Methods effect, that is, arguably not relevant to assessing the proportion of variance that would be accounted for by Methods. However, it does not seem logical to ignore the variability associated with individuals given it is individuals and not schools who take the ACT. Thus, the SPSS partial eta squared statistics must be interpreted with considerable caution as they may be ignoring variability that should be considered in evaluating effects.

5. Why this should be called an "intraclass correlation" may seem a bit obscure because we are used to thinking of squared correlations as indicating proportions of variance accounted for. However, the intraclass correlation is not the correlation between a predictor variable and the dependent variable but reflects the extent to which members of the same group or class tend to act alike–the greater the group or class effect, the greater the similarity of members within a group relative to cross-group similarity. In fact, the intraclass correlation can be defined as the ordinary correlation expected over replications of a study between any two arbitrarily selected observations Y_{ij} and $Y_{i,j}$ (where $i \neq i'$) from the same group (i.e., both from group j) (cf. Scheffé, 1959, p. 223). The rationale leading to the intraclass correlation, which was developed before Fisher's analysis of variance but has come to be used to described the effects of random factors in ANOVA, is clearly explained by Snedecor and Cochran (1980, p. 243ff.). Intraclass correlations also have applications in studies of reliability where the classes are defined as repeated observations on the same individual, and where the index may be taken to indicate the extent of reliability or reproducability of a measure (cf. Rosner, 1995, p. 517ff.; Cicchetti, 1994). Those intraclass correlations are denoted "ICC" (see p. 563ff.; cf. Bird, 2002; McGraw & Wong, 1996), but here we use ρ_I, a Greek letter (cf., Kirk, 1995; Scheffé, 1959; Winer, Brown, & Michels, 1991, p. 126) to suggest that it is a population parameter to be estimated, and subscripted by "I" to indicate this is an intraclass correlation rather than a correlation of Y with another variable.

6. Winer et al. (1991, p. 97) discuss a modification of this formula that corrects for bias. Its use is recommended when sample sizes are small. However, when the total N is reasonably large, say 30 or more, the adjustment will not be very substantial. For example, in the current numerical example, where $N = 60$, the corrected estimate of the square of f_{rand} would be .191 instead of .200.

7. When the nested factor is a fixed factor, it is not necessary that the number of levels per nest or that the number of observations per cell be held constant. Unbiased estimates of effects and exact tests can be obtained. However, in the more typical case when the nested factor is random, having numbers of levels of the nested factor or unequal n's (which is referred to as having an "unbalanced" design) causes problems. As Neter, Wasserman, and Kutner (1985) comment, "Serious complications are encountered in the unbalanced case and no exact test

for treatment effects can be made" (p. 989). A classic discussion of alternative approaches to dealing with the problem are discussed in Searle (1971, Ch. 10 and 11). Because nested factors often occur in observational studies where there is less opportunity for control, e.g. the number of fifth grade classrooms (nested) in one school may not be the same as in another school, the messier, unbalanced situation in practice occur more often than not. An introduction to modern methods for analyzing such data is presented in Chapters 15 and 16.

8. While such tree diagrams are most useful with designs that are completely hierarchical they also can be used in a design having a mixture of nested and crossed factors. Although there is no single correct method of constructing such visual representations, our advice would be to place the factor or factors within which other factors are nested at the top of the diagram and then place the levels of the nested factor immediately below this. Any other factors that are crossed with the nested factor could then be placed at the bottom of the hierarchy. This strategy has the advantage of suggesting at the top of the diagram which effects will be made more variable by their subsuming what will usually be a random nested factor. Also, this method results in the total number of levels of the nested factor, which is sometimes a source of confusion, being enumerated just once rather than having to be listed multiple times. An example of such a diagram for a more complex design is presented in the solution to Exercise 10 at the end of the chapter.

9. Of course, a nested design will have fewer degrees of freedom than a completely crossed design where one factor has as many levels as the total number of different levels of the nested factor included in the nested design. For example, referring back to Figure 10.3 (where a nested design was seen to be equivalent to a crossed design with missing cells), if the comparison were made to a 2×4 crossed design with no missing cells, the completely crossed design would have 7 between-group degrees of freedom as opposed to just 3 between-group degrees of freedom in a nested design where the four different levels of factor B were divided up into two different nests, each of which appeared at only one level of A. Again, one has to be careful to remember that we are using b, when factor B is nested, to designate the number of levels per nest, not the total number of different levels adding across nests.

CHAPTER 11

1. Even with only six subjects, the sample correlation of 0.96 is statistically significant at the .005 level (two-tailed). Thus, we have strong evidence that the errors are correlated in the population.

2. The models may appear to be slightly different, but in fact the difference is really just notational. In Chapter 7, the full model for a two-way factorial design was written as

$$Y_{ijk} = \mu + \alpha_j + \beta_k + (\alpha\beta)_{jk} + \varepsilon_{ijk}$$

In the repeated measures design, we have

$$Y_{ij} = \mu + \alpha_j + \pi_i + (\pi\alpha)_{ij} + \varepsilon_{ij}$$

Notice that π_i (the subject effect) is analogous to β_k in the earlier model, because "subject" is now the second factor in the design. Also, we only need two subscripts now instead of three because with only one observation per cell, there is no need to allow for variation within a cell.

3. An equivalent approach would be to obtain the sum of squares for the condition effect from the difference between the sum of squared errors of the models in Equations 20 and 21:

$$Y_{ij} = \mu + \alpha_j + \pi_i + (\pi\alpha)_{ij} + \varepsilon_{ij} \qquad (20)$$

$$Y_{ij} = \mu + \pi_i + (\pi\alpha)_{ij} + \varepsilon_{ij} \qquad (21)$$

Then, from Chapter 10, the denominator sum of squares would be the difference between the sum of squared errors of the models in Equations 20 and 22:

$$Y_{ij} = \mu + \alpha_j + \pi_i + (\pi\alpha)_{ij} + \varepsilon_{ij} \qquad (20)$$

$$Y_{ij} = \mu + \alpha_j + \pi_i + \varepsilon_{ij} \qquad (22)$$

However, the resultant F value would be identical to the value obtained more simply by directly comparing the models of Equations 22 and 23 as shown in the text.

4. Consistent with the discussion in Chapter 1, the validity of this study might be strengthened if there were a second group of children with whom we were comparing this group. We will discuss analysis of data from such a design in Chapters 12 and 14.

5. In fact, the within-groups assumption is in an important sense identical to the between-groups assumption. If we rewrite Equation 22 as $Y_{ij} - \pi_i = \mu + \alpha_j + \varepsilon_{ij}$, the right-hand side of the model is the same as that for a one-way between-subjects design. Indeed, McNemar (1969) has shown that the mixed-model ANOVA produces the same results as would a between-subjects ANOVA on $Y_{ij} - \overline{Y}_{i.}$. Notice that this between-subjects ANOVA uses an adjusted score as the dependent variable. Specifically, the adjustment results from subtracting out the person (i.e., subject) effect represented by $\overline{Y}_{i.}$. However, a between-subjects ANOVA requires homogeneous variances across the treatment levels for the dependent variable. Within treatment level j, the variance of the adjusted dependent variable is given by $\mathrm{Var}(Y_{ij} - \overline{Y}_{i.}) = \sigma_{\varepsilon_j}^2 + \sigma_\pi^2 - (2/a)\sum_l \mathrm{Cov}(Y_{ij}, Y_{il})$.

   Comparison of this formula with Equation 29 of the text shows that they both involve variances and covariances. Indeed, it turns out that the treatment-difference variance of Equation 29 is equal for every pair of groups if and only if the above variance is a constant for every group. Thus, the homogeneity of treatment-difference variance assumption is equivalent to the between-subjects assumption of homogeneity of variance for the adjusted scores $Y_{ij} - \overline{Y}_{i.}$.

6. In fact, it is possible to perform a statistical test to assess the presence of differential carryover. Differential carryover is indicated when the sum of each subject's two scores in one group is different from the sum in the other group. Notice that in our example (Table 11.15), the mean sum in group 1 is only 30, whereas in group 2 it is 40. However, Brown (1980) shows that the test of differential carryover frequently lacks power, so that differential carryover may go undetected even when it exists in the population. When differential carryover does exist, an unbiased estimate of treatment effects can still be obtained by comparing scores at time 1. On this basis, we stated that our best guess is that the true treatment effect here equals 10. Although this capability offers some solace, notice that when we use only time 1 scores, we effectively have a between-subjects design, so any possible advantages of the within-subjects design have been lost.

7. The digram-balanced Latin square design provides unbiased estimates of treatment effects even in the presence of differential carryover, if carryover effects persist only into the next time point (Fleiss, 1986, p. 281). However, in much behavioral research, it is likely that carryover effects are more persistent, in which case estimates of treatment effects are again biased.

CHAPTER 12

1. Although it is usually true that analysis of two-way designs begins with tests of the main effects and interaction, an important alternative in some situations is to perform tests of planned comparisons. When the research hypotheses are sufficiently explicit, power can potentially be increased by focusing tests on these questions instead of testing more global main effects or interactions.

2. We acknowledge that even the expressions shown in Table 12.2 are laborious to calculate by hand; although we assume that most actual calculations will be left to the computer, we nevertheless believe that the expressions shown in Table 12.2 enhance understanding of the meaning of each effect in the model. It may be instructive to compare the "General Expression for SS" column in Table 12.2 to the same column in Table 8.11. The expression for each effect is the same in the two tables, except that S in Table 12.2 has replaced C in Table 8.11, and there are only three levels of summation in Table 12.2 because there is only one score per cell.

3. As in the between-subjects factorial design, we might want to qualify our interpretation of the main effects here because of the statistically significant interaction. Nevertheless, the main-effect tests are still correct tests of average differences. As in the between-subjects design, the question is, Are these averages directly interpretable when we know that the individual simple effects are different? For the current numerical example, we proceed under the assumption that marginal means are still of interest despite the significant interaction.

4. Notice that Equation 10 is of the same basic form as Equation 9. However, the b term that was included in Equation 9 does not appear in Equation 10. The reason is that the contrast in Equation 9 compares marginal means, each of which is based on nb scores, whereas the contrast in Equation 10 compares cell means, each of which is based on n scores. If the contrast in Equation 9 were rewritten in terms of individual cell means, it would be identical to Equation 10.

5. Note that although the F values are the same, the sums of the squares are not. The sums of squares computed from the data in Table 12.7 are one-half those shown in Table 12.5 because the one-way analysis for Table 12.7 does not take into account the fact that these scores are themselves means, averaged over the two levels of B. However, the same F value is obtained because the ratio of MS_A to $MS_{A \times S}$ is still the same in both cases.

6. Huynh (1978) presents a very general procedure for calculating $\hat{\varepsilon}$ and $\tilde{\varepsilon}$ in complex designs, with any combination of between-subjects and within-subjects factors. However, the procedure requires the use of matrix algebra, so we do not describe it here.

7. In fact, sequence might interact with condition, in which case a between-subjects design might be preferred. However, we continue to discuss the example as a within-subjects design.

8. Another question that may be of interest here is the extent to which scores are generalizable across raters. In other words, while the quasi-F allows for the raters factor to be random, it does not address the question of generalizability, which may be of interest in its own right. Readers interested in learning more about generalizability theory should consult Brennan (1983) and Shavelson, Webb, and Burstein (1986).

9. Of course, these two groups might differ on other variables in addition to age, in which case the Chapter 9 discussion on comparing nonequivalent groups becomes relevant.

10. Greenwald (1976) provides an interesting comparison of the ecological validity of context effects in between- and within-subjects designs. Either may be more valid than the other, depending on the nature of the factors. Readers who are faced with a choice between the two types of designs are urged to read Greenwald's article.

11. We might want to qualify our interpretation of the angle main effect because the interaction of angle and age is statistically significant. However, as we stated in Note 3, tests of comparisons of angle are still correct tests of average angle differences, where the average is calculated over the two age groups. The issue here is whether we should be describing average angle differences or angle differences within each age group (i.e., simple effects). In our opinion, the answer depends on the specific goals of the study. For the purposes of our example, we assume that average angle differences are of interest despite the statistically significant interaction.

12. A more efficient way to use $MS_{B \times S/A_j}$ is to use PROC SORT and BY commands in SAS or to use SORT CASES and SPLIT FILE in SPSS.

13. Two points are relevant here. First, it is interesting to notice that Equation 31 follows from an equality among the sums of squares:

$$\sum_{k=1}^{b} SS_{S/A \text{ at } B_k} = SS_{S/A} + SS_{B \times S/A}$$

The sum of squares for the b simple-effects tests of S/A at each level of B equals the sum of squares for the main effect of S/A plus the sum of squares for the interaction of S/A with B. Second, $MSWCELL$ can be regarded as a weighted average of $MS_{S/A}$ and $MS_{B \times S/A}$:

$$MSWCELL = \frac{(N - a)MS_{S/A} + (b - 1)(N - a)MS_{B \times S/A}}{(N - a) + (b - 1)(N - a)}$$

14. This statement assumes that the SAS analysis is conducted using the REPEATED statement in PROC GLM and that the SPSS analysis is conducted using the WSFACTORS statement in MANOVA.

15. Of course, as always, we cannot affirm the null hypothesis. That is to say, we would not want to conclude here that we have shown that there is absolutely no age difference in the angle quadratic trend. Such a conclusion would be especially misguided in our example, where the power for detecting a difference whose magnitude is of theoretical importance may be low because of the rather small sample sizes.

16. If there were an unequal number of subjects at the different levels of A, $MS_{B \times S/A}$ would be a weighted average of these four components. The weight for a component at level A_j would be equal to $(n_j - 1)/(N - a)$, where N represents the total number of subjects.

17. As we will see in Chapter 14, technically if there are b levels of the B factor, the covariance matrices that must be identical to one another have $b - 1$ rows and $b - 1$ columns, each corresponding to a degree of freedom of the B effect.

18. When one or more additional factors are random, error terms must be chosen differently to account for these additional sources of variance.

19. In fact, summing the squared errors shown in Table 12.23 produces a value of 114.97 instead of 114.88. The discrepancy is due to rounding error and could be reduced by retaining more digits in the predicted values.

CHAPTER 13

1. As in the between-subjects design, it is generally impossible prior to examining the data to formulate a single comparison that can completely account for all mean differences when there are more than 2 groups. Recall

that with a means, there are $a - 1$ degrees of freedom, and hence $a - 1$ independent ways in which means may differ. However, as in the between-subjects design, it is possible after examining the data to formulate a post hoc comparison that will completely account for all mean differences. As we will see later in the chapter, however, in the within-subjects design, the coefficients of this optimal comparison are determined not just by the sample means but also by the sample covariance matrix as well.

2. This symbol is identical to the symbol that is used to represent the absolute value of a number. Hence, it must be kept in mind whether the term inside the vertical lines is a number or a matrix. The meaning should be clear from the context and the boldface type used to represent a matrix.

3. The quantity $(a - 1)(a - 2)/2$ is the number of pairs that exist among $a - 1$ D variables. For example, when $a = 4$, there are three D variables, and $(4 - 1)(4 - 2)/2 = 3$ pairs: D_1 and D_2, D_1, and D_3, and D_2 and D_3. On the other hand, if $a = 5$, four D variables are required, and there are $(5 - 1)(5 - 2)/2 = 6$ pairs: D_1 and D_2, D_1 and D_3, D_1 and D_4, D_2 and D_3, D_2 and D_4, and D_3 and D_4.

4. The determinant of a 3×3 matrix of the form

$$\begin{vmatrix} a & d & e \\ d & b & f \\ e & f & c \end{vmatrix} = a(bc - f^2) + d(ef - cd) + e(df - be)$$

5. Because of rounding error, multiplying a number in column 1 of Table 13.14 by 24 may not exactly reproduce the corresponding number in column 2. However, any discrepancy is due to the presentation of only three decimal places for the slope values. if enough decimal places were shown, the relationship would be exact.

6. The approach we used here of calculating a regression slope for each subject and then performing an analysis on the slopes has received considerable attention in the last few years as a general methodology for handling complex problems in analyzing longitudinal data. Chapter 15 provides an introduction to this approach for analyzing longitudinal data.

7. Notice that this equality requires that the contrasts be orthonormal. When nonnormalized linear and quadratic trend variables were used, the full matrix we found had diagonal values of 32 and 44, which obviously fail to sum to 23.3333. Not only must the contrasts be normalized, but they must also form an orthogonal set for this equality to hold.

8. AVERF is an abbreviation for average F. Notice that the numerator of the mixed-model F is an average of the two diagonal elements of $\mathbf{E}^*(\mathbf{R}) - \mathbf{E}^*(\mathbf{F})$. Similarly, the denominator is an average of the diagonal elements of $\mathbf{E}^*(\mathbf{F})$ divided by $n - 1$. The mixed-model F is also an average of the F values for the individual orthonormal F values, if a pooled error term is used (we discuss the use of a pooled error term shortly).

9. For technical reasons, this statement is only approximately true. Although the numerators of the F statistics in Equations 36 and 37 are identical and the denominators have the same expected value under sphericity, the mean F values will not be literally identical, because the expected value of a ratio does not necessarily equal the ratio of the expected values. Under the null hypothesis, the expected value of an F statistic is $df_{denom}/(df_{denom} - 2)$. Thus, the expected value of the F statistic will be slightly larger for the multivariate approach than for the mixed-model approach.

10. As a technical point, it should be acknowledged that the multivariate approach requires a normality assumption that is theoretically more restrictive than the normality assumption of the mixed-model approach. Specifically, the multivariate approach assumes not only that each individual variable has a normal distribution but also that the joint distribution of the variables is multivariate normal. However, this additional assumption is unlikely to be of practical importance, both because univariate normality typically implies multivariate normality in practice and because the Type I error rate is robust to the degree of nonnormality that usually occurs in practice (see Bray & Maxwell, 1985, for a review of the robustness literature).

11. When n is less than a, the $\mathbf{E}^*(\mathbf{F})$ matrix for the full model is necessarily singular. As a result, its determinant equals zero; because the determinant appears in the denominator of the F statistic, the F is undefined in this situation.

CHAPTER 14

1. Although it is usually true that analysis of two-way designs begins with tests of the main effects and interaction, an important alternative in some situations is to perform tests of planned comparisons. When the research hypotheses are sufficiently explicit, power may be increased by focusing tests on these questions instead of testing more global main effects or interactions.

2. Although all scores are doubled, the F value is unchanged, because $s_{D_1}^2$ (in the denominator of the F) is quadrupled, exactly offsetting the quadrupling of $\overline{D}_1^2$. Thus, using coefficients of ± 1 is functionally equivalent to using coefficients of $\pm .5$.

3. As always, these comparisons must be linearly independent.

4. Of course, we must be careful not to literally accept the null hypothesis. Although the test of the noise by quadratic trend of angle component was nonsignificant, we should not conclude that this component is exactly zero in the population.

5. You should be able to convince yourself that these contrasts are indeed orthogonal, by applying the test for orthogonality that was presented in Chapter 4.

6. The data for this example were originally presented in Tables 12.7 and 12.15.

7. With unequal n, these two different definitions result in different tests of the within-subjects main effect. The general issue here is whether to perform tests of unweighted or weighted marginal means, which you may recall was an issue we discussed in considerable detail in Chapter 7. Our general preference is for tests of unweighted means; as of this writing, all major statistical packages (e.g., SAS and SPSS) produce a test of the unweighted marginal mean by default in the split-plot design. However, as we discussed in Chapter 7, there may be occasions where a test of the weighted marginal means is more appropriate. We will see later that the only difference in the tests concerns whether the sample grand mean $\overline{D}$ is calculated as an unweighted or as a weighted mean across the levels of A, the between-subjects factor.

8. Notice that with unequal n, $\overline{D}$ of Equation 45 is the weighted sample mean because the weighted sample mean is the least-squares estimator of μ in the restricted model of Equation 44.

9. With unequal n, either $\sum_{j=1}^{a} \alpha_j$ or $\sum_{j=1}^{a} n_j \alpha_j$ can be constrained to equal zero. The former occurs when μ is unweighted, and the latter occurs when μ is weighted. In addition, with either equal or unequal n, for technical reasons it may be preferable to regard the constraint that the α_j parameters sum to zero as leading to the definition that α_j equals $\mu_j - \mu$, instead of the definition leading to the constraint.

10. The estimator $\hat{\alpha}_j = \overline{D}_j - \overline{D}$ is identical to the estimator we obtained in the full model containing μ (Equation 43) because the constraint that $\sum_{j=1}^{a} \alpha_j = 0$ was also imposed in that model. Were it not for this constraint, however, we could estimate α_j with $\overline{D}_j$ in the restricted model, in which case the errors of the full and restricted models would be identical, so the comparison of models would not be meaningful. Thus, the constraint we have imposed makes it possible to compare the models meaningfully because the constrained α_j parameters have the same meaning in both models. Lunneborg and Abbott (1983, pp. 196–197) provide details of constrained least-squares estimation.

11. If an experimenter decides to test the weighted mean, then $\overline{D}$ in the numerator of Equation 49 is the sample weighted mean. Otherwise, $\overline{D}$ is the unweighted mean. As usual, with equal n, the weighted and unweighted means are identical.

12. The only exception to this statement is when the design is "doubly multivariate," meaning that more than one dependent variable exists at each and every level of the repeated factor. For example, in the perceptual study, we might have two variables, number of errors and reaction time, for each subject in all three angle conditions. We would then form one M variable for number of errors and a second M variable for reaction time. See Hertzog and Rovine (1985) for more information.

13. Although the numerator degrees of freedom are exactly what we would expect based on df_F and df_R, the denominator degrees of freedom are different. As we will see in more detail later in the chapter, denominator degrees of freedom in the multivariate approach do not always follow rules developed in the univariate case.

14. If we had unequal n, the least-squares estimates of μ_1 and μ_2 would be the weighted grand means $\overline{D}_1$ and $\overline{D}_2$. Notice that each weighted grand mean is simply the mean for that D variable averaged over all N subjects, irrespective of group membership.

15. The technical reason is that when $a = 2$, the magnitude of the interaction can be measured with a single eigenvalue. When $a > 2$, more than one eigenvalue exists, and a different form of the test statistic must be used.

16. The reason involves the matrix that results from subtracting the $E(F)$ matrix from the $E(R)$ matrix. When $a = 2$, this matrix has a rank equal to 1 (regardless of the value of b), so the matrix has only one nonzero eigenvalue. When $a > 2$ (and $b > 2$), the rank of the matrix exceeds 1, and there is more than one nonzero eigenvalue. A different form of the F test is necessary to account for these multiple nonzero eigenvalues.

17. Most multivariate statistics textbooks provide an introduction to matrix algebra, which includes coverage of matrix multiplication and the inverse of a matrix. Some examples of such books are Green (1978), Harris (1985), Marascuilo and Levin (1983), Stevens (1986), Tabachnick and Fidell (1983), and Tatsuoka (1988). For our purposes, it suffices to state that multiplying H by the inverse of T is analogous to division of ordinary numbers. The result is similar to $SS_{\text{effect}}/SS_{\text{total}}$, but the multiplication process for the two matrices is affected by the correlations among the variables. It turns out (cf. Bray & Maxwell, 1985) that the Pillai–Bartlett trace

V equals the sum of the ratios $SS_{\text{effect}}/SS_{\text{total}}$ for the s discriminant variates that can be formed. As a result, V ranges between 0 and s because we are summing s ratios, each of which is between 0 and 1. Larger values of V are associated with larger effects.

18. A complete theoretical explanation of the parameter s is beyond the scope of this book. However, s turns out to be equal to the rank of the $\mathbf{H}$ matrix (where $\mathbf{H} = \mathbf{E(R)} - \mathbf{E(F)}$), so s is the number of nonzero eigenvalues of the $\mathbf{H}$ matrix. All four multivariate test statistics are based on these eigenvalues. However, they differ in how they combine these eigenvalues; so when $s > 1$, the four test statistics are generally somewhat different. On the other hand, when $s = 1$, there is no need to combine multiple eigenvalues, and all four test statistics agree.

19. At first glance, this process of adding and subtracting matrices seems very different from what we have done before, where the error term was based on all subjects. However, in fact, the underlying logic is identical. To demonstrate this equivalence, let's compare Equations 66 and 67. One difference is that each place where $\mathbf{E(F)}_j$ appears in Equation 66, $\mathbf{E(F)}$ takes its place in Equation 67. As a consequence, denominator degrees of freedom increase from $n_j - b + 1$ to $N - a - b + 2$. In addition, there is an apparent departure from previous logic because $\mathbf{E(R)}_j$ in Equation 66 has been replaced by $\mathbf{E(F)} + \mathbf{E(R)}_j - \mathbf{E(F)}_j$ in Equation 67. To understand why the logic is in fact the same, we must understand the origin of the $\mathbf{E(R)}_j$ term in Equation 66. In fact, a more general equation can be written in terms of the $\mathbf{H}$ and $\mathbf{E}$ matrices that we discussed in connection with the Pillai–Bartlett trace statistic. For example, a general expression for an F statistic to test the effect of B at A_j could be written as

$$F = \frac{(|\mathbf{E} + \mathbf{H}| - |\mathbf{E}|)/(b - 1)}{|\mathbf{E}|/df_{\mathbf{E}}}$$

where $\mathbf{E}$ is an appropriately chosen error matrix. $\mathbf{H}$ is the hypothesis matrix, so for testing B at A_j, $\mathbf{H}$ would be given by $\mathbf{H} = \mathbf{E(R)}_j - \mathbf{E(F)}_j$. We have discussed two choices for $\mathbf{E}$. First, suppose we decide to use $\mathbf{E(F)}_j$ as our error matrix. Then, the above expression for the F statistic can be written as

$$F = \frac{\left(|\mathbf{E(F)}_j + \mathbf{E(R)}_j - \mathbf{E(F)}_j| - |\mathbf{E(F)}_j|\right)/(b - 1)}{|\mathbf{E(F)}_j|/(n_j - b + 1)}$$

However, $\mathbf{E(F)}_j + \mathbf{E(R)}_j - \mathbf{E(F)}_j$ simply equals $\mathbf{E(R)}_j$, so we can simplify this F statistic as

$$F = \frac{\left(|\mathbf{E(R)}_j| - |\mathbf{E(F)}_j|\right)/(b - 1)}{|\mathbf{E(F)}_j|/\left(n_j - b + 1\right)}$$

which is identical to Equation 66. Second, suppose that we decide to use $\mathbf{E(F)}$ as our error term. Then, the general expression for the F statistic can be written as

$$F = \frac{\left(|\mathbf{E(F)} + \mathbf{E(R)}_j - \mathbf{E(F)}_j|\right) |\mathbf{E(F)}|/(b - 1)}{|\mathbf{E(F)}|/(N - a - b + 2)}$$

No further simplification is possible, because $\mathbf{E(F)}$ and $\mathbf{E(F)}_j$ do not cancel out, unlike $\mathbf{E(F)}_j$ and $\mathbf{E(F)}_j$ when $\mathbf{E(F)}_j$ is the error matrix. As a result, we are left with the more complex expression of Equation 67. However, in fact both Equations 66 and 67 follow the same logic, and both are based on the more general expression given here in this note. For the sake of caution, we should add that even this more general expression is appropriate only when $s = 1$.

20. We should emphasize that simple-effects tests conducted with a pooled error term are not robust to violations of the homogeneity assumption regardless of which of the four multivariate test statistics is used. Indeed, because the simple-effects test is effectively performed for a one-way within-subjects design, all four test statistics yield exactly the same F value. Although there is some evidence to suggest that the Pillai–Bartlett trace statistic is generally more robust to violations of homogeneity than are the other three statistics, this finding applies only to omnibus tests, such as the A × B interaction.

21. Recall that, in general, mean square within is a weighted average of the individual $s^2_{D_{2j}}$ terms, where the weight for level j of the A factor equals $(n_j - 1)/(N - a)$.

22. For technical reasons, if $s > 1$ (as it might be for testing an interaction contrast), this statement is only true if the Roy–Bose greatest characteristic root is used as the test statistic. See Bird and Hadzi–Pavlovic (1983) for further information.

CHAPTER 15

1. In reality the default method of estimation in SAS PROC MIXED as well as in most other multilevel software packages such as HLM is a variation of maximum likelihood technically known as restricted maximum likelihood (usually abbreviated as REML). For this reason, all references to maximum likelihood in this chapter as well as Chapter 16 technically refer to REML. Further details about this distinction are available in Verbeke and Molenburgh (2000).

2. Although the value of 135.35 is not a direct outcome of the ANOVA approach, it can nevertheless be calculated from the ANOVA output. Table 10.3 shows the relationship between expected mean squares and variance components. In the mixed model, the expected mean square for subjects will be given by

$$E(MS_{\text{subject}}) = \sigma_\varepsilon^2 + a\,\sigma_\pi^2$$

where a is the number of levels of the fixed factor. The expected mean square for residual (or error) will be given by

$$E(MS_{\text{residual}}) = \sigma_\varepsilon^2$$

From these two expressions, we can then obtain an estimate of the subject variance by subtracting MS_{residual} from MS_{subject} and dividing the result by a. In the McCarthy data, Table 15.2 shows that MS_{residual} has a value of 60.79, and MS_{subject} equals 602.18. Subtracting and dividing by 4 (a, the number of levels of A in this example) yields a value of 135.35, which is identical to the estimated subject variance produced directly by the maximum likelihood approach.

3. In reality PROC MIXED generates 4 indicator variables, but it then effectively restricts one of the parameters associated with an effect to equal zero. In other words, 1 of the 4 indicator variables is essentially eliminated when the parameter associated with it is set equal to zero, thus effectively yielding 3 indicator variables. Appendix B-1 provides more detail on parameters in PROC GLM (as well as PROC MIXED).

4. The specification of denominator degrees of freedom in the general linear mixed model is a topic still undergoing statistical research at the time of this writing. By default, PROC MIXED uses what is called a "containment method" to calculate degrees of freedom. However, there is some evidence to suggest that a better option may be to use a Satterthwaite alternative, which can be requested by specifying "ddfm = satterth" as an option in the model statement. Yet another option recently incorporated in PROC MIXED at the time of this writing is a procedure developed by Kenward and Roger. Ongoing research will likely lead to more informed decisions about the best methods for determining denominator degrees of freedom.

5. There is a long history in the psychometric literature of methodological difficulties associated with attempts to correlate initial status with rate of change. In particular, error of measurement at the initial time point creates two biases: (1) a negative bias, that makes the observed correlation more negative than the correlation between true scores, and (2) a bias that makes the observed correlation closer to zero than the correlation between true scores. In general, these two biases can either operate in the same direction, or they can operate in opposite directions, which is one reason this has proven to be such a difficult problem. Random effects modeling provides a solution to this problem by directly providing an estimate of the correlation between true scores, not observed scores. For more information, the interested reader is encouraged to consult Bryk and Raudenbush (1987).

6. Although a z test (known more formally as a Wald test) can be performed to test the variance of a random effect, there can be technical problems with such a test. The basic problem is that the z test relies on normality, but if the null hypothesis is true, the sampling distribution of the estimate parameter will be skewed, because the true value of the parameter is at the boundary of the sampling distribution. Verbeke and Molenberghs (1997) describe this problem and its implications, as well as possible solutions.

7. The restricted maximum likelihood approach used by PROC MIXED does not literally involve forming a ratio of mean squares, so in this respect it is not quite correct technically to discuss the error term chosen by PROC MIXED. However, our example illustrates that in the case of a balanced design, the results obtained by PROC MIXED are identical to those that would be obtained by traditional methods when the error method used in those methods is consistent with the random effects specified by PROC MIXED.

8. Table 15.5 shows effects based on a reference cell coding approach, where the fourth time point serves as the reference cell. See Appendix B for more information about the reference cell method.

9. Technically, all that is actually required is that some individuals have as many as three data points. One of the benefits of the maximum likelihood approach is that the analysis can also include individuals who have only two or even one wave of data as long as some individuals have the stipulated minimum number of waves.

10. Covariances of errors will not always equal covariances of the original scores. However, equality holds here because any given error is simply the deviation of the original score from the mean of the scores at that time point. Because we are subtracting a constant from all subjects's scores at each time point, the covariance remains the same as for the original scores themselves. Similarly, the correlation matrix for the errors that appears as Table 15.9 is identical to the correlation matrix for the scores themselves, which was presented in Chapter 11 as Table 11.10.

11. To be entirely accurate, we should point out that we reported a p value of .1525 in Chapter 13, ever so slightly different from the p value of .1528 we report here. The difference apparently reflects a tiny difference in the algorithms SPSS and SAS use to calculate p values in an F distribution, because the value of .1525 was obtained from SPSS MANOVA.

12. The value of 196.14 has been rounded off to 2 decimal places, but it can be proven mathematically that the mean diagonal element of the covariance matrix will be exactly equal to the sum of the variance due to subjects and the residual variance.

13. Ramsey and Schafer (1997, pp. 343–349) provide an especially readable account of the rationale for Schwarz's Bayesian Information Criterion. Verbeke and Molenberghs (1997, 2000) present several examples of using AIC and BIC (also labeled as SBC) for model selection within the domain of mixed models.

CHAPTER 16

1. One possible option when confronted with unequal sample sizes would be to change the unit of analysis. In our gender example, one could calculate a mean severity score for each trainee, yielding scores of 40, 50, and 48 for the three males, and scores of 62, 54, and 64 for the three females. A one-way ANOVA on these 6 scores produces an F value of 10.50, with 1 numerator and 4 denominator degrees of freedom, exactly the same as we obtained using $MS_{B/A}$ as an error term. Such equivalence will hold as long as sample sizes are equal, which might seem to suggest that this approach could be used even with unequal n. While it would still be simple to calculate an F value using this strategy even if sample sizes were unequal, we would almost certainly have violated an assumption in the process. Recall that ANOVA assumes that the variance of scores is a constant. However, if some of the mean scores we calculate are based on small sample sizes and others are based on large sample sizes, we would expect the scores based on small samples to be more variable than the scores based on large samples. Thus, we would be guilty of violating a basic ANOVA assumption. Instead, it is preferable to use the maximum likelihood approach, which takes into account the sample sizes of the various cells and does not require equal n.

2. Two further points can be made here. First, there are a variety of ways in which the fixed portion of the model might be written. For example, an alternative parameterization to the one we show here would be a cell means model, where the intercept term would be omitted from the model. Yet another possibility would be a reference cell model. See Appendix B for descriptions of these and other models. Second, there is also more than one way to represent the random effects in the model. As we will see when we introduce SAS PROC MIXED for these data, equivalent results can be obtained by parameterizing the model with a single Z intercept term or with indicator variables to represent different trainees.

3. As we discussed in Chapter 15, at the time of writing this book there are a limited variety of software packages that include procedures for using the maximum likelihood approach to analyze data from nested designs. Most of the choices require specialized stand-alone packages. We have chosen to illustrate SAS PROC MIXED in this chapter in large part because we expect it to be the most widely available option for performing these analyses.

4. An alternative coding would be to use the values 1 through 6. This approach produces identical results to those shown here. Notice that regardless of which method of coding is used, it is necessary to be explicit that trainee is nested within gender. We will see momentarily that we do so in PROC MIXED by expressing the nested relationship as trainee(gender), which implies that levels of the trainee factor are nested under the gender factor.

5. There are some situations where the effects of specific trainees (or other similar nested units) might be of great interest. For example, an educational psychologist might want to identify specific schools with especially positive or negative effects. Although such individual effects are not literally parameters in the mixed model, it is nevertheless possible to use PROC MIXED to obtain estimates of these individual effects. See Littell, Milliken, Stroup, and Wolfinger (1996) or SAS documentation for additional details.

6. As we have discussed earlier in the chapter (see especially footnote 4), there would be two different ways of coding classroom for PROC MIXED in this situation: (1) numbering classrooms consecutively within

condition, or (2) numbering classrooms consecutively regardless of condition. Whether or not the number of classrooms differs from one condition to another, these two approaches will produce the same results as long as the classroom factor is consistently expressed as nested under the condition factor by expressing the classroom effect as room(cond).

7. We say there may be "at least" these two reasons to consider including teaching skill in the model, because we may also be interested in the question of whether teaching skill interacts with the intervention. For example, perhaps the intervention is only effective in the hands of a highly skilled teacher. We could assess evidence for such interactions by including not just a predictor variable for teaching skill, but also a cross-product term of teaching skill and treatment condition.

8. One drawback of limiting ourselves to a single subscript is that the Equation 8 model might be misread to say that each student has his or own population mean value μ_i. In reality, the values associated with μ_i reflect classroom means. For example, suppose that the first four students are in classroom 1 and further suppose we could somehow know that classroom 1 has a population mean of 28. It would then follow that μ_1, μ_2, μ_3, and μ_4, would all be equal to 28. The important point to notice here is that several different students have the same value of μ_i, because μ_i depends not on the individual student, but instead on the student's classroom.

9. Notice that we cannot be certain that statistical power is increased by including teaching skill in the model, because statistical power depends on population parameters. It appears that β_2 (see Equation 10) is nonzero based on a p value of .0089, but even so the specific value obtained in this particular sample may have been larger than the true population value, in which case the power of the condition effect test in the population could actually be less when we include teaching skill than when we omit it.

10. The level 1 model shown in Equation 12 allows each classroom to have not just its own intercept but also its own slope. In this respect, it is actually equivalent to the first full model we present in the extension to Chapter 9:

$$\text{Full}: \quad Y_{ij} = \mu + \alpha_j + \beta_j X_{ij} + \varepsilon_{ij} \qquad \text{(9E.1, repeated)}$$

Notice that this model differs from the model given by Equation 9.1 in that the slope parameter now includes a j subscript, indicating that each group is allowed to have its own slope. Because the Equation 9E.1 model allows each group to have both a unique intercept and a unique slope, it is equivalent to the level-1 model shown in Equation 12 of this chapter.

11. Even if sample sizes were equal in all 6 classrooms, it does not generally follow that the two-step approach is equivalent to maximum likelihood, because the precision of the slope and intercept estimates depends not only on sample size but also on the variance of the predictor (cognitive ability) within each classroom. Notice that even if the study is designed so as to obtain equal sample sizes, it would be unusual to obtain data where the predictor had exactly the same variance within each classroom. Thus, models that include additional level-1 predictors typically need to be fit with maximum likelihood analysis.

12. The precision of the slope estimate can be seen by examining the formula for the standard error of the slope:

$$SE = \frac{\sigma_\varepsilon}{\sqrt{SS_X}}$$

where σ_ε is the residual standard deviation, and SS_X is the sum of squares for the predictor variable. The sum of squares equals the sample size times the variance, so both the sample size and the variance of scores on the predictor influence the precision of the slope estimate. Notice that the precision is related to the issue of restriction in range of the predictor. If the range of the predictor is restricted, the precision of the slope estimate will suffer. In our inductive reasoning example, the SS_X values for the three control classrooms are 155, 37.33, and 76.8, respectively. Even though the first classroom has the smallest number of students, its SS_X is the largest because there is much more heterogeneity in cognitive ability in this classroom than in either of the others. Notice that this exemplifies the point made in footnote 11 that the maximum likelihood analysis takes into account not just sample size but more generally precision in deriving parameter estimates.

13. As we discussed in Chapter 15, the PROC MIXED commands for obtaining this information are COVTEST and CL. Issuing these commands for our data reveals that the within-condition covariance between the slope and the intercept is not statistically significant for these data. Thus, it is plausible that the slope and intercept are uncorrelated in the population. Of course, once again, this test probably has very low power because of the small number of classrooms as well as the small number of students per classroom.

Appendix D

Solutions to Selected Exercises

CHAPTER 1

1. As discussed in the text, the Baconian view that the whole process of science can be purely objective and empirical is flawed with regard to:
   a. *Data collection*—Preexisting ideas of what is interesting and relevant necessarily influence the scientist's decisions about what to study.
   b. *Data analysis*—Selecting the most appropriate means for summarizing the collected data involves the judgment of the scientist, and although precise rules can be stated for certain steps of the process once a procedure has been decided upon, critical preliminary decisions, such as what statistical hypotheses should be tested and how, are certainly debatable.
   c. *Data interpretation*—The task of discovering theoretical mechanisms appropriate for explaining any particular phenomenon is not accomplished by following a specified set of logical rules.

3. The logical problem in the suggestion that a materialist monism is necessitated by empirical findings can be stated succinctly: one does not prove the nonexistence of nonempirical entities by empirical methods. To suggest that a materialistic monist position is necessitated by empirical findings is to fall into the logical error of begging the question, that is, of using as a premise of an argument the conclusion the argument is trying to prove. In the present case, the erroneous argument takes the following forms as a solution to the problem of determining what exists:
   1. One can use empirical observation of material entities to determine what exists.
   2. With these methods, one observes only material entities.
   3. Therefore, all that exists is material.

   The argument rests on the premise stated in the first proposition, which is valid only if the conclusion stated in the third proposition is correct. Examples of this kind of argument in the history of psychology are given by Robinson (1981, Chapter 9).

   For our purposes, the general methodological lesson to be learned concerns the relationship between assumptions and conclusions. One must presuppose certain principles—for example, regarding the uniformity of nature—in order to do science; the validity of the conclusions one draws from data will rest on the validity of those presuppositions, but one's findings will not ensure or necessitate the validity of those presuppositions. Similarly, within statistics, conclusions reached are valid *under certain assumptions*. For example, under the assumption of homogeneity of within-group variances across groups, a statistical test may suggest that the means of two groups are different, but the test of means will say nothing about the validity of the homogeneity of variance assumption. As another example, and to anticipate developments in Chapter 2, the probability value associated with a test statistic assumes that a particular hypothesis is true, but it does *not* inform you of the probability that the hypothesis presupposed is true (cf. Exercise 5 at the end of Chapter 2).

9. The contrapositive of an assertion, in general, is that the negation of the conclusion of the assertion implies the negation of the antecedent condition assumed in the assertion. Thus, the contrapositive of the learning theorist's assertion is, "If partially reinforced animals do not persist longer in responding during extinction than continuously reinforced animals, then frustration theory is *not* correct."

10. Because students in the U.S. are not randomly assigned to public vs. Catholic high schools, you should not conclude from a difference between means on a mathematics achievement test that it is the education provided by the Catholic high schools that caused the scores of the Catholic students to be higher. One would be concerned as to whether there was a selection bias operating. The attribution of the cause of the difference to the nature of the high school education would be made more compelling if other information were to be presented showing that public and Catholic students were comparable on other background variables that could reasonably be viewed as contributing causes of mathematics achievement. In fact, it turns out, as Wolfle (1987) reports, that there are large preexisting differences between the two groups of students on variables that would predict higher mathematics achievement for the Catholic students even if the mathematics instruction they received was the same as that received by the public school students. For example, the mothers and fathers of the Catholic students had higher levels of education and socioeconomic status, on the average, than the parents of the public school students. Within each group of students, these variables were related to students' achievement, and fathers' educational level in particular was predictive of higher mathematics achievement. This kind of information about selection factors operating makes the effectiveness of the high school education per se less compelling an explanation of the 3-point difference in mathematics achievement scores.

CHAPTER 2

5. False. The p value is the probability of the observed (or more extreme) results, given that you assume that the results are due to chance. The question, on the other hand, asserts that the p value is the probability that "chance," or the null hypothesis, is the correct explanation of the results. The distinction is an important one.

The point can be underscored by using conditional probability notation. The p value is a probability of the form: Pr (data | null hypothesis), that is, the probability that data having particular characteristics will occur, assuming that the null hypothesis is true. However, p values are frequently misunderstood as indicating Pr (null hypothesis | data), that is, the probability that the null hypothesis is true, given the data (see Bakan, 1966). Arriving at such a probability requires far more knowledge than is typically available in a scientific investigation—for example, what are the alternative hypotheses that are possible, and for each, what is the prior probability that it is true and the probability of obtaining the data if it were true? Thus, although one may wish that the probability of the truth of a particular hypothesis could be determined on the basis of the results of a study, that is not the information yielded by a Fisherian hypothesis test.

7. Decisions about whether the staff member's performance is significantly different from chance can be made by carrying out Fisher's exact test. To this end it is convenient to summarize the obtained results as a 2×2 table, where the columns correspond to the actual categories of patients and the rows indicate the staff member's judgments about who was released early. Thus, "5 out of 6 correct" would be indicated by the following table:

		Actual		
		Released	Not Released	
Judged	Released	5	1	6
	Not Released	1	5	6
		6	6	12

Following the logic used in the tea-tasting example, there are $_6C_5 \cdot _6C_1$ ways of choosing 5 out of the 6 actually "released" patients and 1 out of the 6 actually "not released" patients, or $6 \cdot 6 = 36$ ways of correctly identifying 5 out of 6 early-release patients. This number must be considered relative to the $_{12}C_6 = (12 \cdot 11 \cdot 10 \cdot 9 \cdot 8 \cdot 7)/(6 \cdot 5 \cdot 4 \cdot 3 \cdot 2 \cdot 1) = 924$ different ways of selecting 6 patients out of the total group of 12. Thus, given that the staff member knew 6 patients were released, the probability that he would identify 5 of those 6 correctly just by guessing is

$$Pr(5 \text{ of } 6 \text{ correct}) = \frac{_6C_5 \cdot _6C_1}{_{12}C_6} = \frac{36}{924} = .039$$

Notice that, with the table arrayed as above with the actual categories corresponding to the columns, the combinations involved in the probability are the number of ways of choosing the number indicated in the first row out of the column total. Thus, the denominator of the probability is the number of ways of choosing the number of patients judged to have been released, that is, the marginal total for the first row or 6, out of the total for the table, 12. Similarly, the numerator involves the product of the number of combinations of ways of choosing the number indicated in the first row cells from the corresponding column totals. Notice also that the numbers chosen (5 and 1) and the sizes of the subgroups from which they are chosen (6 and 6) in the numerator must sum to, respectively, the number chosen (6) and the total sample size (12) in the denominator.

To determine a significance level, one needs to compute the probability not only of the obtained results but also of every other outcome that provides as much or more evidence of association (cf. Hays, 1994). Clearly, getting all 6 correct would be stronger evidence of an association between the actual categories and the staff member's judgments than that obtained. The probability of this occurring would be computed similarly:

$$Pr(6 \text{ of } 6 \text{ correct}) = \frac{{}_6C_6 \cdot {}_6C_0}{{}_{12}C_6} = \frac{1 \cdot 1}{924} = \frac{1}{924} = .001$$

The problem also requests that a *two-tailed* test be performed. To carry out a two-tailed test, one needs to consider the possibility of judgments that are predominantly incorrect but that are as strongly indicative of an association between the actual and judged classifications (albeit in the opposite direction) as the obtained results. (In actual practice, neither the staff member nor you might be persuaded that you owe him money if his judgments were surprisingly worse than would be expected by chance. Nonetheless, carrying out two-tailed tests here allows an important pedagogical point to be made about when the two tails of the distribution used in Fisher's exact test will be symmetrical.) It turns out that, when either the column totals are equal to each other or the row totals are equal to each other, the problem is perfectly symmetrical. For example, the probability of getting 5 of 6 incorrect is the same as the probability of getting 5 of 6 correct. Thus, the probability of results as good as or better than those obtained can be doubled to obtain a final answer that may be interpreted as having a two-tailed significance. To illustrate this and to summarize the answer for the current example, we have

$$Pr(\text{results as extreme as or more extreme than those obtaineed})$$

$$= Pr(5 \text{ of } 6 \text{ or } 6 \text{ of } 6 \text{ correct}) + Pr(1 \text{ of } 6 \text{ or } 0 \text{ of } 6 \text{ correct})$$

$$= \left(\frac{36}{924} + \frac{1}{924}\right) + \left(\frac{36}{924} + \frac{1}{924}\right) = .04 + .04 = .08$$

Because the significance level of .08 is greater than the specified alpha level of .05, you conclude the results are not significant. You do not owe the staff member any money.

If the staff member had identified 5 of 6 early-release patients out of a total set of 15, the computed probability would of course be different. The obtained results in such a case could be summarized as follows:

		Actual		
		Released	Not Released	
	Released	5	1	6
Judged	Not Released	1	8	9
		6	9	15

The probability of these results is

$$Pr(5 \text{ of } 6 \text{ correct, out of } 15) = \frac{{}_6C_5 \cdot {}_9C_1}{{}_{15}C_6} = \frac{6 \cdot 9}{5005} = \frac{54}{5005} = .0108$$

The one outcome that would be better would be to classify all 6 correctly:

$$Pr(6 \text{ of } 6 \text{ correct, out of } 15) = \frac{{}_6C_6 \cdot {}_9C_0}{{}_{15}C_6} = \frac{1}{5005} = .0002$$

Thus, the probability of results as good as or better than those obtained is

$$Pr(5 \text{ of } 6 \text{ or } 6 \text{ of } 6, \text{ out of } 15) = \frac{54 + 1}{5005} = .0110$$

Now, since both row totals are unequal and column totals are unequal, one cannot simply double probabilities to get a significance level but must examine probabilities of predominantly incorrect classifications to see if they are as extreme as the probabilities of these predominantly correct classifications. Again treating the marginal totals as fixed, we might first consider the likelihood of getting 5 out of 6 incorrect, as we did before. The corresponding table would be

		Actual		
		Released	*Not Released*	
	Released	1	5	6
Judged	Not Released	5	4	9
		6	9	15

The probability of these results is

$$Pr(1 \text{ of } 6 \text{ correct, out of } 15) = \frac{{}_6C_1 \cdot {}_9C_5}{{}_{15}C_6} = \frac{6 \cdot 126}{5005} = \frac{756}{5005} = .1510$$

This value is considerably larger than the .0108 probability of classifying 5 of 6 *correctly*. In effect, increasing the number of patients who were not released results in there being many more ways of being wrong, making this a more probable outcome. Because the probability of 5 of 6 incorrect is less extreme, we do not need to consider it in determining the significance level of the outcome.

We also need to consider the possibility of being totally incorrect by chance alone; perhaps that outcome would be as improbable as what was observed. Being totally incorrect would mean choosing 0 of the 6 actual early-release patients and instead selecting all 6 from the 9 who were not released. The probability of this outcome is

$$Pr(0 \text{ of } 6 \text{ correct, out of } 15) = \frac{{}_6C_0 \cdot {}_9C_6}{{}_{15}C_6} = \frac{1 \cdot 84}{5005} = \frac{84}{5005} = .0168$$

Thus the probability of missing them all is also a more likely outcome in this situation than getting 5 of 6 correct by chance alone.

This means that the only other chance outcome that is as extremely unlikely as or more extremely unlikely than the observed outcome is correctly identifying all the early-release patients. Thus, in this case the two-tailed probability associated with the observed results turns out to be the same as the one-tailed probability, namely .0110. We would conclude that 5 of 6 correct identifications out of a set of 15 is compelling evidence for the staff member's claim. In this case, he could collect on his bet.

10. a. The observed sum of differences is 372, that is, $22 + 34 + 38 + 38 + 12 + 3 + 55 + 29 + 76 + 23 - 17 + 39 = 372$.

  b. 2^{12} or 4096 assignments of signs to differences are possible.

  c. (1) When all 12 differences are assigned positive values, the largest possible sum of 406 results; e.g., $372 - (-17) + 17 = 406$.

   (2) If either or both of the absolute differences that are less than 17 were negative, one would obtain a sum in between the maximal sum of 406 and the observed sum of 372. There are three such sums—one when 3 has the only negative sign, one when 12 has the only negative sign, and one when both 3 and 12 are negative:

Case	*Sum*
"3" negative	$406 - 3 - 3 = 400$
"12" negative	$406 - 12 - 12 = 382$
"3" and "12" negative	$406 - 3 - 12 - 3 - 12 = 376$

   (3) We have enumerated the 5 assignments of signs that result in sums greater than or equal to the observed sum of 372. If all 12 signs were reversed in each of these 5 assignments, the 5 most extremely negative sums possible would be obtained, namely, $-372, -406, -400, -382,$ and -376. Thus, 10 of the 4096 possible assignments of signs to the obtained differences result in sums at least as large in absolute value as the obtained sum.

    Since the probability of obtaining a sum at least as extreme as that observed is only 10/4096 or .0024, one would reject the null hypothesis that it was equally likely that sums would be preceded by negative as by positive signs. Thus, it appears on the basis of this experiment that the enriched environment caused an increase in the size of the cortex.

11. a. Several issues regarding Darwin's design may be commented on and related to the four kinds of validity discussed in Chapter 1. The most important relate to his basic design strategy, which was to attempt to achieve an unbiased and precise experiment by comparing each cross-fertilized plant against a matched self-fertilized plant under conditions controlled to be as equal as possible. As Darwin was well aware, many factors, besides the independent variable encapsulated in the two seeds for a pair, would influence the height the plants ultimately achieved. Thus he attempted to achieve a valid experiment by trying to ensure that the plants experienced equal soil fertility, illumination, and watering. That he would be unable to achieve exact equality in such conditions, even within a pair of plants, is evident not only logically but in the data we have to analyze, as we shall see.

One can think of the environmental conditions for each potential plant site as being predetermined. Certainly Darwin was aware of some of the relevant factors, such as amount of watering, and just as certainly there were factors he could not assess, such as air currents around the plants. The internal validity of the experiment would have been ensured had Darwin, once the plots were divided into 15 pairs of locations where environmental conditions were thought to be similar within a pair of locations, randomly assigned the cross-fertilized plant to one location and the matched self-fertilized plant to the other paired location. As it was, the internal validity of the experiment has to rest on the presumption that Darwin knew enough not to bias conditions in favor of the cross-fertilized plants by the particular set of sites to which he assigned them. Lack of perfect knowledge of the relevant causes virtually ensures some inadvertent biasing of the true difference between the plant types.

Less critical concerns relate to external and construct validity. That Darwin attempted to equalize conditions not only within pairs of plants but across pairs as well results in diminished external validity. The fact that the precision of a matched-pairs experiment is much more closely tied to the similarity of conditions within a pair than across pairs seemed not to be appreciated. Allowing differences among pairs of sites would have permitted greater statistical generalization to a wider variety of conditions. In terms of construct validity, presumably the height of the plant was an indicant of the strength or hardiness or productivity of the plant, and other measures of the plant may have been more appropriate for specific purposes of interest.

b. (1) As shown in the table of data in the answer to part (b) (2), 13 of the 15 differences in columns II and III favor the cross-fertilized plant. If cross-fertilization had no effect, each of the 15 differences would have a .5 probability of being positive, and one would expect $.5(15) = 7.5$ differences on the average to favor cross-fertilization. One can determine if the observed number of differences favoring cross-fertilization is significantly different from this expected number by using the binomial probability formula, namely,

$$Pr(r \text{ successes}) = {}_nC_r\, p^r (1-p)^{n-r}$$

where r is the required number of successes, n is the number of trials, and p is the probability of success. Here a success is defined as a difference favoring cross-fertilization, and each difference constitutes a trial or an opportunity for a success. The statistical significance here is determined by the "sign test" which simply computes the binomial probability of results at least as extreme as those observed. The probability of 13 or more differences favoring cross-fertilization is

$Pr(13 \text{ or more successes})$

$$= {}_{15}C_{13}\left(\tfrac{1}{2}\right)^{13}\left(1-\tfrac{1}{2}\right)^2 + {}_{15}C_{14}\left(\tfrac{1}{2}\right)^{14}\left(1-\tfrac{1}{2}\right)^1 + {}_{15}C_{15}\left(\tfrac{1}{2}\right)^{15}\left(1-\tfrac{1}{2}\right)^0$$

$$= \left[\frac{15!}{13!2!} + \frac{15!}{14!1!} + \frac{15!}{15!0!}\right]\left(\tfrac{1}{2}\right)^{15}$$

$$= [105 + 15 + 1]\frac{1}{32,768} = \frac{121}{32,768} = .00369$$

Given the symmetry of the distribution under the null hypothesis that $p = .5$, the probability of 2 or fewer successes is also .00369. Thus, the significance of the observed number of differences equals the probability of the observed or more extreme results:

$$Pr(2 \text{ or fewer successes, or 13 or more successes}) = .00369 + .00369$$

$$= .00738$$

Since this is considerably less than .05, we would reject the null hypothesis that the probability of a difference favoring cross-fertilization is .5.

(2) The simplest possible parametric test appropriate for these data is a matched-pairs t test. The test is carried out as a one-sample t test on the differences shown next.

Crossed	Self-fertilized	Difference
$23\frac{4}{8}$	$17\frac{3}{8}$	$6\frac{1}{8}$
12	$20\frac{3}{8}$	$-8\frac{3}{8}$
21	20	1
22	20	2
$19\frac{1}{8}$	$18\frac{3}{8}$	$\frac{6}{8}$
$21\frac{4}{8}$	$18\frac{5}{8}$	$2\frac{7}{8}$
$22\frac{1}{8}$	$18\frac{5}{8}$	$3\frac{4}{8}$
$20\frac{3}{8}$	$15\frac{2}{8}$	$5\frac{1}{8}$
$18\frac{2}{8}$	$16\frac{4}{8}$	$1\frac{6}{8}$
$21\frac{5}{8}$	18	$3\frac{5}{8}$
$23\frac{2}{8}$	$16\frac{2}{8}$	7
21	18	3
$22\frac{1}{8}$	$12\frac{6}{8}$	$9\frac{3}{8}$
23	$15\frac{4}{8}$	$7\frac{4}{8}$
12	18	-6
Mean difference, $\overline{D}$		2.617
Standard deviation, s_D		4.718

We wish to test the null hypothesis that the population mean difference μ_D is 0. We can do so by using the test statistic (see Weinberg & Abramowitz, 2002, p. 302)

$$t = \frac{\overline{D} - \mu_D}{s_{\overline{D}}}$$

where $\overline{D}$ is the mean difference score, and $s_{\overline{D}}$ is the estimated standard error of the mean and is defined as

$$s_{\overline{D}} = \frac{s_D}{\sqrt{n}}$$

Here we have

$$s_{\overline{D}} = \frac{4.718}{\sqrt{15}} = \frac{4.718}{3.873} = 1.218$$

and

$$t = \frac{\overline{D} - \mu_D}{s_{\overline{D}}} = \frac{2.617 - 0}{1.218} = 2.148$$

which just exceeds the critical t value of 2.145 for a two-tailed test with 14 degrees of freedom and α of .05. In particular, the p value associated with an observed t of 2.148 is .0497. The p value for the parametric t test is in this case considerably less extreme than the p value for the nonparametric sign test of part (b)(1). This will not in general be the case. The sign test ignores the magnitude of the differences and thus in effect treats them all as equal. The t test of course uses a mean that reflects all the differences, and in these data the two negative differences happen to be two of the largest differences in the set and thus bring down the mean more than they would if they were only average in absolute value. So, since the two negative differences are large ones, the evidence in favor of cross-fertilization is less compelling when appraised using a procedure that considers the magnitude of the disconfirming evidence in these two cases. In a sense, the sign test makes the evidence appear stronger than it really is by not taking into account the fact that the differences that do favor self-fertilization in these data are large ones.

(3) The assumption required for the sign test is only that the trials or replications or pairs of plants included in the experiment are independent of each other. In the case of the t test, one not only assumes that the differences are independent of each other but also that, over replications of the study, the differences would be distributed as a normally distributed random variable.

(4) Carrying out a randomization test for these data requires consideration of the mean difference resulting from each of the 32,768 possible assignments of signs to the 15 observed differences. The significance level for a two-tailed randomization test is simply twice the proportion of these mean differences that are equal to or greater than the observed mean of 2.617. Although only two of the observed differences were negative, because these were large scores, there are many combinations of signs (including some with as many as six negative signs being assigned to small differences) that result in mean differences larger than 2.617. Enumeration of these is very tedious, but Fisher (1935/1971, p. 46) reports that 863 of the 32,768 mean differences are at least this large and positive, and so the significance level of the randomization test is $2(863/32,768) = 2(.02634) = .0527$.

The only assumptions required by the randomization test are that the differences are independent of each other and that not only their signs but their magnitudes are meaningful. Notice that all three of the tests make the assumption of independence, and we are not assured by Darwin's procedures that this was achieved. Because of the lack of random assignment, it is conceivable that some factor was inadvertently confounded with the type of fertilization. Any causal factor that Darwin's procedures made systematically different across levels of the independent variable would thus invalidate all three tests. To take a blatant example, if all the cross-fertilized plants were given a more southerly exposure than the self-fertilized member of the pair, and if southerly exposure is good for plant growth, then the difference scores would not be independent.

The hypothesis tested by the randomization test is that the observed set of signed differences arose by a process of assigning a $+$ or $-$ sign with equal likelihood to each of the absolute differences observed. Because of the lack of random assignment, we cannot be assured that this test or the others are valid. However, assuming the test's validity, we have only marginal evidence for the difference between the two kinds of fertilization, since the results fail to reach the conventional .05 level. These data would need to be combined with other similar results to make the case compelling.

c. Although the mean of Galton's differences in column VIII is necessarily the same as the mean of the differences between the original pairs of plants in columns II and III, the mean difference is made to appear far too reliable by the re-pairing of the data. In essence, the differences in column VIII make it look as though Darwin had far greater control over his experimental material than he did. In particular, the data as arranged in columns VI and VII imply that Darwin knew enough to control the factors affecting the height of plants to such an extent that, if one member of a pair were the tallest of its type, the other member of the pair would also be the tallest in *its* series. Despite his best efforts to achieve homogeneous pairs of plants, Darwin in fact was not able to approach this degree of control. Rather than the correlation approaching $+1$ as implied by columns VI and VII, the correlation of the heights of the original pairs was actually negative, $r = -.338$. Perhaps because of competition for resources between plants planted close together, all of Darwin's efforts to achieve homogeneous plants within pairs were not sufficient in that the taller one member of a pair in his data, the shorter the other member is expected to be.

Carrying out the computations for a matched-pairs t test on the rearranged data, we find that the standard deviation s_D of the differences in column VIII is only 1.9597. This yields a standard error of 0.5060 and a t value as follows:

$$ t = \frac{2.617}{0.516} = 5.171 $$

The probability of a result this large occurring, given that the null hypothesis is true, is less than 2 in 10,000 or .0002. Similarly, when a randomization test is performed on the differences in column VIII, the significance level is extreme, with only 46 of the 32,678 mean differences being as large as or larger in absolute value than the one obtained, implying $p = .0014$.

Thus, the mean difference by Galton's approach is made to appear so reliable that it would occur only on the order of 10 times in 10,000 replications if there were no effect of cross-fertilization. In fact, results as extreme as those obtained would occur 5 times in 100 by chance alone, or on the order of 500 times in 10,000 replications. Galton's rearrangement in effect makes the evidence appear 50 times more compelling than it really is.

CHAPTER 3

5. False. MS_B is an estimate of the variance of the individual scores in the population. It is, however, based on the variability among the sample means. In particular, in an equal-n design, MS_B is n times the variance of the sample means, or n times the quantity that estimates the variance of the sampling distribution of sample means.

7. False. Although in one-way designs it is most often the case that E_R will equal SS_{Total}, this will not always be the case. E_R equals SS_{Total} when the restriction being tested is that the means of all groups are equal. In other cases E_R could be either larger or smaller than SS_{Total}, depending on the restriction of interest.

8. The loss function used to solve estimation problems in this book is to summarize the errors by squaring each one and summing them over all observations. Parameters are estimated so as to minimize such losses, that is, to satisfy the least squares criterion.

10. a. Although 24 animals were used in Experiment 2, because they represent 12 pairs of litter mates whose cortex weights are expected to be positively correlated, there are only 12 independent observations. The information from each pair can be summarized as a difference score that we may denote D_i, as shown below. (The error scores on the right are used in the answer to part (d).)

Experiment #2

Exp.	Con.	D_i	$e_{i_F}^2 = D_i - \overline{D}$	$e_{i_F}^2$	$e_{i_R}^2 = D_i^2$
707	669	38	−7	49	1444
740	650	90	45	2025	8100
745	651	94	49	2401	8836
652	627	25	−20	400	625
649	656	−7	−52	2704	49
676	642	34	−11	121	1156
699	698	1	−44	1936	1
696	648	48	3	9	2304
712	676	36	−9	81	1296
708	657	51	6	36	2601
749	692	57	12	144	3249
691	618	73	28	784	5329
				10,690	34,990

b. The full model for the 12 difference scores might be written

$$D_i = \mu_D + \varepsilon_i$$

c. Here we want to test the null hypothesis (restriction) that the mean difference score μ_D is zero. The restricted model incorporating this constraint is

$$D_i = 0 + \varepsilon_i$$

d. The estimated parameter value for the full model is the sample mean of the difference scores $\overline{D}$, which here is 45. Subtracting this from the observed differences, we obtain the error scores e_{i_F} for the full model shown in the preceding data table. Squaring these errors and summing yields $E_F = 10{,}690$, as shown. Alternatively, if one were computing E_F using a hand calculator having a single-key standard deviation function, one could compute E_F as $(n-1)s_D^2$. Here $n = 12$, and $s_D = 31.374$, and consequently

$$E_F = (12-1)(31.174)^2 = 11(971.818) = 10{,}690$$

Since there are no parameters to estimate in the restricted model, the errors are the differences between the observed difference scores and 0, or simply the observed difference scores themselves. Thus, the values of $e_{i_R}^2$ are as shown in the rightmost column of the table part (a) and sum to 34,990. Alternatively, one could obtain $E_R - E_F$ as the sum over all observations of the squared differences of the predictions of the two models (see Equation 3.64), that is

$$E_R - E_F = \sum_{\text{all obs}} (\hat{Y}_F - \hat{Y}_R)^2 = \sum_i (\overline{D} - 0)^2 = n\overline{D}^2 = 12 \cdot 45^2 = 12 \cdot 2025 = 24{,}300$$

and so

$$E_R = E_F + 24{,}300 = 10{,}690 + 24{,}300 = 34{,}970$$

e. The full model requires estimation of one parameter, and the restricted model none, so $df_F = n - 1 = 12 - 1 = 11$ and $df_R = n = 12$. Thus we have

$$F = \frac{(E_R - E_F)/(df_R - df_F)}{E_F/df_F} = \frac{(34{,}990 - 10{,}690)/(12 - 11)}{10{,}690/11} = \frac{24{,}300/1}{971.818} = 25.005$$

which exceeds the critical value of 19.7 from Table A-2 for an F with 1 and 11 degrees of freedom at $\alpha = .001$.

f. On the basis of the test in part (e), we reject the restricted model. That is, we conclude that it is not reasonable to presume that the population mean cortex weight is the same for experimental as for control animals. Or stated positively, we conclude that being raised in an enriched (as opposed to a deprived) environment results in rats that have heavier cortexes.

g. The data from the three experiments can again be summarized by using difference scores. We will use these differences to compare the following two models:

$$\text{Full model}: \quad D_{ij} = \mu_j + \varepsilon_{ij_F}$$

$$\text{Restricted model}: \quad D_{ij} = \mu + \varepsilon_{ij_R}$$

The parameter estimates for the full model are the mean difference scores for the three experiments, $\overline{D}_1 = 26$, $\overline{D}_2 = 45$, and $\overline{D}_3 = 31$. Subtracting these from the observed differences yields the errors and squared errors shown next.

	Experiment 1			Experiment 2			Experiment 3	
D_{i1}	e_{i1}	e_{i1}^2	D_{i2}	e_{i2}	e_{i2}^2	D_{i3}	E_{13}	e_{i3}^2
33	7	49	38	−7	49	22	−9	81
32	6	36	90	45	2025	34	3	9
16	−10	100	94	49	2401	38	7	49
6	−20	400	25	−20	400	58	27	729
24	−2	4	−7	−52	2704	12	−19	361
17	−9	81	34	−11	121	3	−28	784
64	38	1444	1	−44	1936	55	24	576
7	−19	361	48	3	9	29	−2	4
89	63	3969	36	−9	81	76	45	2025
−2	−28	784	51	6	36	23	−8	64
11	−15	225	57	12	144	−17	−48	2304
15	−11	121	73	28	784	39	8	64
Σ 312		7574	540		10,690	372		7050
$\overline{D}_j$ 26			45			31		
s_j 26.240			31.174			25.316		

Thus, the sum of squared errors for the full model is

$$E_F = \sum_j \sum_i e_{ij}^2 = 7574 + 10{,}690 + 7050 = 25{,}314$$

Equivalently we could use the standard deviations (see Equation 3.62) as follows:

$$E_F = (n-1)\sum_j s_j^2 = (12-1)(26.240^2 + 31.174^2 + 25.316^2)$$

$$= 11(688.546 + 971.818 + 640.909)$$

$$= 7574.006 + 10{,}689.998 + 7049.999$$

$$= 25{,}314.003$$

This would enable us to obtain the same result within rounding errors.

The numerator sum of squares for our test statistic may be obtained by taking n times the sum of squared deviations of group means around the grand mean (see Equation 3.58). Because the grand mean $\overline{D}$, the estimate of the restricted model's population mean, is here $(26 + 45 + 31)/3 = 34$, we have

$$E_R - E_F = n\sum_{j=1}^{a}(\overline{D}_j - \overline{D})^2$$

$$= 12[(26-34)^2 + (45-34)^2 + (31-34)^2]$$

$$= 12[(-8)^2 + (11)^2 + (-3)^2]$$

$$= 12.[64 + 121 + 9] = 12.194 = 2328$$

The full model with its three parameters has $N - a = 36 - 3 = 33$ degrees of freedom. The restricted model requires estimation of only one mean, so $df_R = N - 1 = 36 - 1 = 35$. Thus, our test statistic may be computed as

$$F = \frac{(E_R - E_F)/(df_R - df_F)}{E_F/df_F} = \frac{2328/(35-33)}{25{,}314/33} = \frac{2328/2}{767.09} = \frac{1164}{767.09} = 1.517.$$

Since this is smaller than the critical value of $F(2,33) =$ approximately 3.3 (either rounding the denominator degrees of freedom down to 30, or interpolating between the table values of 3.32 and 3.23 for 30 and 40 denominator degrees of freedom, respectively), we cannot reject the restricted model. The time of year when the experiments were run did not seem to affect the magnitude of the effect of the environment on the cortex weights.

11. a. Designating the experimental group as group 1 and the control group as group 2, we wish to test the restriction $\mu_1 = \mu_2$ by comparing the following models:

$$\text{Full model:} \quad Y_{ij} = \mu_j + \varepsilon_{ij_F}$$

$$\text{Restricted model:} \quad Y_{ij} = \mu + \varepsilon_{ij_R}$$

The parameter estimates for the full model are the group sample means, that is, $\hat{\mu}_1 = \overline{Y}_1 = 702$ and $\hat{\mu}_2 = \overline{Y}_2 = 657$, whereas for the restricted model the single population mean is estimated by the grand mean, that is, $\hat{\mu} = \overline{Y} = 679.5$. The errors for the full model are as follows:

	Experimental Group			Control Group		
	Y_{i1}	e_{i1}	e_{i1}^2	Y_2	e_{i2}	e_{i2}^2
	707	5	25	669	12	144
	740	38	1444	650	−7	49
	745	43	1849	651	−6	36
	652	−50	2500	627	−30	900
	649	−53	2809	656	−1	1
	676	−26	676	642	−15	225
	699	−3	9	698	41	1681
	696	−6	36	648	−9	81
	712	10	100	676	19	361
	708	6	36	657	0	0
	749	47	2209	692	35	1225
	691	−11	121	618	−39	1521
$\sum$			11,814			6224
$\overline{Y}_j$	702			657		
s_j	32.772			23.787		

Thus,

$$E_F = \sum_j \sum_i e_{ij}^2 = 11{,}814 + 6224 = 18{,}038$$

and

$$E_R - E_F = n \sum_j (\overline{Y}_j - \overline{Y})^2 = 12[(702 - 679.5)^2 + (657 - 679.5)^2]$$

$$= 12[(22.5)^2 + (-22.5)^2] = 12[506.25 + 506.25]$$

$$= 12{,}150$$

which means $E_R = E_F + 12{,}150 = 18{,}038 + 12{,}150 = 30{,}188$. Because at the moment we are acting as if the observations within a pair are independent, we have $df_F = n - a = 24 - 2 = 22$ and $df_R = N - 1 = 24 - 1 = 23$. Thus, our test statistic is

$$F = \frac{(E_R - E_F)/(df_R - df_F)}{E_F/df_F} = \frac{12{,}150/(23 - 22)}{18{,}038/22} = \frac{12{,}150}{819.909} = 14.819$$

which just exceeds the critical F of 14.4 for 1 and 22 degrees of freedom at $\alpha = .001$.

b. Certainly, we have strong evidence ($p < .001$) against the null hypothesis in both the independent groups analysis conducted for the current problem and the matched pairs analysis conducted in parts (a)-(f) of the previous problem. However, closer inspection reveals that there is slightly less evidence against the restricted model here. If p values were computed by a statistical computer program, we would see that, in the current analysis, we have $p = .0009$ associated with $F(1, 22) = 14.819$ here, whereas $p = .0004$ for $F(1, 11) = 25.005$ in Exercise 10(e). There are two main differences in the analyses that are relevant. The more important difference is in the magnitude of E_F, which appears in the denominator of our test statistic. E_F in the independent groups analysis is 68.7% larger than E_F in the matched pairs analysis (18,038 vs. 10,690) and is responsible for the F being 68.7% larger in the matched pairs analysis than in the independent groups analysis. This sum of squared errors will be smaller (and hence the F larger) in the matched pairs analysis whenever the pairs of scores are positively correlated, which they are here, $r = .4285$. This within-pair predictability of scores allows us to reduce our errors and results in more sensitive tests, as we discuss extensively in Part III of the text.

A secondary difference in the analysis is in the denominator degrees of freedom, which determine the particular F distribution used to determine the significance of the observed F. As df_F increases, the critical value required to declare a result significant at a given p value decreases. While for larger values of n this decrease is trivial, for relatively small n the difference in critical F's is noticeable, particularly for very small p values. For example, for $p = .05$, the critical F of 4.84 for 1 and 11 degrees of freedom is 13% larger than the critical F of 4.30 for 1 and 22 degrees of freedom, but for $p = .001$, the critical

F is 37% larger in the matched pairs case (19.7 vs. 14.4). Even so, the matched pairs analysis is more compelling here because the cost of having fewer degrees of freedom is more than outweighed by the benefit of reduced error variability.

12. a. To standardize the observed difference between means of $702 - 657 = 45$ mg, we need to determine an estimate of the within-group standard deviation as indicated in Equations 3.83 through 3.86. The corresponding pooled estimate of the within-group variance was determined in the answer to the preceding question to be 819.909. Thus, the estimated standard deviation is

$$S = \sqrt{E_F/df_F} = \sqrt{819.909} = 28.634$$

This implies that the difference in mean cortex weights is more than one and a half standard deviations:

$$\hat{d} = \frac{\overline{Y}_1 - \overline{Y}_2}{S} = \frac{45}{28.634} = 1.572$$

b. The proportion of the total sum of squares accounted for by the between-group differences is, from Equation 3.90 and the results of the preceding problem,

$$R^2 = \frac{E_R - E_F}{E_R} = \frac{12,150}{30,188} = .4025$$

A corrected estimate of the proportion of variability in the population accounted for by group membership is provided by $\hat{\omega}^2$ as defined in Equation 91:

$$\hat{\omega}^2 = \frac{(E_R - E_F) - (a-1)(E_F/df_F)}{E_R + (E_F/df_F)} \tag{3.91}$$

$$= \frac{12,150 - (1)(819.909)}{30,188 + 819.909} = \frac{11,330.091}{31,007.909} = .3654$$

14. Given $\mu_1 = 21$, $\mu_2 = 24$, $\mu_3 = 30$, $\mu_4 = 45$, and $\sigma_\varepsilon = 20$, we need to compute σ_m and f, as indicated in Equations 3.88 and 3.89; where $\mu = (\sum \mu_j)/a = (21 + 24 + 30 + 45)/4 = 120/4 = 30$:

$$\sigma_m = \sqrt{\frac{\sum_j (\mu_j - \mu)^2}{a}}$$

$$= \sqrt{\frac{(21 - 30)^2 + (24 - 30)^2 + (30 - 30)^2 + (45 - 30)^2}{4}}$$

$$= \sqrt{\frac{81 + 36 + 0 + 225}{4}} = \sqrt{\frac{342}{4}} = \sqrt{85.5} = 9.2466$$

$$f = \frac{\sigma_m}{\sigma_\varepsilon} = \frac{9.2466}{20} = .4623$$

From this, we may obtain ϕ for trial values of n, using Equation 3.100, and determine the resulting power from Table A-11. With $n = 9$ per group, we would have

$$\phi = f\sqrt{n} = .4623\sqrt{9} = .4623(3) = 1.3869,$$

which would result in $df_F = 4(9-1) = 4 \cdot 8 = 32$. However, the vertical line above a ϕ of 1.4 for the chart with 3 numerator degrees of freedom intersects the power curve for 30 denominator degrees of freedom at a height corresponding to just less than a power of .60. Thus, we need to try a larger value for n. If we were to increase n to 16, we would have

$$\phi = f\sqrt{n} = .4623\sqrt{16} = .4623(4) = 1.8492$$

which for $df_F = 4(16 - 1) = 60$ would result in a power of over .86. Because this is more than the required power, we would decrease n. A computation with $n = 14$ yields

$$\phi = .4623\sqrt{14} = .4623(3.7417) = 1.7298$$

$$df_F = 4(14 - 1) = 52$$

and a power of approximately .80.

18. a. Given the grand mean here is $(3.65 + 4.90)/2 = 4.225$, we can estimate the effect parameter for the first group as: $\hat{\alpha}_1 = \overline{Y}_1 - \overline{Y} = 3.65 - 4.225 = -.575$

and then given the value of $\hat{\alpha}_j^2$ is the same for all 40 observations, we can compute SS_B as

$$E_R - E_F = n\sum_{j=1}^{2}\hat{\alpha}_j^2 = N\hat{\alpha}_1 = 40 \cdot (-.575)^2 = 13.225$$

Next, noting the equal n in the two groups, we can compute MS_W using Equation 3.63 simply as the average of the two variances:

$$\frac{E_F}{df_F} = \frac{\sum s_j^2}{a} = \frac{1.57^2 + 2.55^2}{2} = \frac{2.46 + 6.50}{2} = 4.48$$

Thus, the value of the test statistic can be computed as:

$$F = \frac{(E_R - E_F)/(df_R - df_F)}{E_F/df_F} = \frac{MS_B}{MS_W} = \frac{N\hat{\alpha}_1^2/(a - 1)}{\sum s_j^2/a}$$

$$= \frac{13.225/1}{4.48} = 2.95, P > .05$$

To compute the estimate of d we need to compute the pooled estimate of the within-group standard deviation as the square root of MS_W:

$$S = \sqrt{\frac{E_F}{df_F}} = \sqrt{MS_W} = \sqrt{4.48} = 2.117$$

Thus we have using Equation 3.84

$$\hat{d} = \frac{\overline{Y}_1 - \overline{Y}_2}{S} = \frac{3.65 - 4.80}{2.117} = -.543$$

Similarly, if the value of $f = \sigma_m/\sigma_\varepsilon$ were computed by using sample values of the effect parameters and within-group standard deviation we would have

$$\hat{f} = \sqrt{\frac{\sum\hat{\alpha}_j^2/a}{\sqrt{MS_W}}} = \frac{\sqrt{[(-.575)^2 + .575^2]/2}}{\sqrt{4.48}} = \frac{.575}{2.117} = .272$$

Thus, we note that f here is $1/2\ d$ and since $f > .25$, it is a medium-sized effect.

b. To determine the sample size required to achieve a power of .80, using $f = .272$, we would compute values of ϕ for various values of n and then read the power value off the chart in Table A-11. Given the results were not significant at $\alpha = .05$ with 20 subjects per group, we might begin by trying a larger value of n. For example, if n were to be 40, we would compute $\phi = f\sqrt{n} = (.272)\sqrt{40} = 1.717$ which would result in a power of approximately .68. By trying still larger values of n we eventually achieve a power of .80 by using $n = 55$, which yields $\phi = f\sqrt{n} = (.272)\sqrt{55} = 2.01$.

c. Computing a revised estimate of effect size adjusted for sampling error using Equation 3.102, we would have, if computed on the basis of the mean squares:

$$f_{adj} = \sqrt{\frac{(a-1)}{N} \frac{(MS_B - MS_W)}{MS_W}}$$

$$= \sqrt{\frac{(2-1)}{40} \frac{13.225 - 4.48}{4.48}} = \sqrt{.0488} = .221$$

Similarly, if we had calculated f_{adj} on the basis of the observed F test we would have arrived at the same answer

$$f_{adj} = \sqrt{\frac{a-1}{N}(F-1)} = \sqrt{\frac{1}{40}(2.95 - 1)} = \sqrt{.0488} = .221$$

Thus the adjusted effect size is almost 20% less than the estimate computed in part b and now falls just short of the cutoff for a medium effect. By trying different values of n we would eventually arrive at $n = 82$, yielding $\phi = 2.00$ and a power of .80. In this case, with a relatively small F value where adjusting for sampling variability results in more of a reduction in estimated effect size, we see that we would need to use 164 total subjects rather than the 110 total subjects suggested by the power analysis in part b. Thus, the total required sample size would be 54 larger than suggested by the power analysis based on the estimate of f using sample values, meaning almost 50% more subjects would be needed than that analysis suggestd.

CHAPTER 3   EXTENSION

1. False. F^* can be more powerful than F when sample sizes are unequal and population variances are also unequal.
7. False. Simulation studies have shown that the Kruskal–Wallis test is sensitive to heterogeneity of variance when sample sizes are unequal. F^* and W are usually better alternatives in this situation.
8. a.

$$F = \frac{\sum_{j=1}^{a} n_j (\bar{Y}_j - \bar{Y})^2/(a-1)}{\sum_{j=1}^{a} (n_j - 1)s_j^2/(N-a)}$$

For these data,

$$\bar{Y} = \frac{(20)(10) + (20)(12) + (50)(14)}{20 + 20 + 50}$$

$$= 12.6667$$

so

$$\sum_{j=1}^{a} n_j(\bar{Y}_j - \bar{Y})^2 = 20[(10 - 12.6667)^2] + 20[(12 - 12.6667)^2]$$

$$+ 50[(14 - 12.6667)^2]$$

$$= 240.00$$

In addition,

$$\sum_{j=1}^{a} (n_j - 1)s_j^2/(N-a) = \frac{19(10) + 19(10) + 49(50)}{87}$$

$$= 32.5287$$

Thus,

$$F = \frac{240.00/2}{32.5287}$$

$$= 3.69$$

b.

$$F^* = \frac{\sum_{j=1}^{a} n_j(\overline{Y}_j - \overline{Y})^2}{\sum_{j=1}^{a}(1 - (n_j/N))s_j^2}$$

We discovered in part (a) that

$$\sum_{j=1}^{a} n_j(\overline{Y}_j - \overline{Y})^2 = 240.00$$

The denominator of F^* equals

$$\sum_{j=1}^{a}(1 - (n_j/N))s_j^2 = \left(1 - \frac{20}{90}\right)(10) + \left(1 - \frac{20}{90}\right)(10) + \left(1 - \frac{50}{90}\right)(50)$$

$$= 7.7778 + 7.7778 + 22.2222$$

$$= 37.7778$$

Thus,

$$F^* = \frac{240.00}{37.7778}$$

$$= 6.35$$

c.

$$W = \frac{\sum_{j=1}^{a} W_j(\overline{Y}_j - \tilde{Y})^2/(a-1)}{[1 + \frac{2}{3}(a-2)\Lambda]}$$

where

$$w_j = n_j/s_j^2$$

$$\tilde{Y} = \sum_{j=1}^{a} w_j\overline{Y}_j / \sum_{j=1}^{a} w_j$$

$$\Lambda = 3\sum_{j=1}^{a}\left[\frac{\left(1 - \left(w_j / \sum_{j=1}^{a} w_j\right)\right)^2}{(n_j - 1)}\right] / (a^2 - 1)$$

For these data,

$$w_1 = 20/10 = 2$$

$$w_2 = 20/10 = 2$$

$$w_3 = 50/50 = 1$$

Further,

$$\tilde{Y} = \frac{2(10) + 2(12) + 1(14)}{2 + 2 + 1}$$

$$= 11.6$$

and

$$\Lambda = \frac{3\left[\left(\left(1 - \frac{2}{5}\right)^2 / 19\right) + \left(\left(1 - \frac{2}{5}\right)^2 / 19\right) + \left(1 - \frac{1}{5}\right)^2 / 49\right)\right]}{(3)^2 - 1}$$

$$= \frac{3(.01895 + .01895 + .01306)}{8}$$

$$= .01911$$

Thus,

$$W = \frac{2(10 - 11.6)^2 + 2(12 - 11.6)^2 + 1(14 - 11.6)^2 / 2}{1 + (2/3)(1)(.01911)}$$

$$= \frac{(5.12 + .32 + 5.76)/2}{1.01274}$$

$$= 5.53$$

d. Yes, the F value obtained in part (a) is substantially lower than either F^* from part (b) or W from part (c). When large samples are paired with large sample variances, as in this example, F will be smaller than F^* or W. When this pattern holds for population variances, F will tend to be conservative, while F^* and W will tend to be robust.

10. The Kruskal–Wallis test provides a nonparametric analysis of these data. The first step in applying the test is to rank order all observations in the entire set of N subjects. Replacing each score with its rank (where $1 =$ lowest and $18 =$ highest) for these data yields the following values.

	Group 1	Group 2	Group 3
	4	11.5	17
	7.5	2	13.5
	3	5	6
	7.5	15	11.5
	13.5	1	16
	9	10	18
Mean Rank	7.4167	7.4167	13.6667

The Kruskal–Wallis test statistic is given by Equation E.7:

$$H = \frac{12}{N(N+1)} \sum_{j=1}^{a} n_j (\overline{R}_j - ((N+1)/2))^2 \tag{E.7}$$

$$= \frac{12}{18(19)} [6(7.4167 - 9.5000)^2 + 6(7.4167 - 9.5000)^2 + 6(13.6667 - 9.5000)^2]$$

$$= (.03509)(26.0408 + 26.0408 + 104.1683)$$

$$= 5.48$$

Because there are tied observations the correction factor T should be applied, where

$$T = 1 - \frac{\sum_{i=1}^{G} (t_i^3 - t_i)}{N^3 - N}$$

There are 3 sets of tied scores (at 7.5, 11.5, and 13.5), so $G = 3$.

In each case, there are two observations tied at the value, so $t_1 = 2$, $t_2 = 2$, and $t_3 = 2$. Thus, the correction factor for these data is

$$T = 1 - \frac{(2^3 - 2) + (2^3 - 2) + (2^3 - 2)}{(18)^3 - 18}$$

$$= 1 - \frac{6 + 6 + 6}{5814}$$

$$= .9969$$

The corrected test statistic H' equals

$$H' = H/T$$

$$= 5.48/.9969$$

$$= 5.50$$

The critical value is a chi-square with $a - 1$, or 2, degrees of freedom. At the .05 level, the critical value is 5.99 (see Appendix Table A.9), so the null hypothesis cannot be rejected.

CHAPTER 4

1. a. $c_1 = 1$, $c_2 = -1$, $c_3 = 0$, $c_4 = 0$
    b. $c_1 = 1$, $c_2 = -.5$, $c_3 = -.5$, $c_4 = 0$
    c. $c_1 = 0$, $c_2 = 1$, $c_3 = 0$, $c_4 = -1$
    d. $c_1 = -\frac{1}{3}$, $c_2 = -\frac{1}{3}$, $c_3 = -\frac{1}{3}$, $c_4 = 1$
3. a.   Testing the contrast for statistical significance involves a four-step process. First, $\hat{\psi}$ must be found from Equation 40:

$$\hat{\psi} = \sum_{j=1}^{a} c_j \bar{Y}_j \qquad (4.40)$$

$$= .5(12) + .5(10) - 1(6)$$

$$= 5$$

Second, the sum of squares associated with the contrast is determined from Equation 39:

$$E_R - E_F = (\hat{\psi})^2 \bigg/ \sum_{j=1}^{a} \left(c_j^2 / n_j \right) \qquad (4.39)$$

$$= (5)^2 \bigg/ \left[\frac{(.5)^2}{10} + \frac{(.5)^2}{10} + \frac{(-1)^2}{10} \right]$$

$$= 25/(.025 + .025 + .100)$$

$$= 166.67$$

Third, the F value for the contrast can be determined from Equation 41:

$$F = \frac{(\hat{\psi})^2}{MS_W \sum_{j=1}^{a} \left(c_j^2 / n_j \right)}$$

From the second step above, we know that

$$(\hat{\psi})^2 \Big/ \sum_{j=1}^{a} \left(c_j^2/n_j\right) = 166.67$$

We are told that $MS_W = 25$, so the F value for the contrast is given by

$$F = \frac{166.67}{25}$$
$$= 6.67$$

Fourth, this F value must be compared to a critical F value. The critical F here has 1 numerator and 27 (i.e., $30 - 3$) denominator degrees of freedom. Appendix Table A.2 shows the critical F for 1 and 26 degrees of freedom or for 1 and 28 degrees of freedom, but not for 1 and 27 degrees of freedom. To be slightly conservative, we will choose the value for 1 and 26 degrees of freedom, which is 4.23. The observed value of 6.67 exceeds the critical value, so the null hypothesis is rejected. Thus, there is a statistically significant difference between the group 3 mean and the average of the group 1 and 2 means.

b. Once again, the same four steps as in part (a) provide a test of the contrast. First, from Equation 40:

$$\hat{\psi} = \sum_{j=1}^{a} c_j \overline{Y}_j \tag{4.40}$$
$$= 1(12) + 1(10) - 2(6)$$
$$= 10$$

Second, from Equation 39:

$$E_R - E_F = (\hat{\psi})^2 \Big/ \sum_{j=1}^{a} \left(c_j^2/n_j\right) \tag{4.39}$$
$$= (10)^2 \Big/ \left[\frac{(1)^2}{10} + \frac{(1)^2}{10} + \frac{(-2)^2}{10}\right]$$
$$= 100/(.1 + .1 + .4)$$
$$= 166.67$$

Third, from Equation 41:

$$F = \frac{(\hat{\psi})^2}{MS_W \sum_{j=1}^{a} \left(c_j^j/n_j\right)} \tag{4.41}$$
$$= \frac{166.67}{25}$$
$$= 6.67$$

Fourth, as in part (a), the critical F value is 4.23. Thus, the null hypothesis is rejected.

c. In part (a), $(\hat{\psi})^2 = 25$. In part (b), $(\hat{\psi})^2 = 100$. Thus, $(\hat{\psi})^2$ is four times larger in part (b) than in part (a). Similarly, in part (a),

$$\sum_{j=1}^{a} c_j^2 = (.5)^2 + (.5)^2 + (-1)^2$$
$$= .25 + .25 + 1.00$$
$$= 1.50.$$

In part (b),

$$\sum_{j=1}^{a} c_j^2 = (1)^2 + (1)^2 + (-2)^2$$
$$= 1 + 1 + 4$$
$$= 6$$

Thus, $\sum_{j=1}^{a} c_j^2$ is four times larger in part (b) than in part (a). The inclusion of the $\sum_{j=1}^{a} c_j^2$ term in Equation 41 guarantees that the F test of a contrast will not be affected by the absolute magnitude of the contrast coefficients. As our result for part (b) shows, all of the contrast coefficients can be multiplied by 2 (or any other constant), without changing the F value for the contrast.

8. a. Because this is a pairwise comparison, Equation 27 provides the simplest expression for the F value for the contrast:

$$F = \frac{n_1 n_2 (\overline{Y}_1 - \overline{Y}_2)^2}{(n_1 + n_2) MS_W} \tag{4.27}$$

We know that $n_1 = 20$, $n_2 = 20$, $\overline{Y}_1 = 6.0$, and $\overline{Y}_2 = 4.0$. To find MS_W, recall that, during the discussion of pooled and separate error terms, it was stated that

$$MS_W = \sum_{j=1}^{a}(n_j - 1)s_j^2 \Big/ \sum_{j=1}^{a}(n_j - 1)$$
$$= \frac{(20 - 1)(3.2)^2 + (20 - 1)(2.9)^2 + (10 - 1)(3.3)^2}{(20 - 1) + (20 - 1) + (10 - 1)}$$
$$= \frac{194.56 + 159.79 + 98.01}{19 + 19 + 9}$$
$$= 9.62$$

Making the appropriate substitutions,

$$F = \frac{(20)(20)(6.0 - 4.0)^2}{(20 + 20)(9.62)}$$
$$= 4.16$$

The critical F here has 1 numerator and 47 (i.e., $50 - 3$) denominator degrees of freedom. Appendix Table A.2 shows the critical F for 1 and 40 degrees of freedom or for 1 and 60 degrees of freedom, but not for 1 and 47 degrees of freedom. To be slightly conservative, we will choose the value for 1 and 40 degrees of freedom, which is 4.08. The observed F value of 4.16 exceeds the critical value, so the null hypothesis is rejected. Thus, there is a statistically significant difference between the means of the cognitive and the behavioral groups.

b. Once again, this is a pairwise comparison, so Equation 27 can be used:

$$F = \frac{n_1 n_2 (\overline{Y}_1 - \overline{Y}_2)^2}{(n_1 + n_2) MS_W} \tag{4.27}$$

where the "1" subscript refers to the cognitive group, and the "2" subscript refers to the control group. Substituting into the formula for F yields

$$F = \frac{(20)(10)(6.0 - 3.8)^2}{(20 + 10)(9.62)}$$
$$= 3.35$$

As in part (a), the critical F value is 4.08. The observed F value is less than the critical value, so the null hypothesis cannot be rejected. The difference between the means of the cognitive and the control groups is not statistically significant.

c. The mean difference between the cognitive and behavioral groups is 2.0; the mean difference between the cognitive and control groups is 2.2. However, the smaller mean difference is statistically significant, while the larger mean difference is not. The reason for this discrepancy is that the smaller mean difference is based on larger samples (viz., samples of 20 and 20, instead of 20 and 10). As a result, the mean difference of 2.0 is based on a more precise estimate than the mean difference of 2.2.

13. a. *Using MS$_W$:*

$$\hat{\psi} = \overline{Y}_3 - \overline{Y}_4$$

$$= -2$$

$$E_R - E_F = (\hat{\psi})^2 \bigg/ \sum_{j=1}^{a} \left(c_j^2 / n_j \right)$$

$$= (-2)^2 \bigg/ \left(\frac{(0)^2}{5} + \frac{(0)^2}{5} + \frac{(1)^2}{5} + \frac{(-1)^2}{5} \right)$$

$$= 10.00$$

$$MS_W = \frac{\sum_{j=1}^{a} s_j^2}{a} \text{(with equal } n, \text{ from Equation 3.63)}$$

$$= \frac{(1+1+9+9)}{4}$$

$$= 5.00$$

Thus,

$$F = \frac{(\hat{\psi})^2}{MS_W \sum_{j=1}^{a} \left(c_j^2 / n_j \right)}$$

$$= \frac{10.00}{5.00}$$

$$= 2.00$$

From Appendix Table A.2, the critical F value for 1 numerator and 16 denominator degrees of freedom is 4.49. Thus, the null hypothesis cannot be rejected.

Using a Separate Error Term:

The F statistic is now given by

$$F = \frac{(\hat{\psi})^2}{\sum_{j=1}^{a} \left(c_j^2 / n_j \right) s_j^2}$$

$$= \frac{(-2)^2}{\frac{(0)^2}{5}(1) + \frac{(0)^2}{5}(1) + \frac{(1)^2}{5}(9) + \frac{(-1)^2}{5}(9)}$$

$$= \frac{4.00}{3.60}$$

$$= 1.11$$

The denominator degrees of freedom of the critical value are given by Equation 43:

$$df = \frac{\left(\sum\limits_{j=1}^{a} c_j^2 s_j^2 / n_j\right)^2}{\sum\limits_{j=1}^{a}\left[\left(c_j^2 s_j^2 / n_j\right)^2 / (n_j - 1)\right]} \tag{4.43}$$

$$= \frac{\left(\dfrac{(0)^2(1)}{5} + \dfrac{(0)^2(1)}{5} + \dfrac{(1)^2(9)}{5} + \dfrac{(-1)^2(9)}{5}\right)^2}{\dfrac{\left(\dfrac{(0)^2(1)}{5}\right)^2}{5-1} + \dfrac{\left(\dfrac{(0)^2(1)}{5}\right)^2}{5-1} + \dfrac{\left(\dfrac{(1)^2(9)}{5}\right)^2}{5-1} + \dfrac{\left(\dfrac{(-1)^2(9)}{5}\right)^2}{5-1}}$$

$$= \frac{(3.60)^2}{0 + 0 + .81 + .81}$$

$$= 8.00$$

The corresponding critical value is 5.32. Thus, the separate error term approach here produces an appreciably smaller observed F and a somewhat larger critical F.

b. *Using MS_W:*

$$\hat{\psi} = \overline{Y}_1 - \overline{Y}_2$$

$$= -2$$

$$E_R - E_F = (\hat{\psi})^2 \Big/ \sum_{j=1}^{a}\left(c_j^2 / n_j\right)$$

$$= (-2)^2 \Big/ \left[\frac{(1)^2}{5} + \frac{(-1)^2}{5} + \frac{(0)^2}{5} + \frac{(0)^2}{5}\right]$$

$$= 10.00$$

$$MS_W = \frac{\sum\limits_{j=1}^{a} s_j^2}{a}$$

$$= \frac{1 + 1 + 9 + 9}{4}$$

$$= 5.00$$

Thus,

$$F = (\hat{\psi})^2 \Big/ MS_W \sum_{j=1}^{a}\left(c_j^2 / n_j\right)$$

$$= \frac{10.00}{5.00}$$

$$= 2.00$$

As in part (a), the critical F value is 4.49, so the null hypothesis cannot be rejected.

Using a Separate Error Term:
The F statistic is now given by

$$F = \frac{(\hat{\psi})^2}{\sum\limits_{j=1}^{a} \left(c_j^2/n_j\right) s_j^2}$$

$$= \frac{(-2)^2}{\dfrac{(1)^2}{5}(1) + \dfrac{(-1)^2}{5}(1) + \dfrac{(0)^2}{5}(9) + \dfrac{(0)^2}{5}(9)}$$

$$= \frac{4.00}{.40}$$

$$= 10.00$$

The denominator degrees of freedom of the critical value are given by Equation 43:

$$df = \frac{\left(\sum\limits_{j=1}^{a} c_j^2 s_j^2/n_j\right)^2}{\sum\limits_{j=1}^{2} \left[\left(c_j^2 s_j^2/n_j\right)^2 \Big/ (n_j - 1)\right]} \tag{4.43}$$

$$= \frac{\left(\dfrac{(1)^2(1)}{5} + \dfrac{(-1)^2(1)}{5} + \dfrac{(0)^2(9)}{5} + \dfrac{(0)^2(9)}{5}\right)^2}{\dfrac{\left(\dfrac{(1)^2(-1)}{5}\right)^2}{5-1} + \dfrac{\left(\dfrac{(1)^2(-1)}{5}\right)^2}{5-1} + \dfrac{\left(\dfrac{(0)^2(9)}{5}\right)^2}{5-1} + \dfrac{\left(\dfrac{(0)^2(9)}{5}\right)^2}{5-1}}$$

$$= \frac{(.40)^2}{.01 + .01 + .00 + .00}$$

$$= 8.00$$

The corresponding critical value is 5.32, so the null hypothesis is rejected. Unlike part (a), the separate error term approach in part (b) produced a substantially larger F value than was obtained using MS_W. The reason is that the separate error term approach takes into account that, in these data, the $\overline{Y}_1$ and $\overline{Y}_2$ estimates are much more precise than are $\overline{Y}_3$ and $\overline{Y}_4$ because of the large differences in within-group variances. Although the separate error term approach necessarily has a larger critical value than does the pooled error term approach, in these data the much larger F value associated with the separate error term approach overrides the slight increase in critical value.

c. *Using MS_W:*

$$\hat{\psi} = \overline{Y}_1 + \overline{Y}_2 - \overline{Y}_3 - \overline{Y}_4$$

(*Note:* Coefficients of ± 1 instead of ± 0.5 are used to simplify calculations.)

$$\hat{\psi} = 4 + 6 - 6 - 8$$

$$= -4$$

$$E_R - E_F = \hat{\psi}^2 \Big/ \sum_{j=1}^{a} \left(c_j^2/n_j\right)$$

$$= (-4)^2 \Big/ \left(\frac{(1)^2}{5} + \frac{(1)^2}{5} + \frac{(-1)^2}{5} + \frac{(-1)^2}{5}\right)$$

$$= 20.00$$

$$MS_W = \sum_{j=1}^{a} s_j^2 \Big/ a$$

$$= \frac{(1+1+9+9)}{4}$$

$$= 5.00.$$

Thus,

$$F = (\hat{\psi})^2/MS_W \sum_{j=1}^{a} \left(c_j^2/n_j \right)$$

$$= \frac{20.00}{5.00}$$

$$= 4.00$$

As in parts (a) and (b), the critical F value is 4.49, so the null hypothesis cannot be rejected.
Using a Separate Error Term:
The F statistic is now given by

$$F = (\hat{\psi})^2 \Big/ \sum_{j=1}^{a} \left(c_j^2/n_j \right) s_j^2$$

$$= \frac{(-4)^2}{\left[\frac{(1)^2}{5}(1) \right] + \left[\frac{(1)^2}{5}(1) \right] + \left[\frac{(-1)^2}{5}(9) \right] + \left[\frac{(-1)^2}{5}(9) \right]}$$

$$= \frac{16.00}{4.00}$$

$$= 4.00$$

The denominator degrees of freedom of the critical value are given by Equation 43:

$$df = \frac{\left(\sum\limits_{j=1}^{a} c_j^2 s_j^2/n_j \right)^2}{\sum\limits_{j=1}^{a} \left[\left(c_j^2 s_j^2/n_j \right)^2 \Big/ (n_j - 1) \right]} \tag{4.43}$$

$$= \frac{\left(\frac{(1)^2(1)}{5} + \frac{(1)^2(1)}{5} + \frac{(-1)^2(9)}{5} + \frac{(-1)^2(9)}{5} \right)^2}{\frac{\left(\frac{(1)^2(1)}{5} \right)^2}{5-1} + \frac{\left(\frac{(1)^2(1)}{5} \right)^2}{5-1} + \frac{\left(\frac{(-1)^2(9)}{5} \right)^2}{5-1} + \frac{\left(\frac{(-1)^2(9)}{5} \right)^2}{5-1}}$$

$$= \frac{(4.00)^2}{.01 + .01 + .81 + .81}$$

$$= 9.76$$

The critical value for 1 numerator and 9 denominator degrees of freedom is 5.12, so the null hypothesis cannot be rejected. Notice that the only difference between the two approaches here is that the critical value is larger for the separate error term approach. In particular, the observed F values are identical for the two approaches. Such equivalence will occur whenever sample sizes are equal and all contrast coefficients are either 1 or −1.

CHAPTER 5

2. a. The Bonferroni procedure should be used because all comparisons are planned, but not every possible pairwise comparison will be tested (see Figure 5.1). In addition, from Table 5.9, it is clear that the

Bonferroni critical value is less than the Scheffé critical value, since the number of contrasts to be tested is less than 8.

b. With 13 subjects per group, the denominator degrees of freedom equal 60 (i.e., $65 - 5$). From Appendix Table A.3, we find that the critical Bonferroni F value for testing 3 comparisons at an experimentwise alpha level of .05 with 60 denominator degrees of freedom is 6.07.

c. Because the comparison of μ_3 versus μ_4 has been chosen post hoc, but all comparisons to be tested are still pairwise, Tukey's method must be used to maintain the experimentwise alpha level (see Figure 5.1).

d. From Appendix Table A.4, we find that the critical q value for 5 groups, 60 denominator degrees of freedom, and $\alpha_{EW} = .05$ equals 3.98. The corresponding critical F value is $(3.98)^2/2$, which equals 7.92.

e. The Bonferroni critical value for testing 3 planned comparisons is substantially lower than the Tukey critical value for testing all pairwise comparisons. Thus, the price to be paid for revising planned comparisons after having examined the data is an increase in the critical value, which will lead to a decrease in power for each individual comparison.

3. a. With equal n, the F statistic for this pairwise comparison is given by

$$F = \frac{n(\overline{Y}_2 - \overline{Y}_4)^2}{2MS_W} \tag{4.28}$$

Further, with equal n, MS_W is the unweighted average of the within-group variances:

$$MS_W = \sum_{j=1}^{a} s_j^2 \Big/ a \tag{3.63}$$

$$= \frac{96 + 112 + 94 + 98}{4}$$

$$= 100$$

Substituting $n = 25$, $\overline{Y}_2 = 46$, $\overline{Y}_4 = 54$, and $MS_W = 100$ into Equation 4.28 yields

$$F = \frac{25(46 - 54)^2}{2(100)}$$

$$= 8.00$$

The Scheffé critical value is given by

$$(a - 1)F_{.05;\ a-1, N-a} \tag{5.22}$$

which for this design implies a critical value of

$$(4 - 1)F_{.05;\ 4-1, 100-4}$$

From Appendix Table A.2, we find that

$$F_{.05;\ 3,60} = 2.76$$

so the Scheffé critical F value is

$$3(2.76) = 8.28$$

Thus, the experimenter is correct that the mean difference is nonsignificant by Scheffé's method.

b. Tukey's WSD can be used to maintain α_{EW} at .05, since the post hoc contrast is pairwise. The value of the observed F is still 8.00, but the Tukey critical F value is given by

$$(q_{.05;\ a, N-a})^2/2 \tag{Table 5.16}$$

For these data, from Appendix Table A.4, the Tukey critical value equals $(3.74)^2/2$, or 6.99. The observed F exceeds the critical F, so the mean difference can be declared statistically significant with Tukey's method. This exercise illustrates the fact that Tukey's method is more powerful than Scheffé's method for testing pairwise comparisons.

5. a. *Using MS_W:*
        We saw in Chapter 4 that the observed F equals 2.00 for this comparison (see the answer to problem 13(a) in Chapter 4). Also, using a pooled error term, there are 16 denominator degrees of freedom. The critical value for testing all pairwise comparisons is given by

$$(q_{.05;\, a, N-a})^2/2 \qquad \text{(Table 5.16)}$$

For these data, from Appendix Table A.4, $q_{.05;\, 4, 16} = 4.05$, so the appropriate Tukey critical value is $(4.05)^2/2 = 8.20$. Because the observed F value is less than the critical F, the contrast is nonsignificant.
Using a Separate Error Term:
We saw in the Chapter 4 answers that the observed F now equals 1.11, and there are now only 8 denominator degrees of freedom. The critical value is now given by

$$(q_{.05;\, 4, 8})^2/2 = (4.53)^2/2$$
$$= 10.26$$

The observed F value is now lower than it was with MS_W as the error term, and the critical value is now higher. Thus, the contrast is also nonsignificant using a separate error term.

   b. *Using MS_W:*
       We saw in the Chapter 4 answers that the observed F value for this contrast is 2.00. Again there are 16 denominator degrees of freedom, so the Tukey critical value is 8.20, and this contrast is also nonsignificant.
       Using a Separate Error Term:
       We saw in the Chapter 4 answers that the observed F value is now 10.00. With 8 denominator degrees of freedom, the Tukey critical value is again 10.26, so the contrast just misses being statistically significant.

   c. The separate error term seems more appropriate, given the wide disparity in sample values. In particular, there is more evidence that μ_1 and μ_2 are different from one another than that μ_3 and μ_4 are. The separate error term reflects this fact, unlike the pooled error term, which regards these two differences as equally significant.

7. a. It is possible to perform the test of the omnibus null hypothesis. Because this set of contrasts is orthogonal, the sums of squares attributable to the three contrasts are additive. As a result, the between-group sum of squares is given by

$$SS_B = SS_{\psi 1} + SS_{\psi 2} + SS_{\psi 3}$$
$$= 75 + 175 + 125$$
$$= 375$$

The observed value of the F statistic then equals

$$F = \frac{SS_B/(a-1)}{MS_W}$$
$$= \frac{375/3}{25}$$
$$= 5.00$$

From Appendix Table A.2, we find that the critical F with 3 and 40 degrees of freedom is 2.84. Thus, the group means are significantly different from one another at the .05 level.

   b. From Equation 4.41, the observed F for a contrast is

$$F = \frac{(\hat{\psi})^2}{MS_W \sum\limits_{j=1}^{a} \left(c_j^2/n_j\right)} \qquad (4.41)$$

However, we know from Equation 4.39 that the term

$$\frac{(\hat{\psi})^2}{\sum_{j=1}^{a} \left(c_j^2/n_j \right)}$$

is simply the sum of squares for the contrast. Thus,

$$F = \frac{SS_\psi}{MS_W}$$

For the data of this problem, we have

$$\psi_1: \quad F = \frac{75}{25} = 3.0$$

$$\psi_2: \quad F = \frac{175}{25} = 7.0$$

$$\psi_3: \quad F = \frac{125}{25} = 5.0$$

The appropriate procedure for maintaining α_{EW} at .05 here is the Bonferroni approach (see Figure 5.1 and Table 5.9). From Appendix Table A.3, we find that the Bonferroni F critical value for testing three contrasts (at $\alpha_{EW} = .05$) with 40 denominator degrees of freedom is 6.24. Thus, only the second contrast can be declared statistically significant, using an experimentwise alpha level of .05.

c. The omnibus observed F value of part (a) equaled 5.00. The three observed F values of part (b) equaled 3.00, 7.00, and 5.00. Thus, the omnibus F value equals the average (i.e., the mean) of the F values for the three contrasts. In general, the omnibus F value can be conceptualized as an average F value, averaging over a set of $a - 1$ orthogonal contrasts. That this is true can be seen from the following algebraic equivalence:

$$
\begin{aligned}
F_{\text{omnibus}} &= \frac{MS_B}{MS_W} \\[2mm]
&= \frac{SS_B/(a-1)}{MS_W} \\[2mm]
&= \frac{\sum\limits_{j=1}^{a-1} SS_{\psi j}/(a-1)}{MS_W} \quad \text{(where the contrasts are orthogonal)} \\[2mm]
&= \left(\sum_{j=1}^{a-1} \frac{SS_{\psi j}}{MS_W} \right) \bigg/ (a-1) \\[2mm]
&= \sum_{j=1}^{a-1} F_{\psi j} \bigg/ (a-1)
\end{aligned}
$$

For a related perspective, see Exercise 9 at the end of Chapter 3.

11. a. In general, the value of the observed F is

$$F = \frac{(E_R - E_F)/(df_R - df_F)}{E_F/df_F}$$

Substituting from Equations 3.58 and 3.63 yields

$$F = \frac{n \sum\limits_{j=1}^{a} (\bar{Y}_j - \bar{Y})^2 \bigg/ (a-1)}{\sum\limits_{j=1}^{a} s_j^2/a}$$

For these data, $n = 11, \overline{Y}_1 = 10, \overline{Y}_2 = 10, \overline{Y}_3 = 22, \overline{Y} = 14, a = 3, s_1^2 = 100, s_2^2 = 196$, and $s_3^2 = 154$. Substituting these values into the expression for the F statistic yields

$$F = \frac{11(16 + 16 + 64)/2}{150}$$

$$= \frac{528}{150}$$

$$= 3.52$$

From Appendix Table A.2, we find that the critical F value for 2 numerator and 30 denominator degrees of freedom at the .05 level is 3.32. Thus, the professor is correct that the null hypothesis can be rejected.

b. With equal n, Equation 4.28 can be used to test pairwise comparisons. For example, the F statistic for comparing the means of groups 1 and 3 is given by

$$F = \frac{n(\overline{Y}_1 - \overline{Y}_3)^2}{2MS_W}$$

For these data, $n = 11, \overline{Y}_1 = 10, \overline{Y}_3 = 22$, and $MS_W = 150$ (from part (a)). Thus, the observed F equals

$$F = \frac{11(10 - 22)^2}{2(150)}$$

$$= 5.28$$

From Appendix Table A.4, we find that the critical value for 3 groups, 30 denominator degrees of freedom, and $\alpha_{EW} = .05$ is 3.49. The corresponding critical F value is $(3.49)^2/2$, or 6.09. Thus, the means of groups 1 and 3 are not significantly different from one another. The exact same conclusion applies to a comparison of groups 2 and 3, and the difference between groups 1 and 2 is obviously nonsignificant. Thus, the professor is correct that none of the pairwise differences are significant.

c. As we pointed out in the chapter, a statistically significant omnibus test result does not necessarily imply that a significant pairwise difference can be found. Instead, a significant omnibus result implies that there is at least one comparison that will be declared significant with Scheffé's method. However, that comparison need not be pairwise. Indeed, using a pooled error term, in this numerical example, the contrast that produces $F_{maximum}$ is a complex comparison with coefficients of 1, 1, and −2. This comparison is statistically significant, even using Scheffé's method to maintain $\alpha_{EW} = .05$ for all possible contrasts.

CHAPTER 6

2. a. With equal n,

$$SS_{linear} = E_R - E_F = n(\hat{\psi}_{linear})^2 \Big/ \sum_{j=1}^{a} c_j^2 \qquad (6.11)$$

The linear contrast coefficients are $c_1 = -3, c_2 = -1, c_3 = 1$, and $c_4 = 3$ (see Appendix Table A.10). Thus,

$$\hat{\psi}_{linear} = -3(10) - 1(20) + 1(30) + 3(40)$$

$$= 100$$

and

$$\sum_{j=1}^{a} c_j^2 = (-3)^2 + (-1)^2 + (1)^2 + (3)^2$$

$$= 20$$

Thus,

$$SS_{\text{linear}} = 10(100)^2/20$$

$$= 5000$$

b.

$$SS_{\text{quadratic}} = n(\hat{\psi}_{\text{quadratic}})^2 \Big/ \sum_{j=1}^{a} c_j^2$$

From Appendix Table A.10, the quadratic contrast coefficients are $c_1 = 1, c_2 = -1, c_3 = -1$, and $c_4 = 1$.
Thus,

$$\hat{\psi}_{\text{quadratic}} = 1(10) - 1(20) - 1(30) + 1(40)$$

$$= 0$$

and

$$\sum_{j=1}^{a} c_j^2 = (1)^2 + (-1)^1 + (-1)^2 + (1)^2$$

$$= 4$$

Thus,

$$SS_{\text{quadratic}} = 10(0)^2/4$$

$$= 0$$

c.

$$SS_{\text{cubic}} = n(\hat{\psi}_{\text{cubic}})^2 \Big/ \sum_{j=1}^{a} c_j^2$$

From Appendix Table A.10, the cubic contrast coefficients are $c_1 = -1, c_2 = 3, c_3 = -3$, and $c_4 = 1$.
Thus,

$$\hat{\psi}_{\text{cubic}} = -1(10) + 3(20) - 3(30) + 1(40)$$

$$= 0$$

and

$$\sum_{j=i}^{a} c_j^2 = (-1)^2 + (3)^2 + (-3)^2 + (1)^2$$

$$= 20$$

Thus,

$$SS_{\text{cubic}} = 10(0)^2/20$$

$$= 0$$

d. Yes, Figure 6.3(a) reflects a pure linear trend, because SS_{linear} is nonzero but $SS_{\text{quadratic}}$ and SS_{cubic} are both zero (that is, all the other $a - 1$ trends are zero).

6. a.

$$F = \frac{SS_{\text{linear}}}{MS_{\text{w}}}$$

We are told that $MS_W = 150$, but we need to calculate SS_{linear}, which we can do from

$$SS_{linear} = n(\hat{\psi}_{linear})^2 \bigg/ \sum_{j=1}^{a} c_j^2$$

For 5 groups, the linear contrast coefficients are $c_1 = -2$, $c_2 = -1$, $c_3 = 0$, $C_4 = 1$, and $c_5 = 2$ (see Appendix Table A.10). Thus,

$$\hat{\psi}_{linear} = -2(80) - 1(83) + 0(87) + 1(89) + 2(91)$$

$$= 28$$

and

$$\sum_{j=1}^{a} c_j^2 = (-2)^2 + (-1)^2 + (0)^2 + (1)^2 + (2)^2$$

$$= 10$$

Thus,

$$SS_{linear} = 15(28)^2/10$$

$$= 1176$$

The value of the F test statistic for the linear trend then equals

$$F = \frac{SS_{linear}}{MS_W}$$

$$= \frac{1176}{150}$$

$$= 7.84$$

The critical F value has 1 and 70 degrees of freedom. From Appendix Table A.2, we find that the critical F with 1 and 60 degrees of freedom (rounding downward) is 4.00 at the .05 level. Thus, the linear trend is statistically significant at the .05 level.

b. To test the omnibus null hypothesis, we must calculate an observed F of the form

$$F = \frac{MS_B}{MS_W}$$

We are told that $MS_W = 150$, but we must find MS_B, which is given by

$$MS_B = SS_B/(a-1)$$

$$= n \sum_{j=1}^{a} (\overline{Y}_j - \overline{Y})^2/(a-1)$$

$$= 15[(80-86)^2 + (83-86)^2 + (87-86)^2 + (89-86)^2 + (91-86)^2]/4$$

$$= 1200/4$$

$$= 300$$

As a result, the observed F is

$$F = \frac{MS_B}{MS_W}$$

$$= \frac{300}{150}$$

$$= 2.00$$

The critical F value has 4 and 70 degrees of freedom. From Appendix Table A.2, we find that the critical F with 4 and 60 degrees of freedom (rounding downward) is 2.53 at the .05 level. Thus, the omnibus null hypothesis cannot be rejected.

c.   The F statistic for the linear trend is

$$F = \frac{SS_{linear}}{MS_W}$$

while the F statistic for the omnibus test is

$$F = \frac{SS_{between}/4}{MS_W}$$

For these data, the linear trend accounts for 98% of the between-group sum of squares (that is, 1176 out of 1200), so that SS_{linear} is almost as large as $SS_{between}$. However, the linear trend is based on 1 degree of freedom, whereas the omnibus test is based on 4 degrees of freedom. In other words, with one parameter, the linear trend model decreases the sum of squared errors by 1176 relative to a restricted model of the form

$$Y_{ij} = \mu + \varepsilon_{ij}$$

On the other hand, the "cell means" model (that is, the full model of the omnibus test) decreases the sum of squared errors by 1200 relative to the same restricted model, but requires three more parameters than does the restricted model to accomplish this reduction. As a consequence, although SS_{linear} is slightly smaller than $SS_{between}$, MS_{linear} is almost four times larger than $MS_{between}$. The same ratio applies to the observed F values.

d.   If in fact the true difference in population means is entirely linear, the observed F value for the linear trend will likely be appreciably larger than the omnibus F value. Thus, statistical power is substantially increased in this situation by planning to test the linear trend. Of course, if the true trend is nonlinear, the planned test of the linear trend may be sorely lacking in power. This same effect may occur for any planned comparison–not just for a linear trend.

e.   Yes, because the omnibus test need not even be performed when planned comparisons have been formulated.

9.   The estimated slope of 2.35 is not accurate. Using Equation 7 to calculate the slope requires that linear trend coefficients be defined as

$$c_j = X_j - \overline{X}, \tag{6.8}$$

which in this problem implies that the coefficients should be

$$
\begin{aligned}
c_1 &= 4 - 7 &= -3 \\
c_2 &= 7 - 7 &= 0 \\
c_3 &= 10 - 7 &= 3
\end{aligned}
$$

The values of $-1, 0$, and 1 from Appendix Table A.10 are proportional to the proper values, but in general they cannot be used to calculate an estimated slope, although they can be used to test the statistical significance of the linear trend. Substituting $c_1 = -3$, $c_2 = 0$, $c_3 = 3$, $\overline{Y}_1 = 5.5$, $\overline{Y}_2 = 7.7$, and $\overline{Y}_3 = 10.2$ into Equations 6 and 7 yields

$$\hat{\psi}_{linear} = \sum_{j=1}^{a} c_j \overline{Y}_j \tag{6.6}$$

$$= -3(5.5) + 0(7.7) + 3(10.2)$$

$$= 14.10$$

$$\hat{\beta}_1 = \hat{\psi}_{linear} \Big/ \sum_{j=1}^{a} c_j^2 \tag{6.7}$$

$$= 14.10/[(-3)^2 + (0)^2 + (3)^2]$$

$$= .78$$

Thus, the correct estimated slope is .78, which is one-third (within rounding error) of the claimed value of 2.35. Now, with a slope of .78, we would expect 10-year-olds to outperform 4-year-olds by approximately 4.68 units, which is virtually identical to the observed difference of 4.70 units.

11. a. The linear trend coefficients shown in Appendix Table A.10 for testing a linear trend with 4 groups are $-3, -1, 1$, and 3. However, Equation 7 requires that the contrast coefficients be defined as

$$c_j = X_j - \overline{X}$$

which for our data implies that

$$c_1 = 1 - 2.5 = -1.5$$
$$c_2 = 2 - 2.5 = -0.5$$
$$c_3 = 3 - 2.5 = 0.5$$
$$c_4 = 4 - 2.5 = 1.5$$

The estimated slope $\hat{\beta}_1$ is calculated from Equation 7 as follows:

$$\hat{\beta}_1 = \hat{\psi}_{\text{linear}} \Big/ \sum_{j=1}^{a} c_j^2 \tag{6.7}$$

The $\hat{\psi}_{\text{linear}}$ term can be calculated from Equation 6:

$$\hat{\psi}_{\text{linear}} = \sum_{j=1}^{a} c_j \overline{Y}_j \tag{6.6}$$
$$= -1.5(6.16) - .5(4.44) + .5(3.44) + 1.5(4.76)$$
$$= -2.60$$

Also,

$$\sum_{j=1}^{a} c_j^2 = (-1.5)^2 + (-.5)^2 + (.5)^2 + (1.5)^2$$
$$= 5.00$$

Substituting the values of -2.60 and 5.00 into Equation 7 yields

$$\hat{\beta}_1 = -2.60/5.00$$
$$= -.52$$

b. The observed F is given by

$$F = \frac{SS_{\text{linear}}}{MS_W}$$

where

$$SS_{\text{linear}} = n(\hat{\psi}_{\text{linear}})^2 \Big/ \sum_{j=1}^{a} c_j^2 \tag{see 6.11}$$
$$= 5(-2.60)^2/5.00$$
$$= 6.760$$

and

$$MS_W = \sum_{j=1}^{a} s_j^2 / a \tag{3.63}$$

$$= (.688 + .228 + .068 + .148)/4$$

$$= .283$$

Therefore,

$$F = \frac{SS_{\text{linear}}}{MS_W}$$

$$= \frac{6.760}{.283}$$

$$= 23.89$$

From Appendix Table A.2, the critical F value with 1 and 16 degrees of freedom is 4.49, so the linear trend is statistically significant at the .05 level.

c. The least squares estimate of the slope parameter is $\hat{\beta}_1 = -52$, which is identical to the value obtained in part (a).

d. The F value of 7.28 (which is the square of $t = -2.698$) is considerably less than the F value of 23.89 obtained in part (b).

e. Yes, in both cases, the sum of squares attributable to the linear trend equals 6.760. Thus, the value of $E_R - E_F$ is the same in the two analyses.

f. The denominator of the F statistic for testing the linear contrast in part (b) was MS_W, which has a value of 0.283 for these data. Because $df_F = 16$ for this analysis, the corresponding error sum of squares is 4.528 ($16 \times .283$). However, the error sum of squares for the regression approach is 16.720, obviously a much larger value. The associated degrees of freedom equal 18, so the denominator of the F statistic using this approach is .929 ($16.720 \div 18$). The larger denominator of the regression approach (relative to testing the contrast, as in part (b)) produces a lower F value.

g. As stated in the text, the "cell means" model is mathematically equivalent to a model that includes all $a - 1$ trends, such as

$$Y_{ij} = \beta_0 + \beta_1 X_{ij} + \beta_2 X_{ij}^2 + \beta_3 X_{ij}^3 + \varepsilon_{ij}$$

when $a = 4$. However, the full model of the regression approach excludes the quadratic and cubic terms. As a result, any quadratic and cubic effects contribute to the error of this model. Specifically,

$$E_{F(\text{regression})} = E_{F(\text{cell means})} + SS_{\text{quadratic}} + SS_{\text{cubic}}$$

It turns out that, for these data,

$$SS_{\text{quadratic}} = 11.552$$

$$SS_{\text{cubic}} = .640$$

Thus,

$$E_{F(\text{regression})} = 4.528 + 11.552 + .640$$

$$= 16.72$$

in agreement with our earlier finding.

h. To the extent that nonlinear trends are nonzero, testing the linear trend using procedures for testing a contrast will yield a larger F value than will the regression approach. Thus, in this situation, using MS_W as the error term increases the test's power. If, on the other hand, the nonlinear trends are truly zero, the regression approach gains an additional $a - 2$ degrees of freedom for the error term. As a result, the critical F value is somewhat lower, and power is somewhat higher. However, this potential advantage is likely to be very small unless a is large relative to N. Thus, unless there are very few subjects at each level of the factor, the use of MS_W as the error term is generally preferable to the use of the error term based on the regression model with X as the single predictor variable. This problem is not unique to trend analysis, nor to differences between ANOVA and regression. Instead, the general point is that, if one fails to include relevant variables in a model, estimates of error variability calculated from that model can seriously overestimate the magnitude of true error (See Appendix B-2).

CHAPTER 7

1. a. (1) From Equation 10, α_j is defined to be

$$\alpha_j = \mu_{j.} - \mu_{..} \qquad (7.10)$$

For these data, the marginal mean for row 1 is

$$\mu_{1.} = \sum_{k=1}^{b} \mu_{1k}/b \qquad \text{(see 7.7)}$$

$$= \sum_{k=1}^{3} \mu_{1k}/3$$

$$= (\mu_{11} + \mu_{12} + \mu_{13})/3$$

$$= (10 + 10 + 10)/3$$

$$= 10$$

Similarly,

$$\mu_{2.} = (12 + 12 + 12)/3$$

$$= 12$$

and

$$\mu_{3.} = (17 + 17 + 17)/3$$

$$= 17$$

In addition, the population grand mean is defined to be

$$\mu_{..} = \sum_{k=1}^{b} \sum_{j=1}^{a} \mu_{jk}/ab \qquad (7.9)$$

$$= \sum_{k=1}^{3} \sum_{j=1}^{3} \mu_{jk}/9$$

$$= (10 + 12 + 17 + 10 + 12 + 17 + 10 + 12 + 17)/9$$

$$= 13$$

Substituting the values for $\mu_{j.}$ and $\mu_{..}$ into Equation 10 yields

$$\alpha_1 = \mu_{1.} - \mu_{..}$$

$$= 10 - 13$$

$$= -3$$

$$\alpha_2 = \mu_{2.} - \mu_{..}$$
$$= 12 - 13$$
$$= -1$$
$$\alpha_3 = \mu_{3.} - \mu_{..}$$
$$= 17 - 13$$
$$= 4$$

(2) The β parameters are obtained in a similar manner, except that now we must focus on column marginal means, instead of row marginal means:

$$\mu_{.1} = (10 + 12 + 17)/3 \qquad\qquad \text{(see 7.8)}$$
$$= 13$$
$$\mu_{.2} = (10 + 12 + 17)/3$$
$$= 13$$
$$\mu_{.3} = (10 + 12 + 17)/3$$
$$= 13$$

Thus, the values of the column main effect β parameters are given by

$$\beta_1 = \mu_{.1} - \mu_{..}$$
$$= 13 - 13$$
$$= 0$$
$$\beta_2 = \mu_{.2} - \mu_{..}$$
$$= 13 - 13$$
$$= 0$$
$$\beta_3 = 13 - 13$$
$$= 0$$

(3) The interaction parameters are defined in terms of the cell means and the other effect parameters:

$$(\alpha\beta)_{jk} = \mu_{jk} - (\mu_{..} + \alpha_j + \beta_k). \qquad\qquad (7.12)$$

For example,

$$(\alpha\beta)_{11} = \mu_{11} - (\mu_{..} + \alpha_1 + \beta_1)$$
$$= 10 - (13 + (-3) + 0)$$
$$= 10 - 10$$
$$= 0$$

For these data, all 9 interaction parameters have a value of zero.

(4) Only the A main effect is nonzero in the population. For these data, simple visual inspection of the cell means shows that the rows differ from one another but the columns do not. In addition, the row differences are identical in each column. The α_j, β_k, and $(\alpha\beta)_{jk}$ parameter values confirm that the B main effect and AB interactions are null in the population.

c.   (1)   From Equation 10, α_j defined to be

$$\alpha_j = \mu_{j.} - \mu_{..} \tag{7.10}$$

For these data, the marginal mean for row 1 is

$$\mu_{1.} = \sum_{k=1}^{b} \mu_{lk}/b \qquad \text{(see 7.7)}$$

$$= \sum_{k=1}^{3} \mu_{lk}/3$$

$$= (\mu_{11} + \mu_{12} + \mu_{13})/3$$

$$= (26 + 22 + 21)/3$$

$$= 23.$$

Similarly,

$$\mu_{2.} = (23 + 19 + 18)/3$$

$$= 20$$

and

$$\mu_{3.} = (17 + 13 + 12)/3$$

$$= 14$$

In addition, the population grand mean is defined to be

$$\mu_{..} = \sum_{k=1}^{b}\sum_{j=1}^{a} \mu_{jk}/ab$$

$$= \sum_{k=1}^{3}\sum_{j=1}^{3} \mu_{jk}/9$$

$$= (26 + 22 + 21 + 23 + 19 + 18 + 17 + 13 + 12)/9$$

$$= 19$$

Substituting the values for $\mu_{j.}$ and $\mu_{..}$ into Equation 10 yields

$$\alpha_1 = \mu_{1.} - \mu_{..}$$

$$= 23 - 19$$

$$= 4$$

$$\alpha_2 = \mu_{2.} - \mu_{..}$$

$$= 20 - 19$$

$$= 1$$

$$\alpha_3 = \mu_{3.} - \mu_{..}$$

$$= 14 - 19$$

$$= -5$$

(2) The β parameters are obtained in a similar manner, except that now we must focus on column marginal means, instead of row marginal means:

$$\mu_{.1} = (26 + 23 + 17)/3$$
$$= 22$$
$$\mu_{.2} = (22 + 19 + 13)/3$$
$$= 18$$
$$\mu_{.3} = (21 + 18 + 12)/3$$
$$= 17$$

Thus, the values of the column main effect β parameters are given by

$$\beta_1 = \mu_{.1} - \mu_{..}$$
$$= 22 - 19$$
$$= 3$$
$$\beta_2 = \mu_{.2} - \mu_{..}$$
$$= 18 - 19$$
$$= -1$$
$$\beta_3 = \mu_{.3} - \mu_{..}$$
$$= 17 - 19$$
$$= -2$$

(3) The interaction parameters are defined in terms of the cell means and the other effect parameters:

$$(\alpha\beta)_{jk} = \mu_{jk} - (\mu_{..} + \alpha_j + \beta_k). \tag{7.12}$$

For example,

$$(\alpha\beta)_{11} = \mu_{11} - (\mu_{..} + \alpha_1 + \beta_1)$$
$$= 26 - (19 + 4 + 3)$$
$$= 26 - 26$$
$$= 0$$

For these data, it turns out that all nine interaction parameters have a value of zero.

(4) The A main effect and the B main effect are nonzero in the population. The nonzero α_j and β_k parameters corroborate the visual impression that rows differ from one another, and so do columns. However, the row differences are the same in all three columns (or, conversely, the column differences are the same in all three rows), which is why the interaction is null in the population.

4. a. From Equation 16, the general form of an estimated row main effect parameter is

$$\hat{\alpha}_j = \overline{Y}_{j.} - \overline{Y}_{..} \tag{7.16}$$

For these data,

$$\hat{\alpha}_1 = [(8 + 10 + 15)/3] - [(8 + 10 + 15 + 9 + 14 + 10 + 13 + 9 + 11)/9]$$
$$= 11 - 11$$
$$= 0$$

$$\hat{\alpha}_2 = [(9 + 14 + 10)/3] - 11$$
$$= 11 - 11$$
$$= 0$$
$$\hat{\alpha}_3 = [(13 + 9 + 11)/3] - 11$$
$$= 11 - 11$$
$$= 0$$

b.
$$SS_A = \sum_{\text{all obs}} \hat{\alpha}_j^2$$

Notice that with equal n, a total of $n\,b$ subjects have an $\hat{\alpha}_j$ value of $\hat{\alpha}_1$, another $n\,b$ subjects have an $\hat{\alpha}_j$ value of $\hat{\alpha}_2$, and so forth. For these data, then, 24 subjects have an $\hat{\alpha}_j$ value of $\hat{\alpha}_1$, 24 have $\hat{\alpha}_2$, and 24 have $\hat{\alpha}_3$. Thus,

$$SS_A = 24\hat{\alpha}_1^2 + 24\hat{\alpha}_2^2 + 24\hat{\alpha}_3^2$$
$$= 24(0)^2 + 24(0)^2 + 24(0)^2$$
$$= 0.$$

c. From Equation 17, the general form of an estimated column main effect parameter is

$$\hat{\beta}_k = \overline{Y}_{.k} - \overline{Y}_{..} \tag{7.17}$$

For these data,

$$\hat{\beta}_1 = [(8 + 9 + 13)/3] - 11$$
$$= 10 - 11$$
$$= -1$$
$$\hat{\beta}_2 = [(10 + 14 + 9)/3] - 11$$
$$= 11 - 11$$
$$= 0$$
$$\hat{\beta}_3 = [(15 + 10 + 11)/3] - 11$$
$$= 12 - 11$$
$$= 1.$$

d.
$$SS_B = \sum_{\text{all obs}} \hat{\beta}_k^2$$

As in part (b), 24 subjects have a $\hat{\beta}_k$ value of $\hat{\beta}_1$, 24 have $\hat{\beta}_2$, and 24 have $\hat{\beta}_3$. Thus,

$$SS_B = 24\hat{\beta}_1^2 + 24\hat{\beta}_2^2 + 24\hat{\beta}_3^2$$
$$= 24(-1)^2 + 24(0)^2 + 24(1)^2$$
$$= 48$$

e. From Equation 18, the general form of an estimated interaction parameter is

$$\widehat{\alpha\beta}_{jk} = \overline{Y}_{jk} - (\overline{Y}_{j.} + \overline{Y}_{.k} - \overline{Y}_{..}) \tag{7.18}$$

For these data,

$$\widehat{\alpha\beta}_{11} = 8 - (11 + 10 - 11)$$
$$= -2$$
$$\widehat{\alpha\beta}_{12} = 10 - (11 + 11 - 11)$$
$$= -1$$
$$\widehat{\alpha\beta}_{13} = 15 - (11 + 12 - 11)$$
$$= 3$$
$$\widehat{\alpha\beta}_{21} = 9 - (11 + 10 - 11)$$
$$= -1$$
$$\widehat{\alpha\beta}_{22} = 14 - (11 + 11 - 11)$$
$$= 3$$
$$\widehat{\alpha\beta}_{23} = 10 - (11 + 12 - 11)$$
$$= -2$$
$$\widehat{\alpha\beta}_{31} = 13 - (11 + 10 - 11)$$
$$= 3$$
$$\widehat{\alpha\beta}_{32} = 9 - (11 + 11 - 11)$$
$$= -2$$
$$\widehat{\alpha\beta}_{33} = 11 - (11 + 12 - 11)$$
$$= -1.$$

f.

$$SS_{AB} = \sum_{\text{all obs}} (\alpha\beta_{jk})^2$$

In general, with equal n, a total of n subjects will have an $\widehat{\alpha\beta}_{jk}$ value of $\widehat{\alpha\beta}_{11}$, n will have a value of $\widehat{\alpha\beta}_{12}$, and so forth. Thus,

$$SS_{AB} = 8[(-2)^2 + (-1)^2 + (3)^2 + (-1)^2 + (3)^2 + (-2)^2 + (3)^2 + (-2)^2 + (-1)^2]$$
$$= 336$$

5. a.

$$SS_A = E_R - E_F = nb \sum_{j=1}^{a} (\overline{Y}_{j.} - \overline{Y}_{..})^2 \tag{7.25}$$

$$= 5(3)[(187 - 193)^2 + (199 - 193)^2]$$

$$= 1080$$

b.

$$SS_A = E_R - E_F = n \sum_{j=1}^{a} (\overline{Y}_j - \overline{Y})^2 \tag{7.26}$$

$$= 15[(187 - 193)^2 + (199 - 193)^2]$$

$$= 1080$$

c. The answers to parts (a) and (b) are the same. This equivalence provides an empirical demonstration of the assertion in Chapter 7 that, in equal n designs, the sum of squares for the A main effect in a factorial design equals the sum of squares due to A in a single factor design when the data are analyzed as if the B factor never existed.

8.   a.   We need to calculate ϕ from the formula given in the problem:

$$\phi = .40\sqrt{n}.$$

Assuming $n = 10$,

$$\phi = .40\sqrt{10}$$
$$= 1.26$$

The chart for $df_{numerator} = 1$ must be consulted. Also, notice that $df_{denominator} = 18$. With $\alpha = .05$, the power appears to be approximately .40.

  b.   With five groups and $n = 10$, ϕ again equals 1.26. Now, however, the chart for $df_{numerator} = 4$ must be consulted with $df_{denominator} = 45$. With $\alpha = .05$, the power appears to be approximately .53.

  c.   In the factorial design, ϕ is calculated from

$$\phi = .40\sqrt{\frac{df_{denominator}}{df_{effect} + 1} + 1}$$

For a main effect in a 2×2 design with $n = 10$,

$$df_{effect} = 1 \qquad\qquad \text{(see 7.28)}$$
$$df_{denominator} = (2)(2)(10 - 1) = 36 \qquad\qquad \text{(see 7.27)}$$

so

$$\phi = .40\sqrt{\frac{36}{2} + 1}$$
$$= 1.74$$

The chart for $df_{numerator} = 1$ must be consulted with $df_{denominator} = 36$. With $\alpha = .05$, the power appears to be approximately .67.

  d.   The power will be the same as in part (c), because $df_{effect} = 1$ for the interaction effect in a 2×2 design (see Equation 7.34).

  e.   Once again, ϕ is calculated from

$$\phi = .40\sqrt{\frac{df_{denominator}}{df_{effect}} + 1}$$

For a main effect in a 3×3 design with $n = 10$,

$$df_{effect} = 2 \qquad\qquad \text{(see 7.28)}$$
$$df_{denominator} = (3)(3)(10 - 1) = 81 \qquad\qquad \text{(see 7.27)}$$

so

$$\phi = .40\sqrt{\frac{81}{2 + 1} + 1}$$
$$= 2.12$$

The chart for $df_{numerator} = 2$ must be consulted with $df_{denominator} = 81$. With $\alpha = .05$, the power appears to be approximately .91.

f. Yet again, ϕ is calculated from

$$\phi = .40\sqrt{\frac{df_{\text{denominator}}}{df_{\text{effect}} + 1} + 1}$$

For an interaction effect in a 3×3 design with $n = 10$,

$$df_{\text{effect}} = 4 \qquad \text{(see 7.34)}$$

$$df_{\text{denominator}} = (3)(3)(10 - 1) = 81 \qquad \text{(see 7.27)}$$

so

$$\phi = .40\sqrt{\frac{81}{4 + 1} + 1}$$

$$= 1.66$$

The chart for $df_{\text{numerator}} = 4$ must be consulted with $df_{\text{denominator}} = 81$. With $\alpha = .05$, the power appears to be approximately .85.

g. Only 2 of the 6 effects in parts (a) through (f) would have a power as high as .8 for detecting a large effect with 10 subjects per cell.

h. Two comments are pertinent here. First, the power of a test is a function not only of the sample size and the effect size (that is, small, medium, or large), but also of the type of design and the type of effect to be tested in that design. Thus, $n = 10$ may be sufficient for some effects in some designs, but not for others. Second, in many cases, $n = 10$ per cell may be too few subjects to have a power of .8 to detect even a large effect, much less a medium or small effect.

11. a. Notice that this student has performed tests of the simple effect of therapy for females and males separately. In each case the sum of squares for therapy can be found from

$$SS_{\text{effect}} = n\sum_{j=1}^{a}(\overline{Y}_j - \overline{Y})^2 \qquad (7.52)$$

where the sample means refer to the means for the specific individuals under consideration. For females, $\overline{Y}_1 = 60, \overline{Y}_2 = 80$, and $n = 10$. Thus, for females,

$$SS_{\text{therapy}} = 10[(60 - 70)^2 + (80 - 70)^2]$$

$$= 2000$$

The observed F value is given by

$$F = \frac{SS_{\text{effect}}/df_{\text{effect}}}{MS_W}$$

$$= \frac{2000/1}{800}$$

$$= 2.50$$

The critical F value with 1 and 36 degrees of freedom is approximately 4.17 (see Appendix Table A.2), so the difference between the therapies is nonsignificant at the .05 level for the females. For males, $\overline{Y}_1 = 40, \overline{Y}_2 = 60$, and $n = 10$, so

$$SS_{\text{therapy}} = 10[(40 - 50)^2 + (60 - 50)^2)$$

$$= 2000$$

The observed F is 2.50, so the difference between the therapies is also nonsignificant for the males.

b. The only difference from part (a) will involve the critical F value, which now equals 4.41, because there are now only 18 denominator degrees of freedom. However, as in part (a), the difference between the therapies is nonsignificant for females and males considered separately.

c. The sum of squares for the therapy main effect is

$$SS_{\text{therapy}} = (10)(2)[(50 - 60)^2 + (70 - 60)^2] \qquad \text{(see 7.25)}$$

$$= 4000$$

As a result,

$$F = \frac{SS_{\text{therapy}}/df_{\text{therapy}}}{MS_{\text{W}}}$$

$$= \frac{4000/1}{800}$$

$$= 5.00$$

As in part (a), the critical F with 1 and 36 degrees of freedom is approximately 4.17. Now, however, the difference between the therapies is statistically significant at the .05 level. Incidentally, for later parts of this problem, it is helpful to note that the interaction sum of squares for these data is exactly zero.

d. As we saw in Chapter 3, the t test can be regarded as a comparison of models of the form

$$\text{Full}: \quad Y_{ij} = \mu_j + \varepsilon_{ij}$$

$$\text{Restricted}: \quad Y_{ij} = \mu + \varepsilon_{ij}$$

Group membership is solely a function of form of therapy, so any effects due to sex appear in the error term of both models. An F test to compare these models would be

$$F = \frac{(E_R - E_F)/(df_R - df_F)}{E_F/df_F}$$

In this situation,

$$df_F = N - a$$

$$= 40 - 2$$

$$= 38$$

and

$$df_R - df_F = 1$$

Further,

$$E_R - E_F = n \sum_{j=1}^{a} (\overline{Y}_j - \overline{Y})^2$$

$$= 20[(50 - 60)^2 + (70 - 60)^2]$$

$$= 4000$$

To calculate the observed F, we must find the sum of squared errors of the full model. However, the errors of this model will include the within-cell errors of the 2×2 factorial design, as well as any effects due to sex. Specifically,

$$E_F = SS_{\text{within}} + SS_{\text{sex}} + SS_{\text{sex by therapy}}$$

For these data,

$$SS_{\text{within}} = df_{\text{within}}MS_W$$
$$= 36(800)$$
$$= 28,800$$
$$SS_{\text{sex}} = (10)(2)[(70-60)^2 + (50-60)^2]$$
$$= 4000$$
$$SS_{\text{sex by therapy}} = 0$$

Thus,

$$E_F = 28,800 + 4000 + 0$$
$$= 32,800$$

The observed F is then

$$F = \frac{4000/1}{32,800/38}$$
$$= 4.63$$

The critical F value with 1 and 38 degrees of freedom is approximately 4.17 (see Appendix Table A.2), so the difference between the therapies is significant at the .05 level. Alternatively, as a t-test, the observed t value of 2.15 exceeds the critical t of approximately 2.04.

e. Testing the therapy main effect in the 2×2 design produced the largest F value for these data, reflecting the fact that this approach will often provide the most powerful test of the difference between the therapies. Tests of simple effects are less powerful than the test of the main effect when there is no interaction, so, generally speaking, main effects should be tested instead of simple effects when the interaction is nonsignificant (see Figure 7.2). In general, it is true that

$$SS_{\text{A within B1}} + SS_{\text{A within B2}} = SS_A + SS_{AB}$$

In our example,

$$SS_{\text{therapy for females}} + SS_{\text{therapy for males}} = SS_{\text{therapy}} + SS_{\text{therapy by sex}}$$

Specifically,

$$2000 + 2000 = 4000 + 0$$

Because there is no interaction here, the sum of squares for each simple effect is only one-half as large as the sum of squares for the main effect. The same ratio occurs for the F values, making the main effect test considerably more powerful than the simple effects tests. It should also be noted that the test of part (d) will be less powerful than the main effect test to the extent that the other factor (in this case, sex) has any effect on the dependent variable. This tendency is illustrated in these data, where the observed F value for the therapy main effect is 5.00, but the observed F corresponding to the t-test approach is 4.63.

17. a. Unweighted marginal means would reflect personality type effects for individuals at a particular stress level. The unweighted row marginal means for these data are

$$\overline{Y}_{1.(U)} = \sum_{k=1}^{b} \overline{Y}_{1k}\big/b$$
$$= (170 + 150)/2$$
$$= 160$$

$$\overline{Y}_{2.(U)} = \sum_{k=1}^{b} \overline{Y}_{2k}\Big/b$$

$$= (140 + 120)/2$$

$$= 130$$

b. If the effect of stress is not taken into account, personality type effects are reflected in weighted marginal means. The weighted row marginal means for these data are

$$\overline{Y}_{1.(W)} = \sum_{k=1}^{b} n_{1k}\overline{Y}_{1k}\Big/\sum_{k=1}^{b} n_{1k}$$

$$= [14(170) + 6(150)]/(14 + 6)$$

$$= 164$$

$$\overline{Y}_{2.(W)} = \sum_{k=1}^{b} n_{2k}\overline{Y}_{2k}\Big/\sum_{k=1}^{b} n_{2k}$$

$$= [6(140) + 14(120)]/(6 + 14)$$

$$= 126$$

Thus, the estimated magnitude of the mean blood pressure difference between personality types, ignoring level of stress, is 38 units. We saw in part (a) that the comparable difference when the effect of stress is taken into account is 30 units. Thus, taking the effect of stress into account lowers the estimated difference between personality types. The reason is that Type A individuals are predominantly found in high-stress environments, while Type B's are more likely to be in low-stress environments, so some of the 38-unit difference found overall between A's and B's may reflect differences in their environments.

20. a. Table 5.17 (in Chapter 5) provides formulas for forming a confidence interval for a contrast. We can conceptualize the current problem as one of planning to test a single contrast, so that $C = 1$. In this situation, Table 5.17 shows that a 95% confidence interval for ψ has the form

$$\hat{\psi} \pm \sqrt{F_{.05;1,\,N-a}}\sqrt{MS_W \sum_{j=1}^{a}\left(c_j^2/n_j\right)}$$

For the Type III sum of squares, ψ is given by

$$\psi = .5\mu_{11} + .5\mu_{12} - .5\mu_{21} - .5\mu_{22}$$

Then,

$$\hat{\psi} = .5\overline{Y}_{11} + .5\overline{Y}_{12} - .5\overline{Y}_{21} - .5\overline{Y}_{22}$$

$$= .5(52) + .5(46) - .5(48) - .5(42)$$

$$= 4.00$$

$$F_{.05;\,1,\,N-a} = F_{.05;\,1,19}$$

$$= 4.38$$

$$\sum_{j=1}^{a}\left(c_j^2/n_j\right) = \frac{(.5)^2}{6} + \frac{(.5)^2}{4} + \frac{(-.5)^2}{8} + \frac{(-.5)^2}{5}$$

$$= .1854$$

Substituting these values, along with $MS_W = 19$ (which we were given in the problem), into the formula for the confidence interval yields

$$4.00 \pm \sqrt{4.38}\sqrt{19(.1854)}$$

which reduces to

$$4.00 \pm 3.93$$

Equivalently, we can be 95% confident that the population difference in unweighted marginal means is between .07 and 7.93. Given an equal number of females and males, we are 95% confident that *CBT* is between .07 and 7.93 points better than *CCT*.

b. We can use the same formula as in part (a), but the contrast coefficients are now defined to be

$$c_1 = \frac{n_{11}n_{21}/n_{+1}}{n_{11}n_{21}/n_{+1} + n_{12}n_{22}/n_{+2}}$$

$$= \frac{(6)(8)/(14)}{(6)(8)/(14) + (4)(5)/9}$$

$$= .61$$

$$c_2 = \frac{n_{12}n_{22}/n_{+2}}{n_{11}n_{21}/n_{+1} + n_{12}n_{22}/n_{+2}}$$

$$= \frac{(4)(5)/9}{(6)(8)/14 + (4)(5)/9}$$

$$= .39$$

$$c_3 = -\frac{n_{11}n_{21}/n_{+1}}{n_{11}n_{21}/n_{+1} + n_{12}n_{22}/n_{+2}}$$

$$= -\frac{(6)(8)/14}{(6)(8)/14 + (4)(5)/9}$$

$$= -.61$$

$$c_4 = -\frac{n_{12}n_{22}/n_{+2}}{n_{11}n_{21}/n_{+1} + n_{12}n_{22}/n_{+2}}$$

$$= -\frac{(4)(5)/9}{(6)(8)/14 + (4)(5)/9}$$

$$= -.39$$

for μ_{11}, μ_{12}, μ_{21}, and μ_{22}, respectively. Thus,

$$\hat{\psi} = .61\overline{Y}_{11} + .39\overline{Y}_{12} - .61\overline{Y}_{21} - .39\overline{Y}_{22}$$

$$= .61(52) + .39(46) - .61(48) + .39(42)$$

$$= .61(52 - 48) + .39(46 - 42)$$

$$= 4.00$$

$$F_{.05;1,N-a} = F_{.05;1,19}$$

$$= 4.38$$

$$\sum_{j=1}^{a}\left(c_j^2/n_j\right) = \frac{(.61)^2}{6} + \frac{(.39)^2}{4} + \frac{(-.61)^2}{8} + \frac{(-.39)^2}{5}$$

$$= .1770$$

Substituting these values along with $MS_W = 19$ into the formula for the confidence interval yields

$$4.00 \pm \sqrt{4.38}\sqrt{19(.1770)}$$

which reduces to

$$4.00 \pm 3.84$$

We can be 95% confident that CBT is between .16 and 7.84 points better than CCT in the population, if we are willing to assume that the difference is the same for females as for males.

c. The contrast corresponding to the Type II sum of squares can be estimated slightly more precisely than the contrast corresponding to the Type III sum of squares. This advantage is the reason the Type II sum of squares is preferable to Type III if there is known to be no interaction in the population.

d. Once again, the confidence interval has the form

$$\hat{\psi} \pm \sqrt{F_{.05;\,1,N-a}} \sqrt{MS_W \sum_{j=1}^{a} \left(c_j^2/n_j\right)}$$

$\hat{\psi}$ is given by

$$\begin{aligned}
\hat{\psi} &= .5\overline{Y}_{11} + .5\overline{Y}_{12} - .5\overline{Y}_{21} - .5\overline{Y}_{22} \\
&= .5(52) + .5(46) - .5(48) - .5(42) \\
&= .61(52 - 48) + .39(46 - 42) \\
&= 4.00
\end{aligned}$$

$$\begin{aligned}
F_{.05;\,1,N-a} &= F_{.05;\,1,16} \\
&= 4.75
\end{aligned}$$

$$\begin{aligned}
\sum_{j=1}^{a} \left(c_j^2/n_j\right) &= \frac{(.5)^2}{4} + \frac{(.5)^2}{4} + \frac{(-.5)^2}{4} + \frac{(-.5)^2}{4} \\
&= .2500
\end{aligned}$$

Substituting these values, along with $MS_W = 19$, into the formula for the confidence interval yields

$$4.00 \pm \sqrt{4.75}\sqrt{19(.2500)}$$

$$4.00 \pm 4.75$$

Thus, we can be 95% confident that CBT is between .75 units worse and 8.75 units better than CCT.

e. The interval computed in part (d) is considerably wider than the intervals we found in parts (a) and (b). In particular, based on the equal n approach, we could not confidently rule out the possibility that CBT is worse than CCT, as we could with the two nonorthogonal approaches. Randomly deleting observations decreases precision and hence lowers the power to detect a true effect.

CHAPTER 8

3. The marginal mean for the Drug Present condition is

$$\begin{aligned}
\mu_{.1.} &= \sum_{l=1}^{c}\sum_{j=1}^{a} \mu_{j1l}/ac \\
&= (180 + 205 + 170 + 190)/4 \\
&= 186.25
\end{aligned}$$

Similarly, the marginal mean for the Drug Absent condition is

$$\begin{aligned}
\mu_{.2.} &= \sum_{l=1}^{c}\sum_{j=1}^{a} \mu_{j2l}/ac \\
&= (200 + 210 + 185 + 190)/4 \\
&= 196.25
\end{aligned}$$

There is a Drug main effect in the population, since mean blood pressure is lower when the Drug is present than when it is absent.

8. The correct answer is (c). Notice that the contrast coefficients for ψ represent an AB interaction, because the A effect at B_1 is compared to the A effect at B_2(see Equation 7.1 for a reminder). Specifically, ψ equals the difference between A_1 and A_2 at B_1 minus the difference between A_1 and A_2 at B_2. Thus, the fact that the estimated value of ψ at C_1 is -8 implies that A_1 minus A_2 is smaller at B_1 than at B_2, for the first level of C. However, because the estimated value of ψ at C_2 is $+8$, A_1 minus A_2 is larger at B_1 than at B_2, for the second level of C. As a result, the AB interaction at C_1 differs from the AB interaction at C_2, suggesting the possibility of a three-way ABC interaction (see Table 8.8). In contrast, the AB interaction would average ψ at C_1 and ψ at C_2 (see Table 8.8), resulting in a value of 0. Thus, there is no evidence here for an AB interaction. Finally, it is impossible to tell whether the simple two-way interactions of A and B at the two levels of C would be significant, without knowing the sample size and MS_W.

10. a. From Table 8.9,

$$\alpha_j = \mu_{j..} - \mu$$

so

$$\hat{\alpha}_j = \overline{Y}_{j..} - \overline{Y}_{...}$$

For these data,

$$\hat{\alpha}_1 = (45 + 55 + 65 + 40 + 40 + 70)/6 - (45 + 55 + 65 + 40 + 40 + 70 + 55$$
$$+ 75 + 65 + 20 + 30 + 40)/12$$
$$= 52.5 - 50.0$$
$$= 2.5$$
$$\hat{\alpha}_2 = (55 + 75 + 65 + 20 + 30 + 40)/6 - 50.0$$
$$= 47.5 - 50.0$$
$$= -2.5$$

Similarly, for the B main effect,

$$\beta_k = \mu_{.k.} - \mu \qquad \text{(see Table 8.9)}$$

so

$$\hat{\beta}_k = \overline{Y}_{.k.} - \overline{Y}_{...}$$

For these data,

$$\hat{\beta}_1 = (45 + 55 + 40 + 20)/4 - 50.0$$
$$= 40.0 - 50.0$$
$$= -10.0$$
$$\hat{\beta}_2 = (55 + 75 + 40 + 30)/4 - 50.0$$
$$= 50.0 - 50.0$$
$$= 0$$
$$\hat{\beta}_3 = (65 + 65 + 70 + 40)/4 - 50.0$$
$$= 60.0 - 50.0$$
$$= 10.0$$

b. The observed F value for the A main effect is given by

$$F = \frac{SS_A/(a-1)}{MS_W}$$

From Table 8.11,

$$SS_A = \sum_{j=1}^{a}\sum_{k=1}^{b}\sum_{l=1}^{c}\sum_{i=1}^{n}\hat{\alpha}_j^2$$

$$= bcn\sum_{j=1}^{a}\hat{\alpha}_j^2$$

$$= (3)(2)(10)[(2.5)^2 + (-2.5)^2]$$

$$= 750.0$$

We know that $a = 2$, so $a - 1 = 1$, and

$$MS_W = \frac{SS_W}{N-a}$$

$$= \frac{86,400}{120-12}$$

$$= 800$$

Thus, the F value for the A main effect is

$$F = \frac{750/1}{800}$$

$$= 0.94$$

The critical F with 1 and 108 degrees of freedom is approximately 4.00 (see Appendix Table A.2), so the A main effect is nonsignificant at the .05 level.
The observed F value for the B main effect is given by

$$F = \frac{SS_B/(b-1)}{MS_W}$$

From Table 8.11,

$$SS_B = \sum_{j=1}^{a}\sum_{k=1}^{b}\sum_{l=1}^{c}\sum_{i=1}^{n}\hat{\beta}_k^2$$

$$= acn\sum_{k=1}^{b}\hat{\beta}_j^2$$

$$= (2)(2)(10)[(-10.0)^2 + (0.0)^2 + (10.0)^2]$$

$$= 8000.0$$

We know that $b = 3$, so $b - 1 = 2$, and we found that $MS_W = 800$. Thus, the F value for the B main effect is

$$F = \frac{8000/2}{800}$$

$$= 5.00$$

The critical F with 2 and 108 degrees of freedom is approximately 3.15 (see Appendix Table A.2), so the B main effect is statistically significant at the .05 level.

c. The following plot is probably the clearest way to picture the three-way interaction:

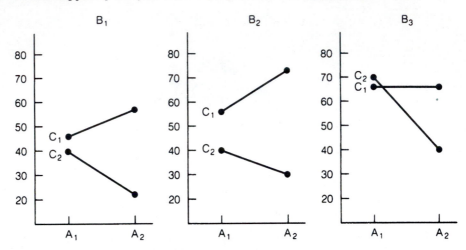

This plot reveals that the AC interaction is the same at every level of B, so there is no evidence of a three-way interaction. To see this explicitly, we will consider the magnitude of the AC interaction at each level of B. Specifically, the following table shows the magnitude of the C_1 mean minus the C_2 mean for both A_1 and A_2, separately for each level of B:

Level of B	$C_1 - C_2$ at A_1	$C_1 - C_2$ at A_2	Difference Between $C_1 - C_2$ at A_1 and $C_1 - C_2$ at A_2
B_1	5	35	−30
B_2	15	45	−30
B_3	−5	25	−30

As the rightmost column shows, the AC interaction is the same at each level of B, so there is no three-way interaction.

11. a.

$$\psi_{C1} = \mu_{111} - \mu_{121} - \mu_{211} + \mu_{221}$$

$$\psi_{C2} = \mu_{112} - \mu_{122} - \mu_{212} + \mu_{222}$$

The contrast for the three-way interaction is

$$\psi_{C1} - \psi_{C2} = \mu_{111} - \mu_{121} - \mu_{211} + \mu_{221} - \mu_{112} + \mu_{122} + \mu_{212} - \mu_{222}$$

b.

$$\psi_{B1} = \mu_{111} - \mu_{112} - \mu_{211} + \mu_{212}$$

$$\psi_{B2} = \mu_{121} - \mu_{122} - \mu_{221} + \mu_{222}$$

The contrast for the three-way interaction is

$$\psi_{B1} - \psi_{B2} = \mu_{111} - \mu_{112} - \mu_{211} + \mu_{212} - \mu_{121} + \mu_{122} + \mu_{221} - \mu_{222}$$

which can be rewritten as

$$\mu_{111} - \mu_{121} - \mu_{211} + \mu_{221} - \mu_{112} + \mu_{122} + \mu_{212} - \mu_{222}$$

c.

$$\psi_{A1} = \mu_{111} - \mu_{112} - \mu_{121} + \mu_{122}$$

$$\psi_{A2} = \mu_{211} - \mu_{212} - \mu_{221} + \mu_{222}$$

The contrast for the three-way interaction is

$$\psi_{A1} - \psi_{A2} = \mu_{111} - \mu_{112} - \mu_{121} + \mu_{122} - \mu_{211} + \mu_{212} + \mu_{221} - \mu_{222}$$

which can be rewritten as

$$\mu_{111} - \mu_{121} - \mu_{211} + \mu_{221} - \mu_{112} + \mu_{122} + \mu_{212} - \mu_{222}$$

d. The contrast coefficients of parts (a), (b), and (c) are identical to one another. This implies that the three interpretations of a three-way interaction are indeed equivalent to one another.

12. a. To find interaction contrasts, corresponding coefficients must be multiplied times one another.

AB:

1	1	0	0	−1	−1	−1	−1	0	0	1	1
0	0	1	1	−1	−1	0	0	−1	−1	1	1

AC:

1	−1	1	−1	1	−1	−1	1	−1	1	−1	1

BC:

1	−1	0	0	−1	1	1	−1	0	0	−1	1
0	0	1	−1	−1	1	0	0	1	−1	−1	1

The three-way interaction contrasts can be found in any of several equivalent ways. For example, the AB contrast coefficients can be multiplied by the C contrast coefficients.

ABC:

1	−1	0	0	−1	1	−1	1	0	0	1	−1
0	0	1	−1	−1	1	0	0	−1	1	1	−1

b. (1) *AB at C_1*

1	0	0	0	−1	0	−1	0	0	0	1	0
0	0	1	0	−1	0	0	0	−1	0	1	0

AB at C_2

0	1	0	0	0	−1	0	−1	0	0	0	1
0	0	0	1	0	−1	0	0	0	−1	0	1

(2) It can be shown that

$$SS_{AB \, at \, C1} + SS_{AB \, at \, C2} = SS_{AB} + SS_{ABC}$$

Thus, the 4 contrasts for AB at C_1 and AB at C_2 would replace the 4 contrats for AB and ABC.

CHAPTER 9

2. The primary considerations are (1) that the covariate correlate with the dependent variable and (2) that the covariate be independent of the treatment factor(s). The first consideration is critical inasmuch as the covariate

is being used to reduce within-cell variability and the strength of the correlation determines the extent of error reduction. The second consideration is important for facilitating interpretation. With the covariate and treatment factor independent, one is assured that the estimate of the treatment effect in a randomized study is unbiased. When the treatment and covariate happen to be correlated, one cannot generally know if the extent of the adjustment for differences on the covariate is too large, too small, or just right.

Two other, secondary considerations that make a covariate desirable are (1) the covariate can be obtained easily and economically, and (2) the process of obtaining the covariate scores does not affect the scores on the dependent variable. The latter possible effect of "testing," if it occurs, can limit the external validity of the study but does not threaten the internal validity of the research.

4. a.   As indicated in Equations 9.1 and 9.2, the models being compared are

$$\text{Full}: \quad Y_{ij} = \mu + \alpha_j + \beta X_{ij} + \varepsilon_{ij}$$

$$\text{Restricted}: \quad Y_{ij} = \mu + \beta X_{ij} + \varepsilon_{ij}$$

b.

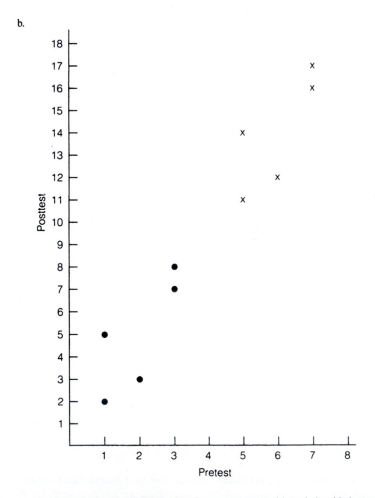

As shown in the preceding plot, there is a very strong positive relationship between the pretest and posttest within each of the two groups. Further, the group with the higher mean on the pretest also has the higher mean on the posttest. Thus, the data follow the pattern discussed in the text (see Figure 9.5(a)) where an apparent treatment effect is due primarily to preexisting differences. It appears in fact that a single regression line would fit all the data nearly as well as separate regression lines for the two groups. Because group membership does not add much to the pretest as a predictor of posttest scores, it appears that the ANCOVA test of the treatment effect would not be significant.

c. Designating groups C and T as groups 1 and 2, and the pretest and posttest as variables X and Y, respectively, we may determine the slope for a group by using Equation 9.11. That is, for each group, we compute the ratio of the sum of cross-products of deviations from the variables' means to the sum of squared deviations on the pretest.

Group C

X_{i1}	$X_{i1} - \overline{X}_1$	Y_{i1}	$Y_{i1} - \overline{Y}_1$	$(X_{i1} - \overline{X}_1)(Y_{i1} - \overline{Y}_1)$	$(X_{i1} - \overline{X}_1)^2$
1	-1	5	0	0	1
3	1	8	3	3	1
3	1	7	2	2	1
1	-1	2	-3	3	1
2	0	3	-2	0	0
$\overline{X}_1 = 2$		$\overline{Y}_1 = 5$		$\sum = 8$	$\sum = 4$

$$b_1 = \frac{\sum_i (X_{i1} - \overline{X}_1)(Y_{i1} - \overline{Y})}{\sum (X_{i1} - \overline{X}_1)^2} = \frac{8}{4} = 2.$$

The computations for group T are carried out similarly:

Group T

X_{i2}	$X_{i2} - \overline{X}_2$	Y_{i2}	$Y_{i2} - \overline{Y}_2$	$(X_{i2} - \overline{X}_2)(Y_{i2} - \overline{Y}_2)$	$(X_{i2} - \overline{X}_2)^2$
5	-1	14	0	0	1
7	1	17	3	3	1
7	1	16	2	2	1
5	-1	11	-3	3	1
6	0	12	-2	0	0
$\overline{X}_2 = 6$		$\overline{Y}_2 = 14$		$\sum = 8$	$\sum = 4$

Since the deviations from the mean in group T are identical here to those in group C, the slopes necessarily are the same:

$$b_2 = \frac{\sum_i (X_{i2} - \overline{X}_2)(Y_{i2} - \overline{Y})}{\sum (X_{i2} - \overline{X}_2)^2} = \frac{8}{4} = 2$$

Although normally these slopes would differ, in this particular example, because $b_1 = b_2 = 2$, it follows that their weighted average b_{W} must also be 2 (see Equation 9.12). Thus, the intercept for each group's regression line in this case will be the same as the intercept computed using the common within-group slope, that is,

$$a_1 = \overline{Y}_1 - b_1\overline{X}_1 = \overline{Y}_1 - b_{\mathrm{W}}\overline{X}_1 = 5 - 2(2) = 5 - 4 = 1$$
$$a_2 = \overline{Y}_2 - b_2\overline{X}_2 = \overline{Y}_2 - b_{\mathrm{W}}\overline{X}_2 = 14 - 2(6) = 14 - 12 = 2$$

The pooled within-group slope we have computed is the estimate of the population slope β in the full model, and the intercepts are the estimates of the combination of parameters $\mu + \alpha_j$ for that group (see Equation 9.18), that is,

$$\hat{\beta} = \beta_{\mathrm{W}} = 2$$
$$\hat{\mu} + \hat{\alpha}_1 = a_1 = 1$$
$$\hat{\mu} + \hat{\alpha}_2 = a_2 = 2$$

Note here that μ is the mean of the intercepts, so $\hat{\mu} = (1 + 2)/2 = 1.5$, and that α_j is the effect of the treatment as indicated by the vertical displacement of the regression line. Here, group 1 results in the regression line's intercept being .5 units lower than the average of the intercepts, and group 2 results in its regression line's intercept being .5 units above the average of the intercepts, that is, $\hat{\alpha}_1 = -.5$ and $\hat{\alpha}_2 = +.5$.

d. We can use our parameter estimates to form the prediction equation for our full model:

$$\hat{Y}_j = a_j + b_W X_{ij} \tag{9.25}$$

That is,

$$\hat{Y}_1 = a_1 + b_W X_{ij} = 1 + 2X_{ij}$$

$$\hat{Y}_2 = a_2 + b_W X_{ij} = 2 + 2X_{ij}$$

Substituting the observed values of X, we obtain the following predictions and errors of prediction, $e_{ij} = Y_{ij} - \hat{Y}_{ij}$:

X	Y	$\hat{Y}$	e	e^2
1	5	3	2	4
3	8	7	1	1
3	7	7	0	0
1	2	3	−1	1
2	3	5	−2	4
5	14	12	2	4
7	17	16	1	1
7	16	16	0	0
5	11	12	−1	1
6	12	14	−2	4
				$\sum = 20 = E_F$

e. As indicated in Equation 3, the predictions of the restricted model are just a linear transformation of the X scores:

$$\hat{Y}_{ij} = \hat{\mu} + \hat{\beta} X_{ij} \tag{9.3}$$

Thus, the overall correlation between Y_{ij} and X_{ij} will be identical to the correlation between Y_{ij} and the prediction of the restricted model. Thus, the proportion of variance accounted for by the restricted model is

$$R_R^2 = r_{XY}^2 = (.95905)^2 = .91978$$

As noted in the statistical tutorial on Regression on the data disk, the sum of squared errors for a model can be expressed simply as the proportion of variance not accounted for by that model times the total sum of squares. Thus we have

$$E_R = (1 - R_R^2)SS_{\text{Total}} = (1 - .91978)254.5 = 20.416.$$

f. We can readily perform the ANCOVA test of treatment effects, using these results for the errors of our models and $df_R = N - 2 = 10 - 2 = 8$ and $df_F = N - (a + 1) = 10 - 3 = 7$. Thus our test statistic is

$$F = \frac{(E_R - E_F)/(df_R - df_F)}{E_F/df_F} = \frac{(20.416 - 20)/(8 - 7)}{20/7} = \frac{.416/1}{2.857} = 0.146$$

Clearly, this is nonsignificant, and we conclude we cannot reject the null hypothesis of no treatment effect here, once we take the pretest scores into account.

9. Power is of course related to the absolute magnitude of the effect you are trying to detect, and this in turn is indicated by the standard deviation of the population means (the numerator of the formula for ϕ given in the problem). Given the population group means provided, the population grand mean is 20, and we have the following standard deviation of means σ_m:

$$\sigma_m = \sqrt{\sum \alpha_j^2 / a} = \sqrt{\sum (\mu_j - \mu)^2 / a}$$

$$= \sqrt{[(10 - 20)^2 + (20 - 20)^2 + (30 - 20)^2]/3}$$

$$= \sqrt{(100 + 0 + 100)/3} = \sqrt{200/3} = \sqrt{66.667}$$

$$= 8.165$$

This fixed characteristic of the population will be the same regardless of the method used to analyze the data. In addition, the degrees of freedom are practically the same for the three approaches. The numerator degrees of freedom are $a - 1 = 3 - 1 = 2$ in each case. The denominator degrees of freedom are $N - a = 30 - 3 = 27$ for the posttest only and gain score analyses, and $N - a - 1 = 26$ for ANCOVA, which requires estimation of a slope parameter as well as a parameter for each of the a groups.

What can vary across the analyses, depending on the correlation between the pretest and the posttest, is the error variance, as indicated in the problem. The error variance in the posttest only analysis, $\sigma_\varepsilon^2 = 20^2 = 400$, is unaffected by this correlation, since information about the pretest is ignored. However, the error variance in the other approaches can be quite different from that in the posttest only approach and in some cases can in fact be larger. For example, when $\rho = 0$, as in part (a), the error variance in the gain score analysis is

$$\sigma_{\varepsilon(\text{gains})}^2 = \sigma_\varepsilon^2 2(1 - \rho) = \sigma_\varepsilon^2 2(1 - 0) = 2(20)^2 = 800$$

On the other hand, the error variance in ANCOVA will be no larger than that in the posttest only analysis and will generally be smaller. For example, when $\rho = .7$, the error variance in ANCOVA is

$$\sigma_{\varepsilon(\text{ANCOVA})}^2 = \sigma_\varepsilon^2 (1 - \rho^2) = (20)^2 (1 - .7^2) = 400(1 - .49) = 400(.51) = 204$$

Carrying out these calculations for the error variances for the various analyses and values of the pretest-posttest correlation yields the following values.

	Error Variance, σ_ε^2		
ρ	Posttest Only	ANCOVA	Gains
0	400	400	800
.3	400	364	560
.5	400	300	400
.7	400	204	240

Given these error variances, we can readily calculate the values of ϕ that we need to determine power using the Pearson–Hartley chart in Table A-11 for $df_{\text{num}} = 2$. For example, for the posttest only design we have

$$\phi = \frac{\sqrt{\sum \alpha_j^2 / a}}{\sigma_\varepsilon / \sqrt{n}} = \frac{8.165}{\sqrt{400}/\sqrt{10}} = \frac{8.165}{20/3.162} = (.408)(3.162) = 1.291$$

Going up vertically from the point on the horizontal axis corresponding to $\phi = 1.291$ for $\alpha = .05$ in the chart, we see that the lines for $df_{\text{denom}} = 20$ and $df_{\text{denom}} = 30$ are around a height of .45 for this ϕ. Thus, power is .45 in the posttest only design for $\rho = 0$; and because is σ_ε^2 not affected by ρ for this analysis, this is the power for all values of ρ.

In the gain score analysis for $\rho = 0$, the inflated error variance results in a smaller ϕ and hence in less power. Specifically,

$$\phi = \frac{\sqrt{\sum \alpha_j^2 / a}}{\sigma_\varepsilon / \sqrt{n}} = \frac{8.165}{\sqrt{800}/\sqrt{10}} = \frac{8.165}{28.284/3.162} = \frac{8.165}{8.944} = .913$$

This value of ϕ is so small that it does not appear on the Pearson–Hartley charts for $\alpha = .05$. However, at the smallest value that does appear of $\phi = 1.0$, the power for 30 denominator degrees of freedom is only barely above .30. Thus the power to detect a smaller effect with 27 degrees of freedom would be even less, although projecting the power curve out to $\phi = .9$ indicates that the power is still only a little below .3.

At the other extreme, when the correlation is .7 and an ANCOVA approach to analysis is used, the relatively small value of σ_ε^2 translates into a large ϕ value and high power:

$$\phi = \frac{\sqrt{\sum \alpha_j^2/a}}{\sigma_\varepsilon/\sqrt{n}} = \frac{8.165}{\sqrt{204}/\sqrt{10}} = \frac{8.165}{14.283/3.162} = \frac{8.165}{4.517} = 1.808$$

Visually interpolating between the curves for 20 and 30 degrees of freedom results in an estimate of .75 power for $df = 26$.

Using these same methods for the other values of ρ yields the following values of ϕ and corresponding estimates of power.

	Approach					
	Posttest Only		ANCOVA		Gains	
	ϕ	Power	ϕ	Power	ϕ	Power
(a) $\rho = 0$	1.291	.45	1.291	.45	.913	.30
(b) $\rho = .3$	1.291	.45	1.353	.50	1.091	.32
(c) $\rho = .5$	1.291	.45	1.491	.58	1.291	.45
(d) $\rho = .7$	1.291	.45	1.808	.75	1.667	.68

e. There are two principal conclusions suggested by these power results. First, the power of the ANCOVA approach is in general larger than that of the posttest only approach, with the extent of the power advantage increasing with the pretest–posttest correlation. Second, the gain score analysis is in general less powerful than the ANCOVA approach and requires a pretest–posttest correlation of .5 to be as powerful as a procedure that ignores the pretest entirely. As the correlation increases beyond $+.5$, the power of the gain score analysis exceeds that of the posttest only approach and approaches that of the ANCOVA approach.

Though not suggested by these results, there are two extreme cases where minor exceptions to these general principles arise. First, if there is no pretest–posttest correlation, the posttest only approach is slightly more powerful than the ANCOVA approach, as a result of having one more degree of freedom. Second, if the pretest–posttest correlation is approximately $+1.0$, the gain score analysis can be slightly more powerful than ANCOVA, again by virtue of having an additional degree of freedom for error.

CHAPTER 10

7. a. Combining the 15 scores for each therapy method into one group, we obtain the following means, standard deviations, and sums of squared deviations from group means.

Method	$\overline{Y}_j$	s_j	$\sum_i (Y_{ij} - \overline{Y}_j)^2$
RET	40	3.3166	154
CCT	42	3.1396	138
BMOD	44	3.0938	134

Thus, the grand mean $\overline{Y}$ is 42, and the sum of squares for the method (A) effect here is

$$SS_A = \sum_j \sum_{i=1}^{15} (\overline{Y}_j - \overline{Y})^2 = 15 \sum_j (\overline{Y}_j - \overline{Y})^2 = 15[(-2)^2 + 0^2 + 2^2]$$

$$= 15[4 + 4] = 120$$

The degrees of freedom for the method effect is $a - 1 = 3 - 1 = 2$. The sum of squares within (or error of the full model) is here

$$SS_W = \sum_j \sum_i (Y_{ij} - \overline{Y}_j)^2 = 154 + 138 + 134 = 426$$

and is based on $a(n - 1) = 3(15 - 1) = 3.14 = 42$ degrees of freedom. Thus, the F for the method effect, analyzed as a one-way design, is

$$F = \frac{SS_A/df_A}{SS_W/df_W} = \frac{120/2}{426/42} = \frac{60}{10.1429} = 5.9155$$

Comparing against the critical F for $\alpha = .01$, $F(2, 42) = 5.16$, the results are declared significant.

b. Approaching the data as a two-way, fixed-effects design, we have the following cell means, standard deviations, and sums of squared deviations from cell means.

Method	Formula	Therapist			
		1	2	3	$\overline{Y}_{j.}$
	$\overline{Y}_{jk}$	38	42	40	40
RET	s_{jk}	2.9155	2.9155	3.3912	
	$\sum_i (Y_{ijk} - \overline{Y}_{jk})^2$	34	34	46	
	$\overline{Y}_{jk}$	41	44	41	42
CCT	s_{jk}	2.4495	3.3912	3.0822	
	$\sum_i (Y_{ijk} - \overline{Y}_{jk})^2$	24	46	38	
	$\overline{Y}_{jk}$	46	44	42	44
BMOD	s_{jk}	2.3452	3.5355	2.3452	
	$\sum_i (Y_{ijk} - \overline{Y}_{jk})^2$	22	50	22	
		41.6667	43.3333	41.0000	

Summary Statistics for Two-Way Design

Thus, the method effect is evaluated using

$$SS_A = \sum_j bn(\overline{Y}_{j.} - \overline{Y})^2 = 3 \cdot 5[(-2)^2 + 0^2 + 2^2] = 15 \cdot 8 = 120$$

$$df_A = a - 1 = 3 - 1 = 2$$

$$SS_W = \sum_i \sum_j \sum_k (Y_{ijk} - \overline{Y}_{jk})^2 = 34 + 34 + 46 + 24 + 46 + 38 + 22 + 50 + 22 = 316$$

$$df_W = ab(n - 1) = 3 \cdot 3(3 - 1) = 9 \cdot 4 = 36$$

Combining these values to compute the F for the method effect, we have

$$F_A = \frac{SS_A/df_A}{SS_W/df_W} = \frac{120/2}{316/36} = \frac{60}{8.7778} = 6.8354$$

We compare this against a critical F for $\alpha = .01$, $F(2, 36) = 5.26$ and again would declare the result statistically significant.

c. Treating the therapist factor as random would imply that the method effect should be compared with a denominator error term corresponding to the method × therapist interaction. The method × therapist interaction sum of squares may be computed from the effect parameters calculated as

$$(\widehat{\alpha\beta})_{jk} = \overline{Y}_{jk} - \overline{Y}_{j.} - \overline{Y}_{.k} + \overline{Y}_{..}$$

For example, $(\widehat{\alpha\beta})_{11} = 38 - 40 - 41.6667 + 42 = -1.6667$. The sum of squares for the method $\times$ therapist effect is then

$$
\begin{aligned}
SS_{AB} &= \sum_i \sum_j \sum_k (\widehat{\alpha\beta})_{jk}^2 = n \sum_j \sum_k (\overline{Y}_{jk} - \overline{Y}_{j.} - \overline{Y}_{.k} + \overline{Y}_{..})^2 \\
&= 5([(-1.6667)^2 + (0.6667)^2 + 1^2 + (-0.6667)^2 + (0.6667)^2 + 0^2 \\
&\quad + (2.3333)^2 + (-1.3333)^2 + (-1)^2] \\
&= 5(13.3333) = 66.6666
\end{aligned}
$$

This is based on $(a-1)(b-1) = (3-1)(3-1) = 4$ degrees of freedom. Thus the test of the method effect, analyzing the data as a two-factor mixed design, yields

$$
F_A = \frac{SS_A/df_A}{SS_{AB}/df_{AB}} = \frac{120/2}{66.6666/4} = \frac{60}{16.6667} = 3.60
$$

However, this is now compared against a critical F with only 2 and 4 degrees of freedom. For $\alpha = .05$, the critical F is 6.94; for .01, it would be 18.00. Thus, treating therapists as a random factor, the method effect does not approach significance.

  d. The sum of squares for the method effect was 120 in each of the three analyses.
  e. The denominator mean square error terms were 10.1429 for the one-way approach, 8.7778 for the two-way fixed effects approach, and 16.6667 for the two-way mixed effects approach. The sum of squares within for the two-way approach removes from the sum of squares within for the one-way approach any variability that can be attributed to B or AB effects. In fact it is the case that

$$
\begin{aligned}
\text{Mean square error term in (a)} &= \frac{SS_{AB} + SS_{AB} + SS_{W(part\ b)}}{df_B + df_{AB} + df_{W(part\ b)}} \\
&= \frac{43.3316 + 66.6666 + 316}{2 + 4 + 36} = \frac{425.9982}{42} = 10.1428
\end{aligned}
$$

The error term for the random effects approach uses the mean square for the AB interaction, which here happens to be larger than either MS_W value.

  f. It is reasonable that Kurtosis obtained different results than Skewed. Kurtosis obtained a smaller F for the method effect yet had to compare it against a larger critical F value since she had fewer degrees of freedom for her error term. In addition, the rationale for evaluating the Method effect is quite different in the mixed effects case than in the fixed effect case. In the mixed effects case the question is, Is the effect of methods large relative to the variability that we would expect to result from randomly selecting therapists for whom the methods effects differ? Because the magnitude of the Method effect varies somewhat over therapists (from an 8-point mean difference for therapist 1 to a 2-point mean difference for therapist 3), it is reasonable to conclude that the variability among the marginal means for methods may just be the result of which therapists happened to be used in the study. However, it is the case (as Skewed found) that, if outcomes with these three therapists are the only ones to which we want to generalize, we can conclude that the three methods would result in different mean outcomes for the population of possible subjects.

10. a. (1) The design may be diagrammed as follows, where C designates cleaning and F filling.

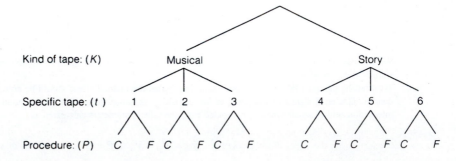

The factor of dental procedure (P) is crossed with the random factor of the specific tape (t), which in turn is nested within levels of the factor of kind of tape (K). "Subjects" of course constitutes a random factor that is nested within combinations of levels of all the other factors. Thus, the basic structure of the design may be labeled as $P \times t/K$.

(2) With three factors, if the factors were completely crossed, there would be 7 effects that could be tested (three main effects, three two-way interactions, and one three-way interaction). However, because here t is nested within K, the t main effect and the tK and PtK interactions cannot be tested. Instead, we can examine the simple effects of factor t within levels of K (that is, t/K) and the simple interactions of factors P and t within levels of K (that is, Pt/K). Thus the testable effects are

Testtable Effect	Verbal Label	Status
P	Procedure main effect	Fixed
K	Kind of tape main effect	Fixed
PK	Procedure $\times$ Kind of tape interaction	Fixed
t/K	Simple effects of specific tape within Kinds of tape	Random
Pt/K	Simple interaction of Procedure $\times$ specific tape within Kinds of tape	Random

The degrees of freedom associated with the main effects of the crossed factors are as usual one less than the number of levels of each factor, and the degrees of freedom for their interaction is equal to the product of the degrees of freedom for the main effects of the factors involved in the interaction. Thus, if P and K are crossed factors with p levels of factor P and k levels of factor K, the main effect of P would have $p - 1$ degrees of freedom, the main effect of K would have $k - 1$ degrees of freedom, and the PK interaction would have $(p - 1)(k - 1)$ degrees of freedom. The tests of the nested factor are carried out as pooled tests of simple effects. For example, carrying out the test of the simple main effects of a factor having t levels nested within each of the k levels of factor K is like carrying out k one-way ANOVAs, each of which would have $t - 1$ degrees of freedom. Thus the pooled test of the simple main effects of factor t within each level of factor K, or the test of the t/K effect, has $k(t - 1)$ degrees of freedom. Similarly, in considering the Pt/K effect, one is pooling k simple interaction effects each of which has $(p - 1)(t - 1)$ degrees of freedom, and so the Pt/K effect has $k(p - 1)(t - 1)$ degrees of freedom.

The error terms for testing these effects can be determined by reference to the preceding diagram and the flowchart in Figure 10.7. Considering first the P main effect, there are no random factors nested under levels of P; but since P is crossed with t, there is an interaction of factor P with the random factor t within each level of K. There is only one such effect, so Pt/K suffices as the error term for testing P. For the main effect of kind of tape, factor K, there is a random factor nested within its levels at the next lowest level of the hierarchy, and thus t/K is selected as the error term. In considering the KP interaction, as explained in the discussion in the main text of the Figure 10.7 flowchart's rule (i), Pt/K is considered to be an interaction of the effect to be tested with a random factor and thus is selected as the error term. Both effects t/K and Pt/K involve all the random factors and so the flowchart implies MS_W is the correct error term. MS_W in a design of this structure is the average of the ptk within-group variances, each of which is based on $n - 1$ degrees of freedom, and so has $ptk(n - 1)$ degrees of freedom.

Thus, the summary of effects, error terms, and degrees of freedom is as follows:

Effect	df_{Effect}	Denominator Error Term	df_{Error}
P	$p - 1 = 2 - 1 = 1$	Pt/K	$k(p - 1)(t - 1) = 2(2 - 1)(3 - 1) = 4$
K	$k - 1 = 2 - 1 = 1$	t/K	$k(t - 1) = 2(3 - 1) = 4$
PK	$(p - 1)(k - 1) = 1 \cdot 1 = 1$	Pt/K	$k(p - 1)(t - 1) = 2(2 - 1)(3 - 1) = 4$
t/K	$k(t - 1) = 2(3 - 1) = 4$	MS_W	$ptk(n - 1) = 2 \cdot 3 \cdot 2(n - 1) = 12 \cdot 4 = 48$
pt/K	$k(p - 1)(t - 1) = 2 \cdot 1 \cdot 2 = 4$	MS_W	$ptk(n - 1) = 2 \cdot 3 \cdot 2(n - 1) = 12 \cdot 4 = 48$

b. Although usually increasing the number of subjects will increase df for the denominator, that is not the case for testing the effect of the kind of tape here. The denominator term for testing the main effect of factor K is t/K and its df depends solely on the number of levels of factors t and K. To increase df for testing the effect of kind of tape, one would need to increase the number of specific tapes of each kind, not the number of subjects. However, increasing n will result in more precise estimates of the means of the levels of K and will thus cause power to increase, even though the critical F value is not affected.

12. a. The type of Feedback (factor F), immediate or delayed, is a fixed factor crossed with the other factors in the design. The type of Concept (factor C), either disjunctive or conjunctive, is also a fixed factor and is crossed with factor F. The specific problem (factor p) is a random factor nested within levels of factor C but crossed with factor F. That is, each problem appears together with only one type of Concept but each problem appears together with all types of feedback. Thus, the basic structure of the design may be labeled $F \times p/C$.

b. Following the same logic as was explained in the answer to problem 10, we arrive at the following 5 testable effects in this design, and the logic of the flowchart of Figure 10.7 leads to the error terms indicated.

Effect	Verbal Label of Effect	Denominator Error Term
F	Feedback main effect	Fp/C
C	Concept main effect	p/C
FC	Feedback $\times$ Concept interaction	Fp/C
p/C	Simple effects of problems within Concepts	MS_W
Fp/C	Simple interaction of Feedback and problems within Concepts	MS_W

c. Let us designate specific levels of the factor of Feedback by $j = 1, 2$, specific levels of the Concept factor by $k = 1, 2$, and the specific problems within a type of Concept by $l = 1, 2, 3, 4$. Thus, we would have the following table of cell and marginal means:

Concept:	Disjunctive (k = 1)				Conjuctive (k = 2)		
Feedback:	Immed. (j = 1)	Delayed (j = 2)	$\overline{Y}_{\cdot 1l}$		Immed. (j = 1)	Delayed (j = 2)	$\overline{Y}_{\cdot 2l}$
Problem 1 ($l = 1$)	3	3	3	Problem 5 ($l = 1$)	1	2	1.5
Problem 2 ($l = 2$)	3	5	4	Problem 6 ($l = 2$)	1	1	1.0
Problem 3 ($l = 3$)	2	6	4	Problem 7 ($l = 3$)	4	5	4.5
Problem 4 ($l = 4$)	4	6	5	Problem 8 ($l = 4$)	0	2	1.0
$\overline{Y}_{j1\cdot}$	3	5	4.0	$\overline{Y}_{j2\cdot}$	1.5	2.5	2.0

The effects of the completely crossed factors of Feedback and Concept can be handled by estimating effect parameters as discussed in Chapters 7 and 8, squaring them, and summing over all observations. Applying this logic to the effects involving the nested factor of problems will require estimating a different set of effects for each of the levels of the Concept factor within which it is nested. Letting α_j, β_k, and $(\alpha\beta)_{jk}$ refer to the main effects of Feedback, Concept, and their interaction, respectively, we can refer to the simple effect of problems within the kth level of Concepts by $\gamma_{l/k}$ and the simple interaction of Feedback by problems within the kth level of Concepts by $\alpha\gamma_{jl/k}$. Thus we can state the Full model here as

$$Y_{ijkl} = \mu + \alpha_j + \beta_k + \alpha\beta_{jk} + \gamma_{l/k} + \alpha\gamma_{jl/k} + \varepsilon_{ijkl}$$

Let us begin our computations with the most straightforward effects of Feedback and Concept. The sums of squares for these completely crossed effects can be obtained very easily from the following summary table of marginal means for the Feedback and Concept factors.

		Concept		$\overline{Y}_{j\cdot\cdot}$	$\hat{\alpha}_j$
		Disjunctive $(k = 1)$	Conjunctive $(k = 2)$		
Feedback:	Immed .$(j = 1)$	3	1.5	2.25	$-.75$
	Delayed $(j = 2)$	5	2.5	3.75	$+.75$
	$\overline{Y}_{\cdot k\cdot}$	4	2.0		
	$\hat{\beta}_k$	$+1$	-1.0		

$$SS_F = \sum_l\sum_k\sum_j\sum_i \hat{\alpha}_j^2 = 4 \cdot 2 \cdot 2\sum_j \hat{\alpha}_j^2 = 16[(-.75)^2 + .75^2] = 16(1.125) = 18$$

$$SS_C = \sum_l\sum_k\sum_j\sum_i \hat{\beta}_k^2 = 4 \cdot 2 \cdot 2\sum_k \hat{\beta}_k^2 = 16[1^2 + (-1)^2] = 32$$

Interaction effects are estimated as usual, that is,

$$\widehat{(\alpha\beta)}_{jk} = \overline{Y}_{jk\cdot} - (\hat{\mu} + \hat{\alpha}_j + \hat{\beta}_k)$$

For example, $\widehat{(\alpha\beta)}_{11} = 3 - (3 - .75 + 1) = 3 - 3.25 = -.25$. Thus, we have

$$\sum_k\sum_j\sum_i \widehat{(\alpha\beta)}_{jk}^2 = 4 \cdot 2\sum_k\sum_j \widehat{(\alpha\beta)}_{jk}^2 = 8[(-.25)^2 + .25^2 + .25^2 + (-.25)^2] = 8 \cdot .25 = 2$$

The sum of squares for the pooled simple effects of the nested factor can be obtained by first estimating the effect parameters for this factor separately at each level of the factor within which it is nested (see Equation 28). We will in essence be computing the sum of squares for a one-way ANOVA of the effects of problem at each level of the Concept factor, and then pooling these sums of squares, i.e,

$$SS_{p/C} = SS_{p \text{ at } C1} + SS_{p \text{ at } C2}$$

The first step is to compute, at each level of the Concept factor, the estimated effects of the nested factor as the difference between the mean for each problem and the marginal mean for that kind of concept. We will thus be computing

$$\hat{\gamma}_{l/1} = \overline{Y}_{\cdot 1l} - \overline{Y}_{\cdot 1\cdot}$$

and

$$\hat{\gamma}_{l/2} = \overline{Y}_{\cdot 2l} - \overline{Y}_{\cdot 2\cdot}$$

as shown below:

Disjunctive		Conjunctive	
$\overline{Y}_{\cdot 1l}$	$\hat{\gamma}_{l/1}$	$\overline{Y}_{\cdot 2l}$	$\hat{\gamma}_{l/2}$
3	-1	1.5	$-.5$
4	0	1.0	-1
4	0	4.5	2.5
5	$+1$	1.0	-1
$\overline{Y}_{\cdot 1\cdot} = 4$		$\overline{Y}_{\cdot 2\cdot} = 2$	

Then we can compute the sum of squares for the pooled simple effects of our nested factor of problems as

$$SS_{P/C} = \sum_l \sum_k \sum_j \sum_i \hat{\gamma}^2_{l/k} = \sum_l \sum_k 2 \cdot 2\hat{\gamma}^2_{l/k}$$

$$= 4[(-1)^2 + 0 + 0 + 1^2] + 4[(-.5)^2 + (-1)^2 + 2.5^2 + (-1)^2]$$

$$= 4(1 + 1) + 4(.25 + 1 + 6.25 + 1) = 4(2) + 4(8.5)$$

$$= 8 + 34 = SS_{p\,at\,C1} + SS_{p\,at\,C2}$$

$$= 42 = SS_{P/C}$$

Similarly, the simple interaction effects of Feedback × Problem are estimated separately at each level of the Concept factor. That is, we compute

$$\widehat{\alpha\gamma}_{jl/1} = \overline{Y}_{j1l} - \overline{Y}_{j1\cdot} - \overline{Y}_{\cdot 1l} + \overline{Y}_{\cdot 1\cdot}$$

and

$$\widehat{\alpha\gamma}_{jl/2} = \overline{Y}_{j2l} - \overline{Y}_{j2\cdot} - \overline{Y}_{\cdot 2l} + \overline{Y}_{\cdot 2\cdot}$$

Estimates of these simple interaction effects are shown in the table below next to the corresponding cell means:

Concept:	Disjunctive (k = 1)					Conjunctive (k = 2)				
Feedback:	Immed· (j = 1)		Delayed (j = 2)		$\overline{Y}_{\cdot 1l}$		Immed. (j = 1)		Delayed (j = 2)		$\overline{Y}_{\cdot 2l}$
	$\overline{Y}_{11l}$	$\widehat{\alpha\gamma}_{11/1}$	$\overline{Y}_{21l}$	$\widehat{\alpha\gamma}_{21/1}$			$\overline{Y}_{12l}$	$\widehat{\alpha\gamma}_{11/2}$	$\overline{Y}_{22l}$	$\widehat{\alpha\gamma}_{21/2}$	
Problem 1 (l = 1)	3	+1	3	−1	3	Problem 5 (l = 1)	1	0	2	0	1.5
Problem 2 (l = 2)	3	0	5	0	4	Problem 6 (l = 2)	1	+.5	1	−.5	1.0
Problem 3 (l = 3)	2	−1	6	+1	4	Problem 7 (l = 3)	4	0	5	0	4.5
Problem 4 (l = 4)	4	0	6	0	5	Problem 8 (l = 4)	0	−.5	2	+.5	1.0
$\overline{Y}_{j1\cdot}$	3		5		4.0	$\overline{Y}_{j2\cdot}$	1.5		2.5		2.0

Then we may compute the pooled sum of squares for the simple interactions of Feedback with Problems as follows:

$$SS_{Fp/C} = \sum_l \sum_k \sum_j \sum_i \widehat{\alpha\gamma}^2_{jl/k} = \sum_l \sum_k \sum_j \sum_{i=1}^{2} [\overline{Y}_{jkl} - (\overline{Y}_{jk\cdot} + \overline{Y}_{\cdot kl} - \overline{Y}_{\cdot k\cdot})]^2$$

$$= \sum_k \left\{ 2 \sum_l \sum_j [\overline{Y}_{jkl} - (\overline{Y}_{jk\cdot} + \overline{Y}_{\cdot kl} - \overline{Y}_{\cdot k\cdot})]^2 \right\}$$

$$= 2[(3-2)^2 + (3-4)^2 + (3-3)^2 + (5-5)^2 + (2-3)^2 + (6-5)^2$$

$$+ (4-4)^2 + (6-6)^2] + 2[(1-1)^2 + (2-2)^2 + (1-.5)^2$$

$$+ (1-1.5)^2 + (4-4)^2 + (5-5)^2 + (0-.5)^2 + (2-1.5)^2]$$

$$= 2[1 + 1 + 0 + 0 + 1 + 1 + 0 + 0] + 2[0 + 0 + .25 + 0 + 0 + .25 + .25]$$

$$= 2(4) + 2(1) = 8 + 2 = SS_{Fp\,at\,c_1} + SS_{Fp\,at\,c_2} = 10 = SS_{Fp/C}$$

To carry out the tests against the error terms outlined in part (b), we only need to determine the degrees of freedom for the various effects. Using lowercase letters to designate the number of levels of a factor, we have the following values:

Source	df
F	$(f-1) = (2-1) = 1$
C	$(c-1) = (2-1) = 1$
FC	$(f-1)(c-1) = (2-1)(2-1) = 1$
p/C	$c(p-1) = 2(4-1) = 2 \cdot 3 = 6$
Fp/C	$c(f-1)(p-1) = 2(2-1)(4-1) = 2 \cdot 1 \cdot 3 = 6$
MS_W	$fcp(n-1) = 2 \cdot 2 \cdot 4(2-1) = 16(1) = 16.$

Thus, we have the following test statistics and critical values at $\alpha = .05$ for our 5 testable effects:

$$F_F = \frac{SS_F/df_F}{SS_{Fp/C}/df_{Fp/C}} = \frac{18/1}{10/6} = 10.8; F_{crit} = F_{1,6} = 5.99; p < .05$$

$$F_C = \frac{SS_C/df_C}{SS_{Fp/C}/df_{p/C}} = \frac{32/1}{42/6} = \frac{32}{7} = 4.57; F_{crit} = F_{1,6} = 5.99; n.s.$$

$$F_{FC} = \frac{SS_{FC}/df_{FC}}{SS_{Fp/C}/df_{Fp/C}} = \frac{2/1}{10/6} = 1.2; F_{crit} = F_{1,6} = 5.99; n.s.$$

$$F_{p/C} = \frac{SS_{p/C}/df_{p/C}}{MS_W} = \frac{42/6}{5} = \frac{7}{5} = 1.4; F_{crit} = F_{6,16} = 2.74; n.s.$$

$$F_{Fp/C} = \frac{SS_{Fp/C}/df_{Fp/C}}{MS_W} = \frac{10/6}{5} = .33; F_{crit} = F_{6,16} = 2.74; n.s.$$

It follows that the only effect for which we have grounds for rejecting the null hypothesis is the main effect of Feedback. Delayed feedback results in more errors being required to reach the criterion performance than immediate feedback.

CHAPTER 11

3. a. From Equation 24, predicted scores for the full model are of the form

$$\hat{Y}_{ij} = \overline{Y}_{\cdot j} + \overline{Y}_{i\cdot} - \overline{Y}_{\cdot\cdot} \tag{11.24}$$

For example,

$$\hat{Y}_{11} = (3+4+2+4+7)/5 + (3+6+4+5)/4 - 4.5$$
$$= 4 + 4.5 - 4.5$$
$$= 4$$

$$\hat{Y}_{12} = (6+7+1+5+6)/5 + (3+6+4+5)/4 - 4.5$$
$$= 5 + 4.5 - 4.5$$
$$= 5$$

$$\hat{Y}_{21} = (3+4+2+4+7)/5 + (4+7+4+8)/4 - 4.5$$
$$= 4 + 5.75 - 4.5$$
$$= 5.25$$

and so forth. Completing similar calculations for all other rows and columns, we find that the predicted scores for the full model are as follows.

	Location			
Subject	1	2	3	4
1	4.00	5.00	3.00	6.00
2	5.25	6.25	4.25	7.25
3	1.25	2.25	0.25	3.25
4	3.25	4.25	2.25	5.25
5	6.25	7.25	5.25	8.25

b. Discrepancies between actual scores and predicted scores are follows.

	Location			
Subject	1	2	3	4
1	−1.00	1.00	1.00	−1.00
2	−1.25	.75	−.25	.75
3	.75	−1.25	.75	−.25
4	.75	.75	−1.25	−.25
5	.75	−1.25	−.25	.75

c. From Equation 25, predicted scores for the restricted model are of the form

$$\hat{Y}_{ij} = \overline{Y}_{i.}$$ (11.25)

For example,

$$\hat{Y}_{11} = \overline{Y}_{1.}$$
$$= (3 + 6 + 4 + 5)/4$$
$$= 4.50$$
$$\hat{Y}_{12} = \overline{Y}_{1.}$$
$$= (3 + 6 + 4 + 5)/4$$
$$= 4.50$$
$$\hat{Y}_{21} = \overline{Y}_{2.}$$
$$= (4 + 7 + 4 + 8)/4$$
$$= 5.75$$

and so forth. Completing similar calculations for all other rows and columns, we find that the predicted scores for the restricted model are as follows.

	Location			
Subject	1	2	3	4
1	4.50	4.50	4.50	4.50
2	5.75	5.75	5.75	5.75
3	1.75	1.75	1.75	1.75
4	3.75	3.75	3.75	3.75
5	6.75	6.75	6.75	6.75

d. Discrepancies between actual scores and predicted scores are as follows.

Subject	Location			
	1	2	3	4
1	−1.50	1.50	−.50	.50
2	−1.75	1.25	−1.75	2.25
3	.25	.75	−.75	1.25
4	.25	1.25	−2.75	1.25
5	.25	−.75	−1.75	2.25

e. The observed F value is

$$F = \frac{(E_R - E_F)/(df_R - df_F)}{E_F/df_F}$$

First, notice that

$$df_R - df_F = a - 1$$
$$= 4 - 1$$
$$= 3$$
$$df_F = (n - 1)(a - 1)$$
$$= (5 - 1)(4 - 1)$$
$$= 12$$

In addition,

$$E_R = (-1.50)^2 + (-1.75)^2 + (.25)^2 + \cdots + (1.25)^2 + (2.25)^2$$
$$= 5.50 + 6.50 + 14.50 + 13.50$$
$$= 40.00$$
$$E_F = (-1.00)^2 + (-1.25)^2 + (.75)^2 + \cdots + (-.25)^2 + (.75)^2$$
$$= 4.25 + 5.25 + 3.25 + 2.25$$
$$= 15.00$$

Thus, the observed F is

$$F = \frac{(40.00 - 15.00)/3}{15.00/12}$$
$$= 6.67$$

For the unadjusted test, there are 3 numerator and 12 denominator degrees of freedom. The critical value at $\alpha = .05$ is 3.49 (see Appendix Table A.2), so there is a statistically significant difference among the locations.

f. The degrees of freedom for the Geisser–Greenhouse lower bound correction are

$$df_{num} = 1$$
$$df_{den} = n - 1 \qquad (11.33)$$
$$= 5 - 1$$
$$= 4$$

The critical F value for 1 numerator and 4 denominator degrees of freedom is 7.71 at the .05 level. Thus, the difference among locations is nonsignificant with the Geisser–Greenhouse lower bound correction.

g. Obviously the simplest way to obtain the value of $\hat{\varepsilon}$ is to rely on a computer program. Nevertheless, we will illustrate its calculation here. The first step is to calculate the covariance matrix for the data. If we let Y_{ij} represent the score of subject i in condition j (i.e., the score in row i and column j of the original data matrix), the element in row j and column k of the covariance matrix is given by

$$E_{jk} = \sum_{i=1}^{n}(Y_{ij} - \overline{Y}_{\cdot j})(Y_{ik} - \overline{Y}_{\cdot k})/n$$

Performing this calculation for our data yields the following matrix:

$$\begin{bmatrix} 2.8 & 2.0 & 1.8 & 3.2 \\ 2.0 & 4.4 & 2.6 & 3.6 \\ 1.8 & 2.6 & 2.8 & 3.0 \\ 3.2 & 3.6 & 3.0 & 4.8 \end{bmatrix}$$

The value of $\hat{\varepsilon}$ then is

$$\hat{\varepsilon} = \frac{a^2(\overline{E}_{jj} - \overline{E}_{..})^2}{(a-1)\left[\left(\sum\sum E_{jk}^2\right) - \left(2a\sum \overline{E}_{j.}^2\right) + \left(a^2\overline{E}_{..}^2\right)\right]}$$

where

$$a = 4$$
$$\overline{E}_{jj} = (2.8 + 4.4 + 2.8 + 4.8)/4 = 3.70$$
$$\overline{E}_{..} = (2.8 + 2.0 + 1.8 + 3.2 + 2.0 + 4.4 + \cdots + 3.0 + 4.8)/16 = 2.95$$
$$\sum\sum E_{jk}^2 = (2.8)^2 + (2.0)^2 + (1.8)^2 + \cdots + (3.0)^2 + (4.8)^2 = 150.48$$
$$\sum \overline{E}_{j.}^2 = (2.45)^2 + (3.15)^2 + (2.55)^2 + (3.65)^2 = 35.75$$

so that

$$\hat{\varepsilon} = \frac{(4)^2(3.70 - 2.95)^2}{(4-1)[(150.48) - (2)(4)(35.75) + (4)^2(2.95)^2]}$$
$$= \frac{9.00}{11.16}$$
$$= .81$$

The adjusted degrees of freedom are

$$df_{\text{num}} = \hat{\varepsilon}(a-1)$$
$$= .81(4-1)$$
$$= 2.43$$
$$df_{\text{den}} = \hat{\varepsilon}(a-1)(n-1)$$
$$= .81(4-1)(5-1)$$
$$= 9.72$$

Rounding down (to be conservative), the critical F value with 2 and 9 degrees of freedom is 4.26 at the .05 level. Thus, the difference among locations is statistically significant at the .05 level with the $\hat{\varepsilon}$-adjusted test, just as it was with the unadjusted test. Using a computer program like SPSS, we can find that the p value for the $\hat{\varepsilon}$-adjusted test is .0125, corroborating the statistical significance at the .05 level.

h. Now that we have calculated $\hat{\varepsilon}$, the value of $\tilde{\varepsilon}$ follows easily from Equation 34:

$$\tilde{\varepsilon} = \frac{n(a-1)\hat{\varepsilon} - 2}{(a-1)[n-1-(a-1)\hat{\varepsilon}]} \qquad (11.34)$$

$$= \frac{5(4-1)(.81) - 2}{(4-1)[5-1-(4-1)(.81)]}$$

$$= \frac{10.15}{4.71}$$

$$= 2.15$$

Because $\tilde{\varepsilon}$ exceeds 1.00 for these data, it is shrunk back to 1.00. As a consequence, the use of the $\tilde{\varepsilon}$ adjustment simply duplicates the unadjusted test for these data.

4. To calculate SS_A and $SS_{A \times S}$, it is helpful to represent the data as in Table 11.3, adding row and column marginal means, in which case we have the following values.

Subject	Condition 1	Condition 2	Marginal Mean
1	8	10	9.00
2	3	6	4.50
3	12	13	12.50
4	5	9	7.00
5	7	8	7.50
6	13	14	13.50
Marginal Mean	8.00	10.00	9.00

Now, the sum of squares for the condition main effect is

$$SS_A = \sum_{j=1}^{a} n(\overline{Y}_{\cdot j} - \overline{Y}_{\cdot \cdot})^2$$

$$= 6[(8-9)^2 + (10-9)^2]$$

$$= 12.00$$

The interaction sum of squares is

$$SS_{A \times S} = \sum_{i=1}^{n}\sum_{j=1}^{a}(Y_{ij} - \overline{Y}_{\cdot j} - \overline{Y}_{i\cdot} + \overline{Y}_{\cdot \cdot})^2$$

$$= (8 - 8.00 - 9.00 + 9.00)^2 + (10 - 10.00 - 9.00 + 9.00)^2$$

$$+ (3 - 8.00 - 4.50 + 9.00)^2 + (6 - 10.00 - 4.50 + 9.00)^2$$

$$+ (12 - 8.00 - 12.50 + 9.00)^2 + (13 - 10.00 - 12.50 + 9.00)^2$$

$$+ (5 - 8.00 - 7.00 + 9.00)^2 + (9 - 10.00 - 7.00 + 9.00)^2$$

$$+ (7 - 8.00 - 7.50 + 9.00)^2 + (8 - 10.00 - 7.50 + 9.00)^2$$

$$+ (13 - 8.00 - 13.50 + 9.00)^2 + (14 - 10.00 - 13.50 + 9.00)^2$$

$$= (0)^2 + (0)^2 + (-.50)^2 + (.50)^2 + (.50)^2 + (-.50)^2 + (-1.00)^2 + (1.00)^2$$

$$+ (.50)^2 + (-.50)^2 + (.50)^2 + (-.50)^2$$

$$= 4.00.$$

b. The observed F value is

$$F = \frac{SS_A/(a-1)}{SS_{A \times S}/(n-1)(a-1)}$$

$$= \frac{12/1}{4/(5)(1)}$$

$$= 15.00$$

c. The F values are identical.
d. Yes, since they yield the same F value.

5. a. To calculate the sums of squares, it is helpful to include row and column marginal means, in which case the original data can be written as follows.

Subject	1	2	3	Marginal Mean
1	10	12	14	12
2	2	5	5	4
3	5	6	10	7
4	12	15	18	15
5	16	17	18	17
Marginal Mean	9	11	13	11

Now, the sum of squares for the condition main effect is

$$SS_A = \sum_{j=1}^{a} n(\bar{Y}_{\cdot j} - \bar{Y}_{\cdot \cdot})^2$$

$$= 5[(9-11)^2 + (11-11)^2 + (13-11)^2]$$

$$= 40$$

The sum of squares for the subject main effect is

$$SS_S = \sum_{j=1}^{n} a(\bar{Y}_{i \cdot} - \bar{Y}_{\cdot \cdot})^2$$

$$= 3[(12-11)^2 + (4-11)^2 + (7-11)^2 + (15-11)^2 + (17-11)^2]$$

$$= 354$$

Finally, the interaction sum of squares is

$$SS_{A \times S} = \sum_{i=1}^{n} \sum_{j=1}^{a} (Y_{ij} - \bar{Y}_{\cdot j} - \bar{Y}_{i \cdot} + \bar{Y}_{\cdot \cdot})^2$$

$$= (10-9-12+11)^2 + (12-11-12+11)^2 + (14-13-12+11)^2$$
$$+ (2-9-4+11)^2 + \cdots + (17-11-17+11)^2$$
$$+ (18-13-17+11)^2$$
$$= (0)^2 + (0)^2 + (0)^2 + (0)^2 + (1)^2 + (-1)^2 + (0)^2 + (-1)^2 + (1)^2 + (-1)^2$$
$$+ (0)^2 + (1)^2 + (1)^2 + (0)^2 + (-1)^2$$
$$= 8$$

b.   The observed F value is

$$F = \frac{SS_A/(a-1)}{SS_{A \times S}/(n-1)(a-1)}$$

$$= \frac{40/2}{8/(4)(2)}$$

$$= 20.00$$

The critical F value at $\alpha = .05$ with 2 numerator and 8 denominator degrees of freedom is 4.46. Thus, the null hypothesis can be rejected.

c.   If these data came from a between-subject design, the between-group sum of squares would be calculated as

$$SS_A = n \sum_{j=1}^{a} (\overline{Y}_j - \overline{Y})^2 \tag{3.58}$$

$$= 5[(9-11)^2 + (11-11)^2 + (13-11)^2]$$

$$= 40$$

$$SS_W = \sum_{j=1}^{a} \sum_{i=1}^{n} (\overline{Y}_{ij} - \overline{Y}_j)^2 \tag{3.65}$$

$$= (10-9)^2 + (2-9)^2 + (5-9)^2 + (12-9)^2 + (16-9)^2 + (12-11)^2$$

$$+ (5-11)^2 + (6-11)^2 + (15-11)^2 + (17-11)^2 + (14-13)^2$$

$$+ (5-13)^2 + (10-13)^2 + (18-13)^2 + (18-13)^2$$

$$= 362$$

First, notice that the main effect sum of squares SS_A is the same whether the data come from a within-subjects design or from a between-subjects design. However, the within-group sum of squares SS_W in the between-subjects design equals the sum of SS_S and $SS_{A \times S}$ in the within-subjects design. In general, it is true that

$$SS_W = SS_S + SS_{A \times S}$$

For these data,

$$362 = 354 + 8$$

d.   The observed F value would be

$$F = \frac{SS_A/(a-1)}{SS_W/(N-a)}$$

$$= \frac{40/2}{362/12}$$

$$= .66$$

The critical F value would be 3.89 (see Appendix Table A.2, for 2 numerator degrees of freedom, 12 denominator degrees of freedom, and $\alpha = .05$), so the null hypothesis could not be rejected.

e.   The consistent individual differences among subjects are captured by SS_S in the within-subjects design. This source of variance does not contribute to the error term, as it would in a between-subjects design. As a result, the within-subjects design provides appreciably greater power than the between-subjects design, when large individual differences exist. Notice that, in this numerical example, the observed F value of 20.00 in the within-subjects design was drastically reduced to a mere .66 in the between-subjects design.

6. a.   The new scores on the adjusted dependent variable $Y_{ij} - \overline{Y}_i.$ are as follows.

	30	36	42	48
	−1	−13	1	13
	−17	−3	7	13
	−8	3	2	3
	−6	−5	2	9
	−3	4	4	−5
	9	6	−5	−10
	2	1	−4	1
	−7	−13	4	16
	−10	10	6	−6
	−5	−1	2	4
	−4	5	−4	3
	−10	−6	9	7
Mean $(\overline{Y}_j)$	−5.00	−1.00	2.00	4.00
$\sum\limits_{i=1}^{n}(Y_{ij} - \overline{Y}_j)^2$	474.00	584.00	220.00	728.00

The observed F value for a one-way between-subjects ANOVA on these data would be

$$F = \frac{(E_R - E_F)/(df_R - df_F)}{E_F/df_F}$$

In this design,

$$E_R - E_F = n\sum_{j=1}^{a}(\overline{Y}_j - \overline{Y})^2 \qquad\qquad (3.58)$$

$$= 12[(-5 - 0)^2 + (-1 - 0)^2 + (2 - 0)^2 + (4 - 0)^2]$$

$$= 552$$

$$E_F = \sum_{j=1}^{a}\sum_{i=1}^{n}(\overline{Y}_{ij} - \overline{Y}_j)^2$$

$$= 474 + 584 + 220 + 728$$

$$= 2006$$

If these data really came from a between-subjects design,

$$df_R = N - 1$$

$$df_F = N - a$$

so

$$df_R - df_F = a - 1$$

For these data, then,

$$df_F = 48 - 4$$

$$= 44$$

$$df_R - df_F = 4 - 1$$

$$= 3$$

Thus, the observed F would be

$$F = \frac{552/3}{2006/44}$$

$$= 4.04$$

With 3 numerator and 44 denominator degrees of freedom, the critical F value at $\alpha = .05$ would be approximately 2.84 (see Appendix Table A.2), so the null hypothesis would be rejected.

b. The F value of 4.04 in part (a) is larger than the F value of 3.03 obtained from Equation 28 in the text. However, notice from Tables 11.8 and 11.9 that, when we regarded these data as coming from a within-subjects design, the error sums of squares were

$$E_R = 2558 \qquad \text{(See Table 11.9)}$$

$$E_F = 2006 \qquad \text{(See Table 11.8)}$$

so

$$E_R - E_F = 552$$

Thus, E_F and $E_R - E_F$ as calculated in the within-subjects design are identical to the value obtained in part (a). However, in the within-subjects design, the degrees of freedom for the restricted and full models are

$$df_R = n(a - 1)$$

$$= 12(4 - 1)$$

$$= 36$$

$$df_F = (n - 1)(a - 1)$$

$$= (12 - 1)(4 - 1)$$

$$= 33$$

Thus, $df_F - df_F = 3$ in both approaches, but $df_F = 33$ for the within-subjects design, whereas $df_F = 44$ in part (a). We can resolve this apparent inconsistency by realizing that the first step in part (a) was to subtract each subject's row marginal mean from each original score. In effect, we have calculated a new dependent variable of the form

$$Y_{ij} - \overline{Y}_{i.}$$

which equals

$$Y_{ij} - \hat{\pi}_i$$

However, there are $n - 1$ independent π_i parameters, so we must increase the number of estimated parameters by $n - 1$. In part (a), we had said

$$df_R = N - 1$$

$$df_F = N - a$$

However, if we count the $n - 1$ additional independent π_i parameters we estimated, the new degrees of freedom become

$$df_R = N - 1 - (n - 1)$$
$$= N - n$$
$$= an - n$$
$$= n(a - 1)$$
$$df_F = N - a - (n - 1)$$
$$= N - a - n + 1$$
$$= an - a - n + 1$$
$$= (a - 1)(n - 1)$$

For our data, then,

$$df_R = n(a - 1)$$
$$= 12(4 - 1)$$
$$= 36$$
$$df_F = (a - 1)(n - 1)$$
$$= (4 - 1)(12 - 1)$$
$$= 33$$

As a result, $df_R - df_F = 3$ and $df_F = 33$. Applying these adjusted degrees of freedom in part (a) would have given us

$$F = \frac{552/3}{2006/33}$$
$$= 3.03$$

in agreement with the F value calculated in the within-subjects design. Thus, the within-subjects ANOVA is identical to a between-subjects ANOVA on $Y_{ij} - \overline{Y}_{i.}$, once we make the proper adjustment in degrees of freedom.

   c. The answers to parts (a) and (b) show that the within-subjects ANOVA can be duplicated by performing a between-subjects ANOVA on $Y_{ij} - \overline{Y}_{i.}$. However, by subtracting $\overline{Y}_{i.}$ from each score, the new scores treat each subject's average score as a baseline. Each new score reflects a subject's performance at level j compared to his or her average performance. In this sense, each subject serves as his or her own control.

9. a. The theoretical minimum value of ε is $1/(a - 1)$. For $a = 3$, this minimum value is .50.
    b. *Minimum* $\varepsilon = 1/(a - 1)$
             $= 1/(4 - 1)$
             $= .33$
    c. *Minimum* $\varepsilon = 1/(a - 1)$
             $= 1/(5 - 1)$
             $= .25$
    d. *Minimum* $\varepsilon = 1/(a - 1)$
             $= 1/(2 - 1)$
             $= 1.00$

11. Unadjusted   Adjusted (see 11.33)
    a. $F_{.05;\,2,28} = 3.34$ $F_{.05;\,1,14} = 4.60$
    b. $F_{.05;\,3,33} = 2.92$ (for $df_{den} = 30$) $F_{.05;\,1,11} = 4.84$
    c. $F_{.05;\,4,60} = 2.53$ $F_{.05;\,1,15} = 4.54$
    d. $F_{.05;\,1,9} = 5.12$ $F_{.05;\,1,9} = 5.12$

CHAPTER 12

6.

Testable	Effects			Error	Term	
Source	df	Source	df		Lower Bound of ε
A	2	$A \times S$	20		.50
B	3	$A \times S$	30		.33
$A \times B$	6	$A \times B \times S$	60		.17

Notice that all three of the error terms have the general form $MS_{\text{effect} \times S}$ (see Equation 12.5, as well as 12.2, 12.3, and 12.4). The degrees of freedom for the three effects are $a - 1$ for A, $b - 1$ for B, and $(a - 1)(b - 1)$ for $A \times B$. The degrees of freedom for each error term equal $n - 1$ times the degrees of freedom of the effect to be tested. In general, the minimum theoretical value of ε for an effect is

$$Minimum\ \varepsilon = 1/df_{\text{effect}}$$

Thus, in the two-way design, the theoretical minimum values are

$$Minimum\ \varepsilon = 1/(a - 1)\ \text{for the } A \text{ main effect}$$

$$Minimum\ \varepsilon = 1/(b - 1)\ \text{for the } B \text{ main effect}$$

$$Minimum\ \varepsilon = 1/(a - 1)(b - 1)\ \text{for the } A \times B \text{ interaction}$$

These theoretical minimum values follow from the dimensions of the covariance matrices used to test these different effects (for example, see Tables 12.8, 12.10, and 12.12).

8. Tests of comparisons using a separate error term always have $n - 1$ denominator degrees of freedom, whether the comparison involves marginal means, cell means, or an interaction contrast (see Equations 12.7 and 12.11, and the subsequent discussion of statistical packages). Thus, with 15 subjects, the denominator degrees of freedom for testing a contrast with a separate error term will equal 14. Thus, the correct answers here are as follows.
   a. 14
   b. 14
   c. 14
   d. 14

12. a. This source table would be appropriate for a 2×2 design with 80 subjects, where both factors were between-subjects. The actual design, however, is a "split-plot" design, where 40 subjects have each been tested twice.
    b. The proper sources, error terms, and degrees of freedom should be as follows (see Tables 12.16 and 12.19).

Source	df
Between-Subjects	
Mood (A)	1
S/A	38
Within-Subjects	
Difficulty (B)	1
Mood $\times$ Difficulty	1
$B \times S/A$	38

Notice that $a = 2$, $b = 2$, and $N = 40$ (see Table 12.16). Thus, the total degrees of freedom sum to 79, as shown in the student's table, but the student's "Within" term fails to distinguish S/A from $B \times S/A$. In addition, $MS_{S/A}$ is the proper error term for testing the B main effect, while $MS_{B \times S/A}$ is the proper error term for testing the B main effect and the $A \times B$ interaction.

c. The sums of squares for the effects shared in common by the two designs will be the same. Thus, the sums of squares for Mood, Difficulty, and Mood × Difficulty are all correct (presuming, of course, that they were calculated correctly in the between-subjects design). Further, it is true that SS_{within} as calculated by the student equals the sum of $SS_{S/A}$ and $SS_{B \times S/A}$:

$$SS_{\text{within}} = SS_{S/A} + SS_{B \times S/A}$$

However, it is impossible to tell from the student's analysis the magnitude of either $SS_{S/A}$ or $SS_{B \times S/A}$ individually. Thus, F values cannot be calculated for any of the effects.

13. a. Mean reaction time scores are as follows.

Younger Subjects	Older Subjects
530	560
470	710
620	560
610	690
600	590
420	750
610	730
650	590
610	780
570	670

b. The F statistic for testing the difference between the mean of the younger subjects and the mean of the older subjects is

$$F = \frac{SS_{\text{between}}/(a-1)}{MS_{\text{W}}}.$$

To calculate this F value, we first find

$$SS_{\text{between}} = n \sum_{j=1}^{a} (\overline{Y}_j - \overline{Y})^2 \qquad \text{(see 3.58)}$$

$$= 10[(569 - 616)^2 + (663 - 616)^2]$$

$$= 44{,}180$$

$$MS_{\text{W}} = \frac{\sum\limits_{j=1}^{a} s_j^2}{a} \qquad \text{(see 3.63)}$$

$$= \frac{5410.00 + 6734.44}{2}$$

$$= 6072.22$$

Finally, notice that $a - 1 = 1$, because $a = 2$. Thus,

$$F = \frac{44{,}180/1}{6072.22} = 7.28$$

The critical value with 1 numerator and 18 denominator degrees of freedom is 4.41 (see Appendix Table A.2), so the Age difference is significant at the .05 level.

c. The two F values are identical (see Table 12.19).

    d. Yes. The test of the between-subjects main effect in a "split-plot" design is equivalent to a between-subjects ANOVA on mean scores (averaged over levels of the within-subjects factor). No sphericity assumption need be made in purely between-subjects designs, so the F test here does not assume sphericity.

14. a. The source table that results from this analysis is as follows.

Source	SS	Df	MS	F
Subjects	460,440	19	24,233.68	
Angle	435,090	2	217,545.00	109.48
Angle × Subjects	75,510	38	1987.11	

Of course, the observed F of 109.48 for the Angle main effect is statistically significant at the .05 level.

    b. The F value in part (a), although still large, is only about three-fourths as large as the F value reported in Table 12.19 for the within-subjects main effect.

    c. Both numerator sums of squares equal 435,090.

    d. The error sum of squares in part (a) equals 75,510. The value reported in Table 12.19 is 54,420. The difference in these two values is 21,090, which equals the sum of squares for the Age by Angle interaction.

    e. No. The degrees of freedom for the Angle by Subjects interaction is 38, whereas the degrees of freedom for Angle by Subjects within Age is 36. The difference equals the degrees of freedom for the Age by Angle interaction. (It also equals the degrees of freedom for the Angle main effect here, because there are only two levels of Age.)

    f. No. The F value for the within-subjects main effect in a "split-plot" design cannot be obtained by simply ignoring the between subjects factor and then performing a one-way within-subjects ANOVA. This latter approach does yield the proper numerator sum of squares for the main effect. However, the denominator sum of squares is not properly calculated with this approach. The reason is that the denominator sum of squares in the "split-plot" design represents the inconsistency of subjects across treatments *within each group*. Ignoring the between-subjects factor, $SS_{A \times S}$ represents inconsistencies across treatments of subjects within groups and between the groups. As we saw in part (d),

$$SS_{A \times S} = SS_{B \times S/A} + SS_{A \times B}$$

To the extent that the between-subjects and the within-subjects factors interact, $SS_{A \times S}$ of the one-way repeated measures design will overestimate the proper measure of inconsistency for assessing the main effect of the within-subjects factor. Instead, the $B \times S/A$ effect of the "split-plot" design will generally provide the proper error term.

15. The following answers can be found in Table 12.20.

    a. Yes, sphericity is assumed.

    b. No, sphericity is not assumed.

    c. Yes, sphericity is assumed.

    d. No, sphericity is not assumed.

    e. Yes, sphericity is assumed.

    f. No, sphericity is not assumed.

20. a. The data are as follows.

Subject	Drug A	Drug B	Drug C	Marginal Mean
1	6	9	3	6.00
2	18	6	12	12.00
3	15	5	12	10.67
4	11	8	14	11.00
5	17	9	9	11.67
6	7	7	7	7.00
Marginal Mean	12.33	7.33	9.50	9.72

The observed F value for these data is

$$F = \frac{SS_A/(a-1)}{SS_{A \times S}/(n-1)(a-1)}$$

where

$$SS_A = \sum_{j=1}^{a} n(\overline{Y}_{.j} - \overline{Y}_{..})^2$$

$$= 6[(12.33 - 9.72)^2 + (7.33 - 9.72)^2 + (9.50 - 9.72)^2]$$

$$= 75.44$$

$$SS_{A \times S} = \sum_{i=1}^{n}\sum_{j=1}^{a} (\overline{Y}_{ij} - \overline{Y}_{.j} - \overline{Y}_{i.} + \overline{Y}_{..})^2$$

$$= (6 - 12.33 - 6.00 + 9.72)^2 + (9 - 7.33 - 6.00 + 9.72)^2 + \cdots$$

$$+ (7 - 9.50 - 7.00 + 9.72)^2$$

$$= (-2.61)^2 + (5.39)^2 + (-2.78)^2 + (3.39)^2 + (-3.61)^2 + (0.22)^2$$

$$+ (1.72)^2 + (-3.28)^2 + (1.56)^2 + (-2.61)^2 + (-0.61)^2 + (3.22)^2$$

$$+ (2.72)^2 + (-0.28)^2 + (-2.44)^2 + (-2.61)^2 + (2.39)^2 + (0.22)^2$$

$$= 127.89$$

In addition, $a = 3$ and $n = 6$, so the observed F is

$$F = \frac{75.44/2}{127.89/(5)(2)}$$

$$= 2.95$$

The critical F value with 2 numerator and 10 denominator degrees of freedom is 4.10 (see Appendix Table A.2), so the null hypothesis cannot be rejected at the .05 level.

b. The F value in part (a) is considerably smaller than the F value of 7.46 reported in the chapter.

c. These values are identical.

d. The denominator sum of squares in part (a) equals 127.89, as compared to a value of only 40.44 in the Latin square analysis.

e. The two denominator sums of squares in part (d) differ by 87.45, which is the same (except for rounding error) as the sum of squares for the time main effect:

$$SS_{A \times S} = SS_{\text{Latin square error}} + SS_{\text{Time}}$$

or, equivalently,

$$SS_{\text{Latin square error}} = SS_{A \times S} - SS_{\text{Time}}$$

f. As the last equation for part (e) shows, the sum of squared errors for the Latin square analysis will be smaller than the sum of squared errors for the ordinary repeated measures design to the extent that Time (that is, sequence) has an effect on subjects' scores. Indeed, the general purpose of a Latin square design and analysis is to control for such effects of time. In the numerical example, the increased statistical power of the Latin square analysis produces a statistically significant treatment effect that would have gone undetected in an ordinary repeated measures analysis.

CHAPTER 13

7. a.

Subject	D_1	D_2	D_3
1	3	1	2
2	3	0	4
3	−1	−1	1
4	1	−3	1
5	−1	−2	2

b. In the full model, the predicted score for each subject on a D variable is the mean of that variable. Thus, here we have

$$\hat{D}_{1i} = \overline{D}_1 = 1$$
$$\hat{D}_{2i} = \overline{D}_2 = -1$$
$$\hat{D}_{3i} = \overline{D}_3 = 2.$$

Errors then equal

$$e_{1i}(F) = D_{1i} - \overline{D}_1$$
$$e_{2i}(F) = D_{2i} - \overline{D}_2$$
$$e_{3i}(F) = D_{3i} - \overline{D}_3$$

The following table presents the errors, squared errors, and cross products for each subject.

Subject	e_1	e_2	e_3	e_1^2	e_2^2	e_3^2	e_1e_2	e_1e_3	e_2e_3
1	2	2	0	4	4	0	4	0	0
2	2	1	2	4	1	4	2	4	2
3	−2	0	−1	4	0	1	0	2	0
4	0	−2	−1	0	4	1	0	0	2
5	−2	−1	0	4	1	0	2	0	0
Sum	0	0	0	16	10	6	8	6	4

c. In the restricted model, the predicted score for each subject on a D variable is zero. Thus, the error for a variable is just the score itself:

$$e_{1i}(R) = D_{1i}$$
$$e_{2i}(R) = D_{2i}$$
$$e_{3i}(R) = D_{3i}.$$

The following table presents the errors, squared errors, and cross products for each subject.

Subject	e_1	e_2	e_3	e_1^2	e_2^2	e_3^2	e_1e_2	e_1e_3	e_2e_3
1	3	1	2	9	1	4	3	6	2
2	3	0	4	9	0	16	0	12	0
3	−1	−1	1	1	1	1	1	−1	−1
4	1	−3	1	1	9	1	−3	1	−3
5	−1	−2	2	1	4	4	2	−2	−4
Sum	5	−5	10	21	15	26	3	16	−6

d. To find the determinant of $\mathbf{E(F)}$, we first write $\mathbf{E(F)}$ in the form of a matrix:

$$\mathbf{E(F)} = \begin{bmatrix} 16 & 8 & 6 \\ 8 & 10 & 4 \\ 6 & 4 & 6 \end{bmatrix}$$

Then, from Footnote 4, the determinant of $\mathbf{E(F)}$ is given by

$$\begin{aligned} |\mathbf{E(F)}| &= 16[(10)(6) - (4)^2] + 8[(6)(4) - (6)(8)] + 6[(8)(4) - (10)(6)] \\ &= 704 - 192 - 168 \\ &= 344. \end{aligned}$$

Similarly, for the restricted model,

$$\mathbf{E(R)} = \begin{bmatrix} 21 & 3 & 16 \\ 3 & 15 & -6 \\ 16 & -6 & 26 \end{bmatrix}$$

so

$$\begin{aligned} |\mathbf{E(R)}| &= 21[(15)(26) - (-6)^2] + 3[(16(-6) - (26(3)] + 16[(3)(-6) - (15)(16)] \\ &= 7434 - 522 - 4128 \\ &= 2784 \end{aligned}$$

e. From Equation 22, the observed F value equals

$$\begin{aligned} F &= \frac{(|\mathbf{E(R)}| - |\mathbf{E(F)}|)/(a - 1)}{|\mathbf{E(F)}|/(n - a + 1)} \\ &= \frac{(2784 - 344)/(4 - 1)}{344/(5 - 4 + 1)} \\ &= 4.73 \end{aligned}$$

(13.22)

The critical F value with 3 numerator and 2 denominator degrees of freedom is 19.2 (see Appendix Table A.2), so the null hypothesis cannot be rejected at the .05 level.

f. (1) From part (b),

$$\sum_{i=1}^{n} e_{1i}^2 = 16.$$

(2) The unexplained sum of squares for e_2 equals

$$\left(1 - r_{e_1 e_2}^2\right) \sum_{i=1}^{n} e_{i2}^2 = (1.00 - .40)(10)$$

$$= 6$$

(3) The unexplained sum of squares for e_3 equals

$$\left(1 - R_{e_3 \cdot e_1, e_2}^2\right) \sum_{i=1}^{n} e_{i3}^2 = (1 - .402778)(6)$$

$$= 3.58333$$

(4) The value of the determinant $|\mathbf{E(F)}|$ equals (except for rounding error) the product of the three values computed in (i), (ii), and (iii):

$$|\mathbf{E(F)}| = 344$$

$$= (16)(6)(3.58333)$$

$$= \left[\sum_{i=1}^{n} e_{1i}^2 \right] \left[(1 - r_{e_1 e_2}^2) \left(\sum_{i=1}^{n} e_{i2}^2 \right) \right] \left[(1 - R_{e_3 \cdot e_1, e_2}^2) \left(\sum_{i=1}^{n} e_{i3}^2 \right) \right]$$

The determinant reflects simultaneously the extent to which the full model fails to explain scores on D_1, D_2, and D_3. Specifically, the determinant equals the product of three sum of squared error terms:

(a) The sum of squared errors for D_1

(b) The unexplained sum of squared errors for D_2 predicted from D_1

(c) The unexplained sum of squared errors for D_3 predicted from D_1 and D_2

In this way, the determinant takes into account the correlations among D_1, D_2, and D_3, and avoids overcounting areas of overlap (see Figure 13.1), in arriving at an index of error for the model.

(5) The value of the determinant $|\mathbf{E(R)}|$ equals (except for rounding error) the product of uncorrected residual sums of squares:

$$|\mathbf{E(R)}| = 2784$$

$$= (21)(14.57143)(9.09804)$$

Thus, the same type of relationship holds for the restricted model as for the full model. As a result, the determinant serves the same purpose for representing the overall magnitude of error in the restricted model as it does in the full model.

g. Equation 6 provides an appropriate test statistic for testing a comparison:

$$F = n\overline{D}^2 / s_D^2 \tag{13.6}$$

The D_3 variable we formed earlier compares locations 1 and 4. From the table we constructed in part (a), we can see that $\overline{D}_3 = 2$ and $s_D^2 = 1.5$. Thus, the observed F value is

$$F = (5)(2)^2 / 1.5$$

$$= 13.33$$

If this is the only planned comparison to be tested, an appropriate critical F value can be found in Appendix Table A.2. With 1 numerator and 4 denominator degrees of freedom, the critical F value is 7.71, so the mean difference between EEG activity at Locations 1 and 4 is statistically significant at the .05 level.

8. a. From Equation 22, the test statistic for the omnibus null hypothesis is

$$F = \frac{(|\mathbf{E(R)}| - |\mathbf{E(F)}|)(a - 1)}{|\mathbf{E(F)}| / (n - a + 1)} \tag{13.22}$$

We are told that $n = 12$. The fact that the $\mathbf{E(F)}$ and $\mathbf{E(R)}$ matrices have two rows and columns implies that $a - 1 = 2$, that is, $a = 3$. Thus, the determinants of $|\mathbf{E(F)}|$ and $\mathbf{E(R)}$ are

$$|\mathbf{E(F)}| = (1584)(704) - (528)^2$$

$$= 836,352$$

$$|\mathbf{E(R)}| = (2784)(1136) - (1248)^2$$

$$= 1,605,120$$

Substituting these values into the formula for the F statistic yields

$$F = \frac{(1,605,120 - 836,352)/2}{836,352/(12 - 3 + 1)}$$

$$= 4.60$$

The critical F value with 2 numerator and 10 denominator degrees of freedom is 4.10 (see Appendix Table A.2), so the null hypothesis can be rejected at the .05 level.

b. Given orthonormal contrasts, the mixed-model F can be written as

$$F = \frac{(tr(\mathbf{E}^*(\mathbf{R})) - tr(\mathbf{E}^*(\mathbf{F})))/(a-1)}{tr(\mathbf{E}^*(\mathbf{F}))/(n-1)(a-1)} \qquad (13.32)$$

For these data,

$$tr(\mathbf{E}^*(\mathbf{R})) = 2784 + 1136$$
$$= 3920$$
$$tr(\mathbf{E}^*(\mathbf{F})) = 1584 + 704$$
$$= 2288$$

Substituting these values, along with $a = 3$ and $n = 12$, into Equation 29 yields

$$F = \frac{(3920 - 2288)/2}{2288/(11)(2)}$$
$$= 7.85$$

The critical F value for 2 numerator and 22 denominator degrees of freedom is 3.44, so the null hypothesis is rejected at the .05 level, using the mixed-model approach.

c. The test statistic for testing a single D variable is given by

$$F = \frac{(E_R - E_F)/(df_R - df_F)}{E_F/df_F}$$

In the one-way within-subjects design,

$$df_R = n$$
$$df_F = n - 1$$

so

$$df_R - df_F = 1$$

Further, E_R and E_F are the entries in row 1 and column 1 of the $\mathbf{E(R)}$ and $\mathbf{E(F)}$ matrices, respectively. For these data,

$$F = \frac{(2784 - 1584)/1}{1584/11}$$
$$= 8.33$$

The critical F value for $\alpha_{PC} = .05$ with 1 numerator and 11 denominator degrees of freedom is 4.84, so the null hypothesis can be rejected.

14. a. The observed F value using the multivariate approach is 7.19. The associated p value is .010, so the null hypothesis is rejected at the .05 level.

b. The observed F value using the mixed-model approach is 3.23. The associated p value is .057, so the null hypothesis cannot be rejected at the .05 level.

c. As discussed at the end of the chapter, the multivariate approach may be more powerful than the mixed-model approach when the homogeneity assumption is violated. It is possible for the mixed-model test to be liberal if the null hypothesis is true, and yet the mixed-model test can be less powerful than the multivariate test when the null hypothesis is false.

16. a. Equation 6 provides the test statistic for testing this contrast:

$$F = n\overline{D}^2/S_D^2 \qquad\qquad (13.6)$$

To work this problem by hand, it is necessary to calculate a D score for each subject. For example, D for subject 1 is

$$D = .56(2) - .54(4) - .02(7)$$
$$= -1.18$$

Using the same formula for all 13 subjects yields the following scores:
$-1.18, .58, -1.64, -1.06, 0, -.10, -2.72, -.52, -1.18, -1.58, -1.56, -2.82, -.52.$
The mean of these 13 scores is $\overline{D} = -1.10$, and the estimated population variance is $S_D^2 = 1.003$. Thus, the observed F value is

$$F = (13)(-1.10)^2/1.003$$
$$= 15.68$$

An appropriate critical value for this post hoc complex comparison is

$$CV = (n-1)(a-1)F_{\alpha FW;a-1,n-a+1}/(n-a+1) \qquad\qquad (13.27)$$
$$= (13-1)(3-1)F_{.05;2,11}/(13-3+1)$$
$$= (12)(2)(3.98)/11$$
$$= 8.68$$

Thus, the null hypothesis can be rejected for this contrast, as we know it should, since this is the maximum contrast, and the omnibus null hypothesis was rejected with the multivariate approach.

  b. This contrast is essentially a comparison of Time 1 versus Time 2. In fact, we might want to test a contrast with coefficients of $1, -1$, and 0, to enhance interpretability.

  c. No. We saw in Problem 12 that the mixed-model omnibus test is nonsignificant for these data. This result would seem to suggest that it would be fruitless to search for a post hoc contrast to test. In fact, however, we saw in part (a) that it is possible to find a statistically significant post hoc contrast by using a separate error term. Thus, we cannot necessarily trust the mixed-model test to inform us as to whether we should pursue tests of post hoc contrasts, if we use a separate error term. However, the multivariate test will be statistically significant if and only if a significant contrast exists when we use a separate error term (remember from Problem 14 that the multivariate test was significant for these data). This agreement (or "coherence") between the multivariate test and the use of a separate error term is a major reason for preferring the multivariate approach to the mixed-model approach.

CHAPTER 14

5. a. The omnibus effects are the A main effect, the B main effect, and the $A \times B$ interaction.

  b. A main effect requires $a - 1$ D variables, or 2 D variables in this particular design. B main effect requires $b - 1$ D variables, or 3 D variables in this particular design. $A \times B$ interaction requires $(a - 1)(b - 1)$ D variables, or 6 D variables in this particular design.

c.

	General From of Degrees of Freedom		Degrees of Freedom in This Design	
Effect	Num	Denom	Num	Denom
A	$a-1$	$n-a+1$	2	18
B	$b-1$	$n-b+1$	3	17
A×B	$(a-1)(b-1)$	$n-[(a-1)(b-1)]$	6	14

8. a. The appropriate multiple comparison procedure for testing all pairwise comparisons of a within-subjects factor is the Bonferroni method. With 3 levels of A, there are 3 pairwise comparisons of the marginal means, so $C=3$. The denominator degrees of freedom equal $n-1$, or 19. From Appendix Table A.3, the value of the critical Bonferroni F is 6.89.

   b. If post hoc complex comparisons were also to be tested, the Roy–Bose procedure would be used, in which case the critical value would be

$$CV = (n-1)(a-1)F_{\alpha FW;a-1,\,n-a+1}/(n-a+1) \qquad (14.31)$$

$$= (20-1)(3-1)F_{.05;\,3-1.20-3+1}/(20-3+1)$$

$$= (19)(2)(3.55)/18$$

$$= 7.49$$

   Notice that the larger critical value here than for the Bonferroni procedure in part (a) reflects the greater protection needed for testing complex comparisons.

   c. Equation 33 provides the appropriate critical value for testing a post hoc interaction contrast:

$$CV = (n-1(a-1)(b-1)F_{\alpha FW;(a-1)(b-1),n-[=(a-1)b-1)]}/(n-[a-1)(b-1)]) \qquad (14.33)$$

$$= (20-1)(3-1)(4-1)F_{.05;\,(3-1)(4-1),20-[(3-1)(4-1)]}/(20-[(3-1)(4-1)])$$

$$= (19)(2)(3)F_{.05;\,6,14}/14$$

$$= (19)(2)(3)(2.85)/14$$

$$= 23.21$$

9. a. At first glance, the answer might seem to be "yes," because the multivariate and mixed-model approaches can yield the same answer for tests involving 1 numerator degree of freedom. However, this agreement occurs only when the error term of the mixed-model approach is $MS_{effect} \times S$. In this problem, the use of this error term would lead to 14 denominator degrees of freedom (that is, $(2-1)$ times $(15-1)$), the same as the multivariate approach. However, the F value reported by the computer program has 98 denominator degrees of freedom. In all likelihood, the computer has used an error term of the form

$$MS_{error} = \frac{SS_{A\times S} + SS_{B\times S} + SS_{A\times B\times S}}{df_{A\times S} + df_{B\times S} + df_{A\times B\times S}}$$

   which indeed leads to 98 denominator degrees of freedom. However, this form of error term is not generally recommended, because it requires a stringent sphericity assumption, even for single degree of freedom tests (see the discussion of Equation 13 in Chapter 12 for further information). The important practical point here is that the multivariate test will give a somewhat different result from the reported result, and the multivariate test is generally to be preferred. In general, then, the mixed-model test will differ from the multivariate test unless the numerator degrees of freedom equal 1 *and* the denominator degrees of freedom equal $n-1$.

11. a. They will always be the same, since the A main effect is a between-subjects effect.

    b. They will necessarily be the same only when $b=2$, because then there is a single D variable, so the multivariate approach yields a univariate test.

    c. The answer here is the same as for part (b). Once again, when $b=2$, the multivariate approach yields a univariate test, and the two approaches yield identical answers.

13. a.   The test statistic for the A main effect is given by Equation 41:

$$F = \frac{\sum\limits_{j=1}^{a} n_j (\overline{M}_j - \overline{M})^2 / (a-1)}{\sum\limits_{j=1}^{a} \sum\limits_{i=1}^{n_j} (M_{ij} - \overline{M}_j)^2 / (N-a)} \tag{14.41}$$

For these data, we know that $a = 3$ and $n_1 = n_2 = n_3 = 20$. Further, the group means on the M variable are

$$\overline{M}_1 = (10 + 12)/2$$
$$= 11$$
$$\overline{M}_2 = (16 + 20)/2$$
$$= 18$$
$$\overline{M}_3 = (16 + 16)/2$$
$$= 16,$$

so

$$\overline{M} = (11 + 18 + 16)/3$$
$$= 15$$

In addition, with equal n,

$$\sum\limits_{j=1}^{a} \sum\limits_{i=1}^{n} (M_{ij} - \overline{M}_j)^2 / (N-a) = \frac{\sum\limits_{j=1}^{a} s_j^2}{a} \tag{see 3.63}$$

$$= \frac{(4)^2 + (6)^2 + (5)^2}{3}$$

$$= 25.67$$

Making the appropriate substitutions into the formula for the F statistic yields

$$F = \frac{20[(11 - 15)^2 + (18 - 15)^2 + (16 - 15)^2]/(3-1)}{25.67}$$

$$= 10.13$$

The critical F value with 2 numerator and 57 denominator degrees of freedom is approximately 3.23 (see Appendix Table A.2), so the A main effect is significant at the .05 level.

b.   The test statistic for the B main effect is given by Equation 49:

$$F = \frac{N\overline{D}^2}{\sum\limits_{j=1}^{a} \sum\limits_{i=1}^{n_j} (D_{ij} - \overline{D}_j)^2 / (N-a)} \tag{14.49}$$

For these data.

$$N = \sum\limits_{j=1}^{a} n_j$$

$$= 20 + 20 + 20$$

$$= 60$$

Further, the grand mean of D can be found as follows:

$$\overline{D} = \frac{\overline{D}_1 + \overline{D}_2 + \overline{D}_3}{3}$$

$$= \frac{(12 - 10) + (20 - 16) + (16 - 16)}{3}$$

$$= 2.00$$

In addition, with equal n,

$$\sum_{j=1}^{a}\sum_{i=1}^{n}(D_{ij} - \overline{D}_j)^2/(N - a) = \frac{\sum_{j=1}^{a} s_j^2}{a} \qquad \text{(see 3.63)}$$

$$= \frac{(6)^2 + (4)^2 + (4)^2}{3}$$

$$= 22.67$$

Substituting these values, along with $a = 3$, into Equation 47 yields

$$F = \frac{60(2.00)^2}{22.67}$$

$$= 10.59$$

The critical F value with 1 numerator and 57 denominator degrees of freedom is approximately 4.08 (see Appendix Table A.2), so the B main effect is significant at the .05 level.

c. The test statistic for the $A \times B$ interaction is given by

$$F = \frac{\sum_{j=1}^{a} n_j(\overline{D}_j - \overline{D})^2/(a - 1)}{\sum_{j=1}^{a}\sum_{i=1}^{n_j}(D_{ij} - \overline{D}_j)^2/(N - a)}$$

For these data, we know that $a = 3$ and that $n_1 = n_2 = n_3 = 20$. Further, as we saw in part (b),

$$\overline{D}_1 = 12 - 10$$

$$= 2$$

$$\overline{D}_2 = 20 - 16$$

$$= 4$$

$$\overline{D}_3 = 16 - 16$$

$$= 0$$

so

$$\overline{D} = (2 + 4 + 0)/3$$

$$= 2$$

In addition, as in part (b), with equal n,

$$\sum_{j=1}^{a}\sum_{j=1}^{n}(D_{ij} - \overline{D}_j)^2/(N - a) = \frac{\sum_{j=1}^{a} s_j^2}{a} \qquad \text{(see 3.63)}$$

$$= \frac{(6)^2 + (4)^2 + (4)^2}{3}$$

$$= 22.67$$

Substituting these values into the formula for the F statistic yields

$$F = \frac{20[(2-2)^2 + (4-2)^2 + (0-2)^2]/(3-1)}{22.67}$$

$$= 3.53$$

The critical F value with 2 numerator and 57 denominator degrees of freedom is approximately 3.23 (see Appendix Table A.2), so the $A \times B$ interaction is significant at the .05 level.

18. It is necessary to realize several facts in order to arrive at the proper critical value. First, this contrast is a within-subjects comparison of cell means. As such, the error term can either be based on those particular cells (see Equation 68), or pooled over levels of the between-subjects factor (see Equation 69). The student decided to pool over levels of the between-subjects factor, so Equation 69 was used to calculate an observed F value. Second, the appropriate critical value to accompany Equation 69 is given by Equation 71:

$$CV = (N-a)(b-1)F_{\alpha FW; b-1, N-a-b+2}/(N-a-b+2) \tag{14.71}$$

From Problem 17, we know that $N = 45$, since the student had 15 subjects in each of his 3 groups. We also know that $a = 3$ and $b = 4$. Finally, we know that $\alpha_{FW} = .05$ here, since he wants to maintain his alpha level at .05 within this level of A. Making these substitutions into Equation 71 yields

$$CV = (45-3)(4-1)F_{.05; 4-1, 45-3-4+2}/(45-3-4+2)$$

$$= (42)(3)F_{.05; 3.40}/40$$

$$= (42)(3)(2.84)/40$$

$$= 8.95$$

Because the observed F value of 4.13 is less than the critical value of 8.95, the contrast is nonsignificant.

20. a. The three-way interaction requires the formation of difference variables for the within-subjects factor. With 4 levels of the within-subjects factor, there will be 3 such D (that is, difference) variables.

   b. Suppose that we label the first D variable as $D1$ and that we represent the score for subject i at level j of the first between-subjects factor and level k of the second between-subjects factor as D_{1ijk}. Then the full model can be written as

$$D_{1ikj} = \mu_1 + \alpha_{ij} + \beta_{1k} + (\alpha\beta)_{1jk} + \varepsilon_{1ijk}$$

The three-way interaction is tested by restricting the two-way $(\alpha\beta)_{1jk}$ parameters for each within-subjects difference variable to be equal to zero. As a consequence, the restricted model for D_1 is given by

$$D_{1ijk} = \mu_1 + \alpha_{1j} + \beta_{1k} + \varepsilon_{1ijk}$$

   c. From Table 14.15, the numerator degrees of freedom will equal pd_H, where p is the number of dependent variables, and d_H is the number of independent restricted parameters per dependent variable. From part (a), we know that there are 3 dependent variables, so $p = 3$. From part (b), the restricted model omitted the $(\alpha\beta)_{1jk}$ parameters. With 3 levels of one factor and 2 levels of the other, the number of independent restricted interaction parameters is $(3-1)(2-1)$, or 2. Thus, $d_H = 2$. The numerator degrees of freedom equal $(3)(2)$, or 6. Notice that this is the same value we would obtain if all three factors were between-subjects, or if all three were within-subjects, or any other combination. Although the denominator degrees of freedom will depend on the particular design (that is, the specific combination of between- and within-subjects factors), the numerator degrees of freedom will be the same regardless of which factors are between-subjects and which are within-subjects.

d. From Table 14.15, we find that the denominator degrees of freedom for the three-way interaction will equal

$$df_{den} = mq - .5pd_H + 1$$

where m is defined as

$$m = N - g + d_H - .5(p + d_H + 1)$$

and q is defined as

$$q = \sqrt{\frac{(pd_H)^2 - 4}{p^2 + d_H^2 - 5}}$$

We know that $p = 3$ and $d_H = 2$ (from part (c)), the total number of subjects is $N = 60$ (that is, 10 subjects for each of the 3×2 cells), and the number of distinct groups of subjects is $g = 6$ (that is, 3×2). Making the appropriate substitutions yields

$$
\begin{aligned}
m &= N - g + d_H - .5(p + d_H + 1) \\
&= 60 - 6 + 2 - .5(3 + 2 + 1) \\
&= 53 \\
q &= \sqrt{\frac{(pd_H)^2 - 4}{p^2 + d_H^2 - 5}} \\
&= \sqrt{\frac{[(3)(2)]^2 - 4}{(3)^2 + (2)^2 - 5}} \\
&= \sqrt{\frac{32}{8}} \\
&= 2
\end{aligned}
$$

Thus, the denominator degrees of freedom equal

$$
\begin{aligned}
df_{den} &= mq - .5pd_H + 1 \\
&= (53)(2) - .5(3)(2) + 1 \\
&= 104
\end{aligned}
$$

CHAPTER 15

4. A model whose only random effect is an intercept term is consistent with a belief that if errors of measurement could be eliminated, each individual's trajectory would be parallel to all other individual's trajectories. In other words, this model implies that everyone is changing at the same rate, because there are no true individual differences in slope (or any other aspect of change). When error variances are assumed to be equal at each time point, this conceptualization also corresponds to the statistical assumption of compound symmetry, which in turn is a special case of sphericity. Thus, from this perspective, the traditional mixed-model analysis methods of Chapters 11 and 12 can be viewed as appropriate when it is plausible that each individual is changing at the same rate over time.

8. The text states that when random as well as fixed trends are included in the model, we generally need two more time points than the order of the highest trend. A linear trend is a first order polynomial, which implies

that we need three time points. As the text explains, two time points would allow us to estimate an intercept and a slope for each person, but our estimates would perfectly fit the observed data. While at first glance this might sound like a benefit, the problem is that a straight line will fit any two data points regardless of the form of the true underlying function. In particular, two data points would not allow us to estimate the error in our model, which may reflect measurement error and/or error in our specification of the true functional form. In any case, without an estimate of error, we cannot test hypotheses and form confidence intervals. Because we are almost always interested in testing hypotheses and/or forming confidence intervals, we need three time points even for a simple case of straight line growth.

11. The multivariate approach usually works well when (a) we have no missing data, (b) all individuals are measured at the same time points, and (c) sample size is not too small. However, if any of these conditions do not hold, other approaches such as those described in this chapter can offer significant benefits. In addition, the multilevel framework we introduce in this chapter also provides a foundation for more complex designs, some of which extend beyond the standard multivariate approaches of Chapters 13 and 14.

13. a. No, the difference in means is nonsignificant, $F(3, 44) = 0.94$, which corresponds to a p value of 0.43.

   b. No, once again the difference in means is nonsignificant, $F(3, 44) = 0.94$, which again corresponds to a p-value of 0.43.

   c. The results in parts a and b are identical to one another. By excluding any random effects in our model in part a, we are not allowing for any systematic individual differences between subjects at all. In other words, we are assuming that obtaining 4 measurements from one child is no different from obtaining 1 measurement from each of 4 different children. In particular, in our data set, we are acting as if we had obtained scores from 48 distinct children. Notice, however, that this is exactly what we would have if the design had been a between-subjects design. Thus, it is not surprising that the results of parts a and b are identical. In general, including random effects in models for longitudinal data allows for systematic individual differences between persons.

   d. The graph would be exactly the same for all 12 individuals. In other words, the model in part a assumes that every person's trajectory is the same (except for error of measurement) as every other person's. Instead of having 12 distinct trajectories, this model assumes that there is only 1 trajectory, and this trajectory is correct for everyone. Notice then that not only are we assuming that everyone is changing at the same rate but in addition that everyone has the same intercept.

   e. This type of graph and thus this type of model rarely seem plausible for longitudinal data in the behavioral and social sciences. Instead, it is virtually guaranteed that systematic individual differences exist between persons, which is typically one of our main reasons for adopting a longitudinal (or within-subjects) design in the first place. Thus, we need to be certain that our statistical models allow for systematic individual differences. A major strength of multilevel models is that their flexibility allows researchers to choose from a variety of ways of modeling such systematic individual differences.

16. a. Fitting a model allowing each day to have its own mean but allowing only a random intercept term yields $F(3, 39) = 1.84$, $p = 0.16$. Thus, the difference between days is nonsignificant at the .05 level. This is exactly the same F value we obtained using the unadjusted univariate approach to repeated measures in Chapter 11.

   b. When no data are missing and every subject is measured at the same time points, the analysis in part a is always identical to the unadjusted approach to repeated measures as described in Chapter 11.

   c. Fitting this model to our data yields $F(3, 26) = 0.80$, $p = 0.51$. The observed F from this model is smaller than the observed F when we allowed only a random intercept term. These two types of analyses will often compare to one another in this way. When we allow the slope as well as the intercept to differ from subject to subject, we are admitting that there may be another source contributing to variability of scores at each time point. To the extent that changes really vary across subjects, we will need stronger evidence to be relatively certain that the changes we observe in our sample will generalize to an entire population of individuals. From a complementary perspective, we know that the F value from the random intercept model will tend to be inflated when individuals differ beyond their intercepts. By also including a random slope term in the model, we reduce the risk that our F value is inflated.

   d. Both the Hotelling-Lawley-McKeon and Hotelling-Lawley-Pillai-Samsom statistics yield $F(3, 11) = 0.81$, $p = 0.52$. This is the same value we obtained using the multivariate approach to repeated measures as described in Chapter 13. This equivalence will hold as long as there are no missing data and each person is measured at the same time points.

   e. These models differ from one another in how they model the covariances among scores over days. However, the models all specify the same fixed effects. Thus, we can use information criteria to help inform the best model for our data. Here we find that the model with a random intercept and slope has the lowest

AIC value, namely 253.7, and thus on this basis is the preferred model. In contrast, the AIC for the model specifying an unstructured covariance matrix is 261.5, and the AIC for the random intercept model is 294.3. The model with a random intercept and slope also has the lowest BIC value of these three models. Blind adherence to these criteria is not advisable, because the criteria themselves are prone to sampling error. For this reason it also makes sense to incorporate theoretical knowledge into our judgment of which model provides the best fit to our data. Of course, that is difficult to do in a hypothetical example, but in many longitudinal studies in the behavioral sciences it is sensible to expect at least random intercept and slope effects.

f. This model yields $F(1, 13) = 1.96$, $p = 0.18$ for the test that mean weight is changing over days. Notice that this result agrees as it must (when the design is balanced and no data are missing) with the test of the linear trend we obtained from the multivariate approach of Chapter 13. Thus, it is plausible that the population mean weight is not changing. From the model our best estimate is that the mean weight gain per day is 0.5643 ounces. The estimated variance of the slope random effect is 2.1897, which implies a standard deviation of 1.48. Thus, our best guess is that slopes have a mean of 0.56 and a standard deviation of 1.48. To find an estimated percentage of infants whose weights are increasing, we need to calculate the z score corresponding to a value of 0. In a distribution with a mean of 0.56 and a standard deviation of 1.48, a raw score of 0 corresponds to a z score of -0.38. If we assume a normal distribution, approximately 65% of scores are above a z score of -0.38. Thus, our best estimate is that just under two thirds of infants are gaining weight. Of course, in such a small sample, we need to realize that there is considerable uncertainty associated with this estimate.

CHAPTER 16

2. a. In principle, "plant" should be regarded as a fixed effect when the organizational psychologist's research question pertains specifically to the two plants included in the study. In this case, the reason for statistical inference (e.g., significance tests and confidence intervals) is that the researcher wants to use the observed sample of workers to infer what would be true for a population of workers. The key point is that the population in this fixed effects design would refer to a population of workers at these two plants. On the other hand, "plant" should be regarded as a random effect when the psychologist wants to make an inference to a broader population of plants, i.e., the desired conclusions apply not just to the two plants in question, but to a broader representation of plants. In the latter case, sampling of plants becomes relevant, because of the desire to use the sample of plants actually included in the study as the basis for inference to a population of plants.

  b. No, this is not a good design. Including only one plant in each condition renders it impossible to estimate variability between plants within each condition. In other words, any difference we observe between the conditions may in reality may reflect a preexisting difference between the plants. Random assignment might seem to solve this problem. It would largely solve the problem (at least with regard to internal validity) if individual workers were randomly assigned to each plant. But more likely in this situation is that at best the plants themselves are randomly assigned to condition. As a result, with a total of only two plants, there is essentially only one "subject" per condition. In particular, recall the F statistic for testing condition effects in a nested design:

$$F = \frac{MS_A}{MS_{B/A}} \tag{16.1}$$

If we have only one plant per condition, it is impossible to calculate $MS_{B/A}$. As a consequence, it is impossible to test the condition effect with only 1 plant per condition.

  c. All other things being equal, obtaining a larger sample of workers at each plant will increase power and precision (of course it is important that these additional workers be sampled at random from the population). However, as we have seen in parts a and b, the critical issue in this design is not the number of workers, but instead the number of plants. If inference is intended to refer to these two specific plants, the study can proceed and including additional workers in the sample would be helpful. However, if inference is intended to refer to a population of plants, increasing the number of workers sampled from these two plants fails to address the problem. The only solution in this case is to sample from more than two plants.

7. As of this writing, the following SAS PROC MIXED syntax provides the desired analysis:

```
proc mixed;
    class room cond;
    model induct = cond cskill cond*cskill/ s;
    random int/subject = room(cond);
    estimate 'condition' cond 1 −1;
```

where "cskill" is the centered version of the skill variable.

The analysis yields the following results. The test for condition is nonsignificant, $F(1, 2)= 7.35$, $p = 0.11$. The test for skill is statistically significant, $F(1,23)= 8.32$, $p = .01$. The test for the interaction of condition and skill is nonsignificant, $F(1,23)= 0.90$, $p = 0.35$. Thus, we can infer that teacher's skill has a positive relationship with students' inductive reasoning scores, but the data do not allow us to make similar statements about condition or the interaction between condition and skill. It is plausible that condition is not related to inductive reasoning and that condition and skill do not interact.

Appendix E

References

Abelson, R. P. (1985). A variance explanation paradox: When a little is a lot. *Psychological Bulletin, 97,* 129–133.

Abelson, R. P. (1995). *Statistics as principled argument.* Hillsdale, NJ: Lawrence Erlbaum Associates.

Abelson, R. P. (1997). On the surprising longevity of flogged horses: Why there is a case for the significance test. *Psychological Science, 8,* 12–15.

Abelson, R. P., & Prentice, D. A. (1997). Contrast tests of interaction hypotheses. *Psychological Methods, 2,* 315–328.

Algina, J., & Keselman, H. J. (1997). Detecting repeated measures effects with univariate and multivariate statistics. *Psychological Methods, 2,* 208–218.

Algina, J., & Olejnik, S. F. (1984). Implementing the Welch–James procedure with factorial designs. *Educational and Psychological Measurement, 44,* 39–48.

Appelbaum, M. I., & Cramer, E. M. (1974). Some problems in the nonorthogonal analysis of variance. *Psychological Bulletin, 81,* 335–343.

Bacon, F. (1928a). Novum organum. In M. T. McClure (Ed.), *Bacon: Selections* (pp. 1–33). New York: Scribner's. (Original work published 1620)

Bacon, F. (1928b). The great instauration. In M. T. McClure (Ed.), *Bacon: Selections* (pp. 269–432). New York: Scribner's. (Original work published 1620)

Bailey, D. F. (1971). *Probability and statistics: Models for research.* New York: Wiley.

Bakan, D. (1966). The test of significance in psychological research. *Psychological Bulletin, 66,* 423–437.

Baker, B. O., Hardyck, C. D., & Petrinovich, L. F. (1966). Weak measurements vs. strong statistics: An empirical critique of S. S. Stevens' proscriptions on statistics. *Educational and Psychological Measurement, 26,* 291–309.

Baril, G. L., & Cannon, J. T. (1995). What *is* the probability that null hypothesis testing is meaningless? *American Psychologist, 50,* 1098–1099.

Barcikowski, R. S. (1973). Optimum sample size and number of levels in a one-way random effects analysis of variance. *Journal of Experimental Education, 41,* 10–16.

Baumeister, R. F., Bratslavsky, E., Muraven, M., & Tice, D. M. (1998). Ego depletion: Is the active self a limited resource? *Journal of Personality and Social Psychology, 74,* 1252–1265.

Beaton, A. E. (1978). Salvaging experiments: Interpreting least squares in non-random samples. *1978 Proceedings of Computer Science and Statistics, 10,* 137–145.

Benjamini, Y., Drai, D., Elmer, G., Kafkafi, N., & Golani, I. (2001). Controlling the false discovery rate in behavior genetics research. *Behavioural Brain Research, 125,* 279–284.

Benjamini, Y., & Hochberg, Y. (1995). Controlling the false discovery rate: A practical and powerful approach to multiple testing. *Journal of the Royal Statistical Society, Series B, 57,* 289–300.

Bennett, E. L., Diamond, M. C., Krech, D., & Rosenzweig, M. R. (1964). Chemical and anatomical plasticity of the brain. *Science, 146,* 610–619.

Berkson, J. (1978). In dispraise of the exact test: Do the marginal totals of the 2×2 table contain relevant information? *Journal of Statistical Planning and Inference, 2,* 27–42.

Bernhardson, C. S. (1975). Type I error rates when multiple comparison procedures follow a significant *F* test of ANOVA. *Biometrics, 31,* 229–232.

Bhaskar, R. (1975). *A realist theory of science.* Bristol, England: Western.

Bhaskar, R. (1982). Emergence, explanation and emancipation. In P. F. Secord (Ed.), *Explaining social behavior: Consciousness, behavior and social structure* (pp. 275–309). Beverly Hills, CA: Sage.

Bien, T. H., Miller, W. R., & Tonigan, J. S. (1993). Brief interventions for alcohol problems: A review. *Addiction, 88,* 315–336.

Bird, K. D. (2002). Confidence intervals for effect sizes in analysis of variance. *Educational and Psychological Measurement, 62,* 197–226.

Bird, K. D., & Hadzi-Pavlovic, D. (1983). Simultaneous test procedures and the choice of a test statistic in MANOVA. *Psychological Bulletin, 93,* 167–178.

Bishop, Y. M. M., Fienberg, S. E., & Holland, P. W. (1975). *Discrete multivariate analysis: Theory and practice.* Cambridge, MA: MIT Press.

Blair, R. C. (1981). A reaction to "Consequences of failure to meet assumptions underlying the fixed effects analysis of variance and covariance." *Review of Educational Research, 51,* 499–507.

Bock, R. D. (1975). *Multivariate statistical methods in behavioral research.* New York: McGraw-Hill.

Boik, R. J. (1979). Interactions, partial interactions, and interaction contrasts in the analysis of variance. *Psychological Bulletin, 86,* 1084–1089.

Boik, R. J. (1981). A priori tests in repeated measures designs: Effects of nonsphericity. *Psychometrika, 46,* 241–255.

Boik, R. J. (1987). The Fisher–Pitman permutation test: A non-robust alternative to the normal theory *F* test when variances are heterogeneous. *British Journal of Mathematical and Statistical Psychology, 40,* 26–42.

Bollen, K. A. (1989). *Structural equations with latent variables.* New York: Wiley.

Boring, E. G. (1950). *A history of experimental psychology.* New York: Appleton-Century-Crofts.

Box, G. E. P. (1954). Some theorems on quadratic forms applied in the study of analysis of variance problems: II. Effects of inequality of variance and of correlation between errors in the two-way classification. *Annals of Mathematical Statistics, 25,* 484–498.

Bradbury, I. (1987). Analysis of variance versus randomization tests—A comparison. *British Journal of Mathematical and Statistical Psychology, 40,* 177–187.

Bradley, J. V. (1968). *Distribution-free statistical tests.* Englewood Cliffs, NJ: Prentice Hall.

Bradley, J. V. (1978). Robustness? *British Journal of Mathematical and Statistical Psychology, 31,* 144–152.

Bratcher, T. L., Moran, M. A., & Zimmer, W. J. (1970). Tables of sample sizes in the analysis of variance. *Journal of Quality Technology, 2,* 391–401.

Bray, J. H., & Maxwell, S. E. (1985). *Multivariate analysis of variance.* Beverly Hills, CA: Sage.

Brennan, R. L. (1983). *Elements of generalizability theory.* Iowa City, IA: American College Testing Program.

Bridgman, P. W. (1927). *The logic of modern physics.* New York: Macmillan.

Bridgman, P. W. (1945). Some general principles of operational analysis. *Psychological Review, 52,* 246–249.

Broad, W., & Wade, N. (1982). *Betrayers of the truth: Fraud and deceit in the halls of science.* New York: Simon & Schuster.

Brown, B. W. (1980). The crossover experiment for clinical trials. *Biometrics, 36,* 69–79.

Brown, H. I. (1977). *Perception, theory and commitment: The new philosophy of science.* Chicago: Precedent.

Brown, M. B., & Forsythe, A. B. (1974). The ANOVA and multiple comparisons for data with heterogeneous variances. *Biometrics, 30,* 719–724.

Browner, W. S., & Newman, T. B. (1987). Are all significant *P* values created equal? *Journal of the American Medical Association, 257,* 2459–2463.

Bryant, J. L., & Paulson, A. S. (1976). An extension of Tukey's method of multiple comparisons to experimental designs with random concomitant variables. *Biometrika, 63,* 631–638.

Bryk, A. S., & Raudenbush, S. W. (1987). Application of hierarchical linear models to assessing change. *Psychological Bulletin, 101,* 147–158.

Bryk, A. S., & Raudenbush, S. W. (1992). *Hierarchical linear models: Applications and data analysis methods.* Newbury Park, CA: Sage.

Busemeyer, J. R. (1980). Importance of measurement theory, error theory, and experimental design for testing the significance of interactions. *Psychological Bulletin, 88,* 237–244.

Campbell, D. T. (1969). Prospective: Artifact and control. In R. Rosenthal & R. L. Rosnow (Eds.), *Artifact in behavioral research* (pp. 351–382). New York: Academic Press.

Campbell, D. T. (1986). Relabeling internal and external validity for applied social scientists. In W. M. K. Trochim (Ed.), *Advances in quasi-experimental design and analysis* (pp. 67–77). San Francisco: Jossey-Bass.

Campbell, D. T., & Fiske, D. W. (1959). Convergent and discriminant validation by the multitrait–multimethod matrix. *Psychological Bulletin, 56,* 81–105.

Campbell, D. T., & Kenny, D. A. (1999). *A primer on regression artifacts.* New York: Guilford.

Campbell, D. T., & Stanley, J. C. (1963). *Experimental and quasi-experimental designs for research.* Chicago: Rand McNally.

Chambers, J. M., Cleveland, W. S., Kleiner, B., & Tukey, P. A. (1983). *Graphical methods for data analysis.* Belmont, CA: Wadsworth.

Chen, R. S., & Dunlap, W. P. (1993). SAS procedures for approximate randomization tests. *Behavior Research Methods, Instruments, & Computers, 25,* 406–409.

Chow, S. L. (1988). Significance test or effect size? *Psychological Bulletin, 103,* 105–110.

Cicchetti, D. V. (1994). Guidelines, criteria, and rules of thumb for evaluating normed and standardized assessment instruments in psychology. *Psychological Assessment, 6,* 284–290.

Clark, H. H. (1973). The language-as-fixed-effect fallacy: A critique of language statistics in psychological research. *Journal of Verbal Learning and Verbal Behavior, 12,* 335–359.

Cleveland, W. S. (1985). *The elements of graphing data.* Belmont, CA: Wadsworth.

Cliff, N. (1996). *Ordinal methods for behavioral data analysis.* Mahwah, NJ: Lawrence Erlbaum Associates.

Clinch, J. J., & Keselman, H. J. (1982). Parametric alternatives to the analysis of variance. *Journal of Educational Statistics, 7,* 207–214.

Cobb, G. W. (1998). *Introduction to design and analysis of experiments.* New York: Springer.

Cochran, W. G. (1957). Analysis of covariance: Its nature and uses. *Biometrics, 13,* 261–281.

Cochran, W. G. (1967). Footnote to an appreciation of R. A. Fisher. *Science, 156,* 1460–1462.

Cochran, W. G., & Cox, G. M. (1957). *Experimental designs.* New York: Wiley.

Cohen, J. (1977). *Statistical power analysis for the behavioral sciences* (Rev. ed.). New York: Academic Press.

Cohen, J. (1983). The cost of dichotomization. *Applied Psychological Measurement, 7,* 249–253.

Cohen, J. (1988). *Statistical power analysis for the behavioral sciences* (2nd ed.). Hillsdale, NJ: Lawrence Erlbaum Associates.

Cohen, J. (1994). The earth is round ($p < .05$). *American Psychologist, 49,* 997–1003.

Cohen, J., & Cohen, P. (1983). *Applied multiple regression/correlation analysis for the behavioral sciences* (2nd ed.). Hillsdale, NJ: Lawrence Erlbaum Associates.

Cohen, J., Cohen, P., West, S. G., & Aiken, L. (2002). *Applied multiple regression/correlation analysis for the behavioral sciences* (3rd ed.). Mahwah, NJ: Lawrence Erlbaum Associates.

Collier, R. O., Jr., Baker, F. B., Mandeville, G. K., & Hayes, T. F. (1967). Estimates of test size for several test procedures based on conventional variance ratios in the repeated measures design. *Psychometrika, 32,* 339–353.

Collingwood, R. G. (1940). *An essay on metaphysics.* Oxford, England: Clarendon.

Conover, W. J., & Iman, R. L. (1981). Rank transformations as a bridge between parametric and nonparametric statistics. *The American Statistician, 35,* 124–129.

Cook, T. D., & Campbell, D. T. (1979). *Quasi-experimentation: Design and analysis issues for field settings.* Chicago: Rand McNally.

Coombs, C. H. (1967). Thurstone's measurement of social values revisited forty years later. *Journal of Abnormal and Social Psychology, 6,* 85–91.

Cramer, E. M., & Appelbaum, M. I. (1980). Nonorthogonal analysis of variance—Once again. *Psychological Bulletin, 87,* 51–57.

Crocker, L. M., & Algina, J. (1986). *Introduction to classical and modern test theory.* New York: Harcourt Brace.

Cronbach, L. J. (1951). Coefficient alpha and the internal structure of tests. *Psychometrika, 16,* 297–334.

Cronbach, L. J. (1957). The two disciplines of scientific psychology. *American Psychologist, 12,* 671–684.

Cronbach, L. J. (1982). *Designing evaluations of educational and social programs.* San Francisco: Jossey-Bass.

Cronbach, L. J., & Meehl, P. E. (1955). Construct validity in psychological tests. *Psychological Bulletin, 52,* 281–302.

Cronbach, L. J., & Snow, R. E. (1977). *Aptitudes and instructional methods: A handbook for research on interactions.* New York: Irvington.

Dallal, G. E. (1988). Statistical microcomputing—Like it is. *The American Statistician, 42,* 212–216.

Dar, R. (1987). Another look at Meehl, Lakatos, and the scientific practices of psychologists. *American Psychologist, 42,* 145–151.

Darlington, R. B. (1973). Comparing two groups by simple graphs. *Psychological Bulletin, 79,* 110–116.

Darlington, R. B. (1990). *Regression and linear models.* New York: McGraw-Hill.

Davidson, M. L. (1972). Univariate versus multivariate tests in repeated measures experiments. *Psychological Bulletin, 77,* 446–452.

Davison, M. L., & Sharma, A. R. (1988). Parametric statistics and levels of measurement. *Psychological Bulletin, 104,* 137–144.

Dawes, R. M. (1975). The mind, the model, and the task. In F. Restle, R. M. Shiffrin, N. J. Castellan, H. R. Lindman, & D. B. Pisoni (Eds.), *Cognitive theory* (Vol. 1, pp. 119–129). Hillsdale, NJ: Lawrence Erlbaum Associates.

Delaney, H. D., & Vargha, A. 2002. Comparing several robust tests of stochastic equality with ordinally scaled variables and small to moderate sized samples. *Psychological Methods, 7,* 485–503

Dewey, J. (1916). *Essays in experimental logic.* Chicago: University of Chicago Press.

Dodd, D. H., & Schultz, R. F. (1973). Computational procedures for estimating magnitude of effect for some analysis of variance designs. *Psychological Bulletin, 79,* 391–395.

Dretzke, B. J., Levin, J. R., & Serlin, R. C. (1982). Testing for regression homogeneity under variance heterogeneity. *Psychological Bulletin, 91,* 376–383.

Dunn, O. J. (1961). Multiple comparisons among means. *Journal of the American Statistical Association, 56,* 52–64.

Dunnett, C. W. (1955). A multiple comparison procedure for comparing several treatments with a control. *Journal of the American Statistical Association, 50,* 1096–1121.

Dunnett, C. W. (1980). Pairwise multiple comparisons in the unequal variance case. *Journal of the American Statistical Association, 75,* 796–800.

Durant, W., & Durant, A. (1961). *The story of civilization: Vol. 7. The age of reason begins.* New York: Simon & Schuster.

Eacker, J. N. (1972). On some elementary philosophical problems of psychology. *American Psychologist, 27,* 553–565.

Edgington, E. S. (1966). Statistical inference and nonrandom samples. *Psychological Bulletin, 66,* 485–487.

Edgington, E. S. (1995). *Randomization tests* (3rd ed.). New York: Dekker.

Efron, B. (1971). Forcing a sequential experiment to be balanced. *Biometrika, 58,* 403–417.

Einstein, A. (1936). Physics and reality. *Journal of the Franklin Institute, 221,* 349–382.

Einstein, A. (1944). Remarks on Bertrand Russell's theory of knowledge. In P. A. Schilpp (Ed.), *The philosophy of Bertrand Russell.* Chicago: Northwestern University.

Einstein, A. (1950). *Out of my later years.* New York: Philosophical Library.

Elashoff, J. D. (2000). *nQuery advisor version 4.0 user's guide.* Los Angeles: Statistical Solutions.

Estes, W. K. (1997). Significance testing in psychology: Some persisting issues. *Psychological Science, 8,* 18–19.

Feinstein, A. R. (2002). *Principles of medical statistics.* Boca Raton, FL: Chapman & Hall.

Fenstad, G. U. (1983). A comparison between the U and V tests in the Behrens–Fisher problem. *Biometrika, 70,* 300–302.

Fessard, A. (1926). Les temps de réaction et leur variabilité, étude statistique. *Annale de Psychologie, 27,* 215–224.

Fidler, F., & Thompson, B. (2001). Computing correct confidence intervals for ANOVA fixed- and random-effects effect sizes. *Educational and Psychological Measurement, 61,* 575–604.

Fine, A. (1987). And not anti-realism either. In J. A. Kourany (Ed.), *Scientific knowledge: Basic issues in the philosophy of science* (pp. 359–368). Belmont, CA: Wadsworth.

Finn, J. D. (1974). *A general model for multivariate analysis.* New York: Holt, Rinehart & Winston.

Fisher, A. C., & Wallenstein, S. (1981). Crossover designs in medical research. In C. R. Buncher & J. Y. Tsay (Eds.), *Statistics in the pharmaceutical industry* (pp. 139–156). New York: Dekker.

Fisher, R. A. (1934). The logic of inductive inference. *Journal of the Royal Statistical Society, 98,* 39–54.

Fisher, R. A. (1955). Statistical methods and scientific induction. *Journal of the Royal Statistical Society (B), 17,* 69–77.

Fisher, R. A. (1971). *Design of experiments.* New York: Hafner. (Original work published 1935)

Fleiss, J. L. (1986). *The design and analysis of clinical experiments.* New York: Wiley.

Fligner, M. A., & Rust, S. W. (1982). A modification of Mood's median test for the generalized Behrens–Fisher problem. *Biometrika, 69,* 221–226.

Forster, K. I., & Dickinson, R. G. (1976). More on the language-as-fixed-effect fallacy: Monte Carlo estimates of error rates for F_1, F_2, F′, and min F′. *Journal of Verbal Learning and Verbal Behavior, 15,* 135–142.

Freedman, D. A., & Lane, D. (1983). Significance testing in a nonstochastic setting. In P. J. Bickel, K. A. Doksum, & J. L. Hodges (Eds.), *A Festschrift for Erich L. Lehmann in honor of his sixty-fifth birthday.* Belmont, CA: Wadsworth.

Freedman, D., Pisani, R., & Purves, R. (1998). *Statistics* (3rd ed.). New York: Norton.

Freund, J. E., & Walpole, R. F. (1980). *Mathematical statistics* (3rd ed.). Englewood Cliffs, NJ: Prentice-Hall.

Frick, R. W. (1996). The appropriate use of null hypothesis testing. *Psychological Methods, 1,* 379–390.

Friedman, L. M., Furberg, C. D., & DeMets, D. L. (1998). *Fundamentals of clinical trials* (3rd ed.). New York: Springer.

Gabriel, K. R., & Hall, W. J. (1983). Rerandomization inferences on regression and shift effects: Computationally feasible methods. *Journal of the American Statistical Association, 78,* 827–836.

Gabriel, K. R., & Hsu, C. F. (1983). Evaluation of the power of rerandomization tests, with applications to weather modification experiments. *Journal of the American Statistical Association, 78,* 766–775.

Gaito, J. (1960). Expected mean squares in analysis of variance procedures. *Psychological Reports, 7,* 3–10.

Gaito, J. (1961). Repeated measurements designs and counterbalancing. *Psychological Bulletin, 58,* 46–54.

Gaito, J. (1980). Measurement scales and statistics: Resurgence of an old misconception. *Psychological Bulletin, 87,* 564–567.

Galecki, A. T. (1994). General class of covariance structures for two or more repeated factors in longitudinal data analysis. *Communications in Statistics—Theory and Methods, 23,* 3105–3119.

Games, P. A. (1973). Type IV errors revisited. *Psychological Bulletin, 80,* 304–307.

Games, P. A. (1983). Curvilinear transformation of the dependent variable. *Psychological Bulletin, 93,* 382–387.

Games, P. A. (1984). Data transformations, power, and skew: A rebuttal to Levine and Dunlap. *Psychological Bulletin, 95,* 345–347.

Games, P. A., & Howell, J. F. (1976). Pairwise multiple comparison procedures with unequal N's and/or variances: A Monte Carlo study. *Journal of Educational Statistics, 1,* 113–125.

Games, P. A., Keselman, H. J., & Rogan, J. C. (1981). Simultaneous pairwise multiple comparison procedures for means when sample sizes are unequal. *Psychological Bulletin, 90,* 594–598.

Gardner, M. (1979). *Mathematical circus.* New York: Knopf.

Gardner, M. R. (1987). Realism and instrumentalism in pre-Newtonian astronomy. In J. A. Kourany (Ed.), *Scientific knowledge: Basic issues in the philosophy of science* (pp. 369–387). Belmont, CA: Wadsworth.

Gardner, P. L. (1975). Scales and statistics. *Review of Educational Research, 45,* 43–57.

Gastorf, J. W. (1980). Time urgency of the Type A behavior pattern. *Journal of Consulting and Clinical Psychology, 48,* 299.

Geisser, S., & Greenhouse, S. W. (1958). An extension of Box's results on the use of the *F* distribution in multivariate analysis. *Annals of Mathematical Statistics, 29,* 885–891.

Gergen, K. J. (2001). Psychological science in a postmodern context. *American Psychologist, 56,* 803–813.

Gholson, B., & Barker, P. (1985). Kuhn, Lakatos, and Lauden: Applications in the history of physics and psychology. *American Psychologist, 40,* 755–769.

Gibbons, J. D. (1971). *Nonparametric statistical inference.* New York: McGraw-Hill.

Gigerenzer, G. (1993). The superego, the ego, and the id in statistical reasoning. In G. Keren & C. Lewis (Eds.), *A handbook for data analysis in the behavioral sciences: Methodological issues.* Hillsdale, NJ: Lawrence Erlbaum Associates.

Gingerich, O. (1973). From Copernicus to Kepler: Heliocentrism as model and as reality. *Proceedings of the American Philosophical Society, 117,* 513–522.

Glass, G. V. (1976). Primary, secondary, and meta-analysis of research. *Educational Researcher, 5,* 3–8.

Glass, G. V., & Hakstian, A. R. (1969). Measures of association in comparative experiments: Their development and interpretation. *American Educational Research Journal, 6,* 401–414.

Glass, G. V., Peckham, P. D., & Sanders, J. R. (1972). Consequences of failure to meet assumptions underlying the analysis of variance and covariance. *Review of Educational Research, 42,* 237–288.

Glass, G. V., & Stanley, J. C. (1970). *Statistical methods in education and psychology.* Englewood Cliffs, NJ: Prentice Hall.

Good, P. (2000). *Permutation tests: A practical guide to resampling methods for testing hypotheses.* New York: Springer.

Graybill, F. A. (1969). *Introduction to matrices with applications in statistics.* Belmont, CA: Wadsworth.

Graybill, F. A. (1976). *Theory and application of the linear model.* North Scituate, MA: Duxbury.

Green, B. F. (1977). A practical interactive program for randomization tests of location. *The American Statistician, 31,* 39–47.

Green, B. F., & Tukey, J. (1960). Complex analysis of variance: General problems. *Psychometrika, 25,* 127–152.

Green, P. E. (1978). *Analyzing multivariate data.* Hinsdale, IL: Dryden.

Green, P. E., & Carroll, J. D. (1976). *Mathematical tools for applied multivariate analysis.* New York: Academic Press.

Green, S. B., Marquis, J. G., Hershberger, S. L., Thompson, M. S., & McCollam, K. M. (1999). The overparameterized analysis of variance model. *Psychological Methods, 4,* 214–233.

Greenwald, A. G. (1975). Consequences of prejudice against the null hypothesis. *Psychological Bulletin, 82,* 1–20.

Greenwald, A. G. (1976). Within-subjects designs: To use or not to use? *Psychological Bulletin, 83,* 314–320.

Greenwald, A. G., Gonzalez, R., Harris, R. J., & Guthrie, D. (1996). Effect sizes and *p* values: What should be reported and what should be replicated? *Psychophysiology, 33,* 175–183.

Grice, G. R. (1966). Dependence of empirical laws upon the source of experimental variation. *Psychological Bulletin, 66,* 488–499.

Gutting, G. (Ed.). (1980). *Paradigms and revolutions: Appraisals and applications of Thomas Kuhn's philosophy of science.* Notre Dame, IN: University of Notre Dame Press.

Hagen, R. L. (1997). In praise of the null hypothesis statistical test. *American Psychologist, 52,* 15–24.

Haig, B. D. (2002). Truth, method, and postmodern psychology. *American Psychologist, 57,* 457–458.

Hale, G. A. (1977). On use of ANOVA in developmental research. *Child Development, 48,* 1101–1106.

Hamilton, B. L. (1976). A Monte Carlo test of the robustness of parametric and nonparametric analysis of covariance against unequal regression slopes. *Journal of the American Statistical Association, 71,* 864–869.

Hamilton, B. L. (1977). An empirical investigation of the effects of heterogeneous regression slopes in analysis of covariance. *Educational and Psychological Measurement, 37,* 701–712.

Hand, D. J., & Taylor, C. C. (1987). *Multivariate analysis of variance and repeated measures: A practical approach for behavioural scientists.* New York: Chapman & Hall.

Harré, R., & Madden, E. H. (1975). *Causal powers: A theory of natural necessity.* Oxford, England: Basil Blackwell.

Harrell, F. E. (2001). *Regression modeling strategies: With applications to linear models, logistic regression, and survival analysis.* New York: Springer-Verlag.

Harris, R. J. (1985). *A primer of multivariate statistics* (2nd ed.). Orlando, FL: Academic Press.

Harris, R. J. (1997). Reforming significance testing via three-value logic. In L. L. Harlow, S. A. Mulaik, & J. H. Steiger (Eds.), *What if there were no significance tests?* Mahwah, NJ: Lawrence Erlbaum Associates.

Hathaway, S. R., & McKinley, J. C. (1940). A multiphasic personality schedule (Minnesota): I. Construction of the schedule. *Journal of Psychology, 10,* 249–254.

Hayes, A. F. (1998). SPSS procedures for approximate randomization tests. *Behavior Research Methods, Instruments, & Computers, 30,* 536–543.

Hays, W. L. (1994). *Statistics* (5th ed.). Ft. Worth: Harcourt Brace College Publishers.

Hedges, L. V. (1981). Distribution theory for Glass's estimator of effect size and related estimators. *Journal of Educational Statistics, 6,* 107–128.

Hedges, L. V. (1982). Estimation of effect size from a series of independent experiments. *Psychological Bulletin, 92,* 490–499.

Hedges, L. V. (1983). A random effects model for effect sizes. *Psychological Bulletin, 93,* 388–395.

Hempel, C. G. (1945). Studies in the logic of confirmation. *Mind, 54,* 1–26, 97–121.

Herr, D. G., & Gaebelein, J. (1978). Nonorthogonal two-way analysis of variance. *Psychological Bulletin, 85,* 207–216.

Hertzog, C., & Rovine, M. (1985). Repeated-measures analysis of variance in developmental research: Selected issues. *Child Development, 56,* 787–809.

Hildebrand, D. K. (1986). *Statistical thinking for behavioral scientists.* Boston: Duxbury.

Hoaglin, D. C., Mosteller, F., & Tukey, J. W. (1983). Introduction to more refined estimators. In D. C. Hoaglin, F. Mosteller, & J. W. Tukey (Eds.), *Understanding robust and exploratory data analysis* (pp. 283–296). New York: Wiley.

Hochberg, Y., & Tamhane, A. C. (1987). *Multiple comparison procedures.* New York: Wiley.

Hoenig, J. M., & Heisey, D. M. (2001). The abuse of power: The pervasive fallacy of power calculations for data analysis. *The American Statistician, 55,* 19–24.

Hofmann, S. G. (2002). More science, not less. *American Psychologist, 57,* 462.

Hogg, R. V., & Craig, A. T. (1978). *Introduction to mathematical statistics* (4th ed.). New York: Macmillan.

Holland, B. S., & Copenhaver, M. D. (1988). Improved Bonferroni-type multiple testing procedures. *Psychological Bulletin, 104,* 145–149.

Hollander, M., & Wolfe, D. A. (1973). *Nonparametric statistical methods.* New York: Wiley.

Howard, G. S., & Conway, C. G. (1986). Can there be an empirical science of volitional action? *American Psychologist, 41,* 1241–1251.

Howard, G. S., Curtin, T. D., & Johnson, A. J. (1991). Point estimation techniques in psychological research: Studies on the role of meaning is self-determined action. *Journal of Counseling Psychology, 38,* 219–226.

Howard, G. S., Maxwell, S. E., & Fleming, K. J. (2000). The proof of the pudding: An illustration of the relative strengths of null hypothesis, meta-analysis and Bayesian analysis. *Psychological Methods, 5,* 315–332.

Howell, D. C., & McConaughy, S. H. (1982). Nonorthogonal analysis of variance: Putting the question before the answer. *Educational and Psychological Measurement, 42,* 9–24.

Hsu, J. C. (1996). *Multiple comparisons: Theory and methods.* New York: Chapman & Hall.

Huber, P. J. (1981). *Robust statistics.* New York: Wiley.

Huberty, C. J. (1987). On statistical testing. *Educational Researcher, 16,* 4–9.

Huberty, C. J. (1991). Historical origins of statistical testing procedures: The treatment of Fisher versus Neyman–Pearson in textbooks. *Journal of Experimental Education, 61,* 317–333.

Huck, S. W., & Sandler, H. M. (1979). *Rival hypotheses: Alternative interpretations of data-based conclusions.* New York: Harper & Row.

Huitema, B. E. (1980). *The analysis of covariance and alternatives.* New York: Wiley.

Huynh, H. (1978). Some approximate tests for repeated measurement designs. *Psychometrika, 43,* 161–175.

Huynh, H., & Feldt, L. S. (1970). Conditions under which mean square ratios in repeated measurements designs have exact *F*-distributions. *Journal of the American Statistical Association, 65,* 1582–1589.

Huynh, H., & Feldt, L. S. (1976). Estimation of the Box correction for degrees of freedom from sample data in randomized block and split-plot designs. *Journal of Educational Statistics, 1,* 69–82.

Huynh, H., & Mandeville, G. K. (1979). Validity conditions in repeated measures designs. *Psychological Bulletin, 86,* 964–973.

Iman, R. L., & Conover, W. J. (1983). *A modern approach to statistics.* New York: Wiley.

Iman, R. L., & Davenport, J. M. (1976). New approximations to the exact distribution of the Kruskal–Wallis test statistic. *Communications in Statistics, Series A, 5,* 1335–1348.

Iman, R. L., Quade, D., & Alexander, D. (1975). Exact probability levels for the Kruskal–Wallis test. In H. L. Harter & D. B. Owen (Eds.), *Selected tables in mathematical statistics.* Providence, RI: American Mathematical Society.

Jennings, J. R. (1987). Editorial policy on analysis of variance with repeated measures. *Psychophysiology, 24,* 474–475.

Jensen, A. R. (1980). *Bias in mental testing.* New York: Free Press.

Jones, L. V., & Tukey, J. W. (2000). A sensible formulation of the significance test. *Psychological Methods, 5,* 411–414.

Judd, C. M., & Kenny, D. A. (1981). *Estimating the effects of social interventions.* Cambridge, England: Cambridge University Press.

Judd, C. M., & McClelland, G. H. (1989). *Data analysis: A model-comparison approach.* Orlando, FL: Harcourt Brace Jovanovich.

Kaiser, L., & Bowden, D. (1983). Simultaneous confidence intervals for all linear contrasts of means with heterogeneous variances. *Communications in Statistics—Theory and Methods, 12,* 73–88.

Kaplan, D. (2000). *Structural equation modeling: Foundations and extensions.* Thousand Oaks, CA: Sage.

Kazdin, A. E. (1980). *Research design in clinical psychology.* New York: Harper & Row.

Kendall, M. G., & Stuart, A. (1973). *The advanced theory of statistics: Vol. 2. Inference and relationship* (3rd ed.). London: Griffin.

Kempthorne, O. (1952). *The design and analysis of experiments.* New York: Wiley.

Kempthorne, O. (1955). The randomization theory of experimental inference. *Journal of the American Statistical Association, 50,* 946–967.

Kempthorne, O. (1979). In dispraise of the exact test: Reactions. *Journal of Statistical Planning and Inference, 3,* 199–213.

Kenny, D. A. (1979). *Correlation and causality.* New York: Wiley.

Kenny, D. A., & Judd, C. M. (1986). Consequences of violating the independence assumption in the analysis of variance. *Psychological Bulletin, 99,* 422–431.

Kepler, J. (1984). A defense of Tycho against Ursus. In N. Jardine (Ed. and Trans.), *The birth of history and philosophy of science: Kepler's defense of Tycho against Ursus, with essays on its provenance and significance.* New York: Cambridge University Press. (Original work published 1601)

Keppel, G. (1973). *Design and analysis: A researcher's handbook.* Englewood Cliffs, NJ: Prentice Hall.

Keppel, G. (1982). *Design and analysis: A researcher's handbook* (2nd ed.). Englewood Cliffs, NJ: Prentice Hall.

Keppel, G. (1991). *Design and analysis: A researcher's handbook* (3rd ed.). Upper Saddle River, NJ: Prentice Hall.

Keselman, H. J., Algina, J., & Kowalchuk, R.K. (2001). The analysis of repeated measures designs: A review. *British Journal of Mathematical and Statistical Psychology, 54,* 1–20.

Keselman, H. J., Algina, J., Kowalchuk, R. K., & Wolfinger, R. D. (1998). A comparison of two approaches for selecting covariance structures in the analysis of repeated measurements. *Communications in Statistics—Simulation and Computation, 27,* 591–604.

Keselman, H. J., Cribbie, R., & Holland, B. (1999). The pairwise multiple comparison multiplicity problem: An alternative approach to familywise and comparisonwise Type I error control. *Psychological Methods, 4,* 58–69.

Keselman, H. J., & Rogan, J. C. (1980). Repeated measures F tests and psychophysiological research: Controlling the number of false positives. *Psychophysiology, 17,* 499–503.

Keselman, H. J., Rogan, J. C., & Feir-Walsh, B. J. (1977). An evaluation of some nonparametric and parametric tests for location equality. *British Journal of Mathematical and Statistical Psychology, 30,* 213–221.

Keselman, H. J., Rogan, J. C., Mendoza, J. L., & Breen, L. J. (1980). Testing the validity conditions of repeated measures F tests. *Psychological Bulletin, 87,* 479–481.

Kirk, R. E. (1966). Practical significance: A concept whose time has come. *Educational and Psychological Measurement, 56,* 746–759.

Kirk, R. E. (1982). *Experimental design: Procedures for the behavioral sciences* (2nd ed.). Monterey, CA: Brooks/Cole.

Kirk, R. E. (1995). *Experimental design: Procedures for the behavioral sciences* (3rd ed.). Pacific Grove, CA: Brooks/Cole.

Klayman, J., & Ha, Y. W. (1987). Confirmation, disconfirmation, and information in hypothesis testing. *Psychological Review, 94,* 211–228.

Kleinbaum, D. G., Kupper, L. L., & Muller, K. E. (1988). *Applied regression analysis and other multivariable methods* (2nd ed.). Boston: PWS-Kent.

Kline, R. B. (1998). *Principles and practice of structural equation modeling.* New York: Guilford.

Koch, S. (1981). The nature and limits of psychological knowledge: Lessons of a century qua "science." *American Psychologist, 36,* 257–269.

Koele, P. (1982). Calculating power in analysis of variance. *Psychological Bulletin, 92,* 513–516.

Kraemer, H. C., & Thiemann, S. (1989). A strategy to use soft data effectively in randomized controlled clinical trials. *Journal of Consulting and Clinical Psychology, 57,* 148–154.

Kramer, C. Y. (1956). Extension of multiple range test to group means with unequal numbers of replications. *Biometrics, 12,* 307–310.

Krathwohl, D. R. (1985). *Social and behavioral science research: A new framework for conceptualizing, implementing, and evaluating research studies.* San Francisco: Jossey-Bass.

Kreft, I., & de Leeuw, J. (1998). *Introducing multilevel modeling.* Thousand Oaks, CA: Sage.

Kreft, I. G. G., de Leeuw, J., & Aiken, L. (1995). The effect of different forms of centering in hierarchical linear models. *Multivariate Behavioral Research, 30,* 1–22.

Kruskal, W. H., & Wallis, W. A. (1952). Use of ranks. *Journal of the American Statistical Association, 47,* 583–621.

Kuder, G. F., & Richardson, M. W. (1937). The theory of the estimation of test reliability. *Psychometrika, 2,* 151–160.

Kuehl, R. O. (2000). *Design of experiments: Statistical principles of research design and analysis.* Pacific Grove, CA: Duxbury/Thomson Learning.

Kuhn, T. S. (1970). *The structure of scientific revolutions* (2nd ed.). Chicago: University of Chicago Press.

Labovitz, S. (1967). Some observations on measurement and statistics. *Social Forces, 46,* 151–160.

Lakatos, I. (1978). Falsification and the methodology of scientific research programs. In J. Worrall & G. Currie (Eds.), *The methodology of scientific research programs: Imre Lakatos philosophical papers* (Vol. 1, pp. 8–101). Cambridge, England; Cambridge University Press.

Lehmann, E. L. (1986). *Testing statistical hypotheses.* New York: Wiley.

Levene, H. (1960). Robust tests for equality of variances. In Olkin, I., Ghurye, S. G., Hoeffding, W., Madow, W. G, & Mann, H. B. (Eds.). *Contributions to probability and statistics: Essays in honor of Harold Hotelling.* Stanford, CA: Stanford University Press, pp. 278–292.

Levin, J. R., & Marascuilo, L. A. (1972). Type IV errors and interactions. *Psychological Bulletin, 78,* 368–374.

Levin, J. R., Serlin, R. C., & Seaman, M. A. (1994). A controlled, powerful multiple-comparison strategy for several situations. *Psychological Bulletin, 115,* 153–159.

Levine, D. W., & Dunlap, W. P. (1982). Power of the *F* test with skewed data: Should one transform or not? *Psychological Bulletin, 92,* 272–280.

Levine, D. W., & Dunlap, W. P. (1983). Data transformation, power, and skew: A rejoinder to Games. *Psychological Bulletin, 93,* 596–599.

Levy, K. J. (1979). Nonparametric large-sample pairwise comparisons. *Psychological Bulletin, 86,* 371–375.

Lewis, D. (1960). *Quantitative methods in psychology.* New York: McGraw-Hill.

Li, G. (1985). Robust regression. In D. C. Hoaglin, F. Mosteller, & J. W. Tukey (Eds.), *Exploring data tables, trends, and shapes* (pp. 281–343). New York: Wiley.

Littell, R. C., Freund, R. J., & Spector, P. C. (1991). *SAS system for linear models* (3rd ed.). Cary, NC: SAS Institute.

Littell, R. C., Milliken, G. A., Stroup, W. W., & Wolfinger, R. D. (1996). *SAS system for mixed models.* Cary, NC: SAS Institute.

Little, R. J., An, H., Johanns, J., & Giordani, B. (2000). A comparison of subset selection and analysis of covariance for the adjustment of confounders. *Psychological Methods, 5,* 459–476.

Little, R. J., & Rubin, D. B. (1987). *Statistical analysis with missing data.* New York: Wiley.

Lix, L. M., & Keselman, H. J. (1995). Approximate degrees of freedom tests: A unified perspective on testing for mean equality. *Psychological Bulletin, 117,* 547–560.

Lix, L. M., Keselman, J. C., & Keselman, H. J. (1996). Consequences of assumption violations revisited: A quantitative review of alternatives to the one-way analysis of variance *F* test. *Review of Educational Research, 66,* 579–619.

Lord, F. M. (1953). On the statistical treatment of football numbers. *American Psychologist, 8,* 750–751.

Lord, F. M. (1967). A paradox in the interpretation of group comparisons. *Psychological Bulletin, 68,* 304–305.

Lubin, A. (1962). The interpretation of significant interaction. *Educational and Psychological Measurement, 21,* 807–817.

Lubinski, D., & Humphreys, L. (1990). Assessing spurious "moderator effects": Illustrated substantively with the hypothesized ("synergistic") relation between spatial and mathematical ability. *Psychological Bulletin, 107,* 385–393.

Lunneborg, C. E., & Abbott, R. D. (1983). *Elementary multivariate analysis for the behavioral sciences: Applications of basic structure.* New York: Elsevier.

MacCallum, R. C., Kim, C., Malarkey, W. B., & Kiecolt-Glaser, J. K. (1997). Studying multivariate change using multilevel models and latent curve models. *Multivariate Behavioral Research, 32,* 215–253.

MacCallum, R. C., & Mar, C. (1995). Distinguishing between moderator and quadratic effects in multiple regression. *Psychological Bulletin, 118,* 405–421.

Mallows, C. L., & Tukey, J. W. (1982). An overview of techniques of data analysis, emphasizing its exploratory aspects. In J. T. deOliveira & B. Epstein (Eds.), *Some recent advances in statistics* (pp. 111–172). London, England: Academic Press.

Manicas, P. T., & Secord, P. F. (1983). Implications for psychology of the new philosophy of science. *American Psychologist, 38,* 339–413.

Mann, H. B., & Whitney, D. R. (1947). On a test of whether one of two random variables is stochastically larger than the other. *The Annals of Mathematical Statistics, 18,* 50–60.

Marascuilo, L. A., & Levin, J. R. (1976). The simultaneous investigation of interaction and nested hypotheses in two-factor analysis of variance designs. *American Educational Research Journal, 13,* 61–65.

Marascuilo, L. A., & Levin, J. R. (1983). *Multivariate statistics in the social sciences: A researcher's guide.* Monterey, CA: Brooks/Cole.

Marascuilo, L. A., & McSweeney, M. (1977). *Nonparametric and distribution-free methods for the social sciences.* Monterey, CA: Brooks/Cole.

Marascuilo, L. A., & Serlin, R. C. (1988). *Statistical methods for the social and behavioral sciences.* New York: Freeman.

Marcus-Roberts, H. M., & Roberts, F. S. (1987). Meaningless statistics. *Journal of Educational Statistics, 12,* 383–394.

Mark, M. M. (1986). Validity typologies and the logic and practice of quasi-experimentation. In W. M. K. Trochim (Ed.), *Advances in quasi-experimental design and analysis* (pp. 47–66). San Francisco: Jossey-Bass.

Matthews, J. N. S. (2000). *An introduction to randomized controlled clinical trials.* New York: Oxford University Press.

Matts, J. P., & Lachin, J. M. (1988). Properties of permuted-block randomization in clinical trials. *Controlled Clinical Trials, 9,* 327–344.

Maxwell, S. E. (1980). Pairwise multiple comparisons in repeated measures designs. *Journal of Educational Statistics, 5,* 269–287.

Maxwell, S. E. (1994). Optimal allocation of assessment time in randomized pretest–posttest designs. *Psychological Bulletin, 115,* 142–152.

Maxwell, S. E. (1998). Longitudinal designs in randomized group comparisons: When will intermediate observations increase statistical power? *Psychological Methods, 3,* 275–290.

Maxwell, S. E., & Arvey, R. D. (1982). Small sample profile analysis with many variables. *Psychological Bulletin, 92,* 778–785.

Maxwell, S. E., Camp, C. J., & Arvey, R. D. (1981). Measures of strength of association. *Journal of Applied Psychology, 66,* 525–534.

Maxwell, S. E., Cole, D. A., Arvey, R. D., & Salas, E. (1991). A comparison of methods of increasing power in randomized between-subjects designs. *Psychological Bulletin, 110,* 328–337.

Maxwell, S. E., & Delaney, H. D. (1985). Measurement and statistics: An examination of construct validity. *Psychological Bulletin, 97,* 85–93.

Maxwell, S. E., & Delaney, H. D. (1993). Bivariate median splits and spurious statistical significance. *Psychological Bulletin, 113,* 181–190.

Maxwell, S. E., Delaney, H. D., & Dill, C. A. (1984). Another look at ANCOVA versus blocking. *Psychological Bulletin, 95,* 136–147.

Maxwell, S. E., Delaney, H. D., & Manheimer, J. M. (1985). ANOVA of residuals and ANCOVA: Correcting an illusion by using model comparisons and graphs. *Journal of Educational Statistics, 10,* 197–209.

Maxwell, S. E., O'Callaghan, M. F., & Delaney, H. D. (1993). Analysis of covariance. In L. K. Edwards (Ed.), *Applied analysis of variance in behavioral science* (pp. 63–104). New York: Dekker.

May, R. B., Hunter, M., & Masson, M. E. J. (1993). NPStat (Version 3.7) [Computer program]. Victoria, Canada: University of Victoria, Department of Psychology.

McCabe, G. P., Jr. (1980). The interpretation of regression analysis results in sex and race discrimination problems. *The American Statistician, 34,* 212–215.

McCall, R. B., & Appelbaum, M. I. (1973). Bias in the analysis of repeated-measures designs: Some alternative approaches. *Child Development, 44,* 401–415.

McClelland, G. H. (2000). Increasing statistical power without increasing sample size. *American Psychologist, 57,* 963–964.

McClelland, G. H., & Judd, C. M. (1993). Statistical difficulties of detecting interactions and moderator effects. *Psychological Bulletin, 114,* 376–390.

McCulloch, C. E., & Searle, S. R. (2001). *Generalized, linear, and mixed models.* New York: Wiley.

McGill, W. J. (1963). Stochastic latency mechanisms. In R. D. Luce, R. R. Bush, & E. Galanter (Eds.), *Handbook of mathematical psychology* (Vol. 1, pp. 309–360). New York: Wiley.

McGraw, K. O., & Wong, S. P. (1992). A common language effect size statistic. *Psychological Bulletin, 111,* 361–365.

McGraw, K. O., & Wong, S. P. (1996). Forming inferences about some intraclass correlation coefficients. *Psychological Methods, 1,* 30–46.

McKinley, J. C., & Hathaway, S. R. (1956). Scale 1 (Hypochondrias). In G. S. Welsh & W. G. Dahlstrom (Eds.), *Basic readings on the MMPI in psychology and medicine* (pp. 64–72). Minneapolis: University of Minnesota Press.

McNemar, Q. (1969). *Psychological statistics* (4th ed.). New York: Wiley.

Meehl, P. E. (1967). Theory-testing in psychology and physics: A methodological paradox. *Philosophy of Science, 34,* 103–115.

Meehl, P. E. (1970a). Nuisance variables and the ex-post-facto design. In M. Radner & S. Winokur (Eds.), *Minnesota studies in the philosophy of science: Vol. 4. Analyses of theories and methods of physics and psychology* (pp. 373–402). Minneapolis: University of Minnesota Press.

Meehl, P. E. (1970b). Psychological determinism and human rationality: A psychologist's reactions to Professor Karl Popper's "Of clouds and clocks." In M. Radner & S. Winokur (Eds.), *Minnesota studies in the philosophy of science: Vol. 4. Analyses of theories and methods of physics and psychology* (pp. 310–372). Minneapolis: University of Minnesota Press.

Meehl, P. E. (1971). High school yearbooks: A reply to Schwarz. *Journal of Abnormal Psychology, 77,* 143–148.

Meehl, P. E. (1978). Theoretical risks and tabular asterisks: Sir Karl, Sir Ronald, and the slow progress of soft psychology. *Journal of Consulting and Clinical Psychology, 46,* 806–834.

Meehl, P. E. (1986). What social scientists don't understand. In D. W. Fiske & R. A. Shweder (Eds.), *Metatheory in social science* (pp. 315–338). Chicago: University of Chicago Press.

Micceri, T. (1989). The unicorn, the normal curve, and other improbable creatures. *Psychological Bulletin, 105,* 156–166.

Michell, J. (1986). Measurement scales and statistics: A clash of paradigms. *Psychological Bulletin, 100,* 398–407.

Miller, R. G. (1981). *Simultaneous statistical inference* (2nd ed.). New York: Springer.

Milligan, G. W., Wong, D. S., & Thompson, P. A. (1987). Robustness properties of nonorthogonal analysis of variance. *Psychological Bulletin, 101,* 464–470.

Mood, A. M., Graybill, F. A., & Boes, D. C. (1974). *Introduction to the theory of statistics* (3rd ed.). New York: McGraw-Hill.

Morley, J. (1955). Auguste Comte. In *Encyclopedia Britannica* (Vol. 6, pp. 190–195). Chicago: Encyclopedia Britannica.

Morrison, D. E., & Henkel, R. E. (Eds.). (1970). *The significance test controversy: A reader.* Chicago: Aldine.

Morrison, D. F. (1976). *Multivariate statistical methods* (2nd ed.). New York: McGraw-Hill.

Morrison, D. F. (1983). *Applied linear statistical methods.* Englewood Cliffs, NJ: Prentice Hall.

Muller, K. E., & Barton, C. N. (1989). Approximate power for repeated-measures ANOVA lacking sphericity. *Journal of the American Statistical Association, 84,* 549–555.

Murray, D. M., & Hannan, P. J. (1990). Planning for the appropriate analysis in school-based drug-use prevention studies. *Journal of Consulting and Clinical Psychology, 58,* 458–468.

Myers, J. L. (1979). *Fundamentals of experimental design* (3rd ed.). Boston: Allyn & Bacon.

Myers, J. L., Dicecco, J. V., White, J. B., & Borden, V. M. (1982). Repeated measurements on dichotomous variables: Q and F tests. *Psychological Bulletin, 92,* 517–525.

Namboodiri, K. (1972). Experimental designs in which each subject is used repeatedly. *Psychological Bulletin, 77,* 54–64.

Namboodiri, K. (1984). *Matrix algebra: An introduction.* Beverly Hills, CA: Sage.

Neter, J., Kutner, M. H., Nachtsheim, C. J., & Wasserman, W. (1996). *Applied linear statistical models* (4th ed.). Chicago: Irwin.

Neter, J., Wasserman, W., & Kutner, M. H. (1985). *Applied linear statistical models: Regression, analysis of variance, and experimental designs.* Homewood, IL: Irwin.

Newton-Smith, W. H. (1981). *The rationality of science.* London: Routledge & Kegan Paul.

Nicewander, W. A., & Price, J. M. (1983). Reliability of measurement and the power of statistical tests. *Psychological Bulletin, 94,* 524–533.

Nickerson, R. S. (2000). Null hypothesis significance testing: A review of an old and continuing controversy. *Psychological Methods, 5,* 241–301.

Noether, G. E. (1976). *Introduction to statistics: A nonparametric approach.* Boston: Houghton Mifflin.

Nunnally, J. C. (1978). *Psychometric theory* (2nd ed.). New York: McGraw-Hill.

Oakes, M. (1986). *Statistical inference: A commentary for the social and behavioral sciences,* New York: Wiley.

O'Brien, R. G. (1981). A simple test for variance effects in experimental designs. *Psychological Bulletin, 89,* 570–574.

O'Brien, R. G. (1998). A tour of UnifyPow: A SAS module/macro for sample-size analysis. *Proceedings of the 23rd SAS Users Group International Conference* (pp. 1346–1355). Cary, NC: SAS Institute. (Updated version available on the Web at www.bio.ri.ccf.org/UnifyPow.all/SUGI98.pdf)

O'Brien, R. G., & Kaiser, M. K. (1985). MANOVA method for analyzing repeated measures designs: An extensive primer. *Psychological Bulletin, 97,* 316–333.

O'Brien, R. G., & Muller, K. E. (1993). Unified power analysis for *t*-tests through multivariate hypotheses. In Edwards, L. K. (Ed.), *Applied analysis of variance in behavioral science* (pp. 297–344). New York: Dekker.

O'Grady, K. E. (1982). Measures of explained variance: Cautions and limitations. *Psychological Bulletin, 92,* 766–777.

Olejnik, S. F., & Algina, J. (1985). A review of nonparametric alternatives to analysis of covariance. *Evaluation Review, 9,* 51–83.

Olejnik, S., & Algina, J. (2000). Measures of effect size for comparative studies: Applications, interpretations, and limitations. *Contemporary Educational Psychology, 25,* 241–286.

Oller, J. W., Jr. (Ed.). (1989). *Language and experience: Classic pragmatism.* Lanham, MD: University Press of America.

Olson, C. L. (1974). Comparative robustness of six tests in multivariate analysis of variance. *Journal of the American Statistical Association, 69,* 894–908.

Olson, C. L. (1976). On choosing a test statistic in multivariate analysis of variance. *Psychological Bulletin, 83,* 579–586.

Oshima, T. C., & Algina, J. (1992). Type I error rates for the James's second order test and Wilcox's H_m test under heteroscedasticity and nonnormality. *British Journal of Mathematical and Statistical Psychology, 45,* 255–263.

Overall, J. E. (1996). How many repeated measurements are useful? *Journal of Clinical Psychology, 52,* 243–252.

Overall, J. E., Spiegel, D. K., & Cohen, J. (1975). Equivalence of orthogonal and nonorthogonal analysis of variance. *Psychological Bulletin, 82,* 182–186.

Overall, J. E., & Woodward, J. A. (1977). Nonrandom assignment and the analysis of covariance. *Psychological Bulletin, 84,* 588–594.

Pearson, E. S., & Please, N. W. (1975). Relation between the shape of population distribution and the robustness of four simple test statistics. *Biometrika, 62,* 223–241.

Pedhazur, E. J. (1982). *Multiple regression in behavioral research: Explanation and prediction* (2nd ed.). New York: Holt, Rinehart & Winston.

Pedhazur, E. J. (1997). *Multiple regression in behavioral research: Explanation and prediction* (3rd ed.). Orlando, FL: Harcourt Brace.

Peirce, C. S. (1878). Illustrations of the logic of science: Second paper—How to make our ideas clear. *Popular Science Monthly, 12,* 286–302.

Pitman, E. J. G. (1937). Significance tests which may be applied to samples from any population: III. The analysis of variance test. *Biometrika, 29,* 322–335.

Popper, K. R. (1968). *The logic of scientific discovery.* London: Hutchinson.

Popper, K. R. (1972). *Objective knowledge: An evolutionary approach.* Oxford, England: Clarendon.

Popper, K. R. (1976). A note on verisimilitude. *British Journal for the Philosophy of Science, 27,* 147–195.

Potthoff, R. F. (1964). On the Johnson–Neyman technique and some extensions thereof. *Psychometrika, 29,* 241–256.

Poulton, E. C. (1975). Range effects in experiments on people. *American Journal of Psychology, 88,* 3–32.

Pruitt, S. D. (1988). *Multimodal assessment of experimentally manipulated affect: An investigation of mood induction with critical controls.* Unpublished master's thesis, University of New Mexico, Albuquerque, NM.

Raaijmakers, J. G. W., Schrijnemakers, J. M. C., & Gremmen, F. (1999). How to deal with "The Language-as-Fixed-Effect Fallacy": Common misconceptions and alternative solutions. *Journal of Memory and Language, 41,* 416–426.

Ramsey, F. L., & Schafer, D. W. (1997). *The statistical sleuth: A course in methods of data analysis.* Belmont, CA: Duxbury.

Rasbash, J., Browne, W., Goldstein, H., Yang, M., Plewis, I., Healy, M., Woodhouse, G., Draper, D., Langford, I., Lewis, T. (2000). *A user's guide to MlwiN.* London: Multilevel Models Project.

Ratzsch, D. (2000). *Philosophy of science* (2nd ed.) Downers Grove, IL: Inter Varsity Press.

Raudenbush, S. W., Bryk, A. S., Cheong, Y. F., & Congdon, R. T. (2000). *HLM 5: Hierarchical linear and nonlinear modeling.* Lincolnwood, IL: Scientific Software International.

Raudenbush, S. W., & Chan, W. (1993). Application of a hierarchical linear model to the study of adolescent deviance in an overlapping cohort design. *Journal of Consulting & Clinical Psychology, 61,* 941–951.

Raykov, T., & Marcoulides, G. A. (2000). *A first course in structural equation modeling.* Mahwah, NJ: Lawrence Erlbaum Associates.

Reichardt, C. S. (1979). The statistical analysis of data from nonequivalent group designs. In T. D. Cook & D. T. Campbell (Eds.), *Quasi-experimentation: Design and analysis issues for field settings* (pp. 147–205). Chicago: Rand McNally.

Rimland, B. (1979). Death knell for psychotherapy? *American Psychologist, 31,* 192.

Robinson, D. N. (1981). *An intellectual history of psychology.* New York: Macmillan.

Robinson, J. (1973). The large-sample power of permutation tests for randomization models. *Annals of Statistics, 1,* 291–296.

Rodgers, J. L., Nicewander, W. A., & Toothaker, L. (1984). Linearly independent, orthogonal, and uncorrelated variables. *The American Statistician, 38,* 133–134.

Rogan, J. C., & Keselman, H. J. (1977). Is the ANOVA *F*-test robust to variance heterogeneity when sample sizes are equal? An investigation via a coefficient of variation. *American Educational Research Journal, 14,* 493–498.

Rogosa, D. R. (1980). Comparing non-parallel regression lines. *Psychological Bulletin, 88,* 307–321.

Rogosa, D. R. (1981). On the relationship between the Johnson–Neyman region of significance and statistical tests of parallel within-group regressions. *Educational and Psychological Measurement, 41,* 73–84.

Rosen, E. (Ed. and Trans.). (1959). *Three Copernican treatises.* New York: Dover.

Rosenbaum, P. R. (2002). *Observational studies* (2nd ed.). New York: Springer.

Rosenthal, R. (1976). *Experimenter effects in behavioral research* (Enlarged ed.). New York: Irvington.

Rosenthal, R. (1987). *Judgment studies: Design, analysis, and meta-analysis.* Cambridge, England: Cambridge University Press.

Rosenthal, R., & Rosnow, R. L. (1991). *Essentials of behavioral research: Methods and data analysis.* New York: McGraw-Hill.

Rosenthal, R., Rosnow, R. L., & Rubin, D. B. (2000). *Contrasts and effect sizes in behavioral research: A correlational approach.* New York: Cambridge University Press.

Rosenthal, R., & Rubin, D. B. (1978). Interpersonal expectancy effects: The first 345 studies. *The Behavioral and Brain Sciences, 3,* 410–415.

Rosenthal, R., & Rubin, D. B. (1982). A simple, general purpose display of magnitude of experimental effect. *Journal of Educational Psychology, 74,* 166–169.

Rosenthal, R., & Rubin, D. B. (1985). Statistical analysis: Summarizing evidence versus establishing facts. *Psychological Bulletin, 97,* 527–529.

Rosner, B. (1995). *Fundamentals of biostatistics* (4th ed.). Belmont, CA: Duxbury.

Rosnow, R. L., & Rosenthal, R. (1989). Statistical procedures and the justification of knowledge in psychological science. *American Psychologist, 44,* 1276–1284.

Rothstein, L. D. (1974). Reply to Poulton. *Psychological Bulletin, 81,* 199–200.

Rouanet, H., & Lépine, D. (1970). Comparison between treatments in a repeated-measures design: ANOVA and multivariate methods. *British Journal of Mathematical and Statistical Psychology, 23,* 147–163.

Rubin, D. B. (1977). Assignment to treatment group on the basis of a covariate. *Journal of Educational Statistics, 2,* 1–26.

Rubin, D. B. (1987). *Multiple imputation for nonresponse in surveys.* New York: Wiley.

Rucci, A. J., & Tweney, R. D. (1980). Analysis of variance and the "second discipline" of scientific psychology: A historical account. *Psychological Bulletin, 87,* 166–184.

Russell, B. (1914). *Our knowledge of the external world as a field for scientific method in philosophy.* London: Allen & Unwin.

Russell, B. (1919a). *Introduction to mathematical philosophy.* London: Allen & Unwin.

Russell, B. (1919b). On propositions. What they are and how they mean. *Aristotelian Society Proceedings, 2,* 1–43.

Russell, B. (1937). *Principles of mathematics.* New York: Norton.

Russell, B. (1950). *Human knowledge: Its scope and limits.* New York: Simon & Schuster.

Rychlak, J. F. (2000). A psychotherapist's lessons from philosophy of science. *American Psychologist, 55,* 1126–1132.

Salmon, W. (1973). Confirmation. *Scientific American, 228,* 75–83.

Santa, J. L., Miller, J. J., & Shaw, M. L. (1979). Using quasi *F* to prevent alpha inflation due to stimulus variation. *Psychological Bulletin, 86,* 37–46.

Satterthwaite, F. E. (1946). An approximate distribution of estimates of variance components. *Biometrics Bulletin, 2,* 110–114.

Sawilowsky, S. S., & Blair, R. C. (1992). A more realistic look at the robustness and Type II error properties of the *t* test to departures from population normality. *Psychological Bulletin, 111,* 352–360.

Scarr, S. (1997). Rules of evidence: A larger context for the statistical debate. *Psychological Science, 8,* 16–17.

Scheffé, H. (1959). *The analysis of variance.* New York: Wiley.

Schmidt, F. L. (1992). What do data really mean? Research findings, meta-analysis and cumulative knowledge in psychology. *American Psychologist, 47,* 1173–1181.

Schmidt, F. L. (1996). Statistical significance testing and cumulative knowledge in psychology: Implications for training of researchers. *Psychological Methods, 1,* 115–129.

Schrader, R. M., & Hettmansperger, T. P. (1980). Robust analysis of variance based upon a likelihood ratio criterion. *Biometrika, 67,* 93–101.

Seaman, M. A., & Serlin, R. C. (1998). Equivalence confidence intervals for two-group comparisons of means. *Psychological Methods, 3,* 403–411.

Searle, S. R. (1966). *Matrix algebra for the biological sciences (Including applications in statistics).* New York: Wiley.

Searle, S. R. (1971). *Linear models.* New York: Wiley.

Searle, S. R. (1987). *Linear models for unbalanced data.* New York: Wiley.

Searle, S. R. (1994). Analysis of variance computing package output for unbalanced data from fixed-effects models with nested factors. *American Statistician, 48,* 148–153.

Senn, S. J. (1989). Covariate imbalance and random allocation in clinical trials. *Statistics in Medicine, 8,* 467–475.

Senn, (1993). *Cross-over trials in clinical research.* New York: Wiley.

Serlin, R. C., & Lapsley, D. K. (1985). Rationality in psychological research: The good-enough principle. *American Psychologist, 40,* 73–83.

Serlin, R. C., & Levin, J. R. (1985). Teaching how to derive directly interpretable coding schemes for multiple regression analysis. *Journal of Educational Statistics, 10,* 223–238.

Shadish, W. R., Cook, T. D., & Campbell, D. T. (2002). *Experimental and quasi-experimental designs for generalized causal inference.* Boston: Houghton Mifflin.

Shavelson, R. J., Webb, N. M., & Burstein, L. (1986). Measurement of teaching. In M. C. Wittrock (Ed.), *Handbook of research on teaching: A project of the American Educational Research Association* (3rd ed.). New York: Macmillan.

Shrout, P. E., & Fleiss, J. L. (1979). Intraclass correlations: Uses in assessing rater reliability. *Psychological Bulletin, 86,* 420–428.

Siegel, S. (1956). *Nonparametric statistics for the behavioral sciences.* New York: McGraw-Hill.

Singer, J. D. (1998). Using SAS PROC MIXED to fit multilevel models, hierarchical models, and individual growth models. *Journal of Educational and Behavioral Statistics, 23,* 323–355.

Smedslund, J. (1988). *Psycho-logic.* New York: Springer.

Smith, M. L., & Glass, G. V. (1977). Meta-analysis of psychotherapy outcome studies. *American Psychologist, 32,* 752–760.

Smith, J. E., Meyers, R. J., & Delaney, H. D. (1998). The Community Reinforcement Approach with homeless alcohol-dependent individuals. *Journal of Consulting and Clinical Psychology, 66,* 541–548.

Snedecor, G. W., & Cochran, W. G. (1980). *Statistical methods* (7th ed.). Ames, IA: Iowa State University Press.

Snijders, T. A. B., & Bosker, R. J. (1994). Modeled variance in two-level models. *Sociological Methods & Research, 22,* 342–363.

Snijders, T. A. B., & Bosker, R. J. (1999). *Multilevel analysis: An introduction to basic and advanced multilevel modeling.* Thousand Oaks, CA: Sage.

Spencer, B. D. (1983). Test scores as social statistics: Comparing distributions. *Journal of Educational Statistics, 8,* 249–269.

StatXact [Computer software] (1995). Cambridge, MA: Cytel Software.

Steiger, J. H., & Fouladi, R. T. (1997). Noncentrality interval estimation and the evaluation of statistical models. In L. L. Harlow, S. A. Mulaik, & J. H. Steiger (Eds.), *What if there were no significance tests?* (pp. 221–257). Mahwah, NJ: Lawrence Erlbaum Associates.

Stevens, S. S. (1946). On the theory of scales of measurement. *Science, 103,* 667–680.

Stevens, S. S. (1951). Mathematics, measurement and psychophysics. In S. S. Stevens (Ed.), *Handbook of experimental psychology* (pp. 1–49). New York: Wiley.

Stigler, S. M. (1986). *The history of statistics: The measurement of uncertainty before 1900.* Cambridge, MA: Belknap.

Stigler, S. M., & Kruskal, W. H. (1999). Normative terminology. In S. M. Stigler (Ed.), *Statistics on the table: The history of statistical concepts and methods* (pp. 403–430). Cambridge, MA: Harvard University Press.

Stout, R. L., Wirtz, P. W., Carbonari, J. P., & Del Boca, F. K. (1994). Ensuring balanced distribution of prognostic factors in treatment outcome research. *Journal of Studies on Alcohol.* [Special issue-Alcoholism treatment matching research: Methodological and clinical approaches]. Supplement 12, Dec. 1994, 70–75.

Strahan, R. F. (1981). Time urgency, Type A behavior, and effect strength. *Journal of Consulting and Clinical Psychology, 49,* 134.

Suppe, F. (1977). *The structure of scientific theories* (2nd ed.). Urbana, IL: University of Illinois Press.

Tabachnick, B. G., & Fidell, L. S. (1983). *Using multivariate statistics.* New York: Harper & Row.

Tatsuoka, M. M. (1988). *Multivariate analysis: Techniques for educational and psychological research* (2nd ed.). New York: Macmillan.

Timm, N. H. (1975). *Multivariate analysis with applications in education and psychology.* Monterey, CA: Brooks/Cole.

Timm, N. H., & Carlson, J. E. (1975). Analysis of variance through full rank models. *Multivariate Behavioral Research Monographs* (No. 75–1).

Titus, H. H. (1964). *Living issues in philosophy.* New York: American Book Company.

Tomarken, A. J., & Serlin, R. C. (1986). Comparison of ANOVA alternatives under variance heterogeneity and specific noncentrality structures. *Psychological Bulletin, 99,* 90–99.

Toothaker, L. E. (1991). *Multiple comparisons for researchers.* Newbury Park, CA: Sage.

Toothaker, L. E., & Chang, H. (1980). On "The analysis of ranked data derived from completely randomized factorial designs." *Journal of Educational Statistics, 5,* 169–176.

Townsend, J. T., & Ashby, F. G. (1984). Measurement scales and statistics: The misconception misconceived. *Psychological Bulletin, 96,* 394–401.

Tukey, J. W. (1953). *The problem of multiple comparisons.* Mimeographed monograph.

Tukey, J. W. (1977). *Exploratory data analysis.* Reading, MA: Addison-Wesley.

Tukey, J. W. (1991). The philosophy of multiple comparisons. *Statistical Science, 6,* 100–116.

Underwood B. J. (1957). *Psychological research.* New York: Appleton-Century-Crofts.

Vargha, A., & Delaney, H. D. (1998). The Kruskal–Wallis test and stochastic homogeneity. *Journal of Educational and Behavioral Statistics, 23,* 195–217.

Vargha, A., & Delaney, H. D. (2000). A critique and modification of the common language effect size measure of McGraw and Wong. *Journal of Educational and Behavioral Statistics, 25,* 101–132.

Vargha, A., Rudas, T., Delaney, H. D., & Maxwell, S. E. (1996). Dichotomization, partial correlation, and conditional independence. *Journal of Educational and Behavioral Statistics, 21,* 264–282.

Vasey, M. W., & Thayer, J. F. (1987). The continuing problem of false positives in repeated measures ANOVA in psychophysiology: A multivariate solution. *Psychophysiology, 24,* 479–486.

Venter, A., & Maxwell, S. E. (1999). Maximizing power in randomized designs when *N* is small. In R. H. Hoyle (Ed.), *Statistical strategies for small sample research* (pp. 31–58). Thousand Oaks, CA: Sage.

Venter, A., Maxwell, S. E., & Bolig, E. (2002). Power in randomized group comparisons: The value of adding a single intermediate timepoint to a traditional pretest–posttest design. *Psychological Methods, 7,* 194–209.

Verbeke, G., & Molenberghs, G. (1997). Case studies. In G. Verbeke & G. Molenberghs (Eds.), *Linear mixed models in practice: A SAS-oriented approach* (pp. 155–189). New York: Springer.

Verbeke, G., & Molenberghs, G. (2000). *Linear mixed models for longitudinal data.* New York: Springer.

Vonesh, E. F. (1983). Efficiency of repeated measure designs versus completely randomized designs based on multiple comparisons. *Communications in Statistics—Theory and Methods, 12,* 289–302.

Vonesh, E. F., & Schork, M. A. (1986). Sample sizes in the multivariate analysis of repeated measurements. *Biometrics, 42,* 601–610.

Wagenaar, W. A. (1969). A note on the construction of digram-balanced Latin squares. *Psychological Bulletin, 72,* 384–386.

Wainer, H. (1999). One cheer for null hypothesis significance testing. *Psychological Methods, 4,* 212–213.

Wainer, H., & Thissen, D. (1993). Graphical data analysis. In G. Keren & C. Lewis (Eds.), *A handbook for data analysis in the behavioral sciences: Methodological issues* (pp. 391–457). Hillsdale, NJ: Lawrence Erlbaum Associates.

Wald, A., & Wolfowitz, J. (1944). Statistical tests based on permutations of the observations. *Annals of Mathematical Statistics, 15*, 358–372.

Wampold, B. E., & Serlin, R. C. (2000). The consequence of ignoring a nested factor on measures of effect size in analysis of variance. *Psychological Methods, 5*, 425–433.

Wei, L. J. (1977). A class of designs for sequential clinical trials. *Journal of the American Statistical Association, 72*, 382–386.

Weinberg, S. L., & Abramowitz, S. K. (2002). *Data analysis for the behavioral sciences using SPSS*. Cambridge, England: Cambridge University Press.

Weisberg, H. I. (1979). Statistical adjustments and uncontrolled studies. *Psychological Bulletin, 86*, 1149–1164.

Welch, B. L. (1938). The significance of the difference between two means when the population variances are unequal. *Biometrika, 29*, 350–362.

Welch, B. L. (1951). On the comparison of several mean values: An alternative approach. *Biometrika, 38*, 330–336.

Wells, G. L., & Windschitl, P. D. (1999). Stimulus sampling and social psychological experimentation. *Personality and Social Psychology Bulletin, 25*, 1115–1125.

West, S. G., Aiken, L. S., & Krull, J. L. (1996). Experimental personality designs: Analyzing categorical by continuous variable interactions. *Journal of Personality, 64*, 1–48.

West, S. G., Biesanz, J. C., & Pitts, S. C. (2000). Causal inference and generalization in field settings: Experimental and quasi-experimental designs. In H. T. Reis & C. M. Judd (Eds.), *Handbook of research methods in social and personality psychology*. New York: Cambridge University Press.

West, S. G., & Sagarin, B. J. (2000). Participant selection and loss in randomized experiments. In Bickman, L. (Ed.), *Research design: Donald Campbell's legacy* (Vol. 2). Thousand Oaks, CA: Sage.

Westfall, P. H., Tobias, R. D., Rom, D., Wolfinger, R. D., & Hochberg, Y. (1999). *Multiple comparisons and multiple tests using the SAS system*. Cary, NC: SAS Institute.

Wherry, R. J. (1931). A new formula for predicting the shrinkage of the coefficient of multiple correlation. *Annals of Mathematical Statistics, 2*, 440–457.

Whitehead, A. N. (1932). *Science and the modern world*. Cambridge, England. Cambridge University Press.

Whitehead, A. N. (1920/1964). *The concept of nature*. Cambridge, England: The University Press.

Wike, E., & Church, J. (1976). Comments on Clark's "The language-as-fixed-effect fallacy." *Journal of Verbal Learning and Verbal Behavior, 15*, 249–255.

Wilcox, R. R. (1985). On comparing treatment effects to a standard when the variances are unknown and unequal. *Journal of Educational Statistics, 10*, 45–54.

Wilcox, R. R. (1987a). New designs in analysis of variance. *Annual Review of Psychology, 38*, 29–60.

Wilcox, R. R. (1987b). *New statistical procedures for the social sciences: Modern solutions to basic problems*. Hillsdale, NJ: Lawrence Erlbaum Associates.

Wilcox, R. R. (1996). *Statistics for the social sciences*. San Diego, CA: Academic Press.

Wilcox, R. R., & Charlin, V. (1986). Comparing medians: A Monte Carlo study. *Journal of Educational Statistics, 11*, 263–274.

Wilcox, R. R., Charlin, V. L., & Thompson, K. L. (1986). New Monte Carlo results on the robustness of the ANOVA F, W, and F^* statistics. *Communications in Statistics–Simulation and Computation, 15*, 933–943.

Wilk, M. B., & Gnanadesikan, R. (1968). Probability plotting methods for the analysis of data. *Biometrika, 55*, 1–17.

Wilkinson, L., & Task Force on Statistical Inference. (1999). Statistical methods in psychology journals: Guidelines and explanations. *American Psychologist, 54*, 594–604.

Willett, J. B. (1989). Some results on reliability for the longitudinal measurement of change: Implications for the design of studies of individual growth. *Educational & Psychological Measurement, 49*, 587–602.

Willett, J. B., & Sayer, A. G. (1994). Using covariance structure analysis to detect correlates and predictors of individual change over time. *Psychological Bulletin, 116*, 363–381.

Willett, J. B., Singer, J. D., & Martin, N. C. (1998). The design and analysis of longitudinal studies of development and psychopathology in context: Statistical models and methodological recommendations. *Development & Psychopathology, 10*, 395–426.

Williams, V. S. L., Jones, L. V., & Tukey, J. W. (1999). Controlling error in multiple comparisons, with examples from state-to-state differences in educational achievement. *Journal of Educational and Behavioral Statistics, 24*, 42–69.

Winer, B. J., Brown, D. R., & Michels, K. M. (1991). *Statistical principles in experimental design*. New York: McGraw-Hill.

Winship, C., & Morgan, S. L. (1999). The estimation of causal effects from observational data. *Annual Review of Sociology, 25*, 659–707.

Woodworth, R. S., & Schlosberg, H. (1954). *Experimental Psychology*. New York: Holt, Rinehart & Winston.

Wu, L. L. (1985). Robust *m*-estimation of location and regression. In N. B. Tuma (Ed.), *Sociological methodology* (pp. 316–388). San Francisco: Jossey-Bass.

Yeaton, W. H., & Sechrest, L. (1981). Meaningful measures of effect. *Journal of Consulting and Clinical Psychology, 49*, 766–767.

Name Index

Page numbers preceded by B, C, *or* D *refer to pages in Appendix B, C, or D, respectively. The letter* T *before a page number denotes pages in the Tutorials on the CD accompanying the book.*

Subject Index

Page numbers preceded by B, C, *or* D *refer to pages in Appendix B, C, or D, respectively. The letter* T *before a page number denotes pages in the Tutorials on the CD accompanying the book.*